CONTENTS

Learning Made Fun

Worm Cookies

 1¾ cups all-purpose flour
 ¾ cup powdered sugar
 ¼ cup unsweetened cocoa powder
 ⅛ teaspoon salt
 1 cup (2 sticks) butter, softened
 1 teaspoon vanilla
 1 tube white frosting

1. Combine flour, sugar, cocoa and salt; set aside. Combine butter and vanilla in large bowl. Beat with electric mixer at medium-low speed until fluffy. Gradually beat in flour mixture until well combined. Cover and chill dough at least 30 minutes before rolling.

2. Preheat oven to 350°F. Form dough into 1½-inch balls. Roll balls gently to form 5- to 6-inch logs about ½ inch thick. Shape into worms 2 inches apart on ungreased cookie sheets.

3. Bake 12 minutes or until set. Let stand on cookie sheets until cooled completely. Create eyes and stripes with white frosting.

Makes about 3 dozen cookies

Butterfly Cookies

  2¼ cups all-purpose flour
  ¼ teaspoon salt
  1 cup sugar
  ¾ cup (1½ sticks) butter, softened
  1 egg
  1 teaspoon vanilla
  1 teaspoon almond extract
  White frosting, assorted food colorings, colored sugars, assorted small decors, gummy fruit and hard candies for decoration

1. Combine flour and salt in medium bowl; set aside.

2. Beat sugar and butter in large bowl at medium speed of electric mixer until fluffy. Beat in egg, vanilla and almond extract. Gradually add flour mixture. Beat at low speed until well blended. Divide dough in half. Cover; refrigerate 30 minutes or until firm.

3. Preheat oven to 350°F. Grease cookie sheets. Roll half of dough on lightly floured surface to ¼-inch thickness. Cut dough with butterfly cookie cutters. Repeat with remaining dough. Transfer cutouts to ungreased cookie sheets.

4. Bake 12 to 15 minutes or until edges are lightly browned. Remove to wire racks; cool completely.

5. Tint portions of white frosting with assorted food colorings. Spread desired colors of frosting over cookies. Decorate as desired.

Makes about 20 to 22 cookies

Honey Bees

- ¾ cup shortening
- ½ cup sugar
- ¼ cup honey
- 1 egg
- ½ teaspoon vanilla
- 2 cups all-purpose flour
- ⅓ cup cornmeal
- 1 teaspoon baking powder
- ½ teaspoon salt
- Yellow and black decorating icings or gels, gummy fruit and decors

1. Beat shortening, sugar and honey in large bowl at medium speed of electric mixer until fluffy. Add egg and vanilla; mix until well blended. Combine flour, cornmeal, baking powder and salt in medium bowl. Add to shortening mixture; mix at low speed until well blended. Shape dough into disc. Wrap in plastic wrap; refrigerate 2 hours or overnight.

2. Preheat oven to 375°F. Divide dough into 24 equal sections. Shape each section into oval-shaped ball. Place 2 inches apart on ungreased cookie sheets.

3. Bake 10 to 12 minutes or until lightly browned. Cool 2 minutes on cookie sheets. Remove to wire racks; cool completely.

4. Decorate cookies with icings, gummy fruit and decors to resemble honey bees.

Makes 2 dozen cookies

Domino Cookies

1 package (20 ounces) refrigerated sugar cookie dough
All-purpose flour (optional)
½ cup semisweet chocolate chips

1. Preheat oven to 350°F. Grease cookie sheets.

2. Remove dough from wrapper according to package directions. Cut dough into 4 equal sections. Reserve 1 section; refrigerate remaining 3 sections.

3. Roll reserved dough to ⅛-inch thickness. Sprinkle with flour to minimize sticking, if necessary. Cut out 9 (2½×1¾-inch) rectangles using sharp knife. Place 2 inches apart on prepared cookie sheets.

4. Score each cookie across middle with sharp knife. Gently press chocolate chips, point side down, into dough to resemble various dominos. Repeat with remaining dough, scraps and chocolate chips.

5. Bake 8 to 10 minutes or until edges are light golden brown. Remove to wire racks; cool completely.   *Makes 3 dozen cookies*

Tip: Use these adorable cookies as a learning tool for kids. They can count the number of chocolate chips in each cookie and arrange them in lots of ways: highest to lowest, numerically or even solve simple math problems. As a treat, they can eat the cookies afterwards.

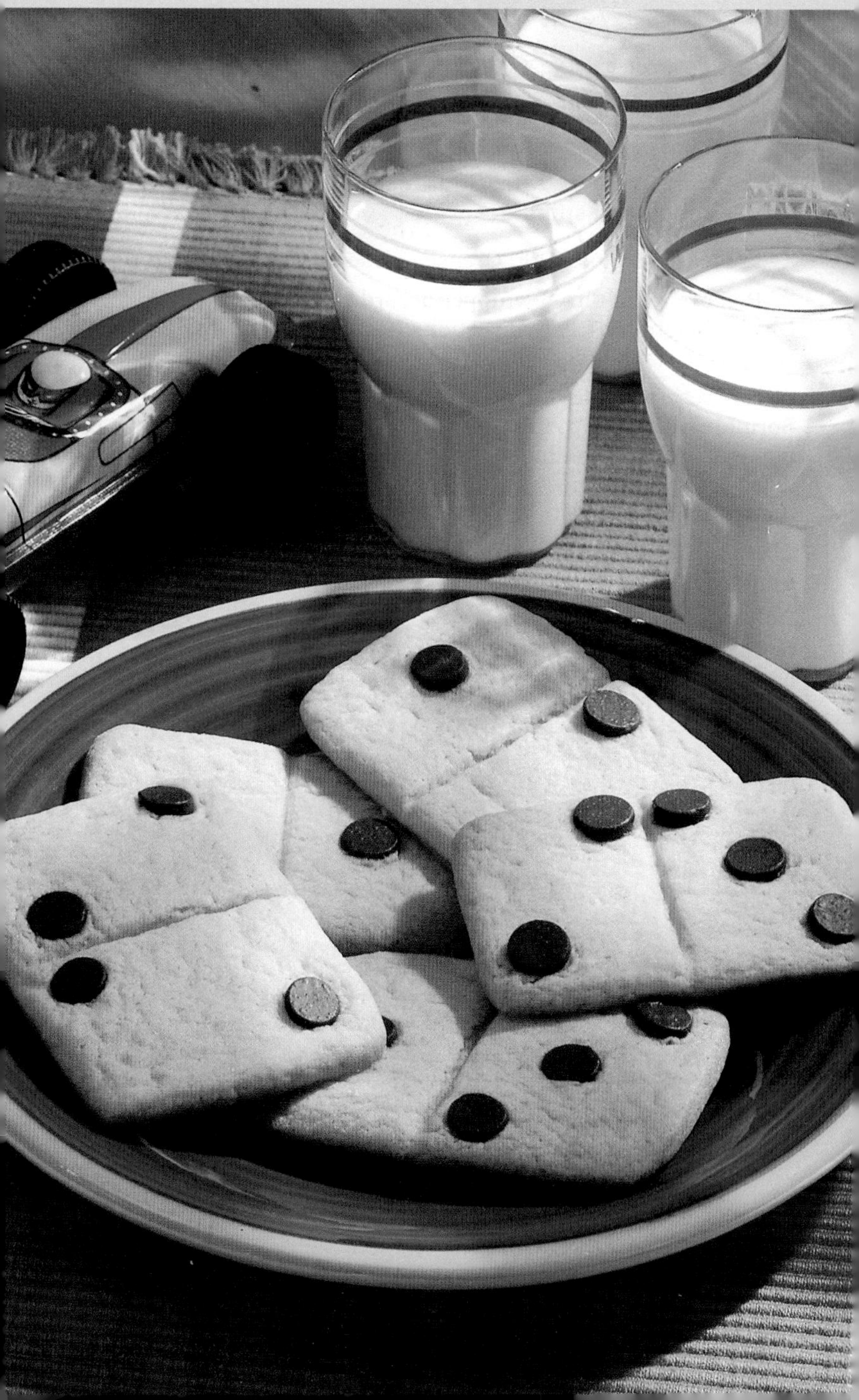

Musical Instrument Cookies

1 package (18 ounces) refrigerated sugar cookie dough

All-purpose flour (optional)

Assorted colored frostings, colored gels, colored sugars, candy and small decors

1. Preheat oven to 350°F. Grease cookie sheets.

2. Remove dough from wrapper according to package directions. Divide dough into 2 equal sections. Reserve 1 section; cover and refrigerate remaining section.

3. Roll reserved dough on lightly floured surface to ¼-inch thickness. Sprinkle with flour to minimize sticking, if necessary. Cut out cookies using about 3½-inch musical notes and instrument cookie cutters. Place cookies 2 inches apart on prepared cookie sheets. Repeat with remaining dough.

4. Bake 10 to 12 minutes or until edges are lightly browned. Remove from oven. Cool on cookie sheets 2 minutes. Remove to wire racks; cool completely.

5. Decorate with colored frostings, gels, sugars and assorted decors as shown in photo.   *Makes about 2 dozen cookies*

hint:

When making cutout cookies, dip the cookie cutters in flour before each use. That way the cookie dough will not stick to the cookie cutters.

Peanut Butter Bears

  2 cups uncooked quick oats
  2 cups all-purpose flour
  1 tablespoon baking powder
  1 cup granulated sugar
  ¾ cup (1½ sticks) butter, softened
  ½ cup creamy peanut butter
  ½ cup packed brown sugar
  ½ cup cholesterol-free egg substitute
  1 teaspoon vanilla
  3 tablespoons miniature chocolate chips

1. Combine oats, flour and baking powder in medium bowl; set aside.

2. Beat granulated sugar, butter, peanut butter and brown sugar in large bowl with electric mixer at medium-high speed until creamy. Add egg substitute and vanilla; beat until light and fluffy. Add oat mixture. Beat on low speed until combined. Cover and refrigerate 1 to 2 hours or until easy to handle.

3. Preheat oven to 375°F.

4. For each bear, shape one 1-inch ball for body and one ¾-inch ball for head. Place body and head together on cookie sheet; flatten slightly. Form 7 small balls for ears, arms, legs and mouth; arrange on bear body and head. Place 2 chocolate chips on each head for eyes; place 1 chocolate chip on each body for belly-button.

5. Bake 9 to 11 minutes or until edges are lightly browned. Cool 1 minute on cookie sheet. Remove to wire racks; cool completely.

Makes 4 dozen cookies

Crayon Cookies

　　1 cup (2 sticks) butter, softened
　　2 teaspoons vanilla
　　½ cup powdered sugar
2¼ cups all-purpose flour
　　¼ teaspoon salt
　　　Assorted paste food colorings
1½ cups chocolate chips
1½ teaspoons shortening

1. Preheat oven to 350°F. Grease cookie sheets.

2. Beat butter and vanilla in large bowl at high speed of electric mixer until fluffy. Add powdered sugar; beat at medium speed until blended. Combine flour and salt in small bowl; add gradually to butter mixture until combine.

3. Divide dough into 10 equal sections. Reserve 1 section; cover and refrigerate remaining 9 sections. Combine reserved section and desired food coloring in small bowl; blend well.

4. Cut dough section in half. Roll each half into 5-inch log. Pinch one end to resemble crayon tip. Place cookies 2 inches apart on prepared cookie sheets. Repeat with remaining 9 sections of dough and desired food colorings.

5. Bake 15 to 18 minutes or until edges are lightly browned. Cool completely on cookie sheets.

6. Combine chocolate chips and shortening in small microwavable bowl. Microwave at HIGH 1 to 1½ minutes, stirring after 1 minute, or until chocolate is melted and smooth. Decorate cookies with chocolate mixture to look like crayons. *Makes 20 cookies*

nutty Footballs

   1 cup (2 sticks) butter, softened
   ½ cup sugar
   1 egg
   ½ teaspoon vanilla
   2 cups all-purpose flour
   ¼ cup unsweetened cocoa powder
   1 cup finely chopped almonds
      Prepared colored decorating icings (optional)
      Prepared white decorating icing

1. Beat butter and sugar in large bowl at medium speed of electric mixer until creamy. Add egg and vanilla; mix until well blended. Combine flour and cocoa; gradually add to butter mixture, beating until well blended. Add almonds; beat until well blended. Shape dough into disc. Wrap in plastic wrap; refrigerate 30 minutes.

2. Preheat oven to 350°F. Lightly grease cookie sheets. Roll out dough on floured surface to ¼-inch thickness. Cut dough with 2½- to 3-inch football-shaped cookie cutter.* Place 2 inches apart on prepared cookie sheets.

3. Bake 10 to 12 minutes or until set. Cool on cookie sheets 1 to 2 minutes. Remove to wire rack; cool completely. Decorate with colored icings, if desired. Pipe white icing onto footballs to make laces.   *Makes 2 dozen cookies*

*To make football shapes without a cookie cutter, shape 3 tablespoonfuls of dough into ovals. Place 3 inches apart on prepared cookie sheets. Flatten ovals to ¼-inch thickness; taper ends. Bake as directed.

Baseball Caps

   1 cup butter (2 sticks), softened
   7 ounces almond paste
   ¾ cup sugar
   1 egg
   1 teaspoon vanilla
   ¼ teaspoon salt
   3 cups all-purpose flour
   Assorted colored decorating icings and colored candies

1. Preheat oven to 350°F. Grease cookie sheets. Beat butter, almond paste, sugar, egg, vanilla and salt in large bowl at high speed of electric mixer until light and fluffy. Add flour all at once; stir just to combine.

2. Roll ¼ of dough on lightly floured surface to ⅛-inch thickness. Cut out 1-inch circles. Place cutouts 2 inches apart on prepared cookie sheets.

3. Shape remaining dough into 1-inch balls.* Place one ball on top of dough circle so about ½ inch of circle sticks out to form bill of baseball cap. Repeat with remaining dough balls and circles.

4. Bake 10 to 12 minutes or until lightly browned. If bills brown too quickly, cut small strips of foil and cover with shiny side of foil facing up. Let cool on cookie sheets 2 minutes. Remove to wire racks; cool completely. Decorate with icings and candies as desired.

Makes about 3 dozen cookies

*Use 1-tablespoon scoop to keep baseball caps uniform in size and professional looking.

Checkerboard Cookie

   1 cup sugar

   ¾ cup (1½ sticks) butter, softened

   2 eggs

   1 teaspoon vanilla

  2¾ cups self-rising flour

    All-purpose flour

    Red and black decorating icings

1. Beat sugar and butter in large bowl at high speed of electric mixer until light and fluffy. Add eggs and vanilla; stir to combine. Add self-rising flour; stir until just combined. Cover and refrigerate 30 minutes.

2. Preheat oven to 350°F. Grease cookie sheets.

3. Roll ¼ of dough on lightly floured surface to ¼-inch thickness. Cut 24 circles with 1-inch round cookie cutter. Place on prepared cookie sheets.

4. Bake 8 to 10 minutes or until cookies turn light golden brown. Cool on cookie sheet 2 minutes. Remove to wire rack; cool completely.

5. Combine scraps of dough with remaining dough. Roll on lightly floured surface to 12-inch square. Place on greased 15½×12-inch cookie sheet.

6. Bake 10 to 12 minutes or until middle does not leave indentation when lightly touched with fingertips. Cool on cookie sheet 5 minutes. Slide checkerboard onto wire rack; cool completely.

7. Divide surface of checkerboard into 8 equal rows containing 8 equal columns. Alternate every other square with red and black icing to create checkerboard. Spread red icing on 12 checker playing pieces and black on remaining 12 checker playing pieces. Allow pieces to stand until icing is set. Place red pieces on black squares and black pieces on red squares. *Makes 1 checkerboard cookie*

Chocolate Spiders

¼ **cup (½ stick) butter, softened**

1 **package (12 ounces) semisweet chocolate chips**

1 **cup butterscotch-flavored chips**

¼ **cup creamy peanut butter**

4 **cups crisp rice cereal**

Chow mein noodles and assorted candies

1. Line baking sheet with waxed paper.

2. Combine butter, chocolate and butterscotch chips in large saucepan; stir over medium heat until chips are melted and mixture is well blended. Remove from heat. Add peanut butter; mix well. Add cereal; stir to evenly coat.

3. Drop mixture by tablespoonfuls, onto prepared baking sheet; insert chow mein noodles for legs and add candies for eyes.

Makes about 3 dozen

Doughnut Hole Spiders: Substitute chocolate-covered doughnut holes for shaped cereal mixture. Insert black string licorice, cut into 1½-inch lengths, into doughnut holes for legs. Use desired color decorating icing to dot onto doughnut holes for eyes.

hint:

To add extra crunch to these delicious cookies, sprinkle in some chopped peanuts when you are stirring in the cereal.

Chip-a-licious

Cookie Pizza

- **1 (18-ounce) package refrigerated sugar cookie dough**
- **2 cups (12 ounces) semi-sweet chocolate chips**
- **1 (14-ounce) can EAGLE BRAND® Sweetened Condensed Milk (NOT evaporated milk)**
- **2 cups candy-coated milk chocolate pieces**
- **2 cups miniature marshmallows**
- **½ cup peanuts**

1. Preheat oven to 375°F. Press cookie dough into 2 ungreased 12-inch pizza pans. Bake 10 minutes or until golden. Remove from oven.

2. In medium saucepan, melt chips with Eagle Brand. Spread over crusts. Sprinkle with chocolate pieces, marshmallows and peanuts.

3. Bake 4 minutes or until marshmallows are lightly toasted. Cool. Cut into wedges.   *Makes 2 pizzas (24 servings)*

Prep Time: 15 minutes
Bake Time: 14 minutes

7 - 6 = 1   4 - 2 = 2   8 - 3 = 5

Peanut Butter Chocolate Chippers

1 cup packed light brown sugar

1 cup creamy or chunky peanut butter

1 large egg

¾ cup milk chocolate chips

Granulated sugar

1. Preheat oven to 350°F.

2. Combine brown sugar, peanut butter and egg in medium bowl; mix until well blended. Add chips; mix well.

3. Roll heaping tablespoonfuls of dough into 1½-inch balls. Place balls 2 inches apart on ungreased cookie sheets.

4. Dip table fork into granulated sugar; press criss-cross fashion onto each ball, flattening to ½-inch thickness.

5. Bake 12 minutes or until set. Let cookies stand on cookie sheets 2 minutes. Remove cookies with spatula to wire racks; cool completely.

Makes about 2 dozen cookies

Note: This simple recipe is unusual because it doesn't contain any flour—but it still makes great cookies!

hint:

These cookies make delicious sandwich cookies, too. Spread the bottoms of half the cookies with your favorite icing, and then top with the remaining cookies. Press the cookies together slightly until the icing is spread between the cookies.

Original Nestlé® Toll House® Chocolate Chip Cookies

2¼ cups all-purpose flour

1 teaspoon baking soda

1 teaspoon salt

1 cup (2 sticks) butter or margarine, softened

¾ cup granulated sugar

¾ cup packed brown sugar

1 teaspoon vanilla extract

2 large eggs

2 cups (12-ounce package) NESTLÉ® TOLL HOUSE® Semi-Sweet Chocolate Morsels

1 cup chopped nuts

PREHEAT oven to 375°F.

COMBINE flour, baking soda and salt in small bowl. Beat butter, granulated sugar, brown sugar and vanilla extract in large mixer bowl until creamy. Add eggs, one at a time, beating well after each addition. Gradually beat in flour mixture. Stir in morsels and nuts. Drop by rounded tablespoon onto ungreased baking sheets.

BAKE for 9 to 11 minutes or until golden brown. Cool on baking sheets for 2 minutes; remove to wire racks to cool completely.

Makes about 5 dozen cookies

Pan Cookie Variation: GREASE 15×10-inch jelly-roll pan. Prepare dough as above. Spread into prepared pan. Bake for 20 to 25 minutes or until golden brown. Cool in pan on wire rack. Makes 4 dozen bars.

Slice and Bake Cookie Variation: PREPARE dough as above. Divide dough in half; wrap in wax paper. Refrigerate for 1 hour or until firm. Shape each half into 15-inch log; wrap in wax paper. Refrigerate for 30 minutes. *(Dough may be stored in refrigerator for up to 1 week or in freezer for up to 8 weeks.)* Preheat oven to 375°F. Cut into ½-inch-thick slices; place on ungreased baking sheets. Bake for 8 to 10 minutes or until golden brown. Cool on baking sheets for 2 minutes; remove to wire racks to cool completely. Makes about 5 dozen cookies.

7 - 6 = 1   4 - 2 = 2   8 - 3 = 5

Chocolate Crackletops

- 2 cups all-purpose flour
- 2 teaspoons baking powder
- 2 cups granulated sugar
- ½ cup (1 stick) butter or margarine
- 4 squares (1 ounce each) unsweetened baking chocolate, chopped
- 4 large eggs, lightly beaten
- 2 teaspoons vanilla extract
- 1¾ cups "M&M's"® Chocolate Mini Baking Bits
- Additional granulated sugar

Combine flour and baking powder; set aside. In 2-quart saucepan over medium heat combine 2 cups sugar, butter and chocolate, stirring until butter and chocolate are melted; remove from heat. Gradually stir in eggs and vanilla. Stir in flour mixture until well blended. Chill mixture 1 hour. Stir in "M&M's"® Chocolate Mini Baking Bits; chill mixture an additional 1 hour.

Preheat oven to 350°F. Line cookie sheets with foil. With sugar-dusted hands, roll dough into 1-inch balls; roll balls in additional granulated sugar. Place about 2 inches apart onto prepared cookie sheets. Bake 10 to 12 minutes. Do not overbake. Cool completely on wire racks. Store in tightly covered container.   *Makes about 5 dozen cookies*

Hershey's "Perfectly Chocolate" Chocolate Chip Cookies

- 2¼ cups all-purpose flour
- ⅓ cup HERSHEY'S Cocoa
- 1 teaspoon baking soda
- ½ teaspoon salt
- 1 cup (2 sticks) butter or margarine, softened
- ¾ cup granulated sugar
- ¾ cup packed light brown sugar
- 1 teaspoon vanilla extract
- 2 eggs
- 2 cups (12-ounce package) HERSHEY'S Semi-Sweet Chocolate Chips
- 1 cup chopped nuts (optional)

1. Heat oven to 375°F.

2. Stir together flour, cocoa, baking soda and salt. Beat butter, granulated sugar, brown sugar and vanilla in large bowl on medium speed of mixer until creamy. Add eggs; beat well. Gradually add flour mixture, beating until well blended. Stir in chocolate chips and nuts, if desired. Drop by rounded teaspoons onto ungreased cookie sheets.

3. Bake 8 to 10 minutes or until set. Cool slightly; remove from cookie sheets to wire rack.   *Makes about 5 dozen cookies*

7 - 6 = 1　4 - 2 = 2　8 - 3 = 5

Dreamy Chocolate Chip Cookies

1¼ cups firmly packed brown sugar

¾ Butter Flavor CRISCO® Stick or ¾ cup Butter Flavor CRISCO® all-vegetable shortening

3 eggs, lightly beaten

2 teaspoons vanilla

1 (4-ounce) package German sweet chocolate, melted, cooled

3 cups all-purpose flour

1 teaspoon baking soda

½ teaspoon salt

1 (11½-ounce) package milk chocolate chips

1 (10-ounce) package premium semisweet chocolate chips

1 cup coarsely chopped macadamia nuts

1. Heat oven to 375°F. Place sheets of foil on countertop for cooling cookies.

2. Combine brown sugar, ¾ cup shortening, eggs and vanilla in large bowl. Beat at low speed of electric mixer until blended. Increase speed to high. Beat 2 minutes. Add melted chocolate. Mix until well blended.

3. Combine flour, baking soda and salt. Add gradually to shortening mixture at low speed.

4. Stir in chocolate chips and nuts with spoon. Drop by rounded tablespoonfuls 3 inches apart onto ungreased baking sheets.

5. Bake at 375°F for 9 to 11 minutes or until set. *Do not overbake.* Cool 2 minutes on baking sheets. Remove cookies to foil to cool completely.   *Makes about 3 dozen cookies*

7 - 6 = 1   4 - 2 = 2   8 - 3 = 5

Peanut Butter and Chocolate Spirals

1 package (20 ounces) refrigerated sugar cookie dough

1 package (20 ounces) refrigerated peanut butter cookie dough

¼ cup unsweetened cocoa powder

⅓ cup peanut butter-flavored chips, chopped

¼ cup all-purpose flour

⅓ cup miniature chocolate chips

1. Remove each dough from wrapper according to package directions.

2. Place sugar cookie dough and cocoa in large bowl; mix with fork to blend. Stir in peanut butter chips.

3. Place peanut butter cookie dough and flour in another large bowl; mix with fork to blend. Stir in chocolate chips. Divide each dough in half; cover and refrigerate 1 hour.

4. Roll each dough on floured surface to 12×6-inch rectangle. Layer each half of peanut butter dough onto each half of chocolate dough. Roll up doughs, starting at long end to form 2 (12-inch) rolls. Wrap in plastic wrap; refrigerate 1 hour.

5. Preheat oven to 375°F. Cut dough into ½-inch-thick slices. Place cookies 2 inches apart on ungreased cookie sheets.

6. Bake 10 to 12 minutes or until lightly browned. Remove to wire racks; cool completely.   *Makes 4 dozen cookies*

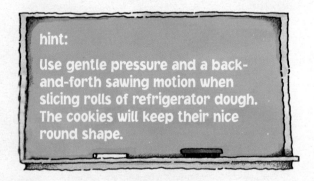

hint:

Use gentle pressure and a back-and-forth sawing motion when slicing rolls of refrigerator dough. The cookies will keep their nice round shape.

7 - 6 = 1   4 - 2 = 2   8 - 3 = 5

Hershey's Milk Chocolate Chip Giant Cookies

¼ cup plus 2 tablespoons butter, softened
½ cup granulated sugar
¼ cup packed light brown sugar
½ teaspoon vanilla extract
1 egg
1 cup all-purpose flour
½ teaspoon baking soda
2 cups (11½-ounce package) HERSHEY'S Milk Chocolate Chips
Frosting (optional)
Ice cream (optional)

1. Heat oven to 350°F. Line two 9-inch round baking pans with foil, extending foil over edges of pans.

2. Beat butter, granulated sugar, brown sugar and vanilla until fluffy. Add egg; beat well. Stir together flour and baking soda; gradually add to butter mixture, beating until well blended. Stir in milk chocolate chips. Spread one half of batter into each prepared pan, spreading to 1 inch from edge. (Cookies will spread to edge when baking.)

3. Bake 18 to 22 minutes or until lightly browned. Cool completely; carefully lift cookies from pans and remove foil. Frost, if desired. Cut each cookie into wedges; serve topped with scoop of ice cream, if desired. *Makes about 12 to 16 servings*

Tip: Bake cookies on the middle rack of the oven, one pan at a time. Uneven browning can occur if baking on more than one rack at the same time.

Hershey's Milk Chocolate Chip Giant Cookie

7 - 6 = 1   4 - 2 = 2   8 - 3 = 5

Colorific Chocolate Chip Cookies

   1 cup (2 sticks) butter or margarine, softened
   ⅔ cup granulated sugar
   ½ cup firmly packed light brown sugar
   1 large egg
   1 teaspoon vanilla extract
   2 cups all-purpose flour
   ¾ teaspoon baking soda
   ¾ teaspoon salt
   1¾ cups "M&M's"® Semi-Sweet Chocolate Mini Baking Bits
   ¾ cup chopped nuts, optional

Preheat oven to 375°F. In large bowl cream butter and sugars until light and fluffy; beat in egg and vanilla. In medium bowl combine flour, baking soda and salt; blend into creamed mixture. Stir in "M&M's"® Semi-Sweet Chocolate Mini Baking Bits and nuts, if desired. Drop by heaping tablespoonfuls about 2 inches apart onto ungreased cookie sheets. Bake 9 to 12 minutes or until lightly browned. Cool 1 minute on cookie sheets; cool completely on wire racks. Store in tightly covered container.   *Makes about 3 dozen cookies*

Hint: For chewy cookies bake 9 to 10 minutes; for crispy cookies bake 11 to 12 minutes.

Pan Cookie Variation: Prepare dough as directed; spread into lightly greased 15×10×1-inch jelly-roll pan. Bake at 375°F for 18 to 22 minutes. Cool completely before cutting into 35 (2-inch) squares. For a more festive look, reserve ½ cup baking bits to sprinkle on top of dough before baking.

Chocolate Chip Cookie Bars

1¼ cups firmly packed light brown sugar

¾ Butter Flavor CRISCO® Stick or ¾ cup Butter Flavor CRISCO® all-vegetable shortening plus additional for greasing

2 tablespoons milk

1 tablespoon vanilla

2 eggs

1¾ cups all-purpose flour

1 teaspoon salt

¾ teaspoon baking soda

1 cup (6 ounces) semisweet chocolate chips

1 cup coarsely chopped pecans* (optional)

*If pecans are omitted, add an additional ½ cup semisweet chocolate chips.

1. Heat oven to 350°F. Grease 13×9-inch baking pan. Place wire rack on countertop for cooling bars.

2. Combine brown sugar, ¾ cup shortening, milk and vanilla in large bowl. Beat at medium speed of electric mixer until well blended. Add eggs; beat well.

3. Combine flour, salt and baking soda. Add to shortening mixture; beat at low speed just until blended. Stir in chocolate chips and nuts, if desired.

4. Press dough evenly onto bottom of prepared pan.

5. Bake at 350°F for 20 to 25 minutes or until lightly browned and firm in the center. *Do not overbake.* Cool completely on cooling rack. Cut into 2×1½-inch bars.   *Makes about 3 dozen bars*

7 − 6 = 1   4 − 2 = 2   8 − 3 = 5

Bake Sale Treats

Ice Cream Cone Cupcakes

   1 package (18¼ ounces) white cake mix plus ingredients
      to prepare

   2 tablespoons nonpareils*

   2 packages (1¾ ounces each) flat-bottomed ice cream cones
      (about 24 cones)

   1 container (16 ounces) vanilla or chocolate frosting

   Candies and other decorations

Nonpareils are tiny, round, brightly colored sprinkles used for cake and cookie decorating.

1. Preheat oven to 350°F.

2. Prepare cake mix according to package directions. Stir in nonpareils.

3. Spoon ¼ cup batter into each ice cream cone.

4. Stand cones on cookie sheet. Bake cones until toothpick inserted into center of cake comes out clean, about 20 minutes. Cool on wire racks.

5. Frost each filled cone. Decorate as desired.

Makes 24 cupcakes

Note: Cupcakes are best served the day they are prepared. Store loosely covered.

Indian Corn

¼ cup butter or margarine

1 package (10.5 ounces) mini marshmallows

Yellow food coloring

8 cups peanut butter and chocolate puffed corn cereal

10 lollipop sticks

1 cup candy-coated chocolate pieces

Tan and green raffia

1. Line large baking sheet with waxed paper; set aside. Melt butter in large heavy saucepan over low heat. Add marshmallows; stir until melted and smooth. Tint with food coloring until desired shade is reached. Add cereal and ½ cup chocolate pieces; stir until evenly coated. Remove from heat.

2. With lightly greased hands, quickly divide mixture into 10 oblong pieces. Push lollipop stick halfway into each oblong piece; shape like ear of corn. Place on prepared baking sheet; press remaining ½ cup chocolate pieces into each "ear." Let treats set.

3. Tie or tape raffia to lollipop sticks to resemble corn husks.

Makes 10 servings

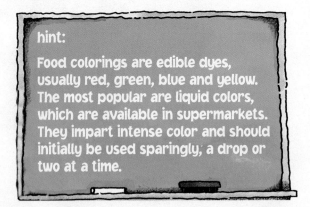

hint:

Food colorings are edible dyes, usually red, green, blue and yellow. The most popular are liquid colors, which are available in supermarkets. They impart intense color and should initially be used sparingly; a drop or two at a time.

Old-Fashioned Cake Doughnuts

3¾ cups all-purpose flour

1 tablespoon baking powder

1 teaspoon ground cinnamon

¾ teaspoon salt

½ teaspoon ground nutmeg

3 eggs

¾ cup granulated sugar

1 cup applesauce

2 tablespoons butter, melted

1 quart vegetable oil

2 cups sifted powdered sugar

3 tablespoons milk

½ teaspoon vanilla

Colored sprinkles (optional)

Combine flour, baking powder, cinnamon, salt and nutmeg in medium bowl. Beat eggs in large bowl with electric mixer at high speed until frothy. Gradually beat in granulated sugar. Continue beating at high speed 4 minutes until thick and lemon colored, scraping down side of bowl once. Reduce speed to low; beat in applesauce and butter.

Beat in flour mixture until well blended. Divide dough into halves. Place each half on large piece of plastic wrap. Pat each half into 5-inch square; wrap in plastic wrap. Refrigerate 3 hours or until well chilled.

To prepare glaze, stir together powdered sugar, milk and vanilla in small bowl until smooth. Cover; set aside.

Roll out 1 dough half to ⅜-inch thickness. Cut dough with floured 3-inch doughnut cutter; repeat with remaining dough. Reserve doughnut holes. Reroll scraps; cut dough again. Pour oil into large Dutch oven. Place deep-fry thermometer in oil. Heat oil over medium heat until thermometer registers 375°F. Adjust heat as necessary to maintain temperature at 375°F.

continued on page 48

White Chocolate Chunk Muffins

2½ cups all-purpose flour

1 cup packed light brown sugar

⅓ cup unsweetened cocoa powder

2 teaspoons baking soda

½ teaspoon salt

1⅓ cups buttermilk

¼ cup plus 2 tablespoons butter, melted

2 eggs, beaten

1½ teaspoons vanilla

1½ cups chopped white chocolate

Preheat oven to 400°F. Grease 12 (3½-inch) large muffin cups; set aside.

Combine flour, sugar, cocoa, baking soda and salt in large bowl. Combine buttermilk, butter, eggs and vanilla in small bowl until blended. Stir into flour mixture just until moistened. Fold in white chocolate. Spoon into prepared muffin cups, filling half full.

Bake 25 to 30 minutes or until toothpicks inserted into centers come out clean. Cool in pan on wire rack 5 minutes. Remove from pan. Cool on wire rack 10 minutes. Serve warm or cool completely.

Makes 12 large muffins

Yuletide Twisters

1 (6-ounce) package premier white baking bars
1 tablespoon plus 1 teaspoon fat-free (skim) milk
1 tablespoon plus 1 teaspoon light corn syrup
8 ounces reduced-salt pretzel twists (about 80)
   Cookie decorations, colored sugar or chocolate sprinkles

1. Line baking sheet with waxed paper; set aside.

2. Melt baking bars in small saucepan over low heat, stirring constantly. Stir in skim milk and corn syrup. Do not remove saucepan from heat.

3. Holding pretzel with fork, dip 1 side of each pretzel into melted mixture to coat. Place, coated side up, on prepared baking sheet; immediately sprinkle with desired decorations. Refrigerate until firm, 15 to 20 minutes.

Makes 10 servings

Chocolate Twisters: Substitute semisweet chocolate chips for premier white baking bars.

Caramel Dippity Do's: Heat 1 cup nonfat caramel sauce and ⅓ cup finely chopped pecans in small saucepan until warm. Pour into small serving bowl. Serve with pretzels for dipping. Makes 8 servings (about 2 tablespoons each).

Chocolate Dippity Do's: Heat 1 cup nonfat hot fudge sauce and ⅓ cup finely chopped pecans or walnuts in small saucepan until warm. Pour into small serving bowl. Serve with pretzels for dipping. Makes 8 servings.

Pretty Posies

1 package (20 ounces) refrigerated sugar cookie dough
Orange and blue or purple food colorings
1 tablespoon colored sprinkles

1. Remove dough from wrapper. Reserve ⅝ of dough. Combine remaining dough, orange food coloring and sprinkles in small bowl; beat at medium speed of electric mixer until well blended. Shape into 7½-inch log. Wrap in plastic wrap; refrigerate 30 minutes or until firm.

2. Combine reserved dough and blue food coloring in large bowl; beat at medium speed of electric mixer until well blended. Shape dough into disc. Wrap with plastic wrap and refrigerate 30 minutes or until firm.

3. Roll out blue dough on waxed paper to 7½×6-inch rectangle on sheet of waxed paper. Place orange log in center of rectangle. Fold blue edges up and around orange log; press seam together. Roll gently to form smooth log. Wrap waxed paper around dough and twist ends to secure. Freeze log 20 minutes.

4. Preheat oven to 350°F. Lightly grease cookie sheets. Remove waxed paper from dough log. Cut log into ¼-inch slices. Place 2 inches apart on prepared cookie sheets. Using 2½-inch flower-shaped cookie cutter, cut slices into flowers; remove and discard dough scraps.

5. Bake 15 to 17 minutes or until edges are lightly browned. Remove to wire rack; cool completely.   *Makes about 1½ dozen cookies*

Jack-O-Lantern Snacks

1 package (8 ounces) cream cheese, softened
Red and yellow food coloring
8 large slices dark pumpernickel bread
1 small green bell pepper
Sliced Genoa salami

1. Place cream cheese in small bowl. Add 8 drops red and 6 drops yellow food coloring to turn cream cheese orange. Mix well and adjust color as desired.

2. Toast bread and allow to cool. Using large pumpkin cookie cutter or metal 1-cup measure, cut round shape from each slice of toast leaving "stem" on top. Spread cream cheese over toast to edges. Cut "stems" from green pepper and place over stem on toast. Cut triangle "eyes" and mouth with several "teeth" from sliced salami. Arrange over each pumpkin toast. *Makes 8 servings*

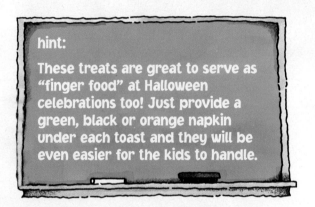

hint:

These treats are great to serve as "finger food" at Halloween celebrations too! Just provide a green, black or orange napkin under each toast and they will be even easier for the kids to handle.

Smushy Cookies

1 package (20 ounces) refrigerated cookie dough, any flavor

All-purpose flour (optional)

Fillings

Peanut butter, multi-colored miniature marshmallows, assorted colored sprinkles, chocolate-covered raisins and caramel candy squares

1. Preheat oven to 350°F. Grease cookie sheets.

2. Remove dough from wrapper according to package directions. Cut into 4 equal sections. Reserve 1 section; refrigerate remaining 3 sections.

3. Roll reserved dough to ¼-inch thickness. Sprinkle with flour to minimize sticking, if necessary. Cut out cookies using 2½-inch round cookie cutter. Transfer to prepared cookie sheets. Repeat with remaining dough, working with 1 section at a time.

4. Bake 8 to 11 minutes or until edges are light golden brown. Remove to wire racks; cool completely.

5. To make sandwich, spread about 1½ tablespoons peanut butter on underside of 1 cookie to within ¼ inch of edge. Sprinkle with miniature marshmallows, sprinkles and candy pieces. Top with second cookie, pressing gently. Repeat with remaining cookies and fillings.

6. Just before serving, place sandwiches on paper towels. Microwave at HIGH 15 to 25 seconds or until fillings become soft.

Makes about 8 to 10 sandwich cookies

Tip: Invite the neighbor kids over on a rainy day to make these fun Smushy Cookies. Be sure to have lots of filling choices available so each child can create their own unique cookies.

Chocolate Bunny Cookies

1 (21-ounce) package DUNCAN HINES® Family-Style
   Chewy Fudge Brownie Mix

1 egg

¼ cup water

¼ cup vegetable oil

1⅓ cups pecan halves (96)

1 container DUNCAN HINES® Creamy Home-Style Dark
   Chocolate Fudge Frosting

White chocolate chips

1. Preheat oven to 350°F. Grease baking sheets.

2. Combine brownie mix, egg, water and oil in large bowl. Stir with spoon until well blended, about 50 strokes. Drop by level tablespoonfuls 2 inches apart on greased baking sheets. Place two pecan halves, flat-side up, on each cookie for ears. Bake at 350°F for 10 to 12 minutes or until set. Cool 2 minutes on baking sheets. Remove to cooling racks. Cool completely.

3. Spread Dark Chocolate Fudge frosting on one cookie. Place white chocolate chips, upside down, on frosting for eyes and nose. Dot each eye with frosting using toothpick. Repeat for remaining cookies. Allow frosting to set before storing cookies between layers of waxed paper in airtight container.

Makes 4 dozen cookies

Tip: For variety, frost cookies with Duncan Hines® Vanilla Frosting and use semisweet chocolate chips for the eyes and noses.

Snack Time

Dipped, Drizzled & Decorated Pretzels

**1 bag chocolate or flavored chips (choose semisweet,
    bittersweet, milk chocolate, green mint, white chocolate,
    butterscotch, peanut butter or a combination)**

1 bag pretzel rods

**Assorted toppings: jimmies, sprinkles, chopped nuts,
    coconut, toasted coconut, cookie crumbs, colored sugars
    (optional)**

Microwave Directions

1. Place chips in microwavable bowl. (Be sure bowl and utensils are completely dry.) Cover with plastic wrap and turn back one corner to vent. Microwave at HIGH for 1 minute; stir. Return to microwave and continue cooking in 30-second intervals until chips are completely melted. Check and stir frequently.

2. Dip one half of each pretzel rod into melted chocolate and decorate, if desired. Roll coated end of several pretzels in toppings. Drizzle others with contrasting color/flavor melted chips. (Drizzle melted chocolate out of spoon while rotating pretzel, to get even coverage.)

3. Place decorated pretzels on cooling rack; set over baking sheet lined with waxed-paper. Let coating harden completely. Do not refrigerate.   *Makes about 2 dozen pretzels*

Super Spread Sandwich Stars

1 Red or Golden Delicious apple, peeled, cored and coarsely chopped

1 cup roasted peanuts

⅓ cup honey

1 tablespoon lemon juice

1 teaspoon ground cinnamon

Sliced sandwich bread

For Super Spread, place chopped apple, peanuts, honey, lemon juice and cinnamon in food processor or blender. Pulse food processor several times until ingredients start to blend, occasionally scraping down the sides with rubber spatula. Process 1 to 2 minutes until mixture is smooth and spreadable.

For Sandwich Stars, use butter knife to spread about 1 tablespoon Super Spread on 2 slices of bread. Stack them together, spread side up. Top with third slice bread. Place cookie cutter on top of sandwich; press down firmly and evenly. Leaving cookie cutter in place, remove excess trimmings with your fingers or a butter knife. Remove cookie cutter. *Makes 1¼ cups spread (enough for about 10 sandwiches)*

Favorite recipe from **Texas Peanut Producers Board**

 duck

 bird

 pig

Quick S'Mores

1 whole graham cracker
1 large marshmallow
1 teaspoon hot fudge sauce

1. Break graham cracker in half crosswise. Place one half on small paper plate or microwavable plate; top with marshmallow.

2. Spread remaining ½ of cracker with fudge sauce.

3. Place cracker with marshmallow in microwave. Microwave at HIGH 12 to 14 seconds or until marshmallow puffs up. Immediately place remaining cracker, fudge side down, over marshmallow. Press crackers gently to even out marshmallow layer. Cool completely.

Makes 1 serving

hint:

S'mores can be made the night before and wrapped in plastic wrap or sealed in a small plastic food storage bag. Store at room temperature until ready to pack in your child's lunch box the next morning.

 duck bird  pig

Take-Along Snack Mix

   1 tablespoon butter or margarine

   2 tablespoons honey

   1 cup toasted oat cereal, any flavor

   ½ cup coarsely broken pecans

   ½ cup thin pretzel sticks, broken in half

   ½ cup raisins

   1 cup "M&M's"® Chocolate Mini Baking Bits

In large heavy skillet over low heat, melt butter; add honey and stir until blended. Add cereal, nuts, pretzels and raisins, stirring until all pieces are evenly coated. Continue cooking over low heat about 10 minutes, stirring frequently. Remove from heat; immediately spread on waxed paper until cool. Add "M&M's"® Chocolate Mini Baking Bits. Store in tightly covered container.

Makes about 3½ cups

 duck  bird  pig

Caramel Popcorn Balls

16 cups plain popped popcorn (do not use buttered popcorn)
1 package (14 ounces) caramels, unwrapped
¼ cup butter
    Pinch of salt
1⅔ cups shredded coconut
1 package (12 ounces) semisweet chocolate chips
10 to 12 lollipop sticks
    Halloween sprinkles and decorations (optional)

1. Place popcorn in large bowl.

2. Place caramels and butter in medium saucepan over low heat. Cook and stir until caramels and butter are melted and smooth, about 5 minutes. Stir in salt and coconut. Remove caramel mixture from heat; pour over popcorn. With large wooden spoon, mix until popcorn is evenly coated. Let cool slightly.

3. Place chocolate chips in microwavable bowl. Microwave at HIGH 1 minute; stir. Microwave at HIGH for additional 30-second intervals until chips are completely melted, stirring after each 30-second interval. Stir until smooth.

4. When popcorn mixture is cool enough to handle, grease hands with butter or nonstick cooking spray. Shape popcorn mixture into baseball-sized balls; place 1 lollipop stick in each ball. Dip each popcorn ball into melted chocolate and roll in Halloween decorations, if desired. Place on waxed paper until chocolate is set.

Makes 10 to 12 balls

Variation: Pour melted chocolate over caramel popcorn mixture; mix by hand until popcorn is coated with chocolate. Spread evenly on baking sheet lined with waxed paper until chocolate is set.

 bunny  doggy  kitty cat

Soft Pretzels

**1 package (16 ounces) hot roll mix plus ingredients
to prepare mix**
1 egg white
2 teaspoons water
2 tablespoons *each* **assorted coatings: coarse salt, sesame
seeds, poppy seeds, dried oregano leaves**

1. Prepare hot roll mix according to package directions.

2. Preheat oven to 375°F. Spray baking sheets with nonstick cooking spray; set aside.

3. Divide dough equally into 16 pieces; roll each piece with hands to form rope, 7 to 10 inches long. Place on prepared cookie sheets; form into desired shape (hearts, wreaths, pretzels, snails, loops, etc.).

4. Beat egg white and water in small bowl until foamy. Brush onto dough shapes; sprinkle each shape with 1½ teaspoons of one coating.

5. Bake until golden brown, about 15 minutes. Serve warm or at room temperature. *Makes 16 servings*

Fruit Twists: Omit coatings. Prepare dough and roll into ropes as directed. Place ropes on lightly floured surface. Roll out, or pat, each rope into rectangle, ¼ inch thick; brush each rectangle with about 1 teaspoon spreadable fruit or preserves. Fold each rectangle lengthwise in half; twist into desired shape. Bake as directed.

Cheese Twists: Omit coatings. Prepare dough and roll into ropes as directed. Place ropes on lightly floured surface. Roll out, or pat, each rope into rectangle, ¼ inch thick. Sprinkle each rectangle with about 1 tablespoon shredded Cheddar or other flavor cheese. Fold each rectangle lengthwise in half; twist into desired shape. Bake as directed.

 duck  bird  pig

Cinnamon Apple Chips

2 cups unsweetened apple juice

1 cinnamon stick

2 Washington Red Delicious apples

1. In large skillet or saucepan, combine apple juice and cinnamon stick; bring to a low boil while preparing apples.

2. With paring knife, slice off ½ inch from tops and bottoms of apples and discard (or eat). Stand apples on either cut end; cut crosswise into ⅛-inch-thick slices, rotating apple as necessary to cut even slices.

3. Drop slices into boiling juice; cook 4 to 5 minutes or until slices appear translucent and lightly golden. Meanwhile, preheat oven to 250°F.

4. With slotted spatula, remove apple slices from juice and pat dry. Arrange slices on wire racks, being sure none overlap. Place racks on middle shelf in oven; bake 30 to 40 minutes until slices are lightly browned and almost dry to touch. Let chips cool on racks completely before storing in airtight container. *Makes about 40 chips*

Tip: There is no need to core apples because boiling in juice for several minutes softens core and removes seeds.

Favorite recipe from **Washington Apple Commission**

Cinnamon Apple Chips

 duck  bird  pig

Perfect Pita Pizzas

    2 whole wheat or white pita bread rounds
    ½ cup spaghetti or pizza sauce
    ¾ cup (3 ounces) shredded part-skim mozzarella cheese
    1 small zucchini, sliced ¼ inch thick
    ½ small carrot, peeled and sliced
    2 cherry tomatoes, halved
    ¼ small green bell pepper, sliced

1. Preheat oven to 375°F. Line baking sheet with foil; set aside.

2. Using small scissors, carefully split each pita bread round around edge; separate to form 2 rounds.

3. Place rounds, rough sides up, on prepared baking sheet. Bake 5 minutes.

4. Spread 2 tablespoons spaghetti sauce onto each round; sprinkle with cheese. Decorate with vegetables to create faces. Bake 10 to 12 minutes or until cheese melts.   *Makes 4 servings*

Pepperoni Pita Pizzas: Prepare pita rounds, partially bake, and top with spaghetti sauce and cheese as directed. Place 2 small pepperoni slices on each pizza for eyes. Decorate with cut-up fresh vegetables for rest of face. Continue to bake as directed.

 bunny  doggy  kitty cat

S'Mores on a Stick

    **1 (14-ounce) can EAGLE BRAND® Sweetened Condensed Milk
(NOT evaporated milk), divided**

1½ cups milk chocolate mini chips, divided

    1 cup miniature marshmallows

11 whole graham crackers, halved crosswise

    **Toppings: chopped peanuts, mini candy-coated chocolate
pieces, sprinkles**

1. Microwave half of Eagle Brand in microwave-safe bowl at HIGH
(100% power) 1½ minutes. Stir in 1 cup chips until smooth; stir in
marshmallows.

2. Spread chocolate mixture evenly by heaping tablespoonfuls onto
11 graham cracker halves. Top with remaining graham cracker
halves; place on waxed paper.

3. Microwave remaining Eagle Brand at HIGH (100% power)
1½ minutes; stir in remaining ½ cup chips, stirring until smooth.
Drizzle mixture over cookies and sprinkle with desired toppings.

4. Let stand for 2 hours; insert a wooden craft stick into center of
each cookie.   *Makes 11 servings*

Prep Time: 10 minutes
Cook Time: 3 minutes

S'Mores on a Stick

Caramel Corn Apple-O's

   7 cups popped butter-flavor microwave popcorn

2¼ cups apple cinnamon cereal rings

   ½ cup chopped dried apples or apricots

   ¼ cup chopped nuts (optional)

   1 package (14 ounces) caramels, unwrapped

   1 to 2 tablespoons water*

   2 tablespoons butter or margarine

      Long cinnamon sticks or wooden craft sticks (optional)

Start with 1 tablespoon water and add more if needed for consistency. Fresher caramels will require less water.

1. Combine popcorn, cereal, apples and nuts, if desired, in large bowl.

2. Microwave caramels, water and butter at HIGH 2½ to 3 minutes, stirring at 1 minute intervals until melted and smooth.

3. Pour caramel over popcorn mixture, tossing with buttered wooden spoon to coat. Let set until just slightly warm.

4. Dampen hands and shape mixture into 8 balls. Shape balls around sticks, if desired. Place on lightly buttered waxed paper until ready to serve.

Makes 8 balls

 duck bird  pig

Bar-o-metrics

Crispy Rice Squares

3 tablespoons Dried Plum Purée (recipe follows) or prepared dried plum butter

1 tablespoon butter or margarine

1 package (10 ounces) marshmallows

6 cups crisp rice cereal

Colored nonpareils

Coat 13×9-inch baking pan with vegetable cooking spray. Heat Dried Plum Purée and butter in Dutch oven or large saucepan over low heat, stirring until butter is melted. Add marshmallows; stir until completely melted. Remove from heat. Stir in cereal until well coated. Spray back of wooden spoon with vegetable cooking spray and pat mixture evenly into prepared pan. Sprinkle with nonpareils. Cool until set. Cut into squares.

Makes 24 squares

Dried Plum Purée: Combine 1⅓ cups (8 ounces) pitted dried plums and ¼ cup plus 2 tablespoons hot water in container of food processor or blender. Pulse on and off until dried plums are finely chopped and smooth. Store leftovers in a covered container in the refrigerator for up to two months. Makes 1 cup.

Favorite recipe from **California Dried Plum Board**

"Everything but the Kitchen Sink" Bar Cookies

- 1 package (18 ounces) refrigerated chocolate chip cookie dough
- 1 jar (7 ounces) marshmallow creme
- ½ cup creamy peanut butter
- 1½ cups toasted corn cereal
- ½ cup miniature candy-coated chocolate pieces

1. Preheat oven to 350°F. Grease 13×9-inch baking pan. Remove dough from wrapper according to package directions.

2. Press dough into prepared baking pan. Bake 13 minutes.

3. Remove baking pan from oven. Drop teaspoonfuls of marshmallow creme and peanut butter over hot cookie base.

4. Bake 1 minute. Carefully spread marshmallow creme and peanut butter over cookie base.

5. Sprinkle cereal and chocolate pieces over melted marshmallow and peanut butter mixture.

6. Bake 7 minutes. Cool completely on wire rack. Cut into 2-inch bars.

Makes 3 dozen bars

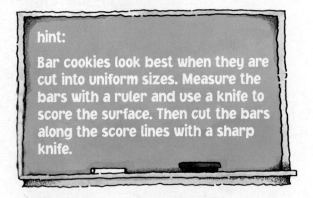

hint:

Bar cookies look best when they are cut into uniform sizes. Measure the bars with a ruler and use a knife to score the surface. Then cut the bars along the score lines with a sharp knife.

Peanut Butter and Jelly Crispies

½ Butter Flavor CRISCO® Stick or ½ cup Butter Flavor CRISCO® all-vegetable shortening plus additional for greasing

½ cup JIF® Crunchy Peanut Butter

½ cup granulated sugar

½ cup firmly packed light brown sugar

1 egg

1¼ cups all-purpose flour

½ teaspoon baking powder

½ teaspoon baking soda

¼ teaspoon salt

2 cups crisp rice cereal

Honey roasted peanuts, finely chopped (optional)

SMUCKER'S® Jelly, any flavor

1. Heat oven to 375°F. Grease 13×9×2-inch pan with shortening. Place wire rack on countertop for cooling bars.

2. Combine ½ cup shortening, peanut butter, granulated sugar and brown sugar in large bowl. Beat at medium speed of electric mixer until well blended. Beat in egg.

3. Combine flour, baking powder, baking soda and salt. Add gradually to creamed mixture at low speed. Beat until well blended. Add cereal. Mix just until blended. Press into greased pan. Sprinkle with nuts, if desired.

4. Score dough into bars about 2¼×2 inches. Press thumb in center of each. Fill indentation with ¼ to ½ teaspoon jelly.

5. Bake at 375°F for 12 to 15 minutes or until golden brown. *Do not overbake.* Remove pan to wire rack. Cool 2 to 3 minutes. Cut into bars. Cool completely. *Makes about 2 dozen bars*

Irish Flag Cookies

1½ cups all-purpose flour

1 teaspoon baking powder

½ teaspoon salt

¾ cup granulated sugar

¾ cup light brown sugar

½ cup (1 stick) butter, softened

2 eggs

2 teaspoons vanilla

1 package (12 ounces) semisweet chocolate chips

Prepared white frosting

Green and orange food coloring

1. Preheat oven to 350°F. Grease 13×9-inch baking pan. Combine flour, baking powder and salt in small bowl; set aside.

2. Beat granulated sugar, brown sugar and butter in large bowl with electric mixer at medium speed until light and fluffy. Beat in eggs and vanilla. Add flour mixture. Beat at low speed until well blended. Stir in chocolate chips. Spread batter evenly into prepared pan. Bake 25 to 30 minutes or until golden brown. Remove pan to wire rack; cool completely. Cut into 3¼×1½-inch bars.

3. Divide frosting among 3 small bowls. Tint 1 with orange food coloring and 1 with green food coloring. Leave remaining frosting white. Frost individual cookies as shown in photo.

Makes 2 dozen cookies

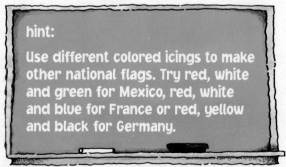

hint:

Use different colored icings to make other national flags. Try red, white and green for Mexico, red, white and blue for France or red, yellow and black for Germany.

Irish Flag Cookies

Yuletide Linzer Bars

1⅓ cups butter, softened

¾ cup sugar

1 egg

1 teaspoon grated lemon peel

2½ cups all-purpose flour

1½ cups whole almonds, ground

1 teaspoon ground cinnamon

¾ cup raspberry preserves

Powdered sugar

Preheat oven to 350°F. Grease 13×9-inch baking pan.

Beat butter and sugar in large bowl at medium speed of electric mixer until creamy. Beat in egg and lemon peel until blended. Mix in flour, almonds and cinnamon until well blended.

Press 2 cups dough onto bottom of prepared pan. Spread preserves over crust. Press remaining dough, a small amount at a time, evenly over preserves.

Bake 35 to 40 minutes until golden brown. Cool in pan on wire rack. Sprinkle with powdered sugar; cut into bars.   *Makes 36 bars*

Candy Bar Bars

¾ cup (1½ sticks) butter or margarine, softened

¼ cup peanut butter

1 cup firmly packed light brown sugar

1 teaspoon baking soda

2 cups quick-cooking oats

1½ cups all-purpose flour

1 egg

1 (14-ounce) can EAGLE BRAND® Sweetened Condensed Milk
(NOT evaporated milk)

4 cups chopped candy bars (such as chocolate-covered
caramel-topped nougat bars with peanuts, chocolate-
covered crisp wafers, chocolate-covered caramel-topped
cookie bars, or chocolate-covered peanut butter cups)

1. Preheat oven to 350°F. In large mixing bowl, combine butter and peanut butter. Add brown sugar and baking soda; beat well. Stir in oats and flour. Reserve 1¾ cups crumb mixture.

2. Stir egg into remaining crumb mixture; press firmly on bottom of ungreased 15×10×1-inch baking pan. Bake 15 minutes.

3. Pour Eagle Brand evenly over baked crust. Stir together reserved crumb mixture and candy bar pieces; sprinkle evenly over top. Bake 25 minutes or until golden. Cool. Cut into bars. Store covered at room temperature.

Makes 4 dozen bars

Prep Time: 20 minutes
Bake Time: 40 minutes

Rocky Road Bars

**2 cups (12-ounce package) NESTLÉ® TOLL HOUSE®
Semi-Sweet Chocolate Morsels, *divided***

1½ **cups all-purpose flour**

1½ **teaspoons baking powder**

1 **cup granulated sugar**

¼ **cup plus 2 tablespoons (¾ stick) butter or margarine,
softened**

1½ **teaspoons vanilla extract**

2 **large eggs**

2 **cups miniature marshmallows**

1½ **cups coarsely chopped walnuts**

PREHEAT oven to 375°F. Grease 13×9-inch baking pan.

MICROWAVE *1 cup* morsels in medium, uncovered, microwave-safe
bowl on HIGH (100%) power for 1 minute. STIR. Morsels may retain
some of their original shape. If necessary, microwave at additional
10- to 15-second intervals, stirring just until morsels are melted. Cool
to room temperature. Combine flour and baking powder in small bowl.

BEAT sugar, butter and vanilla in large mixer bowl until crumbly.
Beat in eggs. Add melted chocolate; beat until smooth. Gradually
beat in flour mixture. Spread batter into prepared baking pan.

BAKE for 16 to 20 minutes or until wooden pick inserted in center
comes out slightly sticky.

REMOVE from oven; sprinkle immediately with marshmallows,
nuts and *remaining* morsels. Return to oven for 2 minutes or just
until marshmallows begin to melt. Cool in pan on wire rack for
20 to 30 minutes. Cut into bars with wet knife. Serve warm.

Makes 2½ dozen bars

Acknowledgments

**The publisher would like to thank the
companies and organizations listed
below for the use of their recipes
and photographs in this publication.**

California Dried Plum Board

Duncan Hines® and Moist Deluxe® are registered
trademarks of Aurora Foods Inc.

Eagle Brand®

Hershey Foods Corporation

© Mars, Incorporated 2004

Nestlé USA

The J.M. Smucker Company

Texas Peanut Producers Board

Washington Apple Commission

Index

METRIC CONVERSION CHART

VOLUME MEASUREMENTS (dry)

1/8 teaspoon = 0.5 mL

1/4 teaspoon = 1 mL

1/2 teaspoon = 2 mL

3/4 teaspoon = 4 mL

1 teaspoon = 5 mL

1 tablespoon = 15 mL

2 tablespoons = 30 mL

1/4 cup = 60 mL

1/3 cup = 75 mL

1/2 cup = 125 mL

2/3 cup = 150 mL

3/4 cup = 175 mL

1 cup = 250 mL

2 cups = 1 pint = 500 mL

3 cups = 750 mL

4 cups = 1 quart = 1 L

VOLUME MEASUREMENTS (fluid)

1 fluid ounce (2 tablespoons) = 30 mL

4 fluid ounces (1/2 cup) = 125 mL

8 fluid ounces (1 cup) = 250 mL

12 fluid ounces (1 1/2 cups) = 375 mL

16 fluid ounces (2 cups) = 500 mL

WEIGHTS (mass)

1/2 ounce = 15 g

1 ounce = 30 g

3 ounces = 90 g

4 ounces = 120 g

8 ounces = 225 g

10 ounces = 285 g

12 ounces = 360 g

16 ounces = 1 pound = 450 g

DIMENSIONS

1/16 inch = 2 mm

1/8 inch = 3 mm

1/4 inch = 6 mm

1/2 inch = 1.5 cm

3/4 inch = 2 cm

1 inch = 2.5 cm

OVEN TEMPERATURES

250°F = 120°C

275°F = 140°C

300°F = 150°C

325°F = 160°C

350°F = 180°C

375°F = 190°C

400°F = 200°C

425°F = 220°C

450°F = 230°C

BAKING PAN SIZES

Utensil	Size in Inches/ Quarts	Metric Volume	Size in Centimeters
Baking or Cake Pan (square or rectangular)	8×8×2	2 L	20×20×5
	9×9×2	2.5 L	23×23×5
	12×8×2	3 L	30×20×5
	13×9×2	3.5 L	33×23×5
Loaf Pan	8×4×3	1.5 L	20×10×7
	9×5×3	2 L	23×13×7
Round Layer Cake Pan	8×1½	1.2 L	20×4
	9×1½	1.5 L	23×4
Pie Plate	8×1¼	750 mL	20×3
	9×1¼	1 L	23×3
Baking Dish or Casserole	1 quart	1 L	—
	1½ quart	1.5 L	—
	2 quart	2 L	—

KIDS' FAVORITE
Classroom Treats

Relax! No need to worry the next time your child comes home from school with news of another classroom party or bake sale fundraiser.

Kids' Favorite Classroom Treats puts over forty great kid-friendly recipes at your fingertips. From holiday specials and snacktime treats to bar cookies and chippers, there are plenty of choices for every occasion throughout the school year.

Manufactured in China.

72406

ISBN 1-4127-2406-6

Publications International, Ltd.
Lincolnwood, IL 60712

PEARSON
INTRAVENOUS DRUG GUIDE
2009-2010

Billie Ann Wilson, RN, PhD

Professor Emerita
School of Nursing
Loyola University New Orleans
New Orleans, Louisiana

Margaret T. Shannon, RN, PhD

Professor Emerita of Nursing
Our Lady of Holy Cross College
New Orleans, Louisiana

Kelly M. Shields, PharmD

Assistant Professor of Pharmacy Practice
Director of Drug Information Center
Raabe College of Pharmacy
Ohio Northern University
Ada, Ohio

PEARSON

Upper Saddle River, New Jersey 07458

Library of Congress Cataloging-in-Publication Data

Wilson, Billie Ann.
  Pearson intravenous drug guide 2009-2010 / Billie Ann Wilson, Margaret
T. Shannon, Kelly M. Shields.
     p. ; cm.
  Includes bibliographical references and index.
  ISBN-13: 978-0-13-114520-7
  1. Injections, Intravenous--Handbooks, manuals, etc. 2.
Drugs--Handbooks, manuals, etc.
    [DNLM: 1. Infusions, Intravenous--Handbooks. 2. Pharmaceutical
Preparations--administration & dosage--Handbooks. QV 735 W746p 2009]
I. Title: Intravenous drug guide 2009-2010. II. Shannon, Margaret T.
III. Shields, Kelly M. IV. Title.
  RM170.W555 2009
  615'.6--dc22

                                        2008018817

Notice: The authors and the publisher of this volume have taken care to
make certain that the doses of drugs and schedules of treatment are correct and compatible with the standards generally accepted at the time of
publication. Nevertheless, as new information becomes available,
changes in treatment and in the use of drugs become necessary. The
reader is advised to carefully consult the instruction and information
material included in the package insert of each drug or therapeutic
agent before administration. This advice is especially important when
using, administering, or recommending new and infrequently used
drugs. The authors and publisher disclaim all responsibility for any liability, loss, injury, or damage incurred as a consequence, directly or indirectly, of the use and application of any of the contents of this volume.

Pearson Education Ltd., London
Pearson Education Singapore, Pte. Ltd.
Pearson Education Canada, Inc., Toronto
Pearson Education—Japan
Pearson Education Australia PTY, Limited
Pearson Education North Asia Ltd., Hong Kong
Pearson Educación de Mexico, S.A. de C.V.
Pearson Education Malaysia, Pte. Ltd.
Pearson Education, Upper Saddle River, New Jersey

Pearson® is a registered trademark of Pearson plc

PRINTED IN THE UNITED STATES OF AMERICA

10   9   8   7   6   5   4   3   2   1

ISBN-10: 0-13-114520-7
ISBN-13: 978-0-13-114520-7

CONTENTS

To

Alvin, Theresa, Ellen, and

Michael, Rick, Kris, and Leah

without whom this work would not have been possible

◆

EDITORIAL REVIEW PANEL

We wish to thank the following individuals for conducting thorough reviews of the drug information in this book for its accuracy, currency, relevance, presentation, accessibility, and use. Their feedback guided us in developing a better book for nurses.

Vicki Jo Sodermark, RN, MSN
Nursing Instructor
Metropolitan Community College
Omaha, NE

Mary Lou Lerma, RN, MSN, CNS
Former Nursing Instructor
University of the Incarnate Word
School of Nursing and Health Professions
San Antonio, TX

Barbara Wilder, DSN, CRNP
Associate Professor
Auburn University School of Nursing
Auburn, AL

PREFACE

Pearson Intravenous Drug Guide 2009–2010 is a current and reliable reference designed to provide comprehensive information needed to make appropriate decisions regarding drug administration. The authors recognize that the decision-making process related to drug administration is a cyclical one. For example, assessments are made both prior to and after drug administration. Thus, nursing diagnoses and interventions may change as a result of an *achieved therapeutic effect, therapeutic failure, manifestation of an adverse effect,* or *demonstration of a learning need.* The authors believe that the users of this drug reference will find that the clear and logical design of the IV drug monographs facilitates decision making and supports the nursing process.

Pearson Intravenous Drug Guide 2009–2010 highlights the critical information nurses need to know in a convenient, easy-to-access format. The goal of the authors is to help nurses:

- find information on dosages, rates of administration, and solution preparation based on age or weight easily;
- access critical dosage adjustment by age, disease, or side effect;
- and provide safe, effective nursing care with clear guidelines for assessment and patient and family teaching.

ORGANIZATION

In this IV drug guide, all drugs are listed alphabetically according to their generic names. Pharmacological classifications are paired with therapeutic classifications for every drug monograph for ease of use by nurse clinicians and students alike. Trade names followed by a maple leaf indicate that brand of the drug is available only in Canada. Each drug is indexed by both its generic and trade names in the back of the guide to make it easier for the user to locate individual drug monographs.

Classifications and Prototype Drugs

The classifications used in this book are based on the system used by the American Hospital Formulary Service (AHFS). This book further classifies drugs by therapeutic uses, enabling the nurse to identify drugs in the same class that have similar indications for use. Thus, the book provides a framework for understanding how drugs in a given class are used in clinical practice. The pharmacologic classification appears immediately after the **Classifications** heading, followed by the

Therapeutic classification. Furthermore, the **Therapeutic Classifications** aid the nurse in assessing and monitoring to evaluate the therapuetic effectiveness of the drug. In general, all drugs in a class will have similar actions, uses, adverse effects, and nursing implications. Therefore, we have selected certain drugs that are representative of a classification or its subclassification—prototype drugs—to aid the nurse in understanding the classification of drugs. Throughout the book, prototype drug monographs are identified with a small icon. The user can refer to the prototype drug to develop a better understanding of drugs that belong within the same classification or subclassification. When a

drug belongs to a classification that has a designated prototype drug, that prototype is identified directly below the therapeutic classification. The table on pages xv–xviii outlines the classification scheme and lists the drug prototype considered to be representative of each class. All prototype drugs are highlighted in bold type in the index for quick identification. Finally, not every drug has a prototype.

AMIODARONE HYDROCHLORIDE

(a-mee´oh-da-rone)

Cordarone

Classification(s): ANTIARRHYTHMIC, CLASS III

Therapeutic: ANTIARRHYTHMIC

Pregnancy Category: D

Pregnancy Category

Drugs may be described as category A, B, C, D, or X according to the risk–benefit ratio for the mother and the fetus, with A being the lowest and X the highest risk. If the FDA pregnancy category is known, it is indicated after the classifications and prototype in each monograph. Refer to *Appendix B, FDA Pregnancy Categories*, for a more complete description of each category.

Controlled Substances

In the United States, controlled substances, such as narcotics, are classified as belonging to one of five Schedules (I to V) according to abuse potential. Schedule I has the highest and Schedule V has the lowest potential for abuse. Refer to *Appendix A, U.S. Schedules of Controlled Substances*, for a more complete description of each schedule.

Uses and Unlabeled Uses

The therapeutic applications of each drug are described in terms of approved, FDA-labeled uses and unlabeled uses. Although currently supported by medical literature, unlabeled uses are those that are not currently approved by the FDA. The unlabeled use is, nevertheless, an accepted use for the drug.

USES Prophylaxis and treatment of life-threatening ventricular arrhythmias and supraventricular arrhythmias, particularly with atrial fibrillation.
UNLABELED USES Conversion of atrial fibrillation to normal sinus rhythm, paroxysmal supraventricular tachycardia, AV nodal reentry tachycardia.

Indication & Dosage

Dosages are listed according to indication or labeled use. One of the hallmarks of this drug guide is the comprehensive dosage information it provides. The guide includes adult, geriatric, and pediatric dosages, as well as dosages for neonates and infants as available from the manufacturer. This section also indicates dosage adjustments for renal impairment (based on creatinine clearance), patients undergoing hemodialysis, hepatic impairment, drug toxicity, and obese patients whenever applicable.

INDICATION & DOSAGE

Symptomatic HIV Infection
Adult: 1–2 mg/kg q4h (1200 mg/day)

Prevention of Maternal–Fetal Transmission
Neonate (over 34 weeks gestation): 1.5 mg/kg q6h × 6 weeks, beginning 8–12 h after birth
Maternal: During labor 2 mg/kg/h loading dose then 1 mg/kg/h until clamping of umbilical cord

Renal Impairment Dosage Adjustment
CrCl less than 15 mL/min: Reduce dose by 50%

Toxicity Dosage Adjustment
Hemoglobin Falls Below 7.5 g/dL or Falls 25% from Baseline: Interrupt therapy
ANC Falls Below 750 Cells/mm³ or Decreases 50% from Baseline: Interrupt therapy

---

Solution Preparation

When **Solution Preparation** differs based on age or weight, specific instructions are provided in these sections.

SOLUTION PREPARATION
- Add contents of 500 mg vial to 100 or 200 mL D5W, NS, D5NS, LR or other compatible solution.
- *Pediatric Patients:* Volume of diluent depends on patient's fluid tolerance. Note that a pediatric injection preparation of 50 mg/mL is available.
- Maximum Concentration: 10 mg/mL
- Note: Color of solution may vary from colorless to light straw color or very pale yellow.

Administration

Drug administration is an important primary role for the nurse. The **Administration** section provides users with comprehensive instructions on how to administer direct, intermittent, and continuous IV medications. Subheadings by age groups are provided, as available from the manufacturer, adding to the ease of locating information by age.

ADMINISTRATION

HIV Infection
- **Intermittent Infusion:** Give calculated dose at a constant rate over 60 min; avoid rapid infusion.

Prevention of Maternal–Fetal Transmission
- *Mother:* Give loading dose over 1 h then continuous infusion at 1 mg/kg/h.
- *Neonate:* Give intermittent infusion at a constant rate over 30 min.

Incompatibilities

This guide provides **Solution/Additive** and **Y-Site** incompatibility for every monograph, where appropriate, to indicate which drugs and solutions should not be mixed with the intravenous drug. This is crucial information for drug administration. Additionally, a *Common Drug IV-Site Compatibility Chart* is located on the last pages of the book.

INCOMPATIBILITIES Solution/additive: Aminophylline, cefamandole, cefazolin, furosemide, quinidine. Y-site: **Aminophylline, ampicillin/sulbactam, argatroban, bivalirudin, cefamandole, cefazolin, ceftazidime, digoxin, drotrecogin, heparin, imipenem/cilastatin, magnesium sulfate, piperacillin, piperacillin/tazobactam, potassium phosphate, sodium bicarbonate, sodium nitroprusside, sodium phosphate.**

Action & *Therapeutic Effect*

Each monograph describes the mechanism by which the specific drug produces physiologic and biochemical changes at the cellular, tissue, and/or organ levels. This information helps the user understand how the drug works in the body and makes it easier to learn its side effects and cautious uses. The *therapeutic effects*, which are set in italics for maximum clarity and ease of use, are the reasons why a drug is prescribed. Therapeutic effectiveness of the drug can be determined by monitoring improvement in the condition for which the drug is prescribed.

> **ACTION & *THERAPEUTIC EFFECT*** Class III antiarrhythmic that also has antianginal and antiadrenergic properties. It acts directly on all cardiac tissues by prolonging duration of action potential and refractory period of cardiac muscle without significantly affecting its resting membrane potential. *By direct action on smooth muscle, it decreases peripheral resistance and increases coronary blood flow. Blocks effects of sympathetic stimulation.*

Contraindications and Cautious Use

Many drugs have contraindications and therefore should not be used in specific conditions, such as during pregnancy or with particular drugs or foods. In other cases, the drug should be used with great caution because of a greater than average risk of untoward effects.

> **CONTRAINDICATIONS** Hypersensitivity to amiodarone, or benzyl alcohol; cardiogenic shock, severe sinus bradycardia, advanced AV block unless a pacemaker is available, severe sinus-node dysfunction or sick sinus syndrome, bradycardia, congenital or acquired QR prolongation syndromes, history of torsade de pointes; severe liver disease; pregnancy (category D), lactation.
> **CAUTIOUS USE** Hepatic disease, cirrhosis; Hashimoto's thyroiditis, hypersensitivity to iodine, goiter, thyrotoxicosis, or history of other thyroid dysfunction; CHF, left ventricular dysfunction; older adults; Fabry disease, especially with visual disturbances; electrolyte imbalance, hypokalemia, hypomagnesemia, hypovolemia; preexisting lung disease, COPD; open heart surgery.

Adverse Effects

Virtually all drugs have adverse side effects that may be bothersome to some individuals but not to others. In each monograph, adverse effects with an incidence of ≥1% are listed by body system or organs. The most common adverse effects appear in *italic* type, whereas those that are life-threatening are <u>underlined</u>. Users of the drug guide will find a key at the bottom of every page as a quick reminder.

ADVERSE EFFECTS (≥1%) **CNS:** Peripheral neuropathy (*muscle weakness, wasting numbness, tingling*), *fatigue*, abnormal gait, dyskinesias, *dizziness*, paresthesia, headache. **CV:** Bradycardia, *hypotension* (IV), <u>sinus arrest, cardiogenic shock</u>, CHF, arrhythmias; AV block. **Special Senses:** *Corneal microdeposits*, blurred vision, optic neuritis, optic neuropathy, permanent blindness, corneal degeneration, macular degeneration, photosensitivity. **GI:** *Anorexia, nausea, vomiting, constipation,* <u>hepatotoxicity</u>. **Metabolic:** Hyperthyroidism or hypothyroidism; may cause neonatal hypo- or hyperthyroidism if taken during pregnancy. **Respiratory:** (Pulmonary toxicity) Alveolitis, pneumonitis (fever, dry cough, dyspnea), interstitial pulmonary fibrosis, *<u>fatal gasping syndrome</u>* with IV in children. **Skin:** Slate-blue pigmentation, *photosensitivity*, rash. **Other:** With chronic use, angioedema.

Diagnostic Test Interference

This section describes the effect of the drug on various diagnostic tests and alerts the nurse to possible misinterpretations of test results when applicable. The name of the specific test altered is highlighted in **_bold italic_** type.

DIAGNOSTIC TEST INTERFERENCE May produce false positive for **_urine 17-hydroxysteroid (17-OHCS)_** determinations in the modified **_Glenn-Nelson_** technique. May produce false-positive results with **_bromophenol blue test reagent_** and with **_sulfosalicylic acid, heat and acetic acid,_** and **_nitric acid ring test_** methods. May result in false increases in theophylline levels due to **_theophylline assay_** interference.

Drug Interactions

Whenever appropriate, this section lists individual drugs, drug classes, foods, and herbs that interact with the drug discussed in the monograph. Drugs may interact to inhibit or enhance one another. Thus, drug interactions may improve the therapeutic response, lead to therapeutic failure, or produce specific adverse reactions. Only drugs, foods, and herbs that have been shown to cause clinically significant and documented interactions with the drug discussed in the monograph are listed in this section. Note that generic drugs appear in **bold** type, and drug classes appear in SMALL CAPS.

> **DRUG INTERACTIONS** Significantly increases **digoxin** levels; enhances pharmacologic effects and toxicities of **disopyramide, procainamide, quinidine, flecainide, lidocaine, lovastatin, simvastatin;** anticoagulant effects of ORAL ANTICOAGULANTS enhanced; **verapamil, diltiazem,** BETA-ADRENERGIC BLOCKING AGENTS may potentiate sinus bradycardia, sinus arrest, or AV block; may increase **phenytoin** levels 2- to 3-fold; **cholestyramine** may decrease amiodarone levels; **fentanyl** may cause bradycardia, hypotension, or decreased output; may increase **cyclosporine** levels and toxicity; **cimetidine** may increase amiodarone levels; **ritonavir** may increase risk of amiodarone toxicity, including cardiotoxicity.

Pharmacokinetics

This section identifies how the drug moves throughout and is disposed of by the body. It lists the mechanisms of absorption, distribution, metabolism, elimination, and half-life when known. It also provides information about onset, peak, and duration of the drug action. Degree of protein binding and hepatic CYP 450 metabolism are provided as available.

> **PHARMACOKINETICS Distribution:** Concentrates in adipose tissue, lungs, kidneys, spleen; crosses placenta. **Metabolism:** Extensively hepatically metabolized; undergoes some enterohepatic cycling. **Elimination:** Excreted chiefly in bile and feces; also excreted in breast milk. **Half-Life:** Biphasic, initial 2.5–10 days, terminal 40–55 days.

Nursing Implications

The **Nursing Implications** section of each drug monograph is formatted in an easy-to-use manner so that all the pertinent information that nurses need is listed under two headings: **Assessment & Drug Effects** and **Patient & Family Education.** Under these headings, the user can quickly and easily identify needed information and incorporate it into the appropriate steps of the nursing process. Before administering a drug, the nurse should read both sections to determine the assessments that should be made before and after administration of the drug, the indicators of drug effectiveness, laboratory tests recommended for individual drugs, and the essential patient and family education related to the drug.

NURSING IMPLICATIONS

Assessment & Drug Effects

▪ Monitor BP carefully during infusion and slow the infusion if significant hypotension occurs; bradycardia should be treated by slowing the infusion or discontinuing if necessary. Monitor heart rate and rhythm and BP until drug response has stabilized. Sustained monitoring is essential because drug has an unusually long half-life.

▪ Report promptly symptomatic bradycardia.

Patient & Family Education

▪ Become familiar with potential adverse reactions and report those that are bothersome to the prescriber.

Monitoring Therapeutic Effectiveness

Therapeutic effectiveness of the drug can be determined by monitoring improvement in the condition for which the drug is prescribed, and by using the **Assessment & Drug Effects** section of the **Nursing Implications.** Drugs have multiple uses or indications. Therefore, it is important to know why a drug is being prescribed for a specific patient (**Uses and Unlabeled Uses**). In the italicized sentences at the end of the **Action & *Therapeutic Effect*** section in all monographs, specific indicators of the effectiveness of the drug are provided. Additionally, in the **Indication and Dosage** table for each drug, the dosages are listed according to the indications for use of the drug. Furthermore, the **Therapeutic** classifications listed within the red box at the beginning of the monograph provides the nurse with further assistance in determining and evaluating the therapeutic effectiveness of the drug.

Appendixes

This IV drug guide includes several helpful appendixes, including *Appendix A, U.S. Schedules of Controlled Substances* and *Appendix B, FDA Pregnancy Categories*. Each drug monograph provides the necessary information for safe and effective intravenous drug administration. The user should read all the information provided. Occasionally, the user will be referred to *Appendix C, Glossary of Key Terms, Clinical Conditions, and Associated Signs and Symptoms*. This unique glossary provides valuable information regarding common assessment findings related to therapeutic effectiveness or ineffectiveness of specific drugs. Finally, other appendixes include *Appendix D, Abbreviations*; *Appendix E, Recommendations for the Safe Handling of Cytotoxic Drugs*; *Appendix F, Toxicity Grades Associated with Chemotherapy*. Appendix E contains the National Institutes of Health (NIH) Guidelines for minimizing the exposure of health-care personnel to cytotoxic agents. Appendix F provides the scales of the National Cancer Institute used to grade toxicity associated with chemotherapy drugs. Drugs requiring adjustments for toxicity are noted within the **Indication & Dosage** sections of the monographs. The required adjustment is indicated by the red subheading **Toxicity Dosage Adjustment** in the table so the nurse can easily locate the correct dosage to use for the patient.

Index

The index in the *Pearson Intravenous Drug Guide 2009–2010* is perhaps the most often-used section in the entire book. All generic and trade drugs are listed in this index. Whenever a trade name is listed, the generic drug monograph is listed in parentheses. Additionally, classifications are listed and identified in SMALL CAPS, whereas all prototype drugs are highlighted in **bold** type. Drugs belonging to various classifications and subclassifications, including therapeutic classes, are also cross-referenced in this index.

PDA VERSION AVAILABLE

For nurses and students who wish to have this critical IV drug information available for download to a PDA, mobile, or hand-held device, the PDA version of *Pearson Intravenous Drug Guide 2009–2010* and other Pearson clinical references are available for purchase at **www.mynursingpda.com**. With just a few clicks, nurses can search for clinical information—such as drugs, lab tests, and more—quickly and easily, right at the point of care. Link to trial versions of this drug guide and other clinical references at **www.mynursingpda.com**.

COMPANION WEBSITE – www.prenhall.com/drugguides

The Companion Website for all Pearson Prentice Hall drug guides is a *bonus* online resource that offers additional information. It includes access to drug updates, links to drug-related sites, drug-related tools, medication administration techniques, drug classifications, principles of pharmacology, common herbal remedies, and more. You can also send the authors your feedback about this intravenous drug guide through this website.

ACKNOWLEDGMENTS

We wish to express our appreciation to our past and present students who have provided the inspiration for this work. It is for these individuals and all who strive for excellence in patient care that this work was undertaken.

Billie Ann Wilson, RN, PhD
Margaret T. Shannon, RN, PhD
Kelly M. Shields, PharmD

Classifications   Prototype

ANTIGOUT AGENT ....Allopurinol

ANTIHISTAMINES
ANTIHISTAMINES (H₁-RECEPTOR ANTAGONIST) ....Diphenhydramine HCl

ANTIINFECTIVES
ANTIBIOTICS
    AMINOGLYCOSIDES...Gentamicin Sulfate
    ANTIFUNGALS..Amphotericin B
        AZOLE ANTIFUNGAL ....Fluconazole
        ECHINOCARDIN ANTIFUNGAL......................Caspofungin
    CARBAPENEM ....Imipenem-Cilastatin
    CEPHALOSPORIN
        FIRST GENERATION ....Cefazolin Sodium
        SECOND GENERATION ....Cefuroxime
        THIRD GENERATION ....Cefotaxime Sodium
    LINCOAMIDE ....Lincomycin Hydrochloride
    MACROLIDES..Erythromycin
    PENICILLIN
        AMINOPENICILLIN ....Ampicillin
        ANTIPSEUDOMONAL PENICILLIN ....Piperacillin
        NATURAL PENICILLIN ....Penicillin G Potassium
    QUINOLONES..Ciprofloxacin
    TETRACYCLINE ....Doxycycline
ANTILEPROSY (SULFONE) AGENT.............................Dapsone
ANTIMALARIAL ....Chloroquine HCl
ANTIPROTOZOAL..Metronidazole
ANTITUBERCULOSIS AGENT,
    ANTIMYCOBACTERIAL ....Rifampin
ANTIVIRAL AGENTS ....Acyclovir

ANTINEOPLASTICS
ALKYLATING AGENT..Cyclophosphamide
ANTIBIOTIC...Doxorubicin HCl
ANTIMETABOLITES
    ANTIMETABOLITE (ANTIFOLATE)...........................Methotrexate
    ANTIMETABOLITE (PURINE ANTAGONIST).............Cladribine
    ANTIMETABOLITE (PYRIMIDINE ANTAGONIST) 5-Fluorouracil
DNA TOPOISOMERASE INHIBITOR ....Topotecan HCl

---

*Based on the American Hospital Formulary Service Pharmacologic–Therapeutic Classification.
†Prototype drugs are highlighted in tinted boxes in this book.
Complete list of drugs for each classification found in classification index starting on p. 691.

Classifications	Prototype

BRONCHODILATORS (RESPIRATORY SMOOTH MUSCLE RELAXANT)
XANTHINE ....Theophylline

CARDIOVASCULAR AGENTS
ANGIOTENSIN-CONVERTING
    ENZYME INHIBITORS..Enalapril
ANTIARRHYTHMIC AGENTS
    CLASS IA ....Procainamide HCl
    CLASS IB ....Lidocaine HCl
    CLASS IC ....Flecainide
    CLASS II ....Propranolol HCl
    CLASS III ....Amiodarone HCl
CALCIUM CHANNEL BLOCKERS................................Verapamil
CARDIAC GLYCOSIDE...Digoxin
ANTIHYPERTENSIVE, CENTRAL-ACTING
    ANTIADRENERGIC..Methyldopa
INOTROPIC AGENT..Inamrinone
NITRATE VASODILATOR ....Nitroglycerin
NONNITRATE VASODILATOR ....Hydralazine HCl

CENTRAL NERVOUS SYSTEM AGENTS
ANALGESICS, ANTIPYRETICS
    NARCOTIC (OPIATE) AGONISTS ....Morphine
    NARCOTIC (OPIATE) AGONIST-ANTAGONIST ......Pentazocine HCl
    NARCOTIC (OPIATE) ANTAGONIST......................Naloxone HCl
    NONSTEROIDAL ANTI-INFLAMMATORY
        DRUGS (NSAID) COX-1 ....Indomethacin
ANESTHETIC
    GENERAL..Thiopental Sodium
    LOCAL (ESTER TYPE) ....Procaine HCl
    LOCAL (AMIDE TYPE)..Lidocaine HCl
ANTICONVULSANTS
    BARBITURATE..Phenobarbital
    BENZODIAZEPINE...Diazepam
    GABA INHIBITOR ....Valproic Acid Sodium
    HYDANTOIN...Phenytoin
ANXIOLYTICS, SEDATIVE-HYPNOTICS
    BARBITURATE..Pentobarbital
    BENZODIAZEPINE...Lorazepam
    NONBENZODIAZEPINE.......................................Zolpidem
    CARBAMATE...Meprobamate
CEREBRAL STIMULANT
    XANTHINE..Caffeine

CLASSIFICATION SCHEME AND PROTOTYPE DRUGS

Classifications   Prototype

ELECTROLYTIC & WATER BALANCE AGENTS
DIURETIC
    LOOP .... Furosemide
    OSMOTIC .... Mannitol
REPLACEMENT SOLUTION .... Calcium Gluconate

ENZYMES
ENZYME REPLACEMENT .... Laronidase
ENZYME INHIBITOR .... Alpha$_1$-Proteinase Inhibitor

GASTROINTESTINAL AGENTS
ANTIEMETIC
    PHENOTHIAZINE .... Prochlorperazine
    5-HT$_3$ ANTAGONIST .... Ondansetron HCl
ANTISECRETORY (H$_2$-RECEPTOR ANTAGONIST .... Cimetidine
PROKINETIC AGENT (GI STIMULANT) .... Metoclopramide HCl
PROTON PUMP INHIBITORS .... Lansoprazole
SALINE CATHARTIC .... Magnesium Hydroxide

HORMONES & SYNTHETIC SUBSTITUTES
ADRENAL CORTICOSTEROID
    GLUCOCORTICOSTEROID .... Prednisolone
ANTIDIABETIC AGENTS
    INSULIN .... Insulin
OXYTOCIC .... Oxytocin
ANTIDIURETIC .... Vasopressin
PROGESTINS .... Progesterone
THYROID AGENTS .... Levothyroxine Sodium
VITAMIN D ANALOG .... Calcitriol

PROSTAGLANDIN .... Epoprostenol

BISPHOSPHONATE (REGULATOR,
    BONE METABOLISM) .... Etidronate Disodium

SOMATIC NERVOUS SYSTEM AGENTS
SKELETAL MUSCLE RELAXANTS
    CENTRAL-ACTING .... Methocarbamol
    DEPOLARIZING .... Succinylcholine Chloride
    NONDEPOLARIZING .... Atracurium

ABATACEPT

(ab-a-ta′sept)

Orencia

Classification(s): IMMUNOLOGIC AGENT, IMMUNOMODULATOR
Therapeutic: ANTIRHEUMATIC
Pregnancy Category: C

USES Management of signs and symptoms of rheumatoid arthritis.

INDICATION & DOSAGE

Rheumatoid Arthritis

Adult: Initial dose *(weight less than 60 kg):* 500 mg; *(weight 60–100 kg):* 750 mg; *(weight over 100 kg):* 1000 mg. Dose should be repeated at 2 and 4 wk then q4wk.

SOLUTION PREPARATION

- *Vial Reconstitution:* Use the supplied silicone-free, disposable syringe with a 18–21 gauge needle to reconstitute the vial. Add 10 mL sterile water for injection to each 250 mg vial to yield 25 mg/mL. To avoid foaming, gently swirl until completely dissolved. Do not shake or vigorously agitate. After dissolving, vent the vial with a needle to dissipate any form. **Must be** further diluted for IV infusion.
- *Further Dilution of Reconstituted Vial:* Further dilute to a total volume of 100 mL. From a 100 mL NS IV bag, remove a volume equal to the total volume of abatacept in the reconstituted vials (e.g., for 2 vials, remove 20 mL). Using the supplied silicone-free syringe, slowly add the reconstituted abatacept to the IV bag and gently mix. The final concentration of the IV solution will be approximately 5 mg/mL, 7.5 mg/mL, or 10 mg/mL depending on whether 2, 3, or 4 vials are used. Discard any unused abatacept.

STORAGE

- Store unopened vials at 2°–8° C (36°–46° F).
- Infuse diluted IV solutions within 24 h of preparation.

ADMINISTRATION

IV Infusion: Use a 0.2–1.2 micron low-protein-binding filter and infuse over 30 min.

INCOMPATIBILITIES Solution/additive: Unknown. **Y-site:** Should not be infused with other agents in the same line.

ACTION & *THERAPEUTIC EFFECT* Abatacept, a selective stimulation modulator, inhibits T-cell (T lymphocyte) proliferation, which is involved in the pathogenesis of rheumatoid arthritis (RA). It decreases T-cell proliferation and inhibits production of cytokines tumor necrosis factor alpha (TNF-

Common adverse effects in *italic*, life-threatening effects underlined: generic names in **bold**; classifications in SMALL CAPS; ♣ Canadian drug name; ● Prototype drug

1

alpha), interferon-gamma, and interleukin-2. It suppresses inflammation, decreases anticollagen antibody production, and reduces antigen-specific production of interferon-gamma. The relationship of these changes to their effects in RA is unknown. *Activated T lymphocytes are found in the synovial fluid of patients with RA. Abatacept is used to reduce activated T lymphocytes and, therefore, S&S of RA by inducing major clinical response, slowing progression of structural damage, and improving physical function in adults with moderately to severely active RA who have had an inadequate response to one or more disease-modifying antirheumatic drugs (DMARDs).*

CONTRAINDICATIONS Known hypersensitivity to abatacept; live vaccines; active infections; co-administration with anakinra; pregnancy (category C); lactation.
CAUTIOUS USE COPD; RA; malignancies.

ADVERSE EFFECTS (≥1%) **Body as a Whole:** Infusion-related reactions, <u>malignancies</u>, hypersensitivity reactions, <u>*infection*</u>. **CNS:** *Headache,* dizziness. **CV:** Hypertension. **GI:** *Nausea,* dyspepsia. **Musculoskeletal:** Back pain, pain in extremity. **Urogenital:** Urinary tract infection. **Respiratory:** *Upper respiratory tract infection, nasopharyngitis,* sinusitis, influenza, bronchitis, cough. **Skin:** Rash.

DRUG INTERACTIONS Use with TNF ANTAGONISTS (ex. adalimumab) increases the risk of serious infection. Avoid use of vaccines until 3 mo after completion of therapy.

PHARMACOKINETICS Half-Life: 13 days. **Distribution:** No significant plasma protein binding.

NURSING IMPLICATIONS

Assessment & Drug Effects

- Prior to initiating treatment with abatacept, screen for latent TB infection with a TB skin test.
- Monitor for S&S of hypersensitivity (e.g., hypotension, urticaria, and dyspnea); discontinue infusion and notify prescriber if any of these occur.
- Monitor for S&S of infection. Withhold drug and notify prescriber if patient develops a serious infection.
- Monitor for deterioration of respiratory status in patients with COPD.

Patient & Family Education

- Report any of the following to a health care provider: Any type of infection, a positive TB skin test, recent vaccination, persistent cough, unexplained weight loss, fever, sore throat, or night sweats.
- Report S&S of an allergic reaction that may develop within 24 h of receiving abatacept (e.g., hives, swollen face, eyelids, lips, tongue, throat, or trouble breathing).
- Do not accept immunizations with live vaccines while taking or within 3 mo of discontinuing abatacept.

- Taking abatacept with TNF-blocker medications (etanercept [Enbrel], adalimumab [Humira], infliximab [Remicade]) is not recommended.

ABCIXIMAB ⊕

(ab-cix′i-mab)
ReoPro
Classification(s): ANTIPLATELET, PLATELET AGGREGATION INHIBITOR
Therapeutic: ANTITHROMBOTIC
Pregnancy Category: C

USES Adjunct to aspirin and heparin for the prevention of acute cardiac ischemic complications in patients undergoing percutaneous transluminal coronary angioplasty (PTCA).
UNLABELED USES Acute MI (with tenecteplase and heparin).

INDICATION & DOSAGE

PTCA

Adult: 10–60 min prior to start of angioplasty, inject 0.25 mg/kg bolus over 5 min followed by continuous infusion of 0.125 mcg/kg/min (up to 10 mcg/min) for next 12 h

SOLUTION PREPARATION

- Do not shake vial. Use a sterile, nonpyrogenic, low-protein-binding 0.20 or 0.22 micron filter when withdrawing drug into syringe from the 2 mg/mL vial **or** when administering abciximab.
- *Direct IV Injection:* No dilution required for bolus dose.
- *Continuous Infusion:* Dilute by injecting 5 mL of abciximab (10 mg) into 250 mL of NS or D5W to yield 39.2 mcg/mL.

STORAGE

- Store vials at 2°–8° C (36°–46° F).
- Discard any unused portion left in vial as well as unused drug at the end of the 12-h infusion.

ADMINISTRATION

- Use an in-line sterile, nonpyrogenic, low-protein-binding 0.20 or 0.22 micron filter if solution was not filtered during preparation.
- **Direct IV Injection:** Give undiluted bolus dose over 5 min followed by continuous drug infusion.
- **Continuous Infusion:** Infuse diluted drug at no more than 15 mL/h (or 10 mcg/min) via an infusion pump over next 12 h.

INCOMPATIBILITIES Solution/additive: Infuse through separate IV line. Do not mix with other drugs. **Y-site:** Infuse through separate IV line.

Common adverse effects in *italic*, life-threatening effects <u>underlined</u>: generic names in **bold**; classifications in SMALL CAPS; ♣ Canadian drug name; ⊕ Prototype drug

ACTION & *THERAPEUTIC EFFECT* Abciximab is a human–murine mono-clonal antibody fragment or Fab (fragment antigen binding) that binds to the glycoprotein IIb/IIIa (GPIIb/IIIa) receptor sites of platelets. *Abciximab inhibits platelet aggregation by preventing fibrinogen, von Willebrand's factor, and other molecules from adhering to GPIIb/IIIa receptor sites of the platelets.*

CONTRAINDICATIONS Hypersensitivity to abciximab or to murine proteins; active internal bleeding; GI or GU bleeding within 6 wk; history of CVA within 2 y or a CVA with severe neurologic deficit; administration of oral anticoagulants unless PT is less than 1.2 times control; thrombocytopenia (less than 100,000 cells/mL); recent major surgery or trauma; intracranial neoplasm, aneurysm, severe hypertension; history of vasculitis; use of dex-tran before or during PTCA.

CAUTIOUS USE Patients weighing less than 75 kg; older adults; history of previous GI disease; recent thrombolytic therapy; PTCA within 12 h of MI; unsuccessful PTCA; PTCA procedure lasting more than 70 min; pregnancy (category C); lactation.

ADVERSE EFFECTS (≥1%) **Body as a Whole:** *Pain,* diaphoresis. **CV:** Hy-potension, chest pain, <u>ventricular tachycardia</u>. **CNS:** *Dizziness,* anxiety, abnormal thinking. **Hematologic:** Anemia, <u>*bleeding*</u>, including intracra-nial, retroperitoneal, and hematemesis; thrombocytopenia.

DRUG INTERACTIONS ORAL ANTICOAGULANTS, NSAIDS, PLATELET AGGREGATION INHIBITORS, **cefamandole, cefoperazone, cefotetan, dipyridamole, ticlopidine, dextran** may increase risk of bleeding.

PHARMACOKINETICS Onset: Greater than 90% inhibition of platelet ag-gregation within 2 h. **Duration:** Approximately 48 h. **Half-Life:** 30 min.

NURSING IMPLICATIONS

Assessment & Drug Effects

- Prior to initiating therapy: Baseline CBC, platelet count, PT, ACT, and aPTT.
- Discontinue therapy immediately & notify prescriber if bleeding or S&S of hypersensitivity occur. Note: Abciximab is a protein solution. Antici-pate hypersensitivity reactions whenever protein solutions are adminis-tered. Have available for immediate use epinephrine, dopamine, theophylline, antihistamines, and corticosteroid. If symptoms of an aller-gic reaction or anaphylaxis appear, stop infusion and institute appropri-ate treatment.
- Monitor for S&S of: Bleeding at all potential sites (e.g., catheter insertion, needle puncture, or cutdown sites; GI, GU, or retroperitoneal sites); hy-persensitivity that may occur any time during administration.
- Monitor vital signs and ECG throughout the infusion period and for sev-eral hours thereafter.
- Lab tests: Monitor Hgb, Hct, platelet count, PT, aPTT, and activated clot-ting time, every 2–4 h during first 24 h.

Common adverse effects in *italic*, life-threatening effects <u>underlined</u>: generic names in **bold**; classifications in SMALL CAPS; ♣ Canadian drug name; ❍ Prototype drug

4

- Avoid or minimize unnecessary invasive procedures and devices to reduce risk of bleeding.
- Elevate head of bed to 30° or less and keep limb straight when femoral artery access is used; following sheath removal, apply pressure for 30 min.

Patient & Family Education

- Report promptly: S&S of bleeding, oozing small amount of blood from IV site is not unusual.
- Minimize all activities that increase the risk of bleeding.

ACETAZOLAMIDE

(a-set-a-zole′a-mide)

Acetazolam ♦, Apo-Acetazolamide ♦

ACETAZOLAMIDE SODIUM

(a-set-a-zole′a-mide)

Classification(s): EYE PREPARATION; CARBONIC ANHYDRASE INHIBITOR
Therapeutic: DIURETIC; ANTICONVULSANT; ANTIGLAUCOMA
Pregnancy Category: C

USES Reduction of intraocular pressure in open-angle glaucoma and secondary glaucoma; preoperative treatment of acute closed-angle glaucoma; drug-induced edema and as adjunct in treatment of edema due to congestive heart failure.
UNLABELED USES Hydrocephalus.

INDICATION & DOSAGE

Glaucoma

Adult: 250–500 mg, may repeat in 2–4 h if needed, up to 1 g/day
Child: 5–10 mg/kg q6h

Edema

Adult: 5 mg/kg or 250–375 mg as a single daily dose; may be given every other day as condition improves
Child: 5 mg/kg or 150 mg/m²/every AM

Anticonvulsant

Adult: 8–30 mg/kg/day in 1–4 divided doses (max: 1 g/day)
Child: 8–30 mg/kg/day in 1–4 divided doses (max: 1 g/day)
Geriatric: Start with lower dose

Common adverse effects in *italic*, life-threatening effects <u>underlined</u>: generic names
in **bold**; classifications in SMALL CAPS; ♦ Canadian drug name; ❷ Prototype drug

5

Renal Impairment Dosage Adjustment

CrCl	Dose	Interval
10–50 mL/min	Normal	q12h
Less than 10 mL/min	Do not use	Do not use
Hemodialysis	Normal	Administer after hemodialysis

SOLUTION PREPARATION

- *Vial Reconstitution:* Reconstitute each 500 mg vial with at least 5 mL of sterile water for injection to yield approximately 100 mg/mL. May be given as prepared direct IV as a bolus dose or further diluted for infusion.
- *Further Dilution of Reconstituted Solution:* Dilute in D5W, NS, or other standard solution for IV infusion. Maximum concentration is 100 mg/mL.

STORAGE

Use reconstituted solution within 12 h of preparation if at room temperature (15°–30° C [59°–86° F]) and within 3 days if refrigerated (2°–8° C [36°–36° F]). Discard unused portion as drug contains no preservatives.

ADMINISTRATION

- **Direct IV Injection:** Give a bolus dose at a rate of 500 mg or fraction thereof over 1 min.
- **Intermittent IV Infusion:** Infuse over 4–8 h.

INCOMPATIBILITIES Solution/additive: AMINO ACIDS. **Y-site: Diltiazem, TPN.**

ACTION & *THERAPEUTIC EFFECT* The mechanism of anticonvulsant action is thought to involve inhibition of CNS carbonic anhydrase. Anticonvulsant property results from retarding abnormal discharge from CNS neurons. Diuretic effect is due to inhibition of carbonic anhydrase activity in proximal renal tubule, preventing formation of carbonic acid, thus decreasing its excretion. Inhibition of carbonic anhydrase in the eye reduces rate of aqueous humor formation with consequent lowering of intraocular pressure. *Has anticonvulsant and diuretic effects; it also lowers intraocular pressure.*

CONTRAINDICATIONS Marked renal and hepatic dysfunction; Addison's disease or other types of adrenocortical insufficiency; hyponatremia, hypokalemia, hyperchloremic acidosis; chronic noncongestive angle-closure glaucoma; pregnancy (category C).

CAUTIOUS USE Hypersensitivity to sulfonamides and derivatives (e.g., thiazides); history of hypercalciuria; diabetes mellitus; gout; patients receiving digitalis; chronic obstructive pulmonary disease (COPD), respiratory acidosis.

ADVERSE EFFECTS (≥1%) **CNS:** Paresthesias, sedation, malaise, disorientation, depression, fatigue, muscle weakness, flaccid paralysis. **Hematologic:** Bone marrow depression with agranulocytosis, hemolytic anemia, aplastic anemia, leukopenia, pancytopenia. **Metabolic:** Metabolic acidosis; electrolyte imbalance. **Ocular:** Transient myopia. **Urogenital:** Glycosuria, urinary frequency, polyuria, dysuria, hematuria, crystalluria. **Other:** Exacerbation of gout, hepatic dysfunction, Stevens Johnson syndrome.

DIAGNOSTIC TEST INTERFERENCE May produce false positive for *urine 17-hydroxysteroid (17-OHCS)* determinations in the modified *Glenn-Nelson* technique. May produce false-positive results with *bromophenol blue test reagent* and with *sulfosalicylic acid, heat and acetic acid,* and *nitric acid ring test* methods. May result in false increases in theophylline levels due to *theophylline assay* interference.

DRUG INTERACTIONS Aspirin and other SALICYLATES: Salicylate toxicity and acetazolamide toxicity (fatigue, lethargy, somnolence, confusion, hyperchloremic, metabolic acidosis). CARDIAC GLYCOSIDES, **arsenic trioxide, droperidol, levomethadyl, quinidine, sotalol:** Decreased excretion of these drugs and increased risk of cardiotoxicity. **Amphetamine, flecainide, methenamine, memantine, mexiletine:** Decreased excretion of these drugs and increased risk of toxicity. ANTIDIABETIC AGENTS, **barbiturates, lithium:** Increased excretion and subtherapeutic effects of these drugs. DIURETICS: Increased diuresis with possible hypokalemia and hyperuricemia. **Topiramate:** May cause renal stones, crystalluria and nephrotoxicity.

PHARMACOKINETICS Onset: 2 min. **Peak:** 15 min. **Duration:** 4–5 h. **Distribution:** Distributed throughout body, concentrating in RBCs, plasma, and kidneys; crosses placenta. **Elimination:** Excreted primarily in urine. **Half-Life:** 2.4–5.8 h.

NURSING IMPLICATIONS

Assessment & Drug Effects

- Prior to initiating therapy: Establish baseline weight initially and daily thereafter when used to treat edema.
- Monitor for S&S of: Mild to severe metabolic acidosis; potassium loss—greatest early in therapy (see hypokalemia in Appendix C).
- Monitor cardiac status especially with concurrent cardiac glycosides.
- Monitor diabetics for loss of glycemic control.
- Lab tests: Baseline CBC and platelet count; blood pH and blood gases (especially with impaired respiratory function), urinalysis, CBC, platelet count, and serum electrolytes periodically during prolonged therapy or concomitant therapy with other diuretics or digitalis.
- Monitor I&O especially when used with other diuretics.
- Concurrent drugs: Monitor diabetics for loss of glycemic control.

Patient & Family Education

- Report promptly: Numbness, tingling, burning, drowsiness, visual problems, sore throat or mouth, unusual bleeding, fever, skin or renal problems.
- Maintain adequate fluid intake to reduce risk of kidney stones.
- Avoid potentially hazardous activities until reaction to drug is known.

Common adverse effects in *italic*, life-threatening effects underlined: generic names in **bold**; classifications in SMALL CAPS; ♣ Canadian drug name; ⊙ Prototype drug

7

ACETYLCYSTEINE

(a-se-til-sis'tay-een)

N-Acetylcysteine, Acetadote

Classification(s): ANTIDOTE

Therapeutic: ACETAMINOPHEN ANTIDOTE

Pregnancy Category: B

USES An antidote for acute acetaminophen poisoning.

INDICATION & DOSAGE

Acetaminophen Toxicity

Adult/Child: **Loading Dose,** 150 mg/kg over 60 min; **First Maintenance Dose,** 50 mg/kg over 4 h; **Second Maintenance Dose,** 100 mg/kg over 16 h (total dose 300 mg/kg over 21 h)

SOLUTION PREPARATION

- Acetylcysteine reacts with certain metals and rubber; use IV equipment made of plastic or glass.
- Drug is supplied in 30 mL vials containing 200 mg/mL. Dilute all required doses in D5W, 1/2NS, or sterile water for injection.
- *IV Solution for Patients 40 kg or More:*
  - *Loading Dose:* Withdraw from vial the volume of drug equal to 150 mg/kg and add to 200 mL IV fluid.
  - *First Maintenance Dose:* Withdraw from vial the volume of drug equal to 50 mg/kg and add to 500 mL IV fluid.
  - *Second Maintenance Dose:* Withdraw from vial the volume of drug equal to 100 mg/kg and add to 1000 mL IV fluid.
- *IV Solution for Patients Less Than 40 kg:* Total IV volume should be **reduced** using the following guidelines:
  - *Loading Dose:* Withdraw from vial the volume of drug equal to 150 mg/kg. Add this to a volume of IV fluid equal to 3–4 mL per kg.
  - *First Maintenance Dose:* Withdraw from vial the volume of drug equal to 50 mg/kg. Add this to a volume of IV fluid equal to 7–8 mL per kg.
  - *Second Maintenance Dose:* Withdraw from vial the volume of drug equal to 100 mg/kg. Add this to a volume of IV fluid equal to 16–17 mL per kg.
- *IV Solution for Small Children:* Individualize the total IV volume to avoid water intoxication and hyponatremia.

STORAGE

Store reconstituted solution for up to 24 h at 15°–30° C (59°–86° F).

ADMINISTRATION

IV Infusion: *Loading Dose:* Infuse over 60 min. *First Maintenance Dose:* Infuse over 4 h. *Second Maintenance Dose:* Infuse over 16 h. Complete all infusions over 21 h.

INCOMPATIBILITIES Y-site: Cefepime, ceftazidime.

ACTION & THERAPEUTIC EFFECT The sulfhydryl groups of acetylcysteine serve as a substrate for the toxic acetaminophen metabolite that depletes the store of the required liver metabolite, glutathione, for proper functioning. It is believed that acetaminophen is hepatotoxic due to the depletion of these glutathione metabolite residues. *Prevents hepatotoxicity after an acute overdose of acetaminophen. Benefits are primarily seen in patients treated within 8–10 h of the overdose.*

CONTRAINDICATIONS Hypersensitivity to acetylcysteine.

CAUTIOUS USE Patients with asthma, older adults, severe hepatic disease, pregnancy (category B), lactation.

ADVERSE EFFECTS (≥1%) **Body as a Whole:** Rash, urticaria, pruritus. **CNS:** Dizziness, drowsiness. **GI:** Nausea, *vomiting*, stomatitis, hepatotoxicity (urticaria). **Respiratory:** <u>Bronchospasm</u>, rhinorrhea, epistaxis.

DRUG INTERACTIONS None known.

PHARMACOKINETICS Metabolism: Deacetylated in liver to cysteine and subsequently metabolized. **Half-Life:** 5.6 h (adult), 11 h (infant).

NURSING IMPLICATIONS

Assessment & Drug Effects

- Discontinue infusion immediately and report to prescriber S&S of hypersensitivity, bronchospasm, or other indicators of respiratory distress. Use particular caution with asthmatics.
- Monitor for fluid overload and signs of hyponatremia (see Appendix C).
- Monitor cardiac status throughout infusion of drug.
- Lab tests: Baseline serum acetaminophen level, ALT & AST, bilirubin, serum electrolytes, BUN, and glucose.

Patient & Family Education

- Report promptly difficulty with clearing the airway or any other respiratory distress.
- Report nausea, as an antiemetic may be indicated.

ACYCLOVIR, ACYCLOVIR SODIUM ⓟ
(ay-sye′kloe-ver)

Zovirax
Classification(s): ANTIVIRAL
Therapeutic: ANTIVIRAL
Pregnancy Category: B

USES Treatment of initial and recurrent mucosal and cutaneous herpes simplex virus (HSV-1 and HSV-2) infections in immunocompromised adults and children and for severe initial episodes of herpes genitalis or

---

Common adverse effects in *italic*, life-threatening effects <u>underlined</u>: generic names in **bold**; classifications in SMALL CAPS; ♣ Canadian drug name; ⓟ Prototype drug

9

varicella-zoster infections in immunocompetent (normal immune system) patients. Treatment of herpes encephalitis or neonatal herpes infection.
UNLABELED USES Prevention of HSV in immunosuppressed HSV-seropositive patients, to reduce risk of CMV infection in bone marrow transplant patients.

INDICATION & DOSAGE

Herpes Simplex Immunocompromised Patient

Adult: 5 mg/kg q8h × 7 days
Child: 10 mg/kg q8h × 7 days

Severe Genital Herpes

Adults/Adolescent: 5 mg/kg q8h × 5 days

Herpes Simplex Encephalitis

Adult/Adolescent: 10 mg/kg q8h × 10 days
Child/Infant (older than 3 mo): 20 mg/kg q8h × 10 days
Neonate/Infant (birth–3 mo): 10 mg/kg q8h × 10 days

Varicella-Zoster

Adult: 10 mg/kg q8h × 7 days
Child: 20 mg/kg q8h × 7 days

Obesity

Use IBW.

Renal Impairment Dosage Adjustment

CrCl	Dose	Interval
25–50 mL/min	Standard	q12h
10–24 mL/min	Standard	q24h
Less than 10 mL/min	Half dose	q24h
Hemodialysis		Administer after hemodialysis

SOLUTION PREPARATION

- **Warning:** Do not reconstitute with bacteriostatic water for injection containing benzyl alcohol.
- *Vial Reconstitution:* Add 10 mL sterile water for injection to the 500-mg vial or 20 mL to the 1000-mg vial to yield 50 mg/mL. Shake well to dissolve. **Must be** further diluted for infusion.
- *Further Dilution of Reconstituted Solution:* Add the volume (mL) of drug equal to the required dose (mg) to 60–150 mL of standard electrolyte or glucose solutions (e.g., NS, LR, D5W).
- Maximum Concentration: 7 mg/mL

STORAGE

- Use reconstituted solution within 12 h. Once further diluted for IV administration, use within 24 h.

- Refrigerated, reconstituted solution may form a precipitate; however, crystals will redissolve at room temperature.
- Store acyclovir powder and reconstituted solutions at controlled room temperature preferably at 15°–25° C (59°–77° F).

ADMINISTRATION

- **Avoid** rapid or bolus IV administration.
- **Intermittent Infusion:** Give at a constant rate over at least 1 h to prevent renal tubular damage.
- Monitor IV flow rate carefully; infusion pump or microdrip infusion set preferred.
- Observe infusion site during infusion and for a few days following infusion for signs of tissue damage.

INCOMPATIBILITIES Solution/additive: Dobutamine, dopamine, pantoprazole. Y-site: Amifostine, amsacrine, aztreonam, cefepime, dobutamine, dopamine, fludarabine, foscarnet, gemcitabine, idarubicin, levofloxacin, ondansetron, piperacillin/tazobactam, sargramostim, TPN, vinorelbine.

ACTION & *THERAPEUTIC EFFECT* Acyclovir is a purine nucleoside analog of guanine. It reduces viral shedding and formation of new lesions and speeds healing time. It interferes with DNA synthesis of herpes simplex virus types 1 and 2 (HSV-1 & HSV-2) and varicella-zoster virus, thereby inhibiting viral replication. *Acyclovir demonstrates antiviral activity against herpes virus simiae, Epstein-Barr (infectious mononucleosis), varicella-zoster and cytomegalovirus, but does not eradicate the latent herpes virus.*

CONTRAINDICATIONS Hypersensitivity to acyclovir and valacyclovir.

CAUTIOUS USE Renal insufficiency; dehydration; seizure disorders or neurological disease; pregnancy (category B).

ADVERSE EFFECTS (≥1%) **CNS:** *Headache,* light-headedness, lethargy, fatigue, tremors, confusion, seizures, dizziness. **GI:** *Nausea, vomiting, diarrhea.* **Urogenital:** Glomerulonephritis, renal tubular damage, <u>acute renal failure</u>. **Skin:** Rash, urticaria, pruritus, burning, stinging sensation, irritation, sensitization. **Other:** Inflammation or phlebitis at injection site, sloughing (with extravasation), <u>thrombocytopenic purpura/hemolytic uremic syndrome</u>.

DRUG INTERACTIONS Probenecid decreases acyclovir elimination; **zidovudine** may cause increased drowsiness and lethargy.

PHARMACOKINETICS Distribution: Distributes into most tissues with lower levels in the CNS; crosses placenta. Limited protein binding. **Metabolism:** Drug is primarily excreted unchanged. **Elimination:** Renally eliminated; also excreted in breast milk. **Half-Life:** 2.5–5 h.

NURSING IMPLICATIONS

Assessment & Drug Effects

- Prior to initiating therapy: Determine baseline renal function (BUN and creatinine).

Common adverse effects in *italic*, life-threatening effects <u>underlined</u>: generic names in **bold**; classifications in SMALL CAPS; ♣ Canadian drug name; ❷ Prototype drug

11

- Monitor for S&S of: Acyclovir-induced neurologic impairment in patients with history of neurologic problems; acute renal failure with concomitant use of other nephrotoxic drugs or preexisting renal disease.
- Monitor for S&S of thrombotic thrombocytopenic purpura/hemolytic-uremic syndrome (i.e., hematuria, acute renal failure, petechiae, confusion, and fever).
- Lab tests: Baseline and periodic renal function studies.
- Report promptly: Elevations of BUN and serum creatinine and decreases in CrCl as they may indicate need for dosage adjustment, discontinuation of drug, or correction of fluid and electrolyte balance.
- Monitor I&O and hydration status. Keep patient adequately hydrated during first 2 h after infusion to maintain sufficient urinary flow and prevent precipitation of drug in renal tubules. Consult prescriber about amount and length of time oral fluids need to be pushed after IV infusion.

Patient & Family Education

- Note: Even after HSV infection is controlled, latent virus can be activated by stress, trauma, fever, exposure to sunlight, sexual intercourse, menstruation, and treatment with immunosuppressive drugs.
- Acyclovir does not prevent transmission of herpes viral infection to sexual partners.

ADENOSINE

(a-den'o-sin)

Adenocard, Adenoscan

Classification(s): ANTIARRHYTHMIC AGENT

Therapeutic: ANTIARRHYTHMIC; DIAGNOSTIC AGENT

Pregnancy Category: C

USES Conversion to sinus rhythm of paroxysmal supraventricular tachycardia (PSVT) including PSVT associated with accessory bypass tracts (Wolff-Parkinson-White syndrome). "Chemical" thallium stress test.

UNLABELED USES Afterload-reducing agent in low-output states; to prevent graft occlusion following aortocoronary bypass surgery; to produce controlled hypotension during cerebral aneurysm surgery.

INDICATION & DOSAGE

Supraventricular Tachycardia

Adult/Adolescent (50 kg or more): 6 mg bolus initially; after 1–2 min may give two additional 12 mg bolus doses for a total of three doses. Do not exceed 12 mg in any one dose.

Neonate/Infant/Child (less than 50 kg): 0.05–1 mg/kg bolus initially; additional doses may be increased by 0.05–1 mg/kg up to maximum of 12 mg dose

---

Common adverse effects in *italic*, life-threatening effects underlined: generic names in **bold**; classifications in SMALL CAPS; ♣ Canadian drug name; ☯ Prototype drug

Thallium Stress Test

Adult: 140 mcg/kg/min (max: 0.84 mg/kg total dose)

SOLUTION PREPARATION

- No dilution is required. Administer as supplied.
- Inspect solution for crystals. If crystals form from refrigeration, dissolve by allowing to warm at room temperature.

STORAGE

Store at room temperature 15°–30° C (59°–86° F). Do not refrigerate, as crystallization may occur. Discard unused portion (contains no preservatives).

ADMINISTRATION

- **Direct IV Injection for Supraventricular Tachycardia:** Give a rapid bolus over 1–2 sec. If given by IV line, administer rapidly as close to insertion site as possible, and follow with a rapid saline flush. Note that slower administration may cause hypotension and reflex tachycardia. Initial dose may be followed by two additional doses at 1–2 min intervals (see **INDICATION & DOSAGE**). If high-level block develops after one dose, **do not repeat** dose.
- **Direct IV Injection for Thallium Stress Test:** Give a bolus dose over 6 min.

ACTION & *THERAPEUTIC EFFECT* Slows conduction through the atrioventricular (AV) and sinoatrial (SA) nodes. Can interrupt the reentry pathways through the AV node. *Restores normal sinus rhythm in patients with paroxysmal supraventricular tachycardia.*

CONTRAINDICATIONS AV block, preexisting second- and third-degree heart block or sick sinus rhythm without pacemaker, since a heart block may result. Ineffective for: Atrial flutter, atrial fibrillation, and ventricular tachycardia.

CAUTIOUS USE Asthmatics, COPD, unstable angina, stenotic valvular disease, hypovolemia, pregnancy (category C), hepatic and renal failure.

ADVERSE EFFECTS (≥1%) **CNS:** Headache, lightheadedness, dizziness, tingling in arms (from IV infusion), apprehension, blurred vision, burning sensation (from IV infusion). **CV:** *Transient facial flushing,* sweating, palpitations, chest pain, atrial fibrillation or flutter. **Respiratory:** Shortness of breath, transient *dyspnea,* chest pressure. **GI:** Nausea, metallic taste, tightness in throat. **Other:** Irritability in children.

DRUG INTERACTIONS Dipyridamole can potentiate the effects of adenosine; **theophylline** will block the electrophysiologic effects of adenosine; **carbamazepine** may increase risk of heart block.

PHARMACOKINETICS Absorption: Rapid uptake by erythrocytes and vascular endothelial cells after IV administration. **Onset:** 20–30 sec. **Metabolism:** Rapid uptake into cells; degraded by deamination to inosine, hypoxanthine, and adenosine monophosphate. **Half-Life:** 10 sec.

Common adverse effects in *italic*, life-threatening effects underlined; generic names in **bold**; classifications in SMALL CAPS; ♣ Canadian drug name; 🅟 Prototype drug

13

NURSING IMPLICATIONS

Assessment & Drug Effects

- Monitor for S&S of bronchospasm in asthma patients. Notify prescriber immediately.
- Use a hemodynamic monitoring system during administration; monitor BP, heart rate and rhythm continuously for several minutes after administration.
- Note: Adverse effects are generally self-limiting due to short half-life (10 sec).
- Note: At the time of conversion to normal sinus rhythm, PVCs, PACs, sinus bradycardia, and sinus tachycardia, as well as various degrees of AV block, are seen on the ECG. These usually last only a few seconds and resolve without intervention.

Patient & Family Education

- Note: Flushing may occur along with a feeling of warmth as drug is injected.

AGALSIDASE BETA

(a-gal'si-dase)

Fabrazyme

Classification(s): ENZYME REPLACEMENT
Therapeutic: LYSOSOMAL ENZYME REPLACEMENT

Pregnancy Category: B

USES Treatment of Fabry disease.

INDICATION & DOSAGE

Fabry Disease
Adult/Child (over 8 y): 1 mg/kg q2wk

SOLUTION PREPARATION

- Bring agalsidase beta vials and supplied diluent (sterile water for injection) to room temperature prior to reconstitution.
- *Vial Reconstitution:* Into each 35 mg vial slowly inject 7.2 mL of sterile water for injection down inside wall of vial. Roll and tilt vial gently to mix but do not shake. Reconstituted vial contains 5 mg/mL of clear, colorless solution. **Must be** further diluted for infusion.
- *Further Dilution of Reconstituted Solution:* Determine the volume (mL) of reconstituted agalsidase beta required for the dose (mg). Remove an equal volume of NS from a 500 mL NS infusion bag. Inject the reconstituted agalsidase beta solution directly into the NS (not into airspace within the infusion bag) to produce a final total volume of 500 mL.

Common adverse effects in *italic*, life-threatening effects <u>underlined</u>: generic names in **bold**; classifications in SMALL CAPS; ♣ Canadian drug name; ◕ Prototype drug

STORAGE

Store refrigerated until needed. Vials are for single use. Discard any unused portion. DO NOT use after expiration date.

ADMINISTRATION

- Give antipyretics prior to infusion.
- **IV Infusion:** An in-line, low-protein-binding, 0.2 micron filter may be used during administration. Initial infusion rate should not exceed 0.25 mg/min (15 mg/h); infuse more slowly if infusion-associated reactions occur. After tolerance to infusion is established, may increase rate in increments of 0.05–0.08 mg/min (increments of 3 to 5 mg/h) for each subsequent infusion.

INCOMPATIBILITIES **Solution/additive:** Do not infuse with other products.

ACTION & *THERAPEUTIC EFFECT* Fabry disease is caused by a deficiency of alpha-galactosidase A resulting in an accumulation of glycosphinolipids in body tissues causing cardiomyopathy, renal failure, and CVA. Agalsidase beta provides an exogenous source of galactosidase A that results in the breakdown of glycosphingolipids, including GL-3. *Reduces globotriaosylceramide (GL-3) deposition in capillary endothelium of the kidney and certain other cell types.*

CONTRAINDICATIONS Safety and efficacy in children less than 16 y have not been established; lactation.

CAUTIOUS USE Hypersensitivity reaction to agalsidase beta or mannitol; compromised cardiac function, mild to severe hypertension; renal impairment; pregnancy (category B).

ADVERSE EFFECTS (≥1%) **Body as a Whole:** *Fever, skeletal pain, pallor, rigors, temperature change sensation,* ataxia, stroke. **CNS:** *Dizziness, headache, paresthesia, anxiety, depression,* vertigo. **CV:** *Chest pain, cardiomegaly, hypertension, hypotension, dependent edema,* bradycardia, heart failure, exacerbation of preexisting arrhythmias. **GI:** *Dyspepsia, nausea, abdominal pain.* **Metabolic:** *Antibody development.* **Musculoskeletal:** *Arthrosis, skeletal pain.* **Respiratory:** *Bronchitis,* bronchospasm, laryngitis, *pharyngitis, rhinitis,* sinusitis, dyspnea. **Skin:** Pruritus, urticaria. **Special Senses:** Hearing loss. **Urogenital:** Testicular pain, nephrotic syndrome.

DRUG INTERACTIONS None known.

PHARMACOKINETICS **Metabolism:** Degraded through peptide hydrolysis. **Elimination:** Renal elimination expected to be a minor pathway. **Half-Life:** 45–102 min.

NURSING IMPLICATIONS

Assessment & Drug Effects

- Monitor for S&S of infusion-related reactions (e.g., hypertension or hypotension, chest pain or chest tightness, dyspnea, fever and chills, headache, abdominal pain, pruritus and urticaria).

- Slow infusion and report promptly to prescriber if infusion reaction occurs. Note that additional antipyretic and/or an antihistamine and oral steroid may reduce the symptoms.
- Monitor cardiac status closely, especially with preexisting heart disease.

Patient & Family Education

- Notify prescriber if you have experienced an unusual reaction to agalsidase beta, agalsidase alfa, mannitol, other drugs, foods, or preservatives.
- Report promptly: Chest pain or chest tightness, rapid heartbeat; shortness of breath or difficulty breathing; depression; dizziness; skin rash, hives or itching; throat tightness; swelling of the face, lips, neck, ears, or extremities.
- Do not drive or engage in other hazardous activities until reaction to drug is known.

ALEFACEPT ℗ᵣ

(a-le′fa-cept)

Amevive

Classification(s): FUSION PROTEIN; IMMUNOLOGIC AGENT, IMMUNOSUPPRESSANT

Therapeutic: ANTIPSORIATIC

Pregnancy Category: B

USES Treatment of moderate to severe chronic plaque psoriasis.

UNLABELED USES Treatment of psoriatic arthritis.

INDICATION & DOSAGE

Chronic Plaque Psoriasis

Adult: 7.5 mg once/wk × 12 wk; may repeat course after 12 wk off therapy if CD4+ T lymphocyte count is above 250 cells/microliter

SOLUTION PREPARATION

- *Vial Reconstitution:* Using the supplied syringe and one of the supplied needles, withdraw 0.6 mL of the supplied diluent (sterile water for injection). Note: Do not reconstitute with other diluents. Keeping the needle pointed at the sidewall of the vial, slowly inject the diluent to yield 7.5 mg/0.5 mL. Gently swirl vial for about 2 min to mix, but do not shake or vigorously agitate. Solution should be clear and colorless to slightly yellow.
- Do not filter reconstituted solution during preparation or administration.

STORAGE

- Store vials of powder away from light at 15°–30° C (59°–86° F).
- Store reconstituted solution for up to 4 h between 2°–8° C (36°–46° F); discard solution not used within 4 h of reconstitution.

ADMINISTRATION

- Administer only if CD4+ T lymphocyte count is at least 250 cells/microliter.
- **Direct IV Injection:** Remove needle used for reconstitution and attach the other supplied needle. Withdraw 0.5 mL (7.5 mg) of the solution into the syringe for direct IV injection. Fill two syringes with 3 mL NS for pre/post flush. Prime the supplied infusion set with 3 mL NS and insert the set into the vein. Attach the syringe with the medication to the infusion set and give as a bolus dose over 5 sec or less. Flush infusion set with 3 mL NS.

INCOMPATIBILITIES Solution/additive: Do not add other medications to solution.

ACTION & *THERAPEUTIC EFFECT* Activation of T cells plays a role in chronic plaque psoriasis. Alefacept is thought to bind to CD2 receptors found on all peripheral T cells and to immunoglobulin receptors on cytotoxic cells, such as natural killer cells. Alefacept blocks further activation of T cells and reduces cellular-mediated destruction of T cells. *Alefacept modulates the immune response by decreasing activation of T cells that are believed to be the key mediators of psoriasis.*

CONTRAINDICATIONS Hypersensitivity to alefacept; CD4+ T lymphocyte count below normal; history of systemic malignancies; patients with HIV; patients with a clinically important infection; serious infections; live or attenuated vaccines; lactation.
CAUTIOUS USE Patients at high risk for malignancies; pregnancy (category B); elderly.

ADVERSE EFFECTS (≥1%) **Body as a Whole:** Secondary malignancies, serious infections, chills, *injection site pain,* injection site inflammation. **CNS:** Dizziness, headache. **GI:** Nausea, vomiting. **Hematologic:** *Lymphopenia,* alefacept antibody formation. **Musculoskeletal:** Myalgia. **Respiratory:** Pharyngitis, increased cough. **Skin:** Pruritus.

DRUG INTERACTIONS Additive immunosuppression with other immunosuppressant drugs (e.g., CORTICOSTEROIDS); LIVE VACCINES increase risk of secondary transmission of infection.

PHARMACOKINETICS Volume of Distribution: 94 mL/kg. **Half-Life:** 270 h.

NURSING IMPLICATIONS

Assessment & Drug Effects

- Prior to initiating therapy: Baseline CD4+ T lymphocyte count. Withhold drug and notify prescriber if not within normal limits.
- Discontinue infusion immediately and institute supportive measures if a serious hypersensitivity reaction occurs.
- Lab tests: Weekly WBC with differential during 12-wk dosing period; periodic liver enzymes. Note: Drug should be discontinued if CD4+ T lymphocyte counts remain below 250 cells/microliter for 1 mo.
- Monitor for and promptly report S&S of infection.

Common adverse effects in *italic*, life-threatening effects <u>underlined</u>: generic names in **bold**; classifications in SMALL CAPS; ♣ Canadian drug name; ✪ Prototype drug

17

Patient & Family Education

- Report promptly: Chest pain or tightness, rapid or irregular heart beat; difficulty breathing or swallowing; swelling of face, tongue, hands, feet or ankles; rapid weight gain; signs of infection (e.g., fever, chills, cough, sore throat, pain or difficulty passing urine); skin rash or itchy skin; severe stomach pain.
- Report persistent nausea, loss of appetite, tiredness, vomiting, abdominal pain, yellowing of skin or eyes, easy bruising, dark urine, or pale stools as these may indicate liver injury.
- Do not accept live or live-attenuated vaccines (e.g., measles, mumps, oral polio) while taking this drug. Avoid contact with people who have recently received the oral polio vaccine.
- Notify prescriber if you become pregnant while taking this drug or within 8 wk of discontinuing drug.

ALEMTUZUMAB

(a-lem'tu-zu-mab)
Campath
Classifications: ANTINEOPLASTIC; MONOCLONAL ANTIBODY
Therapeutic: ANTINEOPLASTIC
Prototype: Basiliximab
Pregnancy Category: C

USES Treatment of B-cell chronic lymphocytic leukemia in patients who have failed fludarabine therapy.
UNLABELED USES Treatment of non-Hodgkin's lymphoma, rheumatoid arthritis, multiple sclerosis.

INDICATION & DOSAGE

B-Cell Chronic Lymphocytic Leukemia

Adult: Start with 3 mg/day; when that is tolerated, increase dose over next 3–7 days to 10 mg/day; when 10 mg/day is tolerated, increase to maintenance dose of 30 mg/day (give 30 mg/day 3 times/wk). Single dose should not exceed 30 mg; cumulative dose should not exceed 90 mg/wk.

Toxicity Adjustment

Toxicity	Modification
First time ANC falls below 250/mcL or platelet count falls below 25,000/mcL	Stop therapy until ANC is at least 500 mcL and platelet count is at least 50,000 mcL, resume at previous dose.
	If therapy is stopped for seven or more days restart at 3 mg and taper up.

Common adverse effects in *italic*, life-threatening effects <u>underlined</u>: generic names in **bold**; classifications in SMALL CAPS; ♣ Canadian drug name; ◍ Prototype drug

Toxicity	Modification
Second time ANC below 250/mcL or platelet count falls below 25,000 mcL	Stop therapy until ANC is at least 500 mcL and platelet count is at least 50,000 mcL, resume at 10 mg dose. If therapy is stopped for seven or more days restart at 3 mg and taper up, do not exceed 10 mg
Third time ANC below 250/mcL or platelet count falls below 25,000 mcL	Stop therapy permanently

Note: Patients starting therapy with baseline ANC of less than 500 mcL or baseline platelet count of less than 25,000 mcL who experience a 50% decrease from baseline should stop therapy until values return to baseline then resume at previous dose. If therapy is stopped for seven or more days restart at 3 mg and taper up.

SOLUTION PREPARATION

- **Do not** shake ampule prior to use. **Must be** diluted prior to use.
- Use a syringe with a sterile, low-protein-binding, non–fiber-releasing, 5-micron filter **either** to withdraw the dose from the ampule **or** to inject the dose into an IV bag with 100 mL NS or D5W.
- Gently invert bag to mix. Infuse within 8 h of mixing. Protect from light. Discard any unused solution.

STORAGE

Store at 2°–8° C (36°–46° F). Discard if ampule has been frozen. Protect from direct light.

ADMINISTRATION

- Withhold drug and notify prescriber if absolute neutrophil count is less than 250/microliter, or platelet count is at or below 25,000/microliter, or the patient has a serious infection.
- Premedication 30 min before the first dose or dose escalation, and as needed, with diphenhydramine 50 mg and acetaminophen 650 mg, is recommended to decrease the incidence of infusion-related reactions.
- **DO NOT** give direct IV as a bolus dose.
- **IV Infusion:** Infuse each dose over 2 h. **Do not** give single doses greater than 30 mg.

INCOMPATIBILITIES Solution/additive: Do not infuse or mix with other drugs.

ACTION & *THERAPEUTIC EFFECT* Monoclonal antibody that attaches to CD52 cell surface antigens on a variety of leukocytes, including normal and malignant B and T lymphocytes, monocytes, and some granulocytes. Proposed mechanism of action is antibody-dependent lysis of leukemic

---

Common adverse effects in *italic*, life-threatening effects <u>underlined</u>: generic names in **bold**; classifications in SMALL CAPS; ♥ Canadian drug name; ● Prototype drug

19

cells following binding to CD52 cell surface antigens. *Initiates antibody-dependent cell lysis, thus inhibiting cell proliferation in chronic lymphocytic leukemia.*

CONTRAINDICATIONS Type I hypersensitivity to alemtuzumab or its components, hamster protein hypersensitivity; serious infection or exposure to viral infections (i.e., herpes or chickenpox), HIV infection; dental work; infection; lactation; pregnancy (category C).

CAUTIOUS USE History of hypersensitivity to other monoclonal antibodies; ischemic cardiac disease, angina, coronary artery disease; dental disease; history of varicella disease; females of childbearing age. Safety and efficacy in children are not established.

ADVERSE EFFECTS (≥1%) **Body as a Whole:** *Infusion reactions (rigors, fever, nausea, vomiting, hypotension, rash, shortness of breath, bronchospasm, chills), fatigue, pain, sepsis, asthenia, edema, herpes simplex, myalgias,* malaise, moniliasis, temperature change sensation, <u>coma, seizures</u>. **CNS:** *Headache, dysesthesias, dizziness, insomnia,* depression, tremor, somnolence, <u>cerebrovascular accident, subarachnoid hemorrhage</u>. **CV:** *Hypotension, tachycardia, hypertension,* <u>cardiac failure, arrhythmias, MI</u>. **GI:** *Diarrhea, nausea, vomiting, stomatitis, abdominal pain, dyspepsia, anorexia,* constipation. **Hematologic:** *Neutropenia, anemia, thrombocytopenia,* purpura, epistaxis, <u>pancytopenia</u>. **Respiratory:** *Dyspnea, cough, bronchitis, pneumonia, pharyngitis,* bronchospasm, rhinitis. **Skin:** *Rash, urticaria, pruritus, increased sweating.* **Other:** Risk of opportunistic infections.

DRUG INTERACTIONS Additive risk of bleeding with ANTICOAGULANTS, NSAIDS, PLATELET INHIBITORS, SALICYLATES. Increased risk of infections with LIVE VACCINES.

PHARMACOKINETICS Half-Life: 12 days.

NURSING IMPLICATIONS

Assessment & Drug Effects

- Alemtuzumab can cause serious, sometimes fatal, infusion-related reactions.
- Discontinue infusion immediately and notify prescriber if any of the following occurs: Hypotension, fever, chills, shortness of breath, bronchospasm, or rash.
- Monitor vital signs frequently during the infusion and for 4 h after the infusion period. Careful monitoring of BP and hypotensive symptoms is especially important in patients with ischemic heart disease and those on antihypertensives.
- Lab tests: Baseline and weekly CBS with differential and platelet counts, or more frequently in the presence of anemia, thrombocytopenia, or neutropenia; periodic blood glucose, serum electrolytes, and alkaline phosphatase.
- Monitor diabetics closely for loss of glycemic control.
- Report promptly S&S of thrombocytopenia (e.g., unusual bleeding, hematuria, or tarry stools).
- Monitor I&O and for S&S of dehydration especially with severe vomiting.

Patient & Family Education

- Do not accept immunizations with live viral vaccines during therapy or if therapy has been recently terminated.
- Men and women should use effective methods of contraception to prevent pregnancy during therapy and for at least 6 mo following therapy.
- Report promptly: Unexplained bleeding, fever, sore throat, flu-like symptoms, S&S of an infection, difficulty breathing, significant GI distress, abdominal pain, fluid retention, or changes in mental status.
- Diabetics should monitor blood glucose levels carefully since loss of glycemic control is a possible adverse reaction.

ALFENTANIL HYDROCHLORIDE

(al-fen'ta-nill)

Alfenta

Classification(s): NARCOTIC (OPIATE) AGONIST
Therapeutic: NARCOTIC ANALGESIC; GENERAL ANESTHETIC
Prototype: Morphine
Pregnancy Category: C   **Controlled Substance:** Schedule II

USES Major component of balanced anesthesia; analgesic, analgesic supplement, and primary anesthetic for induction of anesthesia when endotracheal and mechanical ventilation are required; component of monitored anesthesia care.

INDICATION & DOSAGE

Monitored Anesthesia Care (MAC)

Adult: Induction of MAC 3–8 mcg/kg; maintenance of MAC: 3–5 mcg/kg q5–20min or 0.25–1 mcg/kg/min; total dose: 3–40 mcg/kg
Geriatric: Reduce dose

Obesity

Dose based on IBW.

Hepatic Impairment Dosage Adjustment

Maintenance doses should be decreased.

SOLUTION PREPARATION

- *Direct IV Injection:* Small volumes may be given direct IV undiluted or diluted in 5 mL of NS (usually given by an MD or CRNA).
- *Continuous Infusion:* Add 20 mL of alfentanil to 230 mL of D5W, D5NS, NS, or LR solution to yield 40 mcg/mL. Note: Alfentanil may be diluted to concentrations of 25–80 mcg/mL.
- Maximum Concentration: 80 mcg/mL

Common adverse effects in *italic*, life-threatening effects <u>underlined</u>: generic names in **bold**; classifications in SMALL CAPS; ♣ Canadian drug name; ⊙ Prototype drug

21

STORAGE

Store at 15°–30° C (59°–86° F). Avoid freezing.

ADMINISTRATION

- **Direct IV Injection:** Give bolus dose over at least 3 min. **DO NOT** administer more rapidly.
- **Continuous Infusion:** Infuse at a rate of 0.25–1 mcg/kg/min. Note: Dose may be individualized.

INCOMPATIBILITIES Y-site: Amphotericin B, lansoprazole, thiopental.

ACTION & *THERAPEUTIC EFFECT* Alfentanil is a narcotic agonist analgesic with rapid onset and short duration of action. CNS effects of alfentanil appear to be related to interaction of drug with opiate receptors. *Analgesia is mediated through changes in the perception of pain at the spinal cord and at higher levels in the CNS. Brief duration of action is advantageous for short surgical procedures, but necessitates incremental injections or continuous infusion for long operations.*

CONTRAINDICATIONS Coagulation disorders; bacteremia; infection at injection site; pregnancy (category C), lactation. Safety in children less than 12 y is not established.

CAUTIOUS USE Older adults; history of pulmonary disease; biliary tract disease.

ADVERSE EFFECTS (≥1%) **Body as a Whole:** Thoracic muscle rigidity, flushing, diaphoresis; extremities feel heavy and warm. **CNS:** Dizziness, euphoria, drowsiness. **CV:** Hypotension, hypertension, tachycardia, bradycardia. **GI:** *Nausea,* vomiting, anorexia, constipation, cramps. **Respiratory:** Apnea, respiratory depression, dyspnea.

DIAGNOSTIC TEST INTERFERENCE Alfentanil may interfere with plasma amylase and lipase measurements for 24 h after administration.

DRUG INTERACTIONS BETA-ADRENERGIC BLOCKERS increase incidence of bradycardia; CNS DEPRESSANTS such as BARBITURATES, TRANQUILIZERS, NEUROMUSCULAR BLOCKING AGENTS, OPIATES, and INHALATION GENERAL ANESTHETICS may enhance the magnitude and duration of cardiovascular and CNS effects; enhancement or prolongation of postoperative respiratory depression also may result from concomitant administration of any of these agents with alfentanil. **Cimetidine, diltiazem, erythromycin, fluconazole** may increase levels and increase length of respiratory depression. **Rifampin** may decrease the efficacy of alfentanil.

PHARMACOKINETICS Onset: 2 min. **Duration:** Injection 30 min; continuous infusion 45 min. **Distribution:** Crosses placenta. **Metabolism:** Completely in liver. **Elimination:** Excreted in breast milk. **Half-Life:** 46–111 min.

NURSING IMPLICATIONS

Assessment & Drug Effects

- Monitor for S&S of increased sympathetic stimulation (arrhythmias) and evidence of depressed postoperative analgesia (tachycardia, pain, pupil-

Common adverse effects in *italic*, life-threatening effects <u>underlined</u>: generic names in **bold**; classifications in SMALL CAPS; ♣ Canadian drug name; ❶ Prototype drug

lary dilation, spontaneous muscle movement) if a narcotic antagonist has been administered to overcome residual effects of alfentanil.
- Monitor vital signs carefully; check for bradycardia, especially if patient is also taking a beta blocker.
- Note: Dizziness, sedation, nausea, and vomiting are common when drug is used as a postoperative analgesic.

Patient & Family Education
- Report unpleasant adverse effects when drug is used for patient-controlled analgesia.
- Rise from bed slowly and call for assistance to ambulate.
- Avoid alcoholic beverages or other CNS depressants for 24 h after outpatient surgery.

ALLOPURINOL

(al-oh-pure′i-nole)
Alloprin A ♣, Aloprim, Purinol ♣
Classification(s): ANTIGOUT AGENT
Therapeutic: ANTIGOUT
Pregnancy Category: C

USES Prophylactically to reduce severity of hyperuricemia associated with antineoplastic and radiation therapies, which greatly increase plasma uric acid levels by promoting nucleic acid degradation.

INDICATION & DOSAGE

Hyperuricemia
Adult: 200–400 mg/m^2/day (max: 600 mg/day) in 1–4 divided doses
Child: 200 mg/m^2/day in 1–4 divided doses

Renal Impairment Dosage Adjustment

CrCl	Dose	Interval
11–20 mL/min	200 mg/day	Normal
3–10 mL/min	100 mg/day	Normal
Less than 3 mL/min	100 mg/day	Extended interval (possibly more than 24 h)
Hemodialysis		Administer after hemodialysis or use 50% supplemental dose

SOLUTION PREPARATION
- *Vial Reconstitution:* Add 25 mL of sterile water for injection to a single dose vial (500 mg) to yield 20 mg/mL. Swirl to dissolve. **Must be** further diluted for infusion.

Common adverse effects in *italic*, life-threatening effects underlined: generic names in **bold**; classifications in SMALL CAPS; ♣ Canadian drug name; ✦ Prototype drug

23

- *Further Dilution of Reconstituted Solution:* Dilute with NS or D5W to a final concentration **not greater than** 6 mg/mL. Example: 10 mL reconstituted solution contains 200 mg of allopurinol. 200 mg (10 mL) added to 50 mL IV solution yields a total volume of 60 mL with a concentration of 3.3 mg/mL.
- Maximum Concentration: 6 mg/mL

STORAGE

Store at 20°–25° C (68°–77° F). Administer within 10 h after reconstitution. Do not refrigerate the reconstituted and/or diluted solution.

ADMINISTRATION

- If administering through Y-site with other compatible drugs, flush before/after with NS.
- **Intermittent Infusion:** Infuse over 30–60 min or longer depending on the total volume being infused.
- When possible, infusion should be initiated 24–48 h before the start of chemotherapy known to cause tumor cell lysis.

INCOMPATIBILITIES Solution/additive: Amikacin, amphotericin B, carmustine, cefotaxime, chlorpromazine, cimetidine, clindamycin, cytarabine, dacarbazine, daunorubicin, diphenhydramine, doxorubicin, doxycycline, droperidol, floxuridine, gentamicin, haloperidol, hydroxyzine, idarubicin, imipenem-cilastatin, mechlorethamine, meperidine, methylprednisolone, metoclopramide, minocycline, nalbuphine, netilmicin, ondansetron, prochlorperazine, promethazine, sodium bicarbonate, streptozocin, tobramycin, vinorelbine.

ACTION & *THERAPEUTIC EFFECT* Allopurinol reduces endogenous uric acid by inhibiting action of xanthine oxidase, the enzyme responsible for formation of uric acid from xanthine. Has no analgesic, antiinflammatory, or uricosuric actions. *Thus, urate pool is decreased by the lowering of both serum and urinary uric acid levels, and hyperuricemia is prevented.*

CONTRAINDICATIONS Hypersensitivity to allopurinol; as initial treatment for acute gouty attacks; idiopathic hemochromatosis (or those with family history); children (except those with hyperuricemia secondary to neoplastic disease and chemotherapy); pregnancy (category C).
CAUTIOUS USE Impaired hepatic or renal function; history of peptic ulcer, lower GI tract disease; bone marrow depression.

ADVERSE EFFECTS (≥1%) **CNS:** Drowsiness, headache, vertigo. **GI:** Nausea, vomiting, diarrhea, abdominal discomfort, indigestion, malaise. **Hematologic:** (Rare) Agranulocytosis, aplastic anemia, bone marrow depression, thrombocytopenia. **Skin:** Urticaria or pruritus, pruritic maculopapular rash, toxic epidermal necrolysis. **Other:** Hepatotoxicity, renal insufficiency.

Common adverse effects in *italic*, life-threatening effects underlined: generic names in **bold**; classifications in SMALL CAPS; ♣ Canadian drug name; ● Prototype drug

DIAGNOSTIC TEST INTERFERENCE Possibility of elevated blood levels of *alkaline phosphatase* and *serum transaminases (AST, ALT)*, and decreased blood *Hct, Hgb, leukocytes.*

DRUG INTERACTIONS Alcohol may inhibit renal excretion of uric acid; **ampicillin, amoxicillin** increase risk of skin rash; enhances anticoagulant effect of **warfarin;** toxicity from **azathioprine, mercaptopurine, cyclophosphamide, cyclosporin** increased; increases hypoglycemic effects of **chlorpropamide;** THIAZIDES increase risk of allopurinol toxicity and hypersensitivity (especially with impaired renal function); ACE INHIBITORS increase risk of hypersensitivity; high-dose vitamin C increases risk of kidney stone formation.

PHARMACOKINETICS Peak: 2–6 h. **Metabolism:** 75–80% to the active metabolite oxypurinol. **Elimination:** Slowly excreted in urine; excreted in breast milk. **Half-Life:** 1–3 h; oxypurinol, 18–30 h.

NURSING IMPLICATIONS

Assessment & Drug Effects

- Withhold drug and report promptly the onset of rash or fever. Life-threatening toxicity syndrome can occur 2–4 wk after initiation of therapy (more common with impaired renal function) and is generally accompanied by malaise, fever, and aching; a diffuse erythematous, desquamating rash; hepatic dysfunction; eosinophilia; and worsening of renal function.
- Monitor for therapeutic effectiveness which is indicated by normal serum and urinary uric acid levels usually by 1–3 wk. Goals of therapy: Lower serum uric acid level gradually to about 6 mg/dL; gradual decrease in size of tophi and absence of new tophaceous deposits (after approximately 6 mo), with consequent relief of joint pain and increased joint mobility.
- Monitor for S&S of an acute gouty attack that is most likely to occur during first 6 wk of therapy.
- Lab tests: Baseline CBC, liver and kidney function tests before therapy is initiated and then monthly, particularly during first few mo; serum electrolytes and urine pH at regular intervals; serum uric acid levels q1–2wk.
- Monitor I&O. Fluid intake sufficient to yield a daily output of at least 2 L in adults and the maintenance of a neutral or, preferably, slightly alkaline urine are desirable.

Patient & Family Education

- Drink enough fluid to produce urinary output of at least 2000 mL/day (fluid intake of at least 3000 mL/day).
- Report diminishing urinary output, cloudy urine, unusual color or odor to urine, pain or discomfort on urination.
- Report promptly the onset of itching or rash. Drug will be discontinued if a skin rash appears, even after weeks of therapy.
- Minimize exposure of eyes to ultraviolet or sunlight, which may stimulate the development of cataracts.
- Do not drive or engage in potentially hazardous activities until response to drug is known.

ALPHA₁-PROTEINASE INHIBITOR (HUMAN) 📵

(pro′ten-ase)

Prolastin, Aralast, Zemaira
Classification(s): ENZYME INHIBITOR
Therapeutic: ENZYME INHIBITOR
Pregnancy Category: C

USES Indicated for chronic replacement therapy in patients with alpha₁-antitrypsin deficiency and demonstrable panacinar emphysema.

INDICATION & DOSAGE

Panacinar Emphysema
Adult: 60 mg/kg once per wk

SOLUTION PREPARATION

- Warm unopened diluent (sterile water for injection) and drug concentrate to room temperature.
- *Vial Reconstitution:* Use the supplied, double needle transfer device to reconstitute. Place one end of the transfer needle in the vial of sterile water for injection supplied by manufacturer and the other end in the powder vial. The diluent will be drawn into the powder vial. Do not shake or invert vial until ready to withdraw contents. Note: More specific directions may be located in the kit supplied by the manufacturer.
- When reconstituted as directed, all products yield solutions that may be administered at the same rate (i.e., 0.08 mL/kg/min).
- Withdraw the required dose with the filter needle (if supplied by manufacturer) and change the needle. Inject into a sterile, **empty** IV minibag or glass bottle. If more than one vial is needed to achieve the required dose, use an aseptic technique to transfer the reconstituted solution from the vials into an empty IV bag or glass bottle.
- Note that the solution **must be** filtered prior to administration **either** with a filter needle or an in-line filter for the IV line (supplied by the manufacturer).

STORAGE

- Store unreconstituted drug at 2°–8° C (35°–46° F). Do not refrigerate after reconstitution. Use within 3 h after reconstituted solution is warmed to room temperature. Discard unused solution.
- Unopened vials **must be** used within 1 mo once removed from refrigeration.

ADMINISTRATION

- Note: Alpha₁-proteinase inhibitor is made from human plasma. Patient should be immunized against hepatitis B before receiving this drug.

Common adverse effects in *italic*, life-threatening effects <u>underlined</u>: generic names
in **bold**; classifications in SMALL CAPS; ♣ Canadian drug name; 📵 Prototype drug

- **IV Infusion:** Infuse at 0.08 mL/kg/min or more slowly as determined by the response and comfort of the patient. Note: The recommended dosage takes about 30 min to administer to a 70 kg person.
- If adverse events occur, reduce the rate or stop the infusion until the symptoms subside. The infusion may then be resumed at a rate tolerated by the subject.

INCOMPATIBILITIES Solution/additive: Do not mix with other agents.

ACTION & *THERAPEUTIC EFFECT* Alpha₁-proteinase inhibitor (alpha₁-PI; alpha₁-antitrypsin) is extracted from plasma and used in patients with panacinar emphysema who have alpha₁-antitrypsin deficiency. Alpha₁-antitrypsin deficiency is a chronic, hereditary, and usually fatal autosomal recessive disorder. *Prevents the progressive breakdown of elastin tissues in the alveoli, thus slowing panacinar emphysema progression.*

CONTRAINDICATIONS Individuals with selective IgA deficiencies; pregnancy (category C), lactation.

CAUTIOUS USE Patients with significant heart disease or other conditions that may be aggravated with slight increases in plasma volume. Safety and efficacy in children are not established.

ADVERSE EFFECTS (≥1%) **Hematologic:** Transient leukocytosis. **CNS:** Dizziness, headache, fever (may be delayed). **Respiratory:** Upper and lower respiratory tract infections. **Other:** Hepatitis B if not immunized, elevated liver function tests.

DRUG INTERACTIONS None known.

PHARMACOKINETICS Distribution: Crosses placenta; distributed into breast milk. **Metabolism:** Undergoes catabolism in the intravascular space; approximately 33% is catabolized per day. **Half-Life:** 4.5–5.2 days.

NURSING IMPLICATIONS

Assessment & Drug Effects

- Administer with caution in patients at risk for circulatory overload as drug causes expansion of plasma volume. Monitor cardiac status throughout therapy.
- Discontinue infusion and notify prescriber immediately if bradycardia or hypotension develop.
- Monitor respiratory status throughout therapy. Assess lung sounds, respiratory rate, and ease of breathing throughout infusion.
- Monitor for delayed fever that may develop up to 12 h after therapy.
- Lab tests: Monitor serum alpha₁-PI level (minimum serum concentration level should be 80 mg/mL), periodic pulmonary functions, and ABGs.

Patient & Family Education

- Report promptly any breathing difficulty.
- Avoid smoking and notify prescriber of any changes in respiratory pattern.

Common adverse effects in *italic*, life-threatening effects <u>underlined</u>: generic names in **bold**; classifications in SMALL CAPS; ♣ Canadian drug name; ⊘ Prototype drug

27

ALPROSTADIL (PGE₁)

(al-pross'ta-dil)

Prostin VR Pediatric

Classification(s): PROSTAGLANDIN

Therapeutic: DUCTUS ARTERIOSUS MAINTENANCE

Prototype: Epoprostenol

Pregnancy Category: C

USES Temporary measure to maintain patency of ductus arteriosus in infants with ductal-dependent congenital heart defects until corrective surgery can be performed.

INDICATION & DOSAGE

To Maintain Patency of Ductus Arteriosus

Neonate: 0.05–0.1 mcg/kg/min, may increase gradually (max: 0.4 mcg/kg/min if necessary)

SOLUTION PREPARATION

- Dilute 1 mL (500 mcg) of alprostadil solution in NS or D5W to a volume appropriate for pump delivery system and infusion rate. For example, a 500 mcg ampule diluted in 250 mL yields 2 mcg/mL; diluted in 100 mL yields 5 mcg/mL; diluted in 50 mL yields 10 mcg/mL; diluted in 25 mL yields 20 mcg/mL.
- Prepare fresh solution every 24 h. Discard unused portions.

STORAGE

Store undiluted solution at 2°–8° C (36°–46° F). Protect from freezing.

ADMINISTRATION

- **IV Infusion:** Infuse at rate of 0.05–0.1 mcg/kg/min up to a maximum of 0.4 mcg/kg/min.
- Reduce infusion rate immediately if arterial pressure drops significantly or if fever occurs.
- Discontinue promptly if apnea or bradycardia occurs.
- After the desired therapeutic response is achieved, reduce infusion rate to provide the lowest possible dosage that maintains the response.

INCOMPATIBILITIES Solution/additive: Do not mix with other agents.

ACTION & *THERAPEUTIC EFFECT* Alprostadil maintains ductal patency by relaxing the smooth muscles of the ductus arteriosus. It is only effective if given prior to complete anatomic closure of the ductus arteriosus. *Preserves ductal patency by relaxing smooth muscle of ductus arteriosus.*

CONTRAINDICATIONS Respiratory distress syndrome (hyaline membrane disease); pregnancy (category C).

Common adverse effects in *italic*, life-threatening effects <u>underlined</u>: generic names in **bold**; classifications in SMALL CAPS; ✦ Canadian drug name; ○ Prototype drug

CAUTIOUS USE Bleeding tendencies; hypersensitivity to alprostadil; sickle cell anemia or trait; cardiovascular disease.

ADVERSE EFFECTS (≥1%) **CNS:** *Fever,* seizures, lethargy. **CV:** *Flushing,* bradycardia, hypotension, syncope, tachycardia; CHF, <u>ventricular fibrillation, shock</u>. **GI:** Diarrhea, gastric regurgitation. **Hematologic:** <u>Disseminated intravascular coagulation (DIC)</u>, thrombocytopenia. **Respiratory:** *Apnea.* **Skin:** Rash on face and arms, alopecia. **Other:** Leg pain.

DRUG INTERACTIONS May increase anticoagulant properties of **warfarin;** ANTIHYPERTENSIVE AGENTS increase risk of hypotension.

PHARMACOKINETICS Onset: 15 min to 3 h. **Metabolism:** Rapidly in lungs. **Elimination:** Through kidneys. **Half-Life:** 5–10 min.

NURSING IMPLICATIONS

Assessment & Drug Effects

▪ Monitor therapeutic effectiveness, which is indicated by increase in blood oxygenation (Po₂), usually evident within 30 min, in infants with cyanotic heart disease. Normal Po₂ for neonates is 60–70 mm Hg. Therapeutic effectiveness is also indicated by increased pH in those with acidosis, increased systemic BP and urinary output, return of palpable pulses, and decreased ratio of pulmonary artery to aortic pressure in infants with restricted systemic blood flow.

▪ Monitor ECG, heart rate, respiratory rate, systemic BP, pulmonary artery and descending aorta pressures, femoral pulse, urinary output, and rectal temperature intermittently throughout the infusion.

▪ Lab tests: Monitor arterial blood gases and arterial blood pH intermittently throughout the infusion.

ALTEPLASE RECOMBINANT ●

(al'te-plase)

Activase, Cathflo Activase

Classification(s): THROMBOLYTIC AGENT, TISSUE PLASMINOGEN ACTIVATOR
Therapeutic: THROMBOLYTIC
Pregnancy Category: C

USES Indicated in selected cases of acute MI, preferably within 6 h of attack for recanalization of the coronary artery; lysis of acute pulmonary emboli; acute ischemic stroke or thrombotic stroke (within 3 h of onset); treatment of acute coronary artery thrombosis in the setting of percutaneous coronary intervention (PCI); reestablishing patency of occluded IV catheter.

UNLABELED USES Lysis of arterial occlusions in peripheral and bypass vessels; DVT.

Common adverse effects in *italic*, life-threatening effects <u>underlined</u>: generic names in **bold**; classifications in SMALL CAPS; ♣ Canadian drug name; ● Prototype drug

29

INDICATION & DOSAGE

Acute MI

Adult:
   Wt of 65 kg or More: 60 mg over first hour, 20 mg/h over second hour, and 20 mg over third hour (for a total of 100 mg over 3 h).
   Wt Less Than 65 kg: 1.25 mg/kg over 3 h (60% of dose over first hour, 20% of dose over second hour, and 20% of dose over third hour).
   Accelerated Schedule (with heparin and aspirin), Wt More Than 67 kg: 15 mg bolus, then 50 mg over next 30 min, then 35 mg over next 60 min.
   Accelerated Schedule (with heparin and aspirin), Wt 67 kg or Less: 15 mg bolus, then 0.75 mg/kg (not to exceed 50 mg) over next 30 min, then 0.50 mg/kg (not to exceed 35 mg) over next 60 min.

Acute Ischemic Stroke/Thrombotic Stroke

Adult: 0.9 mg/kg over 60 min with 10% of dose as an initial bolus over 1 min (max: 90 mg)

Pulmonary Embolism

Adult: 100 mg infused over 2 h

Reopen Occluded IV Catheter

Adult/Child (wt greater than 30 kg): Instill 2 mg/2 mL into dysfunctional catheter for 2 h. May repeat once if needed.
Child:
   2 y or Older and 10–29 kg: Instill 110% of internal lumen volume with 1 mg/ mL concentration (max 2 mg). May repeat if function not restored within 2 h.
   Less Than 2 y and Less Than 10 kg: 0.5 mg diluted in a volume to fill the lumen of the catheter

SOLUTION PREPARATION

- *50-mg Vial Reconstitution:* Do not use if vacuum in vial has been broken. Use a large-bore needle (e.g., 18 gauge) and **do not** prime needle with air. Dilute contents of the alteplase vial with sterile water for injection supplied by manufacturer. Direct stream of sterile water into the lyophilized cake. Slight foaming is usual. Allow to stand until bubbles dissipate. Resulting concentration is 1 mg/mL. May be given as prepared or further diluted.
- *100-mg Vial Reconstitution:* Use materials supplied by manufacturer (Note: The 100-mg vial does not contain a vacuum). Keep the vial of sterile water for injection upright and insert the transfer device into the center of the stopper. Hold the vial of alteplase upside-down and push the center of the vial stopper down on transfer device. Invert the two vials so that alteplase is on the bottom. Allow the sterile water to flow into the alteplase vial. Separate the alteplase vial and gently swirl to dissolve the powder. **DO NOT SHAKE.** Resulting concentration is 1 mg/mL. May be given as prepared or further diluted.

- *Further Dilution of Reconstituted Solution:* The 50-mg and 100-mg vials may be further diluted immediately before administration with an equal volume of NS or D5W to a concentration of 0.5 mg/mL.

STORAGE

Reconstituted drug is stable for 8 h refrigerated or at controlled room temperature (2°–30° C; 36°–86° F). Since there are no preservatives, discard any unused solution after that time.

ADMINISTRATION

- Administer as soon as possible after the thrombotic event, preferably within 6 h.

Acute MI

- **Direct IV Injection & Infusion:** Give 60% of total dose in the first hour for acute MI, with 6–10% given by direct bolus injection over 1–2 min and remainder of first dose infused over hour 1. Follow with second dose (20% of total) over hour 2, and third dose (20% of total) over hour 3.
- See **INDICATION & DOSAGE** information for accelerated schedule.

Acute Ischemic Stroke

- **Direct IV Injection & Infusion:** Give 5 mg bolus dose over 1 min, then infuse the remainder of the 0.75 mg/kg dose over 60 min.
- Do not exceed a total dose of 100 mg. Higher doses have been associated with intracranial bleeding.
- Follow infusion of drug by flushing IV tubing with 30–50 mL of NS or D5W.

Pulmonary Embolism

- **IV Infusion:** Infuse entire dose over a 2 h period.

Catheter Occlusion

- *Adult/Child (wt greater than 30 kg):* Instill 2 mg/2 mL into catheter for 2 h. May repeat once if needed.
- *Child (2 y or older and 10–29 kg):* Instill 110% of internal lumen volume with 1 mg/mL concentration (max: 2 mg). May repeat if function not restored within 2 h.
- *Child (less than 2 y and less than 10 kg):* Instill 0.5 mg diluted in a volume to fill the lumen of the catheter.

INCOMPATIBILITIES Solution/additive: Dobutamine, dopamine, heparin. Y-site: Bivalirudin, dobutamine, dopamine, heparin, nitroglycerin.

ACTION & *THERAPEUTIC EFFECT* This recombinant DNA-derived form of human tissue-type plasminogen activator (t-PA) is a thrombolytic agent. The agent t-PA promotes thrombolysis by forming the active proteolytic enzyme plasmin. *Plasmin is capable of degrading fibrin, fibrinogen, and Factors V, VIII, and XII.*

CONTRAINDICATIONS Active internal bleeding; history of cerebrovascular accident; recent (within 2 mo) intracranial or interspinal surgery or

Common adverse effects in *italic*, life-threatening effects <u>underlined</u>: generic names in **bold**; classifications in SMALL CAPS; ♣ Canadian drug name; ◐ Prototype drug

31

trauma, intracranial neoplasm; arteriovenous malformation; bleeding disorders; severe uncontrolled hypertension; likelihood of left heart thrombus; acute pericarditis; bacterial endocarditis; severe liver or renal dysfunction; septic thrombophlebitis; current use of oral anticoagulants; pregnancy (category C).

CAUTIOUS USE Recent major surgery (within 10 days); cerebral vascular disease; recent GI or GU bleeding; recent trauma; renal impairment; hypertension; age greater than 75; hemorrhagic ophthalmic conditions; lactation.

ADVERSE EFFECTS (≥1%) **Hematologic:** Internal and superficial bleeding (cerebral, retroperitoneal, GU, GI).

DRUG INTERACTIONS ANTICOAGULANTS may increase bleeding risk, **nitroglycerin** may decrease therapeutic effect.

PHARMACOKINETICS Peak: 5–10 min after infusion completed. **Duration:** Baseline values restored in 3 h. **Metabolism:** In liver. **Elimination:** In urine. **Half-Life:** 26.5 min.

NURSING IMPLICATIONS

Assessment & Drug Effects

- Prior to initiating therapy: Baseline coagulation tests including aPTT, bleeding time, PT, TT, INR, **must be** done.
- Discontinue infusion immediately and notify prescriber if dysrhythmias occur.
- Monitor for S&S of excess bleeding q15min for the first hour of therapy, q30min for second to eighth hour, then q8h. Monitor vital signs frequently. Perform neurological checks throughout drug infusion q30min and every hour for the first 8 h after infusion. Continue monitoring vital signs until laboratory reports confirm anticoagulant control. Patient is at risk for post-thrombolytic bleeding for 2–4 days after intracoronary alteplase treatment.
- Lab tests: Baseline coagulation tests including aPTT, bleeding time, PT, TT, INR; baseline Hct, Hgb, and platelet counts, in case of bleeding. Draw Hct following drug administration to detect possible blood loss.
- Protect patient from invasive procedures because spontaneous bleeding occurs twice as often with alteplase as with heparin. IM injections are contraindicated. Also prevent physical manipulation of patient during thrombolytic therapy to prevent bruising.
- Keep patient in bed while receiving this medication.
- Report signs of bleeding: Gum bleeding, epistaxis, hematoma, spontaneous ecchymoses, oozing at catheter site, increased pain from internal bleeding. Stop the infusion, then resume when bleeding stops.
- Use the radial artery to draw ABGs. Pressure to puncture sites, if necessary, should be maintained for up to 30 min.

Patient & Family Education

- Report immediately a sudden, severe headache.
- Report blood in urine and bloody or tarry stools.
- Report any signs of bleeding or oozing from cuts or places of injection.
- Remain quiet and on bedrest while receiving this medicine.

AMIFOSTINE

(am-i-fos'teen)

Ethyol

Classification(s): CYTOPROTECTIVE AGENT

Therapeutic: TISSUE PROTECTION

Pregnancy Category: C

USES Reduction of the cumulative renal toxicity associated with cisplatin, xerostomia.

UNLABELED USES Reduction of paclitaxel toxicity.

INDICATION & DOSAGE

Renal Protection

Adult: 910 mg/m^2 once daily, prior to chemotherapy

Reduction of Xerostomia

Adult: 200 mg/m^2 prior to radiation therapy

SOLUTION PREPARATION

Vial Reconstitution: Add 9.7 mL of NS to a single-dose, 500-mg vial to yield 50 mg/mL. May be further diluted with NS to a range of 5–40 mg/mL.

STORAGE

Store reconstituted solution at room temperature (25° C; 77° F) for 5 h or refrigerate up to 24 h.

ADMINISTRATION

- Do not administer to patients who are hypotensive or dehydrated. Keep supine during IV infusion.
- Give antiemetics, adequately hydrate, and defer antihypertensive drugs for 24 h prior to administration.
- **IV Infusion for Renal Protection:** Infuse over no more than 15 min, beginning 30 min before chemotherapy; place patient in supine position prior to and during infusion.
- **IV Infusion for Xerostomia:** Begin 15–30 min before radiation and infuse over 3 min.

INCOMPATIBILITIES Solution/additive: Do not mix with any solutions other than NS. **Y-site: Acyclovir, amphotericin B, chlorpromazine, cisplatin, ganciclovir, hydroxyzine, prochlorperazine.**

ACTION & *THERAPEUTIC EFFECT* Amifostine reduces cytotoxic damage induced by radiation or antineoplastic agents in well-oxygenated cells. Protective effects appear to be mediated by the formation of a metabolite of amifostine that removes free radicals from normal cells exposed to cisplatin. *Amifostine is cytoprotective in the kidney, bone marrow, and GI*

Common adverse effects in *italic*, life-threatening effects <u>underlined</u>: generic names in **bold**; classifications in SMALL CAPS; ♣ Canadian drug name; ● Prototype drug

mucosa, but not in the brain or spinal cord. The cytoprotection results in decreased myelosuppression and peripheral neuropathy.

CONTRAINDICATIONS Sensitivity to aminothiol compounds or mannitol; patients with potentially curable malignancies; hypotensive patients or those who are dehydrated; pregnancy (category C), lactation.
CAUTIOUS USE Patients at risk for hypocalcemia; cardiovascular disease (i.e., arrhythmias, CHF, TIA, CVA).

ADVERSE EFFECTS (≥1%) **CV:** *Transient reduction in blood pressure.* **GI:** *Nausea, vomiting.* **Other:** Infusion reactions (flushing, feeling of warmth or coldness, chills, dizziness, somnolence, hiccups, sneezing), hypocalcemia, hypersensitivity reactions.

DRUG INTERACTIONS ANTIHYPERTENSIVES could cause or potentiate hypotension.

PHARMACOKINETICS Onset: 5–8 min. **Metabolism:** Rapidly in liver to active free thiol metabolite. **Elimination:** Renally excreted. **Half-Life:** 8 min.

NURSING IMPLICATIONS
Assessment & Drug Effects
Treatment for Renal Protection:
- Patient **must be** adequately hydrated before initiation of infusion.
- Monitor BP every 5 min during infusion.
- Discontinue infusion immediately if systolic BP drops significantly from baseline (e.g., baseline SBP [drop]):
  - SBP less than 100 mm [drop 20 mm]
  - SBP 100–119 [drop 25 mm]
  - SBP 120–139 [drop 30 mm]
  - SBP 140–179 [drop 40 mm]
  - SBP equal to 180 or higher [drop 50 mm]
- Place patient flat with legs raised and administer a NS solution using a separate IV line. If BP returns to normal within 5 min and patient is asymptomatic, the infusion may be restarted to complete the dose.
- Lab tests: Periodic serum calcium.
- Monitor for S&S of hypocalcemia (see Appendix C) and fluid balance if vomiting is significant.
- Monitor I&O throughout therapy.

Treatment for Xerostomia:
- Monitor BP before and immediately after the infusion and as needed.

Patient & Family Education
- Remain supine through infusion period.
- Report promptly: Chills, difficulty breathing, rash, itching, tightness of the throat or chest, feelings of dizziness or faintness.

Common adverse effects in *italic*, life-threatening effects <u>underlined</u>: generic names in **bold**; classifications in SMALL CAPS; ♣ Canadian drug name; ◑ Prototype drug

AMIKACIN SULFATE

(am-i-kay'sin)

Amikin

Classification(s): ANTIBIOTIC, AMINOGLYCOSIDE
Therapeutic: ANTIBACTERIAL
Prototype: Gentamicin
Pregnancy Category: C

USES Primarily for short-term treatment of serious infections of respiratory tract, bones, joints, skin, and soft tissue, CNS (including meningitis), peritonitis burns, recurring urinary tract infections (UTIs).

UNLABELED USES Intrathecal or intraventricular administration, in conjunction with IV dosage.

INDICATION & DOSAGE

Moderate to Severe Infections

Adult: 5–7.5 mg/kg loading dose, then 7.5 mg/kg q12h (max: 15 mg/kg/day) for 7–10 days

Child: 5–7.5 mg/kg loading dose, then 5–7.5 mg/kg q8h for 7–10 days (max: 1.5 g/day)

Infant/Neonate (over 7 days): 10 mg/kg loading dose, then 7.5 mg/kg q12h for 7–10 days

Uncomplicated UTI

Adult: 250 mg q12h

Obesity

Calculate dose based on IBW.

Renal Impairment Dosage Adjustments

CrCl	Dose	Interval
Over 60 mL/min	Normal	q8h
40–60 mL/min	Normal	q12h
20–39 mL/min	Half dose	q24h
Less than 20 mL/min	Loading dose then monitor closely	
Hemodialysis		Administer after hemodialysis or $^2/_3$ as supplemental dose

SOLUTION PREPARATION

- Add contents of 500 mg vial to 100 or 200 mL D5W, NS, D5NS, LR or other compatible solution.

Common adverse effects in *italic*, life-threatening effects <u>underlined</u>: generic names in **bold**; classifications in SMALL CAPS; ♣ Canadian drug name; ◑Prototype drug

35

- *Pediatric Patients:* Volume of diluent depends on patient's fluid tolerance. Note that a pediatric injection preparation of 50 mg/mL is available.
- Maximum Concentration: 10 mg/mL
- Note: Color of solution may vary from colorless to light straw color or very pale yellow.

STORAGE

Store at 15°–30° C (59°–86° F).

ADMINISTRATION

- Patient should be well-hydrated prior to infusion.
- **Intermittent Infusion:** Infuse a single dose (*including loading dose*) over at least 30–60 min. Increase infusion time to 1–2 h for infants.
- Monitor infusion rate carefully. A rapid rise in serum amikacin level can cause respiratory depression (neuromuscular blockade) and other signs of toxicity.

INCOMPATIBILITIES Solution/additive: **Aminophylline, amphotericin B, ampicillin,** CEPHALOSPORINS, **chlorothiazide, heparin,** PENICILLINS, **phenytoin, thiopental, vitamin B complex with C.** Y-site: **Allopurinol, amphotericin B, azithromycin, hetastarch, propofol, thiopental.**

ACTION & *THERAPEUTIC EFFECT* Appears to inhibit protein synthesis in bacterial cell and is usually bactericidal. *Effective against a wide range of gram-negative bacteria, including many strains resistant to other aminoglycosides. Also effective against penicillinase- and non–penicillinase-producing* Staphylococcus.

CONTRAINDICATIONS History of hypersensitivity or toxic reaction with an aminoglycoside antibiotic; pregnancy (category C), lactation.

CAUTIOUS USE Impaired renal function; eighth cranial (auditory) nerve impairment; preexisting vertigo or dizziness, tinnitus, or dehydration; fever; older adults; premature infants, neonates, and infants; myasthenia gravis; parkinsonism; hypocalcemia.

ADVERSE EFFECTS (≥1%) **CNS:** Neurotoxicity: drowsiness, unsteady gait, weakness, clumsiness, paresthesias, tremors, convulsions, peripheral neuritis. **Special Senses:** *Auditory–ototoxicity,* high-frequency hearing loss, complete hearing loss (occasionally permanent), tinnitus, ringing or buzzing in ears. **Vestibular:** Dizziness, ataxia. **GI:** Nausea, vomiting, <u>hepatotoxicity</u>. **Metabolic:** Hypokalemia, hypomagnesemia. **Skin:** Skin rash, urticaria, pruritus, redness. **Urogenital:** Oliguria, urinary frequency, hematuria, <u>tubular necrosis</u>, azotemia. **Other:** Superinfections.

DRUG INTERACTIONS ANESTHETICS, SKELETAL MUSCLE RELAXANTS have additive neuromuscular blocking effects; **acyclovir, amphotericin B, bacitracin, capreomycin,** CEPHALOSPORINS, **colistin, cisplatin, carboplatin, methoxyflurane, polymyxin B, vancomycin, furosemide, ethacrynic acid** increase risk of ototoxicity and nephrotoxicity.

PHARMACOKINETICS Peak: 30 min. **Distribution:** Does not cross blood–brain barrier; crosses placenta; accumulates in renal cortex. **Elimination:**

Common adverse effects in *italic*, life-threatening effects <u>underlined</u>: generic names in **bold**; classifications in SMALL CAPS; ♣ Canadian drug name; ❶ Prototype drug

94–98% excreted renally in 24 h, remainder in 10–30 days. **Half-Life:** 2–3 h (adults), 4–8 h (neonates).

NURSING IMPLICATIONS

Assessment & Drug Effects

- Prior to initiating therapy: C&S before initial dose (start therapy pending results).
- Baseline vestibulocochlear nerve function; with treatment over 10 days, weekly audiograms, and vestibular tests strongly advised.
- Lab tests: Baseline and periodic renal function tests (more frequent CrCl in the presence of impaired renal function, in neonates, and in the older adult); peak and trough concentrations intermittently during therapy (peak 30–90 min after infusion and trough just prior to the next dose); note that prolonged high trough (greater than 8 mcg/mL) or peak (greater than 30–35 mcg/mL) levels are associated with toxicity.
- Report promptly: Indicators of declining renal function; respiratory tract infections and other symptoms indicative of superinfections and notify prescriber should they occur.
- Monitor for S&S of ototoxicity [primarily involves the cochlear (auditory) branch; high-frequency deafness usually appears first and can be detected only by audiometer]. Report auditory symptoms (tinnitus, roaring noises, sensation of fullness in ears, hearing loss) and vestibular disturbances (dizziness or vertigo, nystagmus, ataxia).
- Monitor I&O: Report oliguria, hematuria, or cloudy urine.
- Keep well hydrated to reduce risk of nephrotoxicity; consult prescriber regarding optimum fluid intake.

Patient & Family Education

- Report promptly any changes in hearing or unexplained ringing/roaring noises or dizziness, and problems with balance or coordination.

AMINOCAPROIC ACID ⊙

(a-mee-noe-ka-proe′ik)

Amicar

Classification(s): HEMOSTATIC
Therapeutic: COAGULATOR
Pregnancy Category: C

USES To control excessive bleeding; also used in urinary fibrinolysis associated with severe trauma, anoxia, shock, urologic surgery, and neoplastic diseases of GU tract.

UNLABELED USES To prevent hemorrhage in hemophiliacs undergoing dental extraction; as a specific antidote for streptokinase or urokinase toxicity; to prevent recurrence of subarachnoid hemorrhage, especially

Common adverse effects in *italic*, life-threatening effects <u>underlined</u>: generic names in **bold**; classifications in SMALL CAPS; ♦ Canadian drug name; ⊙ Prototype drug

37

when surgery is delayed; for management of amegakaryocytic thrombo-cytopenia; and to prevent or abort hereditary angioedema episodes.

INDICATION & DOSAGE

Hemostatic

Adult: 4–5 g during first hour, then 1–1.25 g hourly for 8 h or until bleeding is controlled (max: 30 g/24 h)
Child: 100–200 mg/kg or 3 g/m^2 during first hour, then 33.3 mg/kg/h or 1 g/m^2/h (max: 18 g/m^2/24 h)

SOLUTION PREPARATION

- Dilute each 1 g (4 mL) in 50 mL of NS, D5W, D5NS, or LR.
- Maximum Concentration: 10 mg/mL

STORAGE

Store in tightly closed containers at 15°–30° C (59°–86° F). Avoid freezing.

ADMINISTRATION

- Use an infusion pump to regulate the infusion rate. Avoid rapid infusion which increases the risk of hypotension, faintness, and bradycardia or other arrhythmias.
- **IV Infusion:** Usual rate is 5 g or a fraction thereof over first hour. (Note: 5 g is typically diluted with 250 mL IV solution.) Infuse each additional dose over 1 h.

INCOMPATIBILITIES Solution/additive: Fructose solution.

ACTION & *THERAPEUTIC EFFECT* Synthetic hemostatic with specific anti-fibrinolysis action. Inhibits plasminogen activator substance, and to a lesser degree plasmin (fibrinolysin), which is concerned with destruction of clots. *Acts as an inhibitor of fibrinolytic bleeding.*

CONTRAINDICATIONS Severe renal impairment; active disseminated intra-vascular clotting (DIC); upper urinary tract bleeding (hematuria); hemophilia; benzyl alcohol hypersensitivity, especially in neonates; paraben hypersensitivity; pregnancy (category C), lactation.
CAUTIOUS USE Cardiac, renal, or hepatic disease; renal impairment; history of pulmonary embolus or other thrombotic diseases; hypovolemia.

ADVERSE EFFECTS (≥1%) **CNS:** Dizziness, malaise, headache, seizures. **CV:** Faintness, orthostatic hypotension; dysrhythmias; thrombophlebitis, thromboses. **Special Senses:** Tinnitus, nasal congestion. Conjunctival erythema. **GI:** Nausea, vomiting, cramps, diarrhea, anorexia. **Urogenital:** Diuresis, dysuria, urinary frequency, oliguria, reddish-brown urine (myoglobinuria), <u>acute renal failure</u>, prolonged menstruation with cramping. **Skin:** Rash.

DIAGNOSTIC TEST INTERFERENCE *Serum potassium* may be elevated (especially in patients with impaired renal function).

DRUG INTERACTIONS ESTROGENS, ORAL CONTRACEPTIVES may cause hypercoagulation.

Common adverse effects in *italic*, life-threatening effects <u>underlined</u>: generic names in **bold**; classifications in SMALL CAPS; ♣ Canadian drug name; ☮ Prototype drug

PHARMACOKINETICS Peak: 2 h. **Distribution:** Readily penetrates RBCs and other body cells. **Elimination:** 80% excreted as unmetabolized drug in 12 h.

NURSING IMPLICATIONS

Assessment & Drug Effects

- Check IV site at frequent intervals for extravasation. Observe for signs of thrombophlebitis. Change site immediately if extravasation or thrombophlebitis occurs (see Appendix C).
- Monitor & report S&S of myopathy: Muscle weakness, myalgia, diaphoresis, fever, reddish-brown urine (myoglobinuria), oliguria, as well as thrombotic complications: Arm or leg pain, tenderness or swelling, Homan's sign, prominence of superficial veins, chest pain, breathlessness, dyspnea. Drug should be discontinued promptly.
- Monitor vital signs and urine output.
- Lab tests: With prolonged therapy, monitor creatine phosphokinase activity and urinalyses for early detection of myopathy.

Patient & Family Education

- Report promptly: Difficulty urinating or reddish-brown urine, arm or leg pain, chest pain, or difficulty breathing.

AMINOPHYLLINE (THEOPHYLLINE ETHYLENEDIAMIDE)

(am-in-off'i-lin)

Classification(s): BRONCHODILATOR; XANTHINE
Therapeutic: BRONCHODILATOR
Prototype: Theophylline
Pregnancy Category: C

USES To prevent and relieve symptoms of acute bronchial asthma and treatment of bronchospasm associated with chronic bronchitis and emphysema.
UNLABELED USES Treatment of apnea and bradycardia in premature infants; as cardiac stimulant and diuretic in treatment of CHF.

INDICATION & DOSAGE

Bronchospasm

Adult: **Loading Dose,** 6 mg/kg; **Maintenance Dose,** *(Nonsmoker):* 0.5 mg/kg/h; *(Smoker):* 0.8 mg/kg/h; *(CHF):* 0.1–0.2 mg/kg/h
Child: **Loading Dose,** 6 mg/kg; **Maintenance Dose,** *(1–9 y):* 1 mg/kg/h; *(over 9 y):* 0.8mg/kg/h
Infant (2–6 mo): 0.5 mg/kg/h *(6–12 mo):* 0.6–0.7 mg/kg/h

Neonatal Apnea

Neonate: **Loading Dose,** 5 mg/kg; **Maintenance Dose,** 5 mg/kg/day divided q12h

---

Common adverse effects in *italic*, life-threatening effects <u>underlined</u>: generic names in **bold**; classifications in SMALL CAPS; ♣ Canadian drug name; ● Prototype drug

Obesity

Dose based on IBW.

SOLUTION PREPARATION

- *Loading Dose:* Dilute required dose in 100–200 mL NS, D5W, or D5/NS.
- *Maintenance Dose:* Dilute required dose in 500–1000 mL NS, D5W, or D5/NS.
- Do not use aminophylline solutions if discolored or if crystals are present.
- Maximum Concentration: 25 mg/mL

STORAGE

Store at 15°–30° C (59°–86° F). Protect from light. Discard any unused portion.

ADMINISTRATION

- **IV Infusion:** Infuse at a rate not to exceed 25 mg/min.
  - *Loading Dose:* Infuse over at least 30 min; do not exceed 25 mg/min.

INCOMPATIBILITIES Solution/additive: Amikacin, bleomycin, CEPHALOSPORINS, **chlorpromazine, ciprofloxacin, clindamycin, dimenhydrinate, dobutamine, doxorubicin, epinephrine, hydralazine, hydroxyzine, insulin, isoproterenol, meperidine, methylprednisolone, morphine, nafcillin, norepinephrine, papaverine, penicillin G, pentazocine, procaine, prochlorperazine, promazine, promethazine, verapamil, vitamin B complex with C, zinc. Y-site: Amiodarone, ciprofloxacin, clarithromycin, dobutamine, fenoldopam, hydralazine, lansoprazole, ondansetron, TPN, vinorelbine, warfarin.**

ACTION & *THERAPEUTIC EFFECT* A xanthine derivative that relaxes smooth muscle in the airways of the lungs, and suppresses the response of the airways to stimuli that constrict them. *It is a respiratory smooth muscle relaxant that results in bronchodilation.*

CONTRAINDICATIONS Hypersensitivity to xanthine derivatives or to ethylenediamine component; cardiac arrhythmias; pregnancy (category C), lactation.

CAUTIOUS USE Severe hypertension, cardiac disease, arrhythmias; impaired hepatic function; diabetes mellitus; hyperthyroidism; glaucoma; prostatic hypertrophy; fibrocystic breast disease; history of peptic ulcer; neonates and young children; patients over 55 y; COPD; acute influenza or patients receiving influenza immunization.

ADVERSE EFFECTS (≥1%) **CNS:** *Nervousness,* restlessness, depression, insomnia, irritability, headache, dizziness, muscle hyperactivity, convulsions. **CV:** Cardiac arrhythmias, tachycardia (with rapid IV), hyperventilation, chest pain, <u>severe hypotension, cardiac arrest.</u> **GI:** *Nausea, vomiting, anorexia,* hematemesis, diarrhea, epigastric pain.

DIAGNOSTIC TEST INTERFERENCE May delay gastric emptying time, and interfere with ***plasma amylase*** and ***lipase*** measurements.

DRUG INTERACTIONS Increases **lithium** excretion, lowering **lithium** levels; **cimetidine,** high-dose **allopurinol** (600 mg/day), **ciprofloxacin, erythromycin,** can significantly increase **theophylline** levels.

PHARMACOKINETICS Peak: 30 min. **Duration:** 4–8 h; varies with age, smoking, and liver function. **Distribution:** Crosses placenta. **Metabolism:** Extensively in liver, by CYP1A2. **Elimination:** Parent drug and metabolites excreted by kidneys; excreted in breast milk. **Half-Life:** 3.7 h (child), 7.7 h (adult).

NURSING IMPLICATIONS

Assessment & Drug Effects

- Monitor for and report promptly S&S of toxicity (generally related to theophylline serum levels over 20 mcg/mL). Observe for hypotension, arrhythmias, and convulsions until serum theophylline stabilizes within the therapeutic range. A sudden, sharp, unexplained rise in heart rate may indicate toxicity.
- Lab tests: Monitor serum theophylline levels closely. Desired range is 10–20 mcg/mL. Note that caffeine can falsely elevate theophylline levels.
- Note: Older adults, acutely ill, and patients with severe respiratory problems, liver dysfunction, or pulmonary edema are at greater risk of toxicity due to reduced drug clearance.
- Note: Children appear more susceptible to CNS-stimulating effects of xanthines (nervousness, restlessness, insomnia, hyperactive reflexes, twitching, convulsions). Dosage reduction may be indicated.

Patient & Family Education

- Report excessive nervousness or insomnia. Dosage reduction may be indicated.
- Note: Dizziness is a relatively common side effect, particularly in older adults; take necessary safety precautions.

AMIODARONE HYDROCHLORIDE ℗

(a-mee′oh-da-rone)

Cordarone

Classification(s): ANTIARRHYTHMIC, CLASS III
Therapeutic: ANTIARRHYTHMIC
Pregnancy Category: D

USES Prophylaxis and treatment of life-threatening ventricular arrhythmias and supraventricular arrhythmias, particularly with atrial fibrillation.
UNLABELED USES Conversion of atrial fibrillation to normal sinus rhythm, paroxysmal supraventricular tachycardia, AV nodal reentry tachycardia.

INDICATION & DOSAGE

Arrhythmias

Adult: **Loading Dose,** 150 mg over the first 10 min then 360 mg over the next 6 h; **Maintenance Dose,** 540 mg (0.5 mg/min) for 18 h; may continue at 0.5 mg/min after first 24 h

Hepatic Impairment Dosage Adjustment

Suggested in severe hepatic impairment.

SOLUTION PREPARATION

- *First Rapid Loading Dose Infusion:* Add 150 mg (3 mL) amiodarone to 100 mL D5W to yield 1.5 mg/mL.
- *Second Loading Dose and Maintenance Infusion First 24 h:* Add 900 mg (18 mL) amiodarone to 500 mL D5W to yield 1.8 mg/mL.
- *Maintenance Infusions After the First 24 h:* Prepare concentrations of 1–6 mg/mL amiodarone.

STORAGE

Store at 15°–30° C (59°–86° F). Protect from light.

ADMINISTRATION

- Note: Correct hypokalemia and hypomagnesemia prior to initiation of therapy.
- Administer using a 0.2 micron in-line filter. Administration through a dedicated central venous line is preferred; concentrations greater than 2 mg/mL infused over longer than 1 h **must be** given through a central venous line.
- **IV Infusions First 24 h:**
  - *First Rapid IV Loading Dose Infusion:* Infuse 150 mg over the first 10 min at a rate of 15 mg/min.
  - *Second IV Loading Dose Infusion:* Over the next 6 h, infuse 360 mg at a rate of 1 mg/min.
  - *IV Maintenance Dose Infusion:* Over the remaining 18 h, infuse 540 mg at a rate of 0.5 mg/min.
- After the first 24 h, infuse maintenance dose of 720 mg/24 h at a rate of 0.5 mg/min.
- Maximum concentration for peripheral infusion is 2 mg/mL.

INCOMPATIBILITIES **Solution/additive:** Aminophylline, cefamandole, cefazolin, furosemide, quinidine. **Y-site:** Aminophylline, ampicillin/sulbactam, argatroban, bivalirudin, cefamandole, cefazolin, ceftazidime, digoxin, drotrecogin, heparin, imipenem/cilastatin, magnesium sulfate, piperacillin, piperacillin/tazobactam, potassium phosphate, sodium bicarbonate, sodium nitroprusside, sodium phosphate.

ACTION & *THERAPEUTIC EFFECT* Class III antiarrhythmic that also has antianginal and antiadrenergic properties. It acts directly on all cardiac tissues by prolonging duration of action potential and refractory period of cardiac

---

Common adverse effects in *italic*, life-threatening effects <u>underlined</u>: generic names in **bold**; classifications in SMALL CAPS; ♣ Canadian drug name; ● Prototype drug

muscle without significantly affecting its resting membrane potential. *By direct action on smooth muscle, it decreases peripheral resistance and increases coronary blood flow. Blocks effects of sympathetic stimulation.*

CONTRAINDICATIONS Hypersensitivity to amiodarone, or benzyl alcohol; cardiogenic shock, severe sinus bradycardia, advanced AV block unless a pacemaker is available, severe sinus-node dysfunction or sick sinus syndrome, bradycardia, congenital or acquired QR prolongation syndromes, history of torsade de pointes; severe liver disease; pregnancy (category D), lactation.

CAUTIOUS USE Hepatic disease, cirrhosis; Hashimoto's thyroiditis, hypersensitivity to iodine, goiter, thyrotoxicosis, or history of other thyroid dysfunction; CHF, left ventricular dysfunction; older adults; Fabry disease, especially with visual disturbances; electrolyte imbalance, hypokalemia, hypomagnesemia, hypovolemia; preexisting lung disease, COPD; open heart surgery.

ADVERSE EFFECTS (≥1%) **CNS:** Peripheral neuropathy (*muscle weakness, wasting numbness, tingling*), *fatigue,* abnormal gait, dyskinesias, *dizziness,* paresthesia, headache. **CV:** Bradycardia, *hypotension* (IV), <u>sinus arrest, cardiogenic shock</u>, CHF, arrhythmias; AV block. **Special Senses:** *Corneal microdeposits,* blurred vision, optic neuritis, optic neuropathy, permanent blindness, corneal degeneration, macular degeneration, photosensitivity. **GI:** *Anorexia, nausea, vomiting, constipation,* <u>hepatotoxicity</u>. **Metabolic:** Hyperthyroidism or hypothyroidism; may cause neonatal hypo- or hyperthyroidism if taken during pregnancy. **Respiratory:** (Pulmonary toxicity) Alveolitis, pneumonitis (fever, dry cough, dyspnea), interstitial pulmonary fibrosis, <u>*fatal gasping syndrome*</u> with IV in children. **Skin:** Slate-blue pigmentation, *photosensitivity,* rash. **Other:** With chronic use, angioedema.

DRUG INTERACTIONS Significantly increases **digoxin** levels; enhances pharmacologic effects and toxicities of **disopyramide, procainamide, quinidine, flecainide, lidocaine, lovastatin, simvastatin;** anticoagulant effects of ORAL ANTICOAGULANTS enhanced; **verapamil, diltiazem,** BETA-ADRENERGIC BLOCKING AGENTS may potentiate sinus bradycardia, sinus arrest, or AV block; may increase **phenytoin** levels 2- to 3-fold; **cholestyramine** may decrease amiodarone levels; **fentanyl** may cause bradycardia, hypotension, or decreased output; may increase **cyclosporine** levels and toxicity; **cimetidine** may increase amiodarone levels; **ritonavir** may increase risk of amiodarone toxicity, including cardiotoxicity.

PHARMACOKINETICS Distribution: Concentrates in adipose tissue, lungs, kidneys, spleen; crosses placenta. **Metabolism:** Extensively hepatically metabolized; undergoes some enterohepatic cycling. **Elimination:** Excreted chiefly in bile and feces; also excreted in breast milk. **Half-Life:** Biphasic, initial 2.5–10 days, terminal 40–55 days.

NURSING IMPLICATIONS

Assessment & Drug Effects

- Monitor BP carefully during infusion and slow the infusion if significant hypotension occurs; bradycardia should be treated by slowing the infu-

Common adverse effects in *italic,* life-threatening effects <u>underlined</u>: generic names in **bold**; classifications in SMALL CAPS; ♣ Canadian drug name; ❶ Prototype drug

43

sion or discontinuing if necessary. Monitor heart rate and rhythm and BP until drug response has stabilized. Sustained monitoring is essential because drug has an unusually long half-life.

- Report promptly symptomatic bradycardia.
- Monitor for S&S of: Adverse effects, particularly conduction disturbances and exacerbation of arrhythmias, in patients receiving concomitant antiarrhythmic therapy (reduce dosage of previous agent by 30–50% several days after amiodarone therapy is started); drug-induced hypothyroidism or hyperthyroidism (see Appendix C), especially during early treatment period; pulmonary toxicity (progressive dyspnea, fatigue, cough, pleuritic pain, fever) throughout therapy.
- Lab tests: Baseline and periodic assessments should be made of liver, lung, and thyroid functions. Drug may cause thyroid function test abnormalities in the absence of thyroid function impairment.
- Report promptly if elevations of AST and ALT persist or if they are 2–3 times above normal baseline readings; dose will be reduced or drug will be withdrawn to prevent hepatotoxicity and liver damage.
- Auscultate chest periodically or when patient complains of respiratory symptoms. Check for diminished breath sounds, rales, pleuritic friction rub; observe breathing pattern. Drug-induced pulmonary function problems **must be** distinguished from CHF or pneumonia.
- Anticipate possible CNS symptoms within a week after amiodarone therapy begins. Proximal muscle weakness, a common side effect, intensified by tremors presents a great hazard to the ambulating patient. Assess severity of symptoms. Supervision of ambulation may be indicated.

Patient & Family Education

- Become familiar with potential adverse reactions and report those that are bothersome to the prescriber.
- When switched to oral amiodarone: Use dark glasses to ease photophobia; follow recommendation for regular ophthalmic exams; wear protective clothing and a barrier-type sunscreen to prevent a photosensitivity reaction (erythema, pruritus); avoid exposure to sun and sunlamps.

AMMONIUM CHLORIDE

(ah-mo'ni-um)

Classification(s): ELECTROLYTIC BALANCE AGENT
Therapeutic: ACIDIFIER; ELECTROLYTE REPLACEMENT
Pregnancy Category: B

USES Treatment of hypochloremic states and metabolic alkalosis.

INDICATION & DOSAGE

Metabolic Alkalosis and Hypochloremic States

Adult/Child: Dose calculated serum Cl deficit, 50% of calculated deficit is administered slowly

SOLUTION PREPARATION
- Dilute each 20 ml vial in 500–1000 mL NS.
- Maximum Concentration: 1–2% ammonium chloride.

STORAGE
- Store at 15°–30° C (59°–86° F). Avoid freezing.
- Concentrated solutions crystallize at low temperatures. Crystals can be dissolved by placing intact container in a warm water bath and warming to room temperature.

ADMINISTRATION
Intermittent Infusion: Infuse at a rate not to exceed 5 mL/min to avoid serious adverse effects (ammonia toxicity) and local irritation and pain.

INCOMPATIBILITIES Solution/additive: Codeine phosphate, dimenhydrinate. Y-site: Warfarin.

ACTION & *THERAPEUTIC EFFECT* Acidifying property is due to conversion of ammonium ion (NH_4^+) to urea in liver with liberation of H^+ and Cl^-. Potassium excretion in kidney also increases acid level of serum H^+ ions, but to a lesser extent. Tolerance to diuretic effect occurs within 2–3 days. *Systemic acidifier in metabolic alkalosis by releasing H^+ ions, which lower pH of the blood.*

CONTRAINDICATIONS Severe renal or hepatic insufficiency; primary metabolic or respiratory acidosis; hyperchloremia.
CAUTIOUS USE Cardiac edema, cardiac insufficiency, pulmonary insufficiency; pregnancy (category B), lactation.

ADVERSE EFFECTS (≥1%) **Body as a Whole:** Most secondary to ammonia toxicity. **CNS:** Headache, depression, drowsiness, twitching, excitability; EEG abnormalities. **CV:** Bradycardia and other arrhythmias. **GI:** Gastric irritation, nausea, vomiting, anorexia. **Metabolic:** Metabolic acidosis, hyperammonia. **Respiratory:** Hyperventilation. **Skin:** Rash. **Urogenital:** Glycosuria. **Other:** Pain and irritation at IV site.

DIAGNOSTIC TEST INTERFERENCE Ammonium chloride may increase *blood ammonia* and *AST,* decrease *serum magnesium* (by increasing urinary magnesium excretion), and decrease *urine urobilinogen.*

DRUG INTERACTIONS Aminosalicylic acid may cause crystalluria; increases urinary excretion of AMPHETAMINES, **flecainide, mexiletine, methadone, ephedrine, pseudoephedrine;** decreased urinary excretion of SULFONYLUREAS, SALICYLATES.

PHARMACOKINETICS Metabolism: In liver to HCl and urea. **Elimination:** Primarily in urine.

NURSING IMPLICATIONS
Assessment & Drug Effects
- Assess IV infusion site frequently for signs of irritation. Change site as warranted.

Common adverse effects in *italic*, life-threatening effects underlined; generic names in **bold**; classifications in SMALL CAPS; ♣ Canadian drug name; Ⓟ Prototype drug

45

- Monitor for S&S of: Metabolic acidosis (mental status changes including confusion, disorientation, coma, respiratory changes including increased respiratory rate and depth, exertional dyspnea); ammonium toxicity (cardiac arrhythmias including bradycardia, irregular respirations, twitching, seizures).
- Lab tests: Baseline and periodic determinations of CO_2 combining power, serum electrolytes, and urinary and arterial pH during therapy to avoid serious acidosis.
- Monitor I&O: Ammonium chloride may have a diuretic effect.

Patient & Family Education
- Report pain at IV injection site.

AMPHOTERICIN B 🅟

(am-foe-ter′i-sin)

Amphocin, Fungizone
Classification(s): ANTIBIOTIC, ANTIFUNGAL
Therapeutic: ANTIFUNGAL
Pregnancy Category: B

USES Used for a wide spectrum of potentially fatal systemic fungal (mycotic) infections.
UNLABELED USES Treatment of candiduria, fungal endocarditis, meningitis, septicemia, fungal infections of urinary bladder and urinary tract, amebic meningoencephalitis, and paracoccidioidomycosis.

INDICATION & DOSAGE

Systemic Infections
Adult: **Test Dose,** 1 mg in 20 mL of D5W; **Maintenance Dose,** 0.25–0.3 mg/kg/day, may gradually increase by 0.125–0.25 mg/kg/day up to 1 mg/kg/day. Max daily dose: 1.5 mg/kg
Child: **Test Dose,** 0.1 mg/kg up to 1 mg in 20 mL of D5W; **Maintenance Dose,** 0.4 mg/kg/day, may increase by 0.25 mg/kg/day to target dose of 0.25–1 mg/kg/day. Max daily dose: 1.5 mg/kg

Renal Impairment Dosage Adjustment
The dose can be reduced or interval extended.

SOLUTION PREPARATION

Typically prepared by pharmacy service due to complex technique required for IV solution preparation.

STORAGE

Solutions prepared for IV infusion (0.1 mg or less amphotericin B per mL) should be used promptly after preparation and should be protected from light during administration.

Common adverse effects in *italic*, life-threatening effects <u>underlined</u>: generic names in **bold**; classifications in SMALL CAPS; ♥ Canadian drug name; 🅟 Prototype drug

ADMINISTRATION

- **ALERT:** Rapid infusion of any amphotericin can cause cardiovascular collapse. If hypotension or arrhythmias develop, interrupt infusion and notify prescriber.
- A separate infusion line is recommended but when given through an existing IV line, flush before and after with D5W.
- Initiate therapy using the most distal vein possible and alternate sites with each dose if possible to reduce the risk of thrombophlebitis.
- *Test Dose:* The recommended concentration is 0.1 mg/mL (1 mg/10 mL). Infuse 1 mg in 20 mL D5W over 10–30 min. Monitor vital signs q30min for 2–4 h.
- *Maintenance Dose:* Infuse **slowly** over a period of 2–6 h (depending on the dose). Use longer infusion time for better tolerance. A 1 micron (or greater) in-line filter may be used.
- Protect IV solution from light during administration if exposed more than 8 h.

INCOMPATIBILITIES Solution/additive: Any **saline-containing solution** (precipitate will form), PARENTERAL NUTRITION SOLUTIONS, **amikacin, calcium chloride, calcium gluconate, chlorpromazine, cimetidine, ciprofloxacin, diphenhydramine, dopamine, edetate calcium disodium, gentamicin, kanamycin, magnesium sulfate, meropenem, metaraminol, methyldopate, penicillin G, polymyxin, potassium chloride, prochlorperazine, ranitidine, streptomycin, verapamil.**
Y-site: AMINOGLYCOSIDES, PENICILLINS, PHENOTHIAZINES, **allopurinol, amifostine, amsacrine, aztreonam, bivalirudin, cefepime, cefpirome, cisatracurium, dexmedetomidine, docetaxel, doxorubicin liposome, enalaprilat, etoposide, fenoldopam, filgrastim, fluconazole, fludarabine, foscarnet, gemcitabine, granisetron, heparin** (flush lines with **D5W**, not **NS**), **hetastarch, lansoprazole, linezolid, melphalan, meropenem, ondansetron, paclitaxel, pemetrexed, piperacillin/tazobactam, propofol, TPN, vinorelbine.**

ACTION & *THERAPEUTIC EFFECT* Exerts antifungal action on both resting and growing cells at least in part by selectively binding to sterols in fungus cell membrane. *Fungistatic at lower doses, and fungicidal at higher concentrations, depending on sensitivity of fungus.*

CONTRAINDICATIONS Hypersensitivity to amphotericin; lactation.
CAUTIOUS USE Severe bone marrow depression; renal function impairment or renal disease; hypokalemia, hypomagnesemia; pregnancy (category B).

ADVERSE EFFECTS (≥1%) **Body as a Whole:** Hypersensitivity (pruritus, urticaria, skin rashes, fever, dyspnea, <u>anaphylaxis</u>); *fever, chills.* **CNS:** Headache, sedation, muscle pain, arthralgia, weakness. **CV:** Hypotension, <u>cardiac arrest</u>. **Special Senses:** Ototoxicity with tinnitus, vertigo, loss of hearing. **GI:** Nausea, vomiting, diarrhea, epigastric cramps, anorexia, weight loss. **Hematologic:** Anemia, thrombocytopenia. **Metabolic:** *Hypokalemia, hypomagnesemia.* **Urogenital:** <u>Nephrotoxicity</u>, urine with low specific gravity. **Skin:** Dry, erythema, pruritus, burning sensation; allergic contact

Common adverse effects in *italic*, life-threatening effects <u>underlined</u>: generic names in **bold**; classifications in SMALL CAPS; ♣ Canadian drug name; ⊚ Prototype drug

47

dermatitis, exacerbation of lesions. **Other:** Pain; arthralgias, thrombophlebitis (IV site), superinfections.

DRUG INTERACTIONS AMINOGLYCOSIDES, **capreomycin, cisplatin, carboplatin, colistin, cyclosporine, mechlorethamine, furosemide, vancomycin** increase the possibility of nephrotoxicity; CORTICOSTEROIDS potentiate hypokalemia; with DIGITALIS GLYCOSIDES, hypokalemia increases the risk of **digitalis** toxicity.

PHARMACOKINETICS Peak: 1–2 h **Duration:** 20 h. **Distribution:** Minimal amounts enter CNS, eye, bile, pleural, pericardial, synovial, or amniotic fluids; similar plasma and urine concentrations. **Elimination:** Excreted renally; can be detected in blood up to 4 wk and in urine for 4–8 wk after discontinuing therapy. **Half-Life:** 24–48 h.

NURSING IMPLICATIONS

Assessment & Drug Effects

- Prior to initiating therapy: Baseline C&S; start drug pending results.
- Report to prescriber and withhold drug if BUN exceeds 40 mg/dL or serum creatinine rises above 3 mg/dL. Dosage should be reduced or drug discontinued until renal function improves.
- Monitor for S&S of local inflammatory reaction or thrombosis at injection site, particularly if extravasation occurs.
- Monitor cardiovascular and respiratory status and observe closely for adverse effects during initial IV therapy.
- If a test dose is given, monitor vital signs every 30 min for 2–4 h.
- Febrile reactions (fever, chills, headache, nausea) occur in 20–90% of patients, usually 1–2 h after beginning infusion, and subside within 4 h after drug is discontinued. The severity of this reaction usually decreases with continued therapy. Keep prescriber informed.
- Lab tests: Baseline C&S prior to initiation of therapy; start drug pending results; baseline and periodic BUN, serum creatinine, creatinine clearance; during therapy periodic CBC, serum electrolytes (especially potassium, magnesium, sodium, and calcium), and LFTs.
- Monitor I&O and weight. Report immediately oliguria, any change in I&O ratio and pattern, or appearance of urine (e.g., sediment, pink or cloudy urine (hematuria), abnormal renal function tests, unusual weight gain or loss.
- Consult prescriber for guidelines on adequate hydration and adjustment of daily dose as a possible means of avoiding or minimizing nephrotoxicity.
- Report promptly evidence of hearing loss or complaints of tinnitus, vertigo, or unsteady gait. Tinnitus may not be a complaint in older adults or the very young. Other signs of ototoxicity (i.e., vertigo or hearing loss) are more reliable indicators of ototoxicity in these age groups.

Patient & Family Education

- Report promptly: Pain or discomfort at IV insertion site; hearing loss, ringing in the ears; dizziness or unsteady gait; decrease in normal daily urinary output.

AMPHOTERICIN B LIPID-BASED

(am-foe-ter′i-sin)

Abelcet, Amphotec, AmBisome
Classification(s): ANTIBIOTIC, ANTIFUNGAL
Therapeutic: ANTIFUNGAL
Prototype: Amphotericin B
Pregnancy Category: B

USES Used for a wide spectrum of potentially fatal systemic fungal (mycotic) infections.
UNLABELED USES Treatment of candiduria, fungal endocarditis, meningitis, septicemia, fungal infections of urinary bladder and urinary tract, amebic meningoencephalitis, and paracoccidioidomycosis.

INDICATION & DOSAGE

Systemic Infections

Abelcet *Adult/Child:* 5 mg/kg/day

Amphotec *Adult/Child:* **Test Dose,** 10 mL of IV infusion solution (1.6–8.3 mg); **Maintenance Dose,** 3–4 mg/kg/day (max: 7.5 mg/kg/day) infused at 1 mg/kg/h

AmBisome *Adult/Child:* 3–5 mg/kg/day

Cryptococcal Meningitis in HIV

AmBisome *Adult:* 6 mg/kg/day infused over 2 h

Leishmaniasis

AmBisome *Adult (immunocompetent):* 3 mg/kg/day on days 1–5, 14, and 21, may repeat if necessary
Adult (immunocompromised): 4 mg/kg/day on days 1–5, 10, 17, 24, 31, and 38

SOLUTION PREPARATION

Each brand of amphotericin is prepared differently according to manufacturer's directions.

Abelcet

▪ Shake the vial gently until the yellow sediment at the bottom disappears. Each mL contains 5 mg of amphotericin. **Must be** diluted for infusion.
▪ Withdraw the required dose using a new 18-gauge needle for each vial needed. Remove the needle from each syringe and replace with the 5-micron filter needle supplied with each vial. Each filter needle may be used to filter the contents of up to four 100-mg vials.

Common adverse effects in *italic*, life-threatening effects <u>underlined</u>: generic names in **bold**; classifications in SMALL CAPS; ♣ Canadian drug name; ⊘ Prototype drug

- Transfer contents of each vial into an IV bag containing enough D5W to yield 1 mg/mL. For pediatric patients and patients with cardiovascular disease, the drug may be diluted to a final concentration of 2 mg/mL.
- Do not dilute with saline solutions or mix with other drugs or electrolytes.
- The IV solution is stable for up to 48 h at 2°–8° C (36°–46° F) and an additional 6 h at room temperature.

AmBisome

- *Vial Reconstitution:* Add 12 mL of sterile water for injection to each vial to yield 4 mg/mL. DO NOT reconstitute or mix with saline or other drugs. Shake well to dissolve. **Must be** further diluted for infusion.
- Withdraw the required dose into a sterile syringe with the 5-micron filter, provided, attached to the syringe. Use only one filter per vial. Inject contents into enough D5W to yield 1–2 mg/mL. Lower concentrations (0.2–0.5 mg/mL) may be used for infants and small children.
- Discard partially used vials. Reconstituted concentrate may be stored for up to 24 h at 2°–8° C (36°–46° F).

Amphotec

- *Vial Reconstitution:* Reconstitute with sterile water for injection only. Using sterile syringe and a 20-gauge needle **without a filter,** rapidly add 10 mL to the 50 mg vial or 20 mL to the 100 mg vial to yield 5 mg/mL. Shake gently rotating the vial until dissolved. The fluid may be opalescent or clear. **Must be** further diluted for infusion.
- Withdraw the required dose and inject into a D5W infusion bag to reach a final concentration of approximately 0.6 mg/mL (acceptable range 0.16 mg/mL to 0.83 mg/mL).
- Refrigerate after reconstitution and dilution at 2°–8° C (36°–46° F) and use within 24 h. **Do not freeze.**

STORAGE

- *Abelcet IV Solution:* Store up to 48 h at 2°–8° C (36°–46° F) and an additional 6 h at room temperature.
- *Amphotec IV Solution:* Store at 2°–8° C (36°–46° F); use within 24 h of preparation.
- *AmBisome IV Solution:* Store at 2°–8° C (36°–46° F); use within 6 h of preparation.

ADMINISTRATION

All Preparations

- **ALERT:** Rapid infusion of any amphotericin can cause cardiovascular collapse. If hypotension or arrhythmias develop, interrupt infusion and notify prescriber.
- A separate infusion line is recommended but when given through an existing IV line, flush before and after with D5W.
- Initiate therapy using the most distal vein possible and alternate sites with each dose if possible to reduce the risk of thrombophlebitis.

Abelcet IV Infusion

- Do not use an in-line filter.
- Infuse total daily dose at 2.5 mg/kg/h.
- Shake IV bag at least q2h to evenly mix solution.

Amphotec IV Infusion

- Do not use an in-line filter.
- *Test Dose:* Infuse over 10–30 min. Monitor vital signs q30min for 2–4 h.
- *Maintenance Dose:* Infuse at 1 mg/kg/h. Infusion time may be shortened but should never be less than 2 h. Infusion time may also be extended for better tolerance.

AmBisome IV Infusion

- An in-line filter may be used for infusion if diameter is not less than 1 micron.
- Infuse total daily dose over 2 h. Infusion time may be shortened if treatment is well tolerated but should never be less than 1 h.
- For pediatric patients a rate of 2.5 mg/kg/h is recommended.

INCOMPATIBILITIES Solution/additive: Any **saline-containing solution** (precipitate will form), PARENTERAL NUTRITION SOLUTIONS. **Y-site:** AMINOGLYCOSIDES, PENICILLINS, PHENOTHIAZINES, **alfentanil, amikacin, ampicillin, ampicillin/sulbactam, atenolol, aztreonam, bretylium, buprenorphine, butorphanol, calcium salts, carboplatin, cefazolin, cefepime, ceftazidime, ceftriaxone, chlorpromazine, cimetidine, cisatracurium, cyclophosphamide, cyclosporine, cytarabine, diazepam, digoxin, diphenhydramine, dobutamine, dopamine, doxorubicin, doxorubicin liposome, droperidol, enalaprilat, esmolol, etoposide, famotidine, fluconazole, fluorouracil, haloperidol, heparin** (flush lines with **D5W**, not **NS**), **hetastarch, hydromorphone, hydroxyzine, imipenem-cilastatin, labetalol, leucovorin, lidocaine, magnesium sulfate, meperidine, mesna, metoclopramide, metoprolol, metronidazole, midazolam, mitoxantrone, morphine, nalbuphine, naloxone, netilmicin, ofloxacin, ondansetron, paclitaxel, phenytoin, piperacillin, piperacillin/tazobactam, potassium chloride, prochlorperazine, promethazine, propranolol, propofol, ranitidine, remifentanil, sodium bicarbonate, ticarcillin/clavulanate, vecuronium, verapamil, vinorelbine.**

ACTION & *THERAPEUTIC EFFECT* Exerts antifungal action on both resting and growing cells at least in part by selectively binding to sterols in fungus cell membrane. *Fungistatic at lower doses, and fungicidal at higher concentrations, depending on sensitivity of fungus.*

CONTRAINDICATIONS Hypersensitivity to amphotericin; lactation.

CAUTIOUS USE Severe bone marrow depression; renal function impairment or renal disease; hypokalemia, hypomagnesemia; pregnancy (category B).

ADVERSE EFFECTS (≥1%) **Body as a Whole:** Hypersensitivity (pruritus, urticaria, skin rashes, fever, dyspnea, <u>anaphylaxis</u>); *fever, chills.* **CNS:** Headache, sedation, muscle pain, arthralgia, weakness. **CV:** Hypotension, <u>cardiac arrest</u>. **Special Senses:** Ototoxicity with tinnitus, vertigo, loss of hearing. **GI:** Nausea, vomiting, diarrhea, epigastric cramps, anorexia, weight loss. **Hematologic:** Anemia, thrombocytopenia. **Metabolic:** *Hypo-*

Common adverse effects in *italic*, life-threatening effects <u>underlined</u>: generic names in **bold**; classifications in SMALL CAPS; ♣ Canadian drug name; ❷ Prototype drug

51

kalemia, hypomagnesemia. **Urogenital:** <u>Nephrotoxicity</u>, urine with low specific gravity. **Skin:** Dry, erythema, pruritus, burning sensation; allergic contact dermatitis, exacerbation of lesions. **Other:** Pain; arthralgias, thrombophlebitis (IV site), superinfections.

DRUG INTERACTIONS AMINOGLYCOSIDES, **capreomycin, cisplatin, carboplatin, colistin, cyclosporine, mechlorethamine, furosemide, vancomycin** increase the possibility of nephrotoxicity; CORTICOSTEROIDS potentiate hypokalemia; with DIGITALIS GLYCOSIDES, hypokalemia increases the risk of **digitalis** toxicity.

PHARMACOKINETICS Peak: 1–2 h. **Duration:** 20 h. **Distribution:** Minimal amounts enter CNS, eye, bile, pleural, pericardial, synovial, or amniotic fluids; similar plasma and urine concentrations. **Elimination:** Excreted renally; can be detected in blood up to 4 wk and in urine for 4–8 wk after discontinuing therapy. **Half-Life:** 24–48 h.

NURSING IMPLICATIONS

Assessment & Drug Effects

- Prior to initiating therapy: Baseline C&S; start drug pending results.
- Report to prescriber and withhold drug if BUN exceeds 40 mg/dL or serum creatinine rises above 3 mg/dL. Dosage should be reduced or drug discontinued until renal function improves.
- Monitor for S&S of local inflammatory reaction or thrombosis at injection site, particularly if extravasation occurs.
- Monitor cardiovascular and respiratory status and observe closely for adverse effects during initial IV therapy.
- If a test dose is given, monitor vital signs every 30 min for at least 4 h.
- Febrile reactions (fever, chills, headache, nausea) occur in 20–90% of patients, usually 1–2 h after beginning infusion, and subside within 4 h after drug is discontinued. The severity of this reaction usually decreases with continued therapy. Keep prescriber informed.
- Lab tests: Baseline C&S prior to initiation of therapy; start drug pending results; baseline and periodic BUN, serum creatinine, creatinine clearance; during therapy periodic CBC, serum electrolytes (especially potassium, magnesium, sodium, calcium), and liver function tests.
- Monitor I&O and weight. Report immediately oliguria, any change in I&O ratio and pattern, or appearance of urine (e.g., sediment, pink or cloudy urine (hematuria), abnormal renal function tests, unusual weight gain or loss.
- Consult prescriber for guidelines on adequate hydration and adjustment of daily dose as a possible means of avoiding or minimizing nephrotoxicity.
- Report promptly evidence of hearing loss or complaints of tinnitus, vertigo, or unsteady gait. Tinnitus may not be a complaint in older adults or the very young. Other signs of ototoxicity (i.e., vertigo or hearing loss) are more reliable indicators of ototoxicity in these age groups.

Patient & Family Education

- Report promptly: Pain or discomfort at IV insertion site; hearing loss, ringing in the ears; dizziness or unsteady gait; decrease in normal daily urinary output.

AMPICILLIN ℗

(am-pi-sill'in)

Novo-Ampicillin ♣

AMPICILLIN SODIUM

Classification(s): ANTIBIOTIC; AMINOPENICILLIN
Therapeutic: ANTIBACTERIAL
Pregnancy Category: B

USES Infections of GU, respiratory, and GI tracts and skin and soft tissues; also gonococcal infections, bacterial meningitis, otitis media, sinusitis, and septicemia and for prophylaxis of bacterial endocarditis. Used parenterally only for moderately severe to severe infections.

INDICATION & DOSAGE

Systemic Infections

Adult/Child (40 kg and over): 250–500 mg q6h
Child/Infant (under 40 kg): 25–50 mg/kg/day divided q6–8h
Neonate: See following table.

Age	Weight	Dose	Interval
Up to 7 days	Up to 2000 g	50 mg/kg/day	q12h
Up to 7 days	Over 2000 g	75 mg/kg/day	q8h
Over 7 days	Less than 1200 g	50 mg/kg/day	q12h
Over 7 days	1200–2000 g	75 mg/kg/day	q8h
Over 7 days	Over 1000 g	100 mg/kg/day	q6h

Meningitis

Adult/Child/Infant: 150–200 mg/kg/day divided q3–4h
Neonate: See following table.

Age	Weight	Dose	Interval
Up to 7 days	Up to 2000 g	100 mg/kg/day	q12h
Up to 7 days	Over 2000 g	150 mg/kg/day	q8h
Over 7 days	Less than 1200 g	100 mg/kg/day	q12h
Over 7 days	1200–2000 g	150 mg/kg/day	q8h
Over 7 days	Over 1000 g	200 mg/kg/day	q6h

Gonorrhea

Adult: 500 mg q8–12h

Common adverse effects in *italic*, life-threatening effects <u>underlined</u>: generic names in **bold**; classifications in SMALL CAPS; ♣ Canadian drug name; ℗ Prototype drug

Bacterial Endocarditis Prophylaxis

Adult: 2 g 30 min before procedure
Child: 50 mg/kg 30 min before procedure (max: 2 g)

Group B Strep Prophylaxis

Adult: 2 g then 1 g q4h until delivery

Renal Impairment Dosage Adjustment

CrCl	Dose	Interval
10–50 mL/min	Normal	q6–12h
Less than 10 mL/min	Normal	q12h
Hemodialysis	Normal	Administer after hemodialysis

SOLUTION PREPARATION

- Wear disposable gloves when handling drug repeatedly; contact dermatitis occurs frequently in sensitized individuals.
- *Vial Reconstitution:* Reconstitute each 250 or 500 mg vial with at least 5 mL of sterile water for injection. Reconstitute each 1 or 2 g vial with 7.4 or 14.8 mL, respectively, of sterile water for injection. May be given direct IV as prepared or further diluted for infusion.
- *Further Dilution of Reconstituted Solution:* Add required dose to 50 mL or more of NS, D5W, D5NS, D5/1/2NS, or LR.

STORAGE

- Store unopened vials at 15°–30° C (59°–86° F) unless otherwise directed. Keep oral preparations tightly covered.
- Solution prepared for direct IV should be given within 1 h of preparation.
- Stability of solution varies with diluent and concentration of solution. NS IV solutions are stable for up to 8 h at room temperature; IV solutions with dextrose should be infused within 4 h if ampicillin concentration is 2 mg/mL or less or within 2 h if concentration if greater.

ADMINISTRATION

- **Direct IV Injection:** Give a 250 or 500 mg dose slowly over 3–5 min. Give a 1 or 2 g dose slowly over at least 10–15 min. For pediatric patients, do not exceed 10 mg/kg/min.
- **Intermittent Infusion:** With solutions of 50–100 mL, set rate according to amount of solution, but not faster than direct IV rate.
- Note: Convulsions may be induced by too rapid administration.

INCOMPATIBILITIES Solution/additive: Do not add to a **dextrose-containing solution** unless entire dose is given within 1 h of preparation. **Aztreonam, cefepime, hydrocortisone, prochlorperazine. Y-site:** **Amphotericin B, epinephrine, fenoldopam, fluconazole, hydralazine, lansoprazole, midazolam, nicardipine, ondansetron, sargramostim, TPN, verapamil, vinorelbine.**

ACTION & *THERAPEUTIC EFFECT* A broad-spectrum, semisynthetic penicillin that is highly bactericidal even at low concentrations, but is inactivated by penicillinase (beta-lactamase). Ampicillin inhibits the third and final stage of bacterial cell wall synthesis by preferentially binding to specific penicillin-binding proteins (PBPs) located inside the bacterial cell wall, thus destroying it. *Its gram-positive spectrum is similar to the natural penicillins, although ampicillin is slightly less active than penicillin G. Ampicillin can also be inactivated by beta-lactamases.*

CONTRAINDICATIONS Hypersensitivity to penicillins; mononucleosis; viral infections including CMV, viral respiratory infections; lymphatic leukemia.
CAUTIOUS USE History of severe reactions to cephalosporins; renal disease; GI disease; history of allergies or allergic conditions such as asthma; pregnancy (category B), lactation.

ADVERSE EFFECTS (≥1%) **Body as a Whole:** Similar to those for penicillin G. Hypersensitivity (pruritus, urticaria, eosinophilia, hemolytic anemia, interstitial nephritis, <u>anaphylactoid reaction</u>); superinfections. **CNS:** Convulsive seizures with high doses. **GI:** *Diarrhea,* nausea, vomiting, <u>pseudomembranous colitis</u>. **Other:** Phlebitis. **Skin:** *Rash.*

DIAGNOSTIC TEST INTERFERENCE Elevated *CPK* levels may result from local skeletal muscle injury following IM injection. *Urine glucose:* High urine drug concentrations can result in false-positive test results with *Clinitest* or *Benedict's* (enzymatic *glucose oxidase methods,* e.g., *Clinistix, Diastix, TesTape,* are not affected). *AST* may be elevated (significance not known).

DRUG INTERACTIONS Allopurinol increases incidence of rash. Effectiveness of the AMINOGLYCOSIDES may be impaired in patients with severe end-stage renal disease. Ampicillin may interfere with the contraceptive action of ORAL CONTRACEPTIVES (**estrogens**).

PHARMACOKINETICS Peak: 5 min. **Duration:** 6–8 h. **Distribution:** Most body tissues; high CNS concentrations only with inflamed meninges; crosses the placenta. **Metabolism:** Minimal hepatic metabolism. **Elimination:** 90% excreted in urine; excreted into breast milk. **Half-Life:** 1–1.8 h.

NURSING IMPLICATIONS

Assessment & Drug Effects

- Prior to initiating therapy: Baseline C&S tests (start drug pending results); determine previous hypersensitivity reactions to penicillins, cephalosporins, and other allergens.
- Note: Sodium content of drug **must be** considered in patients on sodium restriction.
- Lab tests: Baseline and periodic assessments of renal, hepatic, and hematologic functions, particularly during prolonged or high-dose therapy.
- Inspect skin daily and instruct patient to do the same. The appearance of a rash should be carefully evaluated to differentiate a nonallergenic ampicillin rash from a hypersensitivity reaction. Report rash promptly to prescriber.
- Note: Incidence of ampicillin rash is higher in patients with infectious mononucleosis or other viral infections, *Salmonella* infections, lymphocytic leukemia, or hyperuricemia or in patients taking allopurinol.

Common adverse effects in *italic*, life-threatening effects <u>underlined</u>: generic names in **bold**; classifications in SMALL CAPS; ♣ Canadian drug name; ● Prototype drug

55

Patient & Family Education

- Note: Ampicillin rash is often nonallergenic and therefore its appearance is not an absolute contraindication to future therapy.
- Report diarrhea to prescriber even after completion of therapy with ampicillin. Give a detailed report regarding onset, duration, character of stools, associated symptoms, temperature, and weight loss (if any).
- Report promptly S&S of superinfection (onset of black, hairy tongue; oral lesions or soreness; rectal or vaginal itching; vaginal discharge; loose, foul-smelling stools; or unusual odor to urine).
- Females using contraceptives with estrogen should consider nonhormonal contraception while on ampicillin.

AMPICILLIN SODIUM AND SULBACTAM SODIUM

(am-pi-sill'in/sul-bak'tam)

Unasyn

Classification(s): ANTIBIOTIC; AMINOPENICILLIN
Therapeutic: ANTIBACTERIAL
Prototype: Ampicillin
Pregnancy Category: B

USES Treatment of infections due to susceptible organisms in skin and skin structures, intra-abdominal infections, and gynecologic infections.

INDICATION & DOSAGE

Systemic Infections
Adult/Child (over 40 kg): 1.5 g (1 g ampicillin, 0.5 g sulbactam) to 3 g (2 g ampicillin, 1 g sulbactam) q6h (max: 4 g/day of sulbactam)
Child (over 1 y): 300 mg/kg/day divided q6h

Renal Impairment Dosage Adjustment

CrCl	Dose	Interval
Over 30 mL/min	Normal	q6–8h
15–29 mL/min	Normal	q12h
5–14 mL/min	Normal	q24h
Hemodialysis	Normal	Administer after hemodialysis

SOLUTION PREPARATION

- *Vial Reconstitution:* Add 3.2 mL of sterile water for injection to each 1.5 g to yield 375 mg/mL (250 mg ampicillin/125 mg sulbactam). **Must be further diluted prior to administration.**

- *Further Dilution of Reconstituted Solution:* Dilute with NS, D5W, D5NS, D5/1/2NS, or LR to a final concentration within the range of 3–45 mg/mL.

STORAGE
- Store powder for injection at 15°–30° C (59°–86° F) before reconstitution.
- Storage times and temperatures vary for different concentrations of reconstituted solution. Consult manufacturer's information.

ADMINISTRATION
- **Direct IV Injection:** Give dose slowly over at least 10–15 min.
- **Intermittent Infusion:** Infuse solutions of less than 50 mL over 10–15 min and solutions of 50–100 mL over 15–30 min. With solutions of 100 mL or more, set rate according to amount of solution but not faster than direct IV rate.
- Convulsions may be induced by too rapid administration.

INCOMPATIBILITIES Solution/additive: Do not add to a **dextrose-containing solution** unless entire dose is given within 1 h of preparation. **Ciprofloxacin. Y-site:** Amiodarone, amphotericin B, ciprofloxacin, idarubicin, lansoprazole, nicardipine, ondansetron, sargramostim.

ACTION & *THERAPEUTIC EFFECT* Ampicillin inhibits the third and final stage of bacterial cell wall synthesis by preferentially binding to specific penicillin-binding proteins (PBPs) located inside the bacterial cell wall, thus destroying the cell wall. Sulbactam inhibits beta-lactamase, thus inhibiting the growth of a wider range of organisms resistant to penicillins and cephalosporins. *Effective against both gram-positive and gram-negative bacteria including those that produce beta-lactamase as well as nonbeta-lactamase producers. Ampicillin without sulbactam is not effective against beta-lactamase producing strains.*

CONTRAINDICATIONS Hypersensitivity to penicillins; mononucleosis; viral infections including CMV, viral respiratory infections; lymphatic leukemia. **CAUTIOUS USE** Hypersensitivity to cephalosporins; renal disease; GI disease; history of allergies or allergic conditions such as asthma; pregnancy (category B), lactation.

ADVERSE EFFECTS (≥1%) **Body as a Whole:** Hypersensitivity (rash, itching, <u>anaphylactoid reaction</u>), fatigue, malaise, headache, chills, edema. **GI:** *Diarrhea, nausea,* vomiting, abdominal distention, candidiasis. **Hematologic:** Neutropenia, thrombocytopenia. **Urogenital:** Dysuria. **CNS:** Seizures. **Other:** Local pain at injection site; thrombophlebitis.

DRUG INTERACTIONS Allopurinol increases incidence of rash; effectiveness of the AMINOGLYCOSIDES may be impaired in patients with severe end stage renal disease; ampicillin may interfere with the contraceptive action of ORAL CONTRACEPTIVES.

PHARMACOKINETICS Peak: Immediate after IV. **Duration:** 6–8 h. **Distribution:** Most body tissues; high CNS concentrations only with inflamed meninges; crosses placenta; appears in breast milk. **Metabolism:** Minimal hepatic metabolism. **Elimination:** In urine. **Half-Life:** 1 h.

NURSING IMPLICATIONS

Assessment & Drug Effects

- Prior to initiating therapy: Baseline C&S tests (start drug pending results); determine previous hypersensitivity reactions to penicillins, cephalosporins, and other allergens.
- Report promptly unexplained bleeding (e.g., epistaxis, purpura, ecchymoses).
- Monitor patient carefully during the first 30 min after initiation of IV therapy for signs of hypersensitivity and anaphylactoid reaction (see Appendix C). Serious anaphylactoid reactions require immediate use of emergency drugs and airway management.
- Lab tests: Periodic renal and hepatic function tests during long-term therapy.
- Observe for and report symptoms of superinfections (see Appendix C). Withhold drug and notify prescriber.
- Monitor I&O ratio and pattern. Report dysuria, urine retention, and hematuria.

Patient & Family Education

- Report promptly chills, wheezing, pruritus (itching), respiratory distress, or palpitations to prescriber immediately.

ANIDULAFUNGIN

(a-ni-dul'a-fun-gin)

Eraxis

Classification(s): ANTIBIOTIC; ECHINOCANDIN ANTIFUNGAL
Therapeutic: ANTIFUNGAL
Prototype: Caspofungin
Pregnancy Category: C

USES Treatment of candidemia and other *Candida* infections. Treatment of esophageal candidiasis.

INDICATION & DOSAGE

Candidemia and Other *Candida* Infections

Adult: 200 mg loading dose on day 1, then 100 mg daily for at least 14 days after last positive culture

Esophageal Candidiasis

Adult: 100 mg loading dose on day 1, then 50 mg daily for at least 14 days (and for at least 7 days after resolution of symptoms)

SOLUTION PREPARATION

- *Vial Reconstitution:* Reconstitute each vial with the supplied, single-use 15-mL vial of diluent (20% [w/w] dehydrated alcohol in water) to yield 3.33 mg/mL. **Must be** further diluted for infusion.

Common adverse effects in *italic*, life-threatening effects underlined: generic names in **bold**; classifications in SMALL CAPS; ♣ Canadian drug name; ⊘ Prototype drug

- *Further Dilution of Reconstituted Solution:* Each 50 mg of reconstituted solution **must be** further diluted with 100 mL NS or D5W.

Dose	Total Volume of IV Fluid	Final Concentration
50 mg	1 reconstituted vial (15 mL) + 100 mL IV fluid = 115 mL total IV solution	0.43 mg/mL
100 mg	2 reconstituted vials (30 mL) + 250 mL IV fluid = 280 mL total IV solution	0.36 mg/mL
200 mg	4 reconstituted vials (60 mL) + 500 mL IV fluid = 560 mL total IV solution	0.36 mg/mL

STORAGE

Store unreconstituted vials, reconstituted vials, and companion diluent vials at 15°–30° C (59°–86° F). Reconstituted vials **must be** further diluted and administered within 24 h.

ADMINISTRATION

IV Infusion: DO NOT give a bolus dose. Flush IV line before/after infusion with D5W or NS. Give at a rate **no greater** than 1.1 mg/min.

Dose	Concentration	Rate Equal to 1.1 mg/min
50 mg	0.43 mg/mL	Infuse at 2.5 mL/min or less
100 mg	0.36 mg/mL	Infuse at 3 mL/min or less
200 mg	0.36 mg/mL	Infuse at 3 mL/min or less

INCOMPATIBILITIES Y-site: Amphotericin B, ertapenem, sodium bicarbonate.

ACTION & *THERAPEUTIC EFFECT* Anidulafungin is a semisynthetic echinocandin with antifungal activity. It inhibits glucan synthase, an enzyme present in fungal cells. Glucan is an essential component of the fungal cell wall; therefore, anidulafungin causes fungal cell death. *Anidulafungin interferes with reproduction and growth of susceptible fungi.*

CONTRAINDICATIONS Hypersensitivity to anidulafungin or another echinocandin antifungal agent; pregnancy (category C), lactation.
CAUTIOUS USE Hepatic impairment. Safety and efficacy in children have not been established.

ADVERSE EFFECTS (≥1%) **Body as a Whole:** Hypersensitivity. **CNS:** Headache. **GI:** Diarrhea, nausea. **Hematologic:** Neutropenia. **Metabolic:** Increased alkaline phosphatase, increased ALT, increased gamma-glutamyl transferase, hypokalemia. **Skin:** Rash.

DRUG INTERACTIONS Cyclosporin increases overall systemic exposure.

PHARMACOKINETICS Distribution: 84% protein bound. **Metabolism:** Nonhepatic degradation to inactive metabolites. **Elimination:** Fecal. **Half-Life:** 27 h.

Common adverse effects in *italic*, life-threatening effects underlined: generic names in **bold**; classifications in SMALL CAPS; ♣ Canadian drug name; ☻ Prototype drug

59

NURSING IMPLICATIONS

Assessment & Drug Effects

- Prior to initiating therapy: C&S for fungal culture.
- Report promptly: S&S of hypersensitivity (e.g., dyspnea, flushing, hypotension, swelling about the face, pruritus, rash, and urticaria) or liver dysfunction (e.g., jaundice, clay-colored stools).
- Discontinue infusion if signs of hypersensitivity appear.
- Monitor cardiac status especially with a preexisting history of dysrhythmias.
- Lab tests: Baseline and periodic liver function tests; periodic CBC with differential and platelet count; periodic serum electrolytes, amylase, and lipase.
- Monitor for S&S: Hypokalemia and hepatic toxicity (see Appendix C).
- Monitor diabetics for loss of glycemic control.

Patient & Family Education

- Report any of the following immediately if experienced during or shortly after infusion: Difficulty breathing, swelling about the face, itching, rash.
- Report S&S of jaundice to the prescriber: Clay-colored stool, dark urine, yellow skin or sclera, unexplained abdominal pain, or fatigue.

APROTININ

(a-pro-ti'nin)

Trasylol

Classification(s): HEMOSTATIC
Therapeutic: COAGULATOR
Prototype: Aminocaproic acid
Pregnancy Category: B

USES Reduction of blood loss in patients undergoing cardiac procedures (cardiopulmonary bypass or coronary artery bypass graft surgery).

INDICATION & DOSAGE

Cardiac Surgery

Adult: **IV Test Dose,** 1 mL (10,000 kallikrein inactivator units [KIU]) given at least 10 min prior to loading dose (observe for signs of an allergic reaction) *Standard Regimen:* **Adult Loading Dose,** 2 million KIU over 20–30 min; add 2 million KIU to the priming fluid of the cardiopulmonary priming pump; constant infusion of 500,000 KIU/h, continue until the patient leaves the OR *Alternate Regimen:* **Adult Loading Dose,** 1 million KIU over 20–30 min; 1 million into pump prime volume; 250,000 KIU/h while in OR

SOLUTION PREPARATION

No dilution is required. Administer as supplied (1 mL = 1.4 mg or 10,000 KIU).

STORAGE

Store at 15°–30° C (59°–86° F).

ADMINISTRATION

- Use central venous catheter exclusively for aprotinin.
- *Test Dose:* Give by direct IV injection over 1 min at least 10 min before loading dose.
- *Loading Dose:* Infuse over 20–30 min.
- **Continuous Infusion:** Infuse at 50 mL/h (70 mg/h or 500,000 KIU/h).

INCOMPATIBILITIES Do not mix with other drugs.

ACTION & *THERAPEUTIC EFFECT* By interaction with certain proteases, aprotinin has an antifibrinolytic effect, a hemostatic stabilizing effect, and a weak anticoagulant effect. *Aprotinin reduces postoperative bleeding in coronary bypass surgery patients by inhibiting fibrinolytic activity while preserving platelet adhesive function, and prolonging postoperative bleeding time.*

CONTRAINDICATIONS Hypersensitivity to aprotinin and bovine products.

CAUTIOUS USE Patients with heparinized blood; patients previously treated with aprotinin; renal impairment, renal failure; pregnancy (category B). Safety and efficacy in children are not established.

ADVERSE EFFECTS (≥1%) **Body as a Whole:** Hypersensitivity reactions (rash, urticaria, <u>anaphylaxis</u>), fever. **CV:** Tachycardia, arrhythmia. **Hematologic:** Thromboembolism. **CNS:** Confusion, insomnia. **Skin:** Rash, urticaria. **Urogenital:** <u>Nephrotoxicity</u> (elevated serum creatinine). **Other:** <u>Bronchospasm</u>.

DRUG INTERACTIONS Heparin results in further prolongation of the whole blood activated clotting time (ACT), aprotinin blocks hypotensive effects of **captopril.**

PHARMACOKINETICS Distribution: Rapidly into the extracellular fluid, then accumulates in proximal renal tubular epithelial cells; crosses placenta; distributed into breast milk. **Metabolism:** Primarily in kidneys to small peptides or amino acids. **Elimination:** By kidneys. **Half-Life:** Initial 0.7 h, terminal 7 h.

NURSING IMPLICATIONS

Assessment & Drug Effects

- Monitor carefully for S&S of hypersensitivity during administration (see Appendix C). If hypersensitivity occurs, immediately discontinue aprotinin and begin emergency treatment to prevent anaphylaxis.
- Monitor cardiac status and pulmonary function carefully during infusion. Patients with a history of hypersensitivity to any allergens or who have previously received aprotinin are at special risk for hypersensitivity.
- Lab tests: After surgery, monitor PTT, ACT, renal function, and LFTs.

Common adverse effects in *italic*, life-threatening effects <u>underlined</u>: generic names in **bold**; classifications in SMALL CAPS; ♣ Canadian drug name; ● Prototype drug

61

ARGATROBAN

(ar-ga'tro-ban)

Classification(s): ANTICOAGULANT; THROMBIN INHIBITOR
Therapeutic: ANTICOAGULANT
Prototype: Lepirudin
Pregnancy Category: C

USES Prophylaxis or treatment of thrombosis in patients with heparin-induced thrombocytopenia (HIT); prophylaxis or treatment of coronary artery thrombosis during percutaneous coronary interventions (PCI) in patients at risk for HIT.
UNLABELED USES Treatment of disseminated intravascular coagulation (DIC).

INDICATION & DOSAGE

Prevention & Treatment of Thrombosis

Adult: 2 mcg/kg/min; may be adjusted to maintain an aPTT of 1.5–3 times baseline (max: 10 mcg/kg/min)

Prophylaxis or Treatment of Coronary Thrombosis during PCI

Adult: Initiate at 25 mcg/kg/min, then give bolus of 350 mcg/kg over 3–5 min, then return to 25 mcg/kg/min by continuous infusion.

ACT	Bolus	Rate Change
Less than 300 sec	150 mcg/kg	Increase to 30 mcg/kg/min
300–450 sec	No bolus	Continue rate of 25 mcg/kg/min
Over 450 sec	No bolus	Reduce to 15 mcg/kg/min

Disseminated Intravascular Coagulation (DIC)

Adult: 0.7 mcg/kg/min continuous infusion

Hepatic Impairment Dosage Adjustment

Initiate therapy at 0.5 mcg/kg/min, adjust to maintain an aPTT of 1.5–3 times baseline (max: 10 mcg/kg/min)

SOLUTION PREPARATION

- Argatroban is supplied in 100 mg/mL vials that **must be** diluted 100-fold prior to infusion.
- Dilute each 2.5 mL vial by mixing with 250 mL of D5W, NS, or LR to yield 1 mg/mL. Mix by repeated inversion of the diluent bag for 1 min.

STORAGE

Diluted solutions are stable for 24 h at 25° C (77° F) in ambient indoor light. Protect from direct sunlight. Store solutions refrigerated at 2°–8° C (36°–46° F) in the dark.

Common adverse effects in *italic*, life-threatening effects <u>underlined</u>: generic names in **bold**; classifications in SMALL CAPS; ♣ Canadian drug name; ● Prototype drug

ADMINISTRATION
Prevention & Treatment of Thrombosis
- **Continuous Infusion:** Before administration, DC heparin and obtain a baseline aPTT. Infuse at 2 mcg/kg/min, or as ordered (lower initial doses are required with hepatic impairment). Check aPTT 2 h after initiation of therapy. After the initial dose, adjust dose (not to exceed 10 mcg/kg/min) until the steady-state aPTT is 1.5–3 times baseline (not to exceed 100 sec). Check aPTT 2 h after initiation of therapy to confirm desired therapeutic range.

Percutaneous Coronary Intervention
- **Direct IV & Continuous Infusion:** Begin infusion at 25 mcg/kg/min, then give a bolus of 350 mcg/kg, via a large bore IV line, over 3–5 min. Follow with a continuous infusion at 25 mcg/kg/min. Check ACT (activated clotting time) 5–10 min after the bolus dose. If the ACT is greater than 450 sec, decrease infusion rate to 15 mcg/kg/min. If ACT is less than 300 sec, give an additional bolus of 150 mcg/kg and increase infusion to 30 mcg/kg/min. Check ACT q5–10min to maintain an ACT level 300–450 sec.

INCOMPATIBILITIES Do not mix with other drugs.

ACTION & *THERAPEUTIC EFFECT* Argatroban is a direct thrombin inhibitor capable of inhibiting the action of both free and clot-bound thrombin. *Reversibly binds to the thrombin active site, thereby blocking the clot-forming activity of thrombin.*

CONTRAINDICATIONS Hypersensitivity to argatroban. Any bleeding including intracranial bleeding, GI bleeding, retroperitoneal bleeding, recent major bleeding. Pregnancy (category C), lactation.
CAUTIOUS USE Diseased states with increased risk of hemorrhaging; severe hypertension; GI ulcerations; hepatic impairment; spinal anesthesia; stroke; unstable angina; surgery, trauma. Safety and effectiveness in children less than 18 y are not established.

ADVERSE EFFECTS (≥1%) **Body as a Whole:** Fever, sepsis, pain, allergic reactions (rare). **CV:** Hypotension, <u>cardiac arrest</u>, ventricular tachycardia. **GI:** Diarrhea, nausea, vomiting, coughing, abdominal pain. **Hematologic:** <u>Major GI bleed</u>, *minor GI bleeding, hematuria, decrease Hgb/Hct*, groin bleed, hemoptysis, brachial bleed. **Respiratory:** Dyspnea. **Urogenital:** UTI.

DRUG INTERACTIONS Heparin results in increased bleeding; may prolong PT with **warfarin;** may increase risk of bleeding with THROMBOLYTICS.

PHARMACOKINETICS Peak: 1–3 h. **Distribution:** Distributes in the extracellular fluid; 54% protein bound. **Metabolism:** In liver by CYP3A4/5. **Elimination:** Primarily excreted in bile (78%). **Half-Life:** 39–51 min.

NURSING IMPLICATIONS
Assessment & Drug Effects
- Monitor cardiovascular status carefully during therapy.
- Monitor for and report S&S of bleeding: Ecchymosis, epistaxis, GI bleeding, hematuria, hemoptysis. Note: Patients with history of GI ulceration, hypertension, recent trauma, or surgery are at increased risk for bleeding.

- Monitor neurologic status and report immediately focal or generalized deficits.
- Lab tests: Baseline and periodic ACT, thrombin time (TT), platelet count, Hgb & Hct; daily INR when argatroban and warfarin are co-administered; periodic stool test for occult blood; urinalysis.

Patient & Family Education

- Report promptly: Unexplained back or stomach pain; black, tarry stools; blood in urine, coughing up blood; difficulty breathing; dizziness or fainting spells; heavy menstrual bleeding; nosebleeds; unusual bruising or bleeding at any site.

ASCORBIC ACID (VITAMIN C)
Ascor L 500

ASCORBATE, SODIUM
(a-skor'bate)

Cenolate, Cevita
Classification(s): VITAMIN
Therapeutic: VITAMIN SUPPLEMENT
Pregnancy Category: C

USES Treatment of scurvy and as a dietary supplement.
UNLABELED USES To acidify urine; to treat idiopathic methemoglobinemia; as adjuvant during deferoxamine therapy for iron toxicity.

INDICATION & DOSAGE

Scurvy Treatment
Adult: 150–250 mg/day in 1–2 doses (max: 2 g)
Child: 100–300 mg/day in divided doses

SOLUTION PREPARATION

Dilution in a large volume of IV solution, such as NS, D5W, D5/NS, LR, is recommended.

STORAGE

Store in airtight, light-resistant, nonmetallic containers, away from heat and sunlight, preferably at 15°–30° C (59°–86° F), unless otherwise specified by manufacturer.

ADMINISTRATION

Continuous & Intermittent Infusion: Infuse at ordered rate as determined by volume of solution to be infused (usually over 4–8 h).

INCOMPATIBILITIES Solution/additive: Aminophylline, bleomycin, erythromycin, nafcillin, sodium bicarbonate, theophylline. Y-site: Etomidate, thiopental.

Common adverse effects in *italic*, life-threatening effects underlined: generic names in **bold**; classifications in SMALL CAPS; ♣ Canadian drug name; ❶ Prototype drug

ACTION & *THERAPEUTIC EFFECT* Water-soluble vitamin essential for synthesis and maintenance of collagen and intercellular ground substance of body tissue cells, blood vessels, cartilage, bones, teeth, skin, and tendons. Humans are unable to synthesize ascorbic acid in the body, therefore, it **must be** consumed daily. *Increases protection mechanism of the immune system, thus supporting wound healing, and resistance to infection.*

CONTRAINDICATIONS Use of sodium ascorbate in patients on sodium restriction; use of calcium ascorbate in patients receiving digitalis; pregnancy (category C).

CAUTIOUS USE Excessive doses in patients with G6PD deficiency; hemochromatosis, thalassemia, sideroblastic anemia, sickle cell anemia; asthmatics; patients prone to gout or renal calculi.

ADVERSE EFFECTS (≥1%) **GI:** Nausea, vomiting, heartburn, diarrhea, or abdominal cramps (high doses). **Hematologic:** Acute hemolytic anemia (patients with deficiency of G6PD); sickle cell crisis. **CNS:** Headache or insomnia (high doses). **Urogenital:** Urethritis, dysuria, crystalluria, hyperoxaluria, or hyperuricemia (high doses). **Other:** Mild soreness at injection site; dizziness and temporary faintness with rapid IV administration.

DIAGNOSTIC TEST INTERFERENCE High doses of ascorbic acid can produce false-negative results for ***urine glucose*** with ***glucose oxidase*** methods (e.g., ***Clinitest, TesTape, Diastix***); false-positive results with ***copper reduction methods*** (e.g., ***Benedict's solution, Clinitest***); and false increases in ***serum uric acid*** determinations (by ***enzymatic methods***). Interferes with ***urinary steroid*** (17-OHCS) determinations (by ***modified Reddy, Jenkins, Thorn procedure***), decreases in ***serum bilirubin,*** and may cause increases in ***serum cholesterol, creatinine,*** and ***uric acid*** (methodologic inferences). May produce false-negative tests for ***occult blood*** in stools if taken within 48–72 h of test.

DRUG INTERACTIONS Large doses may attenuate hypoprothrombinemic effects of ORAL ANTICOAGULANTS; SALICYLATES may inhibit ascorbic acid uptake by leukocytes and tissues, and ascorbic acid may decrease elimination of SALICYLATES.

PHARMACOKINETICS Distribution: Widely distributed to body tissues; crosses placenta; distributed into breast milk. **Metabolism:** Metabolized in liver. **Elimination:** Rapidly excreted from body in urine when plasma level exceeds renal threshold of 1.4 mg/dL.

NURSING IMPLICATIONS

Assessment & Drug Effects
- Lab tests: Periodic Hct & Hgb, serum electrolytes.
- Monitor for S&S of acute hemolytic anemia and sickle cell crisis in predisposed patients.

Patient & Family Education
- High doses of vitamin C are not recommended during pregnancy.
- Take large doses of vitamin C in divided amounts because the body uses only what is needed at a particular time and excretes the rest in urine.

Common adverse effects in *italic*, life-threatening effects <u>underlined</u>: generic names in **bold**; classifications in SMALL CAPS; ♣ Canadian drug name; ● Prototype drug

65

- Megadoses can interfere with absorption of vitamin B$_{12}$.
- Note: Vitamin C increases the absorption of iron when taken at the same time as iron-rich foods.

ASPARAGINASE

(a-spar'a-gi-nase)

Elspar, Kidrolase A, L-asparaginase

Classification(s): ANTINEOPLASTIC, ANTIMETABOLITE
Therapeutic: ANTINEOPLASTIC
Pregnancy Category: C

USES In combination with other antineoplastic agents to treat acute lymphocytic leukemia (ALL).
UNLABELED USES Other leukemias, lymphosarcoma, and (intra-arterially) treatment of hypoglycemia due to pancreatic islet cell tumor.

INDICATION & DOSAGE

Acute Lymphocytic Leukemia: Induction Regimens

Adult (sole induction): 200 IU/kg/day for 28 days, *or* 1000 IU/kg/day for days 22–32 (along with prednisone and vincristine)
Child: 1000 IU/kg/day × 10 days starting day 22 (along with prednisone and vincristine)

Desensitization Protocol

Schedule begins with 1 IU, then double the dose q10min until the accumulated total matches the planned dose. See package insert for detailed dosing.

SOLUTION PREPARATION

Vial Reconstitution: Add 5 mL of NS to the 10,000 IU (international unit) vial to yield 2000 IU/mL. Shake well to promote dissolution of powder. Avoid vigorous shaking. Use within 8 h.

STORAGE

Store sealed vial of lyophilized powdèr below 8° C (46° F) unless otherwise directed by manufacturer. Store reconstituted solutions and solutions diluted for IV infusion at 2°–8° C (36°–46° F) for up to 8 h; then discard.

ADMINISTRATION

- *Preinfusion Skin Test:* An intradermal skin test is usually performed prior to initial dose and when drug is readministered after an interval of a week or more; allergic reactions are unpredictable. The skin test solution may be prepared as follows: Reconstitute a 10,000-IU vial with 5 mL of NS to yield 2,000 IU/mL; next withdraw 0.1 mL and inject it

Common adverse effects in *italic*, life-threatening effects <u>underlined</u>: generic names in **bold**; classifications in SMALL CAPS; ♣ Canadian drug name; ● Prototype drug

into another vial containing 9.9 mL of NS, yielding a skin test solution of approximately 20 IU/mL. Use 0.1 mL of this solution (about 2 IU) for the intradermal skin test. Observe test site for at least 1 h for evidence of positive reaction (wheal, erythema). A negative skin test, however, does not preclude possibility of an allergic reaction.

- **IV Infusion:** Infuse required dose over at least 30 min into tubing of an already free-flowing infusion of NS or D5W. Use a 5-micron filter to remove gelatinous, fiber-like particles that can develop in solution on standing.

INCOMPATIBILITIES   Data not available; do not mix with other drugs.

ACTION & *THERAPEUTIC EFFECT*   A highly toxic drug with a low therapeutic index. Catalyzes hydrolysis of asparagine to aspartic acid and ammonia, thus depleting extracellular supply of an amino acid essential to synthesis of DNA and other nucleoproteins in cancer cells. *Reduced availability of asparagine causes death of tumor cells, since unlike normal cells, tumor cells are unable to synthesize their own supply. Resistance to cytotoxic action develops rapidly; therefore, this is not an effective treatment for solid tumors and not recommended for maintenance therapy.*

CONTRAINDICATIONS   History of or existing pancreatitis; chickenpox (existing or recent illness or exposure), herpetic infection; acute bronchospasm, hypotension, urticaria; pregnancy (category C), lactation.

CAUTIOUS USE   Liver impairment; diabetes mellitus; infections; history of urate calculi or gout; anticoagulant therapy; antineoplastic or radiation therapy; impaired hepatic function; renal disease.

ADVERSE EFFECTS   (≥1%) **Body as a Whole:** Hypersensitivity (*skin rashes, urticaria,* respiratory distress, <u>anaphylaxis</u>), chills, fever, <u>fatal hyperthermia</u>, perspiration, weight loss. **CNS:** Depression, fatigue, lethargy, drowsiness, confusion, agitation, hallucinations, dizziness, Parkinson-like syndrome with tremor and progressive increase in muscle tone. **GI:** *Severe vomiting, nausea,* anorexia, abdominal cramps, diarrhea, acute pancreatitis, liver function abnormalities. **Urogenital:** Uric acid nephropathy, azotemia, proteinuria, <u>renal failure</u>. **Hematologic:** *Reduced clotting factors* (especially V, VII, VIII, IX), *decreased circulating platelets and fibrinogen,* leukopenia. **Metabolic:** Hyperglycemia, glycosuria, polyuria, hypoalbuminemia, hypocalcemia, hyperuricemia. **Other:** Flank pain, infections.

DIAGNOSTIC TEST INTERFERENCE   Asparaginase may interfere with *thyroid function* tests: Decreased total *serum thyroxine* and increased *thyroxine-binding globulin index;* pretreatment values return within 4 wk after drug is discontinued.

DRUG INTERACTIONS   Decreased hypoglycemic effects of SULFONYLUREAS, **insulin**; increased potential for toxicity if asparaginase is given concurrently or immediately before CORTICOSTEROIDS, **vincristine;** blocks antitumor effect of **methotrexate** if given concurrently or in close proximity.

PHARMACOKINETICS Distribution: Distributed primarily into intravascular space (80%) and lymph; low levels in CSF, pleural and peritoneal flu-

Common adverse effects in *italic*, life-threatening effects <u>underlined</u>: generic names in **bold**; classifications in SMALL CAPS; ♣ Canadian drug name; ◐ Prototype drug

67

ids. **Metabolism:** Unknown. **Elimination:** Small amounts found in urine. **Half-Life:** 8–30 h.

NURSING IMPLICATIONS

Assessment & Drug Effects

- Have immediately available: Personnel, drugs, and equipment for treating allergic reaction (which may range from urticaria to anaphylactic shock) whenever drug is administered, including skin testing.
- Monitor for S&S of hypersensitivity or anaphylactoid reaction (see Appendix C) during drug administration. Anaphylaxis usually occurs within 30–60 min after dose has been given and is more likely with intermittent administrations, particularly at intervals of 7 days or more.
- Monitor I&O and maintain adequate fluid intake.
- Evaluate CNS function (general behavior, emotional status, level of consciousness, thought content, motor function) before and during therapy.
- Lab tests: Periodic serum amylase, serum calcium blood glucose, coagulation factors, ammonia and uric acid levels, hepatic and renal function tests, peripheral blood counts, and bone marrow function; liver function tests at least twice weekly during therapy.
- Monitor diabetics for loss of glycemic control.
- Monitor for and report S&S of hyperammonemia: Anorexia, vomiting, lethargy, weak pulse, depressed temperature, irritability, asterixis, seizures, coma.
- Anticipate possible prolonged or exaggerated effects of concurrently given drugs or their toxicity because of potential serious hepatic dysfunction that reduces enzymatic detoxification of other drugs. Report incidence promptly.
- Watch for neurotoxic reaction (25% of patients) that usually appears within the first few days of therapy. It is manifested by tiredness and changing levels of consciousness (ranging from confusion to coma).
- Note: Protect from infection during first several days of treatment when circulating lymphoblasts decrease markedly and leukocyte counts may fall below normal.
- Report sudden severe abdominal pain with nausea and vomiting, particularly if these symptoms occur after medication is discontinued (may indicate pancreatitis).
- Note: Therapeutic response will most likely be accompanied by some toxicity in all patients; toxicity is reportedly greater in adults than in children.

Patient & Family Education

- Notify prescriber without delay if nausea or vomiting makes it difficult to take all prescribed medication.
- Report promptly S&S of infection: Chills, fever, aches, sore throat; onset of unusual bleeding, bruising, petechiae, melena, skin rash or itching, yellowed skin and sclera, joint pain, puffy face, or dyspnea; continued loss of weight, onset of foot and ankle swelling.
- Do not drive or operate equipment that requires alertness and skill. Exercise caution with potentially hazardous activities. These effects can continue several weeks after last dose of the drug.

ATENOLOL

(a-ten'oh-lole)

Apo-Atenolol ♣, Tenormin
Classification(s): BETA-ADRENERGIC ANTAGONIST
Therapeutic: ANTIHYPERTENSIVE
Prototype: Propranolol
Pregnancy Category: D

USES Myocardial infarction.

INDICATION & DOSAGE

MI

Adult: 5 mg initially; if tolerated repeat dose in 10 min; then switch to PO

SOLUTION PREPARATION

May be given undiluted or diluted in 10–50 mL of NS, D5W, D5/NS, D5/1/2NS, or 1/2NS.

STORAGE

Store in tightly closed, light-resistant container at 15°–30° C (59°–86° F) unless otherwise directed.

ADMINISTRATION

Direct IV Injection: Give a bolus dose over 5 min. Do not exceed 1 mg/min.

INCOMPATIBILITIES **Y-site:** Amphotericin B cholesteryl complex.

ACTION & *THERAPEUTIC EFFECT* Mechanisms for antihypertensive action include central effect leading to decreased sympathetic outflow to periphery, reduction in renin activity with consequent suppression of the renin-angiotensin-aldosterone system, and competitive inhibition of catecholamine binding at beta-adrenergic receptor sites. *Reduces rate and force of cardiac contractions (negative inotropic action); cardiac output is reduced as well as systolic and diastolic BP. Atenolol decreases peripheral vascular resistance both at rest and with exercise.*

CONTRAINDICATIONS Sinus bradycardia, greater than first-degree AV heart block, uncompensated heart failure, cardiogenic shock, peripheral vascular disease, Raynaud's disease, hypotension; abrupt discontinuation, pulmonary edema; abrupt discontinuation, acute bronchospasm; pregnancy (category D), lactation.

CAUTIOUS USE Hypertensive patients with CHF controlled by digitalis and diuretics, vasospastic angina (Prinzmetal's angina); ventricular dysfunction, asthma, bronchitis, emphysema, and COPD; major depression; diabetes mellitus; impaired renal function, dialysis; myasthenia gravis; pheochromocytoma, hyperthyroidism, thyrotoxicosis; older adults.

Common adverse effects in *italic*, life-threatening effects <u>underlined</u>: generic names in **bold**; classifications in SMALL CAPS; ♣ Canadian drug name; ♦ Prototype drug

69

ADVERSE EFFECTS (≥1%) **CNS:** Dizziness, vertigo, light-headedness, syncope, fatigue or weakness, lethargy, drowsiness, insomnia, mental changes, depression. **CV:** *Bradycardia, hypotension, CHF,* cold extremities, leg pains, dysrhythmias. **GI:** Nausea, vomiting, diarrhea. **Respiratory:** Pulmonary edema, dyspnea, <u>bronchospasm</u>. **Other:** May mask symptoms of hypoglycemia; decreased sexual ability.

DRUG INTERACTIONS NSAIDS may decrease hypotensive effects; may increase **lidocaine** levels and toxicity; pharmacologic and toxic effects of both atenolol and **verapamil** are increased. **Prazosin, terazosin** may increase severe hypotensive response to first dose of atenolol.

PHARMACOKINETICS Peak: 5 min. **Duration:** 24 h. **Distribution:** Does not readily cross blood–brain barrier. **Metabolism:** No hepatic metabolism. **Elimination:** 85% excreted in urine. **Half-Life:** 6–7 h (adults), 15 h (neonates).

NURSING IMPLICATIONS

Assessment & Drug Effects

- Monitor cardiac and respiratory status continuously. Check apical pulse, BP, respirations, and peripheral circulation throughout dosage adjustment period.
- Withhold medication and notify prescriber of any of the following: Sinus bradycardia, heart block greater than first degree, cardiogenic shock, or overt cardiac failure.

Patient & Family Education

- Make position changes slowly and in stages, particularly from recumbent to upright posture.

ATRACURIUM BESYLATE

(a-tra-kyoor′ee-um)

Tracrium

Classification(s): SKELETAL MUSCLE RELAXANT, NONDEPOLARIZING
Therapeutic: NEUROMUSCULAR BLOCKER
Prototype: Tubocurarine
Pregnancy Category: C

USES Adjunct for general anesthesia to produce skeletal muscle relaxation during surgery; to facilitate endotracheal intubation. Especially useful for patients with severe renal or hepatic disease, limited cardiac reserve, and in patients with low or atypical pseudocholinesterase levels.

INDICATION & DOSAGE

Skeletal Muscle Relaxation

Adult/Child (2 y or older): 0.4–0.5 mg/kg initial bolus, then (as needed) 0.08–0.1 mg/kg bolus 20–45 min after the first dose and q15–25min thereafter; reduce dose by $^1/_3$ if used with isoflurane or enflurane
Child (1 mo–2 y): 0.3–0.4 mg/kg

Mechanical Ventilation

Adult: 5–9 mcg/kg/min by continuous infusion

SOLUTION PREPARATION

- *Direct IV Injection:* No dilution required for bolus dose.
- *Continuous Infusions:* Dilute to a maximum concentration of 0.5 mg/mL in NS, D5W or D5/NS. Example: 1 mL (10 mg) of atracurium in 99 mL IV solution yields 0.1 mg/mL (100 mcg/mL)

STORAGE

Store at 2°–8° C (36°–46° F) to preserve potency unless otherwise directed. Avoid freezing.

ADMINISTRATION

- **Direct IV Injection:** Give initial bolus dose over 30–60 sec.
- **Continuous Infusion:** Infuse at a rate required to maintain desired effect.
- Do not mix in same syringe or administer through same needle as used for alkaline solutions [incompatible with alkaline solutions (e.g., barbiturates)].

INCOMPATIBILITIES Solution/additive: **Lactated Ringer's, aminophylline, cefazolin, herparin, quinidine, ranitidine, sodium nitroprusside.** Y-site: **Diazepam, propofol, thiopental.**

ACTION & *THERAPEUTIC EFFECT* Inhibits neuromuscular transmission by binding competitively with acetylcholine to muscle end-plate receptors inducing skeletal muscle paralysis. *Given in general anesthesia only after unconsciousness has been induced by other drugs. Adjunct therapy with intubation.*

CONTRAINDICATIONS Myasthenia gravis; pregnancy (category C), lactation. **CAUTIOUS USE** When appreciable histamine release would be hazardous (as in asthma or anaphylactoid reactions, significant cardiovascular disease); neuromuscular disease (e.g., Eaton-Lambert syndrome); carcinomatosis; electrolyte or acid–base imbalances; dehydration; impaired pulmonary function.

ADVERSE EFFECTS (≥1%) **CV:** Bradycardia, tachycardia. **Respiratory:** <u>Respiratory depression</u>. **Other:** Increased salivation, <u>anaphylaxis</u>.

DRUG INTERACTIONS GENERAL ANESTHETICS increase magnitude and duration of neuromuscular blocking action; AMINOGLYCOSIDES, **bacitracin, poly-**

Common adverse effects in *italic*, life-threatening effects <u>underlined</u>: generic names in **bold**; classifications in SMALL CAPS; ♣ Canadian drug name; ◉ Prototype drug

71

myxin B, clindamycin, lidocaine, parenteral magnesium, quinidine, quinine, trimethaphan, verapamil increase neuromuscular blockade; DIURETICS may increase or decrease neuromuscular blockade; **lithium** prolongs duration of neuromuscular blockade; NARCOTIC ANALGESICS present possibility of additive respiratory depression; **succinylcholine** increases onset and depth of neuromuscular blockade; **phenytoin** may cause resistance to or reversal of neuromuscular blockade.

PHARMACOKINETICS Onset: 2 min. **Peak:** 3–5 min. **Duration:** 60–70 min. **Distribution:** Well distributed to tissues and extracellular fluids; crosses placenta; distribution into breast milk unknown. **Metabolism:** Rapid non-enzymatic degradation in bloodstream. **Elimination:** 70–90% excreted in urine in 5–7 h. **Half-Life:** 20 min.

NURSING IMPLICATIONS

Assessment & Drug Effects

▪ Evaluate degree of neuromuscular blockade and muscle paralysis to avoid risk of overdosage by qualified individual using peripheral nerve stimulator.

▪ Monitor BP, pulse, and respirations and evaluate patient's recovery from neuromuscular blocking (curare-like) effect as evidenced by ability to breathe naturally or to take deep breaths and cough, keep eyes open, lift head keeping mouth closed, adequacy of hand-grip strength. Notify prescriber if recovery is delayed.

▪ Lab tests: Baseline serum electrolytes, acid–base balance, and renal function as part of preanesthetic assessment.

▪ Note: Recovery from neuromuscular blockade usually begins 35–45 min after drug administration and is almost complete in about 1 h. Recovery time may be delayed in patients with cardiovascular disease, edematous states, and in older adults.

ATROPINE SULFATE ⓟ

(a′troe-peen)

Atropen

Classification(s): ANTICHOLINERGIC; ANTIMUSCARINIC; ANTIARRHYTHMIC
Therapeutic: ANTISECRETORY; ANTIARRHYTHMIC
Pregnancy Category: C

USES To suppress salivation, perspiration, and respiratory tract secretions; to reduce incidence of laryngospasm, reflex bradycardia arrhythmia, and hypotension during general anesthesia; sinus bradycardia or asystole; for management of selected patients with symptomatic sinus bradycardia and associated hypotension and ventricular irritability; for diagnosis of sinus node dysfunction and in evaluation of coronary artery disease during atrial pacing; for management of chronic symptomatic sinus node dysfunction.

INDICATION & DOSAGE

Preanesthesia

Adult: 0.4–0.6 mg 30–60 min before surgery
Child (less than 5 kg): 0.04 mg/kg; greater than 5 kg, 0.03 mg/kg 30–60 min before surgery (max: 0.4 mg)

Bradyarrhythmia

Adult: 0.5 mg q2–3min (max total dose: 3 mg)
Child: 0.01–0.03 mg/kg for 1–2 doses

Organophosphate Antidote

Adult: 1–2 mg q5–60min until muscarinic signs and symptoms subside (may need up to 50 mg)
Child: 0.05 mg/kg q10–30min until muscarinic signs and symptoms subside

SOLUTION PREPARATION

May be given undiluted or diluted in up to 10 mL of sterile water for injection.

STORAGE

Store at room temperature 15°–30° C (59°–86° F) in protected airtight, light-resistant containers unless otherwise directed by manufacturer.

ADMINISTRATION

Direct IV Injection: Give 1 mg or fraction thereof over 1 min directly into a Y-site.

INCOMPATIBILITIES Solution/additive: **Pantoprazole.**

ACTION & *THERAPEUTIC EFFECT* Acts by selectively blocking all muscarinic responses to acetylcholine (ACh), whether excitatory or inhibitory. Antisecretory action suppresses sweating, lacrimation, salivation, and secretions from nose, mouth, pharynx, and bronchi. Blocks vagal impulses to heart with resulting decrease in AV conduction time, increase in heart rate and cardiac output, and shortened PR interval. *Atropine is a potent bronchodilator when bronchoconstriction has been induced by parasympathomimetics. Suppresses nasopharyngeal and respiratory secretions. Increases heart rate and cardiac output.*

CONTRAINDICATIONS Hypersensitivity to belladonna alkaloids; synechiae; angle-closure glaucoma; parotitis; obstructive uropathy, e.g., bladder neck obstruction caused by prostatic hypertrophy; intestinal atony, paralytic ileus, obstructive diseases of GI tract, severe ulcerative colitis, toxic megacolon; tachycardia secondary to cardiac insufficiency or thyrotoxicosis; during an acute MI, acute hemorrhage; myasthenia gravis; pregnancy (category C), lactation.
CAUTIOUS USE Hypertension, hypotension; coronary artery disease, CHF, tachyarrhythmias; gastric ulcer, GI infections, hiatal hernia with reflux

---

Common adverse effects in *italic*, life-threatening effects <u>underlined</u>: generic names in **bold**; classifications in SMALL CAPS; ♣ Canadian drug name; ☻ Prototype drug

esophagitis; hyperthyroidism; chronic lung disease; hepatic or renal disease; older adults; debilitated patients; autonomic neuropathy, spastic paralysis, brain damage in children; patients exposed to high environmental temperatures; patients with fever.

ADVERSE EFFECTS (≥1%) **CNS:** Headache, ataxia, dizziness, excitement, irritability, convulsions, drowsiness, fatigue, weakness; mental depression, confusion, disorientation, hallucinations. **CV:** Hypertension or hypotension, ventricular tachycardia, palpitation, paradoxical bradycardia, AV dissociation, atrial or <u>ventricular fibrillation</u>. **GI:** Dry mouth with thirst, dysphagia, loss of taste; nausea, vomiting, constipation, delayed gastric emptying, antral stasis, paralytic ileus. **Urogenital:** Urinary hesitancy and retention, dysuria, impotence. **Skin:** Flushed, dry skin; anhidrosis, rash, urticaria, contact dermatitis, allergic conjunctivitis, fixed-drug eruption. **Special Senses:** Mydriasis, blurred vision, photophobia, increased intraocular pressure, cycloplegia, eye dryness, local redness.

DIAGNOSTIC TEST INTERFERENCE *Upper GI series:* Findings may require qualification because of anticholinergic effects of atropine (reduced gastric motility and delayed gastric emptying). *PSP excretion test:* Atropine may decrease urinary excretion of PSP (phenolsulfonphthalein).

DRUG INTERACTIONS Amantadine, ANTIHISTAMINES, TRICYCLIC ANTIDEPRESSANTS, **quinidine, disopyramide, procainamide** add to anticholinergic effects. **Levodopa** effects decreased. **Methotrimeprazine** may precipitate extrapyramidal effects. Antipsychotic effects of PHENOTHIAZINES are decreased due to decreased absorption.

PHARMACOKINETICS Peak: 2–4 min. **Duration:** Inhibition of salivation 4 h; mydriasis 7–14 days. **Distribution:** Distributed in most body tissues; crosses blood–brain barrier and placenta. **Metabolism:** Metabolized in liver. **Elimination:** 77–94% excreted in urine in 24 h. **Half-Life:** 2–3 h.

NURSING IMPLICATIONS

Assessment & Drug Effects

- Monitor vital signs. HR is a sensitive indicator of patient's response to atropine. Be alert to changes in quality, rate, and rhythm of HR and respiration and to changes in BP and temperature.
- Initial paradoxical bradycardia following IV atropine usually lasts only 1–2 min; it most likely occurs when IV is administered slowly (more than 1 min) or when small doses (less than 0.5 mg) are used. Postural hypotension occurs when patient ambulates too soon after parenteral administration.
- Monitor I&O, especially in older adults and patients who have had surgery (drug may contribute to urinary retention). Have patient void before giving atropine.
- Monitor CNS status. Older adults and debilitated patients sometimes manifest drowsiness or CNS stimulation (excitement, agitation, confusion) with usual doses of drug or other belladonna alkaloids.
- Monitor infants, small children, and older adults for "atropine fever" (hyperpyrexia due to suppression of perspiration and heat loss), which increases the risk of heatstroke.

Patient & Family Education

- Follow measures to relieve dry mouth: Adequate hydration; small, frequent mouth rinses with tepid water; meticulous mouth hygiene.
- Drug cadrowsiness, sensitivity to light, blurring of near vision, and temporarily impairs ability to judge distance. Avoid driving and other activities requiring visual acuity and mental alertness.

AZATHIOPRINE

(ay-za-thye'oh-preen)

Classification(s): IMMUNOLOGIC AGENT; IMMUNOSUPPRESSANT
Therapeutic: IMMUNOSUPPRESSANT
Prototype: Cyclosporine
Pregnancy Category: D

USES Adjunctive agent to prevent rejection of kidney allografts, usually with other immunosuppressants.

INDICATION & DOSAGE

Renal Transplantation

Adult: 3–5 mg/kg/day initially, may be able to reduce to 1–3 mg/kg/day; transfer to PO therapy

Obesity

Doses calculated on IBW.

Renal Impairment Dosage Adjustment

CrCl	Dose	Interval
10–50 mL/min	75% of normal dose	Normal
Less than 10 mL/min	50% of normal dose	Normal
Hemodialysis	Normal	Administer after hemodialysis

SOLUTION PREPARATION

- *Vial Reconstitution:* Add 10 mL sterile water for injection to the each 100 mg and swirl until dissolved. May be given as prepared or may be further diluted.
- *Further Dilution of Reconstituted Solution:* Dilute in 50 mL NS, D5W, or D5/NS.

STORAGE

- Reconstituted solution may be stored at room temperature but **must be** used within 24 h after reconstitution (contains no preservatives).
- Store vials at 15°–30° C (59°–86° F).

Common adverse effects in *italic*, life-threatening effects <u>underlined</u>: generic names in **bold**; classifications in SMALL CAPS; ♣ Canadian drug name; ☯ Prototype drug

ADMINISTRATION

IV Infusion: Typical infusion time is 30–60 min or longer but may infuse over a range of 5 min to 8 h. If longer infusion time is ordered, the final volume of the IV solution is increased appropriately.

INCOMPATIBILITIES Data not available; do not mix with other drugs.

ACTION & *THERAPEUTIC EFFECT* Precise mechanism of immunosuppressant and antiinflammatory actions not determined. Antagonizes purine metabolism and appears to inhibit DNA, RNA, and normal protein synthesis in rapidly growing cells. *Suppresses T cell effects before transplant rejection.*

CONTRAINDICATIONS Hypersensitivity to azathioprine or mercaptopurine; clinically active infection, immunization of patient or close family members with live virus vaccines; anuria; pancreatitis; patients receiving alkylating agents (increased risk of neoplasms), concurrent radiation therapy; pregnancy (category D), lactation.

CAUTIOUS USE Impaired kidney and liver function; patients receiving cadaver kidney; myasthenia gravis.

ADVERSE EFFECTS (≥1%) **Body as a Whole:** Hypersensitivity (skin eruptions, rash, arthralgia). **GI:** Nausea, vomiting, anorexia, esophagitis, diarrhea, steatorrhea, hepatitis with elevations in bilirubin, alkaline phosphatase, AST, ALT, biliary stasis, toxic hepatitis. **Hematologic:** <u>Bone marrow depression</u>, thrombocytopenia, leukopenia, anemia, <u>agranulocytosis</u>, pancytopenia. **Other:** *Secondary infection (immunosuppression);* dysarthria, alopecia; carcinogenic and teratogenic potential reported.

DIAGNOSTIC TEST INTERFERENCE Azathioprine may decrease plasma and ***urinary uric acid*** in patients with gout.

DRUG INTERACTIONS Allopurinol increases effects and toxicity of azathioprine by reducing metabolism of the active metabolite; **allopurinol** doses should be decreased by one third or one fourth; **tubocurarine** and other NONDEPOLARIZING SKELETAL MUSCLE RELAXANTS may reverse or inhibit neuromuscular blocking effects.

PHARMACOKINETICS Distribution: Crosses placenta. **Metabolism:** Extensively in liver to active metabolite mercaptopurine. **Elimination:** Eliminated in urine. **Half-Life:** 3 h.

NURSING IMPLICATIONS

Assessment & Drug Effects

- Monitor for toxicity as drug has a high toxic potential. Because it may have delayed action, dosage should be reduced or drug withdrawn at the first indication of an abnormally large or persistent decrease in leukocyte or platelet count to avoid irreversible bone marrow depression.
- Monitor vital signs. Report signs of infection.
- Lab tests: CBC, including Hgb and platelet counts, prior to and at least weekly during first month of therapy, twice monthly during second and third months, and monthly, or more frequently thereafter, if indicated (e.g., by dosage or therapy changes); kidney function tests (urine protein, urine electrolytes, CrCl, serum creatinine, BUN) periodically.

Common adverse effects in *italic*, life-threatening effects <u>underlined</u>: generic names in **bold**; classifications in SMALL CAPS; ♣ Canadian drug name; ◯ Prototype drug

- Monitor I&O ratio; note color, character, and specific gravity of urine. Report an abrupt decrease in urinary output or any change in I&O ratio.
- Monitor for signs of abnormal bleeding [easy bruising, bleeding gums, petechiae, purpura, melena, epistaxis, dark urine (hematuria), hemoptysis, hematemesis]. If thrombocytopenia occurs, invasive procedures should be withheld, if possible.

Patient & Family Education

- Avoid contact with anyone who has a cold or other infection and report signs of impending infection. Exercise scrupulous personal hygiene because infection is a constant hazard of immunosuppressive therapy.
- Practice birth control during therapy and for 4 mo after drug is discontinued. This drug is associated with potential hazards in pregnancy.
- Do not receive/take vaccinations or other immunity-conferring agents during therapy because they may precipitate unusually severe reactions due to the immunosuppressive effects of the drug.

AZITHROMYCIN

(a-zi-thro-mye'sin)

Zithromax

Classification(s): ANTIBIOTIC; MACROLIDE

Therapeutic: ANTIBACTERIAL

Prototype: Erythromycin

Pregnancy Category: B

USES Community acquired pneumonia, pelvic inflammatory disease.
UNLABELED USES Bronchitis, *Helicobacter pylori* gastritis.

INDICATION & DOSAGE

Bacterial Infections

Adult: 500 mg daily for at least 2 days then switch to PO

Renal Impairment Dosage Adjustment

Dose adjustment may be required.

SOLUTION PREPARATION

- *Vial Reconstitution:* Add 4.8 mL of sterile water for injection to the 500-mg vial and shake until dissolved. Final concentration is 100 mg/mL. **Must be** further diluted for infusion.
- *Further Dilution of Reconstituted Solution:* Use D5W, D5/NS, 1/2NS or other compatible IV solution for dilution. To produce a concentration of 1 mg/mL, add 5 mL (500 mg) of reconstituted solution to 500 mL of IV solution. To produce a concentration of 2 mg/mL, add 5 mL (500 mg) of reconstituted solution to 250 mL of IV solution.

Common adverse effects in *italic*, life-threatening effects underlined: generic names in **bold**; classifications in SMALL CAPS; ♣ Canadian drug name; ● Prototype drug

77

STORAGE
Store diluted drug for 24 h at or below 30° C (86° F) or for 7 days under 5° C (41° F).

ADMINISTRATION
- **DO NOT** give a bolus injection.
- **IV Infusion:** Rate of administration depends on the dilution of the IV solution. Infuse 1 mg/mL over 3 h. Infuse 2 mg/mL over 1 h.

INCOMPATIBILITIES Y-site: Amikacin, aztreonam, cefotaxime, ceftazidime, ceftriaxone, cefuroxime, ciprofloxacin, clindamycin, famotidine, fentanyl, furosemide, gentamicin, imipenem/cilastatin, ketorolac, levofloxacin, morphine, ondansetron, piperacillin/tazobactam, potassium, ticarcillin/clavulanate, tobramycin.

ACTION & *THERAPEUTIC EFFECT* A macrolide antibiotic that reversibly binds to the 50S ribosomal subunit of susceptible organisms and consequently inhibits protein synthesis within the bacteria. *Effective for treatment of mild to moderate infection.*

CONTRAINDICATIONS Hypersensitivity to azithromycin, erythromycin, or any of the macrolide antibiotics.

CAUTIOUS USE Older adults or debilitated persons, hepatic or renal impairment; GI disease; ventricular arrhythmias, QT prolongation; UV exposure; pregnancy (category B), lactation.

ADVERSE EFFECTS (≥1%) **CNS:** Headache, dizziness. **GI:** Nausea, vomiting, diarrhea, abdominal pain; hepatotoxicity, mild elevations in liver function tests.

DIAGNOSTIC TEST INTERFERENCE Liver function tests: Reversible, asymptomatic elevations in *liver enzymes (AST, ALT, gamma glutamyl transferase, alkaline phosphatase)* have been reported in some patients treated with azithromycin.

DRUG INTERACTIONS May increase toxicity of **dihydroergotamine, ergotamine.**

PHARMACOKINETICS Peak: 2.5–4 h. **Distribution:** Extensively distributed to most tissues including sputum, blister, and vaginal secretions; tissue concentrations are often higher than serum concentrations. **Metabolism:** Metabolized in liver. **Elimination:** 5–12% of dose is excreted in urine. **Half-Life:** 60–70 h.

NURSING IMPLICATIONS

Assessment & Drug Effects
- Monitor for and report loose stools or diarrhea, since pseudomembranous colitis (see Appendix C) **must be** ruled out.
- Lab tests: Monitor PT and INR closely with concurrent warfarin use.

Patient & Family Education
- Direct sunlight (UV) exposure should be minimized during therapy with drug.
- Report onset of loose stools or diarrhea.

Common adverse effects in *italic*, life-threatening effects underlined: generic names in **bold**; classifications in SMALL CAPS; ♣ Canadian drug name; ☺ Prototype drug

AZTREONAM

(az-tree′oh-nam)

Azactam

Classification(s): ANTIBIOTIC; CARBAPENEM
Therapeutic: ANTIBACTERIAL
Prototype: Imipenem-Cilastatin
Pregnancy Category: B

USES Gram-negative infections of urinary tract, lower respiratory tract, skin and skin structures; and for intra-abdominal and gynecologic infections, septicemia, and as adjunctive therapy for surgical infections.

INDICATION & DOSAGE

Urinary Tract Infection

Adult: 0.5–1 g q8–12h

Moderate to Severe Infections

Adult: 1–2 g q8–12h (max: 8 g/24 h)
Child: 30 mg/kg/day q6–8h

Renal Impairment Dosage Adjustment

After normal loading dose.

CrCl	Dose	Interval
10–30 mL/min	50% of dose	Normal
Less than 10 mL/min	25% of dose	Normal
Hemodialysis	12.5% of dose	Administer after hemodialysis

SOLUTION PREPARATION

- *Vial Reconstitution:* Add 6–10 mL of sterile water for injection to a single-dose vial. Immediately shake vial until solution is dissolved. Reconstituted solutions are colorless to light straw yellow and turn slightly pink on standing. May be given direct IV as prepared or further diluted for IV infusion.
- *Further Dilution of Reconstituted Solution:* Dilute each 1 g of reconstituted aztreonam in at least 50 mL of D5W, NS, or other compatible solution to yield a concentration not to exceed 20 mg/mL.

STORAGE

Solutions for IV infusion **must be** used within 48 h following constitution if kept at 15°–30° C (59°–86° F) or within 7 days if refrigerated at 2°–8° C (36°–46° F).

ADMINISTRATION

- **Direct IV Injection:** Give bolus dose over 3–5 min.

Common adverse effects in *italic*, life-threatening effects underlined: generic names in **bold**; classifications in SMALL CAPS; ♣ Canadian drug name; ❷ Prototype drug

- **Intermittent Infusion:** Infuse over 20–60 min. If given through Y-site, flush before and after with compatible IV solution. Ensure that entire dose is given.

INCOMPATIBILITIES Solution/additive: Ampicillin, metronidazole, nafcillin. **Y-site:** Acyclovir, amphotericin B, amphotericin B cholesteryl complex, amsacrine, azithromycin, chlorpromazine, daunorubicin, ganciclovir, lansoprazole, lorazepam, metronidazole, mitomycin, mitoxantrone, streptozocin.

ACTION & *THERAPEUTIC EFFECT* Differs structurally from other beta-lactam antibiotics (penicillins and cephalosporins). Acts by inhibiting synthesis of the third and final stage of bacterial cell wall synthesis by specifically binding to penicillin-binding proteins (PBP) located in the cell wall. This results in bacteria cell death. *Spectrum of activity limited to aerobic, gram-negative bacteria. There appears to be little cross-allergenicity with penicillins and cephalosporins.*

CONTRAINDICATIONS Viral infections; lactation.

CAUTIOUS USE History of hypersensitivity reaction to penicillin, cephalosporins, or other penicillin derivatives; impaired renal or hepatic function, elderly; pregnancy (category B).

ADVERSE EFFECTS (≥1%) **Body as a Whole:** Hypersensitivity (urticaria, eosinophilia, <u>anaphylaxis</u>). **CNS:** Headache, dizziness, confusion, paresthesias, insomnia, seizures. **GI:** Nausea, *diarrhea,* vomiting, elevated liver function tests. **Hematologic:** Eosinophilia. **Special Senses:** Tinnitus, nasal congestion, sneezing, diplopia. **Skin:** Rash, purpura, erythema multiforme, exfoliative dermatitis, diaphoresis; petechiae, pruritus. **Other:** Phlebitis, thrombophlebitis, pain at injection sites, superinfections (gram-positive cocci), vaginal candidiasis.

DIAGNOSTIC TEST INTERFERENCE Aztreonam may cause transient elevations of *liver function tests,* increases in *PT* and *PTT,* minor changes in *Hgb,* and positive *Coombs' test.*

DRUG INTERACTIONS Imipenem-cilastatin, cefoxitin may be antagonistic, **probenecid** slows renal elimination of aztreonam.

PHARMACOKINETICS Distribution: Widely distributed including synovial and blister fluid, bile, bronchial secretions, prostate, bone, and CSF; crosses placenta; distributed into breast milk in small amounts. **Metabolism:** Not extensively metabolized. **Elimination:** 60–70% excreted in urine within 24 h. **Half-Life:** 1.6–2.1 h.

NURSING IMPLICATIONS
Assessment & Drug Effects

- Prior to initiating therapy: C&S before initial dose (start therapy pending results).
- Determine previous hypersensitivity reactions to penicillins, cephalosporins, and other allergens prior to therapy.
- Inspect IV injection sites daily for signs of inflammation. Pain and phlebitis occur in a significant number of patients.

- Monitor for S&S of opportunistic infections (e.g., diarrhea, rectal or vaginal itching or discharge, fever, cough).
- Lab tests: Baseline and periodic LFTs, and renal function tests particularly in older adults and in those with history of renal impairment.

Patient & Family Education
- Report promptly diarrhea, rectal or vaginal itching or discharge, skin rash).
- IV therapy may cause a change in taste sensation. Report interference with eating.

BASILIXIMAB

(bas-i-lix′i-mab)
Simulect
Classification(s): IMMUNOLOGIC AGENT, IMMUNOSUPPRESSANT
Therapeutic: IMMUNOSUPPRESSANT
Pregnancy Category: B

USES Prophylaxis of acute renal transplant rejection.

INDICATION & DOSAGE

Prophylaxis for Transplant Rejection
Adult/Child (35 or more kg): 20 mg within 2 h of transplant surgery then 20 mg 4 days after surgery
Child (less than 35 kg): 10 mg 2 h before surgery then 10 mg 4 days after transplant

SOLUTION PREPARATION
- *Vial Reconstitution:* Add 2.5 mL or 5 mL sterile water for injection to the 10 mg or 20 mg vial, respectively. Rock vial gently to dissolve. May be given as prepared direct IV as a bolus dose or further diluted for infusion.
- *Further Dilution of Reconstituted Solution:* Use NS or D5W to dilute the 10 mg dose to a volume of 25 mL or the 20 mg dose to a volume of 50 mL in NS or D5W. Invert IV bag to dissolve but do not shake. The resulting solution has a concentration of 2.5 mg/mL.
- Discard if diluted solution is colored or has particulate matter. Use IV solution immediately.

STORAGE
- The diluted solution may be stored at room temperature for 4 h or at 2°–8° C (36°–46° F) for 24 h. Discard after 24 h.
- Store undiluted drug at 2°–8° C (36°–46° F).

Common adverse effects in *italic*, life-threatening effects <u>underlined</u>: generic names in **bold**; classifications in SMALL CAPS; ♣ Canadian drug name; ◎ Prototype drug

81

B

ADMINISTRATION
- **Direct IV Injection:** Give bolus dose over 20–30 sec.
- **IV Infusion:** Infuse the ordered dose over 20–30 min.

INCOMPATIBILITIES Data not available; do not mix with other drugs.

ACTION & *THERAPEUTIC EFFECT* Immunosuppressant agent that is an interleukin-2 receptor monoclonal antibody produced by recombinant DNA technology. Binds to and blocks interleukin-2R-alpha chain (CD-25 antibodies) on surface of activated T lymphocytes. *Binding to CD-25 antibodies inhibits a critical pathway in the immune response of the lymphocytes involved in allograft rejection.*

CONTRAINDICATIONS Hypersensitivity to mannitol or murine protein; serious infection or exposure to viral infections (e.g., chickenpox, herpes zoster); lactation.

CAUTIOUS USE History of untoward reactions to dacliximab or other monoclonal antibodies; pregnancy (category B).

ADVERSE EFFECTS (≥1%) **Body as a Whole:** Pain, peripheral edema, edema, fever, viral infection, asthenia, arthralgia, acute hypersensitivity reactions with any dose. **CNS:** Headache, tremor, dizziness, insomnia, paresthesias, agitation, depression. **CV:** Hypertension, chest pain, hypotension, arrhythmias. **GI:** Constipation, nausea, diarrhea, abdominal pain, vomiting, dyspepsia, moniliasis, flatulence, GI hemorrhage, melena, esophagitis, erosive stomatitis. **Hematologic:** Anemia, thrombocytopenia, thrombosis, polycythemia. **Respiratory:** Dyspnea, URI, cough, rhinitis, pharyngitis, bronchospasm. **Skin:** Poor wound healing, acne. **Urogenital:** Dysuria, UTI, albuminuria, hematuria, oliguria, frequency, renal tubular necrosis, urinary retention. **Other:** Cataract, conjunctivitis. **Metabolic:** Hyperkalemia, hypokalemia, hyperglycemia, hyperuricemia, hypophosphatemia, hypocalcemia, increased weight, hypercholesterolemia, acidosis.

DRUG INTERACTIONS May have additive effects with other IMMUNOSUPPRESSANTS.

PHARMACOKINETICS Duration: 36 days. **Distribution:** Binds to interleukin-2R-alpha sites on lymphocytes. **Half-Life:** 7.2 days (adults), 7–11 days (children).

NURSING IMPLICATIONS
Assessment & Drug Effects
- Monitor carefully for and immediately report S&S of or anaphylactoid reaction (see Appendix C). Note: Anaphylaxis has occurred both upon first exposure and upon reexposure after several months.
- Monitor vital signs and report S&S of opportunistic infections.
- Lab tests: Baseline CBC with differential, renal function tests, and LFTs.

Patient & Family Education
- Report any distressing adverse effects.
- Avoid vaccination for 2 wk following last dose of drug.

BENZTROPINE MESYLATE

B

(benz'troe-peen)

Cogentin

Classification(s): ANTICHOLINERGIC AGENT

Therapeutic: ANTIPARKINSON

Pregnancy Category: C

USES To relieve extrapyramidal symptoms associated with neuroleptic drugs, e.g., haloperidol (Haldol), phenothiazines, thiothixene (Navane), Parkinsonism, acute dystonia.

INDICATION & DOSAGE

Extrapyramidal Reactions

Adult: 1–4 mg 1–2 times daily as needed

Child (over 3 y): 1–2 mg daily

Parkinsonism

Adult: 1–2 mg daily

Acute Dystonia

Adult: 1–2 mg daily

SOLUTION PREPARATION

No dilution is required. Administer as supplied.

STORAGE

Store at 15°–30° C (59°–86° F).

ADMINISTRATION

Direct IV Injection: Give 1 mg or a fraction thereof over 1 min.

INCOMPATIBILITIES Syringe: **Haloperidol.**

ACTION & *THERAPEUTIC EFFECT* Synthetic centrally acting muscarinic-receptor antagonist agent. Blocks dopamine reuptake and storage in CNS cells, thus prolonging the effects of dopamine deficiency. *Helps control tremor but is less effective for treating rigidity.*

CONTRAINDICATIONS Narrow angle glaucoma; myasthenia gravis; obstructive diseases of GU and GI tracts; tendency to tachycardia; tardive dyskinesia; BPH; children less than 3 y, pregnancy (category C).

CAUTIOUS USE Older adults or debilitated patients; autonomic neuropathy; patients with poor mental outlook, mental disorders; enlarged prostate; hypertension, tachycardia, cardiac disease; older children; lactation.

ADVERSE EFFECTS (≥1%) **CNS:** *Sedation,* drowsiness, dizziness, paresthesias; agitation, irritability, restlessness, nervousness, insomnia, hallucinations,

---

Common adverse effects in *italic*, life-threatening effects <u>underlined</u>: generic names in **bold**; classifications in SMALL CAPS; ♣ Canadian drug name; ☻ Prototype drug

83

delirium, mental confusion, toxic psychosis, muscular weakness, ataxia, inability to move certain muscle groups. **CV:** Palpitation, tachycardia, flushing. **Special Senses:** Blurred vision, mydriasis, photophobia. **GI:** Nausea, vomiting, *constipation, dry mouth,* distention, paralytic ileus. **Urogenital:** Dysuria.

DRUG INTERACTIONS Alcohol, CNS DEPRESSANTS have additive sedation and depressant effects; **amantadine,** TRICYCLIC ANTIDEPRESSANTS, MAO INHIBITORS, PHENOTHIAZINES, **procainamide, quinidine** have additive anticholinergic effects and cause confusion, hallucinations, paralytic ileus.

PHARMACOKINETICS Onset: Within 15 min. **Duration:** 6–10 h.

NURSING IMPLICATIONS

Assessment & Drug Effects

- Assess therapeutic effectiveness. Clinical improvement may not be evident for 2–3 days after oral drug is started.
- Monitor I&O ratio and pattern.
- Closely monitor for appearance of S&S of onset of paralytic ileus including intermittent constipation, abdominal pain, diminution of bowel sounds on auscultation, and distention.
- Monitor for and report muscle weakness or inability to move certain muscle groups. Dosage reduction may be needed.
- Supervise ambulation and use falls precautions as necessary.
- Report immediately S&S of CNS depression or stimulation. These usually require interruption of drug therapy.

Patient & Family Education

- Do not drive or engage in potentially hazardous activities until response to drug is known. Seek help walking as necessary.
- Avoid alcohol and other CNS depressants because they may cause additive drowsiness. Do not take OTC cold, cough, or hay fever remedies unless approved by prescriber.
- Report difficulty in urination or infrequent voiding.
- Sugarless gum, hard candy, and rinsing mouth with tepid water will help dry mouth.

BETAMETHASONE SODIUM PHOSPHATE/BETAMETHASONE ACETATE

(bay-ta-meth'a-sone)

Betnesol ♣, Celestone

Classification(s): ADRENAL CORTICOSTEROID; GLUCOCORTICOID
Therapeutic: ANTIINFLAMMATORY
Prototype: Hydrocortisone
Pregnancy Category: C

USES Reduces serum calcium in hypercalcemia, suppresses undesirable inflammatory or immune responses, and produces temporary remission in nonadrenal disease.

UNLABELED USES Prevention of neonatal respiratory distress syndrome (hyaline membrane disease).

INDICATION & DOSAGE

Antiinflammatory Agent
Adult: Up to 9 mg/day as sodium phosphate

SOLUTION PREPARATION
May be given undiluted direct IV (typical) or further diluted in D5W or NS.

STORAGE
Store at 15°–30° C (59°–86° F).

ADMINISTRATION
- **Direct IV Injection:** Give required dose over 1 min.
- **IV Infusion:** Give at a rate determined by the total amount of IV fluid in which drug is dissolved.

INCOMPATIBILITIES **Solution/additive:** Data not available; do not mix with other drugs. **Y-site:** Data not available; do not mix with other drugs.

ACTION & *THERAPEUTIC EFFECT* Synthetic, long-acting glucocorticoid with strong immunosuppressive, antiinflammatory, and metabolic actions. *Relieves antiinflammatory manifestations and is an immunosuppressive agent.*

CONTRAINDICATIONS In patients with systemic fungal infections; acne vulgaris, acne rosacea, or perioral dermatitis; Cushing's syndrome, vaccines; measles; pregnancy (category C), lactation.

CAUTIOUS USE Ocular herpes simplex; concomitant use of aspirin; osteoporosis; diverticulitis, nonspecific ulcerative colitis, abscess or other pyrogenic infection, peptic ulcer disease; CHF, hypertension; renal or hepatic insufficiency; glaucoma; myasthenia gravis.

ADVERSE EFFECTS (≥1%) Most adverse effects are dose and treatment duration dependent. **Body as a Whole:** Hypersensitivity or <u>anaphylactoid reactions; aggravation or masking of infections</u>; malaise, weight gain, obesity. **CNS:** Vertigo, headache, increased intracranial pressure with papilledema (usually after discontinuation of medication), mental disturbances, aggravation of preexisting psychiatric conditions, insomnia. **CV:** Hypertension; syncopal episodes, thrombophlebitis, thromboembolism or fat embolism, palpitation, tachycardia, necrotizing angiitis; CHF. **Endocrine:** Suppressed linear growth in children, decreased glucose tolerance; hyperglycemia, manifestations of latent diabetes mellitus; hypocorticism; amenorrhea and other menstrual difficulties. **Special Senses:** Posterior subcapsular cataracts (especially in children), glaucoma, exophthalmos, increased intraocular pressure with optic nerve damage, perforation of the globe, fungal infection of the cornea, decreased or blurred vision. **Metabolic:** Hypocalcemia; *sodium and fluid retention;* hypokalemia and hypokalemic alkalosis; negative nitrogen balance. **GI:** *Nausea,* increased appetite, ulcerative esophagitis, pancreatitis, abdominal distention, peptic

Common adverse effects in *italic*, life-threatening effects <u>underlined</u>: generic names in **bold**; classifications in SMALL CAPS; ♣ Canadian drug name; ◑ Prototype drug

85

B

ulcer with perforation and hemorrhage, melena; decreased serum concentration of vitamins A and C. **Hematologic:** Thrombocytopenia. **Musculoskeletal:** Osteoporosis, compression fractures, muscle wasting and weakness, tendon rupture, aseptic necrosis of femoral and humeral heads (all resulting from long-term use). **Skin:** *Impaired wound healing;* petechiae, ecchymosis, easy bruising; suppression of skin test reaction, hyper/hypopigmentation. **IV Site:** Pain, irritation, necrosis, atrophy, sterile abscess; Charcot-like arthropathy following intra-articular use; burning and tingling in perineal area (after IV injection).

DIAGNOSTIC TEST INTERFERENCE May increase serum *cholesterol, blood glucose,* serum *sodium, uric acid* (in acute leukemia) and *calcium* (in bone metastasis). It may decrease serum *calcium, potassium, PBI, thyroxin (T4), triiodothyronine (T3)* and reduce *thyroid I 131* uptake. It increases *urine glucose* level and *calcium* excretion; decreases *urine 17-OHCS* and *17-KS* levels. May produce false-negative results with *nitroblue tetrazolium test* for systemic bacterial infection and may suppress reactions to skin tests.

DRUG INTERACTIONS BARBITURATES, **phenytoin**, **rifampin** may reduce pharmacologic effect of betamethasone by increasing its metabolism. May decrease effectiveness of LIVE VACCINES.

PHARMACOKINETICS Onset: Rapid. **Peak:** Unknown. **Half-Life:** Unknown.

NURSING IMPLICATIONS

Assessment & Drug Effects
▪ Assess therapeutic effectiveness. Following IV administration response occurs within several hours and persists for 3–7 days.

Patient & Family Education
▪ Monitor weight at least weekly.

BEVACIZUMAB

(be-va-ci-zu′mab)

Avastin

Classifications: ANTINEOPLASTIC, MONOCLONAL ANTIBODY
Therapeutic: ANTINEOPLASTIC
Pregnancy Category: C

USES Metastatic colorectal cancer; non–small-cell lung cancer.
UNLABELED USES Metastatic renal cell cancer, breast cancer, prostate cancer.

INDICATION & DOSAGE

Metastatic Colorectal Cancer

Adult: 5 or 10 mg/kg q14days until disease progression; in conjunction with other chemotherapy agents

Non–Small-Cell Lung Cancer
Adult: 15 mg/kg q3wk

SOLUTION PREPARATION
Do not shake vial(s). Calculate the required dose (mg) and withdraw from the vial(s) the desired volume (mL) of drug. Dilute in 100 mL of NS. DO NOT use IV solutions containing dextrose. Discard any unused drug remaining in the vial.

STORAGE
Store diluted solution at 2°–8° C (36°–46° F) for up to 8 h. Store vials at 2°–8° C (36°–46° F) and protect from light. Do not shake vials.

ADMINISTRATION
IV Infusion: Do not administer a direct IV bolus dose. Infuse *first dose* over 90 min; if well tolerated, infuse *second dose* over 60 min; if well tolerated, infuse all *subsequent doses* over 30 min.

INCOMPATIBILITIES Solution/additive: Dextrose-containing solutions. **Y-site: Dextrose**-containing solutions.

ACTION & *THERAPEUTIC EFFECT* Blocks endothelial cell proliferation and new blood vessel formation in tumor cells. Its mechanism results from binding to vascular endothelial growth factor (VEGF) and preventing the interaction of VEGF with its receptors on the surface of endothelial cells. *Believed to cause reduction of microvascularization in the tumor, thus inhibiting the progression of metastatic disease.*

CONTRAINDICATIONS Nephrotic syndrome; active bleeding; recent hemoptysis; surgery within 28 days; severe arterial thromboembolic event; dental work within 20 days; neonates; GI perforation; pregnancy (category C), lactation. Safety and effectiveness in children are not established.
CAUTIOUS USE Hypersensitivity to bevacizumab; hypertension, history of arterial thromboembolic, cardiovascular, or cerebrovascular disease; elderly; renal disease.

ADVERSE EFFECTS (≥1%) **Body as a Whole:** *Asthenia,* pain, <u>wound dehiscence</u>. **CNS:** Syncope, headache, dizziness, confusion, abnormal gait, <u>leukoencephalopathy</u>. **CV:** DVT, *hypertension,* heart failure, intra-abdominal thrombosis, <u>cerebrovascular events</u>. **GI:** Abdominal pain, *diarrhea,* constipation, nausea, vomiting, anorexia, stomatitis, dyspepsia, weight loss, flatulence, dry mouth, colitis, <u>gastrointestinal perforation</u>. **Hematologic:** *Leukopenia, neutropenia,* thrombocytopenia, <u>hemorrhage</u>, *thromboembolism*. **Metabolic:** Hypokalemia, hyperbilirubinemia. **Musculoskeletal:** Myalgia. **Respiratory:** Upper respiratory infection, epistaxis, dyspnea, <u>hemoptysis</u>. **Skin:** Exfoliative dermatitis, alopecia. **Special Senses:** Taste disorder, increased tearing. **Urogenital:** *Proteinuria,* urinary frequency/urgency.

DRUG INTERACTIONS None reported at this time.

PHARMACOKINETICS Half-Life: 20 days (11–50 days).

Common adverse effects in *italic*, life-threatening effects <u>underlined</u>: generic names in **bold**; classifications in SMALL CAPS; ✚ Canadian drug name; ◍ Prototype drug

87

B

NURSING IMPLICATIONS

Assessment & Drug Effects

- Monitor for S&S of an infusion reaction (hypersensitivity); infusion should be interrupted in all patients with severe infusion reactions and appropriate therapy instituted.
- Withhold drug and report promptly S&S of CHF, hemorrhage (e.g., epistaxis, hemoptysis, or GI bleeding), or unexplained abdominal pain.
- Monitor BP; if hypertension develops, monitor more frequently, even after discontinuation of bevacizumab.
- Lab tests: Baseline CBC with differential and platelet count; baseline and periodic urinalysis for proteinuria and 24 h urine if protein 2+ or greater.
- Evaluate all wound sites for possible delayed healing or dehiscence.
- Monitor for dizziness, lightheadedness, or loss of balance. Take appropriate safety measures.

Patient & Family Education

- Report any of the following to the prescriber: Bloody or black, tarry stool; changes in patterns of urination; swelling of legs or ankles; increased shortness of breath; severe abdominal pain; change in mental awareness, inability to talk or move one side of the body.
- Women of childbearing age should use effective birth control while receiving bevacizumab and for up to 6 mo following completion of treatment.

BIVALIRUDIN

(bi-val'i-ru-den)

Angiomax

Classification(s): ANTICOAGULANT; THROMBIN INHIBITOR
Therapeutic: ANTITHROMBOTIC
Prototype: Lepirudin
Pregnancy Category: B

USES Used with aspirin as an anticoagulant in patients undergoing PTCA, PCI, and patients at risk for HIT undergoing PCI.
UNLABELED USES Preventing DVT.

INDICATION & DOSAGE

Anticoagulation

Adult: 0.75 mg/kg bolus (5 min after the bolus an ACT should be performed and 0.3 mg/kg given if needed); followed by 1.75 mg/kg/h for the duration of the procedure and up to 4 h postprocedure, may continue at 0.2 mg/kg/h up to 20 h if needed; intended for use with aspirin 300–325 mg

Renal Impairment Dosage Adjustment

Bolus dose is not adjusted.

CrCl	Dose (Infusion Rate)
30–59 mL/min	1.75 mg/kg/h
Less than 30 mL/min	1 mg/kg/h
Hemodialysis	0.25 mg/kg/h

SOLUTION PREPARATION

- *Vial Reconstitution:* Add 5 mL of sterile water for injection to each 250 mg vial; gently swirl until dissolved. **Must be** further diluted before administration.
- *Further Dilution of Reconstituted Vial for IV Bolus and Infusion at 1.75 mg/kg/h:* Dilute each reconstituted vial in 50 mL of D5W or NS to yield 5 mg/mL.
- *Further Dilution of Reconstituted Vial for Low Dose Infusion at 0.2 mg/kg/h:* Dilute each reconstituted vial in 500 mL of D5W or NS to yield 0.5 mg/mL.

STORAGE

Store reconstituted vials refrigerated at 2°–8° C (35.6°–46.4° F) for up to 24 h. Store diluted concentrations between 0.5 mg/mL and 5 mg/mL at 15°–30° C (59°–86° F), for up to 24 h.

ADMINISTRATION

- **Direct IV Injection:** Give bolus dose over 3–5 sec.
- **Initial IV Infusion:** Calculate the rate at 1.75 mg/kg/h.
- **Subsequent Low-dose IV Infusion:** Calculate the rate at 0.2 mg/kg/h.

Wt in lb	Wt in kg	Bolus of 0.75 mg/kg (using 5 mg/mL)	Initial Infusion of 1.75 mg/kg/h (using 5 mg/mL)	Low-dose Infusion of 0.2 mg/kg/h (using 0.5 mg/mL)
95–103	43–47	7 mL	16 mL/h	18 mL/h
106–114	48–52	7.5 mL	17.5 mL/h	20 mL/h
117–125	53–57	8 mL	19 mL/h	22 mL/h
128–136	58–62	9 mL	21 mL/h	24 mL/h
139–147	63–67	10 mL	23 mL/h	26 mL/h
150–158	68–72	10.5 mL	24.5 mL/h	28 mL/h
161–169	73–77	11 mL	26 mL/h	30 mL/h
172–180	78–82	12 mL	28 mL/h	32 mL/h
183–191	83–87	13 mL	30 mL/h	34 mL/h
194–202	88–92	13.5 mL	31.5 mL/h	36 mL/h

Common adverse effects in *italic*, life-threatening effects underlined: generic names in **bold**; classifications in SMALL CAPS; ♣ Canadian drug name; ◐ Prototype drug

89

Wt in lb	Wt in kg	Bolus of 0.75 mg/kg (using 5 mg/mL)	Initial Infusion of 1.75 mg/kg/h (using 5 mg/mL)	Low-dose Infusion of 0.2 mg/kg/h (using 0.5 mg/mL)
205–213	93–97	14 mL	33 mL/h	38 mL/h
216–224	98–102	15 mL	35 mL/h	40 mL/h
227–235	103–107	16 mL	37 mL/h	42 mL/h
238–246	108–112	16.5 mL	38.5 mL/h	44 mL/h
249–257	113–117	17 mL	40 mL/h	46 mL/h
260–268	118–122	18 mL	42 mL/h	48 mL/h
271–279	123–127	19 mL	44 mL/h	50 mL/h
282–290	128–132	19.5 mL	45.5 mL/h	52 mL/h
293–301	133–137	20 mL	47 mL/h	54 mL/h
304–312	138–142	21 mL	49 mL/h	56 mL/h
315–323	143–147	22 mL	51 mL/h	58 mL/h
326–334	148–152	22.5 mL	52.5 mL/h	60 mL/h

INCOMPATIBILITIES Y-site: Alteplase, amiodarone, amphotericin B, chlorpromazine, diazepam, high dose dobutamine, prochlorperazine edisylate, reteplase, streptokinase, vancomycin.

ACTION & *THERAPEUTIC EFFECT* Direct inhibitor of thrombin. Capable of inhibiting the action of both free and clot-bound thrombin. *Reversibly binds to the thrombin active site, thereby blocking the thrombogenic activity of thrombin.*

CONTRAINDICATIONS Hypersensitivity to bivalirudin; cerebral aneurysm, intracranial hemorrhage; patients with increased risk of bleeding (e.g., recent surgery, trauma, CVA, GI bleeding); lactation. Safety and efficacy in children are not established.

CAUTIOUS USE Asthma or allergies; blood dyscrasia or thrombocytopenia; GI ulceration, diverticulitis, inflammatory bowel disease; chronic renal disease; serious hepatic disease; hypertension, aneurysm; peptic ulcer disease; renal impairment; pregnancy (category B).

ADVERSE EFFECTS (≥1%) **Body as a Whole:** *Back pain,* pain, fever. **CV:** *Hypotension,* hypertension, bradycardia. **GI:** *Nausea,* vomiting, dyspepsia, abdominal pain. **Hematologic:** Bleeding. **CNS:** *Headache,* anxiety, nervousness. **Urogenital:** Urinary retention, pelvic pain. **Other:** Injection site pain.

DRUG INTERACTIONS May have additive effect with other ANTICOAGULANTS.

PHARMACOKINETICS Duration: 1 h. **Distribution:** No protein binding. **Metabolism:** Proteolytic cleavage and renal metabolism. **Elimination:** Renal. **Half-Life:** 25 min.

Common adverse effects in *italic*, life-threatening effects underlined: generic names in **bold**; classifications in SMALL CAPS; ♣ Canadian drug name; ❷ Prototype drug

NURSING IMPLICATIONS

Assessment & Drug Effects

- Monitor cardiovascular status carefully during therapy.
- Monitor for and report S&S of bleeding: Ecchymosis, epistaxis, GI bleeding, hematuria, hemoptysis.
- Patients with history of GI ulceration, hypertension, recent trauma or surgery are at increased risk for bleeding.
- Monitor neurologic status and report immediately: Focal or generalized deficits.
- Lab tests: Baseline and periodic ACT (activated clotting time), aPTT, PT, INR, thrombin time (TT), plasma fibrinopeptide A (especially in unstable angina), platelet count, Hgb and Hct; periodic serum creatinine, stool for occult blood, urinalysis.

Patient & Family Education

- Report any of the following immediately: Unexplained back or stomach pain; black, tarry stools; blood in urine, coughing up blood; difficulty breathing; dizziness or fainting spells; heavy menstrual bleeding; nosebleeds; unusual bruising or bleeding at any site.

BLEOMYCIN SULFATE

(blee-oh-mye'sin)

Blenoxane

Classification(s): ANTINEOPLASTIC; ANTIBIOTIC
Therapeutic: ANTINEOPLASTIC
Prototype: Doxorubicin
Pregnancy Category: D

USES As single agent or in combination with other chemotherapeutic agents, as adjunct to surgery and radiation therapy. Squamous cell carcinomas of head, neck, penis, cervix, and vulva; lymphomas (including reticular cell sarcoma, lymphosarcoma, Hodgkin's); testicular carcinoma; malignant pleural effusions.
UNLABELED USES *Mycosis fungoides* and *Verruca vulgaris* (common warts), AIDS-related Kaposi's sarcoma.

INDICATION & DOSAGE

Squamous Cell Carcinoma, Testicular Carcinoma, Lymphomas
Adult/Child: 10–20 units/m² or 0.25–0.5 units/kg 1–2 times/wk (max: 300–400 units)

Renal Impairment Dosage Adjustment
10–50 mL/min: Use 75% of dose; *less than 10mL/min:* Use 50% of dose

SOLUTION PREPARATION

- Wear protective gloves and prevent contact with skin.

Common adverse effects in *italic*, life-threatening effects underlined: generic names in **bold**; classifications in SMALL CAPS; ♥ Canadian drug name; ◐ Prototype drug

91

B

- *Vial Reconstitution:* Using sterile water for injection or NS, add 5 mL to each 15 unit vial and 10 mL to each 30 unit vial. May be given as prepared or further diluted for infusion.
- *Further Dilution of Reconstituted Vial:* Add contents of vial to 50–100 mL of NS. Do use any solution containing D5W.

STORAGE
Store unopened vials at 2°–8° C (36°–46° F). Diluted solution may be stored for 26 h at 15°–30° C (59°–86° F).

ADMINISTRATION
- **Direct IV Injection:** Give each 15 units or fraction thereof over 10 min through Y-tube of free-flowing IV.
- **IV Infusion:** Give over 15–30 min or longer as the volume of IV fluid dictates.

INCOMPATIBILITIES Solution/additive: Aminophylline, ascorbic acid, cefazolin, diazepam, hydrocortisone, methotrexate, mitomycin, nafcillin, penicillin G, terbutaline.

ACTION & *THERAPEUTIC EFFECT* Has intense cytotoxic effects by binding directly to DNA. By unclear mechanism, blocks DNA, RNA, and protein synthesis. *A mixture of cytotoxic antibiotics that has strong affinity for skin and lung tumor cells, in contrast to its low affinity for cells in hematopoietic tissue.*

CONTRAINDICATIONS History of hypersensitivity to bleomycin; vaccination; pregnancy (category D), lactation; children less than 1 y.

CAUTIOUS USE Compromised hepatic, renal, or pulmonary function; previous cytotoxic drug or radiation therapy; women of childbearing age; peripheral vascular disease; children greater than 1 y.

ADVERSE EFFECTS (≥1%) **Body as a Whole:** Hypersensitivity (<u>anaphylactoid reaction</u>); *mild febrile reaction.* **CNS:** Headache, mental confusion. **GI:** Stomatitis, ulcerations of tongue and lips, anorexia, nausea, vomiting, diarrhea, weight loss. **Hematologic:** Thrombocytopenia, leukopenia, (rare). **Respiratory:** <u>Pulmonary toxicity</u> (dose- and age-related); interstitial pneumonitis, pneumonia, or fibrosis. **Skin:** Diffuse alopecia (reversible), *hyperpigmentation, pruritic erythema,* vesiculation, acne, thickening of skin and nail beds, *patchy hyperkeratosis*, striae, peeling, bleeding. **Other:** Pain at tumor site; phlebitis; necrosis at injection site, shivering.

DRUG INTERACTIONS Other ANTINEOPLASTIC AGENTS increase bone marrow toxicity; decreases effects of **digoxin, phenytoin,** avoid use with LIVE VACCINES.

PHARMACOKINETICS Distribution: Concentrates mainly in skin, lungs, kidneys, lymphocytes, and peritoneum. **Elimination:** 60–70% recovered in urine as parent compound. **Half-Life:** 2 h.

NURSING IMPLICATIONS
Assessment & Drug Effects
- Test dose in lymphoma patients: Anaphylactoid reaction may occur immediately or several hours after first or second dose, especially in lym-

---

Common adverse effects in *italic*, life-threatening effects <u>underlined</u>: generic names in **bold**; classifications in SMALL CAPS; ♣ Canadian drug name; ● Prototype drug

phoma patients (10%). Monitor closely for at least 24 h (vital signs, auscultation of chest, careful observations). If there is no acute reaction (hypotension, hyperpyrexia, chills, confusion, wheezing, cardiopulmonary collapse), the regular dosage schedule will be initiated.

- Monitor vital signs. Febrile reaction (mild chills and fever) is relatively common and it usually occurs within the first few hours after administration of a large single dose and lasts about 4–12 h. Reaction tends to become less frequent with continued drug administration, but can recur at any time.
- Monitor for and report any of the following: Unexplained bleeding or bruising; evidence of deterioration of renal function (changed I&O ratio and pattern, decreasing creatinine clearance, weight gain or edema); evidence of pulmonary toxicity (nonproductive cough, chest pain, dyspnea).
- Lab tests: Baseline and periodic creatinine clearance.
- Note: Stomatitis can be a dose-limiting factor because oral ulcerations may interfere with adequate nutrient intake, leading to severe debilitation. Consult prescriber if an oral local anesthetic is indicated. Apply 10 min before meals to take effect so that patient can eat with less pain.
- Check weight at regular intervals under standard conditions. Weight loss and anorexia may persist a long time after therapy has been discontinued.
- Report symptoms of skin toxicity (hypoesthesia, urticaria, tender swollen hands) promptly. May develop in second or third week of treatment and after 150–200 units of bleomycin have been administered. Therapy may be discontinued.

Patient & Family Education

- Avoid OTC drugs during antineoplastic treatment period unless approved by prescriber.
- Report skin irritation which may not develop for several weeks after therapy begins.
- Hyperpigmentation may occur in areas subject to friction and pressure, skin folds, nail cuticles, scars, and intramuscular sites.

BORTEZOMIB

(bor-te-zo'mib)

Velcade

Classification(s): ANTINEOPLASTIC AGENT; PROTEOSOME INHIBITOR
Therapeutic: ANTINEOPLASTIC
Pregnancy Category: D

USES Treatment of relapsed or refractory multiple myeloma or mantle cell lymphoma in patients who have failed one prior therapy.
UNLABELED USES Non-Hodgkin's lymphoma.

Common adverse effects in *italic*, life-threatening effects underlined; generic names in **bold**; classifications in SMALL CAPS; ♣ Canadian drug name; ❷ Prototype drug

93

INDICATION & DOSAGE

Multiple Myeloma/Mantle Cell Lymphoma
Adult: 1.3 mg/m^2 twice weekly for 2 wk (days 1, 4, 8, and 11) followed by a 10-day rest period (days 12–21); at least 72 h should elapse between consecutive doses

Toxicity Adjustment
Hematologic: Withhold dose at onset of grade 3 or grade 4 hematologic toxicities; after symptom resolution may restart with a 25% dose reduction

Neuropathic Pain (on National Cancer Institute Common Toxicity Criteria)	Modification
Grade 1 with pain Grade 2	Reduce dose to 1 mg/m^2
Grade 2 with pain Grade 3	Withhold therapy until symptom resolution then start with 0.7 mg/m^2 once weekly
Grade 4	Stop therapy permanently

SOLUTION PREPARATION
- Wear protective gloves and prevent contact with skin.
- *Vial Reconstitution:* Reconstitute 3.5 mg vial with 3.5 mL of NS to yield 1 mg/mL. Discard if not clear and colorless.

STORAGE
- Store unopened vials at 15°–30° C (59°–86° F). Protect from light.
- Use within 8 h of reconstitution. May store up to 8 h in a syringe; however, total storage time must not exceed 8 h when exposed to normal indoor lighting.

ADMINISTRATION
Direct IV Injection: Give a bolus dose over 3–5 sec. Flush before/after with NS.

INCOMPATIBILITIES Solution/additive: Data not available; do not mix with other drugs.

ACTION & *THERAPEUTIC EFFECT* Bortezomib is a reversible inhibitor of 26S proteasome, which is responsible for regulation of protein expression and degradation of damaged or obsolete proteins within the cell. Its activity is critical to activation or suppression of cellular functions including the cell cycle, oncogene expression, and apoptosis. Malignant cells are much more sensitive to the effects of proteasome inhibition than normal cells. *Proteasome inhibition may reverse some of the changes that allow proliferation of malignant cells and suppress apoptosis (programmed cell death) in malignant cells.*

CONTRAINDICATIONS Hypersensitivity to bortezomib, boron, or mannitol; pregnancy (category D); lactation. Safety and effectiveness in children are not established.

CAUTIOUS USE Peripheral neuropathy; history of syncope, dehydration, hypotension; concurrent antihypertensive drugs; history of allergies, asthma; preexisting electrolyte or acid–base disturbances, especially hypokalemia or hyponatremia; liver disease; myelosuppression, renal impairment; history of peripheral neuropathy or other neurologic disorders; GI toxicities.

ADVERSE EFFECTS (≥1%) **Body as a Whole:** *Asthenia, weakness, fatigue, malaise, fever, dehydration, peripheral neuropathy, rigors, herpes zoster.* **CNS:** *Insomnia, headache, paresthesia, dizziness, anxiety.* **CV:** *Edema, hypotension, orthostatic hypotension.* **GI:** *Nausea, vomiting, diarrhea, anorexia, abdominal pain, constipation, dyspepsia, dysphagia.* **Hematologic:** *Thrombocytopenia, neutropenia, anemia.* **Musculoskeletal:** *Arthralgia, musculoskeletal pain, bone pain, myalgia, back pain, muscle cramps.* **Respiratory:** *Dyspnea, cough, upper respiratory infection.* **Skin:** *Rash, pruritus.* **Special Senses:** *Blurred vision, diplopia.*

DRUG INTERACTIONS Hypoglycemia and hyperglycemia have been reported with ANTIDIABETIC AGENTS; ANTIHYPERTENSIVE AGENTS may exacerbate hypotension; ANTICOAGULANTS, **antithymocyte globulin,** NSAIDS, PLATELET INHIBITORS, **aspirin,** THROMBOLYTIC AGENTS may increase risk of bleeding.

PHARMACOKINETICS Metabolism: In the liver primarily by CYP3A4. **Half-Life:** 9–15 h.

NURSING IMPLICATIONS

Assessment & Drug Effects

- Monitor for and report S&S of neuropathy (e.g., hyperesthesia, hypoesthesia, paresthesia, discomfort or neuropathic pain).
- Monitor postural vital signs for orthostatic hypotension.
- Monitor I&O and assess for S&S of dehydration or electrolyte imbalance if vomiting and/or diarrhea develop.
- Lab tests: Frequent CBC with platelet count; baseline and periodic LFTs; frequent blood glucose in diabetics.

Patient & Family Education

- Report promptly any of the following: Dizziness, light-headedness or fainting spells; numbness, tingling, or other unusual sensations; signs of infection (e.g., fever, chills, cough, sore throat); bruising, pinpoint red spots on the skin; black, tarry stools, nosebleeds, or any other sign of bleeding.
- Do not drive or engage in other hazardous activities until reaction to drug is known.
- Females should use reliable methods of contraception to avoid pregnancy while on this drug.

BRETYLIUM TOSYLATE

(bre-til′ee-um)

Bretylate ♣

Common adverse effects in *italic*, life-threatening effects <u>underlined</u>: generic names in **bold**; classifications in SMALL CAPS; ♣ Canadian drug name; ◯ Prototype drug

95

B

Classifications: ANTIARRHYTHMIC, CLASS III
Therapeutic: ANTIARRHYTHMIC
Prototype: Amiodarone
Pregnancy Category: C

USES Short-term prophylaxis and treatment of ventricular fibrillation; life-threatening arrhythmias such as ventricular fibrillation not responsive to conventional therapy [e.g., lidocaine, procainamide, direct current (cardioversion)].

INDICATION & DOSAGE

Ventricular Fibrillation
Adult: 5 mg/kg rapid IV injection, may increase to 10 mg/kg and repeat q15–30min (max: 30 mg/kg/day); may also give by continuous infusion at 1–2 mg/min
Child: 5 mg/kg, may repeat q15–30min (max: 30 mg/kg)

Renal Impairment Dosage Adjustment
CrCl 10–50 mL/min: Use 25–50% of dose; *CrCl less than 10 mL/min:* Use 25% of dose

SOLUTION PREPARATION
- *Direct IV Injection:* No dilution required for bolus dose.
- *Continuous IV Infusion:* Dilute in at least 50 mL of NS or D5W. See chart.

STORAGE
Store unopened vials at 15°–30° C (59°–86° F).

ADMINISTRATION
- **Direct IV Injection:** Give rapid bolus dose.
- **Continuous IV Infusion:** Give at a constant rate of 1–2 mg/min. See following chart.

Guidelines for Continuous Maintenance Infusion

Amount of Bretylium	Vol IV Fluid (mL)	Total Volume (mL)	IV Solution Concentration (mg/mL)	Needed Dose (mg/min)	IV Rate (mL/h)
2 g (40 mL)	500	540	3.7	1	16
				1.5	24
				2	32
1 g (20 mL)	250	270	3.7	1	16
				1.5	24
				2	32

Common adverse effects in *italic*, life-threatening effects <u>underlined</u>: generic names in **bold**; classifications in SMALL CAPS; ♣ Canadian drug name; ◉ Prototype drug

Amount of Bretylium	Vol IV Fluid (mL)	Total Volume (mL)	IV Solution Concentration (mg/mL)	Needed Dose (mg/min)	IV Rate (mL/h)
1 g (20 mL)	500	520	1.9	1	32
				1.5	47
				2	63
500 mg (10 mL)	250	260	1.9	1	32
				1.5	47
				2	63
500 mg (10 mL)	50	60	8.3	1	7
				1.5	11
				2	14

INCOMPATIBILITIES Solution/additive: Dobutamine, pantoprazole, phenytoin, procainamide. **Y-site:** Amphotericin B cholesteryl, propofol, warfarin.

ACTION & *THERAPEUTIC EFFECT* Suppresses ventricular fibrillation by direct action on the myocardium and ventricular tachycardia by adrenergic blockade. Shortly after administration, norepinephrine is released from adrenergic postganglionic nerve terminals, resulting in a moderate increase in BP, heart rate, and ventricular irritability. Subsequently (1–2 h), drug-induced release and reuptake of norepinephrine are blocked, leading to a state resembling surgical sympathectomy. *Suppresses arrhythmias with a reentry mechanism and decreases dispersion of ectopic foci. PR, QT, and QRS intervals are unchanged. Because onset of desired action is delayed, bretylium is not a first-line antiarrhythmic agent.*

CONTRAINDICATIONS Not for use in life-threatening refractory ventricular arrhythmias; pregnancy (category C).

CAUTIOUS USE Digitalis-induced arrhythmias, patients with fixed cardiac output (e.g., severe aortic stenosis or severe pulmonary hypertension because profound hypotension may result), sinus bradycardia, patients on digitalis maintenance, angina pectoris; impaired renal function, renal disease; lactation.

ADVERSE EFFECTS (≥1%) **CV:** Both supine and postural *hypotension*, syncope, transitory hypertension, bradycardia, increased frequency of PVCs, exacerbation of digitalis-induced arrhythmias. **CNS:** *Headache, confusion, dizziness*, vertigo, lightheadedness, faintness. **GI:** *Nausea, vomiting* (particularly with rapid IV). **Respiratory:** Respiratory depression.

DIAGNOSTIC TEST INTERFERENCE *Urinary VMA, epinephrine,* and *norepinephrine* levels may be decreased during bretylium therapy.

Common adverse effects in *italic*, life-threatening effects <u>underlined</u>: generic names in **bold**; classifications in SMALL CAPS; ✤ Canadian drug name; ⊘ Prototype drug

97

B

DRUG INTERACTIONS Lidocaine, procainamide, quinidine, propranolol may antagonize antiarrhythmic effects and compound hypotension; ANTIHYPERTENSIVE AGENTS will add to hypotensive effects; DIGITALIS GLYCOSIDES may worsen arrhythmias through **digitalis** toxicity, MACROLIDE ANTIBIOTICS, QUINOLONE ANTIBIOTICS, PHENOTHIAZINES, **ranolazine, vardenafil, ziprasidone** increase the risk of cardiac arrhythmias.

PHARMACOKINETICS Onset: 6–20 min. **Peak:** 6–9 h. **Duration:** 6–24 h. **Distribution:** Does not cross blood–brain barrier. **Metabolism:** Not metabolized. **Elimination:** 70–80% excreted in urine in 24 h. **Half-Life:** 4–17 h.

NURSING IMPLICATIONS

Assessment & Drug Effects

▪ Anticipate vomiting. IV administration is associated with a high incidence of nausea and vomiting. These side effects can be minimized by slower administration of drug.

▪ Establish baseline readings and monitor BP and ECG when drug is administered. Observe for initial transient rise in BP, increased heart rate, PVCs and other arrhythmias, or worsening of existing arrhythmias, which may occur within a few minutes to 1 h after drug administration. Initial effect of hypertension is usually followed within 1 h by a fall in supine BP and by orthostatic hypotension.

▪ Use supine position until patient develops tolerance to hypotensive effect of bretylium (generally in several days). Hypotension can occur in the supine position, particularly in patients with severely compromised cardiac function. It may not readily respond to therapy (e.g., vasopressors, fluids); early reporting is essential.

▪ Raise or lower head of bed slowly; advise patient to make position changes slowly in order to prevent orthostatic hypotension.

▪ Monitor I&O, particularly in patients with impaired renal function.

Patient & Family Education

▪ Make position changes slowly. If allowed to be out of bed, dangle legs for a few minutes before standing, but do not stand still for prolonged periods.

BROMPHENIRAMINE MALEATE

(brome-fen-ir′a-meen)

Classification(s): ANTIHISTAMINE; H$_1$-RECEPTOR ANTAGONIST
Therapeutic: ANTIHISTAMINE
Prototype: Diphenhydramine
Pregnancy Category: C

USES Symptomatic treatment of allergic manifestations.

INDICATION & DOSAGE

Allergy

Adult: 5–20 mg q6–12h (max: 40 mg/24 h)

SOLUTION PREPARATION

May be given undiluted direct IV or diluted in 10 mL D5W or NS.

STORAGE

Store in tightly covered container at 15°–30° C (59°–86° F) unless otherwise directed.

ADMINISTRATION

Direct IV Injection: Give bolus dose slowly over 1 min to a recumbent patient.

INCOMPATIBILITIES Solution/additive: Radio-contrast media **(diatrizoate, iothalamate), insulin, pentobarbital.**

ACTION & *THERAPEUTIC EFFECT* Antihistamine that competes with histamine at H_1-receptor sites on effector cells of the upper respiratory system, thus blocking histamine-mediated responses. *Effective against upper respiratory symptoms and allergic manifestations.*

CONTRAINDICATIONS Hypersensitivity to antihistamines; acute asthma; pregnancy (category C), lactation; newborns.
CAUTIOUS USE Older adults; prostatic hypertrophy; narrow-angle glaucoma; history of asthma, COPD; severe hepatic disease; seizure disorders; cardiovascular or renal disease; hyperthyroidism.

ADVERSE EFFECTS (≥1%) **Body as a Whole:** Hypersensitivity reaction (urticaria, increased sweating, <u>agranulocytosis</u>). **CNS:** *Sedation,* drowsiness, dizziness, headache, disturbed coordination. **GI:** Dry mouth, throat, and nose, stomach upset, constipation. **Special Senses:** Ringing or buzzing in ears. **Skin:** Rash, photosensitivity.

DIAGNOSTIC TEST INTERFERENCE May cause false-negative ***allergy skin tests.***

DRUG INTERACTIONS Alcohol and other CNS DEPRESSANTS add to sedation.

PHARMACOKINETICS Peak: 3–9 h. **Duration:** Up to 48 h. **Distribution:** Crosses placenta. **Elimination:** 40% excreted in urine within 72 h; 2% in feces. **Half-Life:** 25 h.

NURSING IMPLICATIONS

Assessment & Drug Effects

- Drowsiness, sweating, transient hypotension, and syncope may follow IV administration; reaction to drug should be evaluated. Keep prescriber informed.
- Note: Older adults tend to be particularly susceptible to drug's sedative effect, dizziness, and hypotension. Most symptoms respond to reduction in dosage.
- Lab tests: Periodic CBC in patients receiving long-term therapy.

Patient & Family Education

- Monitor for an acute hypersensitivity reaction that is manifested by high fever, chills, and possible development of ulcerations of mouth and

---

Common adverse effects in *italic*, life-threatening effects <u>underlined</u>: generic names in **bold**; classifications in SMALL CAPS; ♣ Canadian drug name; ☯ Prototype drug

99

throat, pneumonia, and prostration. Patient should seek medical attention immediately.
- Do not drive a car or other potentially hazardous activities until response to drug is known.
- Do not take alcoholic beverages or other CNS depressants (e.g., tranquilizers, sedatives, pain or sleeping medicines) without consulting prescriber.

BUMETANIDE

(byoo-met′a-nide)

Classification(s): FLUID AND WATER BALANCE AGENT; LOOP DIURETIC
Therapeutic: DIURETIC
Prototype: Furosemide
Pregnancy Category: C

USES Edema associated with CHF; hepatic or renal disease, including nephrotic syndrome. May be used concomitantly with a potassium-sparing diuretic.

INDICATION & DOSAGE

Edema
Adult: 0.5–1 mg over 1–2 min, repeated q2–3h prn (max: 10 mg/day)

SOLUTION PREPARATION
May be given undiluted direct IV (typical) or diluted in D5W, NS, or LR for infusion.

STORAGE
Diluted infusion should be used within 24 h after preparation. Store in tight, light-resistant container at 15°–30° C (59°–86° F) unless otherwise directed.

ADMINISTRATION
- **Direct IV Injection:** Give bolus dose over 1–2 min.
- **IV Infusion:** Give over 5 min or at a rate ordered by prescriber.

INCOMPATIBILITIES Solution/additive: Dobutamine. Y-site: Fenoldopam, midazolam.

ACTION & *THERAPEUTIC EFFECT* Sulfonamide derivative structurally related to furosemide; diuretic activity is 40 times greater, however, and duration of action is shorter than that of furosemide. Causes both potassium and magnesium wastage. Inhibits sodium and chloride reabsorption by direct action on proximal ascending limb of the loop of Henle. Also appears to inhibit phosphate and bicarbonate reabsorption. *Produces only mild hypotensive effects at usual diuretic doses. Controls formation of edema.*

CONTRAINDICATIONS Hypersensitivity to bumetanide or to other sulfonamides; anuria, markedly elevated BUN; severe renal disease; diabetes

Common adverse effects in *italic*, life-threatening effects <u>underlined</u>: generic names in **bold**; classifications in SMALL CAPS; ♣ Canadian drug name; ✪ Prototype drug

mellitus; hepatic coma; acute MI, ventricular arrhythmias, severe electrolyte deficiency; pregnancy (category C), lactation.
CAUTIOUS USE History of hypersensitivity to furosemide; hepatic cirrhosis, history of gout; elderly.

ADVERSE EFFECTS (≥1%) **Body as a Whole:** Sweating, glycosuria. **CNS:** Dizziness, headache, weakness, fatigue. **CV:** Hypotension, ECG changes, chest pain, *hypovolemia.* **GI:** Nausea, vomiting, abdominal or stomach pain, GI distress, diarrhea, dry mouth. **Metabolic:** *Electrolyte imbalance,* hyperglycemia. **Musculoskeletal:** Muscle cramps, muscle pain, stiffness or tenderness; arthritic pain. **Special Senses:** Ear discomfort, ringing or buzzing in ears, impaired hearing.

DRUG INTERACTIONS AMINOGLYCOSIDES, **cisplatin** increase risk of ototoxicity; bumetanide increases risk of hypokalemia-induced **digoxin** toxicity; NONSTEROIDAL ANTIINFLAMMATORY DRUGS (NSAIDS) may attenuate diuretic and hypotensive response; **probenecid** may antagonize diuretic activity; bumetanide may decrease renal elimination of **lithium; sotalol** may increase risk of cardiotoxicity.

PHARMACOKINETICS Onset: 40 min. **Peak:** 0.5–2 h. **Duration:** 4–6 h. **Distribution:** Extensive protein binding; distributed into breast milk. **Metabolism:** Partially in liver. **Elimination:** 80% excreted in urine in 48 h, 10–20% excreted in feces. **Half-Life:** 60–90 min.

NURSING IMPLICATIONS

Assessment & Drug Effects

- Monitor I&O and report onset of oliguria or other changes in I&O ratio and pattern promptly.
- Monitor weight, BP, and pulse rate. Assess for hypovolemia by taking BP and pulse rate while patient is lying, sitting, and standing. Older adults are particularly at risk for hypovolemia with resulting thrombi and emboli.
- Lab tests: Baseline and periodic serum electrolytes, blood studies, LFTs, BUN, uric acid (especially with a history of gout), and blood glucose.
- Monitor for S&S of hypomagnesemia and hypokalemia (see Appendix C) especially in those receiving digitalis or who have CHF, hepatic cirrhosis, ascites, diarrhea, or potassium-depleting nephropathy.
- Monitor patients with hepatic disease carefully for fluid and electrolyte imbalances, which can precipitate encephalopathy (inappropriate behavior, altered mood, impaired judgment, confusion, drowsiness, coma).
- Question patient about hearing difficulty or ear discomfort. Patients at risk of ototoxic effects include those receiving the drug IV at high doses, those with severely impaired renal function, and those receiving other potentially ototoxic or nephrotoxic drug.
- Monitor diabetics for loss of glycemic control.

Patient & Family Education

- Report symptoms of electrolyte imbalance to prescriber promptly (e.g., weakness, dizziness, fatigue, faintness, confusion, muscle cramps, headache, paresthesias).

Common adverse effects in *italic*, life-threatening effects underlined: generic names in **bold**; classifications in SMALL CAPS; ♣ Canadian drug name; ✺ Prototype drug

101

B

- Report S&S of ototoxicity promptly to prescriber (see Appendix C).
- Monitor blood glucose for loss of glycemic control if diabetic.

BUPRENORPHINE HYDROCHLORIDE

(byoo-pre-nor'feen)

Buprenex
Classification(s): NARCOTIC (OPIATE) AGONIST-ANTAGONIST
Therapeutic: NARCOTIC ANALGESIC
Prototype: Pentazocine
Pregnancy Category: C   **Controlled Substance:** Schedule III

USES Treatment of moderate to severe pain.
UNLABELED USES To reverse fentanyl-induced anesthesia.

INDICATION & DOSAGE

Postoperative Pain

Adult/Adolescent (over 12 y): 0.3 mg q6h, additional dose may be given in 30–60 min if needed
Geriatric: 0.15 mg q6h prn
Child (2–12 y): 2–6 mcg/kg q4–6h prn

SOLUTION PREPARATION

- *Direct IV Infusion:* No dilution is required. Administer as supplied.
- *IV Infusion:* Dilute each 1 mL (0.3 mg) ampule in 50 mL of D5W, NS, D5NS, or LR to yield 6 mcg/mL.

STORAGE

Store unopened vials refrigerated at 15°–30° C (59°–86° F), but do not freeze.

ADMINISTRATION

- **Direct IV Injection:** Give bolus dose slowly over at least 3 min directly into a vein or tubing of freely flowing, compatible IV solution.
- **IV Infusion:** Give by slow infusion over at least 3 min or longer depending on volume of IV solution.
- *Adults & Children 13 y and older:* If a repeat dose is required, give 30–60 min after first dose. Use particular caution with the elderly, debilitated patients, those with respiratory disease, and those using other CNS depressants.

INCOMPATIBILITIES Solution/additive: Diltiazem, floxacillin, furosemide, lorazepam. Y-site: Amphotericin B cholesteryl sulfate complex, doxorubicin liposome, lansoprazole.

ACTION & *THERAPEUTIC EFFECT* Opiate agonist-antagonist with agonist activity approximately 30 times that of morphine and antagonist activity equal to or up to 3 times greater than that of naloxone. Respiratory depression occurs infrequently, probably due to drug's opiate antagonist activity. Psychologic and limited physical dependence develops infrequently; tolerance to drug rarely develops. *Dose-related analgesia results from a high affinity of buprenorphine for mu-opioid receptors and as an antagonist at the kappa-opiate receptors in the CNS. Naloxone is also an antagonist at the mu-opioid receptor.*

CONTRAINDICATIONS Hypersensitivity to buprenorphine or naloxone; pregnancy (category C), lactation; children less than 2 y.

CAUTIOUS USE Patients with history of opiate use; compromised respiratory function [e.g., chronic obstructive pulmonary disease (COPD), cor pulmonale, decreased respiratory reserve, hypoxia, hypercapnia, or preexisting respiratory depression]; concomitant use of other respiratory depressants; hypothyroidism, myxedema, Addison's disease; severe renal or hepatic impairment; geriatric or debilitated patients; acute alcoholism, delirium tremens; prostatic hypertrophy, urethral stricture; comatose patient; patients with CNS depression, head injury, or intracranial lesion; biliary tract dysfunction.

ADVERSE EFFECTS (≥1%) **CNS:** *Sedation, drowsiness,* dizziness, vertigo, *headache,* amnesia, euphoria, asthenia, *insomnia, pain* (when used for withdrawal), *withdrawal symptoms.* **CV:** Hypotension, vasodilation. **Special Senses:** Miosis. **GI:** *Nausea,* vomiting, diarrhea, *constipation.* **Respiratory:** Respiratory depression, hyperventilation. **Skin:** Pruritus, injection site reactions, *sweating.*

DRUG INTERACTIONS Alcohol, OPIATES, CNS DEPRESSANTS, BENZODIAZEPINES augment CNS depression; AZOLE ANTIFUNGALS (e.g., **fluconazole**), MACROLIDE ANTIBIOTICS (e.g., **erythromycin**), and PROTEASE INHIBITORS (e.g., **saquinavir**) may increase buprenorphine levels.

PHARMACOKINETICS Onset: 10–30 min. **Peak:** 1 h. **Duration:** 6–10 h. **Metabolism:** In liver (CYP3A4) to active metabolite norbuprenorphine. **Elimination:** 70% eliminated in feces and 30% in urine. **Half-Life:** 2.2 h.

NURSING IMPLICATIONS

Assessment & Drug Effects

- Monitor for excessive sedation.
- Monitor respiratory status during therapy, especially when used with other CNS depressants. Respiratory depression is about equal to that produced by 10 mg of morphine, but onset is slower, and if it occurs, it lasts longer.
- Note: Respiratory depression in the healthy adult plateaus or may even decrease in severity with doses more than 1.2 mg because of antagonist activity of the drug.
- Monitor I&O ratio and pattern as urinary retention is a potential adverse effect.
- Lab tests: Baseline LFTs and renal function tests.
- Supervise ambulation and institute falls precautions as needed; drowsiness occurs in the majority of those taking this drug.

Common adverse effects in *italic*, life-threatening effects underlined: generic names in **bold**; classifications in SMALL CAPS; ♣ Canadian drug name; ● Prototype drug

103

Patient & Family Education

- Do not drive or engage in other potentially hazardous activities until response to drug is known.
- Do not use alcohol or other CNS depressing drugs without consulting prescriber. An additive effect exists between buprenorphine hydrochloride and other CNS depressants, including alcohol.

BUSULFAN

(byoo-sul'fan)

Busulfex

Classification(s): ANTINEOPLASTIC; ALKYLATING AGENT

Therapeutic: ANTINEOPLASTIC
Prototype: Cyclophosphamide
Pregnancy Category: D

USES Stem cell transplant conditioning.
UNLABELED USES Allogenic bone transplantation in patients with acute nonlymphocytic leukemia.

INDICATION & DOSAGE

Stem Cell Transplant Conditioning

Adult: (used with cyclophosphamide) 0.8 mg/kg IBW or ABW (whichever is lower) q6h × 4 days

Obesity

In severely obese patients use adjusted ideal body weight = IBW + 0.25 × (actual weight − IBW).

SOLUTION PREPARATION

- Determine the volume of the required dose. Prepare a volume of NS or D5W IV solution that is 10 times the volume of busulfan needed. This will ensure that the final concentration of busulfan is greater than or equal to 0.5 mg/mL.
- Using a 5 micron nylon filter (supplied), withdraw the needed dose of busulfan. Remove needle and filter and use a new, nonfiltered needle to add busulfan to a volume of IV fluid 10 times greater than the volume of busulfan. (Always add busulfan to IV fluid rather than IV fluid to busulfan.) Mix by inverting the IV bag several times.

STORAGE

IV solution is stable for 8 h at room temperature. IV infusion **must be** completed within 8 h.

ADMINISTRATION

- Premedicate with phenytoin to minimize seizure risk. When a different anti-convulsant **must be** used, plasma busulfan levels should be monitored.

- Premedicate with an antiemetic prior to the first dose of busulfan and continue on a fixed schedule during the busulfan administration period.
- **Intermittent Infusion:** Infuse via a central venous catheter over 2 h. Flush line before/after infusion with at least 5 mL D5W or NS.

INCOMPATIBILITIES Data not available; do not mix with other drugs.

ACTION & *THERAPEUTIC EFFECT* Potent cytotoxic alkylating agent that may be mutagenic, or carcinogenic, and is cell cycle nonspecific. Reduces total granulocyte mass but has little effect on lymphocytes and platelets except in large doses. May cause widespread epithelial cellular dysplasia, severe enough to make it difficult to interpret exfoliative cytologic examinations. *Causes cell death by acting predominantly on slowly proliferating stem cells by inducing cross linkage in DNA, thus blocking DNA replication.*

CONTRAINDICATIONS Therapy-resistant chronic lymphocytic leukemia; lymphoblastic crisis of chronic myelogenous leukemia; bone marrow depression, immunizations (patient and household members), chickenpox (including recent exposure), herpetic infections; pregnancy (category D), lactation. **CAUTIOUS USE** Men and women in childbearing years; history of gout or urate renal stones; hepatic disease; prior irradiation or chemotherapy.

ADVERSE EFFECTS (≥1%) **Hematologic:** Major toxic effects are related to bone marrow failure; agranulocytosis (rare), pancytopenia, thrombocytopenia, leukopenia, *anemia.* **Urogenital:** Flank pain, renal calculi, uric acid nephropathy, acute renal failure, gynecomastia, testicular atrophy, azoospermia, impotence, sterility in males, ovarian suppression, menstrual changes, amenorrhea (potentially irreversible), menopausal symptoms. **Respiratory:** Irreversible pulmonary fibrosis ("busulfan lung"). **Skin:** Alopecia, hyperpigmentation. **Other:** Endocardial fibrosis, dizziness, cholestatic jaundice, infections.

DIAGNOSTIC TEST INTERFERENCE Busulfan may decrease ***urinary 17-OHCS*** excretion, and may increase ***blood and urine uric acid*** levels. Drug-induced cellular dysplasia may interfere with interpretation of ***cytologic studies.***

DRUG INTERACTIONS Probenecid, sulfinpyrazone may increase uric acid levels.

PHARMACOKINETICS Peak: 4 h. **Duration:** 4 h. **Metabolism:** Metabolized in liver. **Elimination:** 10–50% excreted in urine within 48 h.

NURSING IMPLICATIONS

Assessment & Drug Effects

- Monitor for therapeutic effectiveness: Normal leukocyte count is usually achieved in about 2 mo.
- Monitor: Vital signs, weight, I&O ratio and pattern.
- Monitor for and report symptoms suggestive of superinfection (see Appendix C), particularly when patient develops leukopenia.
- Lab test: Baseline Hgb, Hct, WBC with differential, platelet count, liver function, kidney function, serum uric acid; repeat at least weekly.
- Avoid invasive procedures during periods of platelet count depression.

Common adverse effects in *italic*, life-threatening effects underlined: generic names in **bold**; classifications in SMALL CAPS; ♣ Canadian drug name; ● Prototype drug

105

Patient & Family Education

- Report promptly (any of the following): Easy bruising or bleeding, cloudy or pink urine, dark or black stools; sore mouth or throat, unusual fatigue, blurred vision, flank or joint pain, swelling of lower legs and feet; yellowing white of eye, dark urine, light-colored stools, abdominal discomfort, or itching (hepatotoxicity).
- Increase fluid intake to 10–12 [8 oz] glasses daily (if allowed) to ensure adequate urinary output.
- Use contraceptive measures during busulfan therapy and for at least 3 mo after drug is withdrawn.

BUTORPHANOL TARTRATE

(byoo-tor'fa-nole)

Stadol

Classification(s): NARCOTIC (OPIATE) AGONIST-ANTAGONIST
Therapeutic: NARCOTIC ANALGESIC
Prototype: Pentazocine
Pregnancy Category: C   **Controlled Substance:** Schedule IV

USES Relief of moderate to severe pain, preoperative or preanesthetic sedation and analgesia, obstetrical analgesia during labor, cancer pain, renal colic, burns.
UNLABELED USES Musculoskeletal and postepisiotomy pain.

INDICATION & DOSAGE

Pain Relief

Adult: 0.5–2 mg q3–4h as needed
Geriatric: 0.25–1 mg q6–8h

Adjunct to Balanced Anesthesia

Adult: 2 mg before induction or 0.5–1 mg in increments during anesthesia

Labor

Adult: 1–2 mg, may repeat in 4 h

Renal Impairment Dosage Adjustment

Use half normal dose and at least 6 h interval

Hepatic Impairment Dosage Adjustment

Use half normal dose and at least 6 h interval

SOLUTION PREPARATION

- Butorphanol is supplied in a sealed delivery system. Exercise care to avoid producing an aerosol spray while preparing syringe for use. Following skin contact, rinse with cool water.
- *Direct IV Injection:* No dilution is required. Administer as supplied.

Common adverse effects in *italic*, life-threatening effects <u>underlined</u>: generic names in **bold**; classifications in SMALL CAPS; ♣ Canadian drug name; ⊙ Prototype drug

B

STORAGE
Store at 25° C (77° F). Protect from light.

ADMINISTRATION
Direct IV Injection: Give slowly at a rate of 2 mg or fraction thereof over 3–5 min.

INCOMPATIBILITIES Y-site: Amphotericin B cholesteryl, lansoprazole, midazolam.

ACTION & *THERAPEUTIC EFFECT* Synthetic, centrally acting analgesic with mixed narcotic agonist and antagonist actions. Acts as agonist on one type of opioid receptor and as a competitive antagonist at others. Site of analgesic action believed to be subcortical, possibly in the limbic system. Respiratory depression does not increase appreciably with higher doses as it does with morphine, but duration of action increases. *Narcotic analgesic that relieves moderate to severe pain with apparently low potential for physical dependence.*

CONTRAINDICATIONS Narcotic-dependent patients; opiate agonist hypersensitivity; pregnancy and prior to labor (category C); children less than 18 y.

CAUTIOUS USE History of drug abuse or dependence; emotionally unstable individuals; head injury, increased intracranial pressure; acute MI, ventricular dysfunction, coronary insufficiency, hypertension; patients undergoing biliary tract surgery; respiratory depression, bronchial asthma, obstructive respiratory disease; and renal or hepatic dysfunction.

ADVERSE EFFECTS (≥1%) **CNS:** Drowsiness, *sedation,* headache, vertigo, dizziness, floating feeling, weakness, lethargy, confusion, light-headedness, insomnia, nervousness, <u>respiratory depression.</u> **CV:** Palpitation, bradycardia. **GI:** Nausea. **Skin:** Clammy skin, tingling sensation, flushing and warmth, cyanosis of extremities, diaphoresis, sensitivity to cold, urticaria, pruritus. **Genitourinary:** Difficulty in urinating, biliary spasm.

DRUG INTERACTIONS Alcohol and other CNS DEPRESSANTS augment CNS and respiratory depression.

PHARMACOKINETICS Onset: 1 min. **Peak:** 4–5 min. **Duration:** 2–4 h. **Distribution:** Crosses placenta; distributed into breast milk. **Metabolism:** Metabolized in liver in inactive metabolites. **Elimination:** Excreted primarily in urine. **Half-Life:** 3–4 h.

NURSING IMPLICATIONS
Assessment & Drug Effects
- Monitor for respiratory depression. Do not administer drug if respiratory rate is less than 12 breaths/min.
- Monitor vital signs. Report marked changes in BP or bradycardia.
- Note: If used during labor or delivery, observe neonate for signs of respiratory depression.
- Note: Drug can induce acute withdrawal symptoms in opiate-dependent patients.
- Schedule gradual withdrawal following chronic administration. Abrupt withdrawal may produce vomiting, loss of appetite, restlessness, abdomi-

---

Common adverse effects in *italic*, life-threatening effects <u>underlined</u>: generic names in **bold**; classifications in SMALL CAPS; ♣ Canadian drug name; ⊙ Prototype drug

107

nal cramps, increase in BP and temperature, mydriasis, faintness. Withdrawal symptoms peak 48 h after discontinuation of drug.

Patient & Family Education

- Lie down to control drug-induced nausea.
- Do not take alcohol or other CNS depressants with this drug without consulting prescriber because of possible additive effects.
- Do not drive or engage in other potentially hazardous activities until response to drug is known.

CAFFEINE CITRATE 💊

(kaf-een')

Cafcit

Classification(s): RESPIRATORY AND CEREBRAL STIMULANT; XANTHINE
Therapeutic: RESPIRATORY AND CEREBRAL STIMULANT
Pregnancy Category: C

USES Apnea of prematurity.
UNLABELED USES Spinal puncture headache.

INDICATION & DOSAGE

Apnea of Prematurity
Neonate (28–33 wk gestation): 20 mg/kg (loading dose) then after 24 h 5 mg/kg/day

SOLUTION PREPARATION

- Each mL of IV solution contains 20 mg caffeine citrate which is equivalent to 10 mg of caffeine base.
- May be diluted in sufficient D5W to allow infusion at the desired rate.

STORAGE

Store at 15°–30° C (59°–86° F).

ADMINISTRATION

- Infusion via syringe infusion pump is recommended.
- *Loading Dose:* Give over 30 min.
- *Maintenance:* Give over at least 10 min.

INCOMPATIBILITIES Y-site: Acyclovir, furosemide, lorazepam, nitroglycerin, oxacillin, pantoprazole.

ACTION & *THERAPEUTIC EFFECT* Xanthine derivative that relaxes smooth muscle by direct action, particularly of bronchi and pulmonary vessels, and stimulates medullary respiratory center with resulting increase in vital capacity. Stimulates myocardium, thereby increasing force of contractions and cardiac output, and stimulates all levels of CNS. *Effective in managing neonatal apnea, and as an adjuvant for pain control in headaches following dural puncture.*

Common adverse effects in *italic*, life-threatening effects <u>underlined</u>: generic names in **bold**; classifications in SMALL CAPS; ♣ Canadian drug name; 💊 Prototype drug

C

CONTRAINDICATIONS Acute MI, symptomatic cardiac arrhythmias, palpitations; peptic ulcer; pulmonary disease; insomnia, panic attacks; pregnancy (category C).

CAUTIOUS USE Diabetes mellitus; hiatal hernia; psychotic disorders; dementia; depressive disorders; hepatic disease; hypertension with heart disease.

ADVERSE EFFECTS (≥1%) **CV:** Tingling of face, flushing, palpitation, tachycardia or bradycardia, ventricular ectopic beats. **GI:** Nausea, vomiting; epigastric discomfort, gastric irritation (oral form), diarrhea, hematemesis, kernicterus (neonates). **CNS:** *Nervousness, insomnia,* restlessness, irritability, confusion, agitation, fasciculations, delirium, twitching, tremors, clonic convulsions. **Respiratory:** Tachypnea. **Special Senses:** Scintillating scotomas, tinnitus. **Urogenital:** Increased urination, diuresis.

DIAGNOSTIC TEST INTERFERENCE Caffeine reportedly may interfere with diagnosis of pheochromocytoma or neuroblastoma by increasing urinary excretion of *catecholamines, VMA,* and *5-HIAA* and may cause false positive increases in *serum urate* (by *Bittner method*).

DRUG INTERACTIONS Cimetidine increases effects of caffeine; increases cardiovascular stimulating effects of BETA-ADRENERGIC AGONISTS; possibly increases **theophylline** toxicity.

PHARMACOKINETICS Peak: 15–45 min. **Distribution:** Crosses blood–brain barrier and placenta. **Metabolism:** In liver by CYP 1A2. **Elimination:** Excreted in urine as metabolites; excreted in breast milk in small amounts. **Half-Life:** 3–5 h in adults, 36–144 h in neonates.

NURSING IMPLICATIONS

Assessment & Drug Effects

- Monitor vital signs closely as large doses may cause intensification rather than reversal of severe drug-induced depressions.
- Observe children closely as they are more susceptible than adults to the CNS effects of caffeine.
- Lab tests: Monitor blood glucose in diabetics. Monitor diabetics for loss of glycemic control.

Patient & Family Education

- Caffeine in large amounts may impair glucose tolerance in diabetics.

CALCITRIOL ⊙

(kal-si-trye′ole)

Calcijex

Classification(s): VITAMIN D ANALOG

Therapeutic: VITAMIN D ANALOG

Pregnancy Category: C

USES Management of hypocalcemia in patients undergoing chronic renal dialysis and in patients with hypoparathyroidism or pseudohypoparathyroidism.

Common adverse effects in *italic*, life-threatening effects <u>underlined</u>: generic names in **bold**; classifications in SMALL CAPS; ♣ Canadian drug name; ⊙ Prototype drug

109

UNLABELED USES Selected patients with vitamin D–dependent rickets, familial hypophosphatemia (vitamin D–resistant rickets); management of hypocalcemia in premature infants.

INDICATION & DOSAGE

Hypocalcemia

Adult: 0.5 mcg 3 times weekly at the end of dialysis, may need up to 3 mcg 3 times weekly
Child: 0.01–0.05 mcg/kg 3 times/wk

Renal Failure without Dialysis

Child: 0.01–0.05 mcg/kg three times weekly

Hemodialysis Dosage Adjustment

Give at the end of a hemodialysis session.

SOLUTION PREPARATION
May be given undiluted direct IV (typical) or diluted in D5W, NS, or LR for infusion.

STORAGE
Store unopened vials at 15°–30° C (59°–86° F). Discard unused IV solution after 24 h.

ADMINISTRATION
- **Direct IV Injection:** Give bolus dose over 30–60 sec. (This is the typical administration procedure.)
- **IV Infusion:** Infuse over 15 min.

INCOMPATIBILITIES Data not available; do not mix with other drugs.

ACTION & *THERAPEUTIC EFFECT* Synthetic form of ergocalciferol (vitamin D_2). In the liver, cholecalciferol (vitamin D_3) and ergocalciferol (vitamin D_2) are enzymatically metabolized to calcifediol, an activated form of vitamin D_3. Calcifediol is biodegraded in the kidney to calcitriol, the most potent form of vitamin D_3. *By promoting intestinal absorption and renal retention of calcium, calcitriol elevates serum calcium levels, decreases elevated blood levels of phosphate and, therefore, parathyroid hormone. Thus it decreases subperiosteal bone resorption and mineralization defects.*

CONTRAINDICATIONS Hypercalcemia or vitamin D toxicity; pregnancy (category C).
CAUTIOUS USE Hyperphosphatemia, renal failure; elderly; patients receiving digitalis glycosides.

ADVERSE EFFECTS (≥1%) **Body as a Whole:** Muscle or bone pain. **CV:** Palpitation. **GI:** Anorexia, nausea, vomiting, dry mouth, thirst, constipation, abdominal cramps, metallic taste. **Metabolic:** Vitamin D intoxication, hypercalcemia, hypercalciuria, hyperphosphatemia. **CNS:** Headache, weakness. **Special Senses:** Blurred vision, photophobia. **Urogenital:** Increased urination.

Common adverse effects in *italic*, life-threatening effects <u>underlined</u>: generic names in **bold**; classifications in SMALL CAPS; ✤ Canadian drug name; ❍ Prototype drug

DRUG INTERACTIONS THIAZIDE DIURETICS may cause hypercalcemia; **calcifediol**-induced hypercalcemia may precipitate arrhythmias in patients receiving DIGITALIS GLYCOSIDES.

PHARMACOKINETICS Onset: 2–6 h. **Peak:** 10–12 h. **Duration:** 3–5 days. **Metabolism:** In liver. **Elimination:** Mainly in feces. **Half-Life:** 3–6 h.

NURSING IMPLICATIONS

Assessment & Drug Effects

- Monitor for hypercalcemia (see Signs & Symptoms, Appendix C). During dosage adjustment period, monitor serum calcium levels carefully to avoid hypercalcemia.
- Lab tests: Baseline and periodic serum calcium and phosphorus (twice weekly during initial treatment); periodic magnesium, alkaline phosphatase, creatinine, 24-h urinary calcium and phosphorus.
- Withhold calcitriol and calcium supplements if hypercalcemia develops. Promptly report to prescriber. Drugs may be reinitiated when serum calcium returns to normal.

Patient & Family Education

- Do not use any other source of vitamin D during therapy, since calcitriol is the most potent form of vitamin D_3. This will avoid the possibility of hypercalcemia.
- Consult prescriber before taking an OTC medication. (Many products contain calcium, vitamin D, phosphates, or magnesium, which can increase adverse effects of calcitriol.)
- Maintain an adequate daily fluid intake unless you have kidney problems, in which case consult your prescriber about fluids.
- Report promptly any of the following signs of vitamin D toxicity: bone or muscle pain, weakness, nausea and constipation, vomiting, headache, dry mouth and metallic taste.

CALCIUM CHLORIDE

(cal'see-um chlor'ide)

Classification(s): ELECTROLYTIC REPLACEMENT SOLUTION
Therapeutic: ELECTROLYTE REPLACEMENT
Prototype: Calcium gluconate
Pregnancy Category: C

USES Treatment of cardiac resuscitation when epinephrine fails to improve myocardial contractions; for treatment of acute hypocalcemia (as in tetany due to parathyroid deficiency, vitamin D deficiency, alkalosis, insect bites or stings, and during exchange transfusions), for treatment of hypermagnesemia, and for cardiac disturbances of hyperkalemia.

INDICATION & DOSAGE

All doses are in terms of *elemental calcium:* 1 g calcium chloride = 272 mg (13.6 mEq) elemental calcium

---

Common adverse effects in *italic*, life-threatening effects <u>underlined</u>: generic names in **bold**; classifications in SMALL CAPS; ♣ Canadian drug name; ⊙ Prototype drug

111

Hypocalcemia

Adult: 0.5–1 g (7–14 mEq) at 1–3 day intervals as determined by patient response and serum calcium levels
Child/Infant: 2.7–5 mg/kg administered slowly
Neonate: Less than 1 mEq/day

Hypocalcemic Tetany

Adult: 4.5–16 mEq prn
Child/Infant: 0.5–0.7 mEq/kg three or four times daily
Neonate: 2.4 mEq/kg/day in divided doses

CPR

Adult: 2–4 mg/kg may repeat in 10 min
Child/Infant: 20 mg/kg, may repeat in 10 min

SOLUTION PREPARATION

- May be given undiluted (10% solution) or diluted (preferred) with an equal volume of NS to produce a 5% solution. May be further diluted to less than 5% for infusion.
- Solution should be warmed to body temperature before administration.

STORAGE

Store at 15°–30° C (59°–86° F).

ADMINISTRATION

- Use a small-bore needle and inject into a large central or deep vein to minimize venous irritation and undesirable reactions. Do not give via a scalp vein catheter.
- Avoid (if possible) using small veins on dorsal surface of hand or foot, or scalp veins in infants.
- Ensure patency prior to injection or infusion as extravasation may cause tissue sloughing.
- **Direct IV Injection:** Give at a rate not to exceed 0.5–1 mL/min or more slowly if irritation develops. Avoid rapid administration as it may cause serious cardiac effects (e.g., bradycardia, arrhythmias, ventricular fibrillation).
- **IV Infusion:** Give at a rate determined by the amount of IV fluid but not to exceed the direct IV rate of 0.5–1 mL/min.

INCOMPATIBILITIES Solution/additive: Amphotericin B, chlorpheniramine, dobutamine, concentration-dependent incompatibility with other ELECTROLYTES, **fat emulsion. Y-site: Amphotericin B cholesteryl complex, propofol, sodium bicarbonate.**

ACTION & *THERAPEUTIC EFFECT* Ionizes readily and provides excess chloride ions that promote acidosis and temporary (1–2 days) diuresis secondary to excretion of sodium. *Rapidly and effectively restores serum calcium levels in acute hypocalcemia of various origins and is an effective cardiac stabilizer under conditions of hyperkalemia or resuscitation.*

CONTRAINDICATIONS Ventricular fibrillation, hypercalcemia, digitalis toxicity, injection into myocardium or other tissue; pregnancy (category C).
CAUTIOUS USE Digitalized patients; sarcoidosis, renal insufficiency, history of renal stone formation; cor pulmonale, respiratory acidosis, respiratory failure; cardiac arrhythmias; dehydration; diarrhea; lactation.

ADVERSE EFFECTS (≥1%) **Body as a Whole:** Tingling sensation. With rapid IV, sensations of heat waves (peripheral vasodilation), fainting. **CV:** (With rapid infusion) hypotension, bradycardia, cardiac arrhythmias, <u>cardiac arrest</u>. **Skin:** Pain and burning at IV site, severe venous thrombosis, necrosis and sloughing (with extravasation).

DRUG INTERACTIONS May enhance inotropic and toxic effects of **digoxin;** antagonizes the effects of **verapamil** and possibly other CALCIUM CHANNEL BLOCKERS.

PHARMACOKINETICS Distribution: Crosses placenta. **Elimination:** Primarily excreted in feces; small amounts excreted in urine, pancreatic juice, saliva, and breast milk.

NURSING IMPLICATIONS
Assessment & Drug Effects
- Monitor BP and ECG during IV administration to detect evidence of hypercalcemia: Decreased QT interval associated with inverted T wave. IV injection may be accompanied by cutaneous burning sensation and peripheral vasodilation, with moderate fall in BP.
- Lab tests: Periodic serum calcium, phosphate, magnesium, and pH.
- Advise ambulatory patient to remain recumbent for 30 min or more depending on response following injection.
- Observe digitalized patients closely since an increase in serum calcium increases risk of cardiac arrhythmias or digitalis toxicity.

Patient & Family Education
- Remain in bed for 15–30 min or more following injection and depending on response.
- Symptoms of mild hypercalcemia, such as loss of appetite, nausea, vomiting, or constipation may occur. Report promptly feeling confused or extremely excited.
- Do not use other calcium supplements during therapy.

CALCIUM GLUCONATE 🅿
(gloo′koe-nate)
Classification(s): ELECTROLYTIC REPLACEMENT SOLUTION
Therapeutic: ELECTROLYTE REPLACEMENT
Pregnancy Category: B

USES Negative calcium balance (as in neonatal tetany, hypoparathyroidism, vitamin D deficiency, alkalosis). Also to overcome cardiac toxicity of

Common adverse effects in *italic*, life-threatening effects <u>underlined</u>: generic names in **bold**; classifications in SMALL CAPS; ♣ Canadian drug name; 🅿 Prototype drug

113

hyperkalemia, for cardiopulmonary resuscitation, to prevent hypocalcemia during transfusion of citrated blood. Also as antidote for magnesium sulfate, for acute symptoms of lead colic, to decrease capillary permeability in sensitivity reactions, and to relieve muscle cramps from insect bites or stings.

UNLABELED USES To antagonize aminoglycoside-induced neuromuscular blockage, and as "calcium challenge" to diagnose Zollinger-Ellison syndrome and medullary thyroid carcinoma.

INDICATION & DOSAGE

All doses are in terms of *elemental calcium:* 1 g calcium gluconate = 90 mg (4.5 mEq, 9.3%) elemental calcium

Hypocalcemia

Adult: 2–15 g/day continuous or divided dose
Child/Infant: 200–500 mg/kg/day (max: 2–3 g/dose)
Neonate: Not more than 0.93 mEq

Hypocalcemic Tetany

Adult: 1–3 grams prn may repeat q6h prn (max: 15 g daily)
Child/Infant: 100–200 mg/kg/dose may repeat q6–8h
Neonate: 100–200 mg followed by 500 mg/kg/day infusion

CPR

Adult: 2.3–3.7 mEq × 1 dose

Hyperkalemia with Cardiac Toxicity

Adult: 500–800 mg (max dose: 3 g)

SOLUTION PREPARATION

- Doses are expressed as milligrams of a 10% (100 mg/mL) solution.
- *Direct IV Injection:* May be given undiluted (10% solution).
- *Intermittent/Continuous Infusion:* May be diluted in up to 1000 mL NS.
- Solution should be at body temperature for infusion.

STORAGE

Store at 15°–30° C (59°–86° F).

ADMINISTRATION

- Use a small-bore needle and inject into a large central or deep vein to minimize venous irritation and undesirable reactions. Do not give via a scalp vein catheter.
- Avoid (if possible) using small veins on dorsal surface of hand or foot, or scalp veins in infants.
- Ensure patency prior to injection or infusion as extravasation may cause tissue sloughing.
- **Direct IV Injection:** Give at a rate not to exceed 0.5 mL/min (or 50-mg/min) or more slowly if irritation develops. Avoid rapid administration as it may cause serious cardiac effects (e.g., bradycardia, arrhythmias, ventricular fibrillation). IV injection should be stopped if patient complains of any discomfort.

- **Intermittent/Continuous Infusion:** Give slowly, not to exceed 2 mL/min (or 200 mg/min). With **pediatric patients,** do not exceed 1 mL /min (100 mg/min).
- Patient should be advised to remain in bed for 15–30 min or more (depending on response) following IV injection.

INCOMPATIBILITIES Solution/additive: Amphotericin B, cefamandole, **dobutamine, floxacillin, methylprednisolone, metoclopramide,** concentration-dependent incompatibility with other ELECTROLYTES, fat emulsions. **Y-site: Amphotericin B cholesteryl complex, fluconazole, indomethacin, lansoprazole, meropenem.**

ACTION & *THERAPEUTIC EFFECT* Calcium gluconate acts like digitalis on the heart, increasing cardiac muscle tone and force of systolic contractions (positive inotropic effect). *Rapidly and effectively restores serum calcium levels in acute hypocalcemia of various origins and effective cardiac stabilizer under conditions of hyperkalemia or resuscitation.*

CONTRAINDICATIONS Ventricular fibrillation, metastatic bone disease, injection into myocardium; renal calculi, hypercalcemia, predisposition to hypercalcemia (hyperparathyroidism, certain malignancies); digitalis toxicity.
CAUTIOUS USE Digitalized patients, renal or cardiac insufficiency, cardiac arrhythmias; dehydration, hyperphosphatemia; diarrhea; sarcoidosis; history of lithiasis, immobilized patients; pregnancy (category B), lactation.

ADVERSE EFFECTS (≥1%) **Body as a Whole:** Tingling sensation. With rapid IV, sensations of heat waves (peripheral vasodilation), fainting. **GI:** PO preparation: Constipation, increased gastric acid secretion. **CV:** (With rapid infusion) hypotension, bradycardia, cardiac arrhythmias, <u>cardiac arrest</u>. **Skin:** Pain and burning at IV site, severe venous thrombosis, necrosis and sloughing (with extravasation).

DIAGNOSTIC TEST INTERFERENCE IV calcium may cause false decreases in ***serum and urine magnesium*** (by ***Titan yellow method***) and transient elevations of ***plasma 11-OHCS*** levels by ***Glenn-Nelson technique***. Values usually return to control levels after 60 min; ***urinary steroid values (17-OHCS)*** may be decreased.

DRUG INTERACTIONS May enhance inotropic and toxic effects of **digoxin; magnesium** may compete for GI absorption; antagonizes the effects of **verapamil** and possibly other CALCIUM CHANNEL BLOCKERS.

PHARMACOKINETICS Absorption: ~30% from small intestine. **Distribution:** Crosses placenta. **Elimination:** Primarily excreted in feces; small amounts excreted in urine, pancreatic juice, saliva, and breast milk.

NURSING IMPLICATIONS

Assessment & Drug Effects

- Monitor ECG during IV administration to detect evidence of hypercalcemia: decreased QT interval associated with inverted T wave.
- Assess for cutaneous burning sensations and peripheral vasodilation, with moderate fall in BP, during direct IV injection.

Common adverse effects in *italic*, life-threatening effects <u>underlined</u>: generic names in **bold**; classifications in SMALL CAPS; ♣ Canadian drug name; ◐ Prototype drug

115

- Observe IV site closely. Extravasation may result in tissue irritation and necrosis.
- Monitor for hypocalcemia and hypercalcemia (see Signs & Symptoms, Appendix C).
- Lab tests: Determine levels of calcium and phosphorus (tend to vary inversely) and magnesium frequently during sustained therapy. Deficiencies in other ions, particularly magnesium, frequently coexist with calcium ion depletion.

Patient & Family Education
- Remain in bed for 15–30 min or more following injection and depending on response.
- Symptoms of mild hypercalcemia, such as loss of appetite, nausea, vomiting, or constipation may occur. Report promptly feeling confused or extremely excited.
- Do not use other calcium supplements during therapy.

CAPREOMYCIN SULFATE

(kap-ree-oh-mye′sin)
Capastat Sulfate
Classification(s): ANTIBIOTIC; ANTITUBERCULOSIS AGENT
Therapeutic: ANTIMYCOBACTERIAL
Prototype: Isoniazid
Pregnancy Category: D

USES Only in conjunction with other appropriate antitubercular drugs in treatment of pulmonary tuberculosis when bactericidal agents, e.g., isoniazid and rifampin, cannot be tolerated or when causative organism has become resistant.

INDICATION & DOSAGE

Tuberculosis
Adult: 1 g/day (not to exceed 20 mg/kg/day) for 60–120 days, then 1 g 2–3 times/wk

Renal Impairment Dosage Adjustment

CrCl	Dose	Interval
25–50 mL/min	Reduce dose by 50%	Normal
10–24 mL/min	Reduce dose by 50%	q48h
Less than 10 mL/min	Reduce dose by 50%	Dose twice weekly

SOLUTION PREPARATION

- *Vial Reconstitution:* Add 2 mL of NS or sterile water for injection to each 1 g vial to yield 370 mg/mL. Allow 2–3 min for drug to dissolve completely. **Must be** further diluted for infusion.

• *Further Dilution of Reconstituted Solution:* Add required dose to 100 mL of NS.

STORAGE

Reconstituted vials may be stored for 48 h at 15°–30° C (59°–86° F) and up to 14 days under refrigeration unless otherwise directed.

ADMINISTRATION

IV Infusion: Give over 60 min. Avoid rapid infusion as neuromuscular blockade may result.

INCOMPATIBILITIES Data not available; do not mix with other drugs.

ACTION & *THERAPEUTIC EFFECT* Polypeptide antibiotic that is bacteriostatic; action mechanism not clear. Should not be used alone. *Bacteriostatic against human strains of* Mycobacterium tuberculosis *and other species of* Mycobacterium. *Effective second-line antimycobacterial used in conjunction with other antitubercular drugs.*

CONTRAINDICATIONS Pregnancy (category D), lactation. Safe use in infants and children not established.

CAUTIOUS USE Renal insufficiency (extreme caution); acoustic nerve impairment; history of allergies (especially to drugs); preexisting liver disease; myasthenia gravis; parkinsonism.

ADVERSE EFFECTS (≥1%) **Skin:** Urticaria, maculopapular rash, photosensitivity. **Hematologic:** Leukocytosis, leukopenia, *eosinophilia*. **CNS:** Neuromuscular blockage (large doses: skeletal muscle weakness, respiratory depression or arrest). **Urogenital:** Nephrotoxicity (long-term therapy), tubular necrosis. **Special Senses:** *Ototoxicity,* eighth nerve (auditory and vestibular) damage. **Metabolic:** Hypokalemia, and other electrolyte imbalances. **Other:** Impaired hepatic function (decreased BSP excretion); IM site reactions: pain, induration, excessive bleeding, sterile abscesses.

DIAGNOSTIC TEST INTERFERENCE *BSP* and *PSP excretion tests* may be decreased.

DRUG INTERACTIONS Increased risk of nephrotoxicity and ototoxicity with AMINOGLYCOSIDES, **amphotericin B, colistin, polymyxin B, cisplatin, vancomycin.**

PHARMACOKINETICS Peak: 1–2 h. **Distribution:** Does not cross blood–brain barrier; crosses placenta; distribution into breast milk unknown. **Elimination:** 52% excreted in urine unchanged in 12 h; small amount excreted in bile. **Half-Life:** 4–6 h.

NURSING IMPLICATIONS

Assessment & Drug Effects

• Lab tests: Baseline and periodic BUN & serum creatinine, LFTs, and serum electrolytes.
• Monitor I&O rates and pattern: Report immediately any change in output or I&O ratio, any unusual appearance of urine. Keep well hydrated to maintain adequate urine output.

Common adverse effects in *italic*, life-threatening effects <u>underlined</u>: generic names in **bold**; classifications in SMALL CAPS; ♣ Canadian drug name; ● Prototype drug

117

C

- Evaluate hearing and balance by audiometric measurements (twice weekly or weekly) and tests of vestibular function (periodically).

Patient & Family Education
- Periodic evaluation of hearing and balance are recommended.
- Report promptly any change in hearing or disturbance of balance. These effects are sometimes reversible if drug is withdrawn promptly when first symptoms appear.
- Ensure that you know about adverse reactions and what to do about them. Report immediately the appearance of any unusual symptom, regardless of how vague it may seem.

CARBOPLATIN

(car-bo-pla'tin)

Paraplatin

Classification(s): ANTINEOPLASTIC; ALKYLATING AGENT
Therapeutic: ANTINEOPLASTIC
Prototype: Cyclophosphamide
Pregnancy Category: D

USES Monotherapy or combination therapy for ovarian cancer.
UNLABELED USES Combination therapy for breast, cervical, colon, endometrial, head and neck, and lung cancer; leukemia, lymphoma, and melanoma.

INDICATION & DOSAGE

Ovarian Cancer

Adult: 360 mg/m^2 once every 4 wk. May be repeated when neutrophil count is at least 2000 mm^3 and platelet count is at least 100,000 mm^3. If neutrophil and platelet counts are lower, dose of carboplatin should be reduced by 50–75% of initial dose. Alternatively, 400 mg/m^2 as a 24-h infusion for 2 consecutive days can be used.

Renal Impairment Dosage Adjustment

CrCl	Dose
41–59 mL/min	250 mg/m^2
16–40 mL/min	200 mg/m^2
Less than 5 mL/min	Unknown
Hemodialysis	Initial dose not to exceed 150 mg/m^2

SOLUTION PREPARATION
- Do not use needles or IV sets containing aluminum.
- Should be prepared immediately before administration.

Common adverse effects in *italic*, life-threatening effects underlined: generic names in **bold**; classifications in SMALL CAPS; ♦ Canadian drug name; ● Prototype drug

- *Vial Reconstitution*: Immediately before use, reconstitute powder with either sterile water for injection, D5W, or NS as follows: 50-mg vial plus 5 mL diluent; 150-mg vial plus 15 mL diluent; 450-mg vial plus 45 mL diluent. All dilutions yield 10 mg/mL. **Must be** further diluted for infusion.
- *Further Dilution of Reconstituted Solution:* May dilute to concentrations as low as 0.5 mg/mL with D5W or NS. Example: Adding 20 mL of diluent to each 10 mg yields 0.5 mg/mL; adding 10 mL to each 10 mg yields 1 mg/mL.

STORAGE
IV solution is stable for 8 h at 25° C (77° F). Store unopened vials at 15°–30° C (59°–86° F). Protect from light.

ADMINISTRATION
- Premedication with a parenteral antiemetic $1/2$ h before and on a scheduled basis thereafter is typical practice.
- **IV Infusion:** Give over 15 min or longer, depending on total amount of solution and patient tolerance. Lengthening duration of administration may decrease nausea and vomiting.

INCOMPATIBILITIES Solution/additive: Sodium bicarbonate, fluorouracil, mesna. Y-site: Amphotericin B cholesteryl complex, lansoprazole.

ACTION & *THERAPEUTIC EFFECT* Carboplatin is a platinum compound that is a chemotherapeutic agent. It produces inter-strand DNA cross-linkages, thus interfering with DNA, RNA, and protein synthesis. Carboplatin is cell-cycle nonspecific, i.e., effective throughout the entire cell life-cycle inducing programmed cell death. *Full or partial activity against a variety of cancers resulting in reduction or stabilization of tumor size; useful in patients with impaired renal function, patients unable to accommodate high-volume hydration, or patients at high risk for neurotoxicity and/or ototoxicity.*

CONTRAINDICATIONS History of severe reactions to carboplatin or other platinum compounds, severe bone marrow depression; significant bleeding; impaired renal function; pregnancy (category D), lactation.
CAUTIOUS USE Use with other nephrotoxic drugs; coagulopathy; previous radiation therapy; renal impairment.

ADVERSE EFFECTS (≥1%) **Body as a Whole:** Hypersensitivity reactions. **GI:** *Mild to moderate nausea and vomiting,* anorexia, hypogeusia, dysgeusia, mucositis, diarrhea, constipation, elevated liver enzymes. **Hematologic:** *Thrombocytopenia, leukopenia, neutropenia, anemia.* **Metabolic:** *Mild hyponatremia, hypomagnesemia, hypocalcemia, and hypokalemia.* **CNS:** Peripheral neuropathy. **Skin:** Rash, alopecia. **Special Senses:** Tinnitus. **Urogenital:** Nephrotoxicity.

DIAGNOSTIC TEST INTERFERENCE Decreased *calcium serum levels;* mild increases in *liver function tests;* decreased levels of *magnesium, potassium,* and *sodium.*

DRUG INTERACTIONS AMINOGLYCOSIDES may increase the risk of ototoxicity and nephrotoxicity. May decrease **phenytoin** levels.

C

PHARMACOKINETICS Onset: 8 wk (2 cycles). **Duration:** 2–16 mo. **Distribution:** Highest concentration is seen in the liver, lung, kidney, skin, and tumors. Not bound to plasma proteins. **Metabolism:** Hydrolyzed in the serum. **Elimination:** Primarily eliminated by the kidneys; 60–80% excreted in urine within 24 h. **Half-Life:** 3 h.

NURSING IMPLICATIONS

Assessment & Drug Effects

- Monitor closely during first 15 min of infusion, since allergic reactions have occurred within minutes of carboplatin administration.
- Lab tests: Baseline and periodic CBC with differential, platelet count, Hgb and Hct; periodic kidney function tests, and serum electrolytes.
- Monitor results of peripheral blood counts. Median nadir occurs at day 21. Leukopenia, neutropenia, and thrombocytopenia are dose related and may produce dose-limiting toxicity.
- Withhold drug and notify prescriber for platelet count less than 100,000/mm³ and neutrophil count less than 2000/mm³.
- Monitor for electrolyte imbalances as carboplatin has been associated with decreases in sodium, potassium, calcium, and magnesium. Special precautions may be warranted for patients on diuretic therapy.
- Monitor for peripheral neuropathy (e.g., paresthesias), ototoxicity, and visual disturbances.
- Monitor persons taking phenytoin for loss of seizure control.

Patient & Family Education

- Learn the range of potential adverse effects. Strategies for nausea prevention should receive special attention.
- Therapy increases the risk of and hemorrhagic complications related to bone marrow suppression. Avoid unnecessary exposure to crowds or infected persons during the nadir period.
- Report paresthesias (numbness, tingling), visual disturbances, or symptoms of ototoxicity (hearing loss and/or tinnitus).

CARMUSTINE

(kar-mus′teen)

BiCNU, Gliadel

Classification(s): ANTINEOPLASTIC; ALKYLATING AGENT
Therapeutic: ANTINEOPLASTIC
Prototype: Cyclophosphamide
Pregnancy Category: D

USES As single agent or in combination with other antineoplastics in treatment of Hodgkin's disease and other lymphomas, melanoma, primary and metastatic tumors of brain, and GI tract malignancies.
UNLABELED USES Treatment of carcinomas of breast and lungs, Ewing's sarcoma, Burkitt's tumor, malignant melanoma, and topically for mycosis fungoides.

INDICATION & DOSAGE

Previously Untreated Patients—Carcinoma
Adult: 150–200 mg/m² q6wk in one dose *or* given over 2 days

Toxicity Adjustment

Toxicity	Modification
ANC 2000–2999/mm³ and platelets 25,000–74,999/mm³ OR WBC nadir 2000–2999 mm³	Reduce dose to 70%
ANC less than 2000/mm³ and platelets less than 25,000/mm³ OR WBC nadir less than 2000/mm³	Reduce dose to 50%

SOLUTION PREPARATION
- Wear disposable gloves; contact of drug with skin can cause burning, dermatitis, and hyperpigmentation.
- *Vial Reconstitution:* Add supplied diluent to the 100 mg vial then further dilute with 27 mL of sterile water for injection to yield a concentration of 3.3 mg/mL. **Must be** further diluted for infusion. Protect from light.
- *Further Dilution of Reconstituted Vial:* Remove the required dose and add to 100–500 mL of D5W. Use a glass IV solution container. Discard any unused solution.

STORAGE
- Store unopened vials at 2°–8° C (36°–46° F).
- Reconstituted solutions may be stored at 2°–8° C (36°–46° F) for 8 h protected from light.
- Signs of decomposition of carmustine in unopened vial: Liquefaction and appearance of oil film at bottom of vial. Discard drug in this condition.

ADMINISTRATION
- Ensure patency prior to administration.
- **IV Infusion:** Infuse a single dose over at least 1 h. Slow infusion over 1–2 h with adequate dilution will reduce pain of administration.
- Avoid starting infusion into dorsum of hand, wrist, or the antecubital veins; extravasation in these areas can damage underlying tendons and nerves leading to loss of mobility of entire limb.

INCOMPATIBILITIES Solution/additive: 5% dextrose, sodium bicarbonate. Y-site: Allopurinol.

ACTION & *THERAPEUTIC EFFECT* Highly lipid-soluble nitrosourea derivative with cell-cycle nonspecific activity against rapidly proliferating cells. Produces cross-linkage of DNA strands, thereby blocking DNA, RNA, and protein synthesis in tumor cells. *Drug metabolites thought to be responsible for antineoplastic activities. Full or partial activity against a variety of cancers resulting in reduction or stabilization of tumor size and increased survival rates.*

CONTRAINDICATIONS History of pulmonary function impairment; recent illness with or exposure to chickenpox or herpes zoster; infection; severe

Common adverse effects in *italic*, life-threatening effects underlined: generic names in **bold**; classifications in SMALL CAPS; ♣ Canadian drug name; ✺ Prototype drug

121

bone marrow depression; decreased circulating platelets, leukocytes, or erythrocytes; pregnancy (category D), lactation.

CAUTIOUS USE Hepatic and renal insufficiency; patient with previous cytotoxic medication, or radiation therapy; history of herpes infections.

ADVERSE EFFECTS (≥1%) **Hematologic:** Delayed <u>myelosuppression</u> (dose-related); thrombocytopenia. **CNS:** Dizziness, ataxia. **Respiratory:** <u>Pulmonary infiltration or fibrosis</u>. **Skin:** Skin flushing and burning pain at injection site, hyperpigmentation of skin (from contact). **Special Senses:** Suffusion of conjunctiva. **GI:** Stomatitis, *nausea, vomiting*.

DRUG INTERACTIONS Cimetidine may potentiate neutropenia and thrombocytopenia.

PHARMACOKINETICS Distribution: Readily crosses blood–brain barrier; CSF concentrations 15–70% of plasma concentrations. **Metabolism:** Rapidly metabolized; metabolic fate not completely known. **Elimination:** 60–70% in urine in 96 h; 6% via lungs, 1% in feces; excreted in breast milk.

NURSING IMPLICATIONS

Assessment & Drug Effects

- Frequently check rate of flow and blood return; palpate injection site for extravasation. If there is any question about patency, line should be restarted. Change infusion site if patient complains of a burning sensation. Ice application over the area may decrease the discomfort.
- Monitor for nausea and vomiting (dose related), which may occur within 2 h after drug administration and persist for up to 6 h. Prior administration of an antiemetic may help to decrease or prevent these adverse effects.
- Lab tests: Baseline CBC with differential and platelet count, repeat blood studies following infusion at weekly intervals for at least 6 wk. Baseline and periodic LFTs and renal function tests.
- Platelet nadir usually occurs within 4–5 wk, and leukocyte nadir within 5–6 wk after therapy is terminated. Thrombocytopenia may be more severe than leukopenia; anemia is less severe.
- Check temperature daily. Avoid use of rectal thermometer to prevent injury to mucosa. An elevation of 0.6° F or more above usual temperature warrants reporting.
- Report promptly symptoms of lung toxicity (cough, shortness of breath, fever), hepatic toxicity (jaundice, dark urine, pruritus, light-colored stools) or renal insufficiency (dysuria, oliguria, hematuria, swelling of lower legs and feet).

Patient & Family Education

- Report burning sensation immediately, as carmustine can cause burning discomfort even in the absence of extravasation.
- Intense flushing of skin may occur during IV infusion. This usually disappears in 2–4 h.
- Carmustine increases the risk of infection and hemorrhage. Be alert to hazardous periods that occur 4–6 wk after a dose of carmustine. If possible, avoid invasive procedures during this period.

Common adverse effects in *italic*, life-threatening effects <u>underlined</u>: generic names in **bold**; classifications in SMALL CAPS; ♣ Canadian drug name; ⊙ Prototype drug

- Report promptly the onset of sore throat, weakness, fever, chills, infection of any kind, or abnormal bleeding (ecchymosis, petechiae, epistaxis, bleeding gums, hematemesis, melena).

CASPOFUNGIN ⦿

(cas-po-fun'gin)

Cancidas

Classification(s): ANTIBIOTIC; ECHINOCANDIN ANTIFUNGAL
Therapeutic: ANTIFUNGAL
Pregnancy Category: C

USES Treatment of invasive aspergillosis in those refractory to or intolerant of other antifungal therapies; empirical therapy for presumed fungal infection with febrile neutropenia; treatment of candidemia and intra-abdominal abscesses, peritonitis, and pleural space infections due to *Candida*.
UNLABELED USES Treatment of esophageal candidiasis with or without oropharyngeal candidiasis (thrush).

INDICATION & DOSAGE

Invasive Aspergillosis, Empirical Therapy, *Candida*

Adult: **Loading Dose,** 70 mg day 1 then 50 mg daily thereafter

SOLUTION PREPARATION
- Allow vial to come to room temperature.
- *Vial Reconstitution:*
  - *70 mg Vial*: Add 10.5 mL of NS, sterile water for injection or bacteriostatic water for injection to yield 7 mg/mL. Mix gently until clear. **Must be** further diluted before infusion.
  - *50 mg Vial:* Add 10.5 mL of NS, sterile water for injection or bacteriostatic water for injection to yield 5 mg/mL. Mix gently until clear. **Must be** further diluted before infusion.
- *Further Dilution of Reconstituted Solution:* Withdraw the required dose of reconstituted solution (see below) and add to 250 mL of NS, 1/2NS, or 1/4NS, or LR. **DO NOT** use diluents or IV solutions containing dextrose.
  - *Loading Dose using 70 mg Vial:* Withdraw 10 mL
  - *Loading Dose using Two 50 mg Vials:* Withdraw 14 mL
  - *Daily Maintenance Dose using 50 mg Vial:* Withdraw 10 mL
  - *Daily Maintenance Dose using 70 mg Vial:* Withdraw 7.1 mL

STORAGE
May store reconstituted solution at 25° C (77° F) for 1 h prior to preparing the IV solution for infusion. Store IV solution for up to 24 h at 25° C (77° F) or below or 48 h at 2°–8° C (36°–46° F).

Common adverse effects in *italic*, life-threatening effects <u>underlined</u>: generic names in **bold**; classifications in SMALL CAPS; ♥ Canadian drug name; ⦿ Prototype drug

123

C

ADMINISTRATION
IV Infusion: Infuse slowly over at least 1 h.

INCOMPATIBILITIES Solution/additive: Any **dextrose**-containing solution. Do not mix or co-infuse with any other medications.

ACTION & *THERAPEUTIC EFFECT* Caspofungin is an antifungal agent that inhibits the synthesis of an integral component of the fungal cell wall of susceptible *Aspergillus* and *Candida* species. *Interferes with reproduction and growth of susceptible fungi.*

CONTRAINDICATIONS Hypersensitivity to any component of this product; mannitol pregnancy (category C); not studied in patients with ESRF, or children less than 18 y.

CAUTIOUS USE Patients with moderate hepatic insufficiency; concomitant use of cyclosporine; cholestasis; lactation.

ADVERSE EFFECTS (≥1%) **Body as a Whole:** <u>Anaphylaxis</u>, chills, *injection site reaction,* sensation of warmth. **CNS:** Headache. **CV:** Sinus tachycardia. **GI:** *Nausea, vomiting,* diarrhea, abdominal pain. **Hematologic/Lymphatic:** *Phlebitis, thrombophlebitis,* vasculitis, anemia. **Hepatic:** Elevated liver enzymes. **Metabolic:** Anorexia, *hypokalemia.* **Musculoskeletal:** Pain, myalgia. **Respiratory:** <u>Acute respiratory distress syndrome</u>, dyspnea. **Skin:** Rash, facial swelling, pruritus.

DRUG INTERACTIONS Cyclosporine increases overall systematic exposure to caspofungin; inducers of drug clearance or mixed inducer/inhibitors (e.g., **carbamazepine, dexamethasone, efavirenz, nelfinavir, nevirapine, phenytoin, rifampin**) can decrease caspofungin levels; caspofungin decreases the overall systematic exposure to **tacrolimus.**

PHARMACOKINETICS Distribution: 97% protein bound. **Metabolism:** Liver and plasma to inactive metabolites. **Elimination:** Equally excreted in urine and feces. **Half-Life:** 9–11 h.

NURSING IMPLICATIONS
Assessment & Drug Effects
- Monitor for S&S of hypersensitivity during IV infusion; frequently monitor IV site for thrombophlebitis.
- Monitor for and report S&S of fluid retention (e.g., weight gain, swelling, peripheral edema), especially with known cardiovascular disease.
- Lab tests: Baseline and periodic LFTs; periodic kidney function tests, serum electrolytes, and CBC with differential, platelet count.
- Monitor blood levels of tacrolimus with concurrent therapy.

Patient & Family Education
- Report promptly any of the following: Facial swelling, wheezing, difficulty breathing or swallowing, tightness in chest, rash, hives, itching, or sensation of excess warmth.

Common adverse effects in *italic*, life-threatening effects <u>underlined</u>: generic names in **bold**; classifications in SMALL CAPS; ♣ Canadian drug name; ◯ Prototype drug

CEFAZOLIN SODIUM ⊕

(sef-a′zoe-lin)

Ancef, Zolicef ✦

Classification(s): ANTIBIOTIC, CEPHALOSPORIN, FIRST GENERATION
Therapeutic: ANTIBACTERIAL
Pregnancy Category: B

USES Severe infections of urinary and biliary tracts, skin, soft tissue, and bone, and for bacteremia and endocarditis caused by susceptible organisms; also perioperative prophylaxis in patients undergoing procedures associated with high risk of infection, e.g., open heart surgery.

INDICATION & DOSAGE

Moderate to Severe Infections

Adult: 250 mg–2 g q8h, up to 2 g q4h (max: 12 g/day)
Child: 25–100 mg/kg/day in 3–4 divided doses, up to 6 g/day (not to exceed adult doses)

Surgical Prophylaxis

Adult: 1–2 g 30–60 min before surgery, then 0.5–1 g q8h

Renal Impairment Dosage Adjustment: *Adult*

CrCl	Dose	Interval
35–54 mL/min	Normal	q8h
11–34 mL/min	Loading dose then 50% of dose	q12h or longer
Less than 10 mL/min	Normal loading dose then 50% of dose	q18–24h or longer

Renal Impairment Dosage Adjustment: *Child*

CrCl	Dose	Interval
40–70 mL/min	Normal loading dose then 7.5–30 mg/kg	q12h
20–39 mL/min	Normal loading dose then 3.125–12.5 mg/kg	q12h
5–19 mL/min	Normal loading dose then 2.5–10 mg/kg	q24h

SOLUTION PREPARATION

- *Vial Reconstitution:* Use sterile water for injection to reconstitute. Add 2 mL to the 500 mg vial to yield 225 mg/mL, or add 2.5 mL to the 1 g vial

Common adverse effects in *italic*, life-threatening effects <u>underlined</u>: generic names in **bold**, classifications in SMALL CAPS; ✦ Canadian drug name; ⊕ Prototype drug

125

C

to yield 330 mg/mL. Shake well to dissolve. **Must be** further diluted before direct injection or infusion.

- *Further Dilution of Reconstituted Solution:*
  - *Direct IV Injection:* Dilute required dose with 5 mL sterile water for injection.
  - *Intermittent Infusion (preferred to reduce incidence of thrombophlebitis):* Dilute required dose of cefazolin in 50–100 mL of D5W, NS, D5NS, LR, or other compatible solution.

STORAGE

- Reconstituted or diluted cefazolin is stable for 24 h at room temperature or for 10 days refrigerated.
- Store unopened vials at 25° C (77° F) and protect from light.

ADMINISTRATION

- **Direct IV Injection:** Give each 1 g or fraction thereof slowly over 3–5 min.
- **Intermittent Infusion:** Infuse over 15–30 min as determined by the amount of solution.
- Use smaller needles, larger veins, and rotate infusion sites to minimize risk of thrombophlebitis.

INCOMPATIBILITIES Solution/additive: AMINOGLYCOSIDES, **atracurium, bleomycin, cimetidine, clindamycin, lidocaine** (when refrigerated), **ranitidine. Y-site: Amiodarone,** AMINOGLYCOSIDES, **amphotericin B cholesteryl complex, cisatracurium, hydromorphone, idarubicin, lansoprazole, pentamidine, vinorelbine.**

ACTION & *THERAPEUTIC EFFECT* Semisynthetic, first-generation cephalosporin with limited antibiotic activity against gram-negative organisms. Bactericidal action results from preferentially binding to one or more of penicillin-binding proteins (PBP) located on cell walls of susceptible organisms. This inhibits final stage of bacterial cell wall synthesis, thus killing the bacterium. *Effective treatment for susceptible gram-positive organisms.*

CONTRAINDICATIONS Hypersensitivity to any cephalosporin and related antibiotics.

CAUTIOUS USE History of penicillin sensitivity, impaired renal function, patients on sodium restriction; coagulopathy; GI disease, colitis; pregnancy (category B).

ADVERSE EFFECTS (≥1%) **Body as a Whole:** <u>Anaphylaxis</u>, fever, eosinophilia, superinfections, seizure (high doses in patients with renal insufficiency). **GI:** *Diarrhea,* anorexia, abdominal cramps. **Skin:** Maculopapular rash, urticaria.

DIAGNOSTIC TEST INTERFERENCE Because of cefazolin's effect on the transfusion ***direct Coombs' test, cross-matching procedures*** and ***hematologic studies*** may be complicated. False-positive ***urine glucose*** determinations are possible with use of ***copper sulfate tests*** (e.g., ***Clinitest*** or ***Benedict's reagent***) but not with ***glucose oxidase tests*** such as ***TesTape, Diastix,*** or ***Clinistix.***

DRUG INTERACTIONS Probenecid decreases elimination of cefazolin.

PHARMACOKINETICS Peak: 5 min. **Distribution:** Poor CNS penetration even with inflamed meninges; high concentrations in bile and in diseased bone; crosses placenta. **Elimination:** 70% excreted unchanged in urine in 6 h; small amount excreted in breast milk. **Half-Life:** 90–130 min.

NURSING IMPLICATIONS

Assessment & Drug Effects

- Prior to initiating therapy: Baseline C&S tests (start drug pending results); determine previous hypersensitivity reactions to penicillins, cephalosporins, and other allergens.
- Closely monitor infusion site for thrombophlebitis.
- If patient has had a reaction to penicillin, be alert to signs of hypersensitivity with use of cefazolin. Prompt attention should be given to onset of signs of hypersensitivity (see Appendix C).
- Lab tests: Periodic BUN & serum creatinine.
- Monitor I&O rates and pattern: Be alert to changes in BUN, serum creatinine. Decreased urine output may indicate nephrotoxicity.
- Promptly report the onset of diarrhea, which may or may not be dose related. It is seen especially in patients with history of drug-related GI disturbances. Pseudomembranous colitis, a potentially life-threatening condition, starts with diarrhea.

Patient & Family Education

- Report promptly any of the following: Signs or symptoms of superinfection (see Appendix C); signs of hemostatic defects (e.g., ecchymoses, petechiae, nosebleed).

CEFEPIME HYDROCHLORIDE

(cef'e-peem)

Maxipime

Classification(s): ANTIBIOTIC, CEPHALOSPORIN, THIRD GENERATION
Therapeutic: ANTIBACTERIAL
Prototype: Cefotaxime sodium
Pregnancy Category: B

USES Uncomplicated and complicated UTI, skin and skin structure infections, pneumonia caused by susceptible organisms; empiric monotherapy for febrile neutropenic patients.

INDICATION & DOSAGE

Mild to Moderate Infections
Adult: 0.5–1 g q12h for 7–10 days

Moderate to Severe Infections
Adult: 1–2 g q12h for 10 days

Common adverse effects in *italic*, life-threatening effects <u>underlined</u>: generic names in **bold**; classifications in SMALL CAPS; ♣ Canadian drug name; ☻ Prototype drug

127

CEFEPIME HYDROCHLORIDE

Febrile Neutropenia
Adult: 2 g q8h for 7 days or until resolution of neutropenia
Child: 50 mg/kg q8h until resolution of neutropenia

UTI/Pneumonia
Child: 50 mg/kg q12h for 7–10 days

Renal Impairment Dosage Adjustment

CrCl	Dose	Interval
30–60 mL/min	Normal	Extend to q12–24h for maintenance doses
11–29 mL/min	Can reduce maintenance dose by 50%	q24h
Less than 11 mL/min	Reduce maintenance dose by 50%	q24h
Hemodialysis	1 g loading dose then 500 mg q24h (except in febrile neutropenia give 1 g q24h)	Extended interval and administer dose after dialysis

SOLUTION PREPARATION

- *Vial Reconstitution:* Reconstitute with D5W, NS, D5/NS, D10W, LR, Normosol-M or –R, or other compatible solution as indicated in the table that follows. Withdraw the required dose and further dilute in 50–100 mL of compatible IV solution.
- *Piggyback Bottle Reconstitution:* Reconstitute with D5W, NS, D5/NS, D10W, LR, Normosol-M or –R, or other compatible solution as indicated in the table that follows. Give without further dilution.
- *ADD-Vantage Vial Reconstitution:* Reconstitute with D5W or NS as indicated in the table that follows. Give without further dilution.
- Maximum Concentration: 160 mg/mL

Container	Amount of Diluent to be Added	Approximate Available Volume	Approximate Final Concentration
500 mg vial	5 mL	5.6 mL	100 mg/mL
1 g vial	10 mL	11.3 mL	100 mg/mL
2 g vial	10 mL	12.5 mL	160 mg/mL
1 g piggyback bottle	50 mL	50 mL	20 mg/mL
	100 mL	100 mL	10 mg/mL
2 g piggyback bottle	50 mL	50 mL	40 mg/mL
	100 mL	100 mL	20 mg/mL

Common adverse effects in *italic*, life-threatening effects underlined: generic names in **bold**; classifications in SMALL CAPS; ✚ Canadian drug name; ✪ Prototype drug

Container	Amount of Diluent to be Added	Approximate Available Volume	Approximate Final Concentration
1 g ADD-Vantage	50 mL	50 mL	20 mg/mL
	100 mL	100 mL	10 mg/mL
2 g ADD-Vantage	50 mL	50 mL	40 mg/mL
	100 mL	100 mL	20 mg/mL

STORAGE
Store reconstituted solution at 20°–25° C (68°–77° F) for 24 h or in refrigerator at 2°–8° C (36°–46° F) for 7 days. Protect from light.

ADMINISTRATION
- **Intermittent Infusion:** Infuse over 30 min.
- With Y-type administration set, discontinue other compatible solutions while infusing cefepime.
- Use smaller needles, larger veins, and rotate infusion sites to minimize risk of thrombophlebitis.

INCOMPATIBILITIES Solution/additive: AMINOGLYCOSIDES, **aminophylline, ampicillin, metronidazole. Y-site: Acetylcysteine, acyclovir, amphotericin B, amphotericin B cholesteryl complex, chlordiazepoxide, chlorpromazine, cimetidine, ciprofloxacin, cisplatin, dacarbazine, daunorubicin, diazepam, diphenhydramine, dobutamine, dopamine, doxorubicin, droperidol, enalaprilat, erythromycin, etoposide, famotidine, filgrastim, floxuridine, ganciclovir, haloperidol, hydroxyzine, idarubicin, ifosfamide, lansoprazole, magnesium sulfate, mannitol, mechlorethamine, meperidine, metoclopramide, midazolam, mitomycin, mitoxantrone, morphine, nalbuphine, nicardipine, ofloxacin, ondansetron, phenytoin, prochlorperazine, promethazine, streptozocin, theophylline, vancomycin, vinblastine, vincristine.**

ACTION & *THERAPEUTIC EFFECT* Cefepime preferentially binds to one or more of the penicillin-binding proteins (PBPs) located on cell walls of susceptible organisms. This inhibits the third and final stage of bacterial cell wall synthesis, thus destroying the bacteria (bactericidal). *Cefepime is similar to third-generation cephalosporins with respect to broad gram-negative coverage; however, it has broader gram-positive coverage than third-generation cephalosporins. It is highly resistant to hydrolysis by most beta-lactamase bacteria.*

CONTRAINDICATIONS Hypersensitivity to cefepime, other cephalosporins, severe reaction to penicillins, or other beta-lactam antibiotics.
CAUTIOUS USE Patients with history of GI disease, particularly colitis, renal insufficiency; pregnancy (category B), lactation.

ADVERSE EFFECTS (≥1%) **Body as a Whole:** Eosinophilia. **GI:** Antibiotic-associated colitis, diarrhea, nausea, oral moniliasis, vomiting, elevated liver function tests (ALT, AST). **CNS:** Headache, fever. **Skin:** Phlebitis, pain, inflammation, rash, pruritus, urticaria. **Urogenital:** Vaginitis.

Common adverse effects in *italic*, life-threatening effects <u>underlined</u>: generic names in **bold**; classifications in SMALL CAPS; ♣ Canadian drug name; ✪ Prototype drug

DIAGNOSTIC TEST INTERFERENCE Positive ***Coombs' test*** without hemolysis. May cause false-positive ***urine glucose test*** with ***Clinitest.***

DRUG INTERACTIONS AMINOGLYCOSIDES may increase risk of nephrotoxicity and have additive/synergistic effects. May decrease efficacy of ORAL CONTRACEPTIVES. **Probenecid** may increase levels.

PHARMACOKINETICS Distribution: 20% protein bound, widely distributed, may cross inflamed meninges; crosses placenta, secreted into breast milk. **Metabolism:** Metabolized in liver. **Elimination:** Excreted in urine. **Half-Life:** 2 h.

NURSING IMPLICATIONS

Assessment & Drug Effects

- Prior to initiating therapy: Baseline C&S tests (start drug pending results); determine previous hypersensitivity reactions to penicillins, cephalosporins, and other allergens.
- Monitor IV site for thrombophlebitis.
- Lab tests: Periodic BUN & serum creatinine.
- Monitor for S&S of hypersensitivity (see Appendix C). Report their appearance promptly and discontinue drug.
- Monitor I&O rates and pattern: Decreased urine output may indicate nephrotoxicity. Be alert to changes in BUN and creatinine clearance.
- Promptly report the onset of diarrhea, which may or may not be dose related. It is seen especially in patients with history of drug-related GI disturbances.
- With concurrent high-dose aminoglycoside therapy, closely monitor for nephrotoxicity and ototoxicity.

Patient & Family Education

- Promptly report any S&S of hypersensitivity, superinfection, and pseudomembranous colitis, a potentially life-threatening condition, that starts with diarrhea.

CEFOPERAZONE SODIUM

(sef-oh-per′a-zone)

Cefobid

Classification(s): ANTIBIOTIC, CEPHALOSPORIN, THIRD GENERATION
Therapeutic: ANTIBACTERIAL
Prototype: Cefotaxime sodium
Pregnancy Category: B

USES Infections of skin and skin structures, urinary tract, respiratory tract; peritonitis and other intra-abdominal infections, pelvic inflammatory disease, endometritis and other infections of the female genital tract; bacterial septicemia.
UNLABELED USES Infections in children less than 12 y.

INDICATION & DOSAGE

Moderate to Severe Infections
Adult: 1–2 g q12h; up to 16 g/day in 2–4 divided doses

Hepatic and Renal Impairment Dosage Adjustment Simultaneously
Reduce total dose to 1–2 g/day

Hemodialysis Dosage Adjustment
Administer dose after dialysis

SOLUTION PREPARATION

- *Vial Reconstitution:* Add 5 mL sterile water for injection to each 1 g. Shake vigorously then let foam dissipate and inspect solution to ensure complete dissolution. **Must be** further diluted in D5W, NS, D5/NS, LR or other compatible solution for infusion.
- *Further Dilution of Reconstituted Solution:*
  - *Intermittent Infusion*: Add required dose to 50–100 mL of IV solution.
  - *Continuous Infusion:* Add required dose to 500 mL of IV solution.
- Maximum Concentration: 50 mg/mL

STORAGE

- Protect sterile powder and piggyback units from light and store at or below 25° C (77° F).
- Reconstituted solutions may be stored in original containers for 24 h at 15°–25° C (59°–77° F); for 5 days at 5° C (41° F) or less.

ADMINISTRATION

- Rapid, direct IV injection is **not** recommended.
- **Intermittent IV:** Infuse over 15–30 min.
- **Continuous IV:** Infuse over 6–24 h.
- Use smaller needles, larger veins, and rotate infusion sites to minimize risk of thrombophlebitis.

INCOMPATIBILITIES Solution/additive: AMINOGLYCOSIDES, **doxapram, kanamycin.** Y-site: AMINOGLYCOSIDES, **amifostine, amphotericin B cholesteryl complex, cisatracurium, diltiazem, dobutamine, doxorubicin liposome, filgrastim, gemcitabine, hetastarch, labetalol, meperidine, ondansetron, pentamidine, sargramostim, vinorelbine.**

ACTION & *THERAPEUTIC EFFECT* Semisynthetic third-generation cephalosporin antibiotic. Preferentially binds to one or more of the penicillin-binding proteins (PBP) located on cell walls of susceptible organisms. This inhibits the third and final stage of bacterial cell wall synthesis, thus killing the bacterium. *Generally active against a wide variety of gram-negative bacteria, including some strains of* Pseudomonas aeruginosa. *Also active against some organisms resistant to first and second generation cephalosporins and some organisms resistant to aminoglycoside antibiotics and penicillins.*

CONTRAINDICATIONS Hypersensitivity to cephalosporins and related beta-lactam antibiotics.

Common adverse effects in *italic*, life-threatening effects <u>underlined</u>: generic names in **bold**; classifications in SMALL CAPS; ♣ Canadian drug name; ⊙ Prototype drug

131

C

CAUTIOUS USE History of hypersensitivity to penicillins, history of allergy, particularly to drugs; hepatic disease; history of colitis or other GI disease; history of bleeding disorders; pregnancy (category B); lactation.

ADVERSE EFFECTS (≥1%) **Body as a Whole:** Fever, eosinophilia, phlebitis (IV site), transient pain (IM site), superinfections. **GI:** Abdominal cramps, bloating, loose stools or *diarrhea,* pseudomembranous colitis, elevated liver function tests (AST, ALT, alkaline phosphatase). **Hematologic:** Abnormal PT/INR and PTT; hypoprothrombinemia. **Skin:** Skin rash, urticaria, pruritus. **Urogenital:** Transient increases in serum creatinine and BUN, oliguria.

DIAGNOSTIC TEST INTERFERENCE Cefoperazone can cause positive direct *Coombs' test,* which may result in interferences with *hematologic studies* and *cross-matching* procedures. False-positive results for *urine glucose* using *copper sulfate tests (Benedict's, Clinitest),* but not with *glucose enzymatic tests,* e.g., *Clinistix, Tes-Tape, Diastix.* Also causes *prolonged prothrombin* twice during therapy.

DRUG INTERACTIONS Alcohol produces disulfiram reaction.

PHARMACOKINETICS Peak: 15–20 min. **Distribution:** Low CNS penetration except with inflamed meninges; highest concentrations in bile; crosses placenta. **Elimination:** 70–75% excreted unchanged in bile in 6–12 h, small amount excreted in breast milk. **Half-Life:** 2 h.

NURSING IMPLICATIONS

Assessment & Drug Effects

- Prior to initiating therapy: Baseline C&S tests (start drug pending results); determine previous hypersensitivity reactions to penicillins, cephalosporins, and other allergens.
- Inspect IV injection site frequently for signs of phlebitis.
- Lab tests: Baseline and periodic PT/INR before and during therapy; periodic BUN & serum creatinine.
- Monitor cefoperazone serum levels (at steady state: 150 mg/mL) in patients with hepatic disease or biliary obstruction who are receiving over 4 g/day, patients with both hepatic and renal disease receiving over 1–2 g/day, and patients with renal impairment on high dose therapy.
- Monitor for signs of hemostatic defects: Nose bleeds, bleeding gums, bloody sputum, hematuria, etc.
- Report promptly onset of loose stools or diarrhea. Most patients respond to replacement of fluids, electrolytes, and proteins. Discontinuation of drug may be required for some patients.

Patient & Family Education

- Do not ingest alcohol within 72 h after drug administration as this will cause a disulfiram-like reaction (see Signs & Symptoms, Appendix C).
- Report promptly any signs or symptoms of superinfection (see Appendix C).

CEFOTAXIME SODIUM ⓟ
(sef-oh-taks'eem)
Claforan
Classification(s): ANTIBIOTIC, CEPHALOSPORIN, THIRD GENERATION
Therapeutic: ANTIBACTERIAL
Pregnancy Category: B

USES Serious infections of lower respiratory tract, skin and skin structures, bones and joints, CNS (including meningitis and ventriculitis), gynecologic and GU tract infections, including uncomplicated gonococcal infections caused by penicillinase-producing *Neisseria gonorrhoeae* (PPNG). Also used to treat bacteremia or septicemia, intra-abdominal infections, and for perioperative prophylaxis.
UNLABELED USES Treatment of disseminated gonococcal infections (gonococcal arthritis-dermatitis syndrome) and as drug of choice for gonococcal ophthalmia caused by PPNG in adults, children, and neonates.

INDICATION & DOSAGE

Moderate to Severe Infections
Adult: 1–2 g q8–12h, up to 2 g q4h (max: 12 g/day)
Child (less than 1 wk): 50 mg/kg q12h; *(1–4 wk):* 50 mg/kg q8h; *(1 mo–12 y):* 50–200 mg/kg/day divided q4–8h (max: 12 g/24h)

Disseminated Gonorrhea
Adult: 1 g q8h

Surgical Prophylaxis
Adult: 1 g 30–90 min before surgery

Renal Impairment Dosage Adjustment
CrCl less than 20 mL/min: Give ¹/₂ normal dose

Hemodialysis Dosage Adjustment
Supplemental dose may be needed

SOLUTION PREPARATION
- Compatible IV solutions include D5W, NS, D5/NS, D5/1/2NS, NS, LR.
- Do not use diluents that contain benzyl alcohol for neonates.
- *Vial Reconstitution:* Add 10 mL sterile water for injection to the 1 or 2 g vial to yield 95 or 180 mg/mL, respectively. May be given as prepared direct IV as a bolus dose or further diluted for infusion.
- *Further Dilution of Reconstituted Solution:*
  - *Intermittent Infusion:* Dilute required dose in 50 or 100 mL of compatible IV solution.
  - *Continuous Infusion:* Dilute required dose in 500–1000 mL compatible IV solution.

Common adverse effects in *italic*, life-threatening effects <u>underlined</u>: generic names in **bold**; classifications in SMALL CAPS; ♣ Canadian drug name; ⓞ Prototype drug

133

- *IV Bottle Reconstitution:* Add 50–100 mL of compatible diluent. Use for intermittent or continuous infusion.
- *ADD-Vantage Vial:* Reconstitute with 50–100 mL of D5W or NS.
- Maximum Concentration: 200 mg/mL

STORAGE

- Protect from excessive light. Darkening of solution does not affect potency.
- Reconstituted solutions may be stored in original containers for 24 h at room temperature; for 10 days under refrigeration at 5° C (41° F) or less; or for at least 13 wk in frozen state.

ADMINISTRATION

- Do not admix cefotaxime with sodium bicarbonate or any fluid with a pH greater than 7.5.
- **Direct IV Injection:** Give over 3–5 min. DO NOT give over less than 3 min.
- **Intermittent Infusion:** Infuse over 20–30 min, preferably via butterfly or scalp vein-type needles.
- **Continuous Infusion:** Infuse over 6–24 h.
- Use smaller needles, larger veins, and rotate infusion sites to minimize risk of thrombophlebitis.

INCOMPATIBILITIES Solution/additive: AMINOGLYCOSIDES, **aminophylline. Y-site: Allopurinol, azithromycin, cisatracurium, filgrastim, fluconazole, gemcitabine, hetastarch, pentamidine, vancomycin.**

ACTION & *THERAPEUTIC EFFECT* Broad-spectrum semi-synthetic third-generation cephalosporin antibiotic. Preferentially binds to one or more of the penicillin-binding proteins (PBP) located on cell walls of susceptible organisms. This inhibits third and final stage of bacterial cell wall synthesis, thus killing the bacteria. *Generally active against a wide variety of gram-negative bacteria including most of the Enterobacteriaceae. Also active against some organisms resistant to first- and second-generation cephalosporins and some organisms resistant to aminoglycoside antibiotics and penicillins.*

CONTRAINDICATIONS Hypersensitivity to cefotaxime or cephalosporin antibiotics.

CAUTIOUS USE History of type I hypersensitivity reactions to penicillin; history of allergy to other beta-lactam antibiotics; coagulopathy; renal impairment; history of colitis or other GI disease; pregnancy (category B).

ADVERSE EFFECTS (≥1%) **Body as a Whole:** Fever, nocturnal perspiration, inflammatory reaction at IV site, phlebitis, thrombophlebitis; pain, induration, and tenderness at IM site; superinfections. **GI:** Nausea, vomiting, *diarrhea,* abdominal pain, colitis, <u>pseudomembranous colitis</u>, anorexia. **Metabolic:** Transient increases in serum AST, ALT, LDH, bilirubin, alkaline phosphatase concentrations. **Skin:** Rash, pruritus.

DIAGNOSTIC TEST INTERFERENCE May cause falsely elevated ***serum or urine creatinine values (Jaffe reaction).*** False-positive reactions for ***urine glucose*** have not been reported using ***copper sulfate reduction methods,*** e.g., ***Benedict's, Clinitest;*** however, since it has occurred with other cephalosporins, it may be advisable to use ***glucose oxidase tests***

Common adverse effects in *italic*, life-threatening effects <u>underlined</u>; generic names in **bold**; classifications in SMALL CAPS; ♥ Canadian drug name; ⊘ Prototype drug

(Clinistix, TesTape, Diastix). Positive direct **antiglobulin (Coombs')
test** results may interfere with **hematologic studies** and **cross-matching
procedures.**

DRUG INTERACTIONS Probenecid decreases renal elimination.

PHARMACOKINETICS Peak: 5 min. **Distribution:** CNS penetration except
with inflamed meninges; also penetrates aqueous humor, ascitic and
prostatic fluids; crosses placenta. **Metabolism:** Partially in liver to active
metabolites. **Elimination:** 50–60% unchanged in urine in 24 h; small
amount excreted in breast milk. **Half-Life:** 1 h.

NURSING IMPLICATIONS
Assessment & Drug Effects
- Prior to initiating therapy: Baseline C&S tests (start drug pending results);
  determine previous hypersensitivity reactions to penicillins, cephalosporins, and other allergens.
- Monitor IV site for phlebitis or extravasation. Rotate IV sites q72h or more
  often if needed.
- Lab tests: Periodic BUN & serum creatinine at regular intervals during
  therapy and for several months after drug has been discontinued; periodic hematologic studies (including PT and aPTT) and LFTs with high
  doses or prolonged therapy.
- Monitor I&O rates and patterns. Report change in I&O especially in patients with impaired renal function or chronic UTI, those receiving high
  dosages or an aminoglycoside concomitantly.
- Report promptly onset of diarrhea. If severe, pseudomembranous colitis
  (see Signs & Symptoms, Appendix C) **must be** ruled out (may occur in
  4–9 days or as long as 6 wk after cephalosporin therapy is discontinued).
  Chronically ill or debilitated older adult patients undergoing abdominal
  surgery are most vulnerable.

Patient & Family Education
- Report promptly early signs or symptoms of superinfection. Superinfections caused by overgrowth of nonsusceptible organisms may occur, particularly during prolonged use.
- Report loose stools or diarrhea.

CEFOTETAN DISODIUM
(sef'oh-tee-tan)
Cefotan
Classification(s): ANTIBIOTIC, CEPHALOSPORIN, SECOND GENERATION
Therapeutic: ANTIBACTERIAL
Prototype: Cefuroxime
Pregnancy Category: B

USES Infections caused by susceptible organisms in urinary tract, lower
respiratory tract, skin and skin structures, bones and joints, gynecologic

Common adverse effects in *italic*, life-threatening effects <u>underlined</u>: generic names
in **bold**; classifications in SMALL CAPS; ♣ Canadian drug name; ⊙ Prototype drug

135

tract; also intra-abdominal infections, bacteremia, and perioperative prophylaxis.

INDICATION & DOSAGE

Moderate to Severe Infections
Adult: 2–4 g q12h–24h

UTI
Adult: 500 mg q12h or 1–4 g/day

Surgical Prophylaxis
Adult/Adolescent: 1–2 g 30–60 min before surgery

Renal Impairment Dosage Adjustment

CrCl	Dose	Interval
Over 30 mL/min	Regular	q12h
10–30 mL/min	Regular	q24h
Less than 10 mL/min	Regular	q48h

Dialysis
Give $^1/_4$ dose q24h on days between sessions, $^1/_2$ dose on day of dialysis.

SOLUTION PREPARATION
- *Vial Reconstitution:* Dilute each 1 g with 10 mL of sterile water for injection. May be given as prepared direct IV as a bolus dose or further diluted for infusion.
- *Further Dilution of Reconstituted Solution:* Dilute each 1 g with 50–100 mL of D5W or NS.

STORAGE
Protect sterile powder from light; store at 22° C (71.6° F) or less. May darken with age, but potency is unaffected. Reconstituted solutions: Stable for 24 h at 25° C (77° F); 96 h when refrigerated at 5° C (41° F); or at least 1 wk when frozen at –20° C (–4° F).

ADMINISTRATION
- **Direct IV Injection:** Give bolus dose over 3–5 min.
- **Intermittent Infusion:** Infuse a single dose over 30 min. May be given through Y-site tubing system through which other compatible IV solutions are infusing.

INCOMPATIBILITIES Solution/additive: AMINOGLYCOSIDES, **heparin, promethazine,** TETRACYCLINES. **Y-site:** AMINOGLYCOSIDES, **cisatracurium, lansoprazole, pemetrexed, promethazine, vancomycin, vinorelbine.**

ACTION & *THERAPEUTIC EFFECT* Semisynthetic beta-lactam antibiotic, classified as a second-generation cephalosporin. Preferentially binds to one or more of the penicillin-binding proteins (PBP) located on cell walls of susceptible organisms. This inhibits third and final stage of bacterial cell wall synthesis, thus killing the bacterium. *Generally less active against susceptible* Staphylococci *than first generation cephalosporins are, but it has a broad spectrum of activity against gram-negative bacteria when compared to first and second generation cephalosporins. It also shows moderate activity against gram-positive organisms. Although it is generally inactive against* Pseudomonas aeruginosa, *it is active against the Enterobacteriaceae and anaerobes.*

CONTRAINDICATIONS Hypersensitivity to cephalosporins and related beta-lactam antibiotics.

CAUTIOUS USE Preexisting coagulopathy; colitis; GI disease; renal impairment; pregnancy (category B), lactation.

ADVERSE EFFECTS (≥1%) **Body as a Whole:** Fever, chills, injection site pain, inflammation, disulfiram-like reaction. **GI:** Nausea, vomiting, *diarrhea,* abdominal pain, antibiotic-associated colitis. **Hematologic:** Thrombocytopenia, prolongation of bleeding time or prothrombin time. **Skin:** Rash, pruritus.

DIAGNOSTIC TEST INTERFERENCE May cause falsely elevated *serum or urine creatinine values (Jaffe reaction).* False-positive reactions for *urine glucose* have not been reported using *copper sulfate reduction methods,* e.g., *Benedict's, Clinitest;* however, since it has occurred with other cephalosporins, it may be advisable to use *glucose oxidase tests (Clinistix, TesTape, Diastix).* Positive direct *antiglobulin (Coombs') test* results may interfere with *hematologic studies* and *cross-matching procedures.*

DRUG INTERACTIONS **Probenecid** decreases renal elimination of cefotetan; **alcohol** produces disulfiram reaction; **chloramphenicol** may affect therapeutic activity.

PHARMACOKINETICS Distribution: Poor CNS penetration; widely distributed to body tissues and fluids, including bile, sputum, prostatic, and peritoneal fluids; crosses placenta. **Elimination:** 51–81% unchanged in urine; 20% in bile; small amount in breast milk. **Half-Life:** 180–270 min.

NURSING IMPLICATIONS

Assessment & Drug Effects

- Prior to initiating therapy: Baseline C&S tests (start drug pending results); determine history of hypersensitivity to cephalosporins and penicillins, and other drug allergies, before therapy begins.
- Lab tests: Periodic hematologic studies (including PT/INR and aPTT) and evaluation of renal function, especially if cefotetan dose is high or if therapy is prolonged in order to recognize symptoms of nephrotoxicity and ototoxicity (see Appendix C).
- Report onset of loose stools or diarrhea. If diarrhea is severe, suspect pseudomembranous colitis (see Appendix C) caused by *Clostridium difficile.* Check temperature. Report fever and severe diarrhea to prescriber; drug should be discontinued.

Common adverse effects in *italic*, life-threatening effects underlined: generic names in **bold**; classifications in SMALL CAPS; ✦ Canadian drug name; ⊘ Prototype drug

137

Patient & Family Education
- Report promptly S&S of superinfection (see Appendix C).
- Report loose stools or diarrhea.

CEFOXITIN SODIUM

(se-fox'i-tin)
Mefoxin
Classification: ANTIBIOTIC, CEPHALOSPORIN, SECOND GENERATION
Prototype: Cefuroxime
Pregnancy Category: B

USES Infections caused by susceptible organisms in the lower respiratory tract, urinary tract, skin and skin structures, bones and joints; also intra-abdominal endocarditis, gynecological infections, septicemia, uncomplicated gonorrhea, and perioperative prophylaxis in prosthetic arthroplasty or cardiovascular surgery.

INDICATION & DOSAGE

Moderate to Severe Infections
Adult: 1–2 g q6–8h
Child (over 3 mo): 80–160 mg/kg/day in 4–6 divided doses (max: 12 g/day)

Life-Threatening Infections
Adult: 2 g q4h

Surgical Prophylaxis
Adult: 2 g 30–60 min before surgery, then 2 g q6h for 24 h
Child: 30–40 mg/kg 30–60 min before surgery, then 30–40 mg/kg q6h for 24 h

Cesarean Survey Prophylaxis
Adult: 2 g after clamping umbilical cord

Renal Impairment Dosage Adjustment

CrCl	Dose	Interval
30–50 mL/min	1–2 g	q8–12h
10–29 mL/min	1–2 g	q12–24h
5–9 mL/min	0.5–1 g	q12–24h
Less than 5 mL/min	0.5–1 g	q24–48h
Hemodialysis		Loading dose of 1–2 g post-dialysis

SOLUTION PREPARATION

- Do not use diluents that contain benzyl alcohol for neonates.
- *Vial/Bottle Reconstitution:* Reconstitute with bacteriostatic water for injection, sterile water for injection, NS, or D5W as indicated in the table that follows. Solution may be cloudy immediately after reconstitution; let stand and it will clear. The reconstituted 1 or 2 g vial may be given as prepared direct IV as a bolus dose or further diluted for infusion.
- *Further Dilution of Reconstituted Solution:*
  - *Intermittent Infusion:* Add required dose to 50–100 mL of compatible IV solution such as D5W, NS, or D5/NS.
  - *Continuous Infusion:* Dilute large doses in 1000 mL of D5W, NS, or D5/NS.
- Maximum Concentration: 200 mg/mL

Container	Amount of Diluent to be Added	Approximate Available Volume	Approximate Final Concentration
1 g vial	10 mL	10.5 mL	95 mg/mL
2 g vial	10 mL	11.1 mL	180 mg/mL
	20 mL	21 mL	95 mg/mL
1 g infusion bottle	50 mL	50 mL	20 mg/mL
	100 mL	100 mL	10 mg/mL
2 g infusion bottle	50 mL	50 mL	40 mg/mL
	100 mL	100 mL	20 mg/mL

STORAGE

- After reconstitution, solution is stable for 24 h at 25° C (77° F); 7 days when refrigerated at 4° C (39° F), or 30 wk when frozen at –20° C (–4° F).
- Powder or solution may darken during storage but this does not affect the drug's potency.
- Reconstituted solution may become discolored (usually light yellow to amber) if exposed to high temperatures; however, potency is not affected. Solution may be cloudy immediately after reconstitution; let stand and it will clear.

ADMINISTRATION

- **Direct IV Injection:** Give bolus dose over 3–5 min.
- **Intermittent Infusion:** Infuse over 15–30 min. Temporarily stop infusion of any other solution at the same site.
- **Continuous Infusion:** Infuse at a rate determine by the total volume of IV solution. Scalp veins are recommended with continuous infusion.
- Use smaller needles, larger veins, and rotate infusion sites to minimize risk of thrombophlebitis.

INCOMPATIBILITIES Solution/additive: AMINOGLYCOSIDES, **ranitidine.** Y-site: AMINOGLYCOSIDES, **cisatracurium, fenoldopam, filgrastim, hetastarch, lansoprazole, pentamidine, vancomycin.**

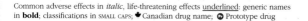

Common adverse effects in *italic*, life-threatening effects <u>underlined</u>: generic names in **bold**; classifications in SMALL CAPS; ♣ Canadian drug name; ❷ Prototype drug

C

ACTION & *THERAPEUTIC EFFECT* Semisynthetic, broad-spectrum beta-lactam antibiotic classified as a second-generation cephalosporin; structurally and pharmacologically related to cephalosporins and penicillins. Preferentially binds to one or more of the penicillin-binding proteins (PBP) located on cell walls of susceptible organisms, thus making it bactericidal. *It shows enhanced activity against a wide variety of gram-negative organisms and is effective for mixed aerobic-anaerobic infections. Considerably less active than most cephalosporins against* Staphylococci.

CONTRAINDICATIONS Hypersensitivity to cefoxitin or cephalosporins; children less than 3 mo.

CAUTIOUS USE History of sensitivity to penicillin, beta-lactam antibiotics, or other allergies, particularly to drugs; impaired renal function; pregnancy (category B).

ADVERSE EFFECTS (≥1%) **Body as a Whole:** Drug fever, eosinophilia, superinfections, local reactions: Pain, tenderness, and induration (IM site), thrombophlebitis (IV site). **GI:** *Diarrhea,* pseudomembranous colitis. **Skin:** Rash, exfoliative dermatitis, pruritus, urticaria. **Urogenital:** Nephrotoxicity, interstitial nephritis.

DIAGNOSTIC TEST INTERFERENCE Cefoxitin causes false-positive (black-brown or green-brown color) *urine glucose* reaction with *copper reduction reagents* such as *Benedict's* or *Clinitest,* but not with *enzymatic glucose oxidase reagents (Clinistix, TesTape).* With high doses, falsely elevated *serum and urine creatinine* (with *Jaffe reaction*) reported. False-positive *direct Coombs' test* (may interfere with *cross-matching procedures* and *hematologic studies*) has also been reported.

DRUG INTERACTIONS Probenecid decreases renal elimination of cefoxitin, AMINOGLYCOSIDES may increase risk of nephrotoxicity.

PHARMACOKINETICS Peak: 5 min. **Distribution:** Poor CNS penetration even with inflamed meninges; widely distributed in body tissues including pleural, synovial, and ascitic fluid and bile; crosses placenta. **Elimination:** 85% excreted unchanged in urine in 6 h, small amount excreted in breast milk. **Half-Life:** 45–60 min.

NURSING IMPLICATIONS

Assessment & Drug Effects

- Prior to initiating therapy: Baseline C&S tests (start drug pending results); determine previous hypersensitivity reactions to penicillins, cephalosporins, and other allergens.
- Inspect infusion site regularly for signs of phlebitis.
- Lab tests: Periodic BUN & serum creatinine.
- Monitor I&O rates and pattern: Nephrotoxicity occurs most frequently in those over 50 y, with impaired renal function, who are the debilitated, and in those receiving high doses or other nephrotoxic drugs.
- Be alert to S&S of superinfections (see Appendix C), which occur more often in older adults, especially when drug has been used for a prolonged period.

- Report promptly onset of diarrhea. If severe, pseudomembranous colitis (see Signs & Symptoms, Appendix C) **must be** ruled out.

Patient & Family Education
- Report promptly S&S of superinfection (see Appendix C), watery or bloody loose stools or severe diarrhea.

CEFTAZIDIME
(sef'tay-zi-deem)

Fortaz, Tazicef
Classification(s): ANTIBIOTIC, CEPHALOSPORIN, THIRD GENERATION
Therapeutic: ANTIBACTERIAL
Prototype: Cefotaxime sodium
Pregnancy Category: B

USES To treat infections of lower respiratory tract, skin and skin structures, urinary tract, bones and joints; also used to treat bacteremia, gynecological, intra-abdominal, and CNS infections (including meningitis).
UNLABELED USES Surgical prophylaxis.

INDICATION & DOSAGE

Moderate to Severe Infections
Adult: 500 mg–2 g q8–12h, up to 2 g q6h
Child/Infant: 30–50 mg/kg/day in 3 divided doses (max: 6 g/day)
Neonate (up to 4 wk): 30 mg/kg q12h

Very Severe Infection
Adult: 2 g q8h

Renal Impairment Dosage Adjustment

CrCl	Dose	Interval
30–50 mL/min	1 g	q12h
15–29 mL/min	1 g	q24h
6–14 mL/min	500 mg	q24h
Less than 5 mL/min	500 mg	q48h
Hemodialysis	1 g	Administer after hemodialysis

SOLUTION PREPARATION

- *Vial Reconstitution:* Add 10 mL of sterile water for injection to the 1 or 2 g vial. Shake to dissolve. May be given as prepared direct IV as a bolus dose or further diluted for infusion.

- *Further Dilution of Reconstituted Solution:* Add the required dose to 50–100 mL of D5W, NS, or LR.
- Maximum Concentration: 200 mg/mL

STORAGE
Protect sterile powder from light. Reconstituted solution is stable 7 days when refrigerated at 4°–5° C (39°–41° F); for 18–24 h when stored at 15°–30° C (59°–86° F).

ADMINISTRATION
- **Direct IV Injection:** Give over 3–5 min.
- **Intermittent Infusion:** Infuse over 15–30 min. If given through a Y-type set, discontinue other solutions during infusion of ceftazidime.
- Use smaller needles, larger veins, and rotate infusion sites every 72 h to minimize risk of thrombophlebitis.

INCOMPATIBILITIES Solution/additive: AMINOGLYCOSIDES, **aminophylline, ciprofloxacin, ranitidine, pantoprazole, sodium bicarbonate. Y-site: Acetylcysteine, amiodarone, amphotericin B cholesteryl complex, amsacrine, azithromycin, clarithromycin, doxorubicin liposome, erythromycin, fluconazole, idarubicin, lansoprazole, midazolam, nicardipine, pentamidine, phenytoin, propofol, sargramostim, vancomycin, warfarin.**

ACTION & *THERAPEUTIC EFFECT* Semisynthetic, third-generation broad-spectrum cephalosporin antibiotic. Preferentially binds to one or more of the penicillin-binding proteins (PBP) located on cell walls of susceptible microbes; this inhibits third and final stage of bacterial cell wall synthesis, leading to cell death of the bacterium. *Third-generation cephalosporins are more active against broad spectrum of organisms that are aerobic gram-negative bacteria than either first- or second-generation agents.*

CONTRAINDICATIONS Hypersensitivity to cephalosporins and related beta-lactam antibiotics; viral diseases.

CAUTIOUS USE Elderly; coagulopathy, renal disease, renal impairment; GI disease; colitis; pregnancy (category B).

ADVERSE EFFECTS (≥1%) **Body as a Whole:** Fever, phlebitis, pain or inflammation at injection site, superinfections. **GI:** Nausea, vomiting, *diarrhea,* abdominal pain, metallic taste, drug-associated <u>pseudomembranous colitis</u>. **Skin:** Pruritus, rash, urticaria. **Urogenital:** Vaginitis, candidiasis.

DIAGNOSTIC TEST INTERFERENCE False-positive reactions for **urine glucose** have been reported using **copper sulfate** (e.g., **Benedict's solution, Clinitest**). **Glucose oxidase tests (Clinistix, TesTape)** are unaffected. May cause positive direct **antiglobulin (Coombs') test** results, which can interfere with **hematologic studies** and transfusion **cross-matching procedures.**

DRUG INTERACTIONS Probenecid decreases renal elimination of ceftazidime.

PHARMACOKINETICS Peak: 1 h. **Distribution:** CNS penetration with inflamed meninges; also penetrates bone, gallbladder, bile, endometrium, heart, skin, and ascitic and pleural fluids; crosses placenta. **Metabolism:** Not metabolized. **Elimination:** 80–90% excreted unchanged in urine in 24 h; small amount excreted in breast milk. **Half-Life:** 25–60 min.

NURSING IMPLICATIONS

Assessment & Drug Effects

- Prior to initiating therapy: Baseline C&S tests (start drug pending results); determine previous hypersensitivity reactions to penicillins, cephalosporins, and other allergens.
- Be alert to onset of rash, itching, and dyspnea. Check patient's temperature. If it is elevated, suspect onset of hypersensitivity reaction (see Appendix C).
- Inspect IV injection site frequently for signs of phlebitis.
- Lab tests: Periodic BUN & serum creatinine; periodic CBC, Hct, serum AST & ALT, bilirubin, and alkaline phosphatase during long-term therapy.
- If administered concomitantly with another antibiotic, monitor renal function and report if symptoms of dysfunction appear (e.g., changes in I&O ratio and pattern, dysuria).
- Monitor for superinfection (see Appendix C).
- Report promptly onset of diarrhea. If severe, pseudomembranous colitis (see Signs & Symptoms, Appendix C) **must be** ruled out.

Patient & Family Education

- Report promptly loose stools or diarrhea, and any signs or symptoms of superinfection (see Appendix C).

CEFTIZOXIME SODIUM

(sef-ti-zox′eem)

Cefizox

Classification(s): ANTIBIOTIC, CEPHALOSPORIN, THIRD GENERATION
Therapeutic: ANTIBACTERIAL
Prototype: Cefotaxime sodium
Pregnancy Category: B

USES Infections caused by susceptible organisms in lower respiratory tract, skin and skin structures, urinary tract, bones and joints; also used to treat intra-abdominal infections, pelvic inflammatory disease, uncomplicated gonorrhea, meningitis (Haemophilus influenzae, Streptococcus pneumoniae), and for surgical prophylaxis.
UNLABELED USES Meningitis caused by Neisseria meningitidis and E. coli.

INDICATION & DOSAGE

Moderate to Severe Infections

Adult: 1 g q8–12h, up to 2 g q4h
Child (over 6 mo): 50 mg/kg q6–8h, up to 200 mg/kg/day

Common adverse effects in *italic*, life-threatening effects <u>underlined</u>: generic names in **bold**, classifications in SMALL CAPS; ♣ Canadian drug name; ❖ Prototype drug

143

UTI

Adult: 500 mg q12h

PID

Adult: 2 g q8h

Life-Threatening Infection

Adult: 3–4 g q8h

Renal Impairment Dosage Adjustment

CrCl	Dose for Infection (Life-Threatening)	Interval
50–79 mL/min	500 mg (0.75–1 g)	q8h
5–49 mL/min	250–500 mg (0.5–1 g)	q12h
0–4 mL/min	250–500 mg (0.5–1 g)	q24–48h
Hemodialysis		Administer regular dose after hemodialysis

SOLUTION PREPARATION

- *Vial Reconstitution:* Reconstitute each 1 g with 10 mL sterile water for injection. Shake well. Reconstituted solutions may range in color from yellow to amber. May be given as prepared direct IV as a bolus dose or further diluted for infusion.
- *Further Dilution of Reconstituted Solution:* Add required dose to 50–100 mL D5W, NS, D5/NS, D5/1/2NS, LR, or other compatible IV solution.

STORAGE

Stable 24 h at room temperature or 96 h if refrigerated (5° C; 41° F).

ADMINISTRATION

- **Direct IV Injection:** Give bolus dose slowly over 3–5 min.
- **Intermittent Infusion:** Infuse over 30 min.
- Use smaller needles, larger veins, and rotate infusion sites to minimize risk of thrombophlebitis.

INCOMPATIBILITIES Solution/additive: Promethazine. Y-site: Filgrastim, lansoprazole, vancomycin.

ACTION & *THERAPEUTIC EFFECT* Semisynthetic third-generation cephalosporin antibiotic. Preferentially binds to one or more of the penicillin-binding proteins (PBP) located on cell walls of susceptible organisms. This inhibits third and final stage of bacterial cell wall synthesis, thus killing the bacterium. *Generally resistant to inactivation by beta-lactamases that act principally as cephalosporinases and penicillinases. Its spectrum includes some gram-positive, but predominately gram-negative organisms.*

CONTRAINDICATIONS Hypersensitivity to ceftizoxime or cephalosporin antibiotics; viral disease. Safe use in infants less than 6 mo not established.

Common adverse effects in *italic*, life-threatening effects <u>underlined</u>: generic names in **bold**; classifications in SMALL CAPS; ♣ Canadian drug name; ⊘ Prototype drug

CAUTIOUS USE Hypersensitivity to penicillin or other beta-lactam antibiotics; coagulopathy; GI disease, colitis; elderly; renal disease, renal impairment; pregnancy (category B); lactation.

ADVERSE EFFECTS (≥1%) **Body as a Whole:** Fever, phlebitis, vaginitis, pain and induration at injection site, paresthesia. **GI:** Nausea, vomiting, diarrhea, <u>pseudomembranous colitis</u>. **Skin:** Rash, pruritus.

DIAGNOSTIC TEST INTERFERENCE Ceftizoxime causes false-positive *direct Coombs' test* (may interfere with *cross-matching procedures* and *hematologic studies*).

DRUG INTERACTIONS Probenecid decreases renal elimination of ceftizoxime.

PHARMACOKINETICS Peak: 1 h. **Distribution:** Crosses placenta. **Metabolism:** Not metabolized. **Elimination:** 80–90% excreted unchanged in urine in 24 h; small amount excreted in breast milk. **Half-Life:** 25–60 min.

NURSING IMPLICATIONS

Assessment & Drug Effects

- Prior to initiating therapy: Baseline C&S test (start drug pending tesults); determine history of hypersensitivity reactions to cephalosporins, penicillin, or other drugs before therapy is instituted.
- Be alert to symptoms of hypersensitivity reaction (see Appendix C). Serious reactions may require emergency measures.
- Inspect IV injection site frequently for signs of phlebitis.
- Lab tests: Periodic BUN & serum creatinine; periodic CBC, Hct, AST, ALT, bilirubin, and alkaline phosphatase during long-term therapy.
- Report promptly onset of diarrhea. If severe, pseudomembranous colitis (see Signs & Symptoms, Appendix C) **must be** ruled out.

Patient & Family Education

- Report loose stools or diarrhea promptly.
- Report any signs or symptoms of hypersensitivity (see Appendix C) promptly.

CEFTRIAXONE SODIUM

(sef-try-ax'one)

Rocephin

Classification(s): ANTIBIOTIC, CEPHALOSPORIN, THIRD GENERATION

Therapeutic: ANTIBACTERIAL

Prototype: Cefotaxime sodium

Pregnancy Category: B

USES Infections caused by susceptible organisms in lower respiratory tract, skin and skin structures, urinary tract, bones and joints; also intra-abdominal infections, pelvic inflammatory disease, uncomplicated gonorrhea, meningitis, and surgical prophylaxis.

Common adverse effects in *italic*, life-threatening effects <u>underlined</u>: generic names in **bold**; classifications in SMALL CAPS; ♣ Canadian drug name; ☻ Prototype drug

145

C

INDICATION & DOSAGE

Moderate to Severe Infections
Adult: 1–2 g q12–24h (max: 4 g/day)
Child: 50–75 mg/kg/day in 2 divided doses (max: 2 g/day)

Meningitis
Adult: 2 g q12h
Child: 100 mg/kg/day in 2 divided doses (max: 4 g/day)

Surgical Prophylaxis
Adult: 1 g 30–120 min before surgery

Renal or Hepatic Impairment Dosage Adjustment
Do not exceed 2 g/day without monitoring.

SOLUTION PREPARATION
- *Vial Reconstitution:* Reconstitute each 250 mg with 2.4 mL of sterile water for injection, D5W, NS, or D5/NS to yield 100 mg/mL. **Must be** further diluted for infusion.
- *Further Dilution of Reconstituted Solution:* Add required dose to 50–100 mL of compatible IV solution (e.g., D5W, NS, or D5/NS). Concentrations of 10–40 mg/mL are recommended for infusion, but lower concentrations may be used.
- Maximum Concentration: 40 mg/mL

STORAGE
Protect sterile powder from light. Store at 15°–25° C (59°–77° F). Reconstituted solutions: Diluent used and concentration of solutions are determinants of stability. See manufacturer's instructions for storage.

ADMINISTRATION
- **Intermittent Infusion:** Infuse over 30 min.
- Use smaller needles, larger veins, and rotate infusion sites to minimize risk of thrombophlebitis.

INCOMPATIBILITIES Solution/additive: Aminophylline, clindamycin, linezolid, metronidazole, theophylline. Y-site: Amphotericin B cholesteryl complex, amsacrine, azithromycin, filgrastim, fluconazole, labetalol, pentamidine, vancomycin, vinorelbine.

ACTION & *THERAPEUTIC EFFECT* Semisynthetic third-generation cephalosporin antibiotic. Preferentially binds to one or more of the penicillin-binding proteins (PBP) located on cell walls of susceptible organisms. This inhibits third and final stage of bacterial cell wall synthesis, thus killing the bacterium. *Similar to other third-generation cephalosporins, it is effective against serious gram-negative organisms, and also penetrates the CSF in concentrations useful in treatment of meningitis.*

CONTRAINDICATIONS Hypersensitivity to ceftriaxone or other cephalosporin antibiotics; viral infections; neonates with hyperbilirubinemia, premature neonates.

Common adverse effects in *italic*, life-threatening effects <u>underlined</u>: generic names in **bold**; classifications in SMALL CAPS; ♣ Canadian drug name; ◍ Prototype drug

CAUTIOUS USE Hypersensitivity to penicillin and beta-lactam antibiotics; coagulopathy, GI disease, colitis; renal disease, renal impairment; pregnancy (category B).

ADVERSE EFFECTS (≥1%) **Body as a Whole:** Pruritus, fever, chills, pain, induration at IM injection site; phlebitis (IV site). **GI:** *Diarrhea*, abdominal cramps, pseudomembranous colitis, biliary sludge. **Urogenital:** Genital pruritus; moniliasis.

DIAGNOSTIC TEST INTERFERENCE Causes prolonged *PT/INR* during therapy.

DRUG INTERACTIONS Probenecid decreases renal elimination of ceftriaxone; effect of **warfarin** may be increased.

PHARMACOKINETICS Distribution: Widely distributed in body tissues and fluids; good CNS penetration, especially with inflamed meninges; crosses placenta. **Metabolism:** Not metabolized. **Elimination:** 33–65% excreted unchanged in urine; also excreted in bile; small amount excreted in breast milk. **Half-Life:** 5–10 h.

NURSING IMPLICATIONS

Assessment & Drug Effects

- Prior to initiating therapy: Baseline C&S tests (start drug pending results); determine previous hypersensitivity reactions to penicillins, cephalosporins, and other allergens.
- Monitor for manifestations of hypersensitivity (see Appendix C). Report their appearance promptly and discontinue drug.
- Inspect IV injection site frequently for signs of phlebitis.
- Lab tests: Periodic BUN & serum creatinine, especially in those with impaired renal function.
- Watch for and report signs of: Petechiae, ecchymotic areas, epistaxis, or any unexplained bleeding. Ceftriaxone appears to alter vitamin K–producing gut bacteria; therefore, hypoprothrombinemic bleeding may occur.
- Report promptly onset of diarrhea. If severe, pseudomembranous colitis (see Signs & Symptoms, Appendix C) **must be** ruled out.

Patient & Family Education

- Report any signs of bleeding.
- Report loose stools or diarrhea promptly.

CEFUROXIME SODIUM ℗

(se-fyoor-ox'eem)

Zinacef

Classification(s): ANTIBIOTIC, CEPHALOSPORIN, SECOND GENERATION
Therapeutic: ANTIBACTERIAL
Pregnancy Category: B

Common adverse effects in *italic*, life-threatening effects underlined: generic names in **bold**, classifications in SMALL CAPS; ♣ Canadian drug name; ℗ Prototype drug

147

USES Infections caused by susceptible organisms in the lower respiratory tract, urinary tract, skin, and skin structures; also used for treatment of meningitis, gonorrhea, and otitis media and for perioperative prophylaxis (e.g., open-heart surgery), early Lyme disease.

INDICATION & DOSAGE

Moderate to Severe Infections
Adult: 750 mg–1.5 g q6–8h
Child: 50–100 mg/kg/day divided q8h (max: 6 g/day)

Bacterial Meningitis
Adult: 1.5–3 g q8h
Child/Infant (over 3 mo): 200–240 mg/kg/day divided q6–8h

Surgical Prophylaxis
Adult/Adolescent: 1.5 g 30–60 min before surgery, then 750 mg q8h for 24 h

Renal Impairment Dosage Adjustment
CrCl 10–20 mL/min: Give q12h; *less than 10 mL/min:* Give q24h

Hemodialysis Dosage Adjustment
Give additional dose post-dialysis.

SOLUTION PREPARATION
- *Vial Reconstitution:* To each 750 mg add 8 mL sterile water for injection, D5W, or NS to yield approximately 90 mg/mL. May be given as prepared direct IV as a bolus dose or further diluted for infusion.
- *Further Dilution of Reconstituted Solution:*
  - *Intermittent Infusion:* Add the required dose to 50–100 mL of compatible solution.
  - *Continuous Infusion:* Add the required dose to 1000 mL of compatible solution.

STORAGE
- Store powder protected from light unless otherwise directed. After reconstitution, store suspension at 2°–30° C (36°–86° F). Discard after 10 days.
- Cefuroxime powder and solutions of the drug may range in color from light yellow to amber without adversely affecting product potency.

ADMINISTRATION
- **Direct IV Injection:** Give bolus dose slowly over 3–5 min.
- **Intermittent Infusion:** Infuse over 30 min.
- **Continuous Infusion:** Infuse over 6–24 h.
- Use smaller needles, larger veins, and rotate infusion sites to minimize risk of thrombophlebitis.

INCOMPATIBILITIES Solution/additive: AMINOGLYCOSIDES, **ciprofloxacin, ranitidine. Y-site:** AMINOGLYCOSIDES, **azithromycin, cisatracurium,**

clarithromycin, filgrastim, fluconazole, midazolam, vancomycin, vinorelbine.

ACTION & *THERAPEUTIC EFFECT* Semisynthetic second-generation cephalosporin antibiotic that preferentially binds to one or more of the penicillin-binding proteins (PBP) located on cell walls of susceptible organisms. This inhibits third and final stage of bacterial cell wall synthesis, thus killing the bacterium. *Resistance against beta-lactamase-producing strains exceeds that of first-generation cephalosporins. Similar to other second-generation cephalosporins, it is more active against gram-negative bacteria than are first-generation cephalosporins.*

CONTRAINDICATIONS Hypersensitivity to cefuroxime and cephalosporin antibiotics; pregnancy (category B), lactation.

CAUTIOUS USE History of allergy, particularly to drugs; hypersensitivity to penicillin or beta-lactam antibiotics; renal insufficiency; history of colitis or other GI disease; potent diuretics.

ADVERSE EFFECTS (≥1%) **Body as a Whole:** Thrombophlebitis (IV site); pain, burning, cellulitis (IM site); superinfections, positive Coombs' test. **GI:** *Diarrhea,* nausea, antibiotic-associated colitis. **Skin:** Rash, pruritus, urticaria. **Urogenital:** Increased serum creatinine and BUN, decreased CrCl.

DIAGNOSTIC TEST INTERFERENCE Cefuroxime causes false-positive (black-brown or green-brown color) ***urine glucose reaction*** with ***copper reduction reagents,*** e.g., ***Benedict's*** or ***Clinitest,*** but not with ***enzymatic glucose oxidase reagents,*** e.g., ***Clinistix, TesTape.*** False-positive ***direct Coombs' test*** (may interfere with ***cross-matching procedures*** and ***hematologic studies***) has been reported.

DRUG INTERACTIONS Probenecid decreases renal elimination of cefuroxime.

PHARMACOKINETICS Distribution: Widely distributed in body tissues and fluids; adequate CNS penetration with inflamed meninges; crosses placenta. **Elimination:** 66–100% excreted in urine in 24 h; excreted in breast milk. **Half-Life:** 1–2 h.

NURSING IMPLICATIONS

Assessment & Drug Effects

- Prior to initiating therapy: Baseline C&S tests (start drug pending results); determine previous hypersensitivity reactions to penicillins, cephalosporins, and other allergens.
- Monitor for manifestations of hypersensitivity (see Appendix C). If any occur, withhold drug and report promptly.
- Inspect IV injection site frequently for signs of phlebitis.
- Lab tests: Periodic BUN & serum creatinine.
- Report promptly onset of diarrhea. If severe, pseudomembranous colitis (see Signs & Symptoms, Appendix C) **must be** ruled out.
- Monitor I&O rates and pattern: Especially important in severely ill patients receiving high doses. Report any significant changes.

Common adverse effects in *italic*, life-threatening effects <u>underlined</u>: generic names in **bold**; classifications in SMALL CAPS; ♣ Canadian drug name; ● Prototype drug

149

Patient & Family Education
- Report loose stools or diarrhea promptly.
- Report any signs or symptoms of hypersensitivity (see Appendix C).

CETUXIMAB
(ce-tux'i-mab)

Erbitux

Classifications: ANTINEOPLASTIC; MONOCLONAL ANTIBODY
Therapeutic: ANTINEOPLASTIC
Pregnancy Category: C

USES Treatment of EGFR-expressing metastatic colorectal cancer in combination with irinotecan in patients who are refractory to irinotecan-based chemotherapy or as monotherapy in patients who are intolerant to irinotecan-based chemotherapy.

INDICATION & DOSAGE

Colorectal Cancer
Adult: Start with 400 mg/m^2 over 2 h; continue with 250 mg/m^2 weekly

Toxicity Adjustment

Toxicity	Modification
1st severe rash	Delay infusion 1–2 wk. If improved, continue therapy; if no improvement, discontinue therapy.
2nd severe rash	Delay infusion 1–2 wk. If improved, continue therapy at 200 mg/m^2; if no improvement, discontinue therapy.
3rd severe rash	Delay infusion 1–2 wk. If improved continue therapy at 150 mg/m^2; if no improvement, discontinue therapy.
4th severe rash	Stop therapy permanently.

SOLUTION PREPARATION
- Do not shake or further dilute vial. Do not mix with other medication.
- Withdraw the required dose and inject into a sterile, evacuated container or bag (i.e., glass, polyolefin, ethylene vinyl acetate, DEHP plasticized PVC, or PVC). Use a new needle for each vial required to achieve the needed dose.
- A syringe and syringe pump may also be used.

STORAGE
- Stable in IV bag for up to 12 h refrigerated and up to 8 h at 20°–25° C (68°–77° F).

Common adverse effects in *italic*, life-threatening effects <u>underlined</u>: generic names in **bold**; classifications in SMALL CAPS; ♣ Canadian drug name; ● Prototype drug

- Store unopened vials at 2°–8° C (36°–46° F). Note: Vials may contain a small amount of easily visible, white particles.

ADMINISTRATION

- Administer with full resuscitation equipment available and under the supervision of a prescriber experienced with chemotherapy.
- Premedication with an H₁-receptor antagonist (e.g., diphenhydramine 50 mg IV) is recommended.
- Do **NOT** give direct IV as a bolus dose. **Must be** given as an infusion with an infusion pump or syringe pump.
- **IV Infusion:** Attach IV container to infusion set with a low-protein-binding 0.22-micron filter. Place the filter as proximal to the patient as possible. Prime line with cetuximab. Control rate with infusion pump. Flush infusion line with NS after the infusion.
  - *Initial Loading Dose:* Infuse over 2 h at a rate not to exceed 5 mL/min.
  - *Weekly Maintenance Dose:* Infuse over 1–2 h at a rate not to exceed 5 mL/min.
- Monitor for an infusion reaction for at least 1 h following completion of infusion. Decrease the rate by 50% for mild-moderate infusion reactions. Use reduced rate for all subsequent infusions.

INCOMPATIBILITIES Solution/additive: Do not mix with other additives. **Y-site:** No data available.

ACTION & *THERAPEUTIC EFFECT* Cetuximab is a recombinant, monoclonal antibody that binds specifically to the epidermal growth factor receptor (EGFR, HER1, c-ErbB-1) on both normal and tumor cells. Binding to the EGFR results in inhibition of cell growth, induction of apoptosis, and decreased vascular endothelial growth factor production. *Over-expression of EGFR is detected in many human cancers, including those of the colon and rectum. Cetuximab inhibits the growth and survival of tumor cells that over-express the EGFR.*

CONTRAINDICATIONS Worsening of preexisting pulmonary edema or interstitial lung disease; pregnancy (category C), lactation within 60 days of using cetuximab. Safety and efficacy in children have not been established.
CAUTIOUS USE Infusion reaction, especially with first time users; history of hypersensitivity to murine proteins or cetuximab; cardiac disease, coronary artery disease; pulmonary disease, pulmonary fibrosis; UV exposure, radiation therapy.

ADVERSE EFFECTS (≥1%) **Body as a Whole:** Infusion reactions (allergic reaction, anaphylactoid reaction, fever, chills, dyspnea, bronchospasm stridor, hoarseness, urticaria, hypotension), *fever,* sepsis, *asthenia, malaise,* pain, infection. **CNS:** *Headache,* insomnia, depression. **CV:** Cardiopulmonary arrest. **GI:** *Nausea, vomiting, diarrhea, abdominal pain, constipation,* stomatitis, dyspepsia. **Hematologic:** Leukopenia, anemia. **Metabolic:** Weight loss, peripheral edema, dehydration, hypomagnesemia, hypokalemia. **Respiratory:** Pulmonary embolism, pulmonary fibrosis (rare), *dyspnea,* cough. **Skin:** *Rash,* alopecia, pruritus. **Urogenital:** Kidney failure.

PHARMACOKINETICS Half-Life: 114 h (75–188 h).

Common adverse effects in *italic*, life-threatening effects underlined: generic names in **bold**; classifications in SMALL CAPS; ♣ Canadian drug name; ❷ Prototype drug

151

C

NURSING IMPLICATIONS

Assessment & Drug Effects

- Discontinue infusion and notify prescriber for S&S of a severe infusion reaction: Chills, fever, bronchospasm, stridor, hoarseness, urticaria, and/or hypotension. Institute supportive measures immediately, including epinephrine, corticosteroids, IV antihistamines, bronchodilators, and oxygen. Carefully monitor until complete resolution of all S&S.
- Monitor pulmonary status and report onset of acute or worsening pulmonary symptoms.
- Lab tests: Periodic CBC with differential, Hct and Hgb.

Patient & Family Education

- During the infusion, report promptly difficulty breathing, wheezing, shortness of breath, hives, faintness and/or dizziness.
- Report promptly any of the following: Eye inflammation, mouth sores, skin rash, redness, or severe dry skin.
- Wear sunscreen and a hat and limit sun exposure while being treated with this drug.

CHLORAMPHENICOL

(klor-am-fen'i-kole)

Chloromycetin, Isopto, Fenicol, Pentamycetin ◆

CHLORAMPHENICOL SODIUM SUCCINATE

Chloromycetin Sodium Succinate
Classification(s): ANTIBIOTIC
Therapeutic: ANTIBACTERIAL
Pregnancy Category: C

USES Severe infections when other antibiotics are ineffective or are contraindicated. Also used in cystic fibrosis antiinfective regimens.

INDICATION & DOSAGE

Serious Infections

Adult: 50 mg/kg/day in 4 divided doses.
Child/Infant: 50–75 mg/kg/day divided q6h (max: 4 g/day)
Neonate: 25–50 mg/kg/day divided q12–24h

Meningitis

Adult/Child: 75–100 mg/kg/day divided q6h

SOLUTION PREPARATION

- *Vial Reconstitution:* To each 1 g, add 10 mL of sterile water for injection or D5W to create a 10% solution. May be given as prepared direct IV as a bolus dose or further diluted for infusion.

Common adverse effects in *italic*, life-threatening effects <u>underlined</u>: generic names in **bold**; classifications in SMALL CAPS; ◆ Canadian drug name; ● Prototype drug

- *Further Dilution of Reconstituted Solution:* Add required dose to 50–100 mL of D5W.
- Maximum Concentration: 100 mg/mL

STORAGE
Solution for infusion may form crystals or a second layer when stored at low temperatures. Solution can be clarified by shaking vial. Do not use cloudy solutions.

ADMINISTRATION
- **Direct IV Injection:** Give over at least 1 min.
- **Intermittent Infusion:** Infuse over 15–30 min.

INCOMPATIBILITIES Solutions/additives: Chlorpromazine, hydroxyzine, metoclopramide, polymyxin B, prochlorperazine, promethazine, TETRACYCLINES, **vancomycin. Y-site: Fluconazole.**

ACTION & *THERAPEUTIC EFFECT* Synthetic broad-spectrum antibiotic principally bacteriostatic but may be bactericidal for certain organisms, or when given in higher concentrations. Believed to act by binding to the 50S ribosome of bacteria and thus interferes with protein synthesis. *Effective against a wide variety of gram-negative and gram-positive bacteria and most anaerobic microorganisms.*

CONTRAINDICATIONS History of hypersensitivity or toxic reaction to chloramphenicol; treatment of minor infections, prophylactic use; typhoid carrier state, history or family history of drug-induced bone marrow depression, concomitant therapy with drugs that produce bone marrow depression; pregnancy (category C); lactation.
CAUTIOUS USE Impaired hepatic or renal function; intermittent porphyria; patients with G6PD deficiency; patient or family history of drug-induced bone marrow depression; premature and full-term infants, children.

ADVERSE EFFECTS (≥1%) **Body as a Whole:** Hypersensitivity, angioedema, dyspnea, fever, anaphylaxis, superinfections, Gray syndrome. **GI:** Nausea, vomiting, diarrhea, perianal irritation, enterocolitis, glossitis, stomatitis, unpleasant taste, xerostomia. **Hematologic:** Bone marrow depression (dose-related and reversible): Reticulocytosis, leukopenia, granulocytopenia, thrombocytopenia, increased plasma iron, reduced Hgb, hypoplastic anemia, hypoprothrombinemia. Non–dose-related and irreversible pancytopenia, agranulocytosis, aplastic anemia, paroxysmal nocturnal hemoglobinuria, leukemia. **CNS:** Neurotoxicity: Headache, mental depression, confusion, delirium, digital paresthesias, peripheral neuritis. **Skin:** Urticaria, contact dermatitis, maculopapular and vesicular rashes, fixed-drug eruptions. **Special Senses:** Visual disturbances, optic neuritis, optic nerve atrophy, contact conjunctivitis.

DIAGNOSTIC TEST INTERFERENCE Possibility of false-positive results for *urine glucose* by *copper reduction methods* (e.g., *Benedict's solution, Clinitest*). Chloramphenicol may interfere with *17-OHCS* (urinary steroid) determinations (modification of *Reddy, Jenkins, Thorn procedure* not affected), with *urobilinogen excretion,* and with responses to *tetanus toxoid* and possibly other active immunizing agents.

DRUG INTERACTIONS The metabolism of **chlorpropamide, dicumarol, phenytoin, tolbutamide** may be decreased, prolonging their activity. **Phenobarbital** decreases chloramphenicol levels. The response to **iron** preparations, **folic acid,** and **vitamin B$_{12}$** may be delayed.

PHARMACOKINETICS Peak: 1 h. **Distribution:** Widely distributed to most body tissues including saliva and ascitic, pleural, and synovial fluid; concentrates in liver and kidneys; penetrates CNS; crosses placenta. **Metabolism:** Primarily inactivated in liver. **Elimination:** Much longer in neonates; metabolite and free drug excreted in urine; excreted in breast milk. **Half-Life:** 1.5–4.1 h.

NURSING IMPLICATIONS

Assessment & Drug Effects

▪ Prior to initiating therapy: Baseline C&S tests (start drug pending results).
▪ Lab tests: Baseline CBC, platelets, serum iron, and reticulocyte cell counts before initiation of therapy, at 48 h intervals during therapy, and periodically thereafter; weekly chloramphenicol blood levels or more frequently with hepatic dysfunction and with therapy for longer than 2 wk (desired concentrations: Peak 10–20 mcg/mL; through 5–10 mcg/mL).
▪ Monitor blood studies. Report promptly leukopenia, thrombocytopenia, or anemia.
▪ Monitor for S&S of peripheral neuropathy.
▪ Monitor I&O ratio or pattern and report any appreciable change.
▪ Monitor diabetics for loss of glycemic control.
▪ Monitor for S&S of Gray syndrome, which has occurred 2–9 days after initiation of high dose chloramphenicol therapy in premature infants and neonates and in children 2 y or younger. Report early signs: Abdominal distention, failure to feed, pallor, changes in vital signs.

Patient & Family Education

▪ A bitter taste may occur 15–20 sec after IV injection; it usually lasts only 2–3 min.
▪ Report immediately sore throat, fever, fatigue, petechiae, nose bleeds, bleeding gums, or other unusual bleeding or bruising, or any other suspicious sign or symptom.
▪ Report promptly S&S of superinfection (see Appendix C).

CHLOROTHIAZIDE

(klor-oh-thye′a-zide)

Diuril

CHLOROTHIAZIDE SODIUM

Diuril

Classification(s): ELECTROLYTE & WATER BALANCE AGENT; THIAZIDE DIURETIC
Therapeutic: DIURETIC
Pregnancy Category: C

Common adverse effects in *italic*, life-threatening effects underlined: generic names in **bold**; classifications in SMALL CAPS; ✦ Canadian drug name; ❂ Prototype drug

USES Adjunctively to manage edema associated with CHF, hepatic cirrhosis, renal dysfunction, corticosteroid, or estrogen therapy.
UNLABELED USES To reduce polyuria of central and nephrogenic diabetes insipidus, to prevent calcium-containing renal stones, and to treat renal tubular acidosis.

INDICATION & DOSAGE

Edema
Adult: 500 mg–1 g/day in 1–2 divided doses

SOLUTION PREPARATION
- *Vial Reconstitution:* Reconstitute the 500 mg vial with at least 18 mL sterile water for injection. May be given as prepared direct IV as a bolus dose or further diluted with D5W or NS for infusion.
- *Further Dilution of Reconstituted Solution:* Add required dose to 50–100 mL D5W or NS.

STORAGE
Store powder vials at 15°–30° C (59°–86° F). Unused reconstituted IV solutions may be stored at room temperature up to 24 h.

ADMINISTRATION
- **Direct IV Injection:** Give at a rate of 500 mg over at least 5 min.
- **Intermittent Infusion:** Give at a rate determined by the amount of IV fluid but not to exceed 500 mg over at least 5 min.
- Monitor IV site closely for extravasation. Thiazide preparations are extremely irritating to the tissues, and great care **must be** taken to avoid extravasation. If infiltration occurs, stop medication, remove needle, and apply ice if area is small.

INCOMPATIBILITIES Solution/additive: Amikacin, chlorpromazine, hydralazine, insulin, morphine, norepinephrine, polymyxin B, procaine, prochlorperazine, promazine, promethazine, streptomycin, triflupromazine, vancomycin. Y-site: TPN.

ACTION & *THERAPEUTIC EFFECT* Thiazide diuretic that has a primary action of diuresis by direct action on the distal convoluted tubules of the nephron. Inhibits reabsorption of sodium, potassium, and chloride ions. Promotes renal excretion of sodium (and water), bicarbonate, and potassium. *Reduces extracellular and intravascular fluid volumes, thus decreasing edema. Antihypertensive mechanism is due to decreased peripheral resistance and reduced blood pressure.*

CONTRAINDICATIONS Hypersensitivity to thiazide or sulfonamides; anuria, renal failure, hypokalemia; jaundiced neonates; SLE; pregnancy (category C).
CAUTIOUS USE History of sulfa allergy; impaired renal or hepatic function or gout; hypercalcemia, diabetes mellitus, older adult or debilitated patients, pancreatitis, sympathectomy.

ADVERSE EFFECTS (≥1%) **Body as a Whole:** Fever, respiratory distress, anaphylactic reaction. **CV:** Irregular heart beat, weak pulse, orthostatic

---

Common adverse effects in *italic*, life-threatening effects underlined: generic names in **bold**; classifications in SMALL CAPS; ♣ Canadian drug name; ♦ Prototype drug

hypotension. **GI:** Vomiting, acute pancreatitis, diarrhea. **Hematologic:** <u>Agranulocytosis</u> (rare), <u>aplastic anemia</u> (rare), asymptomatic hyperuricemia, hyperglycemia, glycosuria, SIADH secretion. **Metabolic:** *Hypokalemia,* hypercalcemia, hyponatremia, hypochloremic alkalosis, elevated cholesterol and triglyceride levels. **CNS:** Unusual fatigue, dizziness, mental changes, vertigo, headache. **Skin:** Urticaria, photosensitivity, skin rash.

DIAGNOSTIC TEST INTERFERENCE Chlorothiazide (thiazides) may cause: Marked increases in **serum amylase** values, decrease in **PBI** determinations; increase in excretion of **PSP;** increase in **BSP retention;** false-negative **phentolamine** and **tyramine** tests; interference with **urine steroid** determinations, and possibly the **histamine test** for pheochromocytoma. Thiazides should be discontinued at least 3 days before **bentiromide test** (thiazides can invalidate test) and before **parathyroid function tests** because they tend to decrease calcium excretion.

DRUG INTERACTIONS Amphotericin B, CORTICOSTEROIDS increase hypokalemic effects of chlorothiazide; the hypoglycemic effects of SULFONYL-UREAS and **insulin** may be antagonized; **cholestyramine, colestipol** decrease chlorothiazide absorption; intensifies hypoglycemic and hypotensive effects of **diazoxide;** increased **potassium** and **magnesium** loss may cause **digoxin** toxicity; decreases **lithium** excretion, increasing its toxicity; increases risk of NSAID-induced renal failure and may attenuate diuresis.

PHARMACOKINETICS Onset: 15 min. **Peak:** 30 min. **Duration:** 2 h. **Distribution:** Distributed throughout extracellular tissue; concentrates in kidney; crosses placenta. **Metabolism:** Does not appear to be metabolized. **Elimination:** Excreted in urine and breast milk. **Half-Life:** 45–120 min.

NURSING IMPLICATIONS

Assessment & Drug Effects

- Monitor for therapeutic effect. Antihypertensive action of a thiazide diuretic requires several days before effects are observed; usually optimum therapeutic effect is not established for 3–4 wk.
- Lab tests: Baseline and periodic CBC with differential, serum electrolytes, CO_2, BUN, creatinine, uric acid, and blood glucose.
- Monitor for hyperglycemia. Thiazide therapy can cause hyperglycemia (see Appendix C) and glycosuria in diabetic and diabetic-prone individuals. Dosage adjustment of hypoglycemic drugs may be required.
- Monitor patients with gout. Asymptomatic hyperuricemia can be produced because of interference with uric acid excretion.
- Establish baseline weight before initiation of therapy. Weigh patient at the same time each a.m. under standard conditions. A gain of more than 1 kg (2.2) within 2 or 3 days and a gradual weight gain over the week's period is reportable. Tell patient to report signs of edema (hands, ankles, pretibial areas).
- Monitor BP closely during early drug therapy.
- Inspect skin and mucous membranes daily for evidence of petechiae in patients receiving large doses and those on prolonged therapy.

Common adverse effects in *italic*, life-threatening effects <u>underlined</u>: generic names in **bold**; classifications in SMALL CAPS; ♣ Canadian drug name; ● Prototype drug

- Monitor I&O rates and patterns: Excessive diuresis or oliguria may cause electrolyte imbalance and necessitate prompt dosage adjustment.
- Monitor patients on digitalis therapy for S&S of hypokalemia (see Appendix C). Even moderate reduction in serum potassium can precipitate digitalis intoxication in these patients.

Patient & Family Education

- Urination will occur in greater amounts and with more frequency than usual, and there will be an unusual sense of tiredness. With continued therapy, diuretic action decreases; hypotensive effects usually are maintained, and sense of tiredness diminishes.
- If orthostatic hypotension is a troublesome symptom (and it may be, especially in the older adult), consult prescriber for measures that will help tolerate the effect and to prevent falling.
- Report to prescriber any illness accompanied by prolonged vomiting or diarrhea.
- Report S&S of hypokalemia, hypercalcemia, or hyperglycemia (see Appendix C).
- Report photosensitivity reaction to prescriber if it occurs. Thiazide-related photosensitivity is considered a photoallergy (radiation changes drug structure and makes it allergenic for some individuals). It occurs $1^1/_2$ –2 wk after initial sun exposure.

CHLORPROMAZINE 🄿

(klor-proe′ma-zeen)

CHLORPROMAZINE HYDROCHLORIDE

Chlorpromanyl ✦, Largactil ✦, Novochlorpromazine ✦, Thorazine
Classification(s): PHENOTHIAZINE
Therapeutic: ANTIEMETIC
Pregnancy Category: C

USES Intractable hiccups, nausea/vomiting during surgery, and as adjunct in treatment of tetanus.

INDICATION & DOSAGE

Tetanus
Adult: 25–50 mg q6–8h
Child: 0.5 mg/kg q6–8h

Nausea and Vomiting during Surgery
Adult/Adolescent: 2 mg q2min prn (max total: 25 mg)
Child/Infant (over 6 mo): 1 mg q2min prn (max total: 0.25 mg/kg)

Intractable Hiccups
Adult/Adolescent: 25–50 mg in 500–1000 mL NS, not to exceed 1 mg/min

Common adverse effects in *italic*, life-threatening effects <u>underlined</u>: generic names in **bold**; classifications in SMALL CAPS; ✦ Canadian drug name; 🄿 Prototype drug

157

SOLUTION PREPARATION

- *Direct IV Injection:* Dilute each 25 mg in 24 mL of NS to yield 1 mg/mL. May be given as prepared direct IV as a bolus dose or further diluted for infusion.
- *Intermittent Infusion:* Required dose may be added to 500–1000 mL of NS for infusion.

STORAGE

Store between 15°–30° C (59°–86° F) protected from light. Discard if solution is markedly discolored (should be colorless to pale yellow).

ADMINISTRATION

- Avoid contact with skin, eyes, and clothing because of the potential for contact dermatitis.
- **Direct IV Injection:** Give 1 mg or fraction thereof over 1 min for adults and over 2 min for children.
- **Intermittent Infusion:** Give slowly at a rate not to exceed 1 mg/min for adults or 1 mg over 2 min for children.
- Keep patient recumbent during infusion and for at least 30 min after administration. Observe closely. Report hypotensive reactions.

INCOMPATIBILITIES Solution/additive: Aminophylline, amphotericin B, ampicillin, chloramphenicol, chlorothiazide, furosemide, methohexital, penicillin G, phenobarbital. Y-site: Allopurinol, amifostine, amphotericin B cholesteryl complex, aztreonam, bivalirudin, cefepime, etoposide, fludarabine, furosemide, lansoprazole, linezolid, melphalan, methotrexate, paclitaxel, piperacillin/ tazobactam, remifentanil, sargramostim.

ACTION & *THERAPEUTIC EFFECT* Phenothiazine derivative with actions at all levels of CNS including actions on hypothalamus and reticular formation produce strong sedation, hypotension, and depressed temperature regulation. Has strong alpha-adrenergic antagonist action. Antiemetic effect due to suppression of the chemoreceptor trigger zone (CTZ). *Has antiemetic effects due to its action on the CTZ.*

CONTRAINDICATIONS Hypersensitivity to phenothiazine drugs; sulfite or benzyl alcohol; withdrawal states from alcohol; comatose states, brain damage, bone marrow depression, Reye's syndrome; children less than 6 mo; pregnancy (category C), lactation.

CAUTIOUS USE Agitated states accompanied by depression, seizure disorders, respiratory impairment due to infection or COPD; glaucoma, diabetes, hypertensive disease, peptic ulcer, prostatic hypertrophy; thyroid, cardiovascular, and hepatic disorders; patients exposed to extreme heat or organophosphate insecticides; previously detected breast cancer.

ADVERSE EFFECTS (≥1%) **Body as a Whole:** Idiopathic edema, muscle necrosis (following IM), SLE-like syndrome, <u>sudden unexplained death</u>. **CV:** Orthostatic hypotension, palpitation, tachycardia, ECG changes (usually reversible): Prolonged QT and PR intervals, blunting of T waves, ST

Common adverse effects in *italic*, life-threatening effects <u>underlined</u>: generic names in **bold**; classifications in SMALL CAPS; ♣ Canadian drug name; ☢ Prototype drug

depression. **GI:** Dry mouth; constipation, <u>adynamic ileus</u>, cholestatic jaundice, aggravation of peptic ulcer, dyspepsia, increased appetite. **Hematologic:** <u>Agranulocytosis</u>, thrombocytopenic purpura, <u>pancytopenia</u> (rare). **Metabolic:** Weight gain, hypoglycemia, hyperglycemia, glycosuria (high doses), enlargement of parotid glands. **CNS:** *Sedation, drowsiness,* dizziness, restlessness, <u>neuroleptic malignant syndrome</u>, tardive dyskinesias, tumor, syncope, headache, weakness, insomnia, reduced REM sleep, bizarre dreams, cerebral edema, convulsive seizures, <u>hypothermia</u>, inability to sweat, depressed cough reflex, *extrapyramidal symptoms,* EEG changes. **Respiratory:** Laryngospasm. **Skin:** Fixed-drug eruption, urticaria, reduced perspiration, contact dermatitis, exfoliative dermatitis, photosensitivity, eczema, anaphylactoid reactions, hypersensitivity vasculitis; hirsutism (long-term therapy). **Special Senses:** Blurred vision, lenticular opacities, mydriasis, photophobia. **Urogenital:** Anovulation, infertility, pseudopregnancy, menstrual irregularity, gynecomastia, galactorrhea, priapism, inhibition of ejaculation, reduced libido, urinary retention and frequency.

DIAGNOSTIC TEST INTERFERENCE Chlorpromazine (phenothiazines) may increase ***cephalin flocculation,*** and possibly other ***liver function tests;*** also may increase ***PBI.*** False-positive result may occur for ***amylase, 5-bydroxyindole acetic acid, porphobilinogens, urobilinogen (Ehrlich's reagent),*** and ***urine bilirubin (Bili-Labstix).*** False-positive or false-negative ***pregnancy test*** results possibly caused by a metabolite of phenothiazines, which discolors urine depending on test used.

DRUG INTERACTIONS Alcohol, CNS DEPRESSANTS increase CNS depression; **phenobarbital** increases metabolism of PHENOTHIAZINES; GENERAL ANESTHETICS increase excitation and hypotension; antagonizes antihypertensive action of **guanethidine;** TRICYCLIC ANTIDEPRESSANTS intensify hypotensive and anticholinergic effects; ANTICONVULSANTS decrease seizure threshold—may need to increase anticonvulsant dose.

PHARMACOKINETICS Duration: 4–6 h. **Distribution:** Widely distributed; accumulates in brain; crosses placenta. **Metabolism:** In liver by CYP 2D6 **Elimination:** Excreted in urine as metabolites; excreted in breast milk. **Half-Life:** Biphasic 2 and 30 h.

NURSING IMPLICATIONS

Assessment & Drug Effects

- Establish baseline BP (in standing and recumbent positions), and pulse, before initiating treatment.
- Monitor BP frequently. Hypotensive reactions, dizziness, and sedation are common during early therapy, particularly in patients on high doses and in the older adult receiving parenteral doses. Patients usually develop tolerance to these adverse effects; however, lower doses or longer intervals between doses may be required.
- Lab tests: Periodic CBC with differential, LFTs, urinalysis, and blood glucose.
- Monitor cardiac status with baseline ECG in patients with preexisting cardiovascular disease.

Common adverse effects in *italic*, life-threatening effects <u>underlined</u>: generic names in **bold**; classifications in SMALL CAPS; ♣ Canadian drug name; ⊘ Prototype drug

159

- Monitor for signs of neuroleptic malignant syndrome (see Appendix C). Report immediately.
- Monitor I&O ratio and pattern: Urinary retention due to mental depression and compromised renal function may occur. If serum creatinine becomes elevated, therapy should be discontinued.
- Monitor for antiemetic effect of chlorpromazine, which may obscure signs of overdosage of other drugs or other causes of nausea and vomiting.
- Report extrapyramidal symptoms that occur most often in patients on high dosage, pediatric patients with severe dehydration and acute infection, older adults, and women.
- Be alert to complaints of diminished visual acuity, reduced night vision, photophobia, and a perceived brownish discoloration of objects. Patient may be more comfortable with dark glasses.
- Monitor diabetics or prediabetics on long-term, high-dose therapy for reduced glucose tolerance and loss of glycemic control.

Patient & Family Education
- May cause pink to red-brown discoloration of urine.
- Wear protective clothing and sunscreen. Photosensitivity associated with chlorpromazine is a phototoxic reaction. Severity of response depends on amount of exposure and drug dose. Exposed skin areas have appearance of an exaggerated sunburn. Report reaction to prescriber.
- Avoid potentially hazardous activities until response to drug is known.

CIDOFOVIR
(cye-do′fo-ver)
Vistide
Classification(s): ANTIVIRAL
Therapeutic: ANTIVIRAL
Prototype: Acyclovir
Pregnancy Category: C

USES Treatment of CMV retinitis in patients with AIDS.

INDICATION & DOSAGE

CMV Retinitis (Induction)
Adult: 5 mg/kg once weekly for 2 wk. Also give 2 g probenecid 3 h prior to infusion and 1 g 8 h after infusion (4 g total).

CMV Retinitis (Maintenance)
Adult: 5 mg/kg once every 2 wk. Also give 2 g probenecid 3 h prior to infusion and 1 g 8 h after infusion (4 g total).

Renal Impairment Dosage Adjustment
If serum Cr increases by 0.3–0.4 then lower dose to 3 mg/kg.

SOLUTION PREPARATION

- *IV Infusion:* Dilute the calculated dose in 100 mL of NS.
- Thoroughly wash any skin area that comes in contact with cidofovir.

STORAGE

Store vials at 20°–25° C (68°–77° F); may store diluted IV solution at 2°–8° C (36°–46° F) for up to 24 h.

ADMINISTRATION

- Note that pre/posttreatment with probenecid is required.
- Prehydrate with IV of 1 L NS infused over 1–2 h immediately before cidofovir infusion. If able to tolerate fluid load, infuse second liter of NS over 1–3 h starting at beginning (or end) of cidofovir infusion.
- **IV Infusion:** Infuse at a constant rate over 1 h using an infusion pump.
- Do not coadminister with other agents with significant nephrotoxic potential.

INCOMPATIBILITIES Data not available; do not mix with other drugs.

ACTION & *THERAPEUTIC EFFECT* Cidofovir, a nucleotide analog, suppresses cytomegalovirus (CMV) replication by inhibiting CMV DNA polymerase. *Cidofovir reduces the rate of viral DNA synthesis of CMV. It is limited for use in treating CMV retinitis in patients with AIDS.*

CONTRAINDICATIONS Hypersensitivity to cidofovir, history of severe hypersensitivity to probenecid or other sulfa-containing medications; severe renal dysfunction; childbearing women and men without barrier contraception; pregnancy (category C); lactation. Safety and effectiveness in children not established.

CAUTIOUS USE Renal function impairment, history of diabetes, myelosuppression, previous hypersensitivity to other nucleoside analogs; older adults.

ADVERSE EFFECTS (≥1%) **Body as a Whole:** Infection, allergic reactions. **GI:** Nausea, vomiting, diarrhea. **Metabolic:** Metabolic acidosis. **Hematologic:** Neutropenia. **CNS:** *Fever, headache,* asthenia. **Respiratory:** Dyspnea, pneumonia. **Special Senses:** Ocular hypotony. **Urogenital:** *Nephrotoxicity, proteinuria.*

DRUG INTERACTIONS AMINOGLYCOSIDES, **amphotericin B, foscarnet, pentamidine, tacrolimus** can increase risk of nephrotoxicity.

PHARMACOKINETICS Duration: Probenecid increases serum levels and area under concentration–time curve. **Elimination:** 80–100% recovered in urine, probenecid delays urinary excretion.

NURSING IMPLICATIONS

Assessment & Drug Effects

- Evaluate concurrent medications. Nephrotoxic drugs are usually discontinued 7 days prior to starting cidofovir.
- Lab tests: Baseline and periodic serum creatinine, urine protein; periodic WBC count with differential prior to each dose.
- Periodically monitor visual acuity and intraocular pressure.
- Monitor for S&S of hypersensitivity (see Appendix C). Report their appearance promptly.

Common adverse effects in *italic,* life-threatening effects <u>underlined</u>: generic names in **bold**; classifications in SMALL CAPS; ♣ Canadian drug name; ◑ Prototype drug

161

Patient & Family Education

- Those taking zidovudine should discontinue or decrease dose to 50% on days of cidofovir administration.
- Initiate or continue regular ophthalmologic exams.
- Be alert to potential adverse reactions caused by probenecid (e.g., headache, nausea, vomiting, hypersensitivity reactions) and cidofovir.
- Women: Use effective contraception during and 1 mo after treatment.
- Men: Use barrier contraception during and 3 mo after treatment.

CIMETIDINE ℗

(sye-met'i-deen)

Novo-Cimetine ♦, Peptol ♦

Classifications: ANTISECRETORY (H₂-RECEPTOR ANTAGONIST)
Therapeutic: ANTIULCER
Pregnancy Category: B

USES Short-term treatment of active duodenal ulcer. Also used for short-term treatment of active benign gastric ulcer, pathologic hypersecretory conditions such as Zollinger-Ellison syndrome.
UNLABELED USES Prophylaxis of stress-induced ulcers, upper GI bleeding, and aspiration pneumonitis, gastroesophageal reflux.

INDICATION & DOSAGE

GI Bleed
Adult: 37.5 mg/h continuous IV

Active Ulcer
Adult: 300 mg q6h

Pathologic Hypersecretory Disease
Adult: 300 mg q6–8h, may increase up to 2400 mg/day

Renal Impairment Dosage Adjustment
CrCl less than 30 mL/min: Dose q12h

Hemodialysis Dosage Adjustment
Give scheduled dose at the end of dialysis.

SOLUTION PREPARATION

- Compatible IV solution include D5W, NS, LR, and combinations thereof.
- *Direct IV Injection:* Dilute 300 mg in 18 mL of D5W or other compatible solution to yield 300 mg/20 mL.
- *Intermittent Infusion:* Dilute 300 mg in 50 mL D5W or other compatible solution.

Common adverse effects in *italic*, life-threatening effects <u>underlined</u>: generic names in **bold**; classifications in SMALL CAPS; ♦ Canadian drug name; ℗ Prototype drug

- *Continuous Infusion:* Dilute in up to 1000 mL of D5W or other compatible solution.

STORAGE
- Store at 15°–30° C (59°–86° F) protected from light.
- IV solutions are stable for 48 h at room temperature when added to commonly used IV solutions for dilution.

ADMINISTRATION
- Note: Rapid infusion increases the risk of arrhythmias and hypotension.
- **Direct IV Injection:** Give 300 mg or fraction thereof over at least 5 min.
- **Intermittent Infusion:** Infuse over 15–20 min.
- **Continuous Infusion:** Infuse a loading dose of 150 mg at the intermittent infusion rate; then infuse remainder equally spaced over 24 h.

INCOMPATIBILITIES Solution/additive: Amphotericin B, cefazolin, chlorpromazine, pentobarbital, phenobarbital, secobarbital. Y-site: Allopurinol, amphotericin B cholesteryl complex, amsacrine, cefepime, indomethacin, lansoprazole, phenytoin, warfarin.

ACTION & *THERAPEUTIC EFFECT* Has high selectivity for histamine H_2-receptors on parietal cells of the stomach and is an H_2-receptor antagonist. By inhibition of histamine at the H_2-receptor sites, it suppresses all phases of daytime and nocturnal basal gastric acid secretion in the stomach. Indirectly reduces pepsin secretion. *Blocks the H_2-receptors on the parietal cells of the stomach, thus decreasing gastric acid secretion, raises the pH of the stomach and, thereby, reduces pepsin secretion.*

CONTRAINDICATIONS Known hypersensitivity to cimetidine or other H_2-receptor antagonists; lactation; children less than 16 y.
CAUTIOUS USE Older adults or critically ill patients; impaired renal or hepatic function; organic brain syndrome; gastric ulcers; immunocompromised patients, pregnancy (category B).

ADVERSE EFFECTS (≥1%) **Body as a Whole:** Fever, transient pain at IM site. **CV:** (Rare) <u>Cardiac arrhythmias and cardiac arrest</u> after rapid IV bolus dose. **GI:** Mild transient diarrhea, severe diarrhea, constipation, abdominal discomfort. **Hematologic:** Increased prothrombin time; neutropenia (rare), thrombocytopenia (rare), <u>aplastic anemia</u>. **Metabolic:** Slight increase in serum uric acid, BUN, creatinine. **Musculoskeletal:** Exacerbation of joint symptoms in patients with preexisting arthritis. **CNS:** Drowsiness, dizziness, light-headedness, depression, headache, reversible confusional states, paranoid psychosis. **Skin:** Rash, <u>Stevens-Johnson syndrome</u>, reversible alopecia. **Urogenital:** Gynecomastia and breast soreness, galactorrhea, reversible impotence.

DIAGNOSTIC TEST INTERFERENCE Cimetidine may cause false-positive *Hemoccult test for gastric bleeding* if test is performed within 15 min of oral cimetidine administration.

DRUG INTERACTIONS Cimetidine decreases the hepatic metabolism of **warfarin, phenobarbital, phenytoin, diazepam, propranolol, lidocaine, theophylline,** increasing their activity and toxicity.

Common adverse effects in *italic*, life-threatening effects <u>underlined</u>: generic names in **bold**; classifications in SMALL CAPS; ♣ Canadian drug name; ◍ Prototype drug

163

C

PHARMACOKINETICS Peak: 1–1.5 h. **Distribution:** Widely distributed; crosses blood–brain barrier and placenta. **Metabolism:** Metabolized in liver by CYP 1A2 and 3A4. **Elimination:** Most of drug excreted in urine in 24 h; excreted in breast milk. **Half-Life:** 2 h.

NURSING IMPLICATIONS

Assessment & Drug Effects

- Monitor HR during first few days of drug regimen. Report bradycardia after IV administration. HR usually returns to normal within 24 h after drug discontinuation.
- Monitor I&O ratio and pattern, particularly in the older adult, severely ill, and in patients with impaired renal function.
- Monitor bowel sounds. Adynamic ileus has been reported in patients receiving cimetidine to prevent and treat stress ulcers.
- Lab tests: Periodic CBC, renal function tests, and LFTs.
- Monitor for and report promptly onset of confusional states, particularly in the older adult or severely ill patient. Symptoms occur within 2–3 days after first dose.
- Check BP if patient complains of severe headache.

Patient & Family Education

- Report breast tenderness, enlargement, or discharge.
- Avoid driving and other potentially hazardous activities until reaction to drug is known.

CIPROFLOXACIN HYDROCHLORIDE ℗

(ci-pro-flox′a-cin)

Cipro IV

Classification(s): ANTIBIOTIC, QUINOLONE
Therapeutic: ANTIBACTERIAL
Pregnancy Category: C

USES UTI, lower respiratory tract infections, skin and skin structure infections, bone and joint infections, GI infection or infectious diarrhea, chronic bacterial prostatitis, nosocomial pneumonia.

INDICATION & DOSAGE

Uncomplicated UTI

Adult: 200 mg q12h × 7–14 days

Complicated UTI

Adult: 400 mg q12h × 7–14 days

Moderate to Severe Systemic Infection

Adult: 200–400 mg q8–12h

Common adverse effects in *italic*, life-threatening effects <u>underlined</u>: generic names in **bold**; classifications in SMALL CAPS; ♣ Canadian drug name; ℗ Prototype drug

Renal Impairment Dosage Adjustment
CrCl less than 30 mL/min: 200–400 mg q18–24h

SOLUTION PREPARATION

- *Intermittent Infusion:* Dilute the 200 mg or 400 mg vial in NS, D5W, D5/1/2NS to a final concentration of 0.5–2 mg/mL. Typical dilutions are 200 mg in 100–250 mL and 400 mg in 250–500 mL.

STORAGE

Reconstituted IV solution is stable for 14 days refrigerated.

ADMINISTRATION

- **Intermittent Infusion:** Infuse slowly over 60 min. Avoid rapid infusion and use of a small vein.
- Discontinue other IV infusion while infusing ciprofloxacin or infuse through another site.

INCOMPATIBILITIES Solution/additive: Aminophylline, amoxicillin, amoxicillin/clavulanate potassium, amphotericin B, ampicillin/sulbactam, ceftazidime, cefuroxime, clindamycin, heparin, metronidazole, piperacillin, sodium bicarbonate, ticarcillin. Y-site: Aminophylline, ampicillin/sulbactam, azithromycin, cefepime, dexamethasone, drotrecogin alfa, furosemide, heparin, hydrocortisone, lansoprazole, magnesium sulfate, methylprednisolone, phenytoin, potassium phospate, propofol, sodium bicarbonate, sodium phosphates, TPN, warfarin.

ACTION & *THERAPEUTIC EFFECT* Synthetic quinolone that is a broad-spectrum bactericidal agent. Inhibits DNA-gyrase, an enzyme necessary for bacterial DNA replication and some aspects of transcription, repair, recombination, and transposition. *Effective against many gram-positive and gram-negative organisms.*

CONTRAINDICATIONS Known hypersensitivity to ciprofloxacin or other quinolones; syphilis; viral infection; tendon inflammation or tendon pain; pregnant women (category C).

CAUTIOUS USE Known or suspected CNS disorders (i.e., severe cerebral arteriosclerosis or seizure disorders); myasthenia gravis; myocardial ischemia, atrial fibrillation, QT prolongation, CHF; GI disease, colitis; CVA; uncorrected hypokalemia; patients receiving theophylline derivatives or caffeine; severe renal impairment and crystalluria during ciprofloxacin therapy; patients on coumarin therapy; children.

ADVERSE EFFECTS (≥1%) **GI:** Nausea, vomiting, diarrhea, cramps, gas, pseudomembranous colitis. **Metabolic:** Transient increases in liver transaminases, alkaline phosphatase, lactic dehydrogenase, and eosinophilia count. **Musculoskeletal:** Tendon rupture, cartilage erosion. **CNS:** Headache, vertigo, malaise, peripheral neuropathy, seizures (especially with rapid IV infusion). **Skin:** Rash, phlebitis, pain, burning, pruritus, and erythema at infusion site. **Special Senses:** *Local burning and discomfort, crystalline precipitate on superficial portion of cornea,* lid margin crusting, scales, foreign body sensation, itching, and conjunctival hyperemia.

Common adverse effects in *italic*, life-threatening effects <u>underlined</u>: generic names in **bold**; classifications in SMALL CAPS; ♣ Canadian drug name; ⊘ Prototype drug

165

DIAGNOSTIC TEST INTERFERENCE Ciprofloxacin does not interfere with *urinary glucose* determinations using cupric sulfate solution or with *glucose oxidase tests;* may cause false positive on *opiate screening tests.*

DRUG INTERACTIONS May increase **theophylline** levels 15–30%; may increase effect of oral ANTIDIABETIC medications; may increase PT for patients on **warfarin.**

PHARMACOKINETICS Peak: 1–2 h. **Distribution:** Widely distributed including prostate, lung, and bone; crosses placenta; distributed into breast milk. **Elimination:** Excreted primarily in urine with some biliary excretion. **Half-Life:** 3.5–4 h.

NURSING IMPLICATIONS

Assessment & Drug Effects

- Prior to initiating therapy: Baseline C&S tests (start drug pending results).
- Report tendon inflammation or pain. Drug should be discontinued.
- Lab tests: Monitor urine pH; it should be less than 6.8, especially in the older adult and patients receiving high dosages of ciprofloxacin, to reduce the risk of crystalluria.
- Monitor I&O ratio and patterns: Patients should be well hydrated; assess for S&S of crystalluria.
- Monitor plasma theophylline concentrations, since ciprofloxacin may prolong theophylline half-life.
- Administration with theophylline derivatives or caffeine can cause CNS stimulation.
- Assess for S&S of GI irritation (e.g., nausea, diarrhea, vomiting, abdominal discomfort) in clients receiving high dosages and in older adults.
- Monitor PT and INR in patients receiving warfarin therapy.
- Assess for S&S of superinfections (see Appendix C).

Patient & Family Education

- Fluid intake of 2–3 L/day is advised, if not contraindicated.
- Report promptly any of the following: Sudden, unexplained joint pain; nausea, diarrhea, vomiting, and abdominal pain or discomfort.
- Use caution with hazardous activities until reaction to drug is known. Drug may cause light-headedness.

CISATRACURIUM BESYLATE

(cis-a-tra-kyoo-ri′um)

Nimbex

Classification(s): SKELETAL MUSCLE RELAXANT, NONDEPOLARIZING
Therapeutic: NEUROMUSCULAR BLOCKING AGENT
Prototype: Atracurium
Pregnancy Category: B

Common adverse effects in *italic*, life-threatening effects <u>underlined</u>: generic names in **bold**; classifications in SMALL CAPS; ◆ Canadian drug name; ◐ Prototype drug

USES Adjunct to general anesthesia to facilitate tracheal intubation and provide skeletal muscle relaxation during surgery or mechanical ventilation.

INDICATION & DOSAGE

Intubation
Adult: 0.15 or 0.20 mg/kg
Child: 0.1–0.15 mg/kg
Infant: 0.15 mg/kg

Maintenance
Adult: 0.03 mg/kg q20min prn *or* 1–2 mcg/kg/min
Child: 1–2 mcg/kg/min

Mechanical Ventilation in ICU
Adult: 3 mcg/kg/min (can range from 0.5 to 10.2 mcg/kg/min)

SOLUTION PREPARATION
- *Direct IV Injection:* No dilution required for bolus dose.
- *IV Infusion:* Dilute 10 mg in 95 mL of compatible IV fluid to yield 0.1 mg/mL. Alternatively, dilute 40 mg in 80 mL of compatible IV solution to yield 0.4 mg/mL. Compatible fluids include D5W, NS, D5/NS, D5/LR.
- *Mechanical Ventilation IV Infusion:* Dilute the contents of the 200 mg vial (i.e., 10 mg/mL) in 1000 mL or 500 mL of D5W, NS, D5/NS, D5/LR to yield 0.2 mg/mL or 0.4 g/mL, respectively.

STORAGE
Refrigerate vials at 2°–8° C (36°–46° F). Protect from light. Diluted solutions may be stored refrigerated or at room temperature for 24 h.

ADMINISTRATION
- Note that 10-mL multiple-dose vials contain benzyl alcohol and should not be used with neonates.
- **Direct IV Injection:** Give a bolus dose over 5–10 sec.
- **IV Infusion:** Adjust the rate based on patient's weight and the concentration of solution used (i.e., 0.1 mg/mL, 0.2 mg/mL, or 0.4 mg/mL).
- Give only by or under supervision of expert clinician familiar with the drug's actions and potential complications.
- Have immediately available personnel and facilities for resuscitation and life support and an antagonist of cisatracurium.

INCOMPATIBILITIES Solution/additive: Ketorolac, propofol (dose dependent). **Y-site: Amphotericin B, amphotericin B cholesteryl complex, ampicillin, cefazolin, cefotaxime, cefotetan, cefuroxime, diazepam, furosemide, ganciclovir, heparin, methylprednisolone, sodium bicarbonate, thiopental, trimethoprim/sulfamethoxazole.**

ACTION & *THERAPEUTIC EFFECT* Cisatracurium is a neuromuscular blocking agent that binds competitively to cholinergic receptors on motor endplate of neurons, antagonizing the action of acetylcholine. *Antagonism of acetylcholine blocks neuromuscular transmission of nerve impulses. This*

Common adverse effects in *italic*, life-threatening effects <u>underlined</u>: generic names in **bold**; classifications in SMALL CAPS; ♣ Canadian drug name; ✪ Prototype drug

action can be reversed or antagonized by acetylcholinesterase inhibitors (e.g., neostigmine).

CONTRAINDICATIONS Hypersensitivity to cisatracurium or other related agents; rapid-sequence endotracheal intubation; infants less than 1 mo.
CAUTIOUS USE History of hemiparesis, electrolyte imbalances, burn patients; pulmonary disease, COPD; neuromuscular diseases (e.g., myasthenia gravis), older adults, renal function impairment; pregnancy (category B), lactation.

ADVERSE EFFECTS (≥1%) **CV:** Bradycardia, hypotension, flushing. **Respiratory:** Bronchospasm. **Skin:** Rash. Effects may be potentiated by GENERAL ANESTHETICS.

PHARMACOKINETICS Onset: Varies with dose from 1.5 to 3.3 min (higher the dose, faster the onset). **Peak:** Varies from 1.5 to 3.3 min (higher the dose, faster to peak). **Duration:** Varies from 46 to 121 min (higher dose, longer recovery time). **Metabolism:** Undergoes Hoffman elimination (pH- and temperature-dependent degradation) and hydrolysis by plasma esterases. **Elimination:** Excreted in urine. **Half-Life:** 22 min.

NURSING IMPLICATIONS

Assessment & Drug Effects
- Use peripheral nerve stimulator to monitor effect of drug.
- Time-to-maximum neuromuscular block is approximately 1 min slower in the older adult.
- Monitor for bradycardia, hypotension, and bronchospasms; monitor ICU patients for spontaneous seizures.

CISPLATIN (cis-DDP, cis-PLATINUM II)
(sis'pla-tin)

Abiplatin ♦, Platinol
Classification(s): ANTINEOPLASTIC; ALKYLATING AGENT
Therapeutic: ANTINEOPLASTIC
Prototype: Cyclophosphamide
Pregnancy Category: D

USES Established combination therapy (cisplatin, vinblastine, bleomycin) in patient with metastatic testicular tumors and with doxorubicin for metastatic ovarian tumors following appropriate surgical or radiation therapy.
UNLABELED USES Carcinoma of endometrium, bladder, head, and neck.

INDICATION & DOSAGE

Testicular Neoplasms
Adult: 20 mg/m^2/day for 5 days q3–4wk for 3 courses

Common adverse effects in *italic*, life-threatening effects underlined: generic names in **bold**; classifications in SMALL CAPS; ♦ Canadian drug name; ⊕ Prototype drug

Ovarian Neoplasms

Adult: With cyclophosphamide: 75–100 mg/m^2 once q4wk; **Single Agent:** 100 mg/m^2 once q4wk

Advanced Bladder Cancer

Adult: 50–75 mg/m^2 q3–4wk

SOLUTION PREPARATION

- Use disposable gloves when preparing cisplatin solutions. If drug accidentally contacts skin or mucosa, wash immediately and thoroughly with soap and water. Do not use any equipment containing aluminum.
- *IV Infusion:* Withdraw required dose and dilute in 2 L D5W & 1/2 or 1/3NS containing 37.5 g mannitol (i.e., or two 1 L bags with 18.75 g mannitol each). **Do not** dilute in plain D5W.
- If solution is not used within 6 h, protect from light.

STORAGE

Store at 15°–25° C (59°–77° F). Do not refrigerate. Protect from light. Once vial is opened, solution is stable for 28 days protected from light or 7 days in fluorescent light.

ADMINISTRATION

- Administered only under supervision of a qualified prescriber experienced in the use of antineoplastics.
- Usually a parenteral antiemetic agent is administered $^{1}/_{2}$ h before cisplatin therapy is instituted and given on a scheduled basis throughout day and night as long as necessary.
- Before the initial dose is given, hydration is started with 1–2 L IV infusion fluid to reduce risk of nephrotoxicity and ototoxicity.
- **IV Infusion:** Infuse 2 L over 6–8 h. Generally, cisplatin should be given no faster than 1 mg/min.

INCOMPATIBILITIES Solution/additive: 5% dextrose, fluorouracil, mesna, metoclopramide, sodium bicarbonate, thiotepa. Y-site: Amifostine, amphotericin B cholesteryl sulfate complex, cefepime, gallium, lansoprazole, piperacillin/tazobactam, thiotepa, TPN.

ACTION & *THERAPEUTIC EFFECT* A heavy metal complex with platinum as the central atom surrounded by 2 chloride atoms and 2 ammonia molecules in the cis-chemical position. Biochemical properties similar to those of alkylating agents. Produces interstrand and intrastrand cross linkage in DNA of rapidly dividing cells, thus preventing DNA, RNA, and protein synthesis. *Cell cycle–nonspecific, i.e., antineoplastic effect occurs throughout the entire cell life cycle.*

CONTRAINDICATIONS History of hypersensitivity to cisplatin or other platinum-containing compounds; impaired renal function; active infection; severe myelosuppression; impaired hearing; history of gout and urate renal stones; renal failure; hypomagnesia; concurrent administration with loop diuretics; Raynaud syndrome; pregnancy (category D). Safe use in children not established, although experimental regimens have been used.

Common adverse effects in *italic*, life-threatening effects <u>underlined</u>: generic names in **bold**; classifications in SMALL CAPS; ♣ Canadian drug name; ⊙ Prototype drug

169

C

CAUTIOUS USE Previous cytotoxic drug or radiation therapy with other ototoxic and nephrotoxic drugs; peripheral neuropathy; hyperuricemia; electrolyte imbalances, moderate renal impairment; hepatic impairment; history of circulatory disorders.

ADVERSE EFFECTS (≥1%) **Body as a Whole:** Anaphylaxis-like reactions. **CV:** Cardiac abnormalities. **GI:** *Marked nausea, vomiting,* anorexia, stomatitis, xerostomia, diarrhea, constipation. **Hematologic:** Myelosuppression (25–30% patients): Leukopenia, thrombocytopenia; hemolytic anemia, hemolysis. **Metabolic:** Hypocalcemia, *hypomagnesemia,* hyperuricemia, elevated AST, SIADH. **CNS:** Seizures, headache; peripheral neuropathies (may be irreversible): Paresthesia, unsteady gait, clumsiness of hands and feet, exacerbation of neuropathy with exercise, loss of taste. **Special Senses:** Ototoxicity (may be irreversible): Tinnitus, hearing loss, deafness, vertigo, blurred vision, changes in ability to see colors (optic neuritis, papilledema). **Urogenital:** Nephrotoxicity.

DRUG INTERACTIONS AMINOGLYCOSIDES, **amphotericin B, vancomycin,** other **nephrotoxic drugs** increase nephrotoxicity and acute renal failure; AMINOGLYCOSIDES, **furosemide** increase risk of ototoxicity; may lower serum levels of **phenytoin.**

PHARMACOKINETICS Peak: Immediately after infusion. **Distribution:** Widely distributed in body fluids and tissues; concentrated in kidneys, liver, and prostate; accumulated in tissues. **Metabolism:** Not known. **Elimination:** 15–50% of dose excreted in urine within 24–48 h. **Half-Life:** 73–290 h.

NURSING IMPLICATIONS

Assessment & Drug Effects

- Obtain baseline ECG and cardiac monitoring during induction therapy because of possible myocarditis or focal irritability.
- Check BP, mental status, pupils, and fundi every hour during therapy. Hydration and mannitol may increase the danger of elevated intracranial pressure (ICP).
- A repeat course of therapy should not be given until (1) serum creatinine is below 1.5 mg/dL; (2) BUN is below 25 mg/dL; (3) platelets at least 100,000/mm³; (4) WBC at least 4000/mm³; (5) audiometric test is within normal limits.
- Monitor urine output and specific gravity for 4 consecutive hours before treatment and for 24 h after therapy. Report if output is less than 100 mL/h or if specific gravity is more than 1.030. A urine output of less than 75 mL/h necessitates medical intervention to avert a renal emergency.
- Lab tests: Baseline and repeated weekly during treatment period serum uric acid, serum creatinine, BUN, urinary CrCl; CBC and platelet counts weekly for 2 wk after each course of treatment; periodic serum electrolytes and LFTs.
- Monitor results of blood studies. The nadirs in platelet and leukocyte counts occur between day 18 and 23 (range: 7.5–45) with most patients recovering in 13–62 days. A decrease in Hgb (more than 2 g/dL) occurs at approximately the same time and with the same frequency.

Common adverse effects in *italic,* life-threatening effects underlined: generic names in **bold**; classifications in SMALL CAPS; ♣ Canadian drug name; ☯ Prototype drug

- Audiometric testing should be performed before the first dose and before each subsequent dose. Suspect ototoxicity if patient manifests tinnitus or difficulty hearing in the high frequency range.
- Monitor for anaphylactoid reactions (particularly in patient previously exposed to cisplatin), which may occur within minutes of drug administration.
- Nephrotoxicity (reported in 28–36% of patients receiving a single dose of 50 mg/m²) usually occurs within 2 wk after drug administration and becomes more severe and prolonged with repeated courses of cisplatin.
- Intractable nausea and vomiting severe enough to warrant discontinuation of drug usually begin 1–4 h after treatment and may last 24 h or persist for up to 1 wk after treatment is ended.
- Monitor and report abnormal bowel elimination pattern. Constipation and the possibility of fecal impaction may be caused by neurotoxicity; diarrhea is a possible response to GI irritation.
- Inspect oral membranes for xerostomia (white patches and ulcerations) and tongue for signs of fungal overgrowth (black, furry appearance).
- Institute infection precautions promptly if a temperature increase of 0.6° F over the previous reading is noted.
- Weigh the patient under standard conditions every day. A gradual ascending weight profile occurring over a period of several days should be reported.

Patient & Family Education

- Continue maintenance of adequate hydration (at least 3000 mL/24 h oral fluid if prescriber agrees) and report promptly: Reduced urinary output, flank pain, anorexia, nausea, vomiting, dry mucosae, itching skin, urine odor on breath, fluid retention, and weight gain.
- Avoid rapid changes in position to minimize risk of dizziness or falling.
- Tingling, numbness, and tremors of extremities, loss of position sense and taste, and constipation are early signs of neurotoxicity. Report their occurrence promptly to prevent irreversibility. Pain with heel walking and difficulty in getting out of bed or chair are late indicators of nerve damage.
- Report tinnitus or any hearing impairment.
- Report promptly evidence of unexplained bleeding and easy bruising.
- Report unusual fatigue, fever, sore mouth and throat, abnormal body discharges.

CLADRIBINE ℗

(cla′dri-been)

Leustatin

Classification(s): ANTINEOPLASTIC; ANTIMETABOLITE, PURINE ANTAGONIST
Therapeutic: ANTINEOPLASTC
Pregnancy Category: D

USES Treatment of hairy cell leukemia, chronic lymphocytic leukemia, non-Hodgkin's lymphomas.
UNLABELED USES Advanced cutaneous T-cell lymphomas, acute myeloid leukemia, autoimmune hemolytic anemia, mycosis fungoides.

C

INDICATION & DOSAGE

Hairy Cell Leukemia
Adult: 0.09 mg/kg/day for 7 days continuous infusion

Chronic Lymphocytic Leukemia/Non-Hodgkin's Lymphoma
Adult: 0.1 mg/kg/day for 7 days continuous infusion; repeated monthly

SOLUTION PREPARATION
- Use disposable gloves and protective clothing when handling the drug. Wash immediately if skin contact occurs.
- *IV Infusion (single daily dose):* Add the required dose to 500 mL of NS.
- *IV Infusion (7-day dose):* The required dose of cladribine is injected into an infusion reservoir using a 0.22 micron filter. An amount of bacteriostatic NS is added through a 0.22 micron filter to bring the total to 100 mL. (Note: Reservoir usually prepared by the pharmacist.)

STORAGE
- Diluted solutions of cladribine may be stored refrigerated for up to 8 h prior to administration.
- Store unopened vials in refrigerator (2°–8° C/36°–46° F), and protect from light.

ADMINISTRATION
- **IV Infusion (single daily dose):** Distribute evenly over 24 h.
- **IV Infusion (7-day dose):** Give through a central line and control by a pump device (e.g., Deltec pump) to deliver 100 mL evenly over 7 days.
- Solutions for cladribine should not be mixed with any other IV drugs or additives, nor administered through an IV line used for other drugs or solutions.

INCOMPATIBILITIES Data not available; do not mix with other drugs.

ACTION & *THERAPEUTIC EFFECT* Cladribine is a synthetic antineoplastic agent with selective toxicity toward certain normal and malignant lymphocytes and monocytes. It accumulates intracellularly, preventing repair of single-stranded DNA breaks and ultimately interfering with cellular metabolism as well as DNA synthesis. *Cladribine is cytotoxic to both actively dividing and quiescent lymphocytes and monocytes, inhibiting both DNA synthesis and repair.*

CONTRAINDICATIONS Hypersensitivity to cladribine; severe bone marrow suppression; pregnancy (category D), lactation.
CAUTIOUS USE Hepatic or renal impairment; previous radiation or chemotherapy treatments. Safety and efficacy in children not established.

ADVERSE EFFECTS (≥1%) **CNS:** Headache, dizziness. **GI:** Nausea, diarrhea. **Hematologic:** <u>*Myelosuppression (neutropenia)*</u>, *anemia,* thrombocytopenia. **Metabolic:** *Fever.* **CNS:** Headache, dizziness. **Urogenital:** Elevated serum creatinine.

DRUG INTERACTIONS Additive risk of bleeding with ANTICOAGULANTS, NSAIDS, PLATELET INHIBITORS, SALICYLATES.

PHARMACOKINETICS Onset: Therapeutic effect 10 days to 4 mo. **Duration:** 7–25-plus mo. **Distribution:** Crosses placenta; distributed into breast milk. **Metabolism:** In malignant leukemias, cladribine is phosphorylated to form active forms, which are subsequently incorporated into cellular DNA. **Half-Life:** Initial 35 min, terminal 6.7 h.

NURSING IMPLICATIONS

Assessment & Drug Effects

- Monitor vital signs during and after drug infusion. Fever over 100° F is common during the 5th to 7th day in patients with hairy cell leukemia, and severe fever (over 104° F) may develop within the first month of therapy.
- Lab tests: Frequent CBC with differential and platelet count; periodic uric acid, BUN and serum, creatinine and LFTs.
- Closely monitor hematologic status; myelosuppression is common during the first month after starting therapy.
- Monitor for and report S&S of infection. Note that within the first month, fever may occur in the absence of infection.
- With high doses of cladribine, monitor for neurologic toxicity (paraparesis/quadriparesis) and acute nephrotoxicity.

Patient & Family Education

- Be fully informed regarding adverse responses to the drug.
- Understand the need for close follow-up during and after treatment with the drug.

CLINDAMYCIN PHOSPHATE ℗ᵣ

(klin-da-mye′sin)
Cleocin Phosphate
Classification(s): ANTIBIOTIC
Therapeutic: ANTIBACTERIAL
Pregnancy Category: B

USES Serious infections when less toxic alternatives are inappropriate.
UNLABELED USES In combination with pyrimethamine for toxoplasmosis in patients with AIDS.

INDICATION & DOSAGE

Moderate to Severe Infections

Adult: 600–1200 mg/day in divided doses (max: 2700 mg/day)
Child/Infant: 20–40 mg/kg/day in divided doses
Neonate: See following table

Age	Weight	Dose	Interval
Up to 7 days	Up to 2000 g	10mg/kg/day	q12h

Common adverse effects in *italic*, life-threatening effects <u>underlined</u>: generic names in **bold**; classifications in SMALL CAPS; ♣ Canadian drug name; ℗ Prototype drug

C

Age	Weight	Dose	Interval
Up to 7 days	Over 2000 g	15 mg/kg/day	q8h
Over 7 days	Less than 1200 g	10 mg/kg/day	q12h
Over 7 days	1200–2000 g	15 mg/kg/day	q8h
Over 7 days	Over 2000 g	20 mg/kg/day	q6–8h

SOLUTION PREPARATION

- *Intermittent Infusion:* Dilute each 18 mg with at least 1 mL of D5W, NS, D5/1/2NS, or other compatible solution. Final concentration should **never exceed** 18 mg/mL. May be further diluted in 50–100 mL of IV solution.
- *Continuous Infusion:* Dilute in 500–1000 mL of compatible IV solution. Final concentration should **never exceed** 18 mg/mL.

STORAGE

May store diluted solutions for 24 h at controlled room temperature.

ADMINISTRATION

- **Never** give a bolus dose.
- **Intermittent Infusion:** Infuse at a rate not to exceed 30 mg/min (see table). **Do not** infuse more than 1200 mg in a single 1-h infusion.
- **Continuous Infusion:** Infuse at 0.75–1.25 mg/min as ordered to maintain serum levels.

Dose	Volume of Diluent	Infusion Time
300 mg	50 mL	10 min
600 mg	50 mL	20 min
900 mg	50–100 mL	30 min
1200 mg	100 mL	40 min

INCOMPATIBILITIES Solution/additive: Aminophylline, BARBITURATES, **calcium gluconate, magnesium sulfate, ceftriaxone, ciprofloxacin, gentamicin, ranitidine. Y-site: Allopurinol, azithromycin, doxapram, filgrastim, fluconazole, idarubicin, lansoprazole.**

ACTION & *THERAPEUTIC EFFECT* Semisynthetic derivative of lincomycin with a greater degree of antibacterial activity. Suppresses protein synthesis by binding to 50 S subunits of bacterial ribosomes, and, therefore. preventing peptide bond formation, which causes bacterial cells to die. *Particularly effective against susceptible strains of anaerobic streptococci as well as aerobic gram-positive cocci.*

CONTRAINDICATIONS History of hypersensitivity to clindamycin or lincomycin; history of regional enteritis, ulcerative colitis, or antibiotic-associated colitis; viral infection.

CAUTIOUS USE History of GI disease, renal or hepatic disease; atopic individuals (history of eczema, asthma, hay fever); older patients greater than 60 y; pregnancy (category B).

Common adverse effects in *italic*, life-threatening effects <u>underlined</u>: generic names in **bold**; classifications in SMALL CAPS; ✦ Canadian drug name; ● Prototype drug

ADVERSE EFFECTS (≥1%) **Body as a Whole:** Fever, serum sickness, sensitization, swelling of face (following topical use), generalized myalgia, superinfections, proctitis, vaginitis, pain, induration, sterile abscess (following IM injections), thrombophlebitis (IV infusion). **CV:** Hypotension (following IM), <u>cardiac arrest</u> (rapid IV). **GI:** *Diarrhea,* abdominal pain, flatulence, bloating, *nausea, vomiting,* <u>pseudomembranous colitis</u>, esophageal irritation, loss of taste, medicinal taste (high IV doses), jaundice, abnormal liver function tests. **Hematologic:** Leukopenia, eosinophilia, <u>agranulocytosis</u>, thrombocytopenia. **Skin:** *Skin rashes,* urticaria, pruritus, irritation.

DIAGNOSTIC TEST INTERFERENCE Clindamycin may cause increases in *serum alkaline phosphatase, bilirubin, creatine phosphokinase (CPK)* from muscle irritation following IM injection; *AST, ALT.*

DRUG INTERACTIONS Chloramphenicol, erythromycin possibly are mutually antagonistic to clindamycin; neuromuscular blocking action enhanced by NEUROMUSCULAR BLOCKING AGENTS.

PHARMACOKINETICS Distribution: Widely distributed except for CNS; crosses placenta; distributed into breast milk. **Metabolism:** Metabolized in liver. **Elimination:** Excreted in urine and feces. **Half-Life:** 2–3 h.

NURSING IMPLICATIONS

Assessment & Drug Effects

- Prior to initiating therapy: Baseline C&S tests (start drug pending results); determine previous hypersensitivity reactions.
- Lab tests: Periodic CBC with differential and platelet count.
- Monitor BP and HR. Advise patient to remain recumbent following drug administration until BP has stabilized.
- Severe diarrhea and colitis, including pseudomembranous colitis, have been associated with oral (highest incidence), parenteral, and topical clindamycin. Report immediately the onset of watery diarrhea, with or without fever; passage of tarry or bloody stools, pus, intestinal tissue, or mucus; abdominal cramps, or ileus.
- Closely observe older adults and chronically ill patients, as they are at a higher risk of developing severe colitis.
- Be alert to signs of superinfection (see Appendix C).

Patient & Family Education

- Report promptly loose stools or diarrhea that may appear within a few days to 2 wk after therapy is begun or up to several weeks following cessation of therapy.
- Do not self-medicate with antidiarrheal preparations. Antiperistaltic agents may prolong and worsen diarrhea by delaying removal of toxins from colon.

CLOFARABINE
(clo-fa-ra'been)
Clolar

Common adverse effects in *italic*, life-threatening effects <u>underlined</u>: generic names in **bold**; classifications in SMALL CAPS; ♣ Canadian drug name; ♦ Prototype drug

175

Classifications: ANTINEOPLASTIC, ANTIMETABOLITE, PURINE ANTAGONIST
Therapeutic: ANTINEOPLASTIC
Prototype: Cladribine
Pregnancy Category: D

USES Treatment of persons 1–21 y of age with relapsed or refractory acute lymphocytic leukemia (ALL) after at least 2 prior regimens.

INDICATION & DOSAGE

Acute Lymphocytic Leukemia
Adult (up to 21 y)/Adolescent/Child (over 1 y): 52 mg/m²/day for 5 days

SOLUTION PREPARATION
IV Infusion: Withdraw required dose from vial using a 0.2 micron filter syringe and further dilute in 100 mL or more of D5W or NS.

STORAGE
Store diluted solution at room temperature. Use within 24 h of mixing.

ADMINISTRATION
- **IV Infusion:** Infuse over 2 h.
- Note: It is recommended that IV fluids be given continuously throughout the 5 days of clofarabine administration do reduce adverse effects.
- Do not give drugs with known renal toxicity during the 5 days of clofarabine administration.

INCOMPATIBILITIES Data not available; do not mix with other drugs.

ACTION & *THERAPEUTIC EFFECT* Clofarabine inhibits DNA repair within cancer cells, thus interfering with mitosis; it also disrupts the mitochondrial membrane, leading to cancer cell death. *Cytotoxic to rapidly proliferating and quiescent cancer cells.*

CONTRAINDICATIONS Severe bone marrow suppression; active infection; pregnancy (category D); lactation.

CAUTIOUS USE Renal or hepatic function impairment; thrombocytopenia; neutropenia; previous chemotherapy or radiation therapy; females of child-bearing age; history of viral infections such as herpes; history of cardiac disease or hypotension.

ADVERSE EFFECTS (≥1%) **CNS:** Anxiety, depression, dizziness, headache, irritability, somnolence. **CV:** *Tachycardia,* pericardial infusion, left ventricular systolic dysfunction (LSVT). **GI:** *Vomiting, nausea, and diarrhea,* abdominal pain, constipation. **Hematologic/Lymphatic:** *Anemia, leukopenia, thrombocytopenia, neutropenia, febrile neutropenia.* **Hepatic:** Jaundice, hepatomegaly. **Metabolic:** Anorexia, decreased appetite, edema, decreased weight. **Musculoskeletal:** Arthralgia, back pain, myalgia. **Respiratory:** Cough, dyspnea, epistaxis, pleural effusion, respiratory distress. **Skin:** Dermatitis, contusion, dry skin, erythema, palmar-plantar erythrodysesthesia syndrome, pruritus. **Body as a Whole:** Increased risk of infection.

PHARMACOKINETICS Distribution: 47% protein bound. **Metabolism:** Negligible. **Elimination:** Primarily eliminated unchanged in the urine. **Half-Life:** 5.2 h.

C

NURSING IMPLICATIONS

Assessment & Drug Effects

- Monitor vital signs frequently during infusion of clofarabine.
- Monitor closely for S&S of capillary leak syndrome or systemic inflammatory response syndrome (e.g., tachypnea, tachycardia, hypotension, pulmonary edema). If either is suspected, immediately DC IV, institute supportive measures and notify prescriber.
- Lab tests: Baseline and periodic CBC and platelet counts (more frequent with cytopenias); frequent LFTs and kidney function test during the 5 days of clofarabine therapy.
- Monitor I&O rates and pattern and watch for S&S of dehydration, including dizziness, lightheadedness, fainting spells, or decreased urine output.
- Withhold drug and notify prescriber if hypotension develops for any reason during 5-day period of drug administration.

Patient & Family Education

- Report any distressing adverse effect of therapy to prescriber.
- Use effective measures to avoid pregnancy while taking this drug.

COLISTIMETHATE SODIUM

(koe-lis-ti-meth′ate)

Coly-Mycin M
Classification(s): ANTIBIOTIC
Therapeutic: ANTIBACTERIAL, URINARY TRACT
Prototype: Trimethoprim
Pregnancy Category: B

USES Particularly for severe, acute and chronic UTIs caused by susceptible strains of gram-negative organisms resistant to other antibiotics. Has been used with carbenicillin for *Pseudomonas* sepsis in children with acute leukopenia.

INDICATION & DOSAGE

Urinary Tract Infections

Adult/Child: 2.5–5 mg/kg/day divided in 2–4 doses (max: 5 mg/kg/day)

Renal Impairment Dosage Adjustment

Serum Cr 1.3–1.5 mg/dL: 2.5–3.8 mg/kg/day in 2 divided doses; *1.6–2.5 mg/dL:* 2.5 mg/kg/day in a single dose or 2 divided doses; *2.6–4 mg/dL:* 1.5 mg/kg q36h

---

Common adverse effects in *italic*, life-threatening effects underlined: generic names in **bold**; classifications in SMALL CAPS; ♣ Canadian drug name; ⊘ Prototype drug

177

SOLUTION PREPARATION

- *Vial Reconstitution:* Add 2 mL of sterile water for injection to the 150-mg vial to yield 75 mg/mL. Swirl vial gently to dissolve.
  - *First Half of Daily Dose:* Give as prepared.
  - *Second Half of Daily Dose:* **Must be** further diluted.
- *Further Dilution of Reconstituted Solution:* Add the remaining half of daily dose to 50 mL or more of D5W, NS, D5/NS, D5/1/2NS, D5/1/4NS, LR or other compatible solution. IV infusion solution should be freshly prepared and used within 24 h.

STORAGE

Reconstituted vial may be stored in refrigerator at 2°–8° C (36°–46° F) or at controlled room temperature of 15°–30° C (59°–86° F). Use within 7 days. Store unopened vials at controlled room temperature.

ADMINISTRATION

- **Direct Intermittent IV Injection:** Give first half of total daily dose slowly over 3–5 min.
- **Continuous Infusion:** Starting 1–2 h after the first half dose has been given, infuse second half of total daily dose over the next 22–23 h.

INCOMPATIBILITIES Solution/additive: Cefazolin, cephapirin, erythromycin, hydrocortisone, hydroxyzine, kanamycin.

ACTION & *THERAPEUTIC EFFECT* Antibacterial activity and overall toxicity are less, but nephrotoxic potential is almost identical with that of polymyxin B. Believed to act by affecting phospholipid component in bacterial cytoplasmic membranes with resulting damage and leakage of essential intracellular components. *Bactericidal against most gram-negative organisms. Not effective against* Proteus *or* Neisseria *species.*

CONTRAINDICATIONS Hypersensitivity to polypeptide antibiotics; concomitant use of drugs that potentiate neuromuscular blocking effect (aminoglycoside antibiotics, other polymyxins, anticholinesterases, curariform muscle relaxants, ether, sodium citrate); nephrotoxic and ototoxic drugs.

CAUTIOUS USE Impaired renal function; myasthenia gravis; older adult patients, infants; pregnancy (category B), lactation.

ADVERSE EFFECTS (≥1%) **Body as a Whole:** Drug fever, pain at IM site. **GI:** GI disturbances. **CNS:** Circumoral, lingual, and peripheral paresthesias; visual and speech disturbances, <u>neuromuscular blockade</u> (generalized muscle weakness, dyspnea, <u>respiratory depression or paralysis</u>), seizures, psychosis. **Respiratory:** <u>Respiratory arrest</u> after IM injection. **Skin:** Pruritus, urticaria, dermatoses. **Special Senses:** Ototoxicity. **Urogenital:** <u>Nephrotoxicity</u>.

DRUG INTERACTIONS Tubocurarine, pancuronium, atracurium, AMINOGLYCOSIDES may compound and prolong respiratory depression; AMINOGLYCOSIDES, **amphotericin B, vancomycin** augment nephrotoxicity.

PHARMACOKINETICS Duration: 8–12 h. **Distribution:** Widely distributed in most tissues except CNS; crosses placenta; distributed into breast milk in low concentrations. **Metabolism:** Metabolized in liver. **Elimination:** 66–75% excreted in urine within 24h. **Half-Life:** 2–3 h.

Common adverse effects in *italic*, life-threatening effects <u>underlined</u>: generic names in **bold**; classifications in SMALL CAPS; ♣ Canadian drug name; ✿ Prototype drug

NURSING IMPLICATIONS

Assessment & Drug Effects

- Prior to initiating therapy: Baseline C&S tests (start drug pending results).
- Report promptly restlessness or dyspnea. Respiratory arrest has been reported after IM administration.
- Lab tests: Baseline and frequent renal function tests. Impaired renal function increases the possibility of nephrotoxicity, apnea, and neuromuscular blockade.
- Monitor I&O ratio and patterns: Decrease in urine output or change in I&O ratio and rising BUN, serum creatinine, and serum drug levels (without dosage increase) are indications of renal toxicity. If they occur, withhold drug and report to prescriber.
- Close monitoring of older adult patients and infants is essential. They are particularly prone to renal toxicity because they tend to have inadequate renal reserves.
- Be alert to neurologic symptoms: Changes in speech and hearing, visual changes, drowsiness, dizziness, ataxia, and transient paresthesias, and keep prescriber informed.
- Monitor closely postoperative patients who have received curariform muscle relaxants, ether, or sodium citrate for signs of neuromuscular blockade (delayed recovery, muscle weakness, depressed respiration).

Patient & Family Education

- Avoid operating a vehicle or other potentially hazardous activities until reaction to drug is known.

CONIVAPTAN HYDROCHLORIDE

(con-i-vap'tin)

Vaprisol

Classification(s): ELECTROLYTIC & WATER BALANCE AGENT; VASOPRESSIN ANTAGONIST
Therapeutic: DIURETIC
Pregnancy Category: C

USES Treatment of euvolemic hyponatremia (e.g., syndrome of inappropriate secretion of antidiuretic hormone, or SIADH) in hospitalized patients.

INDICATION & DOSAGE

Euvolemic Hyponatremia

Adult: 20 mg loading dose followed by 20 mg IV over 24 h. May repeat 20 mg/day for 1–3 days, or may titrate up to 40 mg/day based on response. Total duration of infusion should not exceed 4 days.

SOLUTION PREPARATION

- Use a filter needle when withdrawing drug from an ampule.

Common adverse effects in *italic*, life-threatening effects <u>underlined</u>: generic names in **bold**; classifications in SMALL CAPS; ✢ Canadian drug name; ◐ Prototype drug

179

- *Loading Dose Infusion:* Withdraw 4 mL (20 mg) from one ampule and add to 100 mL of D5W. Gently invert the bag several times to mix.
- *Initial Maintenance Infusion:* Withdraw 4 mL (20 mg) from one ampule and add to 250 mL of D5W. Gently invert the bag several times to mix.
- *Maximum Maintenance Dose Infusion:* Withdraw 8 mL (40 mg) from two ampules and add to 250 mL of D5W. Gently invert the bag several times to mix.

STORAGE
Store vials at 25° C (77° F). Ampules should be stored in the original container and protected from light until ready for use. After diluting with D5W, the solution should be used immediately, with infusion completed within 24 h of mixing.

ADMINISTRATION
- Give via a large vein and change infusion site every 24 h.
- *Loading Dose:* Infuse over 30 min.
- *Maintenance Dose:* Infuse over 24 h.
- Discontinue infusion immediately and notify prescriber of a rise in serum sodium greater than 12 mEq/L/24 h. DO NOT resume infusion if serum sodium continues to rise. Infusion may be resumed ONLY if hyponatremia persists or reoccurs and patient demonstrates no indication of neurologic impairment. If the serum sodium rises too slowly, the dose may be titrated up to 40 mg over 24 h.

INCOMPATIBILITIES Solution/additive: **Lactated Ringer's solution, sodium chloride 0.9%.**

ACTION & *THERAPEUTIC EFFECT* Conivaptan is a vasopressin receptor (V2) antagonist that reduces the effect of vasopressin in the kidney, thus increasing the excretion of free water into the renal collecting ducts. *Conivaptan increases urine output and decreases urine osmolality in patients with euvolemic hyponatremia, thus restoring serum sodium balance.*

CONTRAINDICATIONS Hypersensitivity to conivaptan; CHF; hyponatremia associated with hypovolemia; hypotension, syncope; concurrent administration of potent CYP3A4 inhibitors such as ketoconazole, itraconazole, ritonavir, etc.; pregnancy (category C), lactation. Safety and efficacy in children not established.
CAUTIOUS USE Renal or hepatic function impairment.

ADVERSE EFFECTS (≥1%) **Body as a Whole:** Cannula-site reaction, *infusion-site reaction,* pain, peripheral edema, pyrexia, *thirst.* **CNS:** Confusional state, *headache,* insomnia. **CV:** <u>Atrial fibrillation</u>, hypertension, hypotension, orthostatic hypotension, phlebitis. **GI:** Constipation, diarrhea, dry mouth, nausea, vomiting. **Hematologic:** Anemia. **Metabolic:** Dehydration, hyperglycemia, hypoglycemia, *hypokalemia,* hypomagnesemia, hyponatremia. **Respiratory:** Pneumonia. **Skin:** Erythema. **Special Senses:** Oral candidiasis.

DRUG INTERACTIONS Compounds that inhibit CYP3A4 (e.g., **ketoconazole, itraconazole, clarithromycin, ritonavir, indinavir**) can increase conivaptan levels. Conivaptan can increase the levels of **digoxin** and drugs that require CYP3A4 for metabolism (e.g., **midazolam,** HMG COA RE-

DUCTASE INHIBITORS, **amlodipine**). **Grapefruit juice** may increase the level of conivaptan. **St. John's wort** may decrease the level of conivaptan.

PHARMACOKINETICS Distribution: 99% protein bound. **Metabolism:** Extensive hepatic metabolism. **Elimination:** Primarily fecal elimination (83%) with minor renal elimination. **Half-Life:** 5 h.

NURSING IMPLICATIONS

Assessment & Drug Effects

- Monitor infusion site for erythema, phlebitis, or other site reaction.
- Monitor vital signs and neurologic status frequently; report immediately S&S of hypernatremia (see Appendix C).
- Lab tests: Baseline and frequent serum sodium, serum potassium, and urine osmolality. A reduction in dose or discontinuation of infusion may be required if the serum sodium rises too rapidly.
- Monitor I&O closely. Effective treatment is accompanied by increased urine output, whereas decreasing urine output and oliguria may indicate developing hypernatremia.
- Concurrent drugs: Monitor digoxin blood levels with concurrent therapy and assess for S&S of digoxin toxicity.

Patient & Family Education

- Report any of the following to a health care provider: Pain at the infusion site, dizziness, confusion, palpitations, swelling of hands or feet.

COSYNTROPIN

(koe-sin-troe'pin)

Cortrosyn
Classification(s): DIAGNOSTIC AGENT
Therapeutic: DIAGNOSTIC AGENT
Prototype: Prednisone
Pregnancy Category: C

USES Diagnostic tool to differentiate primary adrenal from secondary (pituitary) adrenocortical insufficiency.

INDICATION & DOSAGE

Rapid Screening Test

Adult/Child (over 2 y): 0.25 mg
Child (under 2 y): 0.125 mg
Neonate: 0.015 mg/kg

SOLUTION PREPARATION

- *Vial Reconstitution*: Add 1.1 mL NS to the 0.25 mg vial to yield 0.25 mg/mL. Further dilute in 2–5 mL of NS. May be given as prepared direct IV as a bolus dose or further diluted for infusion.

Common adverse effects in *italic*, life-threatening effects <u>underlined</u>: generic names in **bold**; classifications in SMALL CAPS; ♣ Canadian drug name; ◉ Prototype drug

181

C

- *Further Dilution of Reconstituted Solution*: Add contents of reconstituted vial to 250 mL of D5W or NS to yield approximately 1 mcg/mL.

STORAGE
Reconstituted solutions remain stable 24 h at room temperature or 21 days at 2°–8° C.

ADMINISTRATION
- **Direct IV Injection:** Give over 2 min.
- **IV Infusion:** Infuse at an approximate rate of 40 mcg/h over 6 h.

INCOMPATIBILITIES Data not available; do not mix with other drugs.

ACTION & *THERAPEUTIC EFFECT* Synthetic polypeptide resembling corticotropin (ACTH) in relation to the first 24 of the 39 amino acids in naturally occurring ACTH. Has less immunologic activity and is associated with less risk of sensitivity than corticotropin. *In patient with normal adrenocortical function, stimulates adrenal cortex to secrete corticosterone, cortisol (hydrocortisone), several weak androgenic substances, and limited amounts of aldosterone.*

CONTRAINDICATIONS History of allergic disorders; scleroderma, osteoporosis; systemic fungal infections; ocular herpes simplex; recent surgery; history of or presence of peptic ulcer; CHF; hypertension; adrenocortical insufficiency and adrenocortical hyperfunction; immunizations, tuberculosis, infections; pregnancy (category C), lactation.

CAUTIOUS USE Multiple sclerosis; acute gouty arthritis; mental disturbances; diabetes; abscess; pyrogenic infections; diverticulitis; renal insufficiency; myasthenia gravis.

ADVERSE EFFECTS (≥1%) **Body as a Whole:** Mild fever. **GI:** Chronic pancreatitis. **Skin:** Pruritus.

DIAGNOSTIC TEST INTERFERENCE Cortisone, hydrocortisone, estrogen, spironolactone, elevated *bilirubin,* and presence of *free Hgb* in plasma may interfere with *plasma cortisol* determinations.

DRUG INTERACTIONS Cortisone, hydrocortisone can exhibit abnormally high baseline values of cortisol, and a decreased response to cosyntropin test.

PHARMACOKINETICS Absorption: Plasma cortisol levels double in 15–30 min. **Peak:** 1 h. **Duration:** 2–4 h. **Distribution:** Unknown; does not cross placenta. **Metabolism:** Unknown.

NURSING IMPLICATIONS

Assessment & Drug Effects
- Normal 17-KS levels in men are 10–25 mg/24 h; in women less than 50 y, 5–15 mg/24 h; and in women over 50 y, 4–8 mg/24 h.
- Normal 17-OHCS levels in men are 5–12 mg/24 h; in women, 3–10 mg/24 h; in children 8–12 y, less than 4.5 mg/24 h; in younger children, 1.5 mg/24 h. Levels may be slightly higher in obese or muscular individuals.

CYCLOPHOSPHAMIDE ⊕

(sye-kloe-foss'fa-mide)

Lyophilized Cytoxan, Neosar, Procytox ♣

Classification(s): ANTINEOPLASTIC; ALKYLATING AGENT

Therapeutic: ANTINEOPLASTIC

Pregnancy Category: C

USES As single agent or in combination with other chemotherapeutic agents in treatment of malignant lymphoma, multiple myeloma, leukemias, mycosis fungoides (advanced disease), neuroblastoma, adenocarcinoma of ovary, carcinoma of breast, or malignant neoplasms of lung.

UNLABELED USES To prevent rejection in homotransplantation; to treat severe rheumatoid arthritis, multiple sclerosis, systemic lupus erythematosus, Wegener's granulomatosis, nephrotic syndrome.

INDICATION & DOSAGE

Neoplasms

Adult: Initial 40–50 mg/kg in divided doses over 2–5 days up to 100 mg/kg; then 10–15 mg/kg q7–10 days *or* 3–5 mg twice weekly

Child: 2–8 mg/kg *or* 60–250 mg/m² in divided doses

Renal Impairment Dosage Adjustment

CrCl 10 mL/min: Give 50% of dose.

Hemodialysis Dosage Adjustment

Administer post-dialysis, give supplemental dose of 35%

SOLUTION PREPARATION

- *Direct IV Injection:* To each 100 mg add 5 mL sterile water for injection or bacteriostatic water for injection (paraben-preserved only) to yield 20 mg/mL. Shake gently to dissolve. (Note: If prepared with sterile water, use within 6 h.) May be given as prepared direct IV as a bolus dose or further diluted for infusion (preferred).
- *Intermittent Infusion:* Further dilute in 100–250 mL D5W, NS, 1/2NS, D5/NS, LR, or other compatible solution.

STORAGE

- Store at or below 25° C (77° F).
- Solutions diluted with sterile water **must be** used within 6 h.
- Solutions diluted with bacteriostatic water (paraben preserved) should be used within 24 h if at room temperature or 6 days if under refrigeration.

ADMINISTRATION

- Prehydration with 500–1000 mL NS is recommended.

Common adverse effects in *italic*, life-threatening effects underlined: generic names in **bold**; classifications in SMALL CAPS; ♣ Canadian drug name; ⊕ Prototype drug

C

- **Direct IV Injection:** Give each 100 mg or fraction thereof over 1 min. Flush with NS before/after injection.
- **Intermittent Infusion:** Infuse each 100 mg or fraction thereof over 10–15 min.

INCOMPATIBILITIES Y-site: Amphotericin B cholesteryl complex, lansoprazole.

ACTION & *THERAPEUTIC EFFECT* Cell-cycle–nonspecific alkylating agent chemically related to the nitrogen mustards. Action mechanism thought to be the result of cross-linkage of DNA strands, thereby blocking synthesis of DNA, RNA, and protein. *Cytotoxic against many neoplastic diseases as well as autoimmune diseases.*

CONTRAINDICATIONS Men and women in childbearing years; serious infections (including chickenpox, herpes zoster); live virus vaccines; myelo-suppression; dehydration; infants; pregnancy (category C), lactation.

CAUTIOUS USE History of radiation or cytotoxic drug therapy; hepatic and renal impairment; elderly; recent history of steroid therapy; bone marrow infiltration with tumor cells; history of urate calculi and gout; patients with leukopenia, thrombocytopenia.

ADVERSE EFFECTS (≥1%) **Body as a Whole:** Transient dizziness, fatigue, facial flushing, diaphoresis, drug fever, <u>anaphylaxis</u>, secondary neoplasia. **GI:** *Nausea, vomiting,* mucositis, *anorexia,* hepatotoxicity, diarrhea. **Hematologic:** <u>Leukopenia</u>, *neutropenia,* acute myeloid leukemia, anemia, thrombophlebitis, interference with normal healing. **Metabolic:** Severe hyperkalemia, SIADH, hyponatremia, weight gain (but without edema) or weight loss, hyperuricemia. **Respiratory:** <u>Pulmonary emboli</u> and edema, pneumonitis, <u>interstitial pulmonary fibrosis.</u> **Skin:** *Alopecia* (reversible), transverse ridging of nails, pigmentation of nail beds and skin (reversible), nonspecific dermatitis, <u>toxic epidermal necrolysis, Stevens-Johnson syndrome.</u> **Urogenital:** <u>Sterile hemorrhagic and nonhemorrhagic cystitis,</u> bladder fibrosis, nephrotoxicity.

DIAGNOSTIC TEST INTERFERENCE Cyclophosphamide suppresses positive reactions to *Candida, mumps, trichophytons,* and *tuberculin PPD skin tests. Papanicolaou (PAP)* smear may be falsely positive.

DRUG INTERACTIONS Succinylcholine, prolonged neuromuscular blocking activity; **doxorubicin** may increase cardiac toxicity.

PHARMACOKINETICS Distribution: Widely distributed, including brain, breast milk; crosses placenta. **Metabolism:** In liver via CYP 3A4. **Elimination:** In urine as active metabolites and unchanged drug. **Half-Life:** 4–6 h.

NURSING IMPLICATIONS

Assessment & Drug Effects

- Lab tests: Baseline and twice weekly total and differential leukocyte count, platelet count, and Hct; baseline and periodic LFTs, kidney function tests, and serum electrolytes. Microscopic urine examinations are recommended after large IV doses.

- If thrombocyte count 100,000/mm³ or lower, assess for bleeding or easy bruising.
- WBC nadir may occur in 2–8 days after first dose but may be as late as 1 mo after a series of several daily doses. Leukopenia usually reverses 7–10 days after therapy is discontinued.
- During severe leukopenic period, protect patient from infection and trauma.
- Report promptly onset of unexplained chills, sore throat, tachycardia.
- Monitor temperature carefully and report an elevation immediately. The development of fever in a neutropenic patient (granulocyte count less than 1000) is a medical emergency.
- Monitor I&O ratio and patterns. PO and IV fluid intake is generally increased to help prevent renal irritation and hemorrhagic cystitis.
- Promptly report hematuria or dysuria.
- Diarrhea may signal onset of hyperkalemia, particularly if accompanied by colicky pain, nausea, bradycardia, and skeletal muscle weakness. These symptoms warrant prompt reporting to prescriber.
- Monitor for hyperuricemia, which occurs commonly during early treatment period in patients with leukemias or lymphoma. Report edema of lower legs and feet; joint, flank, or stomach pain.

Patient & Family Education
- Alopecia occurs in about 33% of patients on cyclophosphamide therapy. Hair loss may be noted 3 wk after therapy begins; regrowth (often differs in texture and color) usually starts 5–6 wk after drug is withdrawn and may occur while on maintenance doses.
- Use adequate means of contraception during and for at least 4 mo after termination of drug treatment.
- Amenorrhea may last up to 1 y after cessation of therapy in 10–30% of women.

CYCLOSPORINE ⓟ

(sye′kloe-spor-een)

Gengraf, Neoral

Classification(s): IMMUNOLOGIC AGENT, IMMUNOSUPPRESSANT
Therapeutic: IMMUNOSUPPRESSANT
Pregnancy Category: C

USES In conjunction with adrenal corticosteroids to prevent organ rejection after kidney, liver, and heart transplants (allografts). Has had limited use in pancreas, bone marrow, and heart/lung transplantations.
UNLABELED USES Sjögren's syndrome, to prevent rejection of heart-lung and pancreatic transplants, ulcerative colitis.

INDICATION & DOSAGE

Prevention of Organ Rejection
Adult/Child: 5–6 mg/kg beginning 4–12 h before transplantation and continued daily after surgery until patient can take oral medication

Common adverse effects in *italic*, life-threatening effects <u>underlined</u>: generic names in **bold**; classifications in SMALL CAPS; ♣ Canadian drug name; ⓞ Prototype drug

185

C

SOLUTION PREPARATION
IV Infusion: Dilute each 1 mL **immediately before** administration in 20–100 mL of D5W or NS. Discard after 24 h.

STORAGE
- Store below 30° C (86° F) and protect from light.
- Discard IV solutions after 24 h.

ADMINISTRATION
IV Infusion: Give by slow infusion over approximately 2–6 h. Rapid IV infusion can result in nephrotoxicity.

INCOMPATIBILITIES Solution/additive: Magnesium sulfate. Y-site: Amphotericin B cholesteryl complex, drotrecogin alfa, TPN.

ACTION & *THERAPEUTIC EFFECT* Immunosuppressant agent derived from extract of a soil fungus. Action in reducing transplant rejection is due to selective and reversible inhibition of the first phase of T-cell activation with T-lymphocytes, which normally stimulate antibody production. *It is used to prevent allograft rejection in transplant patients.*

CONTRAINDICATIONS Hypersensitivity to cyclosporine or to ingredients in commercially available formulations, e.g., Cremophor (polyoxyl 35 castor oil); recent contact with or bout of chickenpox, herpes zoster; administration of live virus vaccines to patient or family members; ocular infection; infants; pregnancy (category C), lactation.
CAUTIOUS USE Renal, hepatic, pancreatic, or bowel dysfunction; biliary tract disease, jaundice, hyperkalemia; electrolyte imbalance, hyperuricemia, hypertension; infection; radiation therapy; older adults; encephalopathy; females of childbearing age; fungal or viral infection; gout; herpes infection; lymphoma, neoplastic disease; malabsorption problems (e.g., liver transplant patients).

ADVERSE EFFECTS (≥1%) **Body as a Whole:** Lymphoma, gynecomastia, chest pain, leg cramps, edema, fever, chills, weight loss, increased risk of skin malignancies in psoriasis patients previously treated with methotrexate, psoralens, or UV light therapy. **CV:** *Hypertension,* MI (rare). **GI:** Gingival hyperplasia, diarrhea, nausea, *vomiting,* abdominal discomfort, anorexia, gastritis, constipation. **Hematologic:** Leukopenia, anemia, thrombocytopenia, *hypermagnesemia, hyperkalemia,* hyperuricemia, *decreased serum bicarbonate,* hyperglycemia. **CNS:** *Tremor,* convulsions, headache, paresthesias, hyperesthesia, flushing, night sweats, insomnia, visual hallucinations, confusion, anxiety, flat affect, depression, lethargy, weakness, paraparesis, ataxia, amnesia. **Skin:** *Hirsutism,* acne, oily skin, flushing. **Special Senses:** Sinusitis, tinnitus, hearing loss, sore throat. **Urogenital:** Urinary retention, frequency, *nephrotoxicity (oliguria).*

DIAGNOSTIC TEST INTERFERENCE *Hyperlipidemia* and abnormalities in *electrophoresis* reported; believed to be due to polyoxyl 35 castor oil (Cremophor) in IV cyclosporine.

DRUG INTERACTIONS AMINOGLYCOSIDES, **danazol, diltiazem, doxycycline, erythromycin, ketoconazole, methylprednisolone, metoclo-**

Common adverse effects in *italic*, life-threatening effects <u>underlined</u>: generic names in **bold**; classifications in SMALL CAPS; ♣ Canadian drug name; ○ Prototype drug

pramide, nicardipine, NSAIDS, **prednisolone, verapamil** may increase cyclosporine levels; **carbamazepine, isoniazid, octreotide, phenobarbital, phenytoin, rifampin** may decrease cyclosporine levels; **acyclovir,** AMINOGLYCOSIDES, **amphotericin B, cimetidine, erythromycin, ketoconazole, melphalan, ranitidine, cotrimoxazole, trimethoprim** may increase risk of nephrotoxicity; POTASSIUM-SPARING DIURETICS, ACE INHIBITORS **(captopril, enalapril)** may potentiate hyperkalemia.

PHARMACOKINETICS Peak: 3–4 h. **Distribution:** Widely distributed; 33–47% distributed to plasma; 41–50% to RBCs; crosses placenta; distributed into breast milk. **Metabolism:** Extensively metabolized in liver by CYPD 3A4, including significant first pass metabolism; considerable enterohepatic circulation. **Elimination:** Primarily eliminated in bile and feces; 6% excreted in urine. **Half-Life:** 19–27 h.

NURSING IMPLICATIONS

Assessment & Drug Effects

- Observe patient for at least 30 min continuously after start of IV infusion, and at frequent intervals thereafter to detect allergic or other adverse reactions.
- Monitor vital signs. Be alert to indicators of local or systemic infection that can be fungal, viral, or bacterial. Also report significant rise in BP.
- Lab tests: Baseline and periodic BUN, serum creatinine, LFTs (serum amylase, bilirubin, alkaline phosphatase), and serum potassium.
- Monitor I&O ratio and pattern: Nephrotoxicity has been reported in about one third of transplant patients. It has occurred in mild forms as late as 2–3 mo after transplantation. In severe form, it can be irreversible, and therefore early recognition is critical.
- Monitor digoxin levels with concurrent therapy.
- Report promptly S&S of infection.

Patient & Family Education

- If possible, see a dentist before start of cyclosporine treatment, and practice good oral hygiene. Inspect mouth daily for white patches, sores, swollen gums.
- Avoid contact with persons who have infections.
- Do not receive vaccines during therapy without consulting prescriber.

CYTARABINE Ⓟ

(sye-tare′a-been)

Cytosar-U, DepoCyt

Classification(s): ANTINEOPLASTIC; ANTIMETABOLITE, PURINE ANTAGONIST
Therapeutic: ANTINEOPLASTIC
Pregnancy Category: D

USES To induce and maintain remission in acute myelocytic leukemia, acute lymphocytic leukemia, and meningeal leukemia and for treatment

---

Common adverse effects in *italic*, life-threatening effects <u>underlined</u>: generic names in **bold**; classifications in SMALL CAPS; ♥ Canadian drug name; Ⓟ Prototype drug

187

C

of lymphomas. Used in combination with other antineoplastics in established chemotherapeutic protocols.

INDICATION & DOSAGE

Leukemias

Adult/Child: 100–200 mg/m² by continuous infusion over 24 h

Renal Impairment Dosage Adjustment

Serum Cr of 1.5–1.9 mg/dL (or 0.5–1.2 mg/dL change from baseline): Reduce to 1 g/m²/dose. *Serum Cr of 2 or more (or greater than 1.2 mg/ dL change):* Do not exceed 100 mg/m²/day

SOLUTION PREPARATION

- *Vial Reconstitution:* Reconstitute with bacteriostatic water for injection (without benzyl alcohol for neonates). Add 5 mL to the 100-mg vial to yield 20 mg/mL, or add 10 mL to the 500-mg vial to yield 50 mg/mL. May be given as prepared direct IV as a bolus dose or further diluted for infusion.
- *Further Dilution of Reconstituted Solution:* Dilute in 100 mL or more of D5W or NS.

STORAGE

Reconstituted solutions may be stored at 15°–30° C (59°–86° F) for 48 h. Discard solutions with a slight haze.

ADMINISTRATION

- **Direct IV Injection:** Give at a rate of 100 mg or a fraction thereof over 3 min through a free-flowing IV tubing.
- **IV Infusion:** Infuse over 30 min or longer depending on the total volume of IV solution.

INCOMPATIBILITIES Solution/additive: **Fluorouracil, gentamicin, heparin, hydrocortisone, insulin, nafcillin, oxacillin, penicillin G.** Y-site: **Allopurinol, amphotericin B cholesteryl sulfate complex, gallium, ganciclovir, lansoprazole, TPN.**

ACTION & *THERAPEUTIC EFFECT* Pyrimidine analog with cell phase specificity affecting rapidly dividing cells in S phase (DNA synthesis). In certain conditions, it prevents development of cell division from G_1 to S phase. Interferes with DNA and RNA synthesis in rapidly growing cells. *Effective antineoplastic agent in rapidly growing cells. It has immunosuppressant properties that are exhibited by obliterated cell-mediated immune responses, such as delayed hypersensitivity skin reactions.*

CONTRAINDICATIONS History of drug-induced myelosuppression; immunization procedures; pregnancy (category D) particularly during first trimester, lactation. Safe use in infants not established.

CAUTIOUS USE Impaired renal or hepatic function; gout; elderly; neurologic disease; drug-induced myelosuppression.

Common adverse effects in *italic*, life-threatening effects <u>underlined</u>: generic names in **bold**; classifications in SMALL CAPS; ♣ Canadian drug name; ◑ Prototype drug

ADVERSE EFFECTS (≥1%) **Body as a Whole:** Weight loss, sore throat, fever, thrombophlebitis and pain at injection site; pericarditis, bleeding (any site); pneumonia. Potentially carcinogenic and mutagenic. **GI:** *Nausea, vomiting,* diarrhea, stomatitis, oral or anal inflammation or ulceration, esophagitis, anorexia, <u>hemorrhage</u>, hepatotoxicity, jaundice. **Hematologic:** *Leukopenia, thrombocytopenia,* anemia, megaloblastosis, myelosuppression (reversible); transient hyperuricemia. **CNS:** Headache, <u>neurotoxicity</u>; peripheral neuropathy, brachial plexus neuropathy; personality change; neuritis; vertigo; lethargy, somnolence; confusion. **Skin:** Rash, erythema, freckling, cellulitis, skin ulcerations, pruritus, urticaria, bulla formation, desquamation. **Special Senses:** Conjunctivitis, keratitis, photophobia. **Urogenital:** Renal dysfunction, urinary retention.

DRUG INTERACTIONS GI toxicity may decrease **digoxin** absorption; decreases AMINOGLYCOSIDES activity against *Klebsiella pneumoniae*.

PHARMACOKINETICS Distribution: Crosses blood–brain barrier in moderate amounts; crosses placenta. **Metabolism:** Metabolized primarily in liver. **Elimination:** 80% excreted in urine in 24 h. **Half-Life:** 1–3 h.

NURSING IMPLICATIONS

Assessment & Drug Effects

- Inspect patient's mouth before the administration of each dose. Toxicity necessitating dosage alterations almost always occurs. Report adverse reactions immediately.
- Lab tests: Daily Hct, platelet counts, total and differential leukocyte counts during initial therapy; periodic serum uric acid and LFTs.
- Hyperuricemia due to rapid destruction of neoplastic cells may accompany cytarabine therapy. To reduce potential for urate stone formation, fluids are forced in excess of 2 L, if tolerated. Consult prescriber.
- Monitor I&O ratio and pattern.
- Monitor body temperature. Be alert to subtle signs of infection, especially low-grade fever, and report promptly.
- When platelet count falls below 50,000/mm³ and neutrophils below 1000/mm³, therapy may be suspended. WBC nadir is usually reached in 5–7 days after therapy has been stopped. Therapy is restarted with appearance of bone marrow recovery and when preceding cell counts are reached.
- Provide good oral hygiene to diminish adverse effects and chance of superinfection. Stomatitis and cheilosis usually appear 5–10 days into the therapy.

Patient & Family Education

- Report promptly protracted vomiting or signs of nephrotoxicity (see Appendix C).
- Flu-like syndrome occurs usually within 6–12 wk after drug administration and may recur with successive therapy. Report chills, fever, achy joints and muscles.
- Report any S&S of superinfection (see Appendix C).

Common adverse effects in *italic*, life-threatening effects <u>underlined</u>: generic names in **bold**; classifications in SMALL CAPS; ♣ Canadian drug name; ✪ Prototype drug

189

CYTOMEGALOVIRUS IMMUNE GLOBULIN (CMVIG, CMV-IVIG)

(cy-to-meg′a-lo-vi-rus)

CytoGam

Classification(s): IMMUNOLOGIC AGENT, IMMUNOGLOBULIN
Therapeutic: IMMUNOGLOBULIN
Prototype: Immune Globulin
Pregnancy Category: C

USES Attenuation of primary cytomegalovirus (CMV) disease associated with kidney transplantation.

UNLABELED USES Prevention of CMV disease in other organ transplants (especially heart) when the recipient is seronegative for CMV and the donor is seropositive.

INDICATION & DOSAGE

Prevention of CMV Disease

Adult: 150 mg/kg within 72 h of transplantation, then 100 mg/kg 2, 4, 6, and 8 wk posttransplant, then 50 mg/kg 12 and 16 wk posttransplant

SOLUTION PREPARATION

IV Infusion: Use a double-ended transfer needle or large syringe to reconstitute with 50 mL sterile water for injection. Enter the vial only once. Gently rotate vial to dissolve; do not shake. Allow 30 min to dissolve powder. Reconstituted solution contains 50 mg/mL. Must begin infusion within 6 h of entering the vial and **must be** completely infused within 12 h since solution contains no preservative.

STORAGE

Reconstituted solution should be started within 6 h and completed within 12 h of preparation. Discard solution if cloudy.

ADMINISTRATION

- CMVIG should be administered through a separate IV line using an infusion pump. Use an in-line, 15 micron filter. A smaller, 0.2 micron filter is acceptable.
- **Initial IV Infusion Following Transplantation:** Infuse at 15 mg/kg/h for first 30 min; if no adverse response, increase to 30 mg/kg/h for next 30 min; if no adverse response, increase to 60 mg/kg/h. **Never** infuse more than 75 mL/h CMVIG. Monitor closely during and after each rate change. If flushing, nausea, back pain, fever, or chills develops, slow or temporarily discontinue infusion. If BP begins to decrease, stop infusion and institute emergency measures.
- **IV Infusion of Subsequent Doses:** Use the technique described for initial infusion. The intervals for increasing the dose from 15 to 30 to 60 mg may be shortened from 30 to 15 min if no adverse response occurs. **Never** infuse more than 75 mL/h CMVIG.

Common adverse effects in *italic*, life-threatening effects <u>underlined</u>: generic names in **bold**; classifications in SMALL CAPS; ♣ Canadian drug name; ○ Prototype drug

INCOMPATIBILITIES Data not available; do not mix with other drugs.

ACTION & *THERAPEUTIC EFFECT* Cytomegalovirus immune globulin (CMVIG) is a preparation of immunoglobulin G (IgG) antibodies derived from a large number of healthy donors with high concentrations of antibodies directed against cytomegalovirus (CMV). *The CMV antibodies attenuate or reduce the incidence of serious CMV disease, such as CMV-associated pneumonia, CMV-associated hepatitis, and concomitant fungi and parasitic superinfections.*

CONTRAINDICATIONS History of previous severe reactions associated with CMVIG or other human immunoglobulin preparations; selective immunoglobulin A (IgA) deficiency; pregnancy (category C).
CAUTIOUS USE Myelosuppression, maltose or sucrose hypersensitivity; cardiac disease; lactation.

ADVERSE EFFECTS (≥1%) **Body as a Whole:** Muscle aches, back pain, <u>anaphylaxis</u> (rare), fever and chills during infusion. **CV:** Hypotension, palpitations. **GI:** Nausea, vomiting, metallic taste. **CNS:** Headache, anxiety. **Respiratory:** Shortness of breath, wheezing. **Skin:** Flushing.

DRUG INTERACTIONS May interfere with the immune response to LIVE VIRUS VACCINES **(BCG, measles/mumps/rubella, live polio),** defer vaccination with LIVE VIRAL VACCINES for approximately 3 mo after administration of CMVIG; revaccination may be necessary if these vaccines were given shortly after CMVIG.

NURSING IMPLICATIONS

Assessment & Drug Effects
- Monitor vital signs preinfusion, before increases in infusion rate, periodically during infusion, and postinfusion.
- Notify prescriber immediately if any of the following occur: Flushing, nausea, back pain, fall in BP, other signs of anaphylaxis.
- Emergency drugs should be available for treatment of acute anaphylactic reactions.
- Monitor for CMV-associated syndromes (e.g., leukopenia, thrombocytopenia, hepatitis, pneumonia) and for superinfections.

Patient & Family Education
- Familiarize yourself with potential adverse effects and know which to report to prescriber.
- Defer vaccination with live viral vaccines for 3 mo after administration of CMVIG.

DACARBAZINE
(da-kar'ba-zeen)
DTIC-Dome
Classification(s): ANTINEOPLASTIC; ALKYLATING AGENT

Common adverse effects in *italic*, life-threatening effects <u>underlined</u>: generic names in **bold**; classifications in SMALL CAPS; ♣ Canadian drug name; ⊙ Prototype drug

191

DACARBAZINE

Therapeutic: ANTINEOPLASTIC
Prototype: Cyclophosphamide
Pregnancy Category: C

USES As single agent or in combination with other antineoplastics in treatment of metastatic malignant melanoma, refractory Hodgkin's disease.
UNLABELED USES Various sarcomas and malignant glucagonoma.

INDICATION & DOSAGE

Metastatic Malignant Melanoma
Adult: 2–4.5 mg/kg/day for 10 days repeated at 4-wk intervals or 250 mg/m^2/day for 5 days repeated at 3-wk intervals

Hodgkin's Disease
Adult: 150 mg/m^2/day × 5 days, repeat at 4 wk intervals

SOLUTION PREPARATION

- Wear gloves when handling this drug. If solution gets into the eyes, wash with soap and water immediately, then irrigate with water or isotonic saline.
- *Vial Reconstitution:* Use sterile water for injection for dilution. Add 9.9 mL to 100 mg or 19.7 mL to 200 mg to yield 10 mg/mL dacarbazine (pH 3.0–4.0). May be given as prepared direct IV as a bolus dose or further diluted for infusion (preferred).
- *Further Dilution of Reconstituted Solution:* Add required dose to 50–250 mL of D5W or NS.

STORAGE
Store reconstituted solution up to 72 h at 4° C (39° F) or at room temperature 15°–30° C (59°–86° F) for up to 8 h. Store reconstituted solution further diluted in D5W or NS for 24 h at 4° C (39° F) or at room temperature for up to 8 h. Protect from light.

ADMINISTRATION

- Administer dacarbazine only to patients under close supervision. Close observation and frequent laboratory studies are required during and after therapy.
- **Direct IV Injection:** Give bolus dose over at least 15 min.
- **IV Infusion (preferred):** Infuse over 30–60 min.
- If possible, avoid using antecubital vein or veins on dorsum of hand or wrist where extravasation could lead to loss of mobility of entire limb. Avoid veins in extremity with compromised venous or lymphatic drainage and veins near joint spaces.
- Monitor injection site frequently and give prompt attention to patient's complaint of swelling, stinging, and burning sensation around injection site. Extravasation can occur painlessly and without visual signs. If extravasation is suspected, infusion should be stopped immediately and restarted in another vein. Report to the prescriber. Prompt institution of local treatment is IMPERATIVE.

Common adverse effects in *italic*, life-threatening effects underlined: generic names in **bold**; classifications in SMALL CAPS; ✚ Canadian drug name; ❷ Prototype drug

INCOMPATIBILITIES Solution/additive: Allopurinol, heparin, hydrocortisone. **Y-site:** Allopurinol, cefepime, heparin, piperacillin/tazobactam.

ACTION & *THERAPEUTIC EFFECT* Cytotoxic agent with alkylating properties is cell-cycle nonspecific. Interferes with purine metabolism, and with RNA and protein synthesis in rapidly proliferating cells. *Has carcinogenic, mutagenic, and teratogenic activities.*

CONTRAINDICATIONS Hypersensitivity to dacarbazine; severe bone marrow depression; pregnancy (category C); lactation.

CAUTIOUS USE Hepatic or renal impairment; previous radiation or chemotherapy.

ADVERSE EFFECTS (≥1%) **Body as a Whole:** Hypersensitivity (erythematosus, urticarial rashes, hepatotoxicity, photosensitivity); facial paresthesia and flushing; flu-like syndrome, myalgia, malaise, anaphylaxis. **CNS:** Confusion, headache, seizures, blurred vision. **GI:** *Anorexia, nausea, vomiting.* **Hematologic:** <u>Severe leukopenia and thrombocytopenia</u>, mild anemia. **Skin:** Alopecia. **Other:** *Pain along injected vein.*

DRUG INTERACTIONS Avoid concurrent administration of LIVE VACCINE.

PHARMACOKINETICS Distribution: Localizes primarily in liver. **Metabolism:** Extensively metabolized in liver by CYP 1A2. **Elimination:** 35–50% excreted in urine in 6 h. **Half-Life:** 5 h.

NURSING IMPLICATIONS

Assessment & Drug Effects

- Monitor IV site carefully for extravasation. Older adults, the very young, comatose, and debilitated patients are especially at risk. Other risk factors include establishing an IV line in a vein previously punctured several times and the use of nonplastic catheters.
- Lab tests: Baseline and periodic CBC with differential, platelet counts, and kidney function tests.
- Withhold therapy and notify prescriber of leukocyte count less than 3000/mm^3 or a platelet count of less than 100,000/mm^3.
- Avoid, if possible, all tests and treatments during platelet nadir requiring needle punctures. Observe carefully and report evidence of unexplained bleeding.
- Monitor I&O ratio and pattern and daily temperature. Renal impairment extends the half-life and increases danger of toxicity. Report symptoms of renal dysfunction and even a slight elevation of temperature.
- Monitor for severe nausea and vomiting that begin within 1 h after drug administration and may last for as long as 12 h.
- Check patient's mouth for ulcerative stomatitis prior to the administration of each dose.

Patient & Family Education

- Report flu-like syndrome that may occur during or even a week after treatment is terminated and last 7–21 days. Symptoms frequently recur with successive treatments.

Common adverse effects in *italic*, life-threatening effects <u>underlined</u>: generic names in **bold**; classifications in SMALL CAPS; ♣ Canadian drug name; ❷ Prototype drug

193

- Avoid prolonged exposure to sunlight or to ultraviolet light during treatment period and for at least 2 wk after last dose. Protect exposed skin with sunscreen lotion (SPF 15) and avoid exposure in midday.
- Report promptly the onset of blurred vision or paresthesia.

D

DACLIZUMAB
(dac'li-zu-mab)
Zenapax
Classification(s): IMMUNOLOGIC AGENT, MONOCLONAL ANTIBODY
Therapeutic: IMMUNOSUPPRESSANT
Pregnancy Category: C

USES Prophylaxis of acute organ rejection in renal transplant.

INDICATION & DOSAGE

Renal Transplant
Adult/Adolescent/Child (11 mo or older): 1 mg/kg no more than 24 h prior to transplant, then repeat every 14 days for 4 more doses

SOLUTION PREPARATION
- *IV Infusion:* Add calculated amount of drug (based on patient's body weight) to 50 mL of NS. Invert infusion bag to dissolve, but do not shake. Discard if diluted solution is colored or has particulate matter.
- Exercise care to ensure sterility as drug contains no antimicrobial agents.

STORAGE
- Use diluted solution immediately or store at room temperature for 4 h or at 2°–8° C (36°–46° F) for 24 h. Discard after 24 h.
- Store unopened vials at 2°–8° C (36°–46° F) and protect from light.

ADMINISTRATION
- Should be administered under supervision of prescriber specializing in immunosuppressive therapy.
- **IV Infusion:** Infuse over 15 min. Do not mix with other drugs in same IV line.

INCOMPATIBILITIES Data not available; do not mix with other drugs.

ACTION & *THERAPEUTIC EFFECT* Immunosuppressant IgG-1 monoclonal antibody produced by recombinant DNA technology. Binds to interleukin-2 (IL-2) receptor complex of lymphocytes. *Daclizumab inhibits IL-2–mediated activation of lymphocytes, which is the major pathway for cellular immune rejection of allografts.*

CONTRAINDICATIONS Hypersensitivity to daclizumab; murine protein hypersensitivity; pregnancy (category C), lactation; infants less than 11 mo.

CAUTIOUS USE Moderate-to-severe renal impairment; allergies, asthma, or history of allergic responses to medications; fungal or herpes infection, lymphoma, neoplastic disease, vaccination, varicella, viral infection.

ADVERSE EFFECTS (≥1%) **Body as a Whole:** Edema (general and in extremities), pain, fever, fatigue, shivering, generalized weakness, arthralgia, myalgia, hypersensitivity reactions. **CNS:** Tremor, headache, dizziness, insomnia, anxiety, depression. **CV:** Chest pain, hypertension, hypotension, tachycardia, thrombosis, bleeding. **GI:** Constipation, nausea, diarrhea, vomiting, abdominal pain, dyspepsia, abdominal distention, epigastric pain, flatulence, gastritis, hemorrhoids. **Urogenital:** Oliguria, dysuria, renal tubular necrosis, hydronephrosis, urinary tract bleeding, renal insufficiency. **Respiratory:** Dyspnea, pulmonary edema, cough, atelectasis, congestion, pharyngitis, rhinitis, hypoxia, rales, abnormal breath sounds, pleural effusion. **Skin:** Impaired wound healing, acne, pruritus, hirsutism, rash, night sweats. **Other:** Diabetes mellitus, dehydration, blurred vision.

DRUG INTERACTIONS Mycophenolate, cyclosporine may increase mortality in patients with infection. **Herbal: Echinacea** may decrease immunosuppressant effects.

PHARMACOKINETICS Duration: 120 days. **Half-Life:** 20 days (Child: 13 days).

NURSING IMPLICATIONS

Assessment & Drug Effects

- Monitor carefully for and immediately report S&S of opportunistic infection or anaphylactoid reaction (see Appendix C).
- Lab tests: Baseline CBC with differential and platelet count, renal function, and LFTs.

Patient & Family Education

- Use effective contraception before beginning daclizumab therapy, during therapy, and for 4 mo after completion of therapy.
- Avoid vaccinations during daclizumab therapy.
- Report promptly any of the following: Chills, fever, difficulty breathing, unexplained weakness.

DACTINOMYCIN

(dak-ti-noe-mye′sin)

Cosmegen

Classification(s): ANTINEOPLASTIC; ANTIBIOTIC

Therapeutic: ANTINEOPLASTIC

Prototype: Doxorubicin

Pregnancy Category: C

USES As single agent or in combination with other antineoplastics or radiation to treat Wilms' tumor, rhabdomyosarcoma, carcinoma of testes

---

Common adverse effects in *italic*, life-threatening effects <u>underlined</u>: generic names in **bold**; classifications in SMALL CAPS; ♣ Canadian drug name; ♠ Prototype drug

195

and uterus, Ewing's sarcoma, solid malignancies, gestational trophoblastic neoplasia, and sarcoma botryoides.

UNLABELED USES Malignant melanoma, Kaposi's sarcoma, osteogenic sarcoma, among others.

INDICATION & DOSAGE

Neoplasms

Adult/Adolescent/Child/Infant (over 6 mo): 25 mcg/kg/day for 5 days max., may repeat at 2–4 wk intervals if tolerated (if patient is obese or edematous, give 400–600 mcg/m²/day to relate dosage to lean body mass)

Malignant Tumor of Testis

Adult/Adolescent/Child/Infant (over 6 mo): 100 mcg/m² × 1 day with other agents

Wilm's Tumor, Childhood Rhabdomyosarcoma, Ewing's Sarcoma, Nephroblastoma

Adult/Adolescent/Child/Infant (over 6 mo): 15 mcg/kg/day × 5 days with other agents

Solid Tumor

Adult/Adolescent/Child (over 6 mo): 50 mcg/kg (lower extremity) or 35 mcg/kg (upper extremity)

Gestational Trophoblastic Neoplasia

Adult/Adolescent/Child/Infant (over 6 mo): 12 mcg/kg/day × 5 days or 500 mcg × 2 days with other agents

SOLUTION PREPARATION

- Use gloves and eye shield when preparing solution. If skin is contaminated, rinse with running water for 10 min; then rinse with buffered phosphate solution. If solution gets into the eyes, wash with water immediately; then irrigate with water or isotonic saline for 10 min.
- *Vial Reconstitution:* Add 1.1 mL sterile water (without preservative) for injection to each 500 mcg vial to yield approximately 500 mcg/mL. May be given as prepared direct IV as a bolus dose or further diluted for infusion.
- *Further Dilution of Reconstituted Solution:* Add the required dose to 50 mL of D5W or NS.

STORAGE

Store drug at 15°–30° C (59°–86° F) unless otherwise directed. Protect from heat and light.

ADMINISTRATION

- **Direct IV Injection:** Use two-needle technique for direct IV. Withdraw calculated dose from vial with one needle, change to new needle to give directly into vein without using an infusion set. Give over 2–3 min.

May give directly into infusing solutions of D5W or NS, or into tubing or side arm of a running IV infusion.

- **IV Infusion:** Infuse diluted solution over 15–30 min.
- Observe injection site frequently; if extravasation occurs, stop infusion immediately. Restart infusion in another vein. Report to prescriber. Institute prompt local treatment to prevent thrombophlebitis and necrosis. If extravasation is suspected, application of ice to the site for 15 minutes 4 times daily for 3 days may be useful.

INCOMPATIBILITIES Y-site: Filgrastim.

ACTION & *THERAPEUTIC EFFECT* Potent cytotoxic cell cycle-nonspecific neoplastic drug. Complexes with DNA, thereby inhibiting DNA, RNA, and protein synthesis. Causes delayed myelosuppression. Potentiates effects of x-ray therapy; the converse also appears likely. *Has antineoplastic properties that result from inhibiting DNA and RNA synthesis in rapidly dividing cells in tumor.*

CONTRAINDICATIONS Acute infections; pregnancy (category C), lactation; infants less than 6 mo.
CAUTIOUS USE Previous therapy with antineoplastics or radiation within 3–6 wk, bone marrow depression; infections; history of gout; impairment of kidney or liver function; obesity; chicken pox, herpes zoster, and other viral infections.

ADVERSE EFFECTS (≥1%) **GI:** *Nausea, vomiting,* anorexia, abdominal pain, diarrhea, proctitis, GI ulceration, *stomatitis,* cheilitis, glossitis, dysphagia, hepatitis. **Hematologic:** Anemia (including <u>aplastic anemia), agranulocytosis, *leukopenia, thrombocytopenia,*</u> pancytopenia, reticulopenia. **Skin:** Acne, desquamation, hyperpigmentation and reactivation of erythema especially over previously irradiated areas, *alopecia* (reversible). **Other:** Malaise, fatigue, lethargy, fever, myalgia, anaphylaxis, gonadal suppression, hypocalcemia, hyperuricemia, thrombophlebitis; *necrosis, sloughing, and contractures at site of extravasation;* hepatitis, hepatomegaly.

DRUG INTERACTIONS Elevated uric acid level produced by dactinomycin may necessitate dose adjustment of ANTIGOUT AGENTS; effects of both dactinomycin and other MYELOSUPPRESSANTS are potentiated; effects of both radiation and dactinomycin are potentiated, and dactinomycin may reactivate erythema from previous radiation therapy; **vitamin K** effects (antihemorrhagic) are decreased, leading to prolonged clotting time and potential hemorrhage.

PHARMACOKINETICS Distribution: Concentrated in liver, spleen, kidneys, and bone marrow; does not cross blood–brain barrier; crosses placenta; distribution into breast milk not known. **Elimination:** 50% excreted unchanged in bile and 10% in urine; only 30% excreted in urine over 9 days. **Half-Life:** 36 h.

NURSING IMPLICATIONS

Assessment & Drug Effects

- Monitor for severe toxic effects that occur with high frequency. Effects usually appear 2–4 days after a course of therapy is stopped and may reach maximal severity 1–2 wk following discontinuation of therapy.

Common adverse effects in *italic*, life-threatening effects <u>underlined</u>: generic names in **bold**; classifications in SMALL CAPS; ♣ Canadian drug name; ❍ Prototype drug

197

D

- Use antiemetic drugs to control nausea and vomiting, which often occur a few hours after drug administration. Vomiting may be severe enough to require intermittent therapy. Observe patient daily for signs of drug toxicity.
- Lab tests: Daily WBC count, platelet counts every 3 days; frequent renal function tests and LFTs.
- Monitor temperature, inspect oral membranes daily for stomatitis and monitor for diarrhea.
- Monitor for severe hematopoietic depression. Report onset of unexplained bleeding, jaundice, and wheezing.
- Be alert to signs of agranulocytosis (see Appendix C). Report to prescriber. Antibiotic therapy, protective isolation, and discontinuation of the antineoplastic are indicated.
- Observe and report symptoms of hyperuricemia (see Appendix C). Urge patient to increase fluid intake up to 3000 mL/day if allowed.

Patient & Family Education
- Infertility is a possible, irreversible adverse effect of this drug.
- Learn preventative measures to minimize nausea and vomiting.
- Alopecia (hair loss) is an anticipated reversible adverse effect of this drug. Seek appropriate supportive guidance.

DANTROLENE SODIUM
(dan'troe-leen)

Dantrium

Classification(s): SKELETAL MUSCLE RELAXANT, CENTRAL-ACTING
Therapeutic: SKELETAL MUSCLE RELAXANT
Prototype: Methocarbamol
Pregnancy Category: C

USES The prophylaxis and management of malignant hyperthermia.

INDICATION & DOSAGE

Malignant Hyperthermia Treatment
Adult/Child: 1 mg/kg direct IV repeated prn up to a total of 10 mg/kg

Malignant Hyperthermia Prophylaxis
Adult: 1.5 mg/kg infusion over 1 h may be repeated

Hepatic Impairment Dosage Adjustment
Do not use in active liver disease.

SOLUTION PREPARATION
- *Vial Reconstitution:* Dilute each 20 mg with 60 mL sterile water without preservatives. Shake until clear. Give as prepared direct IV without further dilution.

- Large volumes used for prophylaxis may be transferred to plastic infusion bags (not glass) for infusion.

STORAGE

Contents of reconstituted vial **must be** protected from direct light and used within 6 h after reconstitution. However, preparation immediately prior to administration is recommended.

ADMINISTRATION

- Ensure IV patency prior to IV injection. Avoid extravasation; solution has a high pH and therefore is extremely irritating to tissue.
- **Direct IV Injection:** Give a rapid bolus dose.
- **IV Infusion:** Infuse over 1 h.

INCOMPATIBILITIES Solution/additive: D5W, normal saline.

ACTION & *THERAPEUTIC EFFECT* Hydantoin derivative with peripheral skeletal muscle relaxant action. Directly relaxes the spastic muscle by interfering with calcium ion release from sarcoplasmic reticulum within skeletal muscle. Clinical doses produce about a 50% decrease in contractility of skeletal muscles. *Relief of spasticity may be accompanied by muscle weakness sufficient to affect overall functional capacity of the patient.*

CONTRAINDICATIONS Active hepatic disease; when spasticity is necessary to sustain upright posture and balance in locomotion or to maintain increased body function; spasticity due to rheumatic disorders; pregnancy (category C), lactation. Safe use in children less than 1 y is not established.

CAUTIOUS USE Impaired cardiac or pulmonary function, muscular sclerosis; neuromuscular disease; myopathy; patients greater than 35 y, especially women.

ADVERSE EFFECTS (≥1%) **Body as a Whole:** Hypersensitivity (pruritus, urticaria, eczematoid skin eruption, photosensitivity, eosinophilic pleural effusion). **CNS:** Drowsiness, *muscle weakness,* dizziness, light-headedness, unusual fatigue, speech disturbances, headache, confusion, nervousness, mental depression, insomnia, euphoria, seizures. **CV:** Tachycardia, erratic BP. **Special Senses:** Blurred vision, diplopia, photophobia. **GI:** *Diarrhea,* constipation, nausea, vomiting, anorexia, swallowing difficulty, alterations of taste, gastric irritation, abdominal cramps, GI bleeding; hepatitis, jaundice, hepatomegaly, <u>hepatic necrosis</u> (all related to prolonged use of high doses). **Urogenital:** Crystalluria with pain or burning with urination, urinary frequency, urinary retention, nocturia, enuresis, difficult erection.

DRUG INTERACTIONS Alcohol and other CNS DEPRESSANTS compound CNS depression; **estrogens** increase risk of hepatotoxicity in women greater than 35 y; **verapamil** and other CALCIUM CHANNEL BLOCKERS increase risk of ventricular fibrillation and cardiovascular collapse.

PHARMACOKINETICS Peak: 5 h. **Distribution:** Crosses placenta. **Metabolism:** In liver. **Elimination:** In urine chiefly as metabolites. **Half-Life:** 8.7 h.

D

NURSING IMPLICATIONS

Assessment & Drug Effects

- Monitor BP and HR frequently during IV infusion.
- Monitor patients with impaired cardiac or pulmonary function closely for CV or respiratory symptoms such as tachycardia, BP changes, difficulty breathing.
- Monitor for and report symptoms of allergy and allergic pleural effusion: Shortness of breath, pleuritic pain, dry cough.
- Lab tests: Baseline and periodic LFTs (alkaline phosphatase, AST, ALT, total bilirubin).

Patient & Family Education

- Dantrolene may weaken arm strength, leg muscles, and impair swallowing. Exercise caution with eating and ambulation.
- Report promptly the onset of jaundice: Yellow skin or sclerae; dark urine, clay-colored stools, itching, abdominal discomfort.
- Do not drive or engage in other potentially hazardous activities until response to drug is known.

DAPTOMYCIN

(dap-to-my'sin)

Cubicin

Classification(s): ANTIBIOTIC
Therapeutic: ANTIBACTERIAL
Pregnancy Category: B

USES Complicated skin and skin structure infections, bacteremia.
UNLABELED USES Treatment of vancomycin-resistant enterococci.

INDICATION & DOSAGE

Infections

Adult: 4 mg/kg q24h for 7–14 days

Bacteremia (*S. aureus*)

Adult: 6 mg/kg × 2–6 wk

Renal Impairment Dosage Adjustment

Skin infection *CrCl less than 30 mL/min:* 4 mg/kg q48h
Bacteremia *CrCl less than 30 mL/min:* 6 mg/kg q48h

Hemodialysis Dosage Adjustment

Dose by CrCl, administer after dialysis.

SOLUTION PREPARATION

- *Vial Reconstitution:* Reconstitute the 250 mg vial or the 500 mg vial with 5 mL or 10 mL, respectively, of NS to yield 50 mg/mL. **Must be** further diluted for infusion.

- *Further Dilution of Reconstituted Solution:* Add the required dose to 50–100 mL of NS.

STORAGE
Store unopened vials in 2°–8° C (36°–46° F). Avoid excessive heat. May store reconstituted, single-use vials or IV solution for 12 h at room temperature or 48 h if refrigerated.

D

ADMINISTRATION
IV Infusion: Infuse over 30 min; if same IV line is used for infusion of other drugs, flush line before/after with NS.

INCOMPATIBILITIES Solution/additive: Dextrose-containing solutions.

ACTION & *THERAPEUTIC EFFECT* Daptomycin is a cyclic lipopeptide antibiotic. It binds to bacterial membranes of gram-positive bacteria causing rapid depolarization of the membrane potential leading to inhibition of protein, DNA, and RNA synthesis and bacterial cell death. *Daptomycin is effective against a broad spectrum of gram-positive organisms, including both susceptible and resistant strains of* S. aureus.

CONTRAINDICATIONS Pseudomembranous colitis; rhabdomyolysis. Safe use in infants, children less than 18 y not known.

CAUTIOUS USE Severe renal or hepatic impairment; end-stage renal impairment; GI disease; myopathy; peripheral neuropathy; history of rhabdomyolysis; elderly; pregnancy (category B); lactation.

ADVERSE EFFECTS (≥1%) **Body as a Whole:** Injection site reactions, fever, fungal infections. **CNS:** Headache, insomnia, dizziness. **CV:** Hypotension, hypertension. **GI:** Constipation, nausea, vomiting, diarrhea, abnormal liver function tests. **Hematologic:** Anemia. **Metabolic:** Elevated CPK. **Musculoskeletal:** Limb pain, arthralgia. **Respiratory:** Dyspnea. **Skin:** Rash, pruritus. **Urogenital:** UTI, renal failure.

PHARMACOKINETICS Metabolism: Site of metabolism not determined. **Elimination:** Primarily renal. **Half-Life:** 8 h.

NURSING IMPLICATIONS
Assessment & Drug Effects
- Prior to initiating therapy: Baseline C&S tests (start drug pending results).
- Monitor for and report: Muscle pain or weakness, especially with concurrent therapy with HMG-CoA reductase inhibitors (statin drugs); S&S of peripheral neuropathy, superinfection such as candidiasis.
- Lab tests: Baseline renal function tests; weekly CPK levels; PT/INR during first few days of daptomycin therapy with concurrent warfarin use; daily blood glucose monitoring in diabetics; serum electrolytes if S&S of hypokalemia or hypomagnesemia (see Appendix C) appear.
- Withhold drug and notify prescriber if S&S of myopathy develop with CPK elevation greater than 1000 units/L (~5 × ULN), or if CPK level is equal to or greater than 10 × ULN.

Common adverse effects in *italic*, life-threatening effects <u>underlined</u>: generic names in **bold**; classifications in SMALL CAPS; ♣ Canadian drug name; ⊘ Prototype drug

Patient & Family Education

- Report promptly any of the following: Muscle pain, weakness or unusual tiredness; numbness or tingling; difficulty breathing or shortness of breath; severe diarrhea or vomiting; skin rash or itching.

D

DARBEPOETIN ALFA

(dar-be-po-e′tin)

ARANESP

Classification(s): HEMATOPOIETIC GROWTH FACTOR
Therapeutic: ANTIANEMIC
Prototype: Epoetin alfa
Pregnancy Category: C

USES Treatment of anemia in patients with chronic renal failure or chemotherapy-associated anemia, treatment of chemotherapy-induced anemia in nonmyeloid malignancies.

INDICATION & DOSAGE

Anemia

Adult: Initially, 0.45 mcg/kg once/wk. Maintenance dose is 0.26–0.65 mcg/kg once/wk

Dosage Adjustment

Pt Response	Dose Adjustment
Hgb increases more than 1 g/dL	Reduce by 25%
Hgb is 12 g/dL	Reduce by 25%
Hgb does not increase by 1 g/dL after 4 wk (with adequate iron)	Increase by 25%

Anemia of Chronic Renal Failure

Adult/Adolescent/Child: 0.45 mcg/kg once/wk

Converting Epoetin Alfa to Darbepoetin

Adults: Estimate the starting dose based on the total weekly dose of epoetin alfa at the time of conversion. If the patient was receiving epoetin alfa 2–3 times/wk, administer darbepoetin alfa once per week; if the patient was receiving epoetin alfa once per week, administer darbepoetin alfa once every 2 wk. The route of administration should be maintained.

Estimated Starting Dose (titrate to maintain target Hgb)

Previous Weekly Dose of Epoetin Alfa (units/wk)	Weekly Darbepoetin Dose (mcg/wk)
1,500 to 2,499 units/wk	6.25 mcg/wk

Common adverse effects in *italic*, life-threatening effects underlined: generic names in **bold**; classifications in SMALL CAPS; ♣ Canadian drug name; ✪ Prototype drug

Previous Weekly Dose of Epoetin Alfa (units/wk)	Weekly Darbepoetin Dose (mcg/wk)
2,500 to 4,999 units/wk	10–12.5 mcg/wk
5,000 to 10,999 units/wk	20–25 mcg/wk
11,000 to 17,999 units/wk	40 mcg/wk
18,000 to 33,999 units/wk	60 mcg/wk
34,000 to 89,999 units/wk	100 mcg/wk
Over 90,000 units/wk	200 mcg/wk

SOLUTION PREPARATION
No dilution is required. Administer as supplied.

STORAGE
Store at 2°–8° C (36°–46° F). Do not freeze or shake. Protect from light.

ADMINISTRATION
- Deficiencies of folic acid or vitamin B$_{12}$ should be corrected prior to initiation of therapy.
- **Direct IV Injection:** Give bolus dose over 1 min. Discard the unused portion remaining in vial.
- Do not shake vial when withdrawing medication and do not use auto-injector for IV administration.
- Do not administer in conjunction with any other drugs or solutions.

INCOMPATIBILITIES Data not available; do not mix with other drugs.

ACTION & _THERAPEUTIC EFFECT_ An erythropoiesis-stimulating protein closely related to erythropoietin. Erythropoietin is produced naturally in the kidney in response to hypoxia, and stimulates red blood cell production in the bone marrow. _Darbepoetin stimulates release of reticulocytes from bone marrow into the blood stream where they mature into RBCs._

CONTRAINDICATIONS Hypersensitivity to darbepoetin, or human albumin; patients with uncontrolled hypertension; pregnancy (category C); children less than 1 y.
CAUTIOUS USE Controlled hypertension; elevated hemoglobin; folic acid or vitamin B$_{12}$ deficiencies; infections; inflammatory or malignant processes; osteofibrosis; occult blood loss, hemolysis; severe aluminum toxicity; bone marrow fibrosis; chronic renal failure; patients not on dialysis; hematologic diseases; lactation.

ADVERSE EFFECTS (≥1%) **Body as a Whole:** Injection site pain, _peripheral edema,_ fatigue, fever, death, chest pain, fluid overload, access infection, access hemorrhage, flu-like symptoms, asthenia, _infection._ **CNS:** _Headache,_ dizziness. **CV:** _Hypertension, hypotension, arrhythmias,_ cardiac arrest, angina, chest pain, vascular access thrombosis, CHF. **GI:** _Nausea, vomiting, diarrhea,_ constipation. **Musculoskeletal:** _Myalgia, arthralgia,_ limb pain, back pain. **Respiratory:** _Upper respiratory infection, dyspnea, cough,_

D

bronchitis. **Skin:** Pruritus. **Other:** Increased risk of thrombotic events and mortality in cancer patients.

DRUG INTERACTIONS Concurrent **epoetin** results in therapeutic duplication.

PHARMACOKINETICS Distribution: Distribution confined primarily to intravascular space. **Elimination:** 10% excreted in urine. **Half-Life:** 21 h IV.

NURSING IMPLICATIONS

Assessment & Drug Effects

- Control BP adequately prior to initiation of therapy and closely monitor and control during therapy. Report immediately S&S of CHF, cardiac arrhythmias, or sepsis. Note that hypertension is an adverse effect that **must be** controlled.
- Notify prescriber of a rapid rise in Hgb as dosage will need to be reduced because of risk of serious hypertension. Note that BP may rise during early therapy as Hgb increases.
- Monitor for and report premonitory neurological symptoms (i.e., aura). The potential for seizures exists during periods of rapid Hgb increase (e.g., greater than 1 g/dL in any 2-wk period).
- Monitor closely and report immediately S&S of thrombotic events (e.g., MI, CVA, TIA), especially for patients with CRF.
- Lab tests: Baseline and periodic transferrin and serum ferritin; Hgb twice weekly until stabilized and maintenance dose is established, then weekly for at least 4 wk, and at regular intervals thereafter; CBC with differential and platelet count at regular interval; periodic BUN, creatinine, serum phosphorus, and serum potassium.

Patient & Family Education

- Risk of seizures is highest during first few months of therapy. Do not drive or engage in other potentially hazardous activity during the first 90 days of therapy because of possible seizure activity.
- Adhere closely to antihypertensive drug regimen and dietary restrictions.
- Monitor BP as directed by prescriber.
- Report promptly any of the following: Chest pain, difficulty breathing, shortness of breath, severe or persistent headache, fever, muscle aches and pains, or nausea.

DAUNORUBICIN HYDROCHLORIDE

(daw-noe-roo'bi-sin)

Cerubidine

DAUNORUBICIN CITRATED LIPOSOMAL

DaunoXome

Classification(s): ANTINEOPLASTIC; ANTIBIOTIC
Therapeutic: ANTINEOPLASTIC
Prototype: Doxorubicin HCl
Pregnancy Category: D

Common adverse effects in *italic*, life-threatening effects <u>underlined</u>: generic names in **bold**; classifications in SMALL CAPS; ♣ Canadian drug name; ◎ Prototype drug

USES To induce remission in acute nonlymphocytic/lymphocytic leukemia, advanced HIV-associated Kaposi's sarcoma.
UNLABELED USES Non-Hodgkin's lymphoma.

INDICATION & DOSAGE

Neoplasms

Adult (less than 60 y): 45 mg/m^2/day on days 1,2,3 of first course then days 1 and 2 of subsequent courses (max: Total cumulative dose 500–600 mg/m^2); *(60 y or over):* 30 mg/m^2/day on days 1, 2, 3 of first course then days 1 and 2 of subsequent courses
Child: As combination therapy; *(over 2 y):* 25 mg/m^2 weekly; *(1–2 y or BSA less than 0.5 m^2):* 1 mg/kg

Kaposi's Sarcoma (DaunoXome)

Adult: 40 mg/m^2 over 1 h, repeat q2wk (withhold therapy if granulocyte count less than 750 cells/mm^3)

Renal Impairment Dosage Adjustment

If serum Cr over 3 mg/dL: Give 50% of dose

Hepatic Impairment Dosage Adjustment

For total bilirubin 1.2–3 mg/dL: Give 50% of dose; *over 3–5 mg/dL:* Give 25% of dose; *over 5 mg/dL:* Omit dose

SOLUTION PREPARATION

- Use gloves during preparation for infusion to prevent skin contact with this drug. If contact occurs, decontaminate skin with copious amounts of water with soap.
- *Daunorubicin HCl Vial Reconstitution:* Add 4 mL sterile water for injection to the 20 mg vial to yield 5 mg/mL. Withdraw the required dose into a syringe containing 10–15 mL of NS. May be given as prepared direct IV as a bolus dose or further diluted for infusion.
  - *Further Dilution of Reconstituted Daunorubicin HCl Solution:* May add to 100 mL of NS for infusion
- *Liposomal Daunorubicin Citrate (DaunoXome) Dilution:* Determine the volume (mL) of drug required. Dilute in an IV bag with an equal amount of D5W to yield 1 mg/mL.

STORAGE

Store reconstituted solution at room temperature (15°–30° C; 59°–86° F) for 24 h and under refrigeration at 2°–8° C (36°–46° F) for 48 h. Protect from light.

ADMINISTRATION

- Avoid extravasation as it can cause severe tissue necrosis.

Daunorubicin HCl

- **Direct IV Injection:** Give over approximately 3 min into the tubing or side arm of a rapidly flowing IV infusion of D5W or NS.
- **IV Infusion:** Infuse over 30–45 min.

Common adverse effects in *italic*, life-threatening effects <u>underlined</u>: generic names in **bold**; classifications in SMALL CAPS; ♣ Canadian drug name; ◯ Prototype drug

205

D

Liposomal Daunorubicin Citrate (DaunoXome) Infusion

- Infuse DaunoXome over 60 min. Do not use a filter with DaunoXome.

INCOMPATIBILITIES Solution/additive: Dexamethasone, heparin. Y-site: Allopurinol, aztreonam, cefepime, fludarabine, lansoprazole, piperacillin/tazobactam.

ACTION & *THERAPEUTIC EFFECT* Cytotoxic and antimitotic anthracycline antibiotic; cell-cycle specific for S-phase of cell division. Mechanism of action is due to rapid interactions with the DNA molecule resulting in inhibition of DNA, RNA, and protein synthesis. *A potent bone marrow suppressant with immunosuppressive properties as well as antineoplastic properties.*

CONTRAINDICATIONS Severe myelosuppression; immunizations (patient, family), and preexisting cardiac disease unless risk-benefit is evaluated; uncontrolled systemic infection; pregnancy (category D), lactation.
CAUTIOUS USE History of gout, urate calculi, hepatic or renal function impairment; older adult patients with inadequate bone reserve due to age or previous cytotoxic drug therapy, tumor cell infiltration of bone marrow; patient who has received potentially cardiotoxic drugs or related antineoplastics.

ADVERSE EFFECTS (≥1%) **Body as a Whole:** Fever. **CNS:** Amnesia, anxiety, ataxia, confusion, hallucinations, emotional lability, tremors. **CV:** Pericarditis, myocarditis, arrhythmias, peripheral edema, CHF, hypertension, tachycardia. **GI:** *Acute nausea and vomiting* (mild), anorexia, *stomatitis,* mucositis, diarrhea (occasionally) hemorrhage. **Urogenital:** Dysuria, nocturia, polyuria, dry skin. **Hematologic:** *Bone marrow depression, thrombocytopenia, leukopenia,* anemia. **Skin:** Generalized *alopecia* (reversible), transverse pigmentation of nails, severe cellulitis or tissue necrosis at site of drug extravasation. **Endocrine:** Hyperuricemia, gonadal suppression.

DRUG INTERACTIONS Avoid LIVE VACCINES.

PHARMACOKINETICS Distribution: Highest concentrations in spleen, kidneys, liver, lungs, and heart; does not cross blood–brain barrier; crosses placenta; distribution into breast milk not known. **Metabolism:** Metabolized in liver to active metabolite. **Elimination:** 25% excreted in urine, 40% in bile. **Half-Life:** 18.5–26.7 h.

NURSING IMPLICATIONS

Assessment & Drug Effects

- Monitor BP, temperature, pulse, and respiratory function during treatment.
- Monitor for S&S of acute CHF that can occur suddenly, especially when total dosage exceeds 550 mg/m².
- Report promptly S&S of hemorrhage or superinfections including elevation of temperature, chills, upper respiratory tract infection, and overgrowth with opportunistic organisms (see Appendix C).
- Lab tests: Baseline and periodic Hct, platelet count, total and differential WBC count, serum uric acid, LFTs including serum bilirubin, and renal function tests.

Common adverse effects in *italic*, life-threatening effects <u>underlined</u>: generic names in **bold**; classifications in SMALL CAPS; ♣ Canadian drug name; ⊘ Prototype drug

- Protect from contact with persons with infections. The most hazardous period is during nadirs of thrombocytes and leukocytes usually reached in 10–14 days.
- Control nausea and vomiting (usually mild) by antiemetic therapy.
- Inspect oral membranes daily. Mucositis may occur 3–7 days after drug is administered.

Patient & Family Education
- Note: Loss of hair is probable; recovery is usual in 6–10 wk.
- Use barrier contraceptives during treatment because this drug is teratogenic. Tell your prescriber immediately if you become pregnant during therapy.
- Note: A transient effect of the drug is to turn urine red on the day of infusion.

DECITABINE

(de-sit′a-bine)

Dacogen

Classification(s): ANTINEOPLASTIC, ANTIMETABOLITE, PYRIMIDINE ANTAGONIST
Therapeutic: ANTINEOPLASTIC
Prototype: 5-Fluorouracil
Pregnancy Category: D

USES Treatment of patients with myelodysplastic syndrome (MDS), including previously treated and untreated patients with de novo and secondary MDS of all French-American-British (FAB) subtypes and intermediate-1, intermediate-2, and high-risk International Prognostic Scoring System (IPSS) groups.
UNLABELED USES Treatment of chronic myelogenous leukemia (CML).

INDICATION & DOSAGE

Myelodysplastic Syndrome

Adult: 15 mg/m^2 q8h for 3 days, repeat q6wk for a minimum of 4 cycles of therapy at 6-wk intervals

Toxicity Adjustment

If hematologic recovery (i.e., ANC equal to or greater than 1000/mm^3 and platelets equal to or greater than 50,000/mm^3) requires more than 6 wk, dosage adjustment is required.

Toxicity	Dosage Adjustment
Requires 6–10 wk to recover hematologic values	Delay cycle 2 wk and reduce dose to 11 mg/m^2 q8h
Serum Cr equal or more than 2 mg/dL	Withhold therapy until resolved

---

Common adverse effects in *italic*, life-threatening effects <u>underlined</u>: generic names in **bold**; classifications in SMALL CAPS; ♣ Canadian drug name; ⊙ Prototype drug

D

Toxicity	Dosage Adjustment
ALT or total bilirubin equal to or more than 2 times ULN	Withhold therapy until resolved
Active or uncontrolled infection	Withhold therapy until resolved

SOLUTION PREPARATION

- Caution should be exercised when handling and preparing decitabine. Procedures for proper handling and disposal of antineoplastic drugs should be applied.
- *Vial Reconstitution:* Reconstitute each vial with 10 mL sterile water for injection to yield approximately 5 mg/mL at pH 6.7–7.3. **Must be** further diluted for infusion.
- *Further Dilution of Reconstituted Solution:* Immediately after reconstitution, dilute with NS, D5W, or LR to a final drug concentration of 0.1–1 mg/mL. Use within 15 min of reconstitution (see **STORAGE**).

STORAGE

Store vials at 15°–30° C (59°– 86° F). Unless used within 15 min of reconstitution, the diluted solution **must be** prepared using cold (2°–8° C) infusion fluids and stored at 2°–8° C (36°–46° F) for up to a maximum of 7 h until administration.

ADMINISTRATION

- Premedicate with standard antiemetic therapy.
- NOTE: Withhold dose and notify prescriber of any of the following: Absolute neutrophil count (ANC) less than 1000/mm³; platelet count less than 50,000/mm³; serum creatinine at 2 mg/dL or higher; ALT, total bilirubin greater than or equal to 2 × ULN; or an active or uncontrolled infection.
- **IV Infusion:** Infuse over 3 h.

INCOMPATIBILITIES Data not available; do not mix with other drugs.

ACTION & *THERAPEUTIC EFFECT* Decitabine is an antimetabolite that exerts antineoplastic effects after its direct incorporation into DNA resulting in inhibition of DNA transferase, thus causing loss of cell differentiation and cell death. *Decitabine-induced changes in neoplastic cells may restore normal function to genes that are critical for control of cellular differentiation and proliferation. Nonproliferating cells are also resistant to the effects of decitabine.*

CONTRAINDICATIONS Hypersensitivity to decitabine; conception within 2 mo of drug use; renal failure patients with CrCl less than 2 mg/mL; liver dysfunction with transaminase greater than 2 × upper limit of normal (ULN), or serum bilirubin greater than 1.5 mg/dL; active infection; pregnancy (category D), lactation. Safety and efficacy in children not established.

CAUTIOUS USE Moderate to severe renal failure; hepatic impairment.

ADVERSE EFFECTS (≥1%) **Body as a Whole:** *Fatigue, pyrexia, Mycobacterium avium* complex infection, peripheral edema, bacteremia, candidal

Common adverse effects in *italic*, life-threatening effects <u>underlined</u>: generic names in **bold**; classifications in SMALL CAPS; ♣ Canadian drug name; ⊙ Prototype drug

infection, cellulitis, injection site reactions, rigors, tenderness, transfusion reaction, sinusitis, staphylococcal infection. **CNS:** <u>Intracranial hemorrhage</u>, anxiety, confusional state, dizziness, headache, hypesthesia, insomnia, pyrexia. **CV:** <u>Cardiorespiratory arrest</u>, cardiac murmur, hypotension. **GI:** *Nausea, vomiting, constipation, diarrhea,* abdominal distention and discomfort, anorexia, dyspepsia, gastroesophageal reflux disease, glossodynia, gingival bleeding, hemorrhoids, lip ulceration, stomatitis, tongue ulceration. **Hematologic:** *Anemia, neutropenia, thrombocytopenia,* hematoma, leukopenia, lymphadenopathy, thrombocythemia. **Metabolic:** *Hyperglycemia,* increased AST, decreased blood albumin, increased blood alkaline phosphatase, altered blood bicarbonate, decreased blood bilirubin, decreased blood chloride, increased blood lactate dehydrogenase, increased blood urea, decreased total protein, dehydration, hyperbilirubinemia, altered potassium levels, hypoalbuminemia, hypomagnesemia, hyponatremia. **Musculoskeletal:** Arthralgia, back pain, chest wall pain, musculoskeletal discomfort, myalgia, pain in limb. **Respiratory:** *Cough,* lung crackles, hypoxia, pharyngitis, pneumonia, pulmonary edema, rales. **Skin:** Alopecia, ecchymosis, erythema, pallor, *petechiae,* pruritus, rash, skin lesion, face swelling, urticaria. **Special Senses:** Blurred vision. **Urogenital:** Dysuria, urinary frequency, urinary tract infection.

DRUG INTERACTIONS Sargramostim and **filgrastim** are contraindicated within 24 h of therapy. LIVE VACCINES are contraindicated during treatment.

PHARMACOKINETICS Distribution: Negligible plasma protein binding. **Half-Life:** 0.2–0.8 h.

NURSING IMPLICATIONS

Assessment & Drug Effects

- Monitor for and report S&S of pulmonary or peripheral edema, cardiac arrhythmias, new-onset depression, or infection.
- Lab tests: CBC with differentials and platelet count prior to each chemotherapy cycle; baseline and periodic LFTs and serum creatinine.
- Avoid IM injections or other invasive procedures, if possible, with platelet counts less than 50,000/mm^3.
- Monitor diabetics for loss of glycemic control.

Patient & Family Education

- Do not accept vaccinations during treatment with decitabine.
- Avoid contact with anyone who recently received the oral poliovirus vaccine.
- Women of childbearing age should avoid becoming pregnant while receiving decitabine.
- Men should not father a child while receiving decitabine and for 2 mo after the end of therapy.
- Report any of the following: Signs of infection such as fever, chills, sore throat; signs of bleeding such as easy bruising, black, tarry stools, blood in the urine; irregular heart rate; significant tiredness or weakness.

Common adverse effects in *italic*, life-threatening effects <u>underlined</u>; generic names in **bold**; classifications in SMALL CAPS; ✦ Canadian drug name; ⊘ Prototype drug

209

DEFEROXAMINE MESYLATE

(de-fer-ox′a-meen)

Desferal

Classification(s): ANTIDOTE, CHELATING AGENT
Therapeutic: ANTIDOTE
Pregnancy Category: C

USES Adjunct in treatment of acute iron intoxication or iron overload.
UNLABELED USES To promote aluminum excretion in aluminum-toxicity.

INDICATION & DOSAGE

Acute Iron Intoxication

Adult: 1 g then 500 mg at 4 h intervals for 2 doses, subsequent doses of 500 mg q4–12h may be given if necessary (max: 6 g/24 h)
Child (3 y or more): 15 mg/kg/h (max: 6 g/24 h)

SOLUTION PREPARATION

- *Vial Reconstitution:* Add 5 mL sterile water for injection for each 500-mg to yield 100 mg/mL. Allow to dissolve completely. Use immediately. **Must be** further diluted for infusion.
- *Further Dilution of Reconstituted Solution:* Withdraw prescribed dose from vial and add to NS, D5W, or LR solution.

STORAGE

Store unreconstituted vials at or below 25° C (77° F). Protect from light.

ADMINISTRATION

- **IV Infusion Adult:**
  - Infuse initial 1000 mg dose at a rate not to exceed 15 mg/kg/h.
  - Infuse two subsequent 500 mg doses at a rate of 125 mg/h.
  - Infuse any additional 500 mg doses over 4–12 h.
  - **DO NOT** infuse more rapidly than 15 mg/kg/h in any circumstance.
- **IV Infusion Child:** Infuse at 15 mg/kg/h.

INCOMPATIBILITIES Solution/admixture: Iron dextran.

ACTION & *THERAPEUTIC EFFECT* Chelating agent with specific affinity for ferric ion and low affinity for calcium. Binds ferric ions to form a stable water-soluble chelate readily excreted by kidneys. *Main effect is removal of iron from ferritin, hemosiderin, and transferrin of patient in iron toxicity.*

CONTRAINDICATIONS Severe renal disease, anuria, pyelonephritis; pregnancy (category C); children less than 3 y of age.
CAUTIOUS USE History of pyelonephritis; primary hemochromatosis; acute infection; lactation.

ADVERSE EFFECTS (≥1%) **Body as a Whole:** Hypersensitivity (generalized itching, cutaneous wheal formation, rash, fever, <u>anaphylactoid reaction</u>). **CV:** Hypotension, tachycardia. **Special Senses:** Decreased hearing; blurred vision, decreased visual acuity and visual fields, color vision abnormalities, night blindness, retinal pigmentary degeneration. **GI:** Abdominal discomfort, diarrhea. **Urogenital:** Dysuria, exacerbation of pyelonephritis, orange-rose discoloration of urine. **Other:** *Pain and induration at injection site.*

DRUG INTERACTIONS Use with **ascorbic acid** increases cardiac risk, **prochlorperazine** may cause loss of consciousness.

PHARMACOKINETICS Distribution: Widely distributed in body tissues. **Metabolism:** Forms nontoxic complex with iron. **Elimination:** Excreted primarily in urine; some excreted in feces.

NURSING IMPLICATIONS

Assessment & Drug Effects

▪ Monitor infusion site closely. If pain and induration occur, move infusion to another site.
▪ Lab tests: Baseline kidney function tests prior to drug administration.
▪ Monitor I&O ratio and pattern. Report any change. Observe stools for blood (iron intoxication frequently causes necrosis of GI tract).

Patient & Family Education

▪ Deferoxamine chelate makes urine turn a reddish color.
▪ Report blurred vision or any other visual abnormality. Periodic ophthalmoscopic examinations and audiometry are advised for patients on prolonged or high-dose therapy for chronic iron overload.

DENILEUKIN DIFTITOX

(den-i-leu′kin dif′ti-tox)

Ontak

Classification(s): ANTINEOPLASTIC, FUSION PROTEIN
Therapeutic: ANTINEOPLASTIC
Pregnancy Category: C

USES Persistent or recurrent T-cell lymphoma.

INDICATION & DOSAGE

T-Cell Lymphoma
Adult: 9 or 18 mcg/kg/day for 5 days, repeat every 21 days

SOLUTION PREPARATION

IV Infusion: Bring vials to room temperature (solution will be clear when room temperature is reached). Swirl to mix, but do not shake. Use only

---

Common adverse effects in *italic*, life-threatening effects <u>underlined</u>: generic names in **bold**; classifications in SMALL CAPS; ♣ Canadian drug name; ● Prototype drug

211

plastic syringe and plastic IV bag. Withdraw the calculated dose and inject it into an empty IV bag. Add **NO MORE THAN** 9 mL sterile saline without preservative to IV bag for each 1 mL of drug. Use within 6 h of preparation.

STORAGE
Store unopened vials in freezer. Prepared solution should be infused within 6 h.

ADMINISTRATION
IV Infusion: Infuse over at least 15 min without an in-line filter. A slower infusion over 30 min may be better tolerated. Stop infusion and notify prescriber if S&S of hypersensitivity occur.

INCOMPATIBILITIES Solution/additive: Do not physically mix with any other drug.

ACTION & *THERAPEUTIC EFFECT* A recombinant DNA cytotoxic protein that is an interleukin-2 receptor-specific protein that acts as an antineoplastic agent against malignant cells that express high-affinity for interleukin-2 (IL-2) receptors on the cell surface. Thus, it inhibits cellular protein synthesis and causes cell death of malignant cells. *Effectiveness is indicated by reduced tumor burden. Interacts with high affinity to IL-2 receptors on the cell surface in certain leukemias and lymphomas.*

CONTRAINDICATIONS Hypersensitivity to denileukin, diphtheria toxin, or interleukin-2; serum albumin levels below 3 g/dL; pregnancy (category C), lactation. Safety and efficacy in children less than 18 y are unknown.
CAUTIOUS USE Cardiovascular disease; peripheral vascular disease, coronary artery disease; elderly; hepatic and renal impairment; preexisting lower levels of serum albumin.

ADVERSE EFFECTS (≥1%) **Body as a Whole:** *Chills, fever, asthenia, infection, pain, headache, chest pain,* flu-like syndrome; injection site reaction; *acute hypersensitivity reaction (hypotension, back pain, dyspnea, vasodilation, rash, chest pain or tightness, tachycardia, dysphagia, syncope, <u>anaphylaxis</u>),* myalgia, arthralgia. **CNS:** *Dizziness, paresthesia, nervousness,* confusion, insomnia. **CV:** *Vascular leak syndrome (hypotension, edema, hypoalbuminemia); hypotension, vasodilation, tachycardia,* thrombotic events, hypertension, arrhythmia. **GI:** *Nausea, vomiting, anorexia, diarrhea,* constipation, dyspepsia, dysphagia. **Hematologic:** *Anemia,* thrombocytopenia, leukopenia. **Metabolic:** *Hypoalbuminemia; transaminase increase; edema; hypocalcemia; weight loss;* dehydration; hypokalemia. **Respiratory:** *Dyspnea, cough, pharyngitis, rhinitis,* lung disorder. **Skin:** *Rash, pruritus, sweating.* **Urogenital:** *Hematuria, albuminuria, pyuria, increased creatinine.*

DRUG INTERACTIONS No clinically significant interactions established.

PHARMACOKINETICS Distribution: Primarily distributed to liver and kidneys. **Metabolism:** Metabolized by proteolytic degradation. **Half-Life:** 70–80 min.

NURSING IMPLICATIONS

Assessment & Drug Effects

- Monitor and notify prescriber immediately for S&S of hypersensitivity or anaphylaxis that occur during/within 24 h of infusion.
- Monitor and notify prescriber immediately for S&S of flu-like syndrome that occur within several hours to days following infusion.
- Monitor outpatients for weight gain, developing edema, or declining BP.
- Notify prescriber immediately for S&S of vascular leak syndrome (e.g., edema PLUS hypotension or hypoalbuminemia) that may occur within 2 wk of infusion.
- Lab tests: Baseline and weekly CBC with differential, platelet count, serum electrolytes, serum albumin, renal function test and LFTs.

Patient & Family Education

- Report promptly S&S of infection.
- Check weight daily and report rapid weight gain or swelling of extremities promptly.
- Report bothersome adverse effects or S&S of infection or flu-like symptoms (e.g., fever, nausea, vomiting, diarrhea, rash).

DESMOPRESSIN ACETATE

(des-moe-pres'sin)

DDAVP

Classification(s): ANTIDIURETIC HORMONE (ADH)
Therapeutic: ANTIDIURETIC
Prototype: Vasopressin
Pregnancy Category: B

USES To control and prevent symptoms and complications of central (neurohypophyseal) diabetes insipidus or temporary polyuria/polydipsia associated with trauma, spontaneous bleeding and bleeding prophylaxis in bleeding disorders.

UNLABELED USES To increase factor VIII activity in selected patients with mild to moderate hemophilia A and in type I von Willebrand's disease or uremia, and to control enuresis in children.

INDICATION & DOSAGE

Diabetes Insipidus

Adult/Adolescent: 2–4 mcg in 2 divided doses

Bleeding Disorders

Adult/Adolescent/Child/Infant (over 3 mo): 0.3 mcg/kg 30 min preop, may repeat in 48 h if needed

Renal Impairment Dosage Adjustment

Do not use if CrCl less than 50 mL/min.

D

SOLUTION PREPARATION

Diabetes Insipidus
- *Direct IV Injection:* No dilution is required. Administer as supplied.

Hemophilia A and von Willebrand's Disease
- *IV Infusion:* Dilute a dose equal to 0.3 mcg/kg in 10 mL of NS (children up to 10 kg) or in 50 mL of NS (children over 10 kg and adults).

STORAGE
Store refrigerated from 2°–8° C (36°–46° F).

ADMINISTRATION

Diabetes Insipidus
- **Direct IV Injection:** Give bolus dose over 30 sec.

Hemophilia A and von Willebrand's Disease
- **IV Infusion:** Infuse over 15–30 min.

INCOMPATIBILITIES Data not available; do not mix with other drugs.

ACTION & *THERAPEUTIC EFFECT* Synthetic analog of the natural human posterior pituitary (antidiuretic) hormone. Has more specific and longer duration of action than antidiuretic hormone and lower incidence of allergic reactions. Reduces urine volume and osmolality of blood in patients with central diabetes insipidus by increasing reabsorption of water by kidney collecting tubules. Produces a dose-related increase in factor VIII (antihemophilic factor) and von Willebrand's factor. *Effective replacement for antidiuretic hormone. Additionally it can shorten or normalize bleeding time, and correct platelet adhesion abnormalities in certain patients with bleeding disorders.*

CONTRAINDICATIONS Nephrogenic diabetes insipidus; type II B von Willebrand's disease; renal failure, renal impairment.

CAUTIOUS USE Coronary artery insufficiency, hypertensive cardiovascular disease; severe CHF; older adults; history of thromboembolic disease; pregnancy (category B).

ADVERSE EFFECTS (≥1%) **Body as a Whole:** Dose related. **CNS:** Transient headache, drowsiness, listlessness. **GI:** Nausea, heartburn, mild abdominal cramps. **Other:** Vulval pain, shortness of breath, slight rise in BP, facial flushing, pain and swelling at injection site.

DRUG INTERACTIONS Demeclocycline, lithium, other VASOPRESSORS may decrease antidiuretic response; **carbamazepine, chlorpropamide, clofibrate** may prolong antidiuretic response.

PHARMACOKINETICS Onset: 15–60 min. **Peak:** 1–5 h. **Duration:** 5–21 h. **Distribution:** Small amount crosses blood–brain barrier; distributed into breast milk. **Half-Life:** 76 min.

NURSING IMPLICATIONS

Assessment & Drug Effects
- Monitor BP and HR closely during IV administration to patients with Hemophilia A and von Willebrand's disease.

- Monitor I&O ratio and pattern. Fluid intake **must be** carefully controlled, particularly in older adults and the very young to avoid water retention and sodium depletion.
- Weigh patient daily and observe for edema. Severe water retention may require reduction in dosage and use of a diuretic.
- Lab tests: Periodic serum sodium, renal function tests, urine and plasma osmolality with diabetes insipidus (an increase in urine osmolality and a decrease in plasma osmolality indicate effectiveness of treatment in diabetes insipidus).

Patient & Family Education
- Adhere closely to all fluid restrictions.

DEXAMETHASONE

(dex-a-meth'a-sone)

Dexamethasone Sodium Phosphate

Classification(s): ADRENAL CORTICOSTEROID

Therapeutic: ANTIINFLAMMATORY

Prototype: Prednisolone

Pregnancy Category: C

USES Adrenal insufficiency, inflammatory conditions, allergic states, collagen diseases, hematologic disorders, cerebral edema, palliative treatment of neoplastic disease, and addisonian shock.

UNLABELED USES As an antiemetic in cancer chemotherapy and to prevent hyaline membrane disease in premature infants.

INDICATION & DOSAGE

Allergies, Inflammation, Neoplasias

Adult: 0.5–0.9 mg/kg/day divided q6–12h, adjusted to patient response
Child: 0.03–0.3 mg/kg/day divided q6–12h adjusted to patient response

Cerebral Edema

Adult: 10 mg followed by 4 mg IM q6h, reduce dose after 2–4 days then taper over 5–7 days
Child: 1–2 mg/kg loading dose, then 1–1.5 mg/kg/day divided q4–6h (max: 16 mg/day)

Shock

Adult: 1–6 mg/kg as a single dose or 40 mg q4–6h if needed or 20 mg bolus then 3 mg/kg/day

SOLUTION PREPARATION

- *Direct IV Injection:* No dilution required for bolus dose.

Common adverse effects in *italic*, life-threatening effects <u>underlined</u>: generic names in **bold**; classifications in SMALL CAPS; ♣ Canadian drug name; ● Prototype drug

215

- *Intermittent Infusion:* Dilute in dextrose or saline solutions for infusion. Use preservative-free solutions with neonates.

STORAGE
Use diluted solutions within 24 h. Store unopened vials at 15°–30° C (59°–86° F) unless otherwise directed.

ADMINISTRATION
- **Direct IV Injection:** Give bolus dose over 30 sec or less.
- **Intermittent Infusion:** Set rate as prescribed or according to amount of solution to infuse (usually 10–30 min).
- Ensure IV patency as drug may cause atrophy and sterile abscess if infused into subcutaneous tissue.

INCOMPATIBILITIES Solution/additive: Daunorubicin, diphenhydramine, doxorubicin, glycopyrrolate, metaraminol, phenobarbital, vancomycin. Y-site: Ciprofloxacin, fenoldopam, idarubicin, midazolam, topotecan.

ACTION & *THERAPEUTIC EFFECT* Long-acting synthetic adrenocorticoid with intense antiinflammatory (glucocorticoid) activity. ***Antiinflammatory action:*** Prevents accumulation of inflammatory cells at sites of infection; inhibits phagocytosis, lysosomal enzyme release, and synthesis of potent mediators of inflammation, prostaglandins, and leukotrienes; reduces capillary dilation and permeability. ***Immunosuppression:*** May be due to prevention or suppression of delayed hypersensitivity immune reaction. *Has antiinflammatory and immunosuppression properties.*

CONTRAINDICATIONS Systemic fungal infection, acute infections, active or resting tuberculosis, vaccinia, varicella, administration of live virus vaccines (to patient, family members), latent or active amebiasis; Cushing's syndrome; neonates or infants less than 1300 g; pregnancy (category C), lactation.
CAUTIOUS USE Herpes simplex; keratitis; GI ulceration; renal disease; diabetes mellitus; hypothyroidism; myasthenia gravis; CHF; cirrhosis; psychic disorders; seizures; coagulopathy.

ADVERSE EFFECTS (≥1%) **CNS:** Euphoria, insomnia, convulsions, increased ICP, vertigo, headache, psychic disturbances. **CV:** CHF, hypertension, *edema*. **Endocrine:** Menstrual irregularities, *hyperglycemia*, cushingoid state, growth suppression in children, hirsutism. **Special Senses:** *Posterior cataract*, increased IOP, glaucoma, exophthalmos. **GI:** Peptic ulcer with possible perforation, abdominal distension, nausea, increased appetite, heartburn, dyspepsia, pancreatitis, <u>bowel perforation</u>, *oral candidiasis.* **Musculoskeletal:** Muscle weakness, loss of muscle mass, <u>vertebral compression fracture</u>, pathologic fracture of long bones, tendon rupture. **Skin:** Acne, *impaired wound healing,* petechiae, ecchymoses, diaphoresis, allergic dermatitis, hypo- or hyperpigmentation, subcutaneous and cutaneous atrophy, burning and tingling in perineal area (following IV injection).

DIAGNOSTIC TEST INTERFERENCE *Dexamethasone suppression test for endogenous depression:* False-positive results may be caused by **al-**

cohol, glutethimide, meprobamate; false-negative results may be caused by high doses of BENZODIAZEPINES (e.g., **chlordiazepoxide and cyproheptadine**), long-term GLUCOCORTICOID treatment, **indomethacin, ephedrine**, ESTROGENS or hepatic enzyme-inducing agents **(phenytoin)** may also cause false-positive results in *test for Cushing's syndrome.*

D

DRUG INTERACTIONS BARBITURATES, **phenytoin, rifampin** increase steroid metabolism—dosage of dexamethasone may need to be increased; **amphotericin B**, DIURETICS compound **potassium** loss; **ambenonium, neostigmine, pyridostigmine** may cause severe muscle weakness in patients with myasthenia gravis; may inhibit antibody response to VACCINES, TOXOIDS.

PHARMACOKINETICS Onset: Rapid onset. **Distribution:** Crosses placenta; distributed into breast milk. **Elimination:** Hypothalamus-pituitary axis suppression: 36–54 h. **Half-Life:** 3–4.5 h.

NURSING IMPLICATIONS

Assessment & Drug Effects

- Monitor and report S&S of Cushing's syndrome (see Appendix C) or other systemic adverse effects.
- Lab tests: Periodic serum electrolytes, lipid profile, blood glucose, and WBC count.
- Monitor diabetics for loss of glycemic control.
- Monitor I&O and daily weight. Assess for peripheral and pulmonary edema.

Patient & Family Education

- Report promptly malaise, muscular weakness or pain, nausea, vomiting, tarry stools, anorexia, hypoglycemic reactions, or mental depression.
- Report changes in appearance and easy bruising to prescriber.
- Note: Hiccups that occur for several hours following each dose may be a complication of high-dose oral dexamethasone.
- Add potassium-rich foods to diet; report signs of hypokalemia (see Appendix C).
- Avoid alcohol as it increases the risk of GI bleeding.
- Note: It is important to prevent exposure to infection, trauma, and sudden changes in environmental factors, as much as possible, because drug is an immunosuppressor.

DEXMEDETOMIDINE HYDROCHLORIDE

(dex-med-e-to′mi-deen)

Precedex

Classification(s): ALPHA-ADRENERGIC AGONIST; SEDATIVE-HYPNOTIC
Therapeutic: SEDATIVE-HYPNOTIC
Prototype: Methoxamine HCl
Pregnancy Category: C

Common adverse effects in *italic*, life-threatening effects underlined: generic names in **bold**; classifications in SMALL CAPS; ♣ Canadian drug name; ✪ Prototype drug

217

DEXMEDETOMIDINE HYDROCHLORIDE

USES Sedation of initially intubated or mechanically ventilated patients.

INDICATION & DOSAGE

Sedation
Adult: 1 mcg/kg loading dose infused over 10 min, then continue with infusion of 0.2–0.7 mcg/kg/h for up to 24 h, adjusted to maintain sedation

Hepatic Impairment Dosage Adjustment
Reduce initial dosage

Renal Impairment Dosage Adjustment
CrCl less than 30 mL/min: Reduce initial dose

SOLUTION PREPARATION
Continuous Infusion: Withdraw 2 mL (200 mcg) of dexmedetomidine and add to 48 mL of NS injection to yield 4 mcg/mL. Shake gently to mix.

STORAGE
Store at 15°–30° C (59°–86° F).

ADMINISTRATION
Continuous Infusion: A loading dose of 1 mcg/kg is infused over 10 min followed by the ordered maintenance infuse of 0.2–0.7 mcg/kg/h over 24 h. **Avoid** rapid bolus dosing. Infuse using a controlled infusion device. Do **not** use administration set containing natural rubber. Do **not** infuse longer than 24 h.

INCOMPATIBILITIES Y-site: **Amphotericin B, diazepam.**

ACTION & *THERAPEUTIC EFFECT* Dexmedetomidine stimulates alpha$_2$-adrenergic receptors in the CNS (primarily in the medulla oblongata) causing inhibition of the sympathetic vasomotor center of the brain. Hemodynamic responses of the heart that are affected by alpha$_2$ receptors are better controlled with dexmedetomidine than with other related drugs (e.g., midazolam). *Sedative properties utilized in intubating patients and for initially maintaining them on a mechanical ventilator.*

CONTRAINDICATIONS Hypersensitivity to dexmedetomidine; labor and delivery, including cesarean section; pregnancy (category C).

CAUTIOUS USE Patients with arrhythmias or cardiovascular disease, uncontrolled hypertension, hypotension; cerebrovascular disease; renal or hepatic insufficiency; signs of light anesthesia; older adults greater than 65 y; lactation. Safety and efficacy in children less than 18 y are unknown.

ADVERSE EFFECTS (≥1%) **Body as a Whole:** Pain, infection. **CV:** *Hypotension,* bradycardia, atrial fibrillation. **GI:** *Nausea,* thirst. **Respiratory:** Hypoxia, pleural effusion, pulmonary edema. **Hematologic:** Anemia, leukocytosis. **Urogenital:** Oliguria.

DRUG INTERACTIONS BARBITURATES, BENZODIAZEPINES, GENERAL ANESTHETICS, OPIATE AGONISTS, ANXIOLYTICS, SEDATIVES/HYPNOTICS, **ethanol,** TRICYCLIC ANTIDEPRESSANTS, **tramadol,** PHENOTHIAZINES, SKELETAL MUSCLE RELAXANTS, **azata-**

D

dine, **brompheniramine, carbinoxamine, chlorpheniramine, clem-astine, cyproheptadine, dexchlorpheniramine, dimenhydrinate, diphenhydramine, doxylamine, hydroxyzine, methdilazine, phenindamine, promethazine** enhance CNS depression, possibly prolonging recovery from anesthesia.

PHARMACOKINETICS Metabolism: Extensively metabolized in the liver (CYP 2A6). **Elimination:** Primarily excreted in urine. **Half-Life:** 2 h.

NURSING IMPLICATIONS

Assessment & Drug Effects

- Monitor for hypertension during loading dose; reduction of loading dose may be required.
- Monitor cardiovascular status continuously; notify prescriber immediately of hypotension or bradycardia (more common in those over 65 y).

DEXRAZOXANE

(dex-ra-zox′ane)

Zinecard

Classification(s): CHELATING AGENT
Therapeutic: CARDIOPROTECTIVE
Pregnancy Category: C

USES Reduction cardiomyopathy associated with a cumulative doxorubicin dose of 300 mg/m².

INDICATION & DOSAGE

Prevention of Cardiomyopathy

Adult: 10 parts dexrazoxane to 1 part doxorubicin (ex. 500 mg/m² for every 50 mg/m² of doxorubicin)

Renal Impairment Dosage Adjustment

CrCl less than 40 mL/min: Use a 5:1 ratio of dexrazoxane to doxorubicin

Hepatic Impairment Dosage Adjustment

Maintain a 10:1 ratio.

SOLUTION PREPARATION

- Wear gloves when handling dexrazoxane. Immediately wash with soap and water if drug contacts skin or mucosa.
- Doxorubicin dose **MUST be** started within 30 min of beginning dexrazoxane infusion or giving bolus injection.
- *Vial Reconstitution:* Add 25 or 50 mL of 0.167 M sodium lactate injection (provided by manufacturer) to the 250- or 500-mg vial, respectively, to produce a 10-mg/mL solution. May be given as prepared direct IV as a bolus dose or further diluted for infusion.

Common adverse effects in *italic*, life-threatening effects underlined: generic names in **bold**; classifications in SMALL CAPS; ♣ Canadian drug name; ✪ Prototype drug

219

- *Further Dilution of Reconstituted Solution:* Dilute with NS or D5W in an IV bag to a concentration of 1.3–5.0 mg/mL for infusion. Examples: Adding the contents of the reconstituted 250 mg vial to an additional 50 mL of IV fluids yields 3.3 mg/mL. Adding the contents of the reconstituted 500 mg vial to an additional 50 mL of IV fluids yields 5 mg/mL.

STORAGE

Store reconstituted solutions for 6 h at 15°–30° C (59°–86° F).

ADMINISTRATION

- **Direct IV Injection:** Give bolus dose slowly.
- **IV Infusion:** Infuse over 10–15 min.

INCOMPATIBILITIES Data not available; do not mix with other drugs.

ACTION & *THERAPEUTIC EFFECT* Derivative of EDTA that readily penetrates cell membranes. It is converted intracellularly to a chelating agent that interferes with iron-mediated free radical generation thought to be partially responsible for one form of cardiomyopathy. *Cardioprotective effect related to its chelating activity.*

CONTRAINDICATIONS Chemotherapy regimens that do not contain anthracycline; pregnancy (category C), lactation.

CAUTIOUS USE Myelosuppression; elderly; prior radiation or chemotherapy; renal failure or impairment. Safety and efficacy in children have not been established.

ADVERSE EFFECTS (≥1%) **All:** Adverse effects of dexrazoxane are difficult to distinguish from those of the chemotherapeutic agents. Pain at injection site, <u>leukopenia, granulocytopenia</u>, and <u>thrombocytopenia</u> appear to occur more frequently with the addition of dexrazoxane than with placebo.

DRUG INTERACTIONS Significant interactions not identified.

PHARMACOKINETICS Distribution: Not bound to plasma proteins. **Metabolism:** Metabolized in liver. **Elimination:** 42% excreted in urine. **Half-Life:** 2–2.5 h.

NURSING IMPLICATIONS

Assessment & Drug Effects

- Monitor cardiac function and assess for signs of HF. Drug does not eliminate risk of doxorubicin cardiotoxicity.
- Lab tests: Baseline and periodic serum iron and zinc, CBC with differential, PT and aPTT, LFTs, and renal function tests.

Patient & Family Education

- Report promptly any of the following: Worsening shortness of breath, swelling extremities, chest pains, or S&S of infection.
- Females using hormonal birth control should add a barrier contraceptive.
- Exercise caution to avoid injury or infection during dexrazoxane therapy.

DEXTRAN 40
(dex'tran)

Gentran 40, 10% LMD, Rheomacrodex
Classification(s): PLASMA VOLUME EXPANDER
Therapeutic: PLASMA VOLUME EXPANDER
Prototype: Albumin
Pregnancy Category: C

D

USES Adjunctively to expand plasma volume and provide fluid replacement in treatment of shock or impending shock. Also used in prophylaxis and therapy of venous thrombosis and pulmonary embolism. Used as priming fluid during extracorporeal circulation.

INDICATION & DOSAGE

Shock
Adult/Adolescent/Child: Up to 20 mL/kg in the first 24 h (doses up to 10 mL/kg/day may be given for a maximum of 4 additional days if needed)

Prophylaxis for Thromboembolic Complications
Adult: 10 mL/kg on the day of operation followed by 500 mL/day for 2–3 days, may continue with 500 mL q2–3day for up to 2 wk if necessary

Priming Fluid
Adult: 10–20 mL/kg added to perfusion circuit (max: 20 mL/kg)

SOLUTION PREPARATION
IV Infusion: Available as a 10% solution with no dilution required. Administer as supplied only if seal is intact, vacuum is detectable, and solution is absolutely clear. Crystals may be dissolved by submerging IV container in warm water.

STORAGE
Store at a constant temperature, preferably 25° C (77° F). Once opened, discard unused portion because dextran contains no preservative.

ADMINISTRATION
▪ **IV Infusion for Emergency Treatment for Shock in Adults:** Infuse first 500 mL rapidly (e.g., 20–40 mL/min); give remaining portion of the daily dose over 8–24 h.
▪ **IV Infusion for Other Indications:** Specific flow rate should be prescribed by prescriber.

INCOMPATIBILITIES Solution/additive: **Amoxicillin, ampicillin, oxacillin, penicillin.**

ACTION & *THERAPEUTIC EFFECT* Low-molecular-weight polysaccharide. As a hypertonic colloidal solution, produces immediate and short-lived ex-

---
Common adverse effects in *italic*, life-threatening effects underlined: generic names in **bold**; classifications in SMALL CAPS; ♣ Canadian drug name; ☻ Prototype drug

221

pansion of plasma volume by increasing colloidal osmotic pressure and drawing fluid from interstitial to intravascular space. *Cardiovascular response to volume expansion includes increased BP, pulse pressure, CVP, cardiac output, venous return to heart, and urinary output.*

CONTRAINDICATIONS Hypersensitivity to dextran solutions; severe renal failure; hypervolemic conditions; severe CHF; significant anemia; hypofibrinogenemia or other marked hemostatic defects including those caused by drugs (e.g., heparin, warfarin); pregnancy (category C), lactation.

CAUTIOUS USE Active hemorrhage; thrombocytopenia; dehydration; moderate chronic liver disease; impaired renal function; patients susceptible to pulmonary edema or CHF.

ADVERSE EFFECTS (≥1%) **Body as a Whole:** Hypersensitivity (mild to generalized urticaria, pruritus, <u>anaphylactic shock</u> (rare), <u>angioedema</u>, dyspnea). **Other:** Renal tubular vacuolization (osmotic nephrosis), stasis, and blocking; oliguria, <u>renal failure</u>; increased AST and ALT, interference with platelet function, prolonged bleeding and coagulation times.

DIAGNOSTIC TEST INTERFERENCE When blood samples are drawn for study, notify laboratory that patient has received dextran. ***Blood glucose:*** False increases (utilizing **ortho-toluidine methods** or **sulfuric** or **acetic acid** hydrolysis). ***Urinary protein:*** False increases (utilizing **Lowry method**). ***Bilirubin assays:*** False increases when alcohol is used. ***Total protein assays:*** False increases using **biuret reagent**. **Rh testing, blood typing** and **crossmatching** procedures: Dextran may interfere with results (by inducing rouleaux formation) when **proteolytic enzyme techniques** are used (**saline agglutination** and **indirect antiglobulin methods** reportedly not affected).

DRUG INTERACTIONS May potentiate **abciximab** anticoagulant effects.

PHARMACOKINETICS Onset: Volume expansion within minutes of infusion. **Duration:** 12 h. **Metabolism:** Degraded to glucose and metabolized to CO_2 and water over a period of a few weeks. **Elimination:** 75% excreted in urine within 24 h; small amount excreted in feces.

NURSING IMPLICATIONS

Assessment & Drug Effects

- Evaluate hydration status before dextran therapy begins. Administration to severely dehydrated patients can result in renal failure.
- If blood is to be administered, draw a cross-match specimen before dextran infusion.
- Monitor CVP as an estimate of blood volume status and a guide for determining dosage. Normal CVP: 5–10 cm H_2O. Observe for S&S of circulatory overload (see Appendix C).
- Monitor vital signs and observe patient closely for at least the first 30 min of infusion. Hypersensitivity reaction is most likely to occur during the first few minutes of administration. Terminate therapy at the first sign of a hypersensitivity reaction (see Appendix C).
- Lab tests: Baseline Hct prior to and after initiation of dextran (dextran usually lowers Hct). Notify prescriber if Hct is depressed below 30% by volume.

222

Common adverse effects in *italic*, life-threatening effects <u>underlined</u>: generic names in **bold**; classifications in SMALL CAPS; ♣ Canadian drug name; ● Prototype drug

- Monitor I&O ratio and check urine specific gravity at regular intervals. Low urine specific gravity may signify failure of renal dextran clearance and is an indication to discontinue therapy.
- Report oliguria, anuria, or lack of improvement in urinary output (dextran usually causes an increase in urinary output). Discontinue dextran at first sign of renal dysfunction.
- High doses are associated with transient prolongation of bleeding time and interference with normal blood coagulation.

Patient & Family Education
- Report immediately S&S of bleeding (e.g., easy bruising, blood in urine, or dark tarry stool).

DEXTRAN 70
(dex'tran)
Macrodex

DEXTRAN 75
Gentran 75
Classification(s): PLASMA VOLUME EXPANDER
Therapeutic: PLASMA VOLUME EXPANDER
Prototype: Albumin
Pregnancy Category: C

USES Primarily for emergency treatment of hypovolemic shock or impending shock caused by hemorrhage, burns, surgery, or other trauma, when whole blood or blood products are not available or when haste precludes cross-matching of blood.
UNLABELED USES Nephrosis, toxemia of pregnancy, and prophylaxis of deep vein thrombosis.

INDICATION & DOSAGE

Shock

Adult: 500 mL administered rapidly (over 15–30 min), additional doses may be given more slowly up to 20 mL/kg in the first 24 h (doses up to 10 mL/kg/day may be given for an additional 4 days if needed)

SOLUTION PREPARATION
IV Infusion: Available as a 6% solution with no dilution required. Administer as supplied only if seal is intact, vacuum is detectable, and solution is absolutely clear. Crystals may be dissolved by submerging IV container in warm water.

STORAGE
Store at a constant temperature, preferably 25° C (77° F). Once opened, discard unused portion because dextran contains no preservative.

Common adverse effects in *italic*, life-threatening effects <u>underlined</u>: generic names in **bold**; classifications in SMALL CAPS; ♣ Canadian drug name; ✪ Prototype drug

D

ADMINISTRATION

- **IV Infusion for Emergency Treatment for Shock in Adults:** Infuse 500–1000 mL at 20–40 mL/min.
- **IV Infusion for Other Indications:** Specific flow rate should be prescribed by prescriber.

INCOMPATIBILITIES Data not available; do not mix with other drugs.

ACTION & *THERAPEUTIC EFFECT* High-molecular-weight polysaccharide. Colloidal properties approximately those of serum albumin. The colloidal osmotic effect of dextran draws fluid into vascular system from interstitial spaces, resulting in increased circulating blood volume and decreased blood viscosity. *Cardiovascular response to volume expansion includes increased BP, pulse pressure, CVP, cardiac output, venous return to heart, and urinary output.*

CONTRAINDICATIONS Known hypersensitivity to dextran solutions; severe bleeding disorders; coagulopathy; severe CHF; severe renal failure; pregnancy (category C), lactation.
CAUTIOUS USE Impaired renal function; thrombocytopenia; pulmonary edema; CHF; pathological GI disorders.

ADVERSE EFFECTS (≥1%) **All:** *Allergic reactions,* urticaria, wheezing, mild hypotension, nausea, vomiting, fever, arthralgia, <u>severe anaphylactoid reaction</u>.

PHARMACOKINETICS Onset: Volume expansion within minutes of infusion. **Duration:** 12 h. **Metabolism:** Degraded to glucose and metabolized to carbon dioxide and water over a period of a few weeks. **Elimination:** 75% excreted in urine within 24 h; small amount excreted in feces.

NURSING IMPLICATIONS

Assessment & Drug Effects

- Evaluate hydration status before dextran therapy begins. Administration to severely dehydrated patients can result in renal failure.
- If blood is to be administered, draw a cross-match specimen before dextran infusion.
- Monitor CVP as an estimate of blood volume status and a guide for determining dosage. Normal CVP: 5–10 cm H_2O. Observe for S&S of circulatory overload (see Appendix C).
- Monitor vital signs and observe patient closely for at least the first 30 min of infusion. Hypersensitivity reaction is most likely to occur during the first few minutes of administration. Terminate therapy at the first sign of a hypersensitivity reaction (see Appendix C).
- Lab tests: Baseline Hct prior to and after initiation of dextran (dextran usually lowers Hct). Notify prescriber if Hct is depressed below 30% by volume.
- Monitor I&O ratio and check urine specific gravity at regular intervals. Low urine specific gravity may signify failure of renal dextran clearance and is an indication to discontinue therapy.

Common adverse effects in *italic*, life-threatening effects <u>underlined</u>: generic names in **bold**; classifications in SMALL CAPS; ♣ Canadian drug name; ✿ Prototype drug

▪ Report oliguria, anuria, or lack of improvement in urinary output (dextran usually causes an increase in urinary output). Discontinue dextran at first sign of renal dysfunction.
▪ High doses are associated with transient prolongation of bleeding time and interference with normal blood coagulation.

Patient & Family Education
▪ Report immediately S&S of bleeding (e.g., easy bruising, blood in urine, or dark tarry stool).

DIAZEPAM ⊘

(dye-az'e-pam)

Diazemuls ✦
Classification(s): ANTICONVULSANT, BENZODIAZEPINE
Therapeutic: ANTIANXIETY; ANTICONVULSANT
Pregnancy Category: D   **Controlled Substance:** Schedule IV

USES Drug of choice for status epilepticus. Also used to alleviate acute withdrawal symptoms of alcoholism, voiding problems in older adults, and adjunctively for relief of skeletal muscle spasm associated with cerebral palsy, paraplegia, athetosis, stiff-man syndrome, tetanus.

INDICATION & DOSAGE

Status Epilepticus
Adult/Adolescent: 5–10 mg, repeat if needed at 10–15 min intervals up to 30 mg, then repeat if needed q2–4h
Child (5 y or over): 1 mg/kg q2–5min (max: 10 mg) may repeat in 2–4 h
Child/Infant (1 mo–5 y): 0.2–0.5 mg slowly q2–5min up to 5 mg
Neonate: 0.1–0.3 mg/kg q15–30min (max: Total dose 2 mg)

Muscle Spasm
Adult/Adolescent/Child (5 y or more): 5–10 mg q3–4h prn (larger dose for tetanus)
Child/Infant (1 mo–5 y): 1–2 mg q3–4h prn

Anxiety
Adult/Adolescent: 2–10 mg, repeat if needed in 3–4 h
Child/Infant (6 mo or over): 0.04–0.3 mg q2–4h (max 0.6 mg/kg/8 h)

Alcohol Withdrawal
Adult: 10 mg then 5–10 mg in 3–4 h

Preoperative
Adult: 5–15 mg 5–10 min before procedure

Common adverse effects in *italic*, life-threatening effects underlined: generic names in **bold**; classifications in SMALL CAPS; ✦ Canadian drug name; ⊘ Prototype drug

SOLUTION PREPARATION

No dilution is required. Administer as supplied and do not dilute or mix with other drugs.

STORAGE

Store at 15°–30° C (59°–86° F). Store emulsion below 25° C (77° F). Protect from light and do not freeze.

ADMINISTRATION

- **Direct IV Injection:** *Adult:* Give bolus dose slowly, over at least 1 min for each 5 mg. *Infant/Child:* Give bolus dose slowly, over at least 3 min (do not exceed 0.25 mg/kg over 3 min).
  - *Emulsified diazepam:* Give emulsion form within 6 h of opening ampule as it contains no preservatives. Use only polyethylene-lined or glass infusion sets. Flush IV line after infusion. If a filter is used, ensure that the pore size is 5 microns or greater.
- Avoid small veins and take extreme care to avoid intra-arterial administration or extravasation. If IV injection cannot be made directly into vein, inject slowly through infusion tubing as close as possible to vein insertion.
- Keep patient recumbent during and for at least 3 h following administration.

INCOMPATIBILITIES Solution/additive: Bleomycin, dobutamine, doxorubicin, epinephrine, fluorouracil, furosemide, glycopyrrolate, nalbuphine, sodium bicarbonate. Y-site: Amphotericin B cholesteryl complex, atracurium, bivalirudin, cefepime, dexmedetomidine, diltiazem, fenoldopam, fluconazole, foscarnet, furosemide, gatifloxacin, heparin, hetastarch, lansoprazole, linezolid, meropenem, oxaliplatin, pancuronium, potassium chloride, propofol, remifentanil, tirofiban, vecuronium, vitamin B complex with C.

ACTION & *THERAPEUTIC EFFECT* Long-acting psychotherapeutic agent; BENZODIAZEPINES act at the limbic, thalamic, and hypothalamic regions of CNS. Depending upon the dosage, it produces CNS depression resulting in sedation, hypnosis, skeletal muscle relaxation, and anticonvulsant activity. *Shortens REM and Stage 4 sleep, but increases total sleep time. Has antianxiety and anticonvulsant properties.*

CONTRAINDICATIONS Shock; coma; acute alcohol intoxication; depressed vital signs; obstetrical patients; pregnancy (category D), lactation.

CAUTIOUS USE Epilepsy, psychoses, mental depression; myasthenia gravis; impaired hepatic or renal function; neuromuscular disease; bipolar disorder, dementia, Parkinson's disease; organic brain syndrome, psychosis, suicidal ideation; drug abuse, addiction-prone individuals; extreme caution in older adults, the very ill, and patients with COPD, or asthma; infants less than 30 days of age.

ADVERSE EFFECTS (≥1%) **Body as a Whole:** Throat and chest pain. **CNS:** *Drowsiness,* fatigue, ataxia, confusion, paradoxic rage, dizziness, vertigo, amnesia, vivid dreams, headache, slurred speech, tremor, EEG changes, tardive dyskinesia. **CV:** Hypotension, tachycardia, edema, <u>cardiovascular</u>

Common adverse effects in *italic*, life-threatening effects <u>underlined</u>: generic names in **bold**; classifications in SMALL CAPS; ♣ Canadian drug name; ⊘ Prototype drug

<u>collapse.</u> **Special Senses:** Blurred vision, diplopia, nystagmus. **GI:** Xerostomia, nausea, constipation, hepatic dysfunction. **Urogenital:** Incontinence, urinary retention, gynecomastia (prolonged use), menstrual irregularities, ovulation failure. **Respiratory:** Hiccups, coughing, <u>laryngospasm</u>. **Other:** Pain, venous thrombosis, phlebitis at injection site.

DRUG INTERACTIONS Alcohol, CNS DEPRESSANTS, ANTICONVULSANTS potentiate CNS depression; **cimetidine** increases diazepam plasma levels, increases toxicity; may decrease antiparkinson effects of **levodopa;** may increase **phenytoin** levels; smoking decreases sedative and antianxiety effects.

PHARMACOKINETICS Onset: 1–5 min. **Duration:** 15 min–1 h. **Distribution:** Crosses blood–brain barrier and placenta; distributed into breast milk. **Metabolism:** Metabolized in liver to active metabolites. **Elimination:** Excreted primarily in urine. **Half-Life:** 20–50 h.

NURSING IMPLICATIONS
Assessment & Drug Effects
- Keep patient on bed rest for 3–4 h post-IV injection.
- Monitor for respiratory depression and apnea especially in the elderly and very ill with limited respiratory reserve.
- Monitor for seizures and other adverse reactions, which are often dose related.
- Observe preventive precautions for suicidal tendencies that may be present in anxiety states accompanied by depression.
- Observe patient closely and monitor vital signs as hypotension, muscular weakness, tachycardia, and respiratory depression may occur.
- Supervise ambulation. Adverse reactions such as drowsiness and ataxia are more likely to occur in older adults, debilitated persons, and those with hypoalbuminemia.
- With concurrent digoxin or phenytoin, monitor blood levels of these drugs closely and assess for S&S of toxicity.

Patient & Family Education
- Avoid alcohol and other CNS depressants. Concomitant use of these agents can cause severe drowsiness, respiratory depression, and apnea.
- Do not drive or engage in other potentially hazardous activities or those requiring mental precision until reaction to drug is known.
- Check with prescriber before taking any OTC drugs.

DIAZOXIDE
(dye-az-ox′ide)

Hyperstat I.V.

Classification(s): VASODILATOR, NONNITRATE

Therapeutic: ANTIHYPERTENSIVE

Prototype: Hydralazine

Pregnancy Category: C

Common adverse effects in *italic*, life-threatening effects <u>underlined</u>: generic names in **bold**; classifications in SMALL CAPS; ♣ Canadian drug name; ● Prototype drug

227

DIAZOXIDE

USES Emergency reduction of BP.

INDICATION & DOSAGE

Severe Hypertension
Adult/Child: 1–3 mg/kg (up to 150 mg/injection), repeat at 5–15 min intervals if necessary

SOLUTION PREPARATION
No dilution is required. Administer as supplied.

STORAGE
Do not give darkened solutions. Store at 2°–30° C (36°–86° F). Protect from light, heat, and freezing.

ADMINISTRATION
- **Direct IV Injection:** Give bolus dose rapidly over 10–30 sec. Keep patient recumbent while receiving IV and for at least 30 min after administration (or up to 10 h when used concurrently with furosemide).
- Check IV injection site frequently. Solution is strongly alkaline. Extravasation of medication into tissues can cause severe inflammatory reaction. Administer drug by peripheral vein ONLY.

INCOMPATIBILITIES Y-site: **Hydralazine, lidocaine, propranolol.**

ACTION & *THERAPEUTIC EFFECT* Rapid-acting thiazide nondiuretic hypotensive and hyperglycemic agent. In contrast to thiazide diuretics, causes sodium and water retention and decreases urinary output, probably because it increases proximal tubular reabsorption of sodium, and decreases glomerular filtration rate. Hypotensive effect may be accompanied by marked reflexive increase in heart rate, cardiac output, and stroke volume; thus cerebral and coronary blood flows are usually maintained. *Reduces peripheral vascular resistance and BP by direct vasodilatory effect on peripheral arteriolar smooth muscles, perhaps by direct competition for calcium receptor sites.*

CONTRAINDICATIONS Hypersensitivity to diazoxide; cerebral bleeding, eclampsia; aortic coarctation; AV shunt, significant coronary artery disease; pheochromocytoma; pregnancy (category C), lactation.
CAUTIOUS USE Diabetes mellitus; impaired cerebral or cardiac circulation; impaired renal function; patients taking corticosteroids or estrogen–progestogen combinations; hyperuricemia, history of gout, uremia; thiazide diuretic hypersensitivity.

ADVERSE EFFECTS (≥1%) **CNS:** Headache, weakness, malaise, *dizziness,* polyneuritis, sleepiness, insomnia, euphoria, anxiety, extrapyramidal signs. **CV:** Palpitations, atrial and ventricular arrhythmias, flushing, shock; *orthostatic hypotension,* CHF, transient hypertension. **Special Senses:** Tinnitus, momentary hearing loss; blurred vision, transient cataracts, subconjunctival hemorrhage, ring scotoma, diplopia, lacrimation, papilledema. **GI:** *Nausea, vomiting,* abdominal discomfort, diarrhea, constipation, ileus, anorexia, transient loss of taste, impaired hepatic function. **Hematologic:** Transient neutropenia, eosinophilia, decreased Hgb/Hct, decreased IgG. **Body as a Whole:** Hypersensitivity (rash, fever, leukopenia); chest and back pain, muscle cramps. **Urogenital:** Decreased urinary output, nephrotic syndrome (reversible), hematuria, increased nocturia, proteinuria, azotemia; inhibition of labor. **Skin:** Pruritus, flushing, monilial dermatitis, herpes, hirsutism; loss of scalp hair, sweating, sensation of warmth, burning, or itching. **Endocrine:** Advance in bone age (children), *hyperglycemia, sodium and water retention, edema,* hyperuricemia, glycosuria, enlargement of breast lump, galactorrhea; decreased immunoglobulinemia, hirsutism.

DIAGNOSTIC TEST INTERFERENCE Diazoxide can cause false-negative response to *glucagon.*

DRUG INTERACTIONS SULFONYLUREAS antagonize effects; THIAZIDE DIURETICS may intensify hyperglycemia and antihypertensive effects; **phenytoin** increases risk of hyperglycemia, and diazoxide may increase **phenytoin** metabolism, causing loss of seizure control; may potentiate effect of **warfarin.**

PHARMACOKINETICS Onset: 30–60 sec. **Peak:** 5 min. **Duration:** 2–12 or more h. **Distribution:** Crosses blood–brain barrier and placenta. **Metabolism:** Partially metabolized in the liver. **Elimination:** Excreted in urine. **Half-Life:** 21–45 h.

NURSING IMPLICATIONS

Assessment & Drug Effects

- Monitor BP q5min for the first 15–30 min or until stabilized, then hourly for balance of drug effect. Assess postural vital signs prior to ambulation.
- Report promptly if BP continues to fall 30 min or more after drug administration.
- Monitor pulse: Tachycardia has occurred immediately following IV; palpitation and bradycardia have also been reported.
- Assess for developing or worsening edema, and observe closely for S&S of CHF (see Appendix C).
- Lab tests: Baseline and periodic CBC, blood glucose, and serum electrolytes particularly in patients with impaired renal function; hypokalemia potentiates hyperglycemic effect of diazoxide.
- Monitor diabetics carefully for loss of glycemic control.
- Report promptly any change in I&O ratio.
- Monitor S&S for up to 7 days for both oral and parenteral forms; essential because of long half-life of diazoxide.

Patient & Family Education

- Note: Drug may cause hyperglycemia and glycosuria in diabetics and diabetic-prone individuals. Closely monitor blood glucose for loss of glycemic control.
- Report palpitations, chest pain, dizziness, fainting, or severe headache.
- Lanugo-type hirsutism occurs frequently, commonly in children and women. It is reversible with discontinuation of drug.

D

DIGOXIN ⊕

(di-jox'in)

Lanoxin
Classification(s): INOTROPIC AGENT, CARDIAC GLYCOSIDE
Therapeutic: ANTIARRHYTHMIC; CARDIOTONIC
Pregnancy Category: A

USES Rapid digitalization and for maintenance therapy in CHF, atrial fibrillation, atrial flutter, paroxysmal atrial tachycardia.

INDICATION & DOSAGE

Digitalizing Dose (give $^1/_2$ dose initially followed by $^1/_4$ at 8–12 h intervals)
Adult: 0.5–1 mg
Child (2–10 y): 20–35 mcg/kg; *(over 10 y):* 8–12 mcg/kg
Infant: 30–50 mcg/kg
Neonate (Preterm): 15–25 mcg/kg; *(Full-term):* 20–30 mcg/kg

Maintenance Dose
Adult: 0.1–0.4 mg/day
Child/Infant: 25–35% of loading dose per day
Neonate: 20–30% of loading dose divided q12h

Obesity
Dose based on IBW.

SOLUTION PREPARATION
May be given undiluted or diluted in 4 mL of sterile water, D5W, or NS for infusion. Once diluted, administer immediately.

STORAGE
Store solution at 25° C (77° F) or at 15°–30° C (59°–86° F).

ADMINISTRATION
- Monitor IV site frequently. Infiltration into subcutaneous tissue can cause local irritation and sloughing.
- **Direct IV Injection:** Give bolus dose over 5 min.

INCOMPATIBILITIES Solution/additive: Dobutamine. Y-site: Amiodarone, amphotericin B cholesteryl complex, fluconazole, foscarnet, propofol.

ACTION & *THERAPEUTIC EFFECT* Widely used cardiac glycoside of *Digitalis lanata*. Acts by increasing the force and velocity of myocardial systolic contraction (positive inotropic effect). It also decreases conduction velocity through the atrioventricular node. *Increases the contractility of the heart muscle (positive inotropic effect). Has antiarrhythmic properties that result from its effects on the AV node.*

Common adverse effects in *italic*, life-threatening effects <u>underlined</u>: generic names in **bold**; classifications in SMALL CAPS; ♣ Canadian drug name; ⊕ Prototype drug

D

CONTRAINDICATIONS Digitalis hypersensitivity, sick sinus syndrome, Wolff-Parkinson-White syndrome; ventricular fibrillation, ventricular tachycardia unless due to CHF. Full digitalizing dose not given if patient has received digoxin during previous week or if slowly excreted cardiotonic glycoside has been given during previous 2 wk.

CAUTIOUS USE Renal insufficiency, hypokalemia, advanced heart disease, cardiomyopathy; acute MI, incomplete AV block, cor pulmonale; hypothyroidism; lung disease; older adults, or debilitated patients; pregnancy (category A); premature and immature infants, children.

ADVERSE EFFECTS (≥1%) **CNS:** Fatigue, muscle weakness, headache, facial neuralgia, mental depression, paresthesias, hallucinations, confusion, drowsiness, agitation, dizziness. **CV:** Arrhythmias, hypotension, <u>AV block</u>. **Special Senses:** Visual disturbances. **GI:** Anorexia, *nausea,* vomiting, diarrhea. **Other:** Diaphoresis, recurrent malaise, dysphagia.

DRUG INTERACTIONS DIURETICS, CORTICOSTEROIDS, **amphotericin B,** LAXATIVES, **sodium polystyrene sulfonate** may cause hypokalemia, increasing the risk of digoxin toxicity; **calcium IV** may increase risk of arrhythmias if administered together with digoxin; **quinidine, verapamil, amiodarone, flecainide** significantly increase digoxin levels, and digoxin dose should be decreased by 50%; **erythromycin** may increase digoxin levels; **succinylcholine** may potentiate arrhythmogenic effects; **nefazodone** may increase digoxin levels.

PHARMACOKINETICS Onset: 5–30 min. **Peak:** 1–5 h. **Duration:** 3–4 days in fully digitalized patient. **Distribution:** Widely distributed; tissue levels significantly higher than plasma levels; crosses placenta. **Metabolism:** Approximately 14% in liver. **Elimination:** 80–90% excreted by kidneys; may appear in breast milk. **Half-Life:** 34–44 h.

NURSING IMPLICATIONS
Assessment & Drug Effects
- Monitor ECG continuously. Note HR/apical pulse before administering drug.
- Withhold medication and notify prescriber if HR/apical pulse falls below ordered parameters (e.g., less than 50 or 60/min in adults and less than 60 or 70/min in children).
- Be familiar with patient's baseline data (e.g., quality of peripheral pulses, blood pressure, clinical symptoms) as a foundation for making assessments.
- Lab tests: Baseline and periodic serum digoxin, potassium, magnesium, and calcium. Draw blood samples for determining plasma digoxin levels at least 6 h after daily dose and preferably just before next scheduled daily dose.
- Monitor for S&S of drug toxicity: In children, cardiac arrhythmias are usually reliable signs of early toxicity. Early indicators in adults (anorexia, nausea, vomiting, diarrhea, visual disturbances) are rarely initial signs in children.
- Monitor I&O ratio during digitalization, particularly in patients with impaired renal function. Also monitor for edema and auscultate chest for rales.
- Monitor serum digoxin levels closely during concurrent antibiotic–digoxin therapy, which can precipitate toxicity because of altered intestinal flora.

Common adverse effects in *italic*, life-threatening effects <u>underlined</u>: generic names in **bold**; classifications in SMALL CAPS; ♣ Canadian drug name; ❂ Prototype drug

231

D

Patient & Family Education
- Report to prescriber if pulse falls below 60 or rises above 110 or if you detect skipped beats or other changes in rhythm, when digoxin is prescribed for atrial fibrillation.
- Report promptly any of the following: Anorexia, nausea, vomiting, diarrhea, or visual disturbances.

DIGOXIN IMMUNE FAB (OVINE)

(di-jox′in)

Digibind, DigiFab
Classification(s): ANTIDOTE
Therapeutic: ANTIDOTE
Pregnancy Category: C

USES Treatment of potentially life-threatening digoxin or digitoxin intoxication in carefully selected patients.

INDICATION & DOSAGE

Serious Digoxin Toxicity Secondary to Overdose
Adult/Child: Dosages vary according to amount of digoxin to be neutralized; dosages are based on total body load or steady state serum digoxin concentrations (see package insert); some patients may require a second dose after several hours

SOLUTION PREPARATION
- *Vial Reconstitution:* Dilute each vial with 4 mL of sterile water for injection to yield 9.5 mg/mL for Digibind and 10 mg/mL for DigiFab; mix gently. May be given as prepared or further diluted for infusion.
- *Further Dilution of Reconstituted Solution:* Dilute with any volume of NS compatible with cardiac status. For those receiving less than 3 mg, dilute to a concentration of 1 mg/mL by adding 34 mL of NS to Digibind or 36 mL of NS to DigiFab.
  - *Infants:* For very small doses for infants, reconstitute to a concentration of 1 mg/mL.
- Maximum Concentration: 10 mg/mL

STORAGE
Use reconstituted solutions promptly or refrigerated at 2°–8° C (36°–46° F) for up to 4 h.

ADMINISTRATION
- **Direct IV Injection:** Give bolus dose ONLY if cardiac arrest is imminent.
- **IV Infusion:** Infuse over 30 min; a 0.22-micron filter is recommended for Digibind and may be used for DigiFab. If infusion-related reactions occur, stop the infusion, notify prescriber; restart infusion only at a slower rate.
- *Administration to Infants:* For very small doses, withdraw dose with a TB syringe for accurate measurement. Closely monitor for fluid overload.

Common adverse effects in *italic*, life-threatening effects <u>underlined</u>: generic names in **bold**; classifications in SMALL CAPS; ♣ Canadian drug name; ⓟ Prototype drug

INCOMPATIBILITIES Data not available; do not mix with other drugs.

ACTION & *THERAPEUTIC EFFECT* Fab contains purified fragments of antibodies specific for digoxin but also effective for digitoxin. Fab acts by selectively complexing with circulating digoxin or digitoxin, thereby preventing drug from binding at receptor sites; the complex is then eliminated in urine. *Digoxin immune Fab is a protein that consists of antibody fragments that are used as an antidote for digitalis toxicity.*

CONTRAINDICATIONS Hypersensitivity to sheep products; renal or cardiac failure; pregnancy (category C), lactation.

CAUTIOUS USE Prior treatment with sheep antibodies or ovine Fab fragments; mannitol hypersensitivity; history of allergies; impaired renal function or renal failure; elderly; lactation.

ADVERSE EFFECTS (≥1%) Adverse reactions associated with use of digoxin immune Fab are related primarily to the effects of **digitalis** withdrawal on the heart (see **NURSING IMPLICATIONS**). Allergic reactions have been rarely reported. Hypokalemia.

DIAGNOSTIC TEST INTERFERENCE Digoxin immune Fab may interfere with ***serum digoxin*** determinations by ***immunoassay tests.***

DRUG INTERACTIONS No clinically relevant interactions have been established.

PHARMACOKINETICS Onset: Less than 1 min after administration. **Elimination:** Excreted in urine over 5–7 days. **Half-Life:** 14–20 h.

NURSING IMPLICATIONS

Assessment & Drug Effects

- Perform skin testing for allergy prior to administration of immune Fab, particularly in patients with history of allergy or who have had previous therapy with immune Fab.
- Keep emergency equipment and drugs immediately available before skin testing is done or first dose is given and until patient is out of danger.
- Monitor for therapeutic effectiveness. S&S of reversal of digitalis toxicity occur in 15–60 min in adults and usually within minutes in children.
- Monitor baseline and frequent vital signs and EGG during administration.
- Lab tests: Baseline and frequent serum potassium, digoxin or digitoxin levels. Note: Serum potassium is particularly critical during first several hours following administration of immune Fab.
- Monitor closely cardiac status as it may deteriorate when inotropic action of digitalis is withdrawn by action of immune Fab. CHF, arrhythmias, and increase in heart rate can occur.

DIHYDROERGOTAMINE MESYLATE

(dye-hye-droe-er-got'a-meen)

D.H.E. 45

Classification(s): ADRENERGIC ANTAGONIST; ERGOT ALKALOID

Common adverse effects in *italic*, life-threatening effects <u>underlined</u>: generic names in **bold**; classifications in SMALL CAPS; ♣ Canadian drug name; ⦿ Prototype drug

233

DIHYDROERGOTAMINE MESYLATE

Therapeutic: ANTIMIGRAINE
Prototype: Ergotamine
Pregnancy Category: X

USES To prevent or abort vascular headache.
UNLABELED USES To treat postural hypotension.

INDICATION & DOSAGE

Migraine Headache
Adult: 1 mg, may be repeated at 1 h intervals to a total 2 mg (max: 6 mg/wk)

SOLUTION PREPARATION
No dilution is required. Administer as supplied.

STORAGE
Store at 15°–30° C (59°–86° F) unless otherwise directed. Protect ampules from heat and light; do not freeze. Discard ampule if solution appears discolored. Discard ampule if solution appears discolored.

ADMINISTRATION
Direct IV injection: Give bolus dose at a rate of 1 mg/min.

INCOMPATIBILITIES Data not available; do not mix with other drugs.

ACTION & *THERAPEUTIC EFFECT* Alpha-adrenergic blocking agent and dihydrogenated ergot alkaloid with direct constricting effect on smooth muscle of peripheral and cranial blood vessels. Its ergot properties acts as a selective serotonin agonist at the 5-HT-1 receptors located on intracranial blood vessels, which may also cause vasoconstriction of large intracranial conductance arteries; this correlates with relief of migraine headaches. *Has somewhat weaker vasoconstrictor action than ergotamine but greater adrenergic blocking activity resulting in relief from migraine headaches.*

CONTRAINDICATIONS History of hypersensitivity to ergot preparations; peripheral vascular disease, coronary heart disease, MI, hypertension; peptic ulcer; severely impaired hepatic or renal function; sepsis; within 48 h of surgery; pregnancy (category X), lactation. Safe use in children less than 6 y is not established.
CAUTIOUS USE Moderate or mild renal or hepatic impairment; obesity; diabetes mellitus; postmenopausal women; male greater than 40 y; pulmonary heart disease; valvular heart disease; smokers.

ADVERSE EFFECTS (≥1%) **CV:** Vasospasm: Coldness, numbness, and tingling in fingers and toes; muscle pains and weakness of legs; precordial distress and pain; transient tachycardia or bradycardia; hypertension (large doses). **GI:** *Nausea, vomiting.* **Body as a Whole:** Dizziness, dysphoria, *localized edema and itching;* ergotism (excessive doses).

DRUG INTERACTIONS BETA BLOCKERS, **erythromycin** increase peripheral vasoconstriction with risk of ischemia; increased **ergotamine** toxicity

Common adverse effects in *italic*, life-threatening effects underlined: generic names in **bold**; classifications in SMALL CAPS; ♣ Canadian drug name; ◐ Prototype drug

with drugs that inhibit CYP3A4 (e.g., PROTEASE INHIBITORS, **amprenavir, ritonavir, nelfinavir, indinavir, saquinavir**), MACROLIDE ANTIBIOTICS **(erythromycin, azithromycin, clarithromycin),** AZOLE ANTIFUNGALS **(ketoconazole, itraconazole, fluconazole, clotrimazole), fluoxetine, fluvoxamine.**

PHARMACOKINETICS Onset: Less than 5 min. **Duration:** 3–4 h. **Distribution:** Probably distributed into breast milk. **Metabolism:** Metabolized in liver (CYP 3A4). **Elimination:** Excreted primarily in urine; some excreted in feces. **Half-Life:** 21–32 h.

NURSING IMPLICATIONS

Assessment & Drug Effects

- Monitor cardiac status, especially when large doses are given.
- Monitor for and report numbness and tingling of fingers and toes, extremity weakness, muscle pain, or intermittent claudication.

Patient & Family Education

- Report immediately if any of the following S&S develop: Chest pain, nausea, vomiting, change in heartbeat, numbness, tingling, pain or weakness of extremities, edema, or itching.

DILTIAZEM

(dil-tye'a-zem)

Cardizem

Classification(s): CALCIUM CHANNEL BLOCKER
Therapeutic: ANTIARRHYTHMIC
Prototype: Verapamil
Pregnancy Category: C

USES Atrial fibrillation, atrial flutter, supraventricular tachycardia.
UNLABELED USES Prevention of reinfarction in non–Q-wave MI.

INDICATION & DOSAGE

Atrial Fibrillation

Adult: 0.25 mg/kg IV bolus over 2 min, if inadequate response, may repeat in 15 min with 0.35 mg/kg, followed by a continuous infusion of 5–10 mg/h (max: 15 mg/h for 24 h)

SOLUTION PREPARATION

- Diltiazem injection (5 mg/mL) may be given undiluted [direct IV] or diluted in D5W, NS, or D5/1/2NS for infusion.
- *Cardizem Lyo-Ject Syringe*: Follow- directions on blister package for reconstitution.

Common adverse effects in *italic*, life-threatening effects <u>underlined</u>: generic names in **bold**; classifications in SMALL CAPS; ♣ Canadian drug name; ⊙ Prototype drug

235

DILTIAZEM

- Dilution of diltiazem injection, monovials, and reconstituted Lyo-Ject syringe: See tables that follow.

Diluent Volume	Quantity of Cardizem Injectable or Lyo-Ject	Concentration	IV Infusion Required Dose	Rate
100 mL	125 mg (25 mL)	1 mg/mL	10 mg/h	10 mL/h
			15 mg/h	15 mL/h
250 mL	250 mg (50 mL)	0.83 mg/mL	10 mg/h	12 mL/h
			15 mg/h	18 mL/h
500 mL	250 mg (50 mL)	0.45 mg/mL	10 mg/h	22 mL/h
			15 mg/h	33 mL/h

Diluent Volume	Quantity of Diltiazem (Number of Monovials)	Concentration	IV Infusion Required Dose	Rate
100 mL	100 mg (1 vial)	1 mg/mL	10 mg/h	10 mL/h
			15 mg/h	15 mg/h
250 mL	200 mg (2 vials)	0.80 mg/mL	10 mg/h	10 mg/h
			15 mg/h	18.8 mL/h
500 mL	200 mg (2 vials)	0.40 mg/mL	10 mg/h	25 mL/h
			15 mg/h	37.5 mL/h

STORAGE
Store single use solution of injection at 2°–8° C (59°–86° F). Store single-use syringe and powder for reconstitution at 15°–30° C (59°–86° F). Reconstituted powder is stable for 24 h.

ADMINISTRATION
- **Direct IV Injection:** Give as a bolus dose over 2 min. A second bolus may be given after 15 min.
- **Continuous Infusion:** Give at a rate 5–15 mg/h (see tables above). Infusion duration longer than 24 h and infusion rate greater than 15 mg/h are **not** recommended.

INCOMPATIBILITIES Solution/additive: Furosemide. Y-site: Acetazolamide, acyclovir, aminophylline, ampicillin, ampicillin/sulbactam, cefoperazone, diazepam, furosemide, hydrocortisone, insulin, lansoprazole, methylprednisolone, mezlocillin, nafcillin, phenytoin, rifampin, sodium bicarbonate, thiopental.

D

ACTION & *THERAPEUTIC EFFECT* Inhibits calcium ion influx through slow channels into cells of myocardial and arterial smooth muscle (both coronary and peripheral blood vessels). As a result, intracellular calcium remains at subthreshold levels insufficient to stimulate cell excitation and contraction. *Slows SA and AV node conduction (antiarrhythmic effect). Dilates coronary arteries and arterioles and inhibits coronary artery spasm; thus myocardial oxygen delivery is increased (antianginal effect). By vasodilation of peripheral arterioles, decreases total peripheral vascular resistance and reduces arterial BP at rest (antihypertensive effect).*

CONTRAINDICATIONS Known hypersensitivity to drug; sick sinus syndrome (unless pacemaker is in place and functioning); second- or third-degree AV block; Wolff-Parkinson-White syndrome, Lown-Ganong-Levine syndrome; acute MI; CHF; left ventricular dysfunction; severe hypotension (systolic less than 90 mm Hg or diastolic less than 60 mm Hg); patients undergoing intracranial surgery; bleeding aneurysms; pregnancy (category C). Safe use in children is not established.

CAUTIOUS USE Sinoatrial nodal dysfunction, sick sinus syndrome; right ventricular dysfunction, severe bradycardia; conduction abnormalities; renal or hepatic impairment; older adults.

ADVERSE EFFECTS (≥1%) **CNS:** *Headache,* fatigue, dizziness, asthenia, drowsiness, nervousness, insomnia, confusion, tremor, gait abnormality. **CV:** Edema, arrhythmias, angina, second- or third-degree AV block, bradycardia, CHF, flushing, hypotension, syncope, palpitations. **GI:** Nausea, constipation, anorexia, vomiting, diarrhea, impaired taste, weight increase. **Skin:** Rash.

DRUG INTERACTIONS BETA BLOCKERS, **digoxin** may have additive effects on AV node conduction prolongation; may increase **digoxin** or **quinidine** or **cyclosporine** levels; **cimetidine** may increase diltiazem levels, thus increasing effects.

PHARMACOKINETICS Distribution: Distributed into breast milk. **Metabolism:** Metabolized in liver (CYP 3A4). **Elimination:** Excreted primarily in urine with some elimination in feces. **Half-Life:** 2 h.

NURSING IMPLICATIONS

Assessment & Drug Effects

- Check BP, HR and ECG before initiation of therapy and monitor particularly during dosage adjustment period.
- Report promptly development of high-degree AV block.
- Lab tests: Baseline and periodic LFTs and renal function tests.
- Monitor for and report S&S of CHF.
- Monitor for headache as an analgesic may be required.
- Supervise ambulation as indicated.

Patient & Family Education

- Make position changes slowly and in stages; light-headedness and dizziness (hypotension) are possible.
- Do not drive or engage in other potentially hazardous activities until reaction to drug is known.

Common adverse effects in *italic*, life-threatening effects <u>underlined</u>: generic names in **bold**; classifications in SMALL CAPS; ♣ Canadian drug name; ⊙ Prototype drug

237

D

DIMENHYDRINATE
(dye-men-hye′dri-nate)
Dimenhydrinate Injection
Classification(s): ANTIHISTAMINE (H₁-RECEPTOR ANTAGONIST)
Therapeutic: ANTIVERTIGO
Prototype: Diphenhydramine
Pregnancy Category: B

USES Prevention and treatment of nausea, vomiting, or vertigo of motion sickness.

INDICATION & DOSAGE

Motion Sickness
Adult: 50 mg as needed (probably q4h)

SOLUTION PREPARATION
Direct IV Injection: **Do not** give undiluted. Dilute each 50 mg in 10 mL of NS.

STORAGE
Store preferably at 20°–25° C (68°–77° F) and protect from light.

ADMINISTRATION
Direct IV Injection: Give each 50 mg or fraction thereof over 2 min.

INCOMPATIBILITIES Solution/additive: Aminophylline, amobarbital, chlorpromazine, glycopyrrolate, hydrocortisone, hydroxyzine, pentobarbital, phenobarbital, phenytoin, prochlorperazine, promazine, promethazine, thiopental.

ACTION & *THERAPEUTIC EFFECT* H₁-receptor antagonist; antiemetic action is thought to involve ability to inhibit cholinergic stimulations in vestibular and associated neural pathways. May inhibit labyrinthine stimulation for up to 3 h. *Has antihistamine, antiemetic, and antivertigo effects.*

CONTRAINDICATIONS Narrow-angle glaucoma, prostatic hypertrophy; GI obstruction; CNS depression; neonates; lactation. Safe use in children less than 6 y is not established.
CAUTIOUS USE Convulsive disorders; asthma, COPD; severe hepatic disease; PKU; history of porphyria; closed angle glaucoma; elderly; pregnancy (category B).

ADVERSE EFFECTS (≥1%) **CNS:** *Drowsiness,* headache, incoordination, dizziness, blurred vision, nervousness, restlessness, *insomnia (especially children).* **CV:** Hypotension, palpitation. **GI:** Dry mouth, nose, throat; anorexia, constipation or diarrhea. **Urogenital:** Urinary frequency, dysuria.

DIAGNOSTIC TEST INTERFERENCE *Skin testing* procedures should not be performed within 72 h after use of an ANTIHISTAMINE.

DRUG INTERACTIONS Alcohol and other CNS DEPRESSANTS enhance CNS depression, drowsiness; TRICYCLIC ANTIDEPRESSANTS compound anticholinergic effects.

PHARMACOKINETICS Duration: 3–6 h. **Distribution:** Distributed into breast milk. **Elimination:** Excreted in urine.

D

NURSING IMPLICATIONS

Assessment & Drug Effects

- Use falls precautions and supervise ambulation; drug produces high incidence of drowsiness.
- Note: Tolerance to CNS depressant effects usually occurs after a few days of drug therapy; some decrease in antiemetic action may result with prolonged use.
- Monitor for dizziness, nausea, and vomiting; these may indicate drug toxicity.

Patient & Family Education

- Do not drive or engage in other potentially hazardous activities until response to drug is known.

DIPHENHYDRAMINE HYDROCHLORIDE 🅿

(dye-fen-hye'dra-meen)

Benadryl

Classification(s): ANTIHISTAMINE; H_1-RECEPTOR ANTAGONIST

Therapeutic: ANTIALLERGY; ANTIVERTIGO

Pregnancy Category: C

USES Allergic conditions, motion sickness, and in treatment of parkinsonism and drug-induced extrapyramidal reactions.

INDICATION & DOSAGE

Allergic Reaction, Antiparkinsonism, Motion Sickness

Adult: 10–50 mg q4–6h (max: 400 mg/day)
Child: 5 mg/kg/day divided into 4 doses (max: 300 mg/day)

SOLUTION PREPARATION

No dilution is required. Administer as supplied.

STORAGE

Store in tightly covered containers at 15°–30° C (59°–86° F). Keep injection formulations in light-resistant containers.

ADMINISTRATION

Direct IV Injection: Give bolus dose at a rate of 25 mg or a fraction thereof over 1 min.

Common adverse effects in *italic*, life-threatening effects <u>underlined</u>: generic names in **bold**; classifications in SMALL CAPS; ♣ Canadian drug name; 🅿 Prototype drug

239

INCOMPATIBILITIES Solution/additive: **Amobarbital, amphotericin B, dexamethasone, iodipamide, methylprednisolone, pentobarbital, phenobarbital, phenytoin, thiopental.** Y-site: **Allopurinol, amphotericin B cholesteryl complex, cefepime, cefmetazole, foscarnet, furosemide, lansoprazole.**

ACTION & *THERAPEUTIC EFFECT* H_1-receptor antagonist and antihistamine with significant anticholinergic activity. Competes for H_1-receptor sites on effector cells, thus blocking histamine release. Effects in parkinsonism and drug-induced extrapyramidal symptoms are apparently related to its ability to suppress central cholinergic activity and to prolong action of dopamine by inhibiting its reuptake and storage. *Has antihistamine, antivertigo, antiemetic, antianaphylactic, antitussive, and antidyskinetic effects.*

CONTRAINDICATIONS Hypersensitivity to antihistamines of similar structure; lower respiratory tract symptoms (including acute asthma); narrow-angle glaucoma; prostatic hypertrophy, bladder neck obstruction; GI obstruction or stenosis; pregnancy (category C), lactation; premature neonates and neonates; use as nighttime sleep aid in children less than 12 y.

CAUTIOUS USE History of asthma; COPD; convulsive disorders; increased IOP; hyperthyroidism; hypertension, cardiovascular disease; hepatic disease; diabetes mellitus; older adults, infants, and young children.

ADVERSE EFFECTS (≥1%) **CNS:** *Drowsiness,* dizziness, headache, fatigue, disturbed coordination, tingling, heaviness and weakness of hands, tremors, euphoria, nervousness, restlessness, insomnia; confusion; (especially in children): Excitement, fever. **CV:** Palpitation, *tachycardia,* mild hypotension or hypertension, <u>cardiovascular collapse</u>. **Special Senses:** Tinnitus, vertigo, dry nose, throat, nasal stuffiness; blurred vision, diplopia, photosensitivity, dry eyes. **GI:** *Dry mouth,* nausea, epigastric distress, anorexia, vomiting, constipation, or diarrhea. **Urogenital:** Urinary frequency or retention, dysuria. **Body as a Whole:** Hypersensitivity (skin rash, urticaria, photosensitivity, <u>anaphylactic shock</u>). **Respiratory:** Thickened bronchial secretions, wheezing, sensation of chest tightness.

DIAGNOSTIC TEST INTERFERENCE In common with other ANTIHISTAMINES, diphenhydramine should be discontinued 4 days prior to ***skin testing*** procedures for allergy because it may obscure otherwise positive reactions.

DRUG INTERACTIONS Alcohol and other CNS DEPRESSANTS, MAO INHIBITORS compound CNS depression.

PHARMACOKINETICS Onset: 15–30 min. **Peak:** 1–4 h. **Duration:** 4–7 h. **Distribution:** Crosses placenta; distributed into breast milk. **Metabolism:** Metabolized in liver; some degradation in lung and kidney. **Elimination:** Mostly excreted in urine within 24 h.

NURSING IMPLICATIONS

Assessment & Drug Effects

- Monitor cardiovascular status especially with preexisting cardiovascular disease.
- Monitor for adverse effects especially in children and the older adult.

- Supervise ambulation and use falls precautions as necessary. Drowsiness is most prominent during the first few days of therapy and often disappears with continued therapy. Older adults are especially likely to manifest dizziness, sedation, and hypotension.

Patient & Family Education
- Do not use alcohol and other CNS depressants because of the possible additive CNS depressant effects with concurrent use.
- Do not drive or engage in other potentially hazardous activities until the response to drug is known.
- Increase fluid intake, if not contraindicated; drug has an atropine-like drying effect (thickens bronchial secretions) that may make expectoration difficult.

DIPYRIDAMOLE
(dye-peer-id′a-mole)
Apo-Dipyridamole ♣
Classifications: ANTIPLATELET AGENT
Therapeutic: DIAGNOSTIC AGENT
Pregnancy Category: B

USES Myocardial perfusion imaging.
UNLABELED USES To reduce rate of reinfarction following MI; to prevent TIAs (transient ischemic attacks) and coronary bypass graft occlusion.

INDICATION & DOSAGE

Imaging
Adult: 0.142 mg/kg/min for 4 min

SOLUTION PREPARATION
Direct IV Injection: Dilute to at least a 1:2 ratio with 1/2NS, NS, or D5W to yield a final volume of 20–50 mL. May be given as prepared direct IV or further diluted for infusion, if needed, to more easily regulate the dosage and rate of infusion.

STORAGE
Store in tightly closed container at 15°–30° C (59°–86° F). Protect injection from direct light.

ADMINISTRATION
- **Direct IV Injection:** Give a single dose over 4 min (0.142 mg/ kg/min).
- **IV Infusion:** Infuse at rate determined by total volume.

INCOMPATIBILITIES Do not mix with other drugs.

ACTION & *THERAPEUTIC EFFECT* Nonnitrate coronary vasodilator that increases coronary blood flow by selectively dilating coronary arteries, thereby

---

Common adverse effects in *italic*, life-threatening effects <u>underlined</u>: generic names in **bold**; classifications in SMALL CAPS; ♣ Canadian drug name; 🔁 Prototype drug

241

increasing myocardial oxygen supply. Exhibits mild inotropic action. Also has antiplatelet activity. *Has coronary vasodilating and antiplatelet effects.*

CONTRAINDICATIONS Safe use in children less than 12 y is not established. **CAUTIOUS USE** Hypotension, anticoagulant therapy; aspirin sensitivity; elderly; severe hepatic dysfunction; syncope; pregnancy (category B), lactation.

ADVERSE EFFECTS (≥1%) Usually dose related, minimal, and transient. **CNS:** Headache, dizziness, faintness, syncope, weakness. **CV:** Peripheral vasodilation, flushing. **GI:** Nausea, vomiting, diarrhea, abdominal distress. **Skin:** Skin rash, pruritus.

DIAGNOSTIC TEST INTERFERENCE May counteract effect of CHOLINESTERASE INHIBITORS.

PHARMACOKINETICS Peak: 45–150 min. **Distribution:** Small amount crosses placenta. **Metabolism:** Metabolized in liver. **Elimination:** Mainly excreted in feces. **Half-Life:** 10–12 h.

NURSING IMPLICATIONS

Assessment & Drug Effects
- Monitor ECG and vital signs. Anticipate an increase in HR with a decrease in BP in the supine position. Report significant hypotension. Return of vital signs to baseline requires 20–60 min.

Patient & Family Education
- Make all position changes slowly and in stages, especially from recumbent to upright posture, if postural hypotension or dizziness is a problem.

DOBUTAMINE HYDROCHLORIDE

(doe-byoo'ta-meen)

Dobutrex

Classification(s): BETA-ADRENERGIC AGONIST
Therapeutic: CARDIAC STIMULANT
Prototype: Isoproterenol
Pregnancy Category: C

USES Inotropic support in short-term treatment of adults with cardiac decompensation due to depressed myocardial contractility (cardiogenic shock) resulting from either organic heart disease or from cardiac surgery.
UNLABELED USES To augment cardiovascular function in children undergoing cardiac catheterization or stress thallium testing.

INDICATION & DOSAGE

Cardiac Decompensation

Adult: 0.5–1 mcg/kg/min then titrate up to 2.5–15 mcg/kg/min (max: 40 mcg/kg/min)
Adolescent/Child: 2–20 mcg/kg/min

Common adverse effects in *italic*, life-threatening effects underlined: generic names in **bold**; classifications in SMALL CAPS; ♣ Canadian drug name; ⊙ Prototype drug

SOLUTION PREPARATION

Continuous Infusion: Concentrate for injection **must be** diluted with **at least** 50 mL of compatible solution (e.g., with D5W, NS, LR, D5/LR, or sodium lactate injection). Further dilution is typical (e.g., 250 mg in 1000 mL yields 250 mcg/mL; 250 mg in 500 mL yields 500 mcg/mL; 250 mg in 250 mL yields 1000 mcg/mL).

STORAGE

Refrigerate reconstituted solution at 2°–15° C (36°–59° F) for 48 h or store for 6 h at room temperature.

ADMINISTRATION

- **Continuous Infusion:** Rate of infusion is determined by body weight. To determine the infusion rate in mL/min: Select the appropriate concentration (mcg/mL) and the ordered rate (mcg/kg/min), then multiply the patient's weight in kg times the IV flow rate (mL/kg/min) as indicated in the table that follows.

IV Rate (mL/kg/min) for Different Concentrations of Dobutamine

Ordered Rate: mcg/kg/min	Concentration 250 mcg/mL IV Flow Rate: mL/kg/min	Concentration 500 mcg/mL IV Flow Rate: mL/kg/min	Concentration 1000 mcg/mL IV Flow Rate: mL/kg/min
0.5	0.002	0.001	0.0005
1	0.004	0.002	0.001
2.5	0.01	0.005	0.0025
5	0.02	0.01	0.005
7.5	0.03	0.015	0.0075
10	0.04	0.02	0.01
12.5	0.05	0.025	0.0125
15	0.06	0.03	0.015
17.5	0.07	0.035	0.0175
20	0.08	0.04	0.02

- Maximum concentration: 5000 mcg/mL

INCOMPATIBILITIES **Solution/additive:** Acyclovir, alteplase, aminophylline, bretylium, bumetanide, calcium chloride, calcium gluconate, diazepam, digoxin, furosemide, heparin, insulin, magnesium sulfate, phenytoin, potassium chloride, potassium phosphate, sodium bicarbonate. **Y-site:** Acyclovir, alteplase, aminophylline, amphotericin B cholesteryl sulfate, cefepime, foscarnet, furosemide, heparin, indomethacin, lansoprazole, pantoprazole, pemetrexed, phytonadione, piperacillin/tazobactam, thiopental, warfarin.

Common adverse effects in *italic*, life-threatening effects underlined: generic names in **bold**; classifications in SMALL CAPS; ✦ Canadian drug name; ●Prototype drug

243

D

ACTION & *THERAPEUTIC EFFECT* Produces inotropic effect primarily by acting on beta-1 myocardial receptors. Increases cardiac output and decreases pulmonary wedge pressure and total systemic vascular resistance with comparatively little or no effect on BP. Additionally it increases conduction through AV node, and has lower potential for precipitating arrhythmias than dopamine. *In CHF or cardiogenic shock, increase in cardiac output enhances renal perfusion and increases renal output as well as renal sodium excretion.*

CONTRAINDICATIONS History of hypersensitivity to other sympathomimetic amines, or sulfites; ventricular tachycardia, idiopathic hypertrophic subaortic stenosis; hypovolemia; pregnancy (category C); children less than 2 y.
CAUTIOUS USE Preexisting hypertension, atrial fibrillation; acute MI; unstable angina, severe coronary artery disease.

ADVERSE EFFECTS (≥1%) **All:** Generally dose related. **CNS:** Headache, tremors, paresthesias, mild leg cramps, nervousness, fatigue (with overdosage). **CV:** *Increased heart rate and BP,* premature ventricular beats, palpitation, *anginal pain.* **GI:** Nausea, vomiting. **Other:** Nonspecific chest pain, shortness of breath.

DRUG INTERACTIONS GENERAL ANESTHETICS (especially **cyclopropane** and **halothane**) may sensitize myocardium to effects of CATECHOLAMINES such as dobutamine and lead to serious arrhythmias—use with extreme caution; BETA-ADRENERGIC BLOCKING AGENTS, e.g., **metoprolol, propranolol,** may make dobutamine ineffective in increasing cardiac output, but total peripheral resistance may increase; MAO INHIBITORS, TRICYCLIC ANTIDEPRESSANTS potentiate pressor effects.

PHARMACOKINETICS Onset: 2–10 min. **Peak:** 10–20 min. **Metabolism:** Metabolized in liver and other tissues by COMT. **Elimination:** Excreted in urine. **Half-Life:** 2 min.

NURSING IMPLICATIONS
Assessment & Drug Effects
- Prior to the initiation of therapy, acidosis and hypovolemia are corrected by appropriate drugs and volume expanders.
- Monitor ECG and BP continuously during administration. At any given dosage level, drug takes 10–20 min to produce peak effects.
- Marked increases in BP (systolic pressure is the most likely to be affected) and HR, or appearance of arrhythmias or other adverse cardiac effects are usually reversed promptly by reduction in dosage.
- Observe patients with preexisting hypertension closely for exaggerated hypotensive response.
- Lab tests: Baseline and periodic serum potassium to assess for hypokalemia.
- Monitor I&O ratio and pattern. Urine output and sodium excretion generally increase because of improved cardiac output and renal perfusion.

Patient & Family Education
- Report promptly anginal pain.

DOCETAXEL

(doc-e-tax′el)

Taxotere

Classification(s): ANTINEOPLASTIC, MITOTIC INHIBITOR, TAXOID

Therapeutic: ANTINEOPLASTIC
Prototype: Paclitaxel
Pregnancy Category: D

D

USES Metastatic breast cancer, metastatic prostate cancer, gastric adeno-carcinoma, head/neck cancer, non–small-cell lung cancer (NSCLC).

INDICATION & DOSAGE

Breast Cancer

Adult: 60–100 mg/m² once every 3 wk (premedicate patients with dexa-methasone 8 mg b.i.d. for 5 days, starting 1 day prior to docetaxel)

Prostate Cancer

Adult: 75 mg/m² every 21 days plus prednisone (5 mg PO twice daily) for 10 cycles (premedicate patients with dexamethasone 8 mg q12h, 3h, and 1h prior to starting docetaxel infusion)

**Non–Small-Cell Lung Cancer/Gastric Adenocarcinoma/
Head and Neck Cancer**

Adult: 75 mg/m² every 3 wk

Hepatic Impairment Dosage Adjustment

AST/ALT		Alkaline Phosphate	Dose Adjustment
Greater than 2.5 up to 5 × ULN	and	2.5 or less × ULN	Reduce dose 20%
Greater than 1.5 up to 5 × ULN	and	Greater than 2.5 up to 5 × ULN	Reduce dose 20%
Greater than 5 × ULN	and/or	Greater than 5 × ULN	Discontinue

Toxicity Adjustment

Indication	Toxicity	Dose Adjustment
Breast Cancer	Neutrophils less than 500 cells/mm³ × 1 wk	Reduce from 100 to 75 mg/m²; then from 75 to 55 if reaction continues
	Severe cutaneous reaction	Reduce from 100 to 75 mg/m²
	Peripheral neuropathy grade 3 or higher	Discontinue treatment

Common adverse effects in *italic*, life-threatening effects <u>underlined</u>: generic names in **bold**; classifications in SMALL CAPS; ♣ Canadian drug name; ⊙ Prototype drug

245

Indication	Toxicity	Dose Adjustment
Breast Cancer (adjuvant)	Febrile neutropenia for more than one cycle OR grade 3 or 4 stomatitis	Reduce dose to 60 mg/m²
	Severe cutaneous reactions	Reduce dose from 75 to 60 mg/m², if reaction does not abate discontinue treatment
Gastric/ Head/Neck Cancer	Febrile neutropenia, prolonged neutropenia, neutropenic infection (despite G-CSF)	Reduce dose from 75 to 60 mg/m², if reaction continues reduce to 45 mg/m²
	Grade 4 thrombocytopenia	Reduce dose from 75 to 60 mg/m²
	Persistent neutrophils below 1,500 cells/mm³ and platelets more than 100,000 cells/mm³	Discontinue treatment
NSCLC	Febrile neutropenia, neutrophils less than 500 cells/mm³ for more than 1 wk, severe cutaneous reactions, grade 3 or 4 nonhematological toxicities	Withhold treatment until resolution of toxicity then reduce from 75 to 55 mg/m²
	Peripheral neuropathy grade 3 or higher	Discontinue treatment
Prostate Cancer	Febrile neutropenia, neutrophils less than 500 cells/mm³ for more than 1 wk, severe cutaneous reactions, or moderate neurosensory signs	Reduce dose from 75 to 60 mg/m², if reaction does not abate discontinue treatment

SOLUTION PREPARATION
- If drug contacts skin during preparation, wash immediately with soap and water.
- *IV Infusion:* Bring vials of concentrate and diluent to room temperature for 5 min; add provided diluent to yield 10 mg/mL. Gently rotate/invert for 45 sec; let stand until surface foam dissipates. Withdraw the required amount of diluted solution and inject into a 250-mL, or larger, bag of NS or D5W; the final concentration should be between 0.3–0.4 mg/mL. Mix completely by manual rotation.

Common adverse effects in *italic*, life-threatening effects <u>underlined</u>: generic names in **bold**; classifications in SMALL CAPS; ♣ Canadian drug name; ☻ Prototype drug

- Use glass or polypropylene bottles or polypropylene or polyolefin plastic bags and polyethylene-lined administration sets. Do not use PVC administration sets or containers.

STORAGE
Refrigerate vials at 2°–8° C (36°–46° F). Protect from light. Use IV infusion solution within 4 h (including the 1 h infusion time).

ADMINISTRATION
IV Infusion: Give at a constant rate over 1 h. Administer after premedication with corticosteroids to prevent hypersensitivity.

INCOMPATIBILITIES Y-site: **Amphotericin B, doxorubicin, methylprednisolone, nalbuphine.**

ACTION & *THERAPEUTIC EFFECT* Docetaxel is a semisynthetic analog of paclitaxel. Potential advantages over paclitaxel are greater antitumor activity and lower toxicity potential. Docetaxel, like paclitaxel, binds to the microtubule network essential for interphase and mitosis of the cell cycle. *Docetaxel stabilizes the microtubules involved in cell division and prevents their normal functioning; this inhibits mitosis in cancer cells.*

CONTRAINDICATIONS Hypersensitivity to docetaxel or other drugs formulated with polysorbate 80, paclitaxel; neutrophil count less than 1500 cells/mm³; biliary tract disease, hepatic disease, jaundice; neutropenia; intramuscular injections; thrombocytopenia; acute infection; pregnancy (category D), lactation.
CAUTIOUS USE Bone marrow suppression, bone marrow transplant patients; CHF; ascites, peripheral edema; pleural effusion; radiation therapy; pulmonary disorders, acute bronchospasm; cardiac tamponade; dental disease, dental work; herpes infection; hypotension; elderly; infection. Safety and effectiveness in children less than 16 y not established.

ADVERSE EFFECTS (≥1%) **CNS:** Paresthesia, pain, burning sensation, weakness, confusion. **CV:** Hypotension, *fluid retention (peripheral edema, weight gain)*, pleural effusion. **GI:** *Nausea, vomiting, diarrhea, stomatitis,* abdominal pain; increased liver function tests (AST or ALT). **Hematologic:** *Neutropenia, leukopenia, thrombocytopenia, anemia*, febrile neutropenia. **Skin:** Rash, localized eruptions, desquamation, *alopecia*, nail changes (hyper/hypopigmentation, onycholysis). **Body as a Whole:** *Hypersensitivity reactions,* infusion site reactions (hyperpigmentation, inflammation, redness, dryness, phlebitis, extravasation).

DRUG INTERACTIONS May interact with other drugs metabolized by the cytochrome P 3A4 system **(cyclosporine, erythromycin, ketoconazole).**

PHARMACOKINETICS **Distribution:** 97% protein bound. **Metabolism:** Metabolized in liver (CYP 3A4). **Elimination:** 80% eliminated in feces, 20% renally excreted. **Half-Life:** 11.1 h.

Common adverse effects in *italic*, life-threatening effects underlined: generic names in **bold**; classifications in SMALL CAPS; ♣ Canadian drug name; ✪ Prototype drug

247

D

NURSING IMPLICATIONS

Assessment & Drug Effects

- Monitor vital signs during infusion and for at least 1 h post-infusion.
- Monitor for S&S of hypersensitivity (see Appendix C), which may develop within a few minutes of initiation of infusion. It is usually not necessary to discontinue infusion for minor reactions (i.e., flushing or local skin reaction).
- Assess throughout therapy and report: cardiovascular dysfunction; respiratory distress; fluid retention; development of neurosensory symptoms; severe, cutaneous eruptions on feet, hands, arms, face, or thorax; and S&S of infection.
- Lab tests: Baseline and periodic CBCs with differential (withhold drug and notify prescriber if platelets are less than 100,000 or neutrophils are less than 1500 cells/mm^3); baseline and prior to each drug cycle: Bilirubin, AST or ALT, and alkaline phosphatase prior to each drug cycle (withhold drug and notify prescriber for elevations of bilirubin or significant elevations of transaminases concurrent with elevations of alkaline phosphatase).

Patient & Family Education

- Learn common adverse effects and measures to control or minimize them when possible. Report immediately any distressing adverse effects.
- Note: It is extremely important to comply with corticosteroid therapy and monitoring of lab values.
- Use effective means of birth control to avoid pregnancy during therapy.

DOLASETRON MESYLATE

(dol-a-se'tron)

Anzemet

Classification(s): ANTIEMETIC, 5-HT$_3$ RECEPTOR ANTAGONIST
Therapeutic: ANTIEMETIC
Prototype: Ondansetron HCl
Pregnancy Category: B

USES Prevention of nausea and vomiting from emetogenic chemotherapy, prevention and treatment of postoperative nausea and vomiting.

INDICATION & DOSAGE

Prevention of Chemotherapy-Induced Nausea and Vomiting

Adult/Child (over 2 y): 1.8 mg/kg or 100 mg administered 30 min prior to chemotherapy (not more than 100 mg/dose)

Pre/Postoperative Nausea and Vomiting

Adult: 12.5 mg 15 min before cessation of anesthesia or when postop nausea and vomiting occurs

---

Child (over 2 y): 0.35 mg/kg (up to 12.5 mg) 15 min before cessation of anesthesia or when postop nausea and vomiting occurs

SOLUTION PREPARATION
May be given undiluted [direct IV] or diluted in 50 mL of any of the following for infusion: NS, D5W, D5/1/2NS, LR.

D

STORAGE
Store at 20°–25° C (66°–77° F) and protect from light. Diluted IV solution may be stored refrigerated up to 48 h.

ADMINISTRATION
* **Direct IV Injection:** Give bolus dose over 30 sec.
* **IV Infusion:** Infuse diluted drug over 15 min.

INCOMPATIBILITIES Solution/additive: **Potassium chloride.**

ACTION & *THERAPEUTIC EFFECT* Dolasetron is a selective serotonin (5-HT_3) receptor antagonist used for control of nausea and vomiting associated with cancer chemotherapy. Serotonin receptors affected by dolasetron are located in the chemoreceptor trigger zone (CTZ) of the brain and peripherally on the vagal nerve terminal. Serotonin, released from the cells of the small intestine, activates $5-HT_3$ receptors located on vagal efferent neurons, thus initiating the vomiting reflex. *Has antiemetic properties that help patients undergoing chemotherapy.*

CONTRAINDICATIONS Hypersensitivity to dolasetron. Safety and efficacy in children less than 2 y are not established.

CAUTIOUS USE Patients who have or may develop prolongation of cardiac conduction intervals, particularly QT_c (i.e., patients with hypokalemia, hypomagnesemia, diuretics, congenital QT syndrome; patients taking antiarrhythmic drugs and high-dose anthracycline therapy, etc.); pregnancy (category B), lactation.

ADVERSE EFFECTS (≥1%) **Body as a Whole:** Fever, fatigue, pain, chills or shivering. **CNS:** *Headache,* dizziness, drowsiness. **CV:** Hypertension. **GI:** *Diarrhea,* increased LFTs, abdominal pain. **Genitourinary:** Urinary retention.

DRUG INTERACTIONS Avoid use with **apomorphine** due to hypotension, **ziprasidone** may prolong QT interval.

PHARMACOKINETICS Peak: 0.6 h. **Distribution:** Crosses placenta, distributed into breast milk. **Metabolism:** Metabolized to hydrodolasetron. Hydrodolasetron is metabolized in the liver by CYP 2D6. **Elimination:** Primarily excreted in urine as unchanged hydrodolasetron. **Half-Life:** 10 min dolasetron, 7.3 h hydrodolasetron.

NURSING IMPLICATIONS
Assessment & Drug Effects
* Prior to initiating therapy, hypokalemia and hypomagnesemia should be corrected.
* Monitor closely cardiac status especially with vomiting, excess diuresis, or other conditions that may result in electrolyte imbalances.

Common adverse effects in *italic*, life-threatening effects <u>underlined</u>: generic names in **bold**, classifications in SMALL CAPS; ♣ Canadian drug name; ○ Prototype drug

249

D

- Monitor ECG, especially in those taking concurrent antiarrhythmic or other drugs that may cause QT prolongation.
- Monitor for and report signs of bleeding (e.g., hematuria, epistaxis, purpura, hematoma).
- Lab tests: Baseline and periodic serum electrolytes; with prolonged therapy, periodic LFTs, aPTT, CBC with platelet count, and alkaline phosphatase.

Patient & Family Education

- Headache requiring analgesic for relief is a common adverse effect.

DOPAMINE HYDROCHLORIDE

(doe'pa-meen)

Classification(s): ALPHA- & BETA-ADRENERGIC AGONIST
Therapeutic: CARDIAC STIMULANT
Prototype: Epinephrine
Pregnancy Category: C

USES To correct hemodynamic imbalance in shock syndrome due to MI (cardiogenic shock), trauma, endotoxic septicemia (septic shock), open heart surgery, and CHF.
UNLABELED USES Hepatorenal syndrome; barbiturate intoxication, bradycardia.

INDICATION & DOSAGE

Shock/Surgery
Adult: 2–5 mcg/kg/min increased gradually up to 20–50 mcg/kg/min if necessary
Adolescent/Child: 1–5 mcg/kg/min increased gradually up to 20 mcg/kg/min

CHF
Adult: 3–10 mcg/kg/min

SOLUTION PREPARATION
- *IV Infusion:* Drug **MUST be** diluted prior to administration in one of the following: D5W, D5NS, D5LR, D5/1/2NS, NS.
  - Dilute 200 mg ampule in 250 mL or 500 mL IV solution to yield 800 mcg/mL or 400 mcg/mL, respectively.
  - Dilute 400 mg ampule in 250 mL or 500 mL IV solution to yield 1600 mcg/mL or 800 mcg/mL, respectively.
  - Dilute 800 mg ampule in 250 mL or 500 mL IV solution to yield 3200 mcg/mL or 1600 mcg/mL, respectively.

STORAGE
Protect dopamine from light. Store reconstituted solution for 24 h at 2°–15° C (36°–59° F) or 6 h at room temperature 15°–30° C.

ADMINISTRATION

- Prior to initiating therapy: Correct hypovolemia, if possible.
- **Continuous Infusion:** Infusion rate is individually titrated to the desired hemodynamic and/or renal response. Flow rate **must be** carefully controlled with a microdrip and/or other reliable metering device to ensure accuracy of flow rate.
- Avoid using small veins for infusion. Monitor infusion continuously for extravasation that can result in tissue sloughing and gangrene. In case of extravasations, stop infusion promptly and remove needle, and notify prescriber. Phentolamine mesylate may be required.

INCOMPATIBILITIES Solution/additive: **Acyclovir, alteplase, amphotericin B, ampicillin, metronidazole, penicillin G, sodium bicarbonate.** Y-site: **Acyclovir, alteplase, amphotericin B cholesteryl complex, cefepime, doxycycline, furosemide, indomethacin, insulin, lansoprazole, sodium bicarbonate, thiopental.**

ACTION & *THERAPEUTIC EFFECT* Major cardiovascular effects produced by direct action on alpha- and beta-adrenergic receptors and on specific dopaminergic receptors in mesenteric and renal vascular beds. Positive inotropic effect on myocardium increases cardiac output with increase in systolic and pulse pressure and little or no effect on diastolic pressure. Improves circulation to renal vascular bed by decreasing renal vascular resistance, thus increasing glomerular filtration rate and urinary output. *Due to its potential for inotropic, chronotropic, and vasopressor effects, dopamine has several clinical uses including decreasing cardiac output as well as correcting hypotension associated with cardiogenic and septic shock. Hemodynamic effects of dopamine are dose dependent.*

CONTRAINDICATIONS Pheochromocytoma; tachyarrhythmias or ventricular fibrillation; pregnancy (category C).

CAUTIOUS USE Patients with history of occlusive vascular disease (e.g., Buerger's or Raynaud's disease); cold injury; CAD; acute MI; diabetic endarteritis, arterial embolism; neonates; lactation.

ADVERSE EFFECTS (≥1%) **CV:** *Hypotension,* ectopic beats, *tachycardia,* anginal pain, palpitation, vasoconstriction (indicated by disproportionate rise in diastolic pressure), cold extremities; less frequent: <u>Aberrant conduction</u>, bradycardia, widening of QRS complex, elevated blood pressure. **GI:** Nausea, vomiting. **CNS:** Headache. **Skin:** Necrosis, tissue sloughing with extravasation, <u>gangrene</u>, piloerection. **Other:** Azotemia, dyspnea, dilated pupils (high doses).

DIAGNOSTIC TEST INTERFERENCE Dopamine may modify test response when histamine is used as a control for ***intradermal skin tests.***

DRUG INTERACTIONS MAO INHIBITORS, ERGOT ALKALOIDS, **furazolidone** increase alpha-adrenergic effects (headache, hyperpyrexia, hypertension); **guanethidine, phenytoin** may decrease dopamine action; BETA BLOCKERS antagonize cardiac effects; ALPHA BLOCKERS antagonize peripheral vasoconstriction; **halothane, cyclopropane** increase risk of hypertension and ventricular arrhythmias.

Common adverse effects in *italic*, life-threatening effects <u>underlined</u>: generic names in **bold**; classifications in SMALL CAPS; ♣ Canadian drug name; ◙ Prototype drug

251

PHARMACOKINETICS Onset: Less than 5 min. **Duration:** Less than 10 min. **Distribution:** Widely distributed; does not cross blood–brain barrier. **Metabolism:** Inactive in the liver, kidney, and plasma by monoamine oxidase and COMT. **Elimination:** Excreted in urine. **Half-Life:** 2 min.

NURSING IMPLICATIONS

Assessment & Drug Effects

- Monitor BP, HR, peripheral pulses, and urinary output at frequent intervals. Precise measurements are essential for accurate titration of dosage.
- Report promptly: Reduced urine flow rate in absence of hypotension; ascending tachycardia; dysrhythmias; disproportionate rise in diastolic pressure (marked decrease in pulse pressure); signs of peripheral ischemia (pallor, cyanosis, mottling, coldness, complaints of tenderness, pain, numbness, or burning sensation).

DOXAPRAM HYDROCHLORIDE

(dox'a-pram)

Dopram

Classification(s): CEREBRAL STIMULANT; RESPIRATORY STIMULANT
Therapeutic: CEREBRAL/RESPIRATORY STIMULANT

Prototype: Caffeine
Pregnancy Category: B

USES Short-term adjunctive therapy to alleviate postanesthesia and drug-induced CNS depression. Also as a temporary measure in hospitalized patients with COPD associated with acute respiratory insufficiency as an aid to prevent elevation of $PaCO_2$ during administration of oxygen. (Not used with mechanical ventilation.)

UNLABELED USES Neonatal apnea refractory to xanthine therapy.

INDICATION & DOSAGE

Postanesthesia CNS Depression

Adult: 0.5–1 mg/kg single injection (not more than 1.5 mg/kg) may repeat q5min up to 2 mg/kg total dose; infusion of 0.5–1 mg/kg (up to 4 mg/kg total dose)

Drug-Induced CNS Depression

Adult: 1–2 mg/kg may repeat in 5 min, then q1–2h until patient awakens [if relapse occurs, resume q1–2h injections (max: total dose 3 g), if no response after priming dose, may give 1–3 mg/min for up to 2 h until patient awakens]

Chronic Obstructive Pulmonary Disease

Adult: 0.5–2 mg/kg OR 1–2 mg/min (max: rate 3 mg/min)

Common adverse effects in *italic*, life-threatening effects underlined: generic names in **bold**; classifications in SMALL CAPS; ♣ Canadian drug name; ◐ Prototype drug

D

SOLUTION PREPARATION
Drug-Induced CNS Depression
- *Direct IV Injection:* Give undiluted.
- *IV Infusion:* Dilute 250 mg (12.5 mL) in 250 mL of D5W or NS.

COPD
- *IV Infusion:* Dilute 400 mg in 180 mL of D5W, D10W, or NS to yield 2 mg/mL.

STORAGE
Store at 15°–30° C (59°–86° F).

ADMINISTRATION
Drug-Induced CNS Depression
- **Direct IV Injection:** Give bolus dose over 5 min.
- **IV Infusion:** Initiate infusion at 5 mg/min then slow to maintenance infusion of 1–3 mg/min. Infusion should not be administered for longer than 2 h.

COPD
- **IV Infusion:** Infuse at 0.5–1.5 mL/min.
- Monitor IV site frequently. Extravasation or use of same IV site for prolonged periods can cause thrombophlebitis (see Appendix C) or tissue irritation.

INCOMPATIBILITIES Solution/additive: **Aminophylline, ascorbic acid,** CEPHALOSPORINS, **dexamethasone, diazepam, folic acid, hydrocortisone, ketamine, methylprednisolone, sodium bicarbonate, thiopental.** Y-site: **Clindamycin.**

ACTION & *THERAPEUTIC EFFECT* Short-acting analeptic capable of stimulating all levels of the cerebrospinal axis. Respiratory stimulation by direct medullary action or by indirect activation of carotid, aortic and other peripheral chemoreceptors increases tidal volume and slightly increases respiratory rate. *Decreases P_{CO_2} and increases P_{O_2} by increasing alveolar ventilation; may elevate BP and pulse rate by stimulation of brain stem vasomotor area. Used to stimulate respiration postanesthesia, for drug-induced CNS depression, and chronic pulmonary disease (COPD) associated with acute hypercapnia.*

CONTRAINDICATIONS Epilepsy and other convulsive disorders; mechanical ventilation; ventilatory mechanism due to muscle paresis, pulmonary fibrosis, flail chest, pneumothorax, airway obstruction, extreme dyspnea, or acute bronchial asthma; severe hypertension, coronary artery disease, uncompensated heart failure, CVA; MAOI; lactation.

CAUTIOUS USE History of bronchial asthma, COPD; cardiac disease, severe tachycardia, arrhythmias, hypertension; hyperthyroidism; pheochromocytoma; head injury, cerebral edema, increased intracranial pressure; peptic ulcer, patients undergoing gastric surgery; acute agitation; pregnancy (category B).

ADVERSE EFFECTS (≥1%) **CNS:** Dizziness, sneezing, apprehension, confusion, *involuntary movements,* hyperactivity, paresthesias; feeling of warmth and burning, especially of genitalia and perineum; flushing,

---

Common adverse effects in *italic,* life-threatening effects <u>underlined</u>: generic names in **bold**; classifications in SMALL CAPS; ♣ Canadian drug name; ❂ Prototype drug

253

sweating, hyperpyrexia, headache, pilomotor erection, pruritus, muscle tremor, rigidity, convulsions, *increased deep-tendon reflexes,* bilateral Babinski sign, *carpopedal spasm,* pupillary dilation, mild delayed narcosis. **CV:** *Mild to moderate increase in BP, sinus tachycardia,* bradycardia, extrasystoles, lowered T waves, PVCs, chest pains, tightness in chest. **GI:** Nausea, vomiting, diarrhea, salivation, sour taste. **Urogenital:** Urinary retention, frequency, incontinence. **Respiratory:** Dyspnea, tachypnea, cough, <u>laryngospasm, bronchospasm</u>, hiccups, rebound hypoventilation, hypocapnia with tetany. **Other:** Local skin irritation, thrombophlebitis with extravasation; decreased Hgb, Hct, and RBC count; elevated BUN; albuminuria.

DRUG INTERACTIONS MAO INHIBITORS, SYMPATHOMIMETIC AGENTS add to pressor effects.

PHARMACOKINETICS Onset: 20–40 sec. **Peak:** 1–2 min. **Duration:** 5–12 min. **Metabolism:** Rapidly metabolized. **Elimination:** Excreted in urine as metabolites.

NURSING IMPLICATIONS

Assessment & Drug Effects

- Monitor carefully and observe accurately: BP, pulse, deep tendon reflexes, airway, and arterial blood gases. All are essential guides for determining minimum effective dosage and preventing overdosage. Make baseline determinations for comparison. Discontinue if sudden hypotension or dyspnea develops.
- Lab tests: Draw arterial Po_2 and Pco_2 and O_2 saturation prior to both initiation of doxapram infusion and oxygen administration in patients with COPD, and then at least q30min during infusion.
- Discontinue doxapram if arterial blood gases show evidence of deterioration and when mechanical ventilation is initiated.
- Observe patient continuously during therapy and maintain vigilance until patient is fully alert (usually about 1 h) and protective pharyngeal and laryngeal reflexes are completely restored.
- Report promptly any adverse effects. Be alert for early signs of toxicity: Tachycardia, muscle tremor, spasticity, hyperactive reflexes.
- Note: A mild to moderate increase in BP commonly occurs.

DOXERCALCIFEROL

(dox-er-kal′si-fe-rol)

Hectorol

Classification(s): VITAMIN D ANALOG
Therapeutic: ANTIHYPERPARATHYROID
Prototype: Calcitriol
Pregnancy Category: B

USES Secondary hyperparathyroidism in patients with chronic kidney disease.

D

INDICATION & DOSAGE

Secondary Hyperparathyroidism

Adult: 4 mcg 3 times/wk at end of dialysis (max: 18 mcg/wk)

Dosage Adjustment

Patient Response	Dosage
iPTH decreases by less than 50% and level at least 300 pg/mL	Increase dose 1–2 mcg q8wk as needed
iPTH decreases 50% or more and level less than 300 pg/mL	Maintain dose
iPTH 100–140 pg/mL	Lower dose by 1 mcg
iPTH less than 100 pg/mL	Stop treatment for one wk then restart with dose 1 mcg lower than previous dose
Hypercalcemia or hyperphosphatemia develops	Stop treatment until values are appropriate, restart with dose of 1 mcg lower than previous dose

SOLUTION PREPARATION

• No dilution is required. Administer as supplied.
• Withdraw appropriate dose from ampule using a filter needle. Change needles before IV injection. Discard any unused portion.

STORAGE

Store unopened ampules at 15°–20° C (59°–77° F).

ADMINISTRATION

Direct IV Injection: Give bolus dose at the end of dialysis sessions.

INCOMPATIBILITIES Data not available; do not mix with other drugs.

ACTION & *THERAPEUTIC EFFECT* Vitamin D$_2$ analog that is activated by the liver. Activated vitamin D is needed for absorption of dietary calcium in the intestine, and for the parathyroid hormone (PTH) which mobilizes calcium from the bone tissue. *Regulates the blood calcium level.*

CONTRAINDICATIONS Hypersensitivity to doxercalciferol or other vitamin D analogs; recent hypercalcemia, recent hyperphosphatemia, hypervitaminosis D.

CAUTIOUS USE Renal or hepatic insufficiency; renal osteodystrophy with hyperphosphatemia, prolonged hypercalcemia; pregnancy (category B), lactation. Safety and efficacy in children are not established.

ADVERSE EFFECTS (≥1%) **Body as a Whole:** Abscess, *headache, malaise,* arthralgia. **CNS:** *Dizziness,* sleep disorder. **CV:** Bradycardia, *edema.* **GI:** Anorexia, constipation, dyspepsia, *nausea, vomiting.* **Respiratory:** *Dyspnea.* **Skin:** Pruritus. **Other:** Weight gain.

Common adverse effects in *italic*, life-threatening effects <u>underlined</u>: generic names in **bold**; classifications in SMALL CAPS; ♣ Canadian drug name; ⊘ Prototype drug

255

DRUG INTERACTIONS MAGNESIUM-CONTAINING ANTACIDS may cause hypermagnesemia; other VITAMIN D ANALOGS may increase toxicity and hypercalcemia.

PHARMACOKINETICS Peak: 11–12 h. **Metabolism:** Activated by CYP 27 to form 1alpha, 25-(OH)$_2$D$_2$ (major metabolite) and 1alpha, 24-dihydroxyvitamin D$_2$ (minor metabolite). **Half-Life:** 32–37 h.

NURSING IMPLICATIONS

Assessment & Drug Effects

▪ Lab tests: Baseline and periodic iPTH, serum calcium, serum phosphorus. Monitor levels weekly during dose titration.
▪ Monitor for S&S of hypercalcemia (see Appendix C).

Patient & Family Education

▪ Do not take antacids without consulting the prescriber.
▪ Notify the prescriber if you become pregnant while taking this drug.
▪ Do not take nonprescription drugs containing magnesium while taking doxercalciferol.
▪ Report S&S of hypercalcemia immediately: Bone or muscle pain, dry mouth with metallic taste, rhinorrhea, itching, photophobia, conjunctivitis, frequent urination, anorexia and weight loss.

DOXORUBICIN HYDROCHLORIDE ⊘

(dox-oh-roo′bi-sin)

Adriamycin, Rubex

DOXORUBICIN LIPOSOME

Doxil

Classification(s): ANTINEOPLASTIC; ANTIBIOTIC
Therapeutic: ANTINEOPLASTIC
Pregnancy Category: D

USES *Conventional Doxorubicin:* To produce regression in neoplastic conditions, including acute lymphoblastic and myeloblastic leukemias, transitional cell bladder cancer, breast cancer, Hodgkin's disease, ovarian cancer, small-cell lung cancer, non-Hodgkin's lymphoma, thyroid cancer, Wilms' tumor, and soft tissue and bone sarcomas. Generally used in combined modalities with surgery, radiation, and immunotherapy. Effective pretreatment to sensitize superficial tumors to local radiation therapy. *Liposome Doxorubicin:* Kaposi's sarcoma, progressive/refractory ovarian cancer, relapsed/refractory multiple myeloma.

INDICATION & DOSAGE

CONVENTIONAL DOXORUBICIN

Acute Lymphatic Leukemia

Adult/Child: 30 mg/m^2 weekly × 4 wk

Acute Myelogenous Leukemia
Adult/Child: 30 mg/m² × 3 days (with cytarabine)

Transitional Bladder Cell Cancer
Adult: 30 mg/m²/dose once monthly

Hodgkin's Disease
Adult/Child: 25 mg/m² days 1 and 15, repeat q28days

Thyroid Cancer
Adult/Child: 60–75 mg/m² q3wk

Other Neoplasms
Adult: 40–50 mg/m² usually in combination with other agents (max: Total cumulative lifetime dose 500–550 mg/m²)
Child: 35–75 mg/m² as single dose, repeat at 21 day interval, or 20–30 mg/m² once weekly (max: Total cumulative lifetime dose 500–550 mg/m²)

Hepatic Impairment Dosage Adjustment
Bilirubin 1.2–3 mg/dL: Reduce dose by 50%; *bilirubin 3–5 mg/dL:* Reduce dose by 75%; *bilirubin over 5 mg/dL:* Stop therapy.

LIPOSOME DOXORUBICIN

Kaposi's Sarcoma
Adult: 20 mg/m² every 3 wk. Infuse over 30 min (do not use in-line filters)

Progressive/Refractory Ovarian Cancer
Adult: 50 mg/m² q4wk, minimum of 4 courses

Relapsed/Refractory Multiple Myeloma
Adult: 45 mg/m² q4wk, up to 6 cycles

Hepatic Impairment Dosage Adjustment
Bilirubin 1.2–3 mg/dL: Reduce dose 50%; *bilirubin 3–5 mg/dL:* Reduce dose by 75%

Toxicity Adjustments

Toxicity	Dosage Adjustment
Palmar-plantar erythodysthesia (grade 1) OR stomatitis (grade 1)	Follow normal schedule unless patient has had grade 3 or 4 before then delay course 2 wk and reduce dose 25%
Palmar-plantar erythodysthesia (grade 2) OR stomatitis (grade 2)	Delay treatment until resolved (grade 0 or 1) up to 2 wk, then if no resolution after 2 wk discontinue therapy
Palmar-plantar erythodysthesia (grade 3 or 4) OR stomatitis (grade 3 or 4)	Delay treatment until resolved (grade 0 or 1) up to 2 wk, then decrease dose by 25%, then if no resolution after 2 wk discontinue therapy

Common adverse effects in *italic*, life-threatening effects underlined: generic names in **bold**; classifications in SMALL CAPS; ♣ Canadian drug name; ⊘ Prototype drug

257

Toxicity	Dosage Adjustment
ANC 1000–1499/mm^3 and platelets 50,000–75,000/mm^3	Wait until ANC is at least 15,000 cells/mm^3 and platelets at least 75,000 cells/mm^3 then restart therapy
ANC 500–999/mm^3 and platelets 25,000–49,999/mm^3	Wait until ANC is at least 15,000 cells/mm^3 and platelets at least 75,000 cells/mm^3 then restart therapy
ANC 1000–1499/mm^3 and platelets 50,000–75,000/mm^3	Wait until NCD is at least 15,000 cells/mm^3 and platelets at least 75,000 cells/mm^3 then restart therapy with a 25% reduction in dose
Patients Also Receiving Bortezomib	
ANC less than 500/mm^3, platelets less than 25,000/mm^3 or Hgb less than 8	If before day 4 of cycle do not administer, if after day 4 reduce dose by 25%

SOLUTION PREPARATION

- Wear gloves and use caution when preparing drug solution. If powder or solution contacts skin or mucosa, wash copiously with soap and water.
- Exposure to doxorubicin during the first trimester of pregnancy can result in losing the fetus

Conventional Doxorubicin

- *Vial Reconstitution:* Add 1 mL of nonbacteriostatic NS for each 2 mg of doxorubicin to yield a final concentration of 2 mg/mL. For each mL of NS added, withdraw an equal volume of air from vial to minimize pressure buildup. Shake to dissolve. May be given as prepared or further diluted in NS or D5W.
- *Doxorubicin Solutions:* Solutions of 2 mg/mL are available that can be further diluted in 50 mL or more of NS or D5W.

Liposome Doxorubicin (Lyophilized Doxorubicin)

- Dilute doses up to 90 mg in 250 mL of D5W and dose greater than 90 mg in 500 mL D5W. Solution will be translucent, but not clear, and will be red in color. DO NOT use filters during preparation or administration.

STORAGE

- Store reconstituted conventional doxorubicin solution for 24 h at room temperature; refrigerated at 4°–10° C (39°–50° F) for 48 h. Protect from sunlight; discard unused solution.
- Store diluted lyophilized doxorubicin refrigerated for 24 h.

ADMINISTRATION

- Avoid using antecubital vein or veins on dorsum of hand or wrist, if possible, where extravasation could damage underlying tendons and nerves. Also avoid veins in extremity with compromised venous or lymphatic drainage.

- Care should be taken to avoid extravasation. Stop infusion, remove IV needle, and notify prescriber promptly if patient complains of stinging or burning sensation at the injection site.

Conventional Doxorubicin

- **Direct IV Injection:** Give bolus dose slowly into Y-site of freely running IV infusion of NS or D5W. If possible, use IV tubing attached to a needle inserted into a large vein with a butterfly needle. Usually infused over 3–5 min. Monitor for red streaking along vein or facial flushing, which indicates need to slow infusion rate.

Liposome Doxorubicin (Lyophilized Doxorubicin)

- DO NOT give bolus injection or undiluted solution.
- **IV Infusion:** Infuse at 1 mg/min initially; may increase rate to complete infusion in 1 h if no adverse reactions occur. Slow infusion rate as warranted if an adverse reaction occurs. Do not use a filter.

INCOMPATIBILITIES Solution/additive: *Conventional Doxorubicin:* **Aminophylline, diazepam, fluorouracil.** Y-site: *Conventional Doxorubicin:* **Allopurinol, amphotericin B cholesteryl sulfate, cefepime, gallium, ganciclovir, lansoprazole, pemetrexed, prochlorperazine, propofol, TPN.** Y-site: *Liposome Doxorubicin:* **Amphotericin B, amphotericin B cholesteryl complex, hydroxyzine, mannitol, meperidine, metoclopramide, mitoxantrone, morphine, paclitaxel, piperacillin/tazobactam, promethazine, sodium bicarbonate.**

ACTION & *THERAPEUTIC EFFECT* Cytotoxic antibiotic with wide spectrum of antitumor activity and strong immunosuppressive properties. Intercalates with pre-formed DNA residues blocking effective DNA and RNA transcription. A potent radiosensitizer capable of enhancing radiation reactions. *Highly destructive to rapidly proliferating cells and slowly developing carcinomas; selectively toxic to cardiac tissue.*

CONTRAINDICATIONS Myelosuppression, thrombocytopenia; impaired cardiac function, obstructive jaundice, previous treatment with complete cumulative doses of doxorubicin or daunorubicin; pregnancy (category D), lactation.

CAUTIOUS USE Impaired hepatic or renal function; patients who have received cyclophosphamide or pelvic irradiation or radiotherapy to areas surrounding heart; history of atopic dermatitis.

ADVERSE EFFECTS (≥1%) **Body as a Whole:** Hypersensitivity (red flare around injection site, erythema, skin rash, pruritus, angioedema, urticaria, eosinophilia, fever, chills, <u>anaphylactoid reaction</u>). **CV:** Serious, <u>irreversible myocardial toxicity with delayed CHF, ventricular arrhythmias, acute left ventricular failure</u>, hypertension, hypotension, cardiomyopathy. **GI:** *Stomatitis,* esophagitis with ulcerations; nausea, vomiting, anorexia, inanition, diarrhea. **Hematologic:** *Severe myelosuppression* (60–85% of patients); <u>*leukopenia (principally granulocytes)*</u>, thrombocytopenia, anemia. **Skin:** Hyperpigmentation of nail beds, tongue, and buccal mucosa (especially in blacks); *complete alopecia* (reversible), hyperpigmentation of dermal creases (especially in children); rash; *recall phenomenon (skin reaction due to prior radiotherapy).* **Other:** Lacrimation, drowsi-

Common adverse effects in *italic*, life-threatening effects <u>underlined</u>: generic names in **bold**; classifications in SMALL CAPS; ✿ Canadian drug name; ❂ Prototype drug

259

D

ness, fever, facial flush with too rapid IV infusion rate, microscopic hematuria, hyperuricemia, *hand-foot syndrome. With extravasation: Severe cellulitis, vesication, tissue necrosis,* lymphangitis, phlebosclerosis.

DRUG INTERACTIONS BARBITURATES may decrease effects of doxorubicin by increasing its hepatic metabolism; **streptozocin** may prolong doxorubicin half-life, agents affecting QT interval (ex. **bepridil, droperidol, erythromycin, haloperidol, methadone,** PHENOTHIAZINES, etc.) may increase risk of cardiac side effects. *Conventional Doxorubicin:* Avoid use with **zidovudine.**

PHARMACOKINETICS Distribution: Widely distributed; does not cross blood–brain barrier; 75% protein binding, does not cross placenta; passes into breast milk. **Metabolism:** Metabolized in liver to active metabolite. **Elimination:** Excreted primarily in bile. **Half-Life:** 30–50 h. *Doxorubicin Liposomal:* **Distribution:** Vascular fluid. **Metabolism:** Metabolized in plasma and liver. **Elimination:** In urine. **Half-Life:** 44–55 h.

NURSING IMPLICATIONS

Assessment & Drug Effects

* Evaluate cardiac function (i.e., ECG, left ventricular ejection fraction, echocardiogram) prior to initiation of therapy, at regular intervals, and at end of therapy.
* Be alert to and report early signs of cardiotoxicity (see Appendix C). Acute life-threatening arrhythmias may occur within a few hours of drug administration.
* Lab tests: Baseline and periodic LFTs, renal function, serum electrolytes, CBC with differential and platelet count throughout therapy.
* Note: The nadir of leukopenia (an expected 1000/mm^3) typically occurs 10–14 days after a single dose, with recovery within 21 days.
* Monitor for thrombocytopenia (platelet count less than 50,000/mm^3) and take precautions to prevent excess bleeding.
* Report promptly objective signs of hepatic dysfunction (jaundice, dark urine, pruritus) or kidney dysfunction (altered I&O ratio and pattern, local discomfort with voiding).
* Promote fastidious oral hygiene, especially before and after meals. Stomatitis, generally maximal in second week of therapy, frequently begins with a burning sensation accompanied by erythema of oral mucosa that may progress to ulceration and dysphagia in 2 or 3 days.
* Report signs of superinfection (see Appendix C) promptly; these may result from antibiotic therapy during leukopenic period.
* Avoid rectal medications and use of rectal thermometer; rectal trauma is associated with bloody diarrhea resulting from an antiblastic effect on rapidly growing intestinal mucosal cells.

Patient & Family Education

* Note: Complete loss of hair (reversible) is an expected adverse effect. It may also involve eyelashes and eyebrows, beard and mustache, pubic and axillary hair. Regrowth of hair usually begins 2–3 mo after drug is discontinued.

▪ Drug turns urine red for 1–2 days after administration.
▪ Keep hands away from eyes to prevent conjunctivitis. Increased tearing for 5–10 days after a single dose is possible.

D

DOXYCYCLINE HYCLATE

(dox-i-sye'kleen)
Doxy
Classification(s): ANTIBIOTIC; TETRACYCLINE
Therapeutic: ANTIBACTERIAL
Pregnancy Category: D

USES Chlamydial and mycoplasmal infections; gonorrhea, syphilis in penicillin-allergic patients; rickettsial diseases; acute exacerbations of chronic bronchitis.
UNLABELED USES Treatment of acute PID, leptospirosis, prophylaxis for rape victims, suppression and chemoprophylaxis of chloroquine-resistant *Plasmodium falciparum* malaria, short-term prophylaxis and treatment of travelers' diarrhea caused by enterotoxigenic strains of *Escherichia coli*. Anthrax postexposure treatment and prophylaxis. Intrapleural administration for malignant pleural effusions.

INDICATION & DOSAGE

Antiinfective
Adult/Adolescent/Child (over 8 y and over 45 kg): 100 mg q12h on day 1, then 200 mg/day
Child (over 8 y and up to 45 kg): 4.4 mg/kg in 1–2 doses on day 1, then 2.2–4.4 mg/kg/day in 1–2 divided doses

Acute Pelvic Inflammatory Disease
Adult: 100 mg q12h until improved then 100 mg PO b.i.d. to complete 14 days (used in combination with cefoxitin or cefotetan)

Anthrax Postexposure
Adult/Adolescent/Child (over 8 y and over 45 kg): 100 mg q12h then switch to PO for a total of 60 days
Child (over 8 y and up to 45 kg): 2.2 mg/kg q12h then switch to PO for a total of 60 days

SOLUTION PREPARATION
▪ *Vial Reconstitution:* Add 10 mL sterile water for injection, D5W, NS, LR, D5LR, or other diluent recommended by manufacturer, to each 100 mg of drug. **Must be** further diluted for infusion.
▪ *Further Dilution of Reconstituted Solution:* Each 100 mg (10 mL) **must be** diluted in 100–1000 mL of compatible infusion solution (e.g., D5W, NS, LR, D5LR) to produce concentrations ranging from 0.1 to 1 mg/mL.

Common adverse effects in *italic*, life-threatening effects <u>underlined</u>: generic names in **bold**; classifications in SMALL CAPS; ♣ Canadian drug name; ⊘ Prototype drug

261

STORAGE

▪ Refrigerate reconstituted solutions for up to 72 h. After this time, infusion **must be** completed within 12 h.

▪ When diluted with LR or D5/LR, infusion **must be** completed within 6 h to ensure adequate stability. Protect all solutions from direct sunlight during infusion.

ADMINISTRATION

Intermittent Infusion: Duration of infusion varies with dose but is usually 1–4 h. Recommended minimum infusion time for 100 mg of 0.5 mg/mL solution is 1 h.

INCOMPATIBILITIES Solution/additive: High dose **meropenem, potassium phosphate.** Y-site: **Allopurinol, heparin, meropenem, pemetrexed, piperacillin/tazobactam.**

ACTION & *THERAPEUTIC EFFECT* Semisynthetic broad-spectrum tetracycline antibiotic derived from oxytetracycline. Is more lipophilic than other tetracyclines, thus allowing it to pass easily through lipid layer of bacteria cell wall where reversible binding to the 30S ribosomal subunits occurs. This blocks the binding of transfer RNA (tRNA) to messenger RNA (mRNA) of the bacteria, resulting in inhibition of bacterial protein synthesis. *Primarily bacteriostatic against both gram-positive and gram-negative bacteria. Similar in effectiveness to tetracycline.*

CONTRAINDICATIONS Sensitivity to any of the tetracyclines; use during period of tooth development including last half of pregnancy; pregnancy (category D); lactation; infants and children less than 8 y (causes permanent yellow discoloration of teeth, enamel hypoplasia, and retardation of bone growth).

CAUTIOUS USE Alcoholism; hepatic disease; GI disease; sulfite hypersensitivity; sunlight (UV) exposure.

ADVERSE EFFECTS (≥1%) **Special Senses:** Interference with color vision. **GI:** Anorexia, *nausea,* vomiting, diarrhea, enterocolitis; esophageal irritation (oral capsule and tablet). **Skin:** Rashes, photosensitivity reaction. **Other:** Thrombophlebitis (IV use), superinfections.

DIAGNOSTIC TEST INTERFERENCE Like other *tetracyclines,* doxycycline may cause false increases in *urinary catecholamines (fluorometric methods);* false decreases in *urinary urobilinogen;* false-negative *urine glucose* with *glucose oxidase methods* (e.g., *Clinistix, TesTape*); parenteral doxycycline (containing ascorbic acid) may cause false-positive determinations using *Benedict's reagent* or *Clinitest.*

DRUG INTERACTIONS Effects of both doxycycline and **desmopressin** antagonized; increases **digoxin** absorption, thus increasing risk of **digoxin** toxicity; **methoxyflurane** increases risk of renal failure.

PHARMACOKINETICS Peak: 1.5–4 h. **Distribution:** Penetrates eye, prostate, and CSF; crosses placenta; distributed into breast milk. **Metabolism:** In GI tract. **Elimination:** 20–30% excreted in urine and 20–40% in feces in 48 h. **Half-Life:** 14–24 h.

NURSING IMPLICATIONS

Assessment & Drug Effects
- Monitor infusion site frequently for phlebitis. Change sites as warranted.
- Report evidence of superinfections, especially candidiasis (see Appendix C).
- Lab tests: Periodic LFTs.

Patient & Family Education
- Avoid exposure to direct sunlight and ultraviolet light during and for 4 or 5 days after therapy is terminated to reduce risk of phototoxic reaction. Phototoxic reaction appears like an exaggerated sunburn. Sunscreens provide little protection.
- Urine may become brown or dark yellow during therapy.

DROPERIDOL
(droe-per'i-dole)

Inapsine

Classification(s): ANESTHETIC, GENERAL; ANTIEMETIC
Therapeutic: ANTIEMETIC
Pregnancy Category: C

USES To reduce nausea and vomiting during surgical and diagnostic procedures.
UNLABELED USES Treatment and prevention of nausea and vomiting associated with chemotherapy.

INDICATION & DOSAGE

Nausea Prevention
Adult/Adolescent: 2.5 mg, additional doses of 1.25 mg may be given
Child (2–12 y): 0.1 mg/kg (max: 2.5 mg)

SOLUTION PREPARATION
No dilution is required. Administer as supplied.

STORAGE
Store at 15°–30° C (59°–86° F), unless otherwise directed by manufacturer. Protect from light.

ADMINISTRATION
- **Direct IV Injection for Adult:** Give a single bolus dose at a rate of 2.5 mg or fraction thereof over 1–2 min.
- **Direct IV Injection for Child:** Give a single bolus dose over at least 2 min.

INCOMPATIBILITIES Solution/additive: BARBITURATES. **Y-site: Allopurinol, amphotericin B cholesteryl complex, cefepime, cefotetan, fluoro-**

D

uracil, foscarnet, furosemide, heparin, lansoprazole, leucovorin, methotrexate, nafcillin, pemetrexed, piperacillin/tazobactam.

ACTION & *THERAPEUTIC EFFECT* Butyrophenone derivative that antagonizes emetic effects of morphine-like analgesics and other drugs that act on chemoreceptor trigger zone (CTZ). Acts primarily at subcortical level to produce sedation. *Sedative property reduces anxiety and motor activity without necessarily inducing sleep; patient remains responsive. Potentiates other CNS depressants. Has antiemetic properties.*

CONTRAINDICATIONS Known or suspected QT prolongation; history of torsades de pointes; known intolerance to droperidol; pregnancy (category C), lactation. Safe use in children less than 2 y is not established.

CAUTIOUS USE Older adult, debilitated, and other poor-risk patients; cardiac disease; cardiac arrhythmias, cardiac bradyarrhythmias; cardiac disease; CHF; Parkinson's disease; hypotension; liver, alcoholism; seizure disorders; renal impairment, renal failure.

ADVERSE EFFECTS (≥1%) **CNS:** *Postoperative drowsiness, extrapyramidal symptoms:* Dystonia, akathisia, oculogyric crisis; dizziness, restlessness, anxiety, hallucinations, mental depression. **CV:** *Hypotension, tachycardia,* irregular heartbeats *(prolonged QTc interval even at low doses).* **Other:** Chills, shivering, <u>laryngospasm, bronchospasm.</u>

DRUG INTERACTIONS Additive effect with CNS DEPRESSANTS, **metoclopramide** may increase extrapyramidal symptoms, closely monitor other drugs affecting QTc interval.

PHARMACOKINETICS Onset: 3–10 min. **Peak:** 30 min. **Duration:** 2–4 h; may persist up to 12 h. **Distribution:** Crosses placenta. **Metabolism:** In liver. **Elimination:** In urine and feces.

NURSING IMPLICATIONS

Assessment & Drug Effects
- Monitor ECG throughout therapy. Report immediately prolongation of QTc interval.
- Monitor vital signs closely. Hypotension and tachycardia are common adverse effects.
- Exercise care in moving medicated patients because of possibility of severe orthostatic hypotension. Avoid abrupt changes in position.
- Observe patients for signs of impending respiratory depression especially when receiving a concurrent narcotic analgesic carefully.
- Observe carefully and report promptly early signs of acute dystonia: Facial grimacing, restlessness, tremors, torticollis, oculogyric crisis. Extrapyramidal symptoms may occur within 24–48 h postoperatively.
- Note: Droperidol may aggravate symptoms of acute depression.

Patient & Family Education
- Use caution when ambulating to prevent falls.
- Do not engage in potentially hazardous activities until reaction to drug is known.

Common adverse effects in *italic*, life-threatening effects <u>underlined</u>: generic names in **bold**; classifications in SMALL CAPS; ♣ Canadian drug name; ⊙ Prototype drug

DROTRECOGIN ALFA (ACTIVATED)
(dro-tree'co-gin)

Xigris

Classification(s): THROMBOLYTIC AGENT, HUMAN PROTEIN C

Therapeutic: ANTITHROMBOTIC
Prototype: Protein C Concentrate (Human)
Pregnancy Category: C

USES Reduction in mortality in patients with severe sepsis and evidence of organ dysfunction.

INDICATION & DOSAGE

Sepsis
Adult: 24 mcg/kg/h continuous infusion for 96 h

SOLUTION PREPARATION
- *Vial Reconstitution:* Prepare immediately prior to use. Reconstitute 5 mg or 20 mg vials with 2.5 mL or 10 mL, respectively, of sterile water for injection to yield approximate concentration of 2 mg/mL. Slowly add sterile water to vial, avoid inverting or shaking vial, gently swirl until powder is completely dissolved. **Must be** further diluted for infusion.
- *Further Dilution of Reconstituted Solution:* Slowly withdraw calculated dose from vial, add to infusion bag of NS by directing stream to side of bag to minimize agitation, then gently invert to mix. Final concentration should be 100–200 mcg/mL. Do not transport infusion bag between locations attached to mechanical pump. Note: When using a syringe pump, solution is typically diluted to a final concentration of 100–1000 mcg/mL.

STORAGE
- Reconstituted vial may be held at 15°–30° C (59°–86° F), but **must be** used within 3 h of preparation.
- Refrigerate solution for IV infusion pump and syringe pump. Infuse each IV pump solution within 24 h and each syringe pump solution within 12 h of preparation.

ADMINISTRATION
Continuous Infusion: Use dedicated IV line or dedicated lumen of central venous catheter. Infuse at a rate of 24 mcg/kg/h over 96 h. Note information under **STORAGE** relative to stability of each type of preparation.

INCOMPATIBILITIES Solution/additive: Do not mix with any other drugs. **Y-site: Amiodarone, ampicillin/sulbactam sodium, ceftazidime, ciprofloxacin, clindamycin, cyclosporine, dobutamine, dopamine, epinephrine, fosphenytoin, furosemide, gentamicin, heparin sodium, human serum albumin, imipenem/cilastatin, insulin human (regular), levofloxacin, magnesium sulfate, metronidazole, midazolam, nitroprusside sodium, norepinephrine bitartrate, piperacillin/tazobactam sodium, potassium phosphate, ranitidine, sodium nitroprusside, ticarcillin/clavulanate, tobramycin sulfate, vancomycin.**

Common adverse effects in *italic*, life-threatening effects <u>underlined</u>: generic names in **bold**; classifications in SMALL CAPS; ♣ Canadian drug name; ⊙ Prototype drug

D

ACTION & *THERAPEUTIC EFFECT* Drotrecogin alfa is a recombinant form of human activated protein C (APC). Protein C deficiencies are found in most septic patients and result in a higher mortality rate. APC exerts antithrombotic and anticoagulant effects by inhibiting clotting Factor Va and VIIIa. APC may exert an antiinflammatory effect by inhibiting human tumor necrosis factor (TNF) produced by monocytes, and by limiting the thrombin-induced inflammatory responses of the endothelial lining of the vasculature. *Drotrecogin alfa possesses anticoagulant, antithrombolytic, profibrinolytic, and antiinflammatory properties.*

CONTRAINDICATIONS Prior hypersensitivity to drotrecogin alfa; chronic severe hepatic disease; active internal bleeding or trauma; recent hemorrhagic stroke (within 3 mo); invasive surgery or invasive procedures; recent intracranial or intraspinal surgery, or severe head trauma (within 2 mo); intracranial neoplasm, lesion, aneurysm, or herniation; presence of an epidural catheter; pregnancy (category C), lactation.

CAUTIOUS USE Immunosuppression; increased risk of bleeding, hypercoagulability; thrombocytopenia; concurrent use of anticoagulants or aspirin; recent ischemic stroke, intracranial aneurysm; children less than 18 y.

ADVERSE EFFECTS (≥1%) **Hematologic:** *Bleeding* (including intracranial).

DIAGNOSTIC TEST INTERFERENCE May affect the ***aPTT assay.*** This interference may result in an apparent Factor concentration that is lower than the true concentration.

DRUG INTERACTIONS ANTICOAGULANTS, NSAIDS, ANTIPLATELET AGENTS may increase risk of bleeding.

PHARMACOKINETICS Absorption: Steady state reached in 2 h. **Duration:** Serum levels undetectable 2 h after end of infusion. **Half-Life:** 1.6 h.

NURSING IMPLICATIONS

Assessment & Drug Effects
- Monitor closely for S&S of hemorrhage. Stop infusion immediately should clinically important bleeding occur.
- Discontinue drotrecogin alfa 2 h prior to invasive procedures with an inherent risk of bleeding. Reinitiation may be reconsidered 12 h after major invasive procedure or immediately after uncomplicated less invasive procedures.
- Lab tests: Monitor closely PT.

Patient & Family Education
- Maintain strict bed rest.

ECULIZUMAB

(e-cul-i-zu'mab)

Soliris

Classification(s): IMMUNOLOGIC AGENT; IMMUNOGLOBULIN; MONOCLONAL ANTIBODY

Therapeutic: IMMUNOGLOBULIN
Prototype: Immune Globulin
Pregnancy Category: C

USES Reduction of hemolysis in patients with paroxysmal nocturnal hemoglobinuria.

INDICATION & DOSAGE

Paroxysmal Nocturnal Hemoglobinuria
Adult: 600 mg q7days × 4 wk (a total of 4 doses); then 900 mg on day 7 after the 4th dose, and then 900 mg q14days thereafter.

SOLUTION PREPARATION
IV Infusion: Dilute to a final concentration of 5 mg/mL in NS, D5/1/2NS, or LR by adding the required volume of eculizumab to an EQUAL volume of IV fluid. Invert bag to mix. *Final infusion volumes:* 600 mg in 120 mL or 900 mg in 180 mL. Allow to come to room temperature prior to infusion.

STORAGE
Store infusion bags for 24 h at 2–8° C (36–46° F).

ADMINISTRATION
- Note: Patients **must be** vaccinated against *Neisseria meningitidis* **at least 2 wk prior to** the first dose of eculizumab. Prior to initiating treatment, patients and prescribers **must be enrolled** in the Soliris™ Safety Registry.
- **IV Infusion:** Do NOT give direct IV. Infuse over 35 min via infusion pump or syringe pump. If infusion is slowed for an infusion reaction, the total infusion time should not exceed 2 h.

INCOMPATIBILITIES Solution/additive/Y-site: Data not available; do not mix with any other drugs or solutions.

ACTION & *THERAPEUTIC EFFECT* A monoclonal antibody (IgG) immunoglobulin molecule that binds with high affinity to complement C5 inhibiting formation of the terminal complement complex, C5b-9. *Inhibition of C5b-9 complement complex prevents complement-mediated hemolysis in those with RBCs deficient in terminal complement inhibitors.*

CONTRAINDICATIONS Serious meningococcal infections; pregnancy (category C); children less than 18 y.
CAUTIOUS USE History of hypersensitivity to protein components; older adults; systemic infection; lactation.

ADVERSE EFFECTS (≥5%) **Body as a Whole:** Herpes simplex infections, influenza-like illness, pain in extremity. **CNS:** *Fatigue, headache.* **GI:** Constipation, *nausea.* **Musculoskeletal:** *Back pain,* myalgia. **Respiratory:** *Cough, nasopharyngitis,* respiratory tract infection, sinusitis.

DRUG INTERACTIONS Clinically significant interactions not known.

PHARMACOKINETICS Half-Life: 272 h.

Common adverse effects in *italic*, life-threatening effects <u>underlined</u>: generic names in **bold**; classifications in SMALL CAPS; ♣ Canadian drug name; ⊕ Prototype drug

267

NURSING IMPLICATIONS

Assessment & Drug Effects

- Monitor for a hypersensitivity reaction throughout infusion and for at least 1 h after completion of the infusion.
- Monitor for early signs of meningococcal infection. Report immediately if an infection is suspected.
- Lab tests: Baseline and periodic serum LDH and RBC blood studies.

Patient & Family Education

- Vaccination may not prevent meningitis. Report immediately any of the following: Moderate to severe headache with nausea or vomiting, stiff neck or stiff back, fever, rash, confusion, severe muscle aches with flu-like symptoms, and sensitivity to light.

EDETATE CALCIUM DISODIUM

(ed'e-tate)

Calcium Disodium Versenate

Classification(s): CHELATING AGENT

Therapeutic: CHELATING AGENT; ANTIDOTE

Pregnancy Category: C

USES Principally as adjunct in treatment of acute and chronic lead poisoning (plumbism). Generally used in combination with dimercaprol (BAL) in treatment of lead encephalopathy or when blood lead level exceeds 100 mcg/dL. Also used to diagnose suspected lead poisoning.

UNLABELED USES Treatment of poisoning from other heavy metals such as chromium, manganese, nickel, zinc, and possibly vanadium; removal of radioactive and nuclear fission products such as plutonium, yttrium, uranium. Not effective in poisoning from arsenic, gold, or mercury.

INDICATION & DOSAGE

Diagnosis of Lead Poisoning

Adult/Child: 500 mg/m^2 (max: 1 g) over 1 h, then collect urine for 24 h (if mcg lead:mg EDTA ratio in urine is over 1, the test is positive)

Treatment of Lead Poisoning

Adult/Child: 1–1.5 g/m^2/day infused over 8–24 h for up to 5 days

Lead Nephropathy/Renal Impairment Dosage Adjustment

Adult: Based on serum creatinine less than 2 mg/dL: 1 g/m^2/day; serum creatinine 2–3 mg/dL: 500 mg/m^2/day; serum creatinine 3.1–4 mg/dL: 500 mg/m^2 q48h; serum creatinine over 4 mg/dL: 500 mg/m^2 per wk. Infuse over 8–24 h for 5 days; may repeat monthly.

SOLUTION PREPARATION
Dilute the 5 mL ampule with 250–500 mL of NS or D5W.

STORAGE
Store at 15°–30° C (59°–86° F).

ADMINISTRATION
- **IV Infusion:** Warning: Rapid IV infusion may be **LETHAL** by suddenly increasing intracranial pressure in those who already have cerebral edema. Infuse total daily dose over 8–12 h. Prescriber should order specific rate.
- Note: Calcium disodium edetate can produce potentially fatal effects when higher than recommended doses are used or when it is continued after toxic effects appear.

INCOMPATIBILITIES Solution/additive: Amphotericin B, hydralazine, lactated Ringer's.

ACTION & *THERAPEUTIC EFFECT* Chelating agent that combines with divalent and trivalent metals to form stable, nonionizing soluble complexes that can be readily excreted by kidneys. Action is dependent on ability of heavy metal to displace less strongly bound calcium in drug molecules. *Chelating agent that binds with heavy metals such as lead to form a soluble complex that can be excreted through the kidney.*

CONTRAINDICATIONS Severe kidney disease, anuria, oliguria, active renal disease; IV use in patients with lead encephalopathy not generally recommended (because of possible increase in intracranial pressure); pregnancy (category C).
CAUTIOUS USE Kidney dysfunction; active tubercular lesions; history of gout; lactation.

ADVERSE EFFECTS (≥1%) **CV:** Hypotension, thrombophlebitis. **GI:** Anorexia, nausea, vomiting, diarrhea, abdominal cramps, cheilosis. **Hematologic:** Transient bone marrow depression, depletion of blood metals. **Urogenital:** <u>Nephrotoxicity</u> (renal tubular necrosis), proteinuria, hematuria. **Body as a Whole:** *Febrile reaction* (excessive thirst, fever, chills, severe myalgia, arthralgia, GI distress), *histamine-like reactions* (flushing, throbbing headache, sweating, sneezing, nasal congestion, lacrimation, postural hypotension, tachycardia).

DIAGNOSTIC TEST INTERFERENCE Edetate calcium disodium may decrease ***serum cholesterol, plasma lipid*** levels (if elevated), and ***serum potassium*** values. ***Glycosuria*** may occur with toxic doses.

DRUG INTERACTIONS No clinically significant interactions established.

PHARMACOKINETICS Onset: 1 h. **Peak:** Peak chelation 24–48 h. **Distribution:** Distributed to extracellular fluid; does not enter CSF. **Metabolism:** Not metabolized. **Elimination:** Chelated lead excreted in urine; 50% excreted in 1 h. **Half-Life:** 20–60 min.

NURSING IMPLICATIONS
Assessment & Drug Effects
- Monitor vital signs and ECG during therapy.

Common adverse effects in *italic*, life-threatening effects <u>underlined</u>: generic names in **bold**; classifications in SMALL CAPS; ♣ Canadian drug name; 🅞 Prototype drug

269

- Determine adequacy of urinary output prior to therapy. This may be done by administering IV fluids before giving first dose.
- Increase fluid intake to enhance urinary excretion of chelates. Avoid excess fluid intake, however, in patients with lead encephalopathy because of the danger of further increasing intracranial pressure. Consult prescriber regarding allowable intake.
- Monitor I&O. Since drug is excreted almost exclusively via kidneys, toxicity may develop if output is inadequate. Stop therapy if urine flow is markedly diminished or absent. Report any change in output or I&O ratio to prescriber.
- Lab tests: Baseline and periodic (during each course of therapy) serum creatinine, calcium, phosphorus, and LFTs. With prolonged therapy: Periodic blood trace element metals (e.g., copper, zinc, magnesium).
- Be alert for occurrence of febrile reaction that may appear 4–8 h after drug infusion (see **ADVERSE EFFECTS**).

Patient & Family Education
- Report promptly lack of urine output over a period of 12 h.

EDROPHONIUM CHLORIDE

(ed-roe-foe′nee-um)

Enlon, Tensilon

Classification(s): CHOLINESTERASE INHIBITOR

Therapeutic: DIAGNOSTIC AGENT

Prototype: Neostigmine

Pregnancy Category: C

USES Differential diagnosis and as adjunct in evaluation of treatment requirements of myasthenia gravis, for differentiating myasthenic from cholinergic crisis, and to reverse neuromuscular blockade produced by overdosage of nondepolarizing skeletal muscle relaxants.

INDICATION & DOSAGE

Myasthenia Gravis Diagnosis

Adult: Prepare 10 mg in a syringe; inject 2 mg over 15–30 sec, if no reaction after 45 sec, inject the remaining 8 mg; may repeat test after 30 min
Child (34 kg or less): 1 mg, if no response after 45 sec, may give 1 mg q30–45sec up to 5 mg; *(over 34 kg):* 2 mg, if no response after 45 sec, may give 1 mg q30–45sec up to 10 mg
Infant: 0.5 mg once

Evaluation of Myasthenia Treatment

Adult: 1–2 mg administered 1 h after last PO dose of anticholinesterase medication

---

Common adverse effects in *italic*, life-threatening effects <u>underlined</u>: generic names in **bold**; classifications in SMALL CAPS; ♣ Canadian drug name; ☻ Prototype drug

Reversal of Neuromuscular Blockade

Adult: 10 mg over 30–45 sec, may give 10 mg every 5–10 min up to total of 40 mg

SOLUTION PREPARATION
May be given undiluted [direct IV] or diluted in D5W or NS for infusion.

STORAGE
Store at 15°–30° C (59°–86° F).

ADMINISTRATION
- Have atropine sulfate immediately available and facilities for endotracheal intubation, tracheostomy, suction, assisted respiration, and cardiac monitoring for treatment of cholinergic reaction.
- **Direct IV Injection:** For diagnosis of MG: Use a TB syringe to inject 2 mg (adult & child over 34 kg) or 1 mg (child 34 kg or less) over 15–30 sec; if no reaction after 45 sec, inject additional 8 mg (adult) or titrate up to a total of 8 mg additional (child over 34 kg) or titrate in 1 mg increments up to a total of 4 mg additional (child 34 kg or less), may repeat test after 30 min. If cholinergic reaction (increased muscle weakness) is obtained after initial 1 or 2 mg, discontinue test and give atropine IV (as ordered).
- **IV Infusion:** Infuse over 1 h.

INCOMPATIBILITIES Solution/additive: Trimetrexate.

ACTION & *THERAPEUTIC EFFECT* Indirect-acting cholinesterase inhibitor that acts as antidote to curariform drugs by displacing them from muscle cell receptor sites, thus permitting resumption of normal transmission of neuromuscular impulses. *Acts as antidote to curariform drugs by displacing them, thus permitting resumption of normal transmission of neuromuscular impulses.*

CONTRAINDICATIONS Hypersensitivity to anticholinesterase agents; cholinesterase inhibitor toxicity; intestinal and urinary obstruction; pregnancy (category C), lactation.

CAUTIOUS USE Sulfite hypersensitivity; bronchial asthma; cardiac arrhythmias, bradycardia; peptic ulcer disease; hypotension; patients receiving digitalis.

ADVERSE EFFECTS (≥1%) **Body as a Whole:** Severe adverse effects uncommon with usual doses. **CNS:** Weakness, muscle cramps, dysphoria, fasciculations, incoordination, dysarthria, dysphagia, convulsions, <u>respiratory paralysis</u>. **CV:** Bradycardia, irregular pulse, hypotension, pulmonary edema. **Special Senses:** Miosis, blurred vision, diplopia, lacrimation. **GI:** Diarrhea, abdominal cramps, nausea, vomiting, excessive salivation. **Respiratory:** Increased bronchial secretions, <u>bronchospasm, laryngospasm</u>, pulmonary edema. **Other:** Excessive sweating, urinary frequency, incontinence.

DRUG INTERACTIONS **Procainamide, quinidine** may antagonize the effects of edrophonium; DIGITALIS GLYCOSIDES increase the sensitivity of the heart to edrophonium; **succinylcholine, decamethonium** may prolong neuromuscular blockade.

PHARMACOKINETICS **Onset:** 30–60 sec. **Duration:** 5–10 min.

Common adverse effects in *italic*, life-threatening effects <u>underlined</u>: generic names in **bold**; classifications in SMALL CAPS; ✚ Canadian drug name; ✱ Prototype drug

271

NURSING IMPLICATIONS

Assessment & Drug Effects

- Monitor vital signs. Observe for signs of respiratory distress. Patients greater than 50 y are particularly likely to develop bradycardia, hypotension, and cardiac arrest.

- Edrophonium test for myasthenia gravis: All cholinesterase inhibitors (anticholinesterases) should be discontinued for at least 8 h before test. Positive response to edrophonium test consists of brief improvement in muscle strength unaccompanied by lingual or skeletal muscle fasciculations.

- Evaluation of myasthenic treatment: *Myasthenic response* (immediate subjective improvement with increased muscle strength, absence of fasciculations; generally indicates that patient requires larger dose of anticholinesterase agent or longer-acting drug); *Cholinergic response* [muscarinic adverse effects (lacrimation, diaphoresis, salivation, abdominal cramps, diarrhea, nausea, vomiting; accompanied by decrease in muscle strength; usually indicates over-treatment with cholinesterase inhibitor)]; *Adequate response* [no change in muscle strength; fasciculations may be present or absent; minimal cholinergic adverse effects (observed in patients at or near optimal dosage level)].

ENALAPRILAT 🅟

(e-nal′a-pri-lat)

Vasotec I.V.

Classification(s): ANGIOTENSIN-CONVERTING ENZYME INHIBITOR
Therapeutic: ANTIHYPERTENSIVE
Pregnancy Category: C in first trimester, D in second and third trimester

USES Malignant, refractory, accelerated, and renovascular hypertension (except in bilateral renal artery stenosis or renal artery stenosis in a solitary kidney).
UNLABELED USES Hypertension or renal crisis in scleroderma.

INDICATION & DOSAGE

Hypertension

Adult: 1.25 mg q6h, may give up to 5 mg q6h in hypertensive emergencies

Renal Impairment Dosage Adjustment

CrCl less than 30 mL/min: Give 0.625 mg q6h

Dialysis

Give post-dialysis.

SOLUTION PREPARATION

May be given undiluted [direct IV] or diluted in 50 mL of D5W, NS, D5NS, D5LR for infusion.

Common adverse effects in *italic*, life-threatening effects <u>underlined</u>: generic names in **bold**; classifications in SMALL CAPS; ♣ Canadian drug name; 🅟 Prototype drug

STORAGE
Stable for 24 h at 15°–30° C (59°–86° F) when added to an IV solution.

ADMINISTRATION
- **Direct IV Injection:** Give bolus dose over least 5 min through a port of a free-flowing infusion of D5W or NS.
- **Intermittent Infusion:** Infuse over 5 min to 1 h. Longer infusion time minimizes risk for severe hypotension.

INCOMPATIBILITIES Y-site: Amphotericin B, amphotericin B cholesteryl complex, cefepime, phenytoin.

ACTION & *THERAPEUTIC EFFECT* Angiotensin-converting enzyme (ACE) inhibitor. ACE catalyzes the conversion of angiotensin I to angiotensin II, a vasoconstrictor substance. Therefore, inhibition of ACE decreases angiotensin II levels, thus decreasing both vasopressor activity and aldosterone secretion. Both actions achieve an antihypertensive effect by suppression of the renin–angiotensin–aldosterone system. ACE inhibitors also reduce peripheral arterial resistance (afterload); pulmonary capillary wedge pressure (PCWP), a measure of preload, pulmonary vascular resistance; and improve cardiac output as well as exercise tolerance. *Antihypertensive effect is related to suppression of the renin-angiotensin-aldosterone system causing vasodilation and, therefore, lower blood pressure. Improvement in cardiac output results in increased exercise tolerance.*

CONTRAINDICATIONS Hypersensitivity to enalapril or captopril. There has been evidence of fetotoxicity and kidney damage in newborns exposed to ACE inhibitors during pregnancy (category C in first trimester, and category D in second and third trimester); infants and children with CrCl less than 30 mL/min/1.73 m^2.

CAUTIOUS USE Renal impairment, renal artery stenosis; patients with hypovolemia, receiving diuretics, undergoing dialysis; hepatic disease, hepatic impairment; bone marrow suppression; patients in whom excessive hypotension would present a hazard (e.g., cerebrovascular insufficiency); CHF; aortic stenosis, cardiomyopathy; diabetes mellitus; lactation.

ADVERSE EFFECTS (≥1%) **CNS:** *Headache, dizziness,* fatigue, nervousness, paresthesias, asthenia, insomnia, somnolence. **CV:** *Hypotension including postural hypotension;* syncope, palpitations, chest pain. **GI:** Diarrhea, nausea, abdominal pain, loss of taste, dyspepsia. **Hematologic:** Decreased Hgb and Hct. **Urogenital:** Acute kidney failure, deterioration in kidney function. **Skin:** Pruritus with and without *rash,* angioedema, erythema. **Metabolic:** Hyperkalemia. **Respiratory:** Cough.

DRUG INTERACTIONS Indomethacin and other NSAIDs may decrease antihypertensive activity; POTASSIUM SUPPLEMENTS, POTASSIUM-SPARING DIURETICS may cause hyperkalemia; may increase **lithium** levels and toxicity.

PHARMACOKINETICS Onset: 15 min. **Peak:** 4 h. **Duration:** 6 h. **Distribution:** Limited amount crosses blood–brain barrier; crosses placenta. **Elimination:** 60% excreted in urine, 33% in feces within 24 h. **Half-Life:** 2 h.

Common adverse effects in *italic*, life-threatening effects underlined: generic names in **bold**; classifications in SMALL CAPS; ♣ Canadian drug name; ◔ Prototype drug

273

NURSING IMPLICATIONS

Assessment & Drug Effects

- Monitor BP closely for therapeutic effectiveness. Peak effects after the first IV dose may not occur for up to 4 h; peak effects of subsequent doses may exceed those of the first.
- Maintain bedrest and monitor BP for the first 3 h after the initial IV dose. First-dose phenomenon (i.e., a sudden exaggerated hypotensive response) may occur within 1–3 h of first IV dose, especially in those with very high BP or on a diuretic. An IV infusion of normal saline for volume expansion may be needed to counteract the hypotensive response. This initial response is not an indicator to stop therapy.
- Report transient hypotension with lightheadedness. Older adults are particularly sensitive to drug-induced hypotension. Supervise ambulation until BP has stabilized.
- Lab tests: Periodic serum potassium and kidney function tests.
- Monitor for S&S of hyperkalemia (see Appendix C). Patients who have diabetes, impaired kidney function, or CHF are at risk of developing hyperkalemia during enalapril treatment.

Patient & Family Education

- When drug is discontinued due to severe hypotension, the hypotensive effect may persist a week or longer after termination because of long duration of drug action.
- Report to prescriber promptly if swelling of face, eyelids, tongue, lips, or extremities occurs. Angioedema is a rare adverse effect and, if accompanied by laryngeal edema, may be fatal.
- Do not drive or engage in other potentially hazardous activities until response to drug is known.

EPHEDRINE SULFATE

(e-fed′rin)

Ectasule, Ephedsol, Vatronol

Classification(s): ALPHA- AND BETA-ADRENERGIC AGONIST
Therapeutic: BRONCHODILATOR; VASOPRESSOR
Prototype: Epinephrine HCl
Pregnancy Category: C

USES For its CNS stimulant actions in treatment of narcolepsy; to improve respiration in narcotic and barbiturate poisoning; to combat hypotensive states, especially those associated with spinal anesthesia; and for temporary support of ventricular rate in Adams-Stokes syndrome.

INDICATION & DOSAGE

Hypotension, Bronchodilation

Adult: 5–25 mg repeat as needed
Child: 2–3 mg/kg/day in 4–6 divided doses (max: 75 mg/24 h)

Common adverse effects in *italic*, life-threatening effects underlined: generic names in **bold**; classifications in SMALL CAPS; ✦ Canadian drug name; ❷ Prototype drug

SOLUTION PREPARATION
No dilution is required. Administer as supplied.

STORAGE
Store at 15°–30° C (59°–86° F) and protect from light.

ADMINISTRATION
Direct IV Injection: Give bolus dose at a rate of 10 mg or fraction thereof over 30–60 sec.

INCOMPATIBILITIES Solution/additive: Hydrocortisone, pentobarbital, phenobarbital, secobarbital, thiopental. Y-site: Thiopental.

ACTION & *THERAPEUTIC EFFECT* Both indirect- and direct-acting sympathomimetic amine. Thought to act indirectly by releasing tissue stores of norepinephrine and directly by stimulation of alpha-, beta$_1$-, and beta$_2$-adrenergic receptors. Like epinephrine, contracts dilated arterioles of nasal mucosa, thus reducing engorgement and edema and facilitating ventilation and drainage. *Ephedrine relaxes bronchial smooth muscle by stimulation of beta$_2$ receptors, relieving mild bronchospasm, improving air exchange, and increasing vital capacity.*

CONTRAINDICATIONS History of hypersensitivity to ephedrine or other sympathomimetics; narrow-angle glaucoma; angina pectoris, coronary insufficiency, chronic heart disease; uncontrolled hypertension, cardiac arrhythmias, cardiomyopathy; hypovolemia; concurrent MAOI therapy; pregnancy (category C), lactation. **CAUTIOUS USE** Hypertension, arteriosclerosis, closed angle glaucoma; diabetes mellitus; hyperthyroidism; prostatic hypertrophy.

ADVERSE EFFECTS (≥1%) **CNS:** Headache, insomnia, *nervousness,* anxiety, tremulousness, giddiness. **CV:** Palpitation, tachycardia, precordial pain, cardiac arrhythmias. **GU:** Difficult or painful urination, acute urinary retention (especially older men with prostatism). **GI:** Nausea, vomiting, anorexia. **Body as a Whole:** Sweating, thirst, overdosage: Euphoria, confusion, delirium, convulsions, pyrexia, hypertension, rebound hypotension, respiratory difficulty. **Skin:** Fixed-drug eruption. **Topical use:** *Burning, stinging,* dryness of nasal mucosa, sneezing, rebound congestion.

DIAGNOSTIC TEST INTERFERENCE Ephedrine is generally withdrawn at least 12 h before ***sensitivity tests*** are made to prevent false-positive reactions.

DRUG INTERACTIONS MAO INHIBITORS, TRICYCLIC ANTIDEPRESSANTS, **furazolidone, guanethidine** may increase alpha-adrenergic effects (headache, hyperpyrexia, hypertension); **sodium bicarbonate** decreases renal elimination of ephedrine, increasing its CNS effects; **epinephrine, norepinephrine** compound sympathomimetic effects; effects of ALPHA- AND BETA-BLOCKERS and ephedrine antagonized.

PHARMACOKINETICS Duration: Bronchodilation 2–4 h; cardiac & pressor effects up to 1 h. **Distribution:** Widely distributed; crosses blood–brain barrier and placenta; distributed into breast milk. **Metabolism:** Small amounts metabolized in liver. **Elimination:** Excreted in urine. **Half-Life:** 3–6 h.

Common adverse effects in *italic*, life-threatening effects underlined: generic names in **bold**; classifications in SMALL CAPS; ♣ Canadian drug name; ◐ Prototype drug

275

NURSING IMPLICATIONS

Assessment & Drug Effects

- Supervise continuously. Take baseline BP and other vital signs. Check BP repeatedly during first 5 min, then q3–5min until stabilized.
- Monitor I&O ratio and pattern, especially in older male patients.

E

EPINEPHRINE ⓟ

(ep-i-ne′frin)

EPINEPHRINE HYDROCHLORIDE

Adrenalin Chloride, Bronkaid Mistometer, Dysne-Inhal, Epifrin, Glaucon, SusPhrine ◆

Classification(s): ALPHA- AND BETA-ADRENERGIC AGONIST
Therapeutic: CARDIAC STIMULANT; VASOPRESSOR
Pregnancy Category: C

USES Hypersensitivity and anaphylactic reactions, syncope due to heart block or carotid sinus hypersensitivity, and to restore cardiac rhythm in cardiac arrest.

INDICATION & DOSAGE

Anaphylaxis

Adult: 0.1–0.25 mg may repeat
Child: 0.01 mL/kg of 1:1000 q10–15min
Neonate: 0.01–0.05 mg/kg may repeat

Cardiac Arrest

Adult: 1 mg q3–5min as needed
Child: 0.01 mg/kg q3–5min as needed

SOLUTION PREPARATION

- The 1:1000 solution contains 1 mg/1 mL. The 1:1000 solution **MUST be** diluted prior to IV administration.
- The 1:10,000 solution contains 0.1 mg/1 mL and may be given undiluted or diluted for infusion.
- *Direct IV Injection:* Dilute each 1 mg of the 1:1000 solution with 10 mL of NS to yield a 1:10,000 solution. May be further diluted for infusion.
- *IV Infusion:* Dilute required dose in 250–500 mL of D5W; 1 mg in 500 mL yields 2 mcg/mL; 1 mg in 250 mL or 2 mg on 500 mL yields 4 mcg/mL.

STORAGE

Protect from light. Deteriorates rapidly. Do not use if solutions turns pink-brown.

ADMINISTRATION

- **Direct IV Injection:** Give each 1 mg over 1 min or longer; may give more rapidly in cardiac arrest.

- **IV Infusion:** Infuse 1–10 mcg/min titrated according to patient's condition.

INCOMPATIBILITIES Solution/additive: Aminophylline, ampicillin, cephapirin, chloramphenicol, hyaluronidase, mephentermine, sodium bicarbonate, warfarin. **Y-site:** Ampicillin, sodium bicarbonate, thiopental.

ACTION & *THERAPEUTIC EFFECT* Catecholamine drug that acts directly on both alpha and beta receptors; it is the most potent activator of alpha receptors. Strengthens myocardial contraction; increases systolic but may decrease diastolic blood pressure; increases cardiac rate and cardiac output. Constricts bronchial arterioles and inhibits histamine release, thus reducing congestion and edema and increasing tidal volume and vital capacity. Relaxes uterine smooth musculature and inhibits uterine contractions. *Imitates all actions of sympathetic nervous system (SNS) except those on arteries of face and sweat glands.*

CONTRAINDICATIONS Hypersensitivity to sympathomimetic amines; narrow-angle glaucoma; hemorrhagic, traumatic, or cardiogenic shock; cardiac dilatation, cerebral arteriosclerosis, coronary insufficiency, arrhythmias, organic heart or brain disease; during second stage of labor; for local anesthesia of fingers, toes, ears, nose, genitalia; pregnancy (category C). **CAUTIOUS USE** Older adult or debilitated patients; prostatic hypertrophy; hypertension; diabetes mellitus; hyperthyroidism; Parkinson's disease; tuberculosis; psychoneurosis; in patients with long-standing bronchial asthma and emphysema with degenerative heart disease; lactation.

ADVERSE EFFECTS (≥1%) **Special Senses:** *Nasal burning or stinging,* dryness of nasal mucosa, sneezing, rebound congestion. *Transient stinging or burning of eyes,* lacrimation, browache, headache, rebound conjunctival hyperemia, allergy, iritis; with prolonged use: Melanin-like deposits on lids, conjunctiva, and cornea; corneal edema; loss of lashes (reversible); maculopathy with central scotoma in aphakic patients (reversible). **Body as a Whole:** *Nervousness,* restlessness, sleeplessness, fear, anxiety, *tremors,* severe headache, cerebrovascular accident, weakness, dizziness, syncope, pallor, sweating, dyspnea. **Digestive:** Nausea, vomiting. **Cardiovascular:** Precordial pain, *palpitations,* hypertension, <u>MI</u>, tachyarrhythmias including <u>ventricular fibrillation</u>. **Respiratory:** Bronchial and <u>pulmonary edema</u>. **Urogenital:** Urinary retention. **Skin:** Tissue necrosis with repeated injections. **Metabolic:** Metabolic acidoses, elevated serum lactic acid, transient elevations of blood glucose. **Nervous System:** Altered state of perception and thought, psychosis.

DRUG INTERACTIONS May increase hypotension in circulatory collapse or hypotension caused by PHENOTHIAZINES, **oxytocin, entacapone.** Additive toxicities with other SYMPATHOMIMETICS **(albuterol, dobutamine, dopamine, isoproterenol, metaproterenol, norepinephrine, phenylephrine, phenylpropanolamine, pseudoephedrine, ritodrine, salmeterol, terbutaline),** MAO INHIBITORS, TRICYCLIC ANTIDEPRESSANTS. ALPHA- AND BETA-ADRENERGIC BLOCKING AGENTS (e.g., **ergotamine, propranolol**) antagonize effects of epinephrine. GENERAL ANESTHETICS increase cardiac irritability.

PHARMACOKINETICS Onset: 3–5 min. **Peak:** 20 min. **Distribution:** Widely distributed; does not cross blood–brain barrier; crosses placenta. **Metab-**

Common adverse effects in *italic*, life-threatening effects <u>underlined</u>: generic names in **bold**, classifications in SMALL CAPS; ♣ Canadian drug name; ● Prototype drug

277

olism: Metabolized in tissue and liver by monoamine oxidase (MAO) and catecholamine-methyltransferase (COMT). **Elimination:** Small amount excreted unchanged in urine; excreted in breast milk.

NURSING IMPLICATIONS

Assessment & Drug Effects

- Careful cardiac monitoring is required. Monitor BP, HR, and respirations closely. Epinephrine may widen pulse pressure. Check BP repeatedly during first 5 min of IV infusion, then q3–5min until stabilized.
- Monitor I&O and report significant changes in ratio.
- Lab tests: Periodic serum potassium and blood glucose.
- Monitor diabetics for loss of glycemic control.

EPIRUBICIN HYDROCHLORIDE

(e-pi-roo'bi-sin)

Ellence

Classification(s): ANTINEOPLASTIC; ANTIBIOTIC
Therapeutic: ANTINEOPLASTIC
Prototype: Doxorubicin HCl
Pregnancy Category: D

USES Adjunctive therapy for axillary node-positive breast cancer.

INDICATION & DOSAGE

Breast Cancer

Adult: 100–120 mg/m² on day 1 of a 3–4 wk cycle or 50–60 mg/m² on day 1 and 8 of a 3–4 wk cycle

Hepatic Impairment Dosage Adjustment

Bilirubin 1.2–3 mg/dL: Give 50% of dose; *bilirubin over 3 mg/dL:* Give 25% of dose

Toxicity Dosage Adjustment

Platelets less than 50,000/mm³, ANC less than 250/mm³, neutropenic fever, grade 3 or 4 hematologic toxicity: Reduce dose by 25%

SOLUTION PREPARATION

No dilution is required. Administer as supplied.

STORAGE

- Store unopened vial between 2°–8° C (36°–46° F). Protect from light.
- Epirubicin is manufactured as a preservative-free ready-to-use solution. The contents of a vial **must be** used within 24 h of first penetrating the rubber stopper. Discard unused solution.

ADMINISTRATION

- **IV Injection:** Give a single dose over 3–20 min. **DO NOT** give by direct IV into a vein. Inject **ONLY** into a port of a freely flowing IV

Common adverse effects in *italic*, life-threatening effects <u>underlined</u>: generic names in **bold**; classifications in SMALL CAPS; ♥ Canadian drug name; ☉ Prototype drug

solution of D5W or NS. Injection time may be extended if red streaking along the vein or facial flushing occur.

- Avoid IV sites that enter small veins or repeated injections into the same vein.
- Monitor IV site closely for S&S of extravasation and if suspected, notify prescriber immediately.
- Note: Pregnant women should **NOT** handle or administer this drug. Wear protective goggles, gowns and disposable gloves and masks when handling this drug. Discard **ALL** equipment used in preparation of this drug in high-risk, waste-disposal bags for incineration. Treat accidental contact with skin or eyes by rinsing with copious amounts of water followed by prompt medical attention.

INCOMPATIBILITIES Solution/additive: ALKALINE SOLUTIONS (including **sodium bicarbonate**), **fluorouracil, heparin.**

ACTION & *THERAPEUTIC EFFECT* Cytotoxic antibiotic with wide spectrum of antitumor activity and strong immunosuppressive properties. Complexes with DNA causing the DNA helix to change shape, thus blocking effective DNA and RNA transcription. *Highly destructive to rapidly proliferating cells. Effectiveness is indicated by tumor regression.*

CONTRAINDICATIONS Hypersensitivity to epirubicin and other related drugs; marked myelosuppression; severely impaired cardiac function, severe cardiac arrhythmias, recent MI; severe hepatic disease, jaundice; previous treatment with maximum doses of epirubicin, doxorubicin, or daunorubicin; pregnancy (category D), lactation; children.
CAUTIOUS USE Arrhythmias; mild or moderate liver dysfunction; severe renal insufficiency or renal failure.

ADVERSE EFFECTS (≥1%) **Body as a Whole:** *Lethargy,* fever. **CV:** Asymptomatic decrease in LVEF, CHF. **GI:** *Nausea, vomiting, mucositis, diarrhea,* anorexia. **Hematologic:** <u>Leukopenia, neutropenia, anemia, thrombocytopenia, AML.</u> **Skin:** *Alopecia, injection site reaction,* rash, itching, skin changes. **Other:** *Amenorrhea, hot flashes, infection, conjunctivitis/keratitis,* <u>secondary acute myelogenous leukemia</u> (related to cumulative dose).

DRUG INTERACTIONS Cimetidine increases epirubicin levels; concomitant use with cardioactive drugs (e.g., CALCIUM CHANNEL BLOCKERS).

PHARMACOKINETICS Distribution: Widely distributed, 77% protein bound, concentrated in red blood cells. **Metabolism:** Extensively metabolized in liver, blood, and other organs. Clearance reduced in patients with hepatic impairment. **Elimination:** Primarily excreted in bile, some urinary excretion; clearance decreases in older adult female patients. **Half-Life:** 33 h.

NURSING IMPLICATIONS

Assessment & Drug Effects

- Withhold drug and notify prescriber of any of the following: Neutrophil count less than 1500/mm³, recent MI, suspicion of severe myocardial insufficiency.

- Before each cycle of therapy, the following are recommended: Left ventricular ejection fraction, ECG and ECHO (especially in the presence of risk factors of cardiac toxicity).
- Monitor cardiac status closely throughout therapy as the risk of developing severe CHF increases rapidly when cumulative doses approach 900 mg/m². Report promptly: Significant ECG change, tachycardia, gallop rhythm; S&S of pleural effusion, pulmonary edema, dependent edema, ascites, or hepatomegaly.
- Lab tests: Before each cycle of therapy, CBC with differential, platelet count, LFTs, and serum creatinine.

Patient & Family Education
- Report any of the following to prescriber immediately: Pain at the site of IV infusion, chest pain, palpitations, shortness of breath or difficulty breathing, sudden weight gain, swelling of hands, feet or legs, or any unexplained bleeding.
- Be aware that your urine may turn red for 1–2 days after receiving this drug. This change is expected and harmless.
- Do not take OTC cimetidine or any other OTC drug without consulting prescriber.
- Use effective means of contraception (both men and women) while on epirubicin therapy.

EPOETIN ALFA (HUMAN RECOMBINANT ERYTHROPOIETIN) ⓟ
(e-po-e-tin)
Epogen, Eprex ◆, Procrit
Classification(s): HEMATOPOIETIC GROWTH FACTOR
Therapeutic: ANTIANEMIC
Pregnancy Category: C

USES Elevates the hematocrit of patients with anemia secondary to chronic kidney failure (CRF); patients may or may not be on dialysis; other anemias related to malignancies and AIDS. Autologous blood donations for anticipated transfusions. Reduces need for blood in anemic surgical patients.

INDICATION & DOSAGE

Anemia

Adult: Start with 50–100 unit/kg/dose until target Hct range of 30–33% (max: 36%) is reached. [Hct should not increase by more than 4 points in any 2-wk period. Rapid increase in Hct increases the risk of serious adverse reactions (hypertension, seizures).] May increase dose if Hct has not increased 5–6 points after 8 wk of therapy. Reduce dose after target range is reached or the Hct increases by over 4 points in any 2-wk period. Dose usually increased or decreased by 25 unit/kg increments.

Child: 50 unit/kg/dose 3 times/wk initially, when Hct increased to 35%, decrease dose by 25 unit/kg/dose until Hct reaches 40%

SOLUTION PREPARATION
- No dilution is required. Administer as supplied.
- Do not shake vial during preparation of dose as drug will be inactivated.
- Vials without preservatives: Enter each vial only once and discard any unused portion.

STORAGE
Store at 2°–8° C (36°–46° F). Do not freeze or shake.

ADMINISTRATION
Direct IV Injection: Give bolus dose over 1 min.

INCOMPATIBILITIES Data not available; do not mix with other drugs.

ACTION & *THERAPEUTIC EFFECT* Human erythropoietin is produced in the kidney and stimulates bone marrow production of RBCs (erythropoiesis) in response to hypoxia and anemia. *Epoetin alpha is a glycoprotein that stimulates RBC production in the bone marrow of severely anemic patients.*

CONTRAINDICATIONS Uncontrolled hypertension and known hypersensitivity to mammalian cell–derived products and albumin (human); pregnancy (category C), lactation; neonates.

CAUTIOUS USE Leukemia, sickle cell disease; coagulopathy; seizure disorders.

ADVERSE EFFECTS (≥1%) **CNS:** Seizures, *headache.* **CV:** *Hypertension.* **GI:** Nausea, diarrhea. **Hematologic:** *Iron deficiency,* thrombocytosis, *clotting of AV fistula.* **Other:** Sweating, bone pain, arthralgias.

DRUG INTERACTIONS No clinically significant interactions established.

PHARMACOKINETICS Onset: 7–14 days. **Metabolism:** Metabolized in serum. **Elimination:** Minimal recovery in urine. **Half-Life:** 4–13 h.

NURSING IMPLICATIONS
Assessment & Drug Effects
- Control BP adequately prior to initiation of therapy and closely monitor and control during therapy. Hypertension is an adverse effect that **must be** controlled.
- Be aware that BP may rise during early therapy as the Hct increases. Report promptly a rapid rise in Hct (greater than 4 points in 2 wk). Dosage will need to be reduced because of risk of serious hypertension.
- Monitor for hypertensive encephalopathy in patients with CRF during period of increasing Hct.
- Monitor for premonitory neurological symptoms (i.e., aura, and report their appearance promptly). The potential for seizures exists during periods of rapid Hct increase (greater than 4 points in 2 wk).
- Monitor closely for thrombotic events (e.g., MI, CVA, TIA), especially for patients with CRF.

- Lab tests: Baseline transferrin and serum ferritin. Periodic aPTT & INR; Hct twice weekly until stabilized in target range (30–33%) and the maintenance dose of epoetin alfa has been determined, then Hct at regular intervals. Periodic CBC with differential and platelet count, BUN and creatinine, phosphorus, and potassium.
- Patients may require additional heparin during dialysis to prevent clotting of the vascular access or artificial kidney.

Patient & Family Education
- Do not drive or engage in other potentially hazardous activity during the first 90 days of therapy because of possible seizure activity.
- Headache is a common adverse effect. Report if severe or persistent as this may indicate developing hypertension.

EPOPROSTENOL SODIUM ⊘

(e-po-pros'te-nol)

Flolan

Classification(s): PROSTAGLANDIN
Therapeutic: PULMONARY ANTIHYPERTENSIVE
Pregnancy Category: B

USES Long-term treatment of primary pulmonary hypertension in NYHA Class III and IV patients.

INDICATION & DOSAGE

Primary Pulmonary Hypertension

Adult: **Acute dose,** Initiate with 2 ng/kg/min, increase by 2 ng/kg/min q15min until dose-limiting effects occur (e.g., nausea, vomiting, headache, hypotension, flushing); **Chronic administration,** Start infusion at 4 ng/kg/min less than the maximum tolerated infusion; if maximum tolerated infusion is less than or equal to 5 ng/kg/min, start maintenance infusion at 50% of maximum tolerated dose

SOLUTION PREPARATION

- *Infusion Pump Selection:* Pump should be small and lightweight; able to infuse in 2 ng/kg/min increments; have occlusion, end of infusion and low battery alarms; be accurate within 6% of programmed rate; and positive-pressure driven with pulse intervals not exceeding 3 min.
- *Vial Reconstitution:* **Must be** reconstituted using supplied sterile diluent for epoprostenol. Must not be mixed with any other medications or solution. Select a concentration compatible with the infusion pump.
  - 3000 ng/mL: Add 5 mL of diluent to one 0.5 mg vial; withdraw 3 mL and add to enough diluent to make a total of 100 mL.
  - 5000 ng/mL: Add 5 mL of diluent to one 0.5 mg vial; withdraw contents of vial and add to enough diluent to make a total of 100 mL.

- 10,000 ng/mL: Add 5 mL of diluent to each of two 0.5 mg vials; withdraw contents of each vial and add to enough diluent to make a total of 100 mL.
- 15,000 ng/mL: Add 5 mL of diluent to a 1.5 mg vial; withdraw contents of vial and add to enough diluent to make a total of 100 mL.
- Note: Anticoagulation therapy is generally initiated along with epoprostenol to reduce the risk of developing thromboembolic disease.

STORAGE
Store unopened vials at 15°–25° C (59°–77° F). Reconstituted solutions **must be** refrigerated and protected from light. Discard unused reconstituted solution after 48 h.

ADMINISTRATION
Continuous Infusion: Infuse at ordered rate using an infusion control device. Avoid abrupt infusion interruption lasting longer than 2–3 min. Infusion **must be** completed within 8 h if at room temperature or 24 h if cold pouch is used with frozen gel pack changed every 12 h.

INCOMPATIBILITIES Solution/additive: Data not available; do not mix with other drugs.

ACTION & *THERAPEUTIC EFFECT* Naturally occurring prostaglandin that reduces right and left ventricular afterload, increases cardiac output, and increases stroke volume through its vasodilation effect. Decreases pulmonary vascular resistance and mean systemic arterial pressure, depending on the dose. *Potent vasodilator of pulmonary and systemic arterial vascular beds.*

CONTRAINDICATIONS Hypersensitivity to epoprostenol or related compounds; chronic use with left ventricular systolic dysfunction in CHF patients; lactation.
CAUTIOUS USE Older adults; concurrent use of hypotensive drugs; pregnancy (category B). Safety and efficacy in children are not established.

ADVERSE EFFECTS (≥1%) **CNS:** *Chills, fever, flu-like syndrome, dizziness,* syncope, *headache, anxiety/nervousness,* hyperesthesia, paresthesia, dizziness. **CV:** *Tachycardia, hypotension, flushing, chest pain,* bradycardia. **GI:** *Diarrhea, nausea, vomiting,* abdominal pain. **Musculoskeletal:** *Jaw pain, myalgia, nonspecific musculoskeletal pain.* **Respiratory:** Dyspnea. **Other:** Dose-limiting effects.

DRUG INTERACTIONS Hypotension if administered with other VASODILATORS or ANTIHYPERTENSIVES.

PHARMACOKINETICS Peak: Approximately 15 min. **Metabolism:** Rapidly hydrolyzed at neutral pH in blood; also subject to enzyme degradation. **Elimination:** 82% in urine. **Half-Life:** Approximately 6 min.

NURSING IMPLICATIONS
Assessment & Drug Effects
- Assess carefully for development of pulmonary edema and monitor ECG during acute dose titration.
- Monitor respiratory and cardiovascular status frequently during entire period of chronic administration.

Common adverse effects in *italic*, life-threatening effects <u>underlined</u>: generic names in **bold**; classifications in SMALL CAPS; ♥ Canadian drug name; ◉ Prototype drug

283

- Monitor for and report recurrence or worsening of symptoms associated with primary pulmonary hypertension (e.g., dyspnea, dizziness, exercise intolerance) or adverse effects of drug; dosage adjustments may be needed.
- Lab tests: Periodic platelet count as warranted.

Patient & Family Education
- Learn correct techniques for storage, reconstitution, and administration of drug, and maintenance of catheter site (see **ADMINISTRATION**).
- Notify prescriber immediately of S&S of worsening primary pulmonary hypertension, adverse drug reactions, and S&S of infection at catheter site or sepsis.

EPTIFIBATIDE
(ep-ti-fib'a-tide)
Integrilin
Classification(s): ANTIPLATELET, PLATELET AGGREGATION INHIBITOR
Therapeutic: ANTITHROMBOTIC
Prototype: Abciximab
Pregnancy Category: B

USES Treatment of acute coronary syndromes (unstable angina, non-Q-wave MI) and patients undergoing percutaneous coronary interventions (PCIs).

INDICATION & DOSAGE

Acute Coronary Syndromes (ACS)
Adult: 180 mcg/kg initial bolus followed by 2 mcg/kg/min until hospital discharge or up to 72 h

PCI
Adult: 180 mcg/kg initial bolus followed by 2 mcg/kg/min for 20–24 h after end of procedure

Renal Impairment Dosage Adjustment
CrCl 10–50 mL/min: Reduce infusion to 1 mcg/kg/min; *CrCl less than 10 mL/min:* Do not use

SOLUTION PREPARATION
No dilution is required. Administer as supplied.

STORAGE
Store unopened vials at 2°–8° C (36°–46° F) and protect from light. Discard any unused portion in opened vial. Vial may be stored at room temperature for up to 2 mo.

ADMINISTRATION
- **Direct IV Injection:** Give bolus dose over 1–2 min.
- **Continuous Infusion:** Begin immediately after bolus dose. Infuse undiluted drug directly from the 100-mL vial (at a rate based on

Common adverse effects in *italic*, life-threatening effects underlined: generic names in **bold**; classifications in SMALL CAPS; ♣ Canadian drug name; ● Prototype drug

patient's weight as indicated in the following chart) using a vented infusion set. May be given in the same IV line with NS or D5NS (either solution may contain up to 60 mEq KCl).

Eptifibatide Infusion Chart

Patient Weight (kg)	(lb)	180 mcg/kg Bolus Volume — From 2 mg/mL vial	2 mcg/kg/min Infusion Volume — From 2 mg/mL vial 100 mL vial	2 mcg/kg/min — From 0.75 mg/mL 100 mL vial	1 mcg/kg/min Infusion Volume — From 2 mg/mL 100 mL vial	1 mcg/kg/min — From 0.75 mg/mL 100 mL vial
37–41	81–91	3.4 mL	2 mL/h	6 mL/h	1 mL/h	3 mL/h
42–46	92–102	4 mL	2.5 mL/h	7 mL/h	1.3 mL/h	3.5 mL/h
47–53	103–117	4.5 mL	3 mL/h	8 mL/h	1.5 mL/h	4 mL/h
54–59	118–130	5 mL	3.5 mL/h	9 mL/h	1.8 mL/h	4.5 mL/h
60–65	131–143	5.6 mL	3.8 mL/h	10 mL/h	1.9 mL/h	5 mL/h
66–71	144–157	6.2 mL	4 mL/h	11 mL/h	2 mL/h	5.5 mL/h
72–78	158–172	6.8 mL	4.5 mL/h	12 mL/h	2.3 mL/h	6 mL/h
79–84	173–185	7.3 mL	5 mL/h	13 mL/h	2.5 mL/h	6.5 mL/h
85–90	186–198	7.9 mL	5.3 mL/h	14 mL/h	2.7 mL/h	7 mL/h
91–96	199–212	8.5 mL	5.6 mL/h	15 mL/h	2.8 mL/h	7.5 mL/h
97–103	213–227	9 mL	6 mL/h	16 mL/h	3 mL/h	8 mL/h
104–109	228–240	9.5 mL	6.4 mL/h	17 mL/h	3.2 mL/h	8.5 mL/h
110–115	241–253	10.2 mL	6.8 mL/h	18 mL/h	3.4 mL/h	9 mL/h
116–121	254–267	10.7 mL	7 mL/h	19 mL/h	3.5 mL/h	9.5 mL/h
Greater than 121	Greater than 267	11.3 mL	7.5 mL/h	20 mL/h	3.7 mL/h	10 mL/h

Common adverse effects in *italic*, life-threatening effects underlined: generic names in **bold**; classifications in SMALL CAPS; ♣ Canadian drug name; ❷ Prototype drug

285

INCOMPATIBILITIES Solution/additive: Furosemide.

ACTION & *THERAPEUTIC EFFECT* Binds to the glycoprotein IIb/IIIa (GP IIb/IIIa) receptor sites of platelets inhibiting their aggregation. *Inhibits platelet aggregation by preventing fibrinogen, von Willebrand's factor, and other molecules from adhering to GP IIb/IIIa receptor sites on platelets.*

CONTRAINDICATIONS Hypersensitivity to eptifibatide; active bleeding; GI or GU bleeding within 6 wk; thrombocytopenia; recent major surgery or trauma; intracranial neoplasm, intracranial bleeding within 6 mo; concurrent administration of another GP IIb/IIIa receptor inhibitor (e.g., abciximab); renal dialysis; severe hypertension (systolic blood pressure greater than 200 mm Hg or diastolic blood pressure greater than 110 mm Hg), aneurysm.

CAUTIOUS USE Hypersensitivity to related compounds (e.g., abciximab, tirofiban, lamifiban); concurrent administration of other anticoagulants; pregnancy (category B), lactation. Safety and effectiveness in children are not established.

ADVERSE EFFECTS (≥1%) **CNS:** Intracranial bleed (rare). **GI:** GI bleeding. **Hematologic:** *Bleeding* (major bleeding 4.4–11%), anemia, thrombocytopenia.

DRUG INTERACTIONS ORAL ANTICOAGULANTS, NSAIDS, **dipyridamole, ticlopidine, dextran** may increase risk of bleeding.

PHARMACOKINETICS Duration: 6–8 h after stopping infusion. **Distribution:** 25% protein bound. **Metabolism:** Minimally metabolized. **Elimination:** 50% excreted in urine. **Half-Life:** 2.5 h.

NURSING IMPLICATIONS

Assessment & Drug Effects

- Prior to infusion determine: PT/aPTT, ACT for those undergoing percutaneous coronary intervention (PCI); Hct or Hgb; platelet count; and serum creatinine.
- Immediately stop infusion of eptifibatide and heparin if bleeding at the arterial access site cannot be controlled by pressure or if the platelet count drops below 100,000/mm³.
- Lab tests: Monitor aPTT & INR (target aPPT, 50–70 sec), and platelet count; during PCI (target ACT, 300–350 sec). Monitor APT or ACT before sheath removal. Do not remove unless apt is less than 45 sec or ACT less than 150 sec.
- Minimize all vascular and other trauma during treatment. When obtaining IV access, avoid using a noncompressible site such as the subclavian vein.
- Monitor vital signs closely. Monitor carefully for and immediately report S&S of bleeding (e.g., femoral artery access site bleeding, intracerebral hemorrhage, GI bleeding).
- Achieve hemostasis at the arterial access site by standard compression for a minimum of 4 h prior to hospital discharge following discontinuation of eptifibatide and heparin.

ERTAPENEM SODIUM

(er-ta-pen'em)

Invanz

Classification(s): ANTIBIOTIC, CARBAPENEM

Therapeutic: ANTIBACTERIAL

Prototype: Imipenem-Cilastatin

Pregnancy Category: B

E

USES Complicated intra-abdominal infections, complicated skin and skin structure infections, community-acquired pneumonia, complicated UTI (including pyelonephritis), and acute pelvic infections due to susceptible bacteria.

INDICATION & DOSAGE

Community-Acquired Pneumonia; Complicated UTI

Adult: 1 g daily for 10–14 days, may switch to appropriate PO antibiotic after 3 days if responding
Child: 15 mg/kg q12h × 10–14 days

Intra-abdominal Infection

Adult: 1 g daily for 5–14 days

Skin and Skin Structure Infections

Adult: 1 g daily for 7–14 days

Acute Pelvic Infections

Adult: 1 g daily for 3–10 days

Renal Impairment Dosage Adjustment

CrCl less than 30 mL/min: Reduce dose to 500 mg daily

SOLUTION PREPARATION

- *Vial Reconstitution:* Reconstitute 1 g vial with 10 mL of sterile water for injection, NS, or bacteriostatic water for injection. Shake well to dissolve.
- *Further Dilution of Reconstituted Solution for Adults and Children 13 y and Older:* Immediately transfer contents of vial to 50 mL of NS injection solution.
- *Further Dilution of Reconstituted Solution for Children 3 mo to 12 y:* Immediately transfer required dose to enough NS injection solution to yield a final concentration of 20 mg/mL or less.
- Complete infusion within 6 h of IV solution preparation.

STORAGE

- Store lyophilized powder above 25° C (77° F).
- May store reconstituted solution at room temperature (not greater than 25° C/77° F) but infusion **must be** completed within 6 h of prepara-

---

tion. May store for 24 h under refrigeration, but **must be** used within 4 h of removal from refrigeration. Do not freeze.

ADMINISTRATION

Intermittent Infusion: Infuse over 30 min. Note that infusion should be completed within 6 h of IV preparation.

INCOMPATIBILITIES Solution/additive: **Dextrose. Y-site:** Do not mix or infuse with any other drugs.

ACTION & *THERAPEUTIC EFFECT* Broad-spectrum carbapenem antibiotic that inhibits the cell wall synthesis of gram-positive and gram-negative bacteria by its strong affinity for penicillin-binding proteins (PBPs) of the bacterial cell wall. This results in destruction of bacteria. *Effective against both gram-positive and gram-negative bacteria. Highly resistant to most bacterial beta-lactamases.*

CONTRAINDICATIONS Hypersensitivity to ertapenem or carbapenem antibiotics; hypersensitivity to amide-type local anesthetics such as lidocaine; hypersensitivity to meropenem or imipenem; previous anaphylactic reaction to beta-lactam antibiotics.

CAUTIOUS USE Renal impairment; history of CNS disorders; history of seizures; hypersensitivity to other beta-lactam antibiotics (penicillins, cephalosporins); hypersensitivity to other allergens; meningitis; pregnancy (category B), lactation (bottle feed during, and for 5 days after therapy ends).

ADVERSE EFFECTS (≥1%) **Body as a Whole:** Phlebitis or thrombosis at injection site, asthenia, fatigue, <u>death</u>, fever, leg pain. **CNS:** Anxiety, altered mental status, dizziness, headache, insomnia. **CV:** Chest pain, hypertension, hypotension, tachycardia, edema. **GI:** Abdominal pain, *diarrhea*, acid regurgitation, constipation, dyspepsia, nausea, vomiting, increased AST and ALT. **Respiratory:** Cough, dyspnea, pharyngitis, rales/rhonchi, and respiratory distress. **Skin:** Erythema, pruritus, rash. **Urogenital:** Vaginitis.

DRUG INTERACTIONS Probenecid decreases renal excretion.

PHARMACOKINETICS Peak: 2.3 h. **Distribution:** 95% protein bound, distributes into breast milk, may cross placenta. **Metabolism:** Hydrolysis of beta-lactam ring. **Elimination:** 80% excreted in urine, 10% in feces. **Half-Life:** 4.5 h.

NURSING IMPLICATIONS

Assessment & Drug Effects

- Prior to initiating therapy: C&S tests (start drug pending results); determine previous hypersensitivity reactions to penicillins, cephalosporins, and other allergens.
- Lab tests: Baseline CrCl and serum creatinine, periodic LFTs and kidney function tests; during prolonged therapy monitor AST, ALT, alkaline phosphatase, CBC, platelet count, and routine blood chemistry.
- Discontinue drug and report promptly S&S of hypersensitivity (see Appendix C).
- Report S&S of superinfection or pseudomembranous colitis (see Appendix C).

Common adverse effects in *italic*, life-threatening effects <u>underlined</u>: generic names in **bold**; classifications in SMALL CAPS; ♣ Canadian drug name; ● Prototype drug

- Monitor for seizures especially in older adults and those with renal insufficiency.

Patient & Family Education
- Learn S&S of hypersensitivity, superinfection, and pseudomembranous colitis (see Appendix C); report any of these to prescriber promptly.

E

ERYTHROMYCIN LACTOBIONATE
(er-ith-roe-mye'sin)
Erythrocin Lactobionate-I.V.
Classification(s): ANTIBIOTIC, MACROLIDE
Therapeutic: ANTIBACTERIAL
Prototype: Erythromycin
Pregnancy Category: B

USES When oral administration is not possible or the severity of infection requires immediate high serum levels.

INDICATION & DOSAGE

Infections
Adult/Child: 15–20 mg/kg/day in 4 divided doses

Legionnaires' Disease
Adult: 1–4 g in divided doses

Pelvic Inflammatory Disease
Adult: 500 mg q6h × 3 days, then convert to PO

SOLUTION PREPARATION
- *Vial Reconstitution:* Add 10 mL sterile water for injection without preservatives to each 500 mg or fraction thereof. Shake vial until drug is completely dissolved. **Must be** further diluted for infusion.
- *Further Dilution of Reconstituted Solution:*
  - *Continuous Infusion* (**preferred**): Dilute each 1 gm in 1000 mL LR or NS. Give within 4 h.
  - *Intermittent Infusion:* Dilute each 1 g in D5W or NS to yield a final concentration of 1–5 mg/mL. Use at least 100 mL of IV solution. Note 1 g in 200 mL yields 5 mg/mL; 1 g in 500 mL yields 2 mg/mL.

STORAGE
Reconstituted solution is stable up to 14 days if refrigerated at 2°–8° C (36°–46° F); use solution diluted for infusion within 8 h.

ADMINISTRATION
- **Intermittent Infusion:** Infuse 1 gm or fraction thereof over 20–60 min. Slow rate if pain develops along course of vein.
- **Continuous Infusion:** Infuse slowly over 6–24 h.

INCOMPATIBILITIES Solution/additive: Dextrose-containing solutions, ascorbic acid, carbenicillin, colistimethate, clindamycin, furosemide, heparin, linezolid, metoclopramide, tetracycline, vitamin B complex with C. **Y-site:** Ceftazidime, fluconazole, heparin.

ACTION & THERAPEUTIC EFFECT Inhibits protein synthesis by binding to the 50s ribosome subunits of susceptible bacteria inhibiting bacterial protein synthesis. *More active against gram-positive than gram-negative bacteria.*

CONTRAINDICATIONS Hypersensitivity to erythromycin or other macrolide antibiotics; concurrent administration with terfenadine or astemizole.

CAUTIOUS USE Impaired liver function; myasthenia gravis; elderly; GI disease, ulcerative colitis; oral anticoagulant use in elderly; pregnancy (category B), lactation.

ADVERSE EFFECTS (≥1%) **Body as a Whole:** *Pain and venous irritation after IV injection;* allergic reactions, <u>anaphylaxis</u> (rare); superinfections. **GI:** *Nausea,* vomiting, diarrhea, *abdominal cramps,* variations in liver function tests following prolonged or repeated therapy.

DRUG INTERACTIONS Serum levels and toxicities of **alfentanil, bexarotene, carbamazepine, cevimeline, cilostazol, clozapine, cyclosporine, disopyramide, estazolam, fentanyl, midazolam, methadone, modafinil, quinidine, sirolimus, digoxin, theophylline, triazolam, warfarin** are increased. **Ergotamine** may increase peripheral vasospasm and may increase risk of arrhythmias.

PHARMACOKINETICS Peak: 1 h. **Distribution:** Concentrates in liver; crosses placenta; distributed into breast milk. **Metabolism:** Metabolized in liver. **Elimination:** Excreted primarily in bile and feces; 12–15% in urine. **Half-Life:** 3–5 h.

NURSING IMPLICATIONS

Assessment & Drug Effects

- Prior to initiating therapy: Baseline C&S tests (start drug pending results).
- Monitor QT interval periodically, especially with high drug doses and in those at risk for cardiac arrhythmias.
- Lab tests: Periodic LFTs with daily high doses or prolonged or repeated therapy.
- Monitor hearing as impairment may occur with large doses of this drug. It may occur as early as the second day and as late as the third week of therapy.
- Monitor for S&S of thrombophlebitis (see Appendix C). IV infusion of large doses is reported to increase risk.

Patient & Family Education

- Notify prescriber immediately of tinnitus, dizziness, or hearing impairment.

Common adverse effects in *italic*, life-threatening effects <u>underlined</u>: generic names in **bold**; classifications in SMALL CAPS; ♣ Canadian drug name; ● Prototype drug

ESMOLOL HYDROCHLORIDE

(ess'moe-lol)

Brevibloc

Classification(s): BETA-ADRENERGIC ANTAGONIST

Therapeutic: ANTIARRHYTHMIC

Prototype: Propranolol

Pregnancy Category: C

USES Supraventricular tachyarrhythmias (SVT) in perioperative and postoperative periods or in other critical situations. Also short-term treatment of noncompensating sinus tachycardia and in the control of heart rate for patients with MI.

UNLABELED USES Moderate postoperative hypertension; treatment of intense transient adrenergic response to surgical stress in cardiac as well as noncardiac surgery.

INDICATION & DOSAGE

Supraventricular Tachyarrhythmias

Adult: 500 mcg/kg loading dose followed by 50 mcg/kg/min × 4 min; if response inadequate, may repeat loading dose followed by 100 mcg/kg/min × 4 min; may continue repeating loading dose and increasing 4-min dose by 50 mcg/kg/min prn (max: 200 mcg/kg/min)

Intraoperative/Postoperative Tachycardia

Adult: 80 mg bolus followed by 150 mcg/kg/min, increase if needed (max: 300 mcg/kg/min)

SOLUTION PREPARATION

- Verify which concentration of esmolol is on hand.
- *Premixed Injection (10 mg/mL or 20 mg/mL):* Solution needs no dilution and may be used as supplied.
- *Concentrate for Injection (250 mg/mL):* **Must be diluted** to a final concentration of 10 mg/mL by adding 2.5 g to 250 mL or 5 g to 500 mL of compatible IV solution (e.g., D5W, D5LR, D5NS, D5/1/2NS, LR).

STORAGE

Diluted infusion solution is stable for at least 24 h at room temperature.

ADMINISTRATION

- **Direct IV Injection:** Give loading dose over 1 min.
- **IV Infusion:** Infuse maintenance dose over 4 min. If response is adequate, continue maintenance infusion. If response is not adequate, repeat loading dose and follow with an increased maintenance infusion of 100 mcg/kg/min. May continue titration cycle with same loading dose while increasing maintenance infusion by 50 mcg/kg/min until desired end point is near. Then omit loading dose and titrate mainte-

Common adverse effects in *italic*, life-threatening effects <u>underlined</u>: generic names in **bold**; classifications in SMALL CAPS; ♣ Canadian drug name; ● Prototype drug

291

E

nance dose up or down by 25 to 50 mcg/kg/min until desired heart rate is reached. Note: Max doses is 200 mcg/kg/min.

- Infusion via a central line is preferred. Avoid butterfly needles and very small veins for infusion.
- Avoid extravasation; sloughing of the skin and necrosis may occur.
- Change injection site if local reaction occurs. IV site reactions (burning, erythema) or diaphoresis may develop during infusion. Both reactions are temporary.

INCOMPATIBILITIES Solution/additive: Diazepam, procainamide, thiopental. **Y-site:** Amphotericin B cholesteryl, furosemide, warfarin.

ACTION & *THERAPEUTIC EFFECT* Ultrashort-acting beta$_1$-adrenergic blocking agent with cardioselective properties. Inhibits agonist effect of catecholamines by competitive binding at beta-adrenergic receptors. Antiarrhythmic properties occur at the AV node. *Since it binds predominantly to beta$_1$-receptors in cardiac tissue, it blocks sympathetically mediated increases in cardiac rate and BP.*

CONTRAINDICATIONS Hypersensitivity to esmolol, heart block greater than first degree, sinus bradycardia, cardiogenic shock; decompensated CHF; acute bronchospasm; pregnancy (category C).
CAUTIOUS USE History of allergy, CHF; pulmonary disease such as bronchial asthma; COPD; pulmonary edema; diabetes mellitus; kidney function impairment; lactation. Safety in children is not established.

ADVERSE EFFECTS (≥1%) **CNS:** Headache, *dizziness,* somnolence, confusion, agitation. **CV:** *Hypotension* (dose related), cold hands and feet, bradyarrhythmias, flushing, myocardial depression. **GI:** Nausea, vomiting. **Respiratory:** Dyspnea, chest pain, rhonchi, <u>bronchospasm</u>. **Skin:** *Infusion site inflammation* (redness, swelling, induration).

DRUG INTERACTIONS May increase **digoxin** IV levels 10–20%; **morphine** IV may increase esmolol levels by 45%; **succinylcholine** may prolong neuromuscular blockade.

PHARMACOKINETICS Onset: Less than 5 min. **Peak:** 10–20 min. **Duration:** 10–30 min. **Metabolism:** Rapidly hydrolyzed by RBC esterases. **Elimination:** Eliminated in urine. **Half-Life:** 9 min.

NURSING IMPLICATIONS

Assessment & Drug Effects

- Monitor BP, pulse, ECG, during esmolol infusion. Hypotension may have its onset during the initial titration phase; thereafter the risk increases with increasing doses. Usually the hypotension experienced during esmolol infusion is resolved within 30 min after infusion is reduced or discontinued.
- Overdose symptoms: Discontinue administration if the following symptoms occur: Bradycardia, severe dizziness or drowsiness, dyspnea, bluish-colored fingernails or palms of hands, seizures.

ESOMEPRAZOLE MAGNESIUM

(e-so-me′pra-zole)

Nexium

Classification(s): PROTON PUMP INHIBITOR

Therapeutic: ANTIULCER

Prototype: Lansoprazole

Pregnancy Category: B

E

USES Erosive esophagitis, gastrointestinal reflux disease (GERD).

INDICATION & DOSAGE

Healing of Erosive Esophagitis, GERD

Adult: 20–40 mg daily

SOLUTION PREPARATION

- *Vial Reconstitution:* Add 5 mL of NS to dissolve. May be given as prepared direct IV as a bolus dose or further diluted for infusion.
- *Further Dilution of Reconstituted Solution:* Add the reconstituted solution to 50 mL of NS, LR, or D5W.

STORAGE

Store reconstituted solution at room temperature up to 30° C (86° F); give within 12 h of reconstitution with NS or LR and within 6 h of reconstitution with D5W.

ADMINISTRATION

- **Direct IV Injection:** Give bolus dose over no less than 3 min.
- **IV Infusion:** Infuse over 10–30 min.

INCOMPATIBILITIES Data not available; do not mix with other drugs.

ACTION & *THERAPEUTIC EFFECT* Isomer of omeprazole that is a weak base that is converted to the active form in the highly acidic environment of the gastric parietal cells. Inhibits the enzyme H^+K^+-ATPase (the acid pump), thus suppressing gastric acid secretion. *Due to inhibition of the H^+K^+-ATPase, esomeprazole substantially decreases both basal and stimulated acid secretion through inhibition of the acid pump in parietal cells.*

CONTRAINDICATIONS Hypersensitivity to esomeprazole magnesium, omeprazole, or other proton pump inhibitors; gastric malignancy; lactation. Safety and efficacy in children are not established.

CAUTIOUS USE Severe renal insufficiency; severe hepatic impairment; treatment for more than a year; gastric ulcers; pregnancy (category B).

ADVERSE EFFECTS (≥1%) **CNS:** Headache. **GI:** Nausea, vomiting, diarrhea, constipation, abdominal pain, flatulence, dry mouth.

DRUG INTERACTIONS May increase **diazepam, phenytoin, warfarin** levels.

Common adverse effects in *italic*, life-threatening effects <u>underlined</u>: generic names in **bold**; classifications in SMALL CAPS; ♣ Canadian drug name; ◎ Prototype drug

293

PHARMACOKINETICS Metabolism: In liver by CYP2C19. **Elimination:** Inactive metabolites excreted in both urine and feces. **Half-Life:** 1.5 h.

NURSING IMPLICATIONS

Assessment & Drug Effects

- Monitor for S&S of adverse CNS effects (vertigo, agitation, depression) especially in severely ill patients.
- Monitor phenytoin levels with concurrent use.
- Monitor INR/PT with concurrent warfarin use.
- Lab tests: Periodic liver function tests, CBC, Hct & Hbg, urinalysis for hematuria and proteinuria.

Patient & Family Education

- Report any changes in urinary elimination such as pain or discomfort associated with urination to prescriber.
- Report severe diarrhea. Drug may need to be discontinued.

ESTROGENS, CONJUGATED

(ess'tro-jenz)

C.E.S. ♣, Premarin
Classification(s): HORMONE; ESTROGEN
Therapeutic: UTERINE BLEEDING
Pregnancy Category: X

USES Abnormal uterine bleeding.

INDICATION & DOSAGE

Abnormal Uterine Bleeding

Adult: 25 mg, repeated in 6–12 h if needed

SOLUTION PREPARATION

Vial Reconstitution: Remove approximately 5 mL of air from the dry-powder vial, then slowly inject the supplied diluent into the vial by aiming it at the side of the vial. Gently agitate to dissolve but DO NOT SHAKE.

STORAGE

Store ampule and reconstituted solution at 2°–8° C (38°–46° F) and protected from light; stable for 60 days. Discard precipitated or discolored solution.

ADMINISTRATION

Direct IV Injection: Give bolus dose slowly at a rate of 5 mg/min. Estrogen solution is compatible with D5W and NS and may be added to IV tubing just distal to the needle if necessary.

Common adverse effects in *italic*, life-threatening effects <u>underlined</u>: generic names in **bold**; classifications in SMALL CAPS; ♣ Canadian drug name; 🅟 Prototype drug

INCOMPATIBILITIES Solution/additive: Ascorbic acid.

ACTION & *THERAPEUTIC EFFECT* Circulating estrogens modulate the pituitary secretion of the gonadotropins, luteinizing hormone (LH), and follicle stimulating hormone (FSH) through a negative feedback mechanism. Estrogens act to reduce the elevated levels of these gonadotropins seen in postmenopausal women. *Binds to intracellular receptors that stimulate DNA and RNA to synthesize proteins responsible for effects of estrogen.*

CONTRAINDICATIONS Breast cancer, except for palliative therapy; vaginal and cervical cancers; endometrial cancer; endometrial hyperplasia; abnormal vaginal bleeding; hepatic disease or cancer; hypercalcemia; ovarian cancer; history of thromboembolic disease; known or suspected pregnancy (category X).

CAUTIOUS USE Hypertension; gallbladder disease; diabetes mellitus; heart failure; kidney dysfunction.

ADVERSE EFFECTS (≥1%) **CNS:** Headache, dizziness, depression, *libido changes.* **CV:** <u>Thromboembolic disorders</u>, hypertension. **GI:** *Nausea,* vomiting, diarrhea, bloating, cholestatic jaundice. **Urogenital:** Mastodynia, spotting, changes in menstrual flow, dysmenorrhea, amenorrhea. **Metabolic:** Reduced carbohydrate tolerance, fluid retention. **Other:** Leg cramps.

DRUG INTERACTIONS BARBITURATES, **carbamazepine, phenytoin, rifampin** decrease estrogen effect by increasing its metabolism; ORAL ANTICOAGULANTS may decrease hypoprothrombinemic effects; interfere with effects of **bromocriptine;** may increase levels and toxicity of **cyclosporine,** TRICYCLIC ANTIDEPRESSANTS, **theophylline;** decrease effectiveness of **clofibrate.**

PHARMACOKINETICS Distribution: Distributed throughout body tissues, especially in adipose tissue; crosses placenta, excreted in breast milk. Bound primarily to albumin. **Metabolism:** Metabolized primarily in liver to glucuronide and sulfate conjugates of estradiol, estrone, and estriol. **Elimination:** Excreted in urine. **Half-Life:** 4–18 h.

NURSING IMPLICATIONS

Assessment & Drug Effects

- Assess for peripheral edema or other signs of fluid retention.
- Assess for S&S of thrombophlebitis.

Patient & Family Education

- Avoid cigarette smoking and remain active to reduce the risk of blood clots.

ETHACRYNIC ACID

(eth-a-krin′ik)

Edecrin

ETHACRYNATE SODIUM
Sodium Edecrin
Classification(s): DIURETIC, LOOP
Therapeutic: DIURETIC
Prototype: Furosemide
Pregnancy Category: B

E

USES Severe edema associated with CHF, hepatic cirrhosis, ascites of malignancy, kidney disease, nephrotic syndrome, lymphedema.
UNLABELED USES As adjunct in therapy of hypertensive crisis complicated by pulmonary edema.

INDICATION & DOSAGE

Edema
Adult: 0.5–1 mg/kg or 50 mg up to 100 mg, may repeat if necessary

SOLUTION PREPARATION
Vial Reconstitution: Add 50 mL of D5W or NS to the 50 mg vial. Vials reconstituted with D5W may turn cloudy; if so, discard the vial. May be given as prepared direct IV as a bolus dose.

STORAGE
Use reconstituted solution within 24 h.

ADMINISTRATION
Direct IV Injection: Give bolus dose at a rate of 10 mg/min. May be given through the tubing of a freely running infusion. If a second IV dose is required, a new site should be selected to prevent thrombophlebitis.

INCOMPATIBILITIES Solution/additive: Hydralazine, procainamide, ranitidine, reserpine, tolazoline, triflupromazine.

ACTION & *THERAPEUTIC EFFECT* Inhibits sodium and chloride reabsorption in proximal tubule and most segments of loop of Henle, promotes potassium and hydrogen ion excretion, and decreases urinary ammonium ion concentration as well as pH of the blood. Promotes calcium elimination in hypercalcemia and nephrogenic diabetes insipidus. Hypotensive effect may be due to hypovolemia secondary to diuresis and in part to decreased vascular resistance. *Rapid and potent diuretic effect. Fluid and electrolyte loss may exceed that caused by thiazides.*

CONTRAINDICATIONS History of hypersensitivity to ethacrynic acid; increasing azotemia, anuria; hepatic coma; severe diarrhea, dehydration, electrolyte imbalance, hypotension; lactation; children, infants, and neonates.
CAUTIOUS USE Hepatic cirrhosis; older adult cardiac patients; diabetes mellitus; history of gout; pulmonary edema associated with acute MI; hyperaldosteronism; nephrotic syndrome; history of pancreatitis; pregnancy (category B).

ADVERSE EFFECTS (≥1%) **CNS:** Headache, fatigue, apprehension, confusion. **CV:** *Postural hypotension* (dizziness, light-headedness). **Metabolic:** Hyponatremia, *hypokalemia,* hypochloremic alkalosis, hypomagnesemia, hypocalcemia, hypercalciuria, hyperuricemia, hypovolemia, hematuria, glycosuria, hyperglycemia, gynecomastia, elevated BUN, creatinine, and urate levels. **Special Senses:** Vertigo, tinnitus, sense of fullness in ears, temporary or permanent deafness. **GI:** Anorexia, diarrhea, nausea, vomiting, dysphagia, abdominal discomfort or pain, GI bleeding (IV use), abnormal liver function tests. **Hematologic:** <u>Thrombocytopenia, agranulocytosis</u> (rare), <u>severe neutropenia</u> (rare). **Skin:** Skin rash, pruritus. **Body as a Whole:** Fever, chills, acute gout; local irritation and thrombophlebitis with IV injection.

DRUG INTERACTIONS THIAZIDE DIURETICS increase potassium loss; increased risk of **digoxin** toxicity from hypokalemia; CORTICOSTEROIDS, **amphotericin B** increase risk of hypokalemia; decreased **lithium** clearance, so increased risk of **lithium** toxicity; SULFONYLUREA effect may be blunted, causing hyperglycemia; ANTIHYPERTENSIVE AGENTS increase risk of orthostatic hypotension; AMINOGLYCOSIDES may increase risk of ototoxicity; **warfarin** potentiates hypoprothrombinemia.

PHARMACOKINETICS Onset: 5 min. **Peak:** 15–30 min. **Duration:** 2 h. **Distribution:** Does not cross CSF. **Metabolism:** Metabolized to cysteine conjugate. **Elimination:** 30–65% excreted in urine; 35–40% excreted in bile. **Half-Life:** 30–70 min.

NURSING IMPLICATIONS

Assessment & Drug Effects

- Monitor IV site closely. Extravasation of IV drug causes local pain and tissue irritation from dehydration and blood volume depletion.
- Monitor BP closely. Rapid, copious diuresis can produce hypotension. Because orthostatic hypotension can occur, supervise ambulation.
- Monitor cardiac status. Diuretic-induced hypovolemia may reduce cardiac output, and electrolyte loss promotes cardiotoxicity in those receiving digitalis (cardiac) glycosides.
- Establish baseline weight prior to start of therapy; weigh patient under standard conditions. Report weight loss or gain in excess of 1 kg (2 lb)/day.
- Monitor I&O ratio. Report promptly excessive diuresis, oliguria, or hematuria.
- Lab tests: Baseline and periodic blood count, serum electrolytes, CO_2, BUN, creatinine, blood glucose, uric acid, and LFTs.
- Observe for and report S&S of electrolyte imbalance: Anorexia, nausea, vomiting, thirst, dry mouth, polyuria, oliguria, weakness, fatigue, dizziness, faintness, headache, muscle cramps, paresthesias, drowsiness, mental confusion. Instruct patient to report these symptoms promptly.
- Report immediately possible signs of thromboembolic complications (see Appendix C).
- Monitor diabetics for loss of glycemic control especially with doses in excess of 200 mg/day.

Patient & Family Education

- Make position changes slowly, particularly from lying to upright posture.
- Report promptly evidence of impaired hearing. Hearing loss may be preceded by vertigo, tinnitus, or fullness in ears; it may be transient, lasting 1–24 h, or it may be permanent.

E

ETOPOSIDE

(e-toe-po'side)

Etopophos, VePesid

Classification(s): ANTINEOPLASTIC; MITOTIC INHIBITOR

Therapeutic: ANTINEOPLASTIC

Prototype: Vincristine

Pregnancy Category: D

USES Treatment of refractory testicular neoplasms, in patients who have already received appropriate surgical, chemotherapeutic, and radiation therapy; for treatment of choriocarcinoma in women and small cell carcinoma of the lung.

UNLABELED USES Hodgkin's and non-Hodgkin's lymphomas, acute myelogenous (nonlymphocytic) leukemia.

INDICATION & DOSAGE

Testicular Carcinoma

Adult: 50–100 mg/m²/day for 5 consecutive days q3–4wk for 3–4 courses or 100 mg/m² on days 1, 3, and 5 q3–4wk for 3–4 courses

Small Cell Lung Carcinoma

Adult: 35 mg/m²/day for 4 consecutive days to 50 mg/m²/day for 5 consecutive days q3–4wk

SOLUTION PREPARATION

- Wear disposable surgical gloves when preparing or disposing of etoposide. Wash immediately with soap and water if skin comes in contact with drug.
- Verify which product is on hand.
  - *Etoposide concentrate for injection:* Each 100 mg **must be** diluted with 250–500 mL of D5W or NS to produce final concentrations of 0.2–0.4 mg/mL. Crystallization is likely to occur with concentrations greater than 0.4 mg/mL. If crystals are present, discard the solution.
  - *Etoposide phosphate:* Add 5 or 10 mL of sterile water for injection, D5W, NS, bacteriostatic water for injection or bacteriostatic NS for injection to yield 20 or 10 mg/mL etoposide, respectively. May be given as prepared or further diluted to as low as 0.1 mg/mL in either D5W or NS.

STORAGE

- *Etoposide concentrate:* The 0.2 mg/mL solution is stable for 96 h and the 0.4 mg/mL solution is stable for 24 h at room temperature.

- Etoposide phosphate solution is stable at room temperature or under refrigeration for 24 h.

ADMINISTRATION

- **IV Infusion:** Infuse slowly over 30–60 min to reduce risk of hypotension and bronchospasm.
- Check IV site frequently during and after infusion. Extravasation can cause thrombophlebitis and necrosis.

E

INCOMPATIBILITIES Y-site: Cefepime, filgrastim, gallium, idarubicin.

ACTION & *THERAPEUTIC EFFECT* Semisynthetic derivative of May apple plant. Produces cytotoxic action by arresting G_2 (resting or premitotic) phase of cell cycle; also acts on S phase of DNA synthesis. High doses cause lysis of cells entering mitotic phase, and lower doses inhibit cells from entering prophase. *Antineoplastic effect is due to its ability to arrest mitosis (cell division).*

CONTRAINDICATIONS Severe bone marrow depression; severe hepatic or renal impairment; existing or recent viral infection, bacterial infection; intraperitoneal, intrapleural, or intrathecal administration; pregnancy (category D), lactation. Safe use in children is not established.

CAUTIOUS USE Impaired kidney or liver function; gout.

ADVERSE EFFECTS (≥1%) **Body as a Whole:** Hypersensitivity (sweating, chills, fever, coryza, tachycardia; throat, back, and general body pain; abdominal cramps, flushing, substernal chest pain, dyspnea, <u>bronchospasm</u>, pulmonary edema, <u>anaphylactoid reaction</u>). **CNS:** Peripheral neuropathy, paresthesias, weakness, somnolence, unusual tiredness, transient confusion. **CV:** Transient hypotension; thrombophlebitis with extravasation. **GI:** *Nausea, vomiting,* dyspepsia, anorexia, diarrhea, constipation, stomatitis. **Hematologic:** <u>*Leukopenia (principally granulocytopenia), thrombocytopenia, severe myelosuppression,*</u> *anemia, pancytopenia, neutropenia.* **Respiratory:** Pleural effusion, bronchospasm. **Skin:** *Reversible alopecia* (can progress to total baldness); radiation recall dermatitis; necrosis, *pain at IV site.*

DRUG INTERACTIONS ANTICOAGULANTS, ANTIPLATELET AGENTS, NSAIDS, **aspirin** may increase risk of bleeding. Do not administer LIVE VACCINES.

PHARMACOKINETICS Peak: 1–1.5 h. **Distribution:** Variable penetration into CSF. **Metabolism:** Probably metabolized in liver. **Elimination:** 44–60% excreted in urine, 2–16% excreted in feces over 3 days. **Half-Life:** 5–10 h.

NURSING IMPLICATIONS

Assessment & Drug Effects

- Be prepared to treat an anaphylactoid reaction (see Appendix C). Stop infusion immediately if the reaction occurs.
- Monitor vital signs during and after infusion. Stop infusion immediately if hypotension occurs.
- Lab tests: Baseline and periodic CBC with differential, LFTs, and kidney function tests.
- Withhold drug and notify prescriber for absolute neutrophil count below 500/mm³ or a platelet count below 50,000/mm³.

Common adverse effects in *italic*, life-threatening effects <u>underlined</u>; generic names in **bold**; classifications in SMALL CAPS; ♣ Canadian drug name; ⊘ Prototype drug

299

- Be alert to S&S of leukopenia (see Appendix C), infection (immunosuppression), and bleeding.
- Protect patient from any trauma that might precipitate bleeding during period of platelet nadir particularly. Withhold invasive procedures if possible.

Patient & Family Education
- Learn possible adverse effects of etoposide, such as blood dyscrasias, alopecia, carcinogenesis.
- Make position changes slowly, particularly from lying to upright position because transient hypotension after therapy is possible.
- Inspect mouth daily for ulcerations and bleeding.

FAMOTIDINE

(fa-moe'ti-deen)

Pepcid

Classification(s): ANTISECRETORY (H₂-RECEPTOR ANTAGONIST)
Therapeutic: ANTIULCER
Prototype: Cimetidine
Pregnancy Category: B

USES Short-term treatment of active duodenal ulcer. Treatment of pathologic hypersecretory conditions (e.g., Zollinger-Ellison syndrome), benign gastric ulcer.
UNLABELED USES Stress ulcer prophylaxis.

INDICATION & DOSAGE

Duodenal Ulcer

Adult: 20 mg q12h
Child: 0.25 mg/kg q12h (max: 40 mg/day)

Renal Impairment Dosage Adjustment

CrCl less than 50 mL/min: 50% of usual dose or usual dose q36–48h

SOLUTION PREPARATION
- *Direct IV Injection:* Dilute each 20 mg to a total volume of 5–10 mL with sterile water for injection, D5W, NS, LR, or other compatible IV solution.
- *Intermittent IV Infusion:* Dilute required dose in 100 mL D5W, NS, LR, or other compatible IV solution.

STORAGE
Store IV solution at 2°–8° C (36°–46° F); reconstituted IV solution is stable for 48 h at room temperature 15°–30° C (59°–86° F).

ADMINISTRATION
- **Direct IV Injection:** Give bolus dose over at least 2 min.
- **Intermittent Infusion:** Infuse over 15–30 min.

Common adverse effects in *italic*, life-threatening effects underlined: generic names in **bold**; classifications in SMALL CAPS; ♣ Canadian drug name; ◯ Prototype drug

INCOMPATIBILITIES Y-site: Amphotericin B cholesteryl complex, azithromycin, cefepime, piperacillin/tazobactam.

ACTION & *THERAPEUTIC EFFECT* A potent competitive inhibitor of histamine at histamine- (H_2) receptor sites in gastric parietal cells. Inhibits basal, nocturnal, meal-stimulated, and pentagastrin-stimulated gastric secretion. *Reduces parietal cell output of hydrochloric acid; thus, detrimental effects of acid on gastric mucosa are diminished.*

CONTRAINDICATIONS Hypersensitivity to famotidine or other H_2-receptor antagonists; sudden GI bleeding; lactation.
CAUTIOUS USE Renal insufficiency, renal failure; PKU; hepatic disease; elderly; pregnancy (category B).

ADVERSE EFFECTS (≥1%) **CNS:** Dizziness, headache, confusion, depression. **GI:** Constipation, diarrhea. **Skin:** Rash, acne, pruritus, dry skin, flushing. **Hematologic:** Thrombocytopenia. **Urogenital:** Increases in BUN and serum creatinine.

DRUG INTERACTIONS May inhibit absorption of **itraconazole** or **ketoconazole.**

PHARMACOKINETICS Peak: 0.5–3 h IV. **Duration:** 10–12 h. **Metabolism:** In liver. **Elimination:** In urine. **Half-Life:** 2.5–4 h.

NURSING IMPLICATIONS
Assessment & Drug Effects
- Monitor for improvement in GI distress.
- Monitor for signs of GI bleeding.
- Monitor for CNS adverse effect in those with impaired renal function.

Patient & Family Education
- Be aware that pain relief may not be experienced for several days after starting therapy.

FAT EMULSION, INTRAVENOUS
(fat e-mul'sion)
Intralipid, Liposyn II, Soyacal
Classification(s): CALORIC AGENT; LIPID EMULSION
Therapeutic: NUTRITIONAL SUPPLEMENT
Pregnancy Category: C

USES Fatty acid deficiency. Also to supply fatty acids and calories in high-density form to patients receiving prolonged TPN therapy who cannot tolerate high dextrose concentrations or when fluid intake **must be** restricted as in renal failure, CHF, ascites.

Common adverse effects in *italic*, life-threatening effects underlined: generic names in **bold**; classifications in SMALL CAPS; ♣ Canadian drug name; ● Prototype drug

301

F

INDICATION & DOSAGE

Prevention of Essential Fatty Acid Deficiency

Adult: 500 mL of 10% or 250 mL of 20% solution twice/wk (max: Rate of 100 mL/h)

Child: 5–10 mL/kg/day twice/wk (max: 3–4 g/kg/day; max: Rate of 100 mL/h)

Calorie Source in Fluid-Restricted Patients

Adult: Up to 2.5 g/kg or 60% of nonprotein calories daily (max: Rate of 100 mL/h)

Child: Up to 4 g/kg or 60% of nonprotein calories daily (max: Rate of 100 mL/h)

Premature Neonate: 0.25–0.5 g/kg/day, increase by 0.25–0.5 g/kg/day (max: 3–4 g/kg/day; max: Infusion rate 0.15 g/kg/h)

SOLUTION PREPARATION

- Do not use if oil appears to be separating out of the emulsion.
- Allow preparations that have been refrigerated to stand at room temperature for about 30 min before using whenever possible.
- Check with a pharmacist before mixing fat emulsions with electrolytes, vitamins, drugs, or other nutrient solutions.

STORAGE

- Discard contents of partly used containers.
- Store Intralipid 10% and Liposyn 10% at room temperature [25° C (77° F) or below]; refrigerate Intralipid 20%. Do not freeze.

ADMINISTRATION

- Give via a separate peripheral site or piggyback into same vein receiving amino acid injection and dextrose mixtures or give by piggyback through a Y-connect or near infusion site so that the two solutions mix only in a short piece of tubing proximal to needle.
- Must hang fat emulsion higher than hyperalimentation solution bottle to prevent backup of fat emulsion into primary line.
- Do not use an in-line filter because size of fat particles is larger than pore size. Control flow rate of each solution by separate infusion pumps.
- **IV Infusion for Adult:**
  - *10% Emulsion:* Infuse at 1 mL/min for first 15–30 min. May increase to 2 mL/min if no adverse reactions.
  - *20% Emulsion:* Infuse at 0.5 mL/min for first 15–30 min. May increase to 2 mL/min if no adverse reactions.
- **IV Infusion for Child:**
  - *10% Emulsion:* Infuse at 0.1 mL/min for first 10–15 min. May increase to 1 g/kg in 4 h if no adverse reactions. Do not exceed 100 mL/h.
  - *20% Emulsion:* Infuse at 0.05 mL/min for first 10–15 min. May increase to 1 g/kg in 4 h if no adverse reactions. Do not exceed 50 mL/h.

- **IV Infusion for Premature Neonate:**
  - Infuse at rate not to exceed 0.15 g/kg/h.
  - Use a constant rate over 20–24 h to reduce risk of hyperlipemia in neonates and premature infants.

INCOMPATIBILITIES Solution/additive: Aminophylline, amphotericin B, ampicillin, calcium chloride, calcium gluconate, gentamicin, hetastarch, penicillin G, phenytoin, ranitidine, vitamin B complex. **Y-site:** Acyclovir, albumin, amphotericin B, cyclosporine, doxorubicin, doxycycline, droperidol, ganciclovir, haloperidol, heparin, hetastarch, hydromorphone, levorphanol, lorazepam, midazolam, minocycline, nalbuphine, ondansetron, pentobarbital, phenobarbital, potassium phosphate, sodium phosphate.

ACTION & *THERAPEUTIC EFFECT* Soybean oil in water emulsion containing egg yolk phospholipids and glycerin. Liposyn 10% is a safflower oil in water emulsion containing egg phosphatides and glycerin. *Used as a nutritional supplement to provide calories and essential fatty acids in deficient patients.*

CONTRAINDICATIONS Hyperlipemia; bone marrow dyscrasias; impaired fat metabolism as in pathological hyperlipemia, lipoid nephrosis, acute pancreatitis accompanied by hyperlipemia; pregnancy (category C).
CAUTIOUS USE Severe hepatic or pulmonary disease; coagulation disorders; anemia; when danger of fat embolism exists; diabetes mellitus; thrombocytopenia; history of gastric ulcer; newborns, premature neonates, infants with hyperbilirubinemia.

ADVERSE EFFECTS (≥1%) **Body as a Whole:** Hypersensitivity reactions (to egg protein), irritation at infusion site. **Hematologic:** Hypercoagulability, thrombocytopenia in neonates. **GI:** *Transient increases in liver function tests, hyperlipemia.* **[Long-Term Administration]** Sepsis, jaundice (cholestasis), hepatomegaly, kernicterus (infants with hyperbilirubinemia), <u>shock</u> (rare).

DIAGNOSTIC TEST INTERFERENCE Blood samples drawn during or shortly after fat emulsion infusion may produce abnormally high *hemoglobin MCH* and *MCHC* values. Fat emulsions may cause transient abnormalities in *liver function tests* and may interfere with estimations of *serum bilirubin* (especially in infants).

DRUG INTERACTIONS No clinically significant interactions established.

NURSING IMPLICATIONS
Assessment & Drug Effects
- Observe patient closely. Acute reactions tend to occur within the first $2^1/2$ h of therapy.
- Lab tests: Baseline values for hemoglobin, platelet count, blood coagulation, LFTs, plasma lipid profile (especially serum triglycerides and cholesterol, free fatty acids in plasma). Repeat 1 or 2 times weekly during therapy in adults; more frequently in children. Obtain daily platelet

Common adverse effects in *italic*, life-threatening effects <u>underlined</u>: generic names in **bold**; classifications in SMALL CAPS; ♣ Canadian drug name; ⊘ Prototype drug

303

counts in neonates during first week of therapy, then every other day during second week, and 3 times a week thereafter.
- Note: Lipemia must clear after each daily infusion. Degree of lipemia is measured by serum triglycerides and cholesterol levels 4–6 h after infusion has ceased.

Patient & Family Education
- Report difficulty breathing, nausea, vomiting, or headache to prescriber.

F

FENOLDOPAM MESYLATE
(fen-ol′do-pam mes′y-late)
Corlopam
Classification(s): VASODILATOR, NONNITRATE
Therapeutic: ANTIHYPERTENSIVE
Pregnancy Category: B

USES Short-term (up to 48 h) management of severe hypertension.

INDICATION & DOSAGE

Severe Hypertension
Adult: 0.1–0.3 mcg/kg/min by continuous infusion for up to 48 h, may increase by 0.05–0.1 mcg/kg/min q15min (dosage range: 0.01–1.6 mcg/kg/min)
Child: 0.2 mcg/kg/min, may increase to 0.3–0.5 mcg/kg/min

SOLUTION PREPARATION
- *Continuous Infusion for Adults:* Dilute to a final concentration of 40 mcg/mL with NS or D5W (see table below).
- *Continuous Infusion for Children:* Dilute to a final concentration of 60 mcg/mL with NS or D5W (see table below).

Dilution Table for Fenoldopam

Amount of Drug	mL of IV Solution	Final Concentration
40 mg (4 mL)	1000 mL	40 mcg/mL
20 mg (2 mL)	500 mL	40 mcg/mL
10 mg (1 mL)	250 mL	40 mcg/mL
30 mg (3 mL)	500 mL	60 mcg/mL
15 mg (1.5 mL)	250 mL	60 mcg/mL
6 mg (0.6 mL)	100 mL	60 mcg/mL

STORAGE
Diluted solution is stable under normal room temperature and light for 24 h. Discard any unused solution after 24 h.

ADMINISTRATION

- **Continuous Infusion:** DO NOT give direct IV or bolus dose. See **INDICATION & DOSAGE** table for infusion rate. Titrate initial dose up or down no more frequently than q15min. Recommended increments for titration are 0.05 to 0.1 mcg/kg/min.
- Use a calibrated mechanical infusion pump.

F

INCOMPATIBILITIES Y-site: **Aminophylline, amphotericin B, ampicillin, bumetanide, cefoxitin, dexamethasone, diazepam, fosphenytoin, furosemide, ketorolac, methohexital, methylprednisolone, pentobarbital, phenytoin, prochlorperazine, sodium bicarbonate, thiopental.**

ACTION & *THERAPEUTIC EFFECT* Rapid-acting vasodilator that is a dopamine D_1-like receptor agonist. Exerts hypotensive effects by decreasing peripheral vascular resistance while increasing renal blood flow, diuresis, and natriuresis. *Indicated by rapid reduction in BP. Decreases both systolic and diastolic pressures.*

CONTRAINDICATIONS Hypersensitivity to fenoldopam. Avoid concomitant use with beta blockers. Children less than 1 y.

CAUTIOUS USE Asthmatic patients; hepatic cirrhosis, portal hypertension, or variceal bleeding; arrhythmias, tachycardia, or angina, particularly unstable angina; elevated IOP; angular-closure glaucoma; hypotension; hypokalemia; acute cerebral infarct or hemorrhage; pregnancy (category B), lactation.

ADVERSE EFFECTS (≥1%) **Body as a Whole:** Injection site reaction, pyrexia, nonspecific chest pain. **CNS:** Headache, nervousness, anxiety, insomnia, dizziness. **CV:** *Hypotension, tachycardia,* T-wave inversion, flushing, postural hypotension, extrasystoles, palpitations, bradycardia, heart failure, ischemic heart disease, <u>MI</u>, angina. **GI:** Nausea, vomiting, abdominal pain or fullness, constipation, diarrhea. **Metabolic:** Increased creatinine, BUN, glucose, transaminases, LDH; hypokalemia. **Respiratory:** Nasal congestion, dyspnea, upper respiratory disorder. **Skin:** Sweating. **Other:** UTI, leukocytosis, bleeding.

DRUG INTERACTIONS Use with BETA-BLOCKERS increases risk of hypotension.

PHARMACOKINETICS Onset: 5 min. **Peak:** 15 min. **Duration:** 15–30 min. **Distribution:** Crosses placenta. **Metabolism:** Conjugated in liver. **Elimination:** 90% excreted in urine, 10% in feces. **Half-Life:** 5 min.

NURSING IMPLICATIONS

Assessment & Drug Effects

- Monitor BP and HR carefully at least q15min or more often as warranted; expect dose-related tachycardia.
- Lab tests: Periodic serum electrolytes (especially serum potassium), BUN and creatinine, LFTs, and blood glucose.

F

FENTANYL CITRATE

(fen'ta-nil)

Duragesic, Sublimaze

Classification(s): ANALGESIC; NARCOTIC (OPIATE) AGONIST

Therapeutic: NARCOTIC ANALGESIC; GENERAL ANESTHETIC

Prototype: Morphine

Pregnancy Category: C   **Controlled Substance:** Schedule II

USES Short-acting analgesic during operative and perioperative periods, as a narcotic analgesic supplement in general and regional anesthesia, and to produce neuroleptic analgesia. Also given with oxygen and a skeletal muscle relaxant (neuroleptic anesthesia) to selected high-risk patients (e.g., those undergoing open heart surgery) when attenuation of the response to surgical stress without use of additional anesthesia agents is important.

INDICATION & DOSAGE

Premedication to Anesthesia

Adult: 25–100 mcg 30–60 min before surgery

Adjunct for Regional Anesthesia

Adult: 50–100 mcg

General Anesthesia

Adult: 2–20 mcg/kg, additional doses of 25–100 mcg as required
Child: 2–3 mcg/kg as needed

SOLUTION PREPARATION

May be given undiluted or diluted in 5 mL of sterile water for injection or NS.

STORAGE

Store at 15°–30° C (59°–86° F) unless otherwise directed. Protect drug from light.

ADMINISTRATION

Direct IV Injection: Give bolus dose over 3–5 min.

INCOMPATIBILITIES Solution/additive: Fluorouracil, lidocaine. Y-site: Azithromycin, phenytoin.

ACTION & *THERAPEUTIC EFFECT* Synthetic, potent narcotic agonist analgesic with pharmacologic actions qualitatively similar to those of morphine, but action is more prompt and less prolonged. Principal actions are analgesia and sedation. Drug-induced alterations in respiratory rate and alveolar ventilation may persist beyond its analgesic effect. *Provides analgesia for moderate to severe pain as well as sedation.*

Common adverse effects in *italic*, life-threatening effects <u>underlined</u>: generic names in **bold**; classifications in SMALL CAPS; ♣ Canadian drug name; ◐ Prototype drug

CONTRAINDICATIONS Patients who have received MAO INHIBITORS within 14 days; myasthenia gravis; labor and delivery; pregnancy (category C); children less than 1 y.

CAUTIOUS USE Head injuries, increased intracranial pressure; older adults; debilitated, poor-risk patients; cardiac disease, angina, hypotension, cardiac arrhythmias; COPD, other respiratory problems; liver and kidney dysfunction; bradyarrhythmias; children over 1 y.

ADVERSE EFFECTS (≥1%) **CNS:** *Sedation,* euphoria, dizziness, diaphoresis, delirium, convulsions with high doses. **CV:** Hypotension, bradycardia, circulatory depression, cardiac arrest. **Special Senses:** Miosis, blurred vision. **GI:** *Nausea,* vomiting, constipation, ileus. **Respiratory:** Laryngospasm, bronchoconstriction, respiratory depression or arrest. **Body as a Whole:** Muscle rigidity, especially muscles of respiration after rapid IV infusion, urinary retention. **Skin:** Rash, contact dermatitis from patch.

DRUG INTERACTIONS CNS DEPRESSANTS potentiate effects; MAO INHIBITORS may precipitate hypertensive crisis.

PHARMACOKINETICS Peak: 3–5 min. **Duration:** 30–60 min. **Metabolism:** In liver (CYP 3A4). **Elimination:** In urine. **Half-Life:** 2–4 h.

NURSING IMPLICATIONS
Assessment & Drug Effects
- Monitor vital signs closely and observe patient for signs of skeletal and thoracic muscle (depressed respirations) rigidity and weakness.
- Watch carefully for respiratory depression and for movements of various groups of skeletal muscle in extremities, eye, and neck during postoperative period. These movements may present patient management problems; report promptly.
- Note: Duration of respiratory depressant effect may be considerably longer than narcotic analgesic effect. Have immediately available oxygen, resuscitative and intubation equipment, and an opioid antagonist such as naloxone.
- Maintain in supine position to prevent orthostatic hypotension.

FILGRASTIM 🔴

(fil-gras′tim)
Neupogen
Classification(s): COLONY STIMULATING FACTOR
Therapeutic: ANTINEUTROPENIC
Pregnancy Category: C

USES To decrease the incidence of infection, as manifested by febrile neutropenia, in patients with nonmyeloid malignancies receiving myelosuppressive anticancer drugs associated with a significant incidence of

Common adverse effects in *italic*, life-threatening effects underlined: generic names in **bold**; classifications in SMALL CAPS; ♣ Canadian drug name; 🔴 Prototype drug

307

severe neutropenia with fever; to decrease neutropenia associated with bone marrow transplant; to treat chronic neutropenia; to mobilize peripheral blood stem cells (PBSCs) for autologous transplantation.

INDICATION & DOSAGE

Neutropenia

Adult/Child: 5 mcg/kg/day, may increase by 5 mcg/kg/day (max: 30 mcg/kg/day)

Bone Marrow Transplant

Adult: 10 mcg/kg/day given 24 h after cytotoxic therapy and 24 h after bone marrow transfusion

Toxicity Adjustment

ANC	Dosage Adjustment
Greater than 1000/mm³ for 3 consecutive days	5 mcg/kg/day
Greater than 1000/mm³ for more than 6 days	Discontinue
Decreases to less than 1000/mm³ for 3 days	Resume discontinued therapy at 5 mcg/kg/day

SOLUTION PREPARATION

- Prior to injection, filgrastim should be warmed to room temperature for up to 6 h.
- Use only one dose per vial; do not reenter the vial. Do not shake vial.
- May dilute with 10–50 mL D5W to yield 15 mcg/mL or greater. If more diluent is used to yield concentrations of 5–15 mcg/mL, 2 mL of 5% human albumin **must be** added for each 50 mL D5W (prior to adding filgrastim) to prevent adsorption to plastic IV infusion materials. Note: Dilutions less than 5 mcg/mL are not recommended.

STORAGE

- Store refrigerated at 2°–8° C (36°–46° F). Do not freeze.
- Avoid shaking and protect from direct sunlight.
- May be allowed to reach room temperature for a maximum of 6 h. Discard any vial left at room temperature for greater than 6 h.

ADMINISTRATION

- Do not administer filgrastim within 24 h before or after cytotoxic chemotherapy.
- Flush IV line before/after with D5W.
- **Intermittent Infusion:** Infuse over 15–30 min.
- **Continuous Infusion:** Infuse over 24 h or less.

INCOMPATIBILITIES Y-site: Amphotericin B, cefepime, cefoperazone, cefotaxime, cefoxitin, ceftizoxime, ceftriaxone, cefuroxime, clinda-

Common adverse effects in *italic*, life-threatening effects <u>underlined</u>: generic names in **bold**; classifications in SMALL CAPS; ♣ Canadian drug name; ✪ Prototype drug

mycin, dactinomycin, etoposide, fluorouracil, furosemide, gentamicin, heparin, imipenem, mannitol, methylprednisolone, metronidazole, mitomycin, piperacillin, prochlorperazine, thiotepa.

ACTION & *THERAPEUTIC EFFECT* Human granulocyte colony-stimulating factor (G-CSF) produced by recombinant DNA technology. Endogenous G-CSF regulates the production of neutrophils within the bone marrow, and primarily affects neutrophil proliferation, differentiation, and selected end-cell functional activity. These include enhanced phagocytic activity and antibody-dependent killing. *Increases neutrophil proliferation and differentiation within the bone marrow.*

CONTRAINDICATIONS Hypersensitivity to *Escherichia coli*–derived proteins, simultaneous administration with chemotherapy, radiation or myeloid cancers; ARDS; pregnancy (category C); children less than 1 y.
CAUTIOUS USE Sickle cell disease; lactation.

ADVERSE EFFECTS (≥1%) **CV:** Abnormal ST segment depression. **Hematologic:** Anemia. **GI:** Nausea, anorexia. **Body as a Whole:** *Bone pain,* hyperuricemia, *fever.*

DIAGNOSTIC TEST INTERFERENCE Elevations in *leukocyte alkaline phosphatase, serum alkaline phosphatase, lactate dehydrogenase,* and *uric acid* have been reported. These elevations appear to be related to increased bone marrow activity.

DRUG INTERACTIONS Clinically significant interactions have not been identified.

PHARMACOKINETICS Onset: 4 h. **Peak:** 1 h. **Elimination:** Probably excreted in urine. **Half-Life:** 1.4–7.2 h.

NURSING IMPLICATIONS

Assessment & Drug Effects
- Prior to initiating therapy: Baseline CBC with differential and platelet count.
- Discontinue filgrastim if absolute neutrophil count exceeds 10,000/mm³ after the chemotherapy-induced nadir. Neutrophil counts should then return to normal.
- Monitor temperature q4h. Incidence of infection should be reduced after administration of filgrastim.
- Lab tests: Twice weekly, or more often, CBC with differential and platelet count; periodic Hct.
- Monitor patients with preexisting cardiac conditions closely. MI and arrhythmias have been associated with a small percent of patients receiving filgrastim.
- Assess degree of bone pain if present. Consult prescriber if nonnarcotic analgesics do not provide relief.

Patient & Family Education
- Report promptly bone pain and, if necessary, request analgesics to control pain.
- Report fever or other signs of infection.

Common adverse effects in *italic*, life-threatening effects <u>underlined</u>: generic names in **bold**; classifications in SMALL CAPS; ♣ Canadian drug name; ⊘ Prototype drug

309

FLUCONAZOLE ℗ℛ
(flu-con'a-zole)
Diflucan
Classification(s): ANTIFUNGAL, AZOLE
Therapeutic: ANTIFUNGAL
Pregnancy Category: C

USES Cryptococcal meningitis and oropharyngeal and systemic candidiasis, both commonly found in AIDS and other immunocompromised patients.

INDICATION & DOSAGE

Oropharyngeal Candidiasis
Adult: 200 mg day 1, then 100 mg/day × 14 days
Child/Infant: 3–6 mg/kg/day × 14 days

Esophageal Candidiasis
Adult: 200 mg day 1, then 100 mg/day × 21 days
Child/Infant: 3–6 mg/kg/day × 21 days

Systemic Candidemia
Adult: 400 mg day 1, then 200 mg/day × 28 days
Child/Infant/Neonate (over 14 days): 6 mg/kg q24h × 28 days
Neonate (0–14 days): 6 mg/kg q72h

Cryptococcal Meningitis
Adult: 400 mg day 1, then 200 mg/day × 10–12 wk
Child/Infant/Neonate (over 14 days): 6–12 mg/kg day 1 then 6–12 mg/kg/day × 10–12 wk
Neonate (0–14 days): 6–12 mg/kg day 1 then 6–12 mg/kg q48h
Premature Neonates (0–14 days): 5–6 mg/kg q72h

Renal Impairment Dosage Adjustment
CrCl 50 mL/min or less (without concurrent dialysis): Give 50% of maintenance dose

Dialysis
Administer full dose post-dialysis.

SOLUTION PREPARATION
No dilution is required. Packaged ready for use as a 2 mg/mL solution. Remove wrapper just prior to use.

STORAGE
Store fluconazole injections between 5°–30° C (41°–86° F). Store *Viaflex Plus* plastic containers between 5°–25° C (41°–77° F).

Common adverse effects in *italic*, life-threatening effects <u>underlined</u>: generic names in **bold**; classifications in SMALL CAPS; ✚ Canadian drug name; ℗ Prototype drug

ADMINISTRATION

Continuous Infusion: Infuse at a maximum rate of 200 mg/h. Give after hemodialysis is completed.

INCOMPATIBILITIES Solution/additive: Trimethoprim/sulfamethoxazole. **Y-site:** Amphotericin B, amphotericin B cholesteryl, ampicillin, calcium gluconate, cefotaxime, ceftazidime, ceftriaxone, cefuroxime, chloramphenicol, clindamycin, diazepam, digoxin, erythromycin, furosemide, haloperidol, hydroxyzine, imipenem/cilastatin, pentamidine, piperacillin, ticarcillin, trimethoprim/sulfamethoxazole.

ACTION & *THERAPEUTIC EFFECT* Fungistatic, but may also be fungicidal depending on concentration. Interferes with formation of ergosterol, the principal sterol in the fungal cell membrane leading to fungal cell death. *Antifungal properties are related to the drug effect on the functioning of fungal cell membrane.*

CONTRAINDICATIONS Hypersensitivity to fluconazole or other azole antifungals; pregnancy (category C); infant less than 14 days.

CAUTIOUS USE AIDS or malignancy; hepatic impairment; structural cardiac disease; history of torsade de pointes; renal impairment or failure; lactation.

ADVERSE EFFECTS (≥1%) **CNS:** Headache. **GI:** Nausea, vomiting, abdominal pain, diarrhea, increase in AST in patients with cryptococcal meningitis and AIDS. **Skin:** Rash.

DRUG INTERACTIONS Increased PT in patients on **warfarin;** may increase **alosetron, bexarotene, phenytoin, cevimeline, cilostazol, cyclosporine, dofetilide, haloperidol, levobupivacaine, modafinil, zonisamide, theophylline** levels and toxicity; hypoglycemic reactions with ORAL SULFONYLUREAS; decreased fluconazole levels with **rifampin, cimetidine;** may prolong the effects of **fentanyl, alfentanil, methadone;** increased ergotamine toxicity with **dihydroergotamine, ergotamine.**

PHARMACOKINETICS Peak: 1–2 h. **Distribution:** Widely distributed, including CSF. **Metabolism:** 11% of dose metabolized in liver. **Elimination:** In urine. **Half-Life:** 20–50 h.

NURSING IMPLICATIONS

Assessment & Drug Effects

- Monitor for allergic response. Patients allergic to other azole antifungals may be allergic to fluconazole.
- Lab tests: Monitor BUN, serum creatinine, and LFTs.
- Monitor for S&S of liver toxicity (see Appendix C).
- Monitor diabetics for loss of glycemic control.
- Concurrent drugs: Monitor for S&S of toxicity from any of the following: Phenytoin, warfarin, theophylline.

Patient & Family Education

- Inform prescriber of all medications being taken.
- Report promptly any of the following: Unexplained fatigue, loss of appetite, nausea, jaundice, itching, abdominal pain, dark-colored urine, or flu-like symptoms.

Common adverse effects in *italic*, life-threatening effects <u>underlined</u>: generic names in **bold**; classifications in SMALL CAPS; ♣ Canadian drug name; ❷ Prototype drug

311

FLUDARABINE

(flu-dar′a-bine)

Fludara

Classification(s): ANTINEOPLASTIC; ANTIMETABOLITE; PURINE ANTAGONIST
Therapeutic: ANTINEOPLASTIC
Prototype: Cladribine
Pregnancy Category: D

USES Treatment of B-cell chronic lymphocytic leukemia (CLL) in patients who fail to respond to a regimen containing at least one standard alkylating agent.

UNLABELED USES Non-Hodgkin's lymphoma; in combination therapy for the treatment of primary resistant or relapsing acute myelogenous leukemia (AML), acute lymphoblastic leukemia (ALL), and secondary AML; cutaneous T-cell lymphoma; macroglobulinemia; myelodysplastic syndrome; prolymphocytic leukemia (PLL); stem-cell transplant preparation.

INDICATION & DOSAGE

Treatment of Unresponsive B-Cell Chronic Lymphocytic Leukemia
Adult: 25 mg/m² daily × 5 days; repeat q28days

Renal Impairment Dosage Adjustment
CrCl 30–70 mL/min: 20% dose reduction; *CrCl less than 30 mL/min:* Should not receive fludarabine

SOLUTION PREPARATION

- Exercise caution in the preparation and handling of fludarabine. Avoid exposure by inhalation or direct contact with skin or mucous membranes.
- *Vial Reconstitution:* Add 2 mL of sterile water for injection to each 50 mg vial to yield 25 mg/mL. The solution should dissolve within 15 sec and have a pH of 7.2–8.2. **Must be** further diluted for infusion.
- *Further Dilution of Reconstituted Solution:* Dilute in 100–125 mL of NS or D5W.

STORAGE

Store unreconstituted vials at 2°–8° C (36°–46° F). Discard any unused reconstituted product.

ADMINISTRATION

IV Infusion: Infuse over 30 min.

INCOMPATIBILITIES Y-site: Acyclovir, amphotericin B, chlorpromazine, daunorubicin, ganciclovir, hydroxyzine, prochlorperazine.

ACTION & *THERAPEUTIC EFFECT* Believed to act by inhibiting DNA polymerase alpha, ribonucleotide reductase, and DNA primase, thus inhibiting DNA synthesis in tumor-sensitive cells. *Fludarabine has cytotoxic effects on lymphocytic leukemia and lymphoma as well as immunosuppressant properties.*

CONTRAINDICATIONS Hypersensitivity to fludarabine; concomitant administration of pentostatin; pregnancy (category D); lactation. Safety and efficacy in children have not been established.

CAUTIOUS USE Renal impairment; patients at risk for tumor lysis syndrome; history of herpes or viral infection.

ADVERSE EFFECTS (≥1%) **Body as a Whole:** *Fever, chills, fatigue, infection, pain,* malaise, diaphoresis, anaphylaxis, hyperglycemia, dehydration. **CNS:** *Weakness,* paresthesia. **CV:** *Edema.* **GI:** *Nausea, vomiting, diarrhea, anorexia, stomatitis,* GI bleeding, esophagitis, mucositis. **Hematologic:** *Neutropenia, thrombocytopenia,* <u>hemolytic anemia</u>. **Musculoskeletal:** Myalgia. **Respiratory:** *Cough, pneumonia, dyspnea,* sinusitis, pharyngitis, upper respiratory tract infection. **Skin:** *Rash,* pruritus. **Special Senses:** Visual disturbance, hearing loss. **Urogenital:** Dysuria, urinary infection, hematuria.

DRUG INTERACTIONS Use with **pentostatin** increases risk of severe pulmonary toxicity. Do not give LIVE VACCINES due to decreased immune response.

PHARMACOKINETICS Metabolism: Rapid conversion to active metabolite (2-fluoro-ara-A). **Elimination:** Renal. **Half-Life:** 7–12 h.

NURSING IMPLICATIONS

Assessment & Drug Effects

▪ Review creatinine clearance values prior to drug administration. Withhold drug and notify prescriber if CrCl less than 30 mL/min.
▪ Monitor for and report S&S of hemolysis, infection, tumor lysis syndrome (e.g., flank pain, hematuria), peripheral neuropathy, or respiratory distress.
▪ Lab tests: Baseline CBC with differential and platelet count, repeat prior to each treatment cycle, and more often as indicated; periodic serum electrolytes, serum uric acid, and renal function tests.

Patient & Family Education

▪ Report promptly any of the following: Fever, chills, cough, sore throat, or other signs of infection; pain or difficulty passing urine; signs of bleeding such as easy bruising, black, tarry stools, nosebleeds; signs of anemia such as excessive weakness, lightheadedness, or confusion; difficulty breathing or shortness of breath; decreased vision; mouth sores or skin rash.
▪ Avoid activities that could cause physical injury and predispose to severe bleeding.
▪ Women of childbearing age should avoid becoming pregnant while receiving fludarabine.

FLUMAZENIL

(flu-ma′ze-nil)

Mazicon ♣, Romazicon
Classification(s): BENZODIAZEPINE ANTAGONIST

FLUMAZENIL

Therapeutic: BENZODIAZEPINE ANTIDOTE
Pregnancy Category: C

USES Complete or partial reversal of sedation induced by benzodiazepine for anesthesia or diagnostic or therapeutic procedures and through overdose.

UNLABELED USES Seizure disorders, alcohol intoxication, hepatic encephalopathy, facilitation of weaning from mechanical ventilation.

INDICATION & DOSAGE

Reversal of Sedation

Adult: 0.2 mg over 15 sec; may repeat 0.2 mg each min for 4 additional doses or a cumulative dose of 1 mg
Child: 0.01 mg/kg may repeat each minute (max dose: 1 mg)

Benzodiazepine Overdose

Adult: 0.2 mg over 30 sec, if no response after 30 sec, then 0.3 mg over 30 sec; may repeat with 0.5 mg each min (max: Cumulative dose of 3 mg)

SOLUTION PREPARATION
May be given direct IV undiluted or diluted in D5W, LR, NS, 1/2NS.

STORAGE
Store at 15°–30° C (59°–86° F). Use all diluted solutions or solutions drawn into a syringe within 24 h of dilution.

ADMINISTRATION
- Ensure patency of IV before administration of flumazenil, since extravasation will cause local irritation.
- Do NOT give as a bolus dose. Give through an IV that is freely flowing into a large vein.
- **Direct IV Injection:**
  - *Reversal of Anesthesia or Sedation:* Give each 0.2 mg dose in small quantities over 15 sec.
  - *Benzodiazepine Overdose:* Give each 0.2 mg dose in small quantities over 30 sec.

INCOMPATIBILITIES Data not available; do not mix with other drugs.

ACTION & *THERAPEUTIC EFFECT* Antagonizes the effects of a benzodiazepine on the CNS, including sedation, impairment of recall as well as psychomotor impairment. *Does not reverse the effects of opioids. Reverses the action of a benzodiazepine.*

CONTRAINDICATIONS Hypersensitivity to flumazenil or to benzodiazepines; patients given a benzodiazepine for control of a life-threatening condition; patients showing signs of cyclic antidepressant overdose; seizure-prone individuals; during labor and delivery; pregnancy (category C); children less than 1 y.

Common adverse effects in *italic*, life-threatening effects underlined: generic names in **bold**; classifications in SMALL CAPS; ♣ Canadian drug name; ⊘ Prototype drug

CAUTIOUS USE Hepatic function impairment; older adults; intensive care patients; head injury; anxiety or pain disorder; drug- and alcohol-dependent patients, and physical dependence upon benzodiazepines; lactation.

ADVERSE EFFECTS (≥1%) **CNS:** Emotional lability, headache, *dizziness,* agitation, *resedation,* seizures, blurred vision. **GI:** *Nausea, vomiting,* hiccups. **Other:** Shivering, pain at injection site, hypoventilation.

DRUG INTERACTIONS May antagonize effects of **zaleplon, zolpidem;** may cause convulsions or arrhythmias with TRICYCLIC ANTIDEPRESSANTS.

PHARMACOKINETICS Onset: 1–5 min. **Peak:** 6–10 min. **Duration:** 2–4 h. **Metabolism:** In the liver to inactive metabolites. **Elimination:** 90–95% excreted in urine, 5–10% in feces within 72 h. **Half-Life:** 54 min.

NURSING IMPLICATIONS

Assessment & Drug Effects

- Monitor carefully respiratory status until risk of resedation is unlikely (up to 120 min). Drug may not fully reverse benzodiazepine-induced ventilatory insufficiency.
- Monitor carefully for seizures and take appropriate precautions.
- Monitor for signs of benzodiazepine withdrawal (e.g., agitation, dysphoria) in drug-dependent patients.

Patient & Family Education

- Do not drive or engage in potentially hazardous activities until at least 18–24 h after discharge following a procedure.
- Do not ingest alcohol or nonprescription drugs for 18–24 h after flumazenil is administered or if the effects of the benzodiazepine persist.

FLUOROURACIL [5-FLUOROURACIL (5-FU)]

(flure-oh-yoor′a-sil)

Fluoroplex
Classification(s): ANTINEOPLASTIC, ANTIMETABOLITE, PYRIMIDINE ANTAGONIST
Therapeutic: ANTINEOPLASTIC
Pregnancy Category: D

USES Systemically as single agent and in combination with other antineoplastics for palliative treatment of carefully selected patients with inoperable neoplasms of breast, colon or rectum, stomach, pancreas, urinary bladder, ovary, cervix, liver. Also topically for solar or actinic keratoses and superficial basal cell carcinoma.
UNLABELED USES To induce repigmentation in vitiligo; actinic cheilitis; malignant effusions; mucosal leukoplakia.

Common adverse effects in *italic*, life-threatening effects <u>underlined</u>: generic names in **bold**; classifications in SMALL CAPS; ◆ Canadian drug name; ◉ Prototype drug

315

INDICATION & DOSAGE

Carcinoma

Adult: 12 mg/kg/day for 4 consecutive days up to 800 mg or until toxicity develops or 12-day therapy, may repeat at 1-mo intervals; if toxicity occurs, 15 mg/kg once weekly can be given until toxicity subsides

Obesity

Dose patient on lean body mass if patient is obese or has significant fluid retention.

F

SOLUTION PREPARATION

- *Safe Handling:* Double-glove with latex gloves, and change the double set after every 30 min of exposure. If a drug spill occurs, change gloves immediately after it is cleaned up.
- May be given undiluted [direct IV] or diluted in D5W or NS for infusion.

STORAGE

Fluorouracil solution is normally colorless to faint yellow. Slight discoloration during storage does not appear to affect potency or safety. Discard dark yellow solution. If a precipitate forms, redissolve drug by heating to 60° C (140° F) and shake vigorously. Allow to cool to body temperature before administration.

ADMINISTRATION

- Ensure patency of IV insertion site before initiating therapy.
- **Direct IV Injection:** Give over 1–2 min. May inject into port of freely flowing infusion.
- **IV Infusion:** Infuse over 2–24 h as prescribed by prescriber.
- Inspect injection site frequently; avoid extravasation. If it occurs, stop infusion and restart in another vein. Ice compresses may reduce danger of local tissue damage from infiltrated solution.

INCOMPATIBILITIES Solution/additive: Carboplatin, chlorpromazine, cisplatin, cytarabine, diazepam, doxorubicin, epirubicin, fentanyl, leucovorin calcium, metoclopramide, morphine. Y-site: Aldesleukin, amphotericin B cholesteryl, droperidol, filgrastim, ondansetron, TPN, topotecan, vinorelbine.

ACTION & *THERAPEUTIC EFFECT* Pyrimidine antagonist and cell-cycle specific antineoplastic agent. Blocks action of enzymes essential to normal DNA and RNA synthesis and may become incorporated in RNA to form a fraudulent molecule; unbalanced growth and death of cell result. Exhibits higher affinity for tumor tissue than healthy tissue. *Highly toxic, especially to proliferative cells in neoplasms, bone marrow, and intestinal mucosa. Low therapeutic index with high potential for severe hematologic toxicity.*

CONTRAINDICATIONS Poor nutritional status; myelosuppression; pregnancy (category D), lactation. Safety and efficacy in children are not established.

Common adverse effects in *italic*, life-threatening effects <u>underlined</u>: generic names in **bold**; classifications in SMALL CAPS; ✦ Canadian drug name; ✪ Prototype drug

CAUTIOUS USE Major surgery during previous month; history of high dose pelvic irradiation, metastatic cell infiltration of bone marrow, previous use of alkylating agents; cardiac disease, CAD, angina; hepatic or renal impairment; men and women of childbearing ages.

ADVERSE EFFECTS (≥1%) **CNS:** Euphoria, acute cerebellar syndrome (dysmetria, nystagmus, ataxia, severe mental deterioration); pustular contact hypersensitivity. **CV:** Cardiotoxicity (rare), angina. **GI:** Anorexia, *nausea, vomiting, stomatitis,* esophagopharyngitis, medicinal taste; *diarrhea,* proctitis. **Hematologic:** Anemia, <u>leukopenia</u>, thrombocytopenia, eosinophilia. **Body as a Whole:** Hypersensitivity: Pustular contact eruption, edema of face, eyes, tongue, legs. **Skin:** SLE-like dermatitis, *alopecia,* photosensitivity, erythema, increased pigmentation, skin dryness and fissuring, pruritic maculopapular rash.

DIAGNOSTIC TEST INTERFERENCE Fluorouracil may increase excretion of *5-hydroxyindoleacetic acid (5-HIAA)* and decrease *plasma albumin* (because of drug-induced protein malabsorption).

DRUG INTERACTIONS Metronidazole may increase general floxuridine toxicity; may increase or decrease serum levels of **phenytoin, fosphenytoin; hydroxyurea** can decrease conversion to active metabolite.

PHARMACOKINETICS Distribution: Distributed to tumor, intestinal mucosa, bone marrow, liver, and CSF; probably crosses placenta. **Metabolism:** Rapidly metabolized in liver. **Elimination:** 15% excreted in urine, 60–80% excreted through lungs as carbon dioxide. **Half-Life:** 16 min.

NURSING IMPLICATIONS

Assessment & Drug Effects

- Prior to initiating therapy: Total and differential WBC counts.
- Withhold drug and notify prescriber if leukopenia occurs (WBC less than 3500/mm^3) or if patient develops thrombocytopenia (platelet count less than 100,000/mm^3). Use protective isolation of patient during leukopenic period.
- Lab tests: Baseline and periodic total and differential WBC counts, Hct, LFTs, and kidney function tests.
- Report promptly signs of abnormal bleeding from any source during thrombocytopenic period (days 7–17); inspect skin for ecchymotic and petechial areas. Protect patient from trauma.
- Report promptly disorientation, confusion, or intractable vomiting.
- Establish baseline body weight and I&O ratio and pattern.
- Inspect patient's mouth daily. Report promptly cracked lips, xerostomia, white patches, and erythema of buccal membranes.
- Report development of maculopapular rash; it usually responds to symptomatic treatment and is reversible.

Patient & Family Education

- Report promptly any of the following: S&S of infection, anorexia, vomiting, nausea, stomatitis, diarrhea, GI bleeding, and difficulty in maintaining balance while ambulating.

Common adverse effects in *italic*, life-threatening effects <u>underlined</u>: generic names in **bold**; classifications in SMALL CAPS; ♣ Canadian drug name; ❷ Prototype drug

317

- Avoid exposure to sunlight or ultraviolet lamp treatments. Protect exposed skin. Photosensitivity usually subsides 2–3 mo after last dose.
- Use contraception during 5-FU treatment. If you suspect you are pregnant, tell your prescriber.

FOLIC ACID (VITAMIN B₉, PTEROYLGLUTAMIC ACID)
(fol'ic)

Apo-Folic ✦, Novofolacid ✦

FOLATE SODIUM
Folvite Sodium
Classification(s): VITAMIN B₉
Therapeutic: VITAMIN B₉ SUPPLEMENT
Pregnancy Category: A

USES Folate deficiency, macrocytic anemia, and megaloblastic anemias associated with malabsorption syndromes, alcoholism, primary liver disease, inadequate dietary intake, pregnancy, infancy, and childhood.

INDICATION & DOSAGE

Therapeutic
Adult: Less than or equal to 1 mg/day
Child: Less than or equal to 1 mg/day

Maintenance
Adult: Less than or equal to 0.4 mg/day
Child (under 4 y): Up to 0.3 mg/day; *(over 4 y):* 0.1 mg/day
Infant: 0.1 mg/day

SOLUTION PREPARATION
May be given undiluted [direct IV] or diluted in compatible IV solution for infusion.

STORAGE
Store at 15°–30° C (59°–86° F) in tightly closed containers protected from light.

ADMINISTRATION
- **Direct IV Injection:** Give at a rate of 5 mg or fraction thereof over 30–60 sec.
- **Continuous Infusion:** Infuse over 30 min or longer.

INCOMPATIBILITIES Solution/additive: Chlorpromazine, dextrose 40% in water, doxapram.

Common adverse effects in *italic*, life-threatening effects <u>underlined</u>: generic names in **bold**; classifications in SMALL CAPS; ✦ Canadian drug name; ⊘ Prototype drug

ACTION & *THERAPEUTIC EFFECT* Vitamin B complex essential for nucleoprotein synthesis and maintenance of normal erythropoiesis. Acts against folic acid deficiency resulting in production of defective DNA leading to megaloblast formation and arrest of bone marrow maturation. *Stimulates production of RBCs, WBCs, and platelets in patients with megaloblastic anemias.*

CONTRAINDICATIONS Folic acid alone for pernicious anemia or other vitamin B₁₂ deficiency states; normocytic, refractory, aplastic, or undiagnosed anemia; neonates.
CAUTIOUS USE Pregnancy (category A).

ADVERSE EFFECTS (≥1%) Reportedly nontoxic. Slight flushing and feeling of warmth following IV administration.

DIAGNOSTIC TEST INTERFERENCE Falsely low *serum folate levels* may occur with *Lactobacillus casei assay* in patients receiving antibiotics such as TETRACYCLINES.

DRUG INTERACTIONS Chloramphenicol may antagonize effects of **folate** therapy; **phenytoin** metabolism may be increased, thus decreasing its levels in **folate**-deficient patients.

PHARMACOKINETICS Distribution: Distributed to all body tissues; high concentrations in CSF; crosses placenta; distributed into breast milk. **Metabolism:** In liver to active metabolites. **Elimination:** Small amounts eliminated in urine in folate-deficient patients; large amounts excreted in urine with high doses.

NURSING IMPLICATIONS

Assessment & Drug Effects

- Concurrent drugs: Monitor for subtherapeutic plasma levels of phenytoin and loss of seizure control.

Patient & Family Education

- Folic acid will correct anemia but will not reverse neurologic problems that develop as a result of pernicious anemia.

FOSCARNET

(fos'car-net)
Foscavir
Classification(s): ANTIVIRAL
Therapeutic: ANTIVIRAL
Pregnancy Category: C

USES CMV retinitis, mucocutaneous HSV, acyclovir-resistant HSV in immunocompromised patients.

Common adverse effects in *italic*, life-threatening effects underlined: generic names in **bold**; classifications in SMALL CAPS; ♣ Canadian drug name; ⊘ Prototype drug

319

UNLABELED USES Other CMV infections, herpes zoster infections in AIDS patients.

INDICATION & DOSAGE

CMV Retinitis

Adult: 60 mg/kg infused over 1 h q8h for 2–3 wk OR 90 mg/kg q12h for 2–3 wk; induction may be repeated if relapse occurs during maintenance therapy

Maintenance Dose

Adult: 90–120 mg/kg/day infused over 2 h

Acyclovir-Resistant HSV in Immunocompromised Patients

Adult: 40 mg/kg q8–12h for up to 3 wk or until lesions heal

Renal Impairment Dosage Adjustment

See package insert.

SOLUTION PREPARATION

- *Central Line:* No dilution is required. Administer as supplied (24 mg/mL).
- *Peripheral Line:* Dilute to 12 mg/mL with D5W or NS.

STORAGE

Use prepared IV solutions within 24 h.

ADMINISTRATION

- Prehydrate with 2.5 L of NS to reduce nephrotoxicity.
- **Direct IV Injection:** Give via an infusion pump at a constant rate NOT to exceed 1 mg/kg/min over the specified period of infusion.

INCOMPATIBILITIES Solution/additive: Lactated Ringer's, acyclovir, amphotericin B, diazepam, digoxin, diphenhydramine, dobutamine, droperidol, ganciclovir, haloperidol, leucovorin, lorazepam, midazolam, pentamidine, phenytoin, prochlorperazine, promethazine, sulfamethoxazole/trimethoprim, TPN, trimetrexate, vancomycin. **Y-site:** Acyclovir, amphotericin B, diazepam, digoxin, diphenhydramine, dobutamine, droperidol, ganciclovir, haloperidol, leucovorin, leucovorin, lorazepam, midazolam, pentamidine, phenytoin, prochlorperazine, promethazine, sulfamethoxazole/trimethoprim, trimetrexate, vancomycin.

ACTION & *THERAPEUTIC EFFECT* Selectively inhibits the viral-specific DNA-polymerases and reverse transcriptases of susceptible viruses, thus preventing elongation of the viral DNA chain. *Acts against cytomegalovirus (CMV), herpes simplex virus types 1 and 2 (HSV-1, HSV-2), human herpesvirus 6 (HHV-6), Epstein-Barr virus (EBV), and varicella-zoster virus (VZV).*

CONTRAINDICATIONS Hypersensitivity to foscarnet; pregnancy (category C), lactation.

CAUTIOUS USE Kidney function impairment; cardiac disease; mineral and electrolyte imbalances; seizures; older adults. Safety and efficacy in children are not established.

ADVERSE EFFECTS (≥1%) **CV:** Thrombophlebitis if infused through a peripheral vein. **CNS:** Tremor, muscle twitching, headache, weakness, fatigue, confusion, anxiety. **Endocrine:** *Hyperphosphatemia,* hypophosphatemia, hypocalcemia. **GI:** Nausea, vomiting, diarrhea. **Urogenital:** Penile ulceration. **Hematologic:** *Anemia,* leukopenia, thrombocytopenia. **Renal:** *Nephrotoxicity* (acute renal failure, tubular necrosis). **Skin:** Fixed drug eruption, rash.

DIAGNOSTIC TEST INTERFERENCE May cause increase or decrease in *se-rum calcium, phosphorus,* and *magnesium.* Decreases *Hct* and *Hgb.* Increased *serum creatinine.*

DRUG INTERACTIONS AMINOGLYCOSIDES, **amphotericin B, vancomycin** may increase risk of nephrotoxicity. **Etidronate, pamidronate, pentamidine** may exacerbate hypocalcemia.

PHARMACOKINETICS Onset: 3–7 days. **Duration:** Relapse usually occurs 3–4 wk after end of therapy. **Distribution:** 3–28% of dose may be deposited in bone; variable penetration into CSF; crosses placenta; distributed into breast milk. **Metabolism:** Not metabolized. **Elimination:** 73–94% excreted in urine. **Half-Life:** 3–4 h.

NURSING IMPLICATIONS

Assessment & Drug Effects

- Monitor for cardiac arrhythmias, especially in presence of known cardiac abnormalities.
- Lab tests: Baseline and frequent serum creatinine, and CrCl; periodic CBC, serum electrolytes.
- Monitor for S&S of electrolyte imbalances.
- Monitor for seizures and take appropriate precautions.
- Question patients regarding local irritation of the penile or vulvovaginal epithelium. If either occurs, increase hydration and better personal hygiene.

Patient & Family Education

- Report perioral tingling, numbness, and paresthesia to prescriber immediately.
- Understand that drug is not a cure for CMV retinitis; regular ophthalmologic exams are necessary.
- Note: Good hydration is important to maintain adequate output of urine.

FOSPHENYTOIN SODIUM

(fos-phen'i-toin)

Cerebyx

Common adverse effects in *italic*, life-threatening effects <u>underlined</u>: generic names in **bold**; classifications in SMALL CAPS; ♣ Canadian drug name; ● Prototype drug

321

Classification(s): ANTICONVULSANT, HYDANTOIN
Therapeutic: ANTICONVULSANT
Prototype: Phenytoin
Pregnancy Category: D

USES Control of generalized convulsive status epilepticus and the prevention and treatment of seizures during neurosurgery, or as a parenteral short-term substitute for oral phenytoin.

UNLABELED USES Antiarrhythmic agent especially in treatment of digitalis-induced arrhythmia; treatment of trigeminal neuralgia (tic douloureux).

INDICATION & DOSAGE

Status Epilepticus

Adult: **IV Loading Dose,** 15–20 mg PE/kg (PE = phenytoin sodium equivalents); **IV Maintenance Dose,** 4–6 mg PE/kg/day

Substitution for Oral Phenytoin Therapy

Adult: Substitute fosphenytoin at the same total daily dose in mg PE as the oral dose at a rate of infusion not greater than 150 mg PE/min

Note: All dosing is expressed in phenytoin sodium equivalents (PE) to avoid the need to calculate molecular weight adjustments between fosphenytoin and phenytoin sodium doses.

SOLUTION PREPARATION
Dilute in D5W or NS to a concentration of 1.5–25 mg PE/mL.

STORAGE
Store at 2°–8° C (36°–46° F); may store at room temperature not to exceed 48 h.

ADMINISTRATION
Direct IV Injection: Give bolus dose at a rate of 100–150 mg PE/min. Give more slowly if patient experiences burning, tingling, or paresthesia.

INCOMPATIBILITIES Y-site: Fenoldopam, midazolam.

ACTION & *THERAPEUTIC EFFECT* Prodrug of phenytoin that converts to the anticonvulsant, phenytoin. Thought to modulate the sodium channels of neurons, calcium flux across neuronal membranes, and enhance the sodium–potassium ATPase activity of neurons and glial cells. *Cellular mechanism of phenytoin is thought to be responsible for the anticonvulsant activity of fosphenytoin.*

CONTRAINDICATIONS Hypersensitivity to hydantoin products; rash, seizures due to hypoglycemia; sinus bradycardia, complete or incomplete heart block; Adams–Stokes syndrome; pregnancy (category D). Safety and efficacy in children are not established.

Common adverse effects in *italic*, life-threatening effects <u>underlined</u>: generic names in **bold**; classifications in SMALL CAPS; ♣ Canadian drug name; ❷ Prototype drug

F

CAUTIOUS USE Impaired liver or kidney function; alcoholism; hypotension, heart block, bradycardia, severe CAD; diabetes mellitus, hyperglycemia; respiratory depression; acute intermittent porphyria; lactation.

ADVERSE EFFECTS (≥1%) **CNS:** Usually dose related. Paresthesia, tinnitus, *nystagmus, dizziness, somnolence, drowsiness,* ataxia, mental confusion, tremors, insomnia, headache, seizures, increased reflexes, dysarthria, intracranial hypertension. **CV:** Bradycardia, tachycardia, asystole, hypotension, hypertension, cardiovascular collapse, cardiac arrest, heart block, ventricular fibrillation, phlebitis. **Special Senses:** Photophobia, conjunctivitis, diplopia, blurred vision. **GI:** *Gingival hyperplasia,* nausea, vomiting, constipation, epigastric pain, dysphagia, loss of taste, weight loss, hepatitis, liver necrosis. **Hematologic:** Thrombocytopenia, leukopenia, leukocytosis, agranulocytosis, pancytopenia, eosinophilia; megaloblastic, hemolytic, or aplastic anemias. **Metabolic:** Fever, hyperglycemia, glycosuria, weight gain, edema, transient increase in serum thyrotropic (TSH) level, hyperkalemia, osteomalacia or rickets associated with hypocalcemia, and elevated alkaline phosphatase activity. **Skin:** Alopecia, hirsutism (especially in young female); rash: Scarlatiniform, maculopapular, urticarial, morbilliform (may be fatal); bullous, exfoliative, or purpuric dermatitis; Stevens–Johnson syndrome, toxic epidermal necrolysis, keratosis, neonatal hemorrhage, *pruritus.* **Urogenital:** Acute renal failure, Peyronie's disease. **Respiratory:** Acute pneumonitis, pulmonary fibrosis. **Musculoskeletal:** Periarteritis nodosum, acute systemic lupus erythematosus, craniofacial abnormalities (with enlargement of lips). **Other:** Lymphadenopathy, injection site pain, chills.

DIAGNOSTIC TEST INTERFERENCE Fosphenytoin may produce lower than normal values for ***dexamethasone*** or ***metyrapone*** tests; may increase ***serum levels*** of ***glucose, BSP,*** and ***alkaline phosphatase*** and may decrease ***PBI*** and ***urinary steroid*** levels.

DRUG INTERACTIONS Alcohol decreases fosphenytoin effects; OTHER ANTICONVULSANTS may increase or decrease fosphenytoin levels; fosphenytoin may decrease absorption and increase metabolism of ORAL ANTICOAGULANTS; fosphenytoin increases metabolism of CORTICOSTEROIDS and ORAL CONTRACEPTIVES, thus decreasing their effectiveness; **amiodarone, chloramphenicol, omeprazole** increase fosphenytoin levels; ANTITUBERCULOSIS AGENTS, **voriconazole** decrease fosphenytoin levels. **Food: Folic acid, calcium, vitamin D** absorption may be decreased by fosphenytoin. **Herbal: Ginkgo** may decrease anticonvulsant effectiveness.

PHARMACOKINETICS Distribution: 95–99% bound to plasma proteins, displaces phenytoin from protein binding sites; crosses placenta, small amount in breast milk. **Metabolism:** Converted to phenytoin by phosphatases; phenytoin is oxidized in liver to inactive metabolites. **Elimination:** Half-life 15 min to convert fosphenytoin to phenytoin, 22 h phenytoin; phenytoin metabolites excreted in urine.

Common adverse effects in *italic*, life-threatening effects underlined: generic names in **bold**; classifications in SMALL CAPS; ♣ Canadian drug name; ⊘ Prototype drug

323

F

NURSING IMPLICATIONS

Assessment & Drug Effects

- Monitor ECG, BP, and respiratory function continuously during and for 10–20 min after infusion.
- Discontinue infusion and notify prescriber if rash appears. Be prepared to substitute alternative therapy to prevent withdrawal-precipitated seizures.
- Lab tests: Periodic CBC with differential, platelet count, serum electrolytes, and blood glucose.
- Allow at least 2 h after IV infusion before monitoring total plasma phenytoin concentration.
- Monitor diabetics for loss of glycemic control.
- Monitor carefully for adverse effects, especially in patients with renal or hepatic disease or hypoalbuminemia.

Patient & Family Education

- Be aware of potential adverse effects. Itching, burning, tingling, or paresthesia are common during and for some time following IV infusion.

FUROSEMIDE ⊙

(fur-oh′se-mide)

Furomide ◆, Lasix, Luramide ◆
Classification(s): DIURETIC, LOOP
Therapeutic: DIURETIC
Pregnancy Category: C

USES Treatment of edema associated with CHF, cirrhosis of liver, and kidney disease, including nephrotic syndrome. Has been used concomitantly with mannitol for treatment of severe cerebral edema, particularly in meningitis.

INDICATION & DOSAGE

Edema

Adult: 20–40 mg in 1 or more divided doses up to 600 mg/day
Child/Infant: 1 mg/kg, may be increased by 1 mg/kg q2h if needed (max: 6 mg/kg/dose)
Neonate: 1–2 mg/kg q12–24h

SOLUTION PREPARATION

May be given undiluted [direct IV] or diluted in NS, LR, or D5W adjusted to a pH above 5.5 or infusion.

STORAGE

Store parenteral solution at controlled room temperature, preferably at 15°–30° C (59°–86° F). Protect from light.

Common adverse effects in *italic*, life-threatening effects <u>underlined</u>: generic names in **bold**; classifications in SMALL CAPS; ◆ Canadian drug name; ⊙ Prototype drug

ADMINISTRATION

- **Direct IV Injection:** Give bolus dose at a rate of 20 mg or a fraction thereof over 1–2 min.
- **Continuous Infusion:** Infuse high doses at a controlled rate of 4 mg/min to decrease risk of ototoxicity.

INCOMPATIBILITIES **Solution/additive:** Amiodarone, buprenorphine, chlorpromazine, diazepam, diphenhydramine, dobutamine, erythromycin, fructose, gentamicin, isoproterenol, meperidine, metoclopramide, milrinone, netilmicin, pancuronium, papaveretum, prochlorperazine, promethazine, quinidine, thiamine. **Y-site:** Amiodarone, amsacrine, azithromycin, chlorpromazine, ciprofloxacin, clarithromycin, diltiazem, dobutamine, dopamine, doxorubicin, droperidol, esmolol, fenoldopam, filgrastim, fluconazole, gemcitabine, gentamicin, hydralazine, idarubicin, labetalol, levofloxacin, meperidine, methocarbamol, metoclopramide, midazolam, milrinone, morphine, netilmicin, nicardipine, ondansetron, quinidine, tetracycline, thiopental, vecuronium, vinblastine, vincristine, vinorelbine, TPN.

ACTION & *THERAPEUTIC EFFECT* Rapid-acting potent sulfonamide "loop" diuretic and antihypertensive. Inhibits reabsorption of sodium and chloride primarily in loop of Henle as well as in proximal and distal renal tubules. Decreases renal vascular resistance and may increase renal blood flow. *A diuretic and antihypertensive that decreases edema and intravascular volume.*

CONTRAINDICATIONS History of hypersensitivity to furosemide or sulfonamides; increasing oliguria, anuria, fluid and electrolyte depletion states; hepatic coma; preeclampsia, eclampsia; pregnancy (category C).

CAUTIOUS USE Older adults; hepatic disease, hepatic cirrhosis; renal disease, nephrotic syndrome; cardiogenic shock associated with acute MI; ventricular arrhythmias, CHF, diarrhea; history of SLE; history of gout; diabetes mellitus; patients receiving digitalis glycosides or potassium-depleting steroids; lactation; infants.

ADVERSE EFFECTS (≥1%) **CV:** Postural hypotension, dizziness with excessive diuresis, acute hypotensive episodes, <u>circulatory collapse</u>. **Metabolic:** Hypovolemia, dehydration, hyponatremia, *hypokalemia,* hypochloremia, metabolic alkalosis, hypomagnesemia, hypocalcemia (tetany), hyperglycemia, glycosuria, elevated BUN, hyperuricemia. **GI:** Nausea, vomiting, oral and gastric burning, anorexia, diarrhea, constipation, abdominal cramping, acute pancreatitis, jaundice. **Urogenital:** Allergic interstitial nephritis, irreversible renal failure, urinary frequency. **Hematologic:** Anemia, leukopenia, thrombocytopenic purpura; <u>aplastic anemia, agranulocytosis</u> (rare). **Special Senses:** Tinnitus, vertigo, feeling of fullness in ears, hearing loss (rarely permanent), blurred vision. **Skin:** Pruritus, urticaria, exfoliative dermatitis, purpura, photosensitivity, porphyria cutanea tarde, necrotizing angiitis (vasculitis). **Body as a Whole:** Increased perspi-

Common adverse effects in *italic*, life-threatening effects <u>underlined</u>: generic names in **bold**; classifications in SMALL CAPS; ♣ Canadian drug name; ⊘ Prototype drug

325

ration; paresthesias; activation of SLE, muscle spasms, weakness; thrombophlebitis, pain at IM injection site.

DIAGNOSTIC TEST INTERFERENCE Furosemide may cause elevations in *BUN, serum amylase, cholesterol, triglycerides, uric acid* and *blood glucose* levels, and may decrease *serum calcium, magnesium, potassium,* and *sodium* levels.

DRUG INTERACTIONS OTHER DIURETICS enhance diuretic effects; with **digoxin** increased risk of toxicity because of hypokalemia; NONDEPOLARIZING NEUROMUSCULAR BLOCKING AGENTS (e.g., **tubocurarine**) prolong neuromuscular blockage; CORTICOSTEROIDS, **amphotericin B** potentiate hypokalemia; decreases **lithium** elimination and increased toxicity; SULFONYLUREAS, **insulin** blunt hypoglycemic effects; NSAIDS may attenuate diuretic effects.

PHARMACOKINETICS Peak: 20–60 min. **Onset:** 5 min. **Duration:** 2 h. **Distribution:** Crosses placenta. **Metabolism:** Small amount metabolized in liver. **Elimination:** 80% excreted in urine; excreted in breast milk. **Half-Life:** 30 min.

NURSING IMPLICATIONS

Assessment & Drug Effects

- Monitor closely BP and vital signs. Sudden death from cardiac arrest has been reported.
- Monitor BP during periods of diuresis and through period of dosage adjustment.
- Monitor for S&S of hypokalemia (see Appendix C).
- Monitor older adults closely during period of brisk diuresis. Sudden alteration in fluid and electrolyte balance may precipitate significant adverse reactions.
- Lab tests: Frequent blood count, serum and urine electrolytes, CO_2, BUN, blood sugar, and uric acid value.
- Monitor I&O ratio and pattern. Report decrease or unusual increase in output. Excessive diuresis can result in dehydration and hypovolemia, circulatory collapse, and hypotension. Excessive dehydration is most likely to occur in older adults, those with chronic cardiac disease on prolonged salt restriction, or those receiving sympatholytic agents.
- Weigh patient daily under standard conditions.
- Monitor urine and blood glucose closely in diabetics and patients with decompensated hepatic cirrhosis. Drug may cause hyperglycemia.

Patient & Family Education

- Report promptly muscle cramps or weakness.
- Make position changes slowly because high doses of antihypertensive drugs taken concurrently may produce episodes of dizziness or imbalance.
- Avoid replacing fluid losses with large amounts of water.
- Adhere to diet recommendations regarding high-potassium foods.
- Avoid prolonged exposure to direct sun.

Common adverse effects in *italic*, life-threatening effects <u>underlined</u>: generic names in **bold**; classifications in SMALL CAPS; ♣ Canadian drug name; ◐ Prototype drug

GALLIUM NITRATE

(gal'li-um)

Ganite

Classification(s): BONE RESORPTION INHIBITOR
Therapeutic: CALCIUM REGULATOR
Pregnancy Category: C

USES Hypercalcemia of malignancy.
UNLABELED USES Paget's disease, painful bone metastases, adjuvant therapy for bladder cancer and lymphomas.

G

INDICATION & DOSAGE

Hypercalcemia

Adult: 100–200 mg/m²/day for 5 days

SOLUTION PREPARATION

Dilute each daily dose with 1000 mL NS (preferred if not contraindicated) or D5W.

STORAGE

Store IV solutions at 15°–30° C (59°–86° F) for 48 h or refrigerated at 2°–8° C (36°–46° F) for 7 days. Discard unused portions.

ADMINISTRATION

- **Continuous IV Infusion:** Infuse over 24 h taking care to avoid rapid infusion. Control rate with infusion pump or micro-drip device.
- Hydrate patient with oral fluids or IV NS to produce a urine output of 2 L/day; maintain adequate hydration prior to and throughout treatment.
- Do not administer concurrently with potentially nephrotoxic drugs.

INCOMPATIBILITIES Y-site: Cisplatin, cytarabine, doxorubicin, haloperidol, hydromorphone.

ACTION & *THERAPEUTIC EFFECT* Exerts a hypocalcemic effect by inhibiting calcium resorption from bone, possibly by reducing the rate of bone metabolism. *Lowers calcium serum levels by inhibiting calcium resorption from bone.*

CONTRAINDICATIONS Severe renal impairment (serum creatinine greater than 2.5 mg/dL); concurrent administration of a nephrotoxic drug (e.g., aminoglycosides, or amphotericin B); pregnancy (category C), lactation.
CAUTIOUS USE Renal function impairment; children.

ADVERSE EFFECTS (≥1%) **CNS:** *Fatigue,* paresthesia, hyperthermia. **CV:** Hypotension. **GI:** *Nausea, vomiting, diarrhea,* anorexia, stomatitis, dysgeusia, mucositis, metallic taste. **Hematologic:** Anemia, granulocytopenia, thrombocytopenia. **Metabolic:** Hypocalcemia, hypophosphatemia, hypomagnesemia. **Urogenital:** Nephrotoxicity, acute renal failure. **Other:** Optic neuritis, maculopapular rash.

Common adverse effects in *italic*, life-threatening effects underlined: generic names in **bold**; classifications in SMALL CAPS; ♣ Canadian drug name; ☉ Prototype drug

327

DRUG INTERACTIONS AMINOGLYCOSIDES, **amphotericin B, vancomycin** increase the risk of nephrotoxicity.

PHARMACOKINETICS Onset: 48 h. **Duration:** 4–14 days after discontinuation of therapy. **Distribution:** Concentrates in tumors; distributed to lung, skin, muscle, and heart with high concentrations in liver and kidney; not known if crosses placenta or is distributed into breast milk. **Metabolism:** Not metabolized. **Elimination:** 35–71% is through kidneys within first 24 h after administration. **Half-Life:** 25–111 h.

NURSING IMPLICATIONS

Assessment & Drug Effects

- Prior to initiating therapy: Baseline serum calcium corrected for serum albumin, serum electrolytes including phosphorus, serum creatinine, BUN, and plasma pH.
- Withhold gallium nitrate and notify prescriber if hypocalcemia occurs or if serum creatinine exceeds 2–2.5 mg/dL.
- Lab tests: Daily serum calcium, frequent serum phosphorus; periodic BUN and serum creatinine throughout therapy.

Patient & Family Education

- Learn S&S of hypocalcemia (see Appendix C). Notify prescriber immediately if any occur.

GANCICLOVIR

(gan-ci'clo-vir)

Cytovene
Classification(s): ANTIVIRAL
Therapeutic: ANTIVIRAL
Prototype: Acyclovir
Pregnancy Category: C

USES CMV retinitis, prophylaxis and treatment of systemic CMV infections in immunocompromised patients including HIV-positive and transplant patients.

INDICATION & DOSAGE

Induction Therapy

Adult/Child (over 3 mo): 5 mg/kg q12h for 14–21 days (doses may range from 2.5–5 mg/kg q8–12h for 10–35 days)

Maintenance Therapy

Adult/Child: 5 mg/kg daily (7 days per wk) or 6 mg/kg daily 5 days per wk

Prevention of CMV Disease in Transplant Recipients

Adult/Child: 5 mg/kg q12h 7–14 days, then 5 mg/kg daily or 6 mg/kg/day 5 days/wk

Common adverse effects in *italic*, life-threatening effects <u>underlined</u>: generic names in **bold**; classifications in SMALL CAPS; ♣ Canadian drug name; ☻ Prototype drug

Renal Impairment Dosage Adjustment

CrCl 50–70 mL/min: Use 50% of dose, *25–50 mL/min:* Use 50% of dose and q24h interval, *10–25 mL/min:* Use 25% of dose and q24h interval

Hemodialysis Dosage Adjustment

Give dose post-dialysis.

SOLUTION PREPARATION

- *Vial Reconstitution:* Add 10 mL of sterile water (supplied) for injection to the 500-mg vial immediately before use to yield 50 mg/mL. **Must be further diluted for infusion.** Shake well to dissolve.
- *Further Dilution of Reconstituted Solution:* Withdraw the ordered amount and add to 100 mL of NS, D5W, or LR (volume less than 100 mL may be used, but the final concentration should be less than 10 mg/mL).
- Avoid direct contact with skin and mucous membranes. Wash thoroughly with soap and water if contact occurs.

STORAGE

Store reconstituted solutions refrigerated at 4° C; use within 12 h. Store infusion solution refrigerated up to 24 h of preparation.

ADMINISTRATION

Intermittent Infusion: Give at a constant rate over 1 h. Avoid rapid infusion or bolus injection.

INCOMPATIBILITIES Solution/additive: Amino acid solutions (TPN), bacteriostatic water for injection, foscarnet. Y-site: Amifostine, amsacrine, aztreonam, cefepime, cytarabine, doxorubicin, fludarabine, foscarnet, gemcitabine, ondansetron, piperacillin/tazobactam, sargramostim, tacrolimus, TPN, vinorelbine.

ACTION & *THERAPEUTIC EFFECT* Ganciclovir is a synthetic purine nucleoside analog that is an antiviral drug active against cytomegalovirus (CMV). It inhibits the replication of CMV DNA. *Sensitive human viruses include CMV, herpes simplex virus-1 and -2 (HSV-1, HSV-2), Epstein-Barr virus, and varicella-zoster virus.*

CONTRAINDICATIONS Hypersensitivity to ganciclovir or acyclovir, infection; severe thrombocytopenia; pregnancy (category C), lactation.
CAUTIOUS USE Renal impairment; older adults; bone marrow suppression; chemotherapy; radiation therapy.

ADVERSE EFFECTS (≥1%) **CNS:** *Fever,* headache, disorientation, mental status changes, ataxia, <u>coma</u>, confusion, dizziness, paresthesia, nervousness, somnolence, tremor. **CV:** Edema, phlebitis. **GI:** *Nausea, diarrhea,* anorexia, elevated liver enzymes. **Hematologic:** <u>*Bone marrow suppression*</u>, *thrombocytopenia, granulocytopenia, eosinophilia, leukopenia,* hyperbilirubinemia. **Metabolic:** Hyperthermia, hypoglycemia. **Urogenital:** Infertility. **Skin:** Rash.

DRUG INTERACTIONS ANTINEOPLASTIC AGENTS, **amphotericin B, didanosine, trimethoprim-sulfamethoxazole (TMP-SMZ), dapsone, pentamidine, probenecid, zidovudine** may increase bone marrow suppression and

Common adverse effects in *italic*, life-threatening effects <u>underlined</u>: generic names in **bold**; classifications in SMALL CAPS; ♣ Canadian drug name; ☻ Prototype drug

329

other toxic effects of ganciclovir; may increase risk of nephrotoxicity from **cyclosporine;** may increase risk of seizures due to **imipenem-cilastatin.**

PHARMACOKINETICS Onset: 3–8 days. **Duration:** Clinical relapse can occur 14 days to 3.5 mo after stopping therapy; positive blood and urine cultures recur 12–60 days after therapy. **Distribution:** Distributes throughout body including CSF, eye, lungs, liver, and kidneys; crosses placenta in animals; not known if distributed into breast milk. **Metabolism:** Not metabolized. **Elimination:** 94–99% of dose is excreted unchanged in urine. **Half-Life:** 2.5–4.2 h.

NURSING IMPLICATIONS

Assessment & Drug Effects

- Inspect IV insertion site throughout infusion for signs and symptoms of thrombophlebitis.
- Withhold drug and notify prescriber for neutrophil count below 500/mm^3 or platelet count below 25,000/mm^3.
- Lab tests: CBC with differential and platelet counts at least every other day during twice-daily dosing and weekly thereafter; daily neutrophil counts with hemodialysis or neutrophil counts less than 1000/mm^3; serum creatinine or creatinine clearance at least every two wk; periodic LFTs.
- Closely monitor renal function in the older adult.

Patient & Family Education

- Drug is not a cure for CMV retinitis; follow regular ophthalmologic examination schedule.
- Drink adequate fluids during therapy. Check with prescriber for appropriate volume of fluids.
- Report promptly unexplained or unusual bleeding.
- Use extra caution to avoid cuts or tissue trauma.
- Use barrier contraception throughout therapy and for at least 90 days afterwards.

GEMCITABINE HYDROCHLORIDE

(gem-ci′ta-been)

Gemzar

Classification(s): ANTINEOPLASTIC; ANTIMETABOLITE, PYRIMIDINE ANTAGONIST
Therapeutic: ANTINEOPLASTIC
Prototype: Fluorouracil
Pregnancy Category: D

USES Locally advanced or metastatic adenocarcinoma of the pancreas, non–small-cell lung cancer, breast cancer.

INDICATION & DOSAGE

Pancreatic Cancer

Adult: 1000 mg/m^2 once weekly for up to 7 wk, followed by 1 wk rest from treatment; may repeat once weekly for 3 of every 4 wk

Common adverse effects in *italic*, life-threatening effects <u>underlined</u>: generic names in **bold**; classifications in SMALL CAPS; ♣ Canadian drug name; ☻ Prototype drug

Non–Small-Cell Lung Cancer

Adult: 1000 mg/m^2 on days 1, 8, 15 of 28-day cycle OR 1250 mg/m^2 on days 1 and 8 of 21-day cycle. Given with cisplatin.

Breast Cancer

Adult: 1250 mg/m^2 on days 1 and 8 of 21-day cycle. Given with paclitaxel.

SOLUTION PREPARATION

- *Vial Reconstitution:* Dilute with NS without preservatives by adding 5 mL or 25 mL to the 200-mg or 1-g vial, respectively, to yield 38 mg/mL. Shake to dissolve. May be given as prepared or further diluted for infusion.
- *Further Dilution of Reconstituted Solution:* Dilute further if necessary with NS to concentrations as low as 0.1 mg/mL.

STORAGE

Store reconstituted solutions unrefrigerated at 20°–25° C (68°–77° F). Use within 24 h of reconstitution.

ADMINISTRATION

IV Infusion: Infuse over 30 min. Infusion time greater than 60 min is associated with increased toxicity.

INCOMPATIBILITIES Y-site: **Acyclovir, amphotericin B, cefoperazone, cefotaxime, furosemide, ganciclovir, imipenem/cilastatin, irinotecan, methotrexate, methylprednisolone, mitomycin, piperacillin, piperacillin/tazobactam, prochlorperazine.**

ACTION & *THERAPEUTIC EFFECT* Pyrimidine analog with cell phase specificity affecting rapidly dividing cells in S phase (DNA synthesis). Interferes with DNA synthesis by inhibiting ribonucleotide reductase, resulting in a reduction in concentration of deoxynucleotides. Additionally, if gemcitabine is incorporated into the DNA strand, it inhibits further growth of the strand. *Induces DNA fragmentation in dividing cells resulting in cell death of tumor cells.*

CONTRAINDICATIONS Hypersensitivity to gemcitabine; severe thrombocytopenia; acute infection; pregnancy (category D), lactation.

CAUTIOUS USE Myelosuppression; renal or hepatic dysfunction; history of bleeding disorders; infection; previous cytotoxic or radiation treatment. Safety and effectiveness in children are not established.

ADVERSE EFFECTS (≥1%) **CNS:** *Fever, flu-like syndrome (anorexia, headache, cough, chills, myalgia),* paresthesias. **GI:** *Nausea, vomiting, diarrhea,* stomatitis, *transient elevations of liver transaminases.* **Hematologic:** <u>*Myelosuppression (anemia, leukopenia, neutropenia, thrombocytopenia)*</u>. **Urogenital:** Mild proteinuria and hematuria. **Other:** *Dyspnea, edema, peripheral edema, infection.*

DRUG INTERACTIONS May increase effect of **warfarin** or ORAL ANTICOAGULANTS.

PHARMACOKINETICS Peak: Peak concentrations reached by 30 min after infusion; lower clearance in women and older adult results in higher concentrations at any given dose. **Distribution:** Crosses placenta, distributed into breast milk. **Metabolism:** Metabolized intracellularly by nucleoside kinases to active diphosphate and triphosphate nucleosides. **Elimination:** 92–98% recovered in urine within 1 wk. **Half-Life:** 32–94 min.

NURSING IMPLICATIONS

Assessment & Drug Effects

- Prior to initiating therapy: Baseline CBC with differential and platelet count.
- Monitor vital signs and report promptly S&S of infection.
- Lab tests: Baseline and periodic CBC with differential and platelet count; periodic renal function tests, and LFTs.
- Concurrent drugs: Monitor closely PT/INR with concurrent warfarin.

Patient & Family Education

- Learn about common adverse effects and measures to control or minimize when possible. Notify prescriber immediately of any distressing adverse effects.
- Fever with flu-like symptoms, rash, and GI distress are very common.

GEMTUZUMAB OZOGAMICIN

(gem-tu′zu-mab)

Mylotarg

Classification(s): ANTINEOPLASTIC, MONOCLONAL ANTIBODY
Therapeutic: ANTINEOPLASTIC
Pregnancy Category: D

USES Treatment of CD33 positive acute myeloid leukemia (AML) in first relapse in patients at least 60 y old.

INDICATION & DOSAGE

Acute Myeloid Leukemia (AML)

Adult: 9 mg/m^2 infused over 2 h, repeat in 14 days

SOLUTION PREPARATION

- *Vial Reconstitution:* Add 5 mL of sterile water for injection to each vial to yield 1 mg/mL. Gently swirl to dissolve. **Must be** further diluted for infusion.
- *Further Dilution of Reconstituted Solution:* Just prior to administration, add the required dose to 100 mL of NS. Cover the IV bag with a UV protectant cover.

Common adverse effects in *italic*, life-threatening effects <u>underlined</u>: generic names in **bold**; classifications in SMALL CAPS; ◆ Canadian drug name; ◌ Prototype drug

STORAGE

Store unopened vials refrigerated at 2°–8° C (36°–46° F). Store reconstituted drug refrigerated at 2°–8° C (36°–46° F) for up to 8 h. Protect vials and solution from light.

ADMINISTRATION

- **Continuous Infusion: DO NOT** give a bolus dose. Infuse over 2 h through a separate IV line with a nonpyrogenic low-protein-binding 0.2 to 1.2 micron filter.
- Acetaminophen 650 mg orally and diphenhydramine 25–50 mg IV are normally given prior to infusion to control adverse effects.

INCOMPATIBILITIES Solution/additive & Y-site: Do not mix with other drugs.

ACTION & *THERAPEUTIC EFFECT* Chemotherapeutic agent composed of recombinant IgG_4 antibodies that bind specifically to CD33 antigens expressed on the surface of leukemic myeloblasts and immature normal cells of myelomonocytic origin. *Cytotoxic to the CD33-positive human leukemia cells in the bone marrow. CD33 antigens are found on the surface of leukemic cells.*

CONTRAINDICATIONS Hypersensitivity to gemtuzumab or anti-CD33 antibody therapy, murine protein hypersensitivity; systemic infections; pregnancy (category D), lactation.

CAUTIOUS USE Hepatic impairment including jaundice; renal dysfunction; pulmonary disease; moderate or severe thrombocytopenia or neutropenia; history of asthma or allergies; concurrent administration with antiplatelet agents or anticoagulants.

ADVERSE EFFECTS (≥1%) **Body as a Whole:** Severe hypersensitivity *anaphylaxis, chills, fever, asthenia, infection, sepsis.* **CV:** *Hypotension,* hypertension, tachycardia. **GI:** *Nausea, vomiting, mucositis, abdominal pain, anorexia, constipation, diarrhea, stomatitis.* **Hematologic:** <u>*Neutropenia, thrombocytopenia, anemia,*</u> *bleeding,* epistaxis, cerebral hemorrhage, hematuria, ecchymosis. **Metabolic:** Hyperglycemia, *hyperbilirubinemia,* abnormal AST, ALT, hypokalemia, hypomagnesemia, increased lactic dehydrogenase. **Musculoskeletal:** Arthralgia. **CNS:** *Headache,* depression, dizziness, *insomnia.* **Respiratory:** Hypoxia, *dyspnea, cough,* pharyngitis, rhinitis, pneumonia, <u>*fatal pulmonary events*</u>. **Skin:** *Rash, herpes simplex, local reactions from infusion, peripheral edema, petechiae.*

DRUG INTERACTIONS No clinically significant interactions established.

PHARMACOKINETICS Metabolism: Hydrolyzed in liver to calicheamicin. **Half-Life:** 45–100 h.

NURSING IMPLICATIONS

Assessment & Drug Effects

- Monitor for S&S of postinfusion syndrome: Fever, chills, and rigors which occur 2–4 h after initiation of infusion; hypotension and dyspnea which may occur during first 24 h after infusion.
- Monitor vital signs during and for at least 2 h after infusion.

Common adverse effects in *italic*, life-threatening effects <u>underlined</u>: generic names in **bold**; classifications in SMALL CAPS; ♣ Canadian drug name; ⊙ Prototype drug

333

- Lab tests: Monitor CBC with differential, platelet count, lymphoblast smears at least weekly; periodic LFTs and routine blood chemistry.

Patient & Family Education

- Avoid exposure to infections and report promptly S&S of infection (e.g., chills, fever, sore throat, lower back or side pain).
- Report unusual bleeding or bruising, black tarry stools, or pinpoint red spots on skin to prescriber immediately.
- Avoid immunizations unless approved by prescriber; avoid contact with anyone who has received oral polio virus vaccine.
- Avoid situations that could result in injury during periods of bone marrow suppression.

G

GENTAMICIN SULFATE ℗

(jen-ta-mye'sin)

Classification(s): ANTIBIOTIC, AMINOGLYCOSIDE
Therapeutic: ANTIBACTERIAL
Pregnancy Category: D

USES Treatment of serious infections of GI, respiratory, and urinary tracts, CNS, bone, skin, and soft tissue (including burns) when other less toxic antimicrobial agents are ineffective or are contraindicated. Has been used in combination with other antibiotics.

UNLABELED USES Prophylaxis of bacterial endocarditis in patients undergoing operative procedures or instrumentation.

INDICATION & DOSAGE

Moderate to Severe Infection

Adult: 1–2 mg/kg loading dose followed by 3–5 mg/kg/day in 3 divided doses
Child: 6–7.5 mg/kg/day in 3 divided doses
Neonate: 2.5 mg/kg/day

Prophylaxis of Bacterial Endocarditis

Adult: 1.5 mg/kg 30 min before procedure; may repeat in 8 h
Child (under 27 kg): 2 mg/kg 30 min before procedure; may repeat in 8 h

Obesity

Dose based on IBW. In morbid obesity use IBW + 0.4 × (TBW − IBW).

Renal Impairment Dosage Adjustment

Reduce dose or extend dosing interval.

SOLUTION PREPARATION

Dilute a single dose with 50–200 mL of D5W or NS. For pediatric patients, amount of infusion fluid may be proportionately smaller

Common adverse effects in *italic*, life-threatening effects <u>underlined</u>: generic names in **bold**; classifications in SMALL CAPS; ♣ Canadian drug name; ℗ Prototype drug

depending on patient's needs but should be sufficient to be infused over the same time period as for adults.

STORAGE
Store all gentamicin solutions between 2°–30° C (36°–86° F) unless otherwise directed by manufacturer.

ADMINISTRATION
Intermittent Infusion: Infuse over 30 min–1 h. May extend infusion time to 2 h in children.

INCOMPATIBILITIES Solution/additive: Fat emulsion, TPN, amphotericin B, ampicillin, carbenicillin, CEPHALOSPORINS, cytarabine, heparin, ticarcillin. **Y-site:** Allopurinol, amphotericin B cholesteryl complex, azithromycin, furosemide, heparin, hetastarch, idarubicin, indomethacin, iodipamide, propofol, warfarin.

G

ACTION & *THERAPEUTIC EFFECT* Broad-spectrum aminoglycoside antibiotic that binds irreversibly to 30S subunit of bacterial ribosomes, blocking a viral step in protein synthesis, and attachment of RNA molecules to bacterial ribosomes resulting in cell death. *Active against a wide variety of aerobic gram-negative, but not anaerobic gram-negative bacteria. Also effective against certain gram-positive organisms, particularly penicillin-sensitive and some methicillin-resistant strains of* Staphylococcus aureus *(MRSA).*

CONTRAINDICATIONS History of hypersensitivity to or toxic reaction with any aminoglycoside antibiotic; concomitant use of other nephrotoxic drugs; severe dehydration; concurrent use of potent diuretics; pregnancy (category D).
CAUTIOUS USE Impaired renal function; history of eighth cranial (acoustic) nerve impairment; preexisting vertigo, dizziness, or tinnitus; dehydration, fever; use in older adults, renal impairment, dehydration; Fabry disease; obesity; neuromuscular disorders: Myasthenia gravis, parkinsonian syndrome; hypocalcemia; heart failure; topical applications to widespread areas; premature infants, neonates, and infants.

ADVERSE EFFECTS (≥1%) **Special Senses:** Ototoxicity (vestibular disturbances, impaired hearing), optic neuritis. **CNS:** Neuromuscular blockade: Skeletal muscle weakness, apnea, respiratory paralysis (high doses); arachnoiditis (intrathecal use). **CV:** Hypotension or hypertension. **GI:** Nausea, vomiting, transient increase in AST, ALT, and serum LDH and bilirubin; hepatomegaly, splenomegaly. **Hematologic:** Increased or decreased reticulocyte counts; granulocytopenia, thrombocytopenia (fever, bleeding tendency), thrombocytopenic purpura, anemia. **Body as a Whole:** Hypersensitivity (rash, pruritus, urticaria, exfoliative dermatitis, eosinophilia, burning sensation of skin, drug fever, joint pains, laryngeal edema, anaphylaxis). **Urogenital:** Nephrotoxicity: Proteinuria, tubular necrosis, cells or casts in urine, hematuria, rising BUN, nonprotein nitrogen, serum creatinine; *decreased creatinine clearance.* **Other:** Local irritation and pain following IM use; thrombophlebitis, abscess, superinfections, syndrome of hypocalcemia (tetany, weakness, hypokalemia, hypomagnesemia). **Topical and Ophthalmic:** Photosensitivity, sensitization, erythema, pruritus; burning, stinging, and lacrimation (ophthalmic formulation).

Common adverse effects in *italic*, life-threatening effects underlined: generic names in **bold**; classifications in SMALL CAPS; ♣ Canadian drug name; ⊘ Prototype drug

335

GENTAMICIN SULFATE

DRUG INTERACTIONS Amphotericin B, capreomycin, cisplatin, methoxyflurane, polymyxin B, vancomycin, ethacrynic acid and furosemide increase risk of nephrotoxicity. GENERAL ANESTHETICS and NEUROMUSCU-
LAR BLOCKING AGENTS (e.g., **succinylcholine**) potentiate neuromuscular blockade. **Indomethacin** may increase gentamicin levels in neonates.

PHARMACOKINETICS Distribution: Widely distributed in body fluids, including ascitic, peritoneal, pleural, synovial, and abscess fluids; poor CNS
penetration; concentrates in kidney and inner ear; crosses placenta.
Metabolism: Not metabolized. **Elimination:** Unchanged in urine; small
amounts accumulate in kidney and are eliminated over 10–20 days; small
amount excreted in breast milk. **Half-Life:** 2–4 h.

NURSING IMPLICATIONS
Assessment & Drug Effects
- Prior to initiating therapy: Baseline C&S tests (start drug pending results)
  and kidney function tests.
- Lab tests: Frequent creatinine clearance and serum drug concentrations
  particularly in those receiving high doses or therapy beyond 10 days, in
  infants and older adults, and those with impaired renal function, fever,
  extensive burns, edema, or obesity.
- Dosages are generally adjusted to maintain peak serum gentamicin concentrations of 4–10 mcg/mL, and trough concentrations of 1–2 mcg/mL.
  Peak concentrations above 12 mcg/mL and trough concentrations above
  2 mcg/mL are associated with toxicity.
- Draw blood for peak serum gentamicin levels 30 min after completion of
  a 30–60 min IV infusion. Draw blood for trough levels just before the
  next dose.
- Monitor I&O. Keep patient well hydrated to prevent chemical irritation of
  renal tubules. Report oliguria, unusual appearance of urine, change in
  I&O ratio or pattern, and presence of edema.
- Check baseline weight and vital signs; determine vestibular and auditory
  function before therapy and at regular intervals. Check vestibular and auditory function again 3–4 wk after drug is discontinued (the time that
  deafness is most likely to occur).
- Report promptly S&S of damage to the eighth cranial nerve. Ototoxic
  effect (see Appendix C) is greatest on the vestibular branch (symptoms:
  Headache, dizziness or vertigo, nausea and vomiting with motion,
  ataxia, nystagmus); however, damage to the auditory branch (tinnitus,
  roaring noises, sensation of fullness in ears, hearing impairment) may
  also occur.
- Watch for S&S of opportunistic infections: Diarrhea, anogenital itching,
  vaginal discharge, stomatitis, glossitis.

Patient & Family Education
- Report promptly any of the following: Hearing impairment, feeling of
  fullness in the ears, dizziness, nausea and vomiting with motion, loss of
  balance.
- Report promptly potential signs of superinfection: Diarrhea, anogenital
  itching, vaginal discharge, sore mouth or tongue.

Common adverse effects in *italic*, life-threatening effects underlined: generic names
in **bold**; classifications in SMALL CAPS; ♣ Canadian drug name; ⊕ Prototype drug

GLUCAGON
(gloo'ka-gon)
GlucaGen
Classification(s): HORMONE; ANTIHYPOGLYCEMIC
Therapeutic: ANTIHYPOGLYCEMIC; DIAGNOSTIC AGENT
Pregnancy Category: B

USES Emergency treatment of severe hypoglycemic reactions in diabetic patients who are unconscious or unable to swallow food or liquids and in psychiatric patients receiving insulin shock therapy. Also radiologic studies of GI tract to relax smooth muscle and thereby allow finer detail of mucosa; to diagnose insulinoma.

UNLABELED USES GI disturbances associated with spasm, cardiovascular emergencies, and to overcome cardiotoxic effects of beta blockers, quinidine, tricyclic antidepressants; as an aid in abdominal imaging.

INDICATION & DOSAGE

Hypoglycemia
Adult: 1 mg, may repeat q5–20min if no response for 1–2 more doses
Child (Over 20 kg): 1 mg; *(under 20 kg):* 20–30 mcg/kg (max: 1 mg/dose); may repeat q5–20min if no response for 1–2 more doses

Insulin Shock Therapy
Adult: 1 mg usually 1 h after coma develops; may repeat in 25 min if no response

Diagnostic Aid to Relax Stomach or Upper GI Tract
Adult: 0.25–2 mg before procedure

Diagnostic Aid for Examination of Colon
Adult: 2 mg before procedure

SOLUTION PREPARATION
Vial Reconstitution: Dilute 1 unit (1 mg) of glucagon with 1 mL of diluent supplied by manufacturer. Roll gently to dissolve. Use immediately after reconstitution of dry powder. Discard any unused portion.

STORAGE
Store unreconstituted vials and diluent at 20°–25° C (68°–77° F).

ADMINISTRATION
Direct IV Injection: Give 1 unit or fraction thereof over 1 min. Do not use a concentration less than 1 unit/mL. May be given through a Y-site of infusion tubing containing D5W (not NS).

INCOMPATIBILITIES Solution/additive: Sodium chloride.

Common adverse effects in *italic*, life-threatening effects underlined: generic names in **bold**; classifications in SMALL CAPS; ♣ Canadian drug name; ◑ Prototype drug

337

ACTION & *THERAPEUTIC EFFECT* Recombinant glucagon identical to natural glucagon produced by alpha cells of islets of Langerhans. Stimulates uptake of amino acids and their conversion to glucose precursors. Promotes lipolysis in liver and adipose tissue with release of free fatty acid and glycerol, which further stimulates ketogenesis and hepatic gluconeogenesis. *Increases blood glucose secondary to gluconeogenesis. Action in hypoglycemia relies on presence of adequate liver glycogen stores.*

CONTRAINDICATIONS Hypersensitivity to glucagon or protein compounds; depleted glycogen stores in liver; insulinoma; pheochromocytoma.
CAUTIOUS USE Cardiac disease; CAD; pregnancy (category B), lactation.

ADVERSE EFFECTS (≥1%) **GI:** Nausea and vomiting. **Body as a Whole:** Hypersensitivity reactions. **Skin:** Stevens-Johnson syndrome (erythema multiforme). **Metabolic:** Hyperglycemia, hypokalemia.

DRUG INTERACTIONS May enhance effect of ORAL ANTICOAGULANTS.

PHARMACOKINETICS Peak: 30 min. **Duration:** 1–1.5 h. **Metabolism:** Metabolized in liver, plasma, and kidneys. **Half-Life:** 3–10 min.

NURSING IMPLICATIONS
Assessment & Drug Effects
▪ Be prepared to give IV glucose if patient fails to respond to glucagon. Notify prescriber immediately.
▪ Patient usually awakens from hypoglycemic coma 5–20 min after glucagon injection. Give PO carbohydrate as soon as possible after patient regains consciousness.
▪ After recovery from hypoglycemic reaction, symptoms such as headache, nausea, and weakness may persist.

Patient & Family Education
▪ Prescriber may request that a responsible family member be taught how to administer glucagon SC or IM for patients with frequent or severe hypoglycemic reactions. Notify prescriber promptly whenever a hypoglycemic reaction occurs so the reason for the reaction can be determined.

GLYCOPYRROLATE
(glye-koe-pye′roe-late)
Robinul
Classification(s): ANTICHOLINERGIC
Therapeutic: GI ANTISPASMODIC; ANTISECRETORY
Prototype: Atropine
Pregnancy Category: B

USES Adjunctive management of peptic ulcer and other GI disorders associated with hyperacidity, hypermotility, and spasm. Also used parenterally as preanesthetic and intraoperative medication and to reverse neuromuscular blockade.

INDICATION & DOSAGE

Peptic Ulcer

Adult: 0.1–0.2 mg as single dose 3–4 times daily

Reversal of Neuromuscular Blockade

Adult/Child: 0.2 mg glycopyrrolate administered with 1 mg of neostigmine or 5 mg pyridostigmine

Preanesthetic

Child: 4–10 mcg/kg q3–4h

G

SOLUTION PREPARATION

No dilution is required. Administer as supplied.

STORAGE

Store at 20°–25° C (68°–77° F).

ADMINISTRATION

Direct IV Injection: Give 0.2 mg or fraction thereof over 1–2 min. May be given through the Y-site of infusion tubing containing D5W, NS, D5/1/2NS, or LR.

INCOMPATIBILITIES Solution/additive: Chloramphenicol, dexamethasone, diazepam, dimenhydrinate, methohexital, methylprednisolone, pentazocine, pentobarbital, secobarbital, sodium bicarbonate, thiopental. Y-site: Propofol.

ACTION & *THERAPEUTIC EFFECT* Synthetic anticholinergic (antimuscarinic) compound with pharmacologic effects similar to those of atropine. Inhibits muscarinic action of acetylcholine on autonomic neuroeffector sites innervated by postganglionic cholinergic nerves. *Inhibits motility of GI tract and genitourinary tract; decreases volume of gastric and pancreatic secretions, saliva, and perspiration.*

CONTRAINDICATIONS Glaucoma; asthma; prostatic hypertrophy, obstructive uropathy; obstructive lesions or atony of GI tract; achalasia; severe ulcerative colitis; myasthenia gravis; BPH, urinary tract obstruction; during cyclopropane anesthesia; children less than 12 y (except parenteral use in conjunction with anesthesia); neonates less than 1 mo old.

CAUTIOUS USE Autonomic neuropathy; hepatic or renal disease; pregnancy (category B), lactation.

ADVERSE EFFECTS (≥1%) **Body as a Whole:** *Decreased sweating,* weakness. **CNS:** Dizziness, drowsiness, overdosage (<u>neuromuscular blockade</u> with curare-like action leading to muscle weakness and <u>paralysis</u> is possible). **CV:** Palpitation, tachycardia. **GI:** *Xerostomia,* constipation. **GU:** *Urinary hesitancy or retention.* **Special Senses:** Blurred vision, mydriasis.

DRUG INTERACTIONS Amantadine, ANTIHISTAMINES, TRICYCLIC ANTIDEPRESSANTS, **quinidine, disopyramide, procainamide** compound anticholinergic effects; decreases **levodopa** effects; **methotrimeprazine** may pre-

Common adverse effects in *italic*, life-threatening effects <u>underlined</u>: generic names in **bold**; classifications in SMALL CAPS; ♣ Canadian drug name; ❍ Prototype drug

339

cipitate extrapyramidal effects; decreases antipsychotic effects (decreased absorption) of PHENOTHIAZINES.

PHARMACOKINETICS Onset: 1 min. **Distribution:** Crosses placenta. **Metabolism:** Minimally metabolized in liver. **Elimination:** 85% excreted in urine. **Half-Life:** 30–70 min (adult), 20–99 min (child), 20–120 min (infant).

NURSING IMPLICATIONS

Assessment & Drug Effects

- Incidence and severity of adverse effects are generally dose related.
- Monitor I&O ratio and pattern particularly in older adults. Watch for urinary hesitancy and retention.
- Monitor vital signs and report any changes in heart rate or rhythm.

Patient & Family Education

- Avoid high environmental temperatures (heat prostration can occur because of decreased sweating).
- Do not drive or engage in other potentially hazardous activities requiring mental alertness until response to drug is known.
- Use good oral hygiene, rinse mouth with water frequently, and use a saliva substitute to lessen effects of dry mouth.

GRANISETRON

(gran'i-se-tron)

Kytril

Classification(s): ANTIEMETIC, 5-HT$_3$ RECEPTOR ANTAGONIST
Therapeutic: ANTIEMETIC
Prototype: Ondansetron
Pregnancy Category: B

USES Prevention of nausea and vomiting associated with initial and repeat courses of emetogenic cancer therapy, including high-dose cisplatin; postoperative nausea and vomiting.

INDICATION & DOSAGE

Chemotherapy-Related Nausea and Vomiting

Adult/Child (over 2 y): 10 mcg/kg beginning at least 30 min before initiation of chemotherapy (up to 40 mcg/kg per dose has been used)

Postoperative Nausea and Vomiting

Adult: 1 mg before anesthesia induction or before reversal of anesthesia

SOLUTION PREPARATION

May be given undiluted [direct IV] or diluted in NS or D5W to a total volume of 20–50 mL for infusion. Prepare infusion at time of administration; do not mix in solution with other drugs.

Common adverse effects in *italic*, life-threatening effects <u>underlined</u>: generic names in **bold**; classifications in SMALL CAPS; ♣ Canadian drug name; ☻ Prototype drug

STORAGE
Store at 15°–30° C (59°–86° F) for 24 h after dilution under normal lighting conditions.

ADMINISTRATION
- **Direct IV Injection:** Give a single dose over 30 sec.
- **IV Infusion:** Infuse diluted drug over 5 min or longer; complete infusion 20–30 min prior to initiation of chemotherapy.

INCOMPATIBILITIES Y-site: Amphotericin B, doxorubicin.

ACTION & *THERAPEUTIC EFFECT* Granisetron is a selective serotonin (5-HT₃) receptor antagonist. Serotonin receptors of the 5-HT₃ type are located centrally in the chemoreceptor trigger zone, and peripherally on the vagal nerve terminals. Serotonin is released from the wall of the small intestine, stimulates the vagal afferent neurons through the serotonin (5-HT₃) receptors, and initiates the vomiting reflex. *Effective selective serotonin (5-HT₃) receptor antagonist for prevention of nausea and vomiting associated with cancer chemotherapy.*

CONTRAINDICATIONS Hypersensitivity to granisetron, benzyl alcohol; GI obstruction; neonates, children less than 2 y.
CAUTIOUS USE Hypersensitivity to ondansetron or similar drugs; liver disease; pregnancy (category B), lactation.

ADVERSE EFFECTS (≥1%) **CNS:** *Headache,* dizziness, somnolence, insomnia, labile mood, anxiety, fatigue. **GI:** Constipation, diarrhea, elevated liver function tests.

DRUG INTERACTIONS Ketoconazole may inhibit metabolism.

PHARMACOKINETICS Duration: Approximately 24 h. **Distribution:** Widely distributed in body tissues. **Metabolism:** Appears to be metabolized in liver. **Elimination:** Excreted in urine. **Half-Life:** 10–11 h in cancer patients, 4–5 h in healthy volunteers.

NURSING IMPLICATIONS

Assessment & Drug Effects
- Monitor the frequency and severity of nausea and vomiting.
- Lab tests: Monitor LFTs; elevated AST and ALT values usually normalize within 2 wk of last dose.
- Assess for headache, which usually responds to nonnarcotic analgesics.

Patient & Family Education
- Headache requiring an analgesic for relief and constipation are common side effects of this drug. Consult prescriber if assistance is needed in managing these adverse effects.

HEMIN
(hee′min)
Panhematin

Common adverse effects in *italic,* life-threatening effects <u>underlined</u>: generic names in **bold**; classifications in SMALL CAPS; ♣ Canadian drug name; ◐ Prototype drug

341

HEMIN

Classification(s): ENZYME INHIBITOR
Therapeutic: PORPHYRIN INHIBITOR
Pregnancy Category: C

USES Recurrent attacks of acute intermittent porphyria (AIP) after an appropriate period of alternate therapy has been tried (i.e., glucose 400 g/day for 1–2 days).

INDICATION & DOSAGE

Acute Intermittent Porphyria

Adult/Adolescent (over 16 y): 1–4 mg/kg/day administered over 10–15 min for 3–14 days; do not repeat dose earlier than q12h (max: 6 mg/kg in 24 h)

SOLUTION PREPARATION

Vial Reconstitution: Immediately before use add 43 mL sterile water for injection to the vial to yield 7 mg/mL. Shake well for 2–3 min to dissolve all particles. Solution will not be transparent. Terminal filtration through a sterile 0.45 micron or smaller filter is recommended.

STORAGE

Refrigerate lyophilized powder at 2°–8° C (36°–46° F) until time of use. Discard any unused reconstituted drug.

ADMINISTRATION

- **IV Infusion:** Infuse a single dose over 10–15 min.
- Administer via a large arm vein or central venous catheter to reduce risk of phlebitis.

INCOMPATIBILITIES Data not available; do not mix with other drugs.

ACTION & *THERAPEUTIC EFFECT* Represses synthesis of porphyrin in liver or bone marrow by blocking production of delta-aminolevulinic acid (ALA) synthetase, an essential enzyme in the porphyrin-heme biosynthetic pathway. *Effective in ameliorating recurrent attacks of acute intermittent porphyria (AIP).*

CONTRAINDICATIONS History of hypersensitivity to hemin; porphyria cutanea tarda; anticoagulation therapy; pregnancy (category C).
CAUTIOUS USE Lactation. Safe use in children less than 16 y is not established.

ADVERSE EFFECTS (≥1%) **Body as a Whole:** *Phlebitis* (when administered into small veins). **Hematologic:** Decreased Hct, anticoagulant effect (prolonged PT, thromboplastin time, thrombocytopenia, hypofibrinogenemia). **Urogenital:** Reversible renal shutdown (with excessive doses).

DRUG INTERACTIONS Potentiates anticoagulant effects of ANTICOAGULANTS; BARBITURATES, ESTROGENS, CORTICOSTEROIDS may antagonize hemin effect.

PHARMACOKINETICS Duration: Up to 5 days in plasma. **Elimination:** Excess amounts eliminated in bile and urine.

NURSING IMPLICATIONS

Assessment & Drug Effects

- Monitor IV site for signs and symptoms of thrombophlebitis (see Appendix C).
- Lab tests: Monitor throughout therapy (decrease in these values indicates favorable clinical response): ALA, UPG (uroporphyrinogen), PBG (porphobilinogen or coproporphyrin).
- Monitor clinical effect of drug therapy by checking patient's symptoms and complaints associated with acute porphyria, which may include depression, insomnia, anxiety, disorientation, hallucinations, psychoses; dark urine, nausea, vomiting, abdominal pain, low back and leg pain, pareses (neuropathy), seizures.
- Monitor I&O and promptly report the onset of oliguria or anuria.

Patient & Family Education

- Notify prescriber of bruising, hematuria, tarry black stools, and nosebleeds.

H

HEPARIN SODIUM ⊕

(hep'a-rin)

Hepalean ♦, Heparin Sodium Lock Flush Solution, Hep-Lock
Classification(s): ANTICOAGULANT
Therapeutic: ANTICOAGULANT
Pregnancy Category: C

USES Prophylaxis and treatment of venous thrombosis, pulmonary embolism, and to prevent thromboembolic complications arising from cardiac and vascular surgery, or acute stage of MI. Also used in treatment of disseminated intravascular coagulation (DIC), atrial fibrillation with embolization, and as an anticoagulant in blood transfusions, extracorporeal circulation, and dialysis procedures.

UNLABELED USES Prophylaxis in hip and knee surgery. Heparin Sodium Lock Flush Solution is used to maintain potency of indwelling IV catheters in intermittent IV therapy or blood sampling. It is not intended for anticoagulant therapy.

INDICATION & DOSAGE

Treatment of Thromboembolism/Thrombosis

Adult: 5000 unit bolus dose, then 20,000–40,000 units infused over 24 h, dose adjusted to maintain desired aPTT
Adult: (Weight based dosing) 80 unit/kg bolus then 18 unit/kg, adjusted for aPTT
Child: 50 unit/kg bolus, 50–100 unit/kg q4h adjusted for aPTT
Child: (Weight based) 75 units/kg then 20 unit/kg/h adjusted for aPTT
Infant/Neonate: 75 units/kg then 28 unit/kg/h adjusted for aPTT

Common adverse effects in *italic*, life-threatening effects <u>underlined</u>: generic names in **bold**; classifications in SMALL CAPS; ♦ Canadian drug name; ⊕ Prototype drug

Myocardial Infarction (with thrombolytic therapy)

Adult: 60 units/kg then 12 units/kg/h (max: 1000 units/h)

Thrombosis Prophylaxis

Adult: **During cardiovascular surgery,** 150–300 units/kg; **During hemodialysis,** 2000–5000 units then 10–20 units/kg/h; **During PCI w/o abciximab,** 60–100 units/kg; **During PCI w/abciximab,** 50–70 units/kg

Open Heart Surgery

Adult: 150–400 units/kg during procedure

H

SOLUTION PREPARATION

- May be given undiluted [direct IV] or diluted in D5W, NS, or LR for infusion.
- *Intermittent Infusion:* Dilute required dose in 50–100 mL NS. Invert IV container several times to ensure adequate mixing.
- *Continuous Infusion:* Dilute required dose in 1000 mL NS. Invert IV container at least 6 times to ensure adequate mixing.

STORAGE

Store at 15°–30° C (59°–86° F). Protect from freezing.

ADMINISTRATION

- Prior to administration, check coagulation test values; if results are above the therapeutic range, notify prescriber for dosage adjustment.
- **Direct IV Injection:** Give bolus dose over 60 sec.
- **Intermittent/Continuous (preferred) Infusion:** Infuse over 4–24 h using an infusion pump.
- Do not use solutions of heparin or heparin lock-flush that contain benzyl alcohol preservative in neonates.

INCOMPATIBILITIES Solution/additive: Alteplase, amikacin, atracurium, ciprofloxacin, codeine, cytarabine, daunorubicin, dobutamine, doxorubicin, erythromycin, gentamicin, haloperidol, hyaluronidase, hydrocortisone, kanamycin, levorphanol, meperidine, methicillin, morphine, netilmicin, polymyxin B, promethazine, sodium lactate, streptomycin, tetracycline, tobramycin, vancomycin. Y-site: Alteplase, amiodarone, amphotericin B cholesteryl complex, amsacrine, ciprofloxacin, clarithromycin, dacarbazine, diazepam, dobutamine, doxorubicin, doxycycline, droperidol, ergotamine, filgrastim, gentamicin, haloperidol, idarubicin, isosorbide, levofloxacin, methotrimeprazine, mexiletine, nitroglycerin, phenytoin, polymyxin B, propafenone, tobramycin, tramadol, triflupromazine, vancomycin, vinorelbine.

ACTION & *THERAPEUTIC EFFECT* Exerts direct effect on the cascade of blood coagulation by enhancing inhibitory actions of antithrombin III (heparin cofactor) on several factors essential to normal blood clotting; it thereby blocks conversion of prothrombin to thrombin and fibrinogen to fibrin. *Inhibits formation of new clots. High molecular weight muco-*

Common adverse effects in *italic*, life-threatening effects <u>underlined</u>: generic names in **bold**; classifications in SMALL CAPS; ✦ Canadian drug name; ❂ Prototype drug

polysaccharide with rapid anticoagulant effect. Does not lyse already existing thrombi but may prevent their extension and propagation.

CONTRAINDICATIONS History of hypersensitivity to heparin (white clot syndrome); active bleeding, bleeding tendencies (hemophilia, purpura, thrombocytopenia); jaundice; ascorbic acid deficiency; inaccessible ulcerative lesions; visceral carcinoma; open wounds, extensive denudation of skin, suppurative thrombophlebitis; advanced kidney, liver, or biliary disease; active tuberculosis; bacterial endocarditis; continuous tube drainage of stomach or small intestines; threatened abortion; suspected intracranial hemorrhage; severe hypertension; recent surgery of eye, brain, or spinal cord; spinal tap; shock; pregnancy (category C), especially the last trimester. **CAUTIOUS USE** Alcoholism; history of allergy (asthma, hives, hay fever, eczema); during menstruation; immediate postpartum period; patients with indwelling catheters; older adults; use of acid-citrate-dextrose (ACD)-converted blood (may contain heparin); patients in hazardous occupations; cerebral embolism.

ADVERSE EFFECTS (≥1%) **Hematologic:** <u>Spontaneous bleeding</u>, *transient thrombocytopenia,* hypofibrinogenemia, "white clot syndrome." **Body as a Whole:** Fever, chills, urticaria, pruritus, skin rashes, itching and burning sensations of feet, numbness and tingling of hands and feet, elevated BP, headache, nasal congestion, lacrimation, conjunctivitis, chest pains, arthralgia, <u>bronchospasm, anaphylactoid reactions</u>. **Endocrine:** Osteoporosis, hypoaldosteronism, suppressed renal function, hyperkalemia; rebound hyperlipidemia (following termination of heparin therapy). **GI:** Increased AST, ALT. **Urogenital:** Priapism (rare). **Skin:** Injection site reactions: pain, itching, ecchymoses, tissue irritation and sloughing; cyanosis and pains in arms or legs (vasospasm), reversible transient alopecia (usually around temporal area).

DIAGNOSTIC TEST INTERFERENCE Notify laboratory that patient is receiving heparin, when a test is to be performed. Possibility of false-positive rise in ***BSP*** test and in ***serum thyroxine;*** and increases in ***resin T$_3$ uptake;*** false-negative ***^{125}I fibrinogen uptake.*** Heparin prolongs ***PT.*** Valid readings may be obtained by drawing blood samples at least 4–6 h after an IV dose (but at any time during heparin infusion).

DRUG INTERACTIONS May prolong PT, which is used to monitor therapy with ORAL ANTICOAGULANTS; **aspirin,** NSAIDS increase risk of bleeding; **nitroglycerin** IV may decrease anticoagulant activity; **protamine** antagonizes effects of heparin. **Herbal: Feverfew, ginkgo, ginger, valerian** may potentiate bleeding.

PHARMACOKINETICS Duration: 2–6 h. **Distribution:** Does not cross placenta; not distributed into breast milk. **Metabolism:** Metabolized in liver and by reticuloendothelial system. **Elimination:** Excreted slowly in urine. **Half-Life:** 90 min.

NURSING IMPLICATIONS
Assessment & Drug Effects
- Note: In general, dosage is adjusted to keep aPTT between 1.5–2.5 times normal control level.

Common adverse effects in *italic*, life-threatening effects <u>underlined</u>: generic names in **bold**; classifications in SMALL CAPS; ♣ Canadian drug name; ❂ Prototype drug

345

- Lab tests: Baseline and periodic blood coagulation tests, Hct, Hgb, and RBC; aPTT after 8 h of continuous IV heparin infusion.
- Draw blood for coagulation test 30 min before each scheduled dose and approximately q4h for patients receiving continuous IV heparin during dosage adjustment period. After dosage is established, tests may be done once daily.
- Patients vary widely in their reaction to heparin; risk of hemorrhage appears greatest in women, all patients over 60 y, and patients with liver disease or renal insufficiency.
- Monitor vital signs. Report fever, drop in BP, rapid pulse, and other S&S of hemorrhage.
- Observe all needle sites daily for hematoma and signs of inflammation (swelling, heat, redness, pain).
- Antidote: Have on hand protamine sulfate (1% solution), which is a specific heparin antagonist.

Patient & Family Education

- Protect from injury and notify prescriber of pink, red, dark brown, or cloudy urine; red or dark brown vomitus; red or black stools; bleeding gums or oral mucosa; ecchymoses, hematoma, epistaxis, bloody sputum; chest pain; abdominal or lumbar pain or swelling; unusual increase in menstrual flow; pelvic pain; severe or continuous headache, faintness, or dizziness.
- Note: Menstruation may be somewhat increased and prolonged; usually, this is not a contraindication to continued therapy if bleeding is not excessive.
- Do not take aspirin or any other OTC medication without prescriber's approval.

HETASTARCH

(het′a-starch)

HES, Hespan, Hydroxyethyl Starch, Hextend

Classification(s): PLASMA EXPANDER
Therapeutic: PLASMA VOLUME EXPANDER
Prototype: Albumin
Pregnancy Category: C

USES Early fluid replacement and plasma volume expansion when whole blood is not available or when there is no time for necessary cross matching. Used to expand plasma volume during cardiopulmonary bypass and in adjunctive treatment of shock. Also used as sedimenting agent in preparation of granulocytes by leukapheresis.
UNLABELED USES As a priming fluid in pump oxygenators for perfusion during extracorporeal circulation and as a cryoprotective agent for long-term storage of whole blood.

INDICATION & DOSAGE

Plasma Volume Expansion
Adult: 500–1000 mL (max: 1500 mL/day)

Common adverse effects in *italic*, life-threatening effects underlined: generic names in **bold**; classifications in SMALL CAPS; ♣ Canadian drug name; ❶ Prototype drug

Leukapheresis

Adult: 250–700 mL infused at a constant fixed ratio of 1:8 to venous whole blood

Renal Insufficiency Dosage Adjustment

CrCl less than 10 mL/min: Use original initial dose, then reduce doses by 25–50%

SOLUTION PREPARATION

No dilution is required. Administer as supplied. Do not use if crystalline precipitate is visible.

STORAGE

Store at room temperature; avoid extremes of heat or cold. Discard partially used bags.

ADMINISTRATION

IV Infusion: Specific flow rate is ordered by prescriber. Rate may be as high as 20 mL/kg/h in acute hemorrhagic shock. Rate is usually reduced in patients with burns or septic shock.

INCOMPATIBILITIES Y-site: *In Lactated Electrolyte Injection:* **Amphotericin B, diazepam, sodium bicarbonate. Y-site:** *In Sodium Chloride 0.9%:* **Amikacin, cefoperazone, cefotaxime, cefoxitin, gentamicin, ranitidine, theophylline, tobramycin.**

ACTION & *THERAPEUTIC EFFECT* Synthetic starch closely resembling human glycogen. Acts much like albumin and dextran but is claimed to be less likely to produce anaphylaxis or to interfere with cross matching or blood typing procedures. Not a substitute for blood or plasma. *In hypovolemia, it increases arterial and venous pressures, heart rate, cardiac output, urine output, and colloidal osmotic pressure. Colloidal osmotic properties are approximately equal to those of human serum albumin.*

CONTRAINDICATIONS Severe bleeding disorders, CHF, renal failure with oliguria and anuria, treatment of shock not accompanied by hypovolemia, intracranial bleeding; pregnancy (category C). Safe use in children is not established.

CAUTIOUS USE Hepatic or renal insufficiency; pulmonary edema in the very young or older adults; patients on sodium restriction.

ADVERSE EFFECTS (≥1%) **CV:** Peripheral edema, <u>circulatory overload, heart failure.</u> **Hematologic:** With large volumes, prolongation of PT, PTT, clotting time, and bleeding time; decreased Hct, Hgb, platelets, calcium, and fibrinogen; dilution of plasma proteins, hyperbilirubinemia, increased sedimentation rate. **Body as a Whole:** Pruritus, <u>anaphylactoid reactions</u> (periorbital edema, urticaria, wheezing), vomiting, mild fever, chills, influenza-like symptoms, headache, muscle pains, submaxillary and parotid glandular swelling.

DRUG INTERACTIONS No clinically significant interactions established.

Common adverse effects in *italic*, life-threatening effects <u>underlined</u>: generic names in **bold**; classifications in SMALL CAPS; ♣ Canadian drug name; ✺ Prototype drug

347

PHARMACOKINETICS Duration: 24–36 h. **Distribution:** Remains in intravascular space. **Metabolism:** Metabolized in reticuloendothelial system. **Elimination:** Excreted in urine with some biliary excretion.

NURSING IMPLICATIONS

Assessment & Drug Effects

▪ Monitor for S&S of hypersensitivity reaction (see Appendix C).
▪ Measure and record I&O. Report oliguria or significant changes in I&O ratio.
▪ Monitor BP and vital signs and observe patient for unusual bruising or bleeding.
▪ Lab tests: Baseline and periodic WBC count with differential, platelet count, and PT & aPTT.
▪ Observe for signs of circulatory overload (see Appendix C).
▪ Report promptly an appreciable drop in Hct or if value approaches 30% by volume. Hct should not be allowed to drop below 30%.

Patient & Family Education

▪ Report promptly any of the following: Difficulty breathing, nausea, chills, headache, itching.

HYDRALAZINE HYDROCHLORIDE ⊕

(hye-dral'a-zeen)

Classification(s): VASODILATOR, NONNITRATE
Therapeutic: ANTIHYPERTENSIVE
Pregnancy Category: C

USES Also in early malignant hypertension and resistant hypertension that persists after sympathectomy.
UNLABELED USES Eclampsia.

INDICATION & DOSAGE

Hypertension

Adult: 10–20 mg q4–6h, may increase to 40 mg

SOLUTION PREPARATION

No dilution is required. Administer as supplied. Use immediately after being drawn into syringe.

STORAGE

Store at 15°–30° C (59°–86° F).

ADMINISTRATION

Direct IV Injection: Give each 10 mg or fraction thereof over 1 min.

INCOMPATIBILITIES Solution/additive: Aminophylline, ampicillin, chlorothiazide, edetate calcium disodium, ethacrynate, hydrocortisone, mephentermine, methohexital, nitroglycerin, pantopra-

zole, phenobarbital, verapamil, D5W, dextrose 10% in Ringer's injection. **Y-site:** Aminophylline, ampicillin, diazoxide, furosemide.

ACTION & *THERAPEUTIC EFFECT* Reduces BP mainly by direct effect on vascular smooth muscles of arterial-resistance vessels, resulting in vasodilation. Hypotensive effect may be limited by sympathetic reflexes that increase heart rate, stroke volume, and cardiac output. *Reduces BP with diastolic response often being greater than systolic response. Vasodilation reduces peripheral resistance and substantially improves cardiac output as well as renal and cerebral blood flow.*

CONTRAINDICATIONS Monotherapy in CHF; mitral valvular rheumatic heart disease, MI, tachycardia. Safe use during pregnancy (category C) not established.

CAUTIOUS USE Coronary artery disease; cerebrovascular accident; SLE; advanced renal impairment (CrCl less than 10 mL/min), use with MAO inhibitors; older adults.

ADVERSE EFFECTS (≥1%) **Body as a Whole:** Hypersensitivity (rash, urticaria, pruritus, fever, chills, arthralgia, eosinophilia, cholangitis, hepatitis, obstructive jaundice). **CNS:** *Headache,* dizziness, tremors. **CV:** *Palpitation,* angina, *tachycardia,* flushing, paradoxical pressor response. **Overdose:** Arrhythmia, shock. **Special Senses:** Lacrimation, conjunctivitis. **GI:** Anorexia, nausea, vomiting, diarrhea, constipation, abdominal pain, paralytic ileus. **Urogenital:** Difficulty in urination, glomerulonephritis. **Hematologic:** Decreased hematocrit and hemoglobin, anemia, agranulocytosis (rare). **Other:** Nasal congestion, muscle cramps, SLE-like syndrome, fixed drug eruption, edema.

DIAGNOSTIC TEST INTERFERENCE Positive ***direct Coombs' tests*** in patients with hydralazine-induced SLE. Hydralazine interferes with ***urinary 17-OHCS*** determinations *(**modified Glenn-Nelson technique**).*

DRUG INTERACTIONS Other ANTIHYPERTENSIVE AGENTS increase hypotensive effects.

PHARMACOKINETICS Peak: 2 h. **Duration:** 2–6 h. **Distribution:** Crosses placenta; distributed into breast milk. **Metabolism:** Metabolized in liver. **Elimination:** 90% rapidly excreted in urine; 10% excreted in feces. **Half-Life:** 2–8 h.

NURSING IMPLICATIONS

Assessment & Drug Effects

- Monitor BP and HR closely. Check every 5 min until it is stabilized at desired level, then every 15 min thereafter throughout hypertensive crisis.
- Lab tests: Baseline antinuclear antibody titer before initiation of therapy and periodically during prolonged therapy; baseline and periodic BUN, creatinine clearance, uric acid, serum potassium, and blood glucose.
- Monitor for S&S of SLE, especially with prolonged therapy.
- Monitor I&O especially in those with renal dysfunction.
- Monitor weight, check for edema, and report weight gain to prescriber.

Patient & Family Education

- Make position changes slowly and avoid standing still, hot baths/showers, strenuous exercise, and excessive alcohol intake.

Common adverse effects in *italic*, life-threatening effects underlined: generic names in **bold**, classifications in SMALL CAPS; ♣ Canadian drug name; ❶ Prototype drug

349

• Do not drive or engage in other potentially hazardous activities until response to drug is known.

HYDROCORTISONE SODIUM SUCCINATE ℗

(hy-dro-cor'ti-sone so-di'um suc'ci-nate)

A-Hydrocort, Solu-Cortef

Classification(s): ADRENAL CORTICOSTEROID
Therapeutic: HORMONE REPLACEMENT
Pregnancy Category: C

USES Replacement therapy in adrenocortical insufficiency. Use as antiinflammatory or immunosuppressive agent largely replaced by synthetic glucocorticoids that have minimal mineralocorticoid activity.

INDICATION & DOSAGE

Adrenal Insufficiency

Adult: 100–500 mg/day, dose may be repeated
Child: 186–280 mcg/kg/day in divided doses

SOLUTION PREPARATION

May be given undiluted direct IV (preferred) or diluted for infusion to 1 mg/mL or less with 100–1000 mL of D5W, NS, or D5NS.

STORAGE

Administer solutions diluted for IV infusion within 24 h.

ADMINISTRATION

• **Direct IV Injection:** Give bolus dose at a rate of 500 mg or fraction thereof over 1 min.
• **Intermittent Infusion:** Infuse over 10 min.

INCOMPATIBILITIES Solution/additive: Amobarbital, ampicillin, bleomycin, colistimethate, dimenhydrinate, doxorubicin, ephedrine, heparin, hydralazine, kanamycin, metaraminol, nafcillin, pentobarbital, phenobarbital, prochlorperazine, promethazine, secobarbital, tetracycline. Y-site: Ciprofloxacin, diazepam, idarubicin, lansoprazole, midazolam, phenytoin, promethazine, sargramostim.

ACTION & *THERAPEUTIC EFFECT* Short-acting synthetic steroid with both glucocorticoid and mineralocorticoid properties that affect nearly all systems of the body. **Antiinflammatory (glucocorticoid) action:** Stabilizes leukocyte lysosomal membranes; inhibits phagocytosis and release of allergic substances; suppresses fibroblast formation and collagen deposition; reduces capillary dilation and permeability; and increases responsiveness of cardiovascular system to circulating catecholamines. **Immunosuppressive action:** Modifies immune response to various stimuli; reduces antibody titers; and suppresses cell-mediated hypersensitivity reactions. **Min-**

eralocorticoid action: Promotes sodium retention, but under certain circumstances (e.g., sodium loading), enhances sodium excretion; promotes potassium excretion; and increases glomerular filtration rate (GFR). **Metabolic action:** Promotes hepatic gluconeogenesis, protein catabolism, redistribution of body fat, and lipolysis. *Has antiinflammatory, immunosuppressive, and metabolic functions in the body.*

CONTRAINDICATIONS Hypersensitivity to glucocorticoids; idiopathic thrombocytopenic purpura (ITP); psychoses; acute glomerulonephritis; viral or bacterial diseases of skin; infections not controlled by antibiotics; active or latent amebiasis; hypercorticism (Cushing's syndrome); smallpox vaccination or other immunologic procedures; acne; pregnancy (category C); child less than 1 y.

CAUTIOUS USE Diabetes mellitus; chronic, active hepatitis; positive for hepatitis B surface antigen; hyperlipidemia; cirrhosis; stromal herpes simplex; glaucoma, tuberculosis of eye; osteoporosis; convulsive disorders; hypothyroidism; diverticulitis; nonspecific ulcerative colitis; fresh intestinal anastomoses; active or latent peptic ulcer; gastritis; esophagitis; thromboembolic disorders; CHF; metastatic carcinoma; hypertension; renal insufficiency; history of allergies; active or arrested tuberculosis; systemic fungal infection; myasthenia gravis; lactation; children.

ADVERSE EFFECTS (≥1%) **Body as a Whole:** Hypersensitivity or <u>anaphylactoid reactions; aggravation or masking of infections</u>; malaise; weight gain, obesity; urogenital urinary frequency and urgency, enuresis increased or decreased motility and number of sperm. **CNS:** Vertigo, headache, nystagmus, ataxia (rare), increased intracranial pressure with papilledema (usually after discontinuation of medication), mental disturbances, aggravation of preexisting psychiatric conditions, insomnia, anxiety, mental confusion, depression. **CV:** Syncopal episodes, thrombophlebitis, thromboembolism or fat embolism, palpitation, tachycardia, necrotizing angiitis, CHF, hypertension edema. **Endocrine:** Suppressed linear growth in children, decreased glucose tolerance, hyperglycemia, manifestations of latent diabetes mellitus, hypocorticism, amenorrhea and other menstrual difficulties, moon facies. **GI:** Cramping, bleeding. **Special Senses:** Posterior subcapsular cataracts (especially in children), glaucoma, exophthalmos, increased intraocular pressure with optic nerve damage, perforation of the globe, fungal infection of the cornea, decreased or blurred vision. **Metabolic:** Hypocalcemia, *sodium* and *fluid retention,* hypokalemia and hypokalemic alkalosis, decreased serum concentration of vitamins A and C, hyperglycemia, hypernatremia. **GI:** *Nausea,* increased appetite, ulcerative esophagitis, pancreatitis, abdominal distention, peptic ulcer with perforation and hemorrhage, melena. **Hematologic:** Thrombocytopenia, polycythemia, ecchymoses. **Musculoskeletal:** Osteoporosis, compression fractures, muscle wasting and weakness, tendon rupture, aseptic necrosis of femoral and humeral heads. **Skin:** Skin thinning and atrophy, *acne, impaired wound healing,* petechiae, ecchymosis, easy bruising, suppression of skin test reaction, hypopigmentation or hyperpigmentation, hirsutism, acneiform eruptions, subcutaneous fat atrophy; allergic dermatitis, urticaria, angioneurotic edema, increased sweating. With parenteral therapy at IV site: pain, irritation, necrosis, atrophy, ster-

Common adverse effects in *italic*, life-threatening effects <u>underlined</u>; generic names in **bold**; classifications in SMALL CAPS; ♣ Canadian drug name; ❂ Prototype drug

351

ile abscess; Charcot-like arthropathy following intraarticular use; burning and tingling in perineal area (after IV injection).

DIAGNOSTIC TEST INTERFERENCE Hydrocortisone (corticosteroids) may increase serum *cholesterol, blood glucose, serum sodium, uric acid* (in acute leukemia) and *calcium* (in bone metastasis). It may decrease *serum calcium, potassium, PBI, thyroxin (T_4), triiodothyronine (T_3)* and *reduce thyroid I 131* uptake. It increases *urine glucose* level and *calcium* excretion; decreases *urine 17-OHCS* and *17-KS* levels. May produce false-negative results with *nitroblue tetrazolium test* for systemic bacterial infection and may suppress reactions to skin tests.

DRUG INTERACTIONS BARBITURATES, **phenytoin, rifampin** may increase hepatic metabolism, thus decreasing cortisone levels; ESTROGENS potentiate the effects of hydrocortisone; NSAIDS compound ulcerogenic effects; **cholestyramine, colestipol** decrease hydrocortisone absorption; DIURETICS, **amphotericin B** exacerbate hypokalemia; ANTICHOLINESTERASE AGENTS (e.g., **neostigmine**) may produce severe weakness; immune response to VACCINES and TOXOIDS may be decreased.

PHARMACOKINETICS Peak: 1 h. **Distribution:** Distributed primarily to muscles, liver, skin, intestines, kidneys; crosses placenta. **Metabolism:** Hepatically metabolized. **Elimination:** HPA suppression 8–12 h; metabolites excreted in urine; excreted in breast milk. **Half-Life:** 1.5–2 h.

NURSING IMPLICATIONS

Assessment & Drug Effects

- Establish baseline and continuing data on BP, weight, fluid and electrolyte balance, and blood glucose.
- Lab tests: Periodic serum electrolytes, blood glucose, Hct and Hgb, platelet count, and WBC with differential.
- Monitor for adverse effects. Older adults and patients with low serum albumin are especially susceptible to adverse effects.
- Be alert to signs of hypocalcemia (see Appendix C).
- Monitor for and report changes in mood and behavior, emotional instability, or psychomotor activity, especially with long-term therapy.
- Be alert to possibility of masked infection and delayed healing (antiinflammatory and immunosuppressive actions).
- Monitor diabetics for loss of glycemic control.

Patient & Family Education

- Avoid alcohol and caffeine; may contribute to steroid-ulcer development in long-term therapy. Do not ignore dyspepsia with hyperacidity. Report symptoms to prescriber and do not self-medicate to find relief.
- Do not use aspirin or other OTC drugs unless prescribed specifically by the prescriber.
- Report promptly slow healing, any vague feeling of being sick, or return to pretreatment symptoms.
- Carry medical identification at all times. It needs to indicate medical diagnosis, drug therapy, and name of prescriber.

HYDROMORPHONE HYDROCHLORIDE

(hye-droe-mor'fone)

Dilaudid, Dilaudid-HP

Classification(s): ANALGESIC; NARCOTIC (OPIATE) AGONIST
Therapeutic: NARCOTIC ANALGESIC
Prototype: Morphine
Pregnancy Category: C   **Controlled Substance:** Schedule II

USES Relief of moderate to severe pain.

INDICATION & DOSAGE

Moderate to Severe Pain
Adult: 1–2 mg q2–3h prn titrate to pain relief

Patient Controlled Analgesia
Adult: 0.2–0.4 mg/demand dose with lock out

Hepatic Impairment Dosage Adjustment
Child-Pugh class B or C: Reduced initial dose

Renal Impairment Dosage Adjustment
Reduced initial dose

SOLUTION PREPARATION

- *Direct IV Injection:* Solution may be given undiluted or diluted in 5 mL of sterile water or NS.
- *IV Infusion:* Solution is typically diluted to 1 mg/mL in D5W, NS, D5NS, D5/1/2NS. Final concentration may be ordered by prescriber.
- *Vial Reconstitution:* Add 25 ml of sterile water for injection to the lyophilized 250 mg vial immediately before use to yield 10 mg/mL. Final concentration for infusion is ordered by prescriber. Discard any unused product as it contains no preservatives.

STORAGE

- A slight discoloration in ampules or multidose vials causes no loss of potency.
- Store in tight, light-resistant containers at 15°–30° C (59°–86° F).

ADMINISTRATION

- **Direct IV Injection:** Give 2 mg or fraction thereof over 3–5 min.
- **IV Infusion:** Rate of infusion **must be** ordered by prescriber.

INCOMPATIBILITIES Solution/additive: Prochlorperazine, sodium bicarbonate, thiopental. **Y-site:** Amphotericin B cholesteryl complex, lansoprazole, minocycline, phenytoin, sargramostim, tetracycline, thiopental.

ACTION & *THERAPEUTIC EFFECT* Semisynthetic derivative structurally similar to morphine but 8–10 times more potent analgesic effect. Has more

Common adverse effects in *italic*, life-threatening effects <u>underlined</u>: generic names in **bold**; classifications in SMALL CAPS; ♣ Canadian drug name; ✪ Prototype drug

353

rapid onset and shorter duration of action than morphine and is reported to have less hypnotic effect. *An effective narcotic analgesic that controls mild to moderate pain.*

CONTRAINDICATIONS Intolerance to opiate agonists; opiate-naïve patients; acute bronchial asthma, COPD, upper airway obstruction, decreased respiratory reserve, severe respiratory depression; pregnancy (category C), lactation. **CAUTIOUS USE** Abrupt discontinuation, alcoholism; angina; biliary tract disease; older adults; epidural administration; GI disease, GI obstruction; head trauma; heart failure; hepatic disease; hypotension, hypovolemia; oliguria, prostatic hypertrophy; pulmonary disease; renal disease, renal impairment; paralytic ileus; increased intracranial pressure; inflammatory bowel disease; labor; latex hypersensitivity; obstetric delivery; bladder obstruction; cardiac arrhythmias, cardiac disease; respiratory depression; seizure disorder, seizures; substance abuse; surgery; ulcerative colitis; urethral stricture, urinary retention; neonates, and infants less than 6 mo, children.

ADVERSE EFFECTS (≥1%) **GI:** Nausea, vomiting, constipation. **CNS:** Euphoria, dizziness, sedation, *drowsiness.* **CV:** Hypotension, bradycardia or tachycardia. **Respiratory:** <u>Respiratory depression</u>. **Special Senses:** Blurred vision.

DRUG INTERACTIONS Alcohol and other CNS DEPRESSANTS compound sedation and CNS depression.

PHARMACOKINETICS Onset: 15 min. **Peak:** 30–90 min. **Duration:** 3–4 h. **Distribution:** Crosses placenta; distributed into breast milk. **Metabolism:** Metabolized in liver. **Elimination:** Excreted in urine. **Half-Life:** 2–3 h.

NURSING IMPLICATIONS

Assessment & Drug Effects

- Note baseline respiratory rate, rhythm, and depth and size of pupils before administration. Respirations of 12/min or less and mitosis are signs of toxicity. Withhold drug and promptly notify prescriber.
- Monitor vital signs at regular intervals. Drug-induced respiratory depression may occur even with small doses and increases progressively with higher doses.
- Assess effectiveness of pain relief 30 min after medication administration.
- Monitor drug effects carefully in older adult or debilitated patients and those with impaired renal and hepatic function.
- Assess effectiveness of cough. Drug depresses cough and sigh reflexes and may induce atelectasis, especially in postoperative patients and those with pulmonary disease.
- Note: Nausea and orthostatic hypotension most often occur in ambulatory patients or when a supine patient assumes the head-up position.
- Monitor I&O ratio and pattern. Assess lower abdomen for bladder distension. Report oliguria or urinary retention.
- Monitor bowel pattern; drug-induced constipation may require treatment.

Patient & Family Education

- Request medication at the onset of pain and do not wait until pain is severe.
- Use caution with activities requiring alertness; drug may cause drowsiness, dizziness, and blurred vision.

HYOSCYAMINE SULFATE

(hye-oh-sye′a-meen)

Levsin

Classification(s): ANTICHOLINERGIC
Therapeutic: ANTISPASMODIC; ANTISECRETORY
Prototype: Atropine
Pregnancy Category: C

USES GI tract relaxation prior to procedure. Also symptomatic relief of biliary and renal colic, as a "drying agent" to relieve symptoms of acute rhinitis, to control preanesthesia salivation and respiratory tract secretions, to treat symptoms of parkinsonism reversal of muscarinic effects.

INDICATION & DOSAGE

GI Relaxation

Adult: 0.25–0.5 mg may require dose q4h

Reversal of Muscarinic Effects

Adult: 0.3–0.6 mg per 0.5–2 mg of neostigmine/physostigmine

Preanesthetic

Adult/Child (over 2 y): 5 mcg/kg 30–60 min before induction of anesthesia

SOLUTION PREPARATION

No dilution is required. Administer as supplied.

STORAGE

Store 15°–30° C (59°–86° F).

ADMINISTRATION

Direct IV Injection: Give bolus dose over 60 sec.

INCOMPATIBILITIES Data not available; do not mix with other drugs.

ACTION & *THERAPEUTIC EFFECT* Competitive inhibitor at autonomic postganglionic cholinergic receptors. It decreases GI motility (smooth muscle tone) in GI, biliary, and urinary tracts. Specific anticholinergic responses are dose-related. *Has both anticholinergic and antispasmodic activity.*

CONTRAINDICATIONS Hypersensitivity to belladonna alkaloids; narrow-angle glaucoma; prostatic hypertrophy; obstructive diseases of GI or GU tract, paralytic ileus or intestinal atony; myasthenia gravis; pregnancy (category C); children less than 2 y.
CAUTIOUS USE Diabetes mellitus; cardiac disease.

ADVERSE EFFECTS (≥1%) **CNS:** Headache, unusual tiredness or weakness, confusion, *drowsiness,* excitement in older adult patients. **CV:** Palpi-

---

Common adverse effects in *italic*, life-threatening effects <u>underlined</u>: generic names in **bold**; classifications in SMALL CAPS; ♣ Canadian drug name; ⊘ Prototype drug

355

tations, tachycardia. **Special Senses:** *Blurred vision,* increased intraocular tension, cycloplegia, mydriasis. **GI:** *Dry mouth, constipation,* paralytic ileus. **Other:** *Urinary retention,* anhidrosis, suppression of lactation.

DRUG INTERACTIONS Amantadine, ANTIHISTAMINES, TRICYCLIC ANTIDEPRESSANTS, **quinidine, disopyramide, procainamide** add anticholinergic effects; decreases **levodopa** effects; **methotrimeprazine** may precipitate extrapyramidal effects; decreases antipsychotic effects of PHENOTHIAZINES.

PHARMACOKINETICS Onset: 2–3 min. **Peak:** 15–30 min. **Duration:** 4–6 h. **Distribution:** Distributed in most body tissues; crosses blood–brain barrier and placenta; distributed in breast milk. **Metabolism:** Metabolized in liver. **Elimination:** Excreted in urine. **Half-Life:** 3.5–13 h.

NURSING IMPLICATIONS

Assessment & Drug Effects
" Monitor urinary output and bowel elimination; may cause constipation.
" Lessen risk of urinary retention by having patient void prior to each dose.
" Assess for dry mouth and recommend good practices of oral hygiene.

Patient & Family Education
" Avoid excessive exposure to high temperatures; drug-induced heatstroke can develop.
" Do not drive or engage in other potentially hazardous activities until response to drug is known.
" Use dark glasses if experiencing blurred vision, but if this adverse effect persists, notify prescriber for dose adjustment or possible drug change.

IBUTILIDE FUMARATE

(i-bu′ti-lide)

Corvert

Classification(s): ANTIARRHYTHMIC AGENT, CLASS III
Therapeutic: ANTIARRHYTHMIC
Prototype: Amiodarone HCl
Pregnancy Category: C

USES Rapid conversion of atrial fibrillation or atrial flutter of recent onset.

INDICATION & DOSAGE

Atrial Fibrillation or Flutter
Adult (less than 60 kg): 0.01 mg/kg, may repeat in 10 min if inadequate response; *(over 60 kg):* 1 mg, may repeat in 10 min if inadequate response

SOLUTION PREPARATION

- *Direct IV Injection:* No dilution required for bolus dose.
- *IV Infusion:* Add contents of 1 mg vial to 50 mL of D5W or NS to yield 0.017 mg/mL.

STORAGE

Store diluted solution up to 24 h at 15°–30° C (59°–86° F) or 48 h refrigerated at 2°–8° C (36°–46° F).

ADMINISTRATION

- **Direct IV Injection/Infusion:** Give a single dose slowly over 10 min.
- Stop injection/infusion as soon as presenting arrhythmia is terminated or with appearance of ventricular tachycardia or marked prolongation of QT or QTc.
- Hypokalemia and hypomagnesemia should be corrected prior to treatment with ibutilide.

INCOMPATIBILITIES Data not available; do not mix with other drugs.

ACTION & *THERAPEUTIC EFFECT* Ibutilide is a Class III antiarrhythmic agent. It prolongs the cardiac action potential and increases both atrial and ventricular refractoriness without affecting conduction (i.e., Class III antiarrhythmic electrophysiologic effects). *Effective for treating recently occurring atrial arrhythmias. Like other Class III antiarrhythmic drugs it may produce proarrhythmic effects that can be life threatening.*

CONTRAINDICATIONS Hypersensitivity to ibutilide; hypokalemia, hypomagnesia; pregnancy (category C). Safe use in children less than 18 y not established.

CAUTIOUS USE History of CHF, ejection fraction of 35% or less, recent MI, prolonged QT intervals, ventricular arrhythmias; renal or liver disease; cardiovascular disorder other than atrial arrhythmias; other drugs that prolong QT interval; lactation.

ADVERSE EFFECTS (≥1%) **CNS:** Headache. **CV:** <u>Proarrhythmic effects (sustained and nonsustained polymorphic ventricular tachycardia)</u>, AV block, bundle branch block, ventricular extrasystoles, hypotension, postural hypotension, bradycardia, tachycardia, palpitations, prolonged QT segment. **GI:** Nausea.

DRUG INTERACTIONS Increased potential for proarrhythmic effects when administered with PHENOTHIAZINES, TRICYCLIC ANTIDEPRESSANTS, **amiodarone, disopyramide, quinidine, procainamide, sotalol** may cause prolonged refractoriness if given within 4 h of ibutilide.

PHARMACOKINETICS Onset: 30 min. **Metabolism:** In liver. **Elimination:** 82% excreted in urine, 19% in feces. **Half-Life:** 6 h (range 2–21 h).

NURSING IMPLICATIONS

Assessment & Drug Effects

- Prior to initiating therapy: Baseline serum potassium and magnesium.
- Monitor for therapeutic effectiveness. Conversion to normal sinus rhythm normally occurs within 30 min of initiation of infusion.

Common adverse effects in *italic*, life-threatening effects <u>underlined</u>: generic names in **bold**; classifications in SMALL CAPS; ✦ Canadian drug name; ✪ Prototype drug

357

- Observe with continuous ECG, BP, and HR monitoring during and for at least 4 h after infusion or until QTc has returned to baseline. Monitor for longer periods with liver dysfunction or if proarrhythmic activity is observed.

Patient & Family Education
- Consult prescriber and understand the potential risks of ibutilide therapy.

IDARUBICIN
(i-da-a-roo'bi-cin)

Idamycin PFS
Classification(s): ANTINEOPLASTIC; ANTIBIOTIC
Therapeutic: ANTINEOPLASTIC
Prototype: Doxorubicin
Pregnancy Category: D

USES In combination with other antineoplastic drugs for treatment of AML.
UNLABELED USES Breast cancer, other solid tumors.

INDICATION & DOSAGE

Acute Myelogenous Leukemia (AML) with Cytarabine
Adult: 8–12 mg/m^2 daily for 3 days

Toxicity Adjustment
Reduce dose 25% if severe mucositis has been experienced

Renal Impairment Dosage Adjustment
Creatinine over 2 mg/dL: Give 75% of dose

Hepatic Impairment Dosage Adjustment
Bilirubin 1.5–5 mg/dL: Give 50% of dose, if over 5 mg/dL do not use drug

SOLUTION PREPARATION
- *Vial Reconstitution:* Reconstitute 5 mg, 10 mg, and 20 mg vials with 5, 10, and 20 mL, respectively, of nonbacteriostatic NS to yield 1 mg/mL. Vials are under negative pressure, therefore, carefully insert needle into vial to reconstitute.
- Gloves, gowns, and goggles are recommended during drug preparation. Wash skin accidentally exposed with soap and water.

STORAGE
Store reconstituted solutions up to 7 days refrigerated at 2°–8° C (36°–46° F) and 72 h at room temperature 15°–30° C (59°–86° F).

ADMINISTRATION
- Ensure that the IV site is patent prior to administering idarubicin.
- **IV Infusion: MUST BE** administered slowly into tubing of free-flowing IV of NS or D5W over 10–15 min.
- If extravasation is suspected, immediately stop infusion, elevate the arm, and apply ice pack for 30 min then q.i.d. for 30 min for 3 days.

Common adverse effects in *italic*, life-threatening effects <u>underlined</u>: generic names in **bold**; classifications in SMALL CAPS; ♦ Canadian drug name; ⊘ Prototype drug

INCOMPATIBILITIES Solution/additive: ALKALINE SOLUTIONS (i.e., **sodium bicarbonate**), **heparin. Y-site:** Acyclovir, allopurinol, ampicillin/sulbactam, cefazolin, cefepime, ceftazidime, clindamycin, dexamethasone, etoposide, furosemide, gentamicin, heparin, hydrocortisone, imipenem/cilastatin, lorazepam, meperidine, methotrexate, mezlocillin, piperacillin/tazobactam, sargramostim, sodium bicarbonate, teniposide, vancomycin, vincristine.

ACTION & *THERAPEUTIC EFFECT* Cytotoxic anthracycline antibiotic with more potency than daunorubicin or doxorubicin; may be less cardiotoxic than other anthracyclines. Idarubicin exhibits inhibitory effects on DNA topoisomerase II, an enzyme responsible for repairing faulty sections of DNA. This results in breaks in the helix of DNA, and thus it affects RNA and protein synthesis in rapidly dividing cells. *Idarubicin exhibits inhibitory effects on DNA and RNA polymerase, thus affecting nucleic acid and protein syntheses in rapidly dividing cells.*

CONTRAINDICATIONS Myelosuppression; hypersensitivity to idarubicin or doxorubicin; pregnancy (category D), lactation; children less than 2 y.
CAUTIOUS USE Impaired renal or hepatic function; patients who have received irradiation or radiotherapy to areas surrounding heart; cardiac disease.

ADVERSE EFFECTS (≥1%) **CV:** CHF, atrial fibrillation, chest pain, <u>MI</u>. **GI:** *Nausea, vomiting, diarrhea, abdominal pain,* mucositis. **Hematologic:** *Anemia, leukopenia,* thrombocytopenia. **Other:** Nephrotoxicity, hepatotoxicity, *alopecia,* rash.

DRUG INTERACTIONS IMMUNOSUPPRESSANTS cause additive bone marrow suppression; ANTICOAGULANTS, NSAIDS, SALICYLATES, **aspirin,** THROMBOLYTIC AGENTS increase risk of bleeding; idarubicin may blunt the effects of **filgrastim, sargramostim.**

PHARMACOKINETICS Onset: Median time to remission 28 days. **Peak:** Serum level 4 h. **Duration:** Serum levels 120 h. **Distribution:** Concentrates in nucleated blood and bone marrow cells. **Metabolism:** In liver to idarubicinol, which may be as active as idarubicin. **Elimination:** 16% excreted in urine; 17% excreted in bile. **Half-Life:** Idarubicin 15–45 h, idarubicinol 45 h.

NURSING IMPLICATIONS

Assessment & Drug Effects

- Monitor infusion site closely, as extravasation can cause severe local tissue necrosis. Note that extravasation can occur without pain at the site. Notify prescriber if pain, erythema, or edema develops at insertion site.
- Lab tests: Periodic LFTs, renal function tests, CBC with differential, coagulation studies, and uric acid.
- Monitor cardiac status closely, especially in older adult patients or those with preexisting cardiac disease.
- Monitor hematologic status carefully; during the period of myelosuppression, patients are at high risk for bleeding and infection.
- Monitor for development of hyperuricemia secondary to lysis of leukemic cells.

Common adverse effects in *italic*, life-threatening effects <u>underlined</u>: generic names in **bold**; classifications in SMALL CAPS; ♣ Canadian drug name; ⊘ Prototype drug

359

Patient & Family Education
- Learn all potential adverse reactions to idarubicin.
- Anticipate possible hair loss.
- Discuss interventions to minimize nausea, vomiting, diarrhea, and stomatitis with health care providers.

IFOSFAMIDE

(i-fos'-fa-mide)

Classification(s): ANTINEOPLASTIC; ALKYLATING AGENT
Therapeutic: ANTINEOPLASTIC
Prototype: Cyclophosphamide
Pregnancy Category: D

USES In combination with other agents in various regimens for germ cell testicular cancer, soft tissue sarcomas, Ewing's sarcoma, and non-Hodgkin's lymphoma. Also for lung and pancreatic sarcoma.

INDICATION & DOSAGE

Antineoplastic

Adult: 1.2 g/m²/day for 5 consecutive days; repeat q3wk or after recovery from hematologic toxicity (platelets at least 100,000/mm³; WBC at least 4,000/mm³)

SOLUTION PREPARATION

- *Vial Reconstitution:* Dilute each 1 g in 20 mL of sterile water or bacteriostatic water to yield 50 mg/mL. Shake well to dissolve. May be given as prepared or further diluted with D5W, NS, or LR to achieve concentrations of 0.6–20 mg/mL.
- Use solution prepared with sterile water within 6 h.

STORAGE

Store reconstituted solution prepared with bacteriostatic solution up to a week at 30° C (86° F) or 6 wk at 5° C (41° F). Solutions prepared with sterile water **must be** used within 6 h.

ADMINISTRATION

- **IV Infusion:** Give slowly over 30 min.
- Note: Mesna is always given concurrently with ifosfamide; never give ifosfamide alone.

INCOMPATIBILITIES Y-site: Cefepime, methotrexate.

ACTION & *THERAPEUTIC EFFECT* Ifosfamide is a chemotherapeutic agent chemically related to nitrogen mustards. The alkylated metabolites of ifosfamide interact with DNA. Antineoplastic or cytotoxic action is primarily due to cross-linking of strands of DNA and RNA as well as inhibition of protein synthesis. *Has effective antineoplastic or cytotoxic action.*

CONTRAINDICATIONS Patients with severe bone marrow depression or who have demonstrated previous hypersensitivity to ifosfamide; dehydration; pregnancy (category D), lactation.

CAUTIOUS USE Impaired renal function, renal failure; hepatic disease; prior radiation or prior therapy with other cytotoxic agents.

ADVERSE EFFECTS (≥1%) **CNS:** *Somnolence, confusion, hallucinations,* coma, dizziness, seizures, cranial nerve dysfunction. **GI:** *Nausea, vomiting,* anorexia, diarrhea, metabolic acidosis, hepatic dysfunction. **Hematologic:** Neutropenia, thrombocytopenia. **Urogenital:** Hemorrhagic cystitis, nephrotoxicity. **Skin:** *Alopecia,* skin necrosis with extravasation.

DRUG INTERACTIONS HEPATIC ENZYME INDUCERS (BARBITURATES, **phenytoin, chloral hydrate**) may increase hepatic conversion of ifosfamide to active metabolites; CORTICOSTEROIDS may inhibit conversion to active metabolites.

PHARMACOKINETICS Distribution: Distributed into breast milk. **Metabolism:** In liver (CYP 3A4). **Elimination:** 70–86% excreted in urine. **Half-Life:** 7–15 h.

NURSING IMPLICATIONS

Assessment & Drug Effects

- Withhold drug and notify prescriber if WBC count is below 2000/mm³ or platelet count is below 50,000/mm³.
- Lab tests: Monitor CBC with differential prior to each dose and at regular intervals; urinalysis prior to each dose for microscopic hematuria.
- Reduce risk of hemorrhagic cystitis by hydrating with 3000 mL of fluid daily prior to therapy and for at least 72 h following treatment to ensure ample urine output.
- Discontinue therapy if any of the following CNS symptoms occur: Somnolence, confusion, depressive psychosis, and hallucinations.

Patient & Family Education

- Void frequently to lessen contact of irritating chemical with bladder mucosa.
- Note: Susceptibility to infection may increase. Avoid people with infection. Notify prescriber of any infection, fever or chills, cough or hoarseness, lower back or side pain, painful or difficult urination.
- Check with prescriber immediately if there is any unusual bleeding or bruising, black tarry stools, or blood in urine or if pinpoint red spots develop on skin.
- Discuss possible adverse effects (e.g., alopecia, nausea, and vomiting) and measures that can minimize them with prescriber.

IMIPENEM-CILASTATIN SODIUM ℗

(i-mi-pen′em sye-la-stat′in)

Primaxin

Classification(s): ANTIBIOTIC, CARBAPENEM
Therapeutic: ANTIBACTERIAL
Pregnancy Category: C

Common adverse effects in *italic*, life-threatening effects <u>underlined</u>: generic names in **bold**; classifications in SMALL CAPS; ✚ Canadian drug name; ℗ Prototype drug

361

USES Treatment of serious infections caused by susceptible organisms in the urinary tract, lower respiratory tract, bones and joints, skin and skin structures; also intra-abdominal, gynecologic, and mixed infections; bacterial septicemia and endocarditis.

INDICATION & DOSAGE

Serious Infections
Adult:

Pt Weight	Mild Infection	Moderate Infection	Life-threatening Infection
At least 70 kg	250 mg q6h	500 mg q6–8h	500 mg q6h
60–69 kg	250 mg q8h	250 mg q6h	250 mg q6h
50–59 kg	125 mg q6h	250 mg q6h	250 mg q6h
40–49 kg	125 mg q6h	250 mg q6–8h	250 mg q6h
30–39 kg	125 mg q8h	125 mg q6h OR 250 mg q8h	250 mg q8h

Child (over 3 mo): 60–100 mg/kg/day in divided doses; *(1–3 mo):* 100 mg/kg/day in divided doses
Neonate (less than 1 wk): 40–50 mg/kg/day in divided doses; *(1 wk or more):* 60–75 mg/kg/day in divided doses

Renal Impairment Dosage Adjustment
CrCl 20–30 mL/min: Dose q8–12h; *less than 20 mL/min:* Dose q12h

SOLUTION PREPARATION
- Caution: IM and IV solutions are NOT interchangeable. Do NOT give IM solution by IV.
- *Vial Reconstitution:* Add 10 mL of D5W, NS, or other compatible infusion solution. Shake well. **Must be** further diluted for infusion.
- *Further Dilution of Reconstituted Solution:* Transfer contents of vial to 100 mL of the IV solution used for reconstitution. After transfer, add another 10 mL of infusion solution to the vial, shake to dissolve, then transfer the remaining contents to the IV container for infusion.

STORAGE
IV solutions retain potency for 4 h at 15°–30° C (59°–86° F) or for 24 h if refrigerated at 4° C (39° F). Avoid freezing.

ADMINISTRATION
- **Intermittent Infusion:** Infuse each 500 mg or fraction thereof over 20–30 min. Infuse larger doses of 750–1000 mg over 40–60 min. **DO NOT** give as a bolus dose.
- Nausea appears to be related to infusion rate (occurs most frequently with 1-g doses), and if it presents during infusion, slow the rate.

Common adverse effects in *italic*, life-threatening effects underlined: generic names in **bold**; classifications in SMALL CAPS; ♣ Canadian drug name; ◐ Prototype drug

INCOMPATIBILITIES Solution/additive: Lactated Ringer's, some dextrose-containing solutions, sodium bicarbonate, TPN. Y-site: Allopurinol, amiodarone, amphotericin B cholesteryl complex, azithromycin, etoposide, fluconazole, gemcitabine, lorazepam, meperidine, midazolam, milrinone, sargramostim, sodium bicarbonate.

ACTION & *THERAPEUTIC EFFECT* Fixed combination of imipenem, a beta-lactam antibiotic, and cilastatin. Action of imipenem is inhibition of mucopeptide synthesis in bacterial cell walls leading to cell death. Cilastatin increases the serum half-life of imipenem. *Effectively used for severe or resistant infections. Acts synergistically with aminoglycoside antibiotics against some isolates of* Pseudomonas aeruginosa *as well as some infections resistant to cephalosporins, penicillins, and aminoglycosides.*

CONTRAINDICATIONS Hypersensitivity to any component of product, multiple allergens; pregnancy (category C).
CAUTIOUS USE Patients with CNS disorders (e.g., seizures, brain lesions, history of recent head injury); renal impairment; seizures; renal failure, renal impairment, renal disease; patients with history of penicillin or cephalosporin allergies; lactation.

ADVERSE EFFECTS (≥1%) **Body as a Whole:** Hypersensitivity (rash, fever, chills, dyspnea, pruritus), weakness, oliguria/anuria, polyuria, polyarthralgia; *phlebitis and pain at injection site,* superinfections. **CNS:** Seizures, dizziness, confusion, somnolence, encephalopathy, myoclonus, tremors, paresthesia, headache. **GI:** *Nausea, vomiting,* diarrhea, <u>pseudomembranous colitis</u>, hemorrhagic colitis, gastroenteritis, abdominal pain, glossitis, heartburn. **Respiratory:** Chest discomfort, hyperventilation, dyspnea. **Skin:** Rash, pruritus, urticaria, candidiasis, flushing, increased sweating, skin texture change, facial edema. **Metabolic:** Hyponatremia, hyperkalemia. **Special Senses:** Transient hearing loss; increased WBC, AST, ALT, alkaline phosphatase, BUN, LDH, creatinine; decreased Hgb, Hct, eosinophilia.

DRUG INTERACTIONS Aztreonam, CEPHALOSPORINS, PENICILLINS may antagonize the antibacterial effects; may alter **cyclosporine** levels.

PHARMACOKINETICS Distribution: Widely distributed; limited concentrations in CSF; crosses placenta; in breast milk. **Elimination:** 70% of dose in urine within 10 h. **Half-Life:** 1 h.

NURSING IMPLICATIONS
Assessment & Drug Effects
- Prior to initiating therapy: Baseline C&S tests (start drug pending results); determine previous hypersensitivity reactions to penicillins, cephalosporins, and other allergens.
- Monitor for S&S of hypersensitivity (see Appendix C). Discontinue drug and notify prescriber if S&S occur.
- Monitor closely patients vulnerable to CNS adverse effects.
- Notify prescriber if focal tremors, myoclonus, or seizures occur; dosage adjustment may be needed.
- Monitor for S&S of superinfection (see Appendix C).

Common adverse effects in *italic*, life-threatening effects <u>underlined</u>: generic names in **bold**; classifications in SMALL CAPS; ♣ Canadian drug name; ● Prototype drug

363

- Report promptly severe diarrhea accompanied by abdominal pain and fever to rule out pseudomembranous colitis (see Appendix C).
- Lab tests: Periodic renal, hematologic, and LFTs.
- Note: Sodium content derived from drug is high; monitor closely those on restricted sodium intake.

Patient & Family Education
- Report promptly: Pruritus, symptoms of respiratory distress, pain or discomfort at IV infusion site, loose stools or diarrhea.

IMMUNE GLOBULIN INTRAVENOUS (IGIV) ⓟ

(im'mune glob'u-lin)

Flebogamma, Gammagard, Gammar-P IV, Gamunex, IGIV, Iveegam, Octagam, Sandoglobulin

Classification(s): IMMUNOLOGIC AGENT, IMMUNOGLOBULIN
Therapeutic: IMMUNOGLOBULIN
Pregnancy Category: C

USES Principally as maintenance therapy in patients unable to manufacture sufficient quantities of IgG antibodies, in patients requiring an immediate increase in immunoglobulin levels, and when IM injections are contraindicated as in patients with bleeding disorders or who have small muscle mass. Also in chronic autoimmune thrombocytopenia and idiopathic thrombocytopenic purpura (ITP). Treatment of primary immunodeficiency disorders associated with defects in humoral immunity.

UNLABELED USES Kawasaki syndrome, chronic lymphocytic leukemia, AIDS, premature and low-birth-weight neonates, autoimmune neutropenia, or hemolytic anemia.

INDICATION & DOSAGE

Immunoglobulin Deficiency

*Dosages vary between brands
Adult/Child:

Product	Dose	Frequency
Gammagard	300–600 mg/kg	q3–4wk
Polygam	100 mg/kg	Monthly
Gammar-P IV (Adult dose)	200–400 mg/kg	q3–4wk
Gammar-P IV (Child dose)	200 mg/kg	q3–4wk
Gamunex	300–600 mg/kg	q3–4wk
Iveegam	200 mg/kg	Monthly

Common adverse effects in *italic*, life-threatening effects <u>underlined</u>: generic names in **bold**; classifications in SMALL CAPS; ♦ Canadian drug name; ⓟ Prototype drug

Product	Dose	Frequency
Panglobulin/Carimune	200 mg/kg (higher dose may be needed)	Monthly (more frequent dose may be needed)
Octagam/Flebogamma	300–600 mg/kg	q3–4wk

Idiopathic Thrombocytopenia Purpura

Adult/Child:

Product	Dose	Frequency
Panglobulin/Carimune	400 mg/kg	Daily × 2–5 days
Gammagard/Polygam	1000 mg/kg	Alternate days for up to 3 doses
Gamunex	1000 mg/kg	2 consecutive days; if sufficient response after one dose, may withhold second dose

Obesity

Dose based on IBW or adjusted IBW

SOLUTION PREPARATION

Immune globulins from various manufacturers are reconstituted according to **specific** guidelines provided by each manufacturer. Reconstitution directions **are not** interchangeable from one brand to another. Refer to manufacturer's directions for information on reconstitution and dilution of the specific product.

STORAGE

- Store as directed by manufacturer for specific product. Avoid freezing. Do not use if cloudy or if product has been frozen.
- Discard partially used vial.

ADMINISTRATION

- **IV Infusion:** Infusion rates vary with product being infused. Refer to manufacturer's directions for the specific product.
- Most preparations require administration through a separate IV tubing with a filter or filter needle (provided by the manufacturer).
- Infusing the drug too rapidly may result in severe hypotension. Use an infusion pump to control rate.

INCOMPATIBILITIES Manufacturers recommend not mixing other drugs with immune globulin.

ACTION & *THERAPEUTIC EFFECT* Sterile concentrated solution containing globulin (primarily IgG) prepared from large pools of normal human plasma of either venous or placental origin and processed by a special technique. *Like hepatitis B immune globulin (H-BIG), contains antibodies specific to*

Common adverse effects in *italic*, life-threatening effects underlined: generic names in **bold**; classifications in SMALL CAPS; ♣ Canadian drug name; ◑ Prototype drug

hepatitis B surface antigen but in lower concentrations. Therefore, not considered treatment of first choice for postexposure prophylaxis against hepatitis B but usually an acceptable alternative when H-BIG is not available.

CONTRAINDICATIONS History of anaphylaxis or severe reaction to human immune serum globulin (IG) or to any ingredient in the formulation and maltose (stabilizing agent) in IV formulations; persons with clinical hepatitis A; IGIV for patients with class-specific anti-IgA deficiencies; pregnancy (category C). **CAUTIOUS USE** Dehydration; diabetes mellitus; children, older adults; hypovolemia; IgA deficiency; infection; renal disease, renal failure, renal impairment; sepsis; sucrose hypersensitivity; vaccination, viral infection, lactation.

ADVERSE EFFECTS (≥1%) **Body as a Whole:** Local inflammatory reaction, erythema, urticaria, angioedema, headache, malaise, fever, arthralgia, nephrotic syndrome, hypersensitivity (fever, chills, anaphylactic shock), infusion reactions (*nausea, flushing, chills,* headache, chest tightness, wheezing, skeletal pain, back pain, abdominal cramps, anaphylaxis), renal dysfunction, renal failure.

DRUG INTERACTIONS May interfere with antibody response to LIVE VIRUS VACCINES (measles/mumps/rubella); give VACCINES 14 days before or 3 mo after IMMUNE GLOBULINS.

PHARMACOKINETICS Peak: 2 days. **Distribution:** Rapidly and evenly distributed to intravascular and extravascular fluid compartments. **Half-Life:** 21–23 days.

NURSING IMPLICATIONS

Assessment & Drug Effects

- Ensure that emergency drugs and appropriate emergency facilities are immediately available for treatment of anaphylaxis or sensitization.
- Monitor vital signs frequently and promptly report falling BP or respiratory distress.
- Monitor for hypersensitivity reactions (see Appendix C) especially in the following situations: Patient is receiving first immune globulin infusion; initial infusion rate is greater than 1 mL/min; last treatment was more than 8 wk earlier.

Patient & Family Education

- Report promptly nausea, chills, headache, or chest tightness; these are indications to slow rate of infusion.
- Avoid vaccination with a live virus until cleared by prescriber to receive that type of vaccination.

INAMRINONE LACTATE 🅟

(in-am'ri-none)

Amrinone

Classification(s): INOTROPIC AGENT; VASODILATOR

Common adverse effects in *italic*, life-threatening effects <u>underlined</u>: generic names in **bold**; classifications in SMALL CAPS; ♣ Canadian drug name; 🅟 Prototype drug

Therapeutic: CARDIAC INOTROPIC
Pregnancy Category: C

USES Short-term management of CHF in patients not adequately controlled by traditional therapy, such as digitalis, diuretics, and vasodilators, and may be used in conjunction with these agents.

INDICATION & DOSAGE

Congestive Heart Failure

Adult: 0.75 mg/kg bolus given slowly over 2–3 min, then start infusion at 5–10 mcg/kg/min; may repeat bolus in 30 min (max: 10 mg/kg/day)

Renal Impairment Dosage Adjustment

CrCl less than 10 mL/min: Give 50–75% of dose

SOLUTION PREPARATION

- *Loading Dose:* May be given undiluted or diluted by adding 1 mL of NS or 1/2NS to each 5 mg (1 mL).
- *IV Infusion:* Dilute 300 mg (60 mL) in 60 mL of NS or 1/2NS to yield 2.5 mg/mL.

STORAGE

- Protect ampules from light.
- Natural color is clear yellow. Discard discolored solutions and those with precipitate.
- Use all diluted solutions within 24 h.

ADMINISTRATION

- **Loading Dose Direct IV Injection:** Give over 2–3 min. May inject into a running D5W infusion through Y-connector.
- **IV Infusion:** Infuse diluted solution at a rate of 5–10 mg/kg/min. Use infusion pump to regulate rate.
- In general, rate of infusion should be slowed or stopped with excessive drop in BP or arrhythmias. Consult prescriber for guidelines.

INCOMPATIBILITIES Solution/additive: **Sodium bicarbonate, dextrose-containing solutions.** Y-site: **Furosemide, sodium bicarbonate.**

ACTION & *THERAPEUTIC EFFECT* A cardiac inotropic agent with vasodilator activity. Mode of action appears to differ from that of the digitalis glycosides and beta-adrenergic stimulants. In patients with depressed myocardial function, it enhances myocardial contractility, increases cardiac output and stroke volume, and reduces right and left ventricular filling pressure, pulmonary capillary wedge pressure (PCWP), and systemic vascular resistance. *It reduces afterload and preload by its direct relaxant effect on vascular smooth muscle. Also produces hemodynamic improvements as well as symptomatic relief in patients with CHF due to ischemic heart disease.*

CONTRAINDICATIONS Hypersensitivity to inamrinone or to bisulfites; severe aortic or pulmonic valvular disease in lieu of appropriate surgery;

acute MI; uncorrected hypokalemia or dehydration; pregnancy (category C). Safe use in children is not established.
CAUTIOUS USE Compromised renal or hepatic function; arrhythmias; hypertrophic subaortic stenosis; decreased platelets; concomitant cardiac glycoside therapy in patients with atrial flutter or fibrillation; lactation.

ADVERSE EFFECTS (≥1%) **Body as a Whole:** Hypersensitivity (pericarditis, pleuritis; myositis with interstitial shadows on chest x-ray and elevated sedimentation rate; vasculitis with nodular pulmonary densities, hypoxemia, ascites, jaundice). **CV:** Hypotension, arrhythmias. **Endocrine:** Nephrogenic diabetes insipidus. **GI:** Nausea, vomiting, anorexia, abdominal cramps, hepatotoxicity. **Hematologic:** Asymptomatic thrombocytopenia.

DRUG INTERACTIONS Possibility of excessive hypotension with **disopyramide.**

PHARMACOKINETICS Onset: 2–5 min. **Peak:** 10 min. **Duration:** About 2 h. **Distribution:** Unknown if it crosses placenta or into breast milk. **Metabolism:** In liver to inactive form. **Elimination:** Primarily in urine. **Half-Life:** 3.6–7.5 h.

NURSING IMPLICATIONS

Assessment & Drug Effects
- Prior to initiating therapy: Baseline serum potassium and platelet count. Correct hypokalemia before and during therapy.
- Monitor infusion site to prevent extravasation.
- Monitor ECG continuously; monitor frequently BP, respirations, kidney output.
- Monitor for therapeutic effectiveness: Increased cardiac output, decreased PCWP, relief of symptoms of CHF. Central venous pressure may be used to assess hypotension and blood volume.
- Allergy alert: IV preparation contains sodium metabisulfite to which some individuals are allergic. Discontinue IV immediately if hypersensitivity reaction occurs.
- Lab tests: Monitor closely platelet count, liver enzymes, serum electrolytes, renal function tests.
- If platelet count falls below 150,000/mm³, report immediately to prescriber; may indicate thrombocytopenia.
- Observe patient closely when drug is withdrawn after prolonged therapy; clinical deterioration may occur within hours.

Patient & Family Education
- Report promptly dizziness, lightheadedness, or S&S of hypersensitivity (see Appendix C).

INDOMETHACIN ℗

(in-doe-meth'a-sin)

Indocin IV

Classification(s): NONSTEROIDAL ANTIINFLAMMATORY DRUG

Common adverse effects in *italic*, life-threatening effects <u>underlined</u>: generic names in **bold**; classifications in SMALL CAPS; ♣ Canadian drug name; ℗ Prototype drug

Therapeutic: PATENT DUCTUS ARTERIOSUS CLOSURE
Pregnancy Category: B (D in third trimester)

USES To close patent ductus arteriosus in the premature infant.

INDICATION & DOSAGE

Close Patent Ductus Arteriosus

Premature Neonate:

Age	Initial	Maintenance
Over 7 days	0.2 mg/kg	If needed, 2 doses of 0.25 mg/kg q12h
2–7 days	0.2 mg/kg	If needed, 2 doses of 0.2 mg/kg q12h
Less than 2 days	0.2 mg/kg	If needed, 1–2 doses of 0.1 mg/kg q12h

SOLUTION PREPARATION
Dilute 1 mg with 1 mL of NS or sterile water for injection **without preservatives.** Resulting concentration (1 mg/mL) may be further diluted with an additional 1 mL for each 1 mg to yield 0.5 mg/mL.

STORAGE
Discard any unused drug, since it contains no preservative.

ADMINISTRATION
- **Direct IV Injection:** Give a single dose over 20–30 min; note that optimal rate for injection has not been clearly established.
- Ensure patency prior to administration and use caution to avoid extravasation or leakage; drug can be irritating to tissue.

INCOMPATIBILITIES Y-site: Amino acid, calcium gluconate, cimetidine, dobutamine, dopamine, gentamicin, levofloxacin, tobramycin, tolazoline.

ACTION & *THERAPEUTIC EFFECT* Potent nonsteroidal compound with antiinflammatory, analgesic, and antipyretic effects. It competes with COX-1 and COX-2 enzymes, thus interfering with formation of prostaglandin. Inhibition of prostaglandins is thought to promote closure of a patent ductus arteriosus in a premature infant. *Promotes closure of a persistent patent ductus arteriosus in a premature infant.*

CONTRAINDICATIONS Allergy to indomethacin, aspirin, or other NSAID; nasal polyps associated with angioedema; history of GI lesions; perioperative pain with CABG; pregnancy (category B; D in third trimester).
CAUTIOUS USE History of psychiatric illness, epilepsy, parkinsonism; impaired renal or hepatic function; uncontrolled infections; coagulation defects, CHF; older adults, persons in hazardous occupations.

ADVERSE EFFECTS (≥1%) **Body as a Whole:** Hypersensitivity (rash, purpura, pruritus, urticaria, angioedema, angiitis, rapid fall in blood pressure,

Common adverse effects in *italic*, life-threatening effects <u>underlined</u>: generic names in **bold**; classifications in SMALL CAPS; ♣ Canadian drug name; ⊘ Prototype drug

369

dyspnea, asthma syndrome in aspirin-sensitive patients), flushing, sweating. **CNS:** Headache, *dizziness,* vertigo, light-headedness, syncope, fatigue, muscle weakness, ataxia, insomnia, nightmares, drowsiness, confusion, coma, convulsions, peripheral neuropathy, psychic disturbances (hallucinations, depersonalization, depression), aggravation of epilepsy, parkinsonism. **CV:** Elevated BP, palpitation, chest pains, tachycardia, bradycardia, CHF. **Special Senses:** Blurred vision, lacrimation, eye pain, visual field changes, corneal deposits, retinal disturbances including macula, *tinnitus,* hearing disturbances, epistaxis. **GI:** *Nausea, vomiting,* diarrhea, anorexia, bloating, abdominal distention, ulcerative stomatitis, proctitis, rectal bleeding, GI ulceration, hemorrhage, perforation, toxic hepatitis. **Hematologic:** Hemolytic anemia, aplastic anemia (sometimes fatal), agranulocytosis, leukopenia, thrombocytopenic purpura, inhibited platelet aggregation. **Urogenital:** Renal function impairment, hematuria, urinary frequency; vaginal bleeding, breast changes. **Skin:** Hair loss, exfoliative dermatitis, erythema nodosum, tissue irritation with extravasation. **Metabolic:** Hyponatremia, hypokalemia, hyperkalemia, hypoglycemia or hyperglycemia, glycosuria (rare).

DIAGNOSTIC TEST INTERFERENCE Increased *AST, ALT, bilirubin, BUN;* positive *direct Coombs' test.*

DRUG INTERACTIONS ORAL ANTICOAGULANTS, **heparin, alcohol** may prolong bleeding time; may increase **lithium** toxicity; effects of **phenytoin,** SALICYLATES, SULFONAMIDES, SULFONYLUREAS increased because of protein-binding displacement; may blunt effects of ANTIHYPERTENSIVES and DIURETICS.

PHARMACOKINETICS Peak: 3 h. **Duration:** 4–6 h. **Metabolism:** In liver. **Elimination:** Primarily in urine. **Half-Life:** 4.5 h.

NURSING IMPLICATIONS

Assessment & Drug Effects

- Withhold drug and notify prescriber if anuria or significant decrease in urine output occurs.
- Monitor closely vital signs and hemodynamic status.
- Lab tests: Periodic renal function tests, LFTs, serum electrolytes, CBC with differential and platelet count, arterial blood gases, BP and HR.
- Monitor closely weight and I&O as significant impairment of renal function is possible; urine output may decrease by 50% or more. Also monitor BUN, serum creatinine, glomerular filtration rate, creatinine clearance, and serum electrolytes.

INFLIXIMAB

(in-flix′i-mab)

Remicade

Classification(s): IMMUNOLOGIC AGENT, IMMUNOMODULATOR
Therapeutic: ANTIINFLAMMATORY
Pregnancy Category: B

Common adverse effects in *italic,* life-threatening effects underlined: generic names in **bold**; classifications in SMALL CAPS; ♣ Canadian drug name; ⊙ Prototype drug

USES Moderately to severely active Crohn's disease, including fistulizing Crohn's disease, rheumatoid arthritis, ankylosing spondylitis, ulcerative colitis.

INDICATION & DOSAGE

Crohn's Disease

Adult: 5 mg/kg, repeat at weeks 2 and 6 for fistulizing disease, then q8wk
Child: 5 mg/kg, repeat at weeks 2 and 6 then 5 mg/kg q8wk

Rheumatoid Arthritis

Adult: 3 mg/kg at weeks 0, 2, and 6 then q8wk (used with methotrexate)

Ulcerative Colitis

Adult: 5 mg/kg at weeks 0, 2, and 6 then 5 mg/kg q8wk

Ankylosing Spondylitis

Adult: 5 mg/kg at weeks 0, 2, and 6 then 5 mg/kg q6wk

Hepatic Impairment Dosage Adjustment

Discontinue use if AST or ALT are 5 times the upper limit of normal or if jaundice develops.

SOLUTION PREPARATION

- *Vial Reconstitution:* Determine the number of vials needed. Add 10 mL of sterile water for injection to each 100 mg vial using a 21-gauge or smaller syringe. Inject against wall of vial, then gently swirl to dissolve but do not shake. Let stand for 5 min. Solution should be colorless to light yellow with a few translucent particles. Discard if particles are opaque. **Must be** further diluted for infusion.
- *Further Dilution of Reconstituted Solution:* Remove from a 250-mL IV bag of NS a volume of NS equal to the volume of reconstituted infliximab to be added to the IV bag. Slowly add the total volume of reconstituted infliximab solution to the infusion bag and gently mix. Infusion concentration should be 0.4 to 4 mg/mL. Begin infusion within 3 h of preparation.

STORAGE

Store unopened vials at 2°–8° C (36°–46° F). Discard any unused reconstituted drug.

ADMINISTRATION

- Prior to infusion, determine if premedication for hypersensitivity reactions has been ordered.
- **IV Infusion:** Infuse over at least 2 h using an infusion set with an in-line, low-protein-binding filter (pore size 1.2 micron or less).
- Flush infusion set before/after with NS to ensure delivery of total drug dose.

INCOMPATIBILITIES Do not infuse with other drugs.

ACTION & *THERAPEUTIC EFFECT* An IgG$_1$-K monoclonal antibody that binds specifically to tumor necrosis factor-alpha (TNF-alpha), a cytokine. Thus, it prevents TNF-alpha from binding to its receptors. (TNF-alpha in-

Common adverse effects in *italic*, life-threatening effects underlined: generic names in **bold**; classifications in SMALL CAPS; ♣ Canadian drug name; ● Prototype drug

371

duces proinflammatory cytokines). Infliximab reduces concentrations of TNF-alpha production resulting in decreased inflammatory process. *Inflix-imab reduces infiltration of inflammatory cells and TNF-alpha production in inflamed areas of the intestine, as seen in Crohn's disease.*

CONTRAINDICATIONS Hypersensitivity to infliximab; CHF; infection, sepsis; murine protein hypersensitivity; lactation.

CAUTIOUS USE History of allergic phenomena or untoward responses to monoclonal antibody preparation; renal or hepatic impairment; multiple sclerosis (potential exacerbation); fungal infection; heart failure, human antichimeric antibody (HACA); leukopenia, thrombocytopenia; immuno-suppressed patients; neoplastic disease; tuberculosis; vaccination; vasculi-tis; neurological disease; neutropenia; seizure disorder, seizures; older adults; pregnancy (category B).

ADVERSE EFFECTS (≥1%) **Body as a Whole:** Fatigue, fever, pain, myalgia, back pain, chills, hot flashes, arthralgia; infusion-related reactions (fever, chills, pruritus, urticaria, chest pain, hypotension, hypertension, dyspnea). Increased risk of opportunistic infections, including tuberculosis. **CNS:** Headache, dizziness, involuntary muscle contractions, paresthesias, vertigo, anxiety, depression, insomnia. **CV:** Chest pain, peripheral edema, hypotension, hypertension, tachycardia, anemia, CHF, pericardial effusion, systemic and cutaneous vasculitis. **GI:** Nausea, diarrhea, abdominal pain, vomiting, constipation, dyspepsia, flatulence, intestinal obstruction, ulcerative stomatitis, increased hepatic enzymes. **Hematologic:** Leukopenia, neutropenia, thrombocytopenia, pancytopenia. **Respiratory:** URI, pharyngitis, bronchitis, rhinitis, coughing, sinusitis, dyspnea. **Skin:** Rash, pruritus, acne, alopecia, fungal dermatitis, eczema, dry skin, increased sweating, urticaria. **Other:** Infections, development of autoantibodies, lupus-like syndrome, conjunctivitis, dysuria, urinary frequency.

DRUG INTERACTIONS May blunt effectiveness of VACCINES given concurrently.

PHARMACOKINETICS Distribution: Distributed primarily to the vascular compartment. **Half-Life:** 9.5 days.

NURSING IMPLICATIONS

Assessment & Drug Effects

- Discontinue IV infusion and notify prescriber for fever, chills, pruritus, urticaria, chest pain, dyspnea, hypo/hypertension.
- Monitor vitals signs q30min or more often as warranted during infusion.
- Monitor for and immediately report S&S of local IV site or more generalized infection.
- Lab tests: Periodic LFTs, CBC with differential and platelet count.

Patient & Family Education

- Report promptly any infection, including past or recent exposure to TB.

INSULIN (REGULAR) 🔵

(in'su-lin)

Humulin R, Novolin R, Regular Insulin

Common adverse effects in *italic*, life-threatening effects <u>underlined</u>: generic names in **bold**; classifications in SMALL CAPS; ♣ Canadian drug name; 🔵 Prototype drug

Classification(s): HORMONE; ANTIDIABETIC AGENT; INSULIN
Therapeutic: ANTIDIABETIC
Pregnancy Category: B

USES Emergency treatment of diabetic ketoacidosis or coma, to promote intracellular shift of potassium in treatment of hyperkalemia.

INDICATION & DOSAGE

Diabetic Ketoacidosis/Hyperosmolar Hyperglycemic State
Adult: 0.15 units/kg followed by 0.1 units/kg/h; dose is adjusted based on plasma glucose levels
Child: 0.1 unit/kg/h; dose is adjusted based on plasma glucose levels

SOLUTION PREPARATION
- *Direct IV Injection:* No dilution is required. Administer as supplied.
- *Continuous Infusion:* Typically diluted in NS or 1/2NS. 100 units added to 1000 mL yields 0.1 units/mL.

STORAGE
Insulin is stable at room temperature up to 1 mo. Avoid exposure to direct sunlight or to temperature extremes [safe range is wide: 5°–38° C (40°–100° F)]. Refrigerate but do not freeze stock supply. Insulin tolerates temperatures above 38° C with less harm than freezing.

ADMINISTRATION
- **Direct IV Injection:** Give bolus dose of 50 units or a fraction thereof over 1 min.
- **Continuous Infusion:** Rate **must be** ordered by prescriber.
- Regular insulin may be adsorbed into the container or tubing when added to an IV infusion solution. Amount lost is variable and depends on concentration of insulin, infusion system, contact duration, and flow rate.

INCOMPATIBILITIES Solution/additive: **Aminophylline, brompheniramine, chlorothiazide, cytarabine, digoxin, dobutamine, pentobarbital, penicillin, phenobarbital, phenytoin, secobarbital, sodium bicarbonate, thiopental.** Y-site: **Dopamine, drotrecogin, labetalol, levofloxacin, norepinephrine.**

ACTION & *THERAPEUTIC EFFECT* Short-acting, clear, colorless solution of exogenous unmodified insulin extracted from beta cells in pork pancreas or synthesized by recombinant DNA technology (human). Enhances transmembrane passage of glucose across cell membranes in muscle and adipose tissue. Promotes conversion of glucose to glycogen in the liver. *It lowers blood glucose levels by increasing peripheral glucose uptake and by inhibiting the liver from changing glycogen to glucose.*

CONTRAINDICATIONS Hypersensitivity to insulin animal protein; children less than 1 y.
CAUTIOUS USE Renal impairment, renal failure; hepatic impairment; fever; thyroid disease; older adults; children and infants; pregnancy (category B).

ADVERSE EFFECTS (≥1%) **Body as a Whole:** Most adverse effects are related to hypoglycemia; <u>anaphylaxis</u> (rare), hyperinsulinemia (*profuse sweating,* hunger, headache, *nausea, tremulousness,* tremors, *palpitation,* tachycardia, weakness, fatigue, nystagmus, circumoral pallor); numb mouth, tongue, and other paresthesias; visual disturbances (diplopia, blurred vision, mydriasis), staring expression, confusion, personality changes, ataxia, incoherent speech, apprehension, irritability, inability to concentrate, personality changes, uncontrolled yawning, loss of consciousness, delirium, hypothermia, convulsions, Babinski reflex, <u>coma.</u> (Urine glucose tests will be negatives.) **CNS:** With overdose, psychic disturbances (i.e., aphasia, personality changes, maniacal behavior). **Metabolic:** Posthypoglycemia or rebound hyperglycemia (Somogyi effect), lipoatrophy and lipohypertrophy of injection sites; insulin resistance. **Skin:** Localized allergic reactions at injection site; generalized urticaria or bullae, lymphadenopathy.

DIAGNOSTIC TEST INTERFERENCE Large doses of insulin may increase urinary excretion of **VMA.** Insulin can cause alterations in ***thyroid function tests*** and ***liver function tests*** and may decrease ***serum potassium*** and ***serum calcium.***

DRUG INTERACTIONS Alcohol, ANABOLIC STEROIDS, MAO INHIBITORS, **guanethidine,** SALICYLATES may potentiate hypoglycemic effects; **dextrothyroxine,** CORTICOSTEROIDS, **epinephrine** may antagonize hypoglycemic effects; **furosemide,** THIAZIDE DIURETICS increase **serum glucose** levels; **propranolol** and other BETA BLOCKERS may mask symptoms of hypoglycemic reaction. **Herbal: Garlic, ginseng** may potentiate hypoglycemic effects.

PHARMACOKINETICS Onset: 15 min. **Peak:** 15–30 min. **Duration:** 30–60 min. **Distribution:** Throughout extracellular fluids. **Metabolism:** In liver with some metabolism in kidneys. **Elimination:** Less than 2% excreted in urine. **Half-Life:** 5–6 min.

NURSING IMPLICATIONS

Assessment & Drug Effects

- Monitor blood glucose values frequently. Therapeutic goal is typically a blood glucose reduction of 50–75 mg/dL/h. When blood glucose reaches 250–300 mg/dL, insulin infusion rate is usually slowed and a separate IV of D5W or D5/1/2NS initiated to prevent hypoglycemia and restore fluid balance.
- Monitor mental status and vital signs at frequent intervals.
- Lab tests: Baseline and hourly blood glucose and urine ketones; frequent arterial blood gases, BUN, serum potassium, sodium and chloride.
- Monitor for hypoglycemia (see Appendix C) throughout and for a period of time after completion of insulin infusion. Report promptly hypoglycemia and/or hypo/hyperkalemia.

Patient & Family Education

- Report immediately S&S of hypoglycemia (see Appendix C).
- Review events that commonly precipitate severe hyperglycemia including physical or emotional stress, physical injury, illness, infection, fever, vomiting, diarrhea, etc.

INTERFERON ALFA-2B

(in-ter-feer′on)

Intron A
Classification(s): IMMUNOLOGIC AGENT, IMMUNOMODULATOR
Therapeutic: ANTINEOPLASTIC
Prototype: Interferon alfa-2a
Pregnancy Category: C

USES Malignant melanoma.
UNLABELED USES Multiple sclerosis.

INDICATION & DOSAGE

Malignant Melanoma
Adult: 20 million units/m² daily for 5 days per wk × 4 wk; maintenance dose is 10 million units/m² given SC weekly × 48 wk

Renal Impairment Dosage Adjustment
Not removed by dialysis.

SOLUTION PREPARATION
- Use only the recombinant powder for injection. Do not use interferon alfa-2b solution.
- Prepare **immediately** before use.
- *Vial Reconstitution:* Select the appropriate number of vials (i.e., 10, 18, or 50 million units) and add to each the 1 mL of diluent supplied by the manufacturer. Gently swirl to dissolve but do not shake. **Must be** further diluted for infusion.
- *Further Dilution of Reconstituted Solution:* Add the required dose to 100 mL of NS. The final concentration should not be less than 10 million units/100 mL.

STORAGE
Store vials at 2°–8° C (36°–46° F). Discard any unused drug in reconstituted vials.

ADMINISTRATION
IV Infusion: Infuse over 20 min. Infusion solution should have been prepared immediately prior to use.

INCOMPATIBILITIES Solution/additive: **Dextrose solutions.**

ACTION & *THERAPEUTIC EFFECT* Interferon (IFN) alfa-2b, one of 4 types of alpha interferons, is a highly purified protein and natural product of human leukocytes formed within 4–6 h after viral stimulation. Produced by recombinant DNA technology (rIFN-A). **Antiviral action:** Reprograms virus-infected cells to inhibit various stages of virus replication. **Antitumor action:** Suppresses cell proliferation. **Immunomodulating action:** Enhances phagocytic activity of macrophages and augments specific cytotox-

Common adverse effects in *italic*, life-threatening effects <u>underlined</u>: generic names in **bold**; classifications in SMALL CAPS; ♣Canadian drug name; ● Prototype drug

375

icity of lymphocytes for target cells. The immune system and the interferon system of defense are complementary. *Has a broad spectrum of antiviral, cytotoxic, and immunomodulating activity (i.e., favorably adjusts immune system to better combat foreign invasion of antigens, cancers, and viruses).*

CONTRAINDICATIONS Hypersensitivity to interferon alfa-2b or to any components of the product; colitis; pancreatitis; neonates; pregnancy (category C), lactation.

CAUTIOUS USE Severe, preexisting cardiac, renal, or hepatic disease; pulmonary disease (e.g., COPD); diabetes mellitus patients prone to ketoacidosis; coagulation disorders; severe myelosuppression; recent MI; previous dysrhythmias.

ADVERSE EFFECTS (≥1%) **Body as a Whole:** *Flu-like syndrome (fever, chills) associated with myalgia and arthralgia,* leg cramps. **CNS:** Depression, nervousness, anxiety, confusion, *dizziness, fatigue,* somnolence, insomnia, altered mental states, ataxia, tremor, paresthesias, *headache.* **CV:** Hypertension, dyspnea, *hot flushes.* **Special Senses:** Epistaxis, pharyngitis, sneezing; abnormal vision. **GI:** Taste alteration, *anorexia,* weight loss, *nausea,* vomiting, stomatitis, *diarrhea,* flatulence. **Hematologic:** Mild thrombocytopenia, transient granulocytopenia, anemia, <u>neutropenia</u>, <u>leukemia</u>. **Skin:** Mild pruritus, mild alopecia, rash, dry skin, herpetic eruptions, nonherpetic cold sores, urticaria.

DRUG INTERACTIONS May increase **theophylline** levels; additive myelosuppression with ANTINEOPLASTICS, **zidovudine** may increase hematologic toxicity, increase **doxorubicin** toxicity, increase neurotoxicity with **vinblastine.** Use with **ribavirin** increases risk of hemolytic anemia; do not use in combination with **ribavirin** if CrCl is less than 50 mL/min.

PHARMACOKINETICS Metabolism: In kidneys. **Half-Life:** 6–7 h.

NURSING MANAGEMENT

Assessment & Drug Effects

- Monitor ECG before and during therapy with those who have a history of CV disease.
- Withhold drug and notify prescriber if platelet count falls below 25,000/mm³.
- Assess hydration status; patient should be well hydrated, especially during initial stage of treatment and if vomiting or diarrhea occurs.
- Lab tests: Baseline and periodic LFTs, CBC with differential and platelet count, Hct & Hgb.
- Monitor for and report ecchymoses, petechiae, and bruising.
- Assess for flu-like symptoms, which may be relieved by acetaminophen (if prescribed).
- Monitor level of GI distress and ability to consume fluids and food.
- Monitor mental status and alertness; implement safety precautions if needed. Patients with CNS or psychiatric disorders are at higher risk for adverse CNS reactions.

Patient & Family Education

- Note: If flu-like symptoms develop, take acetaminophen as advised by prescriber and take interferon at bedtime.

- Note: Fertile, nonpregnant women need to use effective contraception.
- Use caution with hazardous activities until response to drug is known.
- Learn about adverse effects and notify prescriber about those that cause significant discomfort.

IRINOTECAN HYDROCHLORIDE

(eye-ri-no′te-can)

Camptosar

Classification(s): ANTINEOPLASTIC, DNA TOPOISOMERASE INHIBITOR
Therapeutic: ANTINEOPLASTIC
Prototype: Topotecan
Pregnancy Category: D

USES Metastatic carcinoma of colon or rectum.

INDICATION & DOSAGE

Metastatic Carcinoma

Adult: 125 mg/m^2 once weekly for 4 wk, then a 2-wk rest period (single agent) OR 350 mg/m^2 q3wk
Adult: (combination with other agents) 125 mg/m^2 days 1, 8, 15, 22 then begin next cycle day 43 OR 180 mg/m^2 days 1, 15, 29 then begin next cycle on day 43

Toxicity Adjustments

See complete prescribing information. Dosage will be reduced or doses omitted based on severity of adverse reactions (NCI's Common Toxicity Criteria).

SOLUTION PREPARATION

- Wash immediately with soap and water if skin contacts drug during preparation.
- Dilute the ordered dose in enough D5W (preferred) or NS to yield a concentration of 0.12–2.8 mg/mL. Typical amount of diluent used is 250–500 mL.

STORAGE

Store undiluted at 15°–30° C (59°–86° F) and protect from light. Use reconstituted solutions within 24 h.

ADMINISTRATION

- Administer only after premedication (at least 30 min prior) with an antiemetic.
- **IV Infusion:** Infuse over 90 min.
- Closely monitor IV site; if extravasation occurs, immediately flush with sterile water and apply ice.

INCOMPATIBILITIES Y-site: **Gemcitabine, pemetrexed.**

ACTION & *THERAPEUTIC EFFECT* Irinotecan is a camptothecin analog that displays antitumor activity by inhibiting the intranuclear enzyme topo-

---

Common adverse effects in *italic*, life-threatening effects <u>underlined</u>: generic names in **bold**; classifications in SMALL CAPS; ♣ Canadian drug name; ● Prototype drug

377

isomerase I, thus inhibiting DNA and RNA synthesis. Topoisomerase I is an essential intranuclear enzyme that relaxes the supercoiled DNA, thus enabling replication and transcription to take place. By inhibiting topoisomerase I, irinotecan and its active metabolite SN-38 cause double-stranded DNA damage during the synthesis (S) phase of DNA production. *Irinotecan inhibits both DNA and RNA synthesis.*

CONTRAINDICATIONS Previous hypersensitivity to irinotecan, topotecan, or other camptothecin analogs; acute infection; diarrhea; pregnancy (category D), lactation. Safety and effectiveness in children are not established.

CAUTIOUS USE Gastrointestinal disorders; myelosuppression; renal or hepatic impairment; history of bleeding disorders; previous cytotoxic or radiation therapy.

ADVERSE EFFECTS (≥1%) **Body as a Whole:** *Asthenia, fever, pain,* chills, edema, abdominal enlargement, back pain. **CNS:** Headache, *insomnia, dizziness.* **CV:** Vasodilation/flushing. **GI:** *Diarrhea (early and late onset), dehydration, nausea, vomiting, anorexia, weight loss, constipation, abdominal cramping and pain,* flatulence, stomatitis, dyspepsia, increased alkaline phosphatase and AST. **Hematologic:** <u>Leukopenia, neutropenia</u>, *anemia.* **Respiratory:** *Dyspnea,* cough, rhinitis. **Skin:** *Alopecia,* sweating, rash.

DRUG INTERACTIONS ANTICOAGULANTS, ANTIPLATELET AGENTS, NSAIDS may increase risk of bleeding; **carbamazepine, phenytoin, phenobarbital** may decrease irinotecan levels, **ketoconazole** increases the risk of side effects. **Herbal: St. John's wort** decreases efficacy.

PHARMACOKINETICS Peak: 1 h. **Distribution:** Irinotecan is 30% bound to plasma proteins; active metabolite SN-38 is 95% protein bound. **Metabolism:** In liver by carboxylesterase enzyme to active metabolite SN-38. **Elimination:** 10 h for SN-38; approximately 20% excreted in urine. **Half-Life:** 10–20 h.

NURSING IMPLICATIONS

Assessment & Drug Effects

- Prior to initiating therapy: Baseline WBC with differential, Hgb, and platelet count.
- Report promptly signs of hematologic toxicity (e.g., neutrophil count less than 1500/mm³, platelet count less than 100,000/mm³.
- Monitor for acute GI distress, especially early diarrhea (within 24 h of infusion), which may be preceded by diaphoresis and cramping, and late diarrhea (more than 24 h after infusion).
- Monitor fluid status especially with vomiting and diarrhea. Report promptly signs of dehydration (e.g., reduced urine output, poor skin turgor, dry mucous membranes).
- Lab tests: Frequent WBC with differential, Hgb, platelet count, coagulation parameters; serum electrolytes during and after periods of diarrhea; periodic LFTs, renal function tests, and blood glucose.
- Monitor for signs of infection especially during times of leukopenia.
- Avoid traumatic procedures during times of thrombocytopenia.

Patient & Family Education

- Notify prescriber immediately when you experience diarrhea, vomiting, and S&S of infection. Diarrhea requires prompt treatment to prevent serious fluid and electrolyte imbalances.
- Report promptly any signs of bleeding including easy bruising, black tarry stools, blood in urine.
- Avoid immunizations unless approved by prescriber.

IRON DEXTRAN
(i′ern dek′stran)

DexFerrum, InFeD

Classification(s): HEMATINIC; IRON PREPARATION
Therapeutic: ANTIANEMIC
Pregnancy Category: C

USES Only in patients with clearly established iron deficiency anemia when oral administration of iron is unsatisfactory or impossible. Each milliliter of iron dextran contains 50 mg elemental iron.

INDICATION & DOSAGE

Iron Deficiency

Adult: Dose is individualized and determined based on patient's weight and hemoglobin (see package insert); do not administer more than 100 mg (2 mL) of iron dextran within 24 h
Child (less than 5 kg): No more than 0.5 mL (25 mg)/day; *(5–10 kg):* no more than 1 mL (50 mg)/day; *(over 10 kg):* no more than 2 mL (100 mg)/day

SOLUTION PREPARATION
No dilution is required. Administer as supplied.

STORAGE
Store at 15°–30° C (59°–86° F).

ADMINISTRATION

- *Test Dose:* A test dose is given before the first IV therapeutic dose. *DexFerrum:* Give test dose of 25 mg (0.5 mL) slowly over 5 min. *InFeD:* Give test dose over 30 sec. Wait 1–2 h and if no adverse reaction occurs, give the remainder of the first dose.
- Have epinephrine (0.5 mL of a 1:1000 solution) immediately available for hypersensitivity emergency.
- Although anaphylactic reactions (see Appendix C) usually occur within a few minutes after injection, it is recommended that 1 h or more elapse before remainder of initial dose is given following test dose.
- **Infusion:** Infuse at a rate not to exceed 50 mg (1 mL) or fraction thereof over 60 sec. Avoid rapid infusion.

Common adverse effects in *italic*, life-threatening effects <u>underlined</u>: generic names in **bold**; classifications in SMALL CAPS; ♣ Canadian drug name; ● Prototype drug

379

INCOMPATIBILITIES Solution/additive: TPN.

ACTION & *THERAPEUTIC EFFECT* A liquid complex of ferric hydroxide with dextran in 0.9% NaCl solution for injection. Reticuloendothelial cells of liver, spleen, and bone marrow dissociate iron from the iron dextran complex. The released ferric ion combines with transferrin and is transported to bone marrow, where it is incorporated into hemoglobin. *Effective in replacement of iron needed in iron deficiency anemia, thus replenishing hemoglobin and depleted iron stores.*

CONTRAINDICATIONS Hypersensitivity to the product; all anemias except iron-deficiency anemia; acute phase of infectious renal disease; pregnancy (category C).

CAUTIOUS USE Rheumatoid arthritis, ankylosing spondylitis; renal disease; SLE; cardiac disease; impaired hepatic function; history of allergies or asthma; lactation.

ADVERSE EFFECTS (≥1%) **Body as a Whole:** Hypersensitivity (urticaria, skin rash, allergic purpura, pruritus, fever, chills, dyspnea, arthralgia, myalgia; <u>anaphylaxis</u>). **CNS:** Headache, shivering, transient paresthesias, syncope, dizziness, <u>coma</u>, seizures. **CV:** *Peripheral vascular flushing (rapid IV), hypotension,* precordial pain or pressure sensation, tachycardia, <u>fatal cardiac arrhythmias, circulatory collapse</u>. **GI:** Nausea, vomiting, transient loss of taste perception, metallic taste, diarrhea, melena, abdominal pain, hemorrhagic gastritis, intestinal necrosis, hepatic damage. **Skin:** Local phlebitis, lymphadenopathy, *pain at injection site.* **Metabolic:** Hemosiderosis, metabolic acidosis, hyperglycemia, reactivation of quiescent rheumatoid arthritis, exogenous hemosiderosis. **Hematologic:** Bleeding disorder with severe toxicity.

DIAGNOSTIC TEST INTERFERENCE Falsely elevated ***serum bilirubin*** and falsely decreased ***serum calcium*** values may occur. Large doses of iron dextran may impart a brown color to serum drawn 4 h after iron administration. ***Bone scans*** involving Tc-99m diphosphonate have shown dense areas of activity along contour of iliac crest 1–6 days after IM injections of iron dextran.

DRUG INTERACTIONS May decrease absorption of oral **iron, chloramphenicol** may decrease effectiveness of iron; a toxic complex may form with **dimercaprol.**

PHARMACOKINETICS Distribution: Crosses placenta; distributed into breast milk. **Metabolism:** In reticuloendothelial system. **Half-Life:** 6 h.

NURSING IMPLICATIONS
Assessment & Drug Effects
- Monitor closely BP and pulse, and assess closely for S&S of anaphylaxis (see Appendix C). Have patient remain in bed for at least 30 min after IV administration to prevent orthostatic hypotension.
- Note that large IV doses are associated with increased frequency of adverse effects.

- Lab tests: Baseline and periodic Hgb, Hct, serum ferritin, transferrin saturation, and reticulocyte count.

Patient & Family Education
- Remain supine until instructed that it is safe to stand.
- Do not take oral iron preparations when receiving IV iron.
- Report promptly any of the following: Backache or muscle ache, chills, dizziness, fever, headache, nausea or vomiting, pain or redness at injection site, skin rash or hives, or difficulty breathing.

IRON SUCROSE INJECTION
(i'ron su'crose)
Venofer
Classification(s): HEMATINIC, IRON PREPARATION
Therapeutic: ANTIANEMIC
Pregnancy Category: B

USES Treatment of iron deficiency anemia in patients with chronic renal failure (with or without concurrent administration of erythropoietin).

INDICATION & DOSAGE

Iron Deficiency Anemia in CDK
Hemodialysis-dependent (HDD-CDK) *Adult:* 100 mg at least 15 min per hemodialysis session (cumulative dose 1,000 mg)
Non–hemodialysis-dependent (NDD-CDK) *Adult:* 200 mg on 5 different occasions within the 14-day period
Peritoneal Dialysis-dependent (PDD-CDK) *Adult:* 300 mg on days 1 and 15 then 400 mg 14 days later

SOLUTION PREPARATION
HDD-CDK Patient: May give 100 mg undiluted [direct IV] or diluted in a maximum of 100 mL NS immediately prior to infusion.
NDD-CDK Patient: May give 200 mg undiluted [direct IV].
PDD-CDK Patient: Dilute 300–400 mg in a maximum of 250 mL of NS.

STORAGE
Store unopened vials preferably at 25° C (77° F), but room temperature is permitted. Discard unused portion in opened vial.

ADMINISTRATION
HDD-CDK Patient
- **Direct IV Injection:** Give 100 mg undiluted bolus dose slowly over 2–5 min.
- **IV Infusion:** Infuse diluted solution over at least 15 min.

Common adverse effects in *italic*, life-threatening effects <u>underlined</u>: generic names in **bold**; classifications in SMALL CAPS; ♣ Canadian drug name; ❷ Prototype drug

381

NDD-CDK Patient
- **Direct IV Injection:** Give 200 mg undiluted bolus dose slowly over 2–5 min.

PDD-CDK Patient
- **IV Infusion:** Infuse diluted solution over 90 min.

INCOMPATIBILITIES Solution/additive: Do not mix with other medications or parenteral nutrition solutions.

ACTION & *THERAPEUTIC EFFECT* A complex of polynuclear iron (III) hydroxide in sucrose. It is dissociated by the reticuloendothelial system (RES) into iron and sucrose. Normal erythropoiesis depends on the concentration of iron and erythropoietin available in the plasma; both are decreased in renal failure. Exogenous administration of erythropoietin increases red blood cell production and iron utilization, contributing to iron deficiency in hemodialized patients. *Increases serum iron level in chronic renal failure patients, and results in increased hemoglobin level.*

CONTRAINDICATIONS Patients with iron overload, hypersensitivity to iron sucrose injection, or for anemia not caused by iron deficiency; hemochromatosis; concomitant use with an oral iron preparation.

CAUTIOUS USE Patients with a history of hypotension; older adults; decreased renal, hepatic, or cardiac function; pregnancy (category B), lactation. Safety and effectiveness in infants or children are not established.

ADVERSE EFFECTS (≥1%) **Body as a Whole:** Fever, pain, asthenia, malaise, <u>anaphylactoid reactions</u>. **Cardiovascular:** *Hypotension,* chest pain, hypertension, hypervolemia. **Digestive:** Nausea, vomiting, diarrhea, abdominal pain, elevated liver function tests. **Musculoskeletal:** *Leg cramps,* muscle pain. **CNS:** Headache, dizziness. **Respiratory:** Dyspnea, pneumonia, cough. **Skin:** Pruritus, injection site reaction.

DRUG INTERACTIONS May reduce absorption of ORAL IRON PREPARATIONS.

PHARMACOKINETICS Peak: 4 wk. **Distribution:** Primarily to blood with some distribution to liver, spleen, bone marrow. **Metabolism:** Dissociated to iron and sucrose in reticuloendothelial system. **Elimination:** Sucrose is eliminated in urine, 5% of iron excreted in urine. **Half-Life:** 6 h.

NURSING IMPLICATIONS

Assessment & Drug Effects

- Withhold drug and notify prescriber when serum ferritin level equals or exceeds established guidelines.
- Stop infusion and notify prescriber for S&S overdosage or infusing too rapidly: Hypotension, edema; headache, dizziness, nausea, vomiting, abdominal pain, joint or muscle pain, and paresthesia.
- Lab tests: Periodic serum ferritin, transferrin saturation, Hct, and Hgb.
- Monitor vital signs closely during and for the first 30 min after initiation of IV therapy for signs of hypersensitivity and anaphylactoid reaction (see Appendix C).

Patient & Family Education

▪ Report any of the following promptly: Itching, rash, chest pain, headache, dizziness, nausea, vomiting, abdominal pain, joint or muscle pain, and numbness and tingling.

ISOPROTERENOL HYDROCHLORIDE ⓟ

(eye-soe-proe-ter′e-nole)

Isuprel

Classification(s): BETA-ADRENERGIC AGONIST
Therapeutic: BRONCHODILATOR; ANTIARRHYTHMIC
Pregnancy Category: C

USES Used as cardiac stimulant in cardiac arrest, carotid sinus hypersensitivity, cardiogenic and bacteremic shock, Adams-Stokes syndrome, or ventricular arrhythmias, bronchospasm during anesthesia. Used in treatment of shock that persists after replacement of blood volume.

INDICATION & DOSAGE

Cardiac Ventricular Arrhythmias

Adult: 0.02–0.06 mg bolus, followed by 0.2–0.2 mg prn OR 5 mcg/min infusion (all dosing titrated to patient response)

AV Block/Bradycardia

Adult: 2–10 mcg/min (minimum dose adjusted to patient response)
Child: 0.1 mcg/kg/min by continuous infusion

Shock/Hypoperfusion

Adult: 0.5–5 mcg/min

Bronchospasm

Adult: 0.01–0.02 mg prn

Cardiac Arrest

Adult: 2–10 mcg/min titrated to patient response

SOLUTION PREPARATION
Adult with AV Block/Arrhythmia/Bradycardia/Cardiac Arrest

▪ *Direct IV Injection:* Dilute 1 mL (0.2 mg) of 1:5000 solution with 9 mL NS or D5W to produce a 1:50,000 (0.02 mg/mL) solution or use 1:50,000 solution undiluted.
▪ *Continuous Infusion:* Dilute 10 mL (2 mg) of 1:5000 solution in 500 mL D5W to produce a 1:250,000 (4 mcg/mL) solution.

Adult with Shock/Hypoperfusion

▪ *IV Infusion:* Dilute 5 mL (1 mg) of 1:5000 solution in 500 mL D5W to produce a 1:500,000 (2 mcg/mL) solution.

Common adverse effects in *italic*, life-threatening effects <u>underlined</u>: generic names in **bold**; classifications in SMALL CAPS; ♣ Canadian drug name; ⓟ Prototype drug

ISOPROTERENOL HYDROCHLORIDE

Adult with Bronchospasm

▪ *Direct IV Injection:* Dilute 1 mL (0.2 mg) of 1:5000 solution with 9 mL NS or D5W to produce a 1:50,000 (0.02 mg/mL) solution or use 1:50,000 solution undiluted.

Child with AV Block/Bradycardia

▪ *Continuous Infusion:* Dilute to a range of 4–12 mcg/mL in 100 mL of D5W or NS.

▪ Maximum Concentration: 20 mcg/mL (0.02 mg/mL)

STORAGE

Isoproterenol solutions lose potency with standing. Discard if precipitate or discoloration is present.

ADMINISTRATION

▪ **Direct IV Injection:** Give bolus dose over at a rate of 0.2 mg or fraction thereof over 1 min. Flush with 15–20 mL NS.

▪ **IV Infusion:** Infusion rate is adjusted according to patient response. Infusion is generally decreased or may be temporarily discontinued if heart rate exceeds 110 bpm, because of the danger of precipitating arrhythmias. Response to therapy **must be** monitored continuously.

INCOMPATIBILITIES Solution/additive: Sodium bicarbonate, aminophylline, carbenicillin, diazepam, furosemide.

ACTION & *THERAPEUTIC EFFECT* Synthetic sympathomimetic amine. Acts directly on beta$_1$-adrenergic receptors with little or no effect on alpha-adrenoreceptors. Stimulation of beta$_2$-adrenoreceptors relaxes bronchospasm and, by increasing ciliary motion, facilitates expectoration of pulmonary secretions. Drug-induced stimulation of beta$_1$-adrenergic receptors results in increased cardiac output and cardiac workload by increasing strength of contraction through positive inotropic and chronotropic effects on the heart. It also shortens AV conduction time and its refractory period in patients with heart block. *Effective in bronchodilation by reversing bronchospasm as well as facilitating removal of bronchial secretion. Increases cardiac output and cardiac workload. Also has antiarrhythmic properties by affecting AV node conduction.*

CONTRAINDICATIONS Preexisting cardiac arrhythmias associated with tachycardia; tachycardia caused by digitalis intoxication, central hyperexcitability, cardiogenic shock secondary to coronary artery occlusion and MI; simultaneous administration with epinephrine; ventricular fibrillation; pregnancy (category C).

CAUTIOUS USE Sensitivity to sympathomimetic amines; older adult and debilitated patients; hypertension; coronary insufficiency and other cardiovascular disorders; angina; renal dysfunction; hyperthyroidism; diabetes; prostatic hypertrophy; glaucoma; tuberculosis; during anesthesia using cyclopropane; lactation.

ADVERSE EFFECTS (≥1%) **CNS:** Headache, mild tremors, nervousness, anxiety, insomnia, excitement, fatigue. **CV:** Flushing, palpitations, tachycardia, unstable BP, anginal pain, ventricular arrhythmias. **GI:** Swelling of parotids (prolonged use), bad taste, buccal ulcerations (sublingual administration), nausea. **Other:** Severe prolonged asthma attack, sweating, bronchial irritation and edema. **Acute Poisoning:** Overdosage, especially after excessive use of aerosols (*tachycardia,* palpitations, nervousness, nausea, vomiting).

DRUG INTERACTIONS Epinephrine and other SYMPATHOMIMETIC AMINES increase effects and cause cardiac toxicity. HALOGENATED GENERAL ANESTHETICS, TRICYCLIC ANTIDEPRESSANTS exacerbate arrhythmias; while BETA BLOCKERS antagonize effects.

PHARMACOKINETICS Metabolism: Action terminated by tissue uptake and metabolized by COMT in liver, lungs, and other tissues. **Elimination:** 40–50% excreted in urine unchanged.

NURSING IMPLICATIONS

Assessment & Drug Effects

* Monitor ECG continuously before and during IV administration. Rate greater than 110 usually indicates need to slow infusion rate or discontinue infusion. Consult prescriber for guidelines. Incidence of arrhythmias is high, particularly when drug is administered to patients with cardiogenic shock or ischemic heart disease, digitalized patients, or to those with electrolyte imbalance.
* Note: Tolerance to bronchodilating effect and cardiac stimulant effect may develop with prolonged use. Once tolerance has developed, continued use can result in serious adverse effects including rebound bronchospasm.
* Monitor I&O: Hourly urine may be advisable as an indicator of tissue perfusion.
* Monitor diabetics for loss of glycemic control.

IXABEPILONE

(ix-a-be-pi′lone)

Ixempra

Classification(s): ANTINEOPLASTIC, MITOTIC INHIBITOR
Therapeutic: ANTINEOPLASTIC
Pregnancy Category: D

USES Treatment of metastatic or locally advanced breast cancer either alone or in combination with capecitabine in patients who have failed therapy with an anthracycline and a taxane. Monotherapy is indicated only if a patient has also failed with capecitabine therapy.

INDICATION & DOSAGE

Breast Cancer

Adult: 40 mg/m^2 over 3 h q3wk

Common adverse effects in *italic*, life-threatening effects underlined: generic names in **bold**; classifications in SMALL CAPS; ♣ Canadian drug name; ◯ Prototype drug

Obesity

Body Surface Area: BSA greater than 2.2 m², dosage should be calculated based on 2.2 m²

Dosage Adjustments

Grade 2 neuropathy 7 days or longer, or grade 3 neuropathy less than 7 days, or grade 3 toxicity other than neuropathy: 32 mg/m²

Neutrophil less than 500 cells/mm³ 7 days or longer, or febrile neutrope-nia, or platelets less than 25,000/mm³ or platelets less than 50,000/mm³ with bleeding: Decrease dose by 20%.

Grade 3 neuropathy 7 days or longer, or disabling neuropathy, or any grade 4 toxicity: Do not administer.

Regimen with a strong CYP3A4 inhibitor: 20 mg/m²

Hepatic Impairment in Monotherapy

AST and ALT less than or equal to 10 × the ULN and bilirubin less than or equal to 1.5 × ULN: 32 mg/m²

AST and ALT less than or equal to 10 × ULN and bilirubin greater than 1.5 × ULN but less than or equal to 3 × ULN: 20–30 mg/m²

AST and ALT greater than 10 × ULN or bilirubin greater than 3 × ULN: Do not administer.

SOLUTION PREPARATION

- Use gloves when handling vials containing ixabepilone.
- *Vial Reconstitution:* Supplied in kit containing a powder vial and dilu-ent vial. Allow kit to come to room temperature for 30 min before reconstitution. Slowly inject diluent into the powder vial to yield 2 mg/mL. Swirl gently and invert vial to dissolve. **Must be** further diluted for infusion.
- *Further Dilution of Reconstituted Solution:* Add required dose to LR solution in DEHP-free bags. Select a volume of LR to produce a final concentration of 0.2–0.6 mg/mL. Mix thoroughly.

STORAGE

- Store kit refrigerated at 2–8° C (36–46° F) in original packaging.
- Reconstituted solution may be stored in the vial for a maximum of 1 h at room temperature/light. Once diluted with lactated Ringer's injec-tion, solution is stable at room temperature/light for 6 h.

ADMINISTRATION

IV Infusion: Use DEHP-free infusion line with a 0.2–1.2 micron in-line filter. Infuse at a rate appropriate to the total volume of solution. Com-plete infusion within 6 h of preparation.

INCOMPATIBILITIES Solution/additive: Diluents other than **lactated Ringer's** injection should not be combined with ixabepilone. **Y-site:** Do not add to Y-site.

ACTION & *THERAPEUTIC EFFECT* Binds directly to microtubules needed to form the spindle required for mitosis of dividing cells. *Blocks cells in the mitotic phase of cell division cycle, thus leading to cancer cell death.*

CONTRAINDICATIONS Hepatic impairment in patients with AST or ALT greater than 10 times ULN, and/or bilirubin greater than 3 times ULN; concomitant use of capecitabine when bilirubin is greater than 1 ULN, or AST or ALT is greater than 2.5 ULN; concomitant use of strong CYP3A4 inhibitors (e.g. itraconazole, saquinavir, etc.) or ixabepilone requires decreased dosage adjustment; grade 4 neuropathy or any other grade 4 toxicity; grade 3 neuropathy (severe) that last 7 days or longer; disabling neuropathy; pregnancy (category D), lactation.

CAUTIOUS USE Hypersensitivity to ixabepilone; monotherapy of patients with hepatic impairment baseline values of AST or ALT greater than 5 times ULN.

ADVERSE EFFECTS (≥1%) **Body as a Whole:** Chest pain, dehydration, edema, *fatigue*, hypersensitivity reactions, pain, *peripheral neuropathy*, pyrexia. **CNS:** Dizziness, *headache*, insomnia. **CV:** Flushing. **GI:** *Abdominal pain, anorexia, constipation, diarrhea,* gastroesophageal reflux disease, *mucositis, nausea, stomatitis, vomiting,* taste disorder. **Hematological:** Anemia, *leukopenia, neutropenia,* thrombocytopenia. **Metabolic:** Weight loss. **Musculoskeletal:** *Arthralgia, myalgia, musculoskeletal pain.* **Respiratory:** Cough, dyspnea, upper respiratory tract infection. **Skin:** *Alopecia,* exfoliation, hyperpigmentation, nail disorder, palmar-plantar erythrodysesthesia syndrome, pruritus, rash. **Special Senses:** Lacrimation.

DRUG INTERACTIONS Inhibitors of CYP3A4 (e.g., HIV PROTEASE INHIBITORS, MACROLIDE ANTIBIOTICS, AZOLE ANTIFUGAL AGENTS) increase the plasma level of ixabepilone. Strong CYP3A4 inducers (e.g., **dexamethasone, phenytoin, carbamazepine, rifampin, rifabutin, phenobarbital**) decrease the plasma level of ixabepilone. **Food: Grapefruit** and **grapefruit juice** increase the plasma level of ixabepilone. **Herbal: St. John's wort** decreases the plasma level of ixabepilone.

PHARMACOKINETICS Distribution: 67–77% protein bound. **Metabolism:** In liver. **Elimination:** Stool (major) and urine (minor). **Half-Life:** 52 h.

NURSING IMPLICATIONS
Assessment & Drug Effects
- Monitor for signs of an infusion-related hypersensitivity reaction.
- Monitor for and promptly report signs of neuropathy.
- Lab tests: Baseline and periodic WBC count with differential, platelet count, LFTs, periodic serum electrolytes.

Patient & Family Education
- Report promptly any of the following: Numbness and tingling of the hands or feet, S&S of infection (e.g., fever of 100.5° F or greater, chills, cough, burning or pain on urination), hives, itching, rash, flushing, swelling, shortness of breath, difficulty breathing, chest tightness or pain, palpitations or unusual weight gain.
- Use effective contraceptive measures to prevent pregnancy.

KANAMYCIN

(kan-a-mye'sin)

Kantrex

Classification(s): ANTIBIOTIC; AMINOGLYCOSIDE
Therapeutic: ANTIBACTERIAL
Prototype: Gentamicin
Pregnancy Category: D

USES For short-term treatment of serious infections.
UNLABELED USES In conjunction with other drugs to treat tuberculosis in patients resistant to conventional therapy.

INDICATION & DOSAGE

Serious Infection

Adult: 5–7.5 mg/kg/day in divided doses q8–12h (not to exceed 15 mg/kg/day)
Child: 15 mg/kg/day in equally divided doses q8–12h

Obesity

Dose based on IBW.

Renal Impairment Dosage Adjustment

CrCl 50–80 mL/min: Give 60–90% of dose; *CrCl 10–50 mL/min:* Give 30–70% of dose or regular dose q12h; *CrCl less than 10 mL/min:* Give 20–30% of dose or regular dose q24–48h

SOLUTION PREPARATION

* *Adult:* Dilute each 500 mg with at least 100 mL NS, D5W, D5NS, or other compatible solution.
* *Child:* Dilute each 2.5–5 mg in 1 mL of NS, D5W, D5NS, or other compatible solution.

STORAGE

Store vials at 15°–30° C (59°–86° F) unless otherwise directed. Some vials may darken with time, but this does not affect potency. Discard partially used vials within 48 h.

ADMINISTRATION

Intermittent Infusion: Infuse over 30–60 min. Use a constant-rate volumetric infusion device for administration to a child.

INCOMPATIBILITIES Solution/additive: Do not mix with other ANTIBIOTICS, **chlorpheniramine, colistimethate, heparin, hydrocortisone, methohexital.**

ACTION & *THERAPEUTIC EFFECT* Broad-spectrum, aminoglycoside antibiotic. It is known that aminoglycosides bind irreversibly to aminoglycoside-binding sites on 30 S ribosomal subunit of bacteria, subsequently inhibiting bacterial protein synthesis. To be bacteriocidal, an aminoglycoside needs to achieve intracellular concentrations in excess of extracellular ones. *Usually bacteriocidal in action. Active against many gram-negative bacteria as well as some gram-positive bacteria. It is not effective against anaerobic gram-negative bacteria.*

CONTRAINDICATIONS History of hypersensitivity to kanamycin or other aminoglycosides; history of drug-induced ototoxicity, preexisting hearing loss, vertigo, or tinnitus; long-term therapy; intraperitoneally to patients under effects of inhalation anesthetics or skeletal muscle relaxants; pregnancy (category D).

CAUTIOUS USE Impaired renal function; older adults, neonates, and infants (immature renal systems); myasthenia gravis; parkinsonian syndrome.

ADVERSE EFFECTS (≥1%) **All:** Dose related. **Body as a Whole:** Eosinophilia, maculopapular rash, pruritus, urticaria, drug fever, <u>anaphylaxis</u>. **CNS:** Dizziness, circumoral and other paresthesias, optic neuritis, peripheral neuritis, headache, restlessness, tremors, lethargy, convulsions; <u>neuromuscular paralysis, respiratory depression</u> (rarely). **Special Senses:** Deafness (can be irreversible), *tinnitus, vertigo* or *dizziness,* ataxia, nystagmus. **GI:** Nausea, vomiting, diarrhea, appetite changes, proctitis. **Hematologic:** Anemia, increased or decreased reticulocytes, granulocytopenia, <u>agranulocytosis</u>, thrombocytopenia, purpura. **Urogenital:** <u>Nephrotoxicity</u>; hematuria, urine casts and cells, proteinuria; elevated serum creatinine and BUN. **Other:** Superinfections; local pain; nodular formation at injection site.

DRUG INTERACTIONS Amphotericin B, cisplatin, methoxyflurane, vancomycin add to nephrotoxicity; GENERAL ANESTHETICS, SKELETAL MUSCLE RELAXANTS add to neuromuscular blocking effects; **capreomycin** compounds ototoxicity and nephrotoxicity; LOOP and THIAZIDE DIURETICS, **carboplatin** may increase risk of ototoxicity.

PHARMACOKINETICS Peak: 1–2 h. **Distribution:** Crosses placenta; distributed into breast milk. **Elimination:** 80–90% excreted in urine within 24 h. **Half-Life:** 2–4 h.

NURSING IMPLICATIONS

Assessment & Drug Effects

- Report promptly signs of renal irritation: Albuminuria, casts, red and white cells in urine, increasing BUN and serum creatinine, decreasing creatinine clearance, oliguria, and edema.
- Lab tests: Baseline and periodic urinalysis, kidney function tests; periodic serum sodium, potassium, calcium, and magnesium; monitor peak and trough serum kanamycin concentrations (peak 30 min after infusion and trough just before the next dose).
- Keep patient well hydrated to prevent chemical irritation of renal tubules.
- Monitor I&O. Report decrease in urine output or change in I&O ratio.
- Determine baseline weight and vital signs and monitor at regular intervals during therapy.
- Report signs of superinfection (see Appendix C).

Common adverse effects in *italic*, life-threatening effects <u>underlined</u>: generic names in **bold**; classifications in SMALL CAPS; ♣ Canadian drug name; ❂ Prototype drug

389

- Monitor for hearing and balance problems; stop drug if ototoxicity occurs. Tinnitus is not a reliable index of ototoxicity in the very elderly.
- Risk of ototoxicity is high in patients with impaired renal function, older adults, poorly hydrated patients, and with therapy for 5 days or longer. Note: Deafness has occurred 2–7 days or more after termination of therapy in patients with impaired renal function.

Patient & Family Education

- Report promptly ototoxic symptoms: Dizziness, hearing loss, weakness, or loss of balance.

KETOROLAC TROMETHAMINE

(ke-tor'o-lac)

Toradol

Classification(s): ANALGESIC, NONSTEROIDAL ANTIINFLAMMATORY DRUG (NSAID)
Therapeutic: ANALGESIC
Prototype: Indomethacin
Pregnancy Category: B

USES *Short-term* management of pain.

INDICATION & DOSAGE

Pain

Adult: 30 mg (15 mg if patient less than 50 kg); can repeat q6h (max use: 5 days)
Geriatric: 15 mg
Child (over 2): Single dose of 0.5 mg/kg (max: 15 mg)

Renal Impairment Dosage Adjustment

Do not use in advanced renal impairment.

SOLUTION PREPARATION

No dilution is required. Administer as supplied.

STORAGE

Store all forms at 15°–30° C (59°–86° F).

ADMINISTRATION

- Correct hypovolemia prior to administration of ketorolac.
- **Direct IV Injection:** Give bolus dose over at least 15 sec. Preferred method is to give through a Y-tube in a free-flowing IV.

INCOMPATIBILITIES Solution/additive: Hydroxyzine, meperidine, morphine, prochlorperazine, promethazine. Y-site: Azithromycin, fenoldopam.

Common adverse effects in *italic*, life-threatening effects underlined: generic names in **bold**; classifications in SMALL CAPS; ♥ Canadian drug name; ☯ Prototype drug

ACTION & *THERAPEUTIC EFFECT* It inhibits synthesis of prostaglandins by inhibiting both COX-1 and COX-2 enzymes, and is a peripherally acting analgesic. *Ketorolac exhibits analgesic, antiinflammatory, and antipyretic activity. Effective in controlling acute postoperative pain.*

CONTRAINDICATIONS Hypersensitivity to ketorolac; individuals with complete or partial syndrome of nasal polyps, angioedema, and bronchospastic reaction to aspirin or other NSAIDs; during labor and delivery; patients with severe renal impairment or at risk for renal failure due to volume depletion; patients with risk of bleeding; active peptic ulcer disease; pre- or intraoperatively; intrathecal or epidural administration; in combination with other NSAIDs; children less than 2 y.

CAUTIOUS USE History of peptic ulcers; impaired renal or hepatic function; older adults; diabetes mellitus; SLE; CHF; debilitated patients; pregnancy (category B).

ADVERSE EFFECTS (≥1%) **CNS:** *Drowsiness,* dizziness, headache. **GI:** *Nausea,* dyspepsia, GI pain, <u>hemorrhage</u>. **Other:** Edema, sweating, pain at injection site.

DRUG INTERACTIONS May increase **methotrexate** levels and toxicity; may increase **lithium** levels and toxicity.

PHARMACOKINETICS Distribution: Passes into breast milk. **Metabolism:** In liver. **Elimination:** In urine. **Half-Life:** 4–6 h.

NURSING IMPLICATIONS

Assessment & Drug Effects

- Monitor urine output in older adults and patients with a history of cardiac decompensation, renal impairment, heart failure, or liver dysfunction as well as those taking diuretics.
- Monitor for S&S of GI distress or bleeding including nausea, GI pain, diarrhea, melena, or hematemesis. GI ulceration with perforation can occur anytime during treatment. Drug decreases platelet aggregation and thus may prolong bleeding time.
- Monitor for fluid retention and edema in patients with a history of CHF.

Patient & Family Education

- Report promptly: S&S of GI ulceration and bleeding (e.g., bloody emesis, black tarry stools).
- Do not drive or engage in potentially hazardous activities until response to drug is known.

LABETALOL HYDROCHLORIDE

(la-bet′a-lole)

Trandate

Classification(s): ANTIHYPERTENSIVE, ALPHA- AND BETA-ADRENERGIC ANTAGONIST

Common adverse effects in *italic*, life-threatening effects <u>underlined</u>: generic names in **bold**; classifications in SMALL CAPS; ♣ Canadian drug name; ☢ Prototype drug

391

LABETALOL HYDROCHLORIDE

Therapeutic: ANTIHYPERTENSIVE
Prototype: Propranolol
Pregnancy Category: B first & second trimester, D third trimester

USES Control of severe hypertension.

INDICATION & DOSAGE

Hypertension

Adult: 20 mg slowly over 2 min, with 40–80 mg q10min if needed up to 300 mg total or 2 mg/min continuous infusion (max: 300 mg total dose)

SOLUTION PREPARATION

- *Direct IV Injection:* No dilution is required. Administer as supplied.
- *Continuous Infusion:* May be diluted in common IV fluids (e.g., D5W, NS, D5NS, LR) for infusion. Examples: 200 mg (40 mL) in 250 mL of IV solution yields 2 mg/3 mL; 300 mg (60 mL) in 240 mL of IV solution yields 1 mg/mL.

STORAGE

Store at 2°–30° C (36°–86° F) unless otherwise advised. Do not freeze.

ADMINISTRATION

- **Direct IV Injection:** Give a 20-mg dose slowly over 2 min.
- **Continuous Infusion:** Typically infused at 2 mg/min. Controlled infusion pump device is recommended for maintaining accurate flow rate during IV infusion.
- Keep patient supine when receiving labetalol. Take BP immediately before administration. Rate is adjusted according to BP response. Slow rate of infusion for rapidly falling BP.

INCOMPATIBILITIES Solution/additive: Sodium bicarbonate, ceftriaxone, tenecteplase. **Y-site:** Amphotericin B cholesteryl complex, cefoperazone, ceftriaxone, furosemide, heparin, lansoprazole, nafcillin, thiopental, warfarin.

ACTION & *THERAPEUTIC EFFECT* Acts as an adrenergic receptor antagonist that combines selective alpha activity and nonselective beta-adrenergic antagonist activity. Alpha blockade results in vasodilation, decreased peripheral resistance, and orthostatic hypotension. It has beta-antagonist effects on the sinus node, AV node, and ventricular muscle, which lead to bradycardia, delay in AV conduction, and depression of cardiac contractility. *Effective in reducing blood pressure by vasodilation and depression of cardiac contractility.*

CONTRAINDICATIONS NSAID or salicylate hypersensitivity; bronchial asthma; uncontrolled cardiac failure, heart block (greater than first degree), cardiogenic shock, severe bradycardia; perioperative CABG pain; pregnancy (category B in first and second trimester and category D in third trimester). Safe use in children is not established.

CAUTIOUS USE Nonallergic bronchospastic disease (COPD); renal disease, renal failure; hepatic disease; well-compensated patients with history of heart failure; acute MI; coronary artery disease; pheochromocytoma; impaired liver function, jaundice; diabetes mellitus; SLE; peripheral vascular disease.

ADVERSE EFFECTS (≥1%) **CNS:** Dizziness, fatigue/malaise, headache, tremors, transient paresthesias (especially scalp tingling), hypoesthesia (numbness) following IV, mental depression, drowsiness, sleep disturbances, nightmares. **CV:** *Postural hypotension,* angina pectoris, palpitation, bradycardia, syncope, pedal or peripheral edema, pulmonary edema, CHF, flushing, cold extremities, arrhythmias, paradoxical hypertension (patients with pheochromocytoma). **Special Senses:** Dry eyes, vision disturbances, nasal stuffiness, rhinorrhea. **GI:** Nausea, vomiting, dyspepsia, constipation, diarrhea, taste disturbances, cholestasis with or without jaundice, increases in serum transaminases, dry mouth. **Urogenital:** Acute urinary retention, difficult micturition, impotence, ejaculation failure, loss of libido, Peyronie's disease. **Respiratory:** Dyspnea, <u>bronchospasm</u>. **Skin:** Rashes of various types, increased sweating, pruritus. **Body as a Whole:** Myalgia, muscle cramps, toxic myopathy, antimitochondrial antibodies, positive antinuclear antibodies (ANA), SLE syndrome, pain at IV injection site.

DIAGNOSTIC TEST INTERFERENCE False increases in ***urinary catecholamines*** when measured by ***nonspecific trihydroxy indole (THI) reaction*** (due to labetalol metabolites) but not with specific ***radioenzymatic*** or ***high-performance liquid chromatography assay techniques.***

DRUG INTERACTIONS Cimetidine may increase effects of labetalol; **glutethimide** decreases effects of labetalol; **halothane** adds to hypotensive effects; may mask symptoms of hypoglycemia caused by ORAL SULFONYLUREAS, **insulin;** BETA AGONISTS antagonize effects of labetalol.

PHARMACOKINETICS Onset: 2–5 min. **Peak:** 5–15 min. **Duration:** 2–4 h. **Distribution:** Crosses placenta; distributed into breast milk. **Metabolism:** In liver (CYP 2D6). **Elimination:** 60% excreted in urine, 40% in bile. **Half-Life:** 3–8 h.

NURSING IMPLICATIONS

Assessment & Drug Effects

- Monitor BP at 5 min intervals for 30 min after infusion; then at 30 min intervals for 2 h; then hourly for about 6 h; and as indicated thereafter.
- Continuous ECG monitoring is recommended to detect myocardial ischemia and arrhythmias.
- Discontinue drug once the desired BP is attained. Maximum hypotensive effect occurs within 15 min after each administration.
- Maintain patient in supine position for at least 3 h after IV administration. Then determine patient's ability to tolerate elevated and upright positions before allowing ambulation. Manage this slowly.
- Monitor diabetic patients closely; drug may mask usual cardiovascular response to acute hypoglycemia (e.g., tachycardia).

Common adverse effects in *italic*, life-threatening effects <u>underlined</u>: generic names in **bold**; classifications in SMALL CAPS; ♣ Canadian drug name; ⊙ Prototype drug

393

Patient & Family Education

- Make all position changes slowly and in stages, particularly from lying to upright position. Older adult patients are especially sensitive to hypotensive effects.
- Do not drive or engage in other potentially hazardous activities until response to drug is known.
- Note: Most adverse effects (e.g., scalp tingling) are mild, transient, and dose related and occur early in therapy.

LANSOPRAZOLE ⓟ

(lan'so-pra-zole)

Prevacid IV

Classification(s): ANTISECRETORY; PROTON PUMP INHIBITOR

Therapeutic: ANTIULCER

Pregnancy Category: B

USES Short-term treatment of erosive esophagitis if unable to take oral formulation.

INDICATION & DOSAGE

Erosive Esophagitis

Adult: 30 mg once daily for up to 7 days

Hepatic Impairment Dosage Adjustment

Dose reduction required in severe hepatic disease.

SOLUTION PREPARATION

- *Vial Reconstitution:* Add 5 mL of sterile water for injection to each 30-mg vial to yield 6 mg/mL. Swirl gently to mix. **Must be** further diluted for infusion.
- *Further Dilution of Reconstituted Solution:* Dilute in 50 mL of NS, LR, or D5W.

STORAGE

- Reconstituted solution can be held for 1 h at 25° C (77° F) before further dilution.
- If diluted in NS or LR for infusion, administer within 24 h. If diluted in D5W for infusion, administer within 12 h.

ADMINISTRATION

- **IV Infusion: Do NOT** give bolus dose direct IV. Infuse over 30 min through the in-line filter provided.
- Use a dedicated line or a Y-site; flush Y-site with NS before and after administration. Immediately stop infusion if precipitation or discoloration occurs.

INCOMPATIBILITIES Y-site: Alfentanil, aminophylline, amphotericin B, ampicillin, ampicillin/sulbactam, aztreonam, buprenorphine, CALCIUM SALTS, carboplatin, cefazolin, cefepime, cefotetan, cefoxitin, ceftazidime, ceftizoxime, chlorpromazine, cimetidine, ciprofloxacin, cisplatin, clindamycin, cyclophosphamide, cytarabine, daunorubicin, diazepam, digoxin, diltiazem, diphenhydramine, dobutamine, dopamine, doxorubicin, droperidol, enalaprilat, esmolol, etoposide, famotidine, fluorouracil, gemcitabine, granisetron, haloperidol, hydrocortisone, hydromorphone, hydroxyzine, imipenem/cilastin, labetalol, leucovorin, levofloxacin, lidocaine, lorazepam, magnesium sulfate, meperidine, mesna, methylprednisolone, metoclopramide, metronidazole, midazolam, milrinone, mitoxantrone, morphine, naloxone, nicardipine, nitroglycerin, ondansetron, pentobarbital, phenobarbital, phenylephrine, phenytoin, POTASSIUM SALTS, procainamide, prochlorperazine, promethazine, propranolol, ranitidine, sodium bicarbonate, sodium phosphates, theophylline, tobramycin, vancomycin, verapamil, vinblastine, vincristine, vinorelbine, zidovudine.

ACTION & *THERAPEUTIC EFFECT* Antisecretory compound that is a gastric acid pump inhibitor. Specifically, it suppresses gastric acid secretion by inhibiting the H^+, K^+-ATPase enzyme [the acid (proton H^+) pump] in the parietal cells of the stomach. *Suppresses gastric acid formation in the stomach.*

CONTRAINDICATIONS Hypersensitivity to lansoprazole; severe hepatic impairment; hypersensitivity to proton pump inhibitors (PPIs); lactation; infants.
CAUTIOUS USE Hepatic disease; pregnancy (category B).

ADVERSE EFFECTS (≥1%) **CNS:** Fatigue, dizziness, headache. **GI:** Nausea, *diarrhea,* constipation, anorexia, increased appetite, increased thirst, elevated serum transaminases (AST, ALT). **Skin:** Rash.

DRUG INTERACTIONS May decrease **theophylline** levels. May interfere with absorption of **ketoconazole, digoxin, ampicillin,** or IRON SALTS.

PHARMACOKINETICS Peak: 1.5–3 h. **Duration:** 24 h. **Distribution:** 97% bound to plasma proteins. **Metabolism:** In liver (CYP 2C19 and CYP 3A4) system. **Elimination:** 14–25% excreted in urine as metabolites; part of dose eliminated in bile and feces. **Half-Life:** 1.5 h.

NURSING IMPLICATIONS

Assessment & Drug Effects
▪ Lab tests: Periodic CBC, LFTs, kidney function tests, and serum gastrin levels.
▪ Concurrent drugs: Monitor PT/INR with warfarin; monitor for therapeutic effectiveness of drugs that require an acid medium for absorption (e.g., digoxin, ampicillin, ketoconazole).

Patient & Family Education
▪ Inform prescriber of significant diarrhea.

LARONIDASE ⦿

(la-ron′i-dase)

Aldurazyme

Classification(s): ENZYME REPLACEMENT

Therapeutic: ENZYME REPLACEMENT THERAPY

Pregnancy Category: B

USES Treatment of Hurler and Hurler-Scheie forms of mucopolysaccharidosis I (MPS I); treatment of moderate to severe Scheie form of MPS I.

INDICATION & DOSAGE

Mucopolysaccharidosis

Adult/Adolescent/Child (over 5 y): 0.58 mg/kg weekly

SOLUTION PREPARATION

- Determine volume of infusion based on the patient's body weight (100 mL if 20 kg or less, or 250 mL if over 20 kg).
- *IV Infusion:* Prepare IV infusion of 0.1% albumin (human) in NS injection as follows:
  1) Remove and discard a volume of NS equal to the volume of albumin to be added to the IV bag. For 100 mL infusion, use 2 mL of 5% albumin or 0.4 mL of 25% albumin. For 250 mL infusion, use 5 mL of 5% albumin or 1 mL of 25% albumin.
  2) Add the appropriate volume of albumin to the IV bag and gently rotate to mix.
  3) Withdraw and discard a volume of fluid from the IV bag equal to the volume of laronidase concentrate to be added.
  4) Slowly withdraw the required amount of laronidase from vials (avoid excessive agitation of vials), then slowly add laronidase to the IV solution. Gently rotate to ensure mixing. Use immediately.

STORAGE

Store unopened vials at 2°–8° C (36°–46° F). Do not freeze or shake. Discard any unused drug.

ADMINISTRATION

- Pretreatment with antipyretics and/or antihistamines 60 min prior to infusion is recommended.
- **IV Infusion:** Infuse initially at 10 mcg/kg/h; may increase q15min during first h, if vital signs are stable, to a max rate of 200 mcg/kg/h. Maintain max rate for remainder of the infusion (2–3 h). Use a PVC set with an in-line, low-protein-binding 0.2 micron filter for infusion.

INCOMPATIBILITIES Solution/additive: Do not recommend mixing or infusing with other drugs.

ACTION & *THERAPEUTIC EFFECT* Laronidase is a recombinant form of human alpha-L-iduronidase used for enzyme replacement therapy in indi-

viduals with mucopolysaccharidosis I (MPS I). This is an inherited lysosomal storage disease caused by deficiency of the enzyme alpha-L-iduronidase. *Replacement therapy for individuals lacking the enzyme alpha-
L-iduronidase in mucopolysaccharidosis I.*

CONTRAINDICATIONS Hypersensitivity to laronidase; children less than 5 y.
CAUTIOUS USE Renal or hepatic dysfunction; history of allergies, asthma;
hypersensitivity to drugs, especially recombinant forms; pregnancy (category B), lactation.

ADVERSE EFFECTS (≥1%) **Body as a Whole:** Infusion reactions (flushing,
fever, headache, rash), injection site pain, hypersensitivity reactions.
CNS: Hyperreflexia, paresthesias. **CV:** Chest pain, hypotension, edema.
Hematologic: Thrombocytopenia. **Respiratory:** Upper respiratory tract infection. **Skin:** Rash.

DRUG INTERACTIONS Drug interaction studies have not been performed.

PHARMACOKINETICS Distribution: Unlikely to cross CNS or into breast
milk. **Half-Life:** 1.5–3.6 h.

NURSING IMPLICATIONS

Assessment & Drug Effects
- Montor vital signs q15min. Monitor for infusion-related reactions. Slow or
  stop infusion and notify prescriber for any of the following: Cough, bronchospasm, dyspnea, urticaria, angioedema, pruritus, or other signs of hypersensitivity.
- Lab tests: Periodic platelet count.

Patient & Family Education
- Report promptly difficulty breathing, rash, or itching.

LEPIRUDIN ℗

(le-pir'u-din)
Refludan
Classification(s): ANTICOAGULANT; THROMBIN INHIBITOR
Therapeutic: ANTITHROMBOTIC
Pregnancy Category: B

USES Anticoagulation in patients with heparin-induced thrombocytopenia (HIT).

INDICATION & DOSAGE

Anticoagulation
Adult: 0.4 mg/kg initial bolus (max: 44 mg) followed by 0.15 mg/kg/h
(max: 16.5 mg/h) for 2–10 days; adjust rate to maintain aPTT of 1.5–2.5

Common adverse effects in *italic*, life-threatening effects <u>underlined</u>: generic names
in **bold**; classifications in SMALL CAPS; ♣ Canadian drug name; ℗ Prototype drug

Renal Impairment Dosage Adjustment

CrCl (mL/min)	Initial Dose	Follow-Up Dose
45–60	0.2 mcg/kg	0.075 mg/kg/h
30–44	0.2 mcg/kg	0.045 mg/kg/h
15–29	0.2 mcg/kg	0.0225 mg/kg/h
Less than 15	Do not use	Do not use

SOLUTION PREPARATION
- *Vial Reconstitution:* Add 1 mL of sterile water for injection or NS to the 50-mg vial. **Must be** further diluted for injection/infusion.
- *Further Dilution of Reconstituted Solution:*
  - *Direct IV Injection:* Withdraw reconstituted solution into a 10-cc syringe and dilute to 10 mL with sterile water for injection, NS or D5W to yield 5 mg/mL.
  - *Continuous Infusion:* Transfer the contents of two reconstituted vials into 250 or 500 mL of D5W or NS to yield of 0.4 or 0.2 mg/mL, respectively.

STORAGE
Diluted solution is stable for 24 h during infusion. Store unopened vials at 2°–25° C (36°–77° F).

ADMINISTRATION
- Withhold drug and notify prescriber if baseline aPTT is greater than 2.5.
- **Direct IV Injection:** Give over 15–20 sec.
- **Continuous Infusion:** Infuse at a rate determined by body weight.

INCOMPATIBILITIES Data not available; do not mix with other drugs.

ACTION & *THERAPEUTIC EFFECT* Highly specific direct inhibitor of thrombin including thrombin entrapped within established clots. One molecule of lepirudin binds to one molecule of thrombin and thereby blocks the thrombogenic activity of thrombin. Increases PT/INR and aPTT values in relation to the dose given. *Has antithrombotic activity. Effectiveness is indicated by measuring the aPTT value of the blood.*

CONTRAINDICATIONS Hypersensitivity to lepirudin; intracranial bleeding; patients with increased risk of bleeding (e.g., recent surgery, CVA, advanced kidney impairment); lactation. Safety and efficacy in children not established. **CAUTIOUS USE** Serious liver injury (e.g., cirrhosis); concomitant administration with streptokinase; renal impairment; pregnancy (category B).

ADVERSE EFFECTS (≥1%) **CNS:** Intracranial bleeding. **CV:** Heart failure, ventricular fibrillation, pericardial effusion, MI. **GI:** Abnormal LFTs. **Hematologic:** Bleeding from injection site, anemia, hematoma, bleeding, hematuria, GI and rectal bleeding, epistaxis, hemothorax, vaginal bleeding. **Respiratory:** Pneumonia, cough, bronchospasm, stridor, dyspnea. **Skin:** Allergic skin reactions. **Body as a Whole:** Sepsis, abnormal kidney function, multiorgan failure.

DRUG INTERACTIONS Warfarin, NSAIDS, SALICYLATES, ANTIPLATELET AGENTS, THROMBOLYTICS increase risk of bleeding.

PHARMACOKINETICS Distribution: Primarily to extracellular compartment. **Metabolism:** By catabolic hydrolysis in serum. **Elimination:** 48% excreted in urine. **Half-Life:** 1.3 h.

NURSING IMPLICATIONS
Assessment & Drug Effects
- Prior to initiating therapy: Baseline BUN and CrCl.
- Use extreme caution with those at increased risk for bleeding.
- Monitor carefully for bleeding events (e.g., from puncture wounds, hematoma, hematuria) and report immediately.
- Lab tests: Baseline aPTT, repeat 4 h after start of therapy and at least once daily (more often with renal or hepatic impairment) thereafter.
- Monitor for S&S of bleeding: Hematuria, melena, hematemesis, etc.
- Do not give oral anticoagulants until lepirudin dose has been reduced and aPTT ratio is lowered to just above 1.5.

Patient & Family Education
- Report any of the following: Easy bruising, nosebleeds, blood in urine, black tarry stools.
- Exercise caution to avoid physical injury.

LEUCOVORIN CALCIUM
(loo-koe-vor'in)
Classification(s): VITAMIN
Therapeutic: ANTIANEMIC; ANTIDOTE
Pregnancy Category: C

USES Folate-deficient megaloblastic anemias due to sprue, pregnancy, and nutritional deficiency when oral therapy is not feasible. Also to prevent or diminish toxicity of methotrexate; treatment of advanced colorectal cancer.

INDICATION & DOSAGE

Megaloblastic Anemia
Adult/Child: Up to 1 mg/day

Leucovorin Rescue for Methotrexate Toxicity
Adult/Child: 10 mg/m² q6h until serum methotrexate levels reduced

Advanced Colorectal Cancer
Adult: 200 mg/m² followed by fluorouracil

SOLUTION PREPARATION
- *Direct IV Injection:* Give 1 mL (3 mg) ampules, which contain benzyl alcohol, undiluted.

- *Vial Reconstitution for IV Infusion:*
  - For doses less than 10 mg/m^2, reconstitute each 50 mg in 5 mL (10 mg per 1 mL in 10 mL) of bacteriostatic water for injection with benzyl alcohol to yield 10 mg/mL. **Must be** further diluted for infusion.
  - For doses 10 mg/m^2 or greater, reconstitute as above, but with sterile water for injection without a preservative to yield 10 mg/mL. **Must be** further diluted for infusion.
- *Further Dilution of Reconstituted Solution:* Dilute in 100–500 mL of IV solutions (e.g., D5W, NS, LR) to yield a concentration of 10–20 mg/mL.

STORAGE

Use solution reconstituted with bacteriostatic water within 7 days. Use solution reconstituted with sterile water for injection immediately. Protect from light.

ADMINISTRATION

- **Direct IV Injection:** Give bolus dose no faster than 160 mg or fraction thereof over 1 min.
- **IV Infusion:** Do not exceed direct IV rate. Infuse more slowly over several hours if the volume of IV solution to be infused is large.

INCOMPATIBILITIES Solution/additive: Fluorouracil. Y-site: Amphotericin B cholesteryl complex, droperidol, foscarnet, lansoprazole, sodium bicarbonate.

ACTION & *THERAPEUTIC EFFECT* A reduced form of folic acid; unlike folic acid, it does not require enzymatic reduction, and therefore is readily available. Functions as an essential cell growth factor. During antineoplastic therapy, it prevents serious toxicity by protecting cells from the action of folic acid antagonists such as methotrexate. *Antidote against folic acid antagonists such as methotrexate.*

CONTRAINDICATIONS Undiagnosed anemia, pernicious anemia, or other megaloblastic anemias secondary to vitamin B$_{12}$ deficiency; intrathecal administration; pregnancy (category C).
CAUTIOUS USE Renal dysfunction; elderly; seizure disorders; lactation.

ADVERSE EFFECTS (≥1%) **Body as a Whole:** Allergic sensitization (urticaria, pruritus, rash, wheezing). **Hematologic:** Thrombocytosis.

DRUG INTERACTIONS May enhance adverse effects of **fluorouracil;** may decrease therapeutic effects of **methotrexate, trimethoprim-sulfamethoxazole.**

PHARMACOKINETICS Onset: Within 30 min. **Duration:** 3–6 h. **Distribution:** Crosses placenta; distributed into breast milk. **Metabolism:** In liver and intestinal mucosa to tetrahydrofolic acid derivatives. **Elimination:** 80–90% in urine, 5–8% in feces.

NURSING IMPLICATIONS

Assessment & Drug Effects

- Monitor neurologic status. Use of leucovorin alone in treatment of pernicious anemia or other megaloblastic anemias associated with vitamin B$_{12}$

deficiency can result in an apparent hematological remission while allowing already present neurologic damage to progress.
- Fluid intake of 3 L daily is recommended.
- Lab tests: Baseline and daily serum creatinine; baseline urine pH, repeat every 6 h as necessary.
- Monitor persons with seizures for loss of seizure control.

Patient & Family Education
- Notify prescriber immediately of S&S of a hypersensitivity reaction (see Appendix C).

LEVOFLOXACIN

(lev-o-flox'a-sin)

Levaquin

Classification(s): ANTIBIOTIC, QUINOLONE
Therapeutic: ANTIBACTERIAL
Prototype: Ciprofloxacin
Pregnancy Category: C

L

USES Treatment of maxillary sinusitis, acute exacerbations of bacterial bronchitis, community-acquired pneumonia, uncomplicated skin/skin structure infections, UTI, acute pyelonephritis caused by susceptible bacteria, acute bacterial sinusitis, chronic bacterial prostatitis, and bacterial conjunctivitis.

INDICATION & DOSAGE

Infections
Adult: 500 mg–750 mg q24h

Community-Acquired Pneumonia
Adult: 750 mg q24h × 5 days

Uncomplicated UTI
Adult: 250 mg q24h × 14 days

Complicated UTI, Pyelonephritis
Adult: 250 mg q24h × 10 days

Acute Bacterial Sinusitis
Adult: 750 mg q24h × 5 days

Chronic Bacterial Prostatitis
Adult: 500 mg q24h × 28 days

Skin & Skin Structure Infections
Adult: 750 mg q24h × 14 days

Common adverse effects in *italic*, life-threatening effects <u>underlined</u>: generic names in **bold**; classifications in SMALL CAPS; ♣ Canadian drug name; ✺ Prototype drug

Renal Impairment Dosage Adjustment

For initial dose of 500 mg adjust as follows: CrCl 20–50 mL/min: 250 mg q24h; *less than 20 mL/min:* 250 mg q48h

For initial dose of 750 mg adjust as follows: CrCl 20–50 mL/min: 750 mg q48h; *CrCl 10–19 mL/min:* 500 mg q48h; *less than 20 mL/min:* 250 mg q48h

SOLUTION PREPARATION

- *Vial Dilution:* Withdraw the desired dose from 500 or 750 mg (25 mg/mL) single-use vial. Add to enough D5W, NS, D5NS, D5LR, or other compatible solutions to produce a concentration of 5 mg/mL [e.g., 500 mg (or 20 mL) added to 80 mL]. Discard any unused drug remaining in the vial.
- *Premix Flexible Container:* No dilution is required. Administer as supplied.

STORAGE

IV solution is stable for 72 h at 25° C (77° F).

ADMINISTRATION

Intermittent Infusion: Do **not** give a bolus dose or infuse too rapidly. Infuse 500 mg or less over 60 min. Infuse 750 mg over at least 90 min.

INCOMPATIBILITIES Y-site: Acyclovir, alprostadil, azithromycin, drotrecogin, furosemide, heparin, indomethacin, insulin, lansoprazole, nitroglycerin, nitroprusside, propofol.

ACTION & *THERAPEUTIC EFFECT* A broad-spectrum fluoroquinolone antibiotic that inhibits topoisomerase IV and DNA-gyrase, enzymes necessary for bacterial replication, transcription, repair, and recombination. *Effective against many aerobic gram-positive and gram-negative organisms.*

CONTRAINDICATIONS Hypersensitivity to levofloxacin and quinolone antibiotics; tendon pain, inflammation or rupture; syphilis; viral infections; phototoxicity; suicidal ideation; psychotic manifestations; manifestations of peripheral neuropathy; hypoglycemic reaction to drug; QT prolongation, hypokalemia; concurrent administration of class IA (e.g., quinidine, procainamide, or class III (e.g., amiodarone, sotalol) antiarrhythmic agents; pregnancy (category C); lactation. Safety and efficacy in children less than 18 y are not established.

CAUTIOUS USE History of suicidal ideation; psychosis; anxiety, confusion, depression; known or suspected CNS disorders predisposed to seizure activity (e.g., severe cerebral atherosclerosis), risk factors associated with potential seizures (e.g., some drug therapy, renal insufficiency), dehydration, renal impairment (CrCl less than 50 ml/min); colitis; cardiac arrhythmias; renal impairment; diabetes; patients receiving theophylline or caffeine; older adults.

ADVERSE EFFECTS (≥1%) **CNS:** *Headache,* insomnia, dizziness. **GI:** Nausea, diarrhea, constipation, vomiting, abdominal pain, dyspepsia. **Skin:** Rash, pruritus. **Special Senses:** Decreased vision, foreign body sensation, transient ocular burning, ocular pain, photophobia. **Urogenital:** Vaginitis. **Body as a Whole:** Injection site pain or inflammation, chest or back pain, fever, pharyngitis. **Other:** Cartilage erosion.

DIAGNOSTIC TEST INTERFERENCE May cause false positive on *opiate screening tests.*

DRUG INTERACTIONS May have additive effect with other agents affecting QT interval; may cause hyper- or hypoglycemia in patients on ORAL HYPOGLYCEMIC AGENTS.

PHARMACOKINETICS Distribution: Penetrates lung tissue, 24–38% protein bound. **Metabolism:** Minimally metabolized in the liver. **Elimination:** Primarily excreted unchanged in urine. **Half-Life:** 6–8 h.

NURSING IMPLICATIONS

Assessment & Drug Effects
- Prior to initiating therapy: Baseline C&S tests (start drug pending results).
- Withhold drug and report promptly: Skin rash or other signs of a hypersensitivity reaction (see Appendix C); CNS symptoms such as seizures, restlessness, confusion, hallucinations, depression; skin eruption following sun exposure; symptoms of colitis such as persistent diarrhea; joint pain, inflammation, or rupture of a tendon; hypoglycemic reaction in diabetic on an oral hypoglycemic agent.
- Monitor diabetics for loss of glycemic control.

Patient & Family Education
- Consume fluids liberally while taking levofloxacin.
- Avoid exposure to excess sunlight or artificial UV light.
- Report promptly tendon pain for inflammation.

LEVORPHANOL TARTRATE

(lee-vor'fa-nole)

Levo-Dromoran

Classification(s): ANALGESIC; NARCOTIC (OPIATE) AGONIST
Therapeutic: ANALGESIC
Prototype: Morphine sulfate
Pregnancy Category: B; D with long-time use or high doses
Controlled Substance: Schedule II

USES To relieve moderate to severe pain. Also preoperatively to allay apprehension.

INDICATION & DOSAGE

Moderate to Severe Pain
Adult: 1 mg q3–6h prn

SOLUTION PREPARATION
May be given direct IV undiluted or diluted in 5 mL of NS or SW.

STORAGE
Store at 10°–30° C (59°–86° F).

ADMINISTRATION
Direct IV Injection: Give bolus dose at rate of 2 mg or fraction thereof over 5 min. AVOID rapid infusion. May inject into Y-site of compatible infusion solution.

INCOMPATIBILITIES Solution/additive: **Aminophylline, ammonium chloride, amobarbital, chlorothiazide, heparin, methicillin, nitrofurantoin, novobiocin, pentobarbital, perphenazine, phenobarbital, phenytoin, secobarbital, sodium bicarbonate, sodium iodide, sulfadiazine, sulfisoxazole diethanolamine, thiopental.**

ACTION & *THERAPEUTIC EFFECT* A potent synthetic morphine derivative with agonist activity only. Reported to cause less nausea, vomiting, and constipation than equivalent doses of morphine, but may produce more sedation, smooth-muscle relaxation, and respiratory depression. *More potent as an analgesic and has a somewhat longer duration of action than morphine.*

CONTRAINDICATIONS Hypersensitivity to levorphanol; labor and delivery, pregnancy (category B, and D with long-time use or high doses), lactation.
CAUTIOUS USE Patients with impaired respiratory reserve, or depressed respirations from another cause (e.g., severe infection, obstructive respiratory conditions, chronic bronchial asthma); patients with head injury or increased intracranial pressure; acute MI, cardiac dysfunction; liver disease, biliary surgery, alcoholism or delirium tremens; liver or kidney dysfunction; hypothyroidism, Addison's disease; toxic psychosis; prostatic hypertrophy, urethral stricture; concurrent use with CNS depressant drugs; older adults, other vulnerable populations.

ADVERSE EFFECTS (≥1%) **CNS:** Euphoria, *sedation, drowsiness,* nervousness, confusion. **CV:** Hypotension, arrhythmias. **GI:** *Nausea,* vomiting, dry mouth, cramps, constipation. **Urogenital:** Urinary frequency, urinary retention, sedation. **Special Senses:** Blurred vision. **Respiratory:** Respiratory depression. **Body as a Whole:** Physical dependence.

DRUG INTERACTIONS Alcohol and other CNS DEPRESSANTS compound sedation and CNS depression.

PHARMACOKINETICS Duration: 6–8 h. **Distribution:** Crosses placenta; distributed into breast milk. **Metabolism:** In liver. **Elimination:** In urine. **Half-Life:** 11–16 h.

NURSING IMPLICATIONS
Assessment & Drug Effects
- Assess degree of pain relief. Drug is most effective when peaks and valleys of pain relief are avoided.
- Monitor bowel function.
- Monitor ambulation, especially in older adult patients.

Patient & Family Education
- Do not drive or engage in other potentially hazardous activities.
- Ambulation may increase frequency of nausea and vomiting.
- Increase fluid and fiber intake to offset constipating effects of the drug.

LEVOTHYROXINE SODIUM (T₄)

(lee-voe-thye-rox'een)

Eltroxin ♦

Classification(s): HORMONE
Therapeutic: THYROID HORMONE REPLACEMENT
Pregnancy Category: A

USES Myxedematous coma or other thyroid dysfunctions demanding rapid replacement, as well as in failure to respond to oral therapy.

INDICATION & DOSAGE

L

Thyroid Replacement

Adult: $^1/_2$ established oral dose (usually 50–100 mcg daily)

Myxedematous Coma

Adult: 200–500 mcg day 1, additional 100–300 mcg on day 2 if needed

SOLUTION PREPARATION

Vial Reconstitution: Add 5 mL of NS for injection to each 100 mcg. Shake well to dissolve. Use immediately.

STORAGE

Store dry powder at 15°–30° C (59°–86° F).

ADMINISTRATION

Direct IV Injection: Give bolus dose over 1 min.

INCOMPATIBILITIES Do not mix with other drugs.

ACTION & *THERAPEUTIC EFFECT* Synthetically prepared levo-isomer of thyroxine (T₄), with similar actions and uses (natural thyroxine determines normal thyroid function). Principal effects include diuresis, loss of weight and puffiness, increased sense of well-being and activity tolerance, and rise of T₃ and T₄ serum levels toward normal. *By replacing decreased or absent thyroid hormone, it restores metabolic rate of a hypothyroid individual.*

CONTRAINDICATIONS Hypersensitivity to levothyroxine; thyrotoxicosis; severe cardiovascular conditions, acute MI; obesity treatment; adrenal insufficiency.

CAUTIOUS USE Cardiac disease, angina pectoris, cardiac arrhythmias, hypertension; diabetes mellitus; older adult, impaired kidney function; pregnancy (category A).

Common adverse effects in *italic*, life-threatening effects underlined: generic names
in **bold**; classifications in SMALL CAPS; ♥ Canadian drug name; ☻ Prototype drug

405

ADVERSE EFFECTS (≥1%) **CNS:** Irritability, nervousness, *insomnia,* headache (pseudotumor cerebri in children), tremors, craniosynostosis (excessive doses in children). **CV:** Palpitations, tachycardia, arrhythmias, angina pectoris, hypertension. **GI:** Nausea, diarrhea, change in appetite. **Urogenital:** Menstrual irregularities. **Body as a Whole:** Weight loss, heat intolerance, sweating, fever, leg cramps.

DRUG INTERACTIONS ORAL ANTICOAGULANTS may potentiate hypoprothrombinemia.

PHARMACOKINETICS Peak: 3–4 wk. **Duration:** 1–3 wk. **Half-Life:** 6–7 days.

NURSING IMPLICATIONS

Assessment & Drug Effects

- Monitor vital signs and neurologic status at frequent intervals.
- Monitor for adverse effects. If metabolism increases too rapidly, especially in older adults and heart disease patients, symptoms of angina or cardiac failure may appear.
- Lab tests: Baseline and periodic serum TSH, total T4 and T3, and free T4 and T3.
- Concurrent drugs: Monitor closely PT/INR and assess for evidence of bleeding with concurrent anticoagulant therapy.

Patient & Family Education

- Learn S&S of hyperthyroidism (see Appendix C); report promptly if they appear.
- Learn how to self-monitor pulse rate. Notify prescriber if rate begins to increase above 100 or if rhythm changes are noted.
- Notify prescriber immediately of signs of toxicity (e.g., chest pain, palpitations, nervousness).

LIDOCAINE HYDROCHLORIDE ⊙

(lye′doe-kane)

Xylocaine, Xylocard ♦
Classification(s): ANTIARRHYTHMIC, CLASS IB
Therapeutic: ANTIARRHYTHMIC, CLASS IB
Pregnancy Category: B

USES Rapid control of ventricular arrhythmias occurring during acute MI, cardiac surgery, and cardiac catheterization and those caused by digitalis intoxication.
UNLABELED USES Refractory status epilepticus.

INDICATION & DOSAGE

Ventricular Arrhythmias

Adult: 50–100 mg bolus at a rate of 20–50 mg/min; may repeat in 5 min, not more than 300 mg/h

---

Common adverse effects in *italic,* life-threatening effects underlined: generic names in **bold**; classifications in SMALL CAPS; ♦ Canadian drug name; ⊙ Prototype drug

Child: 1 mg/kg bolus dose, then 30 mcg/kg/min infusion

SOLUTION PREPARATION
- Ensure that product is labeled for "IV Use."
- *Direct IV Injection:* No dilution is required. Administer as supplied.
- *IV Infusion:* Use D5W (preferred), D5NS, D5/1/2NS, LR for infusion.
  - *For adult:* Add 1 g to 250 or 500 mL to yield 2 or 4 mg/mL, respectively.
  - *For child:* Add 120 mg to 100 mL to yield 1.2 mg/mL

STORAGE
Discard partially used solutions of lidocaine without preservatives. Stable for 24 h in D5W.

ADMINISTRATION
- **Direct IV Injection:** Give at a rate of 50 mg or fraction thereof over 1 min.
- **IV Infusion:** Use microdrip and infusion pump.
  - *Adult:* Infuse at 1–4 mg/min.
  - *Child:* Infuse at 30 mcg/kg/min.

INCOMPATIBILITIES Solution/additive: Cefazolin, methohexital, phenytoin, propofol. **Y-site:** Amphotericin B cholesteryl complex, lansoprazole, phenytoin, thiopental.

ACTION & *THERAPEUTIC EFFECT* Exerts antiarrhythmic action (Class IB) by suppressing automaticity in His-Purkinje system. Combines with fast sodium channels in myocardial cell membranes, which inhibits sodium influx into cells and decreases ventricular depolarization, automaticity, and excitability during diastole. *Suppresses automaticity in His-Purkinje system of the heart and elevates electrical stimulation threshold of ventricle during diastole.*

CONTRAINDICATIONS History of hypersensitivity to amide-type local anesthetics; application or injection of lidocaine anesthetic in presence of severe trauma or sepsis; blood dyscrasias; supraventricular arrhythmias; Stokes-Adams syndrome untreated sinus bradycardia; severe degrees of sinoatrial, atrioventricular, and intraventricular heart block.

CAUTIOUS USE Liver or kidney disease; CHF; marked hypoxia, respiratory depression; hypovolemia, shock; myasthenia gravis; debilitated patients, older adults; family history of malignant hyperthermia (fulminant hypermetabolism); pregnancy (category B).

ADVERSE EFFECTS (≥1%) **CNS:** Drowsiness, dizziness, light-headedness, restlessness, confusion, disorientation, irritability, apprehension, euphoria, wild excitement, numbness of lips or tongue and other paresthesias including sensations of heat and cold, chest heaviness, difficulty in speaking, difficulty in breathing or swallowing, muscular twitching, tremors, psychosis. With high doses: Convulsions, respiratory depression and arrest. **CV:** With high doses, hypotension, bradycardia, conduction disorders including heart block, cardiovascular collapse, cardiac arrest. **Special Senses:** Tinnitus, decreased hearing; blurred or double vision, impaired color perception. **Skin:** Site of topical application may develop erythema, edema. **GI:** Anorexia, nausea, vomiting. **Body as a Whole:** Excessive per-

Common adverse effects in *italic*, life-threatening effects underlined: generic names in **bold**; classifications in SMALL CAPS; ♣ Canadian drug name; ⦿ Prototype drug

407

spiration, soreness at injection site, local thrombophlebitis (with prolonged infusion), hypersensitivity reactions (urticaria, rash, edema, <u>anaphylactoid reactions</u>).

DIAGNOSTIC TEST INTERFERENCE Increases in *creatine phosphokinase (CPK)* level may occur for 48 h after dose and may interfere with test for presence of MI.

DRUG INTERACTIONS BARBITURATES decrease lidocaine activity; **cimetidine,** BETA BLOCKERS, **quinidine** increase pharmacologic effects of lidocaine; **phenytoin** increases cardiac depressant effects; **procainamide** compounds neurologic and cardiac effects.

PHARMACOKINETICS Onset: 45–90 sec. **Duration:** 10–20 min. **Distribution:** Crosses blood–brain barrier and placenta; distributed into breast milk. **Metabolism:** In liver (CYP 3A4 and 2D6). **Elimination:** In urine. **Half-Life:** 1.5–2 h.

NURSING IMPLICATIONS

Assessment & Drug Effects

- Stop infusion immediately if ECG indicates excessive cardiac depression (e.g., prolongation of PR interval or QRS complex and the appearance or aggravation of arrhythmias).
- Monitor BP and ECG constantly; assess respiratory and neurologic status frequently to avoid potential overdosage and toxicity.
- Auscultate lungs for basilar rales, especially in patients who tend to metabolize the drug slowly (e.g., CHF, cardiogenic shock, hepatic dysfunction).
- Monitor for neurotoxic effects (e.g., drowsiness, dizziness, confusion, paresthesias, visual disturbances, excitement, behavioral changes).
- Lab tests: Periodic serum electrolytes, kidney function tests, and blood pH.

Patient & Family Education

- Use caution when ambulation is permitted. Report promptly dizziness or lightheadedness.

LINCOMYCIN HYDROCHLORIDE

(lin-koe-mye′sin)

Lincocin
Classification(s): ANTIBIOTIC
Therapeutic: ANTIBACTERIAL
Prototype: Clindamycin
Pregnancy Category: B

USES Reserved for treatment of serious infections caused by susceptible bacteria in penicillin-allergic patients or patients for whom penicillin is inappropriate.

INDICATION & DOSAGE

Infections

Adult: 600 mg–1 g q8–12h
Child/Infant (over 1 mo): 10–20 mg/kg/day divided q8–12h

Renal Impairment Dosage Adjustment

25–30% of normal dose

SOLUTION PREPARATION

Compatible IV solutions include D5W, D10W, D5NS, D10NS. Dilute as follows: Each 1 g or fraction thereof in 100 mL; 2 g in 200 mL, 3 g in 300 mL, and 4 g in 400 mL.

STORAGE

Store at 20°–25° C (68°–77° F).

ADMINISTRATION

Intermittent Infusion: Infuse at a rate of 1 g per h.

INCOMPATIBILITIES Solution/additive: **Carbenicillin, kanamycin, methicillin, penicillin G, phenytoin.**

ACTION & ***THERAPEUTIC EFFECT*** Binds to the 50 S ribosomal subunits of bacteria, and inhibits protein synthesis, eventually resulting in inhibition of bacterial cell growth or bacterial cell death. Antibacterial activity primarily results from inhibition of peptide bond formation. *Bacteriostatic or bacteriocidal depending on concentration used and sensitivity of organism. Effective against most of the common gram-positive pathogens, particularly streptococci, pneumococci, and staphylococci. Also effective against many anaerobic bacteria.*

CONTRAINDICATIONS Previous hypersensitivity to lincomycin and clindamycin; impaired liver function; known monilial infections (unless treated concurrently); use in newborns less than 1 mo; lactation.
CAUTIOUS USE Impaired kidney function; history of GI disease, particularly colitis; history of liver, endocrine, or metabolic diseases; history of asthma, hay fever, eczema, drug, or other allergies; older adult patients; pregnancy (category B).

ADVERSE EFFECTS (≥1%) **Body as a Whole:** Hypersensitivity (pruritus, urticaria, skin rashes, exfoliative and vesiculobullous dermatitis, angioedema, photosensitivity, <u>anaphylactoid reaction</u>, serum sickness); superinfections (proctitis, pruritus ani, vaginitis); vertigo, dizziness, headache, generalized myalgia, thrombophlebitis; pain at injection site. **CV:** Hypotension, syncope, <u>cardiopulmonary arrest</u> (particularly after rapid IV). **GI:** Glossitis, stomatitis, *nausea, vomiting,* anorexia, decreased taste acuity, unpleasant or altered taste, abdominal cramps, *diarrhea,* acute enterocolitis, <u>pseudomembranous colitis (potentially fatal)</u>. **Hematologic:** Neutropenia, leukopenia, <u>agranulocytosis</u>, thrombocytopenic purpura, <u>aplastic anemia</u>. **Special Senses:** Tinnitus.

DRUG INTERACTIONS Tubocurarine, pancuronium may enhance neuromuscular blockade.

PHARMACOKINETICS Duration: 14 h. **Distribution:** High concentrations in bone, aqueous humor, bile, and peritoneal, pleural, and synovial fluids; crosses placenta; distributed into breast milk. **Metabolism:** Partially metabolized in liver. **Elimination:** In urine and feces. **Half-Life:** 5 h.

NURSING IMPLICATIONS

Assessment & Drug Effects

- Prior to initiating therapy: Baseline C&S tests (start drug pending results).
- Examine IV injection site daily for signs of inflammation.
- Monitor BP and HR. Keep patient recumbent following drug administration until BP stabilizes.
- Monitor closely and report changes in bowel frequency. Withhold drug and notify prescriber of significant diarrhea.
- Lab tests: Periodic LFTs, kidney function tests, and CBC during prolonged drug therapy.
- Superinfections by nonsusceptible organisms are most likely to occur when duration of therapy exceeds 10 days (see Appendix C).

Patient & Family Education

- Notify prescriber immediately of symptoms of hypersensitivity (see Appendix C).
- Report promptly of the onset of perianal irritation, diarrhea, or blood and mucus in stools. Diarrhea, acute colitis, or pseudomembranous colitis (see Appendix C) may occur up to several weeks after cessation of therapy.

LINEZOLID

(lin-e-zo'lid)

Zyvox, Zyvoxam ♦
Classification(s): ANTIBIOTIC
Therapeutic: ANTIBACTERIAL
Pregnancy Category: C

USES Treatment of vancomycin-resistant *Enterococcus faecium* (VREF), nosocomial pneumonia, complicated and uncomplicated skin and skin structure infections, community-acquired pneumonia due to susceptible gram-positive organisms.

INDICATION & DOSAGE

Vancomycin-Resistant *Enterococcus faecium*
Adult/Adolescent: 600 mg q12h × 14–28 days
Child/Infant: 10 mg/kg q8h × 14–28 days

Common adverse effects in *italic*, life-threatening effects <u>underlined</u>: generic names in **bold**; classifications in SMALL CAPS; ♦ Canadian drug name; ❂ Prototype drug

Nosocomial or Community-Acquired Pneumonia, Complicated Skin Infections

Adult/Adolescent: 600 mg q12h × 10–14 days
Child/Infant: 10 mg/kg q8h × 10–14 days

SOLUTION PREPARATION

IV solution is supplied in a single-use, ready-to-use infusion bag. Remove from protective wrap immediately prior to use. Check for minute leaks by firmly squeezing bag. Discard if leaks are detected.

STORAGE

Store at 25° C (77° F) preferred; 15°–30° C (59°–86° F) permitted. Protect from light and keep bottles tightly closed.

ADMINISTRATION

Intermittent Infusion: Infuse over 30–120 min. If IV line is used to infuse other drugs, flush before and after with D5W, NS, or LR.

INCOMPATIBILITIES Solution/additive: Ceftriaxone, erythromycin, trimethoprim-sulfamethoxazole. Y-site: Amphotericin B, ceftriaxone, chlorpromazine, diazepam, pentamidine, phenytoin.

ACTION & *THERAPEUTIC EFFECT* Synthetic antibiotic of the oxazolidinone group that binds to a site on the bacterial 23S ribosomal RNA of the bacteria, which prevents the bacterial RNA translation process. *Bacteriocidal against gram-positive, gram-negative, and anaerobic bacteria. Bacteriostatic against enterococci and staphylococci, and bacteriocidal against streptococci.*

CONTRAINDICATIONS Hypersensitivity to linezolid; pregnancy (category C), lactation. Safety and effectiveness in children less than 2 y not established.

CAUTIOUS USE History of thrombocytopenia, thrombocytopenia; patients on MAOI, serotonin reuptake inhibitors, or adrenergic agents; active alcoholism; anemia; bleeding; bone marrow suppression; cardiac arrhythmias, cardiac disease; cerebrovascular disease; chemotherapy; coagulopathy; colitis, diarrhea; hypertension; hyperthyroidism; leukopenia; MI; radiographic contrast administration; spinal anesthesia; surgery; phenylketonuria; carcinoid syndrome; lactation.

ADVERSE EFFECTS (≥1%) **Body as a Whole:** Fever. **GI:** Diarrhea, nausea, vomiting, constipation, taste alteration, abnormal LFTs, tongue discoloration. **Hematologic:** Thrombocytopenia, leukopenia. **CNS:** Headache, insomnia, dizziness. **Skin:** Rash. **Urogenital:** Vaginal moniliasis.

DRUG INTERACTIONS MAO INHIBITORS may cause hypertensive crisis; **pseudoephedrine** may cause elevated BP; may cause **serotonin** syndrome with SELECTIVE SEROTONIN REUPTAKE INHIBITORS.

PHARMACOKINETICS Distribution: 31% protein bound. **Metabolism:** By oxidation. **Elimination:** Primarily excreted in urine. **Half-Life:** 6–7 h.

NURSING IMPLICATIONS

Assessment & Drug Effects

- Prior to initiating therapy: Baseline C&S tests (start drug pending results).

Common adverse effects in *italic*, life-threatening effects <u>underlined</u>: generic names in **bold**; classifications in SMALL CAPS; ♣ Canadian drug name; ☯ Prototype drug

411

- Monitor for S&S of: Bleeding, hypertension, or superinfection (see Appendix C), especially pseudomembranous colitis that begins with diarrhea.
- Lab tests: Weekly CBC, including platelet count and Hgb & Hct, in those at risk for bleeding or with more than 2 wk of linezolid therapy.

Patient & Family Education

- Report promptly: Onset of diarrhea; easy bruising or bleeding of any type; blurred vision or any other change in vision.
- Avoid foods and beverages high in tyramine (e.g., aged, fermented, pickled, or smoked foods, and beverages). See Information for Patients provided by the manufacturer.
- Do not take OTC cold remedies or decongestants without consulting prescriber.

LIOTHYRONINE SODIUM (T₃)
(lye-oh-thye'roe-neen)

Triostat
Classification(s): HORMONE
Therapeutic: THYROID HORMONE REPLACEMENT
Prototype: Levothyroxine sodium
Pregnancy Category: A

USES Treatment of myxedema coma.

INDICATION & DOSAGE

Myxedema

Adult: 25–50 mcg, may repeat between 4 and 12 h after previous dose. Target dose over 65 mcg/day (max: 100 mcg/day).

SOLUTION PREPARATION
No dilution is required. Administer as supplied.

STORAGE
Store at 15°–30° C (59°–86° F) and protect from light.

ADMINISTRATION
Direct IV Injection: Give bolus dose of 10 mcg or fraction thereof over 1 min.

INCOMPATIBILITIES Data not available; do not mix with other drugs.

ACTION & *THERAPEUTIC EFFECT* Synthetic form of natural thyroid hormone. Shares actions and uses of thyroid but has more rapid action and more rapid disappearance of effect, permitting quick dosage adjustment, if necessary. *Replacement therapy for absent or decreased thyroid hormone. Principal effect is an increase in metabolic rate of all body tissues.*

Common adverse effects in *italic*, life-threatening effects underlined: generic names in **bold**; classifications in SMALL CAPS; ♣ Canadian drug name; ● Prototype drug

CONTRAINDICATIONS Hypersensitivity to liothyronine; thyrotoxicosis; obesity treatment; severe cardiovascular conditions, acute MI, uncontrolled hypertension; adrenal insufficiency.
CAUTIOUS USE Angina pectoris; hypertension; diabetes mellitus; impaired kidney function; renal failure; older adult; pregnancy (category A), lactation.

ADVERSE EFFECTS (≥1%) **Endocrine:** Result from overdosage evidenced as S&S of hyperthyroidism (see Appendix C). **Musculoskeletal:** Accelerated rate of bone maturation in children.

DRUG INTERACTIONS Epinephrine, norepinephrine increase risk of cardiac insufficiency; ORAL ANTICOAGULANTS may potentiate hypoprothrombinemia; may increase required dose of **insulin.**

PHARMACOKINETICS Duration: Up to 72 h. **Distribution:** Gradually released into tissue cells. **Half-Life:** 6–7 days.

NURSING IMPLICATIONS

Assessment & Drug Effects
- Monitor CV status with frequent BP and HR assessments.
- Lab tests: Baseline and periodic serum TSH, total T4 and T3, and free T4 and T3.
- Withhold drug and report promptly onset of S&S of hyperthyroidism (see Appendix C).
- Concurrent drugs: Monitor PT/INR in those receiving anticoagulants.
- Monitor diabetics for loss of glycemic control.

Patient & Family Education
- Learn S&S of hyperthyroidism (see Appendix C); report promptly if they appear.
- Learn how to self-monitor pulse rate. Notify prescriber if rate begins to increase above 100 or if rhythm changes are noted.
- Notify prescriber immediately of signs of toxicity (e.g., chest pain, palpitations, nervousness).

LORAZEPAM 🄿

(lor-a'ze-pam)

Ativan

Classification(s): ANTICONVULSANT; SEDATIVE-HYPNOTIC; BENZODIAZEPINE
Therapeutic: ANTICONVULSANT; SEDATIVE-HYPNOTIC
Pregnancy Category: D   **Controlled Substance:** Schedule IV

USES Used for preanesthetic medication to produce sedation and to reduce anxiety and recall of events related to day of surgery; for management of status epilepticus.
UNLABELED USES Chemotherapy-induced nausea and vomiting.

Common adverse effects in *italic*, life-threatening effects <u>underlined</u>: generic names in **bold**; classifications in SMALL CAPS; ♣ Canadian drug name; 🄿 Prototype drug

INDICATION & DOSAGE

Surgery Premedication
Adult: 0.044 mg/kg (max: 2 mg) 15–20 min before surgery

Status Epilepticus
Adult: 4 mg injected slowly at 2 mg/min; may repeat dose once if inadequate response after 10–15 min

SOLUTION PREPARATION
Prepare lorazepam immediately before use. Dilute with an equal volume of sterile water for injection, D5W, or NS.

STORAGE
Keep parenteral preparation in refrigerator; do not freeze. Protect from light.

ADMINISTRATION
- Ensure patency of IV before drug administration. Take every precaution to prevent perivascular extravasation.
- **Direct IV Injection:** Give directly into vein or into IV infusion tubing at rate not to exceed 2 mg/min.

INCOMPATIBILITIES Solution/additive: Buprenorphine, dexamethasone, D5W. Y-site: Aldesleukin, aztreonam, buprenorphine, fluconazole, foscarnet, gallium, idarubicin, imipenem/cilastin, lansoprazole, omeprazole, ondansetron, sargramostim, sufentanil, thiopental, TPN with albumin.

ACTION & *THERAPEUTIC EFFECT* Most potent of the available benzodiazepines. Effects (anxiolytic, sedative, hypnotic, and skeletal muscle relaxant) are mediated by the inhibitory neurotransmitter GABA. Action sites: thalamic, hypothalamic, and limbic levels of CNS. *Antianxiety agent that also causes mild suppression of REM sleep, while increasing total sleep time.*

CONTRAINDICATIONS Known sensitivity to benzodiazepines; acute narrow-angle glaucoma; primary depressive disorders or psychosis; COPD; sleep apnea; coma, shock, acute alcohol intoxication; dementia; children less than 12 y; pregnancy (category D), lactation.

CAUTIOUS USE Renal or hepatic impairment; renal failure; organic brain syndrome; myasthenia gravis; narrow-angle glaucoma; pulmonary disease; mania; psychosis; history of seizure disorders; suicidal tendency; GI disorders; older adult and debilitated patients; limited pulmonary reserve.

ADVERSE EFFECTS (≥1%) **Body as a Whole:** Usually disappear with continued medication or with reduced dosage. **CNS:** Anterograde amnesia, *drowsiness, sedation,* dizziness, weakness, unsteadiness, disorientation, depression, sleep disturbance, restlessness, confusion, hallucinations. **CV:** Hypertension or hypotension. **Special Senses:** Blurred vision, diplopia; depressed hearing. **GI:** Nausea, vomiting, abdominal discomfort, anorexia.

DRUG INTERACTIONS Alcohol, CNS DEPRESSANTS, ANTICONVULSANTS potentiate CNS depression; **cimetidine** increases lorazepam plasma levels, increases toxicity; lorazepam may decrease antiparkinsonism effects of **levodopa;** may increase **phenytoin** levels.

PHARMACOKINETICS Onset: 1–5 min. **Duration:** 12–24 h. **Distribution:** Crosses placenta; distributed into breast milk; 91% protein bound. **Metabolism:** Glucuronidated by liver. **Elimination:** In urine. **Half-Life:** 10–20 h (adult).

NURSING IMPLICATIONS

Assessment & Drug Effects

- Have equipment for maintaining patent airway immediately available before starting IV administration.
- Monitor respirations frequently (q5–15min). Elderly patients are especially susceptible to respiratory depression.
- Patients older than 50 y may have more profound and prolonged sedation with IV lorazepam than younger patients. Monitor closely.
- Maintain bed rest for a minimum of 3 h postinfusion. Assess steadiness and gait when ambulation is permitted.
- Supervise ambulation of older adult patients for at least 8 h after lorazepam injection to prevent injury.

Patient & Family Education

- Use caution when ambulating as it may take up to 8 h before the risk of falls is significantly diminished.
- Do not consume alcoholic beverages nor drive or engage in other hazardous activities for a least 24–48 h.

LYMPHOCYTE IMMUNE GLOBULIN

(lymph'o-site)

Antithymocyte Globulin, ATG, Atgam
Classification(s): IMMUNOLOGIC AGENT, IMMUNOGLOBULIN
Therapeutic: IMMUNOSUPPRESSANT
Prototype: Immune globulin
Pregnancy Category: C

USES Primarily to prevent or delay onset or to reverse acute renal allograft rejection, aplastic anemia.
UNLABELED USES T-cell malignancy, acute and chronic graft-vs-host disease, and to prevent rejection of skin allografts.

Common adverse effects in *italic*, life-threatening effects <u>underlined</u>: generic names in **bold**; classifications in SMALL CAPS; ♦ Canadian drug name; ❷ Prototype drug

415

LYMPHOCYTE IMMUNE GLOBULIN

INDICATION & DOSAGE

Renal Allotransplantation

Adult: 10–30 mg/kg/day
Adolescent/Child (over 10 y): 5–25 mg/kg/day

Prevention of Allograft Rejection

Adult: 15 mg/kg/day for 14 days followed by 15 mg/kg every other day for 14 days

Treatment of Allograft Rejection

Adult: 10–15 mg/kg/day for 14 days followed by 15 mg/kg every other day for up to 21 doses if needed

Aplastic Anemia

Adult/Child: 10–20 mg/kg/day for 8–14 days followed by 10–20 mg/kg every other day for 7 doses

SOLUTION PREPARATION

IV Infusion: Withdraw required dose of ATG concentrate and inject into IV solution container of NS or 1/2NS. Invert IV container during injection of ATG to prevent its contact with air inside container. Use enough IV solution to create a concentration of 4 mg/mL or less. Gently rotate to mix but do not shake.

STORAGE

Total storage time for diluted solutions: NO MORE than 12 h (including storage time and actual infusion time). Refrigerate ampules and diluted solutions (if prepared before time of infusion) at 2°–8° C (35°–46° F). Do not freeze.

ADMINISTRATION

- *Intradermal Skin Test:* Test is done to rule out allergy to the drug before first dose. Inject 0.1 mL of a 1:1000 dilution (5 mcg equine IgG in normal saline) and a saline control. If local reaction occurs (wheal or erythema more than 10 mm) or if there is pseudopod formation, itching, or local swelling, use caution during infusion.
- **IV Infusion:** Infuse through a tubing with an in-line 0.2–1.0 micron filter. IV should be infusing into a high-flow vein to decrease potential for phlebitis and thrombosis. Give over at least 4 h (usually 4–8 h). Must finish infusion within 12 h of preparation. Discontinue infusion if systemic reaction develops (generalized rash, tachycardia, dyspnea, hypotension, anaphylaxis).

INCOMPATIBILITIES Data not available; do not mix with other drugs.

ACTION & *THERAPEUTIC EFFECT* An immunoglobulin (IgG) and lymphocyte-selective immunosuppressant derived from horse serum that has been immunized with human thymus lymphocytes. During rejection of allografts, human leukocyte antigens (HLAs) bind to peptides and form complexes. Helper T-lymphocytes activate these complexes and produce interleukins, cytotoxic T-cells, and natural killer cells, which results in destruction of transplanted tissue. Antithymocyte globulin (ATG) reduces the number of circulating T-lymphocytes, altering T-cell activation, and cytotoxic function. *Alters the formation of T-lymphocytes (killer cells) and reduces their number, thus reversing acute allograft rejection. As with other immunosuppressant agents, carcinogenicity of this drug may be expressed.*

CONTRAINDICATIONS Hypersensitivity to other equine gamma globulin preparations; history of previous systemic reaction to antithymocytic globulin (ATG); hemorrhagic diatheses; leporine protein hypersensitivity; use in kidney transplant patient not receiving a concomitant immunosuppressant; fungal or viral infections; pregnancy (category C), lactation.

CAUTIOUS USE Hypotension; infection, leukopenia, lymphoma, neoplastic disease, thrombocytopenia, vaccination, varicella; children (experience limited).

ADVERSE EFFECTS (≥1%) **CNS:** Headache, paresthesia, seizures. **CV:** Peripheral thrombophlebitis, hypotension, <u>hypertension</u>. **GI:** Nausea, vomiting, diarrhea, stomatitis, hiccups, epigastric pain, abdominal distension. **Hematologic:** *Leukopenia, thrombocytopenia.* **Musculoskeletal:** Arthralgia, myalgias, chest or back pain. **Respiratory:** Dyspnea, <u>laryngospasm, pulmonary edema</u>. **Skin:** *Rash, pruritus,* urticaria, wheal and flare. **Body as a Whole:** *Chills, fever,* night sweats, pain at infusion site, hyperglycemia, systemic infection, wound dehiscence; <u>anaphylaxis,</u> *serum sickness,* herpes simplex virus reactivation.

DRUG INTERACTIONS Azathioprine, CORTICOSTEROIDS, and IMMUNOSUPPRESSANTS increase degree of immunosuppression.

PHARMACOKINETICS Distribution: Poorly distributed into lymphoid tissues (spleen, lymph nodes); probably crosses placenta and into breast milk. **Elimination:** About 1% of dose is excreted in urine. **Half-Life:** Approximately 6 days.

NURSING IMPLICATIONS

Assessment & Drug Effects

- Observe patient carefully; allergic reaction can occur even when skin test is negative.
- Discontinue infusion and initiate appropriate therapy promptly with onset of anaphylactic response (respiratory distress; pain in chest, flank, back; hypotension, anxiety).
- Monitor carefully BP, vital signs, and patient's complaints during entire administration period. Prompt treatment is indicated for observed and reported symptoms of anaphylaxis (incidence: 1%), serum sickness, or allergic response. Always have available at the bedside equipment for assisted respiration, epinephrine, antihistamines, corticosteroid, and vasopressor.
- Watch closely for S&S of serum sickness: Fever, malaise, arthralgia, nausea, vomiting, lymphadenopathy, and morbilliform eruptions on trunk and extremities. Rash begins as asymptomatic pale pink macules in periumbilical region, axilla, and groin, then rapidly becomes generalized, ery-

Common adverse effects in *italic*, life-threatening effects <u>underlined</u>: generic names in **bold**; classifications in SMALL CAPS; ♣ Canadian drug name; ◑ Prototype drug

417

thematous, and confluent. Bands of progressive erythema along the sides of hands, fingers, feet, toes, and at margins of palm or plantar skin are characteristic. In ATG-induced serum sickness, when platelet count is low, petechiae and purpura rapidly replace rash distribution over the body. Petechial areas are especially noticeable on legs but also on palms and soles. Serum sickness usually occurs 6–18 days after initiation of therapy; may occur during drug administration or when treatment is stopped.
- Lab tests: Periodic CBC with differential and platelet count.
- Monitor carefully for S&S of thrombocytopenia, concurrent infection, and leukopenia; patient usually receives concomitant corticosteroids and anti-metabolites.
- Monitor patient's temperature and attend to complaints of sore throat or rhinorrhea. Report to prescriber; ATG treatment may be stopped.

Patient & Family Education
- Notify prescriber immediately of pain in chest, flank, or back; chills; pruritus; or night sweats.

L

MAGNESIUM SULFATE
(mag-nes'i-um)

Classification(s): ELECTROLYTE REPLACEMENT SOLUTION
Therapeutic: ELECTROLYTE REPLACEMENT; ANTICONVULSANT
Prototype: Magnesium hydroxide
Pregnancy Category: A

USES To control seizures in toxemia of pregnancy, epilepsy, and acute nephritis and for prophylaxis and treatment of hypomagnesemia.
UNLABELED USES To inhibit premature labor (tocolytic action) and as adjunct in hyperalimentation, to alleviate bronchospasm of acute asthma, to reduce mortality post-MI.

INDICATION & DOSAGE

Seizures
Adult: 1 g, may need to repeat dose

Preeclampsia, Eclampsia
Adult: 4–5 g slowly, then 5 g IM in alternate buttocks q4h

Hypomagnesemia
Adult: Severe, 5 g infused over 3 h
Child: 25–50 mg/kg q4–6h prn (max single dose: 2000 mg)

Total Parenteral Nutrition
Adult: 0.5–3 g/day
Child/Infant: 0.25–1.25 g/day

Common adverse effects in *italic*, life-threatening effects <u>underlined</u>: generic names in **bold**; classifications in SMALL CAPS; ♣ Canadian drug name; ❂ Prototype drug

SOLUTION PREPARATION

Direct IV Injection/IV Infusion: Solutions of 20% or less may be given undiluted. Dilute more concentrated solutions to 20% (200 mg/mL) or less with D5W or NS.

STORAGE

Store at 15°–30° C (59°–86° F).

ADMINISTRATON

- **Direct IV Injection:** Give bolus dose over at least 1 min. May give through Y-site.
- **IV Infusion:** Infuse over 4 h. Do not exceed the direct rate.

INCOMPATIBILITIES Solution/additive: 10% fat emulsion, amphotericin B, calcium, chlorpromazine, clindamycin, cyclosporine, dobutamine, hydralazine, polymyxin B, procaine, prochlorperazine, sodium bicarbonate. Y-site: Amiodarone, amphotericin B cholesteryl complex, cefepime, ciprofloxacin, haloperidol. lansoprazole.

ACTION & *THERAPEUTIC EFFECT* Acts as a CNS depressant and also as a depressant of smooth, skeletal, and cardiac muscle function. Anticonvulsant properties thought to be produced by CNS depression, principally by decreasing amount of acetylcholine liberated from motor nerve terminals, thus producing peripheral neuromuscular blockade. *Effective as a CNS depressant, smooth muscle relaxant, and anticonvulsant in labor and delivery, and cardiac disorders.*

CONTRAINDICATIONS Myocardial damage; AV heart block; cardiac arrest except for certain arrhythmias; hypermagnesemia; GI obstruction; 2 h preceding delivery.
CAUTIOUS USE Renal disease; renal failure; renal impairment; acute MI; digitalized patients; concomitant use of other CNS depressants, neuromuscular blocking agents, or cardiac glycosides.

ADVERSE EFFECTS (≥1%) **Body as a Whole:** Flushing, sweating, extreme thirst, sedation, confusion, depressed reflexes or no reflexes, muscle weakness, flaccid paralysis, hypothermia. **CV:** Hypotension, depressed cardiac function, complete heart block, circulatory collapse. **Respiratory:** Respiratory paralysis. **Metabolic:** Hypermagnesemia, hypocalcemia, dehydration, electrolyte imbalance including hypocalcemia with repeated laxative use.

DRUG INTERACTIONS NEUROMUSCULAR BLOCKING AGENTS add to respiratory depression and apnea.

PHARMACOKINETICS Duration: 30 min. **Distribution:** Crosses placenta; distributed into breast milk. **Elimination:** In kidneys.

NURSING IMPLICATIONS

Assessment & Drug Effects

- Observe frequently, monitoring temperature, BP, and HR q10–15min or more often if indicated.

Common adverse effects in *italic*, life-threatening effects <u>underlined</u>: generic names in **bold**; classifications in SMALL CAPS; ♣ Canadian drug name; ☉ Prototype drug

419

- Monitor respiratory rate closely. Withhold drug and report immediately if rate falls below 12.
- ECG monitoring is recommended for digitalized patients as they are at high risk for cardiac conduction abnormalities, especially heart block.
- Test patellar knee-jerk reflex before each repeated dose. Depression or absence of deep tendon reflexes is a useful index of early magnesium intoxication. Report promptly depressed or absent reflex.
- Lab tests: Baseline and periodic serum magnesium, calcium, and phosphorus levels.
- Monitor for early indicators of magnesium toxicity (hypermagnesemia) such as cathartic effect, profound thirst, feeling of warmth, sedation, confusion, depressed deep tendon reflexes, and muscle weakness.
- Check urinary output, especially in patients with impaired kidney function. Therapy is generally not continued if urinary output is less than 100 mL during the 4 h preceding each dose.
- Observe newborns of mothers who received magnesium sulfate within a few hours of delivery for signs of toxicity, including respiratory and neuromuscular depression.
- Observe patients receiving drug for hypomagnesemia for improvement in these signs of deficiency: Irritability, choreiform movements, tremors, tetany, twitching, muscle cramps, tachycardia, hypertension, psychotic behavior.
- Have calcium gluconate readily available in case of magnesium sulfate toxicity.

Patient & Family Education
- Report promptly: Profound thirst, feeling of warmth, sedation, confusion, depressed deep tendon reflexes, and muscle weakness.

MANNITOL ⓟ

(man'i-tole)

Osmitrol

Classification(s): ELECTROLYTIC AND WATER BALANCE AGENT; DIURETIC, OSMOTIC
Therapeutic: DIURETIC
Pregnancy Category: C

USES To promote diuresis in acute kidney failure following cardiovascular surgery, severe traumatic injury, surgery in presence of severe jaundice, hemolytic transfusion reaction. Also used to reduce elevated intraocular (IOP) and intracranial pressure (ICP), to promote excretion of toxic substances, to relieve symptoms of pulmonary edema.

INDICATION & DOSAGE

Acute Kidney Failure
Adult: **IV Test Dose,** 0.2 g/kg over 3–5 min, if partial response over 2–3 h, may repeat test dose 1 time. If response still negative, do not use.

Child: **IV Test Dose,** 0.2 g/kg (max: 12.5 g) over 3–5 min; **Positive Response,** Urine flow of 1 mL/kg/h for 1–2 h

Oliguria Treatment

Adult: 50–100 g as 15–20% solution

Edema, Ascites

Adult: 100 g as a 10–20% solution over 2–6 h

Elevated IOP or ICP

Adult: 1.5–2 g/kg as a 15–25% solution over 30–60 min

Acute Chemical Toxicity

Adult: 100–200 g depending on urine output

SOLUTION PREPARATION

No dilution is required. Administer as supplied.

STORAGE

Store at 15°–30° C (59°–86° F) unless otherwise directed. Avoid freezing.

ADMINISTRATION

- Ensure patency of IV site prior to infusion
- **IV Infusion:** Infuse a single dose over 30–90 min.
- *Oliguria:* A test dose is given over 3–5 min to check adequacy of kidney function. Satisfactory response is output of at least 30–50 mL/h over 2–3 h. IV rate is adjusted to maintain urine flow at 30–50 mL/h with a single dose usually infused over at least 90 min.
- Use a 5 micron in-line IV filter when infusing concentrations of 15% or higher as they have a tendency to crystallize.

INCOMPATIBILITIES **Solution/additive: Furosemide, imipenem-cilastatin, meropenem, potassium chloride, sodium chloride, whole blood. Y-site: Cefepime, doxorubicin liposome, filgrastim, pantoprazole.**

ACTION & *THERAPEUTIC EFFECT* In large doses, increases rate of electrolyte excretion by the kidney, particularly sodium, chloride, and potassium. Induces diuresis by raising osmotic pressure of glomerular filtrate, thereby inhibiting tubular reabsorption of water and solutes. Reduces elevated intraocular and cerebrospinal pressures by increasing plasma osmolality, thus inducing diffusion of water from these fluids back into plasma and extravascular space. *Parenteral osmotic diuretic that reduces intracranial pressure, cerebral edema, intraocular pressure, and promotes diuresis, thus preventing or treating oliguria.*

CONTRAINDICATIONS Anuria; severe renal failure with azotemia or increasing oliguria; marked pulmonary congestion or edema; hypovolemia; severe CHF; metabolic edema; organic CNS disease, intracranial bleeding; shock, severe dehydration; history of allergy; concomitantly with blood; pregnancy (category C), lactation.
CAUTIOUS USE Older adult; electrolyte imbalance.

Common adverse effects in *italic*, life-threatening effects <u>underlined</u>: generic names in **bold**; classifications in SMALL CAPS; ♣ Canadian drug name; ◯ Prototype drug

421

ADVERSE EFFECTS (≥1%) **CNS:** Headache, tremor, convulsions, dizziness, transient muscle rigidity. **CV:** Edema, CHF, angina-like pain, hypotension, hypertension, thrombophlebitis. **Eye:** Blurred vision. **GI:** Dry mouth, nausea, vomiting. **Urogenital:** Marked diuresis, urinary retention, nephrosis, uricosuria. **Metabolic:** *Fluid and electrolyte imbalance,* especially <u>hyponatremia</u>; dehydration, acidosis. **Other:** With extravasation (local edema, skin necrosis; chills, fever, allergic reactions).

DRUG INTERACTIONS Increases urinary excretion of **lithium,** SALICYLATES, BARBITURATES, **imipramine, potassium.**

PHARMACOKINETICS Onset: 1–3 h diuresis; 30–60 min IOP; 15 min ICP. **Duration:** 4–6 h IOP; 3–8 h ICP. **Distribution:** Confined to extracellular space; does not cross blood–brain barrier except with very high plasma levels in the presence of acidosis. **Metabolism:** Small quantity metabolized to glycogen in liver. **Elimination:** Rapidly excreted by kidneys. **Half-Life:** 100 min.

NURSING IMPLICATIONS

Assessment & Drug Effects

- Take care to avoid extravasation. Observe injection site for signs of inflammation or edema.
- Monitor vital signs closely. Report significant changes in BP and signs of HF.
- Lab tests: Baseline and periodic serum electrolytes and kidney function tests.
- Take accurate daily weight.
- Measure I&O accurately and record to achieve proper fluid balance.
- Monitor for possible indications of fluid and electrolyte imbalance (e.g., thirst, muscle cramps or weakness, paresthesias, and signs of CHF).
- Be alert to the possibility that a rebound increase in ICP sometimes occurs about 12 h after drug administration. Patient may complain of headache or confusion.

Patient & Family Education

- Report any of the following: Thirst, muscle cramps or weakness, paresthesia, dyspnea, or headache.
- Family members should immediately report any evidence of confusion.

MECHLORETHAMINE HYDROCHLORIDE

(me-klor-eth′a-meen)

Mustargen

Classification(s): ANTINEOPLASTIC; ALKYLATING AGENT
Therapeutic: ANTINEOPLASTIC
Prototype: Cyclophosphamide
Pregnancy Category: D

USES Generally confined to non-terminal stages of neoplastic disease. As single agent or in combination in treatment of Hodgkin's disease (stages III and IV), lymphosarcoma, mycosis fungoides, polycythemia vera, bronchogenic carcinoma, chronic myelocytic or chronic lymphocytic leukemia. Also for intrapleural, intrapericardial, and intraperitoneal palliative treatment of metastatic carcinoma resulting in effusion.

INDICATION & DOSAGE

Advanced Hodgkin's Disease
Adult: 6 mg/m^2 on day 1 and 8 of a 28-day cycle

Other Neoplasms
Adult: 0.4 mg/kg given as a single dose or in divided doses of 0.1–0.2 mg/kg/day, may repeat course in 3–6 wk

Obesity
Dose based on IBW.

SOLUTION PREPARATION
- Wear surgical gloves during preparation and administration of solution. Avoid inhalation of vapors and powder and contact of drug with eyes and skin.
- Flush contaminated area immediately if drug contacts the skin. Use copious amounts of water for at least 15 min, followed by 2% sodium thiosulfate solution. Irritation may appear after a latent period. Irrigate immediately if eye contact occurs. Use copious amounts of NS followed by ophthalmologic examination as soon as possible.
- *Vial Reconstitution:* Immediately before use add 10 mL sterile water for injection or NS to the 10 mg vial to yield 1 mg/mL. With needle still in stopper, shake vial several times to dissolve. Discard if solution is colored or has drops of moisture. Withdraw dose into syringe and administer immediately.

STORAGE
Store unopened vials at 15°–30° C (59°–86° F). Protect from light.

ADMINISTRATION
- Ensure patency of IV site prior to beginning infusion.
- **Direct IV Injection:** Give slowly over 3–5 min through tubing or side-arm of freely flowing IV infusion. Flush with running IV solution for 2–5 min to clear tubing of any remaining drug.
- Be alert for extravasation. Treat promptly with subcutaneous or intradermal injection with isotonic sodium thiosulfate solution (1/6 molar) and application of ice compresses intermittently for a 6–12 h period to reduce local tissue damage and discomfort. Tissue induration and tenderness may persist 4–6 wk, and tissue may slough.

INCOMPATIBILITIES Solution/additive: 5% dextrose in water, normal saline, methohexital. Y-site: Allopurinol, cefepime.

ACTION & *THERAPEUTIC EFFECT* Analog of mustard gas and standard of reference for nitrogen mustards. Forms highly reactive carbonium ion, which causes cross-linking and abnormal base-pairing in DNA, thereby in-

---

terfering with DNA replication and RNA and protein synthesis. Cell-cycle nonspecific inhibitor of DNA and RNA synthesis. *Antineoplastic agent that simulates actions of x-ray therapy, but nitrogen mustards produce more acute tissue damage and more rapid recovery.*

CONTRAINDICATIONS Myelosuppression; infectious granuloma; known infectious diseases, acute herpes zoster; intracavitary use with other systemic bone marrow suppressants; pregnancy (category D), lactation.

CAUTIOUS USE Bone marrow infiltration with malignant cells, chronic lymphocytic leukemia; men or women of childbearing age; use with x-ray treatment or other chemotherapy in alternating courses.

ADVERSE EFFECTS (≥1%) **CNS:** Neurotoxicity: vertigo, tinnitus, headache, drowsiness, peripheral neuropathy, light-headedness, paresthesias, cerebral deterioration, coma. **GI:** Stomatitis, xerostomia, anorexia, *nausea, vomiting,* diarrhea. **Hematologic:** Leukopenia, *thrombocytopenia,* lymphocytopenia, <u>agranulocytosis</u>, *anemia,* hyperheparinemia. **Skin:** Pruritus, hyperpigmentation, herpes zoster, alopecia. **Urogenital:** Amenorrhea, azoospermia, chromosomal abnormalities, hyperuricemia. **Body as a Whole:** Weakness, hypersensitivity reactions. *With extravasation: painful inflammatory reaction, tissue sloughing, thrombosis, thrombophlebitis.*

DRUG INTERACTIONS May reduce effectiveness of ANTIGOUT AGENTS by raising serum **uric acid** levels; may prolong neuromuscular blocking effects of **succinylcholine;** may potentiate bleeding effects of ANTICOAGULANTS, SALICYLATES, NSAIDS, PLATELET INHIBITORS.

PHARMACOKINETICS Metabolism: Rapid hydrolysis and demethylation. **Elimination:** In urine. **Half-Life:** Less than 1 min.

NURSING IMPLICATIONS

Assessment & Drug Effects

- Monitor IV site frequently and change site if patency is questionable.
- Establish baseline data for body weight, I&O ratio and pattern, and hematology labs.
- Record daily weight. Alert prescriber to sudden or slow, steady weight gain.
- Lab tests: Periodic CBC with differential and platelet count, and serum uric acid levels.
- Monitor and record patient's fluid losses carefully. Prolonged vomiting and diarrhea can produce volume depletion.
- Report immediately petechiae, ecchymoses, or abnormal bleeding from GI tract and buccal membranes. Keep injections and other invasive procedures to a minimum during period of thrombocytopenia.
- Report symptoms of agranulocytosis (e.g., unexplained fever, chills, sore throat, tachycardia, and mucosal ulceration).
- Note and record state of hydration of oral mucosa, condition of gingiva, teeth, tongue, mucosa, and lips.

Patient & Family Education

- Report promptly any signs of bleeding.

- Use caution to prevent falls or other traumatic injuries, especially during periods of low platelet counts.
- Increase fluid intake up to 3000 mL/day, if allowed, to minimize risk of kidney stones.
- Report promptly: Flank or joint pain, swelling of lower legs and feet, changes in voiding pattern.
- Avoid exposure to people with infection, especially upper respiratory tract infections.

MELPHALAN

(mel'fa-lan)

Alkeran

Classification(s): ANTINEOPLASTIC; ALKYLATING AGENT
Therapeutic: ANTINEOPLASTIC
Prototype: Cyclophosphamide
Pregnancy Category: D

USES For palliative treatment of multiple myeloma and other neoplasms, including Hodgkin's disease and carcinomas of breast and ovary.
UNLABELED USES Polycythemia vera.

INDICATION & DOSAGE

Multiple Myeloma
Adult: 16 mg/m^2 q2wk for 4 doses

SOLUTION PREPARATION

- *Vial Reconstitution:* **Rapidly** inject 10 mL of provided diluent into the vial to yield 5 mg/mL. Shake vigorously until clear. **Must be** further diluted **immediately** for infusion.
- *Further Dilution of Reconstituted Solution:* Add to enough NS to yield a concentration of 0.45 mg/mL or less. Note: 45 mg in 100 mL yields 0.45 mg/mL.

STORAGE

- Do not refrigerate reconstituted solution prior to infusion.
- Store at 15°–30° C (59°–86° F) in light-resistant, airtight containers.

ADMINISTRATION

- Ensure patency of IV site prior to beginning infusion.
- **IV Infusion:** Infuse over at least 15 min. Infusion **must be** completed within 60 min of reconstitution because both reconstituted and diluted solutions are unstable.

INCOMPATIBILITIES Solution/additive: **5% dextrose in water, lactated Ringer's, normal saline.** Y-site: **Amphotericin B, chlorpromazine.**

ACTION & *THERAPEUTIC EFFECT* Forms a highly reactive carbonium ion that causes cross-linking and abnormal base-pairing in DNA, thereby interfering with DNA replication as well as RNA and protein synthesis. *Antineoplastic effects of melphalan result from its activity against both resting and rapidly dividing tumor cells. Also has strong immunosuppressive and myelosuppressive effects.*

CONTRAINDICATIONS Severe bone marrow suppression; hepatic disease; renal impairment, renal failure; severe electrolyte imbalance; pregnancy (category D); men and women of childbearing age; lactation.
CAUTIOUS USE Recent treatment with other chemotherapeutic agents; concurrent administration with radiation therapy; severe anemia, neutropenia, or thrombocytopenia.

ADVERSE EFFECTS (≥1%) **Hematologic:** <u>Leukopenia, agranulocytosis, thrombocytopenia</u>, anemia, acute non-lymphatic leukemia. **Body as a Whole:** Uremia, angioneurotic peripheral edema. **GI:** Nausea, vomiting, stomatitis. **Skin:** Temporary alopecia. **Respiratory:** Pulmonary fibrosis.

DRUG INTERACTIONS Increases risk of nephrotoxicity with **cyclosporine, cimetidine** may decrease efficacy.

PHARMACOKINETICS Peak: 2 h. **Distribution:** Widely distributed to all tissues. **Metabolism:** By spontaneous hydrolysis in plasma. **Elimination:** 25–50% excreted in feces, 25–30% in urine. **Half-Life:** 1.5 h.

NURSING IMPLICATIONS
Assessment & Drug Effects
- Monitor IV site frequently and change site if patency is questionable.
- Lab tests: Monitor WBC and platelet counts 2–3 times/wk during dosage adjustment period; determine WBC each week for 6–8 wk during maintenance therapy. Monitor serum uric acid levels.
- Monitor laboratory reports to anticipate leukopenic and thrombocytopenic periods.
- A degree of myelosuppression is maintained during therapy so as to keep leukocyte count in range of 3000–3500/mm³.
- Assess for flank and joint pain that may signal onset of hyperuricemia.

Patient & Family Education
- Report promptly: Fever, profound weakness, chills, tachycardia, cough, sore throat, changes in kidney function, or joint pain.

MEPERIDINE HYDROCHLORIDE
(me-per'i-deen)
Demerol, Pethadol ♦, Pethidine Hydrochloride ♦
Classification(s): ANALGESIC, NARCOTIC (OPIATE) AGONIST
Therapeutic: NARCOTIC ANALGESIC
Prototype: Morphine
Pregnancy Category: B (D at term) **Controlled Substance:** Schedule II

Common adverse effects in *italic*, life-threatening effects <u>underlined</u>: generic names in **bold**; classifications in SMALL CAPS; ♦ Canadian drug name; ◉ Prototype drug

USES Relief of moderate to severe pain, for preoperative medication, for support of anesthesia, and for obstetric analgesia.

INDICATION & DOSAGE

Moderate to Severe Pain

Adult: 50–150 mg q3–4h prn
Child: 1–1.75 mg/kg q3–4h (max: equal to or lesser than 100 mg q4h) prn

Anesthesia

Adult: 1 mg continuous infusion or 10 mg prn

Hepatic/Renal Impairment Dosage Adjustment

Adjust based on response.

SOLUTION PREPARATION

- *Direct IV Injection:* Dilute 50 mg in at least 5 mL of NS or sterile water to yield 10 mg/mL.
- *IV Infusion:* Dilute to a concentration of 1–10 mg/mL in NS, D5W, or other compatible solution.

STORAGE

Store at 15°–30° C (59°–86° F) in tightly closed, light-resistant containers unless otherwise directed by manufacturer.

ADMINISTRATION

- **Direct IV Injection:** Give over 3–5 min at a rate not to exceed 25 mg/min.
- **IV Infusion:** Infuse through a controlled infusion device at a rate not to exceed 25 mg/min.

INCOMPATIBILITIES Solution/additive: Aminophylline, BARBITURATES, **furosemide, heparin, methicillin, morphine, phenytoin, sodium bicarbonate. Y-site: Allopurinol, amphotericin B cholesteryl complex, cefepime, cefoperazone, doxorubicin liposome, furosemide, idarubicin, imipenem/cilastatin, lansoprazole, mezlocillin, minocycline, tetracycline.**

ACTION & *THERAPEUTIC EFFECT* Synthetic morphine-like compound. Opiates do not alter the pain threshold of afferent nerve endings, nor do they affect conductance of impulses along peripheral nerves. Analgesia is mediated through changes in the perception of pain at the spinal cord (mu_2-, delta-, kappa-receptors) and higher levels in the CNS (mu_1- and $kappa_3$ receptors). *Control of moderate to severe pain.*

CONTRAINDICATIONS Hypersensitivity to meperidine; convulsive disorders; acute abdominal conditions prior to diagnosis; MAOI therapy; pregnancy prior to labor [(category B), at term (category D)].
CAUTIOUS USE Head injuries, increased intracranial pressure; asthma and other respiratory conditions; supraventricular tachycardias; prostatic hypertrophy; urethral stricture; glaucoma; older adult or debilitated patients; impaired kidney or liver function; hypothyroidism, Addison's disease.

ADVERSE EFFECTS (≥1%) **Body as a Whole:** *Pruritus,* urticaria, skin rashes, wheal and flare over IV site, profuse perspiration. **CNS:** *Dizziness,* weakness, euphoria, dysphoria, *sedation,* headache, uncoordinated muscle movements, disorientation, decreased cough reflex, miosis, corneal anesthesia, <u>respiratory depression</u>. Toxic doses: Muscle twitching, tremors, hyperactive reflexes, excitement, hypersensitivity to external stimuli, agitation, confusion, hallucinations, dilated pupils, <u>convulsions</u>. **CV:** Facial flushing, light-headedness, hypotension, syncope, palpitation, bradycardia, tachycardia, <u>cardiovascular collapse, cardiac arrest (toxic doses)</u>. **GI:** Dry mouth, *nausea,* vomiting, *constipation,* biliary tract spasm. **Urogenital:** Oliguria, urinary retention. **Respiratory:** <u>Respiratory depression in newborn, bronchoconstriction</u> (large doses). **Skin:** Phlebitis, tissue irritation. **Metabolic:** Increased levels of serum amylase, BSP retention, bilirubin, AST, ALT.

DIAGNOSTIC TEST INTERFERENCE High doses of meperidine may interfere with ***gastric emptying studies*** by causing delay in gastric emptying.

DRUG INTERACTIONS MAO INHIBITORS, **selegiline** may cause excessive and prolonged CNS depression, convulsions, cardiovascular collapse. **Alcohol** and other CNS DEPRESSANTS, **cimetidine** cause additive sedation and CNS depression; AMPHETAMINES may potentiate CNS stimulation; **phenytoin** may increase toxic metabolites.

PHARMACOKINETICS Onset: 5 min. **Duration:** 2 h. **Distribution:** Crosses placenta; distributed into breast milk. **Metabolism:** In liver. **Elimination:** Excreted in urine. **Half-Life:** 3–5 h.

NURSING IMPLICATIONS

Assessment & Drug Effects

- Assess patient's need for prn medication. Record time of onset, duration, and quality of pain.
- Note respiratory rate, depth, and rhythm. Withhold drug and notify prescriber if respirations are 12/min or below; or, if breathing is shallow, consult prescriber before administering drug.
- Monitor vital signs closely. Heart rate may increase markedly and hypotension may occur. Meperidine may cause severe hypotension in postoperative patients and those with depleted blood volume.
- Monitor I&O and report suspected urinary retention.
- Monitor bowel function and report constipation.

Patient & Family Education

- Be aware that nausea, vomiting, dizziness, and faintness associated with fall in BP are more pronounced when walking than when lying down (these symptoms may also occur in patients without pain who are given meperidine). Symptoms are aggravated by the head-up position.
- Make position changes slowly and in stages to minimize risk of orthostatic hypotension and dizziness.
- Do not drive or engage in potentially hazardous activities until any drowsiness and dizziness have passed.

MEROPENEM

(mer-o'pe-nem)

Merrem IV

Classification(s): ANTIBIOTIC, CARBAPENEM

Therapeutic: ANTIBACTERIAL

Prototype: Imipenem

Pregnancy Category: B

USES Complicated appendicitis and peritonitis, bacterial meningitis caused by susceptible bacteria, complicated skin infections, intra-abdominal infections, skin/soft tissue infections.

UNLABELED USES Febrile neutropenia.

INDICATION & DOSAGE

Intra-Abdominal Infections

Adult/Child (over 50 kg): 1 g q8h

Child/Infant (over 3 mo and less than 50 kg): 20 mg/kg q8h (max: 1 g q8h)

Bacterial Meningitis

Adult/Child (over 50 kg): 2 g q8h

Child/Infant (over 3 mo and less than 50 kg): 40 mg/kg q8h (max: 2 g q8h)

Complicated Skin Infection

Adult/Child (over 50 kg): 500 mg q8h

Child/Infant (over 3 mo and less than 50 kg): 10 mg/kg q8h (max: 500 mg q8h)

Renal Impairment Dosage Adjustment

CrCl (mL/min)	Dosage	Interval
26–50	Normal	q12h
10–25	$^1/_2$ dose	q12h
Less than 10	$^1/_2$ dose	q24h

SOLUTION PREPARATION

- *Vial Reconstitution:* Add 10 or 20 mL sterile water for injection to the 500-mg or 1-g vial, respectively, to yield approximately 50 mg/mL. Shake to dissolve and let stand until clear. May be given as prepared direct IV as a bolus dose or further diluted for infusion.
- *Further Dilution of Reconstituted Solution:* Add required dose to 50–250 mL of D5W, NS, D5NS or other compatible solution.

STORAGE

Store undiluted at 15°–30° C (59°–86° F). Diluted IV solutions should generally be used within 1 h of preparation.

Common adverse effects in *italic*, life-threatening effects <u>underlined</u>: generic names in **bold**; classifications in SMALL CAPS; ♣ Canadian drug name; ⊘ Prototype drug

429

ADMINISTRATION
- **Direct IV Injection:** Give bolus doses of 5–20 mL over 3–5 min.
- **Intermittent IV Infusion:** Infuse over 15–30 min.

INCOMPATIBILITIES Solution/additive: 5% dextrose in water, lactated Ringer's, mannitol, amphotericin B, metronidazole, multivitamins, sodium bicarbonate. **Y-site:** Amphotericin B, diazepam, doxycycline, metronidazole, ondansetron, zidovudine.

ACTION & *THERAPEUTIC EFFECT* Broad-spectrum carbapenem antibiotic that inhibits the cell wall synthesis of gram-positive and gram-negative bacteria by its strong affinity for penicillin-binding proteins of bacterial cell wall. *Effective against both gram-positive and gram-negative bacteria. High resistance to most bacterial beta-lactamases.*

CONTRAINDICATIONS Hypersensitivity to meropenem, other carbapenem antibiotics including imipenem, penicillins, cephalosporins, or other beta-lactams. Safety and effectiveness in infants less than 50 kg not established. **CAUTIOUS USE** History of asthma or allergies, renal impairment, renal disease; epileptics, history of neurologic disorders; older adult; pregnancy (category B), lactation.

ADVERSE EFFECTS (≥1%) **GI:** Diarrhea, nausea, vomiting, constipation. **Other:** Inflammation at injection site, phlebitis, thrombophlebitis. **CNS:** Headache. **Skin:** Rash, pruritus, diaper rash. **Body as a Whole:** Apnea, oral moniliasis, sepsis, shock. **Hematologic:** Anemia.

DRUG INTERACTIONS Probenecid will delay meropenem excretion; may decrease **valproic acid** serum levels.

PHARMACOKINETICS Distribution: Attains high concentrations in bile, bronchial secretions, cerebrospinal fluid. **Metabolism:** Undergoes renal and extrarenal metabolism via dipeptidases or nonspecific degradation. **Elimination:** Primarily in urine. **Half-Life:** 0.8–1 h.

NURSING IMPLICATIONS

Assessment & Drug Effects
- Prior to initiating therapy: Baseline C&S tests (start drug pending results); determine previous hypersensitivity reactions to penicillins, cephalosporins, and other allergens.
- Lab tests: Periodic LFTs and kidney function tests; periodic serum sodium with sodium-restricted patients.
- Discontinue drug and immediately report S&S of hypersensitivity (see Appendix C).
- Report S&S of superinfection or pseudomembranous colitis (see Appendix C).
- Monitor for seizures, especially in older adults and those with renal insufficiency.

Patient & Family Education
- Learn S&S of hypersensitivity, superinfection, and pseudomembranous colitis; report any of these to prescriber promptly.

MESNA

(mes'na)

Mesnex
Classification(s): DETOXIFYING AGENT
Therapeutic: DETOXIFYING AGENT
Pregnancy Category: B

USES Prophylaxis for ifosfamide-induced hemorrhagic cystitis. Not effective in preventing hematuria due to other pathologic conditions such as thrombocytopenia.

UNLABELED USES Reduces the incidence of cyclophosphamide-induced hemorrhagic cystitis.

INDICATION & DOSAGE

Ifosfamide-Induced Hemorrhagic Cystitis

Adult: Dose = 20% of ifosfamide dose given 15 minutes before ifosfamide administration and 4 and 8 h after ifosfamide administration

M

SOLUTION PREPARATION

- *Note:* To be effective, mesna **must be** administered with each dose of ifosfamide.
- *Direct IV Injection:* Add 4 mL of D5W, NS, or LR to each 100 mg of mesna to yield 20 mg/mL.

STORAGE

- Discard any unused portion of the ampule because drug oxidizes on contact with air.
- Refrigerate diluted solutions or use within 6 h of mixing even though diluted solutions are chemically and physically stable for 24 h at 25° C (77° F).
- Store unopened ampule at 15°–30° C (59°–86° F) unless otherwise specified.

ADMINISTRATION

Direct IV Injection: Give bolus dose over 60 sec.

INCOMPATIBILITIES Solution/additive: Carboplatin, cisplatin, ifosfamide with epirubicin. Y-site: Amphotericin B cholesteryl complex, lansoprazole.

ACTION & *THERAPEUTIC EFFECT* Detoxifying agent used to inhibit the hemorrhagic cystitis induced by ifosfamide. Analogous to the physiological cysteine-cystine system. *Reacts chemically with urotoxic ifosfamide metabolites, resulting in their detoxification, and thus significantly decreases the incidence of hematuria.*

CONTRAINDICATIONS Hypersensitivity to mesna or other thiol compounds; neonates; lactation.

Common adverse effects in *italic*, life-threatening effects underlined: generic names in **bold**; classifications in SMALL CAPS; ♣ Canadian drug name; ● Prototype drug

CAUTIOUS USE Autoimmune diseases; infants; pregnancy (category B) and only if the benefits clearly outweigh any possible risk to fetus.

ADVERSE EFFECTS (≥1%) **GI:** *Bad taste in mouth, soft stools,* nausea, vomiting.

DIAGNOSTIC TEST INTERFERENCE May produce a false-positive result in test for *urinary ketones.*

DRUG INTERACTIONS May decrease the effect of **warfarin.**

PHARMACOKINETICS Metabolism: Rapidly oxidized in liver to active metabolite dimesna; dimesna is further metabolized in kidney. **Elimination:** 65% excreted in urine within 24 h. **Half-Life:** Mesna 0.36 h, dimesna 1.17 h.

NURSING IMPLICATIONS

Assessment & Drug Effects
- Monitor urine for hematuria. Note that some patients treated with mesna along with ifosfamide still develop hematuria.
- Be aware that a false-positive test for urinary ketones may arise in patients treated with mesna. In this test, a red-violet color develops that, with the addition of glacial acetic acid, will turn to violet.

M

Patient & Family Education
- Mesna prevents ifosfamide-induced hemorrhagic cystitis; it will not prevent or alleviate other adverse reactions or toxicities associated with ifosfamide therapy.
- Report any unusual or allergic reactions to prescriber.
- Check with prescriber before using any new prescription or OTC medicine.

METHADONE HYDROCHLORIDE

(meth′a-done)

Dolophine

Classification(s): ANALGESIC, NARCOTIC (OPIATE) AGONIST
Therapeutic: NARCOTIC ANALGESIC; DETOX AGENT
Prototype: Morphine
Pregnancy Category: C   **Controlled Substance:** Schedule II

USES To relieve severe pain; for detoxification and temporary maintenance treatment in hospital.

INDICATION & DOSAGE

Pain

Adult: 2.5–10 mg q8–12h prn (opiate naïve patient)

Detoxification Program

Adult: Based on oral usage (use 2:1 oral to injection ratio)

Renal Impairment Dosage Adjustment
CrCl less than 10 mL/min: Use 50–75% of normal dose.

SOLUTION PREPARATION
Direct IV Injection: No dilution required for bolus dose. May be diluted in 1–5 mL of NS to facilitate administration.

STORAGE
Store at 15°–30° C (59°–86° F) in tight, light-resistant containers.

ADMINISTRATION
Direct IV Injection: Give bolus dose over approximately 5 min.

INCOMPATIBILITIES Y-site: Phenytoin.

ACTION & *THERAPEUTIC EFFECT* Methadone is a synthetic narcotic analgesic similar to morphine. It is a CNS depressant that is effectively used in withdrawal treatment from heroin addiction. *Relieves severe pain and manages withdrawal therapy from narcotics.*

CONTRAINDICATIONS Severe pulmonary disease, COPD; obstetric analgesia; pregnancy (category C).
CAUTIOUS USE History of QT prolongation; liver, kidney, or cardiac dysfunction.

ADVERSE EFFECTS (≥1%) **CNS:** *Drowsiness,* light-headedness, dizziness, hallucinations. **GI:** Nausea, vomiting, dry mouth, *constipation.* **Body as a Whole:** Transient fall in BP, bone and muscle pain. **Urogenital:** Impotence. **Respiratory:** Respiratory depression.

DRUG INTERACTIONS Alcohol and other CNS DEPRESSANTS, **cimetidine** add to sedation and CNS depression; AMPHETAMINES may potentiate CNS stimulation; with MAO INHIBITORS, **selegiline, furazolidone** causes excessive and prolonged CNS depression, convulsions, cardiovascular collapse.

PHARMACOKINETICS Peak: 1–2 h. **Distribution:** Crosses placenta and into breast milk. **Metabolism:** In liver (CYP 3A4). **Elimination:** In urine. **Half-Life:** 15–25 h.

NURSING IMPLICATIONS
Assessment & Drug Effects
- Evaluate patient's continued need for methadone for pain. Adjustment of dosage and lengthening of between-dose intervals may be possible.
- Monitor respiratory status. Principal danger of overdosage, as with morphine, is extreme respiratory depression.
- Be aware that because of the cumulative effects of methadone, abstinence symptoms may not appear for 36–72 h after last dose and may last 10–14 days. Symptoms are usually of mild intensity (e.g., anorexia, insomnia, anxiety, abdominal discomfort, weakness, headache, sweating, hot and cold flashes).
- Observe closely for recurrence of respiratory depression during use of narcotic antagonists such as naloxone, naltrexone, and levallorphan to

Common adverse effects in *italic*, life-threatening effects <u>underlined</u>: generic names in **bold**; classifications in SMALL CAPS; ♣ Canadian drug name; ❷ Prototype drug

433

terminate methadone intoxication. Since antagonist action is shorter (1–3 h) than that of methadone (which is 36–48 h or more), repeated doses for 8–24 h may be required.

Patient & Family Education

- Be aware that orthostatic hypotension, sweating, constipation, drowsiness, GI symptoms, and other transient adverse effects of therapeutic doses appear to be more prominent in ambulatory patients. Most adverse effects disappear over a period of several weeks.
- Make position changes slowly, particularly from lying down to upright position; sit or lie down if you feel dizzy or faint.
- Do not drive or engage in potentially hazardous activities until response to drug is known.

METHOCARBAMOL ⊕

(meth-oh-kar′ba-mole)

Robaxin

Classification(s): SKELETAL MUSCLE RELAXANT, CENTRAL-ACTING
Therapeutic: SKELETAL MUSCLE RELAXANT
Pregnancy Category: C

USES Management of discomfort associated with acute musculoskeletal disorders and as adjunct in management of neuromuscular manifestations of tetanus.

INDICATION & DOSAGE

Acute Musculoskeletal Disorders

Adult/Adolescent: 1 g q8h in divided doses

Tetanus

Adult: 1–3 g, then 1–2 g dose, may be repeated q6h
Child: 15 mg/kg repeated q6h as needed (up to 1.8 g/m^2/day for 3 consecutive days)

SOLUTION PREPARATION

May be given undiluted [direct IV] or diluted in up to 250 mL of NS or D5W for infusion.

STORAGE

Store at 15°–30° C (59°–86° F). Do not refrigerate IV solutions.

ADMINISTRATION

- **Direct IV Injection:** Give at a rate of 300 mg or fraction thereof over 1 min or longer.

- **IV Infusion:** Infuse at a rate consistent with the amount of IV fluid but do not exceed the direct rate.
- Keep patient recumbent during, and for at least 15 min after, IV injection in order to reduce possibility of orthostatic hypotension and other adverse reactions.
- Take care to avoid extravasation of IV solution, which may result in thrombophlebitis and sloughing.

INCOMPATIBILITIES Y-site: Furosemide.

ACTION & *THERAPEUTIC EFFECT* Exerts skeletal muscle relaxant action by depressing multisynaptic pathways in the spinal cord and possibly by sedative effect. *No direct action on skeletal muscles; effects are on multisynaptic pathways in spinal cord that control muscular spasm.*

CONTRAINDICATIONS Comatose states; CNS depression; acidosis; kidney dysfunction; older adults; pregnancy (category C), lactation.
CAUTIOUS USE Epilepsy; females of childbearing age; renal disease, renal failure, renal impairment; seizure disorder; children less than 16 y.

ADVERSE EFFECTS (≥1%) **Body as a Whole:** Fever, <u>anaphylactic reaction</u>, flushing, syncope, convulsions. **Skin:** Urticaria, pruritus, rash, thrombophlebitis, pain, sloughing (with extravasation). **Special Senses:** Conjunctivitis, blurred vision, nasal congestion. **CNS:** *Drowsiness, dizziness, lightheadedness,* headache. **CV:** Hypotension, bradycardia. **GI:** Nausea, metallic taste. **Hematologic:** Slight reduction of white cell count with prolonged therapy. **Renal:** Polyethylene glycol in the injection may increase preexisting acidosis and urea retention in patients with renal impairment.

DIAGNOSTIC TEST INTERFERENCE Methocarbamol may cause false increases in ***urinary 5-HIAA*** (with ***nitrosonaphthol reagent***) and ***VMA (Gitlow method).***

DRUG INTERACTIONS Alcohol and other CNS DEPRESSANTS enhance CNS depression.

PHARMACOKINETICS Peak: 1–2 h. **Distribution:** Crosses placenta. **Metabolism:** In liver. **Elimination:** In urine. **Half-Life:** 1–2 h.

NURSING IMPLICATIONS

Assessment & Drug Effects
- Monitor vital signs closely during IV infusion.
- Lab tests: Periodic renal function tests and WBC counts during prolonged therapy (3 days or longer).
- Supervise ambulation following administration.

Patient & Family Education
- Make position changes slowly, particularly from lying down to upright position; dangle legs before standing.
- Avoid activities requiring mental alertness and physical coordination until response to drug is known.
- Urine may darken to brown, black, or green on standing.

Common adverse effects in *italic*, life-threatening effects <u>underlined</u>: generic names in **bold**; classifications in SMALL CAPS; ✦ Canadian drug name; ● Prototype drug

435

METHOHEXITAL SODIUM

(meth-oh-hex'i-tal)

Brevital Sodium

Classification(s): ANESTHETIC, GENERAL; BARBITURATE

Therapeutic: GENERAL ANESTHETIC

Prototype: Thiopental

Pregnancy Category: B   **Controlled Substance:** Schedule IV

USES Induction of anesthesia, as supplement for other anesthetics, and as general anesthetic for brief operative procedures.

INDICATION & DOSAGE

Induction of Anesthesia

Adult: 50–120 mg at a rate of 1 mL (5 mg) q5min, 20–40 mg q4–7min prn

SOLUTION PREPARATION

- Prepare a 1% solution (10 mg/mL) by diluting with sterile water for injection, D5W, or NS.
- Use only clear, colorless solutions. Do not allow contact with rubber stoppers or parts of syringes treated with silicone because solution is incompatible with acid solutions (see **INCOMPATIBILITIES**).

STORAGE

Store drug in sterile water for injection at room temperature for at least 6 wk. Solutions prepared with isotonic NS or D5W are stable for **only** about 24 h.

ADMINISTRATION

- Patient should be recumbent as drop in BP may occur in susceptible patients receiving drug in upright position.
- **Direct IV Injection:** Give bolus dose over 5–10 sec.

INCOMPATIBILITIES Solution/additive: Atropine, chlorpromazine, cimetidine, clindamycin, droperidol, fentanyl, hydralazine, kanamycin, lidocaine, mechlorethamine, methyldopa, prochlorperazine, promazine, promethazine, streptomycin, tubocurarine. Y-site: Fenoldopam.

ACTION & *THERAPEUTIC EFFECT* Rapid, ultra-short-acting barbiturate anesthetic agent. More potent than thiopental but has less cumulative effect and shorter duration of action, and recovery is more rapid. *Induces brief general anesthesia without analgesia by depression of the CNS.*

CONTRAINDICATIONS Hypersensitivity to methohexital sodium; agranulocytosis; barbiturate hypersensitivity; hepatic encephalopathy; intra-arterial administration; shock, heart failure, PVD, severe hypo- and hypertension; respiratory depression; infants less than 1 mo; neonates.

CAUTIOUS USE Adrenal insufficiency, anemia, carbamazepine hypersensitivity; hydantoin hypersensitivity; cardiac disease, COPD; uncontrolled asthma, status asthmaticus, sleep apnea, respiratory insufficiency, CNS depression; depression, ethanol intoxication; exfoliative dermatitis; hepatic disease; older adult; neuromuscular disease; obesity; porphyria; pulmonary disease; renal disease, uremia, renal impairment; seizure disorders, status epilepticus, seizures; shock; pregnancy (category B), labor.

ADVERSE EFFECTS (≥1%) **CV:** Hypotension, cardiac arrhythmias, cardiac arrest. **Musculoskeletal:** Muscle spasm. **CNS:** Postoperative psychomotor impairment that persists for 24 h, anxiety, drowsiness, emergent delirium, restlessness, and seizures. **Respiratory:** Bronchospasm, cough, hiccups, respiratory depression, apnea, dyspnea, respiratory arrest. **Skin:** Phlebitis and nerve injury adjacent to the injection site, local irritation, edema, ulceration, necrosis.

DRUG INTERACTIONS Alcohol and other CNS DEPRESSANTS enhance CNS depression.

PHARMACOKINETICS Distribution: Crosses CNS, placenta and excreted in breast milk. **Metabolism:** Oxidized in liver. **Elimination:** Primarily excreted in urine.

M

NURSING IMPLICATIONS
Assessment & Drug Effects
- Hiccups are common, particularly with rapid injection; they sometimes persist after anesthesia.
- Keep equipment for assisting respiration and administration of oxygen readily available in the event of respiratory distress.

METHOTREXATE SODIUM ⓟ
(meth-oh-trex'ate)

MTX

Classification(s): ANTINEOPLASTIC AGENT; ANTIMETABOLITE, ANTIFOLATE
Therapeutic: ANTINEOPLASTIC; IMMUNOSUPPRESSANT
Pregnancy Category: X

USES To maintain or induce remission in neoplastic diseases. Effective in treatment of gestational choriocarcinoma and hydatidiform mole, for acute and subacute leukemias and leukemic meningitis, especially in children. Used in lymphosarcoma; in certain inoperable tumors of head, neck, and pelvis, mycosis fungoides and to treat severe psoriasis unresponsive to other forms of therapy, rheumatoid arthritis.
UNLABELED USES Psoriatic arthritis, SLE, polymyositis, immunosuppressant in kidney transplantation.

Common adverse effects in *italic*, life-threatening effects underlined: generic names in **bold**; classifications in SMALL CAPS; ♣ Canadian drug name; ⓟ Prototype drug

437

INDICATION & DOSAGE

Leukemia

Adult/Adolescent/Child: **Loading Dose,** 3.3 mg/m²/day; **Maintenance Dose,** 2.5 mg/kg q14days

Osteosarcoma

Adult/Child: 12 g/m², dose repeated at weeks 4, 5, 6, 7, 11, 12, 15, 16, 29, 39, 44, 45

Psoriasis

Adult: 10–25 mg/wk, doses may be adjusted (do not exceed 30 mg/wk)

Renal Impairment Dosage Adjustment

If CrCl less than 80 mL/min: Reduce dose; *if CrCl less than 50 mL/min:* Consider alternative agent.

SOLUTION PREPARATION

- *Vial Reconstitution:* Immediately before use add 2 mL of NS or D5W to each 5 mg to yield 2.5 mg/mL. Reconstitute 1 g high-dose vial with 19.4 mL D5W or NS to yield 50 mg/mL; **must be** further diluted for infusion.
- *Further Dilution of Reconstituted Solution:* Dilute contents of 1 g high-dose vial in D5W or NS to a concentration of 25 mg/mL or less.

STORAGE

Preserve drug in tight, light-resistant container.

ADMINISTRATION

- **Direct IV Injection:** Give bolus dose at rate of 10 mg or fraction thereof over 60 sec.
- **IV Infusion:** Infuse over 1–4 h or as prescribed.

INCOMPATIBILITIES Solution/additive: Bleomycin, metoclopramide, prednisolone. Y-site: Chlorpromazine, droperidol, gemcitabine, idarubicin, ifosfamide, midazolam, nalbuphine, promethazine, propofol.

ACTION & *THERAPEUTIC EFFECT* Antimetabolite and folic acid antagonist. Blocks folic acid participation in nucleic acid synthesis, thereby interfering with mitotic process. Rapidly proliferating tissues (malignant cells, bone marrow) are sensitive to interference of the mitotic process by methotrexate. *In psoriasis, reproductive rate of epithelial cells is higher than in normal cells. Induces remission slowly; use often preceded by other antineoplastic therapies. Also has immunosuppressant effects.*

CONTRAINDICATIONS Hepatic and renal insufficiency; concomitant administration of hepatotoxic drugs and hematopoietic depressants; alcohol; ultraviolet exposure to psoriatic lesions; preexisting blood dyscrasias; men and women of childbearing age; pregnancy (category X), lactation.

CAUTIOUS USE Infections; peptic ulcer, ulcerative colitis; very young or old patients; cancer patients with preexisting bone marrow impairment; poor nutritional status.

ADVERSE EFFECTS (≥1%) **CNS:** *Headache,* drowsiness, blurred vision, dizziness, aphasia, hemiparesis; arachnoiditis; mental confusion, tremors, ataxia, coma. **GI:** <u>Hepatotoxicity</u>, GI ulcerations and hemorrhage, *ulcerative stomatitis, glossitis, gingivitis,* pharyngitis, nausea, vomiting, diarrhea, <u>hepatic cirrhosis</u>. **Urogenital:** Defective oogenesis or spermatogenesis, nephropathy, hematuria, menstrual dysfunction, infertility, abortion, fetal defects. **Hematologic:** *Leukopenia, thrombocytopenia,* anemia, <u>marked myelosuppression, aplastic bone marrow</u>, telangiectasis, thrombophlebitis at intra-arterial catheter site, hypogammaglobulinemia, and hyperuricemia. **Skin:** Erythematous rashes, pruritus, urticaria, folliculitis, vasculitis, photosensitivity, depigmentation, hyperpigmentation, alopecia. **Body as a Whole:** Malaise, undue fatigue, systemic toxicity (after intrathecal and intra-arterial administration), chills, fever, decreased resistance to infection, septicemia, osteoporosis, metabolic changes precipitating diabetes and <u>sudden death, pneumonitis, pulmonary fibrosis</u>.

DRUG INTERACTIONS Acitretin, alcohol, azathioprine, sulfasalazine increase risk of hepatotoxicity; **chloramphenicol, etretinate,** SALICYLATES, NSAIDS, SULFONAMIDES, SULFONYLUREAS, **phenylbutazone, phenytoin,** TETRACYCLINES, **PABA, penicillin, probenecid** may increase methotrexate levels with increased toxicity; **folic acid** may alter response to methotrexate. May increase **theophylline** levels; **cholestyramine** enhances methotrexate clearance. Avoid LIVE VACCINES due to immunosuppressant activity.

PHARMACOKINETICS Peak: 0.5–2 h. **Distribution:** Widely distributed with highest concentrations in kidneys, gallbladder, spleen, liver, and skin; minimal passage across blood–brain barrier; crosses placenta; distributed into breast milk. **Metabolism:** In liver. **Elimination:** Excreted primarily in urine. **Half-Life:** 2–4 h.

NURSING IMPLICATIONS

Assessment & Drug Effects
- Monitor for and report ulcerative stomatitis with glossitis and gingivitis, often the first signs of toxicity. Inspect mouth daily; report patchy necrotic areas, bleeding and discomfort, or overgrowth (black, furry tongue).
- Lab tests: Baseline and weekly LFTs, kidney function tests, CBC with differential, and platelet count; periodic plasma glucose.
- Monitor diabetics for loss of glycemic control.
- Monitor I&O ratio and pattern. Keep patient well hydrated (about 2000 mL/24 h).
- Prevent exposure to infections or colds during periods of leukopenia. Be alert to onset of agranulocytosis (cough, extreme fatigue, sore throat, chills, fever) and report symptoms promptly.
- Be alert for and report symptoms of thrombocytopenia (e.g., ecchymoses, petechiae, epistaxis, melena, hematuria, vaginal bleeding, slow and protracted oozing following trauma).

Patient & Family Education
- Avoid or moderate alcohol ingestion, which increases the incidence and severity of methotrexate hepatotoxicity.

Common adverse effects in *italic*, life-threatening effects <u>underlined</u>: generic names in **bold**; classifications in SMALL CAPS; ♣ Canadian drug name; ✪ Prototype drug

439

- Practice fastidious mouth care to prevent infection, provide comfort, and maintain adequate nutritional status.
- Do not self-medicate with vitamins. Some OTC compounds may include folic acid (or its derivatives), which alters methotrexate response.
- Use contraceptive measures during and for at least 8 wk following therapy.
- Avoid exposure to sunlight and ultraviolet light. Wear sunglasses and sunscreen.

METHYLDOPA ⓟ
(meth-ill-doe′pa)

METHYLDOPATE HYDROCHLORIDE
(meth-ill-doe′pate)

Classification(s): ANTIHYPERTENSIVE, CENTRAL-ACTING, ALPHA-ADRENERGIC AGONIST
Therapeutic: ANTIHYPERTENSIVE
Pregnancy Category: B

M

USES For treatment of hypertensive crises but is not preferred because of its slow onset of action.

INDICATION & DOSAGE

Hypertensive Crisis
Adult: 250–500 mg q6h, may be increased up to 1 g q6h
Child: 20–40 mg/kg/day in divided doses (max: 65 mg/kg/day or 3 g/day, whichever is less)

Renal Impairment Dosage Adjustment
CrCl 10–50 mL/min: Normal dose q8–12h; *CrCl under 10 mL/min:* Normal dose q12–24h.

SOLUTION PREPARATION
Dilute in 100–200 mL of D5W, as needed, to yield 10 mg/mL.

STORAGE
Store at 15°–30° C (59°–86° F).

ADMINISTRATION
Intermittent Infusion: Infuse over 30–60 min.

INCOMPATIBILITIES Solution/additive: **Amphotericin B, hydrocortisone, methohexital, tetracycline.** Y-site: **Fat emulsion.**

ACTION & *THERAPEUTIC EFFECT* Structurally related to catecholamines. Has weak neurotransmitter properties; inhibits decarboxylation of dopa,

thereby reducing concentration of dopamine, a precursor of norepinephrine. Reduces renal vascular resistance; maintains cardiac output without acceleration, but may slow heart rate; tends to support sodium and water retention. *Lowers standing and supine BP, and unlike adrenergic antagonists, is not so prone to produce orthostatic hypotension, diurnal BP variations, or exercise hypertension.*

CONTRAINDICATIONS Active liver disease (hepatitis, cirrhosis); pheochromocytoma; blood dyscrasias; pregnancy (category B).
CAUTIOUS USE History of impaired liver or kidney function or disease; renal failure; autoimmune disease; cardiac disease; angina pectoris; Parkinson's disease; history of mental depression; young or older adult patients.

ADVERSE EFFECTS (≥1%) **Body as a Whole:** Hypersensitivity (*Fever,* skin eruptions, ulcerations of soles of feet, flu-like symptoms, lymphadenopathy, eosinophilia). **CNS:** *Sedation, drowsiness,* sluggishness, headache, weakness, fatigue, dizziness, vertigo, *decrease in mental acuity,* inability to concentrate, amnesia-like syndrome, parkinsonism, mild psychoses, depression, nightmares. **CV:** Orthostatic hypotension, syncope, bradycardia, myocarditis, edema, weight gain *(sodium and water retention),* paradoxic hypertensive reaction. **GI:** Diarrhea, constipation, abdominal distension, malabsorption syndrome, nausea, vomiting, dry mouth, sore or black tongue, sialadenitis, abnormal liver function tests, jaundice, hepatitis, hepatic necrosis (rare). **Hematologic:** *Positive direct Coombs' test* (common especially in African-Americans), granulocytopenia. **Special Senses:** *Nasal stuffiness.* **Endocrine:** Gynecomastia, lactation, *decreased libido, impotence,* hypothermia (large doses), positive tests for lupus and rheumatoid factors. **Skin:** Granulomatous skin lesions.

DIAGNOSTIC TEST INTERFERENCE Methyldopa may interfere with *serum creatinine* measurements using *alkaline picrate method, AST* by *colorimetric methods,* and *uric acid* measurements by *phospho tungstate method* (with high methyldopa blood levels); it may produce false elevations of *urinary catecholamines* and increases in *serum amylase* in methyldopa-induced sialadenitis.

DRUG INTERACTIONS AMPHETAMINES, TRICYCLIC ANTIDEPRESSANTS, PHENOTHIAZINES, BARBITURATES may attenuate antihypertensive response; methyldopa may inhibit effectiveness of **ephedrine; haloperidol** may exacerbate psychiatric symptoms; with **levodopa** may result in additive hypotension, increased CNS toxicity, especially psychosis; increases risk of **lithium** toxicity; **methotrimeprazine** causes excessive hypotension; MAO INHIBITORS may cause hallucinations; **phenoxybenzamine** may cause urinary incontinence.

PHARMACOKINETICS Peak: 4–6 h. **Duration:** 10–16 h. **Distribution:** Crosses placenta, distributed into breast milk. **Metabolism:** In liver and GI tract. **Elimination:** Excreted primarily in urine. **Half-Life:** 1.7 h.

NURSING IMPLICATIONS

Assessment & Drug Effects

▪ Check BP and pulse at least q30min until stabilized and observe for adequacy of urinary output.

- Take BP at regular intervals in lying, sitting, and standing positions during period of dosage adjustment.
- Lab tests: Baseline and period serum electrolytes.
- Supervision of ambulation in older adults and patients with impaired kidney function; both are particularly likely to manifest orthostatic hypotension with dizziness and light-headedness.
- Monitor I&O. Report oliguria and changes in I&O ratio. Weigh patient daily, and check for edema because methyldopa favors sodium and water retention.

Patient & Family Education
- Make position changes slowly, particularly from lying down to upright posture; dangle legs a few minutes before standing.
- Be aware that transient sedation, drowsiness, mental depression, weakness, and headache commonly occur during first 24–72 h of therapy or whenever dosage is increased. Symptoms tend to disappear with continuation of therapy or dosage reduction.

METHYLERGONOVINE MALEATE

(meth-ill-er-goe-noe'veen)

Methergine

Classification(s): ERGOT ALKALOID
Therapeutic: OXYTOCIC
Prototype: Ergotamine
Pregnancy Category: C

USES Postpartum atony, subinvolution, and hemorrhage. With full obstetric supervision, may be used during second stage of labor (IV not commonly used).

INDICATION & DOSAGE

Postpartum Hemorrhage
Adult: 0.2 mg q2–4h (max: 5 doses)

SOLUTION PREPARATION
May be given direct IV undiluted or diluted in 5 mL of NS.

STORAGE
Store at 15°–30° C (59°–86° F) unless otherwise directed. Protect from light.

ADMINISTRATION
Direct IV Injection: Give 0.2 mg or fraction thereof over 60 sec.

INCOMPATIBILITIES Data not available; do not mix with other drugs.

ACTION & *THERAPEUTIC EFFECT* Ergot alkaloid that induces rapid, sustained tetanic uterine contraction that shortens third stage of labor and reduces blood loss. *Administered after delivery of the placenta. It minimizes the risk of postpartal hemorrhage.*

CONTRAINDICATIONS Hypersensitivity to ergot preparations; to induce labor or use prior to delivery of placenta; threatened spontaneous abortion; prolonged use; uterine sepsis; hypertension; toxemia; angina; arteriosclerosis; CAD; dysfunctional uterine bleeding; preeclampsia, eclampsia; hypertension; MI; neonates; PVD; Raynaud's disease; sepsis; stroke; thromboangiitis obliterans; thrombophlebitis; pregnancy (category C), lactation.

CAUTIOUS USE Diabetes mellitus; hepatic disease; migraine headaches; renal failure, renal impairment; pulmonary disease.

ADVERSE EFFECTS (≥1%) **GI:** *Nausea, vomiting.* **CV:** Severe hypertensive episodes, bradycardia. **Body as a Whole:** Allergic phenomena including <u>shock</u>, ergotism.

DRUG INTERACTIONS PARENTERAL SYMPATHOMIMETICS, other ERGOT ALKALOIDS, TRIPTANS add to pressor effects and carry risk of hypertension; PROTEASE INHIBITORS, **itraconazole** may increase the risk of toxicity.

PHARMACOKINETICS Duration: 45 min. **Distribution:** Into breast milk. **Metabolism:** Slowly metabolized in liver. **Elimination:** Mainly in feces, small amount in urine. **Half-Life:** 0.5–2 h.

NURSING IMPLICATIONS

Assessment & Drug Effects

- Monitor vital signs (particularly BP) and uterine response during and after administration of methylergonovine until stabilized (about 1–2 h).
- Notify prescriber if BP suddenly increases or if there are frequent periods of uterine relaxation.

Patient & Family Education

- Report severe cramping or increased bleeding.

METHYLPREDNISOLONE SODIUM SUCCINATE

(meth-ill-pred-niss'oh-lone)

A-Methapred, Solu-Medrol

Classification(s): ADRENAL CORTICOSTEROID
Therapeutic: ANTIINFLAMMATORY
Prototype: Prednisolone
Pregnancy Category: C

USES An antiinflammatory agent in the management of acute and chronic inflammatory diseases, for palliative management of neoplastic diseases, and for control of severe acute and chronic allergic processes. High-dose, short-term therapy: Management of acute bronchial asthma, prevention of fat embolism in patient with long-bone fracture.

INDICATION & DOSAGE

Inflammation/Inflammatory Disease

Adult: 10–40 prn then adjust to patient need
Child: 0.5–1.7 mg/kg/day divided q6–12h; adjust to patient need

Asthma

Adult/Adolescent: 40–80 mg in divided doses until peak flow reaches 70%
Child: 1 mg/kg (up to 60 mg) in divided doses until peak flow reaches 70%

Obesity Dosage Adjustment

Dose based on IBW or ABW, whichever is lower.

SOLUTION PREPARATION

- *Vial Reconstitution:* Available in ACT-O-Vials with supplied diluent. Use only the supplied diluent or bacteriostatic water for injection with benzyl alcohol when reconstituting drug. May be given as prepared after initial dilution or further diluted for infusion. Note: **DO NOT** use preparations with benzyl alcohol for neonates or premature infants.
- *Further Dilution of Reconstituted Solution:* Add required dose to a suitable amount of D5W, NS, D5NS, or D5/1/2NS. Recommended dilution is 0.25 mg/mL.

STORAGE

- Discard IV solution after 48 h.
- Store vials at 15°–30° C (59°–86° F). Do not freeze.

ADMINISTRATION

- **Direct IV Injection (preferred):** Give each 500 mg or fraction thereof over 2–3 min.
- **Intermittent Infusion:** Infuse over 15–30 min.

INCOMPATIBILITIES Solution/additive: Dextrose 5%/sodium chloride 0.45%, aminophylline, calcium gluconate, glycopyrrolate, metaraminol, nafcillin, penicillin G sodium. Y-site: Allopurinol, amsacrine, ciprofloxacin, cisatracurium (high concentration), **diltiazem, docetaxel, etoposide, fenoldopam, filgrastim, gemcitabine, lansoprazole, ondansetron, paclitaxel, potassium chloride, propofol, sargramostim, vinorelbine.**

ACTION & *THERAPEUTIC EFFECT* Intermediate-acting synthetic adrenal corticosteroid with similar glucocorticoid activity as hydrocortisone; has considerably fewer sodium and water retention effects than hydrocortisone. It inhibits phagocytosis, and release of allergic substances. Also modifies immune response of the body to various stimuli. *Has antiinflammatory and immunosuppressive properties.*

CONTRAINDICATIONS Systemic fungal infections; use of solutions with benzyl alcohol preservative for premature infants or neonates; pregnancy (category C), lactation.

Common adverse effects in *italic*, life-threatening effects <u>underlined</u>: generic names in **bold**; classifications in SMALL CAPS; ♣ Canadian drug name; ♦ Prototype drug

CAUTIOUS USE Cushing's syndrome; GI disease, GI ulceration; hepatic disease; renal disease; hypertension; varicella, vaccinia; CHF; diabetes mellitus; glaucoma; coagulopathy; emotional instability or psychotic tendencies.

ADVERSE EFFECTS (≥1%) **CNS:** Euphoria, headache, insomnia, confusion, psychosis. **CV:** CHF, edema. **GI:** Nausea, vomiting, peptic ulcer. **Musculoskeletal:** Muscle weakness, delayed wound healing, muscle wasting, osteoporosis, aseptic necrosis of bone, spontaneous fractures. **Endocrine:** Cushingoid features, growth suppression in children, carbohydrate intolerance, hyperglycemia. **Special Senses:** Cataracts. **Hematologic:** Leukocytosis. **Metabolic:** Hypokalemia.

DRUG INTERACTIONS Amphotericin B, furosemide, THIAZIDE DIURETICS increase potassium loss; with ATTENUATED VIRUS VACCINES, may enhance virus replication or increase vaccine adverse effects; **isoniazid, phenytoin, phenobarbital, rifampin** decrease effectiveness of methylprednisolone.

PHARMACOKINETICS Metabolism: In liver. **Half-Life:** Greater than 3.5 h.

NURSING IMPLICATIONS
Assessment & Drug Effects
- Monitor BP, especially in those with preexisting hypertension.
- Lab tests: Periodic LFTs, kidney function tests, thyroid function tests, CBC, serum electrolytes, serum glucose, and total cholesterol.
- Monitor for S&S of hypokalemia (see Appendix C).
- Monitor diabetics for loss of glycemic control.

Patient & Family Education
- Avoid exposure to persons in contact with chickenpox or measles.
- Report promptly: Edema, rapid weight gain, dark tarry stools, fever, joint pain, muscle weakness, unexplained fatigue, dizziness, fainting, nausea, or loss of appetite.

METOCLOPRAMIDE HYDROCHLORIDE ⊕

(met-oh-kloe-pra′mide)

Emex ✦, Maxeran ✦, Reglan
Classification(s): PROKINETIC AGENT
Therapeutic: GI STIMULANT
Pregnancy Category: B

USES Management of diabetic gastric stasis (gastroparesis); to prevent nausea and vomiting associated with emetogenic cancer chemotherapy (e.g., cisplatin, dacarbazine) or surgery; to facilitate intubation of small bowel.

INDICATION & DOSAGE

Diabetic Gastroparesis
Adult: 10 mg q.i.d. a.c. and at bedtime

Common adverse effects in *italic*, life-threatening effects <u>underlined</u>: generic names in **bold**; classifications in SMALL CAPS; ✦ Canadian drug name; ⊕ Prototype drug

445

Small-Bowel Intubation, Radiologic Examination

Adult: 10 mg administered over 1–2 min
Child (less than 6 y): 0.1 mg/kg; *(6–14 y):* 2.5–5 mg

Chemotherapy-Induced Emesis

Adult: 1–2 mg/kg 30 min before antineoplastic administration; may repeat q2h for 2 doses, then q3h for 3 doses if needed

Postoperative Nausea/Vomiting

Adult: 10–20 mg near end of surgery, may repeat q4-6h prn

Renal Impairment Dosage Adjustment

CrCl less than 40 mL/min: Reduce the dose by 50%.

SOLUTION PREPARATION

- *Direct IV Injection:* Doses of 10 mg or less may be given undiluted.
- *IV Infusion:* Doses greater than 10 mg should be diluted in at least 50 mL of NS (preferred), D5W, D5/1/2NS, LR or other compatible solution.

STORAGE

- Discard open ampules; do not store for future use. Diluted solutions are stable for 24 h in normal light and 48 h protected from light.
- Store unopened at 15°–30° C (59°–86° F). Protect from light.

ADMINISTRATION

- **Direct IV Injection:** Give over 1–2 min or longer (in pediatric patients).
- **IV Infusion:** Infuse slowly over at least 15 min.

INCOMPATIBILITIES Solution/additive: Cisplatin, dexamethasone, erythromycin, floxacillin, fluorouracil, furosemide, lorazepam, methotrexate, penicillin G potassium, sodium bicarbonate, TETRA-CYCLINES. **Y-site: Allopurinol, amphotericin B cholesteryl complex, amsacrine, cefepime, doxorubicin liposome, furosemide, lansoprazole, propofol, TPN.**

ACTION & *THERAPEUTIC EFFECT* Potent central dopamine receptor antagonist that increases resting tone of esophageal sphincter as well as tone and amplitude of upper GI contractions. As a result, gastric emptying and intestinal transit are accelerated with little effect, if any, on gastric, biliary, or pancreatic secretions. Antiemetic action results from drug-induced elevation of CTZ threshold and enhanced gastric emptying. *In diabetic gastroparesis, it is indicated for relief of anorexia, nausea, vomiting, and persistent fullness after meals. Effective as an antiemetic agent for use during chemotherapy.*

CONTRAINDICATIONS Sensitivity or intolerance to metoclopramide; uncontrolled seizures; concurrent use of drugs that can cause extrapyramidal symptoms; pheochromocytoma; mechanical GI hemorrhage; GI obstruction or perforation; ileus; suicidal ideation; history of breast cancer.
CAUTIOUS USE CHF, cardiac disease; sulfite hypersensitivity, asthma; hypokalemia; hypertension; depression, history of suicidal tendencies; hepatic disease; infertility; methemoglobin reductase deficiency; Parkinson's dis-

ease; kidney dysfunction; GI hemorrhage; G6PD deficiency; procainamide hypersensitivity; seizure disorder, seizures; tardive dyskinesia; history of intermittent porphyria; neonates, pregnancy (category B), lactation.

ADVERSE EFFECTS (≥1%) **CNS:** *Mild sedation, fatigue, restlessness,* agitation, headache, insomnia, disorientation, *extrapyramidal symptoms* (acute dystonic type), neurologic malignant syndrome with injection. **GI:** Nausea, constipation, *diarrhea,* dry mouth, altered drug absorption. **Skin:** Urticarial or maculopapular rash. **Body as a Whole:** Glossal or periorbital edema. **Hematologic:** Methemoglobinemia. **Endocrine:** Galactorrhea, gynecomastia, amenorrhea, impotence. **CV:** <u>Hypertensive crisis</u> (rare).

DIAGNOSTIC TEST INTERFERENCE Metoclopramide may interfere with *gonadorelin test* by increasing *serum prolactin* levels.

DRUG INTERACTIONS Alcohol and other CNS DEPRESSANTS add to sedation; ANTICHOLINERGICS, OPIATE ANALGESICS may antagonize effect on GI motility; PHENOTHIAZINES may potentiate extrapyramidal symptoms; may decrease absorption of **acetaminophen, aspirin, atovaquone, diazepam, digoxin, lithium, tetracycline;** may antagonize the effects of **amantadine, bromocriptine, levodopa, pergolide, ropinirole, pramipexole;** may cause increase in extrapyramidal and dystonic reactions with PHENOTHIAZINES, THIOXANTHENES, **droperidol, haloperidol, loxapine, metyrosine;** may prolong neuromuscular blocking effects of **succinylcholine.**

PHARMACOKINETICS Onset: 1–3 min. **Peak:** 1–2 h. **Duration:** 1–3 h. **Distribution:** To most body tissues including CNS; crosses placenta; distributed into breast milk. **Metabolism:** Minimally in liver. **Elimination:** 95% in urine, 5% in feces. **Half-Life:** 2.5–6 h.

NURSING IMPLICATIONS

Assessment & Drug Effects

- Monitor vital signs and report promptly irregular HR or changes in BP.
- Report promptly the onset of restlessness, involuntary movements, facial grimacing, rigidity, or tremors. Extrapyramidal symptoms are most likely to occur in children, young adults, and the older adult and with high-dose treatment of vomiting associated with cancer chemotherapy. Symptoms can take months to regress.
- Lab tests: Periodic serum electrolytes.
- Monitor for possible hypernatremia and hypokalemia (see Appendix C), especially if patient has CHF or cirrhosis.
- Adverse reactions associated with increased serum prolactin concentration (galactorrhea, menstrual disorders, gynecomastia) usually disappear within a few weeks or months after drug treatment is stopped.

Patient & Family Education

- Avoid driving and other potentially hazardous activities for a few hours after drug administration.
- Avoid alcohol and other CNS depressants.
- Report promptly: Trembling hands, facial grimacing, or other unusual movements.

Common adverse effects in *italic*, life-threatening effects <u>underlined</u>: generic names in **bold**; classifications in SMALL CAPS; ♣ Canadian drug name; ◑ Prototype drug

447

METOPROLOL TARTRATE

(me-toe′proe-lole)

Apo-Metoprolol ✦, Betaloc ✦, Lopressor
Classification(s): BETA-ADRENERGIC ANTAGONIST
Therapeutic: REINFARCTION PROPHYLAXIS
Prototype: Propranolol
Pregnancy Category: C

USES Reduce the risk of mortality after an MI.

INDICATION & DOSAGE

Myocardial Infarction
Adult: 5 mg q2min for 3 doses, followed by PO therapy of 50 mg q6h

SOLUTION PREPARATION
No dilution is required. Administer as supplied.

STORAGE
Store at 15°–30° C (59°–86° F). Protect from heat, light, and moisture.

ADMINISTRATION
Direct IV Injection: Give bolus dose at a rate of 5 mg over 60 sec.

INCOMPATIBILITIES **Y-site:** **Amphotericin B cholesteryl complex.**

ACTION & *THERAPEUTIC EFFECT* Beta-adrenergic blocking agent with preferential effect on beta$_1$ receptors located primarily on cardiac muscle. At higher doses, metoprolol also inhibits beta$_2$ receptors located chiefly on bronchial and vascular musculature. Antihypertensive action may be due to competitive antagonism of catecholamines at cardiac adrenergic neuron sites, drug-induced reduction of sympathetic outflow to the periphery, and to suppression of renin activity. *Reduces heart rate and cardiac output at rest and during exercise; lowers both supine and standing BP, slows sinus rate and decreases myocardial automaticity. Antianginal effect is like that of propranolol.*

CONTRAINDICATIONS Cardiogenic shock, sinus bradycardia, heart block greater than first degree, overt cardiac failure, right ventricular failure secondary to pulmonary hypertension; pregnancy (category C). Safety in children is not established.
CAUTIOUS USE Impaired liver or kidney function; cardiomegaly, CHF controlled by digitalis and diuretics; AV conduction defects; bronchial asthma and other bronchospastic diseases; history of allergy; thyrotoxicosis; diabetes mellitus; peripheral vascular disease.

ADVERSE EFFECTS (≥1%) **Body as a Whole:** Hypersensitivity (erythematous rash, fever, headache, muscle aches, sore throat, <u>laryngospasm</u>, respiratory distress). **CNS:** *Dizziness, fatigue, insomnia,* increased dreaming, mental depression. **CV:** *Bradycardia,* palpitation, cold extremities, Raynaud's phenomenon, intermittent claudication, angina pectoris, CHF, intensification of AV block, AV dissociation, <u>complete heart block, cardiac arrest.</u> **GI:** Nausea, *heartburn,* gastric pain, diarrhea or constipation, flatulence. **Hematologic:** Eosinophilia, thrombocytopenic and nonthrombocytopenic purpura, <u>agranulocytosis</u> (rare). **Skin:** Dry skin, pruritus, skin eruptions. **Special Senses:** Dry mouth and mucous membranes. **Metabolic:** Hypoglycemia. **Respiratory:** Bronchospasm (with high doses), *shortness of breath.*

DIAGNOSTIC TEST INTERFERENCE In common with other beta blockers, metoprolol may cause elevated ***BUN*** and ***serum creatinine levels*** (patients with severe heart disease), elevated ***serum transaminase, alkaline phosphatase, lactate dehydrogenase,*** and ***serum uric acid.***

DRUG INTERACTIONS BARBITURATES, **rifampin** may decrease effects of metoprolol; **cimetidine, methimazole, propylthiouracil,** ORAL CONTRACEPTIVES may increase effects of metoprolol; additive bradycardia with **digoxin;** effects of both metoprolol and **hydralazine** may be increased; **indomethacin** may attenuate hypotensive response; BETA AGONISTS and metoprolol are mutually antagonistic; **verapamil** may increase risk of heart block and bradycardia.

PHARMACOKINETICS Peak: 20 min. **Distribution:** Crosses blood–brain barrier and placenta; distributed into breast milk. **Metabolism:** Extensively metabolized in liver (CYP 2D6). **Elimination:** In urine. **Half-Life:** 3–4 h.

NURSING IMPLICATIONS

Assessment & Drug Effects

- Monitor BP, HR, and ECG continuously during IV administration. Report to prescriber significant changes in rate, rhythm, or variations in BP.
- Monitor for HF (especially with left ventricular dysfunction) and AV block that may result from depressed AV node conduction.
- Lab tests: Monitor CBC, blood glucose, LFTs and kidney function tests.
- Monitor I&O, daily weight; auscultate for pulmonary rales.
- Monitor closely patients with thyrotoxicosis since drug masks signs of hyperthyroidism (see Appendix C). Abrupt withdrawal may precipitate thyroid storm.

Patient & Family Education

- Report promptly dizziness or excessive drowsiness.
- Monitor blood glucose (diabetics) for loss of glycemic control. Drug may mask some symptoms of hypoglycemia (e.g., BP and HR changes) and prolong hypoglycemia. Be alert to other possible signs of hypoglycemia not affected by metoprolol and report to prescriber if present: Sweating, fatigue, hunger, inability to concentrate.
- Report immediately to prescriber the onset of problems with breathing.

- If discharged on oral metoprolol, do not abruptly stop taking the medication. Sudden withdrawal can result in increase in anginal attacks and MI in patients with angina pectoris and thyroid storm in patients with hyperthyroidism.
- Do not alter established dosage regimen; compliance is very important.

METRONIDAZOLE ℗

(me-troe-ni′da-zole)

Flagyl IV
Classification(s): ANTIBIOTIC
Therapeutic: ANTIBACTERIAL
Pregnancy Category: B

USES Treatment of serious infections caused by susceptible anaerobic bacteria in intra-abdominal infections, skin infections, gynecologic infections, septicemia, and for both pre- and postoperative prophylaxis, bacterial vaginosis.

INDICATION & DOSAGE

Anaerobic Infections

Adult: 15 mg/kg then 7.5 mg/kg q6h (max: 4 g/day)
Child/Infant: 30 mg/kg/day divided q6h (max: 4 g/day)
Neonate:

Age	Weight	Dose
Over 7 days	Over 2000 g	30 mg/kg/day (divided q12h)
Over 7 days	1200–2000 g	15 mg/kg/day (divided q12h)
Up to 7 days	Over 2000 g	15 mg/kg/day (divided q12h)
Up to 7 days	1200–2000 g	7.5 mg/kg q24h
Up to 28 days	Less than 1200 g	7.5 mg/kg q48h

Pelvic Inflammatory Disease

Adult/Adolescent: 500 mg q8h (in combination with other antibiotics)

SOLUTION PREPARATION

- Single-dose flexible containers (500 mg/100 mL) are ready for use without further dilution.
- *Flagyl IV Vial Reconstitution:* Sequence for preparing solution (important): (1) reconstitution with 4.4 mL sterile water or NS; (2) dilution in IV solution to yield 8 mg/mL in NS, D5W, or LR; (3) pH neutralization with approximately 5 mEq sodium bicarbonate injection for each 500 mg of Flagyl IV used. Avoid use of aluminum-containing equipment

when manipulating IV product (including syringes equipped with aluminum needles or hubs).

STORAGE

- Note: Precipitation occurs if neutralized solution is refrigerated. Use diluted and neutralized solution within 24 h of preparation.
- Store at 15°–30° C (59°–86° F); protect from light. Reconstituted Flagyl IV is chemically stable for 96 h when stored below 30° C (86° F) in room light. Diluted and neutralized IV solutions containing Flagyl IV should be used within 24 h of mixing.

ADMINISTRATION

Intermittent Infusion: Infuse slowly at a rate of one dose per 1 h.

INCOMPATIBILITIES Solution/additive: Amoxicillin/clavulanate, aztreonam, dopamine, meropenem, TPN. Y-site: Amphotericin B cholesteryl complex, aztreonam, drotrecogin alfa, filgrastim, lansoprazole, meropenem, pantoprazole, warfarin.

ACTION & *THERAPEUTIC EFFECT* Synthetic compound with direct trichomonacidal and amebicidal activity as well as antibacterial activity against anaerobic bacteria and some gram-negative bacteria. *Has direct trichomonacidal and amebicidal activity. Exhibits antibacterial activity against obligate anaerobic bacteria, gram-negative anaerobic bacilli, and Clostridia. Most aerobic bacteria are resistant.*

CONTRAINDICATIONS Blood dyscrasias; active CNS disease; lactation.
CAUTIOUS USE Coexistent candidiasis; seizure disorders; heart failure; older adults; severe hepatic disease; renal impairment, renal failure; alcoholism, liver disease; pregnancy (category B).

ADVERSE EFFECTS (≥1%) **Body as a Whole:** Hypersensitivity (rash, urticaria, pruritus, flushing), fever, fleeting joint pains, overgrowth of *Candida*. **CNS:** Vertigo, headache, ataxia, confusion, irritability, depression, restlessness, weakness, fatigue, drowsiness, insomnia, paresthesias, sensory neuropathy (rare). **GI:** *Nausea*, vomiting, anorexia, epigastric distress, abdominal cramps, diarrhea, constipation, dry mouth, metallic or bitter taste, proctitis. **Urogenital:** Polyuria, dysuria, pyuria, incontinence, cystitis, decreased libido, dyspareunia, dryness of vagina and vulva, sense of pelvic pressure. **Special Senses:** Nasal congestion. **CV:** ECG changes (flattening of T wave).

DIAGNOSTIC TEST INTERFERENCE Metronidazole may interfere with certain chemical analyses for *AST,* resulting in decreased values.

DRUG INTERACTIONS ORAL ANTICOAGULANTS potentiate hypoprothrombinemia; **alcohol** may elicit disulfiram reaction; oral solutions of **citalopram, ritonavir; lopinavir/ritonavir,** and IV formulations of **sulfamethoxazole; trimethoprim, SMX-TMP, nitroglycerin** may elicit disulfiram reaction due to the alcohol content of the dosage form; **disulfiram** causes acute psychosis; **phenobarbital** increases metronidazole metabolism; may increase **lithium** levels; **fluorouracil, azathioprine** may cause transient neutropenia.

Common adverse effects in *italic*, life-threatening effects <u>underlined</u>: generic names in **bold**; classifications in SMALL CAPS; ♣ Canadian drug name; ⊕ Prototype drug

451

PHARMACOKINETICS Peak: 1–3 h. **Distribution:** Widely to most body tissues, including CSF, bone, cerebral and hepatic abscesses; crosses placenta; in breast milk. **Metabolism:** 30–60% in liver. **Elimination:** 77% in urine; 14% in feces within 24 h. **Half-Life:** 6–8 h.

NURSING IMPLICATIONS

Assessment & Drug Effects

- Withhold drug and notify prescriber for symptoms of CNS toxicity (see Appendix C). Monitor especially for seizures and peripheral neuropathy (e.g., numbness and paresthesia of extremities).
- Lab tests: Baseline and periodic total and differential WBC counts, especially if a second course is necessary.
- Monitor for S&S of sodium retention, especially in patients on corticosteroid therapy or with a history of CHF.
- Concurrent drugs: Monitor patients on lithium for lithium toxicity.
- Report promptly appearance of candidiasis or its becoming more prominent with therapy.

Patient & Family Education

- Do not drink alcohol during therapy; may induce a disulfiram-type reaction (see Appendix C). Avoid alcohol or alcohol-containing medications for at least 48 h after treatment is completed.
- Urine may appear dark or reddish brown (especially with higher than recommended doses).
- Report symptoms of candidal overgrowth: Furry tongue, color changes of tongue, glossitis, stomatitis; vaginitis, curd-like, milky vaginal discharge; proctitis.

M

MICAFUNGIN

(my-ca-fun′gin)

Mycamine

Classification(s): ANTIBIOTIC; ANTIFUNGAL

Therapeutic: ANTIFUNGAL

Prototype: Caspofungin

Pregnancy Category: C

USES Treatment of patients with esophageal candidiasis, and for prophylaxis of *Candida* infections in patients undergoing hematopoietic stem cell transplantation.

UNLABELED USES Treatment of pulmonary *Aspergillus* infection.

INDICATION & DOSAGE

Esophageal Candidiasis

Adult: 150 mg daily × 10–30 days

Candidiasis Prophylaxis in Hematopoietic Stem Cell Transplantation Patients
Adult: 50 mg/day over 1 h × 18 days

SOLUTION PREPARATION

- *Vial Reconstitution:* Add 5 mL NS (without a bacteriostatic agent) to the 50 mg or 100 mg vial to yield 10 mg/mL or 20 mg/mL, respectively. Gently swirl, but **do not shake,** to dissolve. Solution should be clear. **Must be** further diluted for infusion.
- *Further Dilution of Reconstituted Solution:* Add required dose to 100 mL NS or D5W.

STORAGE

Store reconstituted vial and IV solution for up to 24 h at 25° C (77° F). Protect from light.

ADMINISTRATION

IV Infusion: Give slowly over 1 h. Flush existing IV line with NS before/after infusion. Protect IV solution from light.

INCOMPATIBILITIES Y-site: Albumin, amiodarone, cisatracurium, diltiazem, dobutamine, epinephrine, regular insulin, labetalol, meperidine, midazolam, morphine, mycophenolate, nesiritide, nicardipine, octreotide, ondansetron, phenytoin, rocuronium, vecuronium.

ACTION & *THERAPEUTIC EFFECT* Micafungin is an antifungal agent that inhibits the synthesis of glucan, an essential component of fungal cell walls. It does not allow *Candida* fungi to replicate. *Has antifungal effects against various species of* Candida.

CONTRAINDICATIONS Hypersensitivity to any component in micafungin; pregnancy (category C); lactation. Safety and efficacy in children less than 18 y are unknown.

CAUTIOUS USE Hepatic and renal dysfunction; older adult.

ADVERSE EFFECTS (≥1%) **CNS:** *Headache,* dizziness, somnolence. **CV:** Flushing, hypertension, phlebitis. **GI:** *Nausea, vomiting, diarrhea*, abdominal pain. **Hematologic/Lymphatic:** Anemia, hemolytic anemia, leukemia, neutropenia, thrombocytopenia. **Hepatic:** Elevated liver enzymes, jaundice. **Metabolic:** Hypocalcemia, hypokalemia, hypomagnesemia. **Skin:** Pruritus, rash. **Body as a Whole:** Injection site pain, pyrexia, rigors.

DRUG INTERACTIONS Micafungin increases levels of **sirolimus** and **nifedipine.**

PHARMACOKINETICS Distribution: 99% protein bound. **Metabolism:** Biotransformation primarily in the liver. **Elimination:** Fecal (major) and renal. **Half-Life:** 14–17 h.

NURSING IMPLICATIONS

Assessment & Drug Effects

- Prior to initiating therapy: Baseline C&S tests (start drug pending results).

- Monitor for S&S of hypersensitivity during IV infusion; frequently monitor IV site for thrombophlebitis.
- Monitor for S&S of hemolytic anemia (i.e., blood in urine, jaundice).
- Lab tests: Periodic LFTs, kidney function tests, serum electrolytes, and CBC.
- Concurrent drugs: Monitor blood levels of sirolimus or nifedipine. If sirolimus or nifedipine toxicity occurs, dosages of these drugs should be reduced.

Patient & Family Education

- Report promptly: Blood in urine, facial swelling, wheezing, difficulty breathing or swallowing, tightness in chest, rash, hives, itching, or sensation of warmth.

MIDAZOLAM HYDROCHLORIDE

(mid'az-zoe-lam)

Classification(s): SEDATIVE-HYPNOTIC, BENZODIAZEPINE
Therapeutic: SEDATIVE-HYPNOTIC
Prototype: Lorazepam
Pregnancy Category: D   **Controlled Substance:** Schedule IV

USES Sedation before general anesthesia, induction of general anesthesia; to impair memory of perioperative events (anterograde amnesia); for conscious sedation prior to short diagnostic and endoscopic procedures; and as the hypnotic supplement to nitrous oxide and oxygen (balanced anesthesia) for short surgical procedures.

INDICATION & DOSAGE

Conscious Sedation

Adult: 1–2.5 mg, may repeat in 2 min prn
Adult Intubated Patients: 0.05–0.2 mg/kg/h by continuous infusion
Neonate: 0.5–1 mcg/kg/min

IV Induction for General Anesthesia

Adult (Premedicated): 0.15–0.35 mg/kg over 20–30 sec, allow 2 min for effect; *(Nonpremedicated):* 0.3–0.35 mg/kg over 20–30 sec, allow 2 min for effect

Preoperative Sedation

Adult/Adolescent: 1–2.5 mg titrated slowly; may repeat after 2 min (total dose usually not more than 5 mg)
Adult (over 60 y): 1–1.5 mg titrated slowly; may repeat after 2 min
Child (6–12 y): 0.025–0.05 mg/kg; may titrate up to 0.4 mg/kg (max: 10 mg)
Child/Infant (6 mo–6 y): 0.05–0.1 mg/kg; may titrate up to 0.6 mg/kg (max: 6 mg)

Common adverse effects in *italic*, life-threatening effects <u>underlined</u>: generic names in **bold**; classifications in SMALL CAPS; ♥ Canadian drug name; ● Prototype drug

SOLUTION PREPARATION
- *Direct IV Injection:* Dilute in D5W or NS to a concentration of 0.25 mg/mL (e.g., 1 mg in 4 mL or 5 mg in 20 mL).
- *IV Infusion:* Add 5 mL of the 5 mg/mL concentration to 45 mL of D5W or NS to yield 0.5 mg/mL.

STORAGE
Store at 15°–30° C (59°–86° F). Therapeutic activity is retained for 2 y from date of manufacture.

ADMINISTRATION
- **Direct IV Injection:**
  - *Sedation:* Give over at least 1 min.
  - *Induction of Anesthesia:* Give over 20–30 sec.
  - *Neonate:* DO NOT give rapid injection to neonate; give dose over at least 2 min.
- **IV Infusion:** Give at a rate based on weight.

INCOMPATIBILITIES Solution/additive: Lactated Ringer's, amoxicillin, dimenhydrinate. **Y-site:** Albumin, amoxicillin, amoxicillin/clavulanate, amphotericin B cholesteryl complex, ampicillin, bumetanide, butorphanol, cefepime, ceftazidime, cefuroxime, clonidine, dexamethasone, drotrecogin alfa, foscarnet, fosphenytoin, furosemide, hydrocortisone, imipenem/cilastatin, lansoprazole, methotrexate, nafcillin, omeprazole, pantoprazole, sodium bicarbonate, thiopental, TPN, trimethoprim/sulfamethoxazole.

ACTION & *THERAPEUTIC EFFECT* Short-acting benzodiazepine that intensifies activity of gamma-aminobenzoic acid (GABA), a major inhibitory neurotransmitter of the brain; it interferes with its reuptake and promotes its accumulation at neuronal synapses. This calms the patient, relaxes skeletal muscles, and in high doses produces sleep. *CNS depressant with muscle relaxant, sedative-hypnotic, anticonvulsant, and amnestic properties.*

CONTRAINDICATIONS Intolerance to benzodiazepines; acute narrow-angle glaucoma; shock, coma; acute alcohol intoxication; intra-arterial injection; shock; status asthmaticus; pregnancy (category D), obstetric delivery, lactation.
CAUTIOUS USE Patient with COPD; chronic kidney failure; cardiac disease; pulmonary insufficiency; dementia; electrolyte imbalance; neuromuscular disease; Parkinson's disease; psychosis; CHF; the older adult; bipolar disorder.

ADVERSE EFFECTS (≥1%) **CNS:** *Retrograde amnesia,* headache, euphoria, drowsiness, excessive sedation, confusion. **CV:** Hypotension. **Special Senses:** Blurred vision, diplopia, nystagmus, pinpoint pupils. **GI:** Nausea, vomiting. **Respiratory:** Coughing, <u>laryngospasm</u> (rare), <u>respiratory arrest</u>. **Skin:** Hives, swelling, burning, pain, induration at injection site, tachypnea. **Body as a Whole:** Hiccups, chills, weakness.

DRUG INTERACTIONS Alcohol, CNS DEPRESSANTS, ANTICONVULSANTS potentiate CNS depression; **cimetidine** increases midazolam plasma levels, increasing its toxicity; may decrease antiparkinsonism effects of **levodopa;** may increase **phenytoin** levels; **smoking** decreases sedative and antianxiety effects.

Common adverse effects in *italic*, life-threatening effects <u>underlined</u>: generic names in **bold**; classifications in SMALL CAPS; ♣ Canadian drug name; ◑ Prototype drug

455

PHARMACOKINETICS Onset: 1–5 min. **Peak:** 20–60 min. **Duration:** Less than 2 h IV. **Distribution:** Crosses blood–brain barrier and placenta. **Metabolism:** In liver (CYP 3A4). **Elimination:** In urine. **Half-Life:** 1–4 h.

NURSING IMPLICATIONS

Assessment & Drug Effects

- Inspect insertion site for redness, pain, swelling, and other signs of extravasation during IV infusion.
- Monitor closely for indications of impending respiratory arrest. Resuscitative drugs and equipment should be immediately available.
- Monitor for hypotension, especially if the patient is premedicated with a narcotic agonist analgesic.
- Monitor vital signs for entire recovery period. In obese patient, half-life is prolonged during IV infusion; therefore, duration of effects is prolonged (i.e., amnesia, postoperative recovery).
- Overdose symptoms include somnolence, confusion, sedation, diminished reflexes, coma, and untoward effects on vital signs.

Patient & Family Education

- Do not drive or engage in potentially hazardous activities until response to drug is known. You may feel drowsy, weak, or tired for 1–2 days after drug has been given.
- Review written instructions to ensure future understanding and compliance. Patient teaching during amnestic period may not be remembered.

M

MILRINONE LACTATE

(mil'ri-none)

Primacor

Classification(s): INOTROPIC AGENT; VASODILATOR
Therapeutic: CARDIAC INOTROPIC
Prototype: Inamrinone
Pregnancy Category: C

USES Short-term management of CHF.
UNLABELED USES Short-term use to increase the cardiac index in patients with low cardiac output after surgery. To increase cardiac function prior to heart transplantation.

INDICATION & DOSAGE

Heart Failure

Adult: **Loading Dose,** 50 mcg/kg IV over 10 min; **Maintenance Dose,** 0.375–0.75 mcg/kg/min

SOLUTION PREPARATION

- *Loading Dose:* May be given undiluted or may dilute each 1 mg in 1 mL NS or 1/2NS.

Common adverse effects in *italic*, life-threatening effects underlined: generic names in **bold**; classifications in SMALL CAPS; ♣ Canadian drug name; ⊙ Prototype drug

- *IV Infusion Maintenance Dose:* Dilute 20 mg of milrinone in D5W, NS, or 1/2NS to yield: 100 mcg/mL with 180 mL IV fluid; 150 mcg/mL with 113 mL IV fluid; 200 mcg/mL with 80 mL IV fluid.

STORAGE
Store at 15°–30° C (59°–86° F).

ADMINISTRATION
- Correct preexisting hypokalemia before administering milrinone. See manufacturer's information for dosage reduction in the presence of renal impairment.
- *Loading Dose:* Give 50 mcg/kg over 10 min.
- **IV Infusion Maintenance Dose:** Give at a rate based on weight. Use a microdrip set and infusion pump.

INCOMPATIBILITIES Solution/additive: Bumetanide, furosemide, procainamide. **Y-site:** Furosemide, imipenem/cilastatin, lansoprazole, procainamide.

ACTION & *THERAPEUTIC EFFECT* Milrinone has positive inotropic action, and is a vasodilator with little chronotropic activity. Has inhibitory action against cyclic-AMP phosphodiesterase in cardiac and smooth vascular muscle, thus increasing cardiac contractility. *By increasing myocardial contractility, it increases cardiac output, decreases pulmonary wedge pressure, and vascular resistance, without increasing myocardial oxygen demand or significantly increasing heart rate.*

CONTRAINDICATIONS Hypersensitivity to milrinone; valvular heart disease; acute MI; pregnancy (category C), lactation. Safety and efficacy in children are not established.
CAUTIOUS USE Older adult; atrial fibrillation, atrial flutter; renal disease, renal impairment, renal failure.

ADVERSE EFFECTS (≥1%) **CV:** Increased ectopic activity, PVCs, ventricular tachycardia, ventricular fibrillation, supraventricular arrhythmias; possible increase in angina symptoms, hypotension.

DRUG INTERACTIONS Disopyramide may cause excessive hypotension.

PHARMACOKINETICS Peak: 2 min. **Duration:** 2 h. **Distribution:** 70% protein bound. **Elimination:** 80–85% unchanged in urine within 24 h. Active renal tubular secretion is primary elimination pathway. **Half-Life:** 1.7–2.7 h.

NURSING IMPLICATIONS
Assessment & Drug Effects
- Monitor ECG during and for several hours following infusion. Supraventricular and ventricular arrhythmias have occurred.
- Monitor BP and promptly slow or stop infusion in presence of significant hypotension. Closely monitor those with recent aggressive diuretic therapy for decreasing blood pressure.
- Lab tests: Baseline and periodic serum electrolytes.
- Monitor fluid and electrolyte status. Hypokalemia should be corrected whenever it occurs during administration.

Patient & Family Education
- Report immediately to prescriber angina that occurs during infusion.
- Be aware that drug may cause a headache, which can be treated with analgesics.

MITOMYCIN

(mye-toe-mye'sin)

Mutamycin, Mytozytrex

Classification(s): ANTINEOPLASTIC; ANTIBIOTIC

Therapeutic: ANTINEOPLASTIC

Prototype: Doxorubicin

Pregnancy Category: D

USES With other chemotherapeutic agents in palliative, adjunctive treatment of disseminated adenocarcinoma of pancreas or stomach. Not recommended to replace surgery or radiotherapy or as a single primary therapeutic agent.

UNLABELED USES Adenocarcinoma of the breast, cervix, head, neck, lung.

INDICATION & DOSAGE

Cancer

Adult/Child: 15–20 mg/m²/day as a single dose q6–8wk, additional doses based on hematologic response

Toxicity Adjustment

Neutrophil count 2000–2999/mm³, platelets 25,000–74,999/mm³: Give 70% of dose.
Neutrophil count less than 2000/mm³, platelets less than 25,000/mm³: Give 50% of dose.

Renal Impairment Dosage Adjustment

CrCl 30–60 mL/min: Use 75% of dose, *CrCl 10–29 mL/min:* Use 50% of dose, *CrCl less than 10 mL/min:* Do not use.

SOLUTION PREPARATION

- *Vial Reconstitution:* Dilute each 5 mg with 10 mL sterile water for injection to yield 500 mcg/mL. Shake to dissolve. If product does not clear immediately, allow to stand at room temperature until solution is obtained. Reconstituted solution is purple. May be given as prepared direct IV or further diluted for infusion.
- *Further Dilution of Reconstituted Solution:* Dilute to concentrations of 20–40 mcg in D5W, NS, or LR.

STORAGE

- Store drug reconstituted with sterile water for injection (500 mcg/mL) for 14 days refrigerated or 7 days at room temperature.
- Stability at room temperature of IV solutions: D5W 3 h, NS 12 h, LR 24 h.

ADMINISTRATION

- Ensure patency of IV site prior to initiating infusion.
- **Direct IV Injection:** Give reconstituted solution over 5–10 min. May be given via Y-site of freely flowing IV.
- **IV Infusion:** Infuse over 10 min or longer as determined by total volume of solution. D5W IV solutions must be infused within 3 h of preparation (see **STORAGE**).
- Monitor IV site closely. Avoid extravasation to prevent extreme tissue reaction (cellulitis) to the toxic drug.

INCOMPATIBILITIES Solution/additive: Dextrose-containing solutions, bleomycin, heparin. Y-site: Aztreonam, cefepime, etoposide, filgrastim, gemcitabine, piperacillin/tazobactam, sargramostim, topotecan, vinorelbine.

ACTION & *THERAPEUTIC EFFECT* Potent antibiotic antineoplastic compound effective in certain tumors unresponsive to surgery, radiation, or other chemotherapeutic agents. It selectively inhibits the synthesis of DNA. At high concentrations of mitomycin, cellular and enzymatic RNA and protein synthesis are also suppressed. *Highly destructive to rapidly proliferating cells and slowly developing carcinomas.*

CONTRAINDICATIONS Hypersensitivity or idiosyncratic reaction; severe bone marrow suppression; thrombocytopenia; coagulation disorders or bleeding tendencies; overhydration; severe renal impairment with CrCl less than 30 mL/min; pregnancy (category D), lactation.

CAUTIOUS USE Renal impairment; myelosuppression; CHF; pulmonary disease or respiratory insufficiency; older adults.

ADVERSE EFFECTS (≥1%) **CNS:** Paresthesias. **GI:** Stomatitis, *nausea, vomiting,* anorexia, hematemesis, diarrhea. **Hematologic:** <u>Bone marrow toxicity</u> (*thrombocytopenia, leukopenia* occurring 4–8 wk after treatment onset), thrombophlebitis, anemia. **Respiratory:** <u>Acute bronchospasm</u>, hemoptysis, dyspnea, nonproductive cough, pneumonia, <u>interstitial pneumonitis</u>. **Skin:** Desquamation; induration, pain, necrosis, cellulitis at injection site; reversible alopecia, purple discoloration of nail beds. **Body as a Whole:** Pain, headache, fatigue, edema. **Urogenital:** <u>Hemolytic uremic syndrome</u>, renal toxicity.

PHARMACOKINETICS Metabolism: Metabolized rapidly in liver. **Elimination:** In urine. **Half-Life:** 23-78 min.

NURSING IMPLICATIONS

Assessment & Drug Effects

- Withhold drug and notify prescriber if serum creatinine is less than 1.7 mg/dL, or if platelet count falls below 150,000/mm³ and WBC is down to 4000/mm³, or if prothrombin or bleeding times are prolonged.
- Lab tests: Baseline and periodic WBC with differential, platelet count, PT, INR, aPTT, Hgb, Hct, and serum creatinine during and for at least 7 wk after treatment.
- Monitor I&O ratio and pattern. Report any sign of impaired kidney function: Change in ratio, dysuria, hematuria, oliguria, frequency, urgency.

Keep patient well hydrated (at least 2000–2500 mL orally daily if tolerated). Drug is nephrotoxic.

- Observe closely for signs of infection. Monitor body temperature frequently.
- Inspect oral cavity daily for signs of stomatitis or superinfection (see Appendix C).

Patient & Family Education

- Report respiratory distress to prescriber immediately.
- Report signs of common cold to prescriber immediately.

MITOXANTRONE HYDROCHLORIDE

(mi-tox′an-trone)

Novantrone

Classification(s): ANTINEOPLASTIC; ANTIBIOTIC; IMMUNOLOGIC AGENT
Therapeutic: ANTINEOPLASTIC; IMMUNOSUPPRESSANT
Prototype: Doxorubicin
Pregnancy Category: D

M

USES In combination with other drugs for the treatment of acute non-lymphocytic leukemia (ANLL) in adults, bone pain in advanced prostate cancer. Reducing neurologic disability and/or the frequency of clinical relapses in patients with multiple sclerosis.

UNLABELED USES Breast cancer, non-Hodgkin's lymphomas.

INDICATION & DOSAGE

Combination Therapy for ANLL

Adult: **IV Induction Therapy,** 12 mg/m^2/day on days 1–3, may need to repeat induction course; **IV Consolidation Therapy,** 12 mg/m^2 on days 1 and 2 (max: Lifetime dose 100–160 mg/m^2)

Prostate Cancer

Adult: 12–14 mg/m^2 q21days

Multiple Sclerosis

Adult: 12 mg/m^2 q3mo (max: Lifetime dose 140 mg/m^2)

SOLUTION PREPARATION

- Use goggles, gloves, and protective gown during drug preparation and administration. If mitoxantrone touches skin, wash immediately with copious amounts of warm water.
- *IV Infusion:* Must be diluted prior to use. Withdraw contents of vial and add to at least 50 mL of D5W or NS. May be diluted to larger volumes to extend infusion time.

STORAGE

- Discard unused portions of diluted solution.

Common adverse effects in *italic*, life-threatening effects <u>underlined</u>: generic names in **bold**; classifications in SMALL CAPS; ♣ Canadian drug name; ⊘ Prototype drug

- Once opened, multiple-use vials may be stored refrigerated at 2°–8° C (35°–46° F) for 14 days.

ADMINISTRATION

- **IV Infusion:** May attach to a Y-site of a freely running IV of D5W or NS and infused over at least 3 min or longer (i.e., 30–60 min) depending on the total volume of IV solution. Tubing should be attached to a butterfly needle in a large vein.
- Monitor infusion site closely. If extravasation occurs, stop infusion and immediately restart in another vein.

INCOMPATIBILITIES **Solution/additive: Heparin, hydrocortisone, paclitaxel. Y-site: Amphotericin B cholesteryl complex, aztreonam, cefepime, doxorubicin liposome, lansoprazole, paclitaxel, pemetrexed, piperacillin/tazobactam, propofol, TPN.**

ACTION & *THERAPEUTIC EFFECT* Non–cell-cycle specific antitumor agent with less cardiotoxicity than doxorubicin. Interferes with DNA synthesis by intercalating with the DNA double helix, thus blocking effective DNA and RNA transcription. *Highly destructive to rapidly proliferating cells in all stages of cell division.*

CONTRAINDICATIONS Hypersensitivity to mitoxantrone; multiple sclerosis; baseline left ventricular ejection fraction (LVEF) less than 50%; myelosuppression; pregnancy (category D), lactation.

CAUTIOUS USE Impaired cardiac function; impaired liver and kidney function; systemic infections.

ADVERSE EFFECTS (≥1%) **CV:** Arrhythmias, decreased left ventricular function, _CHF_, tachycardia, ECG changes, <u>MI</u> (occurs with cumulative doses of greater than 80–100 mg/m^2), edema, <u>increased risk of cardiotoxicity.</u> **GI:** *Nausea, vomiting,* diarrhea, <u>hepatotoxicity</u>. **Hematologic:** <u>*Leukopenia, thrombocytopenia*</u>. **Other:** Discolors urine and sclera a blue-green color. **Skin:** Mild phlebitis, blue skin discoloration, alopecia.

DRUG INTERACTIONS May impair immune response to VACCINES such as influenza and pneumococcal infections. May have increased risk of infection with **yellow fever vaccine.**

PHARMACOKINETICS **Distribution:** Rapidly taken up by tissues and slowly released into plasma, 95% protein bound. **Metabolism:** In liver. **Elimination:** Primarily in bile. **Half-Life:** 37 h.

NURSING IMPLICATIONS

Assessment & Drug Effects

- Monitor IV insertion site. Transient blue skin discoloration may occur at site if extravasation has occurred.
- Monitor cardiac functioning throughout course of therapy; report signs and symptoms of CHF or cardiac arrhythmias.
- Lab tests: Baseline and period LFTs, CBC with differential; periodic serum uric acid.

Common adverse effects in *italic*, life-threatening effects <u>underlined</u>: generic names in **bold**; classifications in SMALL CAPS; ♣ Canadian drug name; ⊕ Prototype drug

461

- Note that, typically, hypouricemic therapy is initiated before antileukemic therapy.

Patient & Family Education
- Expect urine to turn blue-green for 24 h after drug administration; sclera may also take on a bluish color.
- Be aware that stomatitis/mucositis may occur within 1 wk of therapy.
- Do not to risk exposure to those with known infections during the periods of myelosuppression.

MIVACURIUM CHLORIDE

(miv-a-cur′i-um)

Mivacron

Classification(s): SKELETAL MUSCLE RELAXANT, NONDEPOLARIZING
Therapeutic: SKELETAL MUSCLE RELAXANT
Prototype: Atracurium
Pregnancy Category: C

USES Adjunct to general anesthesia, to facilitate tracheal intubation, and to provide skeletal muscle relaxation during surgery or mechanical ventilation.

INDICATION & DOSAGE

Tracheal Intubation and Mechanical Ventilation

Adult/Adolescent (healthy): **IV Loading Dose,** 0.15–0.25 mg/kg given over 5–15 sec (over 60 sec in patients with cardiovascular disease); **IV Maintenance Dose,** 0.1 mg/kg generally q15min; **IV Continuous Infusion,** Initial infusion of 9–10 mcg/kg/min, then 6–7 mcg/kg/min
Child (healthy, 2–12 y): **IV Loading Dose,** 0.2 mg/kg given over 5–15 sec (range: 0.09–0.2 mg/kg) then 14 mcg/kg/min

Obesity

Use IBW.

Renal Impairment Dosage Adjustment

Decrease infusion rates by up to 50%.

Hepatic Impairment Dosage Adjustment

May decrease infusion rate up to 50%.

SOLUTION PREPARATION

Direct IV Injection/Infusion: Add 3 mL of D5W, NS, D5NS, LR, or D5LR to each 1 mL mivacurium to yield 0.5 mg/mL.

STORAGE

Store diluted solution at 5°–25° C (41°–77° F) for up to 24 h.

Common adverse effects in *italic*, life-threatening effects <u>underlined</u>: generic names in **bold**; classifications in SMALL CAPS; ♣ Canadian drug name; ⦿ Prototype drug

ADMINISTRATION

- *Loading Dose:*
  - **Direct IV Injection:** Give bolus dose over 5–15 sec (60 sec in those with CV disease).
- **Continuous Infusion:** Give at the rate determined by weight. (Refer to manufacturer's infusion rate tables for examples.)

INCOMPATIBILITIES Data not available; do not mix with other drugs.

ACTION & *THERAPEUTIC EFFECT* Short-acting, skeletal muscle relaxant that combines competitively to cholinergic receptors on the motor neuron end-plate. Antagonizes action of acetylcholine, and blocks neuromuscular transmission. Neuromuscular blocking action is readily reversible with an anticholinesterase agent. *Blocks nerve impulse transmission, which results in skeletal muscle relaxation and paralysis.*

CONTRAINDICATIONS Allergic reactions to mivacurium or its ingredients; pregnancy (category C), lactation; children less than 2 y; neonates.

CAUTIOUS USE Kidney function impairment; liver function impairment; older adult patients; pulmonary disease, COPD.

ADVERSE EFFECTS (≥1%) **CV:** Transient decrease in arterial BP, hypotension, increases and decreases in heart rate. **Skin:** *Transient flushing about the face, neck, and/or chest* (especially with rapid administration).

DRUG INTERACTIONS GENERAL ANESTHETICS may enhance the degree of neuromuscular blockade produced by mivacurium. AMINOGLYCOSIDES, TETRACYCLINES, **bacitracin,** POLYMYXINS, **lincomycin, clindamycin, colistin, magnesium salts, lithium,** LOCAL ANESTHETICS, **procainamide,** and **quinidine** may enhance the neuromuscular blockade.

PHARMACOKINETICS Peak: 2–6 min. **Duration:** 25–30 min in adults, 8–16 min in children. **Distribution:** Limited tissue distribution. **Metabolism:** Rapidly hydrolyzed by plasma cholinesterase.

NURSING IMPLICATIONS

Assessment & Drug Effects

- Assess patients with neuromuscular disease carefully and adjust drug dosage using a peripheral nerve stimulator when they experience prolonged neuromuscular blocks.
- Monitor hemodynamic status carefully in patients with significant cardiovascular disease or those with potentially greater sensitivity to release of histamine-type mediators (e.g., asthma).
- Monitor for significant drop in BP because overdose may increase the risk of hemodynamic adverse effects.

MORPHINE SULFATE 🅟

(mor'feen)

Astramorph PF, DepoDur, Duramorph, Infumorph, Epimorph ♦, Statex ♦

Classification(s): ANALGESIC; NARCOTIC (OPIATE) AGONIST

Common adverse effects in *italic*, life-threatening effects underlined: generic names in **bold**; classifications in SMALL CAPS; ♦ Canadian drug name; 🅟 Prototype drug

463

Therapeutic: NARCOTIC ANALGESIC
Pregnancy Category: C (D with long-term use or high dose, or use close to term)   **Controlled Substance:** Schedule II

USES Symptomatic relief of severe pain after nonnarcotic analgesics have failed and as preanesthetic medication; also used to relieve dyspnea of acute left ventricular failure and pulmonary edema and pain of MI.

INDICATION & DOSAGE

Pain Relief

Adult: 2.5–15 mg/70 kg q2–4h or 0.8–10 mg/h by continuous infusion, may increase prn to control pain or 5–10 mg given via epidural q24h; **Epidural,** (*DepoDur* only) 10–15 mg as single dose 30 min before surgery (max: 20 mg)
Child/Infant (6 mo or older): 0.05–0.1 mg/kg q4h or 0.025–2.6 mg/kg/h by continuous infusion (max: 10 mg/dose)
Neonate/Infant (less than 6 mo): 0.05 mg/kg q4–8h (max: 0.1 mg/kg/dose) or 0.01–0.02 mg/kg/h

Renal Impairment Dosage Adjustment

CrCl 10–50 mL/min: Use 75% of dose, if lower use 50% of dose.

SOLUTION PREPARATION

- *Direct IV Injection:* Dilute 2–10 mg in at least 5 mL of sterile water for injection.
- *Continuous Infusion:* Dilute in an appropriate amount of D5W. Typical concentrations range from 0.1 mg/mL to 1 mg/mL. Higher concentrations (usually not in excess of 5 mg/mL) may be used if fluid volume restriction is required.

STORAGE

Store at 15°–30° C (59°–86° F). Avoid freezing. Refrigerate suppositories. Protect all formulations from light.

ADMINISTRATION

- **Direct IV Injection:** Give a single dose over 4–5 min. Avoid rapid administration.
- **Continuous Infusion:** Use a controlled infusion device and adjust rate according to patient response as ordered.

INCOMPATIBILITIES Solution/additive: Alteplase, aminophylline, amobarbital, chlorothiazide, fluorouracil, heparin, meperidine, nitrofurantoin, pentobarbital, perphenazine, phenobarbital, phenytoin, sodium bicarbonate, thiopental. Y-site: Acyclovir, amphotericin B cholesteryl complex, azithromycin, cefepime, doxorubicin liposome, gallium, lansoprazole, minocycline, phenytoin, sargramostim, tetracycline.

ACTION & *THERAPEUTIC EFFECT* Natural opium with agonist activity by binding with the same receptors as endogenous opioid peptides. Narcotic

Common adverse effects in *italic*, life-threatening effects <u>underlined</u>: generic names in **bold**; classifications in SMALL CAPS; ♣ Canadian drug name; ☻ Prototype drug

agonist effects are identified with 3 locations of receptors: Analgesia at supraspinal level, euphoria, respiratory depression, and physical dependence; analgesia at spinal level, sedation and miosis; and dysphoric, hallucinogenic, and cardiac stimulant effects. *Controls severe pain; also used as an adjunct to anesthesia.*

CONTRAINDICATIONS Hypersensitivity to opiates; increased intracranial pressure; convulsive disorders; acute alcoholism; acute bronchial asthma, chronic pulmonary diseases, severe respiratory depression; chemical-irritant induced pulmonary edema; prostatic hypertrophy; diarrhea caused by poisoning until the toxic material has been eliminated; undiagnosed acute abdominal conditions; following biliary tract surgery and surgical anastomosis; pancreatitis; acute ulcerative colitis; severe liver or renal insufficiency; Addison's disease; hypothyroidism; pregnancy (category C; D in long-term use or when high dose is used, or close to term); during labor for delivery of a premature neonate; premature neonates.

CAUTIOUS USE Toxic psychosis; cardiac arrhythmias, cardiovascular disease; emphysema; kyphoscoliosis; cor pulmonale; severe obesity; reduced blood volume; very old, very young, or debilitated patients; labor.

ADVERSE EFFECTS (≥1%) **Body as a Whole:** Hypersensitivity [pruritus, rash, urticaria, edema, hemorrhagic urticaria (rare), <u>anaphylactoid reaction</u> (rare)], sweating, skeletal muscle flaccidity; cold, clammy skin, hypothermia. **CNS:** Euphoria, insomnia, disorientation, visual disturbances, dysphoria, paradoxic CNS stimulation (restlessness, tremor, delirium, insomnia), convulsions (infants and children); decreased cough reflex, drowsiness, dizziness, deep sleep, coma, continuous intrathecal infusion may cause granulomas leading to paralysis. **Special Senses:** Miosis. **CV:** Bradycardia, palpitations, syncope; flushing of face, neck, and upper thorax; orthostatic hypotension, <u>cardiac arrest</u>. **GI:** *Constipation,* anorexia, dry mouth, biliary colic, *nausea,* vomiting, elevated transaminase levels. **Urogenital:** Urinary retention or urgency, dysuria, oliguria, reduced libido or potency (prolonged use). **Other:** Prolonged labor and respiratory depression of newborn. **Hematologic:** Precipitation of porphyria. **Respiratory:** <u>Severe respiratory depression</u> (as low as 2–4/min) or <u>arrest</u>; pulmonary edema.

DIAGNOSTIC TEST INTERFERENCE False-positive ***urine glucose*** determinations may occur using ***Benedict's solution. Plasma amylase*** and ***lipase*** determinations may be falsely positive for 24 h after use of morphine; ***transaminase levels*** may be elevated.

DRUG INTERACTIONS CNS DEPRESSANTS, SEDATIVES, BARBITURATES, BENZODIAZEPINES, and TRICYCLIC ANTIDEPRESSANTS potentiate CNS depressant effects. Use MAO INHIBITORS cautiously; they may precipitate hypertensive crisis. PHENOTHIAZINES may antagonize analgesia. Use with **alcohol** may lead to potentially fatal overdoses.

PHARMACOKINETICS Peak: 20 min. **Distribution:** Crosses blood–brain barrier and placenta; distributed in breast milk. **Metabolism:** Primarily in liver. **Elimination:** 90% of drug and metabolites excreted in urine in 24 h; 7–10% excreted in bile.

NURSING IMPLICATIONS

Assessment & Drug Effects

- Obtain baseline respiratory rate, depth, and rhythm before administering the drug. Respirations of 12/min or below and miosis are signs of toxicity. Withhold drug and report to prescriber.
- Assess vital signs at regular intervals. Morphine-induced respiratory depression may occur even with small doses, and it increases progressively with higher doses.
- Observe patient closely to be certain pain relief is achieved. Record relief of pain and duration of analgesia.
- Be alert to elevated pulse or respiratory rate, restlessness, anorexia, or drawn facial expression that may indicate need for analgesia.
- Differentiate among restlessness as a sign of pain and the need for medication, restlessness associated with hypoxia, and restlessness caused by morphine-induced CNS stimulation (a paradoxic reaction that is particularly common in older adult patients).
- Encourage changes in position, deep breathing, and coughing (unless contraindicated) at regularly scheduled intervals. Narcotic analgesics also depress cough and sigh reflexes and thus may induce atelectasis, especially in postoperative patients.
- Be alert for nausea and orthostatic hypotension (with light-headedness and dizziness) in ambulatory patients or when a supine patient assumes the head-up position or in patients not experiencing severe pain.
- Monitor I&O ratio and pattern. Report oliguria or urinary retention. Morphine may dull perception of bladder stimuli; therefore, encourage the patient to void at least q4h. Palpate lower abdomen to detect bladder distention.

Patient & Family Education

- Do not smoke or ambulate without assistance after receiving drug.
- Use caution or avoid tasks requiring alertness (e.g., driving a car) until response to drug is known since morphine may cause drowsiness, dizziness, or blurred vision.

MOXIFLOXACIN HYDROCHLORIDE

(mox-i-flox'a-sin)

Avelox

Classification(s): ANTIBIOTIC; QUINOLONE
Therapeutic: ANTIBACTERIAL
Prototype: Ciprofloxacin
Pregnancy Category: C

USES Treatment of acute bacterial sinusitis, acute bacterial exacerbation of chronic bronchitis, community-acquired pneumonia, skin and skin structure infections, bacterial conjunctivitis, complicated skin infections.

INDICATION & DOSAGE

Acute Bacterial Sinusitis, Acute Bacterial Exacerbation of Chronic Bronchitis, Community-Acquired Pneumonia, Skin Infections
Adult: 400 mg daily × 5–14 days

Complicated Skin Infection
Adult: 400 mg daily × 7–21 days

SOLUTION PREPARATION
Avelox (400 mg) is supplied in ready-to-use 250 mL IV bags. No further dilution is necessary.

STORAGE
Store at 15°–30° C (59°–86° F). Do not refrigerate.

ADMINISTRATION
IV Infusion: Infuse over 60 min. AVOID RAPID OR BOLUS DOSE.

INCOMPATIBILITIES Data not available; do not mix with other drugs.

ACTION & *THERAPEUTIC EFFECT* Moxifloxacin is a synthetic broad-spectrum antibiotic belonging to the fluoroquinolone class of drugs. It inhibits DNA gyrase, an enzyme required for DNA replication, transcription, repair, and recombination of bacterial DNA. *It is a broad-spectrum bactericidal agent against both gram-positive and gram-negative organisms.*

CONTRAINDICATIONS Hypersensitivity to moxifloxacin or other quinolones; moderate to severe hepatic insufficiency; syphilis; patients with history of prolonged QT_C interval on ECG, history of ventricular arrhythmias, atrial fibrillation, hypokalemia, bradycardia, acute myocardial ischemia, acute MI, patients receiving Class IA or Class III antiarrhythmic drugs, history of torsade de pointes; tendon pain; viral infection; pregnancy (category C), lactation.
CAUTIOUS USE CNS disorders; cerebrovascular disease; colitis, diarrhea, GI disease; diabetes mellitus; mild or moderate heart insufficiency; myasthenia gravis; seizure disorder; sunlight (UV) exposure.

ADVERSE EFFECTS (≥1%) **CNS:** Dizziness, headache, peripheral neuropathy. **GI:** Nausea, diarrhea, abdominal pain, vomiting, taste perversion, abnormal liver function tests, dyspepsia. **Musculoskeletal:** Tendon rupture, cartilage erosion.

DIAGNOSTIC TEST INTERFERENCE May cause false positive on *opiate screening tests.*

DRUG INTERACTIONS Atenolol, erythromycin, ANTIPSYCHOTICS, TRICYCLIC ANTIDEPRESSANTS, **quinidine, procainamide, amiodarone, sotalol** may cause prolonged QT_C interval.

PHARMACOKINETICS Distribution: 50% protein bound. **Metabolism:** In liver. **Elimination:** Unchanged drug: 20% in urine, 25% in feces; metabolites: 38% in feces, 14% in urine. **Half-Life:** 12 h.

Common adverse effects in *italic*, life-threatening effects underlined: generic names in **bold**; classifications in SMALL CAPS; ✦ Canadian drug name; ❂ Prototype drug

467

NURSING IMPLICATIONS

Assessment & Drug Effects

- Prior to initiating therapy: Baseline C&S tests (start drug pending results); determine previous hypersensitivity reactions to quinolones.
- Note: Do not administer to persons with QT_c prolongation, hypokalemia, or those receiving Class IA or Class III antiarrhythmic drugs. ECG monitoring may be indicated.
- Monitor for and report promptly adverse CNS effects, including peripheral neuropathy, or signs of hypersensitivity (see Appendix C).
- Lab tests: Baseline and periodic CBC with differentia, serum potassium (especially with history of hypokalemia).
- Monitor diabetics for loss of glycemic control.
- Increased seizure potential is possible, especially when history of seizure exists. Monitor closely.

Patient & Family Education

- Report promptly: Itching, swelling about the face or neck, rash.
- Drink fluids liberally, unless directed otherwise.
- Report promptly: Pain, burning, tingling or numbness in feet and/or hands.

- Avoid engaging in hazardous activities until reaction to drug is known.
- Avoid excessive exposure to direct sunlight or UV light to minimize risk of photosensitivity.

MYCOPHENOLATE MOFETIL

(my-co-phen'o-late mo'fe-till)

CellCept

Classification(s): IMMUNOLOGIC AGENT, IMMUNOSUPPRESSANT
Therapeutic: IMMUNOSUPPRESSANT
Prototype: Cyclosporine
Pregnancy Category: C

USES Prophylaxis of organ rejection in patients receiving allogenic kidney, liver, or heart transplants.
UNLABELED USES Treatment of rheumatoid arthritis and psoriasis.

INDICATION & DOSAGE

Prophylaxis for Kidney/Liver Transplant Rejection

Adult: Start within 24 h of transplant, 1 g b.i.d. in combination with corticosteroids and cyclosporine

Prophylaxis for Heart/Liver Transplant Rejection

Adult: 1.5 g b.i.d. started within 24 h of transplant

Common adverse effects in *italic*, life-threatening effects <u>underlined</u>: generic names in **bold**; classifications in SMALL CAPS; ♦ Canadian drug name; ☻ Prototype drug

SOLUTION PREPARATION

- Avoid skin contact. Wash thoroughly with soap and water if contact occurs. Rinse with copious plain water following eye contact.
- *Vial Reconstitution:* Add 14 mL D5W to each vial. **Must be** further diluted for infusion.
- *Further Dilution of Reconstituted Solution:* Dilute each 500 mg with an additional 70 mL of D5W to yield 6 mg/mL.

STORAGE

Store vials at 15°–30° C (59°–86° F). Use reconstituted solution immediately.

ADMINISTRATION

IV Infusion: Infuse slowly over at least 2 h. Avoid rapid injection.

INCOMPATIBILITIES Data not available; do not mix with other drugs.

ACTION & *THERAPEUTIC EFFECT* Prodrug of mycophenolic acid (MPA) with immunosuppressant properties; inhibits T- and B-lymphocyte proliferation responses, thus it inhibits antibody formation, and blocks the generation of cytotoxic T-lymphocyte cells. It also suppresses antibody formation by B-lymphocytes. It may inhibit recruitment of B-leukocytes into the sites of inflammation and graft rejection in transplant patients. *Antirejection effects are attributed to decreased number of activated lymphocytes in the graft site.*

CONTRAINDICATIONS Hypersensitivity to mycophenolate mofetil, mycophenolic acid, polysorbate 80; vaccination, varicella; severe neutropenia; live attenuated vaccines; pregnancy (category C), lactation. Safety and efficacy in children have not been established.

CAUTIOUS USE Viral or bacterial infections; presence or history of carcinoma; bone marrow suppression; active peptic ulcer disease; cholestasis; gallbladder disease; GI disease, severe diarrhea; malabsorption syndromes; hepatic encephalopathy, hepatic or renal impairment, renal failure, uremia; older adults; herpes infection, infection; hypoalbuminemia; PKU; lactase deficiency; females of childbearing age.

ADVERSE EFFECTS (≥1%) **CNS:** *Headache, tremor,* insomnia, dizziness, weakness. **CV:** *Hypertension.* **Endocrine:** Hyperglycemia, hypercholesterolemia, hypophosphatemia, hypokalemia, hyperkalemia, *peripheral edema.* **GI:** *Diarrhea, constipation, nausea,* anorexia, vomiting, *abdominal pain, dyspepsia.* **Urogenital:** *UTI, hematuria,* renal tubular necrosis, burning, frequency, vaginal burning or itching, vaginal bleeding, kidney stones. **Hematologic:** *Leukopenia, anemia, thrombocytopenia,* hypochromic anemia, leukocytosis. **Respiratory:** *Respiratory infection, dyspnea,* increased cough, pharyngitis. **Skin:** Rash. **Body as a Whole:** Leg or hand cramps, bone pain, myalgias, *sepsis (bacterial, fungal, viral).*

DRUG INTERACTIONS Acyclovir, ganciclovir may increase mycophenolate serum levels. Mycophenolate may decrease protein binding of **phenytoin** or **theophylline,** causing increased serum levels. Synergistic with **cyclosporine.**

PHARMACOKINETICS Onset: 4 wk. **Metabolism:** In liver to active form, mycophenolic acid. **Elimination:** 87% excreted in urine. **Half-Life:** 11 h.

Common adverse effects in *italic*, life-threatening effects underlined: generic names in **bold**; classifications in SMALL CAPS; ♣ Canadian drug name; ⊕ Prototype drug

469

NURSING IMPLICATIONS

Assessment & Drug Effects

- Prior to initiating therapy: Baseline CBC with differential.
- Withhold dose and notify prescriber if neutropenia develops (ANC less than 1.3×10^3/mcL).
- Lab tests: Weekly CBC for first month, biweekly for second and third months, then once per month for first year; periodic kidney function tests, LFTs, serum electrolytes, lipase, amylase, blood glucose, and routine urinalysis.
- Monitor for and report any S&S of sepsis or infection.

Patient & Family Education

- Report promptly S&S of infection, such as UTI or respiratory infection, or signs of bleeding (e.g., black tarry stools, blood in urine, easy bruising).
- Report all troubling adverse reactions (e.g., blood in urine and swelling in arms and legs) as soon as possible.
- Women should use effective contraception during and for 6 wk after treatment is completed.

M

NAFCILLIN SODIUM

(naf-sill'in)

Classification(s): ANTIBIOTIC, PENICILLIN, NATURAL
Therapeutic: ANTIBACTERIAL
Prototype: Penicillin G potassium
Pregnancy Category: B

USES Primarily, infections caused by penicillinase-producing *Staphylococci*.

INDICATION & DOSAGE

Staphylococcal Infections

Adult: 500 mg–1 g q4h (max: 12 g/day)
Child: 50–200 mg/kg/day divided q4–6h (max: 12 g/day)
Neonate:

Age	Weight	Dose
Over 7 days	Under 2000 g	100 mg/kg/day divided q6h
Over 7 days	1200–2000 g	75 mg/kg/day divided q8h
Up to 7 days	Over 2000 g	75 mg/kg/day divided q8h
Up to 7 days	1200–2000 g	50 mg/kg/day divided q12h
Up to 28 days	Less than 1200 g	50 mg/kg/day divided q12h

Common adverse effects in *italic*, life-threatening effects underlined: generic names in **bold**; classifications in SMALL CAPS; ♣ Canadian drug name; ⊘ Prototype drug

SOLUTION PREPARATION
- *ADD-Vantage Drug Delivery System:* Vials must be used with the ADD-Vantage diluent containers of NS 50 mL or 100 mL. See manufacturer's instructions for reconstitution.
- *Vial Reconstitution:* Add 1.7 mL of sterile water for injection or NaCl to each 500 mg to yield 250 mg/mL. Shake vigorously to dissolve. **Must be** further diluted for infusion.
- *Further Dilution of Reconstituted Vial:*
  - *Direct IV Injection:* Add 15–30 mL of D5W, NS, or 1/2NS.
  - *Intermittent Infusion:* Add required dose to 100–150 mL of D5W, NS, or 1/2NS.
  - *Continuous Infusion:* Add required dose to a volume of IV solution that maintains concentration of drug between 2–40 mg/mL.

STORAGE
Store vials at 20°–25° C (68°–77° F). Discard reconstituted solution after 24 h.

ADMINISTRATION
- **Direct IV Injection:** Give over at least 10 min.
- **Intermittent Infusion:** Infuse over 30–90 min.
- **Continuous Infusion:** Infuse at ordered rate.

INCOMPATIBILITIES Solution/additive: **Aminophylline, ascorbic acid, aztreonam, bleomycin, cytarabine, gentamicin, hydrocortisone, methylprednisolone, promazine. Y-site: Diltiazem, droperidol, insulin regular, labetalol, midazolam, nalbuphine, pentazocine, vancomycin, verapamil.**

N

ACTION & *THERAPEUTIC EFFECT* Semisynthetic, acid-stable, penicillinase-resistant penicillin. Mechanism of bactericidal action is by interfering with synthesis of mucopeptides essential to formation and integrity of bacterial cell wall leading to bacterial cell lysis. *Effective against both penicillin-sensitive and penicillin-resistant strains of* Staphylococcus aureus. *Also active against pneumococci and group A beta-hemolytic streptococci. Highly active against penicillinase-producing staphylococci but less potent than penicillin G against penicillin-sensitive microorganisms.*

CONTRAINDICATIONS Hypersensitivity to penicillins, cephalosporins, and other allergens.

CAUTIOUS USE History of or suspected atopy or allergy (eczema, hives, hay fever, asthma); GI disease; hepatic disease; pregnancy (category B), lactation.

ADVERSE EFFECTS (≥1%) **Body as a Whole:** Drug fever, <u>anaphylaxis</u>. **GI:** Nausea, vomiting, *diarrhea*. **Hematologic:** Eosinophilia, thrombophlebitis; neutropenia (long-term therapy). **Metabolic:** Hypokalemia (with high doses). **Skin:** Urticaria, pruritus, rash, pain and tissue irritation. **Urogenital:** Allergic interstitial nephritis.

DIAGNOSTIC TEST INTERFERENCE Nafcillin in large doses can cause false-positive **urine protein** tests using **sulfosalicylic acid method.**

DRUG INTERACTIONS May antagonize hypoprothrombinemic effects of **warfarin. Probenecid** increases serum concentrations.

PHARMACOKINETICS Peak: 15 min. **Distribution:** Distributes into CNS with inflamed meninges; crosses placenta; distributed into breast milk, 90% protein bound. **Metabolism:** Enters enterohepatic circulation. **Elimination:** Primarily in bile; 10–30% in urine. **Half-Life:** 1 h.

NURSING IMPLICATIONS

Assessment & Drug Effects

- Prior to initiating therapy: Baseline C&S tests (start drug pending results); determine previous hypersensitivity reactions to penicillins, cephalosporins, and other allergens.
- Inspect IV site for inflammatory reaction. Also check IV site for leakage; in the older adult patient especially, loss of tissue elasticity with aging may promote extravasation around the needle.
- Lab tests: Baseline and periodic WBC with differential; periodic LFTs, and kidney function tests with nafcillin therapy longer than 2 wk.
- Determine IV sodium intake for patients with sodium restriction. Nafcillin sodium contains approximately 3 mEq of sodium per g.
- Monitor for and report allergic reactions. Rash is the most common reaction.
- Be alert for signs of bacterial or fungal superinfections (see Appendix C) in patients on prolonged therapy.

Patient & Family Education

- Report promptly S&S of infection or bleeding.

NALBUPHINE HYDROCHLORIDE

(nal′byoo-feen)

Nubain

Classification(s): ANALGESIC; NARCOTIC (OPIATE) AGONIST-ANTAGONIST
Therapeutic: NARCOTIC ANALGESIC
Prototype: Pentazocine
Pregnancy Category: C

USES Symptomatic relief of moderate to severe pain. Also preoperative sedation analgesia and as a supplement to surgical anesthesia.

INDICATION & DOSAGE

Moderate to Severe Pain

Adult: 10–20 mg q3–6h prn (max: 160 mg/day)

Surgery Anesthesia Supplement

Adult: 0.3–3 mg/kg then 0.25–0.5 mg/kg as required

SOLUTION PREPARATION
No dilution is required. Administer as supplied.

STORAGE
Store at 15°–30°C (59°–86°F). Avoid freezing.

ADMINISTRATION
Direct IV Injection: Give at a rate of 10 mg or fraction thereof over 3–5 min.

INCOMPATIBILITIES Solution/additive: Diazepam, dimenhydrinate, ketorolac, pentobarbital, promethazine, thiethylperazine. Y-site: Allopurinol, amphotericin B cholesteryl complex, cefepime, docetaxel, methotrexate, nafcillin, pemetrexed, piperacillin/tazobactam, sargramostim, sodium bicarbonate.

ACTION & *THERAPEUTIC EFFECT* Synthetic narcotic analgesic with agonist and weak antagonist properties. Analgesic potency is approximately equal to that produced by equivalent doses of morphine. Produces respiratory depression about equal to that of morphine; however, in contrast to morphine, doses greater than 30 mg produce no further respiratory depression. Antagonistic potency is approximately one fourth that of naloxone. *Analgesic action relieves moderate to severe pain with apparently low potential for dependence,*

CONTRAINDICATIONS History of hypersensitivity to nalbuphine; opiate agonists; pregnancy (category C). Prolonged use during pregnancy could result in neonatal withdrawal.

CAUTIOUS USE History of emotional instability or drug abuse; head injury, increased intracranial pressure; cardiac disease; impaired respirations; COPD; GI disorders; impaired kidney or liver function; MI; biliary tract surgery; lactation.

ADVERSE EFFECTS (≥1%) **CV:** Hypertension, hypotension, bradycardia, tachycardia, flushing. **GI:** Abdominal cramps, bitter taste, *nausea, vomiting,* dry mouth. **CNS:** *Sedation, dizziness,* nervousness, depression, restlessness, crying, euphoria, dysphoria, distortion of body image, unusual dreams, confusion, hallucinations; numbness and tingling sensations, headache, vertigo. **Respiratory:** Dyspnea, asthma, <u>respiratory depression</u>. **Skin:** Pruritus, urticaria, burning sensation, *sweaty, clammy skin*. **Special Senses:** Miosis, blurred vision, speech difficulty. **Urogenital:** Urinary urgency.

DRUG INTERACTIONS Alcohol and other CNS DEPRESSANTS add to CNS depression.

PHARMACOKINETICS Onset: 2–3 min. **Peak:** 30 min. **Duration:** 3–6 h. **Distribution:** Crosses placenta. **Metabolism:** In liver. **Elimination:** In urine. **Half-Life:** 5 h.

NURSING IMPLICATIONS

Assessment & Drug Effects

- Assess respiratory rate before/after drug administration. Withhold drug and notify prescriber if respiratory rate falls below 12.
- Monitor for allergic response in persons with sulfite sensitivity.
- Administer with caution to patients with hepatic or renal impairment.

- Monitor ambulation as nalbuphine may produce drowsiness.
- Monitor for respiratory depression of newborn if drug is used during labor and delivery.

Patient & Family Education

- Do not drive or engage in potentially hazardous activities until response to drug is known.

NALMEFENE HYDROCHLORIDE

(nal′me-feen)

Revex

Classification(s): NARCOTIC (OPIATE) ANTAGONIST
Therapeutic: NARCOTIC ANTAGONIST
Prototype: Naloxone
Pregnancy Category: B

USES Complete or partial reversal of opioid drug effects, management of opioid overdose.

INDICATION & DOSAGE

Reversal of Postoperative Opioid Depression (use 100 mcg/mL strength)

Adult: 0.25 mcg/kg followed by 0.25 mcg/kg incremental doses q2–5min until desired degree of reversal or 1 mcg/kg cumulative dose is reached

Known/Suspected Opioid Overdose (use 1 mg/mL)

Adult (for nonopioid-dependent patients): 0.5 mg/70 kg, may repeat with 1 mg/70 kg 2–5 min later; *(for opioid-dependent patients):* 0.1 mg/70 kg, if no evidence of withdrawal in 2 min, continue with 0.5 mg/70 kg, may repeat with 1 mg/70 kg 2–5 min later (doses above 1.5 mg/70 kg not likely to be more effective)

SOLUTION PREPARATION

- No dilution is required. Administer as supplied.
- **Caution:** Check the concentration available for use. When using the 100 mcg/mL concentration, calculate the volume of a dose equal to 0.25 mcg/kg by multiplying the weight in kilograms by 0.0025. When using the 1 mg/mL concentration, calculate the volume of a dose equal to 0.1, 0.5, or 1 mg/70 kg by dividing the weight in kilograms by 70, then multiplying that result by the number of milligrams ordered per 70 kg.

STORAGE

Store at 15°–30° C (59°–86° F).

ADMINISTRATION

Direct IV Injection: Give over 15–30 sec. With kidney failure, give over 60 sec.

Common adverse effects in *italic*, life-threatening effects underlined: generic names in **bold**; classifications in SMALL CAPS; ♣ Canadian drug name; ☻ Prototype drug

INCOMPATIBILITIES Data not available; do not mix with other drugs.

ACTION & *THERAPEUTIC EFFECT* Opiate antagonist that has no opioid agonist activity; also has no pharmacologic activity when given in the absence of an opioid agonist. *Prevents or reverses the effects of opiates, including respiratory depression, sedation, and hypotension; these effects are dose related.*

CONTRAINDICATIONS Hypersensitivity to nalmefene. Safety and efficacy in children are not established.
CAUTIOUS USE Patients at high cardiovascular risk or who have received potential cardiotoxic drugs; patients with known physical dependence on opioids; renal or hepatic impairment; pregnancy (category B), lactation.

ADVERSE EFFECTS (≥1%) **Body as a Whole:** Fever, chills. **CV:** Tachycardia, hypotension, hypertension, pulmonary edema, ventricular arrhythmias (especially in patients with preexisting cardiovascular disease). **GI:** *Nausea, vomiting,* diarrhea, dry mouth, dyspepsia, elevation of liver function tests. **CNS:** Dizziness, headache, irritability, tremor, paresthesias, confusion, paranoia, drowsiness, fatigue, vertigo, agitation, nervousness. **Special Senses:** Blurred vision.

DRUG INTERACTIONS Potential risk of seizures when combined with **flumazenil.**

PHARMACOKINETICS Onset: 2–5 min. **Peak:** 5 min. **Duration:** 4–8 h. **Distribution:** Approximately 45% protein bound; blocks more than 80% of brain opioid receptors within 5 min; distributed into breast milk of rats. **Metabolism:** In liver by glucuronidation. **Elimination:** Primarily in urine, 17% in feces. **Half-Life:** 8.5–10.8 h.

NURSING IMPLICATIONS
Assessment & Drug Effects
- Monitor carefully for reversal of opioid depression within 2–5 min of an IV dose.
- Note: If recurrent respiratory depression occurs following the reversal, titrate the dose again to avoid over-reversal.
- Monitor cardiovascular status closely, assessing for changes in blood pressure and heart rate and development of arrhythmias.
- Monitor for withdrawal symptoms, especially in those with opioid dependence.

NALOXONE HYDROCHLORIDE ⊘

(nal-ox'one)

Narcan

Classification(s): NARCOTIC (OPIATE) ANTAGONIST
Therapeutic: NARCOTIC ANTAGONIST
Pregnancy Category: C

Common adverse effects in *italic*, life-threatening effects <u>underlined</u>: generic names in **bold**; classifications in SMALL CAPS; ♣ Canadian drug name; ⊘ Prototype drug

475

USES Narcotic overdosage; complete or partial reversal of narcotic depression, challenge for suspected opioid dependence. Drug of choice when nature of depressant drug is not known and for diagnosis of suspected acute opioid overdosage.

UNLABELED USES Shock and to reverse alcohol-induced or clonidine-induced coma or respiratory depression.

INDICATION & DOSAGE

Opiate Overdose
Adult: 0.4–2 mg, may repeat q2–3min up to 10 mg if necessary
Child (5 y or older and at least 20 kg): 2 mg, may repeat q2–3min if needed
Child/Infant (less than 20 kg): 0.01–0.1 mg/kg, may repeat q2–3min (up to 10 mg) if necessary
Neonate: 0.01 mg/kg, may repeat q2–3min

Postoperative Opiate Depression
Adult: 0.1–0.2 mg, may repeat q2–3min
Child: 0.005–0.01 mg/kg, may repeat q2–3min

Challenge for Opioid Dependence
Adult: 0.2 mg, observe for 30 sec for S&S of withdrawal; if no S&S then 0.6 mg and observe for 20 min

SOLUTION PREPARATION
- *Direct IV Injection:* Give undiluted.
- *IV Infusion:* Dilute 2 mg in 500 mL of D5W or NS to yield 4 mcg/mL (0.004 mg/mL).

STORAGE
- Use IV solutions within 24 h.
- Store at 15°–30° C (59°–86° F). Protect from excessive light.

ADMINISTRATION
- **Direct IV Injection:** Give bolus dose over 10–15 sec.
- **IV Infusion:** Adjust rate according to patient response.

INCOMPATIBILITIES Y-site: Amphotericin B cholesteryl complex, lansoprazole.

ACTION & *THERAPEUTIC EFFECT* Analog of oxymorphone that is also a "pure" narcotic antagonist, essentially free of agonistic (morphine-like) properties. Thus, it produces no significant analgesia, respiratory depression, psychotomimetic effects, or miosis when administered in the absence of narcotics and possesses potent narcotic antagonist action. *Reverses the effects of opiates, including respiratory depression, sedation, and hypotension.*

CONTRAINDICATIONS Hypersensitivity to naloxone, naltrexone, nalmefene; respiratory depression due to nonopioid drugs; substance abuse; pregnancy (category C) (other than labor).

Common adverse effects in *italic*, life-threatening effects <u>underlined</u>: generic names in **bold**; classifications in SMALL CAPS; ♣ Canadian drug name; ⊙ Prototype drug

CAUTIOUS USE Neonates and children; known or suspected narcotic dependence; brain tumor, head trauma, increased ICP; history of substance abuse; cardiac irritability; seizure disorders; lactation.

ADVERSE EFFECTS (≥1%) **Body as a Whole:** Reversal of analgesia, tremors, hyperventilation, slight drowsiness, sweating. **CV:** Increased BP, tachycardia. **GI:** Nausea, vomiting. **Hematologic:** Elevated partial thromboplastin time.

DRUG INTERACTIONS Reverses analgesic effects of NARCOTIC (OPIATE) AGONISTS and NARCOTIC (OPIATE) AGONIST-ANTAGONISTS.

PHARMACOKINETICS **Onset:** 2 min. **Duration:** 45 min. **Distribution:** Crosses placenta. **Metabolism:** In liver. **Elimination:** In urine. **Half-Life:** 60–90 min.

NURSING IMPLICATIONS

Assessment & Drug Effects

- Monitor closely; duration of action of some narcotics may exceed that of naloxone. Keep prescriber informed; repeat naloxone dose may be necessary.
- May precipitate opiate withdrawal if administered to a patient who is opiate dependent.
- Note: Narcotic abstinence symptoms induced by naloxone generally start to diminish 20–40 min after administration and usually disappear within 90 min.
- Monitor respirations and other vital signs.
- Monitor surgical and obstetric patients closely for bleeding. Naloxone has been associated with abnormal coagulation test results.
- Observe for reversal of analgesia, which may be manifested by nausea, vomiting, sweating, tachycardia.

Patient & Family Education

- Report to prescriber postoperative pain that emerges after administration of this drug.

NATALIZUMAB

(na-tal′-i-zu-mab)

Tysabri

Classification(s): IMMUNOLOGIC AGENT, MONOCLONAL ANTIBODY

Therapeutic: ANTIINFLAMMATORY

Prototype: Basiliximab

Pregnancy Category: C

USES Treatment of relapsing forms of multiple sclerosis, inducing and maintaining remission in Crohn's disease.

Common adverse effects in *italic*, life-threatening effects underlined: generic names in **bold**; classifications in SMALL CAPS; ♣ Canadian drug name; ● Prototype drug

477

INDICATION & DOSAGE

Multiple Sclerosis/Crohn's Disease
Adult: 300 mg infused over 1 h every 4 wk

SOLUTION PREPARATION
- Before and after dilution, solution should be colorless and clear to slightly opaque. Do not use if the solution has visible particles, flakes, color, or is cloudy.
- Withdraw 300 mg (15 mL) from the vial and add to 100 mL of NS. Do not use with any other diluent. Gently invert the bag to mix; do not shake. The IV solution must be used within 8 h.

STORAGE
Store IV solution for up to 8 h at 2°–8° C (36°–46° F). Allow solution to warm to room temperature before administration.

ADMINISTRATION
- **IV Infusion:** Infuse over 1 h. Do not give a bolus dose. Flush IV line before/after with NS.
- Stop infusion immediately if S&S of hypersensitivity appear.

INCOMPATIBILITIES Solution/additive/Y-site: Do not mix or infuse with other drugs.

ACTION & *THERAPEUTIC EFFECT* Natalizumab is a recombinant immunoglobulin-G_4 (IgG_4) monoclonal antibody thought to interfere with the migration of lymphocytes and monocytes into the CNS endothelium of patients with multiple sclerosis. It reduces inflammation and demyelination of CNS white matter. *Inhibition of T-cell infiltration into the brain is thought to impede the demyelinating process of multiple sclerosis. It reduces relapses and occurrence of brain lesions and plaque formation. Natalizumab is also thought to attenuate T-lymphocyte–mediated intestinal inflammation in Crohn's disease and possibly ulcerative colitis.*

CONTRAINDICATIONS Prior hypersensitivity to natalizumab; murine protein hypersensitivity; progressive multifocal leukoencephalopathy; active infection; females of childbearing age; pregnancy (category C), lactation; children less than 18 y.

CAUTIOUS USE Co-administration with other immunosuppressive medication; diabetes mellitus, immunocompromised patients; exposure to infection or tuberculosis.

ADVERSE EFFECTS (≥1%) **Body as a Whole:** Anaphylaxis (rare, usually within 2 h of infusion), infections, fatigue, rigors, risk of progressive multifocal leukoencephalopathy. **CNS:** Depression, headache, syncope, tremor. **CV:** Chest discomfort. **GI:** Abdominal discomfort, abnormal liver function tests. **Hematologic:** Local bleeding from infusion site. **Musculoskeletal:** Arthralgia. **Respiratory:** Pneumonia. **Skin:** Acute urticaria. **Urogenital:** Urinary frequency, irregular menstruation, amenorrhea, dysmenorrhea. **Other:** Infusion-related reactions (headache, dizziness, fatigue, hypersensitivity reactions, urticaria, pruritus, and rigors).

DRUG INTERACTIONS May reduce the effectiveness of VACCINES and TOXOIDS; may increase risk of infection with IMMUNOSUPPRESSANTS.

PHARMACOKINETICS Half-Life: 11 days.

NURSING IMPLICATIONS

Assessment & Drug Effects

- During IV infusion and for 1–2 h after: Monitor closely for S&S of hypersensitivity (e.g., urticaria, dizziness, fever, rash, chills, pruritus, nausea, flushing, hypotension, dyspnea, and chest pain).
- Monitor neurologic status frequently. Report promptly any emerging S&S of dysfunction.
- Lab tests: Baseline and periodic CBC with differential.

Patient & Family Education

- Report promptly any of the following during/after IV infusion: Difficulty breathing, wheezing or shortness of breath, swelling or tightness about the neck and throat, chest pain, skin rash or hives.
- Report promptly S&S of infection (e.g., cough, fever, chills, or sore throat).

NELARABINE

(nel-ar′a-been)

Arranon

Classification(s): ANTINEOPLASTIC, ANTIMETABOLITE, PYRIMIDINE ANTAGONIST
Therapeutic: ANTINEOPLASTIC
Prototype: 5-Fluorouracil
Pregnancy Category: D

USES Treatment of patients with T-cell acute lymphoblastic leukemia/lymphoma.

INDICATION & DOSAGE

Adult T-Cell Leukemia/Lymphoma

Adult: 1500 mg/m^2 on days 1, 3, and 5, repeated every 21 days
Child: 650 mg/m^2 every day for 5 days, repeated every 21 days

Toxicity Adjustment

Grade 2 or Higher Neurologic Toxicity: Discontinue therapy.
Hematologic Toxicities: Delay therapy.

SOLUTION PREPARATION

- Use gloves and protective clothing to prevent skin contact.
- No dilution is required. Administer as supplied. Transfer the required dose to a PVC or glass container for infusion.

Common adverse effects in *italic*, life-threatening effects <u>underlined</u>: generic names in **bold**; classifications in SMALL CAPS; ♣ Canadian drug name; ❂ Prototype drug

479

STORAGE

Store vials at 15°–30° C (59°–86° F). Nelarabine is stable in PVC bags or glass infusion containers for 8 h up to 30° C.

ADMINISTRATION

- **IV Infusion:**
  - *Adult:* Infuse over 2 h.
  - *Child:* Infuse over 1 h.
- Standard IV hydration, urine alkalinization, and prophylaxis with allopurinol are advised to manage hyperuricemia in those at risk for tumor lysis syndrome.
- Withhold drug and notify prescriber for neurologic adverse events of NCI Common Toxicity Criteria grade 2 or greater.

INCOMPATIBILITIES Data not available; do not mix with other drugs.

ACTION & *THERAPEUTIC EFFECT* Nelarabine inhibits DNA synthesis in lymphoblastic T-cells of acute leukemia and lymphoma. *The incorporation of a nelarabine metabolite in the leukemic blast cells halts DNA synthesis and causes cell death.*

CONTRAINDICATIONS Severe bone marrow suppression; older adults; pregnancy (category D), lactation.
CAUTIOUS USE Severe renal impairment, renal failure; hepatic impairment.

ADVERSE EFFECTS (≥1%) **Body as a Whole:** Abnormal gait, *fatigue, pyrexia,* rigors. **CNS:** *Asthenia,* ataxia, *dizziness, headache, hypoesthesia, neuropathy, paresthesia, somnolence,* tremor. **CV:** Chest pain, *edema,* hypotension, *petechiae,* sinus tachycardia. **GI:** Abdominal pain, *constipation, diarrhea, nausea, vomiting,* stomatitis. **Hematologic/Lymphatic:** *Anemia, neutropenia, thrombocytopenia,* increased risk of infection. **Hepatic:** AST levels increased. **Metabolic:** Anorexia, dehydration, hyperglycemia. **Musculoskeletal:** Arthralgia, back pain, muscular weakness, *myalgia,* pain in extremities. **Respiratory:** *Cough, dyspnea, pleural effusion,* epistaxis, wheezing.

PHARMACOKINETICS Distribution: Extensive. **Metabolism:** Bioactivation to ara-GTP, oxidized to uric acid. **Elimination:** Renal. **Half-Life:** 3 h (active metabolite).

NURSING IMPLICATIONS

Assessment & Drug Effects

- Monitor for and report immediately S&S of adverse CNS effects, including altered mental status (e.g., confusion, severe somnolence), seizures, and peripheral neuropathy (e.g., numbness, paresthesias, motor weakness, ataxia, paralysis). Note: Previous or concurrent treatment with intrathecal chemotherapy or previous craniospinal irradiation may increase risk of CNS toxicity.
- Monitor for S&S of bleeding, especially with platelet counts less than 50,000/mm³.
- Lab tests: Baseline and periodic CBC with differential and platelet count; periodic serum electrolytes, serum uric acid, LFTs and renal function tests.
- Monitor diabetics for loss of glycemic control.

Patient & Family Education
- Do not drive or engage in potentially hazardous activities until response to drug is known.
- Report any of the following to the prescriber: Seizures; tingling or numbness in hands and feet; problems with fine motor coordination; unsteady gait and increased weakness with ambulating; fever or other signs of infections.
- Use effective contraceptive measures to avoid pregnancy while taking this drug.

NEOSTIGMINE METHYLSULFATE ⓟ

(nee-oh-stig′meen)

Prostigmin

Classification(s): CHOLINESTERASE INHIBITOR
Therapeutic: ANTIMYASTHENIC; ANTIDOTE
Pregnancy Category: C

USES Myasthenia gravis; and to reverse the effects of nondepolarizing muscle relaxants (e.g., tubocurarine).
UNLABELED USES Diagnosis of myasthenia gravis.

INDICATION & DOSAGE

Reversal of Nondepolarizing Neuromuscular Blockade

Adult: 0.5–2.5 mg slowly, may repeat (max total dose: 5 mg)
Child: 0.025–0.08 mg/kg/dose
Infant: 0.025–0.1 mg/kg/dose

Myasthenia Gravis

Adult: 0.5–2 mg q1–3h
Child: 0.01–0.04 mg/kg q2–4h

Renal Impairment Dosage Adjustment

CrCl 10–50 mL/min: Use 50% of dose; *CrCl less than 10 mL/min:* Use 25% of dose.

SOLUTION PREPARATION
No dilution is required. Administer as supplied.

STORAGE
Store at 15°–30° C (59°–86° F).

ADMINISTRATION
Direct IV Injection: Give 0.5 mg or a fraction thereof over 1 min.

INCOMPATIBILITIES Data not available; do not mix with other drugs.

Common adverse effects in *italic*, life-threatening effects <u>underlined</u>: generic names in **bold**; classifications in SMALL CAPS; ♣ Canadian drug name; ⓟ Prototype drug

ACTION & *THERAPEUTIC EFFECT* Produces reversible cholinesterase inhibition or inactivation. Has direct stimulant action on voluntary muscle fibers and possibly on autonomic ganglia and CNS neurons. Allows intensified and prolonged effect of acetylcholine at cholinergic synapses (basis for use in myasthenia gravis). *Produces generalized cholinergic response including miosis, increased tonus of intestinal and skeletal muscles, constriction of bronchi and ureters, slower pulse rate, and stimulation of salivary and sweat glands.*

CONTRAINDICATIONS Hypersensitivity to neostigmine, cholinergics, or bromides; cholinesterase inhibitor toxicity; GI obstruction; ileus; bradycardia, hypotension; mechanical obstruction of intestinal or urinary tract; peritonitis; administration with other cholinergic drugs; pregnancy (category C), lactation.

CAUTIOUS USE Recent ileorectal anastomoses; epilepsy, seizure disorders; bronchial asthma; hepatic disease; bradycardia, recent coronary occlusion, cardiac arrhythmias; vagotonia; hyperthyroidism; renal failure, renal impairment, renal disease; peptic ulcer.

ADVERSE EFFECTS (≥1%) **Body as a Whole:** Muscle cramps, *fasciculations*, twitching, pallor, fatigability, generalized weakness, paralysis, agitation, fear, <u>death</u>. **CV:** Tightness in chest, bradycardia, hypotension, elevated BP. **GI:** *Nausea,* vomiting, eructation, epigastric discomfort, abdominal cramps, diarrhea, involuntary or difficult defecation. **CNS:** CNS stimulation. **Respiratory:** *Increased salivation* and bronchial secretions, sneezing, cough, dyspnea, diaphoresis, respiratory depression. **Special Senses:** Lacrimation, miosis, blurred vision. **Urogenital:** Difficult micturition.

DRUG INTERACTIONS Succinylcholine decamethonium may prolong phase I block or reverse phase II block; neostigmine antagonizes effects of **tubocurarine; atracurium, vecuronium, pancuronium; procainamide, quinidine, atropine** antagonize effects of neostigmine.

PHARMACOKINETICS Onset: 10–30 min. **Peak:** 20–30 min. **Distribution:** Not reported to cross placenta or appear in breast milk. **Metabolism:** In liver. **Elimination:** 80% of drug and metabolites excreted in urine within 24 h. **Half-Life:** 50–90 min.

NURSING IMPLICATIONS

Assessment & Drug Effects

- Check HR before giving drug to bradycardic patients. If below 60/min or other established parameter, consult prescriber. Atropine will be ordered to restore heart rate.
- Monitor respiration, maintain airway or assisted ventilation, and give oxygen as indicated, when used as antidote for tubocurarine or other nondepolarizing neuromuscular blocking agents (usually preceded by atropine). Respiratory assistance is continued until recovery of respiration and neuromuscular transmission is assured.
- Monitor HR, respiration, and BP during period of dosage adjustment in treatment of myasthenia gravis.
- Report promptly and record accurately the onset of myasthenic symptoms and drug adverse effects in relation to last dose in order to assist prescriber in determining lowest effective dosage schedule.

- Note carefully time of muscular weakness onset. It may indicate whether patient is in cholinergic or myasthenic crisis: Weakness that appears approximately 1 h after drug administration suggests cholinergic crisis (overdose) and is treated by prompt withdrawal of neostigmine and immediate administration of atropine. Weakness that occurs 3 h or more after drug administration is more likely due to myasthenic crisis (underdose or drug resistance) and is treated by more intensive anticholinesterase therapy.
- Record drug effect and duration of action. S&S of myasthenia gravis relieved by neostigmine include lid ptosis; diplopia; drooping facies; difficulty in chewing, swallowing, breathing, or coughing; and weakness of neck, limbs, and trunk muscles.
- Manifestations of neostigmine overdosage often appear first in muscles of neck and those involved in chewing and swallowing, with muscles of shoulder girdle and upper extremities affected next.
- Report to prescriber if patient does not urinate within 1 h after first dose when used to relieve urinary retention.

Patient & Family Education
- Be aware that regulation of dosage interval is extremely difficult; dosage must be adjusted for each patient to deal with unpredictable exacerbations and remissions.
- Keep an accurate record of your response to drug. Learn how to recognize adverse effects, how to modify dosage regimen according to your changing needs, or how to administer atropine if necessary.
- Be aware that certain factors may require an increase in size or frequency of dose (e.g., physical or emotional stress, infection, menstruation, surgery), whereas remission requires a decrease in dosage.
- Some patients become refractory to neostigmine after prolonged use and require change in dosage or medication.

NESIRITIDE
(nes-ir'i-tide)

Natrecor
Classification(s): ATRIAL NATRIURETIC PEPTIDE HORMONE
Therapeutic: DIURESIS
Pregnancy Category: C

USES Acute treatment of decompensated CHF in patients who have dyspnea at rest or with minimal activity.

INDICATION & DOSAGE

Acute Decompensated CHF
Adult: 2 mcg/kg bolus administered over 60 sec, followed by a continuous infusion of 0.01 mcg/kg/min (0.1 mL/kg/h) (max: 0.03 mcg/kg/min). Monitor blood pressure closely. If hypotension occurs, the dose

Common adverse effects in *italic*, life-threatening effects <u>underlined</u>: generic names in **bold**; classifications in SMALL CAPS; ♣ Canadian drug name; ⊙ Prototype drug

483

should be reduced or discontinued. The infusion can subsequently be restarted at a dose that is reduced by 30% (with no bolus administration) after stabilization of hemodynamics.

SOLUTION PREPARATION

▪ *Vial Reconstitution:* Add to one 1.5 mg vial 5 mL of IV solution removed from a 250 mL bag of selected diluent (i.e., D5W, NS, D5/1/2NaCl, D5/1/4NaCl). Rock the vial gently so that all surfaces, including the stopper, contact the diluent ensuring complete reconstitution. Do not shake the vial. **Must be further diluted for bolus dose and for infusion.**

▪ *Further Dilution of Reconstituted Solution:* Add the entire contents of the vial to the 250 mL IV bag to yield approximately 6 mcg/mL. Invert the bag several times to mix completely.

STORAGE

▪ Use IV solution within 24 h.
▪ Store at controlled room temperature at 20°–25° C (68°–77° F) or refrigerated.

ADMINISTRATION

▪ **Direct IV Injection of Bolus Dose:** The bolus dose must be withdrawn from the prepared infusion bag. Determine dose as follows: Bolus volume (mL) = (0.33) × (patient weight in kg). Give the bolus dose over 60 sec through an IV port in the tubing.

▪ **Continuous Infusion:** Prime the IV tubing with the prepared solution prior to connecting to the vascular access port. Infuse remainder of IV infusion immediately following the bolus dose. Determine the infusion rate as follows: Flow rate (mL/h) = (0.1) × (patient weight in kg).

INCOMPATIBILITIES Solution/additive: **Promethazine.** Y-site: **Bumetanide, enalaprilat, ethacrynic acid, furosemide, heparin, hydralazine, regular insulin, micafungin.**

ACTION & *THERAPEUTIC EFFECT* Nesiritide is a human B-type natriuretic peptide (hBNP), produced by recombinant DNA, which mimics the actions of human atrial natriuretic hormone (ANH). ANH is secreted by the right atrium when atrial blood pressure increases. Nesiritide, like ANH, inhibits antidiuretic hormone (ADH) by increasing urine sodium loss by the kidney and triggering formation of a large volume of diluted urine. *Effective in decreasing fluid overload and decreasing dyspnea at rest in patients with acute decompensated congestive heart failure (CHF).*

CONTRAINDICATIONS Hypersensitivity to nesiritide; patients with a systolic blood pressure less than 90 mm Hg; cardiogenic shock; patients with low cardiac filling pressures; patients who should not receive vasodilators, such as those with significant valvular stenosis; restrictive or obstructive cardiomyopathy, pericardial perfusion, constrictive pericarditis, and pericardial tamponade; pregnancy (category C), lactation. Safety and efficacy in pediatric patients have not been established.

CAUTIOUS USE Concurrent administration of ACE inhibitors or vasodilators.

ADVERSE EFFECTS (≥1%) **Body as a Whole:** Headache, back pain, catheter pain, fever, injection site pain, leg cramps. **CNS:** Insomnia, dizziness, anxiety, confusion, paresthesia, somnolence, tremor. **CV:** *Hypotension,* ventricular tachycardia, ventricular extrasystoles, angina, bradycardia, tachycardia, atrial fibrillation, AV node conduction abnormalities. **GI:** Abdominal pain, nausea, vomiting. **Respiratory:** Cough, hemoptysis, apnea. **Skin:** Sweating, pruritus, rash. **Special Senses:** Amblyopia. **Renal:** Renal failure in acutely decompensated heart failure patients.

DRUG INTERACTIONS Additive effects with ANTIHYPERTENSIVES.

PHARMACOKINETICS Onset: 15 min. **Duration:** Greater than 60 min depending on dose. **Metabolism:** Proteolytic cleavage, proteolysis. **Half-Life:** 18 min.

NURSING IMPLICATIONS

Assessment & Drug Effects

- Prior to initiating therapy: Establish hypotension parameters.
- Monitor hemodynamic parameters (e.g., BP, PCWP, HR, ECG) throughout therapy. Notify prescriber immediately if systolic BP less than 90 mm Hg.
- Reduce the dose or withhold the drug if hypotension occurs during administration. Reinitiate infusion only after hypotension is corrected. Subsequent doses following a hypotensive episode are usually reduced by 30% and given without a prior bolus dose.
- Lab tests: Baseline and periodic serum creatinine.

NICARDIPINE HYDROCHLORIDE

(ni-car'di-peen)

Cardene

Classification(s): CALCIUM CHANNEL BLOCKER
Therapeutic: ANTIHYPERTENSIVE AGENT
Pregnancy Category: C

USES Treatment of hypertension, when PO therapy is not viable.

INDICATION & DOSAGE

Hypertension

Adult: **Initiation of Therapy in a Drug-Free Patient,** 5 mg/h initially, increase dose by 2.5 mg/h q15min (max: 15 mg/h); **For Severe Hypertension,** 4–7.5 mg/h; **For Postop Hypertension,** 10–15 mg/h initially, then 1–3 mg/h

Substitute for Oral Nicardipine

Adult: 20 mg q8h for PO = 0.5 mg/h; 30 mg q8h for PO = 1.2 mg/h; 40 mg q8h for PO = 2.2 mg/h

SOLUTION PREPARATION
Dilute each 25 mg ampule with 240 mL of D5W, NS, D5/1/2NS, 1/2NS or other compatible solution to yield 0.1 mg/mL.

STORAGE
- Store at 20°–25° C (68°–77° F). Protect ampules from light.
- IV solutions are stable for 24 h at room temperature.

ADMINISTRATION
- **IV Infusion:** Usually initiated at 50 mL/h (5 mg/h) with rate increases of 25 mL/h (2.5 mg/h) q5–15min up to a maximum of 150 mL/h. Infusion is usually slowed to 30 mL/h once the target BP is reached.
- *Substitute for Oral Doses:* Oral 20 mg q8h, IV equivalent is 0.5 mg/h; oral 30 mg q8h, IV equivalent is 1.2 mg/h; oral 40 mg q8h, IV equivalent is 2.2 mg/h.

INCOMPATIBILITIES Solution/additive: Sodium bicarbonate. **Y-site:** Ampicillin, ampicillin/sulbactam, cefoperazone, furosemide, heparin, thiopental.

ACTION & *THERAPEUTIC EFFECT* Calcium channel blocker that inhibits the transmembrane influx of calcium ions into cardiac muscle and smooth muscle, thus affecting contractility. Selectively affects vascular smooth muscle more than cardiac muscle; relaxes coronary vascular smooth muscle with little or no negative inotropic effect. *Significantly decreases systemic vascular resistance. Therefore, it reduces BP at rest and during isometric and dynamic exercise.*

CONTRAINDICATIONS Hypersensitivity to nicardipine; advanced aortic stenosis; cardiogenic shock; hypotension; pregnancy (category C), lactation.
CAUTIOUS USE CHF; renal and hepatic impairment; severe bradycardia; older adult; GERD; hiatal hernia; renal disease, acute stoke; acute myocardial infarction.

ADVERSE EFFECTS (≥1%) **CNS:** Dizziness or headache, fatigue, anxiety, depression, paresthesias, insomnia, somnolence, nervousness. **CV:** Pedal edema, hypotension, flushing, palpitations, tachycardia, increased angina. **GI:** Anorexia, nausea, vomiting, dry mouth, constipation, dyspepsia. **Skin:** Rash, pruritus. **Body as a Whole:** Arthralgia or arthritis.

DRUG INTERACTIONS Adenosine prolongs bradycardia. **Amiodarone** may cause sinus arrest and AV block. **Benazepril** blunts increase in heart rate and increase in plasma **norepinephrine** and **aldosterone** seen with nicardipine. BETA BLOCKERS cause hypotension and bradycardia. Concomitant nicardipine and **cyclosporine** result in significant increase in **cyclosporine** serum concentrations 1–30 days after initiation of nicardipine therapy; following withdrawal of nicardipine, **cyclosporine** levels decrease. **Magnesium,** when used to retard premature labor, may cause severe hypotension and neuromuscular blockade.

PHARMACOKINETICS Onset: 1 min. **Peak:** 0.5–2 h. **Duration:** 3 h. **Distribution:** 95% protein bound; distributed in breast milk. **Metabolism:** Rapidly and extensively metabolized in liver (CYP 3A4); there is an active metabolite that has less than 1% activity of parent compound. **Elimination:** 35% in feces, 60% in urine; elimination not affected by hemodialysis. **Half-Life:** 8.6 h.

NURSING IMPLICATIONS

Assessment & Drug Effects

- Monitor infusion site and change site q12h if peripheral veins are used.
- Establish baseline data before treatment is started including BP, pulse, and lab values of liver and kidney function.
- Monitor BP carefully during initiation and titration of dosage. Hypotension with or without an increase in heart rate may occur.
- Avoid too rapid reduction in either systolic or diastolic pressure during parenteral administration.
- Discontinue infusion and notify prescriber if hypotension or tachycardia develop.
- Observe for large peak and trough differences in BP. Initially, measure BP at peak effect (1–2 h after dosing) and at trough effect (8 h after dosing).

Patient & Family Education

- Report any increase in frequency, duration, and severity of angina.
- Rise slowly from a recumbent position to minimize risk of hypotension.
- Notify prescriber if any of the following occur: Irregular heart beat, shortness of breath, swelling of the feet, pronounced dizziness, nausea.

N

NITROGLYCERIN ⊕

(nye-troe-gli′ser-in)

Classification(s): VASODILATOR, NITRATE
Therapeutic: ANTIANGINAL
Pregnancy Category: C

USES Used to control BP in perioperative hypertension, CHF associated with acute MI; to produce controlled hypotension during surgical procedures, and to treat angina pectoris in patients who have not responded to nitrate or beta-blocker therapy.

INDICATION & DOSAGE

Angina

Adult: Start with 5 mcg/min and titrate q3–5min until desired response (up to 200 mcg/min)
Child: 0.25–0.5 mcg/kg/min, titrate by 1 mcg/kg/min q3–5min (max: 5 mg/kg/min)

SOLUTION PREPARATION

- Nitroglycerin is available undiluted and premixed in D5W IV solutions of varying concentrations.

Common adverse effects in *italic*, life-threatening effects <u>underlined</u>: generic names in **bold**; classifications in SMALL CAPS; ✚ Canadian drug name; ⊕ Prototype drug

- *IV Infusion from Concentrate:* Use **only** non-PVC plastic or glass bottles and manufacturer-supplied IV tubing. Withdraw contents of one vial (25 or 50 mg) into syringe and inject **immediately** into 500 mL of IV solution to minimize contact with plastic; yields 50 mcg/mL or 100 mcg/mL. If less fluid is desired, add 5 mg to 100 mL to yield 50 mcg/mL. Other concentrations within the range of 25–400 mcg/mL may be used. Do not exceed 400 mcg/mL.

STORAGE
Store diluted solution at room temperature for up to 24 h.

ADMINISTRATION
- **Continuous Infusion:** Infuse by an infusion pump. IV dosage titration requires careful and continuous hemodynamic monitoring.
- Check to see if patient has topical NTG applied to skin or NTG patch before starting IV infusion. The patch (or ointment) is usually removed to prevent overdosage.
- Be aware that when switching from IV to transdermal nitroglycerin, the IV infusion rate is reduced by 50% with simultaneous application of 5 mg/24 h or 10 mg/24 h transdermal patch.

INCOMPATIBILITIES Solution/additive: Caffeine, hydralazine, phenytoin. Y-site: Alteplase, levofloxacin.

ACTION & *THERAPEUTIC EFFECT* Organic nitrate and potent vasodilator that relaxes vascular smooth muscle after conversion to nitric oxide that leads to dose-related dilation of both venous and arterial blood vessels. Promotes peripheral pooling of blood, reduction of peripheral resistance, and decreased venous return to the heart. Both left ventricular preload and afterload are reduced and myocardial oxygen consumption is decreased. *Therapeutic doses may reduce systolic, diastolic, and mean arterial BP; heart rate is usually slightly increased. Produces antianginal, antiischemic, and antihypertensive effects.*

CONTRAINDICATIONS Hypersensitivity, idiosyncrasy, or tolerance to nitrates; severe anemia; head trauma, increased ICP; hypotension, uncorrected hypovolemia, constrictive pericarditis, pericardial tamponade; pregnancy (category C).

CAUTIOUS USE Severe liver or kidney disease; conditions that cause dry mouth; early MI; lactation.

ADVERSE EFFECTS (≥1%) **CNS:** *Headache,* apprehension, blurred vision, weakness, vertigo, dizziness, faintness. **CV:** *Postural hypotension,* palpitations, tachycardia (sometimes with paradoxical bradycardia), increase in angina, syncope, and circulatory collapse. **GI:** Nausea, vomiting, involuntary passing of urine and feces, abdominal pain, dry mouth. **Hematologic:** Methemoglobinemia (high doses). **Skin:** Cutaneous vasodilation with flushing, rash, exfoliative dermatitis, anaphylactoid reaction characterized by oral mucosal and conjunctival edema. **Body as a Whole:** Muscle twitching, pallor, perspiration, cold sweat.

DIAGNOSTIC TEST INTERFERENCE Nitroglycerin may cause increases in determinations of ***urinary catecholamines*** and ***VMA;*** may interfere with the *Zlatkis-Zak color reaction,* causing a false report of decreased *serum cholesterol.*

DRUG INTERACTIONS Alcohol, ANTIHYPERTENSIVE AGENTS compound hypotensive effects; may antagonize **heparin** anticoagulation. Vasodilating effects may be enhanced by **sildenafil, vardenafil,** or **tadalafil,** so this combination should be avoided.

PHARMACOKINETICS Distribution: Widely distributed; not known if distributes to breast milk. **Metabolism:** Extensively in liver. **Elimination:** Inactive metabolites excreted in urine. **Half-Life:** 1–4 min.

NURSING IMPLICATIONS

Assessment & Drug Effects

- Administer IV nitroglycerin with extreme caution to patients with hypotension or hypovolemia since the IV drug may precipitate a severe hypotensive state.
- Continuous cardiac monitoring is required throughout therapy. Monitor patient closely for dysrhythmias.
- Supervise ambulation as needed, especially with older adult or debilitated patients. Postural hypotension may occur even with small doses of nitroglycerin. Patients may complain of dizziness or weakness due to postural hypotension.
- Be alert for overdose symptoms: Hypotension, tachycardia; warm, flushed skin becoming cold and cyanotic; headache, palpitations, confusion, nausea, vomiting, moderate fever, and paralysis. Tissue hypoxia leads to coma, convulsions, cardiovascular collapse. Death can occur from asphyxia.
- Concurrent drugs: Monitor frequently aPTT values with heparin use.

Patient & Family Education

- Change position slowly and avoid prolonged standing. Dizziness, lightheadedness, and syncope (due to postural hypotension) occur most frequently in older adults.
- Report promptly blurred vision or dry mouth.
- Report any increase in frequency, duration, or severity of anginal attack.

N

NITROPRUSSIDE SODIUM

(nye-troe-pruss′ide)

Nitropress

Classification(s): VASODILATOR, NONNITRATE
Therapeutic: ANTIHYPERTENSIVE
Prototype: Hydralazine
Pregnancy Category: C

USES Short-term, rapid reduction of BP in hypertensive crises and for producing controlled hypotension during anesthesia to reduce bleeding.
UNLABELED USES Refractory CHF or acute MI.

INDICATION & DOSAGE

Hypertensive Crisis
Adult: 0.3–0.5 mcg/kg/min (usually 3 mcg/kg/min) (max: 10 mcg/kg/min)
Child: 1 mcg/kg/min (usually 3 mcg/kg/min) (max: 5 mcg/kg/min)

SOLUTION PREPARATION
- *Vial Reconstitution:* Add 2–3 mL of sterile water for injection or D5W to each 50 mg vial. **Must be** further diluted for infusion. Following reconstitution, solutions usually have faint brownish tint; if solution is highly colored, do not use it. Protect from light.
- *Further Dilution of Reconstituted Solution:* Add contents of vial to 250 mL D5W to yield 200 mcg/mL or 500 mL D5W to yield 100 mcg/mL. Lower concentrations may be preferred, depending on patient weight. Promptly wrap container with aluminum foil or other opaque material to protect drug from light.

STORAGE
Store reconstituted solutions at 15°–30° C (59°–86° F) protected from light; stable for 24 h.

ADMINISTRATION
- **Continuous Infusion:** Infuse **only** via controlled device that will allow precise measurement of flow rate required to lower BP. Give at the rate required to lower BP, usually between 0.5–10 mcg/kg/min. **DO NOT** exceed the maximum dose of 10 mcg/kg/min nor give this dose for longer than 10 min. See the following table for specific infusion guidelines.

Nitroprusside Infusion Guidelines

Weight		Concentration 200 mcg/mL Rate (mL/h)		Concentration 100 mcg/mL Rate (mL/h)		Concentration 50 mcg/mL Rate (mL/h)	
kg	lb	Initial	Max	Initial	Max	Initial	Max
20	44	2	60	4	120	7	240
30	66	3	90	5	180	11	360
40	88	4	120	7	240	14	480
50	110	5	150	9	300	18	600
60	132	5	180	11	360	22	720
70	154	6	210	13	420	25	840
80	176	7	240	14	480	29	960
90	198	8	270	16	540	32	1,080
100	220	9	300	18	600	36	1,200

INCOMPATIBILITIES Solution/additive: Amiodarone, propafenone. Y-**site:** Cisatracurium, haloperidol, levofloxacin.

ACTION & *THERAPEUTIC EFFECT* Potent, rapid-acting hypotensive agent with effects similar to those of nitrates. Acts directly on vascular smooth muscle to produce peripheral vasodilatation, with consequently marked lowering of arterial BP, associated with slight increase in heart rate, mild decrease in cardiac output, and moderate lowering of peripheral vascular resistance. *Effective antihypertensive agent used for rapid reduction of high blood pressure.*

CONTRAINDICATIONS Compensatory hypertension, as in atriovenous shunt or coarctation of aorta, and for control of hypotension in patients with inadequate cerebral circulation; pregnancy (category C), lactation.

CAUTIOUS USE Hepatic insufficiency; hypothyroidism; severe renal impairment; hyponatremia; older adult patients with low vitamin B_{12} plasma levels or with Leber's optic atrophy.

ADVERSE EFFECTS (≥1%) **Body as a Whole:** Diaphoresis, apprehension, restlessness, muscle twitching, retrosternal discomfort; <u>thiocyanate toxicity</u> (profound hypotension, tinnitus, blurred vision, fatigue, metabolic acidosis, pink skin color, absence of reflexes, faint heart sounds, loss of consciousness). **CV:** <u>Profound hypotension</u>, palpitation, increase or transient lowering of pulse rate, bradycardia, tachycardia, ECG changes. **GI:** Nausea, retching, abdominal pain. **Metabolic:** Increase in serum creatinine, fall or rise in total plasma cobalamins. **CNS:** Headache, dizziness. **Special Senses:** Nasal stuffiness. **Other:** Irritation at infusion site.

DRUG INTERACTIONS Additive effects with ANTIHYPERTENSIVE drugs.

PHARMACOKINETICS Onset: Within 2 min. **Duration:** 1–10 min after infusion is terminated. **Metabolism:** Rapidly converted to cyanogen in erythrocytes and tissue, which is metabolized to thiocyanate in liver. **Elimination:** In urine primarily as thiocyanate. **Half-Life:** (Thiocyanate): 2.7–7 days.

NURSING IMPLICATIONS
Assessment & Drug Effects
- Monitor constantly to titrate IV infusion rate to BP response.
- Relieve adverse effects by slowing IV rate or by stopping drug; minimize adverse effects by keeping patient supine.
- Report promptly if BP begins to rise after drug infusion rate is decreased or infusion is discontinued.
- Monitor I&O.
- Lab tests: Monitor blood thiocyanate level in patients receiving prolonged treatment or in patients with severe kidney dysfunction (levels usually are not allowed to exceed 10 mg/dL). Determine plasma cyanogen level following 1 or 2 days of therapy in patients with impaired liver function.

NOREPINEPHRINE BITARTRATE
(nor-ep-i-nef'rin)
Levarterenol, Levophed, Noradrenaline

Classification(s): ALPHA- AND BETA-ADRENERGIC AGONIST
Therapeutic: VASOCONSTRICTOR; INOTROPIC
Prototype: Epinephrine
Pregnancy Category: C

USES To restore BP in certain acute hypotensive states such as shock, sympathectomy, pheochromocytomectomy, spinal anesthesia, poliomyelitis, MI, septicemia, blood transfusion, and drug reactions. Also as adjunct in treatment of cardiac arrest.

INDICATION & DOSAGE

Hypotension

Adult: Initial 0.5–1 mcg/min titrate to response usual range 8–30 mcg/min
Child: 0.05–0.1 mcg/kg/min titrate to response (max: 1–2 mcg/kg/min)

SOLUTION PREPARATION

Add contents of a 4 mL ampule (4 mg) to 1000 mL of D5W or D5NS to yield 4 mcg/mL. More concentrated solutions (e.g., 4 mg in 500 mL to yield 8 mcg/mL) may be used based on fluid requirements. Protect from light.

STORAGE

Store at 15°–30° C (59°–86° F) and protect from light.

ADMINISTRATION

- Ensure patency of IV site prior to administration.
- **IV Infusion:** Initial rate of infusion is 2–3 mL/min (8–12 mcg/min), then titrated to maintain BP, usually 0.5–1 mL/min (2–4 mcg/min). Usually give at the slowest rate possible required to maintain BP. Use an infusion control device.
- Check IV site frequently for evidence of extravasation: Blanching along course of infused vein (may occur without obvious extravasation), cold, hard swelling around injection site. Antidote for extravasation ischemia: Phentolamine, 5–10 mg in 10–15 mL NS injection, is infiltrated throughout affected area (using syringe with fine hypodermic needle) as soon as possible.
- If therapy is to be prolonged, change infusion sites at intervals to allow effect of local vasoconstriction to subside. Avoid abrupt withdrawal; when therapy is discontinued, infusion rate is slowed gradually.

INCOMPATIBILITIES Solution/additive: Aminophylline, amobarbital, ampicillin, whole blood, cephapirin, chlorothiazide, chlorpheniramine, diazepam, pentobarbital, phenobarbital, phenytoin, sodium bicarbonate, sodium iodide, streptomycin, thiopental, warfarin. Y-site: Insulin, thiopental.

ACTION & *THERAPEUTIC EFFECT* Direct-acting sympathomimetic amine identical to the body catecholamine, norepinephrine. Acts directly and predominantly on alpha-adrenergic receptors; little action on beta receptors except in heart (beta$_1$ receptors). Causes vasoconstriction and cardiac stimulation; also has powerful constrictor action on resistance and capacitance blood vessels. *Peripheral vasoconstriction and moderate inotropic stimulation of heart result in increased systolic and diastolic blood pressure, myocardial oxygenation, coronary artery blood flow, and workload of heart.*

CONTRAINDICATIONS Use as sole therapy in hypovolemic states, except as temporary emergency measure; mesenteric or peripheral vascular thrombosis; profound hypoxia or hypercarbia; use during cyclopropane or halothane anesthesia; hypertension; hyperthyroidism; MAOI therapy; pregnancy (category C).
CAUTIOUS USE Severe heart disease; older adult patients; within 14 days of MAOI therapy; patients receiving tricyclic antidepressants; lactation.

ADVERSE EFFECTS (≥1%) **Body as a Whole:** Restlessness, anxiety, *tremors,* dizziness, weakness, insomnia, pallor, plasma volume depletion, edema, hemorrhage, intestinal, renal, or <u>hepatic necrosis</u>, retrosternal and pharyngeal pain, profuse sweating. **CV:** Palpitation, hypertension, reflex bradycardia, <u>fatal arrhythmias</u> (large doses), severe hypertension. **GI:** Vomiting. **Metabolic:** Hyperglycemia. **CNS:** Headache, violent headache, <u>cerebral hemorrhage</u>, convulsions. **Respiratory:** Respiratory difficulty. **Skin:** Tissue necrosis at injection site (with extravasation). **Special Senses:** Blurred vision, photophobia.

DRUG INTERACTIONS ALPHA AND BETA BLOCKERS antagonize pressor effects; ERGOT ALKALOIDS, **furazolidone, guanethidine, methyldopa,** TRICYCLIC ANTIDEPRESSANTS may potentiate pressor effects; **halothane, cyclopropane** increase risk of arrhythmias.

PHARMACOKINETICS Onset: Very rapid. **Duration:** 1–2 min after termination of infusion. **Distribution:** Localizes in sympathetic nerve endings; crosses placenta. **Metabolism:** In liver and other tissues by catecholamine o-methyl transferase and monoamine oxidase. **Elimination:** In urine.

NURSING IMPLICATIONS

Assessment & Drug Effects

- Monitor constantly while patient is receiving norepinephrine: Baseline BP and HR before start of therapy, then q2min from initiation of drug until stabilization occurs at desired level, then every 5 min during drug administration.
- Adjust flow rate to maintain BP at low normal (usually 80–100 mm Hg systolic) in normotensive patients. In previously hypertensive patients, systolic BP is generally maintained no higher than 40 mm Hg below preexisting systolic level.
- Observe closely and record mental status (index of cerebral circulation), skin temperature of extremities, and color (especially of earlobes, lips, nail beds) in addition to vital signs.
- Monitor I&O. Urinary retention and kidney shutdown are possibilities, especially in hypovolemic patients. Urinary output is a sensitive indicator of the degree of renal perfusion. Report decrease in urinary output or change in I&O ratio.

Common adverse effects in *italic*, life-threatening effects <u>underlined</u>: generic names in **bold**; classifications in SMALL CAPS; ♣ Canadian drug name; ⊙ Prototype drug

493

- Be alert to patient's complaints of headache, vomiting, palpitation, arrhythmias, chest pain, photophobia, and blurred vision as possible symptoms of overdosage. Reflex bradycardia may occur as a result of rise in BP.
- Continue to monitor vital signs and observe patient closely after cessation of therapy for clinical sign of circulatory inadequacy.

NORMAL SERUM ALBUMIN, HUMAN 🄿

(al-byoo′min)

Albuminar, Albutein, Buminate, Plasbumin
Classification(s): PLASMA EXPANDER
Therapeutic: PLASMA VOLUME EXPANDER
Pregnancy Category: C

USES To restore plasma volume and maintain cardiac output in hypovolemic shock; for prevention and treatment of cerebral edema; as adjunct in exchange transfusion for hyperbilirubinemia and erythroblastosis fetalis; to increase plasma protein level in treatment of hypoproteinemia; and to promote diuresis in refractory edema. Also used for blood dilution prior to or during cardiopulmonary bypass procedures. Has been used as adjunct in treatment of adult respiratory distress syndrome (ARDS).

INDICATION & DOSAGE

Emergency Volume Replacement
Adult: 25 g, may repeat in 15–30 min if necessary (max: 250 g)

Colloidal Volume Replacement (Nonemergency)
Child: 12.5 g, may repeat in 15–30 min if necessary

Hypoproteinemia
Adult: 50–75 g (max: 2 mL/min)
Child: 25 g (max: 2 mL/min)

SOLUTION PREPARATION

Normal serum albumin, 5%, is infused without further dilution. Normal serum albumin, 25%, may be infused undiluted or diluted in NS or D5W (with sodium restriction). Note: 5% solution = 5 g/100 mL; 25% solution = 25 g/mL

STORAGE

- Store at temperature not to exceed 37° C (98.6° F).
- Use solution within 4 h, once container is opened, because it contains no preservatives or antimicrobials. Discard unused portion.

ADMINISTRATION

- **IV Infusion:**
  - *Hypovolemic Shock:* Infuse initially as rapidly as necessary to restore blood volume. As blood volume approaches normal, rate should be

Common adverse effects in *italic*, life-threatening effects underlined; generic names in **bold**, classifications in SMALL CAPS; ♣ Canadian drug name; 🄿 Prototype drug

reduced to avoid circulatory overload and pulmonary edema. Give 5% albumin at rate not exceeding 2–4 mL/min. Give 25% albumin at a rate not to exceed 1 mL/min.

- *Normal Blood Volume:* Infuse 5% albumin human at a rate not to exceed 5–10 mL/min; give 25% albumin at a rate not to exceed 2 or 3 mL/min.
- *Child:* Usual rate is 25–50% of adult rate.

INCOMPATIBILITIES **Solution/additive:** Amino acids, verapamil. **Y-site:** Fat emulsion, midazolam, vancomycin, verapamil.

ACTION & *THERAPEUTIC EFFECT* Obtained by fractionating pooled venous and placental human plasma, which is then sterilized by filtration and heated to minimize possibility of transmitting hepatitis B virus or HIV. Risk of sensitization is reduced because it lacks cellular elements and contains no coagulation factors, Rh factor, or blood group antibodies. Its property as a plasma volume expander results from increasing the osmotic pressure of plasma. *Expands volume of circulating blood by osmotically shifting tissue fluid into general circulation.*

CONTRAINDICATIONS Hypersensitivity to albumin; severe anemia; cardiac failure, within 24 h of severe burns; heart failure; patients with normal or increased intravascular volume; pregnancy (category C).

CAUTIOUS USE Low cardiac reserve; pulmonary disease; absence of albumin deficiency; liver or kidney failure; dehydration; hypertension; restricted sodium intake; hypernatremia.

ADVERSE EFFECTS (≥1%) **Body as a Whole:** Fever, chills, flushing, increased salivation, headache, back pain. **Skin:** Urticaria, rash. **CV:** Circulatory overload, pulmonary edema (with rapid infusion); hypotension, hypertension, dyspnea, tachycardia. **GI:** Nausea, vomiting.

DIAGNOSTIC TEST INTERFERENCE False rise in *alkaline phosphatase* when albumin is obtained partially from pooled placental plasma (levels reportedly decline over period of weeks).

DRUG INTERACTIONS No clinically significant interactions established.

PHARMACOKINETICS **Half-Life:** 21 days.

NURSING IMPLICATIONS

Assessment & Drug Effects

- Monitor BP, pulse and respiration, and IV albumin flow rate. Adjust flow rate as needed to avoid too rapid a rise in BP.
- Lab tests: Baseline and periodic plasma albumin, total serum protein, Hgb, Hct, and serum electrolytes.
- Observe closely for S&S of circulatory overload and pulmonary edema (see Appendix C). If S&S appear, slow infusion rate just sufficiently to keep vein open, and report immediately to prescriber.
- Monitor I&O ratio and pattern. Report changes in urinary output. Increase in colloidal osmotic pressure usually causes diuresis, which may persist 3–20 h.

Common adverse effects in *italic*, life-threatening effects <u>underlined</u>: generic names in **bold**; classifications in SMALL CAPS; ♣ Canadian drug name; ⊘ Prototype drug

495

- Withhold fluids completely during succeeding 8 h, when albumin is given to patients with cerebral edema.

Patient & Family Education
- Report chills, nausea, headache, or back pain to prescriber immediately.

OCTREOTIDE ACETATE

(oc-tre′o-tide)

Sandostatin, Sandostatin LAR depot

Classification(s): SOMATOSTATIN ANALOGUE

Therapeutic: ANTIDIARRHEAL

Pregnancy Category: B

USES Symptomatic treatment of severe diarrhea and flushing episodes associated with metastatic carcinoid tumors. Also watery diarrhea associated with vasoactive intestinal peptide (VIP) tumors, acromegaly.

UNLABELED USES Acromegaly associated with pituitary tumors, fistula drainage, variceal bleeding.

INDICATION & DOSAGE

Carcinoid Syndrome

Adult: 100–600 mcg/day in 2–4 divided doses, titrate to response

VIP Tumors (VIPoma)

Adult: 200–300 mcg/day in 2–4 divided doses, titrate to response

Renal Impairment Dosage Adjustment

Dialysis: Reduce dose.

SOLUTION PREPARATION

May be given undiluted [direct IV] or diluted in 50–200 mL D5W or NS for infusion.

STORAGE

- Use IV solutions within 24 h.
- Discard multiple use vials 14 days after opening.

ADMINISTRATION

- **Direct IV Injection:** Give bolus dose over 3–5 min. In **emergency** (e.g., carcinoid crisis) may give rapid IV bolus over 60 sec.
- **Intermittent Infusion:** Infuse over 15–30 min.

INCOMPATIBILITIES Solution/additive: Fat emulsion, regular insulin. Y-site: Pantoprazole.

ACTION & *THERAPEUTIC EFFECT* A long-acting peptide that mimics the natural hormone somatostatin. Suppresses secretion of serotonin, pancreatic peptides, gastrin, vasoactive intestinal peptide, insulin, glucagon, secretin, and motilin. *Stimulates fluid and electrolyte absorption from GI tract, prolongs intestinal transit time, and also inhibits the growth hormone.*

CONTRAINDICATIONS Hypersensitivity to octreotide.
CAUTIOUS USE Cholelithiasis, renal impairment, dialysis; hepatic disease; cardiac disease; diabetes; hypothyroidism; pregnancy (category B), lactation.

ADVERSE EFFECTS (≥1%) **CNS:** Headache, fatigue, dizziness. **GI:** *Nausea, diarrhea,* abdominal pain and discomfort. **Metabolic:** Hypoglycemia, hyperglycemia, increased liver transaminases, hypothyroidism (after long-term use). **Body as a Whole:** Flushing, edema, injection site pain.

DRUG INTERACTIONS May decrease **cyclosporine** levels; may alter other drug and nutrient absorption because of alterations in GI motility.

PHARMACOKINETICS Peak: 0.4 h. **Duration:** Up to 12 h. **Metabolism:** 68% metabolized in liver. **Elimination:** In urine. **Half-Life:** 1.5 h.

NURSING IMPLICATIONS
Assessment & Drug Effects
- Monitor fluid and electrolyte balance, as octreotide stimulates fluid and electrolyte absorption from GI tract.
- Monitor vitals signs, especially BP.
- Monitor bowel function, including bowel sounds and stool consistency.
- Report S&S of gallbladder dysfunction or pancreatitis.
- Lab tests: Periodic blood glucose, LFTs, and serum electrolytes.
- Monitor for hypoglycemia and hyperglycemia (see Appendix C), because octreotide may alter the balance between insulin, glucagon, and growth hormone.
- Monitor diabetics for loss of glycemic control.

Patient & Family Education
- Report promptly: Abdominal pain that may indicate gallbladder disease or pancreatitis.
- Make position changes slowly to minimize risk of orthostatic hypotension.

ONDANSETRON HYDROCHLORIDE 🄟
(on-dan′si-tron)
Zofran
Classification(s): ANTIEMETIC; 5-HT₃ ANTAGONIST
Therapeutic: ANTIEMETIC
Pregnancy Category: B

USES Prevention of nausea and vomiting associated with initial and repeated courses of cancer chemotherapy, including high-dose cisplatin; postoperative nausea and vomiting.
UNLABELED USES Treatment of hyperemesis gravidarum.

INDICATION & DOSAGE

Prevention of Chemotherapy-Induced Nausea and Vomiting

Adult: 32 mg or three 0.15 mg/kg doses starting 30 min before chemotherapy then 4 and 8 h after

Child/Adolescent (6 mo–18 y): 0.15 mg/kg infused over 15 min beginning 30 min before start of chemotherapy, then 4 and 8 h after first dose

Postoperative Nausea and Vomiting

Adult: 4 mg injected prior to anesthesia induction or once postoperatively if patient experiences nausea/vomiting shortly after surgery

Child (2–12 y and over 40 kg): 4 mg dose

Child (1 mo–12 y and less than 40 kg): 0.1 mg/kg dose

Hepatic Impairment Dosage Adjustment

Child-Pugh class C: Maximum dose 8 mg/day

SOLUTION PREPARATION

May be given undiluted [direct IV] or diluted in 50 mL of D5W or NS for infusion.

STORAGE

Store vials at 2°–30° C (36°–86° F) and protect from light. Stable for 48 h after dilution at room temperature with normal light.

ADMINISTRATION

Postop N&V

▪ **Direct IV Injection:** Give bolus dose over at least 30 sec, 2–5 min preferred.

Chemo-Induced N&V

▪ **IV Infusion:** Infuse over 15 min. When three separate doses are administered, infuse each over 15 min.

▪ *Note:* Premixed ondansetron injection is administered by infusion only.

INCOMPATIBILITIES Solution/additive: Meropenem. Y-site: Acyclovir, allopurinol, aminophylline, amphotericin B, amphotericin B cholesteryl complex, ampicillin, ampicillin/sulbactam, amsacrine, cefepime, cefoperazone, fluorouracil, furosemide, ganciclovir, lansoprazole, lorazepam, meropenem, methylprednisolone, pemetrexed, piperacillin, sargramostim, sodium bicarbonate.

ACTION & *THERAPEUTIC EFFECT* Selective serotonin (5-HT$_3$) receptor antagonist. Serotonin receptors are located centrally in the chemoreceptor trigger zone (CTZ), and peripherally on the vagal nerve terminals. Serotonin is released from the wall of the small intestine and stimulates the vagal efferent nerves through these receptors, and initiates the vomiting reflex. *Prevents nausea and vomiting associated with cancer chemotherapy and anesthesia.*

CONTRAINDICATIONS Hypersensitivity to ondansetron.

CAUTIOUS USE Hepatic disease; QT prolongation; PKU; pregnancy (category B), lactation.

ADVERSE EFFECTS (≥1%) **CNS:** Dizziness and light-headedness, *headache, sedation.* **GI:** *Diarrhea,* constipation, dry mouth, transient increases in liver aminotransferases and bilirubin. **Body as a Whole:** Hypersensitivity reactions.

DRUG INTERACTIONS Rifampin may decrease ondansetron levels, **ziprasidone** may cause QT prolongation.

PHARMACOKINETICS Peak: 1–1.5 h. **Metabolism:** In liver (CYP 3A4). **Elimination:** 44–60% in urine within 24 h; approximately 25% in feces. **Half-Life:** 3 h.

NURSING IMPLICATIONS

Assessment & Drug Effects

- Monitor fluid and electrolyte status. Diarrhea, which may cause fluid and electrolyte imbalance, is a potential adverse effect of the drug.
- Monitor cardiovascular status, especially in patients with a history of coronary artery disease. Rare cases of tachycardia and angina have been reported.
- Lab tests: Periodic serum electrolytes as needed.

Patient & Family Education

- Be aware that headache requiring an analgesic for relief is a common adverse effect.
- Make positions changes slowly and in stages to minimize risk of orthostatic hypotension.
- Exercise caution with ambulation or any hazardous activity as ondansetron may cause dizziness, drowsiness, or blurred vision.

ORPHENADRINE CITRATE

(or-fen'a-dreen)

Norflex

Classification(s): SKELETAL MUSCLE RELAXANT, CENTRAL-ACTING
Therapeutic: SKELETAL MUSCLE RELAXANT
Prototype: Methocarbamol
Pregnancy Category: C

USES To relieve muscle spasm discomfort associated with acute musculoskeletal conditions.

INDICATION & DOSAGE

Muscle Spasm

Adult: 60 mg, may repeat q12h if needed

SOLUTION PREPARATION

No dilution is required. Administer as supplied.

Common adverse effects in *italic*, life-threatening effects <u>underlined</u>: generic names in **bold**; classifications in SMALL CAPS; ♣ Canadian drug name; ❂ Prototype drug

499

STORAGE
Store at 15°–30° C (59°–86° F) and protect from light.

ADMINISTRATION
Direct IV Injection: Give bolus dose at a rate of 60 mg (2 mL) over 5 min. with patient in supine position. Keep supine for 5–10 min postinjection.

INCOMPATIBILITIES Data not available; do not mix with other drugs.

ACTION & *THERAPEUTIC EFFECT* Tertiary amine anticholinergic agent and central-acting skeletal muscle relaxant. Relaxes tense skeletal muscles indirectly, possibly by analgesic action or by atropinelike central action. *Relieves skeletal muscle spasm.*

CONTRAINDICATIONS Narrow-angle glaucoma; pyloric or duodenal obstruction, stenosing peptic ulcers; prostatic hypertrophy or bladder neck obstruction; myasthenia gravis; cardiospasm (megaloesophagus); tachycardia; pregnancy (category C). Safe use in the pediatric age group is not established.
CAUTIOUS USE History of tachycardia, cardiac decompensation, arrhythmias, renal disease, renal impairment; coronary insufficiency; lactation.

ADVERSE EFFECTS (≥1%) **CNS:** *Drowsiness,* weakness, headache, dizziness; mild CNS stimulation (high doses: Restlessness, anxiety, tremors, confusion, hallucinations, agitation, tachycardia, palpitation, syncope). **Special Senses:** Increased ocular tension, dilated pupils, blurred vision. **GI:** *Dry mouth,* nausea, vomiting, abdominal cramps, constipation. **Urogenital:** *Urinary hesitancy* or retention. **Body as a Whole:** Hypersensitivity [pruritus, urticaria, rash, <u>anaphylactic reaction</u> (rare)].

DRUG INTERACTIONS Propoxyphene may cause increased confusion, anxiety, and tremors; may worsen schizophrenic symptoms, or increase risk of tardive dyskinesia with **haloperidol;** additive CNS depressant with ANXIOLYTICS, SEDATIVES, HYPNOTICS, **butorphanol, nalbuphine,** OPIATE AGONISTS, **pentazocine, tramadol; cyclobenzaprine** may increase anticholinergic effects.

PHARMACOKINETICS Peak: 2 h. **Duration:** 4–6 h. **Distribution:** Rapidly distributed in tissues; crosses placenta. **Metabolism:** In liver. **Elimination:** In urine. **Half-Life:** 14 h.

NURSING IMPLICATIONS

Assessment & Drug Effects
- Report complaints of mouth dryness, urinary hesitancy or retention, headache, tremors, GI problems, palpitation, or rapid pulse as dosage reduction or drug withdrawal may be indicated.
- Monitor therapeutic drug effect: With parkinsonism, orphenadrine reduces muscular rigidity but has little effect on tremors. Some reduction in excessive salivation and perspiration may occur, and patient may appear mildly euphoric.
- Lab tests: Periodic CBC with differential, kidney function tests, and LFTs with prolonged therapy.

- Monitor elimination patterns. Older adults are particularly sensitive to anticholinergic effects (urinary hesitancy, constipation); observe closely.

Patient & Family Education
- Relieve mouth dryness by frequent rinsing with clear tepid water, increasing noncaloric fluid intake, sugarless gum, or lemon drops. If these measures fail, a saliva substitute may help.
- Do not drive or engage in potentially hazardous activities until response to drug is known.
- Avoid concomitant use of alcohol and other CNS depressants; these may potentiate depressant effects.

OXACILLIN SODIUM

(ox-a-sill'in)

Bactocill

Classification(s): ANTIBIOTIC, PENICILLIN, NATURAL
Therapeutic: ANTIBACTERIAL
Prototype: Penicillin G
Pregnancy Category: B

USES Infections caused by susceptible staphylococci.

INDICATION & DOSAGE

0

Staphylococcal Infections

Adult/Adolescent/Child (over 40 kg): 250 mg–1 g q4–6h (max: 12 g/day)
Child (up to 40 kg): 100–200 mg/kg/day divided q4–6h (max: 12 g/day)
Neonate:

Age	Weight	Dose
Over 7 days	Over 2000 g	100 mg/kg/day divided q6h
Over 7 days	1200–2000 g	75 mg/kg/day divided q8h
Over 7 days	Less than 1200 g	50 mg/kg/day divided q12h
7 days or less	Over 2000 g	75 mg/kg/day divided q8h
7 days or less	2000 g or less	50 mg/kg/day divided q12h

SOLUTION PREPARATION

- *Vial Reconstitution:* To each 500 mg or fraction thereof add 5 mL of sterile water for injection or NS to yield 250 mg/1.5 mL. May be given as prepared direct IV as a bolus dose or further diluted for infusion.
- *Further Dilution of Reconstituted Solution:*
  - *Intermittent/Continuous Infusion:* Dilute required dose in 50–1000 mL of D5W, NS, D5NS, LR or other compatible IV solutions.
- *Note:* Available as premixed frozen solution for infusion.

Common adverse effects in *italic*, life-threatening effects <u>underlined</u>: generic names in **bold**; classifications in SMALL CAPS; ♣ Canadian drug name; ⊙ Prototype drug

501

STORAGE

- Thawed IV solution is stable for 48 h at 15°–30° C (59°–86° F) and for 21 days refrigerated.
- Reconstituted solutions are stable for 6 h.

ADMINISTRATION

- **Direct IV Injection:** Give at a rate of 1 g or fraction thereof over 10 min.
- **Intermittent Injection:** Infuse over 15–30 min.
- **Continuous Infusion:** Infuse over 6 h.

INCOMPATIBILITIES Solution/additive: Caffeine citrate, cephalothin, cytarabine, erythromycin, hyaluronidase, hydrocortisone, nitrofurantoin, pentobarbital, phenobarbital, TETRACYCLINES, **warfarin. Y-site: Caffeine citrate, sodium bicarbonate, verapamil.**

ACTION & *THERAPEUTIC EFFECT* Semisynthetic, acid-stable, penicillinase-resistant penicillin. Oxacillin inhibits final stage of bacterial cell wall synthesis by preferentially binding to specific penicillin-binding proteins (PBPs) located within the bacterial cell wall. This leads to destruction of the bacterial cell wall and cell death. *Highly active against most penicillinase-producing staphylococci bacteria, and is generally ineffective against gram-negative bacteria and methicillin-resistant staphylococci (MRSA).*

CONTRAINDICATIONS Hypersensitivity to penicillins or cephalosporins.

CAUTIOUS USE History of or suspected atopy or allergy (hives, eczema, hay fever, asthma); history of GI disease; hepatic disease; renal disease; pregnancy (category B), lactation (may cause infant diarrhea); premature infants, neonates.

ADVERSE EFFECTS (≥1%) **Body as a Whole:** Thrombophlebitis, superinfections, wheezing, sneezing, fever, <u>anaphylaxis</u>. **GI:** Nausea, vomiting, flatulence, *diarrhea,* hepatocellular dysfunction (elevated AST, ALT, hepatitis). **Hematologic:** Eosinophilia, leukopenia, thrombocytopenia, granulocytopenia, <u>agranulocytosis</u>; neutropenia (reported in children). **Skin:** Pruritus, rash, urticaria. **Urogenital:** Interstitial nephritis, transient hematuria, albuminuria, azotemia (newborns and infants on high doses).

DIAGNOSTIC TEST INTERFERENCE Oxacillin in large doses can cause false-positive ***urine protein tests*** using ***sulfosalicylic acid methods.***

DRUG INTERACTIONS Serum concentrations are enhanced by concurrent use of **probenecid.**

PHARMACOKINETICS Peak: 15 min. **Distribution:** Distributes into CNS with inflamed meninges; crosses placenta; distributed into breast milk, 90% protein bound. **Metabolism:** Enters enterohepatic circulation. **Elimination:** Primarily in urine, some in bile. **Half-Life:** 0.5–1 h.

NURSING IMPLICATIONS

Assessment & Drug Effects

- Prior to initiating therapy: Baseline C&S tests (start drug pending results); determine previous hypersensitivity reactions to penicillins, cephalosporins, and other allergens.

- Withhold drug and report promptly S&S that resemble viral hepatitis or general signs of hypersensitivity: Hives, rash, fever, nausea, vomiting, abdominal discomfort, anorexia, malaise, jaundice (with dark yellow to brown urine, light-colored or clay-colored stools, pruritus).
- Lab tests: Periodic LFTs, CBC with differential and platelet count, and urinalysis.
- Report promptly S&S of superinfections (see Appendix C).

Patient & Family Education
- Promptly report: Rash, shortness of breath, nausea, or the onset of diarrhea.
- Females using oral contraceptives should add a barrier contraceptive during oxacillin therapy.

OXALIPLATIN

(ox-a-li-pla′tin)

Eloxatin
Classification(s): ANTINEOPLASTIC; ALKYLATING AGENT
Therapeutic: ANTINEOPLASTIC
Prototype: Cyclophosphamide
Pregnancy Category: D

USES Metastatic cancer of colon and rectum.
UNLABELED USES Non–small-cell lung cancer, non-Hodgkin's lymphoma, ovarian cancer.

INDICATION & DOSAGE

Metastatic Colon or Rectal Cancer
Adult: 85 mg/m^2 infused over 120 min once every 2 wk for 6 mo

Toxicity Adjustment

For Advanced Colorectal Cancer Treatment	
Persistent grade 2 neurosensory	Reduce dose to 65 mg/m^2
Grade 3 neurosensory	Discontinue therapy
Grade 3–4 gastrointestinal or hematologic toxicity	Reduce dose to 65 mg/m^2
For Stage III Colorectal Cancer	
Persistent grade 2 neurosensory	Reduce dose to 75 mg/m^2
Grade 3 neurosensory	Discontinue therapy
Grade 3–4 gastrointestinal or hematologic toxicity	Reduce dose to 75 mg/m^2

Renal Impairment Dosage Adjustment
CrCl less than 19 mL/min: Omit dose or change therapy.

Common adverse effects in *italic*, life-threatening effects underlined: generic names in **bold**; classifications in SMALL CAPS; ♣ Canadian drug name; ● Prototype drug

503

SOLUTION PREPARATION

- *Vial Reconstitution:* NEVER reconstitute with NS or any solution containing chloride. Add 10 mL or 20 mL of sterile water for injection or D5W to the 50 mg vial or the 100 mg vial, respectively. **Must be** further diluted for infusion.
- *Further Dilution of Reconstituted Solution:* Add the required dose to 250–500 mL of D5W for infusion.

STORAGE

- Store reconstituted solution up to 24 h under refrigeration at 2°–8° C (36°–46° F).
- After final dilution, the IV solution may be stored for 6 h at room temperature [20°–25° C (68°–77° F)] or up to 24 h under refrigeration.

ADMINISTRATION

- Premedication with an antiemetic is recommended.
- **IV Infusion:** Do NOT use needles or infusion sets containing aluminum parts. Give over 120 min with frequent monitoring of the IV insertion site.
- Flush infusion line with D5W before/after administration of any other medication.
- Discontinue at the first sign of extravasation and restart IV in a different site.

INCOMPATIBILITIES Solution/additive: CHLORIDE-CONTAINING SOLUTIONS, ALKALINE SOLUTIONS, including **sodium bicarbonate, 5-fluorouracil (5-FU). Y-site:** ALKALINE SOLUTIONS, including **sodium bicarbonate, 5-FU, diazepam.**

ACTION & *THERAPEUTIC EFFECT* Oxaliplatin forms inter- and intra-strand DNA cross-links. These cross-links inhibit DNA replication and transcription. The cytotoxicity of oxaliplatin is cell-cycle nonspecific. *Antitumor activity of oxaliplatin in combination with 5-fluorouracil (5-FU) has antiproliferative activity against colon carcinoma that is greater than either compound alone.*

CONTRAINDICATIONS History of known allergy to oxaliplatin or other platinum compounds; myelosuppression; pregnancy (category D), lactation. Safety and effectiveness in children are not established.

CAUTIOUS USE Renal impairment, because clearance of ultrafilterable platinum is decreased in mild, moderate, and severe renal impairment; hepatic impairment; older adults.

ADVERSE EFFECTS (≥1%) **Body as a Whole:** *Fever, edema, pain,* allergic reaction, arthralgia, rigors. **CNS:** *Fatigue, neuropathy, headache,* dizziness, insomnia. **CV:** Chest pain. **GI:** *Diarrhea, nausea, vomiting, anorexia, stomatitis, constipation, abdominal pain,* reflux, dyspepsia, taste perversion, mucositis, flatulence. **Hematologic:** *Anemia, leukopenia, thrombocytopenia,* neutropenia, thromboembolism. **Metabolic:** Hypokalemia, dehydration. **Respiratory:** *Dyspnea, cough,* rhinitis, pharyngitis, epistaxis, hiccup. **Skin:** Flushing, rash, alopecia, injection site reaction. **Urogenital:** Dysuria.

DRUG INTERACTIONS AMINOGLYCOSIDES, **amphotericin B, vancomycin,** and other NEPHROTOXIC DRUGS may increase risk of renal failure.

Common adverse effects in *italic*, life-threatening effects underlined; generic names in **bold**; classifications in SMALL CAPS; ♣ Canadian drug name; ● Prototype drug

PHARMACOKINETICS Distribution: More than 90% protein bound. **Metabolism:** Rapid and extensive nonenzymatic biotransformation. **Elimination:** Primarily in urine. **Half-Life:** 391 h.

NURSING IMPLICATIONS

Assessment & Drug Effects

- Monitor for S&S of hypersensitivity (e.g., rash, urticaria, erythema, pruritus; rarely, bronchospasm and hypotension). Withhold drug and notify prescriber if any of these occur.
- Monitor insertion site. Extravasation may cause local pain and inflammation that may be severe and lead to complications, including necrosis.
- Monitor for and promptly report S&S of coagulation disorders including GI bleeding, hematuria, and epistaxis.
- Monitor for and promptly report S&S of peripheral neuropathy (e.g., paresthesia, dysesthesia; hypoesthesia in the hands, feet, perioral area, or throat; jaw spasm; abnormal tongue sensation; dysarthria; eye pain; and chest pressure). Symptoms may be precipitated or exacerbated by exposure to cold temperature or cold objects.
- Lab tests: Before each administration cycle, WBC count with differential, hemoglobin, platelet count, and blood chemistries (including ALT, AST, bilirubin, and creatinine); baseline and periodic renal functions.
- Do not apply ice to oral mucous membranes (e.g., mucositis prophylaxis) during the infusion of oxaliplatin as cold temperature can exacerbate acute neurological symptoms.

Patient & Family Education

- Use effective methods of contraception while receiving this drug.
- Avoid cold drinks, use of ice, and cover exposed skin prior to exposure to cold temperature or cold objects.
- Do not drive or engage in potentially hazardous activities until response to drug is known.
- Report any of the following: Difficulty writing, buttoning, swallowing, walking; numbness, tingling, or other unusual sensations in extremities; nonproductive cough or shortness of breath; fever, particularly if associated with persistent diarrhea or other evidence of infection.
- Report promptly S&S of a bleeding disorder such as black tarry stool, coke-colored or frankly bloody urine, bleeding from the nose or mucous membranes.

OXYMORPHONE HYDROCHLORIDE

(ox-i-mor'fone)

Numorphan

Classification(s): ANALGESIC, NARCOTIC (OPIATE) AGONIST
Therapeutic: NARCOTIC ANALGESIC
Prototype: Morphine
Pregnancy Category: C   **Controlled Substance:** Schedule II

USES Relief of moderate to severe pain, preoperative medication, obstetric analgesia, support of anesthesia, and relief of anxiety in patients with dyspnea associated with acute ventricular failure and pulmonary edema.

INDICATION & DOSAGE

Moderate to Severe Pain

Adult: 0.5 mg initially then switch to alternate route

SOLUTION PREPARATION

May be given direct IV undiluted or diluted in 5 mL sterile water for injection or NS.

STORAGE

Protect from light. Store in refrigerator at 2°–15° C (36°–59° F).

ADMINISTRATION

Direct IV Injection: Give at a rate of 0.5 mg over 2–5 min.

INCOMPATIBILITIES Data not available; do not mix with other drugs.

ACTION & *THERAPEUTIC EFFECT* Structurally and pharmacologically related to morphine. Analgesic action against moderate to severe pain with mild sedation and, unlike morphine, has little antitussive action. *Effective in relief of moderate to severe pain.*

CONTRAINDICATIONS Pulmonary edema resulting from chemical respiratory irritants. Safe use during pregnancy (category C), or in children less than 12 y, is not established.

CAUTIOUS USE Alcoholism; biliary tract disease; bladder obstruction; severe pulmonary disease, respiratory insufficiency, COPD; depression; older adults; lactation.

ADVERSE EFFECTS (≥1%) **GI:** *Nausea, vomiting, euphoria.* **CNS:** *Dizziness,* lightheadedness, sedation. **Respiratory:** Respiratory depression (see morphine), apnea, respiratory arrest. **Body as a Whole:** Sweating, coma, shock. **CV:** Cardiac arrest, circulatory depression.

DRUG INTERACTIONS Alcohol and other CNS DEPRESSANTS add to CNS depression; **propofol** increases risk of bradycardia.

PHARMACOKINETICS Onset: 5–10 min. **Peak:** 1–1.5 h. **Duration:** 3–6 h. **Distribution:** Crosses placenta. **Metabolism:** In liver. **Elimination:** In urine.

NURSING IMPLICATIONS

Assessment & Drug Effects

- Monitor respiratory rate. Withhold drug and report promptly if rate falls below 12 breaths per minute.
- Supervise ambulation and advise patient of possible light-headedness. Older adults and debilitated patients are most susceptible to CNS depressant effects of drug.
- Evaluate patient's continued need for narcotic analgesic. Prolonged use can lead to dependence of morphine type.

- Medication contains sulfite and may precipitate a hypersensitivity reaction in susceptible patient.

Patient & Family Education
- Use caution when walking because of potential for injury from dizziness.

OXYTOCIN INJECTION 🅟

(ox-i-toe′sin)

Pitocin

Classification(s): OXYTOXIC AGENT
Therapeutic: ANTIHEMORRHAGIC; OXYTOXIC
Pregnancy Category: X

USES To initiate or improve uterine contraction at term; management of inevitable, incomplete, or missed abortion; stimulation of uterine contractions during third stage of labor; stimulation to overcome uterine inertia; control of postpartum hemorrhage and promotion of postpartum uterine involution. Also used to induce labor in cases of maternal diabetes, preeclampsia, eclampsia, and erythroblastosis fetalis.

INDICATION & DOSAGE

0

Labor Induction

Adult: 0.5–2 milliunits/min, may increase by 1–2 milliunits/min q15–60min (max: 20 milliunits/min); dose is decreased when labor is established. **High dose regimen,** 6 milliunits/min, may increase by 6 milliunits/min q15–60min until contraction pattern established

Postpartum

Adult: Infuse a total of 10–40 units at a rate of 20–40 milliunits/min after delivery

Incomplete Abortion

Adult: 10–20 milliunits/min

SOLUTION PREPARATION

- *IV Infusion:* Before withdrawing oxytocin for preparation of IV infusion, rotate bottle gently to distribute medicine throughout solution.
  - *Inducing Labor:* Add 10 units (1 mL) to 1 L of D5W, NS, LR or D5NS to yield 10 milliunits/mL.
  - *Postpartum Bleeding/Incomplete Abortion:* Add 10–40 units (1–4 mL) to 1 L of D5W, NS, LR or D5NS to yield 10–40 milliunits/mL.

STORAGE

Store at 15°–30° C (59°–86° F).

Common adverse effects in *italic*, life-threatening effects underlined: generic names
in **bold**; classifications in SMALL CAPS; ♣ Canadian drug name; 🅟 Prototype drug

507

ADMINISTRATION

- **IV Infusion:** Use an infusion pump for accurate control of infusion rate.
  - *Inducing Labor:* Initially infuse 0.5–2 milliunits/min; increase by 1–2 milliunits/min at 30–60 min intervals.
  - *Postpartum Bleeding:* Initially infuse 10–40 milliunits/min, then adjust to control uterine atony.
  - *Incomplete Abortion:* Infuse 10–20 milliunits/min. Do not exceed 30 units in 12 h.

INCOMPATIBILITIES Solution/additive: Fibrinolysin, norepinephrine, prochlorperazine, warfarin.

ACTION & *THERAPEUTIC EFFECT* Synthetic, water-soluble polypeptide identical pharmacologically to the oxytocic hormone released by posterior pituitary. By direct action on myofibrils, produces phasic contractions characteristic of normal delivery. Uterine sensitivity to oxytocin increases during gestation period and peaks sharply before parturition. *Effective in initiating and improving uterine contractions at term.*

CONTRAINDICATIONS Hypersensitivity to oxytocin; significant cephalopelvic disproportion, unfavorable fetal position or presentations that are undeliverable without conversion before delivery, obstetric emergencies in which benefit-to-risk ratio for mother or fetus favors surgical intervention, fetal distress in which delivery is not imminent, prematurity, placenta previa, prolonged use in severe toxemia or uterine inertia, hypertonic uterine patterns, previous surgery of uterus or cervix including cesarean section, conditions predisposing to thromboplastin or amniotic fluid embolism (dead fetus, abruptio placentae), grand multiparity, invasive cervical carcinoma, primipara greater than 35 y of age, past history of uterine sepsis or of traumatic delivery, intranasal route during labor, simultaneous administration of drug by two routes.
CAUTIOUS USE Concomitant use with cyclopropane anesthesia or vasoconstrictive drugs.

ADVERSE EFFECTS (≥1%) **Body as a Whole:** Fetal trauma from too rapid propulsion through pelvis, <u>fetal death</u>, anaphylactic reactions, postpartum hemorrhage, precordial pain, edema, cyanosis or redness of skin. **CV:** Fetal bradycardia and arrhythmias, maternal cardiac arrhythmias, hypertensive episodes, <u>subarachnoid hemorrhage</u>, increased blood flow, <u>fatal afibrinogenemia</u>, ECG changes, PVCs, <u>cardiovascular spasm and collapse</u>. **GI:** Neonatal jaundice, maternal nausea, vomiting. **Endocrine:** ADH effects leading to severe water intoxication and hyponatremia, hypotension. **CNS:** Fetal <u>intracranial hemorrhage</u>, anxiety. **Respiratory:** Fetal hypoxia, maternal dyspnea. **Urogenital:** Uterine hypertonicity, tetanic contractions, <u>uterine rupture</u>, pelvic hematoma.

DRUG INTERACTIONS VASOCONSTRICTORS cause severe hypertension; **cyclopropane anesthesia** causes hypotension, maternal bradycardia, arrhythmias.

PHARMACOKINETICS Duration: 1 h. **Distribution:** Distributed throughout extracellular fluid; small amount may cross placenta. **Metabolism:** Rapidly destroyed in liver and kidneys. **Elimination:** Small amounts excreted unchanged in urine. **Half-Life:** 3–5 min.

NURSING IMPLICATIONS

Assessment & Drug Effects

- Establish baseline maternal BP and other vital signs, weight, strength, duration, and frequency of contractions, as well as fetal heart tone and rate, before instituting treatment.
- Monitor fetal heart rate and maternal BP and pulse at least q15min during infusion period; evaluate tonus of myometrium during and between contractions. Report significant changes to prescriber as they occur.
- Stop infusion to prevent fetal anoxia, turn patient on her side, and notify prescriber if contractions are prolonged (occurring at less than 2-min intervals) and if monitor records contractions above 50 mm Hg or if contractions last 90 seconds or longer. Stimulation will wane rapidly within 2–3 min. Oxygen administration may be necessary.
- If local or regional (caudal, spinal) anesthesia is being given to the patient receiving oxytocin, be alert to the possibility of hypertensive crisis (sudden intense occipital headache, palpitation, marked hypertension, stiff neck, nausea, vomiting, sweating, fever, photophobia, dilated pupils, bradycardia or tachycardia, constricting chest pain).
- Monitor I&O closely. If patient is receiving drug by prolonged IV infusion, watch for symptoms of water intoxication (drowsiness, listlessness, headache, confusion, anuria, weight gain). Report changes in alertness and orientation and changes in I&O ratio (i.e., marked decrease in output with excessive intake).
- Check fundus frequently during the first few postpartum hours and several times daily thereafter.

Patient & Family Education

- Be aware of purpose and anticipated effect of oxytocin.
- Report promptly severe headache.

PACLITAXEL ⊕

(pac-li-tax′el)

Abraxane, Taxol

Classification(s): ANTINEOPLASTIC, MITOTIC INHIBITOR, TAXOID
Therapeutic: ANTINEOPLASTIC

Pregnancy Category: X

USES Ovarian cancer, breast cancer, Kaposi's sarcoma, non–small-cell lung cancer (NSCLC).
UNLABELED USES Other solid tumors, leukemia, melanoma.

INDICATION & DOSAGE

Ovarian Cancer, NSCLC

Adult: 135 mg/m^2 repeated q3wk

Breast Cancer

Taxol *Adult:* 175–250 mg/m^2 over 3 h q3wk

Abraxane *Adult:* 260 mg/m^2 over 30 min q3wk

Kaposi's Sarcoma

Adult: 135 mg/m^2 infused over 3 h q3wk or 100 mg/m^2 infused over 3 h q2wk

Toxicity Adjustment

If neutrophil count below 500/mm^3 for 7 days: Reduce dose 20%; *if severe peripheral neuropathy:* Reduce dose 20%

Hepatic Impairment Dosage Adjustment

Reduce dose 50%

SOLUTION PREPARATION

▪ Follow institutional or standard guidelines for preparation, handling, and disposal of cytotoxic agents. Following skin contact, wash immediately with soap and water.

Dilution of Conventional Paclitaxel

▪ *IV Infusion:* Do not use equipment or devices containing polyvinyl chloride (PVC) in preparation of infusion. Dilute to a final concentration of 0.3–1.2 mg/mL in any of the following: D5W, NS, D5NS, or D5W in lactated Ringer's solution. The prepared solution may be hazy, but this does not indicate a loss of potency.

Abraxane Vial Reconstitution

▪ *IV Infusion:* Slowly inject 20 mL NS over at least 1 min onto the inside wall of the vial to yield 5 mg/mL. DO NOT inject directly into the cake powder. Allow vial to sit for at least 5 min, then gently swirl for at least 2 min to completely dissolve. If foaming occurs, let stand for at least 15 min until foam subsides. If particulates or settling are visible, gently invert vial to ensure complete resuspension prior to use. Remove the required dose and inject into an empty, sterile, PVC or non-PVC type IV bag.

STORAGE

▪ Conventional solutions diluted for infusion are stable at room temperature (approximately 25° C/77° F) for up to 27 h.

▪ Reconstituted Abraxane should be used immediately but may be kept refrigerated for up to 8 h if needed.

ADMINISTRATION

▪ Premedicate as follows (except with Abraxane) to avoid severe hypersensitivity: Dexamethasone 20 mg (10 mg with AIDS-related Kaposi's sarcoma) PO/IV 12 & 6 h prior to infusion; diphenhydramine 50 mg IV

30–60 min prior to infusion; and cimetidine 300 mg or ranitidine 50 mg IV 30 min before infusion.

- Do not administer to patients with AIDS-related Kaposi's sarcoma unless neutrophil count is at least 1000/mm³; for all others, do not administer unless neutrophil count is at least 1500/mm³.
- Ensure patency of IV prior to infusion.

Conventional Paclitaxel

- **IV Infusion:** Infuse over 3 h through IV tubing containing an in-line (0.22 micron or less) filter. Do not use equipment containing PVC.

Abraxane

- **IV Infusion:** DO NOT use an in-line filter. Infuse over 30 min.

INCOMPATIBILITIES Solution/additive: PVC bags and **infusion sets** should be avoided (except with **Abraxane**) due to leaching of DEHP (plasticizer). Do not mix with any other medications. **Y-site: Amphotericin B, amphotericin B cholesteryl sulfate, chlorpromazine, doxorubicin liposome, hydroxyzine, methylprednisolone, mitoxantrone.**

ACTION & *THERAPEUTIC EFFECT* Normal functioning microtubules within a cell are essential for cell shape and organelles present within cells. During cell division paclitaxel is an antimicrotubule agent that interferes with the microtubule network essential for interphase and mitosis. This induces abnormal spindle formation and multiple asters during mitosis. *Interferes with growth of rapidly dividing cells, including cancer cells, and eventually causes cell death.*

CONTRAINDICATIONS *Taxol:* Hypersensitivity to paclitaxel; baseline neutrophil count less than 1500 cells/mm³; with AIDS-related Kaposi's sarcoma baseline neutrophil count less than 1000 cells/mm³. *Abraxane:* Baseline neutrophil count less than 1500 cells/mm³; pregnancy (category D), lactation.

CAUTIOUS USE Cardiac arrhythmias, cardiac disease; impaired liver function, alcoholism; older adults; peripheral neuropathy. Safety and efficacy in children are not established.

ADVERSE EFFECTS (≥1%) **CV:** Ventricular tachycardia, ventricular ectopy, *transient bradycardia,* chest pain. **CNS:** Fatigue, headaches, *peripheral neuropathy,* weakness, seizures. **GI:** *Nausea, vomiting,* diarrhea, taste changes, *mucositis,* elevations in serum triglycerides. **Hematologic:** <u>Neutropenia</u>, anemia, <u>thrombocytopenia</u>. **Body as a Whole:** *Hypersensitivity reactions (hypotension, dyspnea with <u>bronchospasm</u>, urticaria, abdominal and extremity pain, diaphoresis, <u>angioedema</u>), myalgias, arthralgias, alopecia.* **Skin:** *Alopecia,* tissue necrosis with extravasation. **Urogenital:** Minor elevations in kidney and liver function tests.

DRUG INTERACTIONS Increased myelosuppression if **cisplatin, doxorubicin** is given before paclitaxel; **ketoconazole** can inhibit metabolism of paclitaxel; additive bradycardia with BETA BLOCKERS, **digoxin, verapamil;** additive risk of bleeding with ANTICOAGULANTS, NSAIDS, PLATELET INHIBITORS (including **aspirin**), THROMBOLYTIC AGENTS.

PHARMACOKINETICS Distribution: More than 90% protein bound; does not cross CSF. **Metabolism:** In liver (CYP 3A4, 2C8). **Elimination:** Feces 70%, urine 14%. **Half-Life:** 1–9 h.

NURSING IMPLICATIONS

Assessment & Drug Effects

- Prior to initiating therapy determine that neutrophil count meets minimum guidelines.
- Assess frequently the patency of a peripheral IV site, as tissue necrosis occurs with extravasation.
- Monitor constantly for hypersensitivity reactions, especially during first and second administrations of paclitaxel. S&S requiring treatment, but not necessarily discontinuation of the drug, include dyspnea, hypotension, and chest pain. Discontinue immediately and manage symptoms aggressively if angioedema and generalized urticaria develop.
- Monitor vital signs frequently, especially during the first hour of infusion. Bradycardia occurs in approximately 12% of patients, usually during infusion. It does not normally require treatment. Cardiac monitoring is indicated for those with severe conduction abnormalities.
- Lab tests: Baseline and periodic CBC with differential and platelet count.
- Monitor for severe neutropenia, which is common but usually of short duration (less than 500/mm³ for less than 7 days) with the nadir occurring about day 11.
- Thrombocytopenia occurs less often and is less severe with the nadir around day 8 or 9. The incidence and severity of anemia increase with exposure to paclitaxel.
- Monitor for peripheral neuropathy, the severity of which is dose dependent. Severe symptoms occur primarily with higher than recommended doses.

Patient & Family Education

- Report promptly S&S of paclitaxel hypersensitivity: Difficulty breathing, chest pain, palpitations, angioedema (subcutaneous swelling usually around face and neck), and skin rashes or itching.
- Be sure to have periodic blood work as prescribed.
- Avoid aspirin, NSAIDs, and alcohol to minimize GI distress.

PALIFERMIN

(pal-i-fer-min)

Kepivance

Classification(s): KERATINOCYTE GROWTH FACTOR (KGF)
Therapeutic: STOMATITIS PREVENTION
Pregnancy Category: C

USES Reduction in incidence and duration of severe stomatitis in patients with hematologic malignancies receiving hematopoietic stem cell therapy.

INDICATION & DOSAGE

Pre-/Postmyelotoxic Therapy

Adult: 60 mcg/kg/day × 3 days pre-/postmyelotoxic therapy; **Premyelotoxic Therapy,** give last dose 24–48 h BEFORE myelotoxic therapy; **Post-
myelotoxic Therapy,** give first dose after, but on same day of, hematopoietic stem cell infusion (but at least 4 days after last premyelotoxic palifermin
dose).

SOLUTION PREPARATION

Vial Reconstitution: Slowly inject 1.2 mL of sterile water for injection into
the vial to yield 5 mg/mL. Swirl gently to dissolve but DO NOT shake.
DO NOT filter during preparation or administration.

STORAGE

Store reconstituted solution at 4°–8° C (36°–46° F) for up to 24 h. Protect
from light.

ADMINISTRATION

Direct IV Injection: Give rapid bolus dose. Flush heparinized IV line
with NS before/after injection.

INCOMPATIBILITIES Solution/additive: Data not available; do not mix
with other drugs. **Y-site: Heparin.**

ACTION & *THERAPEUTIC EFFECT* Palifermin is a recombinant human keratinocyte growth factor (KGF) that specifically binds to a KGF receptor
expressed only in epithelial cells. *Palifermin is cytoprotective and stimulates epithelial cell proliferation and differentiation, thus reducing stomatitis formation in patients treated for hematologic malignancies.*

CONTRAINDICATIONS Hypersensitivity to *E. coli*-derived proteins, palifermin, or any other component of the product; pregnancy (category C).
Safety and efficacy in pediatric patients or patients with nonhematologic
malignancies are not established.

CAUTIOUS USE Lactation.

ADVERSE EFFECTS (≥1%) **Body as a Whole:** *Fever*, arthralgia. **CNS:** Pain,
dysesthesia. **CV:** Edema, hypertension. **GI:** Mouth discoloration, taste alteration. **Metabolic:** Increased amylase, increased lipase. **Skin:** *Rash, erythema, pruritus, edema.*

DRUG INTERACTIONS Do not administer within 24 h of beginning neoplastic treatment.

PHARMACOKINETICS Half-Life: 4.5 h (range 3.3–5.7 h).

NURSING IMPLICATIONS

Assessment & Drug Effects

- Monitor for manifestations of hypersensitivity (see Appendix C). If any
  occur, withhold drug and report promptly.

P

- Monitor for and report to prescriber mucocutaneous adverse effects, including rash, erythema, edema, pruritus, oral/perioral dysesthesia, and tongue discoloration or thickening.

Patient & Family Education

- Report promptly (any of the following): Skin rash or itching, unusual sensations in mouth, tongue discoloration or thickening, and alteration of taste.

PALONOSETRON

(pal-o-no′si-tron)

Aloxi

Classification(s): ANTIEMETIC, 5-HT₃ ANTAGONIST
Therapeutic: ANTIEMETIC
Prototype: Ondansetron
Pregnancy Category: B

USES Prevention of acute and delayed nausea and vomiting associated with highly emetogenic cancer chemotherapy.

INDICATION & DOSAGE

Prevention of Chemotherapy-Induced Nausea and Vomiting

Adult: 0.25 mg 30 min prior to chemotherapy

SOLUTION PREPARATION

No dilution is required. Administer as supplied.

STORAGE

Store at room temperature of 15°–30° C (59°–86° F). Protect from light.

ADMINISTRATION

Direct IV Injection: Give bolus dose over 30 sec. Flush line with NS before/after administration.

INCOMPATIBILITIES Data not available; do not mix with other drugs.

ACTION & *THERAPEUTIC EFFECT* Selectively blocks serotonin 5-HT₃ receptors found centrally in the chemoreceptor trigger zone (CTZ) of the hypothalamus, and peripherally at vagal nerve endings in the intestines. *Prevents acute chemotherapy-induced nausea and vomiting associated with initial and repeat courses of moderately or highly emetogenic chemotherapy.*

CONTRAINDICATIONS Hypersensitivity to palonosetron; lactation; children less than 18 y.
CAUTIOUS USE Dehydration; cardiac arrhythmias, QT prolongation; electrolyte imbalance; pregnancy (category B).

ADVERSE EFFECTS (≥1%) **CNS:** Headache, anxiety, dizziness. **GI:** Constipation, diarrhea, abdominal pain.

DRUG INTERACTIONS Can cause profound hypotension with **apomorphine.**

PHARMACOKINETICS Metabolism: In liver (CYP 2D6, 1A2, 3A4). **Elimination:** Primarily renal. **Half-Life:** 40 h.

NURSING IMPLICATIONS
Assessment & Drug Effects
- Monitor closely cardiac status especially in those taking diuretics or otherwise at risk for hypokalemia or hypomagnesemia, with congenital QT syndrome, or patients taking antiarrhythmic or other drugs that lead to QT prolongation.

Patient & Family Education
- Report promptly any of the following: Difficulty breathing, wheezing, or shortness of breath; palpitations or chest tightness; skin rash or itching; swelling of the face, tongue, throat, hands, or feet.

PAMIDRONATE DISODIUM ◎
(pa-mi'dro-nate)

Aredia

Classification(s): BISPHOSPHONATE (REGULATORY, BONE METABOLISM)
Therapeutic: BONE RESORPTION INHIBITOR; ANTIHYPERCALCEMIC
Pregnancy Category: D

P

USES Hypercalcemia of malignancy and Paget's disease, bone metastases in multiple myeloma.
UNLABELED USES Primary hyperparathyroidism, osteoporosis.

INDICATION & DOSAGE

Moderate Hypercalcemia of Malignancy (corrected calcium over 12–13.5 mg/dL)
Adult: 60–90 mg infused over 4–24 h, may repeat in 7 days

Severe Hypercalcemia of Malignancy (corrected calcium over 13.5 mg/dL)
Adult: 90 mg infused over 4–24 h, may repeat in 7 days

Paget's Disease
Adult: 30 mg once daily for 3 days (90 mg total)

Metastases in Multiple Myeloma
Adult: 90 mg once monthly

Renal Impairment Dosage Adjustment
May extend infusion time

PAMIDRONATE DISODIUM

SOLUTION PREPARATION
- *Vial Reconstitution:* Add 10 mL sterile water for injection to reconstitute the 30 or 90 mg vial to yield 3 or 9 mg/ mL, respectively. Allow to completely dissolve. **Must be** further diluted for infusion.
- *Further Dilution of Reconstituted Solution or Injection Concentrate:* Dilute required dose in D5W, NS, or 1/2NS as follows:
  - For hypercalcemia of malignancy, use 1000 mL
  - For Paget's disease and multiple myeloma, use 500 mL
  - For breast cancer bone metastases, use 250 mL

STORAGE
Refrigerate reconstituted pamidronate solution at 2°–8° C (36°–46° F). The IV solution may be stored at room temperature. Both are stable for 24 h.

ADMINISTRATION
- **IV Infusion:**
  - Hypercalcemia of Malignancy: infuse over 2–24 h
  - Paget's Disease and Multiple Myeloma: infuse over 4 h
  - Breast Cancer Bone Metastases: infuse over 2 h
- Use an infusion pump to regulate the infusion rate. Avoid rapid infusion, which may cause renal damage.

INCOMPATIBILITIES Solution/additive: CALCIUM-CONTAINING SOLUTIONS (including **lactated Ringer's**).

ACTION & *THERAPEUTIC EFFECT* A bone resorption inhibitor thought to reduce the flow of calcium from resorbing bone into the bloodstream. May also inhibit osteoclast activity, thus contributing to inhibition of bone resorption. Does not inhibit bone formation or mineralization. *Reduces bone turnover and, when used in combination with adequate hydration, it increases renal excretion of calcium and reduces serum calcium concentrations.*

CONTRAINDICATIONS Hypersensitivity to pamidronate; breast cancer; severe renal disease; hypercalcemia; hypercholesterolemia; polycythemia; prostatic cancer, pregnancy (category D). Safety and effectiveness in children are not established.
CAUTIOUS USE Heart failure; nephrosis or nephrotic syndrome, moderate renal disease, chronic kidney failure; hepatic disease, cholestasis; peripheral edema; prostate hypertrophy; lactation.

ADVERSE EFFECTS (≥1%) **Body as a Whole:** *Fever with or without rigors* generally occurs within 48 h and subsides within 48 h despite continued therapy; *thrombophlebitis at injection site;* general malaise lasting for several weeks; transient increase in bone pain. **Metabolic:** *Hypocalcemia.* **GI:** Nausea, abdominal pain, *epigastric discomfort.* **CV:** Hypertension. **Skin:** Rash.

DRUG INTERACTIONS Concurrent use of **foscarnet** may further decrease serum levels of ionized **calcium.**

PHARMACOKINETICS Absorption: 50% of dose is retained in body. **Onset:** 24–48 h. **Peak:** 6 days. **Duration:** 2 wk–3 mo. **Distribution:** Accumulates in bone; once deposited, remains bound until bone is remodeled. **Metabolism:** Not metabolized. **Elimination:** 50% excreted in urine unchanged. **Half-Life:** 28 h.

NURSING IMPLICATIONS

Assessment & Drug Effects

- Assess IV injection site for thrombophlebitis.
- Monitor vital signs. Be aware that drug fever, which may occur with pamidronate use, is self-limiting, usually subsiding in 48 h even with continued therapy.
- Lab tests: Baseline and periodic serum calcium and phosphate levels, CBC with differential, Hct & Hgb, and kidney function tests.
- Monitor for S&S of hypocalcemia, hypokalemia, hypomagnesemia, and hypophosphatemia.
- Monitor I&O and hydration status. Patient should be adequately hydrated, without fluid overload.
- Monitor for seizures especially in those with a preexisting seizure disorder.

Patient & Family Education

- Be aware that transient, self-limiting fever with/without chills may develop.
- Generalized malaise, which may last for several weeks following treatment, is an anticipated adverse effect.
- Report promptly tingling, numbness, and paresthesia. These are signs of hypocalcemia.

PANCURONIUM BROMIDE

(pan-kyoo-roe'nee-um)

Classification(s): SKELETAL MUSCLE RELAXANT, NONDEPOLARIZING
Therapeutic: SKELETAL MUSCLE RELAXANT
Prototype: Atracurium
Pregnancy Category: C

USES Adjunct to anesthesia to induce skeletal muscle relaxation, management of patients undergoing mechanical ventilation.

INDICATION & DOSAGE

Skeletal Muscle Relaxation

Adult/Child/Infant: 0.04–0.1 mg/kg initial dose, may give additional doses of 0.01 mg/kg at 30–60 min intervals
Neonate: 0.02 mg/kg test dose

Obesity

Dose based on IBW.

SOLUTION PREPARATION

May be given undiluted [direct IV] or diluted in D5W, NS, LR, D5NS, or D5/1/2NS.

Common adverse effects in *italic*, life-threatening effects <u>underlined</u>: generic names in **bold**; classifications in SMALL CAPS; ♣ Canadian drug name; ❷ Prototype drug

STORAGE

Refrigerate at 2°–8° C (36°–46° F). Do not freeze. Use IV solutions within 48 h.

ADMINISTRATION

- **Direct IV Injection:** Give bolus dose over 30–90 sec.
- Use a test dose of 0.02 mg/kg in neonates prior to IV injection.

INCOMPATIBILITIES Solution/additive: Furosemide. Y-site: Diazepam, thiopental.

ACTION & *THERAPEUTIC EFFECT* Synthetic curariform nondepolarizing neuromuscular blocking agent that produces little or no histamine release or ganglionic blockade; thus, it does not cause bronchospasm or hypotension. Produces skeletal muscle relaxation or paralysis by competing with acetylcholine at cholinergic receptor sites on skeletal muscle endplate, thus blocking nerve impulse transmission. *Induces skeletal muscle relaxation or paralysis.*

CONTRAINDICATIONS Hypersensitivity to pancuronium or bromides; tachycardia; pregnancy (category C).

CAUTIOUS USE Debilitated patients; dehydration; myasthenia gravis; neuromuscular disease; pulmonary, liver, or kidney disease; fluid or electrolyte imbalance; lactation.

ADVERSE EFFECTS (≥1%) **CV:** *Increased pulse rate and BP,* ventricular extrasystoles. **Skin:** Transient acneiform rash, burning sensation along course of vein. **Body as a Whole:** Salivation, skeletal muscle weakness, <u>respiratory depression</u>.

DIAGNOSTIC TEST INTERFERENCE Pancuronium may decrease *serum cholinesterase* concentrations.

DRUG INTERACTIONS GENERAL ANESTHETICS increase neuromuscular blocking and duration of action; AMINOGLYCOSIDES, **bacitracin, polymyxin B, clindamycin, lidocaine,** parenteral **magnesium, quinidine, quinine, trimethaphan, verapamil** increase neuromuscular blockade; DIURETICS may increase or decrease neuromuscular blockade; **lithium** prolongs duration of neuromuscular blockade; NARCOTIC ANALGESICS add to respiratory depression; **succinylcholine** increases onset and depth of neuromuscular blockade; **phenytoin** may cause resistance to or reversal of neuromuscular blockade.

PHARMACOKINETICS Onset: 30–45 sec. **Peak:** 2–3 min. **Duration:** 60 min. **Distribution:** Well distributed to tissues and extracellular fluids; crosses placenta in small amounts. **Metabolism:** Small amount metabolized in liver. **Elimination:** Primarily in urine. **Half-Life:** 2 h.

NURSING IMPLICATIONS

Assessment & Drug Effects

- Assess cardiovascular and respiratory status continuously.
- Observe patient closely for residual muscle weakness and signs of respiratory distress during recovery period. Monitor BP and vital signs. Peripheral nerve stimulator may be used to assess the effects of pancuronium and to monitor restoration of neuromuscular function.
- Note: Consciousness is not affected by pancuronium. Patient will be awake and alert but unable to speak.

Common adverse effects in *italic*, life-threatening effects <u>underlined</u>: generic names in **bold**; classifications in SMALL CAPS; ✦ Canadian drug name; ● Prototype drug

PANTOPRAZOLE SODIUM

(pan-to'pra-zole)

Protonix IV

Classification(s): PROTON PUMP INHIBITOR
Therapeutic: ANTIULCER
Prototype: Lansoprazole
Pregnancy Category: B

USES Short-term treatment of erosive esophagitis associated with gastroesophageal reflux disease (GERD), hypersecretory disease.
UNLABELED USES Peptic ulcer disease.

INDICATION & DOSAGE

Erosive Esophagitis
Adult: 40 mg daily × 7–10 days

Hypersecretory Disease
Adult: 80 mg q8–12h; adjust based on acid output

SOLUTION PREPARATION

- *Vial Reconstitution:* To each 40 mg vial add 10 mL NS to yield approximately 4 mg/mL. May be given as prepared over 2 minutes or further diluted for infusion over 15 minutes.
- *Further Dilution of Reconstituted Solution:* Add the 40 or 80 mg dose to 90 or 80 mL, respectively, of D5W, NS, or LR IV fluid. The resulting concentration will be 0.4 mg/mL or 0.8 mg/mL.

STORAGE

The reconstituted solution may be stored for up to 6 h at 15°–30° C (59°–86° F) before infusion or further dilution. The diluted 100 mL solution may be stored for up to 24 h at room temperature.

ADMINISTRATION

- **IV Infusion:** Infuse through a dedicated line or flushed IV line before/after each dose with D5W, NS, or LR. Rate of infusion depends on concentration:
  - Infuse the 4 mg/mL concentration over at least 2 min.
  - Infuse the 0.4 or 0.8 mg/mL concentration over 15 min.

INCOMPATIBILITIES Solution/additive: Solutions containing **zinc. Y-site: Acyclovir, dobutamine, esmolol, mannitol, midazolam,** MULTIVITAMINS, **octreotide, zinc.**

ACTION & *THERAPEUTIC EFFECT* Gastric acid pump inhibitor that belongs to a class of antisecretory compounds. Gastric acid secretion is decreased by inhibiting the H^+, K^+-ATPase enzyme system responsible for acid production. *Specifically, pantoprazole suppresses gastric acid secretion by inhibiting the acid (proton H^+) pump in the parietal cells.*

Common adverse effects in *italic*, life-threatening effects underlined: generic names in **bold**; classifications in SMALL CAPS; ♣ Canadian drug name; ☻ Prototype drug

519

CONTRAINDICATIONS Hypersensitivity to pantoprazole or other proton pump inhibitors (PPIs); lactation.
CAUTIOUS USE Mild to moderate hepatic insufficiency; severe hepatic insufficiency; cirrhosis; pregnancy (category B). Safety and effectiveness in children less than 18 y are not established.

ADVERSE EFFECTS (≥1%) **GI:** Diarrhea, flatulence, abdominal pain. **CNS:** Headache, insomnia. **Skin:** Rash.

DRUG INTERACTIONS Increases INR with **warfarin,** reduces efficacy of **ritonavir** and **atazanavir.**

PHARMACOKINETICS Peak: 2.4 h. **Distribution:** 98% protein bound. **Metabolism:** In liver by CYP2C19. **Elimination:** 71% in urine, 18% in feces. **Half-Life:** 1 h.

NURSING IMPLICATIONS

Assessment & Drug Effects
- Monitor for and report promptly S&S of angioedema or a severe skin reaction.
- Lab tests: Urea breath test 4–6 wk after completion of therapy.
- Concurrent drugs: Monitor closely PT/INR with concurrent warfarin.

Patient & Family Education
- Report promptly if any of the following occur: Peeling, blistering, or loosening of skin; skin rash, hives, or itching; swelling of the face, tongue, or lips; difficulty breathing or swallowing.

P

PAPAVERINE HYDROCHLORIDE
(pa-pav'er-een)

Classification(s): VASODILATOR, NONNITRATE
Therapeutic: VASODILATOR
Prototype: Hydralazine
Pregnancy Category: C

USES Primarily for relief of cerebral and peripheral ischemia associated with arterial spasm and MI complicated by arrhythmias.

INDICATION & DOSAGE

Cerebral and Peripheral Ischemia
Adult: 30–120 mg q3h as needed

SOLUTION PREPARATION
May be given direct IV undiluted or diluted in an equal volume of sterile water for injection. DO NOT dilute with LR, as a precipitate will form.

STORAGE
Store undiluted at 15°–30° C (59°–86° F) and protect from light.

ADMINISTRATION
Direct IV Injection: Give slowly over 1–2 min. AVOID rapid injection.

INCOMPATIBILITIES Solution/additive: Aminophylline, heparin, lactated Ringer's.

ACTION & *THERAPEUTIC EFFECT* Exerts nonspecific direct spasmolytic effect on smooth muscles unrelated to innervation. Action is especially pronounced on coronary, cerebral, pulmonary, and peripheral arteries when spasm is present. Acts directly on myocardium, depresses conduction and irritability, and prolongs refractory period. *Relaxes smooth muscle of the heart and promotes relaxation of the vascular smooth muscles.*

CONTRAINDICATIONS Complete AV block; Parkinson's disease treated with levodopa; pregnancy (category C). Safe use in children not established.

CAUTIOUS USE Glaucoma; myocardial depression, QT prolongation, angina pectoris; recent stroke; lactation.

ADVERSE EFFECTS (≥1%) **Body as a Whole:** General discomfort, facial flushing, sweating, weakness, coma. **CNS:** Dizziness, drowsiness, headache, sedation. **CV:** Slight rise in BP, paroxysmal tachycardia, transient ventricular ectopic rhythms, AV block, arrhythmias. **GI:** Nausea, anorexia, constipation, diarrhea, abdominal distress, dry mouth and throat, hepatotoxicity (jaundice, eosinophilia, abnormal liver function tests); with rapid IV administration, respiratory depression, fatal apnea. **Skin:** Pruritus, skin rash. **Special Senses:** Diplopia, nystagmus. **Urogenital:** Priapism.

DRUG INTERACTIONS May decrease **levodopa** effectiveness; **morphine** may antagonize smooth muscle relaxation effect of papaverine.

PHARMACOKINETICS Peak: 1–2 h. **Metabolism:** In liver. **Elimination:** In urine chiefly as metabolites. **Half-Life:** 90 min.

NURSING IMPLICATIONS

Assessment & Drug Effects
- Monitor pulse, respiration, and BP. If significant changes are noted, withhold medication and report promptly to prescriber.
- Lab tests: Periodic LFTs. Hepatotoxicity (thought to be a hypersensitivity reaction) is reversible with prompt drug withdrawal.

Patient & Family Education
- Notify prescriber if any adverse effect persists or if GI symptoms, jaundice, or skin rash appear. Liver function tests may be indicated.
- Do not drive or engage in potentially hazardous activities until response to drug is known. Alcohol may increase drowsiness and dizziness.

PARICALCITOL

(par-i-cal′ci-tol)

Zemplar

Classification(s): VITAMIN D ANALOG

Therapeutic: ANTIHYPERPARATHYROID AGENT

Prototype: Calcitriol

Pregnancy Category: C

USES Prevention and treatment of secondary hyperparathyroidism associated with chronic renal failure (CRF).

INDICATION & DOSAGE

CRF-Associated Secondary Hyperparathyroidism

Adult: 0.04 mcg/kg–0.1 mcg/kg (max: 0.24 mcg/kg), no more than every other day during dialysis; adjust based on iPTH

Child: 0.04–0.08 mcg/kg 3 times/wk during dialysis, dose based on iPTH

SOLUTION PREPARATION

No dilution is required. Administer as supplied.

STORAGE

Store at 25° C (77° F). Discard unused portion of a single-dose vial.

ADMINISTRATION

Direct IV Injection: Give bolus dose anytime during dialysis.

INCOMPATIBILITIES Data not available; do not mix with other drugs.

ACTION & *THERAPEUTIC EFFECT* Synthetic vitamin D analog that reduces parathyroid hormone (PTH) activity levels in chronic renal failure (CRF) patients. Lowers serum levels of calcium; serum calcium concentration multiplied by serum phosphate concentration cross product value may increase. In addition, it decreases the parathyroid hormone as well as bone resorption in some patients. *Effectiveness indicated by iPTH levels less than 1.5–3 times the nonuremic upper limit of normal.*

CONTRAINDICATIONS Hypersensitivity to paricalcitol; hypercalcemia; evidence of vitamin D toxicity; concurrent administration of phosphate preparations and vitamin D; pregnancy (category C); children less than 5 y.

CAUTIOUS USE Severe liver disease; concurrent administration of digitalis; abnormally low levels of PTH; lactation.

ADVERSE EFFECTS (≥1%) **Body as a Whole:** Chills, feeling unwell, fever, flu-like symptoms, sepsis, edema. **CNS:** Lightheadedness. **CV:** Palpitations. **GI:** Dry mouth, <u>GI bleeding</u>, *nausea,* vomiting. **Respiratory:** Pneumonia. **Metabolic:** Hypercalcemia.

DRUG INTERACTIONS Hypercalcemia may increase risk of **digoxin** toxicity; may increase **magnesium** absorption and toxicity in renal failure.

PHARMACOKINETICS Distribution: More than 99% protein bound. **Metabolism:** Via CYP 3A4. **Elimination:** In feces (74%). **Half-Life:** 15 h.

NURSING IMPLICATIONS

Assessment & Drug Effects

- Monitor for S&S of hypercalcemia (see Appendix C).
- Lab tests: Serum calcium and phosphate 2 times a wk during initiation of therapy, then monthly; serum PTH q3mo; periodic serum magnesium, alkaline phosphatase, 24-urinary calcium and phosphate. Increase frequency of lab tests during dosage adjustments.
- Withhold drug and promptly report if hypercalcemia occurs.
- Concurrent drugs: Monitor for digoxin toxicity if serum calcium level is elevated.

Patient & Family Education

- Report promptly: Weakness, anorexia, nausea, vomiting, abdominal cramps, diarrhea, muscle or bone pain, or excessive thirst.
- Adhere strictly to dietary regimen of calcium supplementation and phosphorus restriction to ensure successful therapy.
- Avoid excessive use of aluminum-containing compounds such as antacids/vitamins.

PEMETREXED

(pe-me-trex′ed)

Alimta

Classification(s): ANTINEOPLASTIC AGENT; ANTIMETABOLITE, ANTIFOLATE
Therapeutic: ANTINEOPLASTIC
Prototype: Methotrexate
Pregnancy Category: D

USES Combination treatment of malignant pleural mesothelioma that is unresectable or in patients who are not surgery candidates; treatment of locally advanced or metastatic non–small-cell lung cancer (NSCLC).
UNLABELED USES Solid tumors, including bladder, breast, colorectal, gastric, head and neck, pancreatic, and renal cell cancers.

INDICATION & DOSAGE

Malignant Mesothelioma, Non–Small-Cell Lung Cancer

Adult: 500 mg/m^2 on day 1 of each 21-day cycle

Toxicity Adjustment

Toxicity	Dosage Adjustment
Platelets less than 50,000/mm^3	Delay tx; then reduce dose by 50%

Common adverse effects in *italic*, life-threatening effects underlined: generic names in **bold**; classifications in SMALL CAPS; ♣ Canadian drug name; ⊘ Prototype drug

523

Toxicity	Dosage Adjustment
ANC less than 500/mm³ and platelets over 50,000/mm³	Delay tx; then reduce dose by 75%
Grade 3 or 4 toxicity	Delay tx; then reduce dose by 75%
Grade 3 or 4 mucositis	Delay tx; then reduce dose 50%
Grade 3 or 4 neurotoxicity	Discontinue therapy

Renal Impairment Dosage Adjustment
Not recommended if CrCl less than 45 mL/min

SOLUTION PREPARATION
- *Vial Reconstitution:* Add 20 mL of preservative-free NS to each 500-mg vial to yield 25 mg/mL. Do not use any other diluent. Swirl gently to dissolve. **Must be** further diluted for infusion.
- *Further Dilution of Reconstituted Solution:* Withdraw the required dose and add to 100 mL of preservative-free NS IV solution. Discard any unused portion.

STORAGE
Store unopened single-use vials at room temperature between 15°–30° C (59°–86° F). The reconstituted drug is stable for up to 24 h at 2°–8° C (36°–46° F) or at 25° C (77° F).

ADMINISTRATION
- **IV Infusion:** Do NOT give a bolus dose. Infuse over 10 min.
- Pre-/posttreatment with folic acid, vitamin B_{12}, and dexamethasone are needed to reduce hematologic and gastrointestinal toxicity, and the possibility of severe cutaneous reactions from pemetrexed.

INCOMPATIBILITIES   Solution/additive: Solutions containing **calcium, lactated Ringer's. Y-site: Amphotericin B, calcium, cefazolin, cefotaxime, cefotetan, cefoxitin, ceftazidime, chlorpromazine, ciprofloxacin, dobutamine, doxorubicin, doxycycline, droperidol, gemcitabine, gentamicin, irinotecan, metronidazole, minocycline, mitoxantrone, nalbuphine, ondansetron, prochlorperazine, tobramycin, topotecan.**

ACTION & *THERAPEUTIC EFFECT* Suppresses tumor growth by inhibiting both DNA synthesis and folate metabolism at multiple target enzymes. *Appears to arrest the cell cycle of rapidly dividing cells, thus inhibiting tumor growth.*

CONTRAINDICATIONS Mannitol hypersensitivity; if creatinine clearance is less than 45 mL/min, renal failure, moderate or severe renal impairment; active infection; vaccines; pregnancy (category D), lactation; children less than 18 y.
CAUTIOUS USE Anemia, thrombocytopenia, neutropenia, dental disease; older adults; hepatic disease, hypoalbuminemia, hypovolemia, dehydration, ascites, pleural effusion.

P

ADVERSE EFFECTS (≥1%) **Body as a Whole:** *Fatigue, fever,* hypersensitivity reaction, edema, myalgia, arthralgia. **CNS:** Neuropathy, *mood alteration, depression.* **CV:** Chest pain, thromboembolism. **GI:** *Nausea, vomiting, constipation, anorexia, stomatitis, diarrhea,* dehydration, dysphagia, esophagitis, odynophagia, increased LFTs. **Hematologic:** *Neutropenia, leukopenia, anemia, thrombocytopenia.* **Respiratory:** *Dyspnea.* **Skin:** *Rash, desquamation,* alopecia. **Urogenital:** *Increases serum creatinine,* renal failure.

DRUG INTERACTIONS Increased risk of renal toxicity with other nephrotoxic drugs **(acyclovir, adefovir, amphotericin B,** AMINOGLYCOSIDES, **carboplatin, cidofovir, cisplatin, cyclosporine, foscarnet, ganciclovir, sirolimus, tacrolimus, vancomycin);** NSAIDS may increase risk of renal toxicity in patients with preexisting renal insufficiency; may cause additive risk of bleeding with ANTICOAGULANTS, PLATELET INHIBITORS, **aspirin,** THROMBOLYTIC AGENTS.

PHARMACOKINETICS Metabolism: Not extensively. **Elimination:** Primarily in urine. **Half-Life:** 3.5 h.

NURSING IMPLICATIONS

Assessment & Drug Effects

- Withhold drug and notify prescriber if the absolute neutrophil count (ANC) is less than 1500 cells/mm^3 or the platelet count is less than 100,000 cells/mm^3, or if the CrCl is less than 45 mL/min.
- Lab tests: Baseline and periodic CBC with differential (monitor for nadir and recovery before each dose on day 8 and 15, respectively, of each cycle); periodic LFTs, serum creatinine, and BUN.
- Report promptly S&S of neuropathy (paresthesia) or thromboembolism.

Patient & Family Education

- Report promptly: Symptoms of anemia (e.g., chest pain, unusual weakness or tiredness, fainting spells, lightheadedness, shortness of breath); symptoms of poor blood clotting (e.g., bruising; red spots on skin; black, tarry stools; blood in urine); symptoms of infection (e.g., fever or chills, cough, sore throat, pain or difficulty passing urine); symptoms of liver problems (e.g., yellowing of skin).
- Do not take nonsteroidal antiinflammatory drugs (NSAIDs) without first consulting the prescriber.

PENICILLIN G POTASSIUM Ⓟ

(pen-i-sill'in)

Megacillin ♣

PENICILLIN G SODIUM

Classification(s): ANTIBIOTIC; PENICILLIN, NATURAL
Therapeutic: ANTIBACTERIAL
Pregnancy Category: B

Common adverse effects in *italic,* life-threatening effects <u>underlined</u>: generic names in **bold**; classifications in SMALL CAPS; ♣ Canadian drug name; Ⓟ Prototype drug

525

USES Moderate to severe systemic infections caused by penicillin-sensitive microorganisms: certain staphylococcal infections; streptococcal infections. Also used as prophylaxis in patients with rheumatic or congenital heart disease.

INDICATION & DOSAGE

Moderate to Severe Infections
Adult/Adolescent: 1.2–24 million units divided q4h
Child: 25,000–400,000 units/kg divided q4–6h
Neonate:

Age	Weight	Dose	Interval
Over 7 days		75,000–200,000 units/ kg/day divided	q6–8h
Up to 7 days	Over 2000 g	75,000 units/kg/day	q8h
Up to 7 days	Up to 2000 g	50,000 units/kg/day	q12h

Renal Impairment Dosage Adjustment
CrCl 10–50 mL/min: Extend interval to q8–12h or reduce dose by 50%;
CrCl less than 10 mL/min: Extend interval to q12–18h or reduce dose by 50% and give q8–12h

SOLUTION PREPARATION
- Available premixed or in dry-powder vials.
- *Vial Reconstitution:* Loosen powder by shaking vial. Add the amount of sterile water for injection or NS specified on the vial. Shake well to dissolve. **Must be** further diluted for infusion.
- *Further Dilution of Reconstituted Solution:* Add required dose to 100–1000 mL of D5W or NS.

STORAGE
- Store dry powder at 15°–30° C (59°–86° F).
- After reconstitution, store solutions for 1 wk under refrigeration.
- Intravenous infusion solutions are stable at 15°–30° C (59°–86° F) for at least 24 h.

ADMINISTRATION
- **Intermittent Infusion:** Infuse over at least 1 h.
- **Continuous Infusion:** Infuse at a rate required to infuse the daily dose in 24 h.
- Note: High doses should be administered slowly to avoid electrolyte imbalance from potassium or sodium content.

INCOMPATIBILITIES Solution/additive: Dextran 40, fat emulsion, aminophylline, amphotericin B, chlorpromazine, dopamine, hydroxyzine, metaraminol, metoclopramide, pentobarbital, prochlorperazine, promazine, sodium bicarbonate, tetracyclines, thiopental.

ACTION & *THERAPEUTIC EFFECT* Acid-labile, penicillinase-sensitive, natural penicillin. Acts by interfering with synthesis of mucopeptides essential to formation and integrity of bacterial cell wall. Action is inhibited by penicillinase. *Antimicrobial spectrum is relatively narrow compared to that of the semisynthetic penicillins. Highly active against gram-positive cocci (e.g., non–penicillinase-producing* Staphylococcus, Streptococcus, *and gram-negative cocci. Also effective against gram-positive bacilli and gram-negative bacilli as well as some strains of* Salmonella *and* Shigella *and spirochetes.*

CONTRAINDICATIONS Hypersensitivity to any of the penicillins or cephalosporins; nausea, vomiting, hypermotility, gastric dilatation; cardiospasm. Use of penicillin G sodium in patients on sodium restriction.

CAUTIOUS USE History of or suspected allergy (asthma, eczema, hay fever, hives); history of allergy to cephalosporins; GI disorders; kidney or liver dysfunction; myasthenia gravis; epilepsy; pregnancy (category B), neonates, young infants. Use during lactation may lead to sensitization of infants.

ADVERSE EFFECTS (≥1%) **Body as a Whole:** Coughing, sneezing, feeling of uneasiness; systemic anaphylaxis, fever, widespread increase in capillary permeability and vasodilation with resulting edema (mouth, tongue, pharynx, larynx), laryngospasm, malaise, serum sickness (fever, malaise, pruritus, urticaria, lymphadenopathy, arthralgia, angioedema of face and extremities, neuritis prostration, eosinophilia), SLE-like syndrome, injection site reactions (pain, inflammation, abscess, phlebitis); superinfections (especially with *Candida* and gram-negative bacteria), neuromuscular irritability (twitching, lethargy, confusion, stupor, hyperreflexia, multifocal myoclonus, localized or generalized seizures, coma). **CV:** Hypotension, circulatory collapse, cardiac arrhythmias, cardiac arrest. **GI:** Vomiting, diarrhea, severe abdominal cramps, nausea, epigastric distress, diarrhea, flatulence, dark discoloration of tongue, sore mouth or tongue. **Urogenital:** Interstitial nephritis, Loeffler's syndrome, vasculitis. **Hematologic:** Hemolytic anemia, thrombocytopenia. **Metabolic:** Hyperkalemia (penicillin G potassium); hypokalemia, alkalosis, hypernatremia, CHF (penicillin G sodium). **Respiratory:** Bronchospasm, asthma. **Skin:** Itchy palms or axilla, pruritus, *urticaria,* flushed skin, *delayed skin rashes* ranging from urticaria to exfoliative dermatitis, Stevens-Johnson syndrome, fixed-drug eruptions, contact dermatitis.

DIAGNOSTIC TEST INTERFERENCE *Blood grouping* and *compatibility tests:* Possible interference associated with penicillin doses greater than 20 million units daily. *Urine glucose:* Massive doses of penicillin may cause false-positive test results with ***Benedict's solution*** and possibly ***Clinitest*** but not with ***glucose oxidase methods*** (e.g., ***Clinistix, Diastix, Tes-Tape***). *Urine protein:* Massive doses of penicillin can produce false-positive results when turbidity measures are used (e.g., ***acetic acid*** and ***heat, sulfo-salicylic acid***); ***Ames reagent*** reportedly not affected. *Urinary PSP excretion tests:* False decrease in urinary excretion of PSP. *Urinary steroids:* Large doses of penicillin may interfere with accurate measurement of ***urinary 17-OHCS*** (***Glenn-Nelson technique*** not affected).

DRUG INTERACTIONS Probenecid decreases renal elimination; penicillin G may decrease efficacy of ORAL CONTRACEPTIVES; **colestipol** decreases

Common adverse effects in *italic*, life-threatening effects underlined: generic names in **bold**; classifications in SMALL CAPS; ♣ Canadian drug name; ❿ Prototype drug

527

penicillin absorption; POTASSIUM-SPARING DIURETICS may cause hyperkalemia with penicillin G potassium.

PHARMACOKINETICS Distribution: Widely distributed; good CSF concentrations with inflamed meninges; crosses placenta; distributed in breast milk. **Metabolism:** 16–30% metabolized. **Elimination:** 60% excreted in urine within 6 h. **Half-Life:** 0.4–0.9 h.

NURSING IMPLICATIONS

Assessment & Drug Effects

- Prior to initiating therapy: Baseline C&S tests (start drug pending results); determine previous hypersensitivity reactions to penicillins, cephalosporins, and other allergens.
- Observe closely for at least 30 min following administration. Rapid appearance of a red flare or wheal at the IV injection site is a possible sign of sensitivity. Also suspect an allergic reaction if patient becomes irritable, has nausea and vomiting, breathing difficulty, or sudden fever. Report immediately.
- Reactions to penicillin may be rapid in onset or may not appear for days or weeks. Reactions are unpredictable and have occurred in those with a negative history of penicillin allergy and also in those with no known prior contact with penicillin.
- Skin rash is the most common type of allergic reaction and should be reported promptly.
- Lab tests: Periodic renal function tests, LFTs, serum electrolytes, CBC with platelet count during high-dose therapy.
- Be alert for neuromuscular irritability in patients receiving in excess of 20 million units/day who have renal insufficiency, hyponatremia, or underlying CNS disease, notably myasthenia gravis or epilepsy. Seizure precautions are indicated. Symptoms usually begin with twitching, especially of face and extremities.
- Monitor I&O, particularly in patients receiving high doses. Report oliguria, hematuria, and changes in I&O ratio. Maintain adequate fluid intake, as dehydration increases the concentration of drug in kidneys and can cause renal irritation and damage.
- Observe closely for signs of toxicity in neonates, young infants, the older adult, and patients with impaired kidney function receiving high-doses, as renal excretion of penicillin is significantly delayed.
- Observe those on high-dose therapy closely for evidence of bleeding, as high doses interfere with platelet aggregation.

Patient & Family Education

- Understand that hypersensitivity reactions may be delayed. Report skin rashes, itching, fever, malaise, and other signs of a delayed allergic reaction.
- Report S&S of superinfection (see Appendix C).

PENTAMIDINE ISOETHIONATE

(pen-tam′i-deen)

Pentacarinat ✦, Pentam 300
Classification(s): ANTIPROTOZOAL
Therapeutic: ANTIPROTOZOAL
Pregnancy Category: C

USES *Pneumocystis jiroveci* (formerly *P. carinii*) pneumonia (PJP) treatment. **UNLABELED USES** African trypanosomiasis and visceral leishmaniasis. (Drug supplied for the latter uses is through the Centers for Disease Control and Prevention, Atlanta, GA.)

INDICATION & DOSAGE

Treatment of *Pneumocystis jiroveci* (formerly *P. carinii*) Pneumonia

Adult/Child/Infant (over 4 mo): 4 mg/kg/day for 14–21 days; infuse IV over 60 min

SOLUTION PREPARATION

- *Vial Reconstitution or Dilution of Concentrate:* Add 3–5 mL sterile water for injection or D5W. **Must be** further diluted for infusion.
- *Further Dilution:* Add required dose to 50–250 mL of D5W.

STORAGE

IV solutions are stable at room temperature for up to 24 h. Protect solution from light.

ADMINISTRATION

IV Infusion: Infuse over 60 min.

P

INCOMPATIBILITIES Y-site: Aldesleukin, CEPHALOSPORINS, **fluconazole, foscarnet, lansoprazole, linezolid.**

ACTION & *THERAPEUTIC EFFECT* Aromatic diamide antiprotozoal drug. Appears to block reproduction of organisms by interfering with nucleotide (DNA, RNA), phospholipid, and protein synthesis. *Effective against the protozoan parasite,* Pneumocystis jiroveci *(formerly* P. carinii*) found in immunocompromised (e.g., AIDS) patients.*

CONTRAINDICATIONS QT prolongation, history of torsades de pointes; pregnancy (category C), lactation.
CAUTIOUS USE Hypertension, hypotension; hyperglycemia, hypoglycemia; pancreatitis; hypocalcemia; blood dyscrasias; liver or kidney dysfunction; diabetes mellitus; asthma; cardiac arrhythmias; children.

ADVERSE EFFECTS (≥1%) **CNS:** Confusion, hallucinations, neuralgia, dizziness, sweating. **CV:** Sudden, severe hypotension, cardiac arrhythmias, ventricular tachycardia, phlebitis. **GI:** Anorexia, nausea, vomiting, pancreatitis, unpleasant taste. **Urogenital:** Acute kidney failure. **Hematologic:** Leukopenia, thrombocytopenia, anemia. **Metabolic:** Hypoglycemia, hypocalcemia, *hyperkalemia.* **Respiratory:** *Cough, bronchospasm,* laryngitis, shortness of breath, chest pain, pneumothorax. **Skin:** Stevens-Johnson syndrome, facial flush, *local reactions at injection site.*

DRUG INTERACTIONS AMINOGLYCOSIDES, **amphotericin B, cidofovir, cisplatin,** cyclosporine, **ganciclovir, vancomycin,** other nephrotoxic drugs increase risk of nephrotoxicity.

PHARMACOKINETICS Distribution: Leaves bloodstream rapidly to bind extensively to body tissues. **Elimination:** 50–66% in urine within 6 h; small amounts found in urine for as long as 6–8 wk. **Half-Life:** 6.5–13.2 h.

NURSING IMPLICATIONS

Assessment & Drug Effects

- Place patient in supine position while receiving the drug. Sudden severe hypotension may develop after a single dose. Monitor BP and HR continuously during the infusion, every half hour for 2 h thereafter, and then every 4 h until BP stabilizes.
- Lab tests: Periodic serum electrolytes, renal function, CBC with differential, platelet count, and blood glucose.
- Monitor I&O ratio and pattern. Be alert and report promptly S&S of impending kidney dysfunction (e.g., changed I&O ratio, oliguria, edema).
- Characteristics of pneumonia in the immunocompromised patient include constant fever, scanty (if any) sputum, dyspnea, tachypnea, and cyanosis.
- Monitor temperature changes and institute measures to lower the temperature as indicated. Fever is a constant symptom in *P. jiroveci* (formerly *P. carinii*) pneumonia, but may be rapidly elevated [as high as 40° C (104° F)] shortly after drug infusion.

Patient & Family Education

- Report promptly increasing respiratory difficulty.
- Monitor blood glucose for loss of glycemic control if diabetic.
- Report any unusual bruising or bleeding. Avoid using aspirin or other NSAIDs.
- Increase fluid intake (if not contraindicated) to 2–3 quarts (liters) per day.

PENTAZOCINE HYDROCHLORIDE ⊙

(pen-taz′oh-seen)

Talwin

Classification(s): ANALGESIC, NARCOTIC (OPIATE) AGONIST-ANTAGONIST

Therapeutic: NARCOTIC ANALGESIC

Pregnancy Category: C   **Controlled Substance:** Schedule IV

USES Relief of moderate to severe pain; also used for preoperative analgesia or sedation, and as supplement to surgical anesthesia.

INDICATION & DOSAGE

Moderate to Severe Pain (Excluding Patients in Labor)

Adult/Adolescent: 30 mg q3–4h (max: 360 mg/days)

Renal Impairment Dosage Adjustment

CrCl 10–50 mL/min: Give 75% of dose, *less than 10 mL/min:* Give 50% of dose

SOLUTION PREPARATION
May be given direct IV undiluted or diluted in 1 mL sterile water for injection for each 5 mg.

STORAGE
Store at 15°–30° C (59°–85° F).

ADMINISTRATION
Direct IV Injection: Give slowly at a rate of 5 mg over 60 sec. AVOID rapid injection.

INCOMPATIBILITIES Solution/additive: **Aminophylline,** BARBITURATES, **sodium bicarbonate. Y-site: Nafcillin.**

ACTION & *THERAPEUTIC EFFECT* Synthetic analgesic with analgesic potency approximately one third that of morphine. Opiates exert their analgesic effects by stimulating specific opiate receptors that produces analgesia, respiratory depression, and euphoria as well as physical dependence. *Effective for moderate to severe pain relief. Acts as weak narcotic antagonist and has sedative properties.*

CONTRAINDICATIONS Hypersensitivity to sulfite; head injury, increased intracranial pressure; emotionally unstable patients, or history of drug abuse, pregnancy (other than labor) (category C), lactation. Safe use in children less than 12 y is not established.
CAUTIOUS USE Impaired kidney or liver function; cardiac disease; COPD, asthma, respiratory depression; biliary surgery; GI obstruction; patients with MI who have nausea and vomiting.

ADVERSE EFFECTS (≥1%) **Body as a Whole:** Flushing, allergic reactions, <u>shock</u>. **CNS:** *Drowsiness,* sweating, *dizziness, light-headedness, euphoria,* psychotomimetic effects, confusion, anxiety, hallucinations, disturbed dreams, bizarre thoughts, euphoria, and other mood alterations. **CV:** Hypertension, palpitation, tachycardia. **GI:** *Nausea, vomiting,* constipation, dry mouth, alterations of taste. **Urogenital:** Urinary retention. **Respiratory:** <u>Respiratory depression</u>. **Skin:** Injection-site reactions (induration, nodule formation, sloughing, sclerosis, cutaneous depression), rash, pruritus. **Special Senses:** Visual disturbances.

DRUG INTERACTIONS CNS DEPRESSANTS add to CNS depression; NARCOTIC ANALGESICS may precipitate narcotic withdrawal syndrome.

PHARMACOKINETICS **Onset:** 2–3 min. **Peak:** 15 min. **Duration:** 1 h. **Distribution:** Crosses placenta. **Metabolism:** Extensively in liver. **Elimination:** In urine; small amount in feces. **Half-Life:** 2–3 h.

Common adverse effects in *italic,* life-threatening effects <u>underlined</u>: generic names in **bold**; classifications in SMALL CAPS; ♣ Canadian drug name; ◑ Prototype drug

531

NURSING IMPLICATIONS

Assessment & Drug Effects

- Monitor vital signs and assess for respiratory depression. Keep supine to minimize adverse effects.
- Monitor for drug-induced CNS depression.
- Be aware that pentazocine may produce acute withdrawal symptoms in some patients who have been receiving opioids on a regular basis.
- Monitor I&O, as drug may cause urinary retention.

Patient & Family Education

- Use caution with ambulation to reduce risk of falling.
- Avoid driving and other potentially hazardous activities until response to drug is known.

PENTOBARBITAL SODIUM

(pen-toe-bar'bi-tal)

Nembutal Sodium, Novopentobarb ◆

Classification(s): SEDATIVE-HYPNOTIC; ANTICONVULSANT, BARBITURATE
Therapeutic: SEDATIVE-HYPNOTIC; ANTICONVULSANT
Pregnancy Category: D   **Controlled Substance:** Schedule II

USES Sedative for preanesthetic medication, induction of general anesthesia, adjunct in manipulative or diagnostic procedures, and emergency control of acute convulsions.

INDICATION & DOSAGE

Sedation/Status Epilepticus

Adult/Adolescent/Child: 10 mg/kg then 0.5–1 mg/kg, adjust for lowest effective dose

SOLUTION PREPARATION

May be given direct IV undiluted or diluted (preferred) in sterile water, D5W, NS, or other compatible IV solutions for infusion. Do not use cloudy solution.

STORAGE

Store at 15°–30° C (59°–86° F) in tightly closed container.

ADMINISTRATION

- Ensure patency prior to injection, as extravasation may cause tissue sloughing.
- **Direct IV Injection:** Give slowly. Do not exceed rate of 50 mg/min.
- Monitor IV injection site closely.
- Do NOT give within 14 days of starting/stopping a MAO inhibitor.

Common adverse effects in *italic*, life-threatening effects <u>underlined</u>: generic names in **bold**; classifications in SMALL CAPS; ◆ Canadian drug name; ⊕ Prototype drug

INCOMPATIBILITIES Solution/additive: Chlorpheniramine, chlorpromazine, cimetidine, codeine, dimenhydrinate, diphenhydramine, droperidol, ephedrine, fentanyl, glycopyrrolate, hydrocortisone, hydroxyzine, inulin, levorphanol, meperidine, methadone, midazolam, morphine, nalbuphine, norepinephrine, penicillin G, pentazocine, perphenazine, phenytoin, promazine, prochlorperazine, promethazine, ranitidine, sodium bicarbonate, streptomycin, succinylcholine, triflupromazine, vancomycin. Y-site: Amphotericin B cholesteryl complex, fenoldopam, lansoprazole, TPN.

ACTION & *THERAPEUTIC EFFECT* Short-acting barbiturate with anticonvulsant properties. Initially, barbiturates suppress REM sleep, but with chronic therapy REM sleep returns to normal. *Effective as a sedative, hypnotic, and anticonvulsant. CNS depression may range from mild sedation to coma, depending on dosage, degree of nervous system excitability, and drug tolerance.*

CONTRAINDICATIONS History of sensitivity to barbiturates; parturition, fetal immaturity; uncontrolled pain; ethanol intoxication; hepatic encephalopathy; porphyria; pregnancy (category D), lactation.

CAUTIOUS USE COPD, sleep apnea; heart failure; mental status changes, suicidality, major depression; neonates; renal impairment, renal failure.

ADVERSE EFFECTS (≥1%) **Body as a Whole:** Drowsiness, lethargy, hangover, paradoxical excitement in the older adult patient. **CV:** Hypotension with rapid IV. **Respiratory:** With rapid IV (<u>respiratory depression, laryngospasm</u>, bronchospasm, <u>apnea</u>).

DRUG INTERACTIONS Phenmetrazine antagonizes effects of pentobarbital; CNS DEPRESSANTS, **alcohol,** SEDATIVES add to CNS depression; MAO INHIBITORS cause excessive CNS depression; **methoxyflurane** creates risk of nephrotoxicity, may decrease effect of warfarin.

PHARMACOKINETICS Onset: 1 min. **Duration:** 15 min. **Distribution:** Crosses placenta. **Metabolism:** In liver. **Elimination:** In urine. **Half-Life:** 4–50 h.

NURSING IMPLICATIONS

Assessment & Drug Effects

- Monitor BP, pulse, and respiration q3–5min during administration. Observe patient closely; maintain airway. Have equipment for artificial respiration immediately available.
- Monitor for hypersensitivity reactions (see Appendix C) especially with a history of asthma or angioedema.
- Monitor for adverse CNS effects, including exacerbation of depression and suicide ideation.
- Monitor those in acute pain, children, the elderly, and debilitated patients for paradoxical excitement and restlessness.
- Lab tests: Periodic pentobarbital levels. Note: Plasma levels greater than 30 mcg/mL may be toxic and 65 mcg/mL and above may be lethal.
- Concurrent drugs: Monitor PT/INR frequently to ensure therapeutic range.

Common adverse effects in *italic*, life-threatening effects <u>underlined</u>: generic names in **bold**; classifications in SMALL CAPS; ♣ Canadian drug name; ⊚ Prototype drug

533

Patient & Family Education

- Exercise caution when driving or operating machinery until reaction to drug is known.
- Avoid alcohol and other CNS depressants for 24 h after receiving this drug.
- Women using oral contraceptives should use an additional, alternative form of contraception.

PHENOBARBITAL SODIUM 🅟

(fee-noe-bar'bi-tal)

Luminal Sodium

Classification(s): ANTICONVULSANT; SEDATIVE-HYPNOTIC; BARBITURATE

Therapeutic: ANTICONVULSANT; SEDATIVE-HYPNOTIC

Pregnancy Category: D   **Controlled Substance:** Schedule IV

USES Seizure disorders, status epilepticus, eclampsia, febrile convulsions in young children. Also used as a sedative in anxiety or tension states and in pediatrics as preoperative and postoperative sedation.

UNLABELED USES Treatment and prevention of hyperbilirubinemia in neonates and in the management of chronic cholestasis; benzodiazepine withdrawal.

INDICATION & DOSAGE

Anticonvulsant

Adult/Adolescent: 1–3 mg/kg/day in divided doses
Child (5–12 y): 3–6 mg/kg/day in divided doses
Child (1–5 y): 6–8 mg/kg/day in divided doses
Infant: 5–6 mg/kg/day in divided doses
Neonates: 3–4 mg/kg/day

Status Epilepticus

Adult/Adolescent/Child: 15–18 mg/kg then 5 mg/kg additional

Renal Impairment Dosage Adjustment

CrCl less than 10 mL/min: Extend interval

Hemodialysis Dosage Adjustment

20–50% dialyzed

SOLUTION PREPARATION

May be given direct IV undiluted or diluted in 10 mL of sterile water for injection.

STORAGE

Store vials at 15°–30° C (59°–86° F).

ADMINISTRATION

- Ensure patency prior to injection, as extravasation may cause tissue sloughing.
- **Direct IV Injection:** Give 60 mg or fraction thereof over at least 60 sec.
- Monitor IV infusion site closely.

INCOMPATIBILITIES Solution/additive: Chlorpromazine, cimetidine, clindamycin, codeine phosphate, dexamethasone, diphenhydramine, erythromycin, ephedrine, hydralazine, hydrocortisone sodium, hydroxyzine, insulin, kanamycin, levorphanol, meperidine, methadone, methylphenidate, morphine, nitrofurantoin, norepinephrine, tetracyclines, pentazocine, pentobarbital, phytonadione, procaine, prochlorperazine, promazine, promethazine, sodium bicarbonate, streptomycin, vancomycin, warfarin. Y-site: Amphotericin B cholesteryl complex, hydromorphone, lansoprazole, TPN with albumin.

ACTION & *THERAPEUTIC EFFECT* Long-acting barbiturate with sedative and hypnotic effects that appear to be due primarily to interference with impulse transmission from the cerebral cortex. This is due to inhibition of the reticular activating system (RAS). *Produces sedative and hypnotic effects with no analgesic properties. Phenobarbital limits spread of seizure activity by increasing threshold for motor cortex stimuli.*

CONTRAINDICATIONS Hypersensitivity to barbiturates; manifest hepatic or familial history of porphyria; severe respiratory or kidney disease; history of previous addiction to sedative hypnotics; alcohol intoxication; uncontrolled pain; renal failure, anuria; pregnancy (category D), lactation.

CAUTIOUS USE Impaired liver, kidney, cardiac, or respiratory function; sleep apnea, COPD; history of allergies; older adult or debilitated patients; patients with fever; hyperthyroidism; seizure disorders; diabetes mellitus or severe anemia; during labor and delivery; patient with borderline hypoadrenal function; young children and neonates.

ADVERSE EFFECTS (≥1%) **Body as a Whole:** Myalgia, neuralgia, CNS depression, coma, and death. **CNS:** *Somnolence,* nightmares, insomnia, "hangover," headache, anxiety, thinking abnormalities, dizziness, nystagmus, irritability, paradoxic excitement and exacerbation of hyperkinetic behavior (in children); confusion or depression or marked excitement (older adult or debilitated patients); ataxia. **CV:** Bradycardia, syncope, hypotension. **GI:** Nausea, vomiting, constipation, diarrhea, epigastric pain, liver damage. **Hematologic:** Megaloblastic anemia, agranulocytosis, thrombocytopenia. **Metabolic:** Hypocalcemia, osteomalacia, rickets. **Musculoskeletal:** Folic acid deficiency, vitamin D deficiency. **Respiratory:** Respiratory depression. **Skin:** Mild maculopapular, morbilliform rash; erythema multiforme, Stevens-Johnson syndrome, exfoliative dermatitis (rare).

DIAGNOSTIC TEST INTERFERENCE BARBITURATES may affect ***bromsulphalein retention tests*** (by enhancing liver uptake and excretion of dye) and increase ***serum phosphatase.***

DRUG INTERACTIONS CNS DEPRESSANTS compound CNS depression; phenobarbital may decrease absorption and increase metabolism of ORAL ANTICOAGULANTS; increases metabolism of CORTICOSTEROIDS, ORAL CONTRACEPTIVES, ANTICONVULSANTS, **digitoxin,** possibly decreasing their effects; ANTIDEPRESSANTS potentiate adverse effects of phenobarbital.

PHARMACOKINETICS Duration: 4–6 h. **Distribution:** 20–45% protein bound; crosses placenta; enters breast milk. **Metabolism:** In liver (CYP 2C19). **Elimination:** In urine. **Half-Life:** 2–6 days.

NURSING IMPLICATIONS

Assessment & Drug Effects

- Observe patients receiving large doses closely for at least 30 min to ensure that sedation is not excessive.
- Keep patient under constant observation and record vital signs at least every hour or more often if indicated.
- Lab tests: Periodic serum phenobarbital, LFTs, CBC with differential and platelet count.
- Monitor serum drug levels. Serum concentrations greater than 50 mcg/mL may cause coma.
- Expect barbiturates to produce restlessness when given to patients in pain because these drugs do not have analgesic action.
- Monitor for paradoxical responses in older adult, debilitated patient, and child [i.e., irritability, marked excitement (inappropriate tearfulness and aggression in child), depression, and confusion].
- Concurrent drugs: Monitor PT/INR and phenytoin levels frequently to ensure therapeutic range.

Patient & Family Education

- Avoid potentially hazardous activities requiring mental alertness until response to drug is known.
- Women using oral contraceptives should use an additional, alternative form of contraception.

PHENTOLAMINE MESYLATE

(fen-tole'a-meen)

Regitine, Rogitine ◆

Classification(s): ANTIHYPERTENSIVE, ALPHA-ADRENERGIC ANTAGONIST
Therapeutic: ANTIHYPERTENSIVE
Prototype: Prazosin
Pregnancy Category: C

USES Diagnosis of pheochromocytoma and to prevent or control hypertensive episodes prior to or during pheochromocytomectomy.
UNLABELED USES Prevention of dermal necrosis and sloughing following IV administration or extravasation of norepinephrine.

INDICATION & DOSAGE

Hypertensive Episode Prevention during Surgery

Adult: 5 mg 1–2 h before surgery, repeat as needed
Child: 0.05–0.1 mg/kg/dose (max: 5 mg/dose)

Pheochromocytoma Diagnosis

Adult: 5 mg
Child: 0.05–0.1 mg/kg (max: 5 mg)

SOLUTION PREPARATION

Vial Reconstitution: Add 1 mL of sterile water for injection for each 5 mg or fraction thereof. May be given as prepared direct IV or further diluted with 5 mL of sterile water for injection. Use immediately.

STORAGE

Use reconstituted solutions immediately. Discard any unused portion.

ADMINISTRATION

Direct IV Injection: Give a single dose over 60 sec.

INCOMPATIBILITIES Data not available; do not mix with other drugs.

ACTION & *THERAPEUTIC EFFECT* Alpha-adrenergic antagonist that competitively blocks alpha-adrenergic receptors, but this action is transient and incomplete. Causes vasodilation primarily by direct action on vascular smooth muscle. It decreases general vascular resistance, and pulmonary arterial pressure. *Prevents hypertension resulting from elevated levels of circulating epinephrine and/or norepinephrine.*

CONTRAINDICATIONS MI (previous or present), coronary artery disease; peptic ulcer disease; pregnancy (category C), lactation.
CAUTIOUS USE Gastritis.

ADVERSE EFFECTS (≥1%) **Body as a Whole:** Weakness, dizziness, flushing, *orthostatic hypotension.* **GI:** *Abdominal pain, nausea, vomiting, diarrhea, exacerbation of peptic ulcer.* **CV:** *Acute and prolonged hypotension, tachycardia, anginal pain,* cardiac arrhythmias, <u>MI</u>, cerebrovascular spasm, <u>shock-like state</u>. **Special Senses:** Nasal stuffiness, conjunctival infection.

DRUG INTERACTIONS May antagonize BP-raising effects of **epinephrine, ephedrine.**

PHARMACOKINETICS Peak: 2 min. **Duration:** 10–15 min. **Elimination:** In urine. **Half-Life:** 19 min.

NURSING IMPLICATIONS

Assessment & Drug Effects

- Test for pheochromocytoma: Keep patient at rest in supine position throughout test, preferably in quiet, darkened room. Prior to drug administration, take BP q10min for at least 30 min to establish that BP has stabilized before IV injection. Record BP immediately after injection and at 30-sec intervals for first 3 min; then at 1-min intervals for next 7 min.

Patient & Family Education

- Avoid sudden changes in position, particularly from reclining to upright posture and dangle legs and exercise ankles and toes for a few minutes before standing to walk.
- Lie down or sit down in head-low position immediately if light-headed or dizzy.

PHENYLEPHRINE HYDROCHLORIDE

(fen-ill-ef'rin)

Neo-Synephrine
Classification(s): ALPHA-ADRENERGIC AGONIST
Therapeutic: VASOPRESSOR, ANTIARRHYTHMIC
Pregnancy Category: C

USES To maintain BP during anesthesia, to treat vascular failure in shock, and to overcome paroxysmal supraventricular tachycardia.

INDICATION & DOSAGE

Severe Hypotension/Shock

Adult: 0.1–0.18 mg/min until BP stabilizes, then 0.04–0.06 mg/min for maintenance

Supraventricular Tachycardia

Adult: 0.25–0.5 mg bolus, then 0.1–0.2 mg doses (max: 1 mg/dose)

SOLUTION PREPARATION

- *Direct IV Injection:* Dilute each 10 mg (1 mL) of 1% solution in 9 mL of sterile water for injection to yield 1 mg/mL.
- *IV Infusion:* Dilute each 10 mg in 500 mL D5W or NS to yield 0.02 mg/mL.

STORAGE

Protect from exposure to air, strong light, or heat, any of which can cause solutions to change color to brown, form a precipitate, and lose potency.

ADMINISTRATION

- Ensure patency prior to injection or infusion, as extravasation may cause tissue sloughing.
- **Direct IV Injection:** Give a single dose over 60 sec.
- **IV Infusion:** Titrate to maintain BP. Use a controlled infusion device.
- Monitor infusion site closely. If extravasation occurs, area should be immediately injected with 5–10 mg of phentolamine (Regitine) diluted in 10–15 mL of NS.

Common adverse effects in *italic*, life-threatening effects underlined: generic names in **bold**; classifications in SMALL CAPS; ♣ Canadian drug name; ✪ Prototype drug

INCOMPATIBILITIES Solution/additive: Phenytoin. Y-site: Lansoprazole, propofol, thiopental.

ACTION & *THERAPEUTIC EFFECT* Potent, synthetic, direct-acting sympathomimetic with strong alpha-adrenergic and weak beta-adrenergic cardiac stimulant actions. *Elevates systolic and diastolic pressures through arteriolar constriction; also constricts capacitance vessels and increases venous return to heart. Rise in BP causes reflex bradycardia.*

CONTRAINDICATIONS Severe coronary disease, severe hypertension, atrial fibrillation, atrial flutter, cardiac arrhythmias; cardiac disease, cardiomyopathy; uncontrolled hypertension; ventricular fibrillation or tachycardia, acute MI, angina; cerebral arteriosclerosis, MAOI; labor and delivery; pregnancy (category C).

CAUTIOUS USE Hyperthyroidism; diabetes mellitus; older adult patients; 21 days before or following termination of MAO inhibitor therapy; lactation.

ADVERSE EFFECTS (≥1%).**CV:** Palpitation, tachycardia, bradycardia (overdosage), extrasystoles, hypertension. **Body as a Whole:** Trembling, sweating, pallor, sense of fullness in head, tingling of extremities, sleeplessness, dizziness, light-headedness, weakness, restlessness, anxiety, precordial pain, *tremor,* severe visceral or peripheral vasoconstriction, necrosis if IV infiltrates.

DRUG INTERACTIONS ERGOT ALKALOIDS, **guanethidine, reserpine,** TRICYCLIC ANTIDEPRESSANTS increase pressor effects of phenylephrine; **halothane, digoxin** increase risk of arrhythmias; MAO INHIBITORS cause hypertensive crisis; **oxytocin** causes persistent hypertension; ALPHA BLOCKERS, BETA BLOCKERS antagonize effects of phenylephrine.

PHARMACOKINETICS Duration: 15–20 min. **Metabolism:** In liver and tissues by monoamine oxidase.

NURSING IMPLICATIONS

Assessment & Drug Effects
- Monitor pulse, BP, and central venous pressure (q2–5min) during administration.
- Monitor for angina and arrhythmias, especially as BP increases.
- Control flow rate and dosage to prevent excessive dosage. Overdose can induce ventricular dysrhythmias.

Patient & Family Education
- Report promptly chest, neck, back or jaw pain.
- Use caution during ambulation until reaction to drug is known.

PHENYTOIN ⊘

(fen'i-toy-in)

Dilantin

Classification(s): ANTICONVULSANT; HYDANTOIN

Therapeutic: ANTICONVULSANT
Pregnancy Category: D

USES To control tonic–clonic (grand mal) seizures, psychomotor and nonepileptic seizures, seizure prophylaxis during surgery.
UNLABELED USES Antiarrhythmic agent, especially in treatment of digitalis-induced arrhythmias.

INDICATION & DOSAGE

Anticonvulsant

Adult: 10–15 mg/kg then 100 mg q6–8h
Child/Infant/Neonate: 15–20 mg/kg loading dose in divided doses

Surgical Seizure Prophylaxis

Adult/Adolescent: 10–20 mg/kg

SOLUTION PREPARATION

- Inspect solution prior to use. Precipitation may be caused by refrigeration, but slow warming to room temperature restores clarity.
- *Direct IV Injection:* Give undiluted. Use only when clear (may be slightly yellowed) without precipitate.

STORAGE

Solution is stable as long as it is clear and without precipitate.

ADMINISTRATION

- Ensure patency prior to injection or infusion, as extravasation may cause tissue sloughing.
- **Direct IV Injection:** Avoid rapid injection. Flush before/after with NS.
  - *Adult:* Give 50 mg or fraction thereof over 1 min (25 mg/min in older adult or when used as antiarrhythmic).
  - *Child/Neonate:* Give 1 mg/kg/min.
- Monitor infusion site closely.

INCOMPATIBILITIES Solution/additive: **5% dextrose, lactated Ringer's, fat emulsion, sodium chloride, amikacin, aminophylline, bretylium, cephalothin, cephapirin, chloramphenicol, chlordiazepoxide, clindamycin, codeine phosphate, diphenhydramine, dobutamine, hydromorphone, insulin, levorphanol, lidocaine, lincomycin, meperidine, metaraminol, methadone, morphine, nitroglycerin, norepinephrine, penicillin G, pentobarbital, phenylephedrine, phytonadione, procaine, prochlorperazine, secobarbital, streptomycin, warfarin.** Y-site: **Amikacin, amphotericin B cholesteryl complex, bretylium, cefepime, ceftazidime, cimetidine, ciprofloxacin, clarithromycin, clindamycin, diltiazem, dobutamine, enalaprilat, fenoldopam, fentanyl, gatifloxacin, heparin, hydromorphone, lansoprazole, lidocaine, linezolid, methadone, morphine, ondansetron, potassium chloride, propofol, sufentanil, tacrolimus, theophylline, TPN, vitamin B complex with C.**

Common adverse effects in *italic*, life-threatening effects <u>underlined</u>: generic names in **bold**; classifications in SMALL CAPS; ♣ Canadian drug name; ◯ Prototype drug

ACTION & *THERAPEUTIC EFFECT* Anticonvulsant action results from elevating the seizure threshold and/or limiting the spread of seizure activity by reducing voltage, frequency, and spread of electrical discharges within the motor cortex. Class IB antiarrhythmic properties similar to those of lidocaine, also a Class IB agent. *Increases seizure activity threshold. Also effective in treating arrhythmias associated with QT prolongation.*

CONTRAINDICATIONS Hypersensitivity to hydantoin products; rash; seizures due to hypoglycemia; sinus bradycardia, complete or incomplete heart block; Adams-Stokes syndrome; pregnancy (category D), lactation.
CAUTIOUS USE Impaired liver or kidney function; alcoholism; blood dyscrasias; hypotension, severe myocardial insufficiency, impending or frank heart failure; older adult, debilitated, gravely ill patients; pancreatic adenoma; diabetes mellitus, hyperglycemia; respiratory depression; acute intermittent porphyria.

ADVERSE EFFECTS (≥1%) **CNS:** Usually dose-related: Nystagmus, *drowsiness,* ataxia, dizziness, mental confusion, tremors, insomnia, headache, seizures. **CV:** Bradycardia, hypotension, underlined{cardiovascular collapse}, ventricular fibrillation, phlebitis. **Special Senses:** Photophobia, conjunctivitis, diplopia, blurred vision. **GI:** *Gingival hyperplasia,* nausea, vomiting, constipation, epigastric pain, dysphagia, loss of taste, weight loss, hepatitis, liver necrosis. **Hematologic:** Thrombocytopenia, leukopenia, leukocytosis, agranulocytosis, pancytopenia, eosinophilia; megaloblastic, hemolytic, or aplastic anemias. **Metabolic:** Fever, hyperglycemia, glycosuria, weight gain, edema, transient increase in serum thyrotropic (TSH) level, osteomalacia or rickets associated with hypocalcemia and elevated alkaline phosphatase activity. **Skin:** Alopecia, hirsutism (especially in young females); rash: scarlatiniform, maculopapular, urticaria, morbilliform; bullous, exfoliative, or purpuric dermatitis; Stevens-Johnson syndrome, toxic epidermal necrolysis, keratosis, neonatal hemorrhage. **Urogenital:** Acute renal failure, Peyronie's disease. **Respiratory:** Acute pneumonitis, pulmonary fibrosis. **Body as a Whole:** Periarteritis nodosum, acute systemic lupus erythematosus, craniofacial abnormalities (with enlargement of lips); lymphadenopathy.

DIAGNOSTIC TEST INTERFERENCE Phenytoin (HYDANTOINS) may produce lower than normal values for ***dexamethasone*** or ***metyrapone tests;*** may increase ***serum levels*** of ***glucose, BSP,*** and ***alkaline phosphatase*** and may decrease ***PBI*** and ***urinary steroid levels.***

DRUG INTERACTIONS Alcohol decreases phenytoin effects; other ANTICONVULSANTS may increase or decrease phenytoin levels; phenytoin may decrease absorption and increase metabolism of ORAL ANTICOAGULANTS; phenytoin increases metabolism of CORTICOSTEROIDS, ORAL CONTRACEPTIVES, and **nisoldipine,** decreasing their effectiveness; **amiodarone, chloramphenicol, omeprazole,** and **ticlopidine** increase phenytoin levels; ANTI-TUBERCULOSIS AGENTS decrease phenytoin levels.

PHARMACOKINETICS Distribution: 95% protein bound; crosses placenta; small amount in breast milk. **Metabolism:** Oxidized in liver to inactive metabolites. **Elimination:** Metabolites excreted by kidneys. **Half-Life:** 22 h.

NURSING IMPLICATIONS

Assessment & Drug Effects

- Continuously monitor ECG and BP during infusion and for an hour afterward. Watch for respiratory depression. Margin between toxic and therapeutic doses is relatively small.
- Lab tests: Periodic serum phenytoin concentration; CBC with differential, platelet count, and Hct and Hgb; serum glucose, serum calcium, and serum magnesium; and LFTs.
- Observe patient closely for neurologic adverse effects. Have on hand oxygen, atropine, vasopressor, assisted ventilation, seizure precaution equipment (mouth gag, nonmetal airway, suction apparatus).
- Monitor diabetics for loss of glycemic control.
- Monitor for S&S of hypocalcemia and hypomagnesemia (see Appendix C).
- Concurrent drug: Monitor thyroid hormone levels with thyroid replacement therapy.

Patient & Family Education

- Avoid potentially hazardous activities until reaction to drug is known.
- Be aware that drug may make urine pink or red to red-brown.

PHYSOSTIGMINE SALICYLATE

(fi-zoe-stig'meen)

Antilirium

Classification(s): CHOLINESTERASE INHIBITOR
Therapeutic: ANTICHOLINERGIC ANTIDOTE
Prototype: Neostigmine
Pregnancy Category: C

USES To reverse anticholinergic toxicities.

INDICATION & DOSAGE

Reversal of Anticholinergic Effects

Adult: 0.5–2 mg repeat q10–30min as needed
Child: 0.02 mg/kg/dose, may repeat q5–10min (max: total dose of 2 mg)

SOLUTION PREPARATION

No dilution is required. Administer as supplied. Note: Use only clear, colorless solutions. Red-tinted solution indicates oxidation, and such solutions should be discarded.

STORAGE

Store at 15°–30° C (59°–86° F).

ADMINISTRATION

- **Direct IV Injection:**
  - *Adult:* Give slowly at a rate of no more than 1 mg/min.

Common adverse effects in *italic*, life-threatening effects <u>underlined</u>: generic names in **bold**; classifications in SMALL CAPS; ♣ Canadian drug name; ● Prototype drug

- *Child:* Give 0.5 mg or fraction thereof over at least 1 min.
- NOTE: Avoid rapid administration, which can cause a cholinergic crisis.

INCOMPATIBILITIES Solution/additive: Phenytoin, ranitidine. **Y-site:** Dobutamine.

ACTION & *THERAPEUTIC EFFECT* Physostigmine is a reversible cholinesterase inhibitor. It competes with acetylcholine (ACE) for its binding site on cholinesterase, thereby potentiating action of ACE on skeletal muscle, GI tract musculature, and on autonomic ganglia in the CNS. *Chief effect is increasing concentration of acetylcholine at cholinergic transmission sites, thus prolonging and exaggerating ACE action. Effective in reversing anticholinergic toxicity.*

CONTRAINDICATIONS Asthma; diabetes mellitus; gangrene, cardiovascular disease; mechanical obstruction of intestinal or urogenital tract; peptic ulcer disease; asthma; any vagotonic state; secondary glaucoma; closed angle glaucoma; inflammatory disease of iris or ciliary body; concomitant use with choline esters (e.g., methacholine, bethanechol) or depolarizing neuromuscular blocking agents (e.g., decamethonium, succinylcholine); pregnancy (category C), lactation.
CAUTIOUS USE Epilepsy; parkinsonism; bradycardia; hyperthyroidism; peptic ulcer; seizure disorders; chronic depression; hypotension.

ADVERSE EFFECTS (≥1%) **Body as a Whole:** *Sweating,* <u>cholinergic crisis (acute toxicity)</u>, hyperactivity, respiratory distress, convulsions. **CNS:** Restlessness, hallucinations, depression, twitching, tremors, *sweating,* weakness, ataxia, convulsions, <u>collapse</u>. **GI:** *Nausea, vomiting, epigastric pain, diarrhea, salivation.* **Urogenital:** Involuntary urination or defecation. **Respiratory:** Dyspnea, bronchospasm, <u>respiratory paralysis, pulmonary edema</u>. **Cardiovascular:** Irregular pulse, palpitation, bradycardia, rise in BP.

DRUG INTERACTIONS Antagonizes effects of **echothiophate, isoflurophate**.

PHARMACOKINETICS Onset: 3–8 min. **Duration:** 0.5–5 h. **Distribution:** Crosses blood–brain barrier. **Metabolism:** In plasma by cholinesterase. **Elimination:** Small amounts excreted in urine. **Half-Life:** 15–40 min.

NURSING IMPLICATIONS

Assessment & Drug Effects

- Monitor closely vital signs and state of consciousness in patients receiving drug for atropine poisoning. Since physostigmine is usually rapidly eliminated, patient can lapse into delirium and coma within 1–2 h; repeat doses may be required.
- Monitor closely for adverse effects related to CNS and for signs of sensitivity to physostigmine. Have atropine sulfate readily available for clinical emergency.
- Withhold drug and notify prescriber for: Bradycardia, excessive salivation, respiratory distress, emesis, frequent urination, or diarrhea.

Common adverse effects in *italic*, life-threatening effects <u>underlined</u>: generic names in **bold**; classifications in SMALL CAPS; ♣ Canadian drug name; ● Prototype drug

543

PHYTONADIONE (VITAMIN K₁)

(fye-toe-na-dye'one)

Classification(s): VITAMIN K
Therapeutic: ANTIHEMORRHAGIC; ANTIDOTE
Pregnancy Category: C

USES Drug of choice as antidote for overdosage of coumarin and indandione oral anticoagulants. Also reverses hypoprothrombinemia secondary to administration of oral antibiotics, quinidine, quinine, salicylates, sulfonamides, excessive vitamin A, and secondary to inadequate absorption and synthesis of vitamin K (as in obstructive jaundice, biliary fistula, ulcerative colitis, intestinal resection, prolonged hyperalimentation). Also prophylaxis of and therapy for neonatal hemorrhagic disease.

INDICATION & DOSAGE

Anticoagulant Overdose (with Serious Bleeding)
Adult: 2.5–10 mg, may repeat parenteral dose after 6–8 h if needed

Other Prothrombin Deficiencies
Adult: 2–25 mg
Child/Infant: 0.5–5 mg

Neonatal Hemorrhagic Disease Prophylaxis
Neonate: 0.5–1 mg

SOLUTION PREPARATION
Dilute a single dose in 10 mL D5W, NS, or D5NS. Protect infusion solution from light by wrapping container with aluminum foil or other opaque material. Use immediately.

STORAGE
- Store ampules at 15°–30° C (59°–86° F).
- Discard any unused solution and contents of open ampule.

ADMINISTRATION
Direct IV Injection: Give at a rate not to exceed 1 mg/min. Note: Solution should be administered immediately after dilution.

INCOMPATIBILITIES Solution/additive: Ascorbic acid, cephalothin, dextran 12%, dobutamine, doxycycline, magnesium sulfate, nitrofurantoin, phenobarbital, ranitidine, thiopental, vancomycin, warfarin. Y-site: Dobutamine.

ACTION & *THERAPEUTIC EFFECT* Fat-soluble substance chemically identical to and with similar activity as naturally occurring vitamin K. Vitamin K is essential for hepatic biosynthesis of blood clotting Factors II, VII, IX, and X. *Promotes liver synthesis of clotting factors.*

Common adverse effects in *italic*, life-threatening effects underlined: generic names in **bold**; classifications in SMALL CAPS; ♣ Canadian drug name; ☯ Prototype drug

CONTRAINDICATIONS Hypersensitivity to phytonadione, benzyl alcohol, or castor oil; severe liver disease; pregnancy (category C).

CAUTIOUS USE Elderly; biliary tract disease, obstructive jaundice, hepatic disease; history of thromboembolic disease; lactation.

ADVERSE EFFECTS (≥1%) **Body as a Whole:** Hypersensitivity or <u>anaphylaxis-like reaction</u>: Facial flushing, cramp-like pains, convulsive movements, chills, fever, diaphoresis, weakness, dizziness, shock, <u>cardiac arrest</u>. **CNS:** Headache (after oral dose), brain damage, <u>death</u>. **GI:** Gastric upset. **Hematologic:** Paradoxic hypoprothrombinemia (patients with severe liver disease), severe hemolytic anemia. **Metabolic:** Hyperbilirubinemia, kernicterus. **Respiratory:** <u>Bronchospasm</u>, dyspnea, sensation of chest constriction, <u>respiratory arrest</u>. **Skin:** Pain at injection site, hematoma, and nodule formation, erythematous skin eruptions (with repeated injections). **Special Senses:** Peculiar taste sensation.

DIAGNOSTIC TEST INTERFERENCE Falsely elevated *urine steroids* (by modifications of *Reddy, Jenkins, Thorn procedure*).

DRUG INTERACTIONS Antagonizes effects of **warfarin.**

PHARMACOKINETICS Onset: 15 min. **Peak:** Hemorrhage usually controlled within 3–8 h; normal prothrombin time may be obtained in 12–14 h after administration. **Distribution:** Concentrates briefly in liver after absorption; crosses placenta; distributed into breast milk. **Metabolism:** Rapidly in liver. **Elimination:** In urine and bile.

NURSING IMPLICATIONS

Assessment & Drug Effects

- Monitor patient constantly. Severe reactions, including fatalities, have occurred during and immediately after IV injection (see **ADVERSE EFFECTS**).
- Lab tests: Baseline and frequent PT/INR.
- Monitor therapeutic effectiveness, which is indicated by shortened PT, INR, bleeding, and clotting times, as well as decreased hemorrhagic tendencies.
- Be aware that patients on large doses may develop temporary resistance to coumarin-type anticoagulants. If oral anticoagulant is reinstituted, larger doses than previously used may be needed initially.

Patient & Family Education

- Maintain consistency in diet and avoid significant increases in daily intake of vitamin K–rich foods when drug regimen is stabilized. Sources rich in vitamin K include asparagus, broccoli, cabbage, lettuce, turnip greens, pork or beef liver, green tea, spinach, watercress, and tomatoes.

PIPERACILLIN SODIUM ⊕

(pi-per′a-sill-in)

Classification(s): ANTIBIOTIC, PENICILLIN, ANTIPSEUDOMONAL

Common adverse effects in *italic*, life-threatening effects <u>underlined</u>: generic names in **bold**; classifications in SMALL CAPS; ♣ Canadian drug name; ⊕ Prototype drug

PIPERACILLIN SODIUM

Therapeutic: ANTIBACTERIAL
Pregnancy Category: B

USES Susceptible organisms that cause gynecologic, skin and skin structure, gonococcal, and streptococcal infections; lower respiratory tract, intraabdominal, and bone and joint infections; septicemia, urinary tract infections. Also prophylactically prior to and during surgery and as empiric antiinfective therapy in granulocytopenic patients.

INDICATION & DOSAGE

Uncomplicated UTI
Adult: 6–8 g/day divided q6–12h

Complicated UTIs
Adult: 8–16 g/day divided q6–8h

Mild to Moderate Infections
Child: 200–300 mg/kg/day divided q4–6h (max: 24 g/day)

Moderate to Severe Infections
Adult/Adolescent: 200–300 mg/kg/day in divided doses

Life-Threatening Infection, *Pseudomonas* Infections
Adult: 12–18 g/day divided q4–6h

Surgical Prophylaxis
Adult: 2 g before procedure then repeat dose during and/or after surgery

Renal Impairment Dosage Adjustment
CrCl 20–40 mL/min: Give q8h; *CrCl less than 20 mL/min:* Give q12h

Hemodialysis Dosage Adjustment
20–50% dialyzable

SOLUTION PREPARATION
- *Vial Reconstitution:* Add 5 mL sterile water or NS for injection for each 1 g or fraction thereof. Shake well until dissolved. May be given as prepared direct IV as a bolus dose or further diluted for infusion.
- *Further Dilution of Reconstituted Solution:* Dilute required dose in 50–100 mL NS, D5W, D5NS, or LR.

STORAGE
- If diluted in LR, **must be** infused within 2 h; other IV solutions and reconstituted solutions stable for 24 h at room temperature and 48 h refrigerated.
- Store powder vials at 15°–30° C (59°–86° F). Note that sunlight may darken powder but does not affect potency.

ADMINISTRATION

- **Direct IV Injection:** Give bolus dose over 3–5 min. Avoid rapid injection.
- **Intermittent Infusion:** Infuse over 30 min.

INCOMPATIBILITIES Solution/additive: AMINOGLYCOSIDES, **ciprofloxacin.** Y-site: AMINOGLYCOSIDES, **amiodarone, amphotericin B cholesteryl complex, cisatracurium, filgrastim, fluconazole, gemcitabine, ondansetron, sargramostim, vancomycin, vinorelbine.**

ACTION & *THERAPEUTIC EFFECT* Piperacillin is a beta-lactam antibiotic and is mainly bactericidal. It inhibits the final stage of bacterial cell wall synthesis by preferentially binding to specific penicillin-binding proteins (PBPs) located inside the bacterial cell wall. This interference with cell wall synthesis promotes loss of membrane integrity and leads to death of the organism. *Extended-spectrum penicillin with antibiotic activity against most gram-negative and many gram-positive anaerobic and aerobic organisms.*

CONTRAINDICATIONS Hypersensitivity to penicillins.

CAUTIOUS USE Liver and kidney dysfunction; hypersensitivity to cephalosporins or carbapenem antibiotics; cystic fibrosis; eczema; asthma; GI disease; pregnancy (category B), lactation.

ADVERSE EFFECTS (≥1%) **Body as a Whole:** Coughing, sneezing, feeling of uneasiness; <u>systemic anaphylaxis</u>, fever, widespread increase in capillary permeability and vasodilation with <u>resulting edema (mouth, tongue, pharynx, larynx), laryngospasm</u>, malaise, serum sickness (fever, malaise, pruritus, urticaria, lymphadenopathy, arthralgia, angioedema of face and extremities, neuritis prostration, eosinophilia), SLE-like syndrome, injection-site reactions (pain, inflammation, abscess, phlebitis), superinfections (especially with *Candida* and gram-negative bacteria), neuromuscular irritability (twitching, lethargy, confusion, stupor, hyperreflexia, multifocal myoclonus, localized or generalized seizures, <u>coma</u>). **CV:** Hypotension, <u>circulatory collapse</u>, cardiac arrhythmias, <u>cardiac arrest</u>. **GI:** Vomiting, diarrhea, severe abdominal cramps, nausea, epigastric distress, diarrhea, flatulence, dark discoloration of tongue, sore mouth or tongue. **Urogenital:** Interstitial nephritis, Loeffler's syndrome, vasculitis. **Hematologic:** Hemolytic anemia, thrombocytopenia. **Metabolic:** Hyperkalemia (penicillin G potassium), hypokalemia, alkalosis, hypernatremia, CHF (penicillin G sodium). **Respiratory:** Bronchospasm, asthma. **Skin:** Itchy palms or axilla, pruritus, *urticaria*, flushed skin, *delayed skin rashes* ranging from urticaria to exfoliative dermatitis, <u>Stevens-Johnson syndrome</u>, fixed-drug eruptions, contact dermatitis.

DRUG INTERACTIONS May increase risk of bleeding with ANTICOAGULANTS; **probenecid** decreases elimination of piperacillin.

PHARMACOKINETICS Peak: 5 min. **Distribution:** Widely distributed with highest concentrations in urine and bile; adequate CSF penetration with inflamed meninges; crosses placenta; distributed into breast milk. **Metabolism:** Slightly metabolized in liver. **Elimination:** Primarily excreted in urine, partly in bile. **Half-Life:** 0.6–1.35 h.

NURSING IMPLICATIONS

Assessment & Drug Effects

- Prior to initiating therapy: Baseline C&S tests (start drug pending results); determine previous hypersensitivity reactions to penicillins, cephalosporins, and other allergens.
- Monitor for hypersensitivity response; discontinue drug and notify prescriber if allergic response noted.
- Monitor for hemorrhagic manifestations because high doses may induce coagulation abnormalities.
- Lab tests: Periodic CBC with differential, platelet count, Hgb and Hct, and serum electrolytes.

Patient & Family Education

- Report significant, unexplained diarrhea.
- Withhold drug and report to prescriber if signs of an allergic reaction develop (e.g., itching, rash, hives).

PIPERACILLIN/TAZOBACTAM

(pi-per'a-cil-lin/taz-o-bac'tam)

Zosyn

Classification(s): ANTIBIOTIC; PENICILLIN, ANTIPSEUDOMONAL
Therapeutic: ANTIBACTERIAL
Prototype: Piperacillin sodium
Pregnancy Category: B

USES Treatment of moderate to severe appendicitis, uncomplicated and complicated skin and skin structure infections, endometritis, pelvic inflammatory disease, or nosocomial or community-acquired pneumonia caused by beta-lactamase-producing bacteria.

INDICATION & DOSAGE

Moderate to Severe Infections

Adult/Adolescent: 3.375 g q6h, infused over 30 min, for 7–10 days
Child/Infant (over 9 mo): 200–300 mg piperacillin component/kg/day divided q8h

Nosocomial Pneumonia

Adult/Adolescent: 4.5 g q6h, infused over 30 min, for 7–14 days

Renal Insufficiency Dosage Adjustment

CrCl 20–40 mL/min: 2.25 g q6h; *less than 20 mL/min:* 2.25 g q8h

Hemodialysis Dosage Adjustment

2.25 g q12h (for nosocomial pneumonia dose q8h); give additional 0.75 g after dialysis session

SOLUTION PREPARATION

- *Vial Reconstitution:* Add 5 mL of D5W, NS, sterile water for injection (max: 50 mL per dose), or other compatible diluent for each 1 g or fraction thereof. Shake well to dissolve. May be given as prepared or further diluted for infusion (preferred).
- *Further Dilution of Reconstituted Solution:* Add required dose to enough IV solution to produce a final volume of 50–150 mL. Acceptable IV solutions: NS, sterile water for injection (max volume: 50 mL per dose), D5W, dextran 6% in NS, and LR only with solution containing EDTA.

STORAGE

Store at 20°–25° C (68°–77° F) prior to reconstitution. Reconstituted and IV solutions are stable for 24 h at 15°–30° C (59°–86° F).

ADMINISTRATION

Intermittent Infusion: Infuse over at least 30 min. Do not administer through a line with another infusion.

INCOMPATIBILITIES Solution/additive: AMINOGLYCOSIDES, **lactated Ringer's, albumin, blood products, solutions containing sodium bicarbonate. Y-site:** Acyclovir, amiodarone, amphotericin B, amphotericin B cholesteryl complex, azithromycin, chlorpromazine, cisatracurium, cisplatin, dacarbazine, daunorubicin, dobutamine, doxorubicin, doxorubicin liposome, doxycycline, droperidol, drotrecogin, famotidine, ganciclovir, gemcitabine, haloperidol, hydroxyzine, idarubicin, miconazole, minocycline, mitomycin, mitoxantrone, nalbuphine, prochlorperazine, promethazine, streptozocin, vancomycin.

ACTION & *THERAPEUTIC EFFECT* Antibacterial combination product consisting of the semisynthetic piperacillin and the beta-lactamase inhibitor tazobactam. Tazobactam component does not decrease the activity of the piperacillin component against susceptible organisms. Tazobactam is an inhibitor of a wide variety of bacterial beta-lactamases. It has little antibacterial activity itself; however, in combination with piperacillin, it extends the spectrum of bacteria that are susceptible to piperacillin. *Two-drug combination has antibiotic activity against an extremely broad spectrum of gram-positive, gram-negative, and anaerobic bacteria.*

CONTRAINDICATIONS Hypersensitivity to piperacillin, tazobactam, penicillins, coagulopathy.

CAUTIOUS USE Hypersensitivity to cephalosporins or beta-lactamase inhibitors such as clavulanic acid and sulbactam; GI disease, colitis; cystic fibrosis; eczema; kidney failure, complicated urinary tract infections; pregnancy (category B), lactation.

ADVERSE EFFECTS (≥1%) **CNS:** Headache, insomnia, fever. **GI:** Diarrhea, constipation, nausea, vomiting, dyspepsia, <u>pseudomembranous colitis</u>. **Skin:** Rash, pruritus, hypersensitivity reactions.

DRUG INTERACTIONS May increase risk of bleeding with ANTICOAGULANTS; **probenecid** decreases elimination of piperacillin.

Common adverse effects in *italic*, life-threatening effects <u>underlined</u>: generic names in **bold**; classifications in SMALL CAPS; ♣ Canadian drug name; ❶ Prototype drug

549

PHARMACOKINETICS Distribution: Distributes into many tissues, including lung, blister fluid, and bile; crosses placenta; distributed into breast milk. **Metabolism:** In liver. **Elimination:** In urine. **Half-Life:** 0.7–1.2 h.

NURSING IMPLICATIONS

Assessment & Drug Effects

- Prior to initiating therapy: Baseline C&S tests (start drug pending results); determine previous hypersensitivity reactions to penicillins, cephalosporins, and other allergens.
- Monitor for hypersensitivity response; discontinue drug and notify prescriber if allergic response noted.
- Monitor for hemorrhagic manifestations because high doses may induce coagulation abnormalities.
- Lab tests: Periodic CBC with differential, platelet count, Hgb and Hct, and serum electrolytes.

Patient & Family Education

- Report significant, unexplained diarrhea.
- Withhold drug and report to prescriber if signs of an allergic reaction develop (e.g., itching, rash, hives).

PLASMA PROTEIN FRACTION

(plas′ma)

Plasmanate, Plasma-Plex, Protenate

Classification(s): PLASMA VOLUME EXPANDER
Therapeutic: PLASMA VOLUME EXPANDER
Prototype: Normal serum albumin, human
Pregnancy Category: C

USES Emergency treatment of hypovolemic shock due to burns, trauma, surgery, infections; temporary measure in treatment of blood loss when whole blood is not available; to replenish plasma protein in patients with hypoproteinemia (if sodium restriction is not a problem).

INDICATION & DOSAGE

Plasma Volume Expansion

Adult: 250–500 mL at a maximum rate of 10 mL/min

SOLUTION PREPARATION

No dilution is required. Administer as supplied.

STORAGE

- Once container is opened, solution should be used within 4 h because it contains no preservatives.
- Discard solutions that have a sediment, appear turbid, or have been frozen.

ADMINISTRATION

- Rate of infusion and volume of total dose will depend on patient's age, diagnosis, degree of venous and pulmonary congestion, and Hct and Hgb.
- As with any oncotically active solution, infusion rate should be relatively slow. See **INDICATION & DOSAGE.**

INCOMPATIBILITIES **Protein hydrolysates** or **solutions containing alcohol.**

ACTION & *THERAPEUTIC EFFECT* Provides plasma proteins that increase colloidal osmotic pressure within the intravascular compartment equal to human plasma; it shifts water from extravascular tissues back into the intravascular space, thus expanding plasma volume. No coagulation factors or gamma globulins are provided. *It is used to maintain cardiac output in the treatment of shock due to various causes. Does not require cross matching.*

CONTRAINDICATIONS Hypersensitivity to albumin; severe anemia; cardiac failure; patients undergoing cardiopulmonary bypass surgery; pregnancy (category C).
CAUTIOUS USE Patients with low cardiac reserve; absence of albumin deficiency; liver or kidney failure.

ADVERSE EFFECTS (≥1%) **GI:** Nausea, vomiting, hypersalivation, headache. **Body as a Whole:** Tingling, chills, fever, cyanosis, chest tightness, backache, urticaria, erythema, <u>shock (systemic anaphylaxis)</u>, circulatory overload, pulmonary edema.

DRUG INTERACTIONS No clinically significant interactions established.

PHARMACOKINETICS Not studied.

NURSING IMPLICATIONS

Assessment & Drug Effects

- Monitor vital signs (BP and pulse). Frequency depends on patient's condition. Flow rate adjustments are made according to clinical response and BP. Slow or stop infusion if patient suddenly becomes hypotensive.
- Report a widening pulse pressure (difference between systolic and diastolic); it correlates with increase in cardiac output.
- Report changes in I&O ratio and pattern.
- Observe patient closely during and after infusion for signs of hypervolemia or circulatory overload (see Appendix C). Report these symptoms immediately to prescriber.
- Make careful observations of patient who has had either injury or surgery in order to detect bleeding points that failed to bleed at lower BP.

POLYMYXIN B SULFATE

(pol-i-mix'in)

Classification(s): ANTIBIOTIC
Therapeutic: ANTIBACTERIAL
Pregnancy Category: B

P

Common adverse effects in *italic*, life-threatening effects <u>underlined</u>: generic names in **bold**; classifications in SMALL CAPS; ♣ Canadian drug name; ⊘ Prototype drug

551

USES In hospitalized patients for treatment of severe acute infections of urinary tract, bloodstream, and meninges.

INDICATION & DOSAGE

Infections

Adult/Child: 15,000–25,000 units/kg/day divided q12h (max: 2 million units/day)
Infant: Up to 40,000 units/kg/day divided q12h

SOLUTION PREPARATION

- *Vial Reconstitution:* Add 5 mL sterile water for injection or NS to 500,000 units to yield 100,000 units/mL. **Must be** further diluted for infusion.
- *Further Dilution of Reconstituted Solution:* Add required dose to 300–500 mL of D5W.

STORAGE

- Protect unreconstituted product and reconstituted solution from light and freezing. Store in refrigerator at 2°–8° C (36°–46° F).
- Parenteral solutions are stable for 1 wk when refrigerated. Discard unused portion after 72 h.

ADMINISTRATION

- **Intermittent Infusion:** Infuse over 60–90 min.
- Inspect injection site often for signs of phlebitis and irritation.

INCOMPATIBILITIES Solution/additive: Amphotericin B, calcium, cefazolin, cephalothin, cephapirin, chloramphenicol, chlorothiazide, heparin, magnesium, nitrofurantoin, prednisolone, tetracycline.

ACTION & *THERAPEUTIC EFFECT* Antibiotic derived from strains of *Bacillus polymyxa*. Binds to lipid phosphates in bacterial membranes and, through cationic detergent action, changes permeability to permit leakage of cytoplasm from the bacterial cell. *Bactericidal against susceptible gram-negative but not gram-positive organisms, particularly most strains of* Escherichia coli, Haemophilus influenzae, Enterobacter aerogenes, *and* Klebsiella pneumoniae.

CONTRAINDICATIONS Hypersensitivity to polymyxin antibiotics; concurrent and sequential use of other nephrotoxic and neurotoxic drugs; concurrent use of skeletal muscle relaxants, ether, or sodium citrate; lactation.
CAUTIOUS USE Impaired kidney function; myasthenia gravis; pregnancy (category B); infant.

ADVERSE EFFECTS (≥1%) **Body as a Whole:** Irritability; facial flushing; ataxia; circumoral, lingual, and peripheral paresthesias (stocking-glove distribution); thrombophlebitis; superinfections; electrolyte disturbances (prolonged use;); <u>anaphylactoid reactions</u> (rare). **CNS:** Drowsiness, dizziness, vertigo, convulsions, coma; <u>neuromuscular blockade</u>; meningeal irritation, increased protein and cell count in cerebrospinal fluid, fever. **Special Senses:** Slurred speech, dysphagia, ototoxicity (vestibular and auditory) with high doses. **GI:** GI disturbances. **Urogenital:** Albuminuria, cylindruria, azotemia, hematuria.

DRUG INTERACTIONS ANESTHETICS and NEUROMUSCULAR BLOCKING AGENTS may prolong skeletal muscle relaxation. AMINOGLYCOSIDES and **amphotericin B** have additive nephrotoxic potential.

PHARMACOKINETICS Distribution: Widely distributed except to CSF, synovial fluid, and eye; does not cross placenta. **Metabolism:** Unknown. **Elimination:** 60% excreted unchanged in urine. **Half-Life:** 4.3–6 h.

NURSING IMPLICATIONS

Assessment & Drug Effects

- Prior to initiating therapy: Baseline C&S tests (start drug pending results).
- Report promptly: Muscle weakness, shortness of breath, dyspnea, depressed respiration.
- Withhold drug and report any of the following: Decreases in urine output (change in I&O ratio), proteinuria, rising BUN, serum creatinine, or serum drug levels (not associated with dosage increase) as these may indicate nephrotoxicity.
- Be alert for respiratory arrest, especially after the first dose. It occurs most commonly in patients with kidney failure and high plasma drug levels and is often preceded by dyspnea and restlessness.
- Lab tests: Baseline and periodic serum electrolytes and kidney function tests; periodic serum drug levels.
- Monitor electrolyte results. Patients with low serum calcium and low intracellular potassium are particularly prone to develop neuromuscular blockade.
- Inspect tongue daily for S&S of superinfection (see Appendix C).
- Monitor I&O and maintain fluid intake sufficient to maintain daily urinary output of at least 1500 mL.

Patient & Family Education

- Report promptly: Difficulty breathing, burning or prickling sensations, numbness, or dizziness.
- Report promptly the onset of stiff neck and headache (possible symptoms of neurotoxic reactions).

POTASSIUM CHLORIDE

(poe-tass'ee-um)

Classification(s): REPLACEMENT SOLUTION
Therapeutic: ELECTROLYTE REPLACEMENT
Pregnancy Category: C

Common adverse effects in *italic*, life-threatening effects <u>underlined</u>: generic names in **bold**; classifications in SMALL CAPS; ♣ Canadian drug name; ⊙ Prototype drug

553

POTASSIUM CHLORIDE

USES To prevent and treat potassium deficit secondary to diuretic or corticosteroid therapy. Also indicated when potassium is depleted by severe vomiting, diarrhea; intestinal drainage, fistulas, or malabsorption; prolonged diuresis, diabetic acidosis. Effective in the treatment of hypokalemic alkalosis.

INDICATION & DOSAGE

Hypokalemia
Adult: Dose based on serum potassium levels, usually not more than 3 mEq/kg (max: 400 mEq/day, monitor higher doses carefully)
Child: Up to 3 mEq/kg/24 h at a rate less than 0.02 mEq/kg/min

SOLUTION PREPARATION
- Add desired dose to 100–1000 mL IV solution (compatible with all standard solutions). Maximum concentration is 80 mEq/1000 mL, but 40 mEq/L is preferred. Invert IV container several times to ensure even distribution.
- Note: **Never** add KCl to an IV bag/bottle in a hanging position.

STORAGE
Store at 15°–30° C (59°–86° F).

ADMINISTRATION
- KCl is **NEVER** given direct IV or in concentrated amounts by any route.
- **IV Infusion:**
  - *Adult:* Typically infused at a rate not to exceed 10 mEq/h. In emergency situations, may be infused very cautiously at a rate up to 40 mEq/h with continuous cardiac monitoring.
  - *Child:* Infuse at a rate not to exceed 0.5–1.0 mEq/kg/h.
- Too rapid infusion may cause **FATAL** hyperkalemia.
- Take extreme care to prevent extravasation and infiltration. At first sign, discontinue infusion and select another site.

INCOMPATIBILITIES Solution/additive: Amoxicillin, amphotericin B, furosemide, pentobarbital, phenobarbital. **Y-site:** Amphotericin B cholesteryl complex, azithromycin, chlordiazepoxide, chlorpromazine, diazepam, ergotamine, lansoprazole, methylprednisolone, phenytoin.

ACTION & *THERAPEUTIC EFFECT* Principal intracellular cation; essential for maintenance of intracellular isotonicity, transmission of nerve impulses, contraction of cardiac, skeletal, and smooth muscles, maintenance of normal kidney function, and for enzyme activity. Plays a prominent role in both formation and correction of imbalances in acid–base metabolism. *Effective in treatment of hypokalemia. Effectiveness measured as serum potassium concentration greater than 3.5 mEq/L.*

CONTRAINDICATIONS Severe renal impairment; severe hemolytic reactions; untreated Addison's disease; crush syndrome; early postoperative oliguria (except during GI drainage); adynamic ileus; acute dehydration; heat cramps, hyperkalemia, patients receiving potassium-sparing diuretics, digitalis intoxication with AV conduction disturbance; pregnancy (category C). **CAUTIOUS USE** Cardiac or kidney disease; systemic acidosis; slow-release potassium preparations in presence of delayed GI transit or Meckel's diverticulum; extensive tissue breakdown (such as severe burns); lactation.

ADVERSE EFFECTS (≥1%) **GI:** *Nausea, vomiting,* diarrhea, abdominal distension. **Body as a Whole:** Pain, mental confusion, irritability, listlessness, paresthesias of extremities, muscle weakness and heaviness of limbs, difficulty in swallowing, <u>flaccid paralysis</u>. **Urogenital:** Oliguria, anuria. **Hematologic:** Hyperkalemia. **Respiratory:** <u>Respiratory distress</u>. **CV:** Hypotension, bradycardia; <u>cardiac depression, arrhythmias, or arrest</u>; altered sensitivity to digitalis glycosides. *ECG changes in hyperkalemia:* Tenting (peaking) of T-wave (especially in right precordial leads), lowering of R with deepening of S waves and depression of RST; prolonged P-R interval, widened QRS complex, decreased amplitude and disappearance of P waves, prolonged Q-T interval, signs of right and left bundle block, <u>deterioration of QRS contour and finally ventricular fibrillation and death</u>.

DRUG INTERACTIONS POTASSIUM-SPARING DIURETICS, ANGIOTENSIN-CONVERTING ENZYME (ACE) INIBITORS may cause hyperkalemia.

PHARMACOKINETICS Elimination: 90% in urine, 10% in feces.

NURSING IMPLICATIONS

Assessment & Drug Effects

- Monitor closely with cardiac monitor. Irregular heartbeat is usually the earliest clinical indication of hyperkalemia.
- Lab test: Baseline and frequent serum electrolytes.
- Monitor I&O ratio and pattern closely. If oliguria occurs (e.g., less than 30 mL/h), stop infusion promptly and notify prescriber.
- Be alert for S&S of hyperkalemia (see Appendix C). The risk of hyperkalemia is increased in older adults because of decremental changes in kidney function.
- Concurrent drug: Monitor for digitalis toxicity or loss of therapeutic effect.

Patient & Family Education

- Report promptly: Mental confusion, muscle weakness, difficulty swallowing, or numbness or tingling in extremities.

PRALIDOXIME CHLORIDE

(pra-li-dox'eem)

2-PAM, Protopam Chloride

Classification(s): ANTICHOLINESTERASE ANTIDOTE

Therapeutic: ANTIDOTE

Pregnancy Category: C

USES As antidote in treatment of poisoning by organophosphate insecticides and pesticides with anticholinesterase activity (e.g., parathion, TEPP, sarin) and to control overdosage by anticholinesterase drugs used in treatment of myasthenia gravis (cholinergic crisis).
UNLABELED USES To reverse toxicity of echothiophate ophthalmic solution.

INDICATION & DOSAGE

Organophosphate Poisoning

Adult: 1–2 g, may repeat after 1 h if muscle weakness not relieved
Child: 20–50 mg/kg, may repeat in 1–2 h if needed

Anticholinesterase Overdose Due to Myasthenia Gravis Drugs

Adult: 1–2 g, followed by increments of 250 mg q5min prn

SOLUTION PREPARATION

- *Vial Reconstitution:* Add 20 mL sterile water for injection to the 1-g vial to yield 50 mg/mL (a 5% solution). Should be further diluted for infusion, but if pulmonary edema is present, may be given without further dilution.
- *Further Dilution of Reconstituted Solution:* Add required dose to 100 mL NS.

STORAGE

Store unopened vials at 20°–25° C (68°–77° F). Reconstituted solutions and IV solutions should be used immediately.

ADMINISTRATION

- **Direct IV Injection of 5% Solution:** In pulmonary edema, give 1 g or fraction thereof over at least 5 min; do not exceed 200 mg/min.
- **IV Infusion (preferred):** Infuse over 15–30 min.
- Stop infusion or reduce rate if hypertension occurs.

INCOMPATIBILITIES Data not available; do not mix with other drugs.

ACTION & *THERAPEUTIC EFFECT* Reactivates cholinesterase inhibited by phosphate esters by displacing the enzyme from its receptor sites; the free enzyme then can resume its function of degrading accumulated acetylcholine, thereby restoring normal neuromuscular transmission. *More active against effects of anticholinesterases at skeletal neuromuscular junction than at autonomic effector sites or in CNS respiratory center; therefore, atropine **must be** given concomitantly to block effects of acetylcholine and its accumulation in these sites.*

CONTRAINDICATIONS Use in poisoning by carbamate insecticide Sevin, inorganic phosphates, or organophosphates having no anticholinesterase activity; pregnancy (category C).
CAUTIOUS USE Myasthenia gravis; asthma; peptic ulcer; severe cardiac disease; renal insufficiency; concomitant use of barbiturates in organophosphorus poisoning; lactation, children.

ADVERSE EFFECTS (≥1%) **CNS:** Dizziness, headache, drowsiness. **GI:** Nausea. **Special Senses:** Blurred vision, diplopia, impaired accommodation. **CV:** Tachycardia, hypertension (dose-related). **Body as a Whole:** Hyperventilation, muscular weakness, <u>laryngospasm</u>, muscle rigidity.

DRUG INTERACTIONS May potentiate the effects of BARBITURATES.

PHARMACOKINETICS Peak: 5–15 min. **Distribution:** Distributed throughout extracellular fluids; crosses blood–brain barrier slowly if at all. **Metabolism:** Probably metabolized in liver. **Elimination:** Rapidly excreted in urine. **Half-Life:** 0.8–2.7 h.

NURSING IMPLICATIONS

Assessment & Drug Effects

- Monitor BP, vital signs, and I&O. Report oliguria or changes in I&O ratio.
- Monitor closely. It is difficult to differentiate toxic effects of organophosphates or atropine from toxic effects of pralidoxime.
- Be alert for and report immediately: Reduction in muscle strength, onset of muscle twitching, changes in respiratory pattern, altered level of consciousness, increases or changes in heart rate and rhythm.
- Observe necessary safety precautions with unconscious patient because excitement and manic behavior reportedly may occur following recovery of consciousness.
- Keep patient under close observation for 48–72 h, particularly when poison was ingested, because of likelihood of continued absorption of organophosphate from lower bowel.
- In patients with myasthenia gravis, overdosage with pralidoxime may convert cholinergic crisis into myasthenic crisis.

P

PROCAINAMIDE HYDROCHLORIDE 🅟

(proe-kane-a′mide)
Procanbid, Pronestyl, Pronestyl SR
Classification(s): ANTIARRHYTHMIC, CLASS IA
Therapeutic: ANTIARRHYTHMIC
Pregnancy Category: C

USES Prophylactically to maintain normal sinus rhythm following conversion of atrial flutter or fibrillation by other methods; to prevent recurrence of paroxysmal atrial fibrillation and tachycardia, paroxysmal AV junctional rhythm, ventricular tachycardia, ventricular and atrial premature contractions. Also cardiac arrhythmias associated with surgery and anesthesia.
UNLABELED USES Malignant hyperthermia.

INDICATION & DOSAGE

Arrhythmias

Adult: 20 mg/min until arrhythmia is controlled (up to 17 mg/kg) then 1–4 mg/min maintenance dose
Child: 15 mg/kg over 30 min

Common adverse effects in *italic*, life-threatening effects <u>underlined</u>: generic names in **bold**; classifications in SMALL CAPS; ♣ Canadian drug name; 🅟 Prototype drug

Renal Impairment Dosage Adjustment

CrCl 35–59 mL/min: Decrease maintenance dose by 30%; *CrCl 15–34 mL/ min:* Reduce maintenance dose by 40–60%

SOLUTION PREPARATION

- *Direct IV Injection:* Dilute each 100 mg with 5–10 mL of D5W or sterile water for injection.
- *IV Infusion:* Add 1 g to 250–500 mL of D5W to yield 4 mg/mL in 250 mL or 2 mg/mL in 500 mL.

STORAGE

- Store solution for up to 24 h at 15°–30° C (59°–86° F) and for 7 days under refrigeration at 2°–8° C (36°–46° F).
- Slight yellowing does not alter drug potency, but discard solution if it is markedly discolored.

ADMINISTRATION

- **Direct IV Injection:** Give at a rate of 20 mg/min. Faster rates (up to 50 mg/min) should be used with caution.
- **IV Infusion:**
  - *Adult:* Infuse at 2–6 mg/min.
  - *Child:* Infuse at 20–80 mcg/kg/min.
- Use an infusion pump with constant monitoring.
- Keep patient in supine position during infusion.

INCOMPATIBILITIES Solution/additive: Bretylium, esmolol, ethacrynate, milrinone, phenytoin, dextrose 5%. Y-site: Inamrinone (amrinone), lansoprazole, milrinone.

ACTION & *THERAPEUTIC EFFECT* Amide analog of procaine hydrochloride with Class IA antiarrhythmic actions. Depresses excitability of myocardium to electrical stimulation, reduces conduction velocity in atria, ventricles, and His-Purkinje system. Increases duration of refractory period, especially in the atria. *Effectively used for atrial arrhythmias; produces slight change in contractility of cardiac muscle and cardiac output; suppresses automaticity of His-Purkinje ventricular muscle.*

CONTRAINDICATIONS Myasthenia gravis; hypersensitivity to procainamide or procaine; blood dyscrasias; bundle branch block; complete AV block, second and third degree AV block unassisted by pacemaker; QT prolongation; pregnancy (category C).

CAUTIOUS USE Patient who has undergone electrical conversion to sinus rhythm; hypotension, cardiac enlargement, bone marrow suppression; CHF, MI, coronary occlusion, ventricular dysrhythmia from digitalis intoxication; hepatic or renal insufficiency; electrolyte imbalance; bronchial asthma; history of SLE.

ADVERSE EFFECTS (≥1%) **CNS:** Dizziness, psychosis. **CV:** Severe hypotension, pericarditis, <u>ventricular fibrillation</u>, AV block, tachycardia, flushing. **Hematologic:** <u>Agranulocytosis with repeated use</u>; thrombocytopenia. **Body as a Whole:** Fever, muscle and joint pain, angioneurotic edema, myalgia. **Skin:** Maculopapular rash, pruritus. erythema, skin rash.

DIAGNOSTIC TEST INTERFERENCE Procainamide increases the *plasma levels of alkaline phosphatase, bilirubin, lactic dehydrogenase, and AST.* It may also alter results of the *edrophonium test.*

DRUG INTERACTIONS Other ANTIARRHYTHMICS add to therapeutic and toxic effects; ANTICHOLINERGIC AGENTS compound anticholinergic effects; ANTIHYPERTENSIVES add to hypotensive effects; **cimetidine** may increase procainamide and **NAPA** levels with increase in toxicity.

PHARMACOKINETICS Distribution: Distributed to CSF, liver, spleen, kidney, brain, and heart; crosses placenta; distributed into breast milk. **Metabolism:** In liver to *N*-acetyl-p-aminophenol (NAPA), an active metabolite (30–60% metabolized to NAPA). **Elimination:** In urine. **Half-Life:** 3 h procainamide, 6 h NAPA.

NURSING IMPLICATIONS

Assessment & Drug Effects

- Monitor continuously ECG and BP during administration. Patients with severe heart, liver, or kidney disease and hypotension are at particular risk for adverse effects.
- Monitor for signs of too-rapid administration of drug (speed shock: irregular pulse, tight feeling in chest, flushed face, headache, loss of consciousness, signs of shock, cardiac arrest).
- Discontinue IV drug temporarily when (1) arrhythmia is interrupted, (2) severe toxic effects are present, (3) QRS complex is excessively widened (greater than 50%), (4) PR interval is prolonged, or (5) BP drops 15 mm Hg or more. Obtain rhythm strip and notify prescriber.
- Ventricular dysrhythmias are usually abolished within a few minutes after IV administration.
- Lab tests: Periodic procainamide levels. Therapeutic blood levels are reached in approximately 24 h if kidney function is normal but are delayed with renal impairment.

Patient & Family Education

- Report promptly chest pain, shortness of breath, or sudden feelings of anxiety.

PROCHLORPERAZINE ⓟ

(proe-klor-per′a-zeen)

Compazine

PROCHLORPERAZINE EDISYLATE

Compazine

Classification(s): ANTIEMETIC, PHENOTHIAZINE
Therapeutic: ANTIEMETIC
Pregnancy Category: C

USES To control severe nausea and vomiting.

INDICATION & DOSAGE

Severe Nausea, Vomiting

Adult: 2.5–10 mg q3–4h (max: 40 mg/day)

SOLUTION PREPARATION

- *Direct IV Injection*: No dilution is required. Administer as supplied.
- *IV Infusion:* Dilute in 50–100 mL of D5W, NS, D5/1/2NS, LR, or other compatible solution.
- Avoid contact with skin; may cause contact dermatitis.

STORAGE

- Store at 15°–30° C (59°–86° F). Protect from light.
- Discard markedly discolored solutions; slight yellowing does not appear to alter potency.

ADMINISTRATION

- **Direct IV Injection:** Give at a maximum rate of 5 mg/min.
- **IV Infusion:** Infuse over 15–30 min. Do not exceed direct IV rate.

INCOMPATIBILITIES Solution/additive: Aminophylline, amphotericin B, ampicillin, calcium gluconate, cephalothin, chloramphenicol, chlorothiazide, dimenhydrinate, epinephrine, erythromycin, furosemide, hydrocortisone, hydromorphone, kanamycin, ketorolac, methohexital, midazolam, morphine, penicillin G sodium, pentobarbital, phenobarbital, tetracycline, thiopental, vancomycin, warfarin. Y-site: Aldesleukin, allopurinol, amifostine, amphotericin B cholesteryl complex, aztreonam, bivalirudin, cefepime, etoposide, fenoldopam, filgrastim, fludarabine, foscarnet, gallium, gemcitabine, lansoprazole, pemetrexed, piperacillin-tazobactam.

ACTION & *THERAPEUTIC EFFECT* Phenothiazine derivative that produces antiemetic effect by suppression of the chemoreceptor trigger zone (CTZ). *Greater antiemetic potency but fewer sedative, hypotensive, and anticholinergic effects than chlorpromazine.*

CONTRAINDICATIONS Hypersensitivity to phenothiazines; bone marrow depression; blood dyscrasias, jaundice; comatose or severely depressed states; children less than 9 kg (20 lb) or 2 y of age; pediatric surgery; short-term vomiting in children or vomiting of unknown etiology; Reye's syndrome or other encephalopathies; history of dyskinetic reactions or epilepsy; pregnancy (category C), lactation.

CAUTIOUS USE Patient with previously diagnosed breast cancer; Parkinson's disease; GI obstruction; hepatic disease; seizure disorders; urinary retention, BPH; children with acute illness or dehydration.

ADVERSE EFFECTS (≥1%) **CNS:** *Drowsiness,* dizziness, *extrapyramidal reactions (akathisia, dystonia or parkinsonism),* persistent tardive dyskinesia, acute catatonia. **CV:** Hypotension. **GI:** Cholestatic jaundice. **Skin:** Contact dermatitis, photosensitivity. **Endocrine:** Galactorrhea, amenorrhea. **Special Senses:** Blurred vision. **Hematologic:** Leukopenia, <u>agranulocytosis</u>.

DRUG INTERACTIONS Alcohol, CNS DEPRESSANTS increase CNS depression; **phenobarbital** increases metabolism of prochlorperazine; GENERAL ANESTHETICS increase excitation and hypotension; antagonizes antihypertensive action of **guanethidine; phenylpropanolamine** poses possibility of sudden death; TRICYCLIC ANTIDEPRESSANTS intensify hypotensive and anticholinergic effects; decreases seizure threshold: ANTICONVULSANT dosage may need to be increased.

PHARMACOKINETICS Distribution: Crosses placenta; distributed into breast milk. **Metabolism:** In liver. **Elimination:** In urine.

NURSING IMPLICATIONS
Assessment & Drug Effects
- Position nauseated patients carefully to prevent aspiration of vomitus; may have depressed cough reflex.
- Monitor vital signs often. Report promptly elevated BP or temperature.
- Most older adult and emaciated patients and children, especially those with dehydration or acute illness, appear to be particularly susceptible to extrapyramidal effects. Be alert to onset of symptoms of pseudoparkinson's and acute dyskinesia.
- Keep in mind that the antiemetic effect may mask toxicity of other drugs or make it difficult to diagnose conditions with a primary symptom of nausea.
- Lab tests: Periodic CBC with differential in long-term therapy.

Patient & Family Education
- Use caution with ambulation and hazardous activities until response to drug is known.
- Avoid alcohol or other CNS depressants after receiving prochlorperazine.
- Be aware that drug may color urine reddish brown. It also may cause the sun-exposed skin to turn gray-blue.
- Protect skin from direct sun's rays and use a sunscreen lotion to prevent photosensitivity reaction.

P

PROMETHAZINE HYDROCHLORIDE
(proe-meth′a-zeen)
Phenergan
Classification(s): PHENOTHIAZINE
Therapeutic: ANTIEMETIC; ANTIHISTAMINE; SEDATIVE-HYPNOTIC
Prototype: Prochlorperazine
Pregnancy Category: C

USES Symptomatic relief of various allergic conditions, to ameliorate and prevent reactions to blood and plasma, and in prophylaxis and treatment of motion sickness, nausea, and vomiting. Preoperative, postoperative, and obstetric sedation and as adjunct to analgesics for control of pain.

INDICATION & DOSAGE

Nausea

Adult: 12.5–25 mg q4–6h prn
Child (greater than 2 y): 6.25–12.5 mg q4–6h prn (max: 25 mg/dose)

Allergies

Adult: 25 mg, repeat in 2 hrs; if necessary, switch to PO
Child (greater than 2 y): Up to 12.5 mg

Sedation

Adult: 25–50 mg/dose
Child (greater than 2 y): 12.5–25 mg/dose

SOLUTION PREPARATION

The 25 mg/mL concentration may be given undiluted. Dilute the 50 mg/mL concentrated in NS to no more than 25 mg/mL (e.g., diluting 50 mg in 4 mL NS yields 10 mg/mL).

STORAGE

- Store at 15°–30° C (59°–86° F) in a tight, light-resistant container unless otherwise directed.
- Inspect parenteral drug before preparation. Discard if it is darkened.

ADMINISTRATION

Direct IV Injection: Give each 25 mg over at least 1 min.

INCOMPATIBILITIES Solution/additive: Aminophylline, ampicillin, carbenicillin, cefazolin, cefotetan, ceftizoxime, chloramphenicol, chlordiazepoxide, chlorothiazide, dexamethasone, dimenhydrinate, furosemide, heparin, hydrocortisone, ketorolac, methicillin, methohexital, nalbuphine, nitrofurantoin, penicillin G sodium, pentobarbital, phenobarbital, thiopental. Y-site: Aldesleukin, allopurinol, amphotericin B cholesteryl complex, cefepime, cefmetazole, cefoperazone, cefotetan, doxorubicin liposome, foscarnet, furosemide, heparin, lansoprazole, methotrexate, piperacillin/tazobactam, TPN.

ACTION & *THERAPEUTIC EFFECT* In common with other antihistamines, promethazine exerts antiserotonin, anticholinergic, and local anesthetic action. Antiemetic action thought to be due to depression of CTZ in medulla. *Long-acting derivative of phenothiazine with marked antihistamine activity and prominent sedative, amnesic, antiemetic, and anti–motion-sickness actions.*

CONTRAINDICATIONS Hypersensitivity to phenothiazines; acute MI, angina, atrial fibrillation, atrial flutter, cardiac arrhythmias, cardiomyopathy, uncontrolled hypertension; MAOI therapy; epilepsy; bone marrow depression; comatose or severely depressed states; child with Reye's syndrome;

hepatic encephalopathy or hepatic diseases; pregnancy (category C), lactation; newborn or premature infants, acutely ill or dehydrated children.
CAUTIOUS USE Impaired liver function; cardiovascular disease; peripheral vascular disease; asthma, acute or chronic respiratory impairment (particularly in children); hypertension; narrow-angle glaucoma; stenosing peptic ulcer, pyloroduodenal obstruction; prostatic hypertrophy; bladder neck obstruction; older adult or debilitated patients; children less than 2 y.

ADVERSE EFFECTS (≥1%) **Body as a Whole:** Deep sleep, coma, convulsions, cardiorespiratory symptoms, extrapyramidal reactions, nightmares (in children), CNS stimulation, abnormal movements. **Respiratory:** Irregular respirations, respiratory depression, apnea. **CNS:** Sedation *drowsiness,* confusion, dizziness, disturbed coordination, restlessness, tremors. **CV:** Transient mild hypotension or hypertension. **GI:** Anorexia, nausea, vomiting, constipation. **Hematologic:** Leukopenia, agranulocytosis. **Special Senses:** *Blurred vision, dry mouth,* nose, or throat. **Skin:** Photosensitivity. **Urogenital:** Urinary retention.

DIAGNOSTIC TEST INTERFERENCE May interfere with *blood grouping in ABO system* and may produce false results with *urinary pregnancy tests (Gravindex,* false-positive; *Prepurex* and *Dap tests,* false-negative). Promethazine can cause significant alterations of *flare response* in *intradermal allergen tests* if performed within 4 days of receiving promethazine.

DRUG INTERACTIONS Alcohol and other CNS DEPRESSANTS add to CNS depression and anticholinergic effects.

PHARMACOKINETICS Onset: 5 min. **Duration:** 2–8 h. **Distribution:** Crosses placenta. **Metabolism:** In liver (CYP2D6, 2B6). **Elimination:** Slowly in urine and feces.

P

NURSING IMPLICATIONS

Assessment & Drug Effects

- Monitor respiratory function in patients with respiratory problems, particularly children. Drug may suppress cough reflex and cause thickening of bronchial secretions.
- Supervise ambulation. Promethazine sometimes produces marked sedation and dizziness.
- Be aware that antiemetic action may mask symptoms of unrecognized disease and signs of drug overdosage as well as dizziness, vertigo, or tinnitus associated with toxic doses of aspirin or other ototoxic drugs.
- Patients in pain may develop involuntary (athetoid) movements of upper extremities following parenteral administration. These symptoms usually disappear after pain is controlled.

Patient & Family Education

- Use caution when ambulating and avoid hazardous activities until response to drug is known.
- Avoid alcohol and other CNS depressants.

PROPOFOL

(pro′po-fol)

Diprivan

Classification(s): ANESTHESIA, GENERAL; SEDATIVE-HYPNOTIC
Therapeutic: GENERAL ANESTHESIA; SEDATION
Prototype: Thiopental
Pregnancy Category: B

USES Induction or maintenance of anesthesia as part of a balanced anesthesia technique; conscious sedation in mechanically ventilated patients.

INDICATION & DOSAGE

Anesthesia

Adult (under 55 y): 40 mg q10sec then 100–200 mcg/kg/min
Adult (55 y or more): 20 mg q10sec then 50–100 mcg/kg/min
Adolescent/Child (over 3 y): 2.5–3.5 mg/kg over 20–30 sec, then 125–300 mcg/kg/min

Conscious Sedation

Adult: 5 mcg/kg/min for at least 5 min, may increase by 5–10 mcg/kg/min q5–10min until desired level of sedation is achieved (may need maintenance rate of 5–80 mcg/kg/min)

SOLUTION PREPARATION

- Use strict aseptic technique to prepare propofol for injection; drug emulsion supports rapid growth of microorganisms.
- Inspect vials for particulate matter and discoloration. Discard if either is noted.
- Shake well before use. Inspect for separation of the emulsion. Do not use if there is evidence of separation of phases of the emulsion.
- *IV Infusion:* May be given undiluted or diluted in D5W to a concentration not less than 2 mg/mL. Use immediately upon dilution.

STORAGE

- Store unopened vial at 4°–22° C (40°–72° F). Refrigeration is not recommended. Protect from light.
- *ICU Sedation:* Discard infusion container and tubing q12h, or if transferred from original container, discard q6h.

ADMINISTRATION

- **IV Infusion:** Use syringe or volumetric pump; rate determined by patient weight. Complete infusion within 6 h.
- Administer immediately after spiking the vial.

INCOMPATIBILITIES Y-site: Amikacin, amphotericin B, ascorbic acid, atracurium, bretylium, calcium chloride, ceftazidime, ciprofloxacin, cisatracurium, diazepam, digoxin, doxorubicin, gentamicin, levoflox-

acin, methotrexate, methylprednisolone, metoclopramide, minocycline, mitoxantrone, netilmicin, phenytoin, tobramycin, verapamil.

ACTION & *THERAPEUTIC EFFECT* Sedative–hypnotic used in the induction and maintenance of anesthesia or sedation. Rapid onset (40 sec) and minimal excitation during induction of anesthesia. *Effectively used for conscious sedation and maintenance of anesthesia.*

CONTRAINDICATIONS Hypersensitivity to propofol or propofol emulsion, which contain soybean oil and egg phosphatide; obstetrical procedures; patients with increased intracranial pressure or impaired cerebral circulation; lactation. Do not use for induction of anesthesia in children less than 3 y. The safe use of propofol for conscious sedation in children has not been established.

CAUTIOUS USE Patients with severe cardiac or respiratory disorders or history of epilepsy or seizures; pregnancy (category B).

ADVERSE EFFECTS (≥1%) **CNS:** Headache, dizziness, *twitching, bucking, jerking, thrashing, clonic/myoclonic movements.* **Special Senses:** Decreased intraocular pressure. **CV:** Hypotension, ventricular asystole (rare). **GI:** Vomiting, abdominal cramping. **Respiratory:** Cough, hiccups, apnea. **Other:** Pain at injection site.

DIAGNOSTIC TEST INTERFERENCE Propofol produces a temporary reduction in ***serum cortisol levels.*** However, propofol does not seem to inhibit adrenal responsiveness to ***ACTH.***

DRUG INTERACTIONS Concurrent continuous infusions of propofol and **alfentanil** produce higher plasma levels of **alfentanil** than expected. CNS DEPRESSANTS cause additive CNS depression.

PHARMACOKINETICS Onset: 9–36 sec. **Duration:** 6–10 min. **Distribution:** Highly lipophilic, crosses placenta, excreted in breast milk. **Metabolism:** Extensively in the liver (by CYP 2B6, 2C9). **Elimination:** Approximately 88% of the dose is recovered in the urine as metabolites. **Half-Life:** 5–12 h.

NURSING IMPLICATIONS
Assessment & Drug Effects
- Monitor hemodynamic status and assess for dose-related hypotension.
- Take seizure precautions. Tonic–clonic seizures have occurred following general anesthesia with propofol.
- Be alert to the potential for drug-induced excitation (e.g., twitching, tremor, hyperclonus) and take appropriate safety measures.
- Provide comfort measures; pain at the injection site is quite common, especially when small veins are used.

PROPRANOLOL HYDROCHLORIDE ℗
(proe-pran'oh-lole)
Apo-Propranolol ✦, Inderal, Novopranol ✦

PROPRANOLOL HYDROCHLORIDE

Classification(s): BETA-ADRENERGIC ANTAGONIST; ANTIARRHYTHMIC, CLASS II
Therapeutic: ANTIARRHYTHMIC
Pregnancy Category: C

USES Management of cardiac arrhythmias.

INDICATION & DOSAGE

Arrhythmia
Adult: 1–3 mg, may repeat q4h

SOLUTION PREPARATION
- *Direct IV Injection:* May be given undiluted or dilute each 1 mg in 10 mL of D5W.
- *Intermittent Infusion:* Dilute a single dose in 50 mL of NS.

STORAGE
Store at 15°–30° C (59°–86° F) in tightly closed, light-resistant containers.

ADMINISTRATION
- **Direct IV Injection:** Give each 1 mg or fraction thereof over 1 min.
- **Intermittent Infusion:** Infuse over 15–20 min.

INCOMPATIBILITIES Y-site: Amphotericin B cholesteryl complex, diazoxide, lansoprazole.

ACTION & *THERAPEUTIC EFFECT* Nonselective beta-blocker of both cardiac and bronchial adrenoreceptors that competes with epinephrine and norepinephrine for available beta-receptor sites. In higher doses, exerts direct quinidine-like effects, which depresses cardiac function including contractility and arrhythmias. Lowers both supine and standing blood pressures in hypertensive patients. *Blocks cardiac effects of beta-adrenergic stimulation; as a result, reduces heart rate, myocardial irritability (Class II antiarrhythmic), and force of contraction, depresses automaticity of sinus node and ectopic pacemaker, and decreases AV and intraventricular conduction velocity.*

CONTRAINDICATIONS Greater than first-degree heart block; CHF (unless caused by tachycardia), right ventricular failure secondary to pulmonary hypertension; ventricular dysfunction; sinus bradycardia, cardiogenic shock, significant aortic or mitral valvular disease; bronchial asthma or bronchospasm, severe COPD, pulmonary edema; abrupt discontinuation; pregnancy (category C).

CAUTIOUS USE Peripheral arterial insufficiency; history of systemic insect sting reaction; patients prone to nonallergenic bronchospasm (e.g., chronic bronchitis, emphysema); major surgery; cerebrovascular disease, stroke; renal or hepatic disease; pheochromocytoma, vasospastic angina; major depression; peripheral vascular disease, Raynaud's disease; older adults; diabetes mellitus; patients prone to hypoglycemia; hyperthyroidism, thyrotoxicosis; surgery; myasthenia gravis; Wolff-Parkinson-White syndrome; lactation.

ADVERSE EFFECTS (≥1%) **Body as a Whole:** Fever; pharyngitis; respiratory distress, weight gain, lupus-like reaction, cold extremities, leg fatigue, arthralgia, <u>anaphylactic/anaphylactoid reactions</u>. **Urogenital:** Impotence or decreased libido. **Skin:** Erythematous, psoriasis-like eruptions; pruritus, <u>Stevens-Johnson syndrome, toxic epidermal necrolysis</u>, erythema multiforme, <u>exfoliative dermatitis</u>, urticaria. Reversible alopecia, hyperkeratoses of scalp, palms, feet; nail changes, dry skin. **CNS:** Drug-induced psychosis, sleep disturbances, depression, *confusion,* agitation, giddiness, lightheadedness, *fatigue,* vertigo, syncope, weakness, *drowsiness,* insomnia, vivid dreams, visual hallucinations, delusions, reversible organic brain syndrome. **CV:** Palpitation, profound *bradycardia,* AV heart block, cardiac standstill, hypotension, angina pectoris, tachyarrhythmia, acute CHF, peripheral arterial insufficiency resembling Raynaud's disease, myotonia, *paresthesia of hands.* **Special Senses:** Dry eyes (gritty sensation), visual disturbances, conjunctivitis, tinnitus, hearing loss, nasal stuffiness. **GI:** Dry mouth, nausea, vomiting, heartburn, diarrhea, constipation, flatulence, abdominal cramps, mesenteric arterial thrombosis, ischemic colitis, pancreatitis. **Hematologic:** Transient eosinophilia, thrombocytopenic or nonthrombocytopenic purpura, <u>agranulocytosis</u>. **Metabolic:** Hypoglycemia, hyperglycemia, hypocalcemia (patients with hyperthyroidism). **Respiratory:** Dyspnea, <u>laryngospasm</u>, bronchospasm.

DIAGNOSTIC TEST INTERFERENCE BETA-ADRENERGIC BLOCKERS may produce false-negative test results in ***exercise tolerance ECG tests,*** and elevations in ***serum potassium, peripheral platelet count, serum uric acid, serum transaminase, alkaline phosphatase, lactate dehydrogenase, serum creatinine, BUN,*** and an increase or decrease in ***blood glucose*** levels in diabetic patients.

DRUG INTERACTIONS PHENOTHIAZINES have additive hypotensive effects. BETA-ADRENERGIC AGONISTS (e.g., **albuterol**) antagonize effects. **Atropine** and TRICYCLIC ANTIDEPRESSANTS block bradycardia. DIURETICS and other HYPOTENSIVE AGENTS increase hypotension. High doses of **tubocurarine** may potentiate neuromuscular blockade. **Cimetidine** decreases clearance, increases effects.

PHARMACOKINETICS Peak: 5 min. **Distribution:** Widely distributed including CNS, placenta, and breast milk. **Metabolism:** Almost completely in liver (CYP1A2, 2D6). **Elimination:** 90–95% in urine as metabolites; 1–4% in feces. **Half-Life:** 2.3 h.

NURSING IMPLICATIONS

Assessment & Drug Effects

- Continuous ECG and BP monitoring is required for IV drug administration.
- Monitor I&O ratio and daily weight as significant indexes for detecting fluid retention and developing heart failure.

- Lab tests: Obtain periodic hematologic, kidney, liver, and cardiac functions when propranolol is given for prolonged periods.
- If patient complains of cold, painful, or tender feet or hands, examine carefully for evidence of impaired circulation. Peripheral pulses may still be present even though circulation is impaired.
- Monitor diabetics for development of hypo- or hyperglycemia. Note that propranolol can mask signs of hypoglycemia.

Patient & Family Education

- Learn usual pulse rate and take radial pulse before each dose. Report to prescriber if pulse is below the established parameter or becomes irregular.
- Diabetics should be aware that propranolol suppresses clinical signs of hypoglycemia (e.g., BP changes, increased pulse rate) and may prolong hypoglycemia.
- Do not drive or engage in potentially hazardous activities until response to drug is known.

PROTAMINE SULFATE

(proe′ta-meen)

Classification(s): ANTIDOTE
Therapeutic: ANTIDOTE; ANTIHEMORRHAGIC
Pregnancy Category: C

USES Antidote for heparin or low molecular weight heparin (LMWH) overdosage (after heparin has been discontinued).

INDICATION & DOSAGE

Antidote for Heparin Overdose

Adult/Child: 1 mg for every 100 units of heparin to be neutralized (max: 100 mg in a 2 h period), give the first 25–50 mg by slow direct IV and the rest over 2–3 h

LMWH Overdose

Adult: 1 mg for every 1 mg of enoxaparin or 1 mg for every 100 units of dalteparin/tinzaparin

SOLUTION PREPARATION

May be given direct IV undiluted or further diluted in 50 mL or more of NS or D5W for infusion.

STORAGE

Store protamine sulfate injection vials at 15°–30° C (59°–86° F). Solutions contain no preservatives and should not be stored.

ADMINISTRATION

- **Direct IV Injection:** Give each 50 mg or fraction thereof slowly over 10–15 min. **NEVER** give more than 50 mg in any 10 min period or 100 mg in any 2 h period.
- **Continuous Infusion:** Do not exceed direct rate. Give over 2–3 h or longer as determined by coagulation studies.

INCOMPATIBILITIES Solution/additive: RADIOCONTRAST MATERIALS, **furosemide, heparin. Y-site: Furosemide,** PENICILLINS, CEPHALOSPORINS.

ACTION & *THERAPEUTIC EFFECT* Because protamine is strongly basic, it combines with strongly acidic heparin to produce a stable complex, thus it neutralizes the anticoagulant effect heparin. *Effective antidote to heparin overdose.*

CONTRAINDICATIONS Hemorrhage not induced by heparin overdosage; pregnancy (category C), lactation.

CAUTIOUS USE Cardiovascular disease; history of allergy to fish; vasectomized or infertile males; history of protamine hypersensitivity in insulin-dependent diabetics.

ADVERSE EFFECTS (≥1%) **CV:** *Abrupt drop in BP* (with rapid IV infusion), bradycardia. **Body as a Whole:** Urticaria, <u>angioedema</u>, pulmonary edema, <u>anaphylaxis</u>, dyspnea, lassitude; transient flushing and feeling of warmth. **GI:** Nausea, vomiting. **Hematologic:** Protamine overdose or "heparin rebound" (hyperheparinemia).

DRUG INTERACTIONS No clinically significant interactions established.

PHARMACOKINETICS Onset: 5 min. **Duration:** 2 h.

NURSING IMPLICATIONS

Assessment & Drug Effects

- Protamine is not recommended if only minor bleeding occurs during heparin therapy because withdrawal of heparin will usually correct minor bleeding within a few hours.
- Monitor BP and pulse q15–30min, or more often if indicated. Continue for at least 2–3 h after each dose, or longer as dictated by patient's condition. Be prepared to treat patient for shock as well as hemorrhage.
- Lab tests: Monitor effect of protamine in neutralizing heparin by aPTT or ACT values. Coagulation tests are usually performed 5–15 min after administration of protamine, and again in 2–8 h if desirable.
- Observe patients undergoing extracorporeal dialysis or patients who have had cardiac surgery carefully for bleeding (heparin rebound). Even with apparent adequate neutralization of heparin by protamine, bleeding may occur 30 min to 18 h after surgery. Monitor vital signs closely. Additional protamine may be required.

PROTEIN C CONCENTRATE (HUMAN) ℗

Ceprotin

Classification(s): THROMBOLYTIC AGENT, HUMAN PROTEIN C

Common adverse effects in *italic*, life-threatening effects <u>underlined</u>: generic names in **bold**; classifications in SMALL CAPS; ♣ Canadian drug name; ℗ Prototype drug

569

PROTEIN C CONCENTRATE (HUMAN)

Therapeutic: THROMBOLYTIC
Pregnancy Category: C

USES Treatment of patients with severe congenital protein C deficiency; protein C replacement therapy for the prevention and treatment of venous thrombosis and purpura fulminans in children and adults.

INDICATION & DOSAGE

Acute Episodes of Venous Thrombosis and Purpura Fulminans and Short-Term Prophylaxis
Adult/Child/Neonate: **Initial dose,** 100–120 units/kg; then 60–80 units/kg q6h × 3; **Maintenance Dose,** 45–60 units/kg q6–12h

SOLUTION PREPARATION

Direct/IV Infusion: Bring powder and supplied diluent to room temperature. Insert supplied double-ended transfer needle into diluent vial, invert, and rapidly insert into protein C powder vial. (If vacuum does not draw diluent into vial, discard.) Remove transfer needle and gently swirl to dissolve. Resulting solution concentration is 100 units/mL and it should be colorless to slightly yellowish, clear to slightly opalescent, and free from visible particles. Withdraw required dose with the supplied filter needle.

STORAGE

Store at room temperature for no more than 3 h after reconstitution. Prior to reconstitution, protect from light.

ADMINISTRATION

- **Direct IV Injection/IV Infusion:**
  - *Adult/Child:* Infuse at 2 mL/min.
  - *Child less than 10 kg:* Infuse at 0.2 mL/kg/min.

INCOMPATIBILITIES Data not available; do not mix with other drugs.

ACTION & *THERAPEUTIC EFFECT* Protein C is a critical element a pathway that provides a natural mechanism for control of the coagulation system. The pathway prevents excess procoagulant responses to activating stimuli. *Protein C is necessary to decrease thrombin generation and intravascular clot formation.*

CONTRAINDICATIONS Pregnancy (category C).
CAUTIOUS USE Hepatic and renal impairment; immunocompromised patients; hypersensitivity to mouse protein; concurrent administration of tissue plasminogen activator (tPA).

ADVERSE EFFECTS (≥1%) **Body as a Whole:** Fever, hyperhidrosis, hypersensitivity reactions (rash, pruritus), restlessness. **CNS:** Lightheadedness. **CV:** Hemothorax, hypotension.

DRUG INTERACTIONS Protein C concentrate can increase bleeding caused by **alteplase, reteplase,** or **tenecteplase.**

PHARMACOKINETICS Peak: 0.5–1 h. **Half-Life:** 9.9 h.

Common adverse effects in *italic*, life-threatening effects underlined: generic names in **bold**; classifications in SMALL CAPS; ♣ Canadian drug name; ❶ Prototype drug

NURSING IMPLICATIONS

Assessment & Drug Effects

- Monitor for and promptly report S&S of bleeding or hypersensitivity reactions.
- Monitor vital signs including BP and temperature.
- Lab tests: Baseline and periodic protein C activity, platelet counts; protein C trough level with acute thrombotic events; frequent serum sodium with renal function impairment.

Patient & Family Education

- Report immediately early signs of hypersensitivity reactions, including hives, generalized itching, tightness in chest, wheezing, difficulty breathing.
- Report immediately any signs of bleeding, including black tarry stools, pink/red-tinged urine, unusual bruising.

PYRIDOSTIGMINE BROMIDE

(peer-id-oh-stig′meen)

Mestinon, Regonol

Classification(s): CHOLINESTERASE INHIBITOR

Therapeutic: ANTIMYASTENIC; ANTIDOTE

Prototype: Neostigmine

Pregnancy Category: C

USES Myasthenia gravis and as an antagonist to nondepolarizing skeletal muscle relaxants (e.g., curariform drugs).

INDICATION & DOSAGE

Myasthenia Gravis

Adult: 2 mg q2–3h

Reversal of Muscle Relaxants

Adult: 10–20 mg immediately preceded by IV atropine or glycopyrrolate

SOLUTION PREPARATION

No dilution is required. Administer as supplied. Do NOT add to IV solutions.

STORAGE

Store at 15°–30° C (59°–86° F). Protect from light and moisture.

ADMINISTRATION

Direct IV Injection: Give at a rate of 0.5 mg over 1 min for myasthenia gravis; 5 mg over 1 min for reversal of muscle relaxants.

INCOMPATIBILITIES Data not available; do not mix with other drugs.

ACTION & *THERAPEUTIC EFFECT* Analog of neostigmine; indirect-acting cholinergic that inhibits cholinesterase activity. Facilitates transmission of im-

---

Common adverse effects in *italic*, life-threatening effects <u>underlined</u>: generic names in **bold**; classifications in SMALL CAPS; ♣ Canadian drug name; ❷ Prototype drug

571

pulses across myoneural junctions by blocking destruction of acetylcholine. *Direct stimulant action on voluntary muscle fibers and possibly on autonomic ganglia and CNS neurons. Produces increased tone in skeletal muscles.*

CONTRAINDICATIONS Hypersensitivity to pyridostigmine; mechanical obstruction of urinary or intestinal tract; bradycardia, hypotension; pregnancy (category C); neonates.

CAUTIOUS USE Hypersensitivity to bromides; bronchial asthma; epilepsy; renal impairment; vagotonia; hyperthyroidism; peptic ulcer; cardiac dysrhythmias.

ADVERSE EFFECTS (≥1%) **Skin:** Acneiform rash. **Hematologic:** Thrombophlebitis. **GI:** *Nausea, vomiting, diarrhea.* **Special Senses:** *Miosis.* **Body as a Whole:** *Excessive salivation and sweating,* weakness, fasciculation. **Respiratory:** Increased bronchial secretion, <u>bronchoconstriction</u>. **CV:** Bradycardia, hypotension.

DRUG INTERACTIONS Atropine NONDEPOLARIZING MUSCLE RELAXANTS antagonize effects of pyridostigmine.

PHARMACOKINETICS Onset: 2–5 min. **Duration:** 3–6 h. **Distribution:** Crosses placenta. **Metabolism:** In liver and in serum and tissue by cholinesterases. **Elimination:** In urine.

NURSING IMPLICATIONS

Assessment & Drug Effects

- Monitor vital signs frequently, especially respiratory rate.
- Observe patient continuously when used as muscle relaxant antagonist. Airway and respiratory assistance **must be** maintained until full recovery of voluntary respiration and neuromuscular transmission is ensured. Complete recovery usually occurs within 30 min.
- Report increasing muscular weakness, cramps, or fasciculations. Failure of patient to show improvement may reflect either underdosage or overdosage.
- Observe patient closely if atropine is used to abolish GI adverse effects or other muscarinic adverse effects because it may mask signs of overdosage (cholinergic crisis): Increasing muscle weakness, which through involvement of respiratory muscles can lead to death.
- Observe for signs of cholinergic reactions (see Appendix C).
- Observe closely neonates of myasthenic mothers who have received pyridostigmine, for difficulty in breathing, swallowing, or sucking.

Patient & Family Education

- Be aware that duration of drug action may vary with physical and emotional stress, as well as with severity of disease.
- Report onset of rash to prescriber. Drug may be discontinued.

PYRIDOXINE HYDROCHLORIDE (VITAMIN B₆)
(peer-i-dox'een)

Classification(s): VITAMIN
Therapeutic: VITAMIN SUPPLEMENT
Pregnancy Category: A (C if greater than RDA)

USES Prophylaxis and treatment of pyridoxine deficiency, as seen with inadequate dietary intake, drug-induced deficiency (e.g., isoniazid, oral contraceptives), and inborn errors of metabolism (vitamin B_6–dependent convulsions or anemia).

INDICATION & DOSAGE

Dietary Deficiency
Adult: 4 mg/kg/day in TPN

Pyridoxine Deficiency Syndrome
Adult: Initial dose up to 600 mg/day may be required; then up to 50 mg/day

SOLUTION PREPARATION
- *Direct IV Injection:* No dilution is required. Administer as supplied.
- *Continuous Infusion:* May be added to most standard IV solutions.

STORAGE
Store at 15°–30° C (59°–86° F) in tight, light-resistant containers. Avoid freezing.

ADMINISTRATION
- **Direct IV Injection:** Give at a rate of 50 mg or fraction thereof over 60 sec.
- **Continuous Infusions:** Give according to ordered rate for infusion.

INCOMPATIBILITIES May be added to most standard IV solutions.

ACTION & *THERAPEUTIC EFFECT* Water-soluble complex of three closely related compounds with B_6 activity. Considered essential to human nutrition, although a deficiency syndrome is not well defined. Converted in body to pyridoxal, a coenzyme that functions in protein, fat, and carbohydrate metabolism and in facilitating release of glycogen from liver and muscle. In protein metabolism, participates in many enzymatic transformations of amino acids and conversion of tryptophan to niacin and serotonin. Aids in energy transformation in brain and nerve cells, and is thought to stimulate heme production. *Evaluated by improvement of B_6 deficiency manifestations: Nausea, vomiting, skin lesions resembling those of riboflavin and niacin deficiency, edema, CNS symptoms, hypochromic microcytic anemia.*

CONTRAINDICATIONS Pregnancy [category A (C if greater than RDA)].
CAUTIOUS USE Renal impairment; neonatal prematurity with renal impairment; cardiac disease.

ADVERSE EFFECTS (≥1%) **Body as a Whole:** Paresthesias, slight flushing or feeling of warmth, temporary burning or stinging pain in injec-

Common adverse effects in *italic*, life-threatening effects underlined: generic names in **bold**; classifications in SMALL CAPS; ♣ Canadian drug name; ✪ Prototype drug

573

tion site. **CNS:** Somnolence seizures (particularly following large doses). **Metabolic:** Low folic acid levels.

DRUG INTERACTIONS Isoniazid, cycloserine, penicillamine, hydralazine and ORAL CONTRACEPTIVES, may increase pyridoxine requirements; may reverse or antagonize therapeutic effects of **levodopa.**

PHARMACOKINETICS Distribution: Stored in liver; crosses placenta. **Metabolism:** In liver. **Elimination:** In urine.

NURSING IMPLICATIONS

Assessment & Drug Effects

- Monitor neurologic status to determine therapeutic effect in deficiency states.
- Record a complete dietary history so poor eating habits can be identified and corrected (a single vitamin deficiency is rare; patient can be expected to have multiple vitamin deficiencies).
- Lab tests: Periodic Hct and Hgb, and serum iron.

Patient & Family Education

- Learn rich dietary sources of vitamin B₆: Yeast, wheat germ, whole grain cereals, muscle and glandular meats (especially liver), legumes, green vegetables, bananas.

QUINIDINE GLUCONATE

(kwin'i-deen sul-fate)

Classification(s): ANTIARRHYTHMIC, CLASS IA
Therapeutic: ANTIARRHYTHMIC; ANTIMALARIAL
Prototype: Procainamide
Pregnancy Category: C

USES Premature atrial, AV junctional, and ventricular contraction; paroxysmal atrial tachycardia, chronic ventricular tachycardia (when not associated with complete heart block); maintenance therapy after electrical conversion of atrial fibrillation or flutter; life-threatening malaria.

INDICATION & DOSAGE (dose of quinidine base)

Atrial Fibrillation or Flutter

Adult: 0.25 mg/kg/min not more than 5–10 mg/kg until converted

Malaria

Adult: 15 mg/kg loading dose over 4 h, then 7.5 mg/kg q8h for a total of 7 days OR 6.25 mg/kg loading dose, then 12.5 mcg/kg/min for 72 h

Renal Impairment Dosage Adjustment

CrCl less than 10 mL/min: Give 75% of dose

Common adverse effects in *italic*, life-threatening effects underlined: generic names in **bold**; classifications in SMALL CAPS; ♥ Canadian drug name; ● Prototype drug

SOLUTION PREPARATION
Dilute 800 mg (10 mL) in at least 40 mL D5W to yield a maximum concentration of 16 mg/mL.

STORAGE
Protect IV solutions from light and heat to prevent brownish discoloration and possibly precipitation.

ADMINISTRATION
- **IV Infusion:** Infuse via infusion pump at a rate not to exceed 16 mg (1 mL)/min.
- Use supine position during drug administration to minimize risk of severe hypotension.

INCOMPATIBILITIES **Solution/additive:** Amiodarone, atracurium, furosemide. **Y-site:** Furosemide, heparin in dextrose.

ACTION & *THERAPEUTIC EFFECT* Class IA antiarrhythmic that depresses myocardial excitability, contractility, automaticity, and conduction velocity, as well as prolongs effective refractory period. Anticholinergic action blocks vagal stimulation of AV node, thus tending to increase ventricular rate, particularly in larger doses. *Depresses myocardial excitability, conduction velocity, and irregularity of nerve impulse conduction.*

CONTRAINDICATIONS Hypersensitivity or idiosyncrasy to quinine or *Cinchona* derivatives; thrombocytopenic purpura resulting from prior use of quinidine; intraventricular conduction defects, complete AV block, ectopic impulses and rhythms due to escape mechanisms; thyrotoxicosis; acute rheumatic fever; subacute bacterial endocarditis, extensive myocardial damage, frank CHF, hypotensive states; myasthenia gravis; digitalis intoxication; pregnancy (category C).

CAUTIOUS USE Incomplete heart block; impaired kidney or liver function; bronchial asthma or other respiratory disorders; potassium imbalance.

ADVERSE EFFECTS (≥1%) **CNS:** Headache, fever, tremors, apprehension, delirium, syncope with sudden loss of consciousness, seizures. **CV:** Hypotension, CHF, widened QRS complex, bradycardia, heart block, atrial flutter, ventricular flutter, fibrillation or tachycardia; quinidine syncope, torsades de pointes. **Special Senses:** Mydriasis, blurred vision, disturbed color perception, reduced visual field, photophobia, diplopia, night blindness, scotomas, optic neuritis, disturbed hearing (tinnitus, auditory acuity). **GI:** *Nausea, vomiting, diarrhea, abdominal pain*, hepatic dysfunction. **Hematologic:** Acute hemolytic anemia (especially in patients with G6PD deficiency), hypoprothrombinemia, leukopenia. Thrombocytopenia, agranulocytosis (both rare). **Body as a Whole:** Cinchonism (nausea, vomiting, headache, dizziness, fever, tremors, vertigo, tinnitus, visual disturbances), angioedema, acute asthma, respiratory depression, vascular collapse. **Skin:** Rash, urticaria, cutaneous flushing with intense pruritus, photosensitivity. **Metabolic:** SLE, hypokalemia.

DRUG INTERACTIONS May increase **digoxin** levels by 50%; **amiodarone** may increase quinidine levels, thus increasing its risk of heart

Common adverse effects in *italic*, life-threatening effects <u>underlined</u>: generic names in **bold**; classifications in SMALL CAPS; ♣ Canadian drug name; ⊘ Prototype drug

575

block; other ANTIARRHYTHMICS, PHENOTHIAZINES, **reserpine** add to cardiac depressant effects; ANTICHOLINERGIC AGENTS add to vagolytic effects; CHOLINERGIC AGENTS may antagonize cardiac effects; ANTICONVULSANTS, BARBITURATES, **rifampin** increase the metabolism of quinidine, thus decreasing its efficacy; CARBONIC ANHYDRASE INHIBITORS, **sodium bicarbonate**, chronic ANTACIDS decrease renal elimination of quinidine, thus increasing its toxicity; **verapamil** causes significant hypotension; may increase hypoprothrombinemic effects of **warfarin. Diltiazem** may increase levels and decrease elimination of quinidine.

PHARMACOKINETICS Distribution: Widely distributed to most body tissues except the brain; crosses placenta; distributed into breast milk. **Metabolism:** In liver (CYP 3A4). **Elimination:** More than 95% in urine, <5% in feces. **Half-Life:** 6–8 h.

NURSING IMPLICATIONS

Assessment & Drug Effects

- Continuous monitoring of ECG and BP is required. Observe patient closely (check sensorium and be alert for any sign of toxicity); determine plasma quinidine concentrations frequently when large doses (more than 2 g/day) are used or when quinidine is given parenterally (i.e., quinidine gluconate).
- Report immediately the following indications for stopping quinidine: (1) Sinus rhythm, (2) widening QRS complex in excess of 25% (i.e., greater than 0.12 sec), (3) changes in QT interval or refractory period, (4) disappearance of P waves, (5) sudden onset of or increase in ectopic ventricular beats (extrasystoles, PVCs), (6) decrease in heart rate to 120 bpm. Also report immediately any worsening of minor side effects.
- Observe patient closely following each dose. Amount of subsequent dose is gauged by response to preceding dose.
- Quinidine can cause unpredictable rhythm abnormalities in the digitalized heart.
- Lab tests: Frequent serum quinidine; periodic blood counts, serum electrolytes, kidney function tests, and LFTs.
- Monitor I&O. Diarrhea occurs commonly during early therapy; most patients become tolerant to this side effect. Evaluate serum electrolytes, acid-base, and fluid balance when symptoms become severe; dosage adjustment may be required.

Patient & Family Education

- Report feeling of faintness. "Quinidine syncope" is caused by quinidine-induced changes in ventricular rhythm resulting in decreased cardiac output and syncope.
- Report hypersensitivity reaction that may appear 3–20 days after drug is started. Fever occurs commonly and may or may not be accompanied by other symptoms.
- Report promptly disturbances in vision, ringing in ears, sense of breathlessness, onset of palpitations, and unpleasant sensation in chest. Be sure to note the time of occurrence and duration of chest symptoms.

QUINUPRISTIN/DALFOPRISTIN
(quin-u-pris′tin/dal′fo-pris-tin)
Synercid
Classification(s): ANTIBIOTIC
Therapeutic: ANTIBACTERIAL
Pregnancy Category: B

USES Serious or life-threatening infections associated with vancomycin resistant *Enterococcus faecium* (VREF) bacteremia; complicated skin and skin structure infections caused by *Staphylococcus aureus* or *Streptococcus pyogenes*.

INDICATION & DOSAGE

Vancomycin-Resistant *Enterococcus faecium*
Adult/Adolescent (over 16 y): 7.5 mg/kg q8h

Complicated Skin and Skin Structure Infections
Adult/Adolescent (over 16 y): 7.5 mg/kg q12h × 7 days

SOLUTION PREPARATION

▪ *Vial Reconstitution:* Reconstitute a single 500 mg vial by adding 5 mL D5W or sterile water for injection to yield 100 mg/mL. Gently swirl to dissolve but **do not** shake. Allow solution to clear. **Must be** further diluted for infusion.
▪ *Further Dilution of Reconstituted Solution:* Withdraw the required dose and add to 100 mL (for central line infusion) or 250–500 mL (for peripheral site infusion) of D5W.

STORAGE
Refrigerate unopened vials. After reconstitution solution is stable for 5 h at room temperature and 54 h refrigerated.

ADMINISTRATION
Intermittent Infusion: Infuse over 1 h. Flush line before/after with D5W. **Do not** use saline.

INCOMPATIBILITIES Solution/additive: **Saline solutions** and **lactated Ringer's solution** (flush lines with **D5W** before infusing other drugs). **Y-site:** Any drugs diluted in **saline.**

ACTION & *THERAPEUTIC EFFECT* Streptogramin (cyclic macrolide) antibiotic that is produced by various streptomyces bacteria. The site of action of quinupristin is the bacterial ribosome. Quinupristin inhibits the late phase of protein synthesis of bacteria, resulting in bacterial cell death. *Indicated by clinical improvement in S&S of infection. Active against gram-positive pathogens including vancomycin-resistant* Enterococcus faecium *(VREF), as well as some gram-negative anaerobes.*

CONTRAINDICATIONS Hypersensitivity to quinupristin/dalfopristin or pristinamycin; other streptogramins; children less than 16 y.

Common adverse effects in *italic*, life-threatening effects underlined: generic names in **bold**; classifications in SMALL CAPS; ♣ Canadian drug name; ❂ Prototype drug

577

CAUTIOUS USE Renal or hepatic dysfunction; pregnancy (category B), lactation.

ADVERSE EFFECTS (≥1%) **Body as a Whole:** Headache, pain, *myalgia, arthralgia.* **GI:** Nausea, diarrhea, vomiting. **Skin:** Rash, pruritus. **Other:** *Inflammation, pain, or edema at infusion site, other infusion site reactions,* thrombophlebitis.

DRUG INTERACTIONS Inhibits CYP 3A4 metabolism of **cyclosporine, midazolam, nifedipine,** PROTEASE INHIBITORS, **vincristine, vinblastine, docetaxel, paclitaxel, diazepam, tacrolimus, carbamazepine, quinidine, lidocaine, disopyramide.**

PHARMACOKINETICS Distribution: Moderately protein bound. **Metabolism:** To several active metabolites. **Elimination:** Primarily in feces (75–77%). **Half-Life:** 3 h quinupristin, 1 h dalfopristin.

NURSING IMPLICATIONS

Assessment & Drug Effects

- Prior to initiating therapy: Baseline C&S tests (start drug pending results).
- Monitor for S&S of infusion site irritation; change infusion site if irritation is apparent.
- Monitor for cutaneous reaction (e.g., pruritus/erythema of neck, face, upper body).
- Lab tests: Periodic WBC with differential, and LFTs (especially with pre-existing hepatic insufficiency).

Patient & Family Education

- Report burning, itching, or pain at infusion site to prescriber.
- Report any sensation of swelling of face and tongue, or difficulty swallowing.

RANITIDINE HYDROCHLORIDE

(ra-nye'te-deen)

Zantac

Classification(s): ANTISECRETORY (H$_2$-RECEPTOR ANTAGONIST)

Therapeutic: ANTIULCER

Prototype: Cimetidine

Pregnancy Category: B

USES Treatment of peptic ulcer disease, treatment of pathologic GI hypersecretory conditions (e.g., Zollinger-Ellison syndrome, systemic mastocytosis).

INDICATION & DOSAGE

Peptic Ulcer Disease

Adult/Adolescent: 50 mg q6–8h; 6.25 mg/h by continuous infusion

---

Common adverse effects in *italic*, life-threatening effects underlined: generic names in **bold**; classifications in SMALL CAPS; ♣ Canadian drug name; ✪ Prototype drug

Pathologic Hypersecretory Conditions

Adult: 1 mg/kg/h, adjusted for gastric output up to 2.5 mg/kg/h **OR** 50 mg q6–8h; higher doses may be necessary (max: 400 mg/day)

Renal Impairment Dosage Adjustment

If CrCl less than 50 mL/min: Dose q18–24h

Hemodialysis Dosage Adjustment

Time dose to administer at the end of dialysis

SOLUTION PREPARATION

- Use NS, D5W, LR, or other compatible IV solution.
- *Direct IV Injection:* Dilute 50 mg to a total volume of 20 mL.
- *Intermittent Infusion:* Dilute 50 mg in 50–100 mL of IV solution.
- *Continuous Infusion:* Dilute total daily dose in 250 mL of IV solution. Final concentration should be no greater than 2.5 mg/mL.

STORAGE

Store diluted solutions at 15°–30° C (59°–86° F) for 48 h.

ADMINISTRATION

- **Direct IV Injection:** Give at a rate of 4 mL/min or 20 mL over not less than 5 min.
- **Intermittent Infusion:** Infuse over 15–20 min.
- **Continuous Infusion:** Infuse over 24 h. Do not exceed 6.25 mg/h.

INCOMPATIBILITIES Solution/additive: **Amphotericin B, atracurium, cefazolin, cefoxitin, ceftazidime, cefuroxime, clindamycin, chlorpromazine, diazepam, ethacrynic acid, hydroxyzine, insulin, methotrimeprazine, midazolam, pentobarbital, phenobarbital, phytonadione.** Y-site: **Amphotericin B cholesteryl complex, hetastarch, insulin, lansoprazole.**

ACTION & *THERAPEUTIC EFFECT* Potent antiulcer drug that competitively and reversibly inhibits histamine action at H_2-receptor sites on parietal cells, thus blocking gastric acid secretion. Indirectly reduces pepsin secretion but appears to have minimal effect on fasting and postprandial serum gastrin concentrations or secretion of gastric intrinsic factor or mucus. *Blocks daytime and nocturnal basal gastric acid secretion stimulated by histamine and reduces gastric acid release in response to food, pentagastrin, and insulin. Shown to inhibit 50% of the stimulated gastric acid secretion.*

CONTRAINDICATIONS Hypersensitivity to ranitidine; acute porphyria.
CAUTIOUS USE Hypersensitivity to H_2-blockers; hepatic and renal dysfunction; renal failure; elderly; PKU; pregnancy (category B), lactation; infants less than 1 mo.

ADVERSE EFFECTS (≥1%) **CNS:** Headache, malaise, dizziness, somnolence, insomnia, vertigo, mental confusion, agitation, depression, hallucinations in older adults. **CV:** Bradycardia (with rapid IV push). **GI:** Constipation, nausea, abdominal pain, diarrhea. **Skin:** Rash. **Hematologic:** Reversible de-

R

Common adverse effects in *italic*, life-threatening effects <u>underlined</u>: generic names in **bold**; classifications in SMALL CAPS; ♣ Canadian drug name; ❷ Prototype drug

579

crease in WBC count, thrombocytopenia. **Body as a Whole:** Hypersensitivity reactions, <u>anaphylaxis</u> (rare).

DIAGNOSTIC TEST INTERFERENCE Ranitidine may produce slight elevations in *serum creatinine* (without concurrent increase in *BUN*); (rare) increases in *AST, ALT, alkaline phosphatase, LDH,* and *total bilirubin.* Produces false-positive tests for *urine protein* with *Multistix* (use *sulfosalicylic acid* instead).

DRUG INTERACTIONS May affect levels of **cefpodoxime, cefuroxime, delavirdine, ketoconazole, itraconazole.**

PHARMACOKINETICS Distribution: Into breast milk. **Metabolism:** In liver. **Elimination:** In urine, with some in feces. **Half-Life:** 2–3 h.

NURSING IMPLICATIONS

Assessment & Drug Effects

- Potential toxicity results from decreased clearance (elimination) and therefore prolonged action; greatest in the older adult patients or those with hepatic or renal dysfunction.
- Lab tests: Periodic LFTs. Monitor creatinine clearance if renal dysfunction is present or suspected.
- Be alert for early signs of hepatotoxicity (low risk and thought to be a hypersensitivity reaction): jaundice (dark urine, pruritus, yellow sclera and skin), elevated transaminases (especially ALT) and LDH.

Patient & Family Education

- Adhere to scheduled periodic laboratory checkups during ranitidine treatment.
- Note that smoking decreases ranitidine efficacy and adversely affects ulcer healing.

R

RASBURICASE

(ras-bur'i-case)

Elitek, Fasturtec ♣

Classification(s): ANTIGOUT AGENT; ANTIMETABOLITE
Therapeutic: ANTIGOUT AGENT
Pregnancy Category: C

USES Initial management of increased uric acid levels secondary to tumor lysis.

INDICATION & DOSAGE

Hyperuricemia

Adult/Child/Infant: 0.15–0.2 mg/kg/day for 5–7 days starting 4–24 h before chemotherapy

Common adverse effects in *italic*, life-threatening effects <u>underlined</u>; generic names in **bold**; classifications in SMALL CAPS; ♣ Canadian drug name; ❂ Prototype drug

SOLUTION PREPARATION

- *Vial Reconstitution:* Add 1 mL of the provided diluent to each 1.5 mg vial and mix by swirling very gently. **Do not shake.** Discard if particulate matter is visible or if product is discolored after reconstitution. **Must be** further diluted for infusion.
- *Further Dilution of Reconstituted Solution:* Remove the required dose from the reconstituted vials and inject into enough NS achieve a final total volume of 50 mL.

STORAGE

Store reconstituted solutions and IV solutions refrigerated for 24 h.

ADMINISTRATION

- **IV Infusion:** Infuse over 30 min. **DO NOT GIVE BOLUS DOSE.**
- Infuse through an **unfiltered** line used for no other medications. If a separate line is not possible, flush the line with at least 15 mL of NS before/after infusion.

INCOMPATIBILITIES Do not mix or infuse with other drugs.

ACTION & *THERAPEUTIC EFFECT* A recombinant urate-oxidase enzyme produced by DNA technology from *Aspergillus flavus*. In humans, uric acid is the final step in the catabolic pathway of purines. Rasburicase catalyzes enzymatic oxidation of uric acid, thus it is only active at the end of the purine catabolic pathway. *Used to manage plasma uric acid levels in pediatric patients with leukemia, lymphoma, and solid tumor malignancies who are receiving anticancer therapy that results in tumor lysis, and therefore elevates plasma uric acid.*

CONTRAINDICATIONS Hypersensitivity to rasburicase; deficiency in glucose-6-phosphate dehydrogenase (G6PD); history of anaphylaxis or hypersensitivity reactions; hemolytic reactions or methemoglobinemia reactions to rasburicase; pregnancy (category C), lactation; children less than 1 mo.
CAUTIOUS USE Patients at risk for G6PD deficiency (e.g., African or Mediterranean ancestry). Safety and efficacy in adults and elderly are unknown.

ADVERSE EFFECTS (≥1%) **Body as a Whole:** *Fever,* sepsis, severe hypersensitivity reactions including anaphylaxis at any time during treatment. **CNS:** *Headache.* **GI:** *Mucositis, vomiting, nausea, diarrhea, abdominal pain.* **Hematologic:** Neutropenia. **Skin:** *Rash.*

DIAGNOSTIC TEST INTERFERENCE May give false elevations for ***uric acid*** if blood sample is left at room temperature.

DRUG INTERACTIONS No clinically significant interactions established.

PHARMACOKINETICS Half-Life: 18 h.

NURSING IMPLICATIONS

Assessment & Drug Effects

- Monitor cardiovascular, respiratory, neurologic, and renal status throughout therapy.

R

- Immediately discontinue IV infusion and institute emergency measures for S&S of anaphylaxis including chest pain, dyspnea, hypotension, and/or urticaria.
- Patients at higher risk for G6PD deficiency (e.g., patients of African or Mediterranean ancestry) should be screened prior to starting therapy, as this deficiency is a contraindication for this drug.
- Lab tests: Baseline and periodic serum uric acid.

Patient & Family Education
- Report immediately any distressing S&S.

REMIFENTANIL HYDROCHLORIDE
(rem-i-fent′a-nil)
Ultiva
Classification(s): NARCOTIC (OPIATE) AGONIST; GENERAL ANESTHESIA
Therapeutic: ANALGESIC; GENERAL ANESTHESIA
Prototype: Morphine
Pregnancy Category: C   **Controlled Substance:** Schedule II

USES Analgesic during induction and maintenance of general anesthesia, as the analgesic component of monitored anesthesia care.

INDICATION & DOSAGE

Analgesia during Anesthesia Induction
Adult: 0.5–1 mcg/kg/min or 1 mcg/kg bolus
Geriatric: Start at 50% normal dose

Analgesia during Anesthesia Maintenance (based on concurrent anesthetic)
Adult: 0.1–2 mcg/kg/min
Geriatric: Start at 50% of normal dose

Analgesic
Adult: 0.1 mcg/kg/min (up to 0.2 mcg/kg/min)

Obesity
Dose based on IBW.

SOLUTION PREPARATION
- *Vial Reconstitution:* Add 1 mL of sterile water for injection, D5W, NS, D5NS, 1/2NS, D5LR to each 1 mg of remifentanil to yield 1 mg/mL. Shake well to dissolve. **Must be** further diluted for infusion.

- *Further Dilution of Reconstituted Solution:* Dilute to a final concentration of 20, 25, 50, or 250 mcg/mL by adding the required dose to the appropriate amount of IV solution. [Example: 1 mL (1 mg) added to 19 mL = 50 mcg/mL]

STORAGE

- Reconstituted solution is stable for 24 h at room temperature unless diluted in LR solution, which is stable for 4 h.
- Store vials of powder at 2°–25° C (36°–77° F).

ADMINISTRATION

- **Direct IV Injection/Infusion:** Give at the ordered rate according to patient's weight.
- Note that bolus doses should NOT be given DURING a continuous infusion of remifentanil.
- Use a controlled infusion pump for administration.
- Clear IV tubing completely of the drug following discontinuation of remifentanil infusion to ensure that inadvertent administration of the drug will not occur at a later time.

INCOMPATIBILITIES Solution/additive: Data not available; do not mix with other drugs. **Y-site: Amphotericin B, amphotericin B cholesteryl complex, cefoperazone, chlorpromazine, diazepam.**

ACTION & *THERAPEUTIC EFFECT* Synthetic, potent narcotic agonist analgesic similar to fentanyl. Rapidly metabolized, therefore respiratory depression is of shorter duration than fentanyl analogs when discontinued. *Used as the analgesic component of an anesthesia regimen.*

CONTRAINDICATIONS Hypersensitivity to fentanyl analogs, epidural or intrathecal administration; pregnancy (category C).

CAUTIOUS USE Head injuries, increased intracranial pressure; older adults, debilitated, morbidly obese, poor-risk patients; COPD, other respiratory problems, bradyarrhythmia; lactation. Safety in labor and delivery has not been demonstrated.

ADVERSE EFFECTS (≥1%) **Body as a Whole:** Muscle rigidity, shivering. **CNS:** Dizziness, headache. **CV:** Hypotension, hypertension, bradycardia. **GI:** *Nausea*, vomiting. **Respiratory:** Respiratory depression, apnea. **Skin:** Pruritus.

DRUG INTERACTIONS Alcohol and other CNS DEPRESSANTS potentiate effects; MAO INHIBITORS may precipitate hypertensive crisis.

PHARMACOKINETICS Duration: 12 min. **Distribution:** 70% protein bound. **Metabolism:** Hydrolyzed by nonspecific esterases in the blood and tissues. **Elimination:** In urine. **Half-Life:** 3–10 min.

NURSING IMPLICATIONS

Assessment & Drug Effects

- Monitor vital signs continuously and report promptly S&S of respiratory distress or respiratory depression, or skeletal and thoracic muscle rigidity and weakness.
- Monitor for adequate postoperative analgesia.

RESPIRATORY SYNCYTIAL VIRUS IMMUNE GLOBULIN (RSV-IVIG)

(res-pir′a-tory sin-cy′ti-al)

RespiGam
Classification(s): IMMUNOLOGIC AGENT; IMMUNOGLOBULIN
Therapeutic: IMMUNOGLOBULIN
Prototype: Immune globulin
Pregnancy Category: C

USES Prevention of serious lower respiratory tract infection caused by RSV in children less than 24 mo with bronchopulmonary dysplasia or history of premature birth; hypervolemia.

INDICATION & DOSAGE

RSV

Child (up to 24 mo)/Infant/Neonate: 750 mg/kg/mo, may repeat monthly as needed

SOLUTION PREPARATION

No dilution is required. Administer as supplied. Do not shake.

STORAGE

- Store vials at 2°–8° C (35°–46° F).
- Begin infusion within 6 h after vial is entered and complete within 12 h.

ADMINISTRATION

- **IV Infusion:** Infuse as 1.5 mL/kg/h for first 15 min, then if clinical condition permits, increase to 3.6 mL/kg/h until end of infusion. Do not shake vial.
- Use a controlled infusion pump.
- Infuse vial contents through a separate IV line if possible; if "piggyback" **must be** used, allowable solutions are dextrose in water and NS. See manufacturer's directions about the permissible ratio of dextrose to RSV-IGIV at the Y-site.

INCOMPATIBILITIES Solution/additive or Y-site: Do not mix with other drugs.

ACTION & *THERAPEUTIC EFFECT* Contains IgG immune globulin antibodies from human plasma. *The preparation contains large amounts of RSV-neutralizing antibodies.*

CONTRAINDICATIONS Previous severe reaction to RespiGam or other human immunoglobulin preparations, selective IgA deficiency; congenital heart disease; hepatic disease; fluid overload; pregnancy (category C).
CAUTIOUS USE Immunodeficiency, AIDS; pulmonary disease; CHF, renal failure.

ADVERSE EFFECTS (≥1%) **Body as a Whole:** Fever, fluid overload. **CV:** Tachycardia, hypertension. **GI:** Vomiting, diarrhea, gastroenteritis. **Respi-**

Common adverse effects in *italic*, life-threatening effects <u>underlined</u>: generic names in **bold**; classifications in SMALL CAPS; ♣ Canadian drug name; ⊙ Prototype drug

ratory: Respiratory distress, wheezing, rales, hypoxia, hypoxemia, tachypnea. **Skin:** Injection site inflammation.

DRUG INTERACTIONS May interfere with immune response to LIVE VIRUS VACCINES (mumps, rubella, measles), may need to repeat vaccine if given within 10 mo of **RespiGam.**

PHARMACOKINETICS Half-Life: 22–28 days.

NURSING IMPLICATIONS

Assessment & Drug Effects

- Monitor closely during and after each IV rate change.
- Assess vital signs and respiratory status prior to infusion, during and after each rate change, and at 30-min intervals until 30 min after infusion is completed, and periodically thereafter for 24 h.
- Slow infusion immediately if S&S of fluid overload appear and report to prescriber.
- Lab tests: Periodic routine blood chemistry, serum electrolytes, blood gases, osmolality.
- Monitor for aseptic meningitis syndrome, which may begin up to 2 days after infusion.

Patient & Family Education

- Be aware of the possibility of aseptic meningitis syndrome; learn S&S to report (headache, drowsiness, fever, photophobia, painful eye movements, muscle rigidity, nausea, vomiting).

RETEPLASE RECOMBINANT

(re'te-plase)

Retavase

Classification(s): THROMBOLYTIC AGENT, TISSUE PLASMINOGEN ACTIVATOR
Therapeutic: THROMBOLYTIC
Prototype: Alteplase
Pregnancy Category: C

R

USES Thrombolysis management of acute MI to reduce the incidence of CHF and mortality.

INDICATION & DOSAGE

Acute MI

Adult: 10 units injected over 2 min; repeat dose in 30 min (20 units total)

SOLUTION PREPARATION

Vial Reconstitution: Use only the diluent, syringe, needle, and dispensing pin provided with reteplase. Withdraw diluent with syringe. Remove needle from syringe, replace with dispensing pin and transfer diluent to

---

Common adverse effects in *italic*, life-threatening effects <u>underlined</u>: generic names in **bold**; classifications in SMALL CAPS; ♣ Canadian drug name; ☻ Prototype drug

585

vial of reteplase. Leave pin and syringe in place in vial and swirl to dissolve. Do NOT shake. When completely dissolved, withdraw 10 mL reteplase solution into syringe. Detach syringe from dispensing pin and replace with a sterile needle for administration.

STORAGE
Store drug kit unopened at 2°–25° C (36°–77° F).

ADMINISTRATION
Direct IV Injection: Flush IV line before & after with 30 mL NS or D5W and do NOT give any other drug simultaneously through the same IV line. Give a single dose evenly over 2 min.

INCOMPATIBILITIES Solution/additive: Heparin. Y-site: Bivalirudin, heparin.

ACTION & *THERAPEUTIC EFFECT* DNA recombinant plasminogen activator (t-PA) that acts as a catalyst in the cleavage of plasminogen to plasmin. Responsible for degrading the fibrin matrix of a clot. *Has antithrombolytic properties.*

CONTRAINDICATIONS Active internal bleeding; history of CVA, recent neurologic surgery or trauma, intracranial neoplasm, or aneurysm, bleeding disorders, severe uncontrolled hypertension; pregnancy (category C).
CAUTIOUS USE Any condition in which bleeding constitutes a significant hazard (i.e., severe hepatic or renal disease, CVA, hypertension, acute pancreatitis, septic thrombophlebitis); lactation. Safety and efficacy in children are not established.

ADVERSE EFFECTS (≥1%) **Hematologic:** *Hemorrhage* (including *intracranial*, GI, genitourinary), anemia. **CV:** Reperfusion arrhythmias.

DIAGNOSTIC TEST INTERFERENCE Causes decreases in ***plasminogen*** and ***fibrinogen,*** making ***coagulation and fibrinolytic tests*** unreliable.

DRUG INTERACTIONS Aspirin, abciximab, dipyridamole, heparin may increase risk of bleeding.

PHARMACOKINETICS Elimination: In urine. **Half-Life:** 13–16 min.

NURSING IMPLICATIONS
Assessment & Drug Effects
- Monitor ECG continuously and monitor carefully for arrhythmias associated with reperfusion.
- Discontinue concomitant heparin immediately if serious bleeding not controllable by local pressure occurs and, if not already given, withhold the second reteplase bolus.
- Monitor carefully all potential bleeding sites; monitor for S&S of internal hemorrhage (e.g., GI, GU, intracranial, retroperitoneal, pulmonary).
- Avoid invasive procedures, arterial and venous punctures, IM injections, and nonessential handling of the patient during reteplase therapy.

Patient & Family Education
- Report promptly: Chest, back, neck or jaw pain; any signs of bleeding.

RH$_0$(D) IMMUNE GLOBULIN
(row)

BayRho-D Full Dose, Rhophylac, WinRho SDF
Classification(s): IMMUNOLOGIC AGENT; IMMUNOGLOBULIN
Therapeutic: IMMUNIZING AGENT
Prototype: Immune Globulin
Pregnancy Category: C

USES To prevent isoimmunization in Rh-negative individuals exposed to Rh-positive RBC. Treatment of idiopathic thrombocytopenia purpura, transfusion/fetomaternal hemorrhage.

INDICATION & DOSAGE

Antepartum Prophylaxis

WinRho SDF *Adult/Adolescent:* 300 mcg at approximately 28 wk gestation; then 120 mcg within 72 h of delivery if infant is Rh-positive
Rhophylac *Adult/Adolescent:* 300 mcg between weeks 28 and 30, then 300 mcg within 72 h of delivery if infant is Rh-positive

Fetomaternal/Transfusion Hemorrhage

Rhophylac *Adult/Adolescent:* 20 mcg/mL fetal blood
WinRho SDF *Adult/Adolescent:* 9 mcg/mL fetal blood up to 600 mcg q8h

Abortion

Rhophylac *Adult/Adolescent:* 300 mcg within 72 h
WinRho SDF *Adult/Adolescent:* 120 mcg within 72 h

Idiopathic Thrombocytopenia Purpura

WinRho SDF *Adult/Child:* 50 mcg/kg, then 25–60 mcg/kg depending on response
Rhophylac *Adult:* 50 mcg/kg

SOLUTION PREPARATION

- No dilution is required for products supplied in liquid form.
- *Vial Reconstitution:* Add 2.5 mL diluent (provided by manufacturer) to each 600 or 1500 international unit (IU) vial; add 8.5 mL diluent (provided by manufacturer) to each 5000 IU vial. Direct stream of diluent to side of vial, swirl to dissolve, do not shake. Concentration of reconstituted vials: 600 IU yields 240 IU/mL, 1500 IU vial yields 600 IU/mL, and 5000 IU vial yields 588 IU/mL.

STORAGE

- Refrigerate commercially prepared solutions. Discard solutions that have been frozen.
- Store powder at 2°–8° C (36°–46° F) unless otherwise directed; avoid freezing.

ADMINISTRATION

Direct IV Injection: Give a single dose over 3–5 min.

INCOMPATIBILITIES Do not mix with other drugs.

ACTION & *THERAPEUTIC EFFECT* Sterile nonpyrogenic gamma globulin solution containing immunoglobulins (IgG) of at least 90% IgG, which provides passive immunity by suppressing active antibody response and formation of anti-Rh$_0$(D) in Rh-negative [Rh$_0$(D)-negative] individuals previously exposed to Rh-positive [Rh$_0$(D)-positive, D^u-positive] blood. *Effective for exposure in Rh-negative women when Rh-positive fetal RBCs enter maternal circulation during third stage of labor, fetal–maternal hemorrhage (as early as second trimester), amniocentesis, or other trauma during pregnancy, termination of pregnancy, and following transfusion with Rh-positive RBC, whole blood, or components (platelets, WBC) prepared from Rh-positive blood.*

CONTRAINDICATIONS Rh$_0$(D)-positive patient; person previously immunized against Rh$_0$(D) factor; severe immune globulin hypersensitivity; bleeding disorders; pregnancy (category C); neonates.
CAUTIOUS USE IgA deficiency.

ADVERSE EFFECTS (≥1%) **Body as a Whole:** Injection site irritation, slight fever, myalgia, lethargy.

DRUG INTERACTIONS May interfere with immune response to LIVE VIRUS VACCINE; should delay use of LIVE VIRUS VACCINES for 3 mo after administration of Rh$_0$(D) immune globulin.

PHARMACOKINETICS Peak: 2 h IV. **Half-Life:** 25 days.

NURSING IMPLICATIONS
Assessment & Drug Effects
- Obtain history of systemic allergic reactions to human immune globulin preparations prior to drug administration.
- Send sample of newborn's cord blood to laboratory for cross-match and typing immediately after delivery and before administration of Rh$_0$(D) immune globulin. Confirm that mother is Rh$_0$(D) and D^u-negative. Infant must be Rh-positive.

Patient & Family Education
- Be aware that administration of Rh$_0$(D) immune globulin (antibody) prevents hemolytic disease of the newborn in a subsequent pregnancy.

RIFAMPIN
(rif′am-pin)
Rifadin, Rofact ✦
Classification(s): ANTIBIOTIC; ANTITUBERCULOSIS AGENT
Therapeutic: ANTIMICROBACTERIAL
Pregnancy Category: C

Common adverse effects in *italic*, life-threatening effects underlined: generic names in **bold**; classifications in SMALL CAPS; ✦ Canadian drug name; ⓟ Prototype drug

USES As adjuvant with other antituberculosis agents in initial treatment and retreatment of clinical tuberculosis.

INDICATION & DOSAGE

Pulmonary Tuberculosis

Adult (HIV-negative): 600 mg daily in conjunction with other antituberculosis agents

Adult (HIV-positive): 10 mg/kg (up to 600 mg) daily × 2 mo then 10 mg/kg/day 2–3 times weekly × 4 mo

Child: 10–20 mg/kg/day (max: 600 mg/day)

Renal Impairment Dosage Adjustment

CrCl less than 10 mL/min: Reduce dose 50%

Hepatic Impairment Dosage Adjustment

Do not exceed 8 mg/kg/day

SOLUTION PREPARATION

- *Vial Reconstitution:* Add 10 mL of sterile water for injection to each 600-mg vial to yield 60 mg/mL. Swirl to dissolve. **Must be** further diluted for infusion.
- *Further Dilution of Reconstituted Solution:* Withdraw the ordered dose and dilute in 500 mL of D5W (preferred) or NS. If absolutely necessary, 100 mL of IV solution may be used.

STORAGE

Use NS solutions within 24 h and D5W solutions within 4 h.

ADMINISTRATION

IV Infusion: Infuse 500 mL solution over 3 h and 100 mL solution over 30 min. Note: A less concentrated solution infused over a longer period is preferred.

R

INCOMPATIBILITIES Solution/additive: Minocycline. Y-site: Diltiazem.

ACTION & *THERAPEUTIC EFFECT* Semisynthetic derivative of rifamycin B, an antibiotic derived from *Streptococcus mediterranei,* with bacteriostatic and bactericidal actions. Inhibits DNA-dependent RNA polymerase activity in susceptible bacterial cells, thereby suppressing RNA synthesis. *Active against* Mycobacterium tuberculosis, M. leprae, Neisseria meningitidis, *as well as a wide range of gram-negative and gram-positive organisms.*

CONTRAINDICATIONS Hypersensitivity to rifampin; obstructive biliary disease; meningococcal disease; intermittent rifampin therapy; pregnancy (category C). Safe use in children less than 5 y is not established.

CAUTIOUS USE Hepatic disease; history of alcoholism; concomitant use of other hepatotoxic agents.

ADVERSE EFFECTS (≥1%) **CNS:** Fatigue, drowsiness, headache, ataxia, confusion, dizziness, inability to concentrate, generalized numbness,

---

pain in extremities, muscular weakness. **Special Senses:** Visual disturbances, transient low-frequency hearing loss, conjunctivitis. **GI:** *Heartburn, epigastric distress, nausea, vomiting, anorexia, flatulence, cramps, diarrhea,* pseudomembranous colitis, *transient elevations in liver function tests* (bilirubin, BSP, alkaline phosphatase, ALT, AST), pancreatitis. **Hematologic:** Thrombocytopenia, transient leukopenia, anemia, including hemolytic anemia. **Body as a Whole:** Hypersensitivity (fever, pruritus, urticaria, skin eruptions, soreness of mouth and tongue, eosinophilia, hemolysis), flu-like syndrome. **Urogenital:** Hemoglobinuria, hematuria, acute renal failure, light-chain proteinuria, menstrual disorders, hepatorenal syndrome (with intermittent therapy). **Respiratory:** Hemoptysis. **Other:** Increasing lethargy, liver enlargement and tenderness, jaundice, brownish-red or orange discoloration of skin, sweat, saliva, tears, and feces; unconsciousness.

DIAGNOSTIC TEST INTERFERENCE Rifampin interferes with *contrast media* used for *gallbladder study;* therefore, test should precede daily dose of rifampin. May also cause retention of *BSP.* Inhibits *standard assays* for *serum folate* and *vitamin B_{12}.*

DRUG INTERACTIONS Alcohol, isoniazid, pyrazinamide, ritonavir, saquinavir increase risk of drug-induced hepatotoxicity); *p*-**aminosalicylic acid (PAS)** decreases concentrations of rifampin; decreases concentrations of **alfentanil, alosetron, alprazolam, amprenavir,** BARBITURATES, BENZODIAZEPINES, **carbamazepine, atovaquone, cevimeline, chloramphenicol, clofibrate,** CORTICOSTEROIDS, **cyclosporine, dapsone, delavirdine, diazepam, digoxin, diltiazem, disopyramide, estazolam, estramustine, fentanyl, fosphenytoin, fluconazole galantamine, indinavir, itraconazole, ketoconazole, lamotrigine, levobupivacaine, lopinavir, methadone, metoprolol, mexiletine, midazolam, nelfinavir,** ORAL SULFONYLUREAS, ORAL CONTRACEPTIVES, **phenytoin,** PROGESTINS, **propafenone, propranolol, quinidine, quinine, ritonavir, sirolimus, theophylline,** THYROID HORMONES, **tocainide, tramadol, verapamil, warfarin, zaleplon,** and **zonisamide,** leading to potential therapeutic failure.

PHARMACOKINETICS Peak: 2–4 h. **Distribution:** Widely distributed, including CSF; crosses placenta; distributed into breast milk. **Metabolism:** In liver to active and inactive metabolites; is enterohepatically cycled. **Elimination:** Up to 30% in urine, 60–65% in feces. **Half-Life:** 3 h.

NURSING IMPLICATIONS

Assessment & Drug Effects

- Prior to initiating therapy: Baseline C&S tests (start drug pending results).
- Monitor IV site frequently for signs of local irritation.
- Lab tests: Periodic LFTs, CBC with platelet count, and serum creatinine. Closely monitor patients with hepatic disease.
- Concurrent drugs: Check PT/INR daily or as necessary to establish and maintain required anticoagulant activity when patient is also receiving an anticoagulant.

Patient & Family Education

- Be aware that drug may impart a harmless red-orange color to urine, feces, sputum, sweat, and tears. Soft contact lenses may be permanently stained.
- Report onset of jaundice, hypersensitivity reactions, and persistence of GI adverse effects to prescriber.
- Use or add barrier contraceptive if using hormonal contraception. Concomitant use of rifampin and oral contraceptives leads to decreased effectiveness of the contraceptive and to menstrual disturbances (spotting, breakthrough bleeding).

RITUXIMAB

(rit-ux′i-mab)

Rituxan

Classification(s): ANTINEOPLASTIC AGENT; IMMUNOMODULATOR

Therapeutic: ANTINEOPLASTIC; ANTIRHEUMATIC

Pregnancy Category: C

USES Relapsed or refractory CD20 positive, B-cell non-Hodgkin's lymphoma, rheumatoid arthritis (with methotrexate).

INDICATION & DOSAGE

Non-Hodgkin's Lymphoma

Adult: 375 mg/m^2 infused at 50 mg/h, may increase infusion rate q30min (max: 400 mg/h, if tolerated), repeat dose on days 8, 15, and 22 (total of 4 doses)

Rheumatoid Arthritis

Adult: 1000 mg on days 1 and 15 (with methotrexate)

SOLUTION PREPARATION

Dilute ordered dose in NS or D5W to a concentration of to 1–4 mg/mL. Examples: 500 mg in 400 mL yields 1 mg/mL; 500 mg in 75 mL yields 4 mg/mL. Gently invert bag to mix. Discard unused portion left in vial.

STORAGE

- Store unopened vials at 2°–8° C (36°–46° F) and protect from light.
- Diluted solutions are stable for 24 h refrigerated and for an additional 24 h at room temperature.

ADMINISTRATION

- **IV Infusion:**
  - *First Dose:* Infuse dose at a rate of 50 mg/h; may increase rate at 50 mg/h increments q30min to maximum rate of 400 mg/h.
  - *Subsequent Doses:* Infuse at a rate of 100 mg/h and increase by 100 mg/h increments q30min up to maximum rate of 400 mg/h.
- Slow or stop infusion if S&S of hypersensitivity appear (see Appendix C).

R

Common adverse effects in *italic*, life-threatening effects <u>underlined</u>: generic names in **bold**; classifications in SMALL CAPS; ♣ Canadian drug name; ☺ Prototype drug

INCOMPATIBILITIES Data not available; do not mix with other drugs.

ACTION & *THERAPEUTIC EFFECT* Monoclonal antibody that binds with the CD20 antigen on the surface of normal and malignant B lymphocytes. B-cells are believed to play a role in the pathogenesis of rheumatoid arthritis and associated chronic synovitis. B-cells may be acting at multiple sites in the autoimmune/inflammatory process including rheumatoid factor and other autoantibody production, antigen presentation, T cell activation, and/or proinflammatory cytokine production. *Rituximab-induced depletion of peripheral B lymphocytes in patients with rheumatoid arthritis (RA) results in a rapid and sustained depletion of circulating and tissue-based (e.g., thymus, spleen) B lymphocytes in non-Hodgkin's lymphoma. Used in combination with methotrexate to reduce signs and symptoms of moderately to severely active RA in adults with an inadequate response to one or more TNF antagonist therapies.*

CONTRAINDICATIONS Hypersensitivity to murine proteins, rituximab, or abciximab; angina, cardiac arrhythmias, cardiac disease; pulmonary disease; chronic lymphocytic leukemia (CLL); lymphoma; severe hypotension; oliguria; rising serum creatinine; viral hepatitis B (HBV); vaccination; pregnancy (category C), lactation.
CAUTIOUS USE Prior exposure to murine-based monoclonal antibodies; history of allergies; asthma and other pulmonary disease (increased risk of bronchospasm); older adults; respiratory insufficiency; CAD; thrombocytopenia; history of cardiac arrhythmias; hypertension, renal impairment. Safety and efficacy in children are not established.

ADVERSE EFFECTS (≥1%) **Body as a Whole:** Angioedema, *fatigue,* asthenia, night sweats, *fever, chills,* myalgia. **CNS:** Headache, dizziness, depression. **CV:** Hypotension, tachycardia, peripheral edema. **GI:** *Nausea,* vomiting, throat irritation, anorexia, abdominal pain, hepatitis B reactivation with <u>fulminant hepatitis, hepatic failure, death</u>. **Hematologic:** <u>Leukopenia, thrombocytopenia, anemia, neutropenia.</u> **Respiratory:** Bronchospasm, dyspnea, rhinitis. **Skin:** Pruritus, rash urticaria. **Other:** Infusion-related reactions: *Fever, chills, rigors, pruritus, urticaria, pain, flushing,* chest pain, hypotension, hypertension, dyspnea, <u>fatal infusion-related reactions</u> have been reported.

DRUG INTERACTIONS ANTIHYPERTENSIVE AGENTS should be stopped 12 h prior to rituximab to avoid excessive hypotension; **cisplatin** may cause additive nephrotoxicity.

PHARMACOKINETICS Duration: 6–12 mo. **Half-Life:** 60–174 h (increases with multiple infusions).

NURSING IMPLICATIONS

Assessment & Drug Effects
- Monitor carefully BP and ECG status during infusion and immediately report S&S of hypersensitivity (e.g., fever, chills, urticaria, pruritus, hypotension, bronchospasms; see Appendix C for others).
- Lab tests: Periodic CBC with differential, peripheral CD20+ B lymphocytes.

Patient & Family Education
- Do not take antihypertensive medication within 12 h of rituximab infusions.
- Note: Use effective contraception during and for up to 12 mo following rituximab therapy.
- Report any of the following experienced during infusion: Itching, difficulty breathing, tightness in throat, dizziness, headache, nausea.

SARGRAMOSTIM (GM-CSF)

(sar-gra'mos-tim)

Leukine

Classification(s): HEMATOPOIETIC GROWTH FACTOR
Therapeutic: HEMATOPOIETIC GROWTH FACTOR; BLOOD FORMER
Prototype: Epoetin alfa
Pregnancy Category: C

USES Myeloid reconstitution after autologous bone marrow transplantation for patients with non-Hodgkin's lymphoma (NHL), acute lymphoblastic leukemia (ALL), and Hodgkin's disease; mobilization of peripheral blood stem cells (PBSCs) for autologous transplantation.

UNLABELED USES To increase WBC counts in AIDS patients; to decrease leukopenia secondary to myelosuppressive chemotherapy; to correct neutropenia in aplastic anemia and in liver and kidney transplantations.

INDICATION & DOSAGE

Autologous Bone Marrow Transplant

Adult: 250 mcg/m²/day infused over 2 h, begin 2–4 h after bone marrow transfusion and not less than 24 h after last dose of chemotherapy or 12 h after last radiation therapy, continue until an ANC of 1500/mm³ is reached for 3 consecutive days

Neutropenia following Chemotherapy

Adult (55 y or older): 250 mcg/m²/day infused over 4 h starting ~day 11 and continue until an ANC of 1500/mm³ is reached for 3 consecutive days or a maximum of 42 days

SOLUTION PREPARATION

- *Vial Reconstitution:* Add 1 mL of sterile water for injection (without preservative) or bacteriostatic water (not to be used for neonates) to the 250 mcg vial to yield 250 mcg/mL. Direct sterile water against side of vial and swirl gently. Avoid excessive or vigorous agitation. Do not shake. **Must be** further diluted for infusion.
- *Further Dilution of Reconstituted Solution:* Add required dose to desired amount of NS. If the final concentration is less than 10 mcg/mL, add albumin (human) to NS before addition of sargramostim. Use 1 mg albumin per 1 mL of NS to give a final concentration of 0.1% albumin.

Common adverse effects in *italic*, life-threatening effects <u>underlined</u>: generic names in **bold**; classifications in SMALL CAPS; ♣ Canadian drug name; ❷ Prototype drug

STORAGE

- Sargramostim vials are single-dose vials, do not reenter or reuse. Discard unused portion.
- If sterile water is used to reconstitute, administer as soon as possible and within 6 h of reconstitution. Vials reconstituted with bacteriostatic water may be stored at 2°–8° C (36°–46° F) for up to 20 days.
- Store unopened vials at 2°–8° C (36°–46° F).

ADMINISTRATION

- **IV Infusion:** Infuse over 2, 4, or 24 h as ordered. Do not use an in-line membrane filter.
- Interrupt infusion and reduce the dose by 50% if: absolute neutrophil count exceeds 20,000/mm^3 or if platelet count exceeds 500,000/mm^3; patient experiences dyspnea. Discontinue infusion if respiratory symptoms worsen. Notify prescriber.

INCOMPATIBILITIES Solution/additive: Do not mix with other drugs. **Y-site:** Acyclovir, amphotericin B, ampicillin, ampicillin/sulbactam, amsacrine, cefonicid, cefoperazone, ceftazidime, chlorpromazine, ganciclovir, haloperidol, hydrocortisone, hydromorphone, hydroxyzine, imipenem/cilastatin, lorazepam, methylprednisolone, mitomycin, morphine, nalbuphine, ondansetron, piperacillin, sodium bicarbonate, tobramycin.

ACTION & *THERAPEUTIC EFFECT* Recombinant human-granulocyte macrophage–colony-stimulating factor (GM-CSF) is produced by recombinant DNA technology in a yeast colony. GM-CSF is a hematopoietic growth factor that stimulates proliferation and differentiation of hematopoietic progenitor cells in the granulocyte–macrophage pathways. *Effectiveness is measured by an increase in the number of mature white blood cells (i.e., neutrophil count).*

CONTRAINDICATIONS Excessive leukemic myeloid blasts in bone marrow or blood; known hypersensitivity to GM-CSF or yeast products; benzyl alcohol; neonates; within 24 h of chemotherapy or radiation treatment; pregnancy (category C), lactation.

CAUTIOUS USE History of cardiac arrhythmias, preexisting cardiac disease, hypoxia, CHF, preexisting fluid retention; pulmonary infiltrates; kidney and liver dysfunction.

ADVERSE EFFECTS (≥1%) **CNS:** Lethargy, malaise, headache, fatigue. **CV:** Abnormal ST segment depression, supraventricular arrhythmias, edema, *hypotension, tachycardia,* <u>pericardial effusion</u>, pericarditis. **Hematologic:** Anemia, *thrombocytopenia.* **GI:** Nausea, vomiting, diarrhea, anorexia. **Body as a Whole:** *Bone pain, myalgia, arthralgias,* weight gain, hyperuricemia, *fever.* **Respiratory:** Pleural effusion. **Skin:** *Rash, pruritus.* **Other:** *First-dose reaction* (some or all of the following symptoms: hypotension, tachycardia, fever, rigors, flushing, nausea, vomiting, diaphoresis, back pain, leg spasms, and dyspnea).

DRUG INTERACTIONS CORTICOSTEROIDS and **lithium** should be used with caution with sargramostim because it may potentiate the myeloproliferative effects.

PHARMACOKINETICS Onset: 3–6 h. **Peak:** 1–2 h. **Elimination:** Probably in urine. **Half-Life:** 80–150 min.

NURSING IMPLICATIONS

Assessment & Drug Effects

- Prior to initiating therapy: Baseline CBC and platelet count, kidney function tests, and LFTs.
- Monitor ECG, as occasional transient supraventricular arrhythmias have occurred during administration, particularly in those with a history of cardiac arrhythmias. Arrhythmias are reversed with discontinuation of drug.
- Monitor closely for respiratory symptoms (dyspnea) during and immediately following infusion, especially in patients with preexisting pulmonary disease.
- Monitor closely patients with preexisting fluid retention, pulmonary infiltrates, or CHF. Peripheral edema, pleural or pericardial effusion has occurred after administration. It is reversible with dose reduction.
- Lab tests: Biweekly CBC with differential, kidney function tests, and LFTs, and liver function biweekly in patients with who have established kidney or liver dysfunction.

Patient & Family Education

- Report promptly any adverse effect (e.g., dyspnea, palpitations, peripheral edema, bone or muscle pain) during or after drug administration.

SCOPOLAMINE HYDROBROMIDE

(skoe-pol′a-meen)

Classification(s): ANTICHOLINERGIC
Therapeutic: ANTISECRETORY; ANTIEMETIC; ANTIVERTIGO
Prototype: Atropine
Pregnancy Category: C

S

USES As preanesthetic medication, for treatment of nausea related to motion sickness.

INDICATION & DOSAGE

Preanesthetic

Adult/Adolescent: 0.3–0.6 mg 45 min before anesthesia induction
Child: 6 mcg/kg q6–8h (max: 0.3 mg/dose)

Motion Sickness

Adult: 0.3–0.6 mg, may be repeated 3–4 times daily
Child: 6 mcg/kg (do not exceed 0.3 mg), may repeat q6–8h

SOLUTION PREPARATION

Dilute required dose with an equal volume of sterile water for injection.

Common adverse effects in *italic*, life-threatening effects <u>underlined</u>: generic names in **bold**; classifications in SMALL CAPS; ♣ Canadian drug name; ⊘ Prototype drug

STORAGE
Store at 15°–30° C (59°–86° F).

ADMINISTRATION
Direct IV Injection: Give a single dose slowly over 2–3 min.

INCOMPATIBILITIES Solution/additive: Methohexital.

ACTION & *THERAPEUTIC EFFECT* Antimuscarinic agent that inhibits the action of acetylcholine (ACh) on postganglionic cholinergic nerves as well as on smooth muscles that lack cholinergic innervation. *Produces CNS depression with marked sedative and tranquilizing effects for use in anesthesia. Effective as a preanesthetic agent to control bronchial, nasal, pharyngeal, and salivary secretions.*

CONTRAINDICATIONS Asthma; hepatitis; toxemia of pregnancy; hypersensitivity to anticholinergic drugs; hypersensitive to belladonna or barbiturates; open angle glaucoma, closed angle glaucoma; GI or urogenital obstructive diseases; severe ulcerative colitis; myasthenia gravis; pregnancy (category C).
CAUTIOUS USE Coronary heart disease, CHF, cardiac arrhythmias, tachycardia, hypertension; infants, children, Down syndrome; patients over 40 y; pyloric obstruction; urinary bladder neck obstruction; autonomic neuropathy; thyrotoxicosis; liver disease; paralytic ileus; GERD, hiatal hernia, ulcerative colitis, gastric ulcer; older adults, parkinsonism; COPD, asthma or allergies; hyperthyroidism; brain damage, spastic paralysis; tartrazine or sulfite sensitivity.

ADVERSE EFFECTS (≥1%) **Body as a Whole:** Fatigue, dizziness, *drowsiness,* disorientation, restlessness, hallucinations, toxic psychosis. **GI:** *Dry mouth and throat, constipation.* **Urogenital:** Urinary retention. **CV:** Decreased heart rate. **Special Senses:** Dilated pupils, photophobia, blurred vision, *local irritation,* follicular conjunctivitis. **Respiratory:** <u>Depressed respiration.</u>

DRUG INTERACTIONS Amantadine, ANTIHISTAMINES, TRICYCLIC ANTIDEPRESSANTS, **quinidine, disopyramide, procainamide** add to anticholinergic effects; decreases **levodopa** effects; **methotrimeprazine** may precipitate extrapyramidal effects; decreases antipsychotic effects (decreased absorption) of PHENOTHIAZINES.

PHARMACOKINETICS Distribution: Crosses placenta; distributed to CNS. **Metabolism:** In liver. **Elimination:** In urine.

NURSING IMPLICATIONS
Assessment & Drug Effects
- Observe patient closely; some patients manifest excitement, delirium, and disorientation shortly after drug is administered until sedative effect takes hold.
- In the presence of pain, scopolamine may cause delirium, restlessness, and excitement unless given with an analgesic.

SODIUM BICARBONATE Na(HCO₃)

(sod'i-um bi-car'bon-ate)

Classification(s): ELECTROLYTIC AND WATER BALANCE AGENT
Therapeutic: ALKALINIZER
Pregnancy Category: C

USES Systemic alkalinizer to correct metabolic acidosis (as occurs in diabetes mellitus, shock, cardiac arrest, or vascular collapse), to minimize uric acid crystallization associated with uricosuric agents, to increase the solubility of sulfonamides, and to enhance renal excretion of barbiturate and salicylate overdosage.

INDICATION & DOSAGE

Cardiac Arrest (in select patients)

Adult: 1 mEq/kg initially, then 0.5 mEq/kg q10min depending on arterial blood gas determinations, give over 1–2 min
Child/Infant: 0.5–1 mEq/kg q10min depending on arterial blood gas determinations, give over 1–2 min

Metabolic Acidosis

Adult/Child: Dose adjusted according to pH, base deficit, $PaCO_2$, fluid limits, and patient response (usually 2–5 mEq/kg)

SOLUTION PREPARATION

- *Direct IV Injection:* May give 4.2% (0.5 mEq/mL) and 5% (0.595 mEq/mL) NaHCO₃ solutions undiluted. Dilute 7.5% (0.892 mEq/mL) and 8.4% (1 mEq/mL) solutions with compatible IV solutions (e.g., D5W, NS, D5NS) to a maximum concentration of 0.5 mEq/mL.
  - *Infants & Children:* Use only 4.2% solution.
- *IV Infusion:* Dilute in D5W, NS, D5NS to a maximum concentration of 0.5 mEg/mL.

STORAGE

Store unopened at 15°–30° C (59°–85° F).

ADMINISTRATION

- Flush line before/after with NS.
- **Direct IV Injection in Cardiac Arrest:**
  - *Adult/Child:* Give over 1–2 min.
  - *Neonate/Infant (less than 2 y):* Use only 4.2% solution and give over 1–2 min. Do not exceed 8 mEq/kg/day.
- **IV Infusion for Metabolic Acidosis:** Usual rate is 2–5 mEq/kg over 4–8 h; do not exceed 50 mEq/h or 1 mEq/kg/min.
- Stop infusion immediately if extravasation occurs. Severe tissue damage has followed tissue infiltration.

INCOMPATIBILITIES Solution/additive: Alcohol 5%, lactated Ringer's, amoxicillin, ampicillin, ascorbic acid, bupivacaine, carboplatin, carmustine, ciprofloxacin, cisplatin, codeine, corticotropin, dobutamine, dopamine, epinephrine, glycopyrrolate, hydromorphone, imipenem-cilastatin, insulin, isoproterenol, labetalol, levorphanol, magnesium sulfate, meperidine, meropenem, methadone, metoclopramide, morphine, nicardipine, norepinephrine, oxytetracycline, penicillin G, pentazocine, pentobarbital, phenobarbital, procaine, promazine, sodium lactate, streptomycin, succinylcholine, tetracycline, thiopental, vancomycin, vitamin B complex with C. **Y-site:** Allopurinol, amiodarone, amphotericin B cholesteryl complex, calcium chloride, ciprofloxacin, cisatracurium, diltiazem, doxorubicin liposome, fenoldopam, hetastarch, idarubicin, imipenem/cilastatin, inamrinone, lansoprazole, leucovorin, lidocaine, midazolam, nalbuphine, ondansetron, oxacillin, sargramostim, verapamil, vincristine, vindesine, vinorelbine.

ACTION & *THERAPEUTIC EFFECT* Short-acting, potent systemic antacid and alkalinizing agent. Rapidly neutralizes gastric acid to form sodium chloride, carbon dioxide, and water. After absorption of sodium bicarbonate, plasma alkali reserve is increased and excess sodium and bicarbonate ions are excreted in urine, thus rendering urine less acid. *Short-acting, potent systemic antacid; rapidly neutralizes systemic acidosis or gastric acid.*

CONTRAINDICATIONS Prolonged therapy with sodium bicarbonate; patients losing chloride (as from vomiting, GI suction, diuresis); hypocalcemia; metabolic alkalosis; respiratory alkalosis; renal insufficiency; peptic ulcer; pregnancy (category C).

CAUTIOUS USE Edema, sodium-retaining disorders; preexisting respiratory acidosis; hyperkalemia; salt-losing nephropathy; heart disease, hypertension; renal disease, renal insufficiency, renal failure; hypokalemia; older adult patients; children less than 2 y.

ADVERSE EFFECTS (≥1%) **GI:** *Belching, gastric distention,* flatulence. **Metabolic:** Metabolic alkalosis; electrolyte imbalance: sodium overload (pulmonary edema), hypocalcemia (tetany), hypokalemia, milk–alkali syndrome, dehydration. **Other:** Hypernatremia, reduction in CSF pressure, <u>intracranial hemorrhage</u>) after rapid IV in neonates. **Skin:** Severe tissue damage following extravasation of IV solution. **Urogenital:** Renal calculi or crystals, impaired kidney function.

DIAGNOSTIC TEST INTERFERENCE Small increase in ***blood lactate levels*** (following IV infusion of sodium bicarbonate); false-positive ***urinary protein*** determinations (using ***Ames reagent, sulfacetic acid,*** heat and ***acetic acid*** or ***nitric acid ring method***); elevated ***urinary urobilinogen levels*** (***urobilinogen*** excretion increases in alkaline urine).

DRUG INTERACTIONS May decrease elimination of **dextroamphetamine, ephedrine, pseudoephedrine, quinidine;** may increase elimination of **chlorpropamide, lithium,** SALICYLATES, TETRACYCLINES.

PHARMACOKINETICS Onset: 15 min. **Duration:** 1–2 h. **Elimination:** In urine within 3–4 h.

NURSING IMPLICATIONS

Assessment & Drug Effects

- Monitor ECG throughout treatment period.
- Monitor for signs of hypokalemia and hypocalcemia.
- Observe for and report S&S of reversal of metabolic acidosis and for signs of alkalosis (over treatment) (see Appendix C). Note that secondary alkalosis is common.
- Lab tests: Frequent blood pH, PO_2, PCO_2, HCO_3^-, and serum electrolytes.

SODIUM FERRIC GLUCONATE COMPLEX

(so'di-um fer'ric glu'co-nate)

Ferrlecit

Classification(s): IRON PREPARATION
Therapeutic: ANTIANEMIC; IRON REPLACEMENT
Pregnancy Category: B

USES Treatment of iron deficiency in patients on chronic hemodialysis and receiving erythropoietin therapy.

INDICATION & DOSAGE

Iron Deficiency in Dialysis Patients

Adult: 125 mg infused over 1 h during each dialysis session
Adolescent/Child (over 6 years): 1.5 mg/kg infused over 1 h (max: 125 mg/dose) during each dialysis session

SOLUTION PREPARATION

- *Direct IV Injection:*
  - *Adult:* May be given undiluted.
  - *Child:* Dilute required dose (1.5 mg/kg) in 25 mL of NS.
- *IV Infusion:* Dilute 125 mg in 100 mL of NS. Use immediately after dilution.

STORAGE

Store unopened ampules at 20°–25° C (68°–77° F).

ADMINISTRATION

- **Direct IV Injection:**
  - *Adult:* Give no faster than 12.5 mg/min.
- **IV Infusion:**
  - *Adult/Child:* Infuse over 1 h.

INCOMPATIBILITIES Solution/additive: Do not mix with any other medications or add to parenteral nutrition solutions.

ACTION & *THERAPEUTIC EFFECT* Stable iron complex used to restore iron loss in chronic kidney failure patients. The use of erythropoietin therapy and blood loss through hemodialysis requires iron replacement. The

Common adverse effects in *italic*, life-threatening effects underlined: generic names in **bold**; classifications in SMALL CAPS; ♣ Canadian drug name; ❷ Prototype drug

599

ferric ion combines with transferrin and is transported to bone marrow where it is incorporated into hemoglobin. *Effectiveness indicated by improved Hgb and Hct, iron saturation as well as serum ferritin levels.*

CONTRAINDICATIONS Any anemias not related to iron deficiency; hypersensitivity to sodium ferric gluconate complex; hemochromatosis, hemosiderosis; hemolytic anemia.

CAUTIOUS USE Benzyl alcohol hypersensitivity; active or suspected infection; preexisting cardiac diseases; older adults; pregnancy (category B), lactation. Safety and efficacy in children less than 6 y are not established.

ADVERSE EFFECTS (≥1%) **Body as a Whole:** Hypersensitivity reaction (cardiovascular collapse, cardiac arrest, bronchospasm, oral/pharyngeal edema, dyspnea, angioedema, urticaria, pruritus). **CV:** Flushing, hypotension.

PHARMACOKINETICS Half-Life: 1–2 h.

NURSING IMPLICATIONS

Assessment & Drug Effects

- Monitor closely for S&S of severe hypersensitivity (see Appendix C).
- Monitor vital signs periodically during administration, as transient hypotension is possible, especially during dialysis.
- Stop infusion immediately and notify prescriber if hypersensitivity is suspected.
- Lab tests: Periodic Hgb, Hct, Fe saturation, serum ferritin.

Patient & Family Education

- Report promptly: Difficulty breathing, itching, flushing, rash, weakness, light-headedness, pain, or any other discomfort during infusion.

STREPTOKINASE

(strep-toe-kye′nase)

Streptase

Classification(s): THROMBOLYTIC AGENT
Therapeutic: THROMBOLYTIC
Prototype: Alteplase
Pregnancy Category: C

USES Acute extensive deep venous thrombosis, acute arterial thrombosis or embolism, acute pulmonary embolus, coronary artery thrombosis, MI, and arteriovenous cannula occlusion.

INDICATION & DOSAGE

Coronary Artery Thrombosis, MI

Adult: 1.5 million international units (IU) infused over 60 min within 6 h of symptoms; **Intracoronary Administration,** 20,000 international units (IU) bolus, followed by 2000 units/min for 60 min (total dose 140,000 units)

Common adverse effects in *italic*, life-threatening effects underlined: generic names in **bold**; classifications in SMALL CAPS; ♣ Canadian drug name; ◐ Prototype drug

Deep Vein Thrombosis, Pulmonary Embolism, Arterial Embolism

Adult: 250,000 international units (IU) over 30 min loading dose, then 100,000 units/h for 24–72 h

Occluded Cannula

Adult: 250,000 international units (IU) in 2 mL over 25–35 min; clamp for 2 h, then aspirate cannula

SOLUTION PREPARATION

- *Vial Reconstitution:* Add 5 mL NS (preferred) or 5 mL D5W to the vial; direct stream against side of vial. Roll or tilt vial to dissolve; avoid shaking to prevent foaming or increase flocculation. **Must be** further diluted for infusion.
- *Further Dilution of Reconstituted Solution:*
  - *Acute MI:* Dilute with NS to a total volume of 45 mL.
  - *Thrombosis/Embolism:* Dilute with NS to a total volume of 90 mL.

STORAGE

- Store unopened vials at 15°–30° C (59°–86° F).
- Store reconstituted solution at 2°–4° C (36°–39° F). Discard after 24 h.

ADMINISTRATION

IV Infusion: Give at rate specified under **INDICATION & DOSAGE** for specific indication (e.g., 1.5 million international units over 60 min for coronary artery thrombosis).

INCOMPATIBILITIES Solution/additive: Dextran. Y-site: Bivalirudin.

ACTION & *THERAPEUTIC EFFECT* Derivative of the beta-hemolytic streptococci. Promotes thrombolysis by activating the conversion of plasminogen to plasmin, the enzyme that degrades fibrin, fibrinogen, and other procoagulant proteins into soluble fragments. Decreases blood and plasma viscosity and erythrocyte aggregation tendency, thus increasing perfusion of collateral blood vessels. *Promotes thrombolysis. The fibrinolytic activity of streptokinase is effective both outside and within the formed thrombus/embolus.*

CONTRAINDICATIONS Streptokinase sensitivity; active internal bleeding; very recent cardiopulmonary resuscitation; recent (within 2 mo) intraspinal, intracranial, intraarterial procedures; intracranial neoplasm; aneurysm or arteriovenous malformation; acute ischemic stroke, history of CVA, severe uncontrolled hypertension (systolic greater than 200, and/or diastolic of 110); history of allergic response to SK; recent streptococcal infection; obstetrical delivery; diabetic hemorrhagic retinopathy; ulcerative colitis, diverticulitis; coagulopathy, any condition in which bleeding presents a hazard or would be difficult to manage because of location; pregnancy (category C). Safety and efficacy in children are not established.

CAUTIOUS USE Patient with preexisting hemostatic deficits; conditions accompanied by risk of cerebral embolism; atrial flutter, atrial fibrillation; septic thrombophlebitis; concomitant use with anticoagulant therapy; uremia; liver failure; severe renal disease; age greater than 75 y; lactation.

Common adverse effects in *italic*, life-threatening effects underlined; generic names in **bold**; classifications in SMALL CAPS; ♣ Canadian drug name; ❶ Prototype drug

601

ADVERSE EFFECTS (≥1%) **Body as a Whole:** *Allergic reactions* (bronchospasm, periorbital swelling, angioneurotic edema, <u>anaphylaxis</u>); urticaria, itching, headache, musculoskeletal pain, flushing, nausea, pyrexia. **Hematologic:** Phlebitis, *bleeding or oozing at sites of percutaneous trauma;* prolonged systemic hypocoagulability; spontaneous bleeding (GI, urogenital, retroperitoneal). **CV:** Unstable blood pressure; reperfusion atrial or <u>ventricular dysrhythmias</u>.

DIAGNOSTIC TEST INTERFERENCE Streptokinase promotes increases in *TT, aPTT,* and *PT.*

DRUG INTERACTIONS ANTICOAGULANTS increase risk of bleeding; **aminocaproic acid** reverses the action of streptokinase.

PHARMACOKINETICS Metabolism: Rapidly cleared from circulation by antibodies. **Distribution:** Does not cross placenta, but antibodies do. **Elimination:** In urine. **Half-Life:** 83 min.

NURSING IMPLICATIONS

Assessment & Drug Effects

- Observe infusion site frequently. If phlebitis occurs, it can usually be controlled by diluting the infusion solution.
- Lab tests: Prior to treatment, baseline control levels for TT, aPTT, PT, Hct, and platelet count. Treatment is delayed until TT and aPTT are less than 2 times the normal control level.
- Check cardiac monitor frequently. Be alert to changes in cardiac rhythm, especially during intracoronary instillation. Dysrhythmias signal need to stop therapy at once.
- Monitor BP. Mild changes can be expected, but report substantial changes (greater than 25 mm Hg). Therapy may be discontinued.
- Check patient's temperature during treatment. A slight elevation, 0.8° C (1.5° F), perhaps with chills, occurs in about one third of the patients. Higher elevations may be treated with acetaminophen.
- Lab tests: Periodic TT, aPTT, PT, Hct, and platelet count. During treatment with SK, TT is generally kept at about 2 times or more baseline value and checked q3–4h.
- Monitor for excessive bleeding q15min for the first hour of therapy, q30min for second to eighth hour, then q8h. Report signs of potential serious bleeding; gum bleeding, epistaxis, hematoma, spontaneous ecchymoses, oozing at catheter site, increased pulse, pain from internal bleeding.

Patient & Family Education

- Report immediately to prescriber symptoms of hypersensitivity (e.g., labored, difficult breathing; hives; itching skin).

STREPTOZOCIN

(strep-toe-zoe'sin)

Zanosar

Common adverse effects in *italic*, life-threatening effects <u>underlined</u>: generic names in **bold**; classifications in SMALL CAPS; ♣ Canadian drug name; ● Prototype drug

Classification(s): ANTINEOPLASTIC; ALKYLATING AGENT
Therapeutic: ANTINEOPLASTIC
Prototype: Cyclophosphamide
Pregnancy Category: D

USES Metastatic islet cell carcinoma of pancreas, as single agent or in combination with fluorouracil.
UNLABELED USES A variety of other malignant neoplasms including metastatic carcinoid tumor or carcinoid syndrome, refractory advanced Hodgkin's disease, and metastatic colorectal cancer.

INDICATION & DOSAGE

Islet Cell Carcinoma of Pancreas

Adult: 500 mg/m^2/day for 5 consecutive days q6wk or 1 g/m^2/wk for 2 wk, then increase to 1.5 g/m^2/wk

Renal Impairment Dosage Adjustment

Use cautiously.

SOLUTION PREPARATION

- Wear gloves to protect against topical exposure. If solution or powder comes in contact with skin or mucosa, promptly flush the area thoroughly with soap and water.
- *Vial Reconstitution:* Add 9.5 mL D5W or NS, to yield 100 mg/mL. Solution will be pale gold. May be further diluted for infusion (typical).
- *Further Dilution of Reconstituted Solution:* Dilute required dose in up to 250 mL of the original diluent.

STORAGE

- Protect reconstituted solution and vials of drug from light. Discard reconstituted solutions after 12 h (contains no preservative and not intended for multidose use).
- Store unopened vials at 2°–8° C (35°–46° F).

ADMINISTRATION

- Ensure patency prior to injection or infusion, as extravasation may cause tissue sloughing.
- **IV Infusion:** Infuse over 15–60 min.
- Inspect IV site frequently for extravasation. If extravasation occurs, stop infusion, apply ice, and contact prescriber regarding further treatment.

INCOMPATIBILITIES Y-site: Allopurinol, aztreonam, cefepime, piperacillin/tazobactam.

ACTION & *THERAPEUTIC EFFECT* Streptozocin is highly toxic and has a low therapeutic index; thus, a clinically effective response is likely to be accompanied by some evidence of toxicity. Inhibits DNA synthesis in both bacterial and mammalian cells and prevents progression of cells into mitosis, affecting all phases of the cell cycle (cell-cycle nonspecific). Appears to

Common adverse effects in *italic*, life-threatening effects <u>underlined</u>: generic names in **bold**; classifications in SMALL CAPS; ♣ Canadian drug name; ☻ Prototype drug

603

have minimal effects on RNA or protein synthesis. *Successful therapy with streptozocin (alone or in combination) produces a biochemical response evidenced by decreased secretion of hormones as well as measurable tumor regression. Thus, serial fasting insulin levels during treatment indicate response to this drug.*

CONTRAINDICATIONS Pregnancy (category D), lactation. Safety in children is not established.

CAUTIOUS USE Renal impairment; hepatic disease, hepatic impairment; patients with history of hypoglycemia, diabetes mellitus.

ADVERSE EFFECTS (≥1%) **CNS:** Confusion, lethargy, depression. **GI:** *Nausea, vomiting,* diarrhea, transient increase in AST, ALT, or alkaline phosphatase; hypoalbuminemia. **Hematologic:** *Mild* to moderate myelosuppression *(leukopenia, thrombocytopenia, anemia).* **Metabolic:** Glucose tolerance abnormalities (moderate and reversible); glycosuria without hyperglycemia, insulin shock (rare). **Urogenital:** Nephrotoxicity: Azotemia, anuria, proteinuria, hypophosphatemia, hyperchloremia; *Fanconi-like syndrome* (proximal renal tubular reabsorption defects, alkaline pH of urine, glucosuria, acetonuria, aminoaciduria); hypokalemia, hypocalcemia. **Other:** Local necrosis following extravasation.

DRUG INTERACTIONS MYELOSUPPRESSIVE AGENTS add to hematologic toxicity; nephrotoxic agents (e.g., AMINOGLYCOSIDES, **vancomycin, amphotericin B, cisplatin**) increase risk of nephrotoxicity; **phenytoin** may reduce cytotoxic effect on pancreatic beta cells.

PHARMACOKINETICS Distribution: Metabolite enters CSF. **Metabolism:** In liver and kidneys. **Elimination:** 70–80% of dose in urine, 1% in feces, and 5% in expired air. **Half-Life:** 35–40 min.

NURSING IMPLICATIONS

Assessment & Drug Effects

- Prior to initiating therapy: Baseline CBC, LFTs, and renal function tests.
- Report evidence of drug-induced declining kidney function promptly; changes are dose related and cumulative. Mild adverse renal effects may be reversible following discontinuation of streptozocin, but nephrotoxicity may be irreversible, severe, or fatal.
- Lab tests: Weekly CBC, LFTs, renal function tests, and serum electrolytes during therapy and for 4 wk after termination of therapy.
- Be alert to early laboratory evidence of kidney dysfunction: Hypophosphatemia, mild proteinuria, and changes in I&O ratio and pattern.
- Platelet and leukocyte nadirs generally occur 1–2 wk after beginning therapy.
- Be alert to symptoms of sepsis and superinfections (leukopenia) or increased tendency to bleed (thrombocytopenia). Myelosuppression is severe in 10–20% of patients and may be cumulative and more severe if patient has had prior exposure to radiation or to other antineoplastics.
- Monitor and record temperature pattern to promptly recognize impending sepsis.

Patient & Family Education

- Inspect site at weekly intervals and report changes in tissue appearance if extravasation occurred during IV infusion.
- Comply with all recommended measures to minimize risk of bleeding. Exercise caution with movement to prevent injury.
- Drink fluids liberally (2000–3000 mL/day). Hydration may protect against drug toxicity effects.
- Report S&S of nephrotoxicity (see Appendix C).
- Do not take aspirin without consulting prescriber.
- Report to prescriber promptly any signs of bleeding: Hematuria, epistaxis, ecchymoses, petechiae.
- Report symptoms that suggest anemia: Shortness of breath, pale mucous membranes and nail beds, exhaustion, rapid pulse.
- Do not breast feed while taking this drug.

SUCCINYLCHOLINE CHLORIDE 🄿

(suk-sin-ill-koe′leen)

Anectine, Quelicin

Classification(s): SKELETAL MUSCLE RELAXANT, DEPOLARIZING
Therapeutic: SKELETAL MUSCLE RELAXANT
Pregnancy Category: C

USES To produce skeletal muscle relaxation as adjunct to anesthesia; to facilitate intubation and endoscopy, to increase pulmonary compliance in assisted or controlled respiration.

INDICATION & DOSAGE

Surgical and Anesthetic Procedures

Adult: 0.3–1.1 mg/kg administered over 10–30 sec, may give additional doses prn
Adolescent/Child: 1–2 mg/kg administered over 10–30 sec, may give additional doses prn

Obesity

Dose based on IBW

SOLUTION PREPARATION

- *Direct IV Injection:* Give undiluted.
- *Intermittent/Continuous Infusion:* Dilute 1 g in 500–1000 mL of D5W, NS, or D5NS.

STORAGE

Refrigerate diluted IV solutions.

ADMINISTRATION

- **Direct IV Injection:** Give a bolus dose over 10–30 sec.

Common adverse effects in *italic*, life-threatening effects underlined: generic names in **bold**; classifications in SMALL CAPS; ♣ Canadian drug name; 🄿 Prototype drug

605

- **Intermittent/Continuous Infusion:** Infuse 0.5–10 mg/min. Do not exceed 10 mg/min.

INCOMPATIBILITIES Solution/additive: Aminophylline, ampicillin, cephalothin, diazepam, epinephrine, hydrocortisone, methicillin, methohexital, nitrofurantoin, oxacillin, oxytetracycline, pentobarbital, sodium bicarbonate, thiopental, warfarin. Y-site: Thiopental.

ACTION & *THERAPEUTIC EFFECT* Synthetic, ultrashort-acting depolarizing neuromuscular blocking agent with high affinity for acetylcholine (ACh) receptor sites. *Initial transient contractions and fasciculations are followed by sustained flaccid skeletal muscle paralysis produced by state of accommodation that develops in adjacent excitable muscle membranes.*

CONTRAINDICATIONS Hypersensitivity to succinylcholine; family history of malignant hyperthermia; burns; trauma; pregnancy (category C).

CAUTIOUS USE Kidney, liver, pulmonary, metabolic, or cardiovascular disorders; myasthenia gravis; dehydration, electrolyte imbalance; patients taking digitalis; severe burns or trauma; fractures; spinal cord injuries; degenerative or dystrophic neuromuscular diseases; low plasma pseudocholinesterase levels (recessive genetic trait, but often associated with severe liver disease, severe anemia, dehydration, marked changes in body temperature, exposure to neurotoxic insecticides, certain drugs); collagen diseases; porphyria; intraocular surgery, glaucoma; during delivery by cesarean section; lactation.

ADVERSE EFFECTS (≥1%) **CNS:** *Muscle fasciculations,* profound and prolonged muscle relaxation, muscle pain. **CV:** *Bradycardia,* tachycardia, hypotension, hypertension, arrhythmias, sinus arrest. **Respiratory:** <u>Respiratory depression</u>, bronchospasm, hypoxia, <u>apnea</u>. **Body as a Whole:** <u>Malignant hyperthermia</u>, increased IOP, excessive salivation, enlarged salivary glands. **Metabolic:** Myoglobinemia, hyperkalemia. **GI:** Decreased tone and motility of GI tract (large doses).

DRUG INTERACTIONS Cyclophosphamide, cyclopropane, echothiophate iodide, halothane, lidocaine, MAGNESIUM SALTS, **methotrimeprazine,** NARCOTIC ANALGESICS, ORGANOPHOSPHAMIDE INSECTICIDES, MAO INHIBITORS, PHENOTHIAZINES, **procaine, procainamide, quinidine, quinine, propranolol** may prolong neuromuscular blockade; DIGITALIS GLYCOSIDES may increase risk of cardiac arrhythmias.

PHARMACOKINETICS Onset: 0.5–1 min. **Duration:** 2–3 min. **Distribution:** Crosses placenta in small amounts. **Metabolism:** In plasma by pseudocholinesterases. **Elimination:** In urine.

NURSING IMPLICATIONS

Assessment & Drug Effects

- Monitor respirations. Transient apnea usually occurs at time of maximal drug effect (1–2 min); spontaneous respiration should return in a few seconds or, at most, 3 or 4 min.
- Have immediately available: Facilities for emergency endotracheal intubation, artificial respiration, and assisted or controlled respiration with oxygen.

- Monitor vital signs and keep airway clear of secretions.
- Lab tests: Baseline serum electrolytes.
- Monitor electrolyte status, as imbalances (particularly potassium, calcium, magnesium) can potentiate effects of neuromuscular blocking agents.

Patient & Family Education
- Patient may experience postprocedural muscle stiffness and pain (caused by initial fasciculations following injection) for as long as 24–30 h.
- Report residual muscle weakness.

SUFENTANIL CITRATE

(soo-fen'ta-nil)

Sufenta

Classification(s): ANALGESIC, NARCOTIC (OPIATE) AGONIST; GENERAL ANESTHETIC
Therapeutic: NARCOTIC ANALGESIC; GENERAL ANESTHETIC
Prototype: Morphine
Pregnancy Category: C   **Controlled Substance:** Schedule II

USES Analgesic supplement in maintenance of balanced general anesthesia and also as a primary anesthetic.

INDICATION & DOSAGE

Adjunct to General Anesthesia

Adult: 1–8 mcg/kg, depending on duration of surgery, may give additional doses of 10–50 mcg if needed

As Primary Anesthetic

Adult: 1–30 mcg/kg administered with 100% oxygen and a muscle relaxant, may give additional doses of 10–50 mcg if needed
Child (less than 12 y): 10–25 mcg/kg administered with 100% oxygen and a muscle relaxant, may give additional doses of 25–50 mcg up to 1–2 mcg/kg/dose if needed

Obesity

Dose based on LBW

SOLUTION PREPARATION
No dilution is required. Administer as supplied.

STORAGE
Store at 15°–30° C (59°–86° F) unless otherwise directed; protect from light.

ADMINISTRATION
Direct IV Injection: Give a bolus dose over 3–5 sec.

INCOMPATIBILITIES Solution/additive: Diazepam, lorazepam, phenobarbital, phenytoin, sodium bicarbonate, sodium chloride. **Y-site:** Lorazepam, phenytoin, thiopental.

ACTION & *THERAPEUTIC EFFECT* Synthetic opioid related to fentanyl with similar pharmacologic actions, but about 7 times more potent. Onset of action and recovery from anesthesia occur more rapidly with sufentanil than with fentanyl. In common with other opiate agonists, sufentanil can cause respiratory depression and suppression of cough reflex. *Effective agent for analgesia as a supplement or a primary anesthesia.*

CONTRAINDICATIONS Hypersensitivity to opiate agonists; pregnancy (category C).

CAUTIOUS USE Pulmonary disease, reduced respiratory reserve; COPD; cardiac disease; increased intracranial pressure; seizure disorders; impaired liver or kidney function; GI disease; lactation.

ADVERSE EFFECTS (≥1%) **CV:** Bradycardia, tachycardia, hypotension, hypertension, arrhythmias. **GI:** Nausea, vomiting, constipation. **Respiratory:** Bronchospasm, *respiratory depression, apnea*. **Body as a Whole:** *Skeletal muscle rigidity (especially of trunk),* chills, *itching,* spasms of sphincter of Oddi, urinary retention.

DRUG INTERACTIONS BETA-ADRENERGIC ANTAGONISTS increase incidence of bradycardia; **alcohol** and other CNS DEPRESSANTS such as BARBITURATES, TRANQUILIZERS, OPIATES, and INHALATION GENERAL ANESTHETICS add to CNS depression; **cimetidine** increases risk of respiratory depression.

PHARMACOKINETICS Onset: 1.5–3 min. **Duration:** 40 min. **Distribution:** Crosses blood–brain barrier. **Metabolism:** In liver (CYP 3A4) and small intestine. **Elimination:** In urine and feces. **Half-Life:** 2–3 h.

NURSING IMPLICATIONS

Assessment & Drug Effects

- Monitor vital signs. Observe for skeletal muscle rigidity, especially of chest wall, and respiratory depression, particularly in older adults, and in patients who are obese, debilitated, or who have received high doses.
- Bear in mind that if naloxone is given to reverse respiratory depression, the duration of sufentanil-induced respiratory depression may exceed the duration of naloxone.

Patient & Family Education

- Avoid activities that require mental alertness for at least 24 h after receiving this drug.

SULFAMETHOXAZOLE-TRIMETHOPRIM (SMZ-TMP)

(sul′fa-meth-ox′a-zole tri-meth′o-prim)

Classification(s): ANTIBIOTIC
Therapeutic: ANTIBACTERIAL
Pregnancy Category: C

USES *Pneumocystis jiroveci* pneumonitis (formerly PCP), *Shigellosis* enteritis, and severe complicated UTIs.
UNLABELED USES Gastrointestinal infections; genital ulcers caused by *Haemophilus ducreyi*.

INDICATION & DOSAGE

Systemic Infections

Adult: 8–10 mg/kg/day divided q6–12h infused over 60–90 min (dose based on TMP component)
Child/Infant (over 2 mo): 6–10 mg/kg/day divided q6–12h infused over 60–90 min (dose based on TMP component)

Pneumocystis jiroveci Pneumonia (formerly PCP)

Adult/Adolescent/Child: 15–20 mg/kg/day divided q6h (dose based on TMP component)

Renal Impairment Dosage Adjustment

CrCl 10–30 mL/min: Reduce dose by 50%; *CrCl less than 10 mL/min:* Reduce by 50–75%

SOLUTION PREPARATION

Solution **must be** diluted. Add contents of 5-mL ampule to 125 mL D5W. Use within 6 h. If less fluid is desired, dilute in 75 or 100 mL and use within 2 h or 4 h, respectively. Discard solution if cloudy or if crystallization appears after mixing.

STORAGE

Store unopened ampule at 15°–30° C (59°–86° F) in dry place protected from light. Do not refrigerate.

ADMINISTRATION

Intermittent Infusion: Infuse over 60–90 min. Avoid bolus or rapid injection. Do not mix other drugs or solutions with IV infusion.

INCOMPATIBILITIES Solution/additive: Stability in **dextrose** and **normal saline** is concentration dependent; **fluconazole, linezolid, verapamil. Y-site: Cisatracurium, fluconazole, foscarnet, midazolam, vinorelbine.**

ACTION & *THERAPEUTIC EFFECT* Fixed combination of sulfamethoxazole (SMZ), an intermediate-acting sulfonamide, and trimethoprim (TMP), a synthetic antiinfective. Both components of the combination are synthetic folate antagonist antiinfectives. Mechanism of action is principally enzyme inhibition, which prevents bacterial synthesis of essential nucleic acids and proteins. *Effective against* Pneumocystis jiroveci *pneumonitis (formerly PCP),* Shigellosis *enteritis, and severe complicated UTIs due to most strains of the* Enterobacteriaceae.

CONTRAINDICATIONS Hypersensitivity to SMZ, TMP, sulfonamides, or bisulfites; carbonic anhydrase inhibitors; group A beta-hemolytic strepto-

Common adverse effects in *italic*, life-threatening effects <u>underlined</u>: generic names in **bold**; classifications in SMALL CAPS; ♣ Canadian drug name; ⊘ Prototype drug

609

coccal pharyngitis; megaloblastic anemia due to folate deficiency; creatinine clearance less than 15 mL/min; G6PD deficiency; hyperkalemia; porphyria; pregnancy (category C); infants less than 2 mo.

CAUTIOUS USE Impaired kidney or liver function; bone marrow depression; possible folate deficiency; severe allergy or bronchial asthma; hypersensitivity to sulfonamide derivative drugs (e.g., acetazolamide, thiazides, tolbutamide).

ADVERSE EFFECTS (≥1%) **Skin:** *Mild to moderate rashes (including fixed drug eruptions),* toxic epidermal necrolysis. **GI:** *Nausea, vomiting,* diarrhea, *anorexia,* hepatitis, pseudomembranous enterocolitis, stomatitis, glossitis, abdominal pain. **Urogenital:** Kidney failure, oliguria, anuria, crystalluria. **Hematologic:** Agranulocytosis (rare), aplastic anemia (rare), megaloblastic anemia, hypoprothrombinemia, thrombocytopenia (rare). **Body as a Whole:** Weakness, arthralgia, myalgia, photosensitivity, allergic myocarditis.

DIAGNOSTIC TEST INTERFERENCE May elevate levels of *serum creatinine, transaminase, bilirubin, alkaline phosphatase.*

DRUG INTERACTIONS May enhance hypoprothrombinemic effects of ORAL ANTICOAGULANTS; may increase **methotrexate** toxicity.

PHARMACOKINETICS Distribution: Widely distributed, including CNS; crosses placenta; distributed into breast milk. **Metabolism:** In liver. **Elimination:** In urine. **Half-Life:** 10–13 h SMZ, 8–10 h TMP.

NURSING IMPLICATIONS

Assessment & Drug Effects

- Be aware IV formulation contains sodium metabisulfite, which produces allergic-type reactions in susceptible patients: Hives, itching, wheezing, anaphylaxis. Susceptibility (low in general population) is seen most frequently in asthmatics or atopic nonasthmatic persons.
- Lab tests: Baseline and periodic urinalysis; CBC with differential, platelet count, BUN and creatinine clearance with prolonged therapy.
- Monitor I&O volume and pattern. Report significant changes to forestall renal calculi formation.
- Older adults are at risk for severe adverse reactions, especially if liver or kidney function is compromised or if certain other drugs are given.
- Be alert for overdose symptoms: Nausea, vomiting, anorexia, headache, dizziness, mental depression, confusion, and bone marrow depression.
- Concurrent drug: Monitor PT and INR in patient also receiving warfarin. Change in warfarin dosage may be indicated.

Patient & Family Education

- Report immediately if rash appears. Other reportable symptoms are sore throat, fever, purpura, jaundice; all are early signs of serious reactions.
- Monitor for and report fixed eruptions to prescriber. This drug can cause fixed eruptions at the same sites each time the drug is administered. Every contact with drug may not result in eruptions.
- Drink 2.5–3 liters (1 liter is approximately equal to 1 quart) daily, unless otherwise directed.

S

TACROLIMUS

(tac-roli-mus)

Prograf

Classification(s): IMMUNOLOGIC AGENT; IMMUNOSUPPRESSANT
Therapeutic: IMMUNOSUPPRESSANT
Prototype: Cyclosporine
Pregnancy Category: C

USES Liver rejection prophylaxis; rejection prophylaxis for other organ transplants (kidney, heart, bone marrow, pancreas, small bowel).
UNLABELED USES Acute organ transplant rejection, severe plaque-type psoriasis.

INDICATION & DOSAGE

Rejection Prophylaxis

Adult/Child: 0.03–0.05 mg/kg/day as continuous IV infusion, start no sooner than 6 h after transplant, continue until patient can take oral therapy

Renal Impairment Dosage Adjustment

Start with lower dose

Hemodialysis Dosage Adjustment

Supplementation not necessary

Hepatic Impairment Dosage Adjustment

Start with lower dose

SOLUTION PREPARATION

Dilute 5 mg/mL ampules with NS or D5W to a concentration of 0.004–0.02 mg/mL (4–20 mcg/mL).

STORAGE

- Store ampules between 5° and 25° C (41° and 77° F).
- Store the diluted infusion in glass or polyethylene containers and discard after 24 h.

ADMINISTRATION

- **Continuous Infusion:** Infuse at a rate based on patient's weight.
- PVC-free tubing is recommended to reduce significant drug absorption onto the tubing, especially at lower concentrations.

INCOMPATIBILITIES Y-site: Acyclovir, ganciclovir.

ACTION & *THERAPEUTIC EFFECT* Inhibits helper T-lymphocytes by selectively inhibiting secretion of interleukin-2, interleukin-3, and interleukin-

---

Common adverse effects in *italic*, life-threatening effects underlined: generic names in **bold**; classifications in SMALL CAPS; ♣ Canadian drug name; ❷ Prototype drug

611

gamma; thus, it reduces transplant rejection. *Inhibits antibody production (thus subduing immune response) by creating an imbalance in favor of suppressor T-lymphocytes.*

CONTRAINDICATIONS Hypersensitivity to tacrolimus or castor oil; pregnancy (category C), lactation.

CAUTIOUS USE Renal or hepatic insufficiency; hyperkalemia; QT prolongation; CHF; diabetes mellitus; gout; history of seizures; hypertension.

ADVERSE EFFECTS (≥1%) **CNS:** *Headache, tremors, insomnia, paresthesia, hyperesthesia* and/or sensations of warmth, circumoral numbness. **CV:** *Mild to moderate hypertension.* **Endocrine:** Hirsutism, *hyperglycemia, hyperkalemia, hypokalemia, hypomagnesemia,* hyperuricemia, decreased serum cholesterol. **GI:** *Nausea, abdominal pain, gas,* appetite changes, *vomiting, anorexia, constipation,* diarrhea, ascites. **Hematologic:** *Anemia, leukocytosis, thrombocytopenia purpura.* **Urogenital:** UTI, oliguria, nephrotoxicity. **Respiratory:** *Pleural effusion, atelectasis, dyspnea.* **Special Senses:** Blurred vision, photophobia. **Skin:** *Flushing, rash, pruritus, skin irritation,* alopecia, erythema, folliculitis, hyperesthesia, <u>exfoliative dermatitis</u>, hirsutism, photosensitivity, skin discoloration, skin ulcer, sweating. **Body as a Whole:** *Pain, fever, peripheral edema.*

DRUG INTERACTIONS Use with **cyclosporine** increases risk of nephrotoxicity. **Erythromycin, metoclopramide** may increase tacrolimus levels; **caspofungin, rifampin** may decrease levels. NSAIDS may lead to oliguria or anuria.

PHARMACOKINETICS Duration: 12 h. **Distribution:** Within plasma, tacrolimus is found primarily in lipoprotein-deficient fraction; 75–97% protein bound; distributed into red blood cells; blood:plasma ratio reported greater than 4; distributed into breast milk. **Metabolism:** Extensively in liver (CYP 3A4). **Elimination:** Primarily in bile. **Half-Life:** 8.7–11.3 h.

NURSING IMPLICATIONS

Assessment & Drug Effects

- Monitor kidney function closely; report elevated serum creatinine or decreased urinary output.
- Monitor for neurotoxicity, and report tremors, changes in mental status, or other signs of toxicity.
- Monitor cardiovascular status and report hypertension.
- Lab tests: Periodic serum electrolytes, blood glucose, uric acid, BUN, and creatinine clearance.

Patient & Family Education

- Be aware of potential adverse effects. Drug can cause diabetes. Report promptly frequent urination or increased thirst or hunger.
- Notify prescriber of S&S of neurotoxicity (i.e., tremors, paresthesia, etc.).
- Women using oral contraceptives should use an alternative form of contraception.

TEMSIROLIMUS

(tem-si-ro-li′mus)

Torisel

Classification(s): ANTINEOPLASTIC

Therapeutic: ANTINEOPLASTIC

Pregnancy Category: D

USES Treatment of advanced renal cell carcinoma.

UNLABELED USES Astrocytoma, mantle cell lymphoma (MCL).

INDICATION & DOSAGE

Renal Cell Carcinoma

Adult: 25 mg every wk

Dosage Adjustment

Regimen with a Strong CYP3A4 Inhibitor: May require dose reduction to 12.5 mg/wk; *Regimen with a Strong CYP3A4 Inducer:* Titrate from 25 mg/ wk to 50 mg/wk based on tolerability

Toxicity Adjustment

Grade 3 or higher toxicity or ANC below 1000/mm^3 or platelets below 75,000/mm^3: Reduce dose by 5 mg/wk until toxicity improves to grade 2 or less (do not reduce dose below 15 mg/wk)

SOLUTION PREPARATION

Dilution of Concentrate: Inject 1.8 mL of supplied diluent into the 25 mg/ mL vial to yield 10 mg/mL. Withdraw the required dose and inject rapidly into a 250 mL DEHP-free container of NS. Invert to mix.

STORAGE

Store at 2°–8° C (36°–46° F). Protect from light. The reconstituted solution is stable for up to 24 h at controlled room temperature. The IV solution should be infused within 6 h of preparation.

ADMINISTRATION

- Premedication with prophylactic IV diphenhydramine 25–50 mg (or similar antihistamine) 30 min before each dose is recommended.
- **IV Infusion:** Infuse over 30–60 min through a DEHP-free infusion line with a 5 micron or less in-line filter. Complete infusion within 6 h of preparation.
- Withhold drug and notify prescriber of an absolute neutrophil count less than 1,000/mm^3 or platelet count less than 75,000/mm^3, or NCI - CTCAE grade 3 or greater adverse reactions.

INCOMPATIBILITIES Solution/additive: Do not add other drugs to temsirolimus IV solutions. **Y-site:** Data not available; do not mix with other drugs.

Common adverse effects in *italic*, life-threatening effects <u>underlined</u>: generic names in **bold**; classifications in SMALL CAPS; ♣ Canadian drug name; ◐ Prototype drug

ACTION & *THERAPEUTIC EFFECT* Inhibits an intracellular protein that controls cell division in renal carcinoma and other tumor cells. *Results in arrest of growth in tumor cells.*

CONTRAINDICATIONS Live vaccines; pregnancy (category D), lactation. Safe use in children has not been established.

CAUTIOUS USE Hypersensitivity to temsirolimus, sirolimus, polysorbate 80, or antihistamines; diabetes mellitus; history of hyperlipemia; respiratory disorders; perioperative period due to potential for abnormal wound healing; CNS tumors (primary or by metastasis) and concomitant use of anticoagulants; hepatic impairment.

ADVERSE EFFECTS (≥1%) **Body as a Whole:** Allergic/hypersensitivity reactions, *asthenia*, chest pain, chills, *edema*, impaired wound healing, infections, pain, pyrexia. **CNS:** Depression, dysgeusia, headache, insomnia. **CV:** Hypertension, thrombophlebitis, venous thromboembolism. **GI:** Abdominal pain, *anorexia*, constipation, diarrhea, fatal bowel perforation, *mucositis, nausea*, vomiting. **Hematological:** Decrease hemoglobin, *leukocytopenia, lymphopenia*, neutropenia, *thrombocytopenia*. **Metabolic:** *Elevated alkaline phosphatase, elevated AST, elevated serum creatinine*, hypokalemia, *hypophosphatemia*, hyperbilirubinemia, *hypercholesterolemia, hyperglycemia, hypertriglyceridemia*, weight loss. **Musculoskeletal:** Arthralgia, back pain, myalgia. **Respiratory:** Cough, dyspnea, epistaxis, interstitial lung disease, pharyngitis, pneumonia, rhinitis, upper respiratory tract infection. **Skin:** Acne, dry skin, nail disorder, pruritus, *rash*. **Special Senses:** Conjunctivitis. **Urogenital:** Urinary tract infection.

DRUG INTERACTIONS AZOLE ANTIFUNGAL AGENTS **(fluconazole, itraconazole, ketoconazole, posaconazole, voriconazole), cyclosporine,** inhibitors of CYP3A4 (PROTEASE INHIBITORS, **clarithromycin, diltiazem**), **mycophenolate mofetil,** and **sunitinib** increase the plasma levels of temsirolimus. Inducers of CYP3A4 **(dexamethasone, rifampin, rifabutin, phenytoin)** decrease the plasma level of temsirolimus. **Food: Grapefruit** and **grapefruit juice** increase the plasma level of temsirolimus. **Herbal: St. John's wort** decreases the plasma level of temsirolimus.

PHARMACOKINETICS Peak: 0.5–2 h. **Metabolism:** In liver. **Elimination:** Primarily in stool. **Half-Life:** 17.3 h.

NURSING IMPLICATIONS

Assessment & Drug Effects

- Monitor for infusion-related reactions during and for at least 1 h after completion of infusion.
- Slow or stop infusion for infusion-related reactions. If infusion is restarted after 30–60 min of observation, slow rate to up to 60 min and continue observation.
- Monitor respiratory status and report promptly dyspnea, cough, S&S of hypoxia, fever.
- Lab tests: Baseline and periodic CBC with differential and platelet count, lipid profile, LFTs, alkaline phosphatase, kidney function tests, serum electrolytes, plasma glucose, ABGs.

- Monitor diabetics for loss of glycemic control.

Patient & Family Education
- Avoid live vaccines and close contact with those who have received live vaccines.
- Use effective contraceptive measures to prevent pregnancy.
- Men with partners of childbearing age should use reliable contraception throughout treatment and for 3 mo after the last dose of temsirolimus.
- Report promptly any of the following: S&S of infection, difficulty breathing, abdominal pain, blood in stools, abnormal wound healing, S&S of hypersensitivity (see Appendix C).

TENECTEPLASE RECOMBINANT

(ten-ecte-plase)

TNKase

Classification(s): THROMBOLYTIC AGENT, TISSUE PLASMINOGEN ACTIVATOR
Therapeutic: THROMBOLYTIC
Prototype: Alteplase
Pregnancy Category: C

USES Reduction of mortality associated with acute myocardial infarction (AMI).

INDICATION & DOSAGE

Acute Myocardial Infarction

Adult:

Weight	Dose
Less than 60 kg	30 mg
60–70 kg	35 mg
70–80 kg	40 mg
80–90 kg	45 mg
Over 90 kg	50 mg

SOLUTION PREPARATION

- *Vial Reconstitution:* Reconstitute only with diluent, syringe, needle, and dispensing system supplied by manufacturer. Read and follow instructions supplied with TwinPak™ Dual Cannula Device. Follow directions supplied with TwinPak™ for proper handling of syringe.
- Withdraw 10 mL of sterile water for injection from the supplied vial; inject entire contents into the TNKase vial directing the diluent stream into the powder. Gently swirl until dissolved but do not shake. The resulting solution contains 5 mg/mL. Withdraw the appropriate dose and discard any unused solution.

Common adverse effects in *italic*, life-threatening effects <u>underlined</u>: generic names in **bold**; classifications in SMALL CAPS; ♣ Canadian drug name; ◐ Prototype drug

615

STORAGE

Store unopened TwinPak™ at or below 30° C (86° F) or under refrigeration at 2°–8° C (36°–46° F).

ADMINISTRATION

Direct IV Injection: Dextrose-containing IV line **must be** flushed with NS before and after bolus. Give as a single bolus dose over 5 sec. The total dose given should not exceed 50 mg.

INCOMPATIBILITIES Solution/additive/Y-site: Dextrose solutions.

ACTION & *THERAPEUTIC EFFECT* Tenecteplase is a third-generation thrombolytic agent with advantages over alteplase: longer half-life, more rapid thrombolysis, and greater fibrin specificity. Additionally, the rate of noncerebral bleeding is less than in alteplase. Activates plasminogen, a substance created by endothelial cells in response to arterial wall injury that contributes to clot formation. Plasminogen is converted to plasmin, which breaks down the fibrin mesh that binds the clot together, thus dissolving the clot. *Effective in producing thrombolysis of a clot involved in a myocardial infarction.*

CONTRAINDICATIONS Active internal bleeding; intracranial or intraspinal surgery with 2 mo; intracranial neoplasm; arteriovenous malformation, or aneurysm; known bleeding diathesis; brain tumor; increased intracranial pressure; coagulopathy; head trauma; stroke; surgery; severe uncontrolled hypertension; pregnancy (category C), lactation.

CAUTIOUS USE Recent major surgery, previous puncture of compressible vessels, CVA, recent GI or GU bleeding, recent trauma; hypertension, mitral valve stenosis, acute pericarditis, bacterial endocarditis; severe liver or kidney disease; hemorrhagic ophthalmic conditions; septic thrombophlebitis or occluded, infected AV cannula; advanced age; concurrent administration of oral anticoagulants, recent administration of GP IIb/IIIa inhibitors, condition involving bleeding. Safety and efficacy in children are not established.

ADVERSE EFFECTS (≥1%) **Hematologic:** <u>Major bleeding</u>, *hematoma,* GI bleed, bleeding at puncture site, hematuria, pharyngeal epistaxis.

DIAGNOSTIC TEST INTERFERENCE Unreliable results for ***coagulation test I*** and measures of ***fibrinolytic activity.***

PHARMACOKINETICS Metabolism: In liver. **Half-Life:** 90–130 min.

NURSING IMPLICATIONS

Assessment & Drug Effects

- Avoid IM injections and unnecessary handling or invasive procedures for the first few hours after treatment.
- Monitor for S&S of bleeding. Should bleeding occur, discontinue concomitant heparin and antiplatelet therapy; notify prescriber.
- Monitor cardiovascular and neurologic status closely. Persons at increased risk for life-threatening cardiac events include those with: A high potential for bleeding, recent surgery, severe hypertension, mitral stenosis and atrial fibrillation, anticoagulant therapy, and advanced age.

- Lab tests: Baseline and 1 h after administration determine cardiac enzymes, circulating myoglobin, cardiac troponin-1, creatine kinase-MB, coagulation studies; Hgb & Hct post-infusion.
- Coagulation parameters may not predict bleeding episodes.

Patient & Family Education
- Report promptly any of the following: A sudden, severe headache; any sign of bleeding; signs or symptoms of hypersensitivity (see Appendix C).
- Stay as still as possible and do not attempt to get out of bed until directed to do so.

THEOPHYLLINE 🅿

(thee-offi-lin)

Classification(s): BRONCHODILATOR; XANTHINE
Therapeutic: BRONCHODILATOR
Pregnancy Category: C

USES Prophylaxis and symptomatic relief of bronchial asthma, as well as bronchospasm associated with chronic bronchitis and emphysema. Also used for emergency treatment of paroxysmal cardiac dyspnea and edema of CHF.

UNLABELED USES Treatment of apnea and bradycardia of premature neonates and to reduce severe bronchospasm associated with cystic fibrosis and acute descending respiratory infection.

INDICATION & DOSAGE

Bronchospasm

Adult/Child: **Loading dose,** 5 mg/kg
Adult: **Maintenance dose,** *(Nonsmoker):* 0.4 mg/kg/h; *(Smoker):* 0.6–0.7 mg/kg/h; *(with CHF or cirrhosis):* 0.2 mg/kg/h
Child: **Maintenance dose,** *(1–9 y):* 0.8–1 mg/kg/h; *(10–12 y):* 0.6–0.7 mg/ kg/h
Infant: **Maintenance dose,** 0.5–0.7 mg/kg/h
Neonate: **Maintenance dose,** 1–1.5 mg/kg q12h

Obesity Dosage Adjustment

Dose based on IBW.

SOLUTION PREPARATION

- *Direct IV Injection/Intermittent Infusion:* Dilute, as needed, to a maximum concentration of 20 mg/mL.
- *Continuous Infusion:* Typically diluted to 0.8 mg/mL with D5W.

STORAGE

Store at 15°–30° C (59°–86° F).

Common adverse effects in *italic*, life-threatening effects underlined: generic names in **bold**; classifications in SMALL CAPS; ♣ Canadian drug name; 🅿 Prototype drug

617

ADMINISTRATION

- **Direct IV Injection/Intermittent Infusion:** Typically infused over 20–30 min. Do NOT EXCEED 20 mg/min.
- **Continuous Infusion:** Infuse at a rate based on patient's weight.

INCOMPATIBILITIES Solution/additive: Ascorbic acid, ceftriaxone, cimetidine, hetastarch. **Y-site:** Cefepime, hetastarch, lansoprazole, phenytoin.

ACTION & *THERAPEUTIC EFFECT* Xanthine derivative that relaxes smooth muscle by direct action, particularly of bronchi and pulmonary vessels, and stimulates medullary respiratory center with resulting increase in vital capacity. Stimulates myocardium, thereby increasing force of contractions and cardiac output, and stimulates all levels of CNS, but to a lesser degree than caffeine. *Effective for relief of bronchospasm in asthmatics, chronic bronchitis, and emphysema.*

CONTRAINDICATIONS Hypersensitivity to xanthines; coronary artery disease or angina pectoris when myocardial stimulation might be harmful; severe renal or liver impairment; pregnancy (category C).
CAUTIOUS USE Compromised cardiac or circulatory function, hypertension; hyperthyroidism; peptic ulcer; prostatic hypertrophy; glaucoma; diabetes mellitus; older adults, children, and neonates.

ADVERSE EFFECTS (≥1%) **CNS:** Stimulation (irritability, restlessness, insomnia, dizziness, headache, tremor, hyperexcitability, muscle twitching, <u>drug-induced seizures</u>). **CV:** Palpitation, *tachycardia,* extrasystoles, flushing, marked hypotension, <u>circulatory failure</u>. **GI:** *Nausea,* vomiting, anorexia, epigastric or abdominal pain, diarrhea, activation of peptic ulcer. **Urogenital:** Transient urinary frequency, albuminuria, kidney irritation. **Respiratory:** Tachypnea, <u>respiratory arrest</u>. **Body as a Whole:** Fever, dehydration.

DIAGNOSTIC TEST INTERFERENCE False-positive elevations of *serum uric acid* (*Bittner* or *colorimetric methods*). **Probenecid** may cause false-high *serum theophylline* readings, and *spectrophotometric methods* of determining *serum theophylline* are affected by furosemide, sulfathiazole, phenylbutazone, probenecid, and theobromine.

DRUG INTERACTIONS Increases **lithium** excretion, lowering **lithium** levels; **cimetidine,** high-dose **allopurinol** (600 mg/day), **tacrine,** QUINOLONES, MACROLIDE ANTIBIOTICS, and **zileuton** can significantly increase theophylline levels; **tobacco** use significantly decreases levels. **Herbal: St. John's wort** may decrease theophylline efficacy.

PHARMACOKINETICS Peak: 30 min. **Duration:** 4–8 h; varies with age, smoking, and liver function. **Distribution:** Crosses placenta. **Metabolism:** Extensively in liver. **Elimination:** Parent drug and metabolites excreted by kidneys; in breast milk.

NURSING IMPLICATIONS

Assessment & Drug Effects

- Observe and report early signs of possible toxicity: Anorexia, nausea, vomiting, dizziness, shakiness, restlessness, abdominal discomfort, irritability, palpitation, tachycardia, marked hypotension, cardiac arrhythmias, seizures.

- Monitor for tachycardia, which may be worse in patients with severe cardiac disease. Conversely, theophylline toxicity may be masked in patients with tachycardia.
- Lab tests: Baseline and periodic serum theophylline. Therapeutic plasma level ranges from 10–20 mcg/mL (a narrow therapeutic range). Levels exceeding 20 mcg/mL are associated with toxicity.
- Monitor drug levels closely in heavy smokers. Cigarette smoking induces CYP 450 activity, decreasing serum half-life and increasing body clearance of theophylline.
- Monitor plasma drug level closely in patients with heart failure, kidney or liver dysfunction, alcoholism, or high fever, as plasma clearance may be reduced.
- Take necessary safety precautions and forewarn older adult patients of possible dizziness during early therapy.
- Monitor **closely** for adverse effects in infants less than 6 mo and premature infants; theophylline metabolism is prolonged, as is the half-life in this age group.

Patient & Family Education
- Limit caffeine intake because it may increase incidence of adverse effects.
- Cigarette smoking may significantly lower theophylline plasma concentration.

THIAMINE HYDROCHLORIDE (VITAMIN B₁)
(thyea-min)
Classification(s): VITAMIN B₁
Therapeutic: VITAMIN B₁ REPLACEMENT THERAPY
Pregnancy Category: A, C if dose is above RDA

USES Treatment and prophylaxis of beriberi, to correct anorexia due to thiamine deficiency states, and in treatment of neuritis associated with pregnancy, pellagra, and alcoholism, including Wernicke-Korsakoff syndrome. Therapy generally includes other members of vitamin B complex, since thiamine deficiency rarely occurs alone. Severe deficiency is characterized by ophthalmoplegia, polyneuropathy, muscle wasting ("dry" beriberi), edema, serous effusions, and CHF ("wet" beriberi).

INDICATION & DOSAGE

Thiamine Deficiency Prophylaxis
Adult: 3 mg every day admixed with TPN

Beriberi
Adult: 5–30 mg every day, then convert to PO
Child/Infant: 10–25 mg every day × 2 wk then convert to PO

Alcohol Withdrawal

Adult: 100 mg/day until PO 50–100 mg/day tolerated

Wernicke's Encephalopathy

Adult: 100 mg/day then 50–100 mg/day until on normal diet

SOLUTION PREPARATION

May be given undiluted [direct IV] or diluted in 1000 mL of standard IV solution for infusion.

STORAGE

Store at 15°–30° C (59°–86° F) in tight, light-resistant, nonmetallic containers. Thiamine is unstable in alkaline solutions (e.g., solutions of acetates, barbiturates, bicarbonates, carbonates, citrates) and neutral solutions.

ADMINISTRATION

- **Direct IV Injection:** Give at a rate of 100 mg over 5 min.
- **IV Infusion:** Infuse at prescribed rate.

INCOMPATIBILITIES Solution/additive: Trimetrexate.

ACTION & *THERAPEUTIC EFFECT* Water-soluble B₁ vitamin and member of B-complex group used for thiamine replacement therapy. Functions as an essential coenzyme in carbohydrate metabolism. *Effectiveness is evidenced by improvement of clinical manifestations of thiamine deficiency: Anorexia, gastric distress, depression, irritability, insomnia, palpitations, tachycardia, loss of memory, paresthesias, muscle weakness and pain, elevated blood pyruvic acid level (diagnostic test for thiamine deficiency), and elevated lactic acid level.*

CONTRAINDICATIONS Pregnancy (category C if dose is above RDA).
CAUTIOUS USE Pregnancy (category A).

ADVERSE EFFECTS (≥1%) **Body as a Whole:** Feeling of warmth, weakness, sweating, restlessness, tightness of throat, angioneurotic edema, <u>anaphylaxis</u>. **Respiratory:** Cyanosis, pulmonary edema. **CV:** <u>Cardiovascular collapse</u>, slight fall in BP following rapid administration. **GI:** GI hemorrhage, nausea. **Skin:** Urticaria, pruritus.

DRUG INTERACTIONS No clinically significant interactions established.

PHARMACOKINETICS Distribution: Widely distributed, including into breast milk. **Elimination:** In urine.

NURSING IMPLICATIONS

Assessment & Drug Effects

- Monitor neurologic status and report S&S of neuropathy.

Patient & Family Education

- Note: Body requirement of thiamine is directly proportional to carbohydrate intake and metabolic rate; requirement increases when diet consists predominantly of carbohydrates.

- Food–drug relationships: Learn about rich dietary sources of thiamine (e.g., yeast, pork, beef, liver, wheat and other whole grains, nutrient-added breakfast cereals, fresh vegetables, especially peas and dried beans).

THIOPENTAL SODIUM 🅿️
(thye-oh-pental)

Pentothal

Classification(s): ANESTHETIC, GENERAL; ANTICONVULSANT, BARBITURATE
Therapeutic: GENERAL ANESTHETIC; ANTICONVULSANT
Pregnancy Category: C   **Controlled Substance:** Schedule III

USES To induce hypnosis and anesthesia prior to or as supplement to other anesthetic agents or as sole agent for brief (15-min) operative procedures. Also used as an anticonvulsant and sedative–hypnotic and for narcoanalysis and narcosynthesis in psychiatric disorders.

INDICATION & DOSAGE

Anesthesia Induction

Adult: 50–100 mg at 20–40 sec intervals; an additional 50 mg may be given if needed
Child: 5–6 mg/kg initially, followed by 1 mg/kg if needed
Infant: 5–8 mg/kg

Convulsions

Adult: 75–125 mg, repeat up to 250 mg

Narcoanalysis

Adult: 100 mg/min until confusion occurs

SOLUTION PREPARATION

- *Vial Reconstitution:* Add 20 mL of sterile water for injection to each 500 mg of powder to yield a 2.5% solution (25 mg/1 mL). May be given as prepared direct IV or further diluted for infusion.
- *Further Dilution of Reconstituted Solution:* Add 20 mL of reconstituted solution to at least 100 mL of NS or D5W. Prepare solution immediately before use.

STORAGE

Store at 15°–30° C (59°–86° F). Avoid excessive heat; protect from freezing. Refrigerate reconstituted solutions and IV solutions and use within 24 h.

ADMINISTRATION

- **Direct IV Injection:** Give each 25 mg over 1 min or more.
- **Continuous Infusion:** Titrate to achieve desired effect.

INCOMPATIBILITIES Solution/additive: Dextrose solutions, lactated Ringer's, 10% dextrose, fructose 10%, amikacin, dimenhydrinate, diphenhydramine, ephedrine, fibrinolysin, hydromorphone, insulin, meperidine, metaraminol, morphine, norepinephrine, penicillin G, prochlorperazine, promazine, promethazine, sodium bicarbonate, succinylcholine. **Y-site:** Alfentanil, ascorbic acid, atracurium, atropine, cisatracurium, diltiazem, dobutamine, dopamine, ephedrine, epinephrine, fenoldopam, furosemide, hydromorphone, labetalol, lidocaine, lorazepam, midazolam, morphine, nicardipine, norepinephrine, pancuronium, phenylephrine, succinylcholine, sufentanil, vecuronium.

ACTION & *THERAPEUTIC EFFECT* Ultra-short–acting barbiturate that induces brief general anesthesia without analgesia by depression of CNS. Loss of consciousness is rapid. Reduction in cardiac output and peripheral vasodilation frequently accompany anesthesia. Rapid redistribution of agent out of brain reduces anesthesia level and increases reflex airway hyperactivity to mechanical stimulation. Muscle relaxation is slight, and reflexes are poorly controlled. *Since analgesia is slight, thiopental is seldom used alone except for brief, minor procedures.*

CONTRAINDICATIONS Hypersensitivity to barbiturates; history of paradoxic excitation; absence of suitable veins for IV administration; status asthmaticus; acute intermittent or other hepatic porphyries; pregnancy (category C).
CAUTIOUS USE Coronary artery disease, hypotension, shock; conditions that may potentiate or prolong hypnotic effect including excessive premedication, liver or kidney dysfunction, myxedema, Addison's disease, severe anemia, increased BUN; increased intracranial pressure; myasthenia gravis; asthma and other respiratory diseases.

ADVERSE EFFECTS (≥1%) **CNS:** Headache, retrograde amnesia, emergence delirium, prolonged somnolence and recovery. **CV:** Myocardial depression, arrhythmias, <u>circulatory depression</u>. **GI:** Nausea, vomiting, regurgitation of gastric contents, rectal irritation, cramping, rectal bleeding, diarrhea. **Respiratory:** <u>Respiratory depression with apnea</u>; hiccups, sneezing, coughing, bronchospasm, <u>laryngospasm</u>. **Body as a Whole:** Hypersensitivity reactions, <u>anaphylaxis</u> (rare), hypothermia, thrombosis and sloughing (with extravasation); salivation, shivering, skeletal muscle hyperactivity.

DIAGNOSTIC TEST INTERFERENCE Thiopental may cause decrease in *I^{123}* and *I^{131} thyroidal uptake* test results.

DRUG INTERACTIONS CNS DEPRESSANTS, **alcohol** potentiate CNS and respiratory depression. PHENOTHIAZINES increase risk of hypotension. **Probenecid** may prolong anesthesia.

PHARMACOKINETICS Onset: 30–60 sec. **Duration:** 10–30 min. **Distribution:** Into muscle and liver; crosses placenta. **Metabolism:** In liver. **Elimination:** In urine. **Half-Life:** 12 min.

Common adverse effects in *italic*, life-threatening effects <u>underlined</u>: generic names in **bold**; classifications in SMALL CAPS; ✦ Canadian drug name; ⊙ Prototype drug

NURSING IMPLICATIONS

Assessment & Drug Effects

- Consult prescriber if extravasation occurs, as IV site will require particular attention to prevent arteritis, neuritis, and skin sloughing.
- Monitor vital signs q3–5min before, during, and after anesthetic administration until recovery and into postoperative period, if necessary.
- Report increases in pulse rate or drop in blood pressure. Hypovolemia, cranial trauma, or premedication with opioids increases potential for apnea and symptoms of myocardial depression (decreased cardiac output and arterial pressure).
- Shivering, excitement, and/or muscle twitching may develop during recovery period if patient is in pain.

Patient & Family Education

- Onset of drug effect is rapid, with loss of consciousness within 30–60 sec.

THIOTEPA

(thye-oh-tepa)

Classification(s): ANTINEOPLASTIC; ALKYLATING AGENT
Therapeutic: ANTINEOPLASTIC
Prototype: Cyclophosphamide
Pregnancy Category: D

USES To produce remissions in malignant lymphomas, including Hodgkin's disease, and adenocarcinoma of breast and ovary. Also in chronic granulocytic and lymphocytic leukemia, superficial papillary carcinoma of the urinary bladder, bronchogenic carcinoma, and in malignant effusions secondary to neoplastic disease of serosal cavities.
UNLABELED USES Prevention of pterygium recurrences following postoperative beta-irradiation; leukemia, malignant meningeal neoplasms.

INDICATION & DOSAGE

Malignant Lymphomas

Adult: 0.3–0.4 mg/kg q1–4wk

SOLUTION PREPARATION

- Avoid exposure of skin and respiratory tract to particles of thiotepa during solution preparation.
- *Vial Reconstitution:* Add 1.5 mL sterile water for injection (supplied) to each 15 mg to yield 10 mg/mL. Filter solution through a 0.22 micron filter prior to administration. Use immediately (do not use if hazy or opaque).

STORAGE

- Store powder for injection and reconstituted solutions at 2°–8° C (35°–46° F); protect from light.

Common adverse effects in *italic*, life-threatening effects <u>underlined</u>: generic names in **bold**; classifications in SMALL CAPS; ♣ Canadian drug name; ❂ Prototype drug

623

- Solutions reconstituted with sterile water only are stable for 8 h under refrigeration.

ADMINISTRATION
Direct IV Injection: Give 60 mg or fraction thereof over 1 min.

INCOMPATIBILITIES **Solution/additive:** Cisplatin. **Y-site:** Cisplatin, filgrastim, minocycline, vinorelbine.

ACTION & *THERAPEUTIC EFFECT* Cell cycle–nonspecific alkylating agent that selectively reacts with DNA phosphate groups to produce chromosome cross-linkage and consequent blocking of nucleoprotein synthesis. Nonvesicant, highly toxic hematopoietic agent. *Myelosuppression is cumulative and unpredictable and may be delayed. Has some immunosuppressive activity.*

CONTRAINDICATIONS Hypersensitivity to thiotepa; acute leukemia; acute infection; pregnancy (category D), lactation.
CAUTIOUS USE Chronic lymphocytic leukemia; myelosuppression produced by radiation; with other antineoplastics; bone marrow invasion by tumor cells; impaired kidney or liver function.

ADVERSE EFFECTS (≥1%) **GI:** Anorexia, nausea, vomiting, stomatitis, ulceration of intestinal mucosa. **Hematologic:** Leukopenia, thrombocytopenia, anemia, pancytopenia. **Skin:** Hives, rash, pruritus. **Urogenital:** Amenorrhea, interference with spermatogenesis. **Body as a Whole:** Headache, febrile reactions, pain and weeping of injection site, hyperuricemia, slowed or lessened response in heavily irradiated area, sensation of throat tightness. **Other:** Reported with intravesical administration: Lower abdominal pain, hematuria, hemorrhagic chemical cystitis, vesical irritability.

DRUG INTERACTIONS May prolong muscle paralysis with **mivacurium;** ANTICOAGULANTS, NSAIDS, SALICYLATES, ANTIPLATELET AGENTS may increase risk of bleeding.

PHARMACOKINETICS **Onset:** Gradual response over several wk. **Metabolism:** In liver. **Elimination:** 60% of dose excreted in urine within 24–72 h.

NURSING IMPLICATIONS
Assessment & Drug Effects
- Monitor closely because most patients will manifest some evidence of toxicity.
- Be aware that because of cumulative effects, maximum myelosuppression may be delayed 3–4 wk after termination of therapy.
- Monitor leukocyte and platelet counts closely. Discontinue therapy (per manufacturer) if leukocyte count falls to 3000/mm^3 or below or if platelet count falls below 150,000/mm^3.
- Lab tests: Weekly Hgb level, WBC with differential, and platelet counts during therapy and for at least 3 wk after therapy is discontinued.

Patient & Family Education
- Menstruating women should be aware of the possibility of amenorrhea (usually reversible in 6–8 mo).

Common adverse effects in *italic*, life-threatening effects <u>underlined</u>: generic names in **bold**; classifications in SMALL CAPS; ✦ Canadian drug name; ⊙ Prototype drug

▪ Report onset of fever, bleeding, a cold or illness—no matter how mild—to prescriber; medical supervision may be necessary.

TICARCILLIN DISODIUM/CLAVULANATE POTASSIUM

(tye-kar-sillin/clav-yoola-nate)

Timentin

Classification(s): ANTIBIOTIC; PENICILLIN, ANTIPSEUDOMONAL
Therapeutic: ANTIBACTERIAL
Prototype: Piperacillin
Pregnancy Category: B

USES Infections of lower respiratory tract and urinary tract and skin and skin structures, infections of bone and joint, and septicemia caused by susceptible organisms. Also mixed infections and as presumptive therapy before identification of causative organism.

INDICATION & DOSAGE

Moderate to Severe Infections

Adult (over 60 kg): 3.1 g q4–6h; *(up to 60 kg):* 200–300 mg/kg/day divided (based on ticarcillin)
Child/Infant (3 mo or more): 200–300 mg/kg/day divided q4–6h (based on ticarcillin)
Infant/Neonates: 200–300 mg/kg/day divided q6–8h (based on ticarcillin)

Renal Impairment Dosage Adjustment

CrCl (mL/min)	Loading Dose	Regular Dose
31–60	3.1 g	2 g q4h
10–30	3.1 g	2 g q8h
Less than 10	3.1 g	2 g q12h

Hemodialysis Dosage Adjustment

2 g q12h, supplement with 3.1 g after dialysis

SOLUTION PREPARATION

▪ *Vial Reconstitution:* Add 13 mL sterile water for injection or NS injection to 3.1 g of powder to yield 200 mg/mL ticarcillin with 6.7 mg/mL clavulanic acid. Shake until dissolved. **Must be** further diluted for infusion.
▪ *Further Dilution of Reconstituted Solution:* Add required dose to desired amount of NS, D5W, or LR IV solution to produce concentrations between 10–100 mg/mL.

T

Common adverse effects in *italic*, life-threatening effects underlined: generic names in **bold**; classifications in SMALL CAPS; ✦ Canadian drug name; ⊘ Prototype drug

625

STORAGE

- Store vial with sterile powder at 21°–24° C (69°–75° F) or colder. If exposed to higher temperature, powder will darken, indicating degradation of clavulanate potassium and loss of potency. Discard vial.
- Store reconstituted solutions for 6 h at room temperature and 72 h refrigerated.

ADMINISTRATION

Intermittent Infusion: Infuse over 30 min.

INCOMPATIBILITIES Solution/additive: Amikacin, doxapram, sodium bicarbonate, tobramycin. **Y-site:** Amphotericin B cholesteryl complex, azithromycin, drotrecogin, lansoprazole, vancomycin.

ACTION & *THERAPEUTIC EFFECT* Extended-spectrum penicillin and fixed combination of ticarcillin disodium with the potassium salt of clavulanic acid, a beta-lactamase inhibitor. Used alone, clavulanic acid antibacterial activity is weak but in combination with ticarcillin, it prevents degradation by beta-lactamase and extends ticarcillin spectrum of activity. *Extends spectrum of activity of ticarcillin against many strains of beta-lactamase–producing bacteria (synergistic effect).*

CONTRAINDICATIONS Hypersensitivity to penicillins or to cephalosporins; coagulopathy.

CAUTIOUS USE Renal impairment; diabetes mellitus; GI disease; asthma; history of allergies; pregnancy (category B).

ADVERSE EFFECTS (≥1%) **Body as a Whole:** Hypersensitivity reactions, pain, burning, swelling at injection site; phlebitis, thrombophlebitis; superinfections. **CNS:** Headache, blurred vision, mental deterioration, convulsions, hallucinations, seizures, giddiness, neuromuscular hyperirritability. **GI:** *Diarrhea, nausea,* vomiting, disturbances of taste or smell, stomatitis, flatulence. **Hematologic:** Eosinophilia, thrombocytopenia, leukopenia, neutropenia, hemolytic anemia. **Metabolic:** Hypernatremia, transient increases in serum AST, ALT, BUN, and alkaline phosphatase; increases in serum LDH, bilirubin, and creatinine and decreased serum uric acid.

DIAGNOSTIC TEST INTERFERENCE May interfere with test methods used to determine ***urinary proteins*** except for tests for urinary protein that use ***bromphenol blue. Positive direct antiglobulin (Coombs') test*** results, apparently caused by clavulanic acid, have been reported. This test may interfere with ***transfusion cross-matching procedures.***

DRUG INTERACTIONS May increase risk of bleeding with ANTICOAGULANTS; **probenecid** decreases elimination of ticarcillin.

PHARMACOKINETICS Distribution: Widely distributed with highest concentrations in urine and bile; crosses placenta; distributed into breast milk. **Metabolism:** Slightly in liver. **Elimination:** In urine. **Half-Life:** 1.1–1.2 h ticarcillin, 1.1–1.5 h clavulanate.

Common adverse effects in *italic*, life-threatening effects <u>underlined</u>: generic names in **bold**; classifications in SMALL CAPS; ♣ Canadian drug name; ❶ Prototype drug

NURSING IMPLICATIONS

Assessment & Drug Effects

- Prior to initiating therapy: Baseline C&S tests (start drug pending results); determine previous hypersensitivity reactions to penicillins, cephalosporins, and other allergens.
- Be aware that serious and sometimes fatal anaphylactoid reactions have been reported in patients with penicillin hypersensitivity or history of sensitivity to multiple allergens.
- Lab tests: Periodic kidney function tests, LFTs, CBC, platelet count, and serum electrolytes during prolonged treatment.
- Monitor cardiac status because of high sodium content of drug.
- Overdose symptoms: This drug may cause neuromuscular hyperirritability or seizures.

Patient & Family Education

- Report urticaria, rashes, or pruritus to prescriber immediately.
- Report frequent loose stools, diarrhea, or other possible signs of pseudomembranous colitis (see Appendix C).

TIGECYCLINE

(ti-ge-cycline)

Tygacil

Classification(s): ANTIBIOTIC

Therapeutic: ANTIBACTERIAL

Pregnancy Category: D

USES Treatment of complicated skin and skin structure infections and complicated intra-abdominal infections.

INDICATION & DOSAGE

Complicated Skin and Intra-Abdominal Infections

Adult: 100 mg initially, followed by 50 mg q12h for 5–14 days

Hepatic Impairment Dosage Adjustment

Adult (Child-Pugh class C): Give 100 mg, followed by 25 mg q12h

SOLUTION PREPARATION

- *Vial Reconstitution:* Add 5.3 mL of NS or D5W to each vial (50 mg) to yield 10 mg/mL. Swirl gently to dissolve; reconstituted solution should be yellow to orange in color. **Must be** further diluted for infusion.
- *Further Dilution of Reconstituted Solution:* After reconstitution, immediately withdraw **exactly** 5 mL of solution from each vial and add to 100 mL of NS or D5W. The maximum concentration in the IV bag should be 1 mg/mL (two 50 mg doses).

T

Common adverse effects in *italic*, life-threatening effects <u>underlined</u>: generic names in **bold**; classifications in SMALL CAPS; ♣ Canadian drug name; ◐ Prototype drug

627

STORAGE
Store IV solutions at room temperature for up to 6 h, or refrigerated for up to 24 h.

ADMINISTRATION
Intermittent Infusion: Infuse over 30–60 min; when using Y-site, flush IV line with NS or D5W before/after infusion.

INCOMPATIBILITIES Y-site: **Amphotericin B, chlorpromazine, methylprednisolone, voriconazole.**

ACTION & *THERAPEUTIC EFFECT* Tigecycline inhibits protein production in bacteria by binding to the 30S ribosomal subunit and blocking entry of transfer RNA molecules into the ribosome of the bacteria. This prevents formation of peptide chains in bacteria, thus interfering with their growth. *Tigecycline is active against a broad spectrum of bacterial pathogens and is bacteriostatic.*

CONTRAINDICATIONS Hypersensitivity to tigecycline; pregnancy (category D) and during tooth development of the fetus; viral infections.
CAUTIOUS USE Severe hepatic impairment (Child-Pugh class C); hypersensitivity to tetracycline; intestinal perforations, intra-abdominal infections; GI disorders; lactation; children less than 18 y.

ADVERSE EFFECTS (≥1%) **CNS:** Asthenia, dizziness, headache, insomnia. **CV:** Hypertension, hypotension, peripheral edema, phlebitis. **GI:** Abdominal pain, constipation, diarrhea, dyspepsia, *nausea, vomiting.* **Hematologic/Lymphatic:** Abnormal healing, anemia, infection, leukocytosis, thrombocythemia. **Metabolic/Nutritional:** Alkaline phosphatase increased, ALT increased, amylase increased, AST increased, bilirubinemia, BUN increased, hyperglycemia, hypokalemia, hypoproteinemia, lactic dehydrogenase increased. **Musculoskeletal:** Back pain. **Respiratory:** Dyspnea, increased cough, pulmonary physical findings. **Skin:** Pruritus, rash, sweating. **Body as a Whole:** Abscess, fever, local reaction to injection, pain.

DRUG INTERACTIONS Increased concentrations of **warfarin** require close monitoring of INR. Efficacy of ORAL CONTRACEPTIVES may be decreased when used in combination with tigecycline.

PHARMACOKINETICS Distribution: 71–89% protein bound. **Metabolism:** Negligible. **Elimination:** Fecal (major) and renal. **Half-Life:** 27 h (single dose); 42 h (multiple doses).

NURSING IMPLICATIONS

Assessment & Drug Effects
- Prior to initiating therapy: Baseline C&S tests (start drug pending results).
- Monitor for hypersensitivity reaction in those with reported tetracycline allergy.
- Monitor for and report S&S of superinfection or pseudomembranous enterocolitis (see Appendix C).
- Lab tests: Periodic serum electrolytes, LFTs, and kidney function tests.
- Concurrent drugs: PT and INT with concurrent anticoagulant therapy.
- Monitor diabetics for loss of glycemic control.

Common adverse effects in *italic*, life-threatening effects <u>underlined</u>: generic names in **bold**; classifications in SMALL CAPS; ♣ Canadian drug name; ● Prototype drug

Patient & Family Education

- Avoid direct exposure to sunlight during therapy, and for several days after therapy is terminated, to reduce risk of photosensitivity reaction.
- Report to prescriber loose stools or diarrhea either during, or shortly after termination of, therapy.
- Women using oral contraceptives should use an additional, alternative form of contraceptive.

TIROFIBAN HYDROCHLORIDE

(tir-o-fiban)

Aggrastat

Classification(s): ANTIPLATELET; PLATELET AGGREGATION INHIBITOR
Therapeutic: ANTITHROMBOTIC
Prototype: Abciximab
Pregnancy Category: B

USES Acute coronary syndromes (unstable angina, MI).

INDICATION & DOSAGE

Acute Coronary Syndrome
Adult: 0.4 mcg/kg/min × 30 min, then 0.1 mcg/kg/min for 12–24 h after angioplasty or arteriectomy

Renal Impairment Dosage Adjustment
CrCl less than 30 mL/min: Reduce dose by 50%

SOLUTION PREPARATION

- Note: Commercially premixed IV tirofiban solutions are available.
- *Dilution of concentrate (250 mcg/mL) to 50 mcg/mL:*
  - 500 mL IV bag of NS or D5W: Withdraw 100 mL of IV solution and replace with 100 mL of IV tirofiban HCl injection. Mix well.
  - 250-mL IV bag of NS or D5W: Withdraw 50 mL of IV solution and replace with 50 mL of tirofiban injection. Mix well.

STORAGE

- Discard unused IV solution 24 h following start of infusion.
- Store unopened containers at 15°–30° C (59°–86° F). Do not freeze and protect from light.

ADMINISTRATION

IV Infusion: An initial loading dose of 0.4 mcg/kg/min for 30 min is usually followed by a maintenance infusion of 0.1 mcg/kg/min.

INCOMPATIBILITIES Y-site: Diazepam, tenecteplase.

ACTION & *THERAPEUTIC EFFECT* Antiplatelet agent that binds to the glycoprotein IIb/IIIa receptor of platelets inhibiting platelet aggregation. *Effec-*

Common adverse effects in *italic*, life-threatening effects <u>underlined</u>: generic names in **bold**; classifications in SMALL CAPS; ♣ Canadian drug name; ⊘ Prototype drug

629

tiveness indicated by minimizing thrombotic events during treatment of acute coronary syndrome.

CONTRAINDICATIONS Active internal bleeding within 30 days; acute pericarditis; aortic dissection; intracranial aneurysm, intracranial mass, coagulopathy; concurrent use with another glycoprotein IIb/IIIa receptor inhibitor (e.g., eptifibatide, abciximab); history of aneurysm or AV malformation; history of intracranial hemorrhage or neoplasm; hypersensitivity to tirofiban; active abnormal bleeding; retinal bleeding; hemorrhagic retinopathy; major surgery or trauma within 3 days; stroke within 30 days; history of hemorrhagic stroke; thrombocytopenia following administration of tirofiban; within 4 h of percutaneous coronary intervention (PCI); lactation.

CAUTIOUS USE Concomitant use with thrombolytic agents or drugs that cause hemolysis; platelet count less than 150,000 mm³; severe renal insufficiency pregnancy (category B). Safety and efficacy in children less than 18 y are unknown.

ADVERSE EFFECTS (≥1%) **Body as a Whole:** Edema, swelling, pelvic pain, vasovagal reaction, leg pain. **CNS:** Dizziness. **CV:** Bradycardia, coronary artery dissection. **GI:** GI bleeding. **Hematologic:** *Bleeding* (major bleeding), anemia, thrombocytopenia. **Skin:** Sweating.

DRUG INTERACTIONS Increased risk of bleeding with ANTICOAGULANTS, NSAIDS, SALICYLATES, ANTIPLATELET AGENTS.

PHARMACOKINETICS Duration: 4–8 h after stopping infusion. **Distribution:** 65% protein bound. **Metabolism:** Minimally metabolized. **Elimination:** 65% in urine, 25% in feces. **Half-Life:** 2 h.

NURSING IMPLICATIONS

Assessment & Drug Effects

- Prior to initiating therapy: Baseline platelet count, Hgb and Hct (within 6 h of infusing loading dose).
- Monitor vital signs closely. Assess for and immediately report S&S of internal or external bleeding.
- Lab tests: Frequent platelet count, Hgb and Hct, aPTT, and ACT.
- Withhold drug and notify prescriber if thrombocytopenia (platelets less than 100,000) is confirmed.
- Wait at least 3–4 h after heparin is stopped and until ACT is less than 180 sec and aPTT is less than 45 sec before removing the femoral catheter sheath.
- Minimize unnecessary invasive procedures and devices to reduce the risk of bleeding.

Patient & Family Education

- Report unexplained pelvic or abdominal pain.

TOBRAMYCIN SULFATE
(toe-bra-myesin)
Classification(s): ANTIBIOTIC, AMINOGLYCOSIDE

Therapeutic: ANTIBACTERIAL
Prototype: Gentamicin sulfate
Pregnancy Category: D

USES Treatment of severe infections caused by susceptible organisms.

INDICATION & DOSAGE

Moderate to Severe Infections
Adult: 3 mg/kg/day divided q8h up to 5 mg/kg/day **OR** 4–7 mg/kg/day single dose
Child (5 y or greater): 2–2.5 mg/kg/day divided q8h
Child/Infant (up to 5 y): 2.5 mg/kg q8h
Neonate:

Age	Weight	Dose
Over 7 days	Over 2000 g	2.5 mg/kg q8h
Over 7 days	1200–2000 g	2.5 mg/kg q8–12h
Up to 7 days	Over 2000 g	2.5 mg/kg q12h
Up to 7 days	1200–2000 g	2.5 mg/kg q12–18h
Preterm 0–4 wk	Less than 1200 g	2.5 mg/kg q18–24h
Preterm	Less than 1000 g	3.5 mg/kg q24h

Cystic Fibrosis
Adult/Child: 2.5–3.5 mg/kg q6–8h

Renal Impairment Dosage Adjustment
Increase interval and reduce dose

Hemodialysis Dosage Adjustment
Administer dose after dialysis and monitor levels

Obesity Dosage Adjustment
Dose based on IBW, in morbid obesity use dosing weight of IBW + 0.4 × (weight – IBW)

SOLUTION PREPARATION
Dilute each dose in 50–100 mL or more of D5W, NS, or D5NS. Final concentration should not exceed 1 mg/mL.

STORAGE
Store at 15°–30° C (59°–86° F) prior to reconstitution. After reconstitution, solution may be refrigerated and used within 96 h. If kept at room temperature, use within 24 h.

ADMINISTRATION
Intermittent Infusion: Infuse over 20–60 min. AVOID rapid infusion.

Common adverse effects in *italic*, life-threatening effects <u>underlined</u>: generic names in **bold**; classifications in SMALL CAPS; ♣ Canadian drug name; ● Prototype drug

631

INCOMPATIBILITIES Solution/additive: Alcohol 5% in dextrose, cefamandole, cefepime, cefoperazone. **Y-site:** Allopurinol, amphotericin B cholesteryl complex, azithromycin, cefoperazone, drotrecogin, heparin, hetastarch, indomethacin, lansoprazole, pemetrexed, propofol, sargramostim.

ACTION & *THERAPEUTIC EFFECT* Tobramycin is a broad-spectrum, aminoglycoside antibiotic derived from *Streptomyces tenebrarius*. It binds irreversibly to one of two aminoglycoside binding sites on the 30 S ribosomal subunit of the bacteria, thus inhibiting protein synthesis. This results in bacterial cell death. *Effective in treatment of gram-negative bacteria. Exhibits greater antibiotic activity against* Pseudomonas aeruginosa *than other aminoglycosides.*

CONTRAINDICATIONS History of hypersensitivity to tobramycin and other aminoglycoside antibiotics; pregnancy (category D).

CAUTIOUS USE Impaired kidney function; renal disease; dehydration; hearing impairment; myasthenia gravis; parkinsonism; concurrent use with other neurotoxic or nephrotoxic agents or potent diuretics; older adults; premature and neonatal infants; lactation.

ADVERSE EFFECTS (≥1%) **CNS:** Neurotoxicity (including ototoxicity), *nephrotoxicity,* increased AST, ALT, LDH, serum bilirubin; anemia, fever, rash, pruritus, urticaria, nausea, vomiting, headache, lethargy, superinfections; hypersensitivity.

DRUG INTERACTIONS ANESTHETICS, SKELETAL MUSCLE RELAXANTS add to neuromuscular blocking effects; **acyclovir, amphotericin B, bacitracin, capreomycin,** CEPHALOSPORINS, **colistin, cisplatin, carboplatin, methoxyflurane, polymyxin B, vancomycin, furosemide, ethacrynic acid** increased risk of ototoxicity, nephrotoxicity.

PHARMACOKINETICS Duration: Up to 8 h. **Distribution:** Crosses placenta; accumulates in renal cortex. **Elimination:** In urine. **Half-Life:** 2–3 h in adults.

NURSING IMPLICATIONS

Assessment & Drug Effects

- Prior to initiating therapy: Baseline C&S tests (start drug pending results).
- Observe closely patient receiving tobramycin because of the high potential for toxicity, even in conventional doses.
- Lab tests: Baseline and periodic kidney function; peak and trough serum tobramycin. Peak concentrations greater than 10 mcg/mL or trough concentrations greater than 2 mcg/mL are not recommended.
- Monitor closely auditory and vestibular functions, particularly with known or suspected renal impairment and with high doses.
- Be aware that drug-induced auditory changes, partial or total, are irreversible and usually bilateral. In cochlear damage, patient may be asymptomatic, and partial or bilateral deafness may continue to develop even after therapy is discontinued.
- Monitor I&O. Report oliguria, changes in I&O ratio, and cloudy or frothy urine (may indicate proteinuria). Keep patient well hydrated to prevent

chemical irritation in renal tubules; older adults are especially susceptible to renal toxicity.

Patient & Family Education
- Report symptoms of superinfections (see Appendix C) to prescriber. Prompt treatment with an antibiotic or antifungal medication may be necessary.
- Report S&S of hearing loss, tinnitus, or vertigo to prescriber.

TOPOTECAN HYDROCHLORIDE ⓟ

(toe-po-teecan)

Hycamtin

Classification(s): ANTINEOPLASTIC, DNA TOPOISOMERASE INHIBITOR

Therapeutic: ANTINEOPLASTIC

Pregnancy Category: D

USES Metastatic ovarian cancer, small-cell lung cancer.

INDICATION & DOSAGE

Metastatic Ovarian Cancer and Small Cell Lung Cancer

Adult: 1.5 mg/m^2 daily for 5 days starting on day 1 of a 21-day course; four courses of therapy recommended

Toxicity Dosage Adjustment

Decrease by 0.25 mg/m^2

Renal Impairment Dosage Adjustment

CrCl 20–39 mL/min: Use 0.75 mg/m^2

Hemodialysis Dosage Adjustment

Supplementation not needed

SOLUTION PREPARATION
- *Vial Reconstitution:* Add 4 mL sterile water for injection to each 4-mg vial with to yield 1 mg/mL. **Must be** further diluted for infusion.
- *Further Dilution of Reconstituted Solution:* Withdraw the required dose and inject into 50–100 mL of NS or D5W.
- If skin contacts drug during preparation, wash immediately with soap and water.

STORAGE

Store vials at 20°–25° C (68°–77° F); protect from light. Reconstituted vials are stable for 24 h.

ADMINISTRATION
- **IV Infusion:** Infuse required dose over 30 min immediately after preparation.

Common adverse effects in *italic*, life-threatening effects <u>underlined</u>: generic names in **bold**; classifications in SMALL CAPS; ♣ Canadian drug name; ⓟ Prototype drug

633

- Initiate therapy only if baseline neutrophil count is at least 1500/mm³ and platelet count is at least 100,000/mm³. Do not give subsequent doses until neutrophil count is at least 1000/mm³, platelet count is at least 100,000/mm³, and Hgb is at least 9.0 mg/dL.

INCOMPATIBILITIES Y-site: Dexamethasone, fluorouracil, mitomycin, pemetrexed.

ACTION & *THERAPEUTIC EFFECT* Antitumor mechanism is related to inhibition of activity of topoisomerase I, an enzyme required for DNA replication. Topoisomerase I is essential for the relaxation of supercoiled double-stranded DNA, which enables replication and transcription to proceed. *Topotecan binds to the DNA-topoisomerase I complex. This permits uncoiling but prevents recoiling of the two strands of DNA, resulting in a permanent break in the DNA strands.*

CONTRAINDICATIONS Previous hypersensitivity to topotecan, irinotecan, or other camptothecin analogs; acute infection; severe bone marrow depression; severe thrombocytopenia; pregnancy (category D), lactation.

CAUTIOUS USE Myelosuppression; severe renal impairment or renal failure; history of bleeding disorders; previous cytotoxic or radiation therapy. Safe use and efficacy in children have not been established.

ADVERSE EFFECTS (≥1%) **Body as a Whole:** *Asthenia, fever, fatigue.* **GI:** *Nausea, vomiting, diarrhea, constipation, abdominal pain, stomatitis, anorexia,* transient elevations in liver function tests. **Hematologic:** <u>*Leukopenia, neutropenia,*</u> anemia, thrombocytopenia. **Respiratory:** *Dyspnea.* **Skin:** *Alopecia.*

DRUG INTERACTIONS Increased risk of bleeding with ANTICOAGULANTS, NSAIDS, SALICYLATES, ANTIPLATELET AGENTS.

PHARMACOKINETICS Distribution: 35% bound to plasma proteins. **Metabolism:** Undergoes pH-dependent hydrolysis. **Elimination:** Approximately 30% in urine. **Half-Life:** 2–3 h.

T

NURSING IMPLICATIONS

Assessment & Drug Effects
- Prior to initiating therapy: Baseline CBC with differential, BUN and CrCl.
- Monitor hydration status, especially with significant vomiting.
- Lab tests: Frequent CBC with differential; periodic ALT, BUN, and CrCl.
- Assess for GI distress, respiratory distress, neurosensory symptoms, and S&S of infection throughout therapy.

Patient & Family Education
- Learn common adverse effects and measures to control or minimize when possible. Immediately report any distressing adverse effects to prescriber.
- Take measures to avoid pregnancy during therapy. Nonhormonal birth control is preferred.

TORSEMIDE

(torse-mide)

Demadex

Classification(s): DIURETIC, LOOP

Therapeutic: DIURETIC

Prototype: Furosemide

Pregnancy Category: B

USES Management of edema associated with CHF, chronic kidney failure, ascites with hepatic cirrhosis.

INDICATION & DOSAGE

Edema

Adult: 10–20 mg once daily, may increase up to 200 mg/day as needed

Hepatic Cirrhosis Ascites

Adult: 5–10 mg once daily administered with an aldosterone antagonist or potassium-sparing diuretic, may increase up to 40 mg/day as needed

SOLUTION PREPARATION

No dilution is required. Administer as supplied.

STORAGE

Store at 15°–30° C (59°–86° F).

ADMINISTRATION

Direct IV Injection: Give bolus dose over 2 min.

INCOMPATIBILITIES Solution/additive: Dobutamine.

ACTION & *THERAPEUTIC EFFECT* Long-acting, potent sulfonamide "loop" diuretic that inhibits reabsorption of sodium and chloride primarily in the loop of Henle as well as in the proximal and distal renal tubules. Binds to the sodium/potassium/chloride carrier in the loop of Henle and in the renal tubules. *Long-acting potent sulfonamide "loop" diuretic and antihypertensive agent.*

CONTRAINDICATIONS Hypersensitivity to torsemide or sulfonamides; anuria, fluid and electrolyte depletion states; acute MI; hepatic coma.

CAUTIOUS USE Renal impairment; ventricular arrhythmias; concurrent use of other ototoxic drugs; gout or hyperuricemia; diabetes mellitus or history of pancreatitis; liver disease; hearing impairment; pregnancy (category B), lactation.

ADVERSE EFFECTS (≥1%) **CNS:** Headache, dizziness, fatigue, insomnia. **CV:** Orthostatic hypotension. **Endocrine:** *Hypokalemia,* hyponatremia, hyperuricemia. **GI:** Nausea, diarrhea. **Skin:** Rash, pruritus. **Body as a Whole:** Muscle cramps, rhinitis.

Common adverse effects in *italic*, life-threatening effects <u>underlined</u>: generic names in **bold**; classifications in SMALL CAPS; ♣ Canadian drug name; 🅿 Prototype drug

635

DRUG INTERACTIONS NSAIDS may reduce diuretic effects. Also see furosemide for potential drug interactions such as increased risk of **digoxin** toxicity due to hypokalemia, prolonged neuromuscular blockade with NEUROMUSCULAR BLOCKING AGENTS, and decreased **lithium** elimination with increased toxicity.

PHARMACOKINETICS Onset: 10 min. **Peak:** Within 60 min. **Duration:** 6–8 h. **Metabolism:** In liver (cytochrome P450). **Elimination:** 80% in bile; 20% in urine. **Half-Life:** 210 min.

NURSING IMPLICATIONS

Assessment & Drug Effects

- Monitor BP often and assess for orthostatic hypotension; assess respiratory status for S&S of pulmonary edema.
- Monitor ECG, as electrolyte imbalances predispose to cardiac arrhythmias.
- Lab tests: Periodic serum electrolytes, uric acid, blood glucose, BUN, and creatinine.
- Monitor I&O with daily weights. Assess for improvement in edema.
- Monitor diabetics for loss of glycemic control.
- Concurrent drugs: Monitor coagulation parameters and lithium levels in patients on concurrent anticoagulant and/or lithium therapy.

Patient & Family Education

- Check weight at least weekly and report abrupt gains or losses to prescriber.
- Understand the risk of orthostatic hypotension.
- Report immediately to prescriber symptoms of hypokalemia (see Appendix C) or hearing loss.
- Monitor blood glucose frequently if diabetic.

TRASTUZUMAB

(tra-stuzu-mab)

Herceptin

Classification(s): ANTINEOPLASTIC; MONOCLONAL ANTIBODY

Therapeutic: ANTINEOPLASTIC

Pregnancy Category: B

USES Metastatic breast cancer in those whose tumors overexpress the human epidermal growth factor receptor 2 (HER2) protein.

INDICATION & DOSAGE

Metastatic Breast Cancer

Adult: 4 mg/kg loading dose then 2 mg/kg weekly

SOLUTION PREPARATION

- *Vial Reconstitution:* Add 20 mL of supplied bacteriostatic water to each 440 mg multidose vial to yield 21 mg/mL. Let stand for 5 min to dissolve. (Note: For patients with a hypersensitivity to benzyl alcohol, reconstitute with sterile water for injection; this solution **must be** used immediately with any unused portion discarded.) **Must be** further diluted for infusion.
- *Further Dilution of Reconstituted Solution:* Withdraw the ordered dose and add to a 250-mL of NS and invert bag to mix. Do not give or mix with dextrose solutions.

STORAGE

Store unopened vials and reconstituted vials at 2°–8° C (36°–46° F). Discard vials reconstituted with bacteriostatic water 28 days after reconstitution.

ADMINISTRATION

IV Infusion: Infuse loading dose (4 mg/kg) over 90 min; infuse subsequent doses (2 mg/kg) over 30 min. Do NOT give IV push or as a bolus dose.

INCOMPATIBILITIES **Solution/additive: Dextrose solution, theophylline;** do not mix or coadminister with other drugs.

ACTION & *THERAPEUTIC EFFECT* Recombinant DNA monoclonal antibody (IgG_1 kappa) that selectively binds to the human epidermal growth factor receptor-2 protein (HER2). *Inhibits growth of human tumor cells that overexpress HER2 proteins.*

CONTRAINDICATIONS Concurrent administration of anthracycline or radiation; lactation during, and for 6 mo following administration of trastuzumab.

CAUTIOUS USE Preexisting cardiac dysfunction; pulmonary disease; previous administration of cardiotoxic therapy (e.g., anthracycline or radiation); older adults; hypersensitivity to benzyl alcohol (preservative in bacteriostatic water); pregnancy (category B).

ADVERSE EFFECTS (≥1%) **Body as a Whole:** *Pain, asthenia, fever, chills,* flu syndrome, allergic reaction, bone pain, arthralgia, <u>hypersensitivity (anaphylaxis, urticaria, bronchospasm, angioedema, or hypotension)</u>, increased incidence of infections, infusion reaction (*chills, fever,* nausea, vomiting, pain, rigors, headache, dizziness, dyspnea, hypotension, rash). **CNS:** *Headache, insomnia, dizziness, paresthesias,* depression, peripheral neuritis, neuropathy. **CV:** <u>CHF</u>, cardiac dysfunction (dyspnea, cough, paroxysmal nocturnal dyspnea, peripheral edema, S3 gallop, reduced ejection fraction), tachycardia, edema, cardiotoxicity. **GI:** *Diarrhea, abdominal pain, nausea, vomiting,* anorexia. **Hematologic:** *Anemia, leukopenia.* **Respiratory:** *Cough, dyspnea,* rhinitis, pharyngitis, sinusitis. **Skin:** *Rash,* herpes simplex, acne.

DRUG INTERACTIONS **Paclitaxel** may increase trastuzumab levels and toxicity.

PHARMACOKINETICS **Half-Life:** 5.8 days.

T

Common adverse effects in *italic*, life-threatening effects <u>underlined</u>; generic names in **bold**; classifications in SMALL CAPS; ♣ Canadian drug name; ❂ Prototype drug

637

NURSING IMPLICATIONS

Assessment & Drug Effects

- Monitor for chills and fever during the first IV infusion; these adverse events usually respond to prompt treatment without the need to discontinue the infusion. Notify prescriber immediately.
- Monitor carefully cardiovascular status at baseline and throughout course of therapy, assessing for S&S of heart failure (e.g., dyspnea, increased cough, PND, edema, S3 gallop). Those with preexisting cardiac dysfunction are at high risk for cardiotoxicity.
- Lab tests: Periodic CBC with differential, platelet count, and Hgb and Hct.

Patient & Family Education

- Report promptly any unusual symptoms (e.g., chills, nausea, fever) during infusion.
- Report promptly any of the following: Shortness of breath, swelling of feet or legs, persistent cough, difficulty sleeping, loss of appetite, abdominal bloating.

TROMETHAMINE

(troe-metha-meen)

Tham

Classification: FLUID AND ELECTROLYTIC BALANCE AGENT
Therapeutic: SYSTEMIC ALKALINIZER
Pregnancy Category: C

USES To prevent or correct metabolic acidosis associated with cardiac bypass surgery and cardiac arrest and to correct excess acidity of stored blood [preserved with acid citrate dextrose (CD)] used in cardiac bypass surgery. (Stored blood has a pH range of 6.8–6.22.)

UNLABELED USES Metabolic acidosis of status asthmaticus and neonatal respiratory distress syndrome.

INDICATION & DOSAGE

Note: Dosage may be estimated from buffer base deficit of extracellular fluid using the following formula as a guide: mL of 0.3–M tromethamine solution required = body weight (kg) × base deficit (mEq/L) × 1.1

Metabolic Acidosis Associated with Cardiac Arrest

Adult: 2–6 g (62–185 mL) of a 0.3–M solution

Systemic Acidosis during Cardiac Bypass Surgery

Adult: 9 mL/kg or approximately 500 mL (18 g) 0.3–M solution; a single dose of up to 1000 mL (36 g) may be necessary in severe acidosis

SOLUTION PREPARATION

No dilution is required. Administer as supplied.

STORAGE
Store unopened at 15°–30° C (59°–86° F).

ADMINISTRATION
- **IV Infusion:** Infuse slowly or add to pump-oxygenator blood or other priming fluid. Give over a period of no less than 1 h.
- Monitor insertion site closely. Perivascular infiltration of the highly alkaline solution may lead to vasospasm, necrosis, and tissue sloughing. Stop infusion if extravasation occurs.
- Treat extravasation with a procaine and hyaluronidase infiltration to reduce vasospasm and to dilute tromethamine remaining in tissues. If necessary, local infiltration of an alpha-adrenergic blocking agent (e.g., phentolamine) into the area may be ordered.

INCOMPATIBILITIES Data not available; do not mix with other drugs.

ACTION & *THERAPEUTIC EFFECT* A proton acceptor that binds cations of fixed or metabolic acids and hydrogen ions of carbonic acid, thus increasing bicarbonate anion (HCO_3^-). It also penetrates the cell membrane to combine with intracellular acid. *Acts as a weak osmotic diuretic, increasing urine pH and excretion of fixed acids, CO_2, and electrolytes. Corrects and prevents metabolic acidosis.*

CONTRAINDICATIONS Anuria, uremia; chronic respiratory acidosis; pregnancy (category C).
CAUTIOUS USE Renal impairment; less than 1 day of therapy.

ADVERSE EFFECTS (≥1%) **Body as a Whole:** *Local irritation,* tissue inflammation, *chemical phlebitis,* extravasation. **Respiratory:** <u>Respiratory depression</u>. **Metabolic:** Transient decrease in blood glucose, hypervolemia, hyperkalemia (with depressed kidney function).

PHARMACOKINETICS Metabolism: No appreciable metabolism. **Elimination:** Rapidly and preferentially by kidneys; 75% within 8 h.

NURSING IMPLICATIONS
Assessment & Drug Effects
- Monitor for signs of hypoxia (see Appendix C). Hypoxia and hypoventilation may result from drug-induced reduction of CO_2 tension (a potent stimulus to breathing), particularly if respiratory acidosis is also present.
- Drug-induced hypoxia is a particular risk with concomitant use of other respiratory depressants or with COPD or impaired kidney function.
- Lab tests: Frequent blood pH, PCO_2, PO_2, bicarbonate, glucose, and electrolytes before, during, and after treatment. Dosage is controlled to raise blood pH to normal limits (arterial: 7.35–7.45) and to correct acid–base imbalance.
- Monitor ECG and serum potassium if drug is given to patient with impaired kidney function (reduced drug elimination). Since hyperkalemia is often associated with metabolic acidosis, be alert to early signs (see Appendix C).
- Be alert for overdose symptoms (from total drug or too-rapid administration): Alkalosis, overhydration, prolonged hypoglycemia, solute overload.

Common adverse effects in *italic*, life-threatening effects <u>underlined</u>: generic names in **bold**; classifications in SMALL CAPS; ♣ Canadian drug name; ⊙ Prototype drug

639

VACCINIA IMMUNE GLOBULIN (VIG-IV)
(vac-cini-a)

Classification(s): IMMUNOLOGIC AGENT; IMMUNOGLOBULIN
Therapeutic: IMMUNOGLOBULIN
Prototype: Immunizing Agent
Pregnancy Category: C

USES Prevention of serious complications of smallpox vaccine; treatment of progressive vaccinia; severe generalized vaccinia; eczema vaccinatum; vaccinia infection in patients with skin conditions; treatment or modification of aberrant infections induced by vaccinia virus.

INDICATION & DOSAGE

Vaccinia
Adults: 100–500 mg/kg

Renal Impairment Dosage Adjustment
Use lowest effective dose (max: 400 mg/kg)

SOLUTION PREPARATION
No dilution is required. Administer as supplied.

STORAGE
Store at 2°–8° C (35°–46° F). After entering the vial, infusion must be started with 6 h and completed with 12 h.

ADMINISTRATION
IV Infusion: Infuse at 1.0 mL/kg/h the first 30 min, increase to 2.0 mL/kg/h the next 30 min, and then increase to 3.0 mL/kg/h until infused. Use in-line filter (0.22 microns), infusion pump, and dedicated IV line [may infuse into a preexisting catheter if it contains NS, D2.5W, D5W, D10W, or D20W (or any combination of these)]. Begin infusion within 6 h of entering the vial. Complete infusion within 12 h of entering the vial.

INCOMPATIBILITIES Data not available; do not mix with other drugs.

ACTION & *THERAPEUTIC EFFECT* Vaccinia immune globulin, VIG (VIG-IV), is an intravenous sterile solution of purified human immunoglobulin G (IgG) with trace amounts of IgA and IgM. It is derived from adult human plasma collected from donors who received booster immunizations with the smallpox vaccine. VIG (VIG-IV) contains high titers of antivaccinia antibodies. *VIG (VIG-IV) is effective in the treatment of smallpox vaccine adverse reactions secondary to continued vaccinia virus replication after vaccination.*

CONTRAINDICATIONS Predisposition to acute renal failure (i.e., preexisting renal insufficiency; diabetes mellitus; volume depletion; sepsis; patients greater than 65 y); postvaccinal encephalitis; pregnancy (category C), lactation; infants less than 2 y.

Common adverse effects in *italic*, life-threatening effects <u>underlined</u>: generic names in **bold**; classifications in SMALL CAPS; ♣ Canadian drug name; ✪ Prototype drug

V

CAUTIOUS USE Concurrent administration of known nephrotoxic drugs; autoimmune disease; cardiomyopathy; cardiac disease.

ADVERSE EFFECTS (≥1%) **Body as a Whole:** Injection site reaction. **CNS:** Dizziness, *headache*. **GI:** Abdominal pain, nausea, vomiting. **Musculoskeletal:** Arthralgia, back pain. **Respiratory:** Upper respiratory infection. **Skin:** Erythema, flushing.

DRUG INTERACTIONS May interfere with the immune response to LIVE VACCINES. Vaccination with LIVE VACCINES should be deferred until approximately 6 mo after administration of VIG-IV.

PHARMACOKINETICS Half-Life: 22 days.

NURSING IMPLICATIONS
Assessment & Drug Effects
- Monitor vital signs continuously during infusion, especially after infusion rate changes.
- Slow infusion rate for any of the following: Flushing, chills, muscle cramps, back pain, fever, nausea, vomiting, arthralgia, and wheezing.
- Withhold infusion, institute supportive measures, and notify prescriber for any of the following: Increase in heart rate, increase in respiratory rate, shortness of breath, rales or other signs of anaphylaxis.
- Have loop diuretic available for management of fluid overload.

Patient & Family Education
- Promptly report any discomfort that develops while drug is being infused.

VALPROATE SODIUM ⊕
(val′pro-ate)

Depacon

Classification(s): ANTICONVULSANT; GAMMA-AMINOBUTYRIC ACID (GABA) INHIBITOR

Therapeutic: ANTICONVULSANT
Pregnancy Category: D

USES Alone or with other anticonvulsants in management of absence (petit mal) and mixed seizures; acute mania.
UNLABELED USES Status epilepticus refractory to IV diazepam, petit mal variant seizures, febrile seizures in children, other types of seizures including psychomotor (temporal lobe), myoclonic, akinetic and tonic–clonic seizures, photosensitivity seizures, and those refractory to other anticonvulsants.

INDICATION & DOSAGE

Management of Seizures, Acute Mania
Adult/Child (over 9 y): 15 mg/kg/day; when total daily dose exceeds 250 mg, divide doses; increase at 1 wk intervals by 5–10 mg/kg/day until seizures are controlled or adverse effects develop (max: 60 mg/kg/day)

Conversion of PO to IV: Give normal dose in divided doses q6h

Hepatic Impairment Dosage Adjustment

Dose reduction recommended

Renal Impairment Dosage Adjustment

Severe renal impairment may require closer monitoring

SOLUTION PREPARATION
Dilute each dose in 50 mL or more of D5W, NS, or LR.

STORAGE
Store unopened at 15°–30° C (59°–86° F). Solutions should be used within 24 h.

ADMINISTRATION
IV Infusion: Infuse a single dose over at least 60 min (at a rate no greater than 20 mg/min). Avoid rapid infusion.

INCOMPATIBILITIES Solution/additive: Data not available; do not mix with other drugs.

ACTION & *THERAPEUTIC EFFECT* Anticonvulsant drug unrelated chemically to other drugs used to treat seizure disorders. Mechanism of action due to the drug's metabolite, valproic acid, may be related to increased bioavailability of the inhibitory neurotransmitter gamma-aminobutyric acid (GABA) to brain neurons. *Depresses abnormal neuron discharges in the CNS, thus decreasing seizure activity.*

CONTRAINDICATIONS Hypersensitivity to valproate sodium; thrombocytopenia, patient with bleeding disorders or liver dysfunction or disease; cirrhosis; pancreatitis; congenital metabolic disorders; those with severe seizures, or on multiple anticonvulsant drugs; AIDS; pregnancy (category D); children less than 2 y for seizures; children less than 18 y for treatment of acute mania.

CAUTIOUS USE History of kidney disease, renal impairment or failure; adjunctive treatment with other anticonvulsants; congenital metabolic disorders; those with severe epilepsy, use as sole anticonvulsant drug; hypoalbuminemia; organic brain syndrome; children greater than 2 y, especially in first 6 mo of therapy.

ADVERSE EFFECTS (≥1%) **CNS:** Breakthrough seizures, *sedation, drowsiness,* dizziness, increased alertness, hallucinations, emotional upset, aggression; <u>deep coma, death (with overdose)</u>. **GI:** *Nausea, vomiting, indigestion (transient),* hypersalivation, anorexia with weight loss, increased appetite with weight gain, abdominal cramps, diarrhea, constipation, <u>liver failure, pancreatitis</u>. **Hematologic:** *Prolonged bleeding time,* leukopenia, lymphocytosis, thrombocytopenia, hypofibrinogenemia, <u>bone marrow depression</u>, anemia. **Skin:** Skin rash, photosensitivity, transient hair loss, curliness or waviness of hair. **Endocrine:** Irregular menses, secondary amenorrhea. **Metabolic:** Hyperammonemia (usually asymptomatic) hyperammonemic encephalopathy in patients with urea cycle disorders. **Respiratory:** Pulmonary edema (with overdose).

DIAGNOSTIC TEST INTERFERENCE Valproic acid, the drug's metabolite, produces false-positive results for *urine ketones,* elevated *AST, ALT, LDH,* and *serum alkaline phosphatase,* prolonged *bleeding time,* altered *thyroid function tests.*

DRUG INTERACTIONS Alcohol and other CNS DEPRESSANTS potentiate depressant effects; other ANTICONVULSANTS, BARBITURATES increase or decrease anticonvulsant and BARBITURATE levels; **haloperidol, loxapine, maprotiline,** MAOIS, PHENOTHIAZINES, THIOXANTHENES, TRICYCLIC ANTIDEPRESSANTS can increase CNS depression or lower seizure threshold; **aspirin, dipyridamole, warfarin** increase risk of spontaneous bleeding and decrease clotting; **clonazepam** may precipitate absence seizures; SALICYLATES, **cimetidine, isoniazid** may increase valproic acid, the drug's metabolite, levels and toxicity. **Mefloquine** can decrease valproic acid, the drug's metabolite, levels; **meropenem** may decrease valproic acid, the drug's metabolite, levels.

PHARMACOKINETICS Distribution: Crosses placenta; distributed into breast milk. **Metabolism:** In liver. **Elimination:** Primarily in urine; small amount in feces and expired air. **Half-Life:** 5–20 h.

NURSING IMPLICATIONS

Assessment & Drug Effects

- Normal therapeutic range: 50–100 mcg/mL.
- Monitor patient alertness, especially with multiple drug therapy for seizure control. Evaluate plasma levels of the adjunctive anticonvulsants as indicators for possible neurologic toxicity.
- Monitor patient carefully during dose adjustments and report promptly presence of adverse effects.
- Monitor for S&S of hepatic dysfunction, including: Anorexia, vomiting, lethargy, fatigue, weakness, jaundice, and facial edema.
- Lab tests: Baseline platelet counts, bleeding time, LFTs, and serum ammonia, then repeat at least q2mo, especially during the first 6 mo of therapy.
- Multiple drugs for seizure control increase the risk of hyperammonemia, marked by lethargy, anorexia, asterixis, increased seizure frequency, and vomiting. Report such symptoms promptly.
- Drug may cause a false-positive test for urine ketones.

Patient & Family Education

- Report promptly if spontaneous bleeding or bruising occurs (e.g., petechiae, ecchymotic areas, otorrhagia, epistaxis, melena).
- Do not drive or engage in potentially hazardous activities until response to drug is known.

V

VANCOMYCIN HYDROCHLORIDE

(van-koe-myesin)

Vancocin
Classification(s): ANTIBIOTIC
Therapeutic: ANTIBACTERIAL
Pregnancy Category: B

VANCOMYCIN HYDROCHLORIDE

USES Parenterally for potentially life-threatening infections in patients allergic, nonsensitive, or resistant to other less toxic antimicrobial drugs.

INDICATION & DOSAGE

Systemic Infections

Adult/Adolescent: 1 g q12h, or 15 mg/kg q12h
Child/Infant (over 1 mo): 30–40 mg/kg/day divided q6–8h
Neonate:

Age	Weight	Dose
Over 7 days	Over 2000 g	10–15 mg/kg q8h
Over 7 days	1200–2000 g	10–15 mg/kg q8–12h
Over 7 days	Less than 1200 g	10–15 mg/kg q12–24h
Up to 7 days	Over 2000 g	10–15 mg/kg q12h
Up to 7 days	1200–2000 g	10–15 mg/kg q12–18h
Up to 7 days	Less than 1200 g	15 mg/kg q24h

Surgical Prophylaxis (in pts allergic to beta-lactams)

Adult/Adolescent/Child (at least 27 kg): 10–15 mg/kg starting 1 h before surgery
Child (less than 27 kg): 20 mg/kg starting 1 h before surgery

Renal Impairment Dosage Adjustment

All doses should be adjusted based on serum concentrations

SOLUTION PREPARATION

- *Vial Reconstitution:* Add 10 mL or 20 mL, respectively, of sterile water for injection to the 500 mg vial or 1 g vial to yield 50 mg/mL. **Must be** further diluted for infusion.
- *Further Dilution of Reconstituted Solution:* Dilute 500 mg in at least 100 mL and 1 g in at least 200 mL of D5W, NS, or LR.

STORAGE

Store reconstituted solutions refrigerated for 96 h. Store IV solutions for 24 h at room temperature.

ADMINISTRATION

- Ensure patency prior to injection or infusion, as extravasation may cause tissue sloughing.
- **Intermittent Infusion:** Give a single dose at a rate of 10 mg/min or a single dose over **not less** than 60 min (whichever is longer).
- Use an infusion pump to regulate the infusion rate. Avoid rapid infusion, which increases the risk of hypotension or transient "red man syndrome."

INCOMPATIBILITIES Solution/additive: Aminophylline, BARBITURATES, **aztreonam** (high concentration), **calcium chloride, chlorampheni-**

col, chlorothiazide, dexamethasone, erythromycin, heparin, methicillin, sodium bicarbonate, warfarin. **Y-site:** Albumin, amphotericin B cholesteryl complex, aztreonam, bivalirudin, cefazolin, cefepime, cefotaxime, cefotetan, cefoxitin, ceftazidime, ceftriaxone, cefuroxime, drotrecogin, foscarnet, gatifloxacin, heparin, idarubicin, lansoprazole, nafcillin, omeprazole, piperacillin/tazobactam, sargramostim, ticarcillin, ticarcillin/clavulanate, warfarin.

ACTION & *THERAPEUTIC EFFECT* Bacteriocidal action is due to inhibition of cell wall biosynthesis and alteration of bacterial cell-membrane permeability and ribonucleic acid (RNA) synthesis. This leads to bacterial cell death. *Active against many gram-positive organisms.*

CONTRAINDICATIONS Known hypersensitivity to vancomycin; allergy to corn or corn products; previous hearing loss; concurrent or sequential use of other ototoxic or nephrotoxic agents.
CAUTIOUS USE Older adults; impaired kidney function, renal failure, renal impairment; concomitant administration of aminoglycosides; hearing impairment; colitis, inflammatory disorders of the intestine; pregnancy (category B), lactation; children; neonates.

ADVERSE EFFECTS (≥1%) **Special Senses:** Ototoxicity (auditory portion of eighth cranial nerve). **Urogenital:** Nephrotoxicity leading to uremia. **Body as a Whole:** Hypersensitivity reactions (chills, fever, skin rash, urticaria, shocklike state), anaphylactoid reaction with vascular collapse, superinfections, severe pain, thrombophlebitis at injection site, generalized tingling following rapid IV infusion. **Hematologic:** Transient leukopenia, eosinophilia. **GI:** Nausea, warmth. **Other:** Injection reaction that includes *hypotension accompanied by flushing and erythematous rash on face and upper body* ("red-neck syndrome") following rapid infusion.

DRUG INTERACTIONS Adds to toxicity of ototoxic and nephrotoxic drugs (AMINOGLYCOSIDES, **amphotericin B, colistin, capreomycin, cidofovir, cisplatin, cyclosporine, foscarnet, ganciclovir, IV pentamidine, polymyxin B, streptozocin, tacrolimus**); may increase risk of lactic acidosis with **metformin.**

PHARMACOKINETICS Peak: 30 min after end of infusion. **Distribution:** Diffuses into pleural, ascitic, pericardial, and synovial fluids; small amount penetrates CSF if meninges are inflamed; crosses placenta. **Elimination:** 80–90% in urine within 24 h. **Half-Life:** 4–8 h.

NURSING IMPLICATIONS

Assessment & Drug Effects

- Prior to initiating therapy: Baseline C&S tests (start drug pending results).
- Monitor BP and heart rate continuously through period of drug administration.
- Lab tests: Baseline and periodic kidney functions tests, LFTs, hematologic studies; serum vancomycin blood levels (peak and trough), especially those over 60 y or with borderline kidney function, in infants and neonates.

Common adverse effects in *italic*, life-threatening effects underlined: generic names in **bold**; classifications in SMALL CAPS; ✚ Canadian drug name; ❖ Prototype drug

645

- Assess hearing. Drug may cause damage to auditory branch (not vestibular branch) of eighth cranial nerve, with consequent deafness, which may be permanent.
- Be aware that serum levels of 60–80 mcg/mL are associated with ototoxicity. Tinnitus and high-tone hearing loss may precede deafness, which may progress even after drug is withdrawn. Older adults and those on high doses are especially susceptible.
- Monitor I&O: Report changes in I&O ratio and pattern. Oliguria or cloudy or pink urine may be a sign of nephrotoxicity (also manifested by transient elevations in BUN, albumin, and hyaline and granular casts in urine).
- Monitor for S&S of superinfections (see Appendix C), especially with prolonged therapy.

Patient & Family Education
- Notify prescriber promptly of ringing in ears.

VASOPRESSIN INJECTION ⊙

(vay-soe-pressin)

Classification(s): ANTIDIURETIC HORMONE
Therapeutic: VASOPRESSOR
Pregnancy Category: C

USES Antidiuretic to treat diabetes insipidus, to dispel gas shadows in abdominal roentgenography, and as prevention and treatment of postoperative abdominal distension.
UNLABELED USES Test for differential diagnosis of nephrogenic, psychogenic, and neurohypophyseal diabetes insipidus; test to elevate ability of kidney to concentrate urine; provocative test for pituitary release of corticotropin and growth hormone; and emergency and adjunct pressor agent in the control of massive GI hemorrhage (e.g., esophageal varices).

INDICATION & DOSAGE

GI Hemorrhage
Adult: 20 units bolus then 0.2–0.4 units/min up to 0.9 units/min

SOLUTION PREPARATION
IV Infusion: Dilute with NS or D5W to a concentration of 0.1–1 units/mL.

STORAGE
Store unopened vials at 15°–30°C (59°–86°F).

ADMINISTRATION
- Ensure patency prior to injection or infusion, as extravasation may cause severe vasoconstriction with tissue necrosis and gangrene.
- **Direct IV Injection:** Give rapid bolus dose.
- **Continuous Infusion:** Titrate dose and rate to patient's response.

Common adverse effects in *italic*, life-threatening effects <u>underlined</u>: generic names in **bold**; classifications in SMALL CAPS; ♣ Canadian drug name; ⊙ Prototype drug

INCOMPATIBILITIES Limited data available; do not mix with other drugs.

ACTION & *THERAPEUTIC EFFECT* Polypeptide hormone extracted from animal posterior pituitaries. Possesses pressor and antidiuretic (ADH) properties, but is relatively free of oxytocic properties. Produces concentrated urine by increasing tubular reabsorption of water (ADH activity), thus reabsorbing up to 90% of the water in the tubules. Causes contraction of smooth muscles of the GI tract as well as the vascular bed, especially capillaries, arterioles, and venules. *Effective in the treatment of diuresis caused by diabetes insipidus.*

CONTRAINDICATIONS Chronic nephritis accompanied by nitrogen retention; ischemic heart disease, PVCs, advanced arteriosclerosis; pregnancy (category C), during first stage of labor, lactation.
CAUTIOUS USE Epilepsy; migraine; asthma; heart failure, angina pectoris; any state in which rapid addition to extracellular fluid may be hazardous; vascular disease; preoperative and postoperative polyuric patients, kidney disease; goiter with cardiac complications; older adults; children.

ADVERSE EFFECTS (≥1%) **Skin:** Rash, urticaria. **Body as a Whole:** <u>Anaphylaxis</u>; *tremor,* sweating, bronchoconstriction, *circumoral and facial pallor,* angioneurotic edema, *pounding in head, water intoxication* (especially with tannate), gangrene at injection site with intra-arterial infusion. **GI:** *Eructations, passage of gas, nausea, vomiting,* heartburn, abdominal cramps, increased bowel movements secondary to excessive use. **CV:** Angina (in patient with coronary vascular disease), <u>cardiac arrest</u>, hypertension, bradycardia, minor arrhythmias, premature atrial contraction, heart block, peripheral vascular collapse, coronary insufficiency, <u>MI</u>, cardiac arrhythmia, pulmonary edema, bradycardia (with intra-arterial infusion). **Urogenital:** Uterine cramps. **Respiratory:** Congestion, rhinorrhea, irritation, mucosal ulceration and pruritus, postnasal drip. **Special Senses:** Conjunctivitis.

DIAGNOSTIC TEST INTERFERENCE Vasopressin increases ***plasma cortisol*** levels.

DRUG INTERACTIONS Alcohol, demeclocycline, epinephrine, heparin, lithium, phenytoin may decrease antidiuretic effects of vasopressin; **guanethidine, neostigmine** increase vasopressor actions; **chlorpropamide, clofibrate, carbamazepine,** THIAZIDE DIURETICS may increase antidiuretic activity.

PHARMACOKINETICS Duration: 30–60 min. **Distribution:** Extracellular fluid. **Metabolism:** In liver and kidneys. **Elimination:** In urine. **Half-Life:** 10–20 min.

NURSING IMPLICATIONS
Assessment & Drug Effects
- Monitor vitals signs frequently. Continuous ECG monitoring is recommended.
- Be alert to the fact that even small doses of vasopressin may precipitate MI or coronary insufficiency, especially in older adult patients. Keep emergency equipment and drugs (antiarrhythmics) readily available.
- Lab tests: Frequent Hct & Hgb, and serum electrolytes.
- Monitor I&O ratio and pattern.

Common adverse effects in *italic*, life-threatening effects <u>underlined</u>: generic names in **bold**; classifications in SMALL CAPS; ♣ Canadian drug name; ● Prototype drug

647

Patient & Family Education

- Be prepared for possibility of anginal attack and have coronary vasodilator available (e.g., nitroglycerin) if there is a history of coronary artery disease. Report to prescriber.

VECURONIUM

(vek-yoo-roenee-um)

Norcuron

Classification(s): SKELETAL MUSCLE RELAXANT, NONDEPOLARIZING
Therapeutic: NEUROMUSCULAR BLOCKING AGENT
Prototype: Atracurium
Pregnancy Category: C

USES Adjunct for general anesthesia to produce skeletal muscle relaxation during surgery. Especially useful for patients with severe kidney disease, limited cardiac reserve, and history of asthma or allergy. Also to facilitate endotracheal intubation.

UNLABELED USES Continuous infusion for facilitation of mechanical ventilation.

INDICATION & DOSAGE

Skeletal Muscle Relaxation

Adult/Child (over 10 y): 0.04–0.1 mg/kg initially, then after 25–40 min, 0.01–0.15 mg/kg q12–15 min continuous infusion (for prolonged procedures)

Child (1–10 y)/Infant: Doses vary greatly, may require slightly higher initial dose

Obesity Dosage Adjustment

Dose based on IBW.

SOLUTION PREPARATION

- *Vial Reconstitution:* Add 10 mL or 20 mL, respectively, of sterile water for injection to the 10 mg or 20 mg vial to yield 1 mg/mL. May be given as prepared direct IV as a bolus dose or further diluted for infusion.
- *Further Dilution of Reconstituted Solution:* Dilute in up to 100 mL D5W, NS, or LR to yield 0.1–0.2 mg/mL.

STORAGE

Refrigerate after reconstitution below 30° C (86° F), unless otherwise directed. Discard solution after 24 h.

ADMINISTRATION

- **Direct IV Injection:** Give bolus dose over 30 sec.
- **Continuous Infusion:** Give at the required rate.

Common adverse effects in *italic*, life-threatening effects <u>underlined</u>: generic names in **bold**; classifications in SMALL CAPS; ♣ Canadian drug name; ● Prototype drug

INCOMPATIBILITIES Y-site: Amphotericin B cholesteryl complex, diazepam, etomidate, furosemide, thiopental.

ACTION & *THERAPEUTIC EFFECT* Intermediate-acting nondepolarizing skeletal muscle relaxant that inhibits neuromuscular transmission by competitively binding with acetylcholine at receptors located on the motor endplate. *Skeletal muscular relaxation results from inhibiting neuromuscular transmission at the motor endplate receptors.*

CONTRAINDICATIONS Hypersensitivity to bromide; pregnancy (category C).

CAUTIOUS USE Severe liver disease; impaired acid–base, fluid and electrolyte balance; severe obesity; adrenal or neuromuscular disease (myasthenia gravis, Eaton-Lambert syndrome); patients with slow circulation time (cardiovascular disease, old age, edematous states); malignant hyperthermia; lactation.

ADVERSE EFFECTS (≥1%) **Body as a Whole:** Skeletal muscle weakness, malignant hyperthermia. **Respiratory:** Respiratory depression.

DRUG INTERACTIONS GENERAL ANESTHETICS increase neuromuscular blockade and duration of action; AMINOGLYCOSIDES, **bacitracin, polymyxin B, clindamycin, lidocaine, parenteral magnesium, quinidine, quinine, trimethaphan, verapamil** increase neuromuscular blockade; DIURETICS may increase or decrease neuromuscular blockade; **lithium** prolongs duration of neuromuscular blockade; NARCOTIC ANALGESICS increase possibility of additive respiratory depression; **succinylcholine** increases onset and depth of neuromuscular blockade; **phenytoin** may cause resistance to or reversal of neuromuscular blockade.

PHARMACOKINETICS Onset: Less than 1 min. **Peak:** 3–5 min. **Duration:** 25–40 min. **Distribution:** Well distributed to tissues and extracellular fluids; crosses placenta; distribution into breast milk unknown. **Metabolism:** Rapid nonenzymatic degradation in bloodstream. **Elimination:** 30–35% in urine, 30–35% in bile. **Half-Life:** 30–80 min.

NURSING IMPLICATIONS

Assessment & Drug Effects

- Lab tests: Baseline serum electrolytes, acid–base balance, kidney function tests, and LFTs.
- Use peripheral nerve stimulator during and following drug administration to avoid risk of overdosage and to identify residual paralysis during recovery period. This is especially indicated when cautious use of drug is specified.
- Monitor vital signs at least q15min until stable, then every 30 min for the next 2 h. Also monitor airway patency until assured that patient has fully recovered from drug effects. Note rate, depth, and pattern of respirations. Obese patients and patients with myasthenia gravis or other neuromuscular disease may have ventilation problems.
- Evaluate patients for recovery from neuromuscular blocking (curare-like) effects as evidenced by ability to breathe naturally or take deep breaths

Common adverse effects in *italic*, life-threatening effects <u>underlined</u>: generic names in **bold**; classifications in SMALL CAPS; ✚ Canadian drug name; ❹ Prototype drug

649

and cough, to keep eyes open, and to lift head keeping mouth closed and by adequacy of hand grip strength. Notify prescriber if recovery is delayed.

- Note: Recovery time may be delayed in patients with cardiovascular disease, edematous states, and in older adults.

VERAPAMIL HYDROCHLORIDE ℗ℜ

(ver-apa-mill)

Isoptin

Classification(s): CALCIUM CHANNEL BLOCKER; ANTIARRHYTHMIC AGENT
Therapeutic: ANTIARRHYTHMIC
Pregnancy Category: C

USES Supraventricular tachyarrhythmias; Prinzmetal's (variant) angina, chronic stable angina; unstable, crescendo or pre-infarctive angina and essential hypertension.
UNLABELED USES Paroxysmal supraventricular tachycardia, atrial fibrillation; prophylaxis of migraine headache; and as alternate therapy in manic depression.

INDICATION & DOSAGE

Supraventricular Tachycardia, Atrial Fibrillation

Adult/Adolescent (over 15 y): 5–10 mg; after 30 min may give 10 mg (max: 20 mg)
Child/Adolescent (up to 15 y): 0.1–0.3 mg/kg (do not exceed 5 mg)
Infant: 0.1–0.2 mg/kg; may repeat after 30 min

Renal Impairment Dosage Adjustment

CrCl less than 10 mL/min: Give 50–75% of dose

Hemodialysis Dosage Adjustment

Supplemental dose not necessary

Hepatic Impairment Dosage Adjustment

In cirrhosis use 20–50% of normal dose

SOLUTION PREPARATION

May be given direct IV undiluted or diluted in 5 mL of sterile water for injection.

STORAGE

Store at 15°–30° C (59°–86° F) and protect from light.

ADMINISTRATION

Direct IV Injection: Give a single dose over 2–3 min.

Common adverse effects in *italic*, life-threatening effects <u>underlined</u>: generic names in **bold**; classifications in SMALL CAPS; ♣ Canadian drug name; ℗ Prototype drug

INCOMPATIBILITIES Solution/additive: **Albumin, aminophylline, amphotericin B, hydralazine, sulfamethoxazole/trimethoprim.** Y-site: **Albumin, amphotericin B cholesteryl complex, ampicillin, lansoprazole, mezlocillin, nafcillin, oxacillin, propofol, sodium bicarbonate.**

ACTION & *THERAPEUTIC EFFECT* Inhibits calcium ion influx through slow channels into cells of myocardial and arterial smooth muscle. Dilates coronary arteries and arterioles and inhibits coronary artery spasm. Decreases and slows SA and AV node conduction without affecting normal arterial action potential or intraventricular conduction. Decreases angina attacks by dilating coronary arteries and inhibiting coronary vasospasms. Dilates peripheral arterioles resulting in decreased total peripheral vascular resistance accompanied by a reduction in BP. *Decreases nodal conduction, thus resulting in an antiarrhythmic effect. Inhibits coronary artery spasms, resulting in controlling angina pain. Decreases total peripheral vascular resistance and, therefore, BP.*

CONTRAINDICATIONS Hypersensitivity to verapamil; severe hypotension (systolic less than 90 mm Hg), cardiogenic shock, cardiomegaly, digitalis toxicity, second- or third-degree AV block; Wolff-Parkinson-White syndrome, including atrial flutter and fibrillation; accessory AV pathway, left ventricular dysfunction, ventricular tachycardia (QRS greater than or equal to 0.12 sec); severe CHF, sinus node disease, sick sinus syndrome (except in patients with functioning ventricular pacemaker); concurrent IV beta adrenergic blocking agents; pregnancy (category C), lactation.

CAUTIOUS USE Duchenne's muscular dystrophy; hepatic and renal impairment; MI followed by coronary occlusion, aortic stenosis; elevated intracranial pressure; infants, neonates.

ADVERSE EFFECTS (≥1%) **CNS:** Dizziness, vertigo, *headache,* fatigue, sleep disturbances, depression, syncope. **CV:** *Hypotension,* congestive heart failure, bradycardia, severe tachycardia, peripheral edema, <u>AV block</u>. **GI:** Nausea, abdominal discomfort, *constipation,* elevated liver enzymes. **Body as a Whole:** Flushing, pulmonary edema, muscle fatigue, diaphoresis. **Skin:** Pruritus.

DIAGNOSTIC TEST INTERFERENCE Verapamil may cause elevations of serum *AST, ALT, alkaline phosphatase.*

DRUG INTERACTIONS BETA BLOCKERS increase risk of CHF, bradycardia, or heart block; significantly increased levels of **digoxin** and **carbamazepine** and toxicity; potentiates hypotensive effects of HYPOTENSIVE AGENTS; levels of **lithium** and **cyclosporine** may be increased, increasing their toxicity; **calcium salts** (IV) may antagonize verapamil effects.

PHARMACOKINETICS Peak: 5 min. **Distribution:** Widely distributed, including CNS; crosses placenta; present in breast milk. **Metabolism:** In liver (CYP 3A4). **Elimination:** 70% in urine; 16% in feces. **Half-Life:** 2–8 h.

NURSING IMPLICATIONS

Assessment & Drug Effects

- Monitor BP and ECG continuously during IV administration. Drug action may be prolonged and incidence of adverse reactions is highest during

IV administration in older adults, patients with impaired kidney function, and patients of small stature.
- Monitor for AV block or excessive bradycardia when infusion is given concurrently with digitalis.
- Lab tests: Baseline and periodic LFTs and kidney function tests.
- Monitor I&O. Renal impairment prolongs duration of action, increasing potential for toxicity and incidence of adverse effects.

Patient & Family Education
- Instruct patient to remain in recumbent position for at least 1 h after dose to diminish effects of transient hypotension.
- Do not drive or engage in potentially hazardous activities until response to drug is known.

VINBLASTINE SULFATE

(vin-blasteen)

Classification(s): ANTINEOPLASTIC; MITOTIC INHIBITOR, VINCA ALKALOID
Therapeutic: ANTINEOPLASTIC
Prototype: Vincristine
Pregnancy Category: D

USES Palliative treatment of Hodgkin's disease and non-Hodgkin's lymphomas, choriocarcinoma, lymphosarcoma, neuroblastoma, mycosis fungoides, advanced testicular germinal cell cancer, histiocytosis, and other malignancies resistant to other chemotherapy. Used singly or in combination with other chemotherapeutic drugs.

INDICATION & DOSAGE

Antineoplastic

Adult: 3.7–10 mg/m^2 once weekly; dose varies based on protocol and may increase incrementally up to 18.5 mg/m^2 if tolerated
Child: 2.5 mg/m^2 once weekly; may increase up to 12.5 mg/m^2 if tolerated

Hepatic Impairment Dosage Adjustment

Bilirubin 1.5–3 mg/dL: Reduce dose 50%; *bilirubin over 3 mg/dL:* Reduce dose 75%

SOLUTION PREPARATION
- Add 10 mL NS to each 10 mg of drug (yields 1 mg/mL). Do not use other diluents.
- Avoid contact with eyes. Severe irritation and persisting corneal changes may occur. Flush immediately and thoroughly with copious amounts of water. Wash both eyes.

STORAGE

Refrigerate reconstituted solution in tight, light-resistant containers up to 30 days without loss of potency.

ADMINISTRATION

- Ensure patency prior to injection or infusion, as extravasation may cause tissue sloughing.
- **Direct IV Injection:** Inject into tubing of running IV infusion of NS or D5W over period of 1 min.
- Stop injection promptly if extravasation occurs. Use applications of moderate heat and local injection of hyaluronidase to help disperse extravasated drug. Restart IV at a different site. Observe injection site for sloughing.

INCOMPATIBILITIES Solution/additive: Furosemide, heparin. Y-site: Cefepime, furosemide, lansoprazole.

ACTION & *THERAPEUTIC EFFECT* Cell cycle–specific drug that interferes with nucleic acid synthesis by arresting proliferating cells in metaphase. It may also interfere with other cellular functions such as phagocytosis and cell mobility. *Interrupts cell cycle in metaphase, thus preventing cell replication of faster replicating tumor cells than normal cells. Exhibits potent myelosuppressive and immunosuppressive properties.*

CONTRAINDICATIONS Severe bone marrow suppression, leukopenia, bacterial infection; men and women of childbearing potential; older adult patients with cachexia or skin ulcers; adynamic ileus; pregnancy (category D), lactation.

CAUTIOUS USE Malignant cell infiltration of bone marrow; obstructive jaundice, hepatic impairment; history of gout; use of small amount of drug for long periods.

ADVERSE EFFECTS (≥1%) **Body as a Whole:** Fever, weight loss, muscular pains, weakness, parotid gland pain and tenderness, tumor site pain, Raynaud's phenomenon. **CNS:** Mental depression, peripheral neuritis, numbness and paresthesias of tongue and extremities, loss of deep tendon reflexes, headache, convulsions. **GI:** Vesiculation of mouth, stomatitis, pharyngitis, anorexia, *nausea, vomiting,* diarrhea, ileus, abdominal pain, constipation, rectal bleeding, hemorrhagic enterocolitis, bleeding of old peptic ulcer. **Hematologic:** Leukopenia, thrombocytopenia and anemia. **Skin:** *Alopecia (reversible),* vesiculation, photosensitivity, phlebitis, cellulitis, and sloughing following extravasation (at injection site). **Urogenital:** Urinary retention, *hyperuricemia,* aspermia. **Respiratory:** Bronchospasm.

DRUG INTERACTIONS Mitomycin may cause acute shortness of breath and severe bronchospasm; may decrease **phenytoin** levels; ALFA INTERFERONS, **erythromycin, itraconazole** may increase toxicity.

PHARMACOKINETICS Distribution: Concentrates in liver, platelets, and leukocytes; poor penetration of blood–brain barrier. **Metabolism:** Partially in liver (CYP 3A4). **Elimination:** In feces and urine. **Half-Life:** 24 h.

NURSING IMPLICATIONS

Assessment & Drug Effects

- Do not administer drug unless WBC count has returned to at least 4000/mm³, even if 7 days have passed.

Common adverse effects in *italic*, life-threatening effects <u>underlined</u>: generic names in **bold**; classifications in SMALL CAPS; ♣ Canadian drug name; ⊚ Prototype drug

653

- Lab tests: Baseline and periodic WBC count. Recovery from leukopenic nadir occurs usually within 7–14 days. With high doses, total leukocyte count may not return to normal for 3 wk.
- Monitor for unexplained bruising or bleeding, which should be promptly reported, even though thrombocyte reduction seldom occurs unless patient has had prior treatment with other antineoplastics.
- Monitor bowel elimination pattern and bowel sounds to recognize severe constipation or paralytic ileus.
- Report promptly if oral mucosa tissue breakdown is noted.

Patient & Family Education

- Be aware that temporary mental depression sometimes occurs on the second or third day after treatment begins.
- Avoid exposure to infection, injury to skin or mucous membranes, and excessive physical stress, especially during leukocyte nadir period.
- Notify prescriber promptly about onset of symptoms of agranulocytosis (see Appendix C).
- Avoid exposure to sunlight unless protected with sunscreen lotion (SPF greater than 12) and clothing.

VINCRISTINE SULFATE ℗

(vin-kristeen)

Classification(s): ANTINEOPLASTIC; MITOTIC INHIBITOR, VINCA ALKALOID
Therapeutic: ANTINEOPLASTIC
Pregnancy Category: D

USES Acute lymphoblastic and other leukemias, Hodgkin's disease, lymphosarcoma, neuroblastoma, Wilms' tumor, lung and breast cancer, reticular cell carcinoma, and osteogenic and other sarcomas.
UNLABELED USES Idiopathic thrombocytopenic purpura, alone or adjunctively with other antineoplastics.

INDICATION & DOSAGE

Antineoplastic

Adult: 1.4 mg/m^2 (max: 2 mg/m^2) at weekly intervals
Child (at least 10 kg): 1.5–2 mg/m^2 at weekly intervals
Child (up to 10 kg): 0.05 mg/kg weekly, then titrate

Hepatic Impairment Dosage Adjustment

Bilirubin 1.5–3 mg/dL: Reduce dose 50%; *bilirubin over 3 mg/dL:* Reduce dose 75%

SOLUTION PREPARATION

- No dilution is required. Administer as supplied.

Common adverse effects in *italic*, life-threatening effects <u>underlined</u>: generic names in **bold**; classifications in SMALL CAPS; ♣ Canadian drug name; ℗ Prototype drug

- Avoid contact with eyes. Severe irritation and persisting corneal changes may occur. Flush immediately and thoroughly with copious amounts of water. Wash both eyes.

STORAGE
Store solution in the refrigerator.

ADMINISTRATION
- Ensure patency prior to injection or infusion, as extravasation may cause tissue sloughing.
- **Direct IV Injection:** Inject into tubing of running infusion over a 1 min period.
- Stop injection promptly if extravasation occurs. Use applications of moderate heat and local injection of hyaluronidase to help disperse extravasated drug. Restart infusion in another vein. Observe injection site for sloughing.

INCOMPATIBILITIES Solution/additive: Furosemide. Y-site: Cefepime, furosemide, idarubicin, lansoprazole, sodium bicarbonate.

ACTION & *THERAPEUTIC EFFECT* Cell cycle–specific vinca alkaloid (obtained from periwinkle plant *Vinca rosea*); analog of vinblastine. Arrests mitosis at metaphase by inhibition of mitotic spindle function, thereby inhibiting cell division. *Induction of metaphase arrest in 50% of tumor cells results in inhibition of cell proliferation.*

CONTRAINDICATIONS Obstructive jaundice; men and women of childbearing potential; patients with demyelinating form of Charcot-Marie-Tooth syndrome; active infection; adynamic ileus; radiation of the liver; pregnancy (category D), lactation.
CAUTIOUS USE Leukopenia; preexisting neuromuscular or neurologic disease; hypertension; hepatic or biliary tract disease; elderly; patients receiving drugs with neurotoxic potential.

ADVERSE EFFECTS (≥1%) **CNS:** *Peripheral neuropathy,* neuritic pain, *paresthesias, especially of hands and feet;* foot and hand drop, sensory loss, athetosis, ataxia, loss of deep tendon reflexes, muscle atrophy, dysphagia, weakness in larynx and extrinsic eye muscles, ptosis, diplopia, mental depression. **Special Senses:** Optic atrophy with blindness; transient cortical blindness, ptosis, diplopia, photophobia. **GI:** Stomatitis, pharyngitis, anorexia, nausea, vomiting, diarrhea, abdominal cramps, *severe constipation (upper-colon impaction), paralytic ileus* (especially in children), rectal bleeding; hepatotoxicity. **Urogenital:** Urinary retention, polyuria, dysuria, SIADH (high urinary sodium excretion, hyponatremia, dehydration, hypotension); uric acid nephropathy. **Skin:** Urticaria, rash, *alopecia,* cellulitis and phlebitis following extravasation (at injection site). **Body as a Whole:** Convulsions with hypertension, malaise, fever, headache, pain in parotid gland area, weight loss. **Metabolic:** Hyperuricemia, hyperkalemia. **CV:** Hypertension, hypotension. **Respiratory:** Bronchospasm.

DRUG INTERACTIONS Mitomycin may cause acute shortness of breath and severe bronchospasm; may decrease **digoxin, phenytoin** levels.

V

PHARMACOKINETICS Distribution: Concentrates in liver, platelets, and leukocytes; poor penetration of blood–brain barrier. **Metabolism:** Partially in liver (CYP 3A4). **Elimination:** Primarily in feces. **Half-Life:** 10–155 h.

NURSING IMPLICATIONS

Assessment & Drug Effects

- Monitor I&O ratio and pattern, BP, and temperature daily.
- Monitor for and report steady weight gain.
- Lab tests: Baseline and periodic serum electrolytes and CBC with differential.
- Assess for hand muscular weakness, and check deep tendon reflexes (depression of Achilles reflex is the earliest sign of neuropathy). Also observe for and report promptly: Mental depression, ptosis, double vision, hoarseness, paresthesias, neuritic pain, and motor difficulties.
- Be aware that neuromuscular adverse effects, most apt to appear in the patient with preexisting neuromuscular disease, usually disappear after 6 wk of treatment. Children are especially susceptible to neuromuscular adverse effects.
- Protect from infection or injury during leukopenic days. Leukopenia occurs in a significant number of patients; leukocyte count in children usually reaches nadir on fourth day and begins to rise on fifth day after drug administration.
- Avoid use of rectal thermometer to prevent injury to rectal mucosa.
- Monitor ability to ambulate and provide support as needed.
- Start a prophylactic regimen against constipation and paralytic ileus at beginning of treatment (paralytic ileus is most likely to occur in young children).

Patient & Family Education

- Notify prescriber promptly of stomach, bone, or joint pain, and swelling of lower legs and ankles.
- Report changes in bowel habit as soon as manifested.
- Report a steady gain or sudden weight change to prescriber.

VINORELBINE TARTRATE

(vin-o-relbeen)

Navelbine

Classification(s): ANTINEOPLASTIC AGENT; MITOTIC INHIBITOR, VINCA ALKALOID

Therapeutic: ANTINEOPLASTIC

Prototype: Vincristine

Pregnancy Category: D

USES Non–small-cell lung cancer.

UNLABELED USES Breast cancer, ovarian cancer, Hodgkin's disease.

INDICATION & DOSAGE

Non–Small-Cell Lung Cancer

Adult: 25–30 mg/m^2 weekly

Hepatic Impairment Dosage Adjustment

Bilirubin 2.1-3 mg/dL: Use 50% of dose; *bilirubin over 3 mg/dL:* Use 25% of dose

Toxicity Dosage Adjustment

Toxicity	Dose Change
ANC 1000–1499	Give 50% of dose
ANC less than 1000	Hold dose; if ANC remains suppressed for 3 wk discontinue drug
Grade 2 neurotoxicity	Discontinue drug
Fever and/or Sepsis or Pt Had Previous Low ANC Requiring a Dose to be Held	
Current ANC at least 15000	Give 75% of dose
Current ANC 1000–1499	Give 37.5% of dose

SOLUTION PREPARATION

- Use caution to prevent contact with skin, mucous membranes, or eyes during preparation.
- *Direct IV Injection:* Dilute each 10 mg in a syringe with either 2 or 5 mL of D5W or NS to yield 3 mg/mL or 1.5 mg/L, respectively.
- *IV Infusion:* Dilute the required dose in an IV bag with D5W, NS, or LR to a final concentration of 0.5–2 mg/mL (example: 10 mg diluted in 19 mL yields 0.5 mg/mL).

STORAGE

Store unopened at 2°–8° C (36°–46° F). Store diluted solutions for up to 24 h refrigerated or at room temperature.

ADMINISTRATION

- Ensure patency prior to injection or infusion, as extravasation may cause tissue sloughing.
- **Direct IV Injection/Infusion:** Give over 6–10 min into the side port closest to an IV bag with free-flowing IV solution; follow by flushing with at least 75–125 mL of IV solution over 10 min.
- Take every precaution to avoid extravasation. If suspected, discontinue IV immediately and begin in a different site.

V

INCOMPATIBILITIES Solution/additive: Acyclovir, aminophylline, amphotericin B, ampicillin, cefazolin, cefoperazone, ceforanide, cefotaxime, cefotetan, ceftazidime, ceftriaxone, cefuroxime, fluorouracil, furosemide, ganciclovir, methylprednisolone, mitomycin, piperacillin, sodium bicarbonate, thiotepa, trimethoprim–sulfamethoxazole. Y-site: Acyclovir, allopurinol, aminophylline, amphotericin B, amphotericin B cholesteryl complex, ampicillin, cefazolin, cefoperazone, cefotetan, ceftriaxone, cefuroxime, fluorouracil, furosemide, ganciclovir, heparin, lansoprazole, methylpredniso-

Common adverse effects in *italic*, life-threatening effects <u>underlined</u>: generic names in **bold**; classifications in SMALL CAPS; ♣ Canadian drug name; ⊙ Prototype drug

657

lone, mitomycin, piperacillin, sodium bicarbonate, thiotepa, tri-methoprim–sulfamethoxazole.

ACTION & *THERAPEUTIC EFFECT* A semisynthetic vinca alkaloid with antineoplastic activity. Inhibits polymerization of tubules into microtubules, which disrupts mitotic spindle formation. *Arrests mitosis at metaphase, thereby inhibiting cell division in cancer cells.*

CONTRAINDICATIONS Hypersensitivity to vinorelbine; infection; severe bone marrow suppression; pregnancy (category D), lactation.

CAUTIOUS USE Hypersensitivity to vincristine or vinblastine; leukopenia, or other indicator(s) of bone marrow suppression; chickenpox or herpes zoster infection; pulmonary disease; hepatic insufficiency; preexisting neurologic or neuromuscular disorders. Safety and efficacy in children are not established.

ADVERSE EFFECTS (≥1%) **CNS:** *Decreased deep tendon reflexes, paresthesia, fatigue, asthenia, peripheral neuropathy,* myalgia, jaw pain. **Hematologic:** *Anemia, <u>neutropenia, granulocytopenia</u>,* thrombocytopenia. **GI:** Paralytic ileus, *constipation, nausea, vomiting, diarrhea,* stomatitis, mucositis, hepatotoxicity (elevated LFT). **Body as a Whole:** *Pain on injection,* venous pain, thrombophlebitis, *alopecia,* myalgia, muscle weakness.

DRUG INTERACTIONS Increased severity of granulocytopenia in combination with **cisplatin;** increased risk of acute pulmonary reactions in combination with **mitomycin; paclitaxel** may increase neuropathy.

PHARMACOKINETICS Distribution: 60–80% bound to plasma proteins (including platelets and lymphocytes); sequestered in tissues, especially lung, spleen, liver, and kidney, and released slowly. **Metabolism:** In liver (CYP 3A4). **Elimination:** Primarily in bile and feces (50%), 10% excreted in urine. **Half-Life:** 42–45 h.

NURSING IMPLICATIONS

Assessment & Drug Effects

- Withhold drug and notify prescriber if the granulocyte count is below 1000 cells/mm^3.
- Monitor for neurologic dysfunction including paresthesia, decreased deep tendon reflexes, weakness, constipation, and paralytic ileus.
- Lab tests: Baseline and periodic CBC with differential; periodic LFTs, kidney function tests, and serum electrolytes.
- Monitor for S&S of infection, especially during period of granulocyte nadir 7–10 days after dosing.

Patient & Family Education

- Be aware of potential and inevitable adverse effects.
- Women should use reliable forms of contraception to prevent pregnancy.
- Report promptly distressing adverse effects, especially symptoms of leukopenia (e.g., chills, fever, cough) and peripheral neuropathy (e.g., pain, numbness, tingling in extremities).
- Report changes in bowel habits as soon as manifested.

VORICONAZOLE

(vor-i-cona-zole)

Vfend

Classification(s): ANTIBIOTIC; ANTIFUNGAL, AZOLE
Therapeutic: ANTIFUNGAL
Prototype: Fluconazole
Pregnancy Category: D

USES Treatment of invasive *Aspergillosis,* esophageal candidiasis, candidemia in nonneutropenic patients and disseminated skin infections, and abdomen, kidney, bladder wall, and wound infections due to *Candida.*

INDICATION & DOSAGE

Aspergillosis

Adult: 6 mg/kg q12h day 1, then 3–4 mg/kg q12h; treatment continues until 7–14 days after symptom resolution

Dose Adjustment for Concomitant Fosphenytoin or Phenytoin

Adult: 6 mg/kg q12h day 1, then 5 mg/kg q12h

Renal Impairment Dosage Adjustment

CrCl less than 50 mL/min: Switch to PO therapy after loading dose

Hepatic Impairment Dosage Adjustment

Child-Pugh class A or B: Reduce maintenance dose by 50%; *Child-Pugh class C:* Avoid use of drug

SOLUTION PREPARATION

- *Vial Reconstitution:* Use a 20 mL syringe to add **exactly 19 mL** of sterile water for injection to each 200 mg vial yield 10 mg/mL. Discard vial if a vacuum does not pull the diluent into vial. Shake until completely dissolved. **Must be** further diluted for infusion.
- *Further Dilution of Reconstituted Solution:* Calculate the required dose of voriconazole based on patient's weight. From a compatible IV solution bag (e.g., NS, D5W, D5NS, D5/1/2NS, LR), withdraw and discard a volume of IV solution equal to the required dose. Inject the calculated dose of voriconazole into the IV bag. The IV solution should have a final voriconazole concentration of 0.5–5 mg/mL. Infuse immediately.
  - Example: A 70 kg patient requires a 420 mg dose (70 kg × 6 mg/kg). A 420 mg dose requires 42 mL of reconstituted solution. Remove 42 mL from a 100 mL bag of IV solution and add the required dose to yield 420 mg in 100 mL or 4.2 mg/mL.

V

STORAGE

Store unopened at 15°–30° C (59°–86° F). Discard unused voriconazole.

Common adverse effects in *italic*, life-threatening effects underlined; generic names in **bold**; classifications in SMALL CAPS; ♣ Canadian drug name; ☻ Prototype drug

659

ADMINISTRATION

Intermittent Infusion: Infuse over 1–2 h at a maximum rate of 3 mg/kg per h. **DO NOT** give a bolus dose.

INCOMPATIBILITIES Solution/additive: Do not dilute with **sodium bicarbonate;** do not mix with any other drugs. **Y-site:** Do not infuse with other drugs.

ACTION & *THERAPEUTIC EFFECT* Inhibits fungal cytochrome P-450 enzymes used for an essential step in fungal ergosterol biosynthesis. The subsequent loss of ergosterol in the fungal cell wall is thought to be responsible for the antifungal activity of voriconazole. *Voriconazole is active against* Aspergillus *and* Candida.

CONTRAINDICATIONS Known hypersensitivity to voriconazole; voriconazole should be avoided in moderate or severe renal impairment (CrCl less than 50 mL/min); severe hepatic impairment; children less than 2 y; history of galactose intolerance; Lapp lactase deficiency or glucose–galactose malabsorption; concurrent use of sirolimus; coadministration of the CYP3A4 substrates pimozide or quinidine; concurrent use of rifampin, rifabutin, carbamazepine and long-acting barbiturates, ergot alkaloids; sunlight (UV) exposure; pregnancy (category D), lactation.
CAUTIOUS USE Mild to moderate hepatic cirrhosis, hepatitis, hepatic disease; renal disease, mild renal impairment; ocular disease; hypersensitivity to other azole antifungal agents such as fluconazole; children greater than 2 y and less than 12 y.

ADVERSE EFFECTS (≥1%) **Body as a Whole:** Peripheral edema, fever, chills. **CNS:** Headache, hallucinations, dizziness. **CV:** Tachycardia, hypotension, hypertension, vasodilation. **GI:** Nausea, vomiting, abdominal pain, abnormal LFTs, diarrhea, cholestatic jaundice, dry mouth. **Metabolic:** Increased alkaline phosphatase, AST, ALT, hypokalemia, hypomagnesemia. **Skin:** Rash, pruritus. **Special Senses:** *Abnormal vision (enhanced brightness, blurred vision, or color vision changes),* photophobia.

DRUG INTERACTIONS Due to significant increased toxicity or decreased activity, the following drugs are CONTRAINDICATED with voriconazole: BARBITURATES, **carbamazepine, efavirenz,** ERGOT ALKALOIDS, **pimozide, quinidine, rifabutin, sirolimus; fosphenytoin, phenytoin, rifampin, ritonavir** may significantly decrease voriconazole levels. PROTEASE INHIBITORS (except **indinavir**) may increase voriconazole toxicity; voriconazole may increase the toxicity of BENZODIAZEPINES, **cyclosporine,** PROTEASE INHIBITORS (except **indinavir**), NONNUCLEOSIDE REVERSE TRANSCRIPTASE INHIBITORS, **omeprazole, tacrolimus, vinblastine, vincristine, warfarin;** NONNUCLEOSIDE REVERSE TRANSCRIPTASE INHIBITORS may increase or decrease voriconazole levels.

PHARMACOKINETICS Absorption: Has a nonlinear pharmacokinetic profile; a small change in dose may cause a large change in serum levels. Steady state not achieved until day 5–6 if no loading dose is given. **Peak:** 1–2 h. **Metabolism:** In liver by (and is an inhibitor of) CYP3A4, 2C9 and 2C19. **Elimination:** Primarily in urine. **Half-Life:** 6 h–6 days, depending on dose.

NURSING IMPLICATIONS

Assessment & Drug Effects

- Monitor visual acuity, visual field, and color perception if treatment continues beyond 28 days.
- Withhold drug and notify prescriber if skin rash develops.
- Monitor cardiovascular status, especially with preexisting CV disease.
- Lab tests: Baseline and periodic LFTs including bilirubin, kidney function tests, especially serum creatinine; periodic CBC with platelet count, Hct & Hgb, serum electrolytes, alkaline phosphatase, blood glucose, and lipid profile.
- Patients who develop abnormal liver function tests during therapy should be monitored for the development of more severe hepatic injury.
- Concurrent drugs: Monitor PT/INR closely with warfarin, as dose adjustments of warfarin may be needed. Monitor frequently blood glucose levels with sulfonylurea drugs, as reduction in the sulfonylurea dosage may be needed. Monitor for and report any of the following: S&S of rhabdomyolysis in patients receiving a statin drug; prolonged sedation in patients receiving a benzodiazepine; S&S of heart block, bradycardia, or CHF in patients receiving a calcium channel blocker.

Patient & Family Education

- Use reliable means of birth control to prevent pregnancy. If you suspect you are pregnant, contact prescriber immediately.
- Do not drive at night while taking voriconazole, as the drug may cause blurred vision and photophobia.
- Do not drive or engage in other potentially hazardous activities until reaction to drug is known.
- Avoid strong, direct sunlight while taking voriconazole.

WARFARIN SODIUM

(warfar-in)

Coumadin Sodium, Warfilone ✦

Classification(s): ANTICOAGULANT

Therapeutic: ANTICOAGULANT

Pregnancy Category: X

W

USES Prophylaxis and treatment of deep vein thrombosis and its extension, pulmonary embolism; treatment of atrial fibrillation with embolization. Also used as adjunct in treatment of coronary occlusion, cerebral transient ischemic attacks (TIAs), and as a prophylactic in patients with prosthetic cardiac valves. Used extensively as rodenticide.

INDICATION & DOSAGE

Anticoagulant

Adult: Usual dose 2–10 mg daily with dose adjusted to maintain target INR

Oral to IV Conversion: Use same dose

Common adverse effects in *italic*, life-threatening effects <u>underlined</u>: generic names in **bold**; classifications in SMALL CAPS; ✦ Canadian drug name; ⊙ Prototype drug

661

SOLUTION PREPARATION
Vial Reconstitution: Add 2.7 mL of sterile water for injection to the 5 mg vial.

STORAGE
Store unopened at 5°–30° C (59°–86° F). Protect from light Reconstituted solution may be stored for 4 h at room temperature.

ADMINISTRATION
Direct IV Injection: Give required dose over 1–2 min.

INCOMPATIBILITIES Solution/additive: Ammonium chloride, 5% dextrose, lactated Ringer's, atropine, calcium chloride, calcium gluconate, chloramphenicol, chlorothiazide, chlortetracycline, erythromycin, methicillin, nitrofurantoin, oxacillin, oxytetracycline, penicillin, pentobarbital, phenobarbital, promethazine, sodium bicarbonate, succinyl chloride, vitamin B with C. **Y-site:** Aminophylline, ammonium chloride, bretylium, ceftazidime, cephalothin, cimetidine, ciprofloxacin, dobutamine, esmolol, gentamicin, labetalol, metronidazole, promazine, lactated Ringer's, vancomycin.

ACTION & *THERAPEUTIC EFFECT* Indirectly interferes with blood clotting by depressing hepatic synthesis of vitamin K–dependent coagulation factors: II, VII, IX, and X. *Deters further extension of existing thrombi and prevents new clots from forming. Has no effect on already synthesized circulating coagulation factors or on circulating thrombi.*

CONTRAINDICATIONS Hemorrhagic tendencies, vitamin C or K deficiency, hemophilia, coagulation factor deficiencies, dyscrasias; active bleeding; open wounds, active peptic ulcer; visceral carcinoma; esophageal varices; malabsorption syndrome; hypertension (diastolic BP greater than 110 mm Hg), cerebral vascular disease; heparin-induced thrombocytopenia (HIT); pericarditis with acute MI; severe hepatic or renal disease; continuous tube drainage of any orifice; subacute bacterial endocarditis; recent surgery of brain, spinal cord, or eye; regional or lumbar block anesthesia; threatened abortion; unreliable patients; pregnancy (category X), lactation.

CAUTIOUS USE Alcoholism; allergic disorders; during menstruation; older adults; senility; psychosis; debilitated patients. Endogenous factors that may increase prothrombin time response (enhance anticoagulant effect): Carcinoma, CHF, collagen diseases, hepatic and renal insufficiency, diarrhea, fever, pancreatic disorders, malnutrition, vitamin K deficiency. Endogenous factors that may decrease prothrombin time response (decrease anticoagulant response): Edema, hypothyroidism, hyperlipidemia, hypercholesterolemia, chronic alcoholism, hereditary resistance to coumarin therapy.

ADVERSE EFFECTS (≥1%) **Body as a Whole:** Major or minor hemorrhage from any tissue or organ; hypersensitivity (dermatitis, urticaria, pruritus, fever). **GI:** Anorexia, nausea, vomiting, abdominal cramps, diarrhea, steatorrhea, stomatitis. **Other:** Increased serum transaminase levels, hepatitis, jaundice, burning sensation of feet, transient hair loss. **Overdosage:** Internal or external bleeding, paralytic ileus; skin necrosis of toes (purple toes syndrome), tip of nose, buttocks, thighs, calves, female breast, abdomen, and other fat-rich areas.

W

Common adverse effects in *italic*, life-threatening effects <u>underlined</u>: generic names in **bold**; classifications in SMALL CAPS; ♣ Canadian drug name; ● Prototype drug

DIAGNOSTIC TEST INTERFERENCE Warfarin (coumarins) may cause alkaline urine to be red-orange; may enhance **uric acid** excretion, cause elevation of **serum transaminases,** and may increase **lactic dehydrogenase** activity.

DRUG INTERACTIONS In addition to the following drugs, many other drugs have been reported to alter the expected response to warfarin. The addition or withdrawal of any drug to an established drug regimen should be made cautiously, with more frequent INR determinations than usual and with careful observation of the patient and dose adjustment as indicated. The following may enhance the anticoagulant effects of warfarin: **Acetohexamide, acetaminophen,** ALKYLATING AGENTS, **allopurinol,** AMINOGLYCOSIDES, **aminosalicylic acid, amiodarone,** ANABOLIC STEROIDS, ANTIBIOTICS (ORAL), ANTIMETABOLITES, ANTIPLATELET DRUGS, **aspirin, asparaginase, capecitabine, celecoxib, chloramphenicol, chlorpropamide, chymotrypsin, cimetidine, clofibrate, co-trimoxazole, danazol, dextran, dextrothyroxine, diazoxide, disulfiram, erythromycin, ethacrynic acid, fluconazole, glucagons, guanethidine,** HEPATOTOXIC DRUGS, **influenza vaccine, isoniazid, itraconazole, ketoconazole,** MAO INHIBITORS, **meclofenamate, mefenamic acid, methyldopa, methylphenidate, metronidazole, miconazole, mineral oil, nalidixic acid, neomycin (oral),** NONSTEROIDAL ANTI-INFLAMMATORY DRUGS, **oxandrolone, plicamycin,** POTASSIUM PRODUCTS, **propoxyphene, propylthiouracil, quinidine, quinine, rofecoxib, salicylates, streptokinase, sulindac,** SULFONAMIDES, SULFONYLUREAS, TETRACYCLINES, THIAZIDES, THYROID DRUGS, **tolbutamide, tricyclic antidepressants, urokinase, vitamin E, zileuton.** The following may increase or decrease the anticoagulant effects of warfarin: **Alcohol** (acute intoxication may increase, chronic alcoholism may decrease effects), **chloral hydrate,** DIURETICS. The following may decrease the anticoagulant effects of warfarin: **Barbiturates, carbamazepine, cholestyramine,** CORTICOSTEROIDS, **corticotropin, ethchlorvynol, glutethimide, griseofulvin,** LAXATIVES, **mercaptopurine,** ORAL CONTRACEPTIVES, **rifampin, spironolactone, vitamin C, vitamin K.**

PHARMACOKINETICS Onset: 2–7 days. **Peak:** 0.5–3 days. **Distribution:** 97% protein bound; crosses placenta. **Metabolism:** In liver (CYP 2C9). **Elimination:** In urine and bile. **Half-Life:** 0.5–3 days.

NURSING IMPLICATIONS

Assessment & Drug Effects

- Prior to initiating therapy: Baseline PT/INR.
- Obtain a CAREFUL medication history prior to start of therapy and whenever altered responses to therapy require interpretation; this is extremely IMPORTANT, since many drugs interfere with the activity of anticoagulant drugs (see **DRUG INTERACTIONS**).
- Lab tests: For maintenance dosage, PT/INR determinations at 1–4-wk intervals depending on patient's response; periodic urinalyses, LFTs. Blood samples should be drawn at 12–18 h after last dose (optimum).
- Note: Patients at greatest risk of hemorrhage include those whose PT/INR are difficult to regulate, who have an aortic valve prosthesis, who are re-

W

ceiving long-term anticoagulant therapy, and older adult and debilitated patients.

Patient & Family Education

- Understand that bleeding can occur even though PT/INR are within therapeutic range. Report promptly if bleeding or signs of bleeding appear: Blood in urine, bright red or black tarry stools, vomiting of blood, bleeding with tooth brushing, blue or purple spots on skin or mucous membrane, round pinpoint purplish red spots (often occur in ankle areas), nosebleed, bloody sputum; chest pain; abdominal or lumbar pain or swelling, profuse menstrual bleeding, pelvic pain; severe or continuous headache, faintness or dizziness; prolonged oozing from any minor injury (e.g., nicks from shaving).
- Report an unusual increase in menstrual bleeding (slightly increased or prolonged). Note: PT/INR are checked at least monthly in menstruating women.
- Use reliable means of birth control to prevent pregnancy. If you suspect you are pregnant, contact prescriber immediately.

ZIDOVUDINE (AZIDOTHYMIDINE, AZT)

(zye-doe'vyoo-deen)

Retrovir

Classification(s): ANTIVIRAL
Therapeutic: ANTIVIRAL
Pregnancy Category: C

USES Patients who are HIV positive and have a CD4 count less than or equal to 500/mm³, asymptomatic HIV infection, early and late symptomatic HIV disease, prevention of perinatal transfer of HIV during pregnancy.
UNLABELED USES Pediatric patients.

INDICATION & DOSAGE

Symptomatic HIV Infection
Adult: 1–2 mg/kg q4h (1200 mg/day)

Prevention of Maternal–Fetal Transmission
Neonate (over 34 weeks gestation): 1.5 mg/kg q6h × 6 weeks, beginning 8–12 h after birth
Maternal: During labor 2 mg/kg/h loading dose then 1 mg/kg/h until clamping of umbilical cord

Renal Impairment Dosage Adjustment
CrCl less than 15 mL/min: Reduce dose by 50%

Toxicity Dosage Adjustment
Hemoglobin Falls Below 7.5 g/dL or Falls 25% from Baseline: Interrupt therapy

W

Common adverse effects in *italic*, life-threatening effects <u>underlined</u>: generic names in **bold**; classifications in SMALL CAPS; ♣ Canadian drug name; ❂ Prototype drug

ANC Falls Below 750 Cells/mm³ or Decreases 50% from Baseline: Interrupt therapy

SOLUTION PREPARATION
Withdraw required dose from vial and dilute with D5W to a concentration not to exceed 4 mg/mL.

STORAGE
Store unopened at 15°–25° C (59°–77° F) and protect from light. Store diluted solutions refrigerated for 24 h.

ADMINISTRATION
HIV Infection
- **Intermittent Infusion:** Give calculated dose at a constant rate over 60 min; avoid rapid infusion.

Prevention of Maternal–Fetal Transmission
- *Mother:* Give loading dose over 1 h then continuous infusion at 1 mg/kg/h.
- *Neonate:* Give intermittent infusion at a constant rate over 30 min.

INCOMPATIBILITIES Solution/additive: Meropenem. **Y-site:** Lansoprazole, meropenem.

ACTION & *THERAPEUTIC EFFECT* Appears to act by being incorporated into growing DNA chains by viral reverse transcriptase, thereby terminating viral replication. *Zidovudine has antiviral action against HIV (human immunodeficiency virus), the causative agent of AIDS (acquired immune deficiency syndrome), LAV (lymphadenopathy-associated virus), and ARV (AIDS-associated retrovirus).*

CONTRAINDICATIONS Life-threatening allergic reactions to any of the components of the drug; lactic acidosis; pregnancy (category C), lactation.
CAUTIOUS USE Impaired renal or hepatic function; alcoholism; anemia; chemotherapy; radiation therapy; bone marrow depression.

ADVERSE EFFECTS (≥1%) **Body as a Whole:** *Fever,* dyspnea, *malaise,* weakness, *myalgia,* myopathy. **CNS:** *Headache,* insomnia, dizziness, paresthesias, mild confusion, anxiety, restlessness, agitation. **GI:** *Nausea,* diarrhea, *vomiting, anorexia,* GI pain. **Hematologic:** <u>Bone marrow depression, granulocytopenia, anemia</u>. **Respiratory:** *Coughing, wheezing.* **Skin:** *Rash,* pruritus, diaphoresis.

DRUG INTERACTIONS **Acetaminophen, ganciclovir, interferon-alfa** may enhance bone marrow suppression; **atovaquone, amphotericin B, aspirin, dapsone, doxorubicin, fluconazole, flucytosine, indomethacin, interferon alfa, methadone, pentamidine, vincristine, valproic acid** may increase risk of AZT toxicity; **probenecid** will decrease AZT elimination, resulting in increased serum levels and thus toxicity; **nelfinavir, rifampin, ritonavir** may decrease AZT concentrations; other ANTIRETROVIRAL AGENTS may cause lactic acidosis and severe hepatomegaly with steatosis; **stavudine, doxorubicin** may antagonize AZT effects.

Z

Common adverse effects in *italic*, life-threatening effects <u>underlined</u>: generic names in **bold**; classifications in SMALL CAPS; ♣ Canadian drug name; ❂ Prototype drug

665

PHARMACOKINETICS Distribution: Crosses blood–brain barrier and placenta; passes into breast milk. **Metabolism:** In liver. **Elimination:** 63–95% in urine. **Half-Life:** 0.5–3 h.

NURSING IMPLICATIONS

Assessment & Drug Effects

- Myelosuppression results in anemia, which commonly occurs after 4–6 wk of therapy, and granulocytopenia in 6–8 wk. Frequently, both respond to dosage adjustment. Significant anemia (Hgb less than 7.5 g/dL or reduction greater than 25% of baseline value), or granulocyte count less than 750/mm^3 (or reduction greater than 50% of baseline) may require treatment and adjustment in therapy.
- Lab tests: Baseline and frequent (at least q2wk) blood counts, CD4 (T$_4$) lymphocyte count, Hgb, and granulocyte count to detect hematologic toxicity.
- Monitor for common adverse effects, especially severe headache, nausea, insomnia, and myalgia.

Patient & Family Education

- Understand that this drug is not a cure for HIV infection; you will continue to be at risk for opportunistic infections.
- Drug does not reduce the risk of transmission of HIV infection through body fluids.

ZOLEDRONIC ACID

(zo-le-dronic)

Zometa, Reclast

Classification(s): BISPHOSPHONATE; REGULATOR, BONE METABOLISM
Therapeutic: BONE RESORPTION INHIBITOR; ANTIHYPERCALCEMIC
Prototype: Pamidronate disodium
Pregnancy Category: D

USES Treatment of hypercalcemia of malignancy, multiple myeloma, and bony metastases from solid tumors; Paget's disease.

INDICATION & DOSAGE

Hypercalcemia of Malignancy

Adult: 4 mg, may consider retreatment if serum calcium has not returned to normal; may repeat after 7 days

Multiple Myeloma and Bony Metastases from Solid Tumors

Adult: 4 mg q3–4 wk

Paget's Disease

Adult: 5 mg

Common adverse effects in *italic*, life-threatening effects <u>underlined</u>: generic names in **bold**; classifications in SMALL CAPS; ◆ Canadian drug name; ◑ Prototype drug

Osteoporosis Treatment

Adult: 5 mg annually

Renal Impairment Dosage Adjustment (use in hypercalcemia)

CrCl (mL/min)	Dosage
50–60	3.5 mg
40–49	3.3 mg
30–39	3 mg
Less than 30	Do not use

SOLUTION PREPARATION

Injection Concentrate: Withdraw required dose from the 4 mg/5 mL vial and dilute in 100 mL of D5W or NS. Do not use lactated Ringer's solution. If not used immediately, refrigerate.

STORAGE

Store at 2°–8° C (36°–46° F) following dilution. **Must be** completely infused within 24 h of dilution.

ADMINISTRATION

- **IV Infusion:** Infuse a single dose over NO LESS than 15 min.
- Do not administer to anyone who is dehydrated or suspected of being dehydrated.

INCOMPATIBILITIES Solution/additive and Y-site: Do not mix or infuse with **calcium-containing solutions** (e.g., **lactated Ringer's**).

ACTION & *THERAPEUTIC EFFECT* Zoledronic acid inhibits bone resorption by inhibiting osteoclastic activity produced by bone tumors and inducing osteoclast apoptosis. Zoledronic acid inhibits various stimulatory factors of osteoclastic activity by bone tumors. *It inhibits osteoclastic activity and skeletal calcium release induced by various stimulatory factors released by bone tumors.*

CONTRAINDICATIONS Hypersensitivity to zoledronic acid or other bisphosphonates; preexisting hypocalcemia; serum creatinine of 0.5 mg/dL; pregnancy (category D), lactation.

CAUTIOUS USE Renal, and/or hepatic, impairment; renal failure; dental work; concurrent administration of aminoglycosides or loop diuretics; multiple myeloma; older adults. Safety and effectiveness of zoledronic acid in children have not been established.

ADVERSE EFFECTS (≥1%) **Body as a Whole:** *Fever,* flu-like syndrome, redness and swelling at injection site, asthenia, chest pain, leg edema, mucositis, rigors. **CNS:** *Insomnia, anxiety, confusion, agitation,* headache, somnolence. **CV:** *Hypotension.* **GI:** *Nausea, vomiting, constipation, abdominal pain, anorexia,* dysphagia. **Hematologic:** *Anemia,* granulocytopenia, thrombocytopenia, <u>pancytopenia</u>. **Metabolic:** *Hypophosphatemia, hypokalemia, hypomagnesemia,* hypocalcemia, dehydration. **Musculoskeletal:** Skeletal

Z

Common adverse effects in *italic*, life-threatening effects <u>underlined</u>: generic names in **bold**; classifications in SMALL CAPS; ♣ Canadian drug name; ◐ Prototype drug

667

pain, arthralgias, osteonecrosis of the jaw in cancer patients. **Respiratory:** *Dyspnea, cough,* pleural effusion. **Skin:** Alopecia, dermatitis. **Urogenital:** Renal deterioration.

DRUG INTERACTIONS LOOP DIURETICS may increase risk of hypocalcemia; **thalidomide** and other NEPHROTOXIC DRUGS may increase risk of renal toxicity.

PHARMACOKINETICS Onset: 4–10 days. **Duration:** 3–4 wk. **Metabolism:** Not metabolized. **Elimination:** In urine. **Half-Life:** 146 h.

NURSING IMPLICATIONS

Assessment & Drug Effects

* Lab tests: Baseline and periodic kidney function tests; periodic ionized calcium or corrected serum calcium (CSC) levels, serum phosphate and magnesium, electrolytes, CBC with differential, Hct and Hgb.
* Notify prescriber immediately of deteriorating renal function as indicated by rising serum creatinine levels over baseline value.
* Withhold zoledronic acid if serum creatinine is not within 10% of the baseline value. Consult prescriber.
* Monitor closely patient's hydration status. Note that loop diuretics should be used with caution due to the risk of hypocalcemia.

Patient & Family Education

* Maintain adequate daily fluid intake. Consult prescriber for guidelines.
* Use reliable means of birth control to prevent pregnancy. If you suspect you are pregnant, contact prescriber immediately.
* Report unexplained weakness, tiredness, irritation, muscle pain, insomnia, or flu-like symptoms.

Z

Common adverse effects in *italic*, life-threatening effects <u>underlined</u>: generic names in **bold**; classifications in SMALL CAPS; ♣ Canadian drug name; ◐ Prototype drug

Appendixes

Schedule I

High potential for abuse and of no currently accepted medical use. Examples: heroin, LSD, marijuana, mescaline, peyote. Not obtainable by prescription but may be legally procured for research, study, or instructional use.

Schedule II

High abuse potential and high liability for severe psychological or physical dependence. Prescription required and cannot be renewed.[a] Includes opium derivatives, other opioids, and short-acting barbiturates. Examples: amphetamine, cocaine, meperidine, morphine, secobarbital.

Schedule III

Potential for abuse is less than that for drugs in Schedules I and II. Moderate to low physical dependence and high psychological dependence. Includes certain stimulants and depressants not included in the above schedules and preparations containing limited quantities of certain opioids. Examples: acetaminophen with codeine, anabolic steroids, paregoric, phendimetrazine. Prescription required.[b]

Schedule IV

Lower potential for abuse than Schedule III drugs. Examples: certain psychotropics (tranquilizers), chlordiazepoxide, diazepam, meprobamate, phenobarbital, zolpidem. Prescription required.[a]

Schedule V

Abuse potential less than that for Schedule IV drugs. Preparations contain limited quantities of certain narcotic drugs; generally intended for antitussive and antidiarrheal purposes and may be distributed without a prescription provided that:

1. Such distribution is made only by a pharmacist.
2. Not more than 240 mL or not more than 48 solid dosage units of any substance containing opium, nor more than 120 mL or not more than 24 solid dosage units of any other controlled substance may be distributed at retail to the same purchaser in any given 48-hour period without a valid prescription order.
3. The purchaser is at least 18 years old.
4. The pharmacist knows the purchaser or requests suitable identification.
5. The pharmacist keeps an official written record of: name and address of purchaser, name and quantity of controlled substance purchased, date of sale, and name/initials of dispensing pharmacist. This record is to be made available for inspection and copying by U.S. officers authorized by the Attorney General.
6. Other federal, state, or local law does not require a prescription order.

Under jurisdiction of the Federal Controlled Substances Act:

[a]Except when dispensed directly by a practitioner, other than a pharmacist, to an ultimate user, no controlled substance in Schedule II may be dispensed without a *written* prescription, except that in emergency situations such drug may be dispensed upon oral prescription and a written prescription must be obtained within the time frame prescribed by law. No prescription for a controlled substance in Schedule II may be refilled.

[b]Refillable up to 5 times within 6 mo, but only if so indicated by prescriber.

◆ APPENDIX B FDA PREGNANCY CATEGORIES

The FDA requires that all prescription drugs absorbed systemically or known to be potentially harmful to the fetus be classified according to one of five pregnancy categories (A, B, C, D, X). The identifying letter signifies the level of risk to the fetus and is to appear in the precautions section of the package insert. The categories described by the FDA are as follows:

Category A

Controlled studies in women fail to demonstrate a risk to the fetus in the first trimester (and there is no evidence of risk in later trimesters), and the possibility of fetal harm appears remote.

Category B

Either animal-reproduction studies have not demonstrated a fetal risk but there are no controlled studies in pregnant women, or animal-reproduction studies have shown an adverse effect (other than a decrease in fertility) that was not confirmed in controlled studies in women in the first trimester (and there is no evidence of a risk in later trimesters).

Category C

Either studies in animals have revealed adverse effects on the fetus (teratogenic or embryocidal effects or other) and there are no controlled studies in women, or studies in women and animals are not available. Drugs should be given only if the potential benefit justifies the potential risk to the fetus.

Category D

There is positive evidence of human fetal risk, but the benefits from use in pregnant women may be acceptable despite the risk (e.g., if the drug is needed in a life-threatening situation or for a serious disease for which safer drugs cannot be used or are ineffective). There will be an appropriate statement in the "warnings" section of the labeling.

Category X

Studies in animals or human beings have demonstrated fetal abnormalities or there is evidence of fetal risk based on human experience, or both, and the risk of the use of the drug in pregnant women clearly outweighs any possible benefit. The drug is contraindicated in women who are or may become pregnant. There will be an appropriate statement in the "contraindications" section of the labeling.

acute dystonia extrapyramidal symptom manifested by abnormal posturing, grimacing, spastic torticollis (neck torsion), and oculogyric (eyeball movement) crisis.

adverse effect unintended, unpredictable, and nontherapeutic response to drug action. Adverse effects occur at doses used therapeutically or for prophylaxis or diagnosis. They generally result from drug toxicity, idiosyncrasies, or hypersensitivity reactions caused by the drug itself or by ingredients added during manufacture (e.g., preservatives, dyes, or vehicles).

afterload resistance that ventricles must work against to eject blood into the aorta during systole.

agranulocytosis sudden drop in leukocyte count; often followed by a severe infection manifested by high fever, chills, prostration, and ulcerations of mucous membrane such as in the mouth, rectum, or vagina.

akathisia extrapyramidal symptom manifested by a compelling need to move or pace, without specific pattern, and an inability to be still.

analeptic restorative medication that enhances excitation of the CNS without affecting inhibitory impulses.

anaphylactoid reaction excessive allergic response manifested by wheezing, chills, generalized pruritic urticaria, diaphoresis, sense of uneasiness, agitation, flushing, palpitations, coughing, difficulty breathing, and cardiovascular collapse.

anticholinergic actions inhibition of parasympathetic response manifested by dry mouth, decreased peristalsis, constipation, blurred vision, and urinary retention.

bioavailability fraction of active drug that reaches its action sites after administration by any route. Following an IV dose, bioavailability is 100%; however, such factors as first-pass effect, enterohepatic cycling, and biotransformation reduce bioavailability of an orally administered drug.

blood dyscrasia pathological condition manifested by fever, sore mouth or throat, unexplained fatigue, easy bruising or bleeding.

cardiotoxicity impairment of cardiac function manifested by one or more of the following: hypotension, arrhythmias, precordial pain, dyspnea, electrocardiogram (ECG) abnormalities, cardiac dilation, congestive failure.

cholinergic response stimulation of the parasympathetic response manifested by lacrimation, diaphoresis, salivation, abdominal cramps, diarrhea, nausea, and vomiting.

Chvostek's sign a sign of tetany seen with hypocalcemia that is demonstrated by an abnormal response to stimulation of facial nerves.

circulatory overload excessive vascular volume manifested by increased central venous pressure (CVP), elevated blood pressure, tachycardia, distended neck veins, peripheral edema, dyspnea, cough, and pulmonary rales.

CNS stimulation excitement of the CNS manifested by hyperactivity, excitement, nervousness, insomnia, and tachycardia.

CNS toxicity impairment of CNS function manifested by ataxia, tremor, incoordination, paresthesias, numbness, impairment of pain or touch sensation, drowsiness, confusion, headache, anxiety, tremors, and behavior changes.

congestive heart failure (CHF) impaired pumping ability of the heart manifested by paroxysmal nocturnal dyspnea, cough, fatigue or dyspnea on exertion, tachycardia, peripheral or pulmonary edema, and weight gain.

Cushing's syndrome fatty swellings in the interscapular area (buffalo hump) and in the facial area (moon face), distension of the abdomen, ecchymoses following even minor trauma, impotence, amenorrhea, high blood pressure, general weakness, loss of muscle mass, osteoporosis, and psychosis.

dehydration decreased intracellular or extracellular fluid manifested by elevated temperature, dry skin and mucous membranes, decreased tissue turgor, sunken eyes, furrowed tongue, low blood pressure, diminished or irregular pulse, muscle or abdominal cramps, thick secretions, hard feces and impaction, scant urinary output, urine specific gravity above 1.030, an elevated hemoglobin.

disulfiram-type reaction Antabuse-type reaction manifested by facial flushing, pounding headache, sweating, slurred speech, abdominal cramps, nausea, vomiting, tachycardia, fever, palpitations, drop in blood pressure, dyspnea, and sense of chest constriction. Symptoms may last up to 24 hours.

enzyme induction stimulation of microsomal enzymes by a drug resulting in its accelerated metabolism and decreased activity. If reactive intermediates are formed, drug-mediated toxicity may be exacerbated.

first-pass effect reduced bioavailability of an orally administered drug due to metabolism in GI epithelial cells and liver or to biliary excretion. Effect may be avoided by use of sublingual tablets or rectal suppositories.

fixed drug eruption drug-induced circumscribed skin lesion that persists or recurs in the same site. Residual pigmentation may remain following drug withdrawal.

half-life ($t_{1/2}$) time required for concentration of a drug in the body to decrease by 50%. Half-life also represents the time necessary to reach steady state or to decline from steady state after a change (i.e., starting or stopping) in the dosing regimen. Half-life may be affected by a disease state and age of the drug user.

heat stroke a life-threatening condition manifested by absence of sweating; red, dry, hot skin; dilated pupils; dyspnea; full bounding pulse; temperature above 40° C (105° F); and mental confusion.

hepatic toxicity impairment of liver function manifested by jaundice, dark urine, pruritus, lightcolored stools, eosinophilia, itchy skin or rash, and persistently high elevations of alanine amino-transferase (ALT) and aspartate aminotransferase (AST).

hyperammonemia elevated level of ammonia or ammonium in the blood manifested by lethargy, decreased appetite, vomiting, asterixis (flapping tremor), weak pulse, irritability, decreased responsiveness, and seizures.

hypercalcemia elevated serum calcium manifested by deep bone and flank pain, renal calculi, anorexia, nausea, vomiting, thirst, constipation, muscle hypotonicity, pathologic fracture, bradycardia, lethargy, and psychosis.

hyperglycemia elevated blood glucose manifested by flushed, dry skin, low blood pressure and elevated pulse, tachypnea, Kussmaul's respirations, polyuria, polydipsia, polyphagia, lethargy, and drowsiness.

hyperkalemia excessive potassium in blood, which may produce lifethreatening cardiac arrhythmias, including bradycardia and heart block, unusual fatigue, weakness or heaviness of limbs, general muscle weakness, muscle cramps, paresthesias, flaccid paralysis of extremities, shortness of breath, nervousness, confusion, diarrhea, and GI distress.

hypermagnesemia excessive magnesium in blood, which may produce cathartic effect, profound thirst, flushing, sedation, confusion, depressed deep tendon reflexes (DTRs), muscle weakness, hypotension, and depressed respirations.

hypernatremia excessive sodium in blood, which may produce confusion, neuromuscular excitability, muscle weakness, seizures, thirst, dry and flushed skin, dry mucous membranes, pyrexia, agitation, and oliguria or anuria.

hypersensitivity reactions excessive and abnormal sensitivity to given agent manifested by urticaria, pruritus, wheezing, edema, redness, and anaphylaxis.

hyperthyroidism excessive secretion by the thyroid glands, which increases basal metabolic rate, resulting in warm, flushed, moist skin; tachycardia, exophthalmos; infrequent lid blinking; lid edema; weight loss despite increased appetite;

frequent urination; menstrual irregularity; breathlessness; hypoventilation; congestive heart failure; excessive sweating.

hyperuricemia excessive uric acid in blood, resulting in pain in flank; stomach, or joints, and changes in intake and output ratio and pattern.

hypocalcemia abnormally low calcium level in blood, which may result in depression; psychosis; hyperreflexia; diarrhea; cardiac arrhythmias; hypotension; muscle spasms; paresthesias of feet, fingers, tongue; positive Chvostek's sign. Severe deficiency (tetany) may result in carpopedal spasms, spasms of face muscle, laryngospasm, and generalized convulsions.

hypoglycemia abnormally low glucose level in the blood, which may result in acute fatigue, restlessness, malaise, marked irritability and weakness, cold sweats, excessive hunger, headache, dizziness, confusion, slurred speech, loss of consciousness, and death.

hypokalemia abnormally low level of potassium in blood, which may result in malaise, fatigue, paresthesias, depressed reflexes, muscle weakness and cramps, rapid, irregular pulse, arrhythmias, hypotension, vomiting, paralytic ileus, mental confusion, depression, delayed thought processes, abdominal distension, polyuria, shallow breathing, and shortness of breath.

hypomagnesemia abnormally low level of magnesium in blood, resulting in nausea, vomiting, cardiac arrhythmias, and neuromuscular symptoms (tetany, positive Chvostek's and Trousseau's signs, seizures, tremors, ataxia, vertigo, nystagmus, muscular fasciculations).

hypophosphatemia abnormally low level of phosphates in blood, resulting in muscle weakness, anorexia, malaise, absent deep tendon reflexes, bone pain, paresthesias, tremors, negative calcium balance, osteomalacia, osteoporosis.

hypothyroidism condition caused by thyroid hormone deficiency that lowers basal metabolic rate and may result in periorbital edema, lethargy, puffy hands and feet, cool, pale skin, vertigo, nocturnal cramps, decreased GI motility, constipation, hypotension, slow pulse, depressed muscular activity, and enlarged thyroid gland.

hypoxia insufficient oxygenation in the blood manifested by dyspnea, tachypnea, headache, restlessness, cyanosis, tachycardia, dysrhythmias, confusion, decreased level of consciousness, and euphoria or delirium.

international normalizing ratio measurement that normalizes for the differences obtained from various laboratory readings in the value for thromboplastin blood level. Used to assess efficacy of oral anticoagulants.

Kussmaul's respirations deep, gasping type of breathing associated with severe metabolic acidosis.

leukopenia abnormal decrease in number of white blood cells, usually below 5000 per cubic millimeter, resulting in fever, chills, sore mouth or throat, and unexplained fatigue.

liver toxicity manifested by anorexia, nausea, fatigue, lethargy, itching, jaundice, abdominal pain, dark-colored urine, and flu-like symptoms.

metabolic acidosis decrease in pH value of the extracellular fluid caused by either an increase in hydrogen ions or a decrease in bicarbonate ions. It may result in one or more of the following: lethargy, headache, weakness, abdominal pain, nausea, vomiting, dyspnea, hyperpnea progressing to Kussmaul's respiration, dehydration, thirst, weakness, flushed face, full bounding pulse, progressive drowsiness, mental confusion, combativeness.

metabolic alkalosis increase in pH value of the extracellular fluid caused by either a loss of acid from the body (e.g., through vomiting) or an increased level of bicarbonate ions (e.g., through ingestion of sodium bicarbonate). It may result in muscle weakness, irritability, confusion, muscle twitching, slow and shallow respirations, and convulsive seizures.

microsomal enzymes drug-metabolizing enzymes located in the endoplasmic reticulum of the liver and other tissues chiefly responsible for oxidative drug metabolism (e.g., cytochrome P450).

myopathy any disease or abnormal condition of striated muscles manifested by muscle weakness, myalgia, diaphoresis, fever, and reddish-brown urine (myoglobinuria) or oliguria.

nephrotoxicity impairment of the nephrons of the kidney manifested by one or more of the following: oliguria, urinary frequency, hematuria, cloudy urine, rising BUN and serum creatinine, fever, graft tenderness or enlargement.

neuroleptic malignant syndrome (NMS) potentially fatal complication associated with antipsychotic drugs manifested by hyperpyrexia, altered mental status, muscle rigidity, irregular pulse, fluctuating BP, diaphoresis, and tachycardia.

orphan drug (as defined by the Orphan Drug Act, an amendment of the Federal Food, Drug, and Cosmetic Act that took effect in January 1983): drug or biological product used in the treatment, diagnosis, or prevention of a rare disease. A rare disease or condition is one that affects fewer than 200,000 persons in the United States, or affects more than 200,000 persons but for which there is no reasonable expectation that drug research and development costs can be recovered from sales within the United States.

ototoxicity impairment of the ear manifested by one or more of the following: headache, dizziness or vertigo, nausea and vomiting with motion, ataxia, nystagmus.

prodrug inactive drug form that becomes pharmacologically active through biotransformation.

protein binding reversible interaction between protein and drug resulting in a drug-protein complex (bound drug) which is in equilibrium with free (active) drug in plasma and tissues. Since only free drug can diffuse to action sites, factors that influence drug-binding (e.g., displacement of bound drug by another drug, or decreased albumin concentration) may potentiate pharmacological effect.

pseudomembranous enterocolitis life-threatening superinfection characterized by severe diarrhea and fever.

pseudoparkinsonism extrapyramidal symptom manifested by slowing of volitional movement (akinesia), mask facies, rigidity

and tremor at rest (especially of upper extremities); and pill rolling motion.

pulmonary edema excessive fluid in the lung tissue manifestied by one or more of the following: shortness of breath, cyanosis, persistent productive cough (frothy sputum may be blood tinged), expiratory rales, restlessness, anxiety, increased heart rate, sense of chest pressure.

renal insufficiency reduced capacity of the kidney to perform its functions as manifested by one or more of the following: dysuria, oliguria, hematuria, swelling of lower legs and feet.

serotonin syndrome manifested by restlessness, myoclonus, mental status changes, hyperreflexia, diaphoresis, shivering, and tremor. Seen with use of multiple serotonin agents simultaneously.

Somogyi effect rebound phenomenon clinically manifested by fasting hyperglycemia and worsening of diabetic control due to unnecessarily large p.m. insulin doses. Hormonal response to unrecognized hypoglycemia (i.e., release of epinephrine, glucagon, growth hormone, cortisol) causes insensitivity to insulin. Increasing the amount of insulin required to treat the hyperglycemia intensifies the hypoglycemia.

superinfection new infection by an organism different from the initial infection being treated by antimicrobial therapy manifested by one or more of the following: black, hairy tongue; glossitis, stomatitis; anal itching; loose, foul-smelling stools; vaginal itching or discharge; sudden fever; cough.

tachyphylaxis rapid decrease in response to a drug after administration of a few doses. Initial drug response cannot be restored by an increase in dose.

tardive dyskinesia extrapyramidal symptom manifested by involuntary rhythmic, bizarre movements of face, jaw, mouth, tongue, and sometimes extremities.

Trousseau's sign muscle spasm resulting from pressure applied to the nerves of the upper arms.

vasovagal symptoms transient vascular and neurogenic reaction marked by pallor, nausea, vomiting, bradycardia, and rapid fall in arterial blood pressure.

water intoxication (dilutional hyponatremia) less than normal concentration of sodium in the blood resulting from excess extracellular and intracellular fluid and producing one or more of the following: lethargy, confusion, headache, decreased skin turgor, tremors, convulsions, coma, anorexia, nausea, vomiting, diarrhea, sternal fingerprinting, weight gain, edema, full bounding pulse, jugular vein distension, rales, signs and symptoms of pulmonary edema.

ABGs	arterial blood gases
ABW	adjusted body weight
a.c.	before meals (*ante cibum*)
ACD	acid–citrate–dextrose
ACE	angiotensin-converting enzyme
ACh	acetylcholine
ACIP	Advisory Committee on Immunization Practices
ACLS	advanced cardiac life support
ACS	acute coronary syndrome
ACT	activated clotting time
ACTH	adrenocorticotropic hormone
AD	Alzheimer's disease
ADD	attention deficit disorder
ADH	antidiuretic hormone
ADLs	activities of daily living
ad libas	as desired (*ad libitum*)
ADP	adenosine diphosphate
ADT	alternate-day drug (administration)
AIDS	acquired immunodeficiency syndrome
AIP	acute intermittent porphyria
ALA	aminolevulinic acid
alpha1-PI	alpha1-proteinase inhibitor
ALS	amyotrophic lateral sclerosis
ALT	alanine aminotransferase (formerly SGPT)
AML	acute myelogenous leukemia
AMP	adenosine monophosphate
ANA	antinuclear antibody(ies)
ANC	absolute neutrophil count
ANH	atrial natriuretic hormone
aPTT	activated partial thromboplastin time
ARC	AIDS-related complex
ARDS	adult respiratory distress syndrome
ARV	AIDS-associated retrovirus
ASHD	arteriosclerotic heart disease
AST	aspartate aminotransferase (formerly SGOT)
AT$_1$	angiotensin II receptor subtype I
AT$_2$	angiotensin II receptor subtype II
ATP	adenosine triphosphate
AV	atrioventricular
b.i.d.	two times a day
BMD	bone mineral density
BMI	body mass index
BMR	basal metabolic rate
BP	blood pressure
BPH	benign prostatic hypertrophy
bpm	beats per minute
BSA	body surface area

BSE	breast self-exam
BSP	bromsulphalein
BT	bleeding time
BUN	blood urea nitrogen
C	centigrade, Celsius
CAD	coronary artery disease
cAMP	cyclic adenosine monophosphate
CBC	complete blood count
cc	cubic centimeter
CDC	Centers for Disease Control and Prevention
CF	cystic fibrosis
cGMP	cyclic guanosine monophosphate
CHF	congestive heart failure
CLL	chronic lymphocytic leukemia
cm	centimeter
CMV	cytomegalovirus-I
CNS	central nervous system
Coll	collyrium (eye wash)
COMT	catecholamine-o-methyl transferase
COPD	chronic obstructive pulmonary disease
COX-2	cyclooxygenase-2
CPK	creatinine phosphokinase
CPR	cardiopulmonary resuscitation
CrCl	creatinine clearance
CRF	chronic renal failure
CRFD	chronic renal failure disease
C&S	culture and sensitivity
CSF	cerebrospinal fluid
CSP	cellulose sodium phosphate
CT	clotting time
CTZ	chemoreceptor trigger zone
CV	cardiovascular
CVA	cerebrovascular accident
CVP	central venous pressure
CYP	cytochrome P450 system of enzymes
D5W	5% dextrose in water
D&C	dilation and curettage
DIC	disseminated intravascular coagulation
DKA	diabetic ketoacidosis
dL	deciliter (100 mL or 0.1 liter)
DM	diabetes mellitus
DMARD	disease-modifying antirheumatic drug
DNA	deoxyribonucleic acid
DPD	dihydropyrimidine dehydrogenase
DTRs	deep tendon reflexes
DVT	deep venous thrombosis
ECG, EKG	electrocardiogram
ECT	electroconvulsive therapy
EEG	electroencephalogram
EENT	eye, ear, nose, throat

e.g.	for example (*exempli gratia*)
EGFR	epidermal growth factor receptor
ENT	ear, nose, throat
EPS	extrapyramidal symptoms (or syndrome)
ER	estrogen receptor
ESRF	end-stage renal failure
F	Fahrenheit
FBS	fasting blood sugar
FDA	Food and Drug Administration
FSH	follicle-stimulating hormone
FTI	free thyroxine index
5-FU	5-fluorouracil
FUO	fever of unknown origin
g	gram
G6PD	glucose-6-phosphate dehydrogenase
GABA	gamma-aminobutyric acid
GERD	gastroesophageal reflux disease
GM-CSF	granulocyte-macrophage colony-stimulating factor
GnRH	gonadotropic releasing hormone
GFR	glomerular filtration rate
GH	growth hormone
GI	gastrointestinal
GPIIb/IIIa	glycoprotein IIb/IIIa
GU	genitourinary
h	hour
HACA	human antichimeric antibody
HbA$_{1C}$	glycosylated hemoglobin
hBNP	human B-type natriuretic peptide
HBV	viral hepatitis B
HCG	human chorionic gonadotropin
Hct	hematocrit
HDL	high-density lipoprotein
HDL-C	high-density-lipoprotein cholesterol
HER	human epidermal growth factor
HF	heart failure
Hgb	hemoglobin
5-HIAA	5-hydroxyindoleacetic acid
HIT	heparin-induced thrombocytopenia
HIV	human immunodeficiency virus
HMG-CoA	3-hydroxy-3-methyl-glutaryl coenzyme A
HPA	hypothalamic–pituitary–adrenocortical (axis)
HPV	human papillomavirus
HR	heart rate
h.s.	nightly or at bedtime (*hora somni*)
HSV-1	herpes simplex virus type 1
HSV-2	herpes simplex virus type 2
5-HT	5-hydroxytryptamine (serotonin receptor)
IBW	ideal body weight
IC	intracoronary
ICP	intracranial pressure

ICU	intensive care unit
ID	intradermal
IFN	interferon
Ig	immunoglobulin
IGF-1	insulin-like growth factor 1
IL	interleukin
IM	intramuscular
INR	international normalized ratio
IOP	intraocular pressure
IPPB	intermittent positive pressure breathing
iPTH	idiopathic parathyroid hormone
IT	intrathecal
ITP	idiopathic thrombocytopenic purpura
IU	international unit
IV	intravenous
JRA	juvenile rheumatoid arthritis
kg	kilogram
KGF	keratinocytic growth factor
17-KGS	17-ketogenic steroids
17-KS	17-ketosteroids
KVO	keep vein open
L	liter
LAV	lymphadenopathy-associated virus
LBW	lean body weight
LDH	lactic dehydrogenase
LDL	low density lipoprotein
LDL-C	low-density-lipoprotein cholesterol
LE	lupus erythematosus
LFT	liver function test
LH	luteinizing hormone
LMWH	low molecular weight heparin
LR	lactated Ringer's
LSD	lysergic acid diethylamide
LTRA	leukotriene receptor antagonist
LVEDP	left ventricular end diastolic pressure
M	molar (strength of a solution)
m^2	square meter (of body surface area)
MAO	monoamine oxidase
MAOI	monoamine oxidase inhibitor
MBD	minimal brain dysfunction
MCH	mean corpuscular hemoglobin
MCHC	mean corpuscular hemoglobin concentration
mCi	millicurie
mcg	microgram (1/1000 of a milligram)
MDI	metered dose inhaler
MDR	minimum daily requirements
mEq	milliequivalent
mg	milligram
MI	myocardial infarction
MIC	minimum inhibitory concentration

min	minute
mL	milliliter (0.001 liter)
mm	millimeter
mo	month
MPA	mycophenolic acid
MPS I	mucopolysaccharidosis I
MRSA	methicillin-resistant *Staphylococcus aureus*
MS	multiple sclerosis
N	normal (strength of a solution)
NADH	reduced form of nicotine adenine dinucleotide
NAPA	*N*-acetyl-p-aminophenol
nb	note well (*nota bene*)
ng	nanogram (1/1000 of a microgram)
NMS	neuroleptic malignant syndrome
NNRTI	nonnucleoside reverse transcriptase inhibitor
NON-PVC	nonpolyvinyl chloride IV bag or tubing
NPN	nonprotein nitrogen
NPO	nothing by mouth
NRTI	nucleoside reverse transcriptase inhibitor
NS	normal saline
NSAID	nonsteroidal antiinflammatory drug
NSCLC	non–small-cell lung cancer
NSR	normal sinus rhythm
NYHA Class I, II, III, IV	New York Heart Association classes of heart failure
OAB	overactive bladder
OC	oral contraceptive
ODT	oral disintegrating tablet
17-OHCS	17-hydroxycorticosteroids
OTC	over the counter (nonprescription)
P450	cytochrome P450 system of enzymes
PABA	*para*-aminobenzoic acid
PAS	*para*-aminosalicylic acid
PAWP	pulmonary artery wedge pressure
PBG	porphobilinogen
PBI	protein-bound iodine
PBP	penicillin-binding protein
PCI	percutaneous coronary intervention
PCP	*Pneumocystis carinii* pneumonia (outdated term; see PJP, *Pneumocystis jiroveci* pneumonia)
PCWP	pulmonary capillary wedge pressure
PDE	phosphodiesterase
PE	pulmonary embolism
PERLA	pupils equal, react to light and accommodation
PG	prostaglandin
PGE$_2$	prostaglandin E$_2$
pH	hydrogen ion concentration
PID	pelvic inflammatory disease
PJP	*Pneumocystis jiroveci* pneumonia (formerly *Pneumocystis carinii* pneumonia)

PKU	phenylketonuria
PMDD	premenstrual dysphoric disorder
PND	paroxysmal nocturnal dyspnea
PO	by mouth or orally (*per os*)
PPI	proton pump inhibitor
PPM	parts per million
prn	when required (*pro re nata*)
PSA	prostate-specific antigen
PSP	phenolsulfonphthalein
PSVT	paroxysmal supraventricular tachycardia
PT	prothrombin time
PTH	parathyroid hormone
PTT	partial thromboplastin time
PUD	peptic ulcer disease
PVC	premature ventricular contraction
PVD	peripheral vascular disease
PZI	protamine zinc insulin
q.i.d.	four times daily
q.o.d.	every other day
RA	rheumatoid arthritis
RAI	radioactive iodine
RAS	reticular activating system
RAST	radioallergosorbent test
RBC	red blood (cell) count
RDA	recommended (daily) dietary allowance
RDS	respiratory distress syndrome
REM	rapid eye movement
rem	radiation equivalent man
RES	reticuloendothelial system
RIA	radioimmunoassay
RL	Ringer's lactate
RNA	ribonucleic acid
ROM	range of motion
RSV	respiratory syncytial virus
RT	reverse transcriptase
RT_3U	total serum thyroxine concentration
S&S	signs and symptoms
SA	sinoatrial
SBE	subacute bacterial endocarditis
SC	subcutaneous
S_{cr}	serum creatinine
sec	second
SGGT	serum gamma-glutamyl transferase
SGOT	serum glutamic–oxaloacetic transaminase (*see* AST)
SGPT	serum glutamic–pyruvic transaminase (*see* ALT)
SIADH	syndrome of inappropriate antidiuretic hormone
SI Units	International System of Units
SK	streptokinase
SLE	systemic lupus erythematosus
SMA	sequential multiple analysis

SNRI	serotonin norepinephrine reuptake inhibitor
SOS	if necessary (*si opus cit*)
sp	species
SPF	sun protection factor
sq	square
SR	sedimentation rate
SRS-A	slow-reactive substance of anaphylaxis
SSRI	selective serotonin reuptake inhibitor
stat	immediately
STD	sexually transmitted disease
STI	sexually transmitted infection
SVT	supraventricular tachyarrhythmias
$t_{1/2}$	half-life
T_3	triiodothyronine
T_4	thyroxine
TCA	tricyclic antidepressant
TG	total triglycerides
TIA	transient ischemic attack
t.i.d.	three times a day (*ter in die*)
TNF	tumor necrosis factor
tPA	tissue plasminogen activator
TPN	total parenteral nutrition
TPR	temperature, pulse, respirations
TSH	thyroid-stimulating hormone
TSS	toxic shock syndrome
TT	thrombin time
Tx	treatment
ULN	upper limit of normal
UPG	uroporphyrinogen
URI	upper respiratory infection
USP	United States Pharmacopeia
USPHS	United States Public Health Service
UTI	urinary tract infection
UV-A, UVA	ultraviolet A wave
VDRL	Venereal Disease Research Laboratory
VEGF	vascular endothelial growth factor
VIG-IV	vaccinia immune globulin-IV
VLDL	very low density lipoprotein
VMA	vanillylmandelic acid
VREF	vancomycin-resistant *Enterococcus faecium*
VRSA	vancomycin-resistant *Staphylococcus aureus*
VS	vital signs
wk	week
WBC	white blood (cell) count
WBCT	whole blood clotting time
y	year

**U.S. Department of Health and Human Services, Public Health Service,
National Institutes of Health: NIH Publication No. 92-2621**

Cytotoxic drugs are toxic compounds and are known to have carcinogenic,
mutagenic, and/or teratogenic potential. With direct contact they may
cause irritation to the skin, eyes, and mucous membranes, and ulceration
and necrosis of tissue. The toxicity of cytotoxic drugs dictates that the exposure of healthcare personnel to these drugs should be minimized. At the
same time, the requirement for maintenance of aseptic conditions must be
satisfied.

Potential Routes of Exposure

These guidelines apply in any setting where cytotoxic drugs are prepared—
including pharmacies, nursing units, clinics, physicians' offices, and the
home healthcare environment. The primary routes of exposure during the
preparation and administration phases are through the inhalation of aero-
solized drug or by direct skin contact.

During drug preparation, a variety of manipulations are performed that
may result in aerosol generation, spraying, and splattering. Examples of
these manipulations include: The withdrawal of needles from drug vials; the
use of syringes and needles or filter straws for drug transfer; the opening of
ampules; and the expulsion of air from the syringe when measuring the
precise volume of a drug.

Pharmaceutical practice calls for the use of aseptic techniques and a sterile
environment. Many pharmacies provide this sterile environment by using a
horizontal laminar flow work bench. However, while this type of unit provides product protection, it may expose the operator and the other room
occupants to aerosols generated during drug preparation procedures.
Therefore, a Class 11 laminar flow (vertical) biological safety cabinet that
provides both product and operator protection is needed for the preparation of cytotoxic drugs. This is accomplished by filtering incoming and
exhaust air through a high-efficiency particulate air (HEPA) filter. It should
be noted that the filters are not effective for volatile materials because they
do not capture vapors and gases. Personnel should be familiar with the
capabilities, limitations, and proper utilization of the biological safety cabinet selected.

During administration, clearing air from a syringe or infusion line and leakage at tubing, syringe, or stopcock connections should be avoided to prevent opportunities for accidental skin contact and aerosol generation.
Dispose of syringes and unclipped needles into a leakproof and puncture-
resistant container.

The disposal of cytotoxic drugs and trace contaminated materials (e.g.,
gloves, gowns, needles, syringes, vials) presents a possible source of exposure to pharmacists, nurses, and physicians as well as to ancillary person-

nel, especially the housekeeping staff. Excreta from patients receiving cytotoxic drug therapy may contain high concentrations of the drug. All personnel should be aware of this source of potential exposure and should take appropriate precautions as established by your hospital or clinic to avoid accidental contact.

The potential risks to pharmacists, nurses, and physicians from repeated contact with parenteral cytotoxic drugs can be effectively controlled by using a combination of specific containment equipment and certain work techniques, which are described in the recommendations sections. For the most part, the techniques are merely an extension of good work practices by healthcare and ancillary personnel, and similar in principle and practice to Universal Precautions being performed. By using these precautions, personnel are better able to minimize possible exposure to cytotoxic drugs.

Safe Preparation of Cytotoxic Drugs

A. Part 1: All procedures involved in the preparation of cytotoxic drugs should be performed in a Class 11, Type A, or Type B laminar flow biological safety cabinet. The cabinet exhaust should be discharged to the outdoors in order to eliminate the exposure of personnel to drugs that may volatilize after retention on filters of the cabinet. The cabinet of choice is a Class 11, Type B, which discharges exhaust to the outdoors and can be obtained with a bag-in/bag-out filter to protect the personnel servicing the cabinet and to facilitate disposal.
Part 2: Alternatively, a Class 11, Type A cabinet can be equipped with a canopy or thimble unit that exhausts to the outdoors. For detailed information about the design, capabilities, and limitations of various types of biological safety cabinets, refer to the National Sanitation Foundation Standard 49 National Science Foundation, Standard 49 for Class 11 (Laminar Flow) Biohazard Cabinetry.

B. The work surface of the safety cabinet should be covered with plastic-backed absorbent paper. This will reduce the potential for dispersion of droplets and spills and facilitate cleanup. This paper should be changed after any overt spill and at the end of each work shift.

C. Personnel preparing the drugs should wear unpowdered latex surgical gloves and a disposable gown with elastic or knit cuffs. Gloves should be changed regularly and immediately if torn or punctured. Protective clothing should not be worn outside of the drug preparation area. Overtly contaminated gowns require immediate removal and replacement. In case of skin contact with any cytotoxic drug, thoroughly wash the affected area with soap and water. However, do not abrade the skin by using a scrub brush. Flush the affected eye(s), while holding back the eyelid(s), with copious amounts of water for at least 15 minutes. Then seek medical evaluation by a physician.

D. Vials containing drugs requiring reconstitution should be vented to reduce the internal pressure with a venting device using a 0.22 micron hydrophobic filter or other appropriate means such as a chemotherapy dispensing pin. This reduces the probability of spraying and spillage.

E. If a chemotherapy dispensing pin is not used, a sterile alcohol pad should be carefully placed around the needle and vial top during withdrawal from the septum.

F. The external surfaces contaminated with a drug should be wiped clean with an alcohol pad prior to transfer or transport.

G. When opening the glass ampule, wrap it, and then snap it at the break point using an alcohol pad to reduce the possibility of injury and to contain the aerosol produced. Use a 5-micron filter needle or straw when removing the drug solution.

H. Syringes and IV bottles containing cytotoxic drugs should be labeled and dated. Before these items leave the preparation area, an additional label reading, "Caution-chemotherapy, Dispose of Properly" is recommended.

I. After completing the drug preparation process, wipe down the interior of the safety cabinet with water (for injection or irrigation) followed by 70% alcohol using disposable towels. All wastes are considered contaminated and should be disposed of properly.

J. Contaminated needles and syringes, IV tubing, butterfly clips, etc., should be disposed of intact to prevent aerosol generation and injury. Do not recap needles. Place these items in a puncture-resistant container along with any contaminated bottles, vials, gloves, absorbent paper, disposable gowns, gauze, and other waste. The container should then be placed in a box labeled, "Cytotoxic waste only," then sealed and disposed of according to federal, state and local requirements. Linens contaminated with drugs, patient excreta, or body fluids should be handled separately.

K. Hands should be washed between glove changes and after glove removal.

L. Cytotoxic drugs are categorized as regulated wastes and, therefore, should be disposed of according to federal, state and local requirements.

Recommended Practices for Personnel Administering Parenteral Cytotoxic Drugs

A. A protective outer garment such as a closed-front surgical-type gown with knit cuffs should be worn. Gowns may be of the disposable or washable variety.

B. Disposable latex surgical gloves should be worn during those procedures where exposure to the drugs may result and when handling patient body fluids or excreta. When bubbles are removed from syringes or IV tubing, an alcohol pad should be placed carefully over the tip of such items in order to collect any of the cytotoxic drugs that may be inadvertently discharged. Discard gloves after each use and wash hands.

C. Contaminated needles and syringes and IV apparatus should be disposed of intact into a labeled, puncture-resistant container in order to minimize aerosol generation and risk of injury. Do not recap needles. The container, as well as other contaminated materials should placed in a box labeled, "Cytotoxic waste only." Linen overtly contaminated with any cytotoxic agent or excreta from a patient within 48 hours following drug administration, may be safely handled by using the procedures prescribed for isolation cases. For example, place the contaminated articles in a "yellow" cloth bag lined with a water-soluble plastic bag and then place into the washing machine. Linens without overt contamination can be handled by routine laundering procedures.

D. In case of skin contact with any cytotoxic drug, thoroughly wash the affected area with soap and water. However, do not abrade the skin by using a scrub brush. Flush the affected eye(s), while holding back the eyelid(s), with copious amounts of water for at least 15 minutes. Then seek medical evaluation by a physician. Always wash hands after removing gloves.

Source: U.S. Department of Health and Human Services, Public Health Service, National Institutes of Health: NIH Publication No. 92-2621, http://dohs.ors.od.nih.gov

◆ APPENDIX F   TOXICITY GRADES ASSOCIATED WITH CHEMOTHERAPY

There are multiple grading scales used to evaluate toxicities associated with drug therapies. The scales range from 1 to 5; the higher the number, the more severe/significant the toxicity. Generally, scales are:

0 = Not present (this is not included in all scales)
1 = Mild side effects
2 = Moderate side effects
3 = Severe side effects
4 = Life-threatening or disabling side effects
5 = Fatal

The National Cancer Institute has developed Common Terminology Criteria for Adverse Events (CTCAE), which standardize the evaluation of toxicities to allow comparisons between various trial results. This grading scale is available at http://ctep.cancer.gov/reporting/ctc.html. The toxicity adjustments provided in the drug monographs reflect this CTCAE scale.

In some cases, patients will experience different toxicities with different grades with the same therapy. For example, for one particular treatment, the side effect of nausea may be graded as 2, while the side effect of neutropenia may be graded as a 4.

Reference:
The National Cancer Institute (2008). *Common terminology criteria for adverse events.* Bethesda, MD: Author. http://ctep.cancer.gov/reporting/ctc.html

BIBLIOGRAPHY

American Hospital Formulary Service (AHFS) Drug Information. 08. Bethesda, MD: American Society of Health-System Pharmacists. 2008.

Bindler R, Howry L. *Prentice Hall Pediatric Drug Guide with Nursing Implications.* Upper Saddle River, NJ: Prentice Hall Health. 2005.

Clinical Pharmacology. http://www.gsm.com. Gold Standard Media. 2008.

Drug Facts and Comparisons. http://factsandcomparisons.com. Version 4.0 online. St. Louis: Wolters Kluwer Health, Inc. 2008.

King Guide to Parenteral Admixtures. Napa, CA: King Guide Publications, Inc. 2005.

Lacy CF, Armstrong LL, Goldman MP, Lance LL. *Drug Information Handbook.* 15th ed. Hudson, OH: Lexi-Comp. 2007.

Micromedex Healthcare Series. Greenwood Village, NJ: Thompson Healthcare. 2008.

Phelps SJ, Hak EB, Cril CM, *Teddy Bear, Pediatric Injectable Drugs.* 8th ed. Bethesda, MD: American Society of Health-System Pharmacists (ASHSP). 2008.

Physicians' Desk Reference. 61st ed. Montvale, NJ: Thompson Healthcare. 2008.

Semla TP, Beizer JL, Higbee MD. *Geriatric Dosage Handbook.* 10th ed. Hudson, OH: Lexi-Comp. 2005.

Trissel LA, *Handbook of Injectable Drugs.* 14th ed. Bethesda, MD: American Society of Health-System Pharmacists. 2007.

USP DI: Advice to Patients. Rockville, MD: US Pharmacopeial Convention. 2007.

USP DI: Drug Information for the Health Care Professional. Rockville, MD: US Pharmacopeial Convention. 2007.

INDEX

INDEX

Drug categories are in SMALL CAPS. Prototypes in **bold.**
Generic drug names are given in parentheses.

Drug categories are in SMALL CAPS. Prototypes in **bold.**
Generic drug names are given in parentheses.

Drug categories are in SMALL CAPS. Prototypes in **bold.**
Generic drug names are given in parentheses.

Drug categories are in SMALL CAPS. Prototypes in **bold.**
Generic drug names are given in parentheses.

INDEX

Drug categories are in SMALL CAPS. Prototypes in **bold.**
Generic drug names are given in parentheses.

Drug categories are in SMALL CAPS. Prototypes in **bold.**
Generic drug names are given in parentheses.

697

Drug categories are in SMALL CAPS. Prototypes in **bold.**
Generic drug names are given in parentheses.

Drug categories are in SMALL CAPS. Prototypes in **bold.**
Generic drug names are given in parentheses.

699

Drug categories are in SMALL CAPS. Prototypes in **bold.**
Generic drug names are given in parentheses.

Drug categories are in SMALL CAPS. Prototypes in **bold.**
Generic drug names are given in parentheses.

701

Drug categories are in SMALL CAPS. Prototypes in **bold.**
Generic drug names are given in parentheses.

Drug categories are in SMALL CAPS. Prototypes in **bold.**
Generic drug names are given in parentheses.

703

Drug categories are in SMALL CAPS. Prototypes in **bold.**
Generic drug names are given in parentheses.

Drug categories are in SMALL CAPS. Prototypes in **bold.**
Generic drug names are given in parentheses.

705

Drug categories are in SMALL CAPS. Prototypes in **bold.**
Generic drug names are given in parentheses.

Drug categories are in SMALL CAPS. Prototypes in **bold.**
Generic drug names are given in parentheses.

707

Drug categories are in SMALL CAPS. Prototypes in **bold.**
Generic drug names are given in parentheses.

Drug categories are in SMALL CAPS. Prototypes in **bold.**
Generic drug names are given in parentheses.

709

Drug categories are in SMALL CAPS. Prototypes in **bold.**
Generic drug names are given in parentheses.

Drug categories are in SMALL CAPS. Prototypes in **bold.**
Generic drug names are given in parentheses.

711

Drug categories are in SMALL CAPS. Prototypes in **bold.**
Generic drug names are given in parentheses.

Drug categories are in SMALL CAPS. Prototypes in **bold.**
Generic drug names are given in parentheses.
713

Drug categories are in SMALL CAPS. Prototypes in **bold.**
Generic drug names are given in parentheses.

	AMINOPHYLLINE	DOBUTAMINE	DOPAMINE	HEPARIN	MEPERIDINE	MORPHINE	NITROGLYCERIN	ONDANSETRON	POTASSIUM
acyclovir		I	I	C	I/C	I/C		I	C
alteplase		I	I	I					
amikacin				I	C	C	I	C	
amino acids (TPN)	I/C	C	C	C	C	C		I	C
aminophylline	C	I	I/C	C	C	C		–	C
amiodarone	I	C	C	I		C			C
ampicillin				C	C	C		I	C
ampicillin/sulbactam				C	C	C		I	
amrinone	C	C	C		C		C		C
aztreonam	C	I	I	C	C	C		C	C
bretylium	C	I	C		C		C		C
bumetanide				C	C	C			
calcium chloride	I	C				C			
cefazolin	C		C	C	C	C		C	
cefoperazone	C	I			I	C		–	
cefotaxime		C	C		C	C		C	
cefotetan	C			C	C	C			
cefoxitin					C	C		C	
ceftazidime	C	I/C	C	C	C	C		C	C
ceftizoxime					C	C		C	
ceftriaxone	C			C	C	C			
cefuroxime	C				C	C		C	
chloramphenicol		C	C		C				
cimetidine	C	C		C	C			C	
ciprofloxacin	I		C	I	C				C
clindamycin	I	C	C	C	C			C	C
dexamethasone	C			C		C		C	C
diazepam		C		I		C			–

COMMON DRUG IV-SITE COMPATIBILITY CHART

	AMINOPHYLLINE	DOBUTAMINE	DOPAMINE	HEPARIN	MEPERIDINE	MORPHINE	NITROGLYCERIN	ONDANSETRON	POTASSIUM
digoxin	I/C		C	C	C	C			C
diltiazem	C	C	C	I/C	C	C	C		C
diphenydramine			C	C	C	C	C	C	C
dobutamine	I	C	C	I/C	C	C	C		C
dopamine		C		C	C	C	C	C	C
doxycycline		C						C	
enalapril/enalaprilat	C	C	C	C		C			C
epinephrine		C	C	C		C			C
eptifibatide		C							
erythromycin	C		C	C	C	C	C		C
esmolol	C	C	C	C		C	C	C	C
famotidine	C		C	C	C	C	C	C	C
filgrastim	C	C		I	I	C	C	C	
fluconazole	C	C	C	C	C	C	C	C	
foscarnet	C	I	C	C	C	C			
fosphenytoin	C	I/C	I/C	C	I/C	I/C	C	I	C
furosemide								I	
ganciclovir									
gentamicin	C	I/C	I/C	I	C	C	C	C	C
heparin		I/C	I/C		C	C		C	
hydrocortisone		C	C	C	C	C	C		
hydromorphone				C		C		C	
imipenem/cilastatin				C	I				
insulin		C		C	C	C			C
isoproterenol	C			I/C		C	C		C
labetolol	C	C	C	C	C	C	C		C
lidocaine		C	C	C		C	C		C
lorazepam			C	C		C	C	I	C

magnesium
meperidine
methylprednisolone
metoclopramide
metoprolol
metronidazole
midazolam
milrinone
morphine
nafcillin
nitroglycerin
nitroprusside
norepinephrine
ondansetron
penicillin G
phenylephrine
phenytoin
piperacillin
piperacillin/tazobactam
potassium Cl
procainamide
propofol
ranitidine
sargramostim
sodium bicarbonate
ticarcillin/clavulanate
tobramycin
trimethoprim-sulfamethoxazole
vancomycin

C = compatible; I = incompatible; I/C = conflicting data.